The Corsini
Encyclopedia *of*
Psychology

The Corsini
Encyclopedia *of*
Psychology

FOURTH EDITION

Volume 3

Edited by

Irving B. Weiner
W. Edward Craighead

WILEY

John Wiley & Sons, Inc.

Published by John Wiley & Sons, Inc., Hoboken, New Jersey.
Published simultaneously in Canada.

Library of Congress Cataloging-in-Publication Data:

The Corsini encyclopedia of psychology / edited by Irving B.
Weiner, W. Edward Craighead.—4th ed.
    v. cm.
  Rev. ed. of: The Corsini encyclopedia of psychology and behavioral science.
3rd ed. New York : Wiley, c2001.
  Includes bibliographical references and index.
  ISBN 978-0-470-17024-3 (cloth, set)
  ISBN 978-0-470-17027-4 (cloth, Volume 3)
  1. Psychology—Encyclopedias. I. Weiner, Irving B. II. Craighead, W. Edward. III.
Corsini encyclopedia of psychology and behavioral science.
  BF31.E52 2010
  150.3—dc22

                                               2009031719

Printed in the United States of America

10 9 8 7 6 5 4 3 2 1

PREFACE

The fourth edition of the *Corsini Encyclopedia of Psychology* contains entries whose utility has endured through several editions and entirely new entries written for this first edition of the twenty-first century. The selected previous entries have been updated to reflect recent conceptualizations and research findings; the new entries, which constitute approximately half of the articles, were commissioned to broaden the coverage of the encyclopedia and to capture a full range of contemporary topics in psychology. For readers previously unfamiliar with a particular topic, related articles are intended to be an informative source of what is most important for them to know about it; for readers already knowledgeable about a topic, articles related to it are intended to provide useful, concise summaries of current knowledge.

Numerous features of the encyclopedia are designed to help readers gain information about topics of interest to them. Most entries are referenced to relevant publications in the psychological literature and include suggested additional readings and cross-references to other articles in the encyclopedia on similar or related topics. Many topics are discussed in more than one entry, to provide additional facts about the topic and identify different ways of looking at it. Along with articles on substantive topics in psychology, this fourth edition of the encyclopedia includes detailed biographies of 63 of the most distinguished persons in the history of psychology. Supplementing these biographies is a special alphabetized section in Volume 4 consisting of brief biographies of 543 other important contributors to psychological theory and research.

Among other special topics, the encyclopedia features entries on the history and current status of psychology in various countries from around the world in which there are active communities of psychologists; numerous articles describing the activities and functions of the major psychological and mental health organizations and societies; and attention to topics of psychological significance in related fields of social work and medicine, with a particular emphasis on psychiatry. With further respect to the breadth of coverage in the encyclopedia, the areas in which numerous specific articles appear include the following:

- Child, adolescent, adult, midlife, and late-life development
- Cognitive, affective, and sensory functions
- Cross-cultural psychology
- Forensic psychology
- Industrial and organizational psychology
- Mental and psychological disorders listed in the DSM, the PDM, and the ICD
- Neuroscience and the biological bases of behavior
- Language and linguistic processes
- Personality processes and interpersonal relationships
- Psychological therapies and psychosocial interventions
- Psychopharmacological treatment methods
- Psychological and neuropsychological assessment methods
- Social and environmental influences on behavior
- Statistical procedures and research methods

After selecting the topics for inclusion in this fourth edition, the editors set about to identify and recruit individuals whose scholarly background and professional experience would enable them to give inquiring readers clear and accurate information about topics of their interest. We believe that we were highly successful in this effort, and we are grateful to the approximately 1,200 authors who contributed articles to these four volumes. We appreciate their knowledge, their literacy, and their tolerance of our editing their work to achieve a consistent format across the large number of articles in the four volumes.

An undertaking of this magnitude involves the cooperation and collaboration of a many of individuals in addition to its authors. We would like first of all to express our gratitude to Patricia Rossi, Wiley Executive Editor in Psychology, who brought us together to work on this project. She has been a wonderful editor, leading and supporting us throughout this process beginning with our first meeting to discuss the encyclopedia, what we would include, and the development and implementation of a plan to bring the publication of the encyclopedia to fruition. It is hard to imagine a better editor with whom one could work. For their essential roles in the preparation and production of the encyclopedia, we would like to thank as well Wiley staff members Kim Nir, Senior Production Editor; Kathleen DeChants, Senior Editorial Assistant; and Ester Mallach, Administrative Assistant.

We are especially grateful to Jennifer Moore for her many activities associated with the production of these volumes. She found addresses (especially e-mail addresses), retyped articles, located missing references for articles, and was generally extremely helpful in our completion of the manuscript. We would also like to express our appreciation to Rebecca Suffness and Ava Madoff, who helped with various aspects of the development of the manuscript.

Finally, we would like to thank four librarians who reviewed our plan for the new edition and provided valuable advice concerning its format and content: Barbara Glendenning of the University of California Berkeley Library; Sally Speller of the New York Public Library; Bruce Stoffel of the Milner Library at Illinois State University; and Michael Yonezawa of the University of Calfornia Riverside Library.

Irving B. Weiner, Tampa, FL
W. Edward Craighead, Atlanta, GA
June, 2009

HOW TO USE THIS ENCYCLOPEDIA

Welcome to this fourth edition of the *Corsini Encyclopedia of Psychology*. Like its predecessors, the fourth edition is organized into four distinct parts. Each of the four volumes begins with frontmatter that includes the entire list of entries for all four volumes and a complete list of the contributing authors and their affiliations. The second part of each volume consists of the actual entries, listed in alphabetical order. Included among these alphabetized entries are biographies of 63 of the most important figures in the history of psychology. Alphabetized entries constitute most of Volumes 1 though 3 and some of Volume 4. As a third part of the encyclopedia, Volume 4 contains a section of brief biographies for 543 other important contributors to psychological theory, research, and practice. Finally, Volume 4 concludes with an Author Index and a Subject Index for the entire four-volume set.

Readers looking for information on a particular topic should first check the list of entries in the frontmatter to see if there is an article on that topic. If so, the article can be found in its alphabetical location. If not, the next place to look is the Subject Index in Volume 4. If the topic is mentioned in the encyclopedia, the Subject Index will identify the particular pages on which the topic is discussed. Readers looking for information about a particular person should also first check the list of entries to see if the person is one of the distinguished individuals for whom there is a biography among the alphabetized entries. If not, the next place to look is the section of Brief Biographies in Volume 4. Should the person not appear in either of these locations, the searcher should turn to the Author Index. If the person is mentioned anywhere in the encyclopedia, the author index will identify the pages on which this mention occurs. In most instances in which persons are mentioned

in an article, some of their publications are included in a list of references accompanying the article.

An important additional source for locating information is in the cross-referencing that appears at the end of most entries. The following cross-references listed with five selected entries illustrate this guide to further information and also speak to the breadth of coverage in the encyclopedia:

Central Nervous System (See also Brain; Neuroscience; Parasympathetic Nervous System; Sympathetic Nervous System)

Cognitive Development (See also Emotional Development; Intellectual Development; Social Cognitive Development)

Major Depressive Disorder (See also Antidepressant Medications; Depression; Depressive Personality Disorder)

Multivariate Methods (See also Analysis of Covariance; Analysis of Variance; Factor Analysis; Multiple Correlation)

Psychotherapy (See also Counseling; Current Psychotherapies; Psychotherapy Research; Psychotherapy Training)

Each of the cross-references accompanying an article has cross-references of its own to related articles. By pursuing the trail of cross-references related to a topic, readers can maximize the amount of information they can get from the encyclopedia.

CORSINI ENCYCLOPEDIA ENTRIES

CONTRIBUTORS

Norman Abeles, Michigan State University

Jonathan S. Abramowitz, University of North Carolina at Chapel Hill

Lyn Y. Abramson, University of Wisconsin-Madison

Philip A. Ackerman, Georgia Institute of Technology

Thomas G. Adams, University of Arkansas

Wayne Adams, George Fox University, Newburg, OR

Howard Adelman, University of California, Los Angeles

Bernard W. Agranoff, University of Michigan

Muninder K. Ahluwalia, Montclair State University

Leona S. Aiken, Arizona State University

Peter Alahi, University of Illinois College of Medicine, Peoria

Anne Marie Albano, Columbia University College of Physicians and Surgeons

John A. Albertini, Rochester Institute of Technology

Amelia Aldao, Yale University

Mark D. Alicke, Ohio University

Daniel N. Allen, University of Nevada Las Vegas

Lauren B. Alloy, Temple University

Carolyn J. Anderson, University of Illinois, Urbana-Champaign

Corey Anderson, Pacific University

Keelah D. Andrews, Wheaton College

Hymie Anisman, Carleton University

Heinz L. Ansbacher, University of Vermont

Martin M. Antony, Ryerson University, Toronto, Canada

Steven J. Anzalone, State University of New York at Binghamton

Robert P. Archer, Eastern Virginia Medical School

Ruben Ardila, National University of Columbia

Eirikur Orn Arnarson, Landspitali University Hospital, Reykjavik, Iceland

Mark Arnoff, University at Albany, SUNY

Jane Ashby, University of Massachusetts Amherst

Gord, J. G. Asmundson, University of Regina, Canada

John A. Astin, California Pacific Medical Center, San Francisco, CA

Martha Augoustinos, University of Adelaide, Australia

Tatjana Ave, University of Chicago

Oksana Babenko, University of Alberta, Canada

Michael Babyak, Duke University Medical Center

Bahador Bahram, University College London, United Kingdom

Clark Baim, Birmingham Institute of Psychodrama, Birmingham, UK

Tatiana N. Balachova, University of Oklahoma Health Sciences Center

Scott A. Baldwin, Brigham Young University

Michael Bambery, University of Detroit Mercy

Albert Bandura, Stanford University

Marie T. Banich, University of Colorado at Boulder

Steven C. Bank, Center for Forensic Psychiatry, Ann Arbor, MI

Jacques P. Barber, University of Pennsylvania

Daniel Barbiero, US National Academy of Sciences

John A. Bargh, Yale University

Blanche Barnes, Mumbai, India

Sean Barns, Binghamton University

Barnaby B. Barratt, Prescott, AZ

Rowland P. Barrett, Warren Alpert Medical School of Brown University

Tammy D. Barry, University of Southern Mississippi

Jennifer L. Bass, The Kinsey Institute, Bloomington, IN

David S. Batey, University of Alabama School of Medicine

C. Daniel Batson, University of Kansas

Steven H. R. Beach, University of Georgia

Theodore P. Beauchaine, University of Washington

Eric Beauregard, Simon Fraser University

Robert B. Bechtel, University of Arizona

Judith S. Beck, Beck Institute for Cognitive Therapy and Research and University of Pennsylvania

Carolyn Black Becker, Trinity University

Deborah C. Beidel, University of Central Florida

Bernard C. Beins, Ithaca College

Mark Beitel, Yale University School of Medicine

Genevieve Belleville, University of Quebec at Montreal, Canada

J. B. Bennett, Texas Christian University

Shannon Bennett, University of California, Los Angeles

Yossef S. Ben-Porath, Kent State University

Gary G. Benston, Ohio State University

Peter M. Bentler, University of California, Los Angeles

Tanya N. Beran, University of Calgary, CA

Stanley Berent, University of Michigan

Kathleen Stassen Berger, Bronx Community College, City University of New York

Arjan Berkeljon, Brigham Young University

Gregory S. Berns, Emory University School of Medicine

Jane Holmes Bernstein, Children's Hospital Boston and Harvard Medical School

David T. R. Berry, University of Kentucky

Michael D. Berzonsky, State University of New York at Cortland

Jeffrey L. Binder, Argosy University/Atlanta

Andri S. Bjornsson, University of Colorado at Boulder

Danielle Black, Northwestern University

Donald W. Black, University of Iowa Roy J. and Lucille A. Carr College of Medicine

Alberto Blanco-Campal, University College Dublin, Ireland

Ricardo D. Blasco, University of Barcelona, Spain

Sidney Bloch, University of Melbourne, Australia

Deborah Blum, University of Wisconsin-Madison

Mark S. Blum, University of Iowa

Anthony F. Bogaert, Brock University, St. Catharines, Canada

G. Anne Bogat, Michigan State University

Johan J. Bolhuis, Utrecht University, The Netherlands

Trevor G. Bond, James Cook University, Australia

Mark W. Bondi, Veterans Administration San Diego Healthcare System and University of California, San Diego

C. Alan Boneau, George Mason University

Hale Bolak Boratav, Istanbul Bilgi University, Turkey

John G. Borkowski, University of Notre Dame

Robert F. Bornstein, Adelphi University

James F. Boswell, Pennsylvania State University

Lyle E. Bourne, Jr., University of Colorado

James N. Bow, Hawthorn Center, Northville, MI

Christopher R. Bowie, Queen's University, Kingston, ON, Canada

Elza Boycheva, Binghamton University

Michelle J. Boyd, Tufts University

Virginia Brabender, Widener University

Paul Bracke, Mountain View, CA

Rom Brafman, Palo Alto, CA

David Brang, University of California, San Diego

Gary G. Brannigan, State University of New York-Plattsburg

Ann D. Branstetter, Missouri State University

Myron L. Braunstein, University of California, Irvine

Jeremy W. Bray, RTI International, Research Triangle Park, NC

Alisha Breetz, American University

Britton W. Brewer, Springfield College

K. Robert Bridges, Pennsylvania State University at New Kensington

Sara K. Bridges, University of Memphis

Arthur P. Brief, University of Utah

John Briere, University of Southern California

Nicholas E. Brink, Coburn, PA University of Colorado

Martin Brodwin, California State University, Los Angeles

Arline L. Bronzaft, City University of New York

Sarah Brookhart, Association for Psychological Science

Alisha L. Brosse, University of Colorado at Boulder

Ronald T. Brown, Temple University

Sheldon S. Brown, North Shore Community College, Danvers, MA

Caroline B. Brown, University of North Carolina at Chapel Hill

Patricia Brownell, Fordham University Graduate School of Social Service

Timothy J. Bruce, University of Illinois College of Medicine, Peoria

Martin Brüne, University of Bochum, Bochum, Germany

Silvina Brussino, National University of Córdoba, Córdoba, Argentina

Angela Bryan, University of New Mexico

Sue A. Buckley, University of Portsmouth, United Kingdom

Kristen A. Burgess, Emory University School of Medicine

M. Michele Burnette, Columbia, SC

Brenda Bursch, David Geffen School of Medicine at UCLA

William Buskist, Auburn University

James N. Butcher, University of Minnesota

Barbara M. Byrne, University of Ottawa, Canada

James P. Byrnes, Temple University

Desiree Caban, Columbia University

John T. Cacioppo, University of Chicago

David J. Cain, Alliant International University, San Diego

Lawrence G. Calhoun, University of North Carolina Charlotte

Amanda W. Calkins, Boston University

Jennifer L. Callahan, University of North Texas

Joseph Cambray, Massachusetts General Hospital, Harvard Medical School

Jenna Cambria, University of Maryland

Jonathan M. Campbell, University of Georgia

Keith Campbell, University of Georgia

Larry D. Campeau, Clarkson University School of Business

Caroline Campion, Tulane University School of Medicine

Tyrone Cannon, University of California, Los Angeles

Claudio Cantalupo, Clemson University

E. J. Capaldi, Purdue University

Rudolf N. Cardinal, University of Cambridge, United Kingdom

Bernardo Carducci, Indiana University Southeast

Leeanne Carey, National Stroke Research Institute, Melbourne, Australia

Jon Carlson, Governors State University

Laura A. Carlson, University of Notre Dame

Malique L. Carr, Pacific Graduate School of Psychology

Sonia Carrillo, University of the Andes, Bogotá, Columbia

Rachel Casas, University of Iowa College of Medicine

Margaret J. Cason, University of Texas at Austin

Wendy J. Caspar, University of Texas at Arlington

Louis G. Castonguay, Pennsylvania State University

Yoojin Chae, University of California, Davis

Kate Chapman, Pennsylvania State University

Stephanie G. Chapman, University of Houston

Susan T. Charles, University of California, Irvine

Cary Cherniss, Rutgers University

Allan Cheyne, University of Waterloo, Canada

Jean Lau Chin, Adelphi University

Jinsoo Chin, University of Michigan

Nehrika Chowli, University of Washington

Joan C. Chrisler, Connecticut College

Shawn E. Christ, University of Missouri-Columbia

Edward R. Christophersen, Children's Mercy Hospitals and Clinics, Kansas City, KS

Charles Clifton, Jr., University of Massachusetts Amherst

W. Glenn Clingempeel, Fayetteville State University

Sam V. Cochran, University of Iowa

Rosemary Cogan, Texas Tech University

Adam B. Cohen, Arizona State University

Barry H. Cohen, New York University

Karen R. Cohen, Canadian Psychological Association

Lisa J. Cohen, Beth Israel Medical Center and Albert Einstein College of Medicine

Taya R. Cohen, Northwestern University

P. T. Cohen-Kettenis, VU University Medical Center, Amsterdam, The Netherlands

Theodore Coladarci, University of Maine

Raymond J. Colello, Virginia Commonwealth University

Frank L. Collins, Jr., University of North Texas

Lillian, Comas-Diaz, Transcultural Mental Health Institute, Washington, DC

David J. Y. Combs, University of Kentucky

Jessica L. Combs, University of Kentucky

Jonathan Comer, Columbia University

Mary Connell, Fort Worth, TX

Daniel F. Connor, University of Connecticut School of Medicine

Michael J. Constatino, Pennsylvania State University

Frederick L. Coolidge, University of Colorado at Colorado Springs

Steven H. Cooper, Harvard Medical School

Stewart Cooper, Valparaiso University

Tori Sacha Cordiano, Case Western Reserve University

David Cordy, University of Iowa College of Medicine

Stanley Coren, University of British Columbia, Canada

Dave Corey, Portland Oregon Police Bureau

Erminio Costa, University of Illinois, Chicago

Stefany Coxe, University of Arizona

Robert J. Craig, Roosevelt University

Benjamin H. Craighead, Salisbury Pediatrics, Salisbury, NC

Margaret C. Craighead, Emory University School of Medicine

W. Edward Craighead, Emory University School of Medicine

Phebe Cramer, Williams College

Michelle G. Craske, University of California, Los Angeles

Candice E. Crerand, Children's Hospital of Philadelphia

Mario Cristancho, University of Pennsylvania School of Medicine

Pilar Cristancho, University of Pennsylvania School of Medicine

Thomas S. Critchfield, Illinois State University

Paul Crits-Christoph, University of Pennsylvania

Katherine B. Crocker, John College, City University of New York

Jessica M. Cronce, Yale University

Julio Eduardo Cruz, University of the Andes, Bogotá, Columbia

Pim Cuijpers, VU University of Amsterdam, The Netherlands

E. Mark Cummings, University of Notre Dame

David Yun Dai, University at Albany, State University of New York

Melita Daley, University of California, Los Angeles

J. P. Das, University of Alberta, Canada

William Davidson II, Michigan State University

Joanne Davila, SUNY Stony Brook

Samuel B. Day, Indiana University

Edward L. Deci, University of Rochester

Gregory DeClue, Sarasota, FL

Patricia J. Deldin, University of Michigan

Patricia R. DeLucia, Texas Tech University

Heath A. Demaree, Case Western Reserve University

Florence L. Denmark, Pace University

M. Ray Denny, Michigan State University

Brendan E. Depue, University of Colorado at Boulder

Leonard R. Derogatis, Sheppard Pratt Hospital and Johns Hopkins University School of Medicine

Paula S. Derry, Paula Derry Enterprises in Health Psychology, Baltimore, MD

Sreedhari D. Desai, University of Utah

Esther Devall, New Mexico State University

Donald A. Dewsbury, University of Florida

Lisa J. Diamond, University of Utah

Milton Diamond, University of Hawaii

Andreas Dick-Niederhauser, University Psychiatry Service, Berne, Switzerland

Adele Diederich, Jacobs University Bremen, Germany

Marc J. Diener, Argosy University, Washington, DC

Volker Dietz, University Hospital Balgrit, Zurich, Switzerland

Nicholas DiFonzo, Rochester Institute of Technology

Raymond A. DiGiuseppe, St. Johns University

Sona Dimidjian, University of Colorado, Boulder

Beth Doll, University of Nebraska Lincoln

Lorah H. Dom, Cincinnati Children's Hospital Medical Center

Aila K. Dommestrup, University of Georgia

John W. Donahue, University of Massachusetts

M. Brent Donnellan, Michigan State University

William I. Dorfman, Nova Southeastern University

William F. Doverspike, Atlanta, GA

Peter W. Dowrick, University of Hawai'i at Manoa

David J. A. Dozois, University of Western Ontario, Canada

Peter A. Drake, DePaul University

Michelle Drefs, University of Calgary, Canada

Clifford J. Drew, University of Utah

Eric Y. Drogin, Harvard Medical School

Dan Du, Tufts University

Rand A. Dublin, Hofstra University

David Dunning, Cornell University

Francis T. Durso, Georgia Institute of Technology

Donald G. Dutton, University of British Columbia, Canada

Joel A. Dvoskin, University of Arizona College of Medicine

Lutz H. Ecksenberger, German Institute for International Educational Research and Johann Wolfgang Goethe University, Frankfort, Germany

Barry A. Edelstein, West Virginia University

Louisa Egan, Yale University

Howard Eichenbaum, Boston University

Steven M. Elias, New Mexico State University

David Elkind, Tufts University

Brigitte Elle, Roskilde University, Roskilde, Denmark

Robert W. Elliott, Aerospace Health Institute, Los Angeles, CA

Roger E. Enfield , West Central Georgia Regional Hospital, Columbus, GA

Jan B. Engelmann, Emory University School of Medicine

Alyssa M. Epstein, University of California, Los Angeles

Jane Epstein, Weill College of Medicine at Cornell University

Franz Etping, University of Florida

Sean Esbjorn-Hargens, John F. Kennedy University, Pleasant Hill, CA

Chris Evans, Nottingham University, United Kingdom

David R. Evans, University of Western Ontario, Canada

Sara W. Feldstein Ewing, University of New Mexico

Carol Falender, University of California, Los Angeles

Jeanne M. Fama, Harvard University Medical School

Qijuan Fang, University of Hawaii at Manoa

Richard F. Farmer, Oregon Research Institute

Jaelyn, R. Farris, University of Notre Dame

Greg A. Febbraro, Counseling for Growth and Change, L.C., Windsor Heights, IA

Laurie Beth Feldman, University at Albany, SUNY

Eva Dreikers Ferguson, Southern Illinois University Edwardsville

Shantel Fernandez, Medical University of South Carolina

Joseph R. Ferarri, Drake University

F. Richard Ferraro, University of North Dakota

Seymour Feshbach, University of California, Los Angeles

Chelsea E. Fiduccia, University of North Texas

Dustin Fife, University of Oklahoma

Ione Fine, University of Washington

Stephen Finn, Center for Therapeutic Assessment, Austin, TX

Michael B. First, Columbia University

Constance T. Fischer, Duquesne University

Kurt W. Fischer, Harvard University

Kelly S. Flanagan, Wheaton College

Debra A. Fleischman, Rush University Medical Center, Chicago

Gordon L. Flett, York University, Canada

Peter Fonagy, University College London, United Kingdom

Rex Forehand, University of Vermont

Joseph P. Forgas, University of New South Wales, Australia

Blaine J. Fowers, University of Miami

Carol A. Fowler, University of Connecticut

Marcel G. Fox, Beck Institute for Cognitive Therapy and Research, Bala Cynwynd, PA

Lisa A. Fraleigh, University of Connecticut School of Medicine

Norah Frederickson, University College London, United Kingdom

Carolyn R. Freeman, McGill University, Canada

Fred Friedberg, Stony Brook University

Harris Friedman, University of Florida

Regan E. Friend, University of Kentucky

W. Otto Friesen, University of Virginia

Irene Hanson Frieze, University of Pittsburgh

Rober H. Friis, California State University Long Beach

Patrick C. Friman, Boys Town, NE

Randy O. Frost, Smith College

Daniel Fulford, University of Miami

K. W. M. Fulford, University of Warwick Medical School and St. Cross College, Oxford, United Kingdom

Wyndol Furman, University of Denver

Karina Royer Gagnier, York University, Toronto, Canada

Rodolfo Galindo, University of California, Merced

David A. Gallo, University of Chicago

Howard N. Garb, Lackland Air Force Base, Texas

Steven J. Garlow, Emory University School of Medicine

Gareth Gaskell, University of York, York, United Kingdom

Marisa Gauger, University of Nevada, Las Vegas

Kurt F. Geisinger, University of Nebraska-Lincoln

Pamela A. Geller, Drexel University

Charles J. Gelso, University of Maryland, College Park

Carol George, Mills College

Mark S. George, Medical University of South Carolina

Melissa R. George, University of Notre Dame

Kenneth J. Gergen, Swarthmore College

Andrew R. Getzfeld, New Jersey City University

Mary Beth Connolly Gibbons, University of Pennsylvania

Uwe Gielen, St. Francis College, Brooklyn, NY

Howard Giles, University of California, Santa Barbara

Charles F. Gillespie, Emory University School of Medicine

Marika Ginsburg-Block, University of Delaware

Richard G. T. Gipps, University of Warwick Medical School, United Kingdom

Todd A. Girard, Ryerson University, Toronto, Canada

James T. Gire, Virginia Military Institute

Thomas A. Glass, Honolulu, Hawaii

David Gleaves, University of Canterbury, New Zealand

Peter Glick, Lawrence University, Appleton, WI

Laraine Masters Glidden, St. Mary's College of Maryland

Lisa Hagen Glynn, University of New Mexico

Juan Carlos Godoy, National University of Córdoba, Córdoba, Argentina

Maurice Godwin, St. Augustine's College, Raleigh, NC

Hillel Goelman, University of British Columbia, Canada

Jerry Gold, Adelphi University

Peter B. Goldblum, Pacific Graduate School of Psychology

Charles Golden, Nova Southeastern University

Marvin R. Goldfried, Stony Brook University

Tina M. Goldstein, University of Pittsburgh

Robert L. Goldstone, Indiana University

Reginald Golledge, University of California Santa Barbara

Juliya Golubovich, Michigan State University

Emily E. Good, Pennsylvania State University

Jeffrey L. Goodi, Uniformed Service of the Health Sciences

Madeline S. Goodkind, University of California, Berkeley

Gail S. Goodman, University of California, Davis

Amanda Gordon, Sydney, Australia

Robert M. Gordon, Allentown, PA

Bernard S. Gorman, Nassau Community College, SUNY and Hofstra University

William Graebner, State University of New York, Fredonia

James W. Grau, Texas A & M University

Melanie Greenaway, Emory University College of Medicine

Lauren M. Greenberg, Drexel University

Martin S. Greenberg, University of Pittsburgh

William A. Greene, Eastern Washington University, Spokane

Shelly F. Greenfield, Harvard Medical School and McLean Hospital

Gregoire, Jacques Gregoire, Catholic University of Louvain, Belgium

Robert Gregory, SUNY Upstate Medical University

Robert J. Gregory, Wheaton College, IL

Bruce Greyson, University of Virginia Health System

Tiffany M. Griffin, University of Michigan

Vladas Griskevicius, University of Minnesota

Robert J. Grissom, San Francisco State University

Marc Grosjean, Leibniz Research Centre for Working Environment and Human Factors, Dortmund, Germany

James J. Gross, Stanford University

Gary Groth Marnat, Pacifica Graduate Institute, Carpinteria, CA

Corey L. Guenther, Ohio University

Bernard Guerin, University of South Australia, Australia

R. E. Gutierrez, Drake University

Russell Haber, University of South Carolina

Michael N. Haderlie, University of Nevada Las Vegas

William K. Hahn, University of Tennessee, Knoxville

William E. Haley, University of Wisconsin-Milwaukee

Judy E. Hall, National Register of Health Service Providers in Psychology

Mark B. Hamner, Medical University of South Carolina

Gregory R. Hancock, University of Maryland, College Park

Leonard Handler, University of Tennessee

Jo-Ida Hansen, University of Minnesota

Rochelle F. Hanson, Medical University of South Carolina

Lisa A. Harlow, University of Rhode Island

Robert J. Harnish, Pennsylvania State University at New Kensington

Robert G. Harper, Baylor College of Medicine

Anton H. Hart, William Alanson White Institute

Stephen D. Hart, Simon Fraser University, Canada

Chrisopher B. Harte, University of Texas at Austin

Glenn Hartelius, California Institute of Integral Studies

Abby B. Harvey, Temple University

Allison Harvey, University of California, Berkeley

Philip Harvey, Emory University School of Medicine

Nadia T. Hasan, University of Akron

David B. Hatfield, Developmental Behavioral Health, Colorado Springs, CO

Elaine Hatfield. University of Hawaii

Louise Hawkley, University of Chicago

Steven C. Hayes, University of Nevada

N. A. Haynie, Honolulu, HI

Alice F. Healy, University of Colorado

Bridget A. Hearon, Boston University

Pamela Heaton, University of London, United Kingdom

Monica Hedges, University of Southern California

Elaine M. Heiby, University of Hawaii at Manoa

Kathleen M. Heide, University of South Florida

Nicole Heilbrun, University of North Carolina at Chapel Hill

Deborah Heiser, State Society on Aging of New York

Janet E. Helms, Boston College

Lynne Henderson, Shyness Institute, Palo Alto, CA

Scott W. Henggeler, Family Service Research Center, Charleston, SC

James M. Hepburn, Waynesburg University

Gregory M. Herek, University of California, Davis

Hubert J. M. Hermans, Radboud University, Nijmegen, The Netherlands

Adriana Hermida, Emory University School of Medicine

Laura Hernandez-Guzman, National Autonomous University of Mexico

Edwin L. Herr, Pennsylvania State University

M. Sandy Hershcovis, University of Manitoba, Canada

Allen K. Hess, Auburn University at Montgomery

Herbert Heuer, University of Dortmund, Germany

Paul L. Hewitt, University of British Columbia, Canada

Richard E. Heyman, Stony Brook University

Ernest R. Hilgard, Stanford University

Thomas T. Hills, Indiana University

Stephen P.Hinshaw, University of California, Berkeley

Stephen C. Hirtle, University of Pittsburgh

Christine Hitchcock, University of British Columbia, Canada

Kristin Hitchcock, Northwestern University

Julian Hochberg, Columbia University

Ralph Hoffman, Yale University

Thomas P. Hogan, University of Scranton

Ronald R. Holden, Queens University, Canada

Lori L. Holt, Carnegie Mellon University

Ryan Holt, California State University at San Bernardino

Phan Y. Hong, University of Wisconsin Oshkosh

Audrey Honig, Los Angeles Count Sheriff's Department

Burt Hopkins, Seattle University

Adam O. Horvath, Simon Fraser University, Canada

Arthur C. Houts, University of Memphis

Robert H. Howland, University of Pittsburgh School of Medicine

Wayne D. Hoyer, University of Texas, Austin

Jeanette Hsu, Veterans Affairs Palo Alto Health System

Charles H. Huber, New Mexico State University

Samuel Hubley, University of Colorado, Boulder

Daniel A. Hughes, Lebanon, PA

Bradley E. Huitema, Western Michigan University

Olivia Y. Hung, Emory University School of Medicine

Scott J. Hunter, University of Chicago

Steven K. Huprich, Eastern Michigan University

Jena Huston, Argosy University, Phoenix, AZ

Kent Hutchison, University of New Mexico

Pamela Hyde, New Zealand Psychological Society, New Zealand

William G. Iacono, University of Minnesota

James R. Iberg, The Focusing Institute, Chicago, IL

Kaori Idemaru, University of Oregon

Stephen S. Ilardi, University of Kansas

Aubrey Immelman, St. John's University, MN

Mary Helen Immordino-Yang, University of Southern California

Rick Ingram, University of Kansas

Kathleen C. Insell, University of Arizona

Thomas R. Insel, National Institute of Mental Health

David Irwin, Drexel University College of Medicine

James S. Jackson, University of Michigan

Russell E. Jackson, California State University at San Marcos

Safia C. Jackson, University of Washington

Frederick M. Jacobsen, Transcultural Mental Health Institute, Washington, DC

Jacob Jacoby, New York University

Jack James, National University of Ireland, Galway, Ireland

Leonard A. Jason, DePaul University

Sharon Rae Jenkins, University of North Texas

Arthur R. Jensen, University of California, Berkeley

David W. Johnson, University of Minnesota

Deborah F. Johnson, University of Southern Maine

James H. Johnson, University of Florida

Kathryn Johnson, Arizona State University

Roger T. Johnson, University of Minnesota

Sheri L. Johnson, University of Miami

Susan K. Johnson, University of North Carolina-Charlotte

Keith S. Jones, Texas Tech University

Staci Jordan, University of Denver

Anthony S. Joyce, University of Alberta, Canada

Julia I. Juechter, Georgia State University

Barbara J. Juhasz, Wesleyan University

Robert M. Julien, Oregon Health Sciences University

James W. Kalat, North Carolina State University

Thomas Kalpakoglou, Institute of Behaviour Research and Therapy, Athens, Greece

Randy W. Kamphaus, Georgia State University

Jan H. Kamphuis, University of Amsterdam, The Netherlands

Anil Kanjee, Human Sciences Research Council, South Africa

Frank R. Kardes, University of Cincinnati

Georgia Karutzos, RTI International, Triangle Research Park, NC

Nadine J. Kaslow, Emory University

Marina Katz, San Diego, CA

Alan S. Kaufman, Yale University School of Medicine

James C. Kaufman, California State University at San Bernardino

Margaret M. Keane, Wellesley College

Terence M. Keane, Boston University School of Medicine

Christopher A. Kearney, University of Nevada, Las Vegas

Pamela K. Keel, University of Iowa

Michael Keesler, Drexel University and Villanova University School of Law

W. Gregory Keilin, University of Texas at Austin

Ken Kelley, University of Notre Dame

Francis D. Kelly, Greenfield, MA

Joan B. Kelly, Corte Madera, CA

Mary E. Kelley, Emory University

John A. Kenard, Temple University

Carrie Hill Kennedy, Kennedy Naval Aerospace Medical Institute, Pensacola, FL

Ray D. Kent, University of Wisconsin

Roy M. Kern, Vytautus Magnus University, Lithuania

Roy P. C. Kessels, Radboud Unversity Nijmegen, The Netherlands

Ronald C. Kessler, Harvard Medical School

Corey L. M. Keyes, Emory University

Kathryn Kidd, Colorado State University

John F. Kihlstrom, University of California, Berkeley

Bruce A. Kimball, USDA/APHIS/NWRC and Monell Chemical Senses Center, Philadelphia, PA

Gregory A. Kimble, Duke University

Douglas Kimmel, City College, City University of New York

Bruce M. King, Clemson University

Cheryl A. King, University of Michigan

D. Brett King, University of Colorado at Boulder

Roger E. Kirk, Baylor University

Ryo Kitado, Queens University, CA

Karen Strom Kitchener, University of Denver

Elena Klaw, San Jose State University

Daniel L. Klein, Stony Brook University

Dena A. Klein, Albert Einstein College of Medicine

Peggy J. Kleinplatz, University of Ottawa, Canada

E. David Klonsky, Stony Brook University

Tracy A. Knight, Western Illinois University

Kenneth A. Kobak, MedAvante Research Institute, Hamilton, NJ

Carolynn S. Kohn, University of the Pacific

George F. Koob, Scripps Research Institute, La Jolla, CA

Sander L. Koole, VU University, Amsterdam, The Netherlands

Mary P.Koss, University of Arizona

Beth A. Kotchick, Loyola College in Maryland

Chrystyna D. Kouros, University of Notre Dame

Margaret Bull Kovera, John Jay College, City University of New York

Robin M. Kowalski, Clemson University

Eileen M. Kranz, Brandeis University

Alan Kraut, Association for Psychological Science

Dennis L. Krebs, Simon Fraser University, Canada

Tina Kretschmer, University of Sussex, United Kingdom

Ann M. Kring, University of California, Berkeley

Stanley Krippner, Saybrook Graduate School, San Francisco, CA

Radhika Krishnamurthy, Florida Institute of Technology

Joachim I. Krueger, Brown University

Robert F. Krueger, Washington University at St. Louis

Romana C. Krycak, University of Missouri-Kansas City

Kathryn Kuehnle, University of South Florida

G. Tarcan Kumkale, Koc University, Istanbul, Turkey

Robert G. Kunzendorf, University of Massachusetts-Lowell

Jung Kwak, University of Wisconsin-Milwaukee

Virginia S. Y. Kwan, Princeton University

Margie E. Lachman, Brandeis University

Michael Lambert, Brigham Young University

Dominque Lamy, Tel Aviv University, Israel

Frank J. Landy, Baruch College, City University of New York

Brittany Lannert, Michigan State University

Molly Larsen, Emory University

Randy J. Larsen, Washington University

Daniel K. Lapsley, University of Notre Dame

Leah Lavelle, University of Chicago

Michael Lavin, Washington, DC

Patrick F. Lavin, Chattanooga, TN

Foluso M. Williams Lawal-Solarin, Emory University

Jay Lebow, Northwestern University

Susan J. Lederman, Queen's University, Kingston, Canada

Courtland C. Lee, University of Maryland at College Park

Erica D. Marshall Lee, Emory University

Sandra R. Leiblum, Robert Wood Johnson Medical School, University of Medicine and Dentistry New Jersey

Martin Leichtman, Leawood, KS

Jacqueline P. Leighton, University of Alberta, Canada

Michael P. Leiter, Acadia University, Nova Scotia, Canada

Larry M. Leitner, Miami University

Alison P. Lenton, University of Edinburgh, Scotland, United Kingodm

Frederick T. L. Leong, Michigan State University

Richard M. Lerner, Tufts University

David Lester, Richard Stockton College, Pamona, NJ

Richard Lettieri, New Center for Psychoanalysis, Los Angeles, CA

L. Stan Leung, University of Western Ontario, Canada

Ronald F. Levant, University of Akron

Allan Levey, Emory University College of Medicine

Karen Z. H. Li, Concordia University, Montreal

Norman P. Li, University of Texas at Austin

Shu-Chen Li, Max Planck Institute for Human Development, Berlin, Germany

Ting-Kai Li, National Institute on Alcohol Abuse and Alcoholism, NIH, Bethesda MD

Peter A. Lichtenberg, Wayne University

Scott O. Lillienfeld, Emory University

Geoff Lindsay, University of Warwick, Coventry, United Kingdom

Roderick C. Lindsay, Queens University, Ontario Canada

Marsha M. Linehan, University of Washington

Carol F. Lippa, Drexel University College of Medicine

Mark D. Litt, University of Connecticut

Roderick J. Little, University of Michigan

John E. Lochman, University of Alabama

John C. Loehlin, University of Texas at Austin

Jeffrey M. Lohr, University of Arkansas

Richard G. Lomax, Ohio State University

Jeffrey D. Long, University of Minnesota

Julie R. Lonoff, Miami University

David Loomis, California State University at San Bernardino

Christopher M. Lootens, University of North Carolina at Greensboro

Jeffrey P. Lorberbaum, Medical University of South Carolina

William R. Lovallo, VA Medical Center and University of Oklahoma Health Sciences Center

Tamara Penix Loverich, Eastern Michigan University

Kristen Lowell, University of North Dakota

Rodney L. Lowman, Lake Superior State University

Sara E. Lowmaster, Texas A&M University

James K. Luiselli, May Institute, Randolph MA

Katarina Lukatela, Brown University Medical School

Ralph W. Lundin, Wheaton, IL

Robert W. Lundin, The University of the South

Desiree Q. Luong, San Jose State University

Steven Jay Lynn, Binghamton University

Shelley M. MacDermind, Purdue University

William M. Mace, Trinity College, Hartford CT

Armando Machado, University of Minho, Portugal

Maya Machunsky, University of Marburg, Germany

Colin M. MacLeod, University of Waterloo, Canada

Joshua W. Madsen, VA San Diego Healthcare System

Jeffrey J. Magnavita, University of Hartford

Brittain L. Mahaffey, University of North Carolina at Chapel Hill

Robert Malgady, Touro College, New York, NY

Jill Malik, Stony Brook University

Thomas E. Malloy, Rhode Island College

Tina Malti, University of Zurich, Switzerland

Valerie Malzer, University of Chicago

Rachel Manber, Stanford University School of Medicine

Jon K. Maner, Florida State University

Jamal K. Mansour, Queens University, Ontario Canada

Amy Jo Marcano-Reik, University of Iowa

Stephanie C. Marcello, University Medicine and Dentistry of New Jersey

Stephen Maren, University of Michigan

Richard S. Marken, University of California at Los Angeles

G. Alan Marlatt, University of Washington

Ronald R. Martin, University of Regina, Canada

Steve Martino, Yale University School of Medicine

Ana P. G. Martins, Purdue University

Melvin H. Marx, N. Hutchinson Island, FL

Joseph D. Matarazzo, Oregon Health Science University

Kenneth B. Matheny, Georgia State University

Nancy Mather, University of Arizona

David Matteo, Drexel University

Brian P. Max, Boston University School of Medicine

Molly Maxfield, University of Colorado at Colorado Springs

Ryan K. May, Marietta College

Richard E. Mayer, University of California, Santa Barbara

Dan Mayton, Lewis-Clark State College

Randi E. McCabe, McMaster University, Hamilton, Ontario, Canada

Robert McCaffrey, State University of New York at Albany

Barry McCarthy, American University

Elizabeth McCauley, University of Washington and Seattle Children's Hospital

Brook McClintic, University of Colorado at Boulder

Allyn McConkey-Russell, Duke University Medical Center

Bridget L. McConnell, State University of New York at Binghamton

Christine McCormick, University of Massachusetts-Amherst

Barbara S. McCrady, University of New Mexico

Robert R. McCrae, National Institute on Aging

James P. McCullough, Jr., Virginia Commonwealth University

Janet L. McDonald, Louisiana State University

Kate L. McDonald, University of Arizona

William M. McDonald, Emory University School of Medicine

Lata M. McGinn, Albert Einstein College of Medicine, Yeshiva University

Eleanor McGlinchey, University of California, Berkeley

F. Dudley McGlynn, Auburn University

Robert E. McGrath, Fairleigh Dickinson University

Ian McGregor, York University, Toronto, Canada

Laura Gale McKee, University of Vermont

John Paul McKinney, Michigan State University

Kathleen McKinney, University of Wyoming

Patrick E. McNight, George Mason University

Kaitlyn McLachlan, Simon Fraser University, Canada

Richard J. McNally, Harvard University

Neil McNaughton, University of Otago, Dunedin, New Zealand

Kateri McRae, Stanford University

Paul W. McReynolds, University of Nevada, Reno

Stephanie K. Meador, Developmental Behavioral Health, Colorado Springs, CO

Heide Meeke, Pacific University

J. Reid Meloy, University of California, San Diego

Ronald Melzack, McGill University, Canada

Dana Menard, University of Ottawa, Canada

Tamar Mendelson, Johns Hopkins Bloomberg School of Public Health

Jorge Mendoza, University of Oklahoma

Douglas S. Mennin, Yale University

Andrew J. Menzel, Florida State University

Jessie Menzel, University of South Florida

Peter F. Merenda, University of Rhode Island

Stanley B. Messer, Rutgers University

Cindy M. Meston, University of Texas at Austin

Lotte Meteyard, University College London, United Kingdom

Alicia E. Meuret, Southern Methodist University

Andrew H. Meyers, University of Memphis

Kristina D. Micheva, Stanford University School of Medicine

Jesse B. Milby, University of Alabama at Birmingham

Alec L. Miller, Albert Einstein College of Medicine

Andrew H. Miller, Emory University School of Medicine

Carlin J. Miller, University of Windsor, Canada

Catherine Miller, Pacific University

Gloria Miller, University of Denver

Joshua D. Miller, University of Georgia

Mark W. Miller, Boston University School of Medicine

Ralph I. Miller, State University of New York at Binghamton

Cindy Miller-Perrin, Pepperdine University

Glenn W. Milligan, The Ohio State University

Theodore Millon, Institute for Advanced Studies in Personology and Psychopathology, Port Jervis, NY

Jon Mills, International Federation for Psychoanalytic Education

Michael Mingroni, Newark, DE

Hamid Mirsalimi, Argosy University, Atlanta

Victor Molinari, University of South Florida

Ivan Molton, University of Washington

Alexandra Monesson, University of Massachusetts, Amherst

Myriam Mongrain, York University, Toronto, Canada

Timothy E. Moore, York University, Toronto, Canada

Nilly Mor, Hebrew University of Jerusalem, Israel

Marlene M. Moretti, Simon Fraser University, Canada

Leslie C. Morey, Texas A&M University

George A. Morgan, Colorado State University

Robert D. Morgan, Texas Tech University

Charles M. Morin, Laval University, Canada

John W. Morin, Center for Offender Rehabilitation and Education, Fort Lauderdale, FL

Daniel G. Morrow, University of Illinois at Urbana-Champaign

Ezequiel Morsella, San Francisco State University and University of California, San Francisco

Susan M. Mosher, Boston University School of Medicine and Department of Veterans Affairs Healthcare System, Boston Campus

Christohper J. Mruk, Bowling Green State University

Paul M. Muchinsky, University of North Carolina at Greensboro

Kim T. Mueser, Dartmouth Medical School

Michael J. Mullard, Pacifica Graduate Institute, Carpinteria, CA

Ricardo F. Munoz, University of California, San Francisco

Anjana Muralidharan, Emory University

Nancy L. Murdock, University of Missouri-Kansas City

Kevin R. Murphy, Pennsylvania State University

Frank B. Murray, University of Delaware

Lisa M. Nackers, University of Florida

Raymond Nairn, New Zealand Psychological Society, New Zealand

James S. Nairne, Purdue University

Julius Najab, George Mason University

Urs M. Nater, University of Zurich, Switzerland

Francis A. Nealon, Rice Diet Program, Durham, NC

Becca Neel, Arizona State University

Sonya Negriff, Cincinnati Children's Hospital Medical Center

Robert A. Neimeyer, University of Memphis

Rosemery O. Nelson-Gray, University of North Carolina at Greensboro

Cory F. Newman, University of Pennsylvania School of Medicine

Thomas C. Neylan, University of California, San Francisco

Arthur M. Nezu, Drexel University

Christine Maguth Nezu, Drexel University

Michael E. R. Nicholls, University of Melbourne, Australia

Pekka Niemi, University of Turku, Finland

Gil G. Noam, Harvard University and McLean Hospital

Pedro J. Nobre, University of Tras-os-Montes e Alto, Douro, Portugal

Samuel S. Norberg, Pennsylvania State University

Jacob N. Norris, Texas Christian University

Brian A. Nosek, University of Virginia

Raymond W. Novaco, University of California, Irvine

Jack Novick, Michigan Psychoanalytic Institute

Kerry Kelly Novick, Michigan Psychoanalytic Institute

David Nussbaum, University of Toronto Scarborough, Canada

Amy K. Nuthall, University of Colorado at Boulder

Michael S. Nystul, New Mexico State University

William H. O'Brien, Bowling Green State University

Lynn E. O'Connor, Wright Institute and University of California, Berkeley

William T. O'Donohue, University of Nevada, Reno

Daniel O'Leary, Stony Brook University

Thomas Oakland, University of Florida

Carmen Oemig, Bowling Green State University

Christin, M. Ogle, University of California, Davis

Sumie Okazaki, University of Illinois at Urbana-Champaign

Piotr Oles, John Paul II Catholic University of Lublin, Lublin, Poland

Kristina R. Olson, Yale University

Eyitayo Onifade, Michigan State University

Jeanne Ellis Ormrod, University of Northern Colorado and University of New Hampshire

Pamela Orpinas, University of Georgia

Ingrid Osbuth, Simon Fraser University, Canada

Marlene, Boston University School of Medicine and Department of Veterans Affairs Healthcare System, Boston Campus

Frank Oswald, University of Heidelberg, Germany

Michael W. Otto, Boston University

Randy K. Otto, University of South Florida

Willis F. Overton, Temple University

Timothy J. Ozechowski, Oregon Research Institute

Steven R. Pacynski, SRCD Research Associate

David C. Palmer, Smith Colleege

Edward L. Palmer, Davidson College

Josefa N. S. Pandeirada, University of Santiago, Portugal

Joyce S. Pang, Nonyang Technological University, Singapore

Mauricio R. Papine, Texas Christian University

Kenneth I. Pargament, Bowling Green State University

Bernadette Park, University of Colorado

Martin Parker, Northwestern University

Fayth Parks, Georgia Southern University

Christopher J. Patrick, University of Minnesota

Diane T. V. Pawluk, Virginia Commonwealth University

Joshua W. Payen, University of North Texas

Joseph J. Pear, University of Manitoba, Canada

Mary Jo Peebles, Bethesda, MD

Daniel Perlman, University of North Carolina Greensboro

Michael G. Perri, University of Florida

Melissa Peskin, University of Pennsylvania

Christopher Peterson, University of Michigan

Jean Sunde Peterson, Purdue University

John Petrila, University of South Florida

Charles S. Peyser, University of the South.

Bruce E. Pfeiffer, University of New Hampshire

Daniel Philip, University of North Florida

Sheridan Phillips, University of Maryland School of Medicine

John Piacentini, University of California, Los Angeles

Jennifer R. Piazza, University of California, Irvine

Wade E. Pickren, Ryerson University, Toronto, Canada

Ralph L. Piedmont, Loyola College in Maryland

Alison Pike, University of Sussex, United Kingdom

Aaron L. Pincus, Pennsylvania State University

Nancy A. Piotrowski, Capella University

William Piper, University of British Columbia, Canada

Thomas G. Plante, Santa Clara University and Stanford University School of Medicine

Ingrid Plath, German Institute for International Educational Research, Frankfort, Germany

John Porcerelli, Wayne State University School of Medicine

Amir Poreh, Cleveland State University

Nicole Porter, DePaul University

Bruno Poucet, Universite de Provence, Marseille, France

Daniel J. Povinelli, University of Louisiana

Michael J. Power, University of Edinburgh, Scotland, United Kingdom

Judith Preissle, University of Georgia

Jose M. Preito, University of Madrid, Spain

George P. Prigatano, St. Joseph's Hospital and Medical Center, Phoenix, AZ

Mitchell J. Prinstein, University of North Carolina at Chapel Hill

Jerilynn C. Prior, University of British Columbia, Canada

Robert W. Proctor, Purdue University

Dennis Proffitt, University of Virginia

Jean Proulx, University of Montreal

Aina Puce, West Virginia University School of Medicine

Tom Pyszczynski, University of Colorado at Colorado Springs

Sara Honn Qualls, University of Colorado at Colorado Springs

Naomi L. Quenk, Analytical Psychology, Ltd., Albuquerque, NM

James Campbell Quick, University of Texas at Arlington

Mark Quigg, University of Virginia

Karen S. Quigley, Department of Veterans Affairs New Jersey Healthcare System, East Orange, NJ and New Jersey Medical School, University of Medicine and Dentistry of New Jersey

Christine A. Rabinek, University of Michigan

Nosheen K. Rahman, Punjab University, Lahore, Pakistan

Joseph S. Raiker, University of Central Florida

Adrian Raine, University of Pennsylvania

Charles Raison, Emory University School of Medicine

Leo Rangell, University of California, Los Angeles

Mark D. Rapport, University of Central Florida

Richard L. Rapson, University of Hawaii

June Rathbone, University College London, England

William J. Ray, Pennsylvania State University

Tenko Raykov, Michigan State University

Keith Rayner, University of California, San Diego

Robert J. Reese, University of Kentucky

William C. Reeves, Centers for Disease Control and Prevention, Atlanta, GA

Lynn P. Rehm, University of Houston

Holly A. Reich, Wheaton College

Tara C. Reich, University of Manitoba, Canada

Charles S. Reichardt, University of Denver

Scott, A. Reid, University of California, Santa Barbara

Jost Reinecke, University of Bielefeld, Germany

Harry T. Reis, University of Rochester

Sally M. Reis, University of Connecticut

Joseph Renzulli, University of Connecticut

Gilbert Reyes, Fielding Graduate University, Santa Barbara, CA

Cecil R. Reynolds, Texas A&M University

William M. Reynolds, Humboldt State University, Arcata, CA

Soo Hyun Rhee, University of Colorado-Boulder

George R. Rhodes, Ola Hou Clinic, Aiea, HI

David C. S. Richard, Rollins College

Jodie Richardson, McGill University

Margaret W. Riddle, University of Denver

Cedar Riener, University of Virginia

Christopher L. Ringwalt, Pacific Institute for Research and Evaluation, Chapel Hill, NC

Evan F. Risko, University of British Columbia, Canada

Lorie A. Ritschel, Emory University School of Medicine

Rostyslaw W. Robak, Pace University

Gary J. Robertson, Tampa, FL

Richard W., University of California, Davis

George H. Robinson, University of North Alabama

Jennifer L. Robinson, University of Texas Health Sciences Center at San Antonio

Kathryn A. Roecklin, University of Vermont

Karin Roelofs, Leiden University, The Netherlands

Lizabeth Roemer, University of Massachusetts, Boston

Ronald Roesch, Simon Fraser University, Canada

Roger Roffman, University of Washington

Richard Rogers, University of North Texas

Kelly J. Rohan, University of Vermont

Michael J. Rohrbaugh, University of Arizona

George Ronan, Central Michigan University

Elsa Ronningstam, Harvard University Medical School

Steven P. Roose, New York State Psychiatric Institute, Columbia University

Robert Rosenthal, University of California, Riverside, and Harvard University

Alan M. Rosenwasser, University of Maine

David H. Rosmarin, Bowling Green State University

William H. Ross, University of Wisconsin at La Crosse

Joseph S. Rossi, University of Rhode Island

Barbara Olasov Rothbaum Emory University School of Medicine

Donald K. Routh, Florida Gulf Coast University

Linda Rubin, Texas Women's University

Jerry W. Rudy, University of Colorado, Boulder

Michael G. Rumsey, U.S. Army Research Institute for the Behavioral and Social Sciences, Arlington, VA

Sandra W. Russ, Case Western Reserve University

Alexandra Rutherford, York University, Canada

Bret R. Rutherford, New York State Psychiatric Institute, Columbia University

Richard M. Ryan, University of Rochester

Jeremy Safran, New School for Social Research

Donald H. Saklofske, University of Calgary, Canada

Morgan T. Sammons, National Register of Health Service Providers in Psychology

Trond Sand, University of Science and Technology and Trondheim University Hospital, Norway

William C. Sanderson, Hofstra University

Jerome Sanes, Alpert Medical School of Brown University

Craig Santerre, VA Puget Sound Health Care System, Seattle Division

Craig Santree, VA Puget Sound Health Care System, Seattle Division

Edward P. Sarafino, College of New Jersey

David B. Sarwer, University of Pennsylvania School of Medicine

William I. Sauser, Jr., Auburn University

Lisa M. Savage, State University of New York at Binghamton

Victoria Savalei, University of California, Los Angeles

Mark L. Savickas, Northeastern Ohio Universities College of Medicine

Douglas J. Scaturo, State University of New York Upstate Medical University and Syracuse VA Medical Center

E. Warner Schaie, Pennsylvania State University

Marcia J., Scherer, University of Rochester Medical Center

Dawn M. Schiehser, Veterans Administration San Diego Healthcare System and University of California, San Diego

Elizabeth A. Schilling, University of Connecticut Health Center

Lindsay J. Schipper, University of Kentucky

Kelly Schloredt, University of Washington and Seattle Children's Hospital

Karen B. Schmaling, University of North Carolina at Charlotte

Frank L. Schmidt, University of Iowa

Klaus Schmidtke, University Hospital Freiburg, Germany

Neal Schmitt, Michigan State University

Kirk J. Schneider, Center for Existential Therapy, San Francisco, CA

Michael E. Schoeny, Institute for Juvenile Research and University of Illinois at Chicago

Joseph E. Schumacher, University of Alabama School of Medicine

Julie A. Schumacher, University of Mississippi Medical Center

Dale H. Schunk, University of North Carolina at Greensboro

Alexander J. Schut, Pennsylvania State University

Alan Schwartz, University of Illinois at Chicago

Eliezer Schwartz, Argosy University Chicago

Jonathan P. Schwartz, University of Houston

Marlene B. Schwartz, Yale University

Stephanie Schwartz, Association for Behavioral and Cognitive Therapies, New York, NY

Julie B. Schweitzer, University of California Davis School of Medicine

Lisa S. Scott, University of Massachusetts, Amherst

Gretchen B. Sechrist, University at Buffalo, State University of New York

Daniel L. Segal, University of Colorado at Colorado Springs

Lauren S. Seifert, Malone College

Stephen Seligman, University of California, San Francisco

Edward P. Serafino, College of New Jersey

Ilene A. Serlin, San Francisco, CA

Michael C. Seto, Center for Addiction and Mental Health and University of Toronto, Canada

William R. Shadish, University of California, Merced

Anne Shaffer, University of Minnesota

David L. Shapiro, Nova Southeastern University

Deane H. Shapiro, University of California School of Medicine, Irvine

Francine Shapiro, Mental Research Institute, Palo Alto, CA

Johanna Shapiro, University of California School of Medicine, Irvine

Josh D. Shapiro, University of California, San Diego

Kenneth J. Shapiro, Animals and Society Institute, Washington Grove, MD

Shauna L. Shapiro, Santa Clara University

Brian A. Sharpless, University of Pennsylvania

Richard J. Shavelson, Stanford University

Erin S. Sheets, Brown University Medical School and Butler Hospital

Anees A. Sheikh. Marquette University

Kenneth J. Sher, University of Missouri

Lonnie R. Sherrod, Fordham University

Alissa Sherry, University of Texas at Austin

Stephanie A. Shields, Pennsylvania State University

Robert Shilkret, Mount Holyoke College

Merton A. Shill, University of Michigan

Varda Shoham, University of Arizona

Lauren B. Shumaker, University of Denver

Kristin Shutts, Harvard University

Jerome Siegel, University of California, Los Angeles

Judith P. Siegel, Silver School of Social Work at New York University

David Silbersweig, Weill College of Medicine at Cornell University

Francisco J. Silva, University of Redlands

Doris K. Silverman, New York, NY

Wendy K. Silverman, Florida International University

Louise Silvern, University of Colorado at Boulder

Marshall L. Silverstein, Long Island University

Steven M. Silverstein, University Medicine and Dentistry of New Jersey

Amy M. Smith Slep, Stony Brook University

Frank L. Small, University of Washington

Colin Tucker Smith, University of Virginia

Gregory T. Smith, University of Kentucky

J. Allegra Smith, University of Colorado

Jeffrey K. Smith, University of Otago, New Zealand

Lisa F. Smith, University of Otago, New Zealand

Nathan Grant Smith, McGill University, Canada

Richard H. Smith, University of Kentucky

Ronald E. Smith, University of Washington

Myriam J. Sollman, University of Kentucky

Roger M. Solomon, Buffalo Center for Trauma and Loss, Buffalo, NY

Subhash R. Sonnad, Western Michigan University

Peter W. Sorenson, University of Minnesota

Elizabeth Soucar, Penndel Mental Health Center, Penndel, CA

Susan C. South, Purdue University

Marion Spengler, Saarland University, Saarbrucken, Germany

Dante Spetter, Tufts University

Eric P. Spiegel, James A. Haley VAMC, Tampa, FL

Charles D. Spielberger, University of South Florida

Robert Spies, Buros Institute of Mental Measurements

Frank M. Spinath, Saarland University, Saarbrucken, Germany

Philip Spinhoven, Leiden University, The Netherlands

Bonnie Spring, Northwestern University

Jayne E. Stake, University of Missouri—St. Louis

Jayne M. Standley, Florida State University

Ursula J. Staudinger, Jacobs University, Bremen, Germany

Jeffrey T. Steedle, Council for Aid to Education, New York, NY

Timothy A. Steenburgh, Indiana Wesleyan University

Rebecca Y. Steer, Emory University

Dana Steidtmann, University of Kansas

Axel Steiger, Max Planck Institute of Psychiatry, Munich, Germany

Howard Steiger, McGill University

Emily Stein, Weill College of Medicine at Cornell University

Jennifer Steinberg, Cognitive and Behavioral Consultants of Westchester, White Plains, NY

Melissa K. Stern, University of Florida

Robert M. Stern, Pennsylvania State University

Michael J. Stevens, Illinois State University

Paul Stey, University of Notre Dame

Timothy R. Stickle, University of Vermont

John M. Stokes, Pace University

Stephen Strack, U.S. Department of Veterans Affairs, Los Angeles, CA

David L. Streiner, University of Toronto, Canada

George Stricker, Argosy University Washington

Natalie Stroupe, University of Kansas

Margaret L. Stubbs, Chatham University, Pittsburgh, PA

Sally J. Styles, Yale University

Peter Suedfeld, University of British Columbia, Canada

Alan Sugarman, University of California, San Diego

Jeff Sugarman, Simon Fraser University, Canada

Jennifer A. Sullivan, Duke University Medical Center

Norman D. Sundberg, University of Oregon

Elizabeth Susman, Pennsylvania State University

Lisa A. Suzuki, New York University

Harvey A. Swadlow, Brown University Medical School

Robert A. Sweet, University of Pittsburgh and VA Pittsburgh Healthcare System

Derek D. Szafranski, University of the Pacific

Brian J. Taber, Oakland University

Raymond Chip Tafrate, Central Connecticut State University

Harold Takooshian, Fordham University

Rebecca L. Tamas, University of Louisville School of Medicine

Junko Tanaka-Matsumi, Kansei Gakuin University, Japan

Sombat Tapanya, Chiang Mai University, Thailand

Steven Taylor, University of British Columbia

Richard G. Tedeschi, University of North Carolina Charlotte

Hedwig Teglasi, University of Maryland

Howard Tennen, University of Connecticut

Lois E. Tetrick, George Mason University

Timothy J. Teyler, Washington State University

Michael E. Thase, University of Pennsylvania School of Medicine

Ryan Thibodeau, St. John Fisher College, Rochester, NY

Jay C. Thomas, Pacific University

J. Kevin Thompson, University of South Florida

Scott M. Thompson, University of Maryland

Travis Thompson, University of Minnesota School of Medicine

B. Michael Thorne, Mississippi State University

Shira Tibon, Bar-Ilan University and Academic College of Tel-Aviv, Yaffo, Israel

Jane G. Tillman, The Austen Riggs Center, Stockbridge, MA

Michael Tobia, Temple University

James Toch, State University of New York at Albany

Patrick H. Tolan, Institute for Juvenile Research and University of Illinois at Chicago

David F. Tolin, Institute of Living, Hartford, CT and Yale University School of Medicine

Jessica L. Tracy, University of British Columbia, Canada

Daniel Tranel, University of Iowa College of Medicine

Michael Treanor, University of Massachusetts, Boston

Warren W. Tryon, Fordham University

Ivy F. Tso, University of Michigan

William T. Tsushima, Straub Clinic and Hospital, Honolulu, HI

Larissa Tsvetkova, St. Petersburg State University, St. Petersburg, Russia

Jane Tucker, New York University

Denis C. Turk, University of Washington

Dio Turner II, University of Nevada, Las Vegas

Rachael Unger, Towson University

Annmarie Urso, State University of New York College at Geneseo

Uma Vaidyanathan, University of Minnesota

Mary M. Valmas, Boston University School of Medicine and Department of Veterans Affairs Healthcare System, Boston Campus

Henk T. van der Molen, Erasmus University Rotterdam, The Netherlands

Judy L. Van Raalte, Springfield College

Rodney D. Vanderploeg, James A. Haley VAMC, Tampa, FL and University of South Florida

Susan M. VanScoyoc, University of Phoenix

Myrna V. Vashcenko, Tufts University

Ruut Veenhoven, Erasmus University Rotterdam, The Netherlands

Beth A. Venzke, Concordia University-Chicago

Mieke Verfaellie, Boston University School of Medicine and VA Boston Healthcare System

Philip E. Vernon, University of Calgary, Canada

Ian Verstegen, Philadelphia, PA

Ryan P. Vetreno, State University of New York at Binghamton

Donald J. Viglione, Alliant International University, San Diego, CA

Penny S. Visser, University of Chicago

Jennifer E. Vitale, Hampden-Sydney College, Hampden-Sydney, VA

Ladislav Volicer, University of South Florida

Nora D. Volkow, National Institute on Drug Abuse

Jennifer Vonk, University of Louisiana

Kim-Phuong, L. Vu, California State University, Long Beach

Paul L. Wachtel, City College and CUNY Graduate Center

Nicholas J. Wade, University of Dundee, Scotland, United Kingdom

Harriet Wadeson, University of Illinois at Chicago

Hans-Werner Wahl, University of Heidelberg, Germany

Howard Wainer, National Board of Medical Examiners

Deward E. Walker, Jr., University of Colorado at Boulder

Elaine F. Walker, Emory University

Stephanie Wallio, VA Connecticut Health Care System and University of Kansas

Roger Walsh, University of California College of Medicine, Irvine

Michael R. Walther, University of Wisconsin-Milwaukee

Alvin Wang, University of Central Florida

Philip S. Wang, National Institute of Mental Health Care Policy

William H. Watson, University of Rochester School of Medicine and Dentistry

Adam Waytz, University of Chicago

Stanley Wearden, West Virginia University

Danny Wedding, University of Missouri-Columbia School of Medicine

Bernard Weiner, University of California, Los Angeles

Karen Colby Weiner, Southfield, Michigan

Irving B. Weiner, University of South Florida

Daniel Weisholtz, Weill College of Medicine at Cornell University

Daniel J. West, Pennsylvania State University

Myrna M. Weissman, College of Physicians and Surgeons and Mailman School of Public Health, Columbia University

Julie C. Weitlauf, Veterans Affairs Palo Alto Health Care System and Stanford University School of Medicine

Barbara J. Wendling, University of Arizona

Kathryn R. Wentzel, University of Maryland, College Park

Michael Wertheimer, University of Colorado at Boulder

Donald Wertlieb, Tufts University

Hans Westmeyer, Free University of Berlin, Germany

Michael G. Wheaton, University of North Carolina at Chapel Hill

Mark E. Wheeler, University of Pittsburgh

Mark A. Whisman, University of Colorado at Boulder

Stephen G. White, University of California, San Francisco

Thomas W. White, Training and Counseling Services, Shawnee Mission, KS

Thomas A. Widiger, University of Kentucky

Donald E. Wiger, Elmo, MN

Allan Wigfield, University of Maryland

Ken Wilber, Integral Institute, Boulder, CO

Sabine Wilhelm, Harvard University Medical School

Douglas A. Williams, University of Winnipeg

Paul Williams, Queens University Belfast, Northern Ireland

Rebecca B. Williamson, The Hague, The Netherlands

Hillary D. Wilson, University of Washington

Janelle Wilson, University of Minnesota Duluth

Michael Windle, Emory University

Idee Winfield, College of Charleston

David L. Wolitzky, New York University

Nina Wong, University of Central Florida

Margaret T. T. Wong-Riley, Medical College of Wisconsin

Diana S. Woodruff-Pak, Temple University

Douglas W. Woods, University of Wisconsin-Milwaukee

Robert F. Woolfolk, Rutgers University

J. Brooke Wright, Wheaton College

Jesse H. Wright, University of Louisville School of Medicine

Li-Tzy-Wu, Duke University Medical Center

Robert E. Wubbolding, Center for Reality Therapy, Cincinnati, OH

Yufang Yang, Chinese Academy of Sciences, Beijing, China

William A. Yost, Arizona State University

Larry J. Young, Emory University School of Medicine

Adam Zagelbaum, Sonoma State University

Patricia A. Zapf, John Jay College of Criminal Justice, City University of New York

Tamika C. H. Zapolski, University of Kentucky

Charles H. Zeanah, Tulane University School of Medicine

Moshe Zeidner, University of Haifa, Israel

Elias A. Zerhouni, National Institutes of Health

Eric A. Zillmer, Drexel University

Philip Zimbardo, Stanford University

Grégoire Zimmerman, University of University of Lausanne, Switzerland

Marvin Zuckerman, University of Delaware

Ofer Zur, Zur Institute, Sonoma, CA

M

MAGNETIC RESONANCE IMAGING

Magnetic resonance imaging (MRI) is a method that provides information on both the anatomy and physiological function of the brain. It is a powerful tool for integrating our current understanding of brain function with models of cognition and emotion. Anatomical MRI provides a picture of brain structure, whereas functional MRI (fMRI) provides information about the physiological function of the brain.

The physics of MRI relies on three magnetic fields. A constant magnetic field, known as the static field, aligns all magnetically sensitive particles uniformly so that perturbations to this static field can be detected. In clinical machines, this magnetic field is generally 1.5 Tesla (T) and 3, 4, or 7 Tesla in "high-field" research machines (as reference, the magnetic field of the earth is 0.0001 T). The perturbation is delivered by a second magnetic field, known as the pulse sequence, which is an oscillating electromagnetic field "tuned" to a set frequency (resonant frequency) of a particular substance, typically hydrogen atoms. The relaxation time, the time it takes for the protons to revert to their original state after this perturbation, is recorded through a radio frequency coil, also known as a receiver coil. Because hydrogen atoms in different substances have different relaxation times, distinct tissues, such as white matter and grey matter, can be differentiated. Information on where in the brain those substances are residing comes from another magnetic field, the gradient field, which varies in intensity over the area being imaged.

Structural MRI is used to examine the anatomy of the brain. For example, it is used to detect regions of decreased tissue volume, such as occurs after brain injury, and it can show changes in white matter, such as increases in myelination during childhood. Recently developed diffusion tensor MRI (DT-MRI) provides information about the structural integrity of nerve fibers as well as patterns of anatomical connectivity. This method works by detecting differences in the degree to which water diffuses along each of the three axes of nerve fibers. The axis along which water diffusion is greatest indicates the main directional orientation of white matter tracts, while the degree of diffusion can provide information on the structural integrity of those tracts. Since white matter tracts connect distant brain regions, this method can be utilized to detect disorders that arise from a partial or complete disconnection between brain regions.

Functional MRI (fMRI) detects local changes in other physiological functions, such as cerebral blood flow and blood oxygenation. The most commonly used fMRI method, known as BOLD (Blood Oxygen Level Dependent), takes advantage of the fact that oxygenated blood and deoxygenated blood have different magnetic properties. Deoxygenated blood disrupts the ability to pick up the magnetic signal from iron contained in hemoglobin of the blood to a greater degree than oxygenated blood. When neurons in a brain region are active, the circulatory system delivers oxygen-rich blood, in fact more than can be extracted by the local tissue. As a result, the relative proportion of deoxygenated blood in that particular region drops, leading to an increased signal from which a measure of brain activation can be derived. This change in signal is a hemodynamic response that peaks approximately 6–8 seconds after neuronal activity starts. As a result, the temporal resolution of fMRI is generally on the order of a couple of seconds, which is sluggish compared to the time scale of neuronal activity.

Because the BOLD method relies on detecting a change in the signal, fMRI typically requires that two conditions be compared: the condition of interest and a baseline condition. The selection of the baseline is critical for interpretation of the results. For example, comparing activity while viewing emotional faces to a baseline of viewing a rudimentary visual stimulus, such as a simple plus sign, will reveal all brain regions involved in processing the visual form, interpreting it as a face, and understanding its emotional significance. On the other hand, comparing activity during the viewing of emotional faces to a baseline of nonemotional faces will isolate those regions that specifically process the emotional information contained in faces.

The use of fMRI in psychological investigations has exploded over the past decade, for a variety of reasons. First and foremost, it allows researchers to identify, in the intact human brain, the entire set of brain regions required for a given cognitive or emotional function. Such information cannot be obtained from other methods linking brain and behavior, such as those that rely on the examination of disrupted behavior in patients with localized brain lesions. Second, fMRI is a noninvasive technique and does not involve high-energy ionizing radiation, as do other brain-imaging methods such as positron emission tomography (PET). As such, multiple scans can be run on a single individual, allowing clinicians and scientists to examine changes in the brain over time, such as those that occur as a result of practice or treatment regimens. Third, fMRI provides excellent spatial resolution relative to other brain imaging methods, allowing the detection of brain activity with an anatomical resolution of 3–5 millimeters. Fourth, the machines and the pulse sequences required to examine brain activation are widely available.

fMRI has provided important information in a number of different arenas. It has revealed the organization of neural tissue for sensory and motor functioning in humans in exquisite detail, building upon and amplifying knowledge that previously was only available through research using monkey physiology. It has provided insights into a whole host of cognitive and emotional processes including attention, memory, language, and spatial processing, as well as moral reasoning, decision making, and the suppression of emotional memories (e.g., Depue, Curran, & Banich, 2007). It has helped to link changes in mental functioning across the lifespan with changes in brain structure and functioning during development (e.g., Giedd, 2008) and as one ages (e.g., Reuter-Lorenz, 2002). Furthermore, it has elucidated the alterations in the functioning of brain systems associated with psychiatric disorders ranging from depression to schizophrenia to post-traumatic stress disorder (Malhi & Lagopoulos, 2007).

The prominence of fMRI in cognitive neuroscience and clinical research has led to much discussion of the method, both within the scientific community and in the popular press. Claims that this method can be used to "read" the mind have been overblown, but ethical issues, such as those regarding personal privacy of inner thought, are worth consideration (see Racine, Bar-Ilan, & Illes, 2005 for a discussion).

The influence of MR technologies in clinical, cognitive, psychological and neuroscientific endeavors shows no sign of abating. Recent technical advances allow imaging of humans at 4 and 7 Tesla, leading to even greater increases in the spatial resolution. New computational and mathematical approaches are extending the method in important ways as well, such as enabling real-time fMRI. Because of the voluminous amount of data acquired, fMRI data analysis is quite time-consuming and occurs after data acquisition. For example, a typical imaging session may involve obtaining data for 30 slices of brain tissue, each providing a 64-by-64 grid of signal intensities, every 2 seconds over the course of 20 minutes.

New methods are allowing these data to be analyzed as they are being collected, so that a participant can "see" activity in specific brain regions and use that information, for example, as a biofeedback signal to control brain activity (DeCharms, 2007). Other methods are being developed that allow the pattern of brain activity to predict an individual's behavior (Spiers & Maguire, 2007). For example, patterns of brain activity are used to predict

when, as an individual travels through a virtual world while lying in the scanner, he or she is looking at the surroundings as compared to navigating through them. These approaches contrast with more standard approaches in which the experimenter controls what the participant is doing during an epoch (e.g., viewing emotional faces vs. non-emotional faces) and then determines which brain regions are differently active during each epoch.

Another recent emphasis in MR imaging has been to examine not simply which brain regions become active during a given task, but also to reveal the functional relationship between them, determining which regions co-activate or appear to influence one another (Rogers et al., 2007). These functional approaches have been combined with evidence drawn from MR-DTI that provides information on the white-matter tract connections between regions. Moreover, fMRI data have been used in conjunction with electrophysiological techniques that provide millisecond-by-millisecond records of brain activity, so that both the location and timing of brain activation can be observed. Finally, in part as a result of the human genome project, fMRI data are also now being combined with data on an individual's genetic make-up to understand variation in brain responses during cognitive and emotional processing (e.g., Hariri & Weinberger, 2003).

In sum, magnetic resonance imaging has had a profound impact on our ability to link specific neural systems to particular cognitive and emotional states, and it has provided new insights into differences among individuals, whether related to their age, genetic make-up, personality, or psychiatric status.

REFERENCES

DeCharms, C. (2007). Reading and controlling human brain activation using real-time functional magnetic resonance imaging. *Trends in Cognitive Sciences, 11*, 473–481.

Depue, B. E., Curran, T., & Banich, M. T. (2007). Prefrontal regions orchestrate suppression of emotional memories via a two-phase process. *Science, 317*, 215–219.

Giedd, J. N. (2008). The teen brain: Insights from neuroimaging. *The Journal of Adolescent Health, 42*, 335–343.

Hariri, A. R., & Weinberger, D. R. (2003). Imaging genomics. *British Medical Bulletin, 65*, 259–270.

Malhi, G. S., & Lagopoulos, J. (2007). Making sense of neuroimaging in psychiatry. *Acta psychiatrica Scandinavica, 117*, 100–117.

Racine, E., Bar-Ilan, O, & Illes, J. (2005). fMRI in the public eye. *Nature Reviews Neuroscience, 6*, 159–164.

Reuter-Lorenz, P. (2002). New visions of the aging mind & brain. *Trends in Cognitive Sciences, 6*, 394–400.

Rogers, B. P., Morgan, V. L., Newton, A. T., & Gore, J. C. (2007). Assessing functional connectivity in the human brain by fMRI. *Magnetic Resonance Imaging, 25*, 1347–1357.

Spiers, H. J., & Maguire, E. (2007). Decoding human brain activity during real-world experiences. *Trends in Cognitive Sciences, 11,* 356–365.

SUGGESTED READINGS

Assaf, Y., & Pasternake, O. (2008). Diffusion tensor imaging (DTI)-based white matter mapping in brain research: A review. *Journal of Molecular Neuroscience, 34,* 51–61.

Bandettini, P. (2007). fMRI today. *International Journal of Psychophysiology, 63,* 138–145.

Mathews, P. M., Honey, G. D., & Bullmore, E. T. (2006). Applications of fMRI in translational medicine and clinical practice. *Nature Reviews Neuroscience, 7,* 732–744.

MARIE T. BANICH
University of Colorado at Boulder

See also: **Cognitive Neuroscience; Neuroimaging**

MAINSTREAMING

Mainstreaming dates back to the very beginnings of the field of special education. As the term implies, mainstreaming means educating students with disabilities alongside students without disabilities in a general education classroom for at least some portion of a school day. Mainstreaming came into widespread use in the late 1960s as professionals and parents called into question the segregation of students with disabilities in U.S. public schools. Professionals argued that special classes for students, particularly those with mental retardation, could not be justified (Dunn, 1968). The purpose of mainstreaming was to ensure that students with disabilities receive individualized planning and support from both general and special education teachers. However, this did not always happen in actual practice. In fact, the term mainstreaming fell from favor when it became associated with placing students with disabilities in general education classes without the necessary support as a means to save money or limit the number of students who could receive specialized services. Such practices gave rise to the term *maindumping.* Although the term *mainstreaming* still remains in limited use today as one way to describe educating students with disabilities in general education settings, other descriptors have come into standard use, including *integration, least restrictive environment,* and *inclusive education.*

With the passage of the federal Education of All Handicapped Children Act in 1975, now the Individuals with Disabilities Education Act (IDEA), the term *least restrictive environment* (LRE) became commonly used in the United States. LRE describes a process by which students with disabilities are placed in educational settings consistent with their individual educational needs. As defined in IDEA, the intent of LRE is to educate students with disabilities with their typical peers to the maximum extent appropriate. A student is removed from the general education setting only when the nature and severity of the disability are such that education in general education classes with supplementary aids or services cannot be achieved satisfactorily. Although the concept of LRE suggests a strong preference for students with disabilities to be educated alongside their typical peers, it also states that this should occur only when appropriate. As such, LRE and mainstreaming are not synonymous. A student's LRE may be any one of a "continuum of placements," ranging from the general education classroom to separate educational environments provided exclusively for students with disabilities. Public schools are required to provide such a continuum for students who cannot be satisfactorily educated in general education classes. Whenever possible, however, students should be educated within or close to the school they would attend if not disabled

As is true with mainstreaming, the concept of LRE has been criticized in recent years (Hardman, Drew, & Egan, 2008). The concern is that, despite LRE's strong preference that students are to be educated with peers who are without disabilities, it also has legitimized and supported the need for more restrictive, segregated settings. Additionally, LRE has created the perception that students with disabilities must "go to" services, rather than having services "come to" them. In other words, as students move farther from the general education class, the resources required to meet their needs increase concomitantly.

Whereas LRE is most often associated with special education in the United States, *integration* is the term that has most often been used to describe programs and services in several other countries throughout the world. For example, Italy mandates by law the integration of students with disabilities into general education classes. Australia may be described as moving toward full integration of these students, while to a lesser extent France, England, and Germany all have major initiatives promoting the integration of students with disabilities in general education settings.

In the United States, the term *integration* is most closely associated with social policy to end separate education for ethnic minority children, specifically students of color. In the landmark *Brown vs. Topeka, Kansas, Board of Education* in 1954, the U.S. Supreme Court ruled that education must be made available to everyone on an equal basis. Separate education for African-American students was ruled as inherently unequal to the education of white students. The increasing use of the term *integration* by many professionals and parents to describe the value of educating students with disabilities alongside their typical peers coincided with the U.S. civil rights movement for people with disabilities of the 1980s, a movement that culminated in the passage of the Americans with Disabilities Act (ADA) in 1990. In fact, ADA moved away from the concept of the least restrictive environment as defined in IDEA, mandating that people with disabilities be placed in integrated settings appropriate to their individual needs.

In today's schools, the most widely used term consistent with the original intent of mainstreaming is *inclusive education*. At its most fundamental level, inclusive education promotes the value of students with disabilities attending the same school they would attend were they not disabled. This value promotes acceptance and belonging, focusing on services and supports coming to students within the natural setting of the general education school and classroom rather than students with disabilities going to services in a segregated environment. In inclusive classrooms, the intent is for every student to be actively involved, socially accepted, and motivated to learn to the best of their ability. To achieve this goal, some professionals have argued the need for specific changes in the educational system (Landers & Weaver, 1997). These include providing inclusive services and supports in a neighborhood school. In a neighborhood school, the proportion of students needing special education is relatively uniform for all schools within a particular area or district. This ratio reflects the proportion of people with disabilities in society at large. Students with disabilities receive the support they need to succeed, and are not segregated into special classes within the school.

Inclusive education may also be defined by the level of participation and support the student receives in the educational setting. Two terms are used to describe this level of participation: *full inclusion* and *partial inclusion*. Full inclusion is an approach whereby students with disabilities receive all instruction in a general education classroom setting; support services come to the student or are "pushed in." Partial inclusion involves students with disabilities receiving most of their instruction in general education settings, but they are "pulled out," or go to another instructional setting when this is appropriate to serve their individual needs.

The success of both full and partial inclusion programs depends on the availability of both formal and natural supports in the general education classroom. Formal supports are those provided by, and funded through, the public school system. These include qualified teachers, paraprofessionals, appropriate curriculum materials, and assistive technology aids. Natural supports in an educational setting most often consist of the student's family and classmates. Natural supports emphasize the relationships among children as friends and learning partners.

REFERENCES

Dunn, M. L. (1968). Special education for the mildly retarded. Is much of it justified? *Exceptional Children, 35,* 229–237.

Hardman, M. L., Drew, C. J., & Egan, N. W. (2008). *Human exceptionality: School, community, and family* (9th ed.). Boston: Houghton Mifflin.

Landers, M. F., & Weaver, M. F. (1997). *Inclusive education: A process not a placement.* Swampscott, MA: Watersun.

MICHAEL L. HARDMAN
SHIRLEY A. DAWSON
University of Utah

See also: Educational Mainstreaming

MAJOR DEPRESSIVE DISORDER

Major depressive disorder (MDD) is characterized by depressed mood or a lack of interest or pleasure in once-enjoyable activities, and associated symptoms (e.g., sleep disturbance; appetite/weight disturbance; difficulty concentrating; feelings of worthlessness or exaggerated guilt). To receive a diagnosis of MDD, at least five symptoms must be present most of the day, nearly every day, for at least two weeks (American Psychiatric Association [APA], 2000).

The lifetime prevalence of MDD (estimated at 16.6%) is higher than that of any other major psychiatric disorder and the 12-month prevalence rate is estimated to be nearly 7% (Kessler et al., 2005; Kessler, Chiu, Demler, & Walters, 2005). Evidence suggests that the prevalence of MDD has been increasing in recent birth cohorts (Lewinsohn, Rohde, Seeley, & Fischer, 1993), whereas the age at first onset has been decreasing (Klerman & Weissman, 1989). Indeed, approximately 20% of college-age young adults have previously experienced an episode of MDD (Lewinsohn, Hops, Roberts, Seeley, & Andrews, 1993). Although episodes of MDD appear to be self-limiting, the disorder is typically episodic, with high rates of relapse/recurrence of the disorder.

Remission and Recovery

Initial research used various definitions of "remission" and "recovery" from MDD. Guidelines were later adopted (Frank et al., 1991) which have increased consistency across studies. Remission was defined as a period during which full criteria for MDD are no longer met, but there are still some significant symptoms (i.e., partial remission), or during which the individual experiences no more than minimal (e.g., two or fewer) symptoms for a specified period of time (i.e., full remission). Recovery is considered to have occurred when full remission persists; researchers generally have adopted either two or six months as the time period to define full recovery.

An episode of major depression appears to be self-limiting, in that most cases remit in approximately six to eight months, even if untreated. Recovery rates appear to be similar across children and adult samples. For example, Kessler and Walters (1998) found that, in a community sample of adolescents and young adults, the average length of the longest episode an individual had suffered was 32.5 weeks. Within one year of onset of a major depressive episode, 78% of adults will have recovered (Keller, Lavori, Rice, Coryell, & Hirschfeld, 1986). Despite the high rate of spontaneous remission of MDD, it must be noted that six to eight months is the average length of episode; therefore, a number of individuals experience significantly longer episodes of depression. The longer an individual suffers from an episode of MDD, the lower the probability of recovery from that episode. The long-term prognosis for individuals who recover more quickly from MDD is also discouraging in that a large proportion will go on to suffer a relapse or recurrence of the disorder.

Relapse and Recurrence

Relapse is a return of depressive symptoms such that the individual once again meets full criteria for MDD during the period of remission, but before recovery. A recurrence, on the other hand, is a new episode of MDD with onset occurring after full recovery from the previous episode (Frank et al., 1991). Although these terms have been defined fairly consistently in research, initial investigations did not differentiate between relapse and recurrence; therefore, these terms will be used interchangeably here.

Research indicates that each new MDD episode increases the risk of suffering another episode in the future; additionally, there is evidence of increasing severity with each new MDD episode, as well as decreased well-time between episodes (Boland & Keller, 2002). Longitudinal research indicates that the risk for recurrence continues many years after episode recovery. Between 25% and 40% of individuals experience a new depressive episode within two years of recovery, approximately 60% have a recurrence within five years, and 85% experience a recurrence within fifteen years following recovery (Lavori, Keller, Mueller, & Scheftner, 1994; Mueller et al., 1999).

A broad body of research has examined risk factors for the onset of depression and recurrence of depression. Although some demographic variables are related to greater lifetime risk for depression, the variables of gender, socioeconomic status, and marital status do not predict MDD recurrence (Burcusa & Iacono, 2007). Clinical variables, including age of onset, comorbid psychopathology, poor social support, personality factors, stressful life, events and negative cognitions have been identified as other risk factors for recurrence.

Psychotherapy Treatment

Research on psychosocial treatments for depression indicates that acute treatment with psychotherapy (e.g., cognitive behavior therapy; interpersonal psychotherapy) provides greater prophylactics against relapse than does pharmacotherapy alone (e.g., Hollon et al., 2005; Klein et al., 1994), and that "maintenance" or "continuation" psychotherapy further protects patients against relapse (e.g., Jarrett et al., 2001). For those individuals who do not receive treatment for their depression, programs designed to be implemented after recovery, and to be independent of acute treatment, may reduce the risk of a future recurrence. Mindfulness-based cognitive therapy (MBCT; Teasdale et al., 2000) and an intervention integrating cognitive behavior therapy and interpersonal therapy (Craighead et al., 2008) have both demonstrated initial empirical support. Given the high cost of depression, and the increasing severity of the disorder with each new episode, additional research regarding the prevention of relapse and recurrence of MDD is clearly warranted.

REFERENCES

American Psychiatric Association. (2000). *Diagnostic and statistical manual of mental disorders* (4th ed., text rev.). Washington, DC: Author.

Boland, R. J., & Keller, M. B. (2002). Course and outcome of depression. In I. H. Gotlib & C. L. Hammen (Eds.), *Handbook of depression*. New York: Guilford Press.

Burcusa, S. L. & Iacono, W. G. (2007). Risk for recurrence in depression. *Clinical Psychology Review 27*, 959–985.

Craighead, W. E., Craighead, L. W., Brosse, A. L., Hauser, M., Madsen, J. W., & Sheets, E. S. (2008). *Prevention of recurrence of major depression among college students*. Manuscript under review.

Frank, E., Prien, R. F., Jarrett, R. B., Keller, M. B., Kupfer, D. J., Lavori, P. W., et al. (1991). Conceptualization and rationale for consensus definitions of terms in major depressive disorder. *Archives of General Psychiatry, 48*, 851–855.

Hollon, S. D., DeRubeis, R. J., Shelton, R. C., Amsterdam, J. D., Salomon, R. M., O'Reardon, J. P., et al. (2005). Prevention of relapse following cognitive therapy vs. medications in moderate to severe depression. *Archives of General Psychiatry, 62*, 417–422.

Jarrett, R. B., Kraft, D., Doyle, J., Foster, B. M., Eaves, G., & Silver, P. C. (2001). Preventing recurrent depression using cognitive therapy with and without a continuation phase. *Archives of General Psychiatry, 58*, 381–388.

Keller, M. B., Lavori, P. W., Rice, J., Coryell, W., & Hirschfeld, R. M. A. (1986). The persistent risk of chronicity in recurrent episodes of nonbipolar major depressive disorder: A prospective follow-up. *American Journal of Psychiatry, 143*, 24–28.

Kessler, R. C., Berglund, P., Demler, O., Jin, R., Merikangas, K. R., & Walters, E. E. (2005). Lifetime prevalence and age-of-onset distributions of DSM-IV disorders in the National Comorbidity Survey Replication. *Archives of General Psychiatry, 62*, 593–602.

Kessler, R. C., Chiu, W. T., Demler, O., & Walters, E. E. (2005). Prevalence, severity, and comorbidity of 12-month DSM-IV disorders in the National Comorbidity Survey Replication. *Archives of General Psychiatry, 62*, 617–627.

Kessler, R. C., & Walters, E. E. (1998). Epidemiology of DSM-III-R major depression and minor depression among adolescents and young adults in the national comorbidity survey. *Depression and Anxiety, 7*, 3–14.

Klein, D. N., Santiago, N. J., Vivian, D., Arnow, B., Blalock, J. A., Dunner, D. L., et al. (2004). Cognitive-behavioral analysis system of psychotherapy as a maintenance treatment for chronic depression. *Journal of Consulting and Clinical Psychology, 72*, 681–688.

Klerman, G. L., & Weissman, M. M. (1989). Increasing rates of depression. *Journal of the American Medical Association, 261*, 2229–2235.

Lavori, P. W., Keller, M. B., Mueller, T. I., & Scheftner, W. (1994). Recurrence after recovery in unipolar major depressive disorder: An observational follow-up study of clinical predictors and somatic treatment as a mediating factor. *International Journal of Methods in Psychiatric Research, 4*, 211–229.

Lewinsohn, P. M., Hops, H., Roberts, R. E., Seeley, J. R., & Andrews, J. A. (1993). Adolescent psychopathology: I. Prevalence and incidence of depression and other DSM-III-R disorders in high school students. *Journal of Abnormal Psychology, 103*, 133–144.

Lewinsohn, P. M., Rohde, P., Seeley, J. R., & Fischer, S. A. (1993). Age-cohort changes in the lifetime occurrence of depression and other mental disorders. *Journal of Abnormal Psychology, 102*, 110–120.

Mueller, T. I., Leon, A. C., Keller, M. B., Solomon, D. A., Endicott, J., Coryell, W., et al. (1999). Recurrence after recovery from major depressive disorder during 15 years of observational follow-up. *American Journal of Psychiatry, 156*, 1000–1006.

Teasdale, J. D., Segal, Z. C., Williams, J. M. G., Ridgeway, V. A., Soulsby, J. M., & Lau, M. A. (2000). Prevention of relapse/recurrence in major depression by mindfulness-based cognitive therapy. *Journal of Consulting and Clinical Psychology, 68*(4), 615–623.

SUGGESTED READINGS

Gotlib, I. H., & Hammen, C. L. (Eds.). (2002). *Handbook of depression.* New York: Guilford Press.

Segal, Z. V., Williams, J. M. G., & Teasdale, J. D. (2002). *Mindfulness-based cognitive therapy for depression: A new approach to preventing relapse.* New York: Guilford Press.

ERIN S. SHEETS
Brown University Medical School and Butler Hospital

ALISHA L. BROSSE
University of Colorado at Boulder

See also: **Antidepressant Medications; Depression; Depressive Personality Disorder**

MALINGERING

Evaluations of mental disorders rely extensively on the assumption of accurate symptom reporting. However, intentional distortions of symptoms by examinees are common during psychological evaluations. The assumption of genuine disclosures becomes particularly questionable in forensic contexts, given the far-reaching consequences of their legal outcomes. The base rates of malingering are substantial but highly variable in forensic evaluations (Rogers, 2008). In civil forensic contexts, base rates of one third are possible when malingering is broadened to include lesser cases of symptom exaggeration.

Terminology

Malingering, as defined by the current *Diagnostic and Statistical Manual of Mental Disorders* (DSM; American Psychiatric Association, 2000, p. 739), is "the intentional production of false or grossly exaggerated physical or psychological symptoms, motivated by external incentives." DSM's operationalization of malingering relies on two key components: (1) gross exaggeration or fabrication and (2) clearly defined motivation (not simply inferred) for external gain. Importantly, the feigned presentations of patients with factitious disorders parallel the first of these key components but differ from the second one, because of these patients' internal motivation to assume a sick role.

Distortions in the pathological direction have been described by a variety of different terms through the literature and should not be used interchangeably with the classification of malingering. Clinical descriptors such as exaggeration, overendorsement, fake-bad, and suboptimum performance typically characterize poorly defined conditions that do not meet the definition of malingering based on both severity of feigning (i.e., they lack the required gross exaggeration or fabrication) and established motivation (i.e., they lack clear evidence of external incentive).

Evaluation of Malingering

Feigning of all reported symptoms and psychological problems is comparatively rare. Most often, a malingerer's clinical presentation is a complex mixture of feigned, honest, and nondisclosed symptomatology. Of critical importance, malingering and genuine mental disorders are not mutually exclusive conditions. Simply put, malingering does not invalidate or rule out the concomitant presence of legitimate symptoms. As an example, a genuinely depressed patient may choose to fabricate symptoms of posttraumatic stress disorder (PTSD) in an effort to receive disability benefits. The result would be a diagnosis of major depressive disorder and the classification of malingering.

Malingerers can feign their clinical presentations in a variety of different ways. They can fabricate psychological symptoms (e.g., depression or psychosis), simulate nonexistent cognitive impairments (e.g., amnesia or mental retardation), or grossly exaggerate physical ailments (e.g., back pain). Additionally, malingerers can also deceive evaluators about the disabling nature of their symptoms. Therefore, clinicians must evaluate the genuineness of symptoms, the actual effects of these symptoms on functioning, and the underlying motivation for the clinical presentation.

Malingering is not a *DSM-IV* diagnosis but rather a V code, or a condition that may be a focus of clinical attention. Accordingly, no formal inclusion or exclusion criteria are provided for the classification of malingering. Instead, *DSM* provides a list of four common characteristics to raise the suspicion of potential malingering. Misuse of these screening items as formal criteria is an erroneous and substandard practice. When tested in forensic practice, they have resulted in devastating errors that have wrongly classified four out of five examinees as malingerers (Rogers, 1990).

Standardized Feigning Measures

Standardized measures do not evaluate malingering per se. Instead, they focus on feigning, previously described as component 1: the gross exaggeration or fabrication of psychological or physical symptoms. They cannot evaluate the complex nature of motivations (i.e., component 2). Therefore, any statement that a particular test indicates malingering raises questions about the examiner's competence.

During the last decade, large advances have been made in testing and validating which methods are effective for the identification of feigning. The state-of-the-art approach uses detection strategies that are characterized by Rogers (2008, p. 16) "as a standardized method, which is conceptually-based and empirically-validated, for systematically differentiating a specific response style (e.g., malingering or defensiveness) from other response styles (e.g., honest responding)." Different detection strategies are needed for each domain of feigning. For example, the detection of feigned mental retardation (Rogers & Bender, 2003) requires very different detection strategies than feigned PTSD (Resnick, West, & Payne, 2008).

Rogers (2008) recently provided a comprehensive review of detection strategies used to evaluate feigning of mental disorders, cognitive impairment, and medical complaints. With empirical support (see Rogers, Jackson, Sewell, & Salekin, 2005; Rogers, 2008), he conceptualized two general categories of detection strategies. Amplified strategies detect feigning based on degree or intensity. A feigner may report an unrealistic number of potentially genuine symptoms. This type of detection capitalizes on the sheer number of symptoms rather than questioning the plausibility of any individual symptom. In direct contrast, implausible strategies examine the likelihood that an individual symptom occurs in genuine patients. For example, certain reported "symptoms" are almost never observed in genuine presentations.

Detection strategies provide a conceptual framework and discriminant validity for psychological measures of malingering. For feigned mental disorders, clinicians should adopt, whenever feasible, a multimethod approach that combines self-administered multiscale inventories with a structured interview approach, such as the Structured Interview of Reported Symptoms. With dozens of validity and feigning scales, clinicians will need a solid foundation regarding their effectiveness and clinical applications. For comprehensive coverage, they are referred to *Clinical Assessment of Malingering and Deception* (Rogers, 2008).

Malingering Research

In evaluating the usefulness of detection strategies and feigning scales, clinicians must have a clear understanding of how feigning and other response styles are researched. Feigning research emphasizes either experimental rigor with excellent internal validity (i.e., simulation designs) or clinical relevance with excellent external validity (i.e., known group comparisons and bootstrapping designs). Of critical importance, clinicians must be able to explain to the court or other referral sources why a particular measure of feigning is valid and accurate for a specific domain (e.g., feigned mental disorders or feigned cognitive impairment).

Valid Research Designs for Feigning

Simulation designs with clinical groups. This analog design randomly assigns participants to experimental (feigning) or control (honest) groups. Either patients are used for random assignment, or a relevant clinical comparison sample is added.

Known-groups comparison. Using the best available methods, patients are independently identified as feigners or genuine responders. Results on psychological measures are compared for the two groups.

Bootstrapping design. When known-groups comparisons are not feasible, systematic decision rules can be applied, based on established cut scores, to determine likely groups of feigners and honest responders. Because of imprecision in cut scores, marginal cases (i.e., an indeterminate category) must be excluded.

Questionable Research Designs

Simulation designs without clinical groups. Without relevant clinical samples, we cannot determine whether evaluations are correctly identifying feigners or wrongly classifying genuine patients. Due to its unknown accuracy, this design should not be used.

Differential prevalence design. Because a greater proportion of forensic than nonforensic cases feign, some researchers assume all forensic referrals are feigners. Given that most research indicates that the large majority of forensic referrals do not feign, this design provides spurious results without any demonstrable accuracy. With spurious results and no known accuracy, it should not be used in research.

The assessment of malingering involves the careful evaluation of feigning via established feigning measures. In addition, extensive interviewing and use of collateral sources are necessary to establish the primary motivations for feigning in order to distinguish malingering from factitious presentations. Importantly, care must be taken not to accept past reports of malingering at face value; some careless clinicians confuse the possibility of malingering (e.g., a financial settlement) with the strong probability of malingering. Because of their consequential nature, determinations of malingering should be comprehensive, including multiple measures and a careful analysis of detection strategies relevant to the appropriate domain.

REFERENCES

American Psychiatric Association. (2000). *Diagnostic and statistical manual of mental disorders* (4th ed., text rev.). Washington, DC: Author.

Aribisi, P., & Ben-Porath, Y. S. (1995). An MMPI-2 infrequent response scale for use with psychopathological populations: The Infrequency-Psychopathology Scale, F(p). *Psychological Assessment*, 7(4), 424–431.

Lees-Haley, P. (1986). Personal injury malingering. *For the Defense*, 28–31.

Resnick, P. J., West, S., & Payne, J. W. (2008). Malingering of post-traumatic disorders. In R. Rogers (Ed.), *Clinical assessment of malingering and deception* (3rd ed., pp.109–127). New York: Guilford Press.

Rogers, R. (1990). Models of feigned mental illness. *Professional Psychology: Research and Practice*, 21(3), 182–188.

Rogers, R. (2008). Detection strategies for malingering and defensiveness. In R. Rogers (Ed.), *Clinical assessment of malingering and deception* (3rd ed., pp. 14–35). New York: Guilford Press.

Rogers, R., & Bender, S. D. (2003). Evaluation of malingering and deception. In A. M. Goldstein (Ed.), *Handbook of psychology: Forensic psychology* (Vol. 11, pp. 109–129). New York: John Wiley & Sons.

Rogers, R., Jackson, R. L., Sewell, K. W., & Salekin, K. L. (2005). Detection strategies for malingering: A confirmatory factor analysis of the SIRS. *Criminal Justice and Behavior*, 32, 511–525.

Rogers, R. Salekin, R., Sewell, K., Goldstein, A., & Leonard, K. (1998). A comparison of forensic and nonforensic malingerers: A prototypical analysis of explanatory models. *Law and Human Behavior*, 22(4), 353–367.

SUGGESTED READING

Rogers, R. (2008). *Clinical assessment of malingering and deception* (3rd ed.). New York: Guilford Press.

JOSHUA W. PAYNE
RICHARD ROGERS
University of North Texas

MANIA (See Bipolar Disorder)

MANIC-DEPRESSIVE DISORDER (See Bipolar Disorder)

MANN-WHITNEY U TEST

The Mann-Whitney U test, which is also known as the Wilcoxon rank sum test, tests for differences between two groups on a single, ordinal variable with no specific distribution (Mann & Whitney, 1947; Wilcoxon, 1945). In contrast, the independent samples t-test, which is also a test of two groups, requires the single variable to be measured at the interval or ratio level, rather than the ordinal level, and to be normally distributed. We accordingly refer to the Mann-Whitney U test as the nonparametric version of the parametric t-test. Both tests require two independently sampled groups and assess whether two groups differ on a single, continuous variable. The two tests, however, differ on the assumed distribution. A nonparametric test assumes no specific distribution, whereas a parametric test assumes a specific distribution. Thus, the Mann-Whitney U is conceptually similar to the t-test for determining whether two sampled groups are from a single population. When data do not meet the parametric assumptions of the t-test, the Mann-Whitney U tends to be more appropriate.

The Mann-Whitney U is intended to determine if two groups (e.g., samples "a" and "b") come from the same population (p), which is a null hypothesis significance test stipulating that both samples are subsets from the same population (i.e., H0: $(a, b) \subseteq p$). To test the null hypothesis, we first combine observations from two groups into a single group and rank the scores from 1 to N, where N is the total sample size ($n_a + n_b = N$). As in all ranking procedures, ties may be handled by either assigning a mean value, the first value, a random value, the maximum value, or the minimum value. The Mann-Whitney U test handles any form of ranking. After ranking, the procedure divides the rank scores by group and computes a sum score for each group (T_a and T_b). Equation 1 shows how both the summed ranked score groups (T_a and T_b) and the group sample sizes combine to calculate the U statistic.

$$\text{If } n_a > n_b : U = T_a - (n_a(n_a + 1))/2 \quad (1)$$
$$\text{If } n_b > n_a : U = T_b - (n_b(n_b + 1))/2$$

The U statistic has a discrete or uniform distribution that provides us with the ability to define a critical value, assign a probability to that value, and then test the null hypothesis. A critical value represents a probability level—typically .05—that helps us rule out chance differences. If the U statistic is greater than the critical value, then we reject the null with the inference that both samples do not come from the same population.

Consider a problem in which we compare rankings between 10 Eastern and 10 Western U.S. colleges. We want to know whether the two samples of twenty colleges come from a single population distribution ($N_{east} = 10$, $N_{west} = 10$). The rankings are as follows: Eastern colleges were ranked 55, 60, 63, 81, 91, 121, 123, 149, 182, and 201, and the Western colleges were ranked 3, 32, 46, 72, 97, 141, 184, 190, 230, and 234. A reranking of the colleges results in the following new sample ranks among the 20 colleges: Eastern colleges are now ranked 4, 5, 6, 8, 9, 11, 12, 14, 15, and 18, whereas the Western colleges are now ranked 1, 2, 3, 7, 10, 13, 16, 17, 19, 20. Using Equation 1, we find $U = 47$ ($p = .85$), and thus we conclude that the rank means do not differ and that the two samples come from the same population.

REFERENCES

Mann, H. B., & Whitney, D. R. (1947). On a test of whether one of two random variables is stochastically larger than the other. *Annals of Mathematical Statistics, 18,* 50–60.

Wilcoxon, F. (1945). Individual comparisons by ranking methods. *Biometrics Bulletin, 1,* 80–83.

SUGGESTED READINGS

Cohen, B. H. (2008). *Explaining psychological statistics* (3rd ed.). Hoboken, NJ: John Wiley & Sons.

Gibbons, J. D. (1993). *Nonparametric statistics: An introduction.* Newbury Park, CA: Sage.

Hollander, M., & Wolfe, D. A. (1999). *Nonparametric statistical methods* (2nd ed.). New York: John Wiley & Sons.

PATRICK E. MCKNIGHT
JULIUS NAJAB
George Mason University

See also: **Kruskal-Wallis Test; Nonparametric Statistical Tests**

MAO INHIBITORS (See Antidepressant Medications)

MARASMUS (See Failure to Thrive)

MARIJUANA (See Cannabis-Related Disorders)

MARITAL DISCORD

The large volume of research on marital discord and the related constructs of marital conflict and marital dissatisfaction attest to the perceived importance of understanding the problems that sometimes arise in marriage. Of the various terms used in this area of inquiry, "marital satisfaction" is the best defined, referring to an evaluation of the relationship or the partner. Because of their clarity and brevity, measures of marital satisfaction play a prominent role in all areas of marital research.

"Marital conflict" is a somewhat broader term than "marital satisfaction" and is used to refer to spousal perceptions, emotions, anticipations, and behavior in relation to some disagreement or area of differing interests. However, marital conflict is not inherently negative and may or may not be associated with marital dissatisfaction. In some cases marital conflict may set the stage for increases in relationship satisfaction, while in others it may be the harbinger of deterioration in the relationship. For this reason, the study of marital conflict is often considered distinct from the study of marital satisfaction, and researchers in this area place considerable importance on direct observation of marital interaction.

"Marital discord" is also a relatively broad term, referring to a state of marital dissatisfaction in conjunction with any of a number of problems that may beset couples and lead to long-standing marital conflict, loss of marital commitment, feelings of estrangement within marriage, or marital dissolution. Because the construct combines a variety of disparate features, measures of marital discord tend to be collections of heterogeneous items. The most comprehensive self-report instrument of marital discord is called the Marital Satisfaction Inventory. This inventory solves the problem of heterogeneous content by assessing each content area using a separate scale. Its primary disadvantage is its overall length of 150 items.

Maintaining the distinctions between different terms used in the area has become increasingly important as research in the area of marital discord has developed. Of particular importance is the distinction between marital satisfaction and marital conflict, as these two constructs may often diverge in their implications. On the other hand, measures of marital satisfaction and measures of marital discord are often highly correlated, and the two terms are sometimes used interchangeably.

Inquiry into the causes, consequences, and correlates of marital discord is driven, in part, by the perceived importance of better understanding the effect of marital discord on numerous processes related to personal and family adjustment. Supporting this perception, much recent research suggests that marital discord and the related constructs of marital dissatisfaction and marital conflict play an important role in individual and family well-being. For example, marital dissatisfaction commonly co-occurs with depression, eating disorders, and some types of alcoholism, as well as physical and psychological abuse of partners. In addition, marital discord and marital dissolution co-vary with problems of delinquency and may presage children's later problems with intimate communication. Recent research has also shown that marital discord predicts longitudinal changes in psychiatric symptomatology, including increased incidence of mood, anxiety, and substance-use disorders among the maritally discordant as well as poorer response to treatment for mood, anxiety, and substance use disorders.

Similarly, marital discord is associated with poorer health and with specific physical illnesses such as cancer, cardiac disease, and chronic pain. Marital interaction studies suggest possible mechanisms that may account for these links showing, for example, that hostile behaviors during conflict relate to alterations in immunological, endocrine, and cardiovascular functioning. Better understanding of marital discord therefore offers the potential for more effective treatment of certain types of individual psychopathology and family difficulty or else offers hope for better managing their sequelae. In addition, increased understanding of marital discord may also prove useful in developing better health maintenance strategies and in the management of chronic health problems.

Inquiry regarding marital discord is also fueled by the perceived importance of developing harmonious marital relationships as an end in itself. Better understanding of marital discord is sought as a way to provide guidance to those attempting to develop interventions to relieve marital discord or to those developing programs to prevent marital distress and divorce. That is, understanding marital discord is potentially important because enhancing marital satisfaction and alleviating marital discord is a desirable goal in its own right. In the past several years, these considerations have led to a substantial increase in attention at the federal and state level to the identification of community level programs that can strengthen marriage and marital relationships.

There has also been inquiry into the structure of marital discord. Recent results using statistical methods to examine patterns indicative of latent categories (i.e., taxa) suggests that there is an underlying categorical difference between discordant and nondiscordant couples. Recent results using the MSI confirmed prior work in finding that marital discord was taxonic, with about 30% of the general population falling into the discordant group.

As these considerations suggest, there is good reason for continuing research on the topic of marital therapy and the development of prevention programs designed to prevent decline in marital satisfaction and the development of marital discord. Because of the need to control for various extraneous effects, randomized clinical trials of various marital therapy programs have been conducted. The results of these trials indicate that substantial benefit may be obtained from several types of marital therapy, including behavioral marital therapy, emotion-focused marital therapy, insight-oriented marital therapy, and cognitive-behavioral marital therapy.

Similarly, promising results have been obtained for divorce prevention programs. However, because of the difficulty in conducting randomized clinical trials on preventative intervention, and the difficulty in reaching couples at greatest risk for developing marital discord and divorcing, many questions about the utility of preventative programs remain unanswered. Further, in early studies of treatment, fewer than half of discordant couples receiving marital therapy remained maritally satisfied at long-term follow-up. More recent outcome research appears to demonstrate somewhat better maintenance, but it is still relatively early in the follow-up process. Likewise, the majority of couples in need of prevention services do not seek them out. Accordingly, there is considerable room for progress in the development of marital interventions and divorce prevention programs.

SUGGESTED READINGS

Beach, S. R. H., Wamboldt, M., Kaslow, N., Heyman, R. E., First, M. B., Underwood, L. G., & Reiss, D. (2006). *Relational processes and DSM-V: Neuroscience, assessment, prevention & intervention.* Washington, DC: American Psychiatric Publishing.

Fincham, F. D., & Bradbury, T. N. (2005). Studying marriages longitudinally. In V. Bengtson et al. (Eds.) *Sourcebook of family theory and research* (pp. 274–276). Newbury Park, CA: Sage.

Fincham, F. D., & Grych, J. H. (2001). *Interparental conflict and child development: Theory, research, and applications.* New York: Cambridge University Press.

Gottman, J. M. (1999). *The marriage clinic.* New York: Norton.

Schmaling, K. B., & Sher, T. G. (2000). *The psychology of couples and illness: Theory, research, & practice.* Washington, DC: APA Press.

STEVEN R. H. BEACH
University of Georgia

See also: **Couples Therapy; Family Therapy; Marriage Counseling**

MARRIAGE COUNSELING

Problems in marriage and other close relationships are widespread. For example, the divorce rate in the United States is approximately 50%. Relationship problems are also among the most common reasons for people seeking mental health services. There is good evidence that marriage counseling is effective in treating relationship problems and a variety of emotional and behavioral disorders.

Treatment of Couple Discord

The most widely researched approach to marriage counseling is cognitive-behavioral couple therapy (CBCT; Epstein & Baucom, 2002). This approach focuses on making positive changes in each partner so that couples have more rewarding and less punishing interactions. The goals of CBCT are (1) to identify and increase the frequency of positive behaviors that each person does to make the partner happier ("caring behaviors"), (2) to teach verbal and nonverbal expressive and receptive communication skills to help couples improve their communication around sharing thoughts and feelings, (3) to teach conflict resolution and problem-solving skills, and (4) to educate partners in the use of various techniques that allow them to identify and modify their negative or maladaptive cognitions about their partner or the relationship.

Another approach to marriage counseling that has been widely studied is emotion-focused therapy (EFT; Johnson, 2004). This approach is based on adult attachment theory, and the model integrates techniques from the experiential and family systems approaches to primarily target attachment insecurity rather than couple discord per se. The goals of EFT are (1) to identify repetitive negative interaction cycles that are the manifestation of attachment insecurities; (2) to reframe these cycles in terms of the underlying attachment needs; and (3) to facilitate the expression and the acceptance of one another's attachment needs. When specific attachment injuries are identified, the therapist attempts to use emotional processing of these injuries to allow the injured partner to move toward a more secure bond.

The effectiveness of these two approaches to marriage counseling has been evaluated in several clinical trials. To summarize the results across studies, researchers have used meta-analysis, which is a summary of previous research that uses quantitative methods to compare outcomes across studies and provide a measure of the magnitude or degree of the impact of the intervention (i.e., an effect size). A meta-analysis of clinical trials comparing CBCT with waiting list control groups in treating couple discord yielded a mean effect size (d) of 0.95, which can be interpreted as indicating that the average couple who received CBCT was better off at the end of treatment than 83% of untreated couples. A meta-analysis of clinical trials comparing EFT with a waiting list control group indicated

that it also has a positive impact on couple discord, with a mean effect size of 1.27, which can be interpreted as indicating that the average couple who received EFT was better off at the end of treatment than 89% of untreated couples (Byrne, Carr, & Clark, 2004).

In addition to these two approaches to marriage counseling that have been evaluated in multiple clinical trials, there are several approaches that have demonstrated positive outcomes in treating couple discord in only one trial. For example, an insight-oriented approach to marriage counseling, which emphasized the interpretation and resolution of conflictual emotional processes related to developmental issues and maladaptive relationship patterns, demonstrated significant gains in couple discord compared to a wait-list control group. The most recently studied approach to marriage counseling is integrative behavioral couple therapy (IBCT), which combines traditional behavioral techniques for promoting change with strategies aimed at fostering emotional acceptance. Interventions aimed at increasing acceptance include encouraging empathic joining around or unified detachment from ongoing relationship problems, building tolerance to responses that problems elicit, and encouraging acceptance of differences. In the largest randomized clinical trial of couple therapy ever conducted, IBCT was compared with CBCT, and results indicated that, although the treatments demonstrated different patterns of change over the course of treatment, the two treatments were equally effective at the end of treatment (Christensen et al., 2004).

Treatment of Mental Health Problems

In addition to treating couple discord, marriage counseling has also been shown to be effective in the treatment of a variety of psychiatric disorders. Research has shown that relationship discord is higher among people with mental-health problems versus those without such problems (see Whisman, 2006). Mental-health problems may negatively affect a person's role functioning, resulting in greater discord in close relationships. Alternatively, relationship problems may act as social stressors, increasing the likelihood of mental health problems. Whether they are the cause or consequence of a disorder, relationship problems are likely to complicate the course of an emotional or behavioral problem, suggesting that marriage counseling, singly or in combination with other treatments, may be effective in the treatment of a range of disorders.

The co-occurrence of couple discord with psychiatric disorders has led to three couple-based treatment strategies for addressing these comorbid difficulties. The first uses marriage counseling to reduce overall couple discord based on the premise that such discord serves as a broad stressor that contributes to the development, exacerbation, or maintenance of mental-health problems. The second strategy involves developing disorder-specific couple interventions that focus on particular relationship processes presumed to directly influence either the co-occurring problems or their treatment. The third couple-based strategy involves partner-assisted interventions in which one partner serves as a "surrogate therapist" or coach in assisting the other partner with individual problems.

Research has documented the effectiveness of couple-based interventions for a broad range of mental-health problems, including alcohol and drug-use disorders, mood disorders, anxiety disorders, and physical aggression (see Snyder, Castellani, & Whisman, 2006). Promising couple-based interventions have also been developed for a variety of other emotional and behavioral problems, including sexual dysfunctions, post-traumatic stress disorder, and borderline personality disorder. For many of these conditions, marriage counseling not only improves the mental health problem, but also reduces couple discord, which may result in lower rates of relapse of psychiatric disorders. Finally, the cost effectiveness of marriage counseling has been shown to compare favorably with individual-based treatments of several disorders.

REFERENCES

Byrne, M., Carr, A., & Clark, M. (2004). The efficacy of behavioral couples therapy and emotionally focused therapy for couple distress. *Contemporary Family Therapy, 26*, 361–387.

Christensen, A., Atkins, D. C., Berns, S., Wheeler, J., Baucom, D. H., & Simpson, L. E. (2004). Traditional versus integrative behavioral couple therapy for significantly and chronically distressed married couples. *Journal of Consulting and Clinical Psychology, 72*, 176–191.

Epstein, N. B., & Baucom, D. H. (2002). *Enhanced cognitive-behavioral therapy for couples: A contextual approach*. Washington, DC: American Psychological Association.

Johnson, S. M. (2004). *The practice of emotionally focused couple therapy: Creating connection* (2nd ed.). New York: Brunner-Routledge.

Snyder, D. K., Castellani, A. M., & Whisman, M. A. (2006). Current status and future directions in couple therapy. *Annual Review of Psychology, 57*, 317–344.

Whisman, M. A. (2006). Role of couples relationships in understanding and treating mental disorders. In S. R. H. Beach, M. Z. Wamboldt, N. J. Kaslow, R. E. Heyman, M. B. First, L. G. Underwood, & D. Reiss (Eds.), *Relational processes and DSM-V: Neuroscience, assessment, prevention, and intervention* (pp. 225–238). Washington, DC: American Psychiatric Publishing, Inc.

SUGGESTED READINGS

Gurman, A. S. (Ed.). (2008). *Clinical handbook of couple therapy*. New York: Guilford Press.

Snyder, D. K., & Whisman, M. A. (Eds.). (2003). *Treating difficult couples: Helping clients with coexisting mental and relationship disorders*. New York: Guilford Press

MARK A. WHISMAN
University of Colorado at Boulder

See also: **Counseling; Couples Therapy; Marital Discord**

MASCULINITY

The dominant psychological perspective on masculinity views gender roles not as biological or even social "givens," but rather as psychologically and socially constructed entities that bring certain advantages and disadvantages. Most importantly, they can change. This perspective acknowledges the biological differences between men and women, but argues that it is not the biological differences of sex that make for masculinity and femininity. These notions are socially constructed from bits and pieces of biological, psychological, and social experience to serve particular purposes. Traditional constructions of gender serve patriarchal purposes; non-traditional constructions, such as Gilmore (1990) described among the Tahitians and the Semai, serve more equalitarian purposes.

The Gender Role Strain paradigm, originally formulated by Joseph Pleck in *The Myth of Masculinity* (1981), is the forerunner in the psychology of masculinity, of social constructionism, and of modern critical thinking about masculinity. This paradigm was formulated before social constructionism emerged as a new perspective on masculinity (Pleck, 1995). It spawned a number of major research programs that have produced important data that have deepened our understanding of the strain men experience when they attempt to live up to the impossible demands of the man role.

Pleck demonstrated that the paradigm that had dominated the research on masculinity for 50 years (1930–1980)—The Gender Role Identity Paradigm—not only poorly accounted for the observed data, but also promoted the bifurcation of society on the basis of stereotyped gender roles. In its place, Pleck proposed the Gender Role Strain Paradigm.

The older Gender Role Identity Paradigm assumed that people have an inner psychological need to have a gender role identity and that optimal personality development hinged on its formation. The extent to which this "inherent" need is met is determined by how completely people embrace their traditional gender role. From such a perspective, the development of appropriate gender role identity is viewed as a failure-prone process; failure for men to achieve masculine gender role identity is thought to result in homosexuality, negative attitudes towards women, or defensive hypermasculinity. The paradigm springs from the same philosophical roots as an "essential" or "nativist" view of sex roles—the notion that for men there is a clear masculine "essence" that is historically invariant.

In contrast, the Gender Role Strain Paradigm proposed the following: (1) contemporary gender roles are contradictory and inconsistent; (2) the proportion of persons who violate gender roles is high; (3) violation of gender roles leads to condemnation and negative psychological consequences; (4) actual or imagined violation of gender roles leads people to overconform to them; (5) violation of gender roles have more severe consequences for males than for females; and (6) certain prescribed gender role traits (e.g., male aggression) are often dysfunctional. In this paradigm, appropriate gender roles are determined by prevailing gender ideology that is operationally defined by gender role stereotypes and norms. These gender roles are imposed on the developing child by parents, teachers, and peers, who represent cultural transmitters who subscribe to the prevailing gender ideology. As noted previously, this paradigm springs from the same philosophical roots as social constructionism—the perspective that notions of "masculinity" and "femininity" are relational, socially constructed, and subject to change.

Masculinity Ideology

Thompson and Pleck (1995) proposed the term *masculinity ideology* to characterize the core construct in the corpus of research assessing attitudes toward men and male roles. Masculinity (or gender) ideology is a very different construct from the older notion of gender orientation. Gender orientation arises out of the Identity Paradigm and "presumes that masculinity is rooted in actual differences between men and women" (Thompson & Pleck, 1995, p. 130). This approach has attempted to assess the personality traits more often associated with men than women, using such instruments as the Bem Sex Role Inventory (Bem, 1974) and the Personal Attribute Questionnaire (Spence & Helmreich, 1978). In contrast, studies of masculinity ideology take a normative approach in which masculinity is viewed as a socially constructed gender ideal for men. The masculine male in the orientation/trait approach is one who possesses particular personality traits, whereas the traditional male in the ideology/normative approach "is one who endorses the ideology that men should have sex-specific characteristics (and women should not)" (Thompson & Pleck, 1995, p. 131). Thompson and Pleck (1995) adduced evidence to support the notion that gender orientation and gender ideologies are independent and have different correlates.

Masculinity Ideologies

The Strain Paradigm asserts that there is no single standard for masculinity nor is there an unvarying masculinity ideology. Rather, since masculinity is a social construction, ideals of manhood may differ for men of different social classes, races, ethnic groups, sexual orientations, life stages, and historical eras. Following Brod (1987), we therefore prefer to speak of masculinity ideolo*gies*. To illustrate, consider these brief descriptions of varying male codes among four ethnic-minority groups in the contemporary United States:

> African-American males have adopted distinctive actions and attitudes known as *cool-pose*.... Emphasizing honor, virility, and physical strength, the Latino male adheres to a code of *machismo*.... The American-Indian male struggles to maintain contact with a way of life and the traditions of elders while faced with economic castration and political trauma.... Asian-American men resolve uncertainty privately in order to save face and surrender personal autonomy to family obligations and needs (Lazur & Majors, 1995, p. 338).

Traditional Masculinity Ideology

Despite the diversity in masculinity ideology in the contemporary United States, Pleck (1995, p. 20) points out that "there is a *particular* constellation of standards and expectations that individually and jointly have various kinds of negative concomitants." It is common to refer to this as "traditional" masculinity ideology, because it was the dominant view prior to the deconstruction of gender that took place beginning in the 1970s.

Traditional masculinity ideology is thought to be a multidimensional construct. Brannon (David & Brannon, 1976) identified four components of traditional masculinity ideology: (1) men should not be feminine (or, as described by Brannon, "no sissy stuff"); (2) men should strive to be respected for successful achievement ("the big wheel"); (3) men should never show weakness ("the sturdy oak"); and (4) men should seek adventure and risk, even accepting violence if necessary ("give 'em hell"). These dimensions are assessed by the Brannon Masculinity Scale (Brannon & Juni, 1984). Levant et al. (1992) developed the Male Role Norms Inventory (MRNI), which defines traditional masculinity ideology in terms of seven dimensions: (1) the requirement to avoid all things feminine; (2) the injunction to restrict one's emotional life; (3) the emphasis on toughness and aggression; (4) the injunction to be self-reliant; (5) the emphasis on achieving status above all else; (6) non-relational, objectifying attitudes toward sexuality; and (7) fear and hatred of homosexuals (see Levant and Richmond, 2007, for more information on the MRNI).

Types of Male Gender Role Strain

Pleck (1995), in an update on the Gender Role Strain Paradigm, pointed out that his original formulation of the paradigm stimulated research on three varieties of masculine gender role strain, which he termed "discrepancy strain," "dysfunction strain," and "trauma strain." Discrepancy strain results when one fails to live up to one's internalized manhood ideal, which, among contemporary adult males, is often a close approximation of the traditional code. Dysfunction strain results even when one fulfills the requirements of the male code, because many of the characteristics viewed as desirable in men can have negative side effects on the men themselves and on those close to them. Trauma strain results from the ordeal of the male role socialization process, which is now recognized as inherently traumatic.

REFERENCES

Bem, S. L. (1974). The measurement of psychological androgyny. *Journal of Personality and Social Psychology, 42*, 155–162.

Brannon, R., & Juni, S. (1984). A scale for measuring attitudes about masculinity. *Psychological Documents, 14*(1). (University Microfilms No. 2612).

Brod, H. (1987). *The making of the masculinities: The new men's studies.* Boston: Unwin Hyman.

David, D., & Brannon, R. (Eds.). (1976). *The forty-nine percent majority: The male sex role.* Reading, MA: Addison-Wesley.

Gilmore, D. (1990). *Manhood in the making: Cultural concepts of masculinity.* New Haven: Yale University Press.

Lazur, R. F., & Majors, R. (1995). Men of color: Ethnocultural variations of male gender role strain. In R. F. Levant & W. S. Pollack (Eds.), *A new psychology of men.* New York: Basic Books.

Levant, R. F., Hirsch, L., Celentano, E., Cozza, T., Hill, S., MacEachern, M., Marty, N., & Schnedeker, J. (1992). The male role: An investigation of norms and stereotypes. *Journal of Mental Health Counseling, 14*, 325–337.

Levant, R. F., & Richmond, K. (2007). A review of research on masculinity ideologies using the Male Role Norms Inventory. *Journal of Men's Studies, 15*, 130–146.

Pleck, J. H. (1981). *The myth of masculinity.* Cambridge, MA: MIT Press.

Pleck, J. H. (1995). The gender role strain paradigm: An update. In R. F. Levant & W. S. Pollack (Eds.), *A new psychology of men* (pp. 11–32). New York: Basic Books.

Spence, J. T., & Helmreich, R. L. (1978). *Masculinity and femininity: Their psychological dimensions, correlates, and antecedents.* Austin: University of Texas Press.

Thompson, E. H., & Pleck, J. H. (1995). Masculinity ideology: A review of research instrumentation on men and masculinities. In R. F. Levant & W. S. Pollack (Eds.), *A new psychology of men* (pp. 129–163). New York: Basic Books.

RONALD F. LEVANT
University of Akron

See also: **Bem Sex Role Inventory; Gender Roles; Psychology of Men**

MASLOW, ABRAHAM (1908–1970)

Abraham Maslow studied with two of the leading Gestalt psychologists, Max Wertheimer and Kurt Koffka, at the New School for Social Research. From these men he got the idea for a holistic psychology. He received all three of his academic degrees from the University of Wisconsin, obtaining his Ph.D. in 1934 along with Carl Rogers, Rollo May, and Charlotte Buhler. His most important books, presenting his humanistic position, include *Motivation and Personality* and *Toward a Psychology of Being.*

Maslow considered his basic approach to psychology to fall within the broad range of humanistic psychology, which he characterized as the Third Force in American Psychology (the other two being behaviorism and psychoanalysis). His main efforts were directed to the field of personality. He believed that psychology had dealt too much with human frailty and not enough with human strengths. In deploring the pessimism of so many psychologists—Freud, for example—Maslow looked to the more positive side of humanity; he believed that human nature was essentially good. As personality unfolded through maturation, the creative powers manifested themselves more clearly. If humans were miserable or neurotic, it was the environment that made them so. Humans were not basically destructive or violent, but became so when their inner nature was twisted or frustrated.

Maslow proposed a theory of motivation that has become extremely popular in humanistic circles. Humans' basic needs or drives could be arranged in a hierarchy, often pictured as a pyramid. At the bottom are the basic physiological needs: hunger and thirst. Next are safety needs: security from attack, avoidance of pain, and freedom from invasion of privacy. On the top of these are needs for love and belonging. Higher up are the needs for self-esteem: feeling good, pride, and confidence. At the top of the hierarchy is the need for self-actualization, a basic driving force for self-fulfillment. This emphasis on self-actualization is shared by many humanistic psychologists.

To understand human nature, Maslow felt it was more profitable to study people who have realized their potentiality rather than those who were psychologically crippled or neurotic. He selected a group of people, some from history, who he felt had reached a considerable degree of self-actualization—such persons are Abraham Lincoln, Thomas Jefferson, Albert Einstein, and Eleanor Roosevelt. In studying them he found certain distinguishing characteristics such as the following: (1) a realistic orientation, (2) acceptance of themselves and others, (3) spontaneity of expression, (4) attitudes that are problem-centered rather than self-centered, (5) independence, (6) identification with humanity, (7) emotional depth, (8) democratic values, (9) a philosophical rather than a caustic sense of humor, (10) transcendence of the environment, and (11) creativity.

SUGGESTED READINGS

Maslow, A. (1954). *Toward a psychology of being*. New York: John Wiley & Sons.

Maslow, A. (1970). *Motivation and personality*. New York: Harper Collins.

Maslow, A. (1971). *The farther reaches of human nature*. New York: Penguin.

RALPH W. LUNDIN
Wheaton, IL

MASOCHISM

It is doubtful whether an increased tolerance for sadism and masochism (S&M) in the sexual behavior of daily life has led to any greater understanding of the phenomenon of masochism. A rather simplistic definition in a medical encyclopedia runs as follows: a glandular insufficiency, especially of the gonads and adrenals, demanding the stimulation of pain before the subject is able to react to sexual stimuli.

Some sexologists of the past, among them Schrenck-Notzing, preferred the term *algolagnia*, emphasizing pleasure in pain, whereas Krafft-Ebing's terms, *sadism* and *masochism*, include pleasure in humiliation, dominance, and submission. Sadism takes its name from the writings and exploits of Donatien Alphonse François, Marquis de Sade, found to have been one of the nine prisoners held in the Bastille when it was stormed in 1789. It denotes a condition in which erotic pleasure is derived from inflicting pain or humiliation. The more puzzling condition of masochism, in which erotic pleasure is obtained from being hurt, restrained, or humiliated, is so named after the writings and activities roughly a century later of the Chevalier Leopold von Sacher-Masoch. The coupling of the two names in sadomasochism is important, as the two conditions are usually present, albeit with one or the other predominating, in one and the same individual. This individual may also display other deviant interests, for instance in fetishism or transvestism. Freud pointed out that the sexuality of infancy is "polymorphously perverse," and some masochists actually visit "Adult Baby" clubs.

Trying to explain masochism without Freud would be like trying to explain gravity without Newton. In 1924 he wrote in *The Economic Problem of Masochism*: "The existence of a masochistic trend in the instinctual life of human beings may justly be described as mysterious from the economic point of view. For if mental processes are governed by the pleasure principle in such a way that their first aim is the avoidance of unpleasantness and the obtaining of pleasure, masochism is incomprehensible. If pain and unpleasantness can be not simply warnings but actually aims, the pleasure principle is paralyzed—it is

as though the watchman over our mental life were put out of action by a drug. Thus masochism appears to us in the light of a great danger, which is in no way true of its counterpart, sadism. We are tempted to call the pleasure principle the watchman over our life rather than merely over our mental life" (p. 159).

Few psychologists would wish to dispute the primacy of the pleasure principle. The whole edifice of behaviorism is built upon it. The fact that masochism is sometimes literally a danger to life itself is attested to by the deaths ensuing on certain rituals of "bondage" and hypoxyphilia (autoerotic asphyxia, sexual arousal by oxygen deprivation): about 50 a year in the United States, according to coroners' records of 35 years ago, and up to 1,000 adult or teenaged victims a year according to more recent FBI statistics; more than 50 deaths recorded in 1994 in Britain; and almost certainly more numerous incidents today.

Sadomasochism is, and always has been, common among the paraphilias, more prevalent in men than in women. The standard practices have not changed since Freud listed them in 1924 (p. 162): "being gagged, bound, painfully beaten, whipped, in some way maltreated, forced into unconditional obedience, dirtied and debased." Many of those engaging in sadomasochistic ritual will tell you that it is all about control and is dictated by the masochist. Their explanations are, however, seldom adequate to the impenetrability of the phenomenon they are addressing. Women who perform sadistic acts for money or to please men are not necessarily sexually excited. Young women who cut their arms with razors do so to obtain relief from psychological distress, not for sexual satisfaction.

The subculture of sadomasochism has seeped into mainstream culture. It has long exercised a considerable influence upon fashion and the visual images and story content of science fiction. Most animated cartoons and slapstick comedies contain sequences where extremely painful happenings are presented for enjoyment. An increasing number of young men and women submit themselves to body piercings and tattooing.

As Freud pointed out, a child will repeat an unpleasant experience in its play in order to gain control of it. The masochist, who has never grown up, recreates not once but many times, the situation he fears in order that he shall not, in retrospect, be its hapless victim but, indeed, its instigator. This is not likely to benefit those in his path! It is not difficult to recognize that his "mishaps" are provocations because he will never apologize or express regret as he would if they were truly inadvertent.

Mervin Glasser has, out of his extensive clinical involvement with sadomasochism at the Portman Clinic, London, identified an important and frequently encountered etiological factor: incomplete individuation. He explains it in terms of a "core complex": a pervasive longing for closeness to another person, amounting to a "merging," which invariably awakens the fear of a permanent loss of self as soon as closeness is offered. The flight to a safe distance brings a sense of isolation and, in a vicious circle, the return of longing for union. Aggression, aroused by this threat of obliteration, cannot be directed towards the potentially engulfing person (originally the mother)—it may, however, be focused on the self, and it may be sexualized and the relationship preserved in sadomasochistic mode. In adulthood, when a "love" relationship ceases to be loving it may flip into its opposite, or end in indifference, or become sadomasochistic.

Many masochists lack a sense of identity apart from that of their family or their childhood background. Any struggle for autonomy that may have started, perhaps with adolescence, has failed. Some not only have an obvious reluctance to achieve satisfaction in conventional sexual intercourse with a partner, which might be a reluctance due to a sense of guilt, but they even fear such a loss of control as the culmination of a punishment ritual. They would rather masturbate alone afterwards. This confirms Glasser's interpretation that the masochist needs to regulate his moving towards or away from his partner, ensuring that he does not lose control of the situation in her presence and expose himself to the danger of being engulfed.

Some masochists describe sexually colored incidents in their childhood involving rubber or plastic articles, and attribute their lifelong interest in rubber or shiny plastic as sexual stimuli to these incidents. Fetishes may bear some resemblance to the "transitional objects" postulated by Donald W. Winnicott. John Bowlby preferred the term "substitute objects," explaining that inanimate objects, such as teddy bears, simply have attachment behavior directed towards them because the attachment figure herself is unavailable. Like her, they are sought particularly when a child is tired or sick or upset. One might perhaps add also that when a child is bored, the physical properties of the substitute object itself might become salient. In a final step, they might become sexual stimuli through masturbation. In pursuit of their fetish, some adolescents and adults find themselves confronted with pornographic literature that leads them into the S&M "scene." What they at first encounter in sex shops as a contiguous interest gradually extends its fascination and becomes central to their deviance. As to the fetishistic paraphernalia on sale in sex shops, a mask or uniform may serve to conceal the ordinary and create a new and powerful identity. As a film censor pointed out, pornography is compromising because it is designed to effect sexual arousal. It infiltrates the imagination, and its addictive property means that it is likely to escalate.

In cases of prolonged illness or severe injury in childhood, the endogenous opioids produced as a biological response to these situations may create an addiction to pain and stress because, as definitively reported by Kosterlitz and Hughes, these opioids are many times more addictive than morphine and other exogenous opiates (Hughes et al., 1975). The receptors to which these neuromodulators bind have been found in many parts of the human body, but chiefly in pain pathways and limbic regions of the brain. They have been implicated in strenuous physical exercise—an "endorphin rush" has now become part of common parlance.

What is firmly established, however, and of prime significance, is that they are, like morphine, both painkilling and addictive. They are produced by pain or stress, and they relieve it by reducing neural excitability. Pleasure, often referred to in the literature as "the reward factor," follows. The practicing masochist is a person for whom "normal" sexual release by means of the genitals is at best problematic. Often, the anus and buttocks are more erotogenic than the genitals. If one looks into the childhood of a masochist, one frequently finds an accident or illness involving intense, protracted, physical pain, or repeated beatings, or a situation causing severe, prolonged stress. These events, usually only the beginning of a series, have not only psychological but also physiological consequences, one of these being the release of endogenous opioids. As painful event succeeds event, what happened at first by ill chance is later engineered. He is addictively seeking pain and in some cases he even knows it and explicitly states it.

Thus the etiology of masochism may be predominantly physical through injury, illness, or stress, predominantly psychological through maternal rejection, parental divorce, or death for which the masochist attributes guilt to himself, or a combination of both through traumatic experiences of emotional attachment as a young child, leading to a loss of confidence in those on whom the child is dependent. Later the masochist entrusts his safety to the "dominant" person, with whom he has entered into a type of contract and whom he therefore judges trustworthy even though he is a stranger. Other etiological factors, both physical and psychological, may be corporal punishment, hospitalization, persecution by or envious hatred of siblings, a puritanical home atmosphere where sexual relations are considered sinful or disgusting, or a bullied and miserable school-life.

Where sadomasochism finds no outlet in sexual activity, it is likely to spill over from sexuality into the personality in the form of rigidity, infantilism, hypocrisy, and passivity. Particularly in women, martyrdom may be a way of transferring guilt to others. As the neurologist and psychiatrist Kurt Goldstein noted, the healthy personality is characterized by flexible functioning, the damaged personality is rigid; healthy functioning is planned and organized, disturbed functioning is mechanical; the healthy person can delay and anticipate the future, the disturbed personality is bound by the past and the immediate present. Defensive or self-deceiving mental processes are compartmentalizing processes, which act to separate feeling, attention, perception, and memory. They therefore place limits on metacognitive monitoring (Main, 1991). The sadomasochist has a sadomasochistic mind-set.

Theodor Reik's is arguably the most accurate depiction of this mind-set after Freud's. He identifies its quintessential characteristics as a predilection for fantasy, the seeking of suspense, and what he calls the demonstrative feature. He seeks the common denominator in the various manifestations of masochism—sexual deviance and personality disorder alike—and finds it in the formula "victory through defeat" (Reik, 1939, 1941). This is indeed the kernel of masochism and there is no doubt that the highly specific victory is total. The man whose aim is to be defeated has achieved a desperate invulnerability.

The masochist who, in each situation life presents, systematically ruins his chances of happiness and success, is locked within a vicious circle of guilt, requiring punishment, punishment affording masochistic satisfaction, thus begetting more guilt, requiring more punishment. The masochist who operates primarily through deviant sexual practices, the "supersensualist," as Sacher-Masoch styled himself, defiantly obtains gratification in spite of every obstacle, every delay, and every embargo. He is characteristically identified with his body. His body and its sensations are his prime preoccupation. Where such a great investment has been made in the body the inevitable deterioration of the body with age is likely to have a devastating effect on the conception of the self. The poignancy of masochism lies, after all, in the fact that it is an abuse of what is most treasured—the self.

Sadomasochism has been described by Otto Kernberg as a continuum—a spectrum would be another metaphor, with feckless theatrical games at one end and sadistic serial killings at the other. The danger comes when preoccupation with immediate physical pleasure takes over, when other human beings are seen only as insensate means of sexual gratification, and this is indissolubly linked with domination. That at the other end of the spectrum, everyday human relations are shot through with covert sadomasochism is, sadly, as irrefutable as saying that *Homo sapiens* is a dangerous species.

Life is surely cruel enough in itself without the deliberate pursuit of cruelty. The pain pathways of the central nervous system evolved as a protective mechanism, not to be misused as a vehicle of sensuality. However, the scripts, the scenarios, enacted by practicing sadomasochists often resemble the make-believe games of children, albeit unhappy children. We must reflect that there is a difference between the person and the behavior he is displaying. Scripts are written by a playwright. Behind the script there is a person or an awareness, not reducible to the awareness portrayed in the script. There may be a person who is striving for catharsis. Masochists have other qualities besides deviance and sometimes, where fantasy is creative as opposed to imprisoning and debilitating, considerable talents or skills, as in the case of Gesualdo, Musorgsky, Bartok, Rousseau, Dostoevsky, Swinburne, C. S. Lewis, T. E. Lawrence, and Yukio Mishima, to mention but a few.

REFERENCES

Freud, S. (1924). The economic problem of masochism. *Standard Edition, 19*, 159–170.

Hughes, J., Smith, T. W., Kosterlitz, H. W., Fothergill, L. A., Morgan, B. A., & Morris, H. R. (1975). Identification of two related pentapeptides from the brain with potent opiate agonist activity. *Nature, 258*, 577–579.

Main, M. (1991). Metacognitive knowledge, metacognitive monitoring, and singular (coherent) vs. multiple (incoherent) models of attachment: Findings and directions for future research. In P. Harris, J. Stevenson-Hinde, & C. Parkes (Eds.), *Attachment across the lifecycle* (pp. 127–159). New York: Routledge.

Reik, T. (1939). The characteristics of masochism. *American Imago, 1*, 26–59.

Reik, T. (1941). *Masochism in modern man.* New York: Farrar and Rinehart.

SUGGESTED READINGS

Giles, J. (2006). Social constructionism and sexual desire. *Journal for the Theory of Social Behaviour, 36*(3), 225–238.

Rathbone, J. (2001). *Anatomy of masochism.* New York: Kluwer Academic/Plenum Publishers.

JUNE RATHBONE
University College London

See also: Sadomasochistic Personality

MASOCHISTIC PERSONALITY (See Sadomasochistic Personality)

MASTURBATION

Masturbation is the term used to signify any type of autoerotic stimulation. Both males and females indulge in stimulation of the genitals for sexual gratification. The term is also applied to an infant's manipulation of the genitals, a common exploratory behavior in the early years. During adolescence, masturbation becomes one of the main sexual outlets, and remains so for many adults. Michael, Gagnon, Laumann, and Kolata (1994) found that among Americans, 60% of men and 40% of women report that they have masturbated during the past year, and 25% of men and 10% of women say they masturbate at least once a week. While estimates vary, depending on the studies cited and the specific approaches used in collecting the data, it is generally accepted that there has been an increase in the acceptance and practice of this behavior in recent years, such that the behavior is reported to occur more frequently than in the past and to be initiated at an earlier age. (Francoeur, 1998; Dekker & Schmidt, 2002).

These changes have occurred irrespective of whether or not the individuals are in a sexual relationship, and regardless of the satisfaction obtained from that relationship.

Of all the areas of sexual behavior, masturbation appears to be subject to wide variation in reported frequency, owing no doubt to the privacy of this behavior and the shame that has traditionally surrounded it. While in earlier historical periods masturbation was considered a sign of depravity or sinfulness, it is more generally accepted today as a common practice among adolescents and adults, both male and female.

REFERENCES

Dekker, A., & Schmidt, G. (2002). Patterns of masturbatory behavior: Changes between the sixties and the nineties. *Journal of Psychology and Human Sexuality. 14*(2/3), 35–48.

Francoeur, R. T. (1998). Autoerotic behaviors and patterns. In R. T. Francoeur, P. B. Koch, & D. L. Weiss (Eds.), *Sexuality in America* (pp. 88–91). New York: Continuum.

Michael, R. T., Gagnon, J. H., Laumann, E. O., & Kolata, G. (1994). *Sex in America: A definitive survey*. Boston: Little, Brown.

JOHN PAUL MCKINNEY
Michigan State University

See also: Sexual Intercourse, Human

MATE SELECTION

"It is a truth universally acknowledged that a single man in possession of a good fortune must be in want of a wife"—so wrote Jane Austen in *Pride and Prejudice*. From classic literature to contemporary screenplays, from the latest celebrity news to office gossip, it is nearly impossible to escape the pervasive topic of romantic relationships. Indeed, the pursuit of mates consumes a significant portion of our time and energy, and for good reason—mates give us companionship, pleasure, comfort, security, and even health benefits. As we discuss in this article, there are two major theoretical perspectives for understanding mate selection. Although these perspectives have different explanations for people's mate choices, both agree that who one selects as a mate depends largely on the type of relationship one seeks and the characteristics one desires.

Theoretical Perspectives

The sociocultural perspective (Eagly & Wood, 1999) focuses on the role of culture and social norms in the development of men's and women's social behavior. Thus, mate selection is typically explained in terms of modern-day societal factors. In contrast, evolutionary theories of human behavior are based on conditions and adaptive problems faced by ancestral humans. From an evolutionary perspective, mate selection is viewed as a process facilitated by multiple psychological adaptations designed to ensure the selection of a mate who will help produce viable offspring (Buss & Schmitt, 1993). Therefore, mate preferences today might reflect heritable psychological mechanisms that have allowed ancestral humans to successfully reproduce over thousands of generations.

Relationship Preferences

People want to be in relationships for various reasons— love, sex, family—and the type of relationship one seeks significantly influences one's mate choices. Long-term relationships, such as marriage, entail significant investment and commitment by both partners, whereas short-term relationships, like one-night stands, tend to be primarily sexual. In general, most women favor long-term relationships, whereas men report a stronger desire for casual sex. To some extent, this may be due to the perpetuation of gender stereotypes. It can also be explained in evolutionary terms. That is, in the ancestral environment, the cost of short-term relationships was higher for a woman, because she could have become pregnant and faced rearing an infant without paternal support. Thus, natural selection may have favored women who desired commitment before sex, thereby ensuring paternal support and increasing their offspring's chances of survival.

Trait Preferences

Mate selection is further based on preferences for certain traits. In general, those who pursue long-term relationships value traits such as kindness, emotional stability, and intelligence, while those who pursue short-term relationships tend to focus on physical attractiveness. Even so, men and women still differ in their trait preferences. For example, numerous studies have shown that, when considering long-term mates, women prefer older men who are high in social status, ambitious, athletic, and dependable, whereas men prefer younger women who are physically attractive. These sex differences in preferences may reflect societal factors, such as women's limited access to status and power, or the media's emphasis on female physical attractiveness. On the other hand, several studies have found the same differences across cultures, suggesting that these differences may be rooted in human nature.

From an evolutionary perspective, sex-specific trait preferences stem from the adaptive problems faced by ancestral men and women. For instance, a major adaptive problem for ancestral women was acquiring adequate resources and protection for their offspring. One solution was to find a long-term mate with ample resources and willingness to support and raise children. This may account for women's reported preferences for social status, employment, education, and physical strength. Another problem was making certain one had healthy offspring who could survive harsh ancestral conditions, even in the absence of paternal support. Therefore, women, especially those pursuing short-term relationships, may have evolved to be attracted to cues of genetic quality. Indeed, research has shown that women are attracted to testosterone-driven features, such as masculinity and symmetry (Thornhill & Gangestad, 1994). Masculinity and symmetry are hypothesized to be an indication of "good genes" in that men who developed masculine features and a symmetrical physique were able to ward off parasites despite the immune-suppressing effects of higher baseline testosterone.

Men faced very different adaptive problems. For example, although a man has the ability to have many offspring with multiple mates, his mating effort would not have led to reproduction if he consistently selected infertile women. Therefore, men have likely evolved to prioritize the identification of traits that indicate a capacity for bearing children (Li, Bailey, Kenrick, & Linsenmeier, 2002). Age is one important factor, as women reach peak fertility in their early 20s. It should come as no surprise then that men tend to prefer women in that age range (Kenrick & Keefe, 1992). Waist-to-hip ratio (WHR) is another characteristic closely linked to fertility. WHR describes body-fat distribution; the lower a woman's WHR, the more fertile she is, and the more attractive men find her to be (Singh, 1993). This appears to be true regardless of body mass.

In summary, mate selection can be viewed from different perspectives, and much research on mate choice has concentrated on relationship and trait preferences. Still, mate selection is a complex process, and there are numerous variables yet to be investigated. For instance, there has been a growing interest in the menstrual cycle in women, which is characterized by fluctuations in baseline levels of female sex hormones (estrogen and progesterone), as well as the male sex hormone testosterone. These fluctuations coincide with specific changes in mating behavior. Evidence suggests that when women in long-term relationships are ovulating, and therefore most likely to conceive, they show increased attraction to masculine, symmetrical men other than their primary partners. That is, women with a proclivity for long-term relationships during other times in their cycle show a "switch" to a short-term strategy during ovulation. Encouraged by findings such as these, mate selection researchers will likely continue to uncover the psychological and biological underpinnings of human mating dynamics.

REFERENCES

Buss, D. M., & Schmitt, D. (1993). Sexual strategies theory: An evolutionary perspective on human mating. *Psychological Review, 100*, 204–232.

Eagly, A. H., & Wood, W. (1999). The origins of sex differences in human behavior: Evolved dispositions versus social roles. *American Psychologist, 54*, 408–433.

Kenrick, D. T., & Keefe, R. C. (1992). Age preferences in mates reflect sex differences in human reproductive strategies. *Behavioral & Brain Sciences, 15*, 75–133.

Li, N. P., Bailey, J. M., Kenrick, D. T., & Linsenmeier, J. A. W. (2002). The necessities and luxuries of mate preferences: Testing the tradeoffs. *Journal of Personality and Social Psychology, 82*, 947–955.

Singh, D. (1993). Adaptive significance of female physical attractiveness: Role of waist-to-hip ratio. *Journal of Personality & Social Psychology, 65*, 293–307.

Thornhill, R., & Gangestad, S. W. (1994). Fluctuating asymmetry and human sexual behavior. *Psychological Science, 5*, 297–302.

SUGGESTED READINGS

Buss, D.M. (2003). *The evolution of desire: Strategies of human mating* (rev. ed.). New York: Basic Books.

Symons, D. (1979). *The evolution of human sexuality*. New York: Oxford University Press.

MARGARET J. CASON
NORMAN P. LI
University of Texas at Austin

See also: Interpersonal Relationships; Love; Sexual Desire

MATHEMATICAL PSYCHOLOGY

Mathematical psychology applies mathematical and statistical methods, formal logic, and computer simulation to investigate psychological phenomena. It aims at building mathematical models in a variety of fields such as learning and memory, perception, and decision making, and at developing quantitative methods and measurement theory to describe behavior. The goal is to find regularities and principles that govern a set of phenomenona. Mathematical modeling has several advantages. First, it forces researchers to give precise definitions and to make clear statements. This requires a high degree of abstraction, because assumptions about underlying processes, relations, and connections between certain aspects of behavior, interactions between experimental variables, and so on are all mapped onto mathematical objects and operations. The language of mathematics minimizes the risk of making contradictory statements in the theory.

Second, mathematical modeling allows derivation of precise predictions from the underlying assumptions, thereby enabling empirical falsification of these assumptions. Furthermore, deriving predictions is particularly important and useful when they are not obvious. Testable predictions may be drawn on in order to decide between competing theories. They are not necessarily quantitative and can also reflect qualitative patterns possibly observable in the data. Third, mathematical modeling brings together theory and data; it facilitates the analysis and interpretation of complex data and helps in generating new hypotheses. Good praxis for mathematical modeling in psychology is to put psychological phenomena, ideas, and problems first, and then to find the adequate methods to solve the specific problem, rather than choosing some mathematical approach and applying it to many, often very different, phenomena. Finally, even rather simple mathematical models often describe data better and are more informative than a statistical test of a verbally phrased hypothesis.

A Short History of Mathematical Psychology

The German philosopher Johann Friedrich Herbart (1776–1841) was one of the first scholars who brought together psychology and mathematics. Developing his mechanics of "Vorstellungen," he saw it as a necessity to apply mathematics to psychology in order to avoid pure speculation. Gustav Theodor Fechner, philosopher and physicist (1801–1877), became famous for his psychophysical approach in which he quite naturally assumed mathematical relations between physically measurable entities and psychological sensations. Further early examples of mathematical modeling in psychology are intelligence measurement (e.g., Spearman's 1904 *General Intelligence*), scaling and attitude measurement (e.g., Thurstone's 1927 *Law of Comparative Judgment*), decision conflicts (e.g., Lewin's 1951 *Field Theory*), and learning (e.g., Hull's 1943 *Principles of Behavior*).

In the 1950s, mathematical psychology started booming, triggered by several publications, in particular by Estes (1950; *Towards a Statistical Theory of Learning*), Hick (1952; *On the Rate of Gain of Information*), Tanner and Swets (1954; *A Decision-theory of Visual Detection*), and Luce and Raiffa (1957; *Games and Decision*). In 1963/1964 the three-volume *Handbook of Mathematical Psychology* was published by Luce, Bush, and Galanter, and in 1964 the first issue of *The Journal of Mathematical Psychology* appeared. By that time, mathematical psychology had become a respected research field and an important, integral part of psychology. In 1966, the *Society for Mathematical Psychology* (SMP) was founded at Stanford University, and in 1971 its European branch, the *European Mathematical Psychology Group* (EMPG), was established in Paris. In the 1970s, several textbooks on mathematical psychology appeared (e.g., Coombs, Dawes, & Tversky, 1970; Laming, 1973), as well as the first volume of the three-volume *Foundations of Measurement* by Krantz, Luce, Suppes, and Tversky (1971), which laid the foundation of an axiomatic approach to measurement.

Until the beginning of the 1970s, stochastic learning theories dominated the field of mathematical psychology. Interest declined when it became obvious that these theories could only describe elementary learning processes and could not be applied to more complex learning structures. Today, mathematical learning theories are actively studied in the fields of machine learning, artificial intelligence, and experimental economics, so that stochastic learning models have experienced a renaissance.

Due to developments in computer science in the 1960s and 1970s, models of complex memory processes, thinking, problem solving, knowledge representation, linguistics, and so on emerged, utilizing the structure and language of programming and leading to symbol-oriented connectionist and network models, as in the work of Newell and Simon and J. Anderson. In the 1980s and 1990s, neural network models for learning, memory, and pattern recognition became widespread (e.g. Rumelhart, McClelland, & the PDP Group). Recently, Bayesian models have become very popular addressing research topics such as learning, perception, motor control, semantic memory, language processing and acquisition, symbolic reasoning, causal learning and inference, and social cognition and inference (see Griffiths, Kemp, & Tenenbaum, 2008). These approaches could be subsumed under mathematical psychology, but they now more often come under the heading of cognitive science.

Although its topics have shifted over the past 50 years, methodology including mathematics, statistics, and measurement is still a major issue of mathematical psychology, and traditionally important topics such as sensation, perceptual processes, psychophysics, judgment and decision-making, games, choice and preference, problem solving, and inference are still major parts of research in mathematical psychology (Falmagne, 2005).

Research Areas

From the preceding, it is obvious that mathematical psychology plays a major role in almost all areas of psychology. It is closely tied to experimental psychology, in that a mathematical model generates predictions that can be tested empirically, and it may even specify the experimental design to obtain these data. On the other hand, the data can reject a model and require a modification of the model's assumption. Mathematical psychology is sometimes divided into content areas (such as learning, memory, and decision making) and often into areas of methodology (such as psychophysics and measurement theory). Here we focus on areas of methodology (see also Townsend, 2008).

Psychophysics. As founded by Fechner in 1860, psychophysics is arguably the earliest area of mathematical psychology and is closely related to data collection. The goal of classical psychophysics was to derive a functional relation between a physically well-defined stimulus and the sensation it triggers (psychophysical function). Fechner derived a logarithmic form for the psychophysical function, whereas Stevens (1957), based on direct scaling techniques, postulated a power law. Modern approaches to classical psychophysics have been developed by Falmagne (1985) and Laming (1997). A recent approach substantially generalizing Fechner's ideas is presented by Dzhafarov and Colonius (2007). The theory of signal detection (SDT) developed by engineers in the 1940–1950s allowed psychophysicists to separate sensitivity from response bias. Its applications now often go beyond the areas of sensation and perception, and SDT notions are being used in theories of categorization, learning, memory, and cognition. Psychophysics today is an active research field and finds applications in neuroscience, physics, and computer science. Good introductions are provided to psychophysics by Gescheider (1997) and to SDT by MacMillan and Creelman (2005).

Measurement theory and scaling. Measuring psychological entities, that is, eventually presenting them as numbers, is far more difficult than measuring physical entities such as length or mass. The measurable entities (e.g., preference, utility) are often not clearly defined and may even change while being measured. Psychological measurement theory is concerned with these problems of measurability, and its goal is to justify various measurement procedures utilizing mathematical means and logic. Conditions of behavioral empirical relations (e.g., whether A is preferred to B) are described via a system of axioms and then mapped onto a numerical system that expresses the properties and relations numerically (e.g., u(A) > u(B)). The questions of particular concern are (1) representability—what are the conditions under which measurement scales can be constructed?; (2) uniqueness—how unique is the scale obtained by a particular measurement procedure?; (3) meaningfulness—what inferences can be made from a particular measurement scale?; and (4) scaling—how are numerical scales constructed and measurement errors taken into account?

This approach is predominantly applied to sensation/perception and to decision making, particularly utility theory and psychologically motivated variations of it, such as prospect theory. This is now an interdisciplinary field involving mathematical psychology, economics, and decision science. Various approaches, such as additive conjoint measurement or random utility models, developed within mathematical psychology, have become highly accepted in economics (see Roberts, (1979).

Psychometrics and test theory. Psychometrics and test theory are concerned with measuring psychological entities such as intelligence and utilize mainly statistical methods. The focus is on developing measurement instruments that can differentiate between individuals or groups. Work in this area has developed into a distinct field of its own and usually is no longer considered a part of mathematical psychology.

Information-processing models. Information-processing models attempt to model what is going on in the brain, with particular respect to the cognitive processes involved, how they interact, and how they lead to observed behavior. Typically, a structure or architecture of subsystems performing mental activity is described. Information processing models are predominately found in all areas of cognitive psychology, including perception, learning, memory, thinking, problem solving, decision making, categorization, judgment, and inference. The models come in a variety of forms. They can be classified as deterministic versus probabilistic, static versus dynamic, or linear versus nonlinear.

For example, sequential sampling models assume that information in a sensory or cognitive system is accumulated sequentially over time, until a preset criterion is reached and a response is initiated. Information here means any changes in the central nervous system that translate perception and cognition into action. Characteristics of the stimulus (e.g., intensity) and the subject (e.g., strategy) may influence the information accumulation process. Sequential sampling models seek to account for both response time and accuracy data in binary choice tasks. They hypothesize that the stimuli (or choice alternatives) can be mapped onto a hypothetical numerical dimension representing the instantaneous level of activation, evidence, or preference. Further, they assume some random fluctuation of this value over time in the course of information accumulation.

Therefore, sequential sampling is described as a stochastic process. This is an example of a probabilistic, dynamic, nonlinear model. The processing assumptions may be modified according to the needs of the particular research area, and the parameters of the process are then interpreted within its conceptual framework. These models, often specified as Poisson counter models, random walks, or diffusion models, have been applied to account for response time and accuracy data in identification and discrimination tasks, to model memory retrieval, for classification tasks, to decision-making tasks, and many more. Townsend and Ashby (1983) and Luce (1986) review sequential sampling models and their applications in psychology, and Busemeyer and Diederich (2009) provide an introduction to cognitive models.

Methodology. A fast-growing area in mathematical psychology is methodology in a broad sense, including model comparison and selection, model complexity, Bayesian hierarchical modeling, statistics, kernel methods, and computer simulations. Models are considered abstractions of complex theories and systems concerned with specific aspects of this complexity. When there is a set of competing models that try to explain a psychological phenomenon, the question is how to decide among the various models, given the data. Several principles and techniques based on these principles have been proposed. The first step is to select models from the class of all possible models. This should be done based on scientific principles explaining the underlying phenomenon (Burnham & Anderson, 2002) and is up to the researcher.

Other selection criteria are goodness of fit, that is, how well can the model predict or describe the data using some likelihood ratio approach, and model complexity measures, usually expressed as the number of free parameters. Model selection techniques take these two criteria into account. For instance, the Akaike information criterion is defined as $AIC = 2k - 2\ln(L)$, where k is the number of parameters in the model and L is the maximized value of the likelihood of the data given the estimated model. The model obtaining the smallest AIC is usually the model selected. Other criteria that have found wide acceptance in mathematical psychology are the Bayesian information criterion (BIC) or the Minimum Description Length (MDL). Two special issues on these topics appeared in the *Journal of Mathematical Psychology* in 2000 and 2006.

Perspectives

Today, most research as well as its application takes place in an interdisciplinary context. Psychologists and cognitive scientists cooperate with researchers from areas such as neuroscience, economics, computer science, and the like. A successful cooperation requires a common language, and formal models often enhance communication. For instance, psychophysics has become increasingly important in neuroscience. Research on decision making is unthinkable without close ties between psychology and economics. Research on vision, learning, categorization, and so forth all involve interdisciplinary approaches. Mathematical psychology is assisting the search to find common ground.

REFERENCES

Burnham, K. P., & Anderson, D. R. (2002). *Model selection and multimodel inference: A practical information-theoretic approach* (2nd ed.). New York: Springer-Verlag.

Busemeyer, J. R., & Diederich, A. (2009). *Cognitive modeling.* London: Sage.

Coombs, C. H., Dawes, R. M., & Tversky, A. (1970). *Mathematical psychology.* Upper Saddle River, NJ: Prentice Hall.

Dzhafarov, E. N., & Colonius, H. (2007). Dissimilarity cumulation theory and subjective metrics. *Journal of Mathematical Psychology, 51*(5), 290–304.

Falmagne, J.-C. (1985). *Elements of psychophysical theory.* New York: Oxford University Press.

Falmagne, J-.C. (2005). Mathematical psychology—A perspective. *Journal of Mathematical Psychology, 49,* 436–439.

Gescheider, G. A. (1997). *Psychophysics: The fundamentals* (3rd ed.). London: Lawrence Erlbaum.

Griffiths, T. L., Kemp, C., & Tenenbaum, J. B. (in press). Bayesian models of cognition. In R. Sun (Ed.), *Cambridge handbook of computational cognitive modeling.* Cambridge, UK: Cambridge University Press.

Laming, D. (1973). *Mathematical psychology.* London: Academic Press.

Laming, D. (1997) *The measurement of sensation.* Oxford, UK: Oxford University Press.

Luce, R. D. (1986). *Response times.* New York: Oxford University Press.

MacMillan, N. A., & Creelman, C. D. (2004). *Detection theory: A user's guide* (2nd ed.). Mahwah, NJ: Lawrence Erlbaum.

Roberts, F. S. (1979). *Measurement theory with applications to decision making, utility and social sciences.* Reading, Mass: Addison-Wesley.

Townsend, J. T. (2008). Mathematical psychology: Prospects for the 21st century: A guest editorial. *Journal of Mathematical Psychology. 28*(1), 1–288.

Townsend, J. T., & Ashby, F. G. (1983). *Stochastic modeling of elementary psychological processes.* Cambridge, UK: Cambridge University Press.

SUGGESTED READINGS

Marley, A. A. J. (Ed.). (1997). *Choice, decision, and measurement: Essays in honor of R. Duncan Luce.* Mahwah, NJ: Lawrence Erlbaum.

Wickens, T. D. (2002). *Elementary signal detection theory.* London: Oxford University Press.

ADELE DIEDERICH
Jacobs University Bremen, Germany

See also: **Information Processing; Psychometrics; Psychophysics**

McNAUGHTON RULE

On January 20, 1843, Daniel McNaughton shot Edmund Drummond. That McNaughton shot the secretary of Sir Robert Peel, the *actus reus*, is indisputable. *Mens rea*, or the concept that an evil mind must be present for criminal culpability, became crystallized in this case. Thus, a guilty person will have an evil mind, but that same mind must be a mind that is free from mental disease or defect.

For two-score years the issue swirling in juridical circles had been what to do with people whose reason was compromised. Reason is the central tenet of Western civilization that emerged from the Dark Ages. Basing justice on the Utilitarian principles of Jeremy Bentham, James Mills, and John Stuart Mills, punishment for a crime works as a deterrent and as society's retribution only if the perpetrator is of sound mind and can know or appreciate the consequences of his or her actions. Absent a sound mind, punishing a person is unjust within utilitarian philosophy. British law recognized that if a person had no more reason than a "wilde beeste," punishing the perpetrator was like whipping a dog for not knowing algebra. Humanistic concepts challenged prevailing ecclesiastically driven views that the mentally ill were inhabited by evil spirits. The emerging principles of a more modern psychiatry began to represent a medical approach to the mentally ill.

In the two decades before the McNaughton case (spelled in various ways due to clerk-of-court and printers' variations such as M'Naghton, McNaughten; his preferred spelling is followed here [see Diamond, 1977]), the cases of Oxford and Hatfield were flashpoints for British justice (West & Walk, 1977). Social policy began to reflect the sense that delusional disorders might well rob the murderous person of Reason, which would compromise one's ability to form evil intent. The McNaughton rule, developed from this legal case, held that the jury should be directed that: "To establish a defence on the ground of insanity it must be clearly proved that, at the time of committing the act, the party accused was labouring under such a defect of reason from disease of the mind, as to not know the nature and quality of the act he was doing, or if he did know it, that he did not know that what he was doing was wrong." (West & Walk, 1977, p. 75, provides a further elaboration of these rules.)

Note that one key element, a sound mind at the time of the crime, is crucial and distinguishes insanity at the time of the crime from competence to confess, to stand trial, and to bear the punishment. Competence to stand trial requires sufficient reason to allow for a person to know the nature of the offense, the individuals in the courtroom, and to be able to meaningfully participate in one's defense. A person could be competent to stand trial yet have been insane at the time of the offense. Alternatively, a person could be sane and criminally responsible at the time of the offense, but now his or her mental illness could lead to an incompetent-to-stand-trial finding. This would result in one being bound to civil authorities (e.g., a mental hospital) until such time as they could be tried.

In the political temper of the times, the McNaughton case set off a volley of arguments that resound to this day. Both the sense that someone might fake a mental illness and the sense that someone can evade just punishment or the retribution to which society is entitled weigh heavily in arguments since McNaughton. Insanity determinations are supposed to draw a line in that fuzzy area of values that deem people responsible or not, moral or not, blameworthy or not, possessing free will or not, able to be deterred or not, and punishable or not for their actions (Stone, 1976). These issues are at the heart of what it means to be civilized, so the few times that this defense is made seem to have resulted in the highest of passions on both sides.

After McNaughton several variants arose. These tests include (1) Irresistible Impulse ("... if by duress of such mental disease, he had so far lost the power to choose between right and wrong ... [that his] free agency [was] destroyed ... connected with such a mental disease ... as to have been the product of it solely" [*Parson v. State*, 1887]); (2) the Durham ("... unlawful act was the product of mental disease or mental defect [*Durham v. United States*, 1954]); and (3) the American Law Institute ("... not responsible ... as a result of mental disease or defect he lacks substantial capacity to appreciate the criminality of his conduct or to conform his conduct to the requirements of law" (Stone, 1976, p. 230). The assassination of John Lennon and the attempt on the life of President Reagan rekindled the debate about the insanity plea. Such pleas as Georgia's "Guilty but Insane" statute also acknowledge the actus reus (guilty) while leaving the mens rea portion intact.

McNaughton governs a bit less than half of the United States population but remains the insanity standard in over half of the states in the United States. Daniel McNaughton was remanded to Bedlam, an asylum for the mentally ill, where he remained for some 20 years. Near the end of his life, he was transferred to Broadmoor, another asylum, where he died on May 3, 1865.

REFERENCES

Diamond, B. L. (1977). On the spelling of Daniel M'Naghten's name (reprinted from the Ohio State Law Journal, 1964, Vol. 25, no. 1). In D. J. Weiss & A. Walk (Eds.), *Daniel McNaughton: His trial and the aftermath* (pp. 86–90). Ashford, Kent, UK: Gaskell Books, Headley Brothers Ltd.

Durham v. United States, 214 F. 2D862, 874–875. [D.C. Cir. 1954].

Parsons v. State, 2 So. 854, 866–67 [Ala. 1887].

Stone, A. A. (1976). *Mental health and the law: A system in transition*. Rockville, MD: National Institute of Mental Health.

West, D. J., & Walk, A. (Eds.). (1977). *Daniel McNaughton: His trial and the aftermath*. Ashford, Kent, UK: Gaskell Books, Headley Brothers Ltd.

SUGGESTED READINGS

Stone, A. A. (1976). *Mental health and the law: A system in transition*. Rockville, MD: National Institute of Mental Health.

Weiner, I. B., & Hess, A. K. (Eds.). (2006). *The handbook of forensic psychology, third edition*. New York: John Wiley & Sons.

West, D. J., & Walk, A. (Eds.). (1977). *Daniel McNaughton: His trial and the aftermath*. Ashford, Kent, UK: Gaskell Books, Headley Brothers Ltd.

ALLEN K. HESS
Auburn University at Montgomery

See also: **Criminal Responsibility; Forensic Psychology**

MEEHL, PAUL E. (1920–2003)

Paul E. Meehl was born in 1920 in Minneapolis, Minnesota. He attended public schools there and received his Ph.D. in clinical psychology from the University of Minnesota in 1945. Among the teachers at Minnesota who shaped his thinking were psychologists D. G. Paterson, William T. Heron, B. F. Skinner, and his advisor, Starke R. Hathaway; philosopher Herbert Feigl; and statisticians A. Treloar and P. O. Johnson.

He became interested in psychoanalysis by reading Karl Menninger's *The Human Mind* and much of Freud in his late teens, but the Minnesota psychology department was behavioristic, statistical, and anti-Freudian. The resulting cognitive conflict led Meehl to try to answer questions in "soft" psychology with rigorous methodological approaches, as reflected in his work on clinical versus actuarial prediction, his criticism of the misuse of the null hypothesis testing in psychology, and his development of new statistical techniques to deal with the problem of classification.

Meehl published, with K. MacCorquodale, animal research on latent learning, and he co-authored, with W. K. Estes and others, *Modern Thinking Theory* (1954), summarizing the Dartmouth Conference on learning theory, which many believed signaled the closing phase of grand general theories of learning. The MacCorquodale and Meehl article, "On a Distinction between Hypothetical Constructs and Intervening Variables," is considered a classic. A philosophically related classic paper (coauthored with L. J. Cronbach) is titled "Construct Validity in Psychological Tests."

His early writings and colloquium lectures on the Minnesota Multiphasic Personality Inventory (MMPI) forced clinicians to take the MMPI seriously; this work included the first analysis of profile patterns, the first theoretical exposition, the first use of actuarial approach to MMPI interpretation, and the identification of the K-factor.

His training analyst, B. C. Glueck, interested him in Rado's theory of schizophrenics and J. C. McKinley taught him that many schizophrenics have neurological aberrations. The clinical knowledge greatly influenced his theory of schizotype: that it is a result of genetic hypokrisia at the neural synapse conjoined with social learning regimes, and that schizophrenia begins its clinical decompensation in a small minority of schizotypes.

In order to test any theory of schizophrenia, Meehl realized that new statistical procedures for classification were needed. This led him to invent the taxometric method and coherent cut kinetics, which is a collection of specific taxometric procedures that provide consistency tests of the underlying coherence of data to tell whether the latent situation is purely dimensional or taxonic. Its importance and application was general and was not confined to detecting schizotype.

Meehl's work ranged widely: he published about animal behavior, learning theory, psychopathology, interview assessment, psychometrics, MMPI scale development and validation, methods of actuarial interpretation, forensic psychology, political behavior, behavior genetics, and philosophy of science. His books include the *Atlas for Clinical Interpretation of the MMPI* (1951, coauthored with S. R. Hathaway), *Clinical vs. Statistical Prediction* (1954), *Psychodiagnosis: Selected Papers* (1973), *Selected Philosophical and Methodological Papers* (1991; edited by C. A. Anderson and K. Gunderson), and *Multivariate Taxometric Procedures: Distinguishing Types from Continua* (1998; coauthored with N. G. Waller).

Meehl served as chairman of the psychology department at Minnesota from 1951–1957. He was cofounder, with Herbert Feigl and Wilfred Sellars, of the Minnesota Center for Philosophy and Science, the prototype for such centers around the world. Until his retirement, he engaged part-time in the practice of psychotherapy (psychoanalytic, and later, rational-emotive). He served as an expert witness in civil and criminal trials and as advisor to the Minnesota legislature. He was a member of the American Psychological Association and served as president in 1962. He was also a member of the National Academy of Arts and Science. He received APA's Distinguished Scientific Contribution Award, Award for Distinguished Professional Contribution to Knowledge, and Award for Outstanding Lifetime Contribution to Psychology; the APA Clinical Division's Distinguished Contributions Award and its 1996 Centennial Award; the APA Division 5 award for Distinguished Lifetime Contribution to Evaluation, Measurement, and Statistics; the Bruno Klopfer Distinguished Contribution Award from the Society for Personality Assessment; the American Board of Professional Psychology's Award for Distinguished Service and Outstanding Contributions to the Profession; the American Psychological Foundation Gold Medal Award for Life Achievement in the Application of Psychology; the Joseph P. Zubin Award for Distinguished Contributions to Psychopathology; the Educational Testing Service Award for Distinguished Service to Measurement; and the Lifetime Achievement Award in Basic and Applied Research in Psychology from the American Association of Applied and Preventive Psychology. He was a William James Fellow of the American Psychological Society and received its James McKeen Cattell Fellow award.

SUGGESTED READINGS

Meehl, P. (1954). *Clinical vs. statistical prediction.* Amsterdam: Jason Aronson.

Meehl, P. (1991). *Selected philosophical and methodological papers.* C. A. Anderson & K. Gunderson (Eds.). Minneapolis: University of Minnesota Press.

Meehl, P., & Waller, N. G. (1991). *Multivariate taxometric procedures: Distinguishing types from continua.* Thousand Oaks, CA: Sage.

STAFF

MEGALOMANIA

The *Oxford English Dictionary* (1978) defines megalomania as "the insanity of self-exaltation; the passion for 'big things'" (p. 308). Megalomania is characterized by an inflated sense of self-esteem and overestimation by persons of their powers and beliefs. Often associated with delusions, psychotic processes, or extreme forms of narcissism, megalomania may refer to delusions of grandeur, with a pathological overvaluation of ideas, or plans for remaking the world in accord with the person's own wishes and fantasies. Representing a form of denial and disavowal of the limitations of the self, of the existence of death, and of the power of the constituted social order, the megalomaniacal state may involve omnipotence and grandiosity taken to an extreme. People suffering from megalomania privilege their thinking to a degree where shared reality is abandoned and attempts are made to dominate others.

An early clinical example of megalomania was demonstrated by Daniel Paul Schreber, who wrote a memoir of his psychosis, which began in 1884 and recurred several times thereafter. Schreber's delusion was of his body being transformed into that of a woman. The expert testimony of Dr. Weber, a psychiatrist evaluating Schreber, gave this description of Schreber: "He is called to redeem the world and to bring back to mankind the lost state of Blessedness. He maintains he has been given this task by direct divine inspiration." (Schreber, 1903, p. 272). In his memoir, Schreber details his sense of being singled out by God to save the world with special knowledge and a privileged position among men. This type of fantastical thinking and belief about oneself is common in megalomania.

A symptom associated with several diagnostic entities, megalomania is not a stand-alone diagnosis in current nosology. Various psychopathologies and etiologies have been put forth to explain megalomania. Examining the case of Schreber, Freud (1911/1958) locates narcissism as a developmental stage between autoerotism and object relations. Megalomania occurs when the ego ideal becomes suffused with regressive wishes for total self-sufficiency and omnipotence, which are fantasies associated with the earliest phase of development. Schizophrenia, paranoia, and melancholia are also linked to the symptom of megalomania, which may in fact be a manic defense against vulnerability and fears of being overpowered by stronger forces, or may be an attempt to deny death. The treatment of megalomania involves addressing the underlying disorder and treating active psychotic or manic states, often with medication. Frequently, character disturbances preponderate and may be addressed through longer-term psychotherapy, although a person with megalomania may not be interested in self-reflection or personal change.

REFERENCES

Freud, S. (1958). Psycho-analytic notes on an autobiographical account of a case of paranoia (dementia paranoids). In J. Strachey (Ed. and Trans.), *The standard edition of the complete psychological works of Sigmund Freud* (Vol. 12, pp. 1–82). London: Hogarth Press. (Original work published in 1911)

Oxford English Dictionary (1978). Megalomania (p. 308). Oxford, UK: Oxford University Press.

Schreber, D. (1955) *Memoirs of my nervous illness* (I. MacAlpine & R. Hunter, Trans. & Eds.). London: Dawson. (Originally published in 1903)

SUGGESTED READING

Scull, Andrew (2005). *Madhouse: A tragic tale of megalomania and modern medicine*. New Haven: Yale University Press.

JANE G. TILLMAN
The Austen Riggs Center, Stockbridge, MA

See also: Delusions; Narcissism

MELANCHOLIA (See Major Depressive Disorder)

MEMORY DISORDERS (See Alzheimer's Disease; Amnesia; Dementia; Late-Life Forgetting)

MEMORY FUNCTIONS

Defined generally, memory is the capacity to preserve and recover information. Yet neither memory's operation nor its structures are easily understood without some consideration of function. Like other biological systems, the capacity to remember evolved because of its fitness-enhancing properties. Memory helped solve adaptive problems that, in turn, increased the chances of survival and genetic transmission. As a result, memory's operating characteristics likely bear the imprints of the specific selection pressures that shaped their development.

For example, seasonal variation in the availability of food leads some birds to store small quantities of food in widely scattered locations. Food-storing birds, such as Clark's nutcrackers and marsh tits, later show a remarkable ability to locate and recover this food during the harsh winter season. In laboratory tests, these birds perform better on some tests of spatial memory, and show larger hippocampal volume, than do other non-storing species (Clayton, 1995). The mechanisms that produce these differences have yet to be identified fully, and learning potentially plays a role in the development of these abilities, but few question the tight functional link between mnemonic ability and the particular environmental and/or selection pressures faced by the organism (Heyes, 2003). To understand how memory works—its "tunings"—it is essential to attend closely to the functional problems that memory needs to solve.

In the human domain, cognitive psychologists historically have given little attention to the functions of memory, choosing instead to focus on the structural properties of memory systems and tasks. It is common for researchers to propose various memory systems, such as working memory, procedural memory, and semantic memory, but without detailed consideration of the specific problems that those systems emerged to solve. Similarly, a great deal is known about how to improve memory—e.g., form a visual image, space repetitions of material, practice retrieval through testing—yet very little is known about how or why these particular sensitivities developed. What were the adaptive problems, ancestral or ontogenetic, that helped shape memory's sensitivity to imagery or to the spacing of repetitions? Anderson and Schooler (1991) have speculated that our memory systems may be tuned to remember how events naturally occur and recur in the environment; this may help to explain how the accessibility of stored material changes with time, but analyses of this sort are rare and capture only a small portion of the ultimate functions of remembering.

What, then, are the true functions of memory? From an evolutionary perspective, of course, one is encouraged to focus on memory's fitness-enhancing properties. Memory mechanisms must be geared especially to helping us perform actions that enhance our reproductive fitness. The emphasis here is placed on memory's ability to increase the adaptive value of behavior in the present, particularly as it applies to survival and reproduction, not simply as a device to recover intact records of the past. The past can never occur again, at least in exactly the same form, so there is questionable adaptive value in designing a system simply to recover the veridical past. Instead, memory processes are likely engineered to use the past in the service of the present, or perhaps to predict the likelihood of events occurring in the future. There is substantial evidence that remembering is a constructive process, a blending of the present with the past (e.g., Schacter & Addis, 2007). In addition, growing behavioral and neural evidence indicates that memories of the past play a vital role in the envisioning of future events (Szpunar & McDermott, 2008).

More controversial, though, is the notion that our memory systems show content-specificity—that is, they are tuned to remember some kinds of information better than others. Psychologists usually appeal to general memory processes, such as encoding, storage, and retrieval, and assume that these processes operate similarly across materials and domains. Successful retention is determined mainly by the degree of "match" between the conditions present at encoding and those existing at the point of the retrieval query (Tulving & Thomson, 1973). Encoding processes establish a memory record that, in turn, determines the range of retrieval cues that will be effective in providing later access to that record (i.e., those cues that match the ones present at encoding). Although some kinds of situations may engender richer or more elaborate memory records, and thus create records that are more likely to be matched in later environments, the memory processes themselves are assumed to be domain-general, or insensitive to content.

Yet from a fitness perspective, not all occurrences are equally important. It is much more important to remember the appearance of a predator, the location of food, or the recent activities of a prospective mate than it is to remember events and activities that do not relate directly to fitness. Indeed, Klein (2007) has argued that the ability to relive past experiences through episodic memory, which may be a uniquely human characteristic, is an evolved adaptation designed specifically to help us interact in the social world. Ancestrally, humans lived in small bands and needed the ability to develop a sense of personal identity and to differentiate effectively among other members of the social group (e.g., track coalitional structure, identify cheaters, develop accurate personality assessments, track the activities of kin versus nonkin); the capacity to remember is a vital ingredient of each of these tasks. One can also imagine memory playing a critical role in navigational abilities—everything from recognizing landmarks to remembering diagnostic weather patterns or relevant constellations.

Empirically, recent evidence indicates that processing information in terms of its relevance to fitness can produce excellent retention—better retention, in fact, than most (if not all) known encoding techniques (Nairne, Thompson, & Pandeirada, 2007). In the relevant experiments, participants were asked to imagine themselves stranded in the grasslands of a foreign land without basic survival materials. They were then given random words and asked to rate the relevance of each to finding steady supplies of food and water and gaining protection from predators. Later, surprise memory tests for the rated materials revealed uniformly high retention. For example, a few seconds of survival processing produced better free recall than established memory encoding procedures such as forming a visual image, self-generating the material, or relating the information to a personal autobiographical memory (Nairne, Pandeirada, & Thompson, 2008). Moreover, it is the fitness relevance of the processing that seems to matter; for example, using a scenario in which participants are asked to imagine gathering food for survival produces better memory than a scenario in which participants are asked to gather food as part of a scavenger hunt. Memory is apparently tuned to remember information that is processed for fitness.

Recognizing the fitness-enhancing properties of memory, however, tells us little about the proximate mechanisms that actually produce behavior. Some evolutionary psychologists have proposed that the mind contains thousands of cognitive adaptations, each uniquely sculpted by nature to solve some specific end (Tooby & Cosmides, 1992). Just like the organs of the body are specialized to perform particular functions—i.e., pump blood, filter impurities, manufacture insulin—so too might mnemonic "organs," be specialized to recognize and retain information particularly relevant to fitness. This "Swiss Army knife" model of the mind allows ample room for memory adaptations, much like those that have been proposed for non-human animals (e.g., birds' abilities to learn the signature songs of conspecifics). At the same time, it is notoriously difficult to establish the existence of true cognitive adaptations (i.e., specialized mechanisms that have been sculpted by the processes of natural selection), so considerable caution needs to be exercised in theory development.

The survival experiments described earlier, along with other work demonstrating that it is comparatively easy for people to associate predatory snakes and spiders with fear-eliciting stimuli (Öhman & Mineka, 2001), are representative of how functional aspects of memory can be explored empirically. One begins by speculating about the adaptive problems that our memory systems need to solve, such as remembering the location of food or predators, and then generating relevant empirical predictions. Presumably, if the adaptive problems are correctly identified, their "footprints" should be found in the operating characteristics of memory processes (e.g., memory is enhanced after survival-based processing). This kind of task analysis, in which one generates a priori empirical predictions based on a consideration of recurrent adaptive problems, helps to circumvent a common criticism of evolutionary psychology—namely, that evolutionary reasoning is often nothing more than a collection of post-hoc "just so" stories (Gould & Lewontin, 1979).

Even if one chooses not to focus on evolutionary determinants of remembering, however, there is still considerable merit in adopting a truly functional perspective. As noted, it is rare for memory researchers to consider function or, more importantly, the role that function potentially plays in the actual design and operation of memory systems. Even if our memory systems are shaped primarily by current or developmentally-based selection pressures, rather than ancestral environments, the act of remembering will still be purposeful and goal-directed. Thinking functionally i.e., asking questions about the "why" of remembering, is apt to open new research pathways and, ultimately, it should provide the necessary empirical and theoretical structure to discover "how" memory operates as well.

REFERENCES

Anderson, J. R., & Schooler, L. J. (1991). Reflections of the environment in memory. *Psychological Science, 2*(6), 396–408.

Clayton, N. S. (1995). Development of memory and the hippocampus: Comparison of food-storing and nonstoring birds on a one-trial associative memory task. *Journal of Neuroscience, 15*(4), 2796–2807.

Gould, S. J., & Lewontin, R. C. (1979). The spandrels of San Marco and the Panglossian paradigm: A critique of the adaptationist programme. *Proceedings of the Royal Society of London— Series B, 205*(1161), 581–598.

Heyes, C. (2003). Four routes of cognitive evolution. *Psychological Review, 110*(4), 713–727.

Klein, S. B. (2007). Phylogeny and evolution: Implications for understanding the nature of a memory system. In H. L. Roediger, Y. Dudai & S. M. Weiss (Eds.), *Science of memory: Concepts* (pp. 377–381). Oxford, UK: Oxford University Press.

Nairne, J. S., Pandeirada, J. N. S., & Thompson, S. R. (2008). Adaptive memory: The comparative value of survival processing. *Psychological Science, 19*(2), 176–180.

Nairne, J. S., Thompson, S. R., & Pandeirada, J. N. S. (2007). Adaptive memory: Survival processing enhances retention. *Journal of Experimental Psychology: Learning, Memory, and Cognition, 33*(2), 263–273.

Öhman, A., & Mineka, S. (2001). Fears, phobias, and preparedness: Toward an evolved module of fear and fear learning. *Psychological Review, 108*(3), 483–522.

Schacter, D. L., & Addis, D. R. (2007). The cognitive neuroscience of constructive memory: Remembering the past and imagining the future. *Philosophical Transactions of the Royal Society (B), 362*, 773–786.

Szpunar, K. K., & McDermott, K. B. (2008). Episodic future thought and its relation to remembering: Evidence from ratings of subjective experience. *Consciousness and Cognition, 17*(1), 330–334.

Tooby, J., & Cosmides, L. (1992). The psychological foundations of culture. In J. H. Barkow, L. Cosmides & J. Tooby (Eds.), *The adapted mind: Evolutionary psychology and the generation of culture* (pp. 19–136). New York: Oxford University Press.

Tulving, E., & Thomson, D. M. (1973). Encoding specificity and retrieval processes in episodic memory. *Psychological Review, 80*(5), 352–373.

SUGGESTED READINGS

Gangestad, S. W., & Simpson, J. A. (Eds.). (2007). *The evolution of mind: Fundamental questions and controversies.* New York: Guilford Press.

Klein, S. B., Cosmides, L., Tooby, J., & Chance, S. (2002). Decisions and the evolution of memory: Multiple systems, multiple functions. *Psychological Review, 109*, 306–329.

Nairne, J. S. (2005). The functionalist agenda in memory research. In A. F. Healy (Ed.), *Experimental cognitive psychology and its applications.* (pp. 115–126). Washington, DC: American Psychological Association.

James S. Nairne
Purdue University

Josefa N. S. Pandeirada
University of Santiago, Portugal

See also: **Declarative Memory; Episodic Memory; Spatial Memory**

MENOPAUSE

Menopause is the permanent end of menstruation or the last menstrual period. It occurs naturally in all women at some time during midlife or is caused by surgery, chemotherapy, or radiation. The average age at the last menstrual period is 51 years for women in industrialized countries, with most women reaching menopause between ages 45 and 55 and the normal range spanning ages 40 to 60. Menopause is defined retroactively after a woman has not had a period for 12 months (although in one large study 5% of women did have another period after this length of time).

The final period is one event in a longer physiological process. Perimenopause is the transitional time leading up to and surrounding menopause. In one study perimenopause averaged 4 years but can range from 0 (i.e., no noticeable changes) to 10 years or more. This is when distressing symptoms are most likely, for example, hot flashes, which are subjective feelings of heat accompanied by measurable changes in body temperature. Postmenopause is the time following the last menstrual period until a woman's death. Possible relationships of menopause to increased vulnerability to a wide range of chronic illnesses, such as heart, bone, and brain disease, have centered on postmenopause.

Perimenopause is defined by the World Health Organization (WHO) as the "period immediately before menopause (when the endocrinological, biological, and clinical features of approaching menopause commence) and the first year after menopause" (WHO Scientific Group, 1996, p. 10). However, there is no consensus about what specific changes causally lead to menopause. Perimenopause is therefore defined by changes observed in the years preceding menopause, especially changes in menstrual flow. The STRAW staging system (Soules, et al., 2001) has several stages for pre-, peri-, and postmenopause. STRAW characterizes the menopausal transition by a progression from irregular to skipped menstrual periods, and by elevations in the hormone FSH (follicle stimulating hormone) during the menstrual cycle early follicular phase. However, many women do not linearly progress from one stage to another, but may go back and forth and may experience symptoms like hot flashes while periods are still regular. Other researchers' definitions of perimenopause include subjective experiences such as hot flashes or a woman's own definition of her stage. Postmenopause, FSH levels are permanently elevated, and estrogen levels permanently sharply decline. There is no consensus about what substages, whether defined by differing hormonal milieus or other criteria, are needed for postmenopause.

The menstrual cycle involves a complicated set of relationships among ovarian hormones, the hypothalamic-pituitary axis, and other brain structures. This system changes in poorly understood ways during perimenopause.

There is dysregulation of former relationships, seemingly erratic or unpredictable changes in hormone levels, and great variability among individuals. For example, regular periods may be observed even when FSH and estrogen levels have changed. Estrogen levels may be variable and on average higher rather than lower (Prior, 1998). At menopause, the ovary has depleted, or nearly depleted, its follicles. Because reproductive hormones like estrogen are manufactured in the follicle, which is a ball of cells surrounding an immature egg, depletion of follicles means that estrogen cannot be made in the ovary. Much lower amounts of estrogen continue to be manufactured in adrenal, fat, and other tissue.

The depletion of follicles is due largely to atresia. At puberty, a girl has on the order of 300,000–500,000 follicles; during each menstrual cycle, only a small number become active, while a far larger number, on the order of 1,000 monthly, simply die. Atresia begins prenatally and continues throughout life, including prior to puberty. One theory is that observed perimenopausal changes are caused when follicles reach a critical low number; this causes changes in levels of another ovarian hormone, inhibin B, which then affects other hormones. Further, aging follicles may not respond normally to chemical signals. Another theory suggests that the aging central nervous system (CNS) becomes less responsive to chemical signals, or that CNS set points that establish relationships among these signals are altered.

The dominant metatheory of the fundamental nature of menopause is the biomedical model, the basic idea of which is that menopause is senescence: The reproductive system stops working because the ovary has aged and stops functioning. A further assumption is that, if ovarian hormones, especially estrogen, are found in lower amounts, this is a deficiency. Menopause is viewed as the central event of midlife, physically and psychologically; estrogen deficiency is the major cause of serious health problems. However, critics have suggested that the idea that reproductive ability is central to women's physical and psychological health reflects gender stereotypes rather than science (see Voda, 1992). A period of post-reproductive, competent adulthood might be part of the human genetic body plan, because menopause appears unique to humans (Derry, 2006). A National Institutes of Health (NIH, 2005) state-of-the-science conference concluded that menopause is natural and healthy and overly medicalized.

Whereas some women experience distressing symptoms, many women do not. A syndrome with a wide range of symptoms, including moodiness, memory problems, hot flashes, and other symptoms, is said to characterize perimenopause. However, in research studies only hot flashes, vaginal dryness, and in some studies insomnia are reliably associated with menopausal status. Research has established that clinical depression is not, as was assumed, a widespread phenomena during menopause, and most women do not find menopause important to their self-definition. A small increase in rates of depression may occur during perimenopause. Research on menopause causing chronic illnesses like bone, brain, and heart disease has had at best ambiguous results, with best evidence for a relationship with bone disease. The Women's Health Initiative clinical trials (Writing Group for the Women's Health Initiative Investigators, 2002), for example, found that treatment with replacement estrogen medications does not lower risk of heart disease.

For social scientists, additional issues include research needed on the role of cultural expectations, coping factors, and other psychological and social factors that contribute to a woman's definition and experience of mature adulthood and menopause.

REFERENCES

Derry, P. (2006). A lifespan biological model of menopause. *Sex Roles, 54*, 393–399.

National Institutes of Health. (2005, March 21–23). NIH state-of-the-science conference statement on management of menopause-related symptoms. *NIH Consensus Statements Scientific Statements, 22*, 1–38.

Prior, J. (1998). Perimenopause: The complex endocrinology of the menopausal transition. *Endocrine Reviews, 19*, 397–428.

Soules, R., Sherman, S., Parrott, E., Rebar, R., Santoro, N., Utian, W., et al. (2001). Executive summary. Stages of reproductive aging workshop (STRAW). *Journal of Women's Health and Gender-Based Medicine, 10*, 843–848.

Voda, A. (1992). Menopause: A normal view. *Clinical Obstetrics and Gynecology, 35*, 923–933.

Writing Group for the Women's Health Initiative Investigators. (2002). Risks and benefits of estrogen plus progestin in healthy postmenopausal women. *Journal of the American Medical Association, 288*, 321–333.

WHO Scientific Group (1996). *Research on the menopause in the 1990s: A report of the WHO Scientific Group.* Geneva, Switzerland: World Health Organization.

SUGGESTED READINGS

Lock, M. (1998). Deconstructing the change: Female maturation in Japan and North America. In R. Shweder (Ed.), *Welcome to middle age!* (pp. 45–74). Studies on successful midlife development, The John D. and Catherine T. MacArthur Foundation series on mental health and development. Chicago: University of Chicago Press.

Prior, J. (1998). Perimenopause: The complex endocrinology of the menopausal transition. *Endocrine Reviews, 19*, 397–428.

PAULA S. DERRY
Paula Derry Enterprises in Health Psychology, Baltimore, MD

See also: **Menstruation**

MENSTRUATION

Menstruation refers to normal vaginal bleeding that is usually monthly. The endometrium (uterus lining) sheds when a woman is not pregnant. The menstrual cycle refers to the time from the menstrual flow until the day before the next bleeding (commonly called a "period") begins, with normal lengths of 21–36 days (van Hooff et al., 1998). Normal flow lasts for 3–5 days, and the total amount of fluid is about 20–40 mL (4–8 soaked regular tampons or menstrual pads). (Hallberg, Hogdahl, Nillson, & Rybo, 1966)

Menstruation is a normal biological phenomenon. However, in many cultures menstruating women are seen as unclean and subject to restrictive beliefs about sexual behavior or participation in religious events. These beliefs can be seen in media coverage of "menstrual suppression" with extended or continuous hormonal contraception (Johnston-Robledo, Barnack, & Wares, 2006).

A young woman in North America has her first menstruation (menarche) about age 12, although between 10 and 14 years is normal. Menstruation continues cyclically for an average of three and a half decades until the final menstrual period at an average age of 51 (normal from 40-58). A woman is menopausal with less than a 10% chance of further flow once she has had a year without menstrual flow (Wallace, Sherman, Bean, Treloar, & Schlabaugh, 1979). Perimenopause refers to the transition to one year beyond the final flow and may begin in regularly cycling women with typical symptoms (cyclic night sweats, shorter cycles, or increased cramps and premenstrual symptoms (Prior, 2005) in women as young as the mid-30s. The duration of perimenopause is not known but is on average four years from irregular periods (about age 47) until menopause. It is a time of change with variable and higher estrogen levels, ovulation disturbances and consequent changes in flow and experiences (Prior, 1998).

The menstrual cycle also describes the cyclic hormonal changes that are orchestrated by coordination of signals from the brain and pituitary with hormones from the ovary. All estrogen produced during a given cycle is made by the cells of one particular "dominant follicle" (larger nest of cells surrounding one egg). This follicle begins to grow during menstrual flow and increases in size and the amount of estrogen it makes to the middle of the cycle. As it enlarges it develops a cyst (small sac) of fluid that may normally grow to 2–3 cm in size. Next, ovulation occurs with cyst rupture and egg extrusion. Following ovulation, cells that lined the follicle form a new body called the corpus luteum that makes progesterone as well as estrogen. If ovulation does not occur, progesterone levels do not rise, and the ovary is left containing a cyst.

Although the typical menstrual cycle is 28 days long, and ovulation ideally occurs on day 14, there is a wide variation in the lengths of menstrual cycles (21–36 days normally) and the timing of ovulation (day 9–25). The luteal phase includes the days following ovulation until the next flow. The normal luteal phase length is usually 14 or more days.

An interested woman can detect three events in an ovulatory menstrual cycle. One is a sustained rise of about 0.22 degrees Celsius in first morning temperature. This rise follows ovulation by about 24 to 48 hours. Progesterone raises the core temperature through its action in the brain. The temperature rise continues until the cycle end. If a woman is pregnant she will not have a period, and her temperature will remain elevated.

The second event occurs before ovulation and is the response of glands at the cervix (opening of uterus into the vagina) to the increasing estrogen. Estrogen stimulates production of clear, stretchy mucus that resembles egg white—this creates an ideal environment in which sperm can swim into the uterus. After ovulation (because progesterone suppresses the cervical glands' production), the stretchy mucus disappears. If there is no ovulation, stretchy mucus may be detected throughout the cycle.

Finally, near the middle of the cycle, a one-day rise in a pituitary hormone called "luteinizing hormone" (LH) can be detected using over-the-counter urine test kits. This test can tell whether a woman is going to ovulate and is used as an aid to fertility. When ovulation occurs late in a menstrual cycle, this is called short luteal phase. It is defined as fewer than 12 days between the LH peak and flow or fewer than 10 days between temperature rise and the next menstruation. Short luteal phase cycles are associated with infertility or early miscarriages. In addition, short luteal phases are associated with risks for low bone density and subsequent osteoporosis. Short luteal phase cycles are common during the first 12 years following menarche and during perimenopause, but may occur at any age.

Menstrual cycle and ovulation changes are caused by physical or emotional stresses, such as examinations at school, psychological abuse, heavy exercise training, decreased food intake, and being ill. The subtlest of these changes is shortening of the luteal phase length. More intense stress may cause anovulation (lack of ovulation) that may occur in a normal or irregular cycle. Several stressors operating together or young gynecological age (number of years following menarche) may cause oligomenorrhea (cycle lengths longer than 36 days). Absence of menstruation for six months is called amenorrhea.

Emotional stress related to worry about gaining weight (called cognitive dietary restraint) in a normal weight woman is relatively common. It is associated with short luteal phase cycles and also with higher urinary excretion of the stress hormone, cortisol, and probably with increased risks for bone loss. A woman's physical and emotional experiences fluctuate during an ovulatory menstrual cycle in concert with hormonal changes. These normal but observable changes are known collectively as molimina. Some use this term for all premenstrual changes, but it may be specific for cycles with normal ovulation. Slowly increasing moderate exercise reduces premenstrual symptoms, as does taking supplemental calcium (1200 mg/d).

The concept of a "premenstrual monster" has become common in recent decades (Chrisler & Levy, 1990), but epidemiological research shows that premenstrual syndrome (PMS) is rare (Ramcharan, Love, Frick, & Goldfien, 1992). Some women experience a premenstrual exaggeration of normal molimina, particularly emotional lability, fluid retention, increased appetite and cravings, and breast tenderness. The *Diagnostic and Statistical Manual* (DSM) currently includes a diagnosis of "premenstrual dysphoric disorder" for premenstrual mood changes. The vast popular and scientific literature on "PMS" has significant methodological problems (Prior, 2002). Many women endorse "PMS" and answer retrospective questionnaires by describing adverse premenstrual experiences. However, prospective daily records often do not confirm these reports. Retrospective questionnaire data may capture stereotypes about what women experience, or may reflect worst rather than usual patterns. Alternatively, women may attribute intense premenstrual emotional experiences to the menstrual cycle, and find other attributions when they occur at other times.

Physiological processes related to exercise performance, lung function, immunology, and bone and insulin metabolism systematically vary across the menstrual cycle. Some medical problems also vary with the menstrual cycle—these are classically called "catamenial" conditions and include migraine headaches, epileptic seizures, and asthma. The hormonally documented research in this area, however, is inadequate.

Adequate or high levels of estrogen with too little or no progesterone are associated with disturbances in flow and cycles—these are common in puberty and perimenopause. Any menstrual period requiring 16 or more soaked regular-sized pads or tampons is abnormal; this increases risk for iron deficiency and anemia (low blood count). Over-the-counter ibuprofen use during heavy flow decreases its volume importantly by about 25% (Lethaby, Augood, & Duckitt, 2002). Menstrual cramps (dysmenorrhea) may occur before and during flow especially in teenagers and women in perimenopause. Dysmenorrhea is effectively prevented by anti-inflammatory medications such as ibuprofen—one tablet needs to be taken at the first feeling of pelvic heaviness and repeated whenever the feeling recurs.

Menstruation may be dismissed as a purely physiological event. However, each culture and each individual gives it specific meaning. As well, the dynamic interdependence of biology and culture play important roles in the link between menstruation and women's health.

REFERENCES

Chrisler, J. C., & Levy, K. B. (1990). The media construct a menstrual monster: A content analysis of PMS articles in the popular press. *Women and Health, 16*, 89–104.

Hallberg, L., Hogdahl, A. M., Nillson, L., & Rybo, G. (1966). Menstrual blood loss—a population study. *Acta Obstetrics and Gynecology Scandinavia, 45*, 320–351.

Johnston-Robledo, I., Barnack, J., & Wares, S. (2006). "Kiss your period good-bye": Menstrual suppression in the popular press. *Sex Roles, 54*, 353–360.

Lethaby, A., Augood, C., & Duckitt, K. (2002). Nonsteroidal anti-inflammatory drugs for heavy menstrual bleeding. *Cochrane Database System Review*, CD000400.

Prior, J. C. (1998). Perimenopause: The complex endocrinology of the menopausal transition. *Endocrine Reviews, 19*, 397–428.

Prior, J. C. (2002). Premenstrual symptoms and signs. In R. E. Weiss & E. T. Weiss (Eds.), *Conn's Current Therapy 2002* (pp. 1078–1080). New York: W.B. Saunders.

Prior, J. C. (2005). Clearing confusion about perimenopause. *British Columbia Medical Journal, 47*, 534–538.

Ramcharan, S., Love, E. J., Frick, G. H., & Goldfien, A. (1992). The epidemiology of premenstrual symptoms in a population-based sample of 2,650 urban women: attributable risk and risk factors. *Journal of Clinical Epidemiology, 45*, 377–392.

van Hooff, M. H., Voorhorst, F. J., Kaptein, M. B., Hirasing, R. A., Koppenaal, C., & Schoemaker, J. (1998). Relationship of the menstrual cycle pattern in 14–17 year old adolescents with gynaecological age, body mass index, and historical parameters. *Human Reproduction, 13*, 2252–2260.

Wallace, R. B., Sherman, B. M., Bean, J. A., Treloar, A. E., & Schlabaugh, L. (1979). Probability of menopause with increasing duration of amenorrhea in middle-aged women. *American Journal of Obstetrics and Gynecology, 135*, 1021–1024.

SUGGESTED READINGS

Centre for Menstrual Cycle and Ovulation Research. http://www.cemcor.ubc.ca/.

Prior, J. C. (1998). Perimenopause: The complex endocrinology of the menopausal transition. *Endocrine Reviews, 19*, 397–428.

Ussher, J. M. (2005). *Managing the monstrous feminine: Regulating the reproductive body.* London: Routledge.

JERILYNN C. PRIOR
CHRISTINE HITCHCOCK
University of British Columbia, Canada

See also: Menopause

MENTAL IMAGERY

The study of mental imagery has generated major disagreement ever since the science of psychology was founded in the nineteenth century. Much of this disagreement, then and now, focuses on whether imaging abilities are representative of universal psychological processes or whether they are indicative of individual differences.

From Nineteenth-Century Introspectionism to Twentieth-Century Behaviorism

The founder of modern psychology—Wilhelm Wundt—introspectively studied the contents of his own mind and concluded that all his thoughts were composed of mentally imaged sensations and that all his percepts were composed of perceived sensations. Contrary to Wundt's position on thinking, the leader of the Würzburg school of imageless thought, Oswald Külpe, discovered some people who were unable to imagine colors but were nevertheless able to reason accurately about them. By way of explanation, Külpe suggested that imageless thinkers and vivid visualizers are equally adept at imageless reasoning and imageless remembering, but that vivid visualizers are more adept at constructing visually imaged sensations from their imageless thoughts and imageless memories.

Consistent with Külpe's suggestion, early twentieth-century studies found that people's ratings of the vividness of their visually imaged sensations did not correlate significantly with either their ability to solve visual problems or their ability to remember visual information. However, the founder of behaviorism, John Watson, used these null correlations to convince the psychological community that mental images have no causal effect on behavior and, hence, can be omitted from scientific psychology. A 50-year hiatus in imagery research ensued.

The Revival of Research on Mental Imagery

In the mid-1960s, imagery research was revived by CUNY professors Sylvan Tomkins, Jerome L. Singer, Sydney Joelson Segal, and John Antrobus; by Arnold Lazarus in South Africa; by Mardi Horowitz in California; by Allan Paivio in Canada; and by Alan Richardson and Peter Sheehan in Australia. In a theoretical challenge to behaviorists' denial of purposive behavior, Tomkins argued that psychologists should "conceptualize a purpose, a goal, or an aim as an Image; that is, a criterion by which feedback is monitored and discrepancies measured until the Image is attained." Transforming behavior therapy into cognitive therapy, Arnold Lazarus showed that exposure to an imaged object of fear is as therapeutic as exposure to the real object. In clinical challenges to Freud's dictum that "happy people never make phantasies, only unsatisfied ones," Singer showed that fantasizing *per se* is not associated with psychopathology, and Horowitz distinguished normal images from hallucinatory images during psychosis and unbidden images following trauma. Moving in new empirical directions, Paivio found that memory for paired words is improved by combining their meanings into a visual image, but did not find that such improvement is positively correlated with image vividness.

In the early 1970s, cognitive psychologists Roger Shepard and Stephen Kosslyn developed problem-solving tasks purportedly requiring the use of visual imagery. On Shepard's prototypical task, research subjects viewed visual pairings of identical or mirror-image stimuli, one of which was rotated between 0 and 180 degrees, and their identification times for identical stimuli increased a fraction of a second for each degree of rotation—as if subjects were mentally rotating one stimulus at a constant speed until it matched the other. On one of Kosslyn's tasks, subjects were presented with the names of two animals and asked to identify the larger animal, and their identification times were faster for animals differing greatly in size (e.g., mouse versus elephant) than for animals differing less dramatically in size (e.g., fox versus rabbit)—as if they were comparing mental images of the two animals and were making quicker comparisons when the size difference was introspectively larger.

Cognitive scientist Zenon Pylyshyn objected that Shepard's mentally rotated images and Kosslyn's mentally compared images had to be constructed from imageless propositions in the central nervous system—propositions containing all of the information necessary to identify the correct answer without constructing any imagery. Furthermore, research showed that subjects' ratings of the vividness of their visual imagery do not correlate significantly with their performance on either Shepard's mental-rotation task or Kosslyn's size-comparison task.

The Theoretical Movement to Objectify Mental Imagery

Given the mounting evidence that the subjective vividness of imagery does not correlate with objective performance on cognitive tasks purportedly requiring imagery, Kosslyn objectified and redefined "imagery" as "the internal representation that is used in information processing, not the experience itself." In the 1980s, Kosslyn and his followers likened this "internal representation" to the objective representation that is generated onto a computer's cathode ray tube (CRT) from underlying information in the central processing unit (CPU). But as critics Janice Keenan and Richard Olson noted, "It is hard to argue that images are functionally distinct representations of knowledge when they are equated with CRTs that can be unplugged without causing any alterations in the processing." In the 1990s, Kosslyn abandoned his computer model and once again redefined the image in objectified terms, this time as a "depictive representation in the brain"—specifically, in cortical area V1, where visual information is represented retinotopically.

Individual Differences in the Subjective Experience of Mental Imagery

Researchers who disfavor any objectification of mental imagery believe that images are subjective experiences, by definition, and that Kosslyn and his followers run the risk of studying imageless processes of visual thinking instead of physiological aspects of mental imagery. The search by subjectivist researchers for objective performance variables that correlate significantly with the subjective vividness of imagery ultimately resulted both in the development of a psychometrically better measure of image vividness and in the discovery of some reliable correlations.

David Marks's Vividness of Visual Imagery Questionnaire (VVIQ), on which 16 visual images are rated for their subjective vividness, has become the most widely used measure of the subjective experience of mental imagery. VVIQ scores indicative of greater image vividness correlate significantly with the effects of imagery on autonomic and bodily responses, as Anees Sheikh has documented, and with performance measures of visual perception and behavioral measures of hypnotic susceptibility, as Stuart McKelvie has documented—but not with performance measures of visual thinking, as reviewed by McKelvie and by Robert Kunzendorf.

The Subjective Experience of Imagery and the Inflation of False Memory

Based on the subjective similarity between imaged sensations and perceived sensations, Marcia Johnson demonstrated that mentally imaging an event inflates the likelihood of later misremembering the event as previously perceived. This imagination inflation effect has become the scientific rallying point for those psychologists who interpret recovered memories of abuse as "false memories."

In subsequent research, however, Michael Nash and others found that greater imagination inflation is statistically associated not with image vividness, but with dissociative tendencies. These are the same tendencies that make it possible for some persons to dissociate from the reality of trauma, to convince themselves that they are just dreaming, memorially to encode the trauma as not real but imaginary, and later to re-experience the trauma as unbidden imagery. To the extent that both imagination inflation and dissociative tendencies are legitimate phenomena, the clinical determination of whether uncovered memories of abuse are real or false ought to be deemed a difficult and sobering endeavor.

The Symbolic Value of Imagery in the Clinic and in the Laboratory

Clinical psychologists tend to be interested in the symbolic content of their patients' imagery, rather than individual differences in vividness as studied by cognitive psychologists. And at the end of the twentieth century, Ernest Hartmann and Robert Kunzendorf developed a new line of research on image symbolism. In clinical episodes that inspired this research, Hartman encountered some recently traumatized patients who had dream images of being overwhelmed by a tidal wave—a wave that not only looked overwhelming at a purely visual level of meaning, but also felt as overwhelming as the traumatic event itself and, at this emotionally deeper level of meaning, appeared to stand for the traumatic event. This led Hartmann and Kunzendorf to hypothesize that images become symbolic not when they take on an additional level of unconscious meaning, as Freudians suggest, but when they take on an additional level of emotional meaning. In accord with this hypothesis, Hartmann and Kunzendorf were able to create symbolic images and symbolic daydreams in the laboratory, by instructing research subjects to generate either a visual image or a daydream while intensifying an unrelated emotion.

Twentieth-Century Directions

As imagery research moves forward in the twenty-first century, the objectivist approach and the subjective-differences approach need to be reconciled one way or another. Whether this reconciliation will be rooted in newfound correlations between the subjective experience of visual imagery and the activation of area V1, or whether it will be rooted in Külpe's suggestion that all cogitations in the visual cortex are imageless thoughts, or whether it will be rooted in new integrative theorizing, is a matter for future research.

REFERENCES

Baddeley, A. D. (1988). Imagery and working memory. In M. Denis, J. Engelkamp, & J. T. E. Richardson (Eds.), *Cognitive and neuropsychological approaches to mental imagery* (pp. 169–180). Dordrecht, The Netherlands: Martinus Nijhoff.

Hartmann, E., Kunzendorf, R. G., Baddour, A., Chapwick, M., Eddins, M., Krueger, C., et al. (2002–2003). Emotion makes daydreams more dreamlike, more symbolic. *Imagination, Cognition, and Personality, 22*(3), 257–276.

Johnson, M. K. (1991). Reflection, reality monitoring, and the self. In R. G. Kunzendorf (Ed.), *Mental imagery* (pp. 3–16). New York: Plenum.

Kosslyn, S. M. (1994). *Image and brain: The resolution of the imagery debate.* Cambridge, MA: MIT Press.

Kunzendorf, R. G., & Reynolds, K. (2004–2005). On the cognitive function of visual images and the development of individual differences. *Imagination, Cognition, and Personality, 24*(3), 245–257.

McKelvie, S. J. (1995). The VVIQ as a psychometric test of individual differences in visual imagery vividness: A critical review and plea for direction. *Journal of Mental Imagery, 19*(3&4), 1–106.

Sheehan, P. (Ed.). (1972). *The function and nature of imagery.* New York: Academic.

Sheikh, A. A. (Ed.). (2003). *Healing images: The role of imagination in health.* Amityville, NY: Baywood.

Singer, J. L. (2006). *Imagery in psychotherapy.* Washington, DC: American Psychological Association.

SUGGESTED READINGS

Finke, R. A. (1989). *Principles of mental imagery.* Cambridge, MA: MIT Press.

Klinger, E. (1990). *Daydreaming.* Los Angeles, CA: Tarcher.

Sheikh, A. A. (Ed.). (2002). *Handbook of therapeutic imagery techniques.* Amityville, NY: Baywood.

ROBERT G. KUNZENDORF
University of Massachusetts–Lowell

ANEES A. SHEIKH
Marquette University

See also: **Cognitive Development; Memory Functions**

MENTAL MEASUREMENTS YEARBOOK (See Buros Mental Measurements Yearbook)

MENTAL RETARDATION

Mental retardation, also known as intellectual disability, is characterized by subaverage general intellectual functioning and impairments in adaptive behavior, both manifested during the developmental years of childhood and adolescence (American Association on Mental Retardation, 2002; American Psychiatric Association, 2000). Intellectual functioning is measured by the Intelligence Quotient (IQ), and, in most instances, an IQ score of lower than 70 meets the criterion for subaverage general intellectual functioning. Definitions of adaptive behavior usually include skills of communication, socialization, and daily living as well as gross and fine motor abilities. Both IQ and adaptive behavior tests are available, have satisfactory reliability and validity, and yield scores that compare individuals with others of the same age. Nevertheless, controversy about their measurement exists, and some critics believe that essential components of intellectual functioning are complex, multidimensional, and not adequately measured by current instruments (Switzky & Greenspan, 2006).

Estimates of the prevalence of mental retardation vary somewhat, but are usually estimated to be approximately 4% of the population, with higher incidence during the school years when much of the diagnosis of individuals with mild intellectual disability occurs (Larson, Lakin, Anderson, Kwak, Lee, & Anerseon, 2001). The causes of mental retardation are many, and their origins can be genetic and/or environmental. Frequently, hereditary or environmental characteristics pose risks that are either amplified or ameliorated by the other. For example, maternal drinking during pregnancy is a risk factor for fetal alcohol syndrome or milder fetal alcohol effects, conditions which are associated with lowered IQ and adaptive behavior problems. However, many pregnant women drink with seemingly no effect on their fetus, suggesting that biological risk is quite varied across individuals.

Prenatal causes of mental retardation are numerous and can arise from gene mutations as, for example, in Tay-Sachs disease; from chromosomal irregularities such as Down syndrome; and from environmental hazards such as the presence of toxins (e.g., alcohol), or an insufficiency of necessary nutritional elements such as maternal folic acid/Vitamin B_{12} that is associated with risk of neural tube defects such as spina bifida or hydrocephalus. Down syndrome, a widely recognized condition involving a number of impairments, including mental retardation, is the result of extra chromosome 21 material; this extra material is almost always from maternal nondisjunction during meiosis that result in three, rather than two, chromosomes 21. This nondisjunction occurs more frequently with advancing maternal age; currently, approximately 1 in 700–800 births of an infant with Down syndrome (National Institute of Child Health and Human Development, 2006).

Although hundreds of causes of mental retardation have been identified, the etiology is unknown in more than 50% of cases and frequently assumed to be complex. For example, many as yet unidentified genes are believed to contribute to overall intellectual ability, and parents with limited intellectual ability are more at risk of having a child with mental retardation than are parents with high intelligence. This risk is likely magnified because of environmental conditions such as the failure to provide an enriching environment.

Perinatal and postnatal insults also can cause mental retardation. Trauma during birth can result in brain damage, and children who are born prematurely and/or are at low birthweight are at greater risk of impaired physical and intellectual disability. Accidental as well as nonaccidental injuries can damage neurobiological systems, as can infections, such as meningitis or encephalitis. Children of poverty are more likely to be exposed to multiple pre-, peri-, and post-natal risk factors that combine to produce a higher cumulative risk for mental retardation.

In some cases, mental retardation can be diagnosed in infancy or even prenatally with the identification of a condition that is always associated with mental retardation. For example, an ultrasound might reveal the development of a fetus with anencephaly (missing much of the brain). More typically, however, the diagnosis comes later

as infants and children fail to meet developmental milestones and lag behind in intellectual areas as well as other areas of development. Even during the early childhood years, though, it is sometimes difficult to differentiate intellectual disabilities from other disabilities such as language impairments, cerebral palsy, and autism. Indeed, some diagnosticians assert that recent increased incidence in autism is the result of many children now receiving that diagnosis rather than a diagnosis of mental retardation.

It is possible to prevent some instances of mental retardation or at least reduce the severity of the disability associated with it. If implemented, total abstinence from maternal alcohol consumption during pregnancy would eliminate fetal alcohol syndrome and the intellectual disabilities that accompany it. When prenatal diagnosis became available, the association of greater Down syndrome risk and older maternal age led to routine recommendations for prenatal screening for women who are 34 years or older. Positive diagnoses are often followed by the voluntary termination of the pregnancy. However, the incidence of Down syndrome has remained high, both because some women choose not to terminate their pregnancies when their screening result is positive, and because most children are born to younger women for whom screening is not routinely recommended.

When a condition associated with mental retardation is identified, it is essential to implement treatments that reduce the severity of the intellectual disability. For example, limiting the intake of phenylalanine to persons with phenylketonuria, a recessive genetic condition, will reduce or even eliminate neurological damage. The diet must be started early in infancy to be maximally effective. Surgical intervention, for example, shunt implantation for children with the neural tube defect of hydrocephalus, can reduce or prevent brain enlargement and the disability that accompanies it.

The diagnosis of mental retardation and the implementation of treatments can be a crisis for families. Research on family reaction and adaptation to living with a son or daughter with mental retardation has shown that after a crisis at the time of diagnosis, most families are resilient, and that they can and do adjust, reporting many satisfactions from their parenting experiences (Glidden & Schoolcraft, 2003). Indeed, parents sometimes become advocates not only for their own children with disabilities, but for others as well.

In addition to the usual parenting responsibilities, mothers and fathers of children with mental retardation often implement a variety of therapeutic and educational interventions that are recommended by professionals. These educational interventions can be effective in helping individuals achieve their maximum potential. The interventions should be started as early as possible, and many states now have programs that focus on identifying infants and toddlers with disabilities and then providing services to them, usually in their home. Many research studies have demonstrated that early intervention programs are most effective if they start early, are intensive, and continue beyond the early childhood years (Dunst, 2007).

Federal legislation, in the form of the Individuals with Disabilities Education Act (IDEA), guarantees that children with mental retardation are entitled to a free and appropriate public education until they reach their 22nd birthday. They may be included in the regular education classroom, in special classes, or in special schools. Children with milder levels of intellectual disability are usually included in the regular classroom with access to special services. Children with more severe learning problems as well as other impairments are more likely to be in special classes or even special schools. However, regardless of the placement, each child is entitled to an individualized education program (IEP) that includes both short- and long-term objectives and services that may involve reading specialists, physical and occupational therapists, speech and language pathologists, and other professionals (Sudhalter, 2007). Programs for adolescents include strategies and skills that will help these children with disabilities and their families navigate the transition to adulthood.

Adults with mental retardation may receive support through a variety of community services. Depending on where the individual fits on the spectrum of severity, these supports may be only occasional and minimal in intensity, or they may be continuous and encompass all aspects of the individual's life. Persons with only mild intellectual disabilities and no other associated impairments may be able to live independently and successfully compete for full-time employment. They may obtain a driver's license, engage in leisure activities with persons who have no intellectual disabilities, and marry and become parents. An estimated half-million adults with mental retardation in the United States have one or more children (Larson, Lakin, Anderson, & Kwak, 2001).

In contrast, when the level of mental retardation is profound and the person may be nonambulatory and have associated sensory disabilities, a high intensity of supports will be likely lifelong (American Association on Mental Retardation, 2002). Nevertheless, appropriate education and training can maximize the individual's capacity and functioning, leading to a higher quality of life. Mastering a task such as self-feeding, or pressing a picture of a glass of water on a picture board, thus communicating a current need to a caretaker, represents an enhanced living situation. Additionally, society can benefit economically when these skills are mastered in that persons who are relatively self-sufficient represent a cost savings.

Although many adults with mental retardation continue to live with their families of origin, other options exist. In addition to living independently, supervised apartments and group homes are available in the community. These living environments require staffing, which is either drop-in (for most apartments) or live-in (for most group homes). Staff members provide support and implement training programs for those adults who are not employed full-time. These programs may involve vocational training and work in a sheltered environment. Ultimately, the goal is for adults to work in the least restrictive environment that their functioning allows. Many employers are aware that adults with mental retardation can be excellent employees, that they are punctual and reliable, and that they are able to follow learned routines. Frequently, job coaches are available to help adults with mental retardation adjust to a new or changed job situation and to educate employers on effective accommodations that may be of benefit (Smith, Weber, Graffam, & Wilson, 2004).

Views of mental retardation are culture- and time-dependent. During the past 50 years, changes in societal attitudes have led to changes in the way we think about and treat individuals with mental retardation in the developed world. Children were frequently banned from public education in the mid-twentieth century, and both children and adults lived in institutions in far greater numbers than they do in the twenty-first century. Civil rights legislation that led to racial integration was also used to fight for the rights of persons with disabilities. Federal and state legislation combined with judicial decision-making helped ensure those rights, and social movements acted to spread their acceptance. The move toward de-institutionalization in the 1960s caused the closure of many institutions, and today, almost all children with mental retardation live with families, and most adults live with other family members or in independent or supported living quarters in the community (Polister, Lakin, Smith, Prouty, & Smith, 2002).

Despite the availability of services for adults with mental retardation, many problems persist. Adequate funding is not always available, especially in times of general economic downturn. Frequently, long waiting lists for group homes and vocational training programs can translate into years of delay until an adult can move on with his or her life. Moreover, because adults with mental retardation may be trusting and less able to analyze attempts by others to exploit them, they are vulnerable to victimization. This vulnerability may be one reason that they are more likely to be arrested, indicted, found guilty, and imprisoned. There is general agreement that they are overrepresented in prison populations, perhaps as much as five times higher than what would be expected given their prevalence. Recent court cases have successfully argued that persons with intellectual disability who are convicted of murder should not be sentenced to death. In 2002, the Supreme Court issued a ruling in *Atkins v. Virginia* that execution of a person with mental retardation violated the eighth amendment of the U.S. Constitution, which bans cruel and unusual punishment.

In sum, as a result of medical and educational advances, and behavioral and family interventions, persons with mental retardation are living longer, are more integrated into the community, and have a larger range of options available to them as life choices. These advances have been accompanied by changed societal attitudes that view persons with intellectual disabilities as human beings that are entitled to the same rights as other individuals.

REFERENCES

Atkins v. Commonwealth of Virginia, 536 U.S. 304 (2002).

American Association on Mental Retardation (2002). *Mental retardation: Definition, classification, and systems of support* (10th ed.). Washington, DC: Author.

American Psychiatric Association (2000). Mental retardation. *Diagnostic and statistical manual of mental disorders* (4th ed., text. rev.). Washington, DC: Author.

Dunst, C. J. (2007). Early intervention for infants and toddlers with developmental disabilities. In S. L. Odom, R. H. Horner, M. E. Snell, & J. Blacher (Eds.), *Handbook of developmental disabilities* (pp. 161–180). New York: Guilford.

Glidden, L. M. & Schoolcraft, S. A. (2003). Depression: Its trajectory and correlates in mothers rearing children with developmental disabilities. *Journal of Intellectual Disability Research, 47*, 250–263.

Larson, S., Lakin, C., Anderson, L., & Kwak, N. (2001). Demographic characteristics of persons with MR/DD living in their own homes or with family members: NHIS-D Analysis. *MR/DD Data Brief 3*(2). Minneapolis, MN: University of Minnesota, Institute on Community Integration, Research and Training Center on Community Living.

Larson, S.A., Lakin, K. C., Anderson, L., Kwak, N., Lee, J. H., & Anderson, D. (2001) Prevalence of mental retardation and developmental disabilities: Estimates from the 1994/1995 National Health Interview Survey Disability Supplements. *American Journal on Mental Retardation, 106*, 231–252.

National Institute of Child Health and Human Development (2006). Facts about Down syndrome. Retrieved June 12, 2008, from http://www.nichd.nih.gov/publications/pubs/downsyndrome.cfm.

Polister, B., Lakin, K. C., Smith, J., Prouty, R., & Smith, G. (2002). Institution residents continue to decrease as community setting residents grow at an accelerating pace. *Mental Retardation, 6*, 488–490.

Smith, K., Webber, L., Graffam, J., & Wilson, C. (2004). Employment and intellectual disability: Achieving successful employment outcomes. In L. M. Glidden (Ed.), *International Review of Research in Mental Retardation* (pp. 261–289).

Sudhalter, V. (2007). The individualized education program: Navigating the IEP development process. In M. M. Mazzocco & J. L. Ross (Eds.), *Neurogenetic developmental disorders Variation of manifestation in childhood*. Cambridge, MA: MIT Press.

Switzky, H. N., & Greenspan, S. (2006). Summary and conclusions: Can so many diverse ideas be integrated? Multiparadigmatic models of understanding mental retardation in the 21st century. In H. W. Weiss & S. Greenspan (Eds.), *What is mental retardation: Ideas for an evolving disability* (rev. ed.). Washington, DC: American Association on Mental Retardation.

SUGGESTED READINGS

Glidden, L. M., & Schoolcraft, S. A. (2007). From diagnosis to adaptation: Optimizing family and child functioning when a genetic diagnosis is associated with mental retardation. In M. M. M. Mazzocco & J. L. Weiss (Eds.), *Neurogenetic developmental disorders: Manifestation and identification in childhood* (pp. 391–413). Cambridge, MA: MIT Press.

Odom, S. L., Horner, R. H., Snell, M. E., & Blacher, J. (Eds.). (2007). *Handbook of developmental disabilities*. New York: Guilford Press.

Switzky, H. N., & Greenspan, G. (Eds.). (2006). *What is mental retardation? Ideas for an evolving disability in the 21st century* (rev. ed.). Washington, DC: American Association on Mental Retardation.

LARAINE MASTERS GLIDDEN
St. Mary's College of Maryland

See also: Intelligence

MENTAL STATUS EXAMINATION

The Mental Status Examination (MSE) is a structured method of observations and inquiry that guides examiners in collecting observable behaviors and manifestations of emotions and cognitions and categorizing them for diagnostic purposes. The MSE does not need to be a standardized test. Its validity and reliability are not based on psychometric properties, but on its simplicity and its consistent sequential inquiry (Rogers, 2001). This method of investigation is relatively independent from the verbal content of an interview, and it is uniquely tuned to the identification of specific behavioral manifestations that are diagnostically and prognostically significant. The MSE can be part of a formal clinical interview or part of any type of interaction with a patient. The MSE method allows the examiner to observe and identify selected targeted behaviors that are specific objectives for intervention.

Categories of Behavioral Observations

The scope of this article does not allow for a comprehensive presentation of the categories of behavioral observations and the guidelines for a complete MSE. The *Psychiatric Mental Status Examination* by Trzepacz and Baker (1993) is a good example of a publication that provides a detailed and structured presentation of the MSE. The following categories of observations present a fundamental outline and sequence for the MSE mode of inquiry (Schwartz, 2005).

General Appearance

Starting a report of MSE findings with a description of the patient by age, sex, race, body type, and quality of personal appearance (nutrition, health, and grooming) allows the reader to have a visual image of the patient. This category includes an observation of patient's state of consciousness (on a continuum from *alert* to *coma*) and the manner and the attitude of the patient toward the examination and the examiner.

Behavior

The examiner evaluates the overall profile of patient's movements and motor activities. Observations are made on patient's gait, frequency and speed of movement, rhythm and coordination of movements, and the presence or absence of abnormal movements (such as agitated motions, tics, pacing, foot tapping).

Affect and Mood

Affect is the underlying emotional tone generated by the appearance of the patient, whereas the feeling state reported by the patient is referred to as mood. The congruity between affect and mood is a valuable source toward differential diagnosis. Affect and mood are observed within the context of the interview. It is expected to observe changes in expression of affect according to the content of the interview. Inappropriateness of mood (e.g., laughing while describing a tragedy) or constriction in range of affect (e.g., the interview is dominated by the same expression of mood) can be valuable diagnostic clues. Relatedness, or the ability of the patient to interact emotionally with the examiner, is an important subject of observations.

Speech and Thought Processes

Maxmen (1986) suggested four categories of observations of speech and thought processes:

1. Quantity of thought or stream of thought is manifested through rhythm of speech, speed of speech production, poverty or richness of speech, and degree of pressure of speech.

2. Continuity of thought refers to the quality of associations between ideas communicated by the patient. Patterns of verbal idiosyncrasies and disturbed linkages between words, phrases, or sentences (such as perseverations, loose associations, flight of ideas, or word approximations) are crucial indicators of various forms of pathology.

3. The content of thoughts is the patient's mode of verbal expression of personal experiences, perceptions, and feelings. Examiners pay attention to delusions, incomprehensible speech, illogical and magical thinking, and expressed obsessions. For example,

delusions, or belief systems without social, cultural, or religious foundations, are characteristic of individuals suffering from schizophrenia.

4. The ability to think symbolically and to conceptualize and generalize is called *abstraction*. Specific patterns of impoverished abstraction abilities are valuable cues differentiating between neurological conditions and various forms of mental illness.

Perceptual Processes

Patients with impaired reality testing consequent to neurological conditions or severe forms of mental illness present sensory and perceptual disorders. Such manifestations of break from reality can also be found temporarily in individuals in states of physical illness, fatigue, or heightened state of arousal. The persistence of a particular pattern of distortion is the diagnostic clue differentiating between a temporary state and a severe pathological condition. Examiners look for hallucinations (perceptions without external stimuli) and illusions (distortions of existing external stimuli).

Orientation

Patients are evaluated in their basic ability to orient themselves in person (asking the patient's name), time (asking to identify the time, day, month, and year of the evaluation session), and place (asking for patient's address or location of the evaluation). Some examiners add to this inquiry orientation to situation (questioning the purpose of the evaluation).

Attention and Concentration

A fully alert patient allows the examiner to evaluate the abilities of attention to a stimulus and concentration on a task. These abilities are prerequisites for the evaluation of various cognitive and intellectual functioning.

Intellectual Functioning

Observations of patient's vocabulary, general fund of information, use of learned material, and abstract thinking are needed to assess intellectual functioning. In addition, observations are made on basic skills of selective attention, perception, memory, language, and motor skills.

Insight and Judgment

The assessment of patients' insight and judgment, the quality of the interview, and patients' overall intelligence allow the examiner to assess the reliability of the evaluation. The prognostic value of the examination depends on its reliability.

Use of the MSE

The MSE is highly adaptive to various therapeutic orientations and specific populations. For example, a psychologist working with a volatile hospitalized patient is interested in this patient's pattern of pressured speech, independent of the content of the patient's verbalization. A neuropsychologist working with a stroke patient is more interested in the person's effortful production of speech. Psychology and psychiatry alike have recognized the practical versatility of the MSE and the adaptability of this approach and technique to various purposes. Rogers (2001) has published one of the best overviews of current uses of many variants of MSEs and their multiple adaptations to specific populations.

Examiners must be highly trained to differentiate between manifestations of mental illnesses, neurological and medical conditions, and consequences of temporary conditions (such as fatigue, sarcasm, humor, intoxication, or intense affect). Examiners also need to be sensitive to the impact of impoverished education and the impact of cultural and language differences on behavioral correlates of mental states.

REFERENCES

Maxmen, J. S. (1986). *Essential psychopathology*. New York: Norton.

Rogers, R. (2001). *Handbook of diagnostic and structured interviewing*. New York/London: Guilford Press.

Schwartz, E. (2005). The Mental Status Examination. In R. J. Craig (Ed.), *Clinical and diagnostic interviewing* (pp. 361–384). New York: Jason Aronson.

Trzepacz, P. T., & Baker, R. W. (1993). *The Psychiatric Mental Status Examination*. New York: Oxford University Press.

ELIEZER SCHWARTZ
Argosy University, Chicago

See also: **Interview Assessment**

META-ANALYSIS

Meta-analysis is a set of methods for integrating findings across studies to reveal the patterns of relations that underlie conflicting research literatures, thus providing a basis for theory development. Meta-analysis can correct for the distorting effects of sampling error, measurement error, and other artifacts that produce the illusion of conflicting findings. The goal in any science is the production of cumulative knowledge, and this implies the development of theories. But before theories can be developed, we must be able to calibrate the relations between variables. Applications of meta-analysis to accumulated research literatures has shown that research findings are not nearly as conflicting as had been thought and that useful and sound general conclusions can be drawn from existing research. During the 1980s and accelerating up to the present, the use of meta-analysis to make sense of research literatures has increased greatly.

Classification of Meta-Analysis Methods

Meta-analysis methods can be divided into three categories: (1) methods that are purely descriptive (and do not address sampling error); (2) methods that address sampling error but not other artifacts; and (3) methods that address both sampling error and other artifacts that distort findings in individual studies.

Purely Descriptive Methods

Glassian Methods

For Glass, the purpose of meta-analysis is descriptive; the goal is to paint a very general and broad picture of a particular research literature (Glass, McGaw, & Smith, 1981). Glassian meta-analysis accepts observed effect sizes at face value and thus implicitly assumes that the observed variability in effect sizes is real and should have some substantive explanation. There is no attention to sampling error variance in the effect sizes. The substantive explanations are sought in the varying characteristics of the studies (e.g., sex or mean age of subjects, length of treatment, and more). Study characteristics that correlate with study effect are examined for their explanatory power. In this method, there is a strongly empirical (nontheory based) approach to determining which aspects of studies should be coded and tested for possible association with study outcomes.

Study Effects Meta-Analysis

This method differs from Glass's procedures in several ways. First, only one effect size from each study is included in the meta-analysis, to ensure statistical independence within the meta-analysis. If a study has multiple dependent measures, those that assess the same construct are combined (usually averaged), and those that assess different constructs are assigned to different meta-analyses. Second, study effects meta-analysis calls for the meta-analyst to make some judgments about study methodological quality and to exclude studies with deficiencies judged serious enough to distort study outcomes. This procedure seeks to calibrate relationships between specific variables rather than to paint a broad Glassian picture of a research area. It is more focused on the kinds of questions that researchers desire answers to. However, this approach is like the Glass method in that it does not acknowledge that much of the variability in study findings is due to sampling error variance. That is, it takes observed correlations and d-values at face value.

Methods Focusing on Sampling Error

Homogeneity Based Methods

Homogeneity based meta-analysis methods have been advocated independently by Hedges (1982b; Hedges & Olkin, 1985) and by Rosenthal and Rubin (1982). Hedges and Rosenthal and Rubin propose that chi-square statistical tests be used to decide whether study outcomes are more variable than would be expected from sampling error alone. If these chi-square tests of homogeneity are not statistically significant, then the population correlation or effect size is accepted as constant across studies and there is no search for moderators.

One problem is that the chi-square test of homogeneity typically has low power to detect variation beyond sampling error, causing the meta-analyst to often conclude that the studies being examined are homogenous when they are not. Under these circumstances, the fixed effects model of meta-analysis is then used in almost all cases. Unlike random effects meta-analysis models, fixed effects models assume zero between-study variability in study parameters, often resulting in underestimates of the relevant standard errors of the mean. This in turn results in confidence intervals that are erroneously narrow. Both Rosenthal and Rubin and Hedges and Olkin have presented random effects meta-analysis models as well as fixed effects methods, but meta-analysts have rarely employed their random effects methods. However, their use is now increasing.

Bare Bones Meta-Analysis

The second approach to meta-analysis that attempts to control only for the artifact of sampling error is bare bones meta-analysis (Hunter, Schmidt & Jackson, 1982; Hunter & Schmidt, 2004). Like the other methods discussed here, this approach can be applied to correlations, d-values, or any other effect size statistic for which the standard error is known. For example, if the statistic is correlations, $\bar{r}$ is first computed. Then the variance of the set of correlations is computed. Next the amount of sampling error variance is computed and subtracted from this observed variance. If the result is zero, then sampling error accounts for all the observed variance, and the r value accurately summarizes all the studies in the meta-analysis. If not, then the square root of the remaining variance is the index of variability remaining around the mean r after sampling error variance is removed. Because there are always other artifacts (such as measurement error) that should be corrected for, the bare bones meta-analysis method is not a complete meta-analysis method.

Psychometric Meta-Analysis

The third type of meta-analysis is psychometric meta-analysis (Hunter & Schmidt, 2004). These methods correct not only for sampling error (an unsystematic artifact) but for other, systematic artifacts, such as measurement error, range restriction or enhancement, dichotomization of measures, and so forth. These other artifacts are said to be systematic because, in addition to creating artifactual variation across studies, they also create systematic downward biases in the results of all studies. For example, measurement error systematically biases all correlations and d-values downward. Psychometric meta-analysis corrects not only for artifactual variation across studies, but also for the downward biases. Psychometric meta-analysis is the only meta-analysis method that takes into account both statistical and measurement artifacts.

Until recently, psychological research literatures appeared conflicting and contradictory. Meta-analysis methods have provided the solution to this problem. Meta-analytic findings have repeatedly shown that there is much less conflict between different studies than had been believed, that coherent, useful, and generalizable conclusions can be drawn from research literatures, and that therefore cumulative knowledge is possible in psychology and the social sciences.

REFERENCES

Glass, G. V. (1976). Primary, secondary, and meta-analysis of research. *Educational Researcher, 5*, 3–8.

Glass, G. V. (1977). Integrating findings: The meta-analysis of research. *Review of Research in Education, 5*, 351–379.

Glass, G. V., McGaw, B., & Smith, M. L. (1981). *Meta-analysis in social research.* Beverly Hills, CA: Sage.

Hedges, L. V. (1982b). Fitting categorical models to effect sizes from a series of experiments. *Journal of Educational Statistics, 7*, 119–137.

Hedges, L. V., & Olkin, I. (1985). *Statistical methods for meta-analysis.* Orlando, FL: Academic Press.

Hunter, J. E., Schmidt, F. L., & Jackson, G. B. (1982). *Meta-analysis: Cumulating research findings across studies.* Beverly Hills, CA: Sage.

Hunter, J. E., & Schmidt, F. L. (1990b). *Methods of meta-analysis: Correcting error and bias in research findings.* Newbury Park, CA: Sage.

Rosenthal, R., & Rubin, D. B. (1982). Comparing effect sizes of independent studies. *Psychological Bulletin, 92*, 500–504.

Frank L. Schmidt
University of Iowa

MEXICO, PSYCHOLOGY IN

Psychology has been taught in Mexico since the late nineteenth century, but professional training did not begin until the 1960s, and licenses were initially issued in the early 1970s. Professional training programs prepare psychologists at the licentiate level. Licentiate level students take courses exclusively in psychology for approximately five years. Although there was only one training program in 1960, at Mexico's National University, there has been a proliferation of training programs during subsequent decades. In Mexico there are several agencies with the authority to open a professional training program: the president of the country or a state governor, state autonomous universities, private universities by incorporating their programs with an autonomous university, and private universities asking for recognition by the federal government. Autonomous universities make their own legal decisions, and the government cannot intervene in those decisions.

Currently there are about 500 psychology training programs in the country, and their curricula are mainly oriented to the teaching of theories, with little attention being given to professional competencies. The license is automatically issued to persons who have completed the professional training programs recognized by the Mexican Ministry of Education. The license to practice psychology is permanent and is rarely revoked. One of the most serious challenges facing Mexican psychology is to change this situation.

Graduate programs usually provide preparation at the master's level for advanced teaching and, more recently, for professional specialization. At the doctorate level graduate programs provide training for researchers.

The Mexican Psychological Society, after conducting a study of professional practice in Mexico, has reported that most psychologists are engaged mainly in clinical or health psychology, followed by industrial-organizational and school psychology. Forensic and community psychology are also becoming popular. Psychologists also work in universities, institutions of higher education, and research organizations. Around 53% of Mexican psychologists work as employees, with only 4% engaged exclusively in private practice. Most of the psychologists interviewed reported working both as employees and in part-time private practice, 81% have a license, and 95% practice in urban areas.

Professional organizations in Mexico can be divided into colleges (*colegios*) and societies. The oldest, largest, and most important national organization in psychology is the Mexican Psychological Society (SMP—Sociedad Mexicana de Psicologia). It was founded in 1950, is the most prestigious psychological organization in Mexico, and maintains scientific and professional exchanges with other Mexican and international organizations. The SMP publishes the *Mexican Journal of Psychology* (MJP), which is its official periodical. The MJP is the leading journal, not only in Mexico, but in Latin America, and it is one of only three psychology journals published in Spanish with an impact factor listed by the Institute of Scientific Information.

In addition, the Mexican Psychological Society has in five successive editions since 1984 developed and published the *Ethics Code of the Psychologist* (*El Código Ético del Psicólogo*, 2002), which encompasses the ethical principles and norms of conduct most widely taught by universities and recognized by Mexican psychologists. This code of ethics has been revised several times on the basis of nationwide surveys of ethical dilemmas reported by Mexican psychologists. Among other activities promoting scientific psychology, the society organizes an annual Mexican Congress of Psychology, which is the largest and most prestigious academic event in Mexico. Although the Mexican Congress was designed to promote scientific exchange among Mexican psychologists, it has become an international event as well, with the participation of distinguished psychologists from Spain and Latin America.

The National Council for Research and Education in Psychology (CNEIP—Consejo Nacional para la Enseñanza e Investigación en Psicología), which is composed of department chairs and deans of schools of psychology, is another important psychological organization. CNEIP covers psychology programs based in mainly public universities, although it also includes private institutions of higher education. CNEIP is the primary organization for accrediting professional training programs. Accreditation of psychology programs at the federal level is currently the responsibility of CNEIP and of a governmental committee, jointly coordinated by the Ministry of Education and the Ministry of Health, that accredits new programs. Other arrangements for financial allocations to find postgraduate programs also play an indirect role in the accreditation process (Hernandez-Guzman & Sanchez-Sosa, 2005).

According to Mexican law, the *colegios* are in charge of regulating psychology as a profession. Among the *colegios*, the Colegio Mexicano de Profesionales de la Psicología (CoMePPsi; Mexican College of Psychology Professionals) and the Colegio Nacional de Psicólogos (CoNaPsi; National College of Psychologists) are the two most widely recognized. CoMePPsi, though recently founded, is currently making progress toward reaching the criteria required by the Mexican Ministry of Education to be accredited to certify professional psychologists.

Mexican psychology faces great challenges related to increasing pressures to regulate professional services. The development of guidelines and criteria for regulating professional practice, specifically with respect to accrediting training programs and certifying individuals, are among the most important activities to be pursued in the near future by Mexican psychologists.

REFERENCES

Hernández-Guzmán, L. & Sánchez-Sosa, J. J. (2005). El aseguramiento de la calidad de los programas de formación en psicología profesional en México [Quality assurance of professional psychology education in Mexico]. *Revista Mexicana de Psicología* [*Mexican Journal of Psychology*], *Número Monográfico Especial Evaluación de la Calidad de los Programas de Psicología* [*Special Issue: Evaluation of the Quality of Psychology Training Programs*], 22(3), 271–286.

Hernandez-Guzman, L. & Sanchez-Sosa, J. J. (2008). Latin America. In J. E. Hall & E. M. Altmaier (Eds.), *Global promise: Quality assurance and accountability in professional psychology* (pp. 109–127). New York: Oxford University Press.

Sociedad Mexicana de Psicología [Mexican Psychological Society]. (2002). *El código ético del psicólogo* [*The ethics code of the psychologist*]. Mexico: Editorial Trillas.

LAURA HERNÁNDEZ-GUZMÁN
National Autonomous University of Mexico

MIDLIFE CRISIS

One of the most common expectations for the middle years of the life course is that there is an inevitable crisis, but research evidence in this regard is mixed (Lachman, 2004). Approximately 26% of the participants over age 40 in the national survey of Midlife in the United States (MIDUS) reported having a midlife crisis. Most life crises, however, were reported to occur before age 40 or after age 50, thus raising questions as to whether a crisis is unique to midlife or to specific birth cohorts (Lachman, 2004).

In one of the earliest discussions of the midlife crisis, Jacques (1965) observed that the midlife crisis in his clinical patients was driven by their fears of impending death. More recent research has shown the usual sources of crises are life events such as illness, marital problems or divorce, job loss, or financial problems, which are not associated only with the midlife period, but occur regularly at other points in the lifespan (Lachman, 2004; Wethington, Kessler, & Pixley, 2004). Personality has been identified as a key factor predisposing some individuals to experience crises at transition points throughout the life course. For example, those who are more neurotic are more prone to have a midlife crisis as well as crises at other times in their lives (Lachman, 2004; Whitbourne & Willis. 2006; Willis & Martin, 2005).

Midlife is often a period of reflection and reevaluation, but crisis may be a misleading description of this review process. Even if life changes are made in midlife, they do not always involve a crisis; they may instead involve careful planning, decisions, and choices about new directions, and they may often lead to growth. In some cases, the process of reevaluation and review may be triggered by an unexpected or undesirable circumstance, such as the death of someone close or loss of a job. Traditionally, a life-review process has been associated with old age. Older adults, when faced with mortality or a sense that time is running out, engage in a reminiscence process, and the outcome may be adaptive (e.g., ego integrity) or may result in distress (e.g., despair), as suggested by Erik Erikson. The main purpose of a review at this late stage of life is to make sense of one's life, to accept it for what it has been, and to move toward a graceful end of life (Neugarten & Datan, 1996).

A life review at midlife can also serve an adaptive function for mental health and positive growth that can have a long-term impact. Stewart and Vandewater (1999) examined the role of the midlife review, which they called the "midlife correction," in relation to well-being and depression outcomes. They found that, in the process of self-reflection during midlife, using regret as a catalyst for productive change was associated with higher well-being in later life.

Instead of the term midlife crisis, some have used the concept of turning points or transitions to describe significant changes in the life trajectory. Such an experience or realization often leads one to reinterpret the past and make changes for the future, as well as to modify the way one feels or thinks about life. Wethington et al. (2004) examined in what areas of life turning points occurred and whether they clustered in midlife. The most common turning points involved the work domain, usually a change in job or career. They were most likely to occur at midlife for men but earlier for women. Turning points or difficult transitions may also occur at other points in the lifespan, as suggested by the notion of a "quarter-life crisis" occurring for those in their mid-20s and early 30s as they struggle to find satisfaction in work and meaningful relationships.

It is likely that being in the middle of the lifespan holds special challenges and opportunities for reflection, advancement, or change, similar to being in the middle of the academic semester or a summer vacation (Lachman & James, 1997). Midlife may provide a critical training ground for aging, and it may offer a window on later life. At midlife we can get a glimpse of things to come while there is still time to do something about them. For example, those who suffer functional limitations and disability in midlife are headed for a rough old age unless they take action. The midlife period often involves demands in multiple domains of work, family, and personal health and well-being. There is a need to juggle and balance multiple spheres of life, at the same time as physical changes associated with aging are becoming more noticeable, which may be associated with increased stress. When we surveyed adults from age 25 to 75 about their most frequent problems, the most common problem reported by those in midlife was not being able to get everything done (Lachman, 2004). There is typically still much time left in the life course, but this realization that there are still goals to accomplish can lead to anxiety and pressure, especially if physical symptoms such as fatigue and pain are present.

Although the incidence of clinical depression peaks in midlife, there is emerging evidence that midlife is often a period of enhanced mastery and competence and that a crisis is not inevitable. Recent research has begun to identify the risk factors for poor mental health outcomes as well the protective factors that can enhance well-being in midlife. Classic views of midlife portray it as a period of turmoil and crisis (Neugarten & Datan, 1996), yet other more recent work has demonstrated consistently that midlife is a period of peak functioning, responsibility, and balance (Lachman, 2004). This is especially important, because the well-being of those in midlife has a widespread impact on those younger and older whom they care for and supervise in the family, workplace, and society at large. A focus on generativity, or the concern for others, is the key task that Erik Erikson identified as central to midlife adjustment (Neugarten and Datan, 1996).

In midlife, life goals shift from a focus on growth to an emphasis on maintenance of functioning and avoidance of losses and decline. It is not necessary to ruminate or dwell on the mistakes of the past or to make radical or drastic changes in one's family or work life. Some in midlife are reflective and take stock of their lives, but others do not.

An adaptive midlife evaluation is aimed at making sense of one's situation, making choices and plans for the present and future, and taking control over aging-related declines through preventive or compensatory behaviors. Changes may be external and objective or internal and subjective. Today, those in the 40–60 age range (i.e., the baby boomers) are the fastest growing segment of the population (Whitbourne & Willis, 2006). There is a burgeoning interest among scholars of the life course and clinicians in helping adults to navigate the middle years successfully. For those who experience a crisis, the emphasis is on how to cope and adjust without major disruptions to one's work and family life. As we learn more about the protective factors for healthy adult development, the association of midlife with crisis may be replaced with midlife competence.

REFERENCES

Jacques, E. (1965). Death and the mid-life crisis. *International Journal of Psychoanalysis, 46,* 502–514.

Lachman, M. E. (2004). Development in midlife. *Annual Review of Psychology, 55,* 305–331.

Lachman, M. E., & James, J. B. (1997). Charting the course of midlife development: An overview. In M. E. Lachman & J. B. James (Eds.), *Multiple paths of midlife development* (pp. 1–17). Chicago: University of Chicago Press.

Neugarten, B. L., & Datan, N. (1996). The middle years. In D. A. Neugarten (Ed.), *The meanings of age: Selected papers of Bernice L. Neugarten* (pp. 135–159). Chicago: University of Chicago Press.

Reid, J. D., & Willis, S. L. (1999). Middle age: New thoughts, new directions. In Willis, S. L., & Reid, J. D. (Eds.) *Life in the middle* (pp. 275–280). San Diego: Academic Press.

Stewart, A. J., & Vandewater, E. A. (1999). "If I had it to do over again … ": Midlife review, midcourse corrections, and women's well-being in midlife. *Journal of Personality and Social Psychology 76,* 270–283.

Wethington, E., Kessler, R. C., & Pixley J. E. (2004). Turning points in adulthood. In O. G. Brim, C. D. Ryff, & R. C. Kessler (Eds.), *How healthy are we?: A national study of well-being at midlife.* Chicago: University of Chicago Press.

Whitbourne, S. K., & Willis, S. L. (Eds.). (2006). *The baby boomers grow up: Contemporary perspectives on midlife.* Mahwah, NJ: Lawrence Erlbaum.

Willis, S. L., & Martin, M. (2005). *Middle adulthood: A lifespan perspective,* Thousand Oaks, CA: Sage.

SUGGESTED READINGS

Brim, O. G., Ryff, C. D. & Kessler, R. C. (Eds.). (2004). *How healthy are we?: A national study of well-being at midlife.* Chicago: University of Chicago Press.

Lachman, M. E. (Ed.). (2001). *Handbook of midlife development.* New York: John Wiley & Sons.

MARGIE E. LACHMAN
EILEEN M. KRANZ
Brandeis University

***See also*: Adulthood and Aging; Human Development; Identity Formation**

MILGRAM, STANLEY (1933–1984)

Stanley Milgram received his Ph.D. in social psychology from Harvard in 1960. He began his career as an Assistant Professor at Harvard, but was denied tenure (some think due to his obedience studies), and he moved to the Graduate Center of the City University of New York where he remained until his death. Using an auditory judgment task rather than the visual judgment task of the original Solomon Asch studies, Milgram compared the conformity levels of Norwegians and Frenchmen and found Norwegians to be more conforming.

His best-known studies were on the dynamics of obedience to authority. In these studies, a subject was commanded to give increasingly higher voltages of electric shock to a learner every time the latter gave a wrong answer on a verbal-learning task. The learner was an actor who feigned increasingly intense suffering with increases in shock levels. Milgram found an unexpectedly high rate of obedience. Milgram conducted more than 20 variations of this basic experiment. A full report of his research program on obedience to authority is found in *Obedience to Authority: An Experimental View*, which has been translated into 11 languages.

From the beginning, the obedience studies were embroiled in controversy—praised by some, vilified by others. Much of the controversy has to do with the ethics of deceiving participants into believing that they may have harmed an innocent human being. The obedience work became one of the best-known pieces of research in social sciences. The 1963 report became a citation class in 1981 and has been reprinted in dozens of anthologies.

Milgram went on to make a number of other original contributions. The following are brief summaries of the principal ones: in 1970 Milgram published the article "The experience of living in cities," in which he introduced the concept of overload as a way to understand urban/rural differences in social behavior. In 1965, Milgram and colleagues introduced an unobtrusive way of measuring community attitudes and opinions. They scattered 400 "lost letters" throughout New Haven—on sidewalks, in phone booths, on car windshields. One hundred were addressed to Friends of the Nazi Party, Friends of the Communist Party, Medical Research Associates, and a Mr. Walter Camp. Although a majority of the latter two were mailed, only a minority of the first two letters were. This technique is the most widely used nonreactive measure of attitudes.

In 1967, Milgram introduced a technique of studying the small-world phenomenon, the not-uncommon situation of meeting someone in San Francisco, for example, who happens to know one's first cousin in Toronto. In the small-world method, a sample of starters are given a packet that needs to reach a designated stranger, the target person, in another city, with the limitation that each person can send it to only someone he or she knows on a first-name basis. Milgram found that among completed chains it typically required only a small number of intermediaries—average ranged from 4.4 to 5.9—for the mail to reach the target. The technique is an important tool of social network researchers (Kadushin, 1989).

An integrative review of the whole corpus of Milgram's work can be found in Blass (1992). Additionally, an updated version of most of Milgram's published writings has been published (Sabini & Silver, 1992), and a symposium exploring Milgram's contributions to social psychology was conducted at the annual convention of the American Psychological Association in Boston in 1990.

SUGGESTED READINGS

Blass, T. (1992). *The man who shocked the world: The life and legacy of Stanley Milgram*. New York: Basic Books.

Milgram, S. (1974). *Obedience to authority: An experimental view*. New York: Harper Perennial.

Milgram, S. (1974). *Psychology in today's world*. Boston: Little, Brown.

Milgram, S., Sabini, J., & Silver, M. (1992). *The individual in a social world: Essays and experiments*. New York: McGraw Hill.

STAFF

MILITARY PSYCHOLOGY

Military psychology is defined as the science and application of human behavior as it relates to the military. The field of military psychology integrates the professional and scientific literature with practical requirements of the military in order to meet the needs of the armed forces and military personnel (Kennedy & Zillmer, 2006). Much of the thinking in the field of military psychology, stimulated by the situational demands of the military, has had a dramatic impact on the overall field of psychology itself, particularly psychological testing, personnel selection, clinical psychology education, aviation psychology, understanding of the human response to trauma, and head-injury rehabilitation. Thus, the origins, history, and development of military psychology and its relationship to the general field of psychology are intertwined.

The growth of U.S. military psychology has developed in spurts, relative to the various military conflicts over time (for a review, see Kennedy & McNeil, 2006). For example, during the Revolutionary War, the Colonials used leaflets to encourage the desertion of frustrated and hungry enlisted British soldiers. During the Civil War soldiers experienced problems with addiction to alcohol, cocaine, morphine, and opium, and what we now know as posttraumatic stress disorder (PTSD) was first described. World War I marked the official birth of military psychology with the commissioning of the first Army psychologists, largely because of the success of psychological testing procedures to assess and select individuals for specific occupations (Yoakum & Yerkes, 1920). Head-injury rehabilitation was born during this war due to war injuries and more effective neurosurgical techniques.

Psychologists were also in high demand during World War II and were involved in the psychology of combat fatigue, aptitude testing, screening results, counterespionage, and propaganda. The Korean War saw psychologists in new frontline positions. The psychological impact of the Vietnam War spurred our understanding of the severity and chronicity of posttraumatic stress disorder; this war also facilitated better addiction treatments and policies for the military. For the first time psychologists were deployed aboard Navy aircraft carriers during the Persian Gulf War. In the current war on global terrorism, psychologists are deployed to battle zones as part of combat stress units wherein they evaluate and manage combat stress on site.

Given the wide variety of military applications, military psychology consists of three distinct subspecialties that can generally be categorized as clinical, research, and operational. These three overarching categories include experimental, industrial/organizational, human factors, cognitive, and the range of clinical psychology services. Although there is significant overlap in duties of military psychologists, each category has specific functions and applications. Clinicians in the military, for example, focus on assessment, diagnosis, intervention, and treatment while promoting the health of service members, their beneficiaries, and any others who may be encountered (e.g., foreign nationals, enemy combatants). Researchers work on projects including the development of test batteries used in selection, the examination of the physical and cognitive effects of sustained and continuous operations, and the long-term effects of combat stress. More recently, military psychologists have been filling unprecedented operational roles pertaining to the Global War on Terror (GWOT). Operational psychology in military organizations is responsive to changing circumstances and requirements, threats, and opportunities to ensure meaningful and relevant support to military commanders. Operational military psychology represents the latest chapter in the development of the field of military psychology. The following sections describe examples of the variety of psychological applications to the military.

Clinical Military Psychology

Clinical psychology as a discipline owes its existence to military psychologists in World War II. Following this war there were too few psychiatrists to meet the mental health needs of veterans. Psychologists stepped in to fill this void, and the first psychology internships were subsequently developed in the Veteran's Administration system (Cranston, 1986). Clinical military psychology is now a diverse field and includes fitness for duty evaluations, inpatient assessment and treatment, psychotherapy, health psychology, neuropsychology, psychopharmacology, suicide risk assessments, and substance abuse and gambling intervention and treatment. There are unique characteristics of practicing clinical psychology in a military environment that differ from traditional clinical roles. These include differences in education and training, the influence of rank on the therapeutic relationship, distinctive limits of confidentiality, ethical issues of multiple relationships (Johnson, Ralph, & Johnson, 2005), dual agency (Jeffrey, Rankin, & Jeffrey, 1992), and unique multicultural training needs (Kennedy, Jones, & Arita, 2007), as well as having to train to provide support in potentially hostile environments.

Effectively addressing combat stress in service members is one of the primary roles of clinical psychologists during wartime. The United States Department of Defense (DoD) currently utilizes the term Combat Stress Reactions (CSRs) to describe the expected, predictable, emotional, intellectual, physical, and/or behavioral reactions of service members who have been exposed to traumatic events in combat or military operations. Reactions to combat stress are thought to be abnormal events, with recovery expected to occur in days with appropriate intervention. Psychologists play a large role in assessing and addressing these responses both on the battlefield and upon return from combat (Campise, Geller, & Campise, 2006).

Clinical psychologists are also responders to natural disasters and other mass traumatic events. Military psychologists are integral players in coordinated responses to trauma and many are experts in the field of post-traumatic intervention and treatment. Given the wide variety of events military psychologists may respond to as a result of their deployability, they are trained to intervene competently for the range of trauma experiences. Different types of trauma require different interventions, and military psychologists are able to treat individual traumas (e.g., military sexual trauma), natural disaster trauma (e.g., hurricanes), combat trauma, and trauma secondary to man-made disasters (e.g., terrorist bombings).

Research Military Psychology

Researchers in the military have historically filled the most traditional psychology functions in the military (Zeidner & Drucker, 1988). Research psychologists continue to be involved in both basic and applied research and act as consultants on a variety of military projects. Although there is some overlap between the psychology specialties, military research psychologists essentially fill three primary roles: those of selection, safety, and acquisition. Selection activities have the longest history and continue to be highly valued and relevant today. Military psychologists create, validate, and norm the various selection batteries used for a variety of jobs. For example, the Navy's aerospace experimental psychologists maintain the Aviation Selection Test Battery for Navy and Marine Corps aviators and flight officers. These unique psychologists have flight status and are provided basic flight training in both fixed wing and rotary wing aircraft in order to competently work with the aviation population. The roles of military research psychologists with regards to safety include optimizing efficient communications and operational risk management. Military psychologists focus on acquisition activities work within human systems integration teams, alongside human factors, cognitive psychologists, and engineers. These teams focus on the interaction between the individual warfighter and the system in question (e.g., cockpit design), thereby optimizing functioning and improving the complex interactions between these forces.

Operational Military Psychology

Operational military psychology encompasses new and emerging roles for psychologists. This field grew largely out of the practice of police psychologists. In contrast to the more traditional aspects of military psychology reviewed above, operational psychology offers a significant paradigm shift for psychologists who may have envisioned their delivery of services as limited to military treatment facilities, academic settings, research laboratories, or medical centers. Operational psychologists may be involved in such activities as assessing terrorists and terrorist threats, conducting evaluations of special operational personnel, conducting indirect assessments during hostage negotiations, preparing psychological autopsies (Gelles, 1995), consulting to interrogations, consulting to counterintelligence and counterterrorism operations (Shumate & Borum, 2006), and monitoring military survival schools in order to enhance safety and training efficacy.

Operational psychologists provide expertise and understanding of human behavior to assist commanders in understanding the enemy and optimizing the performance of military personnel. As military organizations transform to remain responsive and relevant to the changing circumstances and requirements, threats, and opportunities of modern warfare, so too are military psychologists adapting and developing new methods to ensure they provide meaningful and relevant support to the operational and strategic needs of military commanders (Staal & Stephenson, 2006). The need for operational psychologists grew rapidly following the events of September 11, 2001, and psychologists have lent their expertise to a variety of wartime dilemmas and national security agencies. Operational psychologists may be found all over the world in intelligence and law enforcement agencies, embedded with special operational personnel, and working at Survival, Evasion, Resistance, and Escape (SERE) schools.

All military psychologists utilize dynamic subspecialties of military psychology to facilitate the support of the military. In doing so, military psychologists continue to pioneer developments in the field and the armed forces provides real-life experience, responsibility, and exposure to psychologists that are seldom available for civilian psychologists. Psychologists are experts in the science of human decision-making. Psychology practice and science can be put to good use in counterterrorism endeavors, law enforcement, and the military. Advancing military psychological science directly and indirectly in these areas benefits the security of our nation as well as the discipline of psychology.

REFERENCES

Campise, R. L., Geller, S. K., & Campise, M. E. (2006). Combat stress. In C. H. Kennedy & E. A. Zillmer (Eds.), *Military psychology: Clinical and operational applications* (pp. 215–240). New York: Guilford Press.

Cranston, A. (1986). Psychology in the veterans administration: A storied history, a vital future. *American Psychologist, 41,* 990–995.

Gelles, M. G. (1995). Psychological autopsy: An investigative aid. In M. I. Weiss & E. M. Weiss (Eds.), *Police psychology into the 21st Century* (pp. 337–355). Hillsdale, N.J.: Lawrence Erlbaum.

Jeffrey, T. B., Rankin, R. J., & Jeffrey, L. K. (1992). In service of two masters: The ethical-legal dilemma faced by military psychologists. *Professional Psychology: Research and Practice, 23,* 91–95.

Johnson, W. B., Ralph, J., & Johnson, S. J. (2005). Managing multiple roles in embedded environments: The case of aircraft carrier psychology. *Professional Psychology: Research and Practice, 36,* 73–81.

Kennedy, C. H., Jones, D. E., & Arita, A. A. (2007). Multicultural experiences of U.S. military psychologists: Current trends and training target areas. *Psychological Services, 4,* 158–167.

Kennedy, C. H., & McNeil, J. A. (2006). A history of military psychology. In C. H. Weiss & E. A. Weiss (Eds.), *Military psychology: Clinical and operational applications* (pp. 1–17). New York: Guilford Press.

Kennedy, C. H., & Zillmer, E. A. (2006). *Military psychology: Clinical and operational applications.* New York: Guilford Press.

Shumate, S., & Borum, R. (2006). Psychological support to defense counterintelligence operations. *Military Psychology, 18,* 283–296.

Staal, M. A., & Stephenson, J. A. (2006). Operational psychology: An emerging subdiscipline. *Military Psychology, 18,* 269–282.

Yoakum, C. S., & Yerkes, R. M. (1920). *Army mental tests.* New York: Henry Holt.

Zeidner, J., & Drucker, A. J. (1988). *Behavioral science in the Army: A corporate history of the Army Research Institute.* Washington, D.C.: Army Research Institute.

SUGGESTED READINGS

Figley, C. R., & Nash, W. P. (2007). Combat stress injury: Theory, research and management. New York: Routledge.

Williams, T. J., & Johnson, W. B. (2006). Operational psychology and clinical practice in operational environments. Special Issue of *Military Psychology, 18,* 261–320.

ERIC A. ZILLMER
Drexel University

CARRIE HILL KENNEDY
Naval Aerospace Medical Institute, Pensacola, FL

MILLER, NEAL E. (1909–2002)

Neal Elgar Miller (born in Milwaukee, Wisconsin, August 3, 1909), was Professor Emeritus of Rockefeller University from 1981 until his death in 2002 and research affiliate at Yale University from 1985 to 2002. He was the first psychologist to receive the National Medal of Science, the nation's highest award for scientific achievement. On February 8, 1965, President Lyndon Johnson presented Miller with the medal, citing him for sustained and imaginative research on principles of learning and motivation and illuminating behavioral analysis of the effects of direct electrical stimulation on the brain.

After receiving his MA at Stanford University in 1932, Miller moved to the Institute of Human Relations at Yale University, where he became involved in applications of experimental psychology techniques to the study of psychiatric patients. At Yale, he was also strongly influenced by C. L. Hull, applying principles of Pavlov's conditioning to Thorndike's trial-and-error learning. Miller went through psychoanalytic training in Vienna in 1935–1936 in Freud's laboratory and later visited Pavlov's laboratory in the U.S.S.R. in order to test the difference hypothesis experimentally; he became an active proponent of a Pavlovian approach toward the study of high nervous functions.

During World War II, Miller served as an officer in charge of psychological research for the Army Air Corps. His unit was responsible for developing some of the first tests for the selection of pilots and objective measures of flying skill.

In 1950, when Miller became professor of psychology at Yale, his interest shifted to the use of a variety of behavioral, physiological, and pharmacological techniques to study mechanisms of motivation and reward. In 1953, with W. Roberts and J. Delgado, Miller performed the first experiments to demonstrate trial-and-error learning, or operant conditioning, motivated by direct stimulation of the brain. With other co-workers, he studied electrical brain stimulation, eliciting eating and drinking and displaying motivational properties of a drive such as hunger or thirst. In other experiments the researchers had shown that eating could be elicited by adrenergic stimulation and drinking by cholinergic stimulation.

Investigating whether visceral responses, such as salivation, heart rate, and blood pressure, could be modified by operant conditioning, Miller started a new chapter in the study of visceral conditioning and stress that became a fundamental problem of his new Laboratory of Physiological Psychology at Rockefeller University, to which he moved in 1966. The general goal of the Miller lab was to coalesce recent advances in the behavioral sciences, neurophysiology, and molecular biology into a unified approach in order to understand how the brain controls behavior. In this direction, his laboratory made a crucial contribution toward clinical psychophysiology and biofeedback research and Miller became a senior member of the group, which founded the Society for Neuroscience, currently an organization of more than 28,000 biomedical scientists and researchers.

In an article in *Science* (July, 1980) describing the emergence of behavioral medicine, it is written that "the most direct precursor of behavior medicine is psychosomatic medicine, a field based on psychoanalytic theories about disease etiology which grew up in the 1950s and 1960s," and that a "schism developed in the field between those who were psychoanalytically oriented and the basic scientists whose roots were in psychobiology. It was the latter group that broke off to define the field of behavioral medicine." This development also mirrors the evolution of Miller's attitudes toward psychogenics and neurogenics, pathogenesis of neuroses, and some somatic diseases. Miller pioneered the application of learning theory to behavioral therapy and the use of chemical and electrical stimulation to analyze the brain's mechanism of behavior, homeostasis, and reinforcement.

Miller won many awards and held outstanding offices and advisory posts. President of the American Psychological Association (APA) in 1960–1961, he was elected the second president of the Society of Neuroscience (1971–1972) and then became the first president of the Academy of Behavioral Medicine Research (1979–1980) and of the Biofeedback Society of America (1980–1981). In 1961 Miller was appointed by President J. F. Kennedy to serve as chairman of the behavioral sciences section in the Life Sciences Panel of the President's Science Advisory Committee. This panel produced a paper on research and science policy, which was widely distributed and influential.

Earlier, in 1959, the APA honored Miller with its Distinguished Scientific Contribution Award, citing him as follows: "For his sustained and imaginative research on the basic principles of learning. Through brilliantly conceived and skillfully executed experiments, he and his students served as a major spearhead in the current breakthrough area of motivation and learning. The importance of his research in extending knowledge is matched by its importance in stimulating the research of others. His influence has been greatly enhanced by his clear reports and reviews, in which he is never afraid to point out the broad implications of his results. In every respect, he is a fortunate model to set up before building up young psychologists."

In the field of applied psychophysiology and biofeedback, Miller's early work with animals contributed more than any other single factor to arouse interest and focus the attention of the scientific community on the new field of biofeedback. In the late 1960s, Miller conducted a series of studies in which he taught curarized rats to control such visceral responses to the autonomic nervous system as blood flows, heartbeat, and stomach contractions. Miller believed that if visceral responses could be made "visible," it would be possible to apply instrumental learning to control and modify them. His dramatic research on self-regulatory control of blood pressure in quadriplegic patients, with B. Brucker, rendered it highly probable that autonomic response systems in human beings could be controlled through biofeedback or operant conditioning without the mediating of the somatic musculature. In 1972, Miller's work was the subject of a two-part *New Yorker* magazine profile by Gerald Jones, later published as a book, *Visceral Learning: Toward a Science of Self-Control*.

A member of the National Academy of Sciences since 1958, Miller was elected to senior membership in its Institute of Medicine in 1983. He was a fellow of the American Philosophical Society and of the New York Academy of Sciences, which elected him an honorary life member in 1976 and an honorary fellow of the British Psychological Society and the Spanish Psychological Society, among others. He served on the editorial boards of *Science* and a number of other journals and is the author of more than 260 scholarly papers, co-author of the volumes of *Frustration and Aggression* (1939), *Social Learning and Imitation* (1941), and *Personality and Psychotherapy* (1950), and the author of *Graphic Communication and the Crisis in Education* (1957) and of *Selected Papers* (1971).

Miller has been awarded honorary Doctor of Science degrees at numerous universities, including the University of Uppsala, Sweden (1977), where he was presented in front of the King as part of the celebration of the university's 500th year. He has also been a great teacher to his profession; a number of his students have gone on to make significant contributions to the fields of behavioral medicine and biofeedback. For example, J. Weiss has shown clearly that digestive system lesions can be produced by stress in rats. P. Cowings has developed a biofeedback technique for the control of nausea associated with motion sickness, and B. Brucker has carried out significant work in the use of biofeedback for the rehabilitation of movement after injury to the central nervous system.

SUGGESTED READINGS

Miller, N. E. (1939). *Frustration and aggression.* New Haven: Yale University Press.

Miller, N. E. (1949). *Social learning and imitation.* New Haven: Yale University Press.

Miller, N. E. (1950). *Personality and psychotherapy.* New Haven: Yale University Press.

Miller, N. E. (1957). *Graphic communication and crisis in education.* New Haven: Yale University Press.

STAFF

MILLON CLINICAL MULTIAXIAL INVENTORY

The Millon Clinical Multiaxial Inventory-III (MCMI-III) (Millon, 2006) is one of nine published measures that operationalize Theodore Millon's (1969, 1996) evolutionary model of personality and psychopathology. Other Millon tests include the Millon Behavioral Medicine Diagnostic and the Millon Adolescent Clinical Inventory. Since its introduction in 1977, the MCMI has become one of the most frequently used instruments for the examination of personality disorders and clinical syndromes. There are over 500 empirical studies based on this measure, as well as seven MCMI-related books. Among personality tests, only the Rorschach and the MMPI-2 have produced more research during the past 15 years. Recent reviews of this literature are available in Choca (2004) and Craig (2005).

Overview

Now in its third edition, the MCMI-III (Millon, 2006) is a 175-item standardized self-report True-False questionnaire. It was designed for adults 18 years of age and older who read at minimally the eighth-grade level and who are being evaluated or treated for mental health problems. It takes most respondents 30 minutes to complete the test. A unique feature of the inventory is that scale scores are standardized against samples of psychiatric patients. For this reason, it is not appropriate for use with nonhelp-seeking nonpatient adults.

Scales and Scoring

Most MCMI-III test items are scored on multiple scales. As a result, this relatively brief measure provides 70 different scale scores: 1 Validity indicator, 3 Modifying indices (Disclosure, Desirability, Debasement), 11 Clinical Personality Patterns (Schizoid, Avoidant, Depressive, Dependent, Histrionic, Narcissistic, Antisocial, Sadistic, Compulsive, Negativistic, Masochistic), 3 Severe Personality Pathology scales (Schizotypal, Borderline, Paranoid), 7 Clinical Syndromes (Anxiety, Somatoform, Bipolar: Manic, Dysthymia, Alcohol Dependence, Drug Dependence, Post-Traumatic Stress), 3 Severe Clinical Syndromes (Thought Disorder, Major Depression, Delusional Disorder), and 42 Grossman Facet scales that measure subcomponents of the 14 clinical and severe personality scales.

Items for the personality and clinical syndrome scales, when endorsed, are given a weight of 2 or 1 depending on whether the characteristic being measured represents a unique feature of the particular personality or clinical syndrome (weight of 2) or represents a feature that is less definitive and likely to be shared with similar personalities or syndromes (weight of 1).

The personality and clinical syndrome scales contain 12 to 24 items each, and the Grossman Facet scales contain 6 to 11 items. The Validity scale contains 3 improbable items designed to detect confused or random responding. The Disclosure scale is a weighted composite of the 11 Clinical Personality Pattern scales, the Desirability scale contains 21 items measuring socially desirable attributes, and the Debasement scale consists of 33 items judged to measure negative personal attributes.

Reliability

Internal reliability of the personality and clinical syndrome scales—a gauge of how consistently items within a scale are endorsed by respondents—is estimated to be $\alpha = .67–.90$ (where $.00 =$ not at all consistent, $1.00 =$ completely consistent). Test-retest stability—which measures the similarity of test score responses over time—is estimated to be $r = .84–.96$ over a period of 5 to 14 days (where 1.00 indicates the highest level of stability; Millon, 2006, pp. 57–59). The Grossman Facet scales, which were first published in 2006, have exhibited internal consistency scores ranging from $\alpha = .48$ to $.85$ (Median $= .73$; Millon, 2006, p. 114). No test-retest data have yet been offered.

Base Rate Scores

MCMI-III personality and clinical syndrome scales were standardized as base rate (BR) scores rather than T scores. T scores were considered inappropriate by Millon (2006), because they assume an underlying normal population distribution, whereas the MCMI-III normative samples consist of psychiatric patients. BR scores reflect the diagnoses of the individuals comprising the normative samples. For the MCMI-III, Millon had experienced clinicians provide multiaxial diagnoses for the patients in the normative groups. By knowing the scores of these patients on the MCMI-III and their clinical diagnoses, Millon was able to create anchor points for his scales that would reflect the prevalence, or BR, of each psychiatric condition. BR scores range from 0 to 115. BR $= 60$ represents the median raw score obtained by all patients (i.e., 50th percentile). BR scores of 75 were assigned to the minimum raw score obtained by patients who met criteria for the particular disorder or syndrome. BR scores of 85 were given to the minimum raw score of patients who were judged to have a particular disorder or condition as their primary problem. For the personality scales, BR scores ≥ 75 signify the presence of clinically significant personality traits, and BR scores ≥ 85 suggest the presence of a disorder. For the clinical syndrome scales, BR scores ≥ 75 indicate the presence of a syndrome, and BR scores ≥ 85 denote the prominence of a particular syndrome.

Normative Samples

There are two MCMI-III normative samples. The first sample consists of 998 psychiatric patients (490 men, 508 women) from the United States and Canada, which Millon (2006) used to develop the MCMI-III scales and which is the sample used to standardize scores for all applications of the test except the assessment of prisoners. A second normative sample ($N = 1,676$) was collected from correctional inmates and was used to standardize MCMI-III scale scores for that population only (Millon, 2003).

When developing the MCMI-III, Millon (2006) divided the psychiatric normative sample into two groups. The first group of 600 patients was used to create scales, and the second group of 398 patients was used for cross-validation to verify accuracy of the standardized scores. Although modest in size, the normative sample represents a broad range of demographic characteristics. Patients were men (54%) and women (46%) from outpatient (52%) and inpatient (26%) settings, as well as correctional facilities (8%). Age range was 18–88, although 80% were between 18 and 45. Most of the patients had completed high school (82%); among these 18% also had a college degree (18%). A notable limitation of the sample is that most subjects were White (86%), with only a small number of Blacks (8%), Hispanics (2%), and all other minorities (4%) represented.

History of the Test

The MCMI-I (Millon, 1983) was based on Theodore Millon's (1969) original model of personality and psychopathology. In that model he proposed three bipolar axes—active-passive, pleasure-pain, self-other—as the basic building blocks of normal and abnormal personality. Conceived in terms of instrumental coping patterns designed to maximize positive reinforcements and avoid punishment, the model crossed the active-passive axis with four reinforcement strategies—detached, dependent, independent, and ambivalent—to derive eight basic personality patterns (asocial, avoidant, submissive, gregarious, narcissistic, aggressive, conforming, negativistic) and three severe variants (schizoid, cycloid, paranoid). Although Millon (1969) did not propose a formal model of clinical syndromes along with his personality taxonomy, he asserted that most or all psychiatric conditions (e.g., major depression, anxiety disorders, psychosis) could be best explained as extensions of personality.

Millon's (1969) strong theoretical interests led him to a test development strategy that was also grounded in theory. Jane Loevinger (1957) had previously proposed that assessment instruments should be built in a three-step process, with theory guiding development and validation in every step. Millon (1983) used Loevinger's strategy to create the MCMI-I, as well as subsequent editions of the instrument.

The three steps of test development and validation described by Loevinger (1957) were called *theoretical-substantive*, *internal-structural*, and *external*. In the theoretical-substantial phase, items were generated for scales in terms of how well they conformed to theory. For the internal-structural phase of development, scales were created to match a set of criteria defined by the theory. For example, Millon's (1969, 1996) model posits that personality scales should have high internal consistency, test-retest reliability, and a theoretically consistent pattern of correlations with other scales. For the third stage of external criterion validation, which is analogous to convergent-discriminant validity, Millon had psychiatric patients complete the final form of the test along with several self-report measures of personality and clinical syndromes. Based on these data he judged that the scales were faithful to his theory, and the test was then published.

The second edition of the measure, the MCMI-II (Millon, 1987), was created to keep pace with changes in the revised third edition of the *Diagnostic and Statistical Manual of Mental Disorders-III-R* (DSM-III-R; American Psychiatric Association [APA], 1987). New scales measuring Self-Defeating and Aggressive-Sadistic personality disorders were developed. A total of 45 items in the MCMI-I were changed, and Millon introduced an item-weighting system whereby prototype items (i.e., those central to the disorder) were given higher scores. He also derived three validity scales. Validation studies were then conducted as described earlier.

The MCMI-III (Millon, 2006) was created to bring the test in line with DSM-IV (APA, 2000). Here 45 of the 175 items in the MCMI-II were changed, two new scales were added (Depressive Personality and Post Traumatic Stress), the item-weighting system was changed from three points to two points, scales were reduced in length, and noteworthy items pertaining to child abuse and eating disorders were added but not scored on any of the scales. Significantly, Millon made sure that most test items directly reflected diagnostic criteria in the DSM-IV.

New Developments

Since the MCMI-III first appeared in 1994, Millon (2006) has conducted a cross-validation study to answer criticism that the original validation of the BR transformations (Millon, 1994, pp. 33–34, 132–134), which was made with the 998 patients in the normative sample, was faulty because independent data were needed to calculate accurate statistics. The second study had 67 clinicians rate the primary diagnoses of 322 psychiatric patients, who independently completed the MCMI-III. Using these data Millon (2006, pp. 87–99) found that the MCMI-III personality and clinical syndrome BR scores were much more accurate in making clinical diagnoses than had been originally estimated.

In 1998 Millon (2003) published a version of the MCMI-III that was normed on correctional inmates. In 2006 the Grossman Facet scales were added. Millon (2006) and his associate, Seth Grossman, factor analyzed the MCMI-III's individual personality scale items using the test's normative sample. Employing an alpha factoring technique with oblique rotation they were able to recover three dimensional elements for each personality, that were later refined into facet subscales using rational and empirical criteria. These assess theoretically related subcomponents of the 14 personality scales. By 2008 the MCMI-III had been translated into eight languages

and was being used for clinical assessment in seven non-English-speaking countries, including Denmark, Italy, and Spain.

REFERENCES

American Psychiatric Association. (1987). *Diagnostic and statistical manual of mental disorders* (3rd ed., rev.) (DSM-III-R). Washington, DC: Author.

American Psychiatric Association. (2000). *Diagnostic and statistical manual of mental disorders* (4th ed., text rev.) (DSM-IV-TR). Washington, DC: Author.

Choca, J. P. (2004). *Interpretive guide to the Millon Clinical Multiaxial Inventory* (3rd ed.). Washington, DC: American Psychological Association.

Craig, R. J. (Ed.) (2005). *New directions in interpreting the Millon Clinical Multiaxial Inventory-III.* Hoboken, NJ: John Wiley & Sons.

Loevinger, J. (1957). Objective tests as instruments of psychological theory. *Psychological Reports, 3,* 635–694.

Millon, T. (1969). *Modern psychopathology.* Philadelphia, PA: Saunders.

Millon, T. (1983). *Millon Clinical Multiaxial Inventory (MCMI) Manual* (3rd ed.). Minneapolis, MN: National Computer Systems.

Millon, T. (1987). *Manual for the MCMI-II* (2nd ed.). Minneapolis, MN: National Computer Systems.

Millon, T. (1994). *Millon Clinical Multiaxial Inventory-III (MCMI-III) manual.* Minneapolis, MN: National Computer Systems.

Millon, T., with Davis, R. D. (1996). *Disorders of personality: DSM-IV and beyond.* New York: John Wiley & Sons.

Millon, T. (2003). *MCMI-III corrections report user's guide* (rev. ed.). Minneapolis, MN: Pearson Assessments.

Millon, T. (2006). *Millon Clinical Multiaxial Inventory-III (MCMI-III) manual* (3rd ed.). Minneapolis, MN: Pearson Assessments.

SUGGESTED READING

Craig, R. J. (2008). Essentials of MCMI-III assessment. In S. Strack (Ed.), *Essentials of Millon inventories assessment* (3rd ed., pp. 1–55). Hoboken, NJ: John Wiley & Sons.

STEPHEN STRACK
U.S. Department of Veterans Affairs,
Los Angeles

See also: **Personality Assessment; Self-Report Inventories**

MINDFULNESS (See Mindlessness-Mindfulness)

MINDLESSNESS-MINDFULNESS

For many of us, the majority of our lives are spent in a state of "mindlessness" or "automatic-pilot" in which we may be actively engaged in several activities, but are largely unaware of the nuances of our experience. In this state we may get from one point to another without really knowing how we got there. Further, being mindless also makes us vulnerable to reacting in ways that are largely habitual and somewhat mechanistic.

Mindfulness is a state that directly contrasts automatic-pilot. It involves bringing one's complete attention to the experience of each moment, rather than being absorbed in the past or the future. It also involves approaching one's experience with a sense of openness, curiosity, and non-judgment, regardless of whether the experience is pleasant or unpleasant. Mindfulness often begins with a simple recognition of one's tendency to be on automatic pilot, and it can be further cultivated and expanded to include an awareness of all phenomena, as they are arising, without the need to control, evaluate, or avoid. These phenomena may be internal, as in thoughts, feelings, and sensations, as well as external.

Mindfulness: Definition and Origins

The term *mindfulness* is a Western psychological term that is used to refer to a practice that was borne out of Eastern philosophy, although many Western contemplative practices include elements of it as well (e.g., contemplative prayer in the Christian tradition). In particular, mindfulness is rooted in the Buddhist practice of Vipassana, which literally translates as "seeing things as they really are." The practice involves formal meditation, which begins with an observation of the breath, and gradually expands to include all aspects of experience. The term *meditation* typically refers to a form of mental training that may involve several techniques, including directing one's attention to a particular object, such as a word, mantra, image, or the sensations of the breath. Whereas the goal of many forms of meditation is to enhance concentration or single-pointed awareness, the goal of Vipassana meditation is not only to calm and settle the mind by paying attention to the breath, but also to harness this unified attentional capacity and direct it toward the contents of the mind itself, thus bringing attention to all aspects of current experience. The traditional practice of Vipassana meditation requires periods of intensive training, often in a residential setting, and under the guidance and supervision of a highly experienced teacher. However, several approaches have begun to translate the core practices of Vipassana into structures and systems that are more applicable to a Western lifestyle.

Thus in the last 10 years or so, mindfulness has gained a great deal of attention in both the popular and the academic psychological literatures. Much of this popularity can be attributed to two developments: (1) the increasing number of Eastern and Western Buddhist teachers who have brought the practices used in cultivating mindfulness to the West; and (2) the scientific interest in objectively understanding mindfulness and its benefits on physical and mental health. In the context of Western psychology, mindfulness has been described as "paying attention in a particular way: on purpose, in the present moment, and nonjudgmentally" (Kabat-Zinn, 1994), as a state of meta-cognitive awareness (awareness of thoughts and feelings as "mental events" (Teasdale, Segal, & Williams, 1995); and as "the non-judgmental observation of the ongoing stream of internal and external stimuli as they arise" (Baer, 2003).

Scientists and scholars have attempted not only to operationally define the construct of mindfulness, so that it may lend itself more readily to scientific inquiry, but also to quantify and measure it. Current self-report measures of mindfulness conceptualize it as being comprised of five different aspects: (1) the ability to observe and attend to one's sensations, thoughts, feelings, and perceptions; (2) the ability to describe and label one's experience with words; (3) nonreactivity to inner experience; (4) nonjudging of experience; and (5) the ability to act with awareness (Baer, Smith, Hopkins, Krietemeyer, & Toney, 2006).

Mindfulness: Research and Clinical Applications

The current list of benefits associated with mindfulness spans the fields of psychology, medicine, and neuroscience. A large number of therapeutic orientations have begun to utilize mindfulness techniques both explicitly and implicitly. Examples include mindfulness-based stress reduction (Kabat-Zinn, 1990), which was designed for the management of chronic pain; mindfulness-based cognitive therapy (Teasdale, Segal, & Williams, 1995), which was designed primarily for the prevention of relapse related to depression; mindfulness-based relapse prevention (Witkiewitz, Marlatt, & Walker, 2005) for substance-use problems; dialectical behavior therapy (Linehan, 1993) for borderline personality disorder; and acceptance and commitment therapy (Hayes, Strosahl, & Wilson, 1999), which has been used for a wide range of psychological problems. Whereas the first three approaches are based largely on formal meditation practices such as sitting and lying down meditation, and yoga, the latter approaches utilize mindfulness techniques within the context of other interventions.

Overall, the therapeutic effects of these interventions have collectively been noted for a variety of problems, including chronic pain, fibromyalgia, stress, anxiety, depressive relapse, and addictive behaviors. Not only do these interventions regard mindfulness as a therapeutic technique, but some of them also view it as an attitude that is embodied by the therapist towards the client. These approaches also emphasize the importance of the therapist's personal practice of meditation.

Several explanations have been put forth to help understand the mechanisms by which these interventions affect outcomes. These include factors such as an increase in nonjudgmental thinking and acceptance; an increased ability to tolerate difficult emotional states; a decrease in distractive, judgmental, and ruminative thoughts; and a decreased tendency to avoid these thoughts (see Baer, 2003).

Within the field of neuroscience, the capacities cultivated by mindfulness practice have been associated with several changes in the brain, including those associated with increased attentional focus, greater regulation of emotional reactions, increased positive affect in both the short and long term, greater response flexibility (the ability to pause before acting), greater modulation of fear and morality, and an increased capacity for empathy and self-awareness (see Siegel, 2007).

Thus the popularity of mindfulness is rapidly expanding and continues to influence several areas of research and psychological treatment. In the past 10 years or so, there has been a proliferation of the literature on mindfulness in both the academic and the popular media. This popularity may to some extent be indicative of a larger movement towards greater health and well-being and a need to counter the "automatic-mode" that currently dominates much of Western society.

REFERENCES

Baer, R. A. (2003). Mindfulness training as a clinical intervention: A conceptual and empirical review. *Clinical Psychology: Science and Practice, 10*, 125–143.

Baer, R. A., Smith, G. T., Hopkins, J., Krietemeyer, J., & Toney, L. (2006). Using self-report assessment methods to explore facets of mindfulness. *Assessment, 13*, 27–45.

Hayes, S. C., Strosahl, K. D., & Wilson, K. G. (1999). *Acceptance and commitment therapy: An experimental approach to behavior change.* New York: Guilford Press.

Kabat-Zinn, J. (1990). *Full catastrophe living: The program of the Stress Reduction Clinic at the University of Massachusetts Medical Center.* New York: Dell.

Kabat-Zinn, J. (1994). *Wherever you go, there you are: Mindfulness meditation in everyday life.* New York: Hyperion.

Linehan, M. M. (1993). *Cognitive–behavioral treatment of borderline personality disorder.* New York: Guilford Press.

Siegel, D. (2007). *The mindful brain.* New York: W. W. Norton.

Teasdale, J. D., Segal, Z., & Williams, J. M. G. (1995). How does cognitive therapy prevent depressive relapse and why should attentional control (mindfulness) training help? *Behavior Research and Therapy, 33*, 25–39.

Witkiewitz, K., Marlatt, G. A., & Walker, D. (2005). Mindfulness-based relapse prevention for alcohol and substance use disorders. *Journal of Cognitive Psychotherapy: An International Quarterly, 19*, 211–228.

Neharika Chawla
G. Alan Marlatt
University of Washington

See also: **Cognitive Therapy; Dialectical Behavior Therapy; Mental Imagery**

MINIMAL BRAIN DYSFUNCTION (See Attention-Deficit/Hyperactivity Disorder)

MINNESOTA MULTIPHASIC PERSONALITY INVENTORY

The original Minnesota Multiphasic Personality Inventory (MMPI) was developed in the 1940s to assess mental health problems in psychiatric and medical settings, and it rapidly became a standard personality instrument (Hathaway & McKinley, 1940). The popularity of this true-false personality inventory was due in large part to its easy-to-use format and to the fact that the scales have well-established validity in assessing clinical symptoms and syndromes (Butcher, 2005). The MMPI underwent a major revision in the 1980s, resulting in two forms of the test: an adult version, the MMPI-2 (Butcher, Dahlstrom, Graham, Tellegen, & Kaemmer, 1989), and an adolescent form, MMPI-A (Butcher et al., 1992). The MMPI-2 is a 567-item inventory comprised of symptoms, beliefs, and attitudes in adults above age 18. The MMPI-A is a 478-item version that is used for assessing young people, age 14–18. This article addresses only the MMPI-2. Together, the MMPI-2 and MMPI-A have become the most widely researched and used clinical assessment instruments in the field of personality assessment.

Assessing Protocol Validity

In some settings such as forensic applications or personnel settings, people may be motivated to present themselves in ways that do not disclose accurate information about themselves. For example, when an individual is being tested to determine sanity in a pretrial criminal evaluation, the person might be exaggerating symptoms. The initial step in MMPI-2 profile interpretation is the important one of determining whether the client has cooperated with the testing to provide an accurate appraisal of his or her personality functioning. Several scales on the MMPI-2 aid clinicians in determining whether a client's item responses provide key personality information or are instead simply reflecting response sets or deceptive motivational patterns that disguise the client's true feelings and motivations (Baer, Wetter, Nichols, Greene, & Berry, 1995). Several validity scales have been developed to evaluate a client's approach to the test. Four of these assessment strategies are the following.

The L Scale

The *L* scale addresses the client's willingness to acknowledge faults or problems. Individuals who score high on *L* are presenting an overly favorable picture of themselves. High scorers are claiming virtue not found among people in general. The *L* scale is particularly valuable in situations like personnel screening or some types of court cases, because people in those settings try to put their best foot forward and present themselves as better adjusted than they really are.

The K Scale

The *K* scale was developed to appraise test defensiveness or the tendency that some people have to minimize problems. In addition, this measure also serves as a means of correcting for defensiveness. That is, if clients are defensive as assessed by this scale, their score on five of the clinical scales are adjusted to compensate for their evasiveness.

The F Scale

The Infrequency scale or *F* scale was developed to assess the tendency of some people to exaggerate their problems or to fake the test by overresponding to extreme items. The items on this scale are very rare or bizarre symptoms. Individuals who endorse a lot of these items tend to exaggerate symptoms on the MMPI-2, perhaps as a way of trying to convince professionals that they need psychological services. As noted earlier, this motivational pattern is also found among individuals with a need to claim problems in order to influence the court in forensic cases. The *F* scale can be elevated for several possible reasons. The profile could be invalid because the client became confused or disoriented or responded in a random manner. High *F* scores are also found among clients who are malingering or producing exaggerated responses in order to falsely claim mental illness (Graham, Watts, & Timbrook, 1991).

TRIN and VRIN Scales

Two measures were developed to assess response inconsistency. These scales are based on the analysis of the individual's responding to the items in a consistent or inconsistent manner. The scales are comprised of item pairs that involve responses that are semantically inconsistent, for example, a pair of items that contain contradictory content that cannot logically be answered in the same direction if the subject is responding consistently to the content.

Assessing Clinical Symptom Patterns

Several types of scales have been developed to evaluate clinical problems. There are three types of scales that address problems in somewhat different ways: the traditional clinical scales and profile codes, the MMPI-2 content scales, and the specific problems or supplemental scales. A scale is a group of items from the MMPI-2 item pool that have been shown to measure certain symptom patterns or personality traits. Each item cluster or scale is normed on a population of normal individuals. This normative group serves as the reference point to which all profiles are compared.

The MMPI-2 Clinical Scales

Hathaway and McKinley developed the original MMPI clinical scales by determining empirically the items that separated clinical patients with clear diagnoses from a sample of nonpatients, or *normals*. For example, they developed scales to assess hypochondriasis (the Hs scale), depression (the D scale), hysteria (the Hy scale), psychopathic deviation (the Pd scale), paranoid thinking (the Pa scale), psychasthenia (the Pt scale), schizophrenia (the Sc scale), and mania (the Ma scale). In addition, two other scales were included on the clinical profile to address problems of sex role identification (the Mf scale) and social introversion and extraversion (the SI scale). Besides interpretation of single clinical scales, elevations on certain scale patterns or configurations of scores (referred to as profile or code types) are interpreted. These profile types result from clients endorsing two or more of the clinical scales.

Content-Based Scales

In the development of MMPI-2, a number of scales that assess the content themes an individual endorses were developed. The content scales are homogeneous item clusters that assess unitary themes and represent clear communication about problems to the practitioner. There are 15 content scales measuring different symptom areas and problems; examples include Antisocial Practices (ASP), Bizarre Mentation (BIZ), and Family Problems (FAM).

Special Scales

Several additional scales have been developed to address specific problems, such as the potential to develop substance abuse problems (the MacAndrew Addiction scale, or MAC-R, and the Addiction Potential scale, or APS) and whether the individual acknowledges having problems with drugs or alcohol (the (Addiction Acknowledgment scale, or AAS). The Marital Distress scale assesses clients' attitudes toward their marital relationship. These special scales allow the practitioner to assess specific problems that are not addressed in the clinical or content scales.

Development of New Scales for the MMPI-2

Since its original publication, psychologists have been developing new scales for the test. In fact, there have actually been more MMPI scales published than there are items on the test. A scale is simply a combination of items that have been thought to measure a personality construct or symptom pattern. Researchers interested in developing MMPI-2-based measures typically provide substantial information about the novel measure's psychometric functioning, validity, and reliability (Butcher, Graham, Kamphuis, & Rouse, 2006). In some instances, new scales have been developed without sufficient empirical research or clear rationale. For example the Restructured Clinical scales (Tellegen et al., 2003) were released for public use, even though the release elicited controversy with respect to these scales having been shown to be highly redundant with existing measures (Rouse, Greene, Butcher, Nichols, & Williams, in press), or having drifted too far from the scales of origin (Butcher, Hamilton, Rouse, & Cumella, 2006), or having been shown to lack sensitivity to assessment of clinical problems (Rogers & Sewell, 2006; Wallace & Liljequist, 2005). Caution in interpreting these measures in assessing clients is needed until sufficient research has delineated their meanings and uses.

How the MMPI-2 Is Used

There are currently many diverse applications for the MMPI-2 for evaluating individuals across a wide variety of settings. Contemporary uses include evaluating clients who are being admitted to an inpatient psychiatric facility, understanding problems and possible treatment resistance of clients entering psychotherapy, providing personality information for therapists to employ in giving the client feedback in psychotherapy, assessing possible personality problems of students applying for a graduate clinical psychology program, measuring behavior problems and symptoms in neuropsychological evaluation of a client with severe head injury, appraising personality factors and psychological adjustment in applicants for an airline pilot position, examining persons who are being tried for murder and are claiming to be not guilty by reason of insanity, and using the test as a research instrument to evaluate the psychological changes in a drug trial. There have been more than 32 translations and adaptations of the MMPI-2 for use in other countries. The items and scales have shown remarkable robustness when used in other languages and cultures (Butcher, 1996).

In summary, the MMPI-2 is a self-report personality inventory that provides the test user with scores on a number of scales. These scales assess response attitudes, mental health symptoms, personality traits, and special problems that the client might be experiencing. The MMPI-2 has been widely validated and is used in numerous settings around the world.

REFERENCES

Baer, R. A., Wetter, M. W., Nichols, D., Greene, R., & Berry, D. T. (1995). Sensitivity of MMPI-2 validity scales to underreporting of symptoms. *Psychological Assessment, 7,* 419–423.

Butcher, J. N. (1996). *International adaptations of the MMPI-2.* Minneapolis: University of Minnesota Press.

Butcher, J. N. (2005). *The MMPI-2: A beginner's guide* (2nd ed.). Washington, DC: American Psychological Association.

Butcher, J. N., Dahlstrom, W. G., Graham, J. R., Tellegen, A. M., & Kaemmer, B. (1989). *Minnesota Multiphasic Personality Inventory-2 (MMPI-2): Manual for administration and scoring.* Minneapolis: University of Minnesota Press.

Butcher, J. N., Graham, J. R., Kamphuis, J., & Rouse, S. (2006). Evaluating MMPI-2 research: Considerations for practitioners. In J. N. Butcher (Ed.), *MMPI-2: The practitioner's handbook* (pp. 15–38). Washington, DC: American Psychological Association.

Butcher, J. N., Hamilton, C. K., Rouse, S. V., & Cumella, E. J. (2006). The deconstruction of the Hy scale of MMPI-2: Failure of RC3 in measuring somatic symptom expression. *Journal of Personality Assessment, 87,* 186–192.

Butcher, J. N., Williams, C. L., Graham, J. R., Tellegen, A., Ben-Porath, Y. S., Archer, R. P., et al. (1992). *Manual for administration, scoring, and interpretation of the Minnesota Multiphasic Personality Inventory for Adolescents: MMPI-A.* Minneapolis: University of Minnesota Press.

Graham, J. R., Watts, D., & Timbrook, R. (1991). Detecting fake-good and fake-bad MMPI-2 profiles. *Journal of Personality Assessment, 57,* 264–277.

Hathaway, S. R., & McKinley, J. C. (1940). A multiphasic personality schedule (Minnesota): 1. Construction of the schedule. *Journal of Psychology, 10,* 249–254.

Rogers, R., & Sewell, K. W. (2006). MMPI-2 at the crossroads: Aging technology or radical retrofitting? *Journal of Personality Assessment, 87,* 175–178.

Rouse, S. V., Greene, R. L., Butcher, J. N., Nichols, D. S., & Williams, C. L. (in press). What do the MMPI-2 restructured clinical scales reliably measure? Answers from multiple research settings. *Journal of Personality Assessment.*

Tellegen, A., Ben-Porath, Y. S., McNulty, J., Arbisi, P., Graham, J. R., & Kaemmer, B. (2003). *MMPI-2: Restructured clinical (RC) scales.* Minneapolis: University of Minnesota Press.

Wallace, A., & Liljequist, L. (2005). A comparison of the correlational structures and elevation patterns of the MMPI-2 restructured clinical (RC) and clinical scales. *Assessment, 12,* 290–294.

SUGGESTED READING

Butcher, J. N. (Ed.). (2006). *MMPI-2: A practitioner's guide.* Washington, DC: American Psychological Association.

JAMES N. BUTCHER
University of Minnesota

MINNESOTA MULTIPHASIC PERSONALITY INVENTORY–ADOLESCENT

The Minnesota Multiphasic Personality Inventory–Adolescent (MMPI-A; Butcher et al., 1992) is an adolescent-specific revision of the original, broadband personality instrument, the Minnesota Multiphasic Personality Inventory (MMPI; Hathaway & McKinley, 1943). The original MMPI, designed primarily for adult clinical assessment, had been applied to evaluate adolescents from the time of its release. The revision to the MMPI-A was prompted by several considerations. First, the passage of nearly five decades since the original test's release made it necessary to develop contemporary adolescent norms. Second, it was apparent that MMPI items did not provide sufficient coverage of adolescent experiences. The accumulated research on adolescent MMPI profiles indicated that adolescent response patterns were quite distinct from those of adults, therefore warranting a developmentally appropriate instrument to achieve interpretive accuracy. The revision effort was undertaken with the goals of updating and refining item content, reducing test length and reading-level demands, developing a uniform set of contemporary adolescent norms, and developing scales to measure adolescent-relevant difficulties such as school- and family-related problems (Archer, 2005; Butcher et al., 1992).

Test Description

The MMPI-A is published by the University of Minnesota Press and distributed by Pearson Assessments. It is intended for assessing psychopathology in adolescents ages 14 through 18 years and requires a sixth-grade reading level. The MMPI-A can be extended downward to carefully selected 12- and 13-year-olds who have adequate reading and comprehension skills. Test norms are based on a national representative sample of 1,620 adolescents (805 boys and 815 girls), with an additional clinical sample of 713 adolescents from Minneapolis treatment centers used to develop new content scales and establish their clinical correlates. MMPI-A raw scores are converted to T scores that have a normative mean of 50 and standard deviation of 10. An empirically determined T-score cutting score of 65 marks the beginning of the clinical range, and T scores in the range of 60–64 denote a subclinical level suitable for interpretation at a more moderate level (Archer, 2005; Archer & Krishnamurthy, 2002).

The test instrument contains 478 items that form the basis for a multitude of scales and subscales measuring a broad range of experiences and difficulties. The initially released version contained 7 validity scales designed to detect aberrant response styles; 10 clinical scales modeled after the original MMPI scales, with 31 subscales to identify their subcomponents; 15 content scales measuring specific areas such as alienation, conduct problems, and low self-esteem; and 6 supplementary scales measuring areas such as substance-abuse problems and immaturity (Butcher et al., 1992). Subsequently, 31 content component scales were added to identify content scale subdomains (e.g., explosive actions versus irritability components of anger), and a new set of Personality Psychopathology-Five (PSY-5) scales have been provided to evaluate core dimensions of personality; these are described in a recent supplement to the MMPI-A manual (Ben-Porath, Graham, Archer, Tellegen, & Kaemmer, 2006).

Test Administration, Scoring, and Interpretation

MMPI-A test administration takes approximately one hour, and the test can be administered in paper-and-pencil format—using the booklet, audio CD, or audiocassette versions—or by computer. A Spanish-language version is available for testing Spanish-speaking adolescents in the United States. Available methods for test scoring include use of hand-scoring templates, computer software or optical scan scoring methods, or use of a mail-in scoring service provided by Pearson Assessments (Archer, 2005; Archer & Krishnamurthy, 2002).

Test interpretation begins with an evaluation of profile validity that includes examining the number of omissions, consistency in responding, and accuracy of self-presentation. Excessive omissions, inconsistency, or response biases in the direction of either overreporting or underreporting problems prohibit further interpretation, and there are empirically derived cutting scores to guide this decision. Subsequent profile interpretation is conducted at several levels. At the single-scale level, clinical, content, supplementary, and PSY-5 scales elevated at or above a T score of 60 are interpreted using scale descriptors, and the clinical scale subscales and content component scales are used to refine these descriptions. At the configural level, clinical scales are organized into two-point codetypes with established clinical correlate descriptions.

In the years since the MMPI-A's initial release, various empirically-based additions have been added to facilitate clinical interpretation. For example, a structural summary form has been developed to enhance interpretive organization and focus (see Archer & Krishnamurthy, 2002), and a critical item list has been developed to alert the test interpreter to clinically significant item responses reflecting potential risk of harm (see Ben-Porath et al., 2006). The interpretive process may thus be facilitated with an examination of salient overarching domains of dysfunction using the MMPI-A structural summary and with review of salient critical items that indicate the need for follow-up.

Resources for test interpretation include the scholarly texts listed in the suggested readings section of this article and test interpretation is also guided by two published volumes that present clinical case analyses (Archer, Krishnamurthy, & Jacobson, 1994; Ben-Porath & Davis, 1996). The test user can also find MMPI-A computer-based interpretive services described in these texts.

Research and Applications

The MMPI-A has been the focus of numerous research studies that have demonstrated its psychometric adequacy and clinical applications. For example, it has been shown to be appropriate for testing ethnic minority adolescents and useful in evaluating special populations such as juvenile delinquents, substance abusers, sexually abused teenagers, and adolescents with eating disorders. MMPI-A results are particularly useful for planning treatment in identifying critical issues related to level of distress and maladjustment, behavioral concerns, and interpersonal functioning. The test results also aid in diagnosis, identifying potential barriers to a favorable treatment response, and selection of intervention methods, and retesting can be useful to evaluate treatment outcomes (Archer & Krishnamurthy, 2002).

At the current time, the MMPI-A has been translated into several languages including Croatian, Dutch, French, Italian, and Korean, and specific Spanish versions are also available for use in Mexico/Central America and Spain, respectively (Archer, 2005). In light of its widespread clinical application and extensive research focus, the MMPI-A may be regarded as a well-established measure of adolescent functioning.

REFERENCES

Archer, R. P. (2005). *MMPI-A: Assessing adolescent psychopathology* (3rd ed.). Mahwah, NJ: Lawrence Erlbaum.

Archer, R. P., & Krishnamurthy, R. (2002). *Essentials of MMPI-A assessment*. Hoboken, NJ: John Wiley & Sons.

Archer, R. P., Krishnamurthy, R., & Jacobson, J. M. (1994). *MMPI-A casebook*. Tampa, FL: Psychological Assessment Resources.

Ben-Porath, Y. S., & Davis, D. L. (1996). *Case studies for interpreting the MMPI-A*. Minneapolis: University of Minnesota Press.

Ben-Porath, Y. S., Graham, J. S., Archer, R. P., Tellegen, A., & Kaemmer, B. (2006). *Supplement to the MMPI-A manual for administration, scoring, and interpretation*. Minneapolis: University of Minnesota Press.

Butcher, J. N., Williams, C. L., Graham, J. R., Archer, R. P., Tellegen, A., Ben-Porath, Y. S., & Kaemmer, B. (1992). *MMPI-A (Minnesota Multiphasic Personality Inventory— Adolescent): Manual for administration, scoring, and interpretation*. Minneapolis: University of Minnesota Press.

Hathaway, S. R., & McKinley, J. C. (1943). *The Minnesota Multiphasic Personality Inventory* (rev. ed.). Minneapolis: University of Minnesota Press.

SUGGESTED READING

Butcher, J. N., & Williams, C. L. (2000). *Essentials of MMPI-2 and MMPI-A interpretation* (2nd ed.). Minneapolis: University of Minnesota Press.

ROBERT P. ARCHER
Eastern Virginia Medical School

RADHIKA KRISHNAMURTHY
Florida Institute of Technology

See also: **Minnesota Multiphasic Personality Inventory; Personality Assessment; Self-Report Inventories**

MISSING DATA

Missing values are a common problem in psychology research. For example, in longitudinal studies, missing data arise because of attrition, that is, subjects dropping out prior to the end of the study. In surveys, some individuals provide no information because of noncontact or refusal to respond (unit nonresponse), or they fail to answer some of the questions because the topics are sensitive or because the information is hard to retrieve (item nonresponse). Information about a variable may be partially recorded, as when information is censored or classified or when time of an event (e.g., death) is not known because an individual is still alive at the termination of the study. Often psychology research involves indexes formed by summing values of particular items; missing data arise if any of the items that form the index is missing. Missing data can also arise by design, for example, when expensive or hard to collect information is recorded for only a subset of study participants.

Properties of missing data methods depend crucially on whether "missingness" depends on variables in the data set. Let Y denote the data matrix if there were no missing values, and $M = (m_{ij})$ the matrix of missing data indicators, with $m_{ij} = 1$ if y_{ij} is missing and $m_{ij} = 0$ if y_{ij} is observed. If the distribution of M does not depend on the data Y, the data are called missing completely at random (MCAR). An MCAR mechanism is plausible in planned missing-data designs, but it is rarely justified in other settings. A less restrictive assumption is that the distribution of M depends only on Y through the values that are observed (say Y_{obs}), and not on the values that are missing (say Y_{mis}). The missing data mechanism is then called missing at random (MAR). With drop-outs in longitudinal studies, data are MAR if dropout depends on observed values prior to drop-out, but it is not MAR if missingness depends on missing values, such as the value of Y at the time of drop-out, if not recorded. If the missing data depend on missing values Y_{mis}, the mechanism is not missing at random (NMAR). Most methods for handling missing data assume MAR, and, if values are likely to be NMAR, it may be best to do a sensitivity analysis to assess the impact of deviations from MAR.

A common default analysis method is complete-case (CC) analysis, also known as *listwise* deletion, in which incomplete cases are discarded and standard analysis methods applied to the complete cases. This analysis may suffice with small amounts of missing data, but it is inefficient when there is considerable information in the incomplete cases, and it is potentially biased when data are not MCAR, since then the complete cases are not a random subsample of the original sample with respect to all variables. The extent of bias depends on the degree of deviation from MCAR, the amount of missing data, and the specifics of the analysis. When data are MAR but not MCAR, a useful modification of CC analysis is to weight the respondents by the inverse of an estimate of the probability of response. This weighting method is commonly used to handle unit nonresponse in surveys. It is less useful for item nonresponse, because it is not well suited to handle general patterns of missing data or the case where there is extensive information in the incomplete cases.

Methods that impute or fill in the missing values have the advantage that, unlike CC analysis, observed values in the incomplete cases are retained. Naïve imputation approaches include imputing unconditional sample means, or carrying forward previously observed values in longitudinal studies. Such methods are easy but not generally recommended, because they can lead to bias, particularly if there are a lot of missing values. Better imputation methods condition imputations on the observed variables in the case. In particular regression imputation, which bases imputations on the predictions from a regression of the missing on the observed variables, is estimated using the complete cases.

Predictions from regression are conditional means, and as such do not preserve the full distribution of the imputed variable. Adding residuals or normal errors to the conditional means creates draws from the predictive distribution, which is advantageous if the full distribution is relevant, as when percentiles of the distribution are being estimated. *Hot deck* methods, which impute values of missing variables from a complete case matched to the incomplete case on observed characteristics, also tend to preserve distributions.

A single imputed value cannot represent all of the uncertainty about which value to impute, so analyses that treat imputed values the same as observed values generally underestimate uncertainty, even if nonresponse is modeled correctly. A modification of imputation that fixes this problem is multiple imputation (MI; see Rubin, 20). Instead of imputing a single set of draws for the missing values, a set of M (say $M = 10$) datasets is created, each containing different sets of draws of the missing values from their predictive distribution. We then analyze each of the M datasets and combine the results using simple multiple imputation combining rules. Often MI is not much more difficult than doing a single imputation, since most of the work is in generating good predictive distributions for the missing values. Important examples include MI for the multivariate normal model, as implemented in programs like PROC MI in SAS, and sequential regression MI (see IVEware, at http://www.isr.umich.edu/src/smp/ive/, or MICE, at http://www.multiple-imputation.com/).

An alternative to imputation is maximum likelihood (ML), which bases inferences on the likelihood function of the incomplete data, derived from a statistical model for the observed data. If the data are MAR, the missing data mechanism can be ignored, and inference based on a model for the data Y. Otherwise a model is required for the joint distribution of Y and M, which is harder to specify. Likelihoods based on incomplete data often have complicated forms and require iterative maximization algorithms like the EM algorithm. Little and Rubin (2002) and Schafer (1997) describes ML estimation for a variety of important models with missing data.

ML is most useful when sample sizes are large. When sample sizes are small, a useful alternative approach is to add a prior distribution for the parameters and compute the posterior distribution of the parameters of interest. The posterior distribution can often be computed by Markov Chain Monte Carlo methods, and it also yields predictions of the missing values that can be used for MI.

SUGGESTED READINGS

Allison, P. D. (2002). *Missing data*. New York: Sage.

Little, R. J. A., & Rubin, D. B. (2002). *Statistical analysis with missing data*, (2nd ed.). Hoboken, NJ: John Wiley & Sons.

Rubin, D. B. (2004). *Multiple imputation for nonresponse in surveys*. Wiley Classics Library. Hoboken, NJ: John Wiley & Sons.

Schafer, J. L. (1997). *Analysis of incomplete multivariate data*. New York: Chapman & Hall/CRC.

RODERICK J. LITTLE
University of Michigan

See also: **Sampling Error**

MOB PSYCHOLOGY

Crowds are defined as "co-acting, shoulder-to-shoulder, anonymous, casual, temporary, and unorganized collectivities" (Brown, 1954, p. 840). According to Floyd Allport (1924), "A crowd is a collection of individuals who are all attending and reacting to some common object, their reactions being of a simple prepotent sort and accompanied by strong emotional responses" (p. 292). Crowds can be subdivided according to whether they are active or passive, the former being a *mob* and the latter an *audience*. Mobs are further classified according to the dominant behavior of participants, whether aggressive, escapist, acquisitive, or expressive.

Aggressive mobs, which include riot and lynch mobs, involve a display of aggression toward persons or objects. The dominant behavior of escapist mobs is one of panic, as during a fire in a theater. Orderly escape is not panic. According to Brown (1954), "Panic is emotional and irrational. The escape behavior of the fear-driven mob must either be maladaptive from the point of view of the individual, or, if personally adaptive, the behavior must ruthlessly sacrifice the interests of others who also seek to escape" (p. 858). Acquisitive mobs are similar to escapist mobs in that both involve a competition for some object that is in short supply—tickets to the theater in the case of the acquisitive mob, and exits from the theater in the case of the escapist mob. Expressive mobs represent a wastebasket category that includes all mobs not in the first three categories. Included here is behavior that can best be described by the obsolete word *revelous*: behavior that might be displayed at religious revivals, sporting events, and rock music concerts.

Although there is no universal agreement among theorists, certain features tend to be attributed to mobs, such as like-mindedness, or "mental homogeneity," and emotionality. Gustav Le Bon (1903), in his classic work, *The Crowd*, explained the mental homogeneity of mobs in terms of "contagion"—a mechanical, disease-like spreading of affect from one member to another. More recent research suggests that contagion is not mechanical, but rather is dependent on a number of conditions. Milgram and Toch (1969) suggest that the mechanism of "convergence" may also account for the seeming mental homogeneity of mobs: likeminded individuals tend to converge and join mobs. Thus, homogeneity precedes rather than follows from membership in the mob. Brown (1954) questioned the homogeneity of aggressive mobs and suggested that the composition of such mobs could be ordered in terms of mob members' readiness to deviate from conventional norms of society. He identified five types of participants, ranging from the "lawless," whose actions trigger the mob, to the "supportive onlookers," who stand on the fringes shouting encouragement.

A central issue in the study of mob behavior is determining why restraints that produce conventional behavior break down when individuals find themselves in a crowd. Two important mechanisms that account for the violation of conventional behavior in crowds are (1) the loss of responsibility through anonymity and (2) the impression of universality. Both mechanisms are enhanced by the size of the crowd. Le Bon (1903) and many others have pointed out that aggressive mob members find it easier to act out their impulses because of the difficulty legal authorities have in singling them out and holding them responsible for their actions. Mob participants will feel safer from legal reprisals in large crowds because the sheer size of the crowd will pose impediments to identification and apprehension by the authorities.

Allport (1924) and more recently Turner and Killian (1957) have contended that an individual is swayed by the mob because of a belief that if everyone else is acting in a certain way, the actions cannot be wrong—the mob simply redefines the norm for correct behavior. In their "emergent norm theory," Turner and Killian (1957) take issue with the causal role of emotional contagion and argue instead that people act the way they do in crowds because the crowd helps to define the situation and the appropriate behavior. In the crowd context, the less anonymous people are to their coacting peers, the greater their conformity to crowd norms. The greater the number of crowd participants, the stronger the impression of universality. Crowd size has different implications for aggressive as opposed to acquisitive and escapist mobs. Whereas in aggressive mobs, a larger number of crowd members enhances beliefs in anonymity and impressions of universality, in acquisitive and escapist mobs, a large number of crowd members increases the competition for scarce resources (e.g., theater tickets, escape exits), thereby amplifying crowd responses.

Until recently, mob psychology has attracted little attention from social psychologists. Thanks to the efforts of Stephen Reicher, interest in the subject has been rekindled. Taking a social identity perspective, Reicher cites evidence from experimental and field studies showing that social identity forms the basis of much of mob behavior. People define themselves in part in terms of the groups to which they belong. Crowd or mob actions represent an expression of this identity. Thus, rather than losing their sense of identity in crowds, mob behavior acts to reaffirm participants' identity.

REFERENCES

Allport, F. H. (1924). *Social psychology*. Boston: Houghton Mifflin.

Brown, R. (1954). Mass phenomena. In G. Lindzey (Ed.), *Handbook of social psychology* (Vol. 2, pp. 833–876). Cambridge, MA: Addison-Wesley.

Le Bon, G. (1903). *The crowd*. London: Unwin.

Milgram, S., & Toch, H. (1969). Collective behavior: Crowds and social movements. In G. Lindzey, & E. Aronson (Eds.), *The handbook of social psychology* (2nd ed., Vol. 4, pp. 507–610). Reading, MA: Addison-Wesley.

Turner, R. H., & Killian, L. M. (1957). *Collective behavior*. Englewood Cliffs, NJ: Prentice-Hall.

SUGGESTED READINGS

Postmes, T., & Spears, R. (1998). Deindividuation and antinormative behavior: A meta-analysis. *Psychological Bulletin, 123*, 238–259.

Reicher, S. (2001). The psychology of crowd dynamics. In M.A. Hogg & S. Tindale (Eds.), *Blackwell handbook of social psychology: Group processes* (pp. 182–208). Malden, MA: Blackwell.

MARTIN S. GREENBERG
University of Pittsburgh

See also: **Conformity**

MODELING

Psychological theories have traditionally emphasized learning through the rewarding and punishing effects that actions produce. Natural endowment provides humans with enabling biological systems but few inborn skills. Competencies must be developed over long periods and altered to fit changing conditions over the life course. Direct experience is a tough teacher, because errors can be highly costly and some types of missteps are deadly. If knowledge and competencies could be acquired only by direct experience, human development would be severely retarded, not to mention unmercifully tedious and perilous. A given culture could never transmit the complexities of its language, mores, social practices, and essential competencies if they had to be shaped laboriously in each new member solely by response consequences, without the benefit of models to exemplify the cultural patterns. The abbreviation of the acquisition process is, therefore, vital for survival as well as for successful human development. Moreover, the constraints of time, resources, and mobility impose severe limits on the situations and activities that can be directly explored for the acquisition of knowledge and competencies.

Humans have evolved an advanced capacity for learning by observation that enables them to develop their knowledge and competencies rapidly from information conveyed by modeling influences. Indeed, virtually all types of behavioral, cognitive, and affective learning resulting from direct experience can be achieved vicariously by observing people's behavior and its consequences for them (Bandura, 1986; Rosenthal, & Zimmerman, 1978).

Much human learning occurs either deliberately or inadvertently by observance of the actual behavior of others in one's social environment and the consequences they experience. However, a great deal of information about human values, styles of thinking, behavior patterns, and societal opportunities and constraints is gained from modeled styles of behavior portrayed symbolically through the electronic mass media (Bandura, 2001). The growing importance of symbolic modeling lies in its tremendous scope and multiplicative power. A single model can transmit new ways of thinking and behaving to multitudes of people in widely dispersed locales. The accelerated development of electronic technologies has vastly expanded the range of models to which members of society are exposed day in and day out. These electronic systems, feeding off telecommunications satellites, have become the dominant vehicle for disseminating symbolic environments (Bandura, 2002). By drawing on these modeled patterns of thought and action, observers transcend the bounds of their immediate environment.

Not only are social practices being widely diffused within societies, but ideas, values, and styles of conduct are being modeled worldwide. The electronic media are coming to play an increasingly influential role in transcultural and sociopolitical change (Bandura, 1997; Braithwaite, 1994). Because the electronic media occupy a large part of people's lives, the study of acculturation in the present electronic age must be broadened to include electronic acculturation.

Mechanisms of Observational Learning

Observational learning is governed by four subfunctions. Attentional processes determine what people selectively observe in the profusion of modeling influences and what information they extract from ongoing modeled events. Observers' preconceptions, cognitive development, interests, and value preferences influence what they explore and how they perceive in what is modeled in the social and symbolic environment.

People cannot be much influenced by modeled events if they do not remember them. A second subfunction concerns cognitive representational processes. Retention involves an active process of transforming and restructuring information about modeled events into rules and conceptions for generating new patterns of behavior. In the third subfunction in observational learning—the behavioral production processes—symbolic conceptions are translated into appropriate courses of action. Skills are usually perfected through a conception-matching process. Conceptions guide the construction and execution of behavior patterns and the behavior is modified as necessary to achieve close correspondence between conception and action.

The fourth major subfunction concerns motivational processes. People do not perform everything they learn.

Performance of styles of behavior acquired through modeling are influenced by three types of incentive motivators—direct, vicarious, and self-produced. People are more likely to adopt observationally learned behavior if it results in valued outcomes for them than if it has unrewarding or punishing effects. The observed detriments and benefits experienced by others influence the performance of modeled patterns in much the same way as do directly experienced consequences. People are motivated by the successes of others who are similar to themselves, but discouraged from pursuing courses of behavior that they have seen often result in adverse consequences. Personal standards of conduct provide a further source of incentive motivation. People pursue activities that they find self-satisfying and that give them a sense of self-worth but reject those of which they personally disapprove.

Abstract Modeling

Social modeling is not merely behavioral mimicry, as is commonly believed. As we have seen, it operates at a higher level of learning. Highly functional patterns of behavior, which constitute the proven skills and established customs of a culture, may be adopted in essentially the same form as they are exemplified. There is little leeway for improvisation on how to drive automobiles. However, in most activities, subskills must be improvised to suit different situations. Modeling influences convey rules for generative and innovative behavior as well. For example, an individual may see others confront moral conflicts involving different matters but apply the same moral standard to them. In abstract modeling, observers extract the principles or standards governing specific judgments differing in content but embodying the same underlying rule. Once people extract the principles, they can use them to judge things and generate new courses of behavior that fit the prototype but go beyond the examples they have seen or heard. Evidence that generative rules of thought and behavior can be created through abstract modeling attests to the broad scope of observational learning (Bandura, 1986; Rosenthal & Zimmerman, 1978).

Modeling can also promote creativity in several ways (Bandura, 1986). Few innovations are entirely new. Rather, creativeness usually involves synthesizing existing knowledge into new ways of thinking and doing things. There is variety in the profusion of social modeling. Innovators select useful elements from different exemplars, improve upon them, synthesize them into new forms, and tailor them to their particular pursuits (Bolton, 1993). Models who exemplify novel perspectives on common problems also foster innovativeness in others, whereas modeled conventional styles of thinking and doing things diminish creativity. In these ways, selective modeling serves as the mother of innovation (Harris & Evans, 1973).

Motivational, Emotional, and Valuational Effects

In addition to cultivating competencies, modeling influences can alter incentive motivation (Bandura, 1986). Seeing others achieve desired outcomes by their efforts can instill motivating outcome expectations in observers that they can secure similar benefits for comparable performances. These motivational effects rest on observers' judgments that they have the efficacy to produce the modeled attainments and that comparable accomplishments will bring them similar beneficial outcomes. By the same token, seeing others punished for engaging in certain activities can instill negative outcome expectations that serve as disincentives.

People are easily aroused by the emotional expressions of others. What gives significance to vicarious emotional influence is that observers can acquire lasting attitudes and emotional and behavioral proclivities toward persons, places, or things that have been associated with modeled emotional experiences. They learn to fear the things that frightened models, to dislike what repulsed them, and to like what gratified them (Bandura, 1992). Fears and intractable phobias are ameliorated by modeling influences that convey information about coping strategies for exercising control over the things that are feared (Bandura, 1997; Williams, 1992). Attitudes and values can similarly be developed and altered vicariously by repeated exposure to modeled preferences. The actions of models can also serve as social prompts that activate, channel, and support previously learned behavior. Thus, the types of models that prevail within a social milieu partly determine which human qualities, from among many alternatives, are selectively encouraged.

During the course of their daily lives, people have direct contact with only a small sector of the physical and social environment. In their daily routines, they travel the same routes, visit the same familiar places, and see the same group of friends and associates. As a result, their conceptions of social reality are greatly influenced by modeled representations of society in the mass media (Bandura, 2009; Gerbner, 1972). The more their conceptions of the world around them depend on portrayals in the media's symbolic environment, the greater is its social impact (Ball-Rokeach & DeFleur, 1976).

Social Diffusion through Symbolic Modeling

Much of the preceding discussion has been concerned mainly with modeling at the individual level. As previously noted, the electronic media are coming to play an increasingly powerful role in transcultural change. In this broader function, symbolic modeling usually serves as the principal conveyer of innovations to widely dispersed areas, especially in early phases of diffusion (Bandura, 2006). Modeling instructs people in new ideas and social practices and designates their functional value.

A number of factors, including perceived self-efficacy to execute the modeled patterns, possession of necessary resources, outcome expectations concerning the costs and benefit of the new styles of behavior in the new milieu, and perceived opportunities and impediments determine whether people will adopt and put into practice what they have learned observationally (Bandura, 1986).

People are enmeshed in networks of relationship. They are not only linked directly by personal relationships. Because acquaintanceships overlap different network clusters, people become linked to each other indirectly by interconnected ties. These multilinked social networks provide diffusion paths for the spread of new ideas, lifestyle patterns, and social practices (Granovetter, 1983; Rogers & Kincaid, 1981).

REFERENCES

Ball-Rokeach, S., & DeFleur, M. (1976). A dependency model of mass media effects. *Communication Research, 3*, 3–21.

Bandura, A. (1986). *Social foundations of thought and action: A social cognitive theory*. Englewood Cliffs, NJ: Prentice-Hall.

Bandura, A. (1992). Social cognitive theory of social referencing. In S. Feinman (Ed.), *Social referencing and the social construction of reality in infancy* (pp. 175–208). New York: Plenum Press.

Bandura, A. (1997). *Self-efficacy: The exercise of control*. New York: Freeman.

Bandura, A. (2002). Growing primacy of human agency in adaptation and change in the electronic era. *European Psychologist, 7*, 2–16.

Bandura, A. (2006). On integrating social cognitive and social diffusion theories. In A. Singhal & J. Dearing (Eds.), *Communication of innovations: A journey with Ev Rogers* (pp. 111–135). Beverley Hills, CA; Sage.

Bandura, A. (2009). Social cognitive theory of mass communications. In J. Bryant & M. B. Olivier (Eds.), *Media effects: Advances in theory and research* (3rd ed.). Mahwah, NJ: Lawrence Erlbaum.

Bolton, M. K. (1993). Imitation versus innovation: Lessons to be learned from the Japanese. *Organizational Dynamics*, 30–45.

Braithwaite, J. (1994). A sociology of modeling and the politics of empowerment. *British Journal of Sociology, 45*, 445–479.

Gerbner, G. (1972). Communication and social environment. *Scientific American, 227*, 153–160.

Granovetter, M. (1983). The strength of weak ties: A network theory revisited. In R. Collins (Ed.), *Sociological theory* (pp. 201–233). San Francisco: Jossey-Bass.

Harris, M. B., & Evans, R. C. (1973). Models and creativity. *Psychological Reports, 33*, 763–769.

Rogers, E. M., & Kincaid, D. L. (1981). *Communication networks: Toward a new paradigm for research*. New York: Free Press.

Rosenthal, T. L., & Zimmerman, B. J. (1978). *Social learning and cognition*. New York: Academic Press.

Williams, S. L. (1992). Perceived self-efficacy and phobic disability. In R. Schwarzer (Ed.), *Self-efficacy: Thought control of action* (pp. 149–176). Washington, DC: Hemisphere.

Albert Bandura
Stanford University

See also: Social Learning Theory

MONOAMINE OXIDASE INHIBITORS (See Antidepressant Medications)

MOOD DISORDERS

Mood disorders refer to conditions involving maladaptive expression of any of three basic emotions—sadness, happiness, and anger—and their corresponding thoughts and actions. These three emotions are usually considered to be naturally adaptive reactions to changes that involve loss, gain, or obstruction, respectively. Adaptive reactions to such changes are associated with an eventual return to a euthymic (neutral or somewhat positive) mood state.

The key to defining mood disorders is developing criteria indicating that the emotion is indeed maladaptive, rather than a normal reaction to the vicissitudes of life. The American Psychiatric Association (APA, 2000) has endorsed criteria to define Mood Disorders in its *Diagnostic and Statistical Manual of Mental Disorders* (DSM).

Although the DSM has a hegemony in defining mood disorders, many of its diagnostic criteria have been criticized for their weak reliability and validity, heavy reliance on subjective Western values, vague symptom definitions, and neglect of the context in which an emotion is experienced (Kirk & Kutchins, 1992). Among other factors, the context includes the intensity, duration, and controllability of the loss, gain, or obstruction; cultural conditions; the skills needed to adjust to change; and whether emotional reaction is in proportion to the situation.

Cultural context must be considered in terms of whether emotions are adaptive or maladaptive. Taking Eastern culture as an example, Chinese patients with significant depressive symptoms tend to attribute their problems to physical discomforts rather than sadness and guilt commonly experienced by Western patients with depression. Compared to the very rare diagnosis of depression in China, many Chinese patients have been diagnosed with neurasthenia (*shenjin shuairuo*; Kleinman, 1986), which is a "nervous exhaustion." Kleinman found that 93% of Chinese patients diagnosed with neurasthenia met the DSM criteria for depression. This difference may be due partly to the strong stigma in Chinese culture about expressing sadness.

Another study examined the differences between Japanese and American students in their experiences of sadness, happiness, and anger. Compared to their American counterparts, Japanese students experienced these emotions with less intensity and had fewer physiological, phenomenological, and verbal reactions (Matsumoto, Kudoh, Scherer, & Wallbott, 1988). The tendency to refrain from feeling and expressing extreme emotions may be reinforced by Japanese culture and is important in maintaining social harmony (*wa*). Therefore, the concepts of adaptive or maladaptive emotions may differ across cultures and caution should be taken in diagnosis.

Sadness versus Major Depressive and Dysthymic Disorder

Sadness is a reaction of sorrow to a loss of something meaningful to the individual. A feeling of sadness can be accompanied by crying, frowning, fatigue, a change in sleep and appetite, a sense of worthlessness or hopelessness, loss of interest in activities that are usually pleasurable, difficulty concentrating, and thoughts about suicide.

Experiencing sadness is an indicator that the individual is capable of valuing aspects of the environment and of oneself that provide a sense of meaning to life. Sadness can be transient and a learning experience if accompanied by awareness of the changes the loss has created, acceptance of the sadness as natural, problem-solving regarding how to go about replacing the loss, and acting on solutions (Hurtado, Fernandez-Ballesteros, Notero, & Heiby, 1995). Adaptive sadness eventually dissipates and one returns to a euthymic mood. How long can one be adaptively sad?

Maladaptive sadness is identified in the DSM (APA, 2000) by a duration that meets temporal criteria for dysphoria (severe sadness) or anhedonia (loss of interest in pleasure) and by several associated thoughts, physical symptoms, and actions. The temporal criterion for major depressive disorder (MDD) is two weeks unless one is grieving the death of a loved one. This time frame is arbitrary and acknowledges only one contextual factor. However, would it be natural for a person to be very sad for more than two weeks when facing other contexts, such as losing a job or being divorced? Consideration of the context is critical to distinguishing sadness that is in proportion to one's situation from sadness that is not. Using DSM criteria for MDD, whether the sadness is veridical to the loss is not considered and can lead to overdiagnosis. For instance, it has been argued that neglect of context has led to a psychopathologizing of natural emotions and overestimates of the prevalence of mood disorders (Horowitz & Wakefield, 2007). Similar concerns relate to dysthymic disorder, which the DSM defines as a milder form of depression with a longer duration (i.e., two years).

Major depressive and dysthymic disorders also may be overdiagnosed in part due to the popularity of antidepressant medications, even though the evidence of their effectiveness is equivocal (Lacasse & Leo, 2005). Pharmaceutical companies encourage consumers to buy these drugs regardless of the reasons for or degree of their sadness. Therefore, the public may become less accepting of normal sadness and seek mood-enhancing altering drugs to eliminate the feeling rather than learn from it.

When sadness is disproportionate to the loss or occurs with no apparent loss and leads to severe disruption of functioning, then the diagnosis of major depressive or dysthymic disorder may help an individual obtain treatment. The use of anti-depressant medication and cognitive-behavior therapy are the most researched types of treatment, with some evidence that psychotherapy is essential for long-term recovery (Fava, Ruini, Rafanelli, Finos, Conti, & Grandi, 2004; Craighead, Sheets, & Brosse, 2006).

Happiness and Anger versus Bipolar and Cyclothymic Disorders

Happiness is a reaction of joy to gaining something of value. Its adaptive function gives a sense of well-being. Happiness is often accompanied by smiling, positive self-esteem, and involvement in pleasurable activities. Anger is a reaction of resentment to facing an obstruction in obtaining something of value. Its adaptive function is to motivate an individual to reach goals. Anger is often accompanied by tensing of brow muscles, adopting offensive and defensive postures, and attributing the cause of the obstruction to an event that must be changed.

Although happiness and anger have distinct adaptive functions, and are experienced and expressed differently, disordered levels of these emotions inexplicably are treated together as manic episodes under bipolar and cyclothymic disorders in the DSM (APA, 2000). A manic episode involves elevated happiness in the form of euphoria or elevated anger in the form of irritability that persists at least a week. As with other temporal criteria in the DSM, one week is an arbitrary time frame that does not consider the context of the emotion. For example, would it be maladaptive for someone who obtained a college degree and won the lottery to feel extremely happy for more than a week? Similarly, would it be maladaptive for someone who was unjustifiably fired from a job and placed in jail to feel extremely angry for more than a week?

Perhaps the heterogeneous definition of a manic episode is one reason why disordered happiness and anger are poorly understood. In addition, although there is a large literature indicating psychosocial determinants of mania, the primary mode of treatment remains medication, and the effectiveness of psychotherapy has less frequently been explored (Riedel, Heiby, & Kopetskie, 2001).

REFERENCES

American Psychiatric Association. (2000). *Diagnostic and statistical manual of mental disorders* (4th ed., text rev.). Washington, DC: Author.

Craighead, W. E., Sheets, E. S., Brosse, A. L., & Ilardi, S. S. (2007). Psychosocial treatments for major depressive disorder. In P. E. Nathan & J. M. Gorman (Eds.), *A guide to treatments that work* (3rd ed., pp. 289–307). New York: Oxford University Press.

Fava, G. A., Ruini, C., Rafanelli, C., Finos, L., Conti, S., & Grandi, S. (2004). Six-year outcome of cognitive behavior therapy for prevention of recurrent depression. *American Journal of Psychiatry, 161*, 1872–1876.

Horowitz, A. V., & Wakefield, J. C. (2007). *The loss of sadness: How psychiatry transformed normal sorrow into depressive disorder.* London: Oxford University Press.

Hurtado, J., Fernandez-Ballesteros, R., Montero, I., & Heiby, E. M. (1995). Multiple correlates of unipolar depression: Contributions from the paradigmatic behavior theory. *Psicologena, 7*, 41–50.

Kirk, S. A., & Kutchins, H. (1992). *The selling of DSM: The rhetoric of science in psychiatry.* New York: Walter de Gruyter.

Kleinman, A. (1986). *Social origins of distress and disease: Depression, neurasthenia, and pain in modern China.* New Haven: Yale University Press.

Lacasse, J. R., & Leo, J. (2005). Serotonin and depression: A disconnect between the advertisements and the scientific literature. *PLoS Medicine, 2*(12), e392.

Matsumoto, D., Kudoh, T., Scherer, K., & Wallbott, H. (1988). Antecedents of and reactions to emotions in the United States and Japan. *Journal of Cross-Cultural Psychology, 19*, 267–286.

Riedel, H. P. R., Heiby, E. M., & Kopetskie, S. (2001). Psychological behaviorism theory of bipolar disorder. *The Psychological Record, 51*, 507–532.

SUGGESTED READINGS

Caplan, P. J. (1995). *They say you're crazy: How the world's most powerful psychiatrists decide who's normal.* New York: Addison-Wesley.

Horowitz, A. V. (2002). *Creating mental illness.* Chicago: University of Chicago Press.

Kazarian, S., & Evans, D. (Eds.). (1998). *Cultural clinical psychology: Theory, research, and practice.* Oxford, UK: Oxford University Press.

Kitayama, S., & Markus, H. R. (Eds.). (1994). *Emotion and culture: Empirical studies of mutual influence.* Washington, DC: American Psychological Association.

ELAINE M. HEIBY
QIJUAN FANG
University of Hawaii at Manoa

See also: Bipolar Disorder; Cyclothymic Disorder; Dysthymic Disorder; Major Depressive Disorder

MOOD STABILIZING MEDICATIONS

As bipolar disorder is a recurrent illness over the lifetime of the patient, a central aspect of its successful treatment is the prevention of new mood episodes rather than simply the stabilization of acute manic or depressive episodes. For decades lithium was the only effective medication available for this purpose. However, not all patients responded to lithium, particularly those with a rapid cycling course of illness (four or more affective episodes per year) or mixed states (meeting criteria for depressive and manic states simultaneously). Over the last 15 years or so, fortunately, many new medications have emerged to greatly expand therapeutic options for our patients. Anticonvulsants such as valproate, carbamazepine, and lamotrigine have all received FDA approvals for treatment of bipolar mood states. This article summarizes the roles that lithium and several anticonvulsants play in the current treatment of mood disorders, with attention to their mechanism of action, indications, dosing, and side effects.

Lithium

Lithium is considered a first-line therapy for bipolar disorder. In the United States, lithium carbonate was approved for the treatment of acute mania in 1970 and for maintenance treatment in 1974. Lithium actions in the brain are highly complex. It acts on multiple neurotransmitters systems including glutamate, gamma-aminobutyric acid (GABA), norepinephrine, and serotonin. Additionally, lithium affects second messenger systems beyond the synapse, such as inhibition of the enzyme inositol monophosphatase (Schatzberg, Cole, & DeBattissta, 2007).

With respect to treatment of acute mania, some of the first placebo-controlled studies conducted in all of medicine were with lithium. Goodwin and Jamison analyzed studies conducted between 1950 and 1970 and found an overall response rate of 78% with lithium in acute mania ($n = 116$) (Goodwin & Jamison, 2007). More recent placebo-controlled studies, when lithium was compared to valproate, have reconfirmed its efficacy (Bowden et al., 1994). Lithium appears to be much less effective, though, in certain subgroups of bipolar patients, such as those with dysphoric mania, mixed states, or a history of substance abuse (Dilsaver, Swann, Shoaib, & Bowers, 1993).

As for maintenance treatment, as early as 1970 Baastrup and colleagues paved the way for this prophylaxis indication in a placebo-controlled trial with 84 patients (50 with bipolar disorder, 34 with recurrent unipolar depression) who had been stable on lithium for periods ranging from one to seven years. Following randomization to lithium or placebo, 21 out of the 39 patients randomized to placebo relapsed, while none of 45 on lithium relapsed. Results were so unequivocal that the investigators terminated the trial early for ethical reasons. Of the 25 patients who relapsed, 9 had unipolar depression, indicating a protective effect for lithium in both conditions (Baastrup, Poulsen, Schou, Thomsen, & Amdison, 1970). Subsequently, several double-blind studies carried out in

Europe and the United States confirmed lithium as an effective prophylaxis in bipolar disorder. In recent times two large placebo-controlled studies in which lithium was compared to the anticonvulsant lamotrigine for maintenance treatment of bipolar disorder reaffirmed its efficacy (Calabrese et al., 2003; Bowden et al., 2003).

Lithium is also efficacious as an add-on augmentation agent in treating unipolar depression when added to existing antidepressant treatment (De Montigny, Grunberg, Mayer, & Deschenes, 1981; Nierenberg et al., 2006). Moreover, and very significant clinically, lithium has demonstrated an antisuicide protective effect. In a meta-analysis comparing 1,389 patients receiving lithium with 2,069 patients on other psychotropics, patients on lithium experienced a 60% reduction of suicide rates (Cipriana, Pretty, Hawton, & Geddes, 2005).

For acute mania lithium is generally commenced at 300 mg 2–3 times daily and titration as needed to achieve blood levels of 0.6–1.2 mEq/L. For maintenance treatment, the dose range is 600–1800 mg daily to obtain levels between 0.6 to 1.2 mEq/L. Common side effects include nausea and diarrhea, which can be minimized by using the lowest effective dose and extended release formulations. Lithium is excreted by the kidneys, and its chronic administration can lead to a condition called nephrogenic diabetes insipidus. This condition is characterized by a decrease in the kidney's ability to concentrate urine due to interference with the effects of intrinsic anti-diuretic hormone (ADH), whose role is to help the kidneys retain water. The practical effects for the patient are symptoms of increased urination (polyuria) and increased thirst (polydypsia). This problem can be managed by dosage adjustment or use of an antidote called amiloride, which, ironically, is also used as a diuretic. More serious renal issues are either acute renal impairment (as an allergic reaction) or a slower insidious reduction in renal function. The former, while rare, necessitates cessation of lithium. The latter can be preempted by regular monitoring (every six months) of kidney function, and possibly additionally protected against by dosing all of the lithium as a single nocturnal dose.

In addition, lithium can induce hypothyroidism. Thyroid function should be monitored every six months on lithium. If it occurs (about 3% of patients), it is easily treated by thyroid replacement hormone. Weight gain, usually mild to moderate, is not uncommon. Side effects that can undercut compliance include cognitive slowing, memory problems, and tremor. Lithium has a narrow therapeutic index of 0.6–1.5 mmol/L, above which toxicity can occur. Maintaining adequate hydration and salt intake in summer months is important for patients.

Valproate

Valproic acid is an antiepileptic used for the treatment of absence seizures, partial seizures, and migraines.

Valproate was the first anticonvulsant to be approved by the FDA for treatment of acute mania (in 1994). A range of different formulations are available, including immediate release valproic acid (Depakene), salts of valproic acid in the form of divalproex sodium (Depakote), and extended release divalproex sodium (Depakote ER). Depakote tends to have less stomach side effects such as nausea compared to Depakene (Schatzberg et al., 2007). Valproate is believed to have gating effects on sodium and calcium channels in neurons with the effect of reducing excitatory effects related to the neurotransmitter glutamate and increasing the inhibitory actions of GABA. It is also believed to have positive neuroprotective effects on neurons and in normalizing circadian rhythms, which are disrupted in bipolar patients.

Several controlled trials have demonstrated valproate's superior efficacy relative to placebo in acute mania (Schatzberg & Nemeroff, 2004). A randomized double blind study comparing divalproex sodium to placebo and lithium in 179 inpatients with acute mania revealed a response rate of 48% for those on divalproex and 49% for those on lithium, versus only 25% for those on placebo (Bowden et al., 1994). The FDA recently approved the use of the extended release formulation divalproex sodium (divalproex ER) based on results from a large randomized, double-blind trial in 377 bipolar I patients, with 48% responding to divalproex ER versus 34% on placebo (Bowden et al., 2006).

Valproate appears particularly effective in patients with mixed states (Dilsaver et al., 1993; Bowden & Singh, 2005), prominent irritability, and a history of poor response to lithium or of multiple prior mood episodes (>8) (Bowden & Singh, 2005).

Surprisingly, valproate has not demonstrated clear benefit for prophylaxis in bipolar disorder. A pivotal trial failed to demonstrate valproate's efficacy in preventing recurrences of mood episodes. This trial, with 372 patients randomized to valproate, lithium, or placebo, yielded negative results, with neither active agent showing superiority over placebo (Bowden et al., 2000). However, it has been commented that this study may have been underpowered in light of the higher than predicted response to placebo, and, if so, it may represent a false negative finding.

In acute treating mania, valproate is dosed at 15–20 mg/kg/day and titrated as needed to reach a level of 45–125 μg/ml. Maintenance levels between 75–100 μg/ml are usually adequate. Common side effects such as gastrointestinal upset (nausea, dyspepsia, diarrhea), sedation, tremor, and weight gain can be alleviated with dose reduction or use of the ER formulation. Decreased platelet (thrombocytopenia) and white cell count (leucopenia) occur occasionally at levels over 125μg/ml, but these decreases are fortunately benign and reverse upon drug discontinuation. Elevation of liver transaminases and hepatitis can occur and represent the main serious risk with valproate. Hence, the American Psychiatric Association (APA) recommends monitoring liver function every 6–12 months and educating patients about symptoms of liver dysfunction. Other relatively uncommon but serious side effects include pancreatitis (1/3,000) and polycystic ovarian syndrome in females (up to 10%).

Carbamazepine

Carbamazepine is an antiepileptic used for generalized tonic-clonic and partial seizures and for trigeminal neuralgia. Even though carbamazepine is also available as a generic, an extended release formulation (Equetro) is the version that has received an FDA indication for treatment of acute mania, in 2005. Carbamazepine antiepileptic properties are related to the blockade of sodium channels. Its mood-stabilizing properties are complex and not entirely understood. Carbamazepine affects multiple neurotransmitter systems including adenosine, norepinephrine, dopamine, serotonin, acetylcholine, GABA, glutamate, substance P, and aspartate. It also affects second messenger systems (Schatzberg & Nemeroff, 2004).

Carbamazepine was approved for the treatment of mania based on two similarly designed, 3-week, double-blind placebo controlled trials. Carbamazepine (200 mg–1600 mg/day) was evaluated in bipolar I patients in a current manic or mixed episode and was found to be more effective than placebo, with the additional benefit of improving depressive symptoms in mixed states (Weisler, Kalali, & Ketter, 2004; Weisler et al., 2005). Additional controlled studies comparing carbamazepine to placebo or to lithium have suggested efficacy for carbamazepine in the prophylaxis of bipolar disorder, but the FDA has not granted an indication for this use, based on the current level of evidence (Schatzberg & Nemeroff, 2004).

Interestingly, certain patient characteristics that have been associated with poor response to lithium have been found to be positive predictors of response to carbamazepine. These include: severe mania, dysphoric symptoms, lack of family history of affective illness, and a history of rapid cycling. However, the response in rapid cyclers now appears to be less than initially reported (Dilsaver et al., 1993; Schatzberg & Nemeroff, 2004).

Doses in the range of 400–1600 mg/day are generally indicated. Serum levels between 6–10 μg/mL are adequate, but there is not a clear correlation between levels and the therapeutic response. Common and transient side effects include sedation, fatigue, nausea, and dizziness. Elevation of liver transaminases and hyponatremia are less common. Stevens Johnson syndrome occurs rarely. Carbamazepine can induce bone marrow suppression, but fortunately very rarely (1:100,000). Benign transient leucopenia may emerge during the first weeks of treatment. Serious adverse effects such as very low white cell counts (agranulocytosis) or aplastic anemia are rare (risk ranging from 1/10,000 to 1/125,000 patients). The APA advises regular monitoring of hepatic and hematologic function including CBC, platelets, and liver transaminases during carbamazepine therapy. In addition, patients should be instructed to seek immediate medical attention if any symptoms of bone marrow suppression such as bleeding, bruising, fever, or infections arise.

Carbamazepine induces a group of hepatic enzymes involved in metabolism called the P-450. This can lower the levels of many other drugs and needs to be factored into the dosing of such medications if carbamazepine is used. The best-known interaction is the effect of carbamazepine in lowering levels of estrogen from the birth control pill and thereby possibly causing contraception failure. Women of childbearing age who take carbamazepine will need a higher estrogen level pill or other contraceptive methods to prevent unintended pregnancy.

Oxcarbamazepine

Oxcarbamazepine is an anticonvulsant used to treat partial seizures. Oxcarbamazepine is structurally related to carbamazepine and, like this compound, it blocks sodium channels. Unlike carbamazepine, however, oxcarbazepine has fewer drug interactions, lacks the worrisome side effects on the bone marrow and the liver, and is better tolerated by most patients. Even though commonly prescribed, oxcarbamazepine has less research evidence for its use in bipolar disorder than the other antiepileptics previously described. Two small randomized double blind studies demonstrated comparable efficacy between oxcarbamazepine and haloperidol and lithium in treating acute mania (Hellewell, 2002).

Doses of oxcarbamazepine from 600–2400 mg/day are generally given in two divided doses. Dose-related side effects such as nausea, sedation, dizziness, headache, ataxia, fatigue, diplopia, and nystagmus are relatively common. Skin rashes and hyponatremia are rare side effects. Oxcarbamazepine is a mild inducer of the P-450 system and therefore has less drug interaction than carbamazepine, but it still can decrease the efficacy of oral contraceptives.

Lamotrigine

Lamotrigine was the third medication to receive FDA approval for the maintenance treatment of bipolar disorder (in 2003, after lithium and olanzapine). Lamotrigine is an anticonvulsant that inhibits sodium dependent channels in neuronal membranes, thus reducing the release of glutamate. In addition, lamotrigine appears to modulate serotonin reuptake (Schatzberg et al., 2007).

Lamotrigine efficacy in the maintenance of bipolar disorder was demonstrated in two pivotal randomized, placebo-controlled studies. One study enrolled bipolar I patients recovering from a depressive episode (Calabrese et al., 2003), and the other enrolled bipolar I patients recovering from a manic or hypomanic episode (Bowden et al., 2003). Subsequent to acute stabilization, patients were randomized to lamotrigine (50 mg, 200 mg, or 400 mg dose groups), lithium (0.8–1.1 mEq/l level), or placebo and followed for up to 18 months. The study outcome was the period of time until patients had a recurrence of any mood episode and needed additional treatment. In both studies lamotrigine was superior to placebo and equally as efficacious as lithium in preventing a new mood episode. Interestingly, lamotrigine showed a better profile in preventing depressive relapses as opposed to manic or hypomanic relapses. Conversely, lithium was more effective in preventing manic or hypomanic relapses than in preventing depressive relapses.

Common side effects of lamotrigine include dizziness, headache, double vision, ataxia, and sedation. A benign maculopapular rash occurs in approximately 10% of patients. In addition, however, a serious rash, Stevens Johnson syndrome, can occur in 1/1,000 cases in adults and 1/100 cases in children. In these cases the rash is a confluent, blistering one that involves skin, mucosa, and generalized symptoms such as fever, malaise, pharyngitis, anorexia, or lymphadenopathy. Patients should be educated about this risk and instructed to stop lamotrigine and seek medical attention immediately if the rash develops. To decrease risk of a serious rash, lamotrigine should be started slowly: 25 mg/day for two weeks, then 50 mg/day for two weeks, and then increasing up to 100 mg. A target dose of 200 mg can be reached as needed. A slower titration is necessary if the patient is already on valproate because of increased risk of rash.

Gabapentin and Topiramate

Initial small open studies on these two anticonvulsants indicated some mood stabilizing properties. Under double-blind conditions, however, they failed to separate from placebo (Pande, Crockatt, Janney, & Werth, 2000), indicating that not all anticonvulsants can be viewed as mood stabilizers. Topiramate, which is indicated for migraine prophylaxis, can be helpful secondarily in mitigating the weight gain that is a common side effect with the mood stabilizer medications we have reviewed here.

In conclusion, therapeutic options for patients have greatly expanded over the last decade. Nevertheless, it remains a challenge to find the best treatment with the least burden of side effects for the individual patient. Flexibility in treatment is a key consideration, as many patients need changes in medication to maintain benefit in concert with fluctuations in mood states over the lifetime course of a mood disorder.

REFERENCES

Baastrup, P. C., Poulsen, J. C., Schou, M., Thomsen, K., & Amdisen, A. (1970, August). Prophylactic lithium: Double blind discontinuation in manic depressive and recurrent depressive disorders. *The Lancet*, 326–330.

Bowden, C. L., Brugger, A. M., Swann, A. C., et al. (1994). Efficacy of divalproex vs. lithium and placebo in the treatment of mania. The Depakote Mania Study Group. *Journal of the American Medical Association, 271*, 918–924.

Bowden, C. L., Calabrese, J. R., McElroy, S. L., Gyulai, L., Wassef, A., Petty, F., et al. (2000). A randomized placebo controlled 12-month trial of divalproex and lithium in bipolar I disorder. *Archives of General Psychiatry, 57*, 481–489.

Bowden, C. L., Calabrese, J. R., Sachs, G., Yathman, L. N., Asghar, S. A., Hompland, M., et al. (2003). A placebo-controlled 18-month trial of lamotrigine and lithium maintenance treatment in recently manic or hypomanic patients with bipolar I disorder. *Archives of General Psychiatry, 60*, 392–400.

Bowden, C. L., & Singh, V. (2005). Valproate in bipolar disorder: 2000 onwards. *Acta Psychiatrica Scandinavica, 426* (Supp.), 13–20.

Bowden, C. L., Swann, A. C., Calabrese, J. R., Rubenfaer, L. M., Wozniak, P. J., & Collings, M. A. (2006). A randomized placebo-controlled multicenter study of divalproex sodium extended release in the treatment of acute mania. *Journal of Clinical Psychiatry, 67*, 1501–1510.

Calabrese, J. R., Bowden, C. L., Sach, G., Yatham, L. N., Behnke, K., Mehtonen, O., et al. (2003). A placebo-controlled 18-month trial of lamotrigine and lithium maintenance treatment in recently depressed patients with bipolar I disorder. *Journal of Clinical Psychiatry, 64*, 1013–1024.

Cipriani, A., Pretty, H., Hawton, K., Geddes, J. R. (2005). Lithium in the prevention of suicidal behavior and all cause mortality in patients with mood disorders: A systematic review of randomized trials. *American Journal of Psychiatry, 16*, 1805–1819.

De Montigny, C., Grunberg, F., Mayer, A., Deschenes, J. P. (1981). Lithium induces rapid relief of depression in tricyclic antidepressant drug non-responders. *British Journal of Psychiatry, 138*, 252–256.

Dilsaver, S. C., Swann, A. C., Shoaib, A. M., Bowers, T. C. (1993). The manic syndrome: Factors which may predict a patient's response to lithium, carbamazepine and valproate. *Journal of Psychiatric Neuroscience, 18*(2), 61–66.

Goodwin, F., & Jamison, K. R. (2007). *Manic depressive illness* (2nd ed.). New York: Oxford University Press.

Hellewell, J. S. E. (2002). Oxcarbazepine (trileptal) in the treatment of bipolar disorders: A review of efficacy and tolerability. *Journal of Affective Disorders, 72*, S23–S24

Kushner, S. F., Khan, A., Lane, R., & Olson, W. H. (2006). Topiramate monotherapy in the management of acute mania: Results of four double-blind placebo-controlled trials. *Bipolar Disorder, 8*, 15–27.

Weisler, R. H., Kalali, A. H., Ketter, T. A., & The SPD417 Study Group. (2004). A multicenter, randomized, double-blind placebo controlled trial of extended-release carbamazepine capsules as monotherapy for bipolar disorder patients with manic or mixed episodes. *Journal of Clinical Psychiatry, 65.* 478–484.

Weisler, R. H., Keck, P. E., Swann, A. C., Cutler, A. J., Ketter, T. A., & Kalali, A. H. (2005). Extended release carbamazepine capsules as monotherapy for acute mania in bipolar disorder: A multicenter, randomized, double blind placebo controlled trial. *Journal of Clinical Psychiatry, 66,* 323–330.

SUGGESTED READING

Thase, M. E., & Denko, T. (2008). Pharmacotherapy of mood disorders. *Annual Review of Clinical Psychology, 4,* 53–91.

PILAR CRISTANCHO
MARIO CRISTANCHO
MICHAEL E. THASE
University of Pennsylvania School of Medicine

See also: Anticonvulsant Medications; Antidepressant Medications; Mood Disorders

MOODS (See Emotions)

MORAL DEVELOPMENT

Moral development involves the process by which people internalize and orient their behavior according to socially sanctioned rules. Three conceptually distinguishable aspects of this developmental process have been highlighted: moral judgment (how one reasons about moral situations), moral behavior (how one acts), and moral emotions (what one feels).

Moral Judgment

Early in the twentieth century, psychologists like James Mark Baldwin and William McDougall began to study the process of moral development. Much contemporary research, however, was inspired by the cognitive-developmental theory of Jean Piaget (1932). According to Piaget's two-stage account, children progress from a heteronomous morality of constraint to an autonomous morality of cooperation. Although the stages differ on a number of dimensions—including employment of expiatory punishment versus restitution, belief in immanent justice, and unilateral obedience to authority—most research has examined whether moral judgments are based on objective consequences or subjective intentions. In general, research supports an age-related shift from an objective to a more subjective (intentional) conception of moral responsibility. The explanation of this finding, however, appears to be more complex than Piaget's referential interpretation: He maintained that younger children fail to differentiate between subjective (mental) and objective phenomena and rely on concrete referents when reasoning about moral situations. Other developmental variables including comprehension, memory, and integration of information may also play a role.

Kohlberg (1958) extended Piaget's two-stage view by postulating that moral rules and principles are progressively internalized throughout adolescence and into adulthood. The theory comprises three general levels of moral reasoning—preconventional, conventional, and postconventional morality. Each level, in turn, is divided into two specific stages (Kohlberg, 1958).

Preconventional morality is externally oriented. At Stage 1, what is right is defined by avoiding punishment and obeying authority. At Stage 2, hedonistic acts that satisfy personal needs determine what is right. Moral decisions at the conventional level are mediated by internalized rules and values. At Stage 3, interpersonal conformity is emphasized; one adheres to rules in order to please and be approved of by significant others. At Stage 4, right is defined in terms of doing one's duty and maintaining the existing social order.

Postconventional reasoners emphasize moral principles with applicability and validity independent from a specific authority or social order. At Stage 5, moral decisions reflect a personal obligation to abide by contractual commitments including implicit societal contracts. People understand the relativistic nature of rules and laws, but realize the need for contractual agreements to ensure equal justice and protect individual rights. Rational considerations about social utility, however, may necessitate subsequent changes and revisions of existing laws. At Stage 6, moral decisions are grounded in self-selected rational ethical principles considered to be universally valid.

The central tenet of Kohlberg's formulation—namely, a fixed moral developmental sequence—has generally been supported by empirical investigations, especially the supposition that preconventional morality is a prerequisite for conventional reasoning and both must precede the development of postconventional morality (Walker, 1989). However, the judgments people make about different moral dilemmas do not consistently reflect the same stage (Krebs & Denton, 2005). Also, the postconventional stages may not necessarily be found in all samples of adolescents or adults, especially Stage 6, which was deleted in the revised scoring method (Colby & Kohlberg, 1987).

Critics have emphasized the role that social-cultural factors may play in promoting postconventional reasoning, especially experiences within the context of a jurisprudence system of justice. Although Kohlberg's model may not provide *the* universal view of moral reasoning, it does seem to be relevant to people living in countries with constitutionally based legal systems.

Moral Behavior

The empirical link between moral cognition and action has been elusive: People can behave the same way for different reasons, and individuals at the same level of moral reasoning may act in different ways. Although some linkages have been reported, relationships between moral reasoning and behavior may not be linear (e.g., Hann, Smith, & Block, 1968). If moral behavior is mediated by moral reasoning, it may be necessary to focus on intra-individual variation over time and situations.

Knowing that people are, for instance, conventional moral reasoners may not be sufficient to predict accurately their behavior; the specific normative rules or values they hold would need to be taken into account. Other relevant factors may include knowing how personally committed people are to translating their reasoning into action, their sense of moral identity (Hardy & Carlo, 2005), and the extent to which they possess the self-regulatory resources to do so. Also, reasoning associated with moral behavior may not always be deliberate and effortful; it may occur automatically without conscious awareness (Haidt, 2001).

In the 1920s, the fundamental issue of moral behavior was addressed by Hartshorne and May. They devised behavioral measures of the extent to which participants would resist the temptation to lie, cheat, and steal in experimental settings. Correlational analyses provided little evidence for a general personality trait of honesty; they advanced the position that moral behavior was situation-specific. Research has continued to support the situation-specificity doctrine of moral behavior (Bersoff, 1999). Of course, not all people yield when confronted by situational temptations and external pressures. Research has highlighted the role that individual differences in self-regulatory resources may play in impulse control, temptation resistance, and self-restraint (Baumeister, Heatherton, & Tice, 1994).

Moral Emotion

The psychoanalytic theory of guilt-motivated morality was presented by Sigmund Freud. Briefly, Freud contended that children experience Oedipal/Electra feelings: They experience an intense love attraction to their opposite-sexed parent. Anxiety and fear of punishment prompts them to introject the same-sexed parent's rules and prohibitions; thus the superego or conscience is formed. In subsequent situations, according to Freud, children experience self-punishment or guilt when tempted to violate these internalized rules. Research indicates, however, that power-assertive parental practices are associated with an externalized morality: children comply with normative standards because they fear detection and/or punishment (Hoffman, 1994). A more internalized morality results when parental discipline is coupled with explanations about the harmful consequences of children's behavior for others. Such practices may contribute to moral development by enhancing children's tendencies to anticipate the consequences of their actions and to empathically experience another's emotional state (Hoffman, 2001).

REFERENCES

Baldwin, J. M. (1897). *Social and ethical interpretations in mental development: A study in social psychology.* New York: Macmillan. (Reprinted, New York: Arno Press, 1973.)

Baumeister, R. F., Heatherton, T. F., & Tice, D. M. (1994). *Losing control: How and why people fail at self-regulation.* San Diego: Academic.

Bersoff, D. (1999). Why good people sometimes do bad things: Motivated reasoning and unethical behavior. *Personality and Social Psychology Bulletin, 25,* 28–38.

Colby, A., & Kohlberg, L. (1987). *The measurement of moral judgment* (Vols. 1–2). New York: Cambridge University Press.

Freud, S. (1950/1925). The passing of the Oedipus complex. In *Collected papers,* Vol. 2. London: Hogarth Press.

Haidt, J. (2001). The emotional dog and its rational tail: A social intuitionist approach to moral judgment. *Psychological Bulletin, 108,* 814–834.

Hann, N., Smith, B., & Block, J. (1968). Moral reasoning of young adults. *Journal of Personality and Social Psychology, 10,* 183–201.

Hardy, S. A., & Carlo, G. (2005). Identity as a source of moral motivation. *Human development, 48,* 232–256.

Hartshorne, H., & May, M. A. (1928-1930). *Studies in the nature of character. Vol. I: Studies in deceit. Vol. II: Studies in self-control. Vol. III: Studies in the organization of character.* New York: Macmillan.

Hoffman, M. L. (1994). Discipline and Internalization. *Developmental Psychology, 30,* 26–28.

Kohlberg, L. (1958). *The development of modes of moral thinking and choice in the years 10 to 16.* Unpublished doctoral dissertation, University of Chicago.

Krebs, D. L., & Denton, K. (2005). Toward a more pragmatic approach to Morality: A critical evaluation of Kohlberg's model. *Psychological Review, 112,* 629–649.

McDougall, W. (1926/1908). *An introduction to social psychology.* Boston: Luce.

Piaget, J. (1965/1932). *The moral judgment of the child.* New York: Free Press.

Walker, L. J. (1989). A longitudinal study of moral reasoning. *Child Development, 60,* 157–166.

SUGGESTED READINGS

Bandura, A. (2002). Selective moral disengagement in the exercise of moral agency. *Journal of Moral Education, 31,* 101–119.

Hart, D. (2005). The development of moral identity. In G. Carlo & C. P. Weiss (eds.), *Nebraska Symposium on Motivation: Moral motivation through the life span* (Vol. 51, pp. 165–196). Lincoln, NE: University of Nebraska Press.

Hoffman, M. L. (2000). *Empathy and moral development: Implications for caring and justice.* New York: Cambridge University Press.

MICHAEL D. BERZONSKY
State University of New York at Cortland

See also: **Human Development; Morality; Socialization**

MORAL TREATMENT

Moral treatment (also called moral therapy) refers to the complex of ideas that came into prominence in Europe and America at the end of the eighteenth century and lasted through the nineteenth century. It maintained that madness (the eighteenth-century term) was not due to a total absence of reason. Thus, the mad were not to be seen as bestial (without reason), but rather as human (following an Enlightenment principle defining reason as human), and thus should be treated as such as much as possible. "Moral" then had the general connotations of today's "psychological"; it contrasted with "medical" therapeutics (although they were often employed together), which, through the eighteenth century, included such things as bleeding, blistering, purges, emetics, opium, and liberal use of physical restraint. In the words of Gerald Grob (1973), the dean of the history of institutional treatment of mental illness in the United States, moral treatment "meant kind, individualized care in a small hospital; resort to occupational therapy, religious exercises, amusements and games; repudiation in large measure of all threats of physical violence; and, only infrequent application of mechanical restraints. Moral treatment, in effect, involved the re-education of the patient within a proper moral atmosphere" (p. 168).

Moral treatment was grounded upon faculty psychology, derived from John Locke's (seventeenth century) associationism and sensationalism, modified by the Scottish "common sense" (or realist) school, which regarded "passions" (as well as intellectual functions) as a faculty. As further modified at the end of the eighteenth century by Phillippe Pinel (who is usually credited with the origination of the term *moral treatment*), bodily disorder, rather than being the cause of mental illness, was seen as the result of such disorder (Tomes, 1984; see also Dain, 1964). At that time most mental illness was seen as "functional," rather than the result of organic lesion; if left untreated for about a year, however, a functional illness could become organic. "Proximate causes" could be nearly anything disturbing in the person's environment, yielding a rich etiologic array (and the reason we see such superficial-seeming causes in nineteenth-century asylum records). Not only was treatment possible, it was thought better to intervene as soon as possible after the disturbing event(s), and, if possible, removal from the source of disturbing sensations should occur. Ideal treatment, it followed, would involve complete control of the person's environment, to control the disturbing sensations. Order would replace the disorder of the person's natural environment; the disordered mind would become ordered again via self-control.

The early asylums of this period, which came to be called "lunacy reform," were founded on principles of moral treatment. For the Americans, the most influential of developments in England and France at the end of the eighteenth century was the work of William Tuke, who founded the York (England) Retreat in 1796. Based on the principles of moral treatment augmented by Quaker humanitarianism, York was a small private institution with a building constructed specifically to implement, as fully as possible, the principles of treatment to be used there. Tuke's work directly influenced the Friends Asylum (founded in 1817) in Frankford, Pennsylvania, and several asylums of this early period. The asylum was to be carefully sited on a large parcel of land (for walks and other recreations) outside of town (later thought to be disordered and disturbing in itself) but close enough for occasional visits by family and friends. By the 1830s, a few state-supported asylums were constructed, a movement that expanded considerably by the time of the Civil War and was helped by the lobbying efforts of legislatures by Dorothea Dix.

Thus, the asylum of the nineteenth century was a purpose-built instrument for moral therapy. The earliest were run by laymen, but by the middle of the nineteenth century, medical men had assumed the reins. Asylum's professionalization predated, by a few years, the founding of the American Medical Association. In 1844, the Association of Medical Superintendents of American Institutions for the Insane (AMSAII) was founded (known later as The American Medico-Psychological Association, and since 1921 as the American Psychiatric Association). Moral therapy was thus combined with medical interventions by the mid-nineteenth century.

The unique architectural form, called the Kirkbride or "linear" plan, which we associate today with the nineteenth-century archipelago of asylums, was codified by Thomas Kirkbride's hospital-building manual of 1854. The plan called for an imposing center structure (administration, admissions, even living quarters for the superintendent and his family in the early days), from which relatively short wards were symmetrically arrayed out, stepped back one from the next, in the overall form of a shallow V. The design, in all its particulars, was based on the ideas of moral therapy. For example, there were to be single rooms (for privacy at night), but residents were not allowed to remain in them all day (to encourage social interactions). Each room had a view of an ordered world, and considerable attention was given to landscaping. Size was to be limited to 250 patients, (in 1866, the AMSAII raised the limit to 600, but these limits were quickly exceeded among the public asylums). By the end of the Civil War, there were 30 such buildings; by 1890, there were 70 (Yanni, 2007). By the time Kirkbride published his second edition (1880), his architectural plan, and moral therapy, had largely been superseded by the "segregate" (or campus) plans of the second half of the nineteenth century, and a return to somatic, rather than psychological, interventions.

Much of the modern history of psychiatry and abnormal psychology has been deeply contested for the past three or four decades, and this is certainly true for moral therapy. The famous image of Pinel casting off the chains of the young woman in the courtyard of Paris's Salpêtrière to usher in the era of moral therapy has long been debunked as at best overly simplistic, and at worst as completely wrong. The earliest Whiggish histories were written by the superintendents themselves (yet this sort of account still appears in many textbooks of abnormal psychology). The first revolt against this approach was stimulated by Michel Foucault in the 1960s: Moral therapy served to confine deviancy, not cure it. Even the term "moral management" (used interchangeably with moral therapy in the late eighteenth and early nineteenth centuries) was transformed in the service of the treatment/incarceration debate: Management followed therapy, historically, as needs for custodial care superseded those of therapy. Subsequent accounts have attempted to be more balanced and have been much more firmly grounded in historical evidence (e.g., Grob, 1973; Tomes, 1984). Even granting the self-serving motivations of the earliest accounts, it does seem that moral therapy was successful with many people before it was overwhelmed by the numbers attracted by its original successes. Ultimately, Dain's (1964) conclusion is persuasive: "Moral management [therapy] was never firmly established in the United States" (p. 205). The optimism of the early nineteenth century that insanity could be cured was gone by that century's end, and a more realistic view has largely remained to this day. Despite some heroic and successful twentieth-century programs of psychological interventions even with the most severely mentally disturbed, somatic (pharmacologic) interventions are grounded in pessimism regarding cure or even longer-term change of behavior.

REFERENCES

Dain, N. (1964). *Concepts of insanity in the United States, 1789–1865.* New Brunswick, NJ: Rutgers University Press.

Grob, G. N. (1973). *Mental institutions in America: Social policy to 1875.* New York: Free Press.

Kirkbride, T. S. (1854). *On the construction, organization and general arrangements of hospitals for the insane.* Philadelphia: Lindsay & Blakiston.

Kirkbride, T. S. (1972). *On the construction, organization, and general arrangements of hospitals for the insane, with some remarks on insanity and its treatment.* New York: Arno Press. (Original work published 1880, Philadelphia: Lippincott)

Tomes, N. (1984). *A generous confidence: Thomas Story Kirkbride and the art of asylum-keeping, 1840–1883.* New York: Cambridge University Press. Reprinted (1994) with a new historiographical essay as *The art of asylum-keeping: Thomas Story Kirkbride and the origins of American psychiatry.* Philadelphia: University of Pennsylvania Press.

Tuke, S. (1813). *Description of the Retreat, an institution near York* .... York, England: W. Alexander. Reprinted (1964) with a new introduction by R. Hunter & I. MacAlpine. London: Dawsons of Pall Mall.

Yanni, C. (2007). *The architecture of madness: Insane asylums in the United States.* Minneapolis: University of Minnesota Press.

SUGGESTED READING

Tomes, N. (1994). The art of asylum-keeping: *Thomas Story Kirkbride and the origins of American psychiatry.* Philadelphia: University of Pennsylvania Press.

ROBERT SHILKRET
Mount Holyoke College

See also: Morality; Residential Treatment

MORALITY

Traditionally, psychologists have focused on the moral development of children and have derived their models from psychoanalytic, social learning, and cognitive-developmental theory. Each of these models focuses on a different aspect of moral development—respectively, conscience, moral behavior, and moral judgment—and defines morality in a different way. In contrast to philosophical theories of ethics, which attempt to derive ultimate moral principles, psychological theories attempt to explain why people conform to moral norms and how they develop a subjective sense of morality. In recent years, psychologists have joined with scholars from other disciplines in attending to the evolution of morality in the human species.

Psychoanalytic Models of Moral Development

Early psychoanalysts advanced an "original sin" model of human nature, based on the assumption that although children are born with selfish, sexual, and aggressive drives (housed in a mental structure called the id), they may acquire the ability to suppress their immoral drives when they acquire a superego, or conscience. Psychoanalysts suggested that during a critical stage in their development, boys feel sexually attracted to their mothers (the Oedipus complex) but fear their fathers (castration anxiety). Boys acquire a superego when they resolve this dilemma by identifying with their fathers and introjecting their morals.

Psychoanalytic models capture important aspects of moral development—in particular, the problems created in families and other groups by the selfish desires of individuals, the value of resolving conflicts of interest, the importance of identification, and the role played by parents in children's acquisition of a conscience. However, Freud's (1925) account of moral development suffers from logical inconsistencies, fails to explain how girls acquire a sense of morality, and has not been supported by research.

Social Learning Models of Moral Development

The focus on social learning models of moral development is on how children learn to behave. Early learning theorists argued that children can be taught to suppress their anti-social urges and to obey rules through the judicious use of rewards and punishments. It might be summed up in the aphorism "Spare the rod and spoil the child." Later social learning theorists argued that children learn to behave in moral ways by imitating, or modeling, the behavior of those they like, respect, and admire. In addition, social learning theorists insisted that, to fully account for the acquisition of morality, theorists must attend to the internal cognitive mechanisms through which children process information and to the mental representations they form of their experiences (Bandura, 1986).

Many studies have supported social learning models of moral development. However, critics have argued that social learning models equate morality with conformity and fail to account for the active role that children play in developing their own autonomous conceptions of morality.

Cognitive Developmental Models of Moral Development

Jean Piaget (1932) founded the cognitive-developmental approach to morality when he observed children playing marbles and asked them to explicate their ideas about such aspects of morality as obeying authority, distributing resources, and punishing misdeeds. To aid in his interviews, Piaget read little stories to children of different ages, and he asked them questions about the behavior of the characters. For example, in one set of stories, Piaget asked children who was naughtier: a boy who broke 1 cup trying to get some jam from a cupboard, or a boy who broke 15 cups accidentally when he opened a door. Piaget concluded that children go through two major phases of moral development. In the first, the heteronomous phase, they conceptualize morality in terms of obedience to authority. In the second, the autonomous phase, they conceptualize morality more in terms of cooperation. Piaget attributed these changes to two interacting factors: (1) cognitive development, especially the development of perspective-taking abilities and moral reasoning, and (2) changes in the social world of children, from one dominated by adults to one comprised mainly of interactions with peers.

In the 1960s, Laurence Kohlberg revised Piaget's model of moral development. In place of Piaget's stories, Kohlberg created a set of complex hypothetical moral dilemmas. For example, in one dilemma, interviewees are asked to decide whether a character should steal an overpriced drug to save his dying wife. Kohlberg was not concerned about the content of children's moral judgments; he was concerned with the structure of their moral reasoning, as manifest in their answers to "why" questions.

In one of the most impressive longitudinal studies in psychology, Kohlberg and his colleagues (Colby & Kohlberg, 1987) retested the children from Kohlberg's early research every 3 years for more than two decades. These investigators concluded that conceptions of morality normally undergo several transformations as they develop, in an invariant sequence, which define stages of moral development. At Stage 1, children conceptualize morality primarily in terms of obedience to authority and avoidance of punishment. At Stage 2, they conceptualize it primarily in terms of instrumental exchanges among equals. At Stage 3, they view it in terms of the Golden Rule, conforming to social norms, and the value of performing one's social roles. At Stage 4, they view morality primarily in terms of upholding the order of their societies. And at Stage 5, they define morality more autonomously in terms of the kinds of universal and reversible principles derived by philosophers of ethics, such as treating others as means, not as ends, and promoting the greatest good for the greatest number.

Kohlberg's model of moral development reigned supreme in psychology for several decades. However, as it came under increasingly close scrutiny, a growing number of scholars, including several of Kohlberg's students and colleagues, took exception to some of its foundational assumptions. The criticism that attracted the most attention was advanced by Carol Gilligan (1982), who claimed that Kohlberg's stage sequence is biased against women. Gilligan argued that Kohlberg downgraded women's care-based moral orientation by classifying care-based moral judgments at Stage 3, while classifying the justice-based moral judgments preferred by men as Stage 4. However, research failed to support these criticisms (Walker, 2006).

Other criticisms were supported by research. In particular, the evidence suggests that (1) Kohlberg conflated the domain of morality with the domain of social conventions; (2) Kohlberg's sequence of stages is biased toward the moral orientation of people from the Western world; (3) Kohlberg's final stages of moral development are meta-theoretical (thinking about thinking) and qualitatively different from his other stages; (4) Kohlberg's model is a model of people's competence, or capacity, to make ideal moral judgments, but people often fail to perform at their level of competence; (5) although people may make structurally consistent, rational moral judgments to the hypothetical moral dilemmas on Kohlberg's test, the moral judgments that people make in their everyday lives are often inconsistent and irrational; (6) people do not process all moral information through one cognitive structure of the whole, but rather they invoke different structures to process information from different domains; (7) Kohlberg's model accounts for only one of several forms of moral judgment and moral reasoning; (8) moral judgment is often inconsistent with moral behavior; (9) in its focus on moral reasoning, Kohlberg's model neglects other sources of morality, such as heuristics and moral emotions; and (10) people may use the forms of moral reasoning that define Kohlberg's stages of moral development for immoral purposes, such as making a good impression and justifying immoral deeds (Krebs & Denton, 2005).

Evolutionary Approaches to Morality

In recent years, psychologists and other scientists have advanced models of how the mental mechanisms that dispose people to behave in moral ways and that endow people with a sense of morality have evolved in the human species. Researchers such as Frans de Waal (2008) have adduced evidence that chimpanzees and other primates show precursors of morality, such as helping members of their groups, sharing food, expressing sympathy, repairing damaged relationships, intervening in disputes, and punishing those who violate social norms. Theorists have argued that moral dispositions evolved in the human species because they enabled early humans to foster their survival and reproductive interests by joining forces with others, helping members of their groups, upholding systems of cooperation, and resolving conflicts of interest in mutually beneficial ways (Krebs, 2008).

Studies guided by evolutionary approaches to morality have found that people react to moral issues in two ways: (1) by interpreting them in a rational manner and deriving moral decisions from structures of moral reasoning, or (2) by deriving moral decisions impulsively, in the heat of the moment, based on moral intuitions and heuristics. Using functional magnetic imaging technology, researchers have given people a variety of trolley problems and assessed the areas of their brains that light up when they make moral decisions. Studies have found that although people believe that the most moral choice is to throw a switch that diverts a train onto a side track containing one person, in order to save the lives of five people on the main track, people do not believe it is right to push a heavy person off a drawbridge to stop a train that otherwise would kill five people. Researchers have found that the idea of pushing a person off a track activates areas of the brain that produce emotional responses, whereas the idea of pulling a switch to divert a train activates areas of the brain that produce rational, utilitarian considerations. The general conclusion from such research is that people often derive their moral decisions in significantly less rational ways than most people assume they do and that reason is a tool that people are disposed to invoke when it best serves their adaptive interests.

REFERENCES

Bandura, A. (1986). *Social foundations of thought and action: A social cognitive theory.* Englewood Cliffs, NJ: Prentice Hall.

Colby, A., & Kohlberg, L. (Eds.). (1987). *The measurement of moral judgment* (Vols. 1–2). Cambridge, England: Cambridge University Press.

De Waal, F. B. M. (2008). Putting the altruism back into altruism: The evolution of empathy. *Annual Review of Psychology, 59,* 279–300.

Freud, S. (1925). *Collected papers.* London: Hogarth Press.

Gilligan, C. (1982). *In a different voice: Psychological theory and women's development.* Cambridge, MA: Harvard University Press.

Krebs, D. L. (2008). Morality: An evolutionary account. *Perspectives on Psychological Science, 3,* 149–172.

Krebs, D. L., & Denton, K. (2005). Toward a more pragmatic approach to morality: A critical evaluation of Kohlberg's model. *Psychological Review, 112,* 629–649.

Piaget, J. (1932). *The moral judgment of the child.* London: Routledge & Kegan Paul.

Walker, L. J. (2006). Gender and morality. In M. Killen & J. G. Smetana (Eds.), *Handbook of moral development* (pp. 93–115). Mahwah, NJ: Lawrence Erlbaum.

SUGGESTED READINGS

Haidt, J. (2001). The emotional dog and its rational tail: A social intuitionist approach to moral judgment. *Psychological Review, 108,* 814–834.

Killen, M., & Smetana, J. (2006). *Handbook of moral development.* Mahwah, NJ: Lawrence Erlbaum.

Krebs, D. L. (2009). *Sources of morality: An evolutionary framework.* New York: Guilford Press.

DENNIS L. KREBS
Simon Fraser University, Canada

MORPHOLOGY

The central focus of those who study morphology is how language users understand complex words and how they create new ones. Compare the two English words *secure* and *insecurity*. The word *secure* cannot be broken down further into meaningful parts. It is morphologically simple. By contrast, *insecurity* is morphologically complex because it consists of three unanalyzable meaningful components (i.e., in + secure + ity), which linguists call morphemes. The study of the patterning of morphemes within a word and how morphemes combine to form new complex words falls within the domain of morphology. Morphemes are meaningful elements and must be distinguished from units of sound, because a simple morpheme may be complex in its sound structure: The simple morpheme *secure* is complex in terms of sound, consisting of two syllables and six phonemes. The study of the sound structure in language processing is well established. Only relatively recently, however, have psycholinguists begun to examine morphology as a window into understanding how we process words.

The first morpheme in *insecurity* is the prefix (in-), which means approximately "not"; the second or stem morpheme is the adjective *secure*; the third or word-final morpheme is the suffix (-ity), which serves to form a noun from the adjective *secure*. The meaning of *insecurity* (viz., "the state of not being secure") is fully predictable from the meaning of its components. It is semantically transparent. The same prefix occurs in many other words, as does its suffix (e.g., inactivity, impartiality). Note, however, that not all adjective stems can combine with morphemes such as *in* or *ity*. For example, the stem *abashed* combines with the affixes *un* and *ness* to form the noun *unabashedness*, whereas *continue* combines with *dis* and *ity* to form the noun *discontinuity*. The fact that nouns like *incontinueness* or *disambiguosity* are impossible also tells us that there are restrictions on how morphemes combine. At the same time, we can understand novel forms such as *unfaxable*. It is the morphologist's job to discover the general principles that underlie our ability to form and understand some complex forms but not others.

Affixes are morphemes that appear before or after the stem morpheme (namely, prefixes and suffixes, respectively). Affixes may vary quite widely in their productivity and in the likelihood that they will appear in new words. Compare the three English suffixes *-ory, -ive* and *-able*, all of which form adjectives from verbs. The first suffix is almost completely unproductive in Modern English; very few new words with this suffix have been added to the language in centuries. The second occurs in such recent words as *adaptive* and *adoptive*. The third is highly productive: innovations such as *unfaxable* are common.

Productivity is usually defined with respect to the extent to which a morpheme is expected to appear in novel forms. For example, if we search a large database for new words (words that do not appear in a large standard dictionary) containing the two morphemes *in-* and *-ity* that we introduced at the beginning of this article, we find very few new words with *in-* (actual examples include *ineliminable* and *inegalitarian*), but many more with *-ity* (actual examples include avuncularity and deviosity). We therefore say that *-ity* is more productive than *in-*. However, sometimes researchers define productivity with respect to the total number of words in which a morpheme appears. Again we find that the affix *able* appears in many more than does the affix *ive*. Analogous to affixes, stem morphemes can differ with respect to their family size, that is, the number of words formed from a particular morpheme stem. For example, many more words are formed from the stem *sist* (i.e., consist, persist, desist, insist, and approximately 31 derivations) than from the stem *flect* (i.e., inflect, deflect, reflect, and approximately 7 derivations).

Depending on whether they can stand alone, morphemes are classified into two basic types: free (e.g., *secure*) and bound (e.g., *in*, *ity*, *fect*). Affixes are bound because they cannot appear in isolation, but must combine with (be bound to) another morpheme to form a word. Repeated additions of bound morphemes allow for the formation of more complex words as affixes pile one onto another. The word *inconclusiveness* contains three bound morphemes as well as a free stem [conclude]; it has been built up in stages from *conclude* by first adding the suffix *-ive* to the verbal stem (with a sound change from *d* to *s*), so as to produce *conclusive*, then the prefix *-in* so as to form *inconclusive*, and finally the suffix *-ness*, resulting in [[in[[conclude]V ive]A]A ness]N.

Note that *in-* cannot combine with *conclude*, but it can combine with *conclusive*. This reflects the strict ordering of stages when complex words are formed. Sometimes, two morphemes can be added to a stem in two different orders, yielding two different meanings. Consider the word *unbalanced*. It can mean either "not balanced" or "deranged." The first meaning results from adding the suffix *–ed* to *balance* and then adding the prefix *un-*, which, when attached to adjectives, means "not." The second meaning results from first adding the prefix *un-* to the verb balance, giving us the verb *unbalance*, which means "derange." When the suffix *–ed* is added to this complex verb, it creates the adjective meaning, hence "deranged."

Finally, among bound morphemes, linguists distinguish inflectional from derivational morphemes. Derivational morphology deals with the way in which distinct words are related to one another; inflectional morphology focuses on the different forms that a word may take, depending on its role in a sentence. English is quite sparse inflectionally, as compared with many other languages (e.g., Classical Greek and most Slavic languages) in which each noun, verb, and adjective has a large number of inflected forms.

The way in which morphemes combine to form complex words also varies across languages. Some languages (e.g., Chinese) have little in the way of combining morphology. Others (e.g., Turkish) are distinctive for the manner in which multiple morphemes occur within a single word. Rules for combining morphemes also vary across languages. In English, morphemes are linked linearly as in words such as *inconclusiveness*. In Hebrew, by contrast, morphemes can be interleaved with one another (e.g., R-G-L combines with -e-e- to form ReGeL, meaning "leg," and with m-a-e- to form mragel, meaning "spy"). The relationship between "legs" and "spies" may seem obscure until one realizes that in biblical times one could spy only by walking around.

Knowledge about words is represented in the mental lexicon. A major research question for psycholinguists is how the mental lexicon represents morphological knowledge. One issue is whether regular forms and irregular forms are represented differently in the mental lexicon. If regularity is defined with respect to form, we can ask whether words with stems that undergo a change in spelling (and sometimes pronunciation) are represented differently from words whose stem is always regular. That is, are forms such as *run* and *ran* represented differently from forms such as *turn* and *turn*ed? Derivation tends to be semantically somewhat unpredictable: *walker* can mean either "one who walks" or "a special support that helps one to walk." If regularity is defined with respect to meaning, a second issue is whether inflected forms such as *concluded* and derived forms such as *conclusive* are represented in the same manner. Similarly, we can ask whether semantically opaque (or ambiguous) forms (e.g., *walker*) as well as semantically transparent morphological relatives (e.g., *talker*) are represented in a like manner in the lexicon. Within the mental lexicon, some theorists express morphological relatedness in terms of representations that are decomposed and share a constituent morpheme. Other theorists express morphological relatedness in terms of graded activation patterns that reflect degree of form and meaning similarity among full forms.

In the psycholinguistic literature, the classic task for exploring morphological knowledge is the lexical decision task. Letter strings are presented and readers must decide whether each is a real word. Reaction time to decide is measured. Words usually are presented in pairs, a prime and then a target. Typically they occur in immediate succession. When both prime and target are fully visible, decision latencies to the target are faster when it is preceded by a prime that is morphologically related (e.g., *turned-turn*) than by a prime that is similar in form (e.g., *turnip-turn*) or meaning (e.g., *rotate-turn*) but not morphologically related. Reduced decision latencies following a morphologically related prime as compared to an unrelated prime is termed *morphological facilitation,* and many psycholinguists interpret the effect as evidence that the same base morpheme or stem was activated by the prime and by the target.

Typically, the magnitude of morphological facilitation in lexical decision and similar tasks is attenuated when the prime is irregular (e.g., *ran-run*) relative to regular (e.g., *turned-turn*), but generally this involves reduced form similarity with its target. Likewise, magnitudes are smaller following derived than inflected primes but typically involve reduced semantic similarity (transparency). Morphological facilitation has been documented in a variety of languages, including those in which morphemes are not generally appended linearly (viz., *nonconcatenative*), such as American Sign and Hebrew, as well as in many in which morphemes are concatenated, such as Bulgarian, Dutch, English, French, German, Greek, Serbian, and Spanish. Properties of word stems that can alter morphological processing in variants of the lexical decision task include productivity of the stem and of the affix in addition to semantic transparency and orthographic similarity.

SUGGESTED READINGS

Aronoff, M. (1994). *Morphology by itself*. Cambridge, MA: MIT Press.

Baayen, R. H., Feldman, L. F., & Schreuder, R. (2006). Morphological influences on the recognition of monosyllabic monomorphemic words. *Journal of Memory and Language, 53,* 496–512.

Booij, G., & van Marle, J. (annual). *Yearbook of morphology*. Dordrecht, the Netherlands: Kluwer.

Feldman, L. B. (2000). Are morphological effects distinguishable from the effects of shared meaning and shared form? *Journal of Experimental Psychology: Learning, Memory and Cognition, 26.*

Feldman, L. B., & Basnight-Brown, D. (2007). Origins of cross-language differences in word recognition. In G. Jarema and G. Libben (Eds.), *The Mental Lexicon Core Perspectives.* Oxford, UK: Elsevier.

Feldman, L. B. (Ed.). (1995). *Morphological aspects of language processing*. Hillsdale, NJ: Lawrence Erlbaum.

Marslen-Wilson, W., Tyler, L., Waksler, R., & Older, L. (1994). Morphology and meaning in the English mental lexicon, *Psychological Review, 101.*

Matthews, P. H. (1991). *Morphology* (2nd ed.). Cambridge, UK: Cambridge University Press.

Moscoso del Prado Martín, F., Kostić, A., & Baayen, R. H. (2004). Putting the bits together: An information-theoretical perspective on morphological processing. *Cognition, 94,* 1–18.

Rueckl, J. G., Mikolinski, M., Raveh, M., Miner, C. S., & Mars, F. (1997). Morphological priming, connectionist networks, and masked fragment completion, *Journal of Memory and Language, 36.*

Zwicky, A., & Spencer, A. (Eds.). (1997). *Handbook of morphology.* Oxford, UK: Blackwell.

LAURIE BETH FELDMAN
MARK ARONOFF
University at Albany, SUNY

See also: **Psycholinguistics**

MOTION PARALLAX AND STRUCTURE FROM MOTION

Motion parallax and structure from motion are two related sources of information for the perception of the shape of 3-D objects and surfaces as well as the layout of objects and surfaces in 3-D scenes. Motion parallax refers to the inverse relation between the speed at which the projection of an object moves across the retina and the distance of the object from the eye. When the head moves horizontally, for example, projections of stationary objects closer than fixation move across the visual field in the direction opposite the head while projections of more distant objects move in the same direction as the head. The same is true for parts of objects or surfaces; the relative speeds with which objects move in the retinal projection provides information about their relative distances in the environment, assuming that the 3-D distances between the objects remain constant. This assumption is known as the *rigidity constraint*. Stationary objects move rigidly when an observer moves, but the validity of a rigidity constraint is less clear for moving objects. If the moving objects are associated with a continuous surface that is moving relative to the observer, a rigidity constraint may be reasonable.

Motion parallax is a perspective cue, in that the extent of projected motion is a function of distance, just as the projected sizes of objects of equal 3-D size vary according to their distance. The motion of the head, or of the objects, must be a pure translation for the inverse relation to be precise and the objects must be close enough so that the differences in their projected speeds are discriminable. Hermann von Helmholtz provided a classic description of this cue in which an observer standing still in a thick wood could not distinguish the separate trees and branches in the scene, but once moving forward could distinguish relative depth as well as in a stereoscopic view. Using random dot displays simulating corrugated surfaces, Rogers and Graham (1979) demonstrated that motion parallax is an effective source of information for surface perception in the absence of all other cues to depth. This was true for parallax produced by active observer head movements relative to a stationary display, and it was also true for parallax produced by moving a display relative to a stationary observer. Looming is an especially important form of motion parallax in which the projection of an object increases in size as it gets closer to the observer.

Structure from motion is an effective source of information for the perception of the shape of 3-D objects. It is distinguished from motion parallax in that it requires rotation and does not depend on the distance between the observer and the object or objects. Rotation of an object in depth changes the orientations of the 3-D distances between parts of the object relative to the line of sight. This results in corresponding changes in the projected distances. These variations in projected distance during rotation occur even in a parallel projection in which a 3-D scene is projected onto a 2-D plane simply by using the X and Y coordinates of each point and disregarding the Z coordinate. Structure from motion has been demonstrated with real objects by Metzger (1934) and by Wallach and O'Connell (1959), who called it the "kinetic depth effect." It has been studied with computer simulations using orthographic projection (e.g., Braunstein, 1962). Computational analyses have demonstrated that the 3-D coordinates of points can be recovered from as few as three views of four noncoplanar points in rigid rotation (Ullman, 1979), but

the applicability of such analyses to human perception has been questioned. Todd (e.g., in Todd & Bressen, 1990) has argued that people cannot integrate information across three views but, instead, use the velocity information in pairs of views to recover depth up to a scale factor. Domini and Braunstein (1998) have proposed that heuristic processes rather than full computational analyses are used. Heuristic processes are efficient computational shortcuts that usually recover good approximations to objective 3-D measurements but do not guarantee accuracy.

Because structure from motion is based on variations in the orientations of distances between points on objects, as opposed to distances from the observer, near-far relationships are ambiguous. Other depth information, such as binocular disparity, and occlusion and relative brightness, can be combined with structure from motion to resolve this ambiguity.

Although based on different geometrical considerations, motion parallax and structure from motion are probably not distinct in human vision. Objects of interest are generally close enough, or at least separated sufficiently in depth relative to their distance from the observer, so that the perspective effects of motion parallax are visible during head movements and while observing moving objects. Structure from motion is present whenever there is rotation. If we fixate on an object off to the side while moving past it, we are inducing a rotation between the eye and the object that may provide structure from motion information. Human observers appear to use the same decoding principles (Johansson, 1970) or heuristic processes (Braunstein, 1994) for motion parallax and structure from motion. The faster moving elements in an artificially generated display may be judged to be closer, even in a parallel projection in which projected speed is not determined by distance from the observer.

The overall motion of objects and surfaces in the visual field that occurs with observer motion is referred to as optic flow, especially in research on heading (the perception of the direction of observer motion). Optic flow is primarily a form of motion parallax, but may also involve rotation. It is closely related to research on time to contact, collision detection, and perceived self-motion or vection with applications to aviation, highway safety, and perceptual changes with age.

REFERENCES

Braunstein, M. L. (1962). Depth perception in rotating dot patterns. *Journal of Experimental Psychology, 64,* 415–420.

Braunstein, M. L. (1994). Decoding principles, heuristics and inference in visual perception. In G. Jansson, S. S. Bergstrom, & Epstein, W. (Eds.), *Perceiving events and objects* (pp. 336–346). Hillsdale, NJ: Lawrence Erlbaum.

Domini, F., & Braunstein, M. L. (1998). Recovery of 3D structure from motion is neither Euclidean nor affine, *Journal of*

Experimental Psychology: Human Perception and Performance, 24, 1273–1295.

Johansson, G. (1970). On theories for visual space perception: A letter to Gibson. *Scandinavian Journal of Psychology, 11,* 67–74. [Reprinted in G. Jansson, S. S. Bergstrom, & Epstein, W. (Eds.). (1994). *Perceiving events and objects.* Hillsdale, NJ: Lawrence Erlbaum.]

Metzger, W. (1934). Tiefenerscheinungen in optischen bewegungsfeldern.(Depth phenomena in optical movement fields). *Psychologische Forschung, 20,* 193–260.

Rogers, B. J., & Graham, M. E. (1979). Motion parallax as an independent cue for depth perception. *Perception, 8,* 125–34.

Todd, J. T., & Bressan, P. (1990). The perception of 3-dimensional affine structure from minimal apparent motion sequences. *Perception & Psychophysics, 48,* 419–430.

Wallach, H., & O'Connell, D. N. (1953). The kinetic depth effect. *Journal of Experimental Psychology, 45,* 205–217.

SUGGESTED READINGS

Andersen, G. J. (1986). Perception of self-motion: Psychophysical and computational approaches. *Psychological Bulletin, 99,* 52–65.

Braunstein, M. L. (1976). *Depth perception through motion.* New York: Academic Press.

Helmholtz, H. (1925/1962). Physiological optics (Vol. 3). In J. P. Southall (Ed.), *Physiological optics.* New York: Dover. (Original work published 1925)

MYRON L. BRAUNSTEIN
University of California, Irvine

See also: Depth Perception; Motion Perception

MOTION PERCEPTION

There have been substantial advances in our understanding of motion perception over the last few decades. These advances include exciting developments in motion perception research within neurophysiology, functional imaging, psychophysics, and computational modeling. To go beyond the overview provided in this article, readers are encouraged to consult detailed summaries available elsewhere (Blake, Sekuler, & Grossman, 2003; Sekuler, Watamaniuk & Blake, 2002).

Our ability to perceive motion serves a number of different functions, perhaps the most obvious of which is being able to perceive the speed and direction of (multiple) objects in our environment, as well as estimating the time until they reach some critical point (e.g., until they collide with us or each other). Because of this function, motion information is critical to our understanding of event sequences, event boundaries, and causality. Motion provides cues as to whether or not something is alive, because animate things move in particular ways that characterize their bodies and agency; as such, the processing of biological motion is thought to be relatively specialized. Motion allows the shape of objects to be distinguished from a background, facilitating object recognition (camouflage is much more effective as camouflage when it is stationary than when it is moving). Motion also serves depth segregation (motion parallax) and provides critical cues to our own path through an environment.

For simplicity, research on motion perception can be roughly divided into the psychophysical experiments that have sought to isolate motion and its critical parameters in perception (independent of objects or environmental context) and those that have explored the way movement through an environment changes the distribution of light on the retina (optic flow), which provides basic information about the observer's world. Optic flow is critically dependent on velocity, and it expands radially from the center of the visual field in the direction of the observer's motion. It has been shown to be a reliable source of information for guiding locomotion (in combination with egocentric motion information from the inner ear), accurately judging the direction of movement through an environment, learning and navigating around objects and complex paths, avoiding collisions, and parsing object structures; a good example of this is how biological motion creates a powerful percept of body shape (Warren, 2004; Sekuler, Watamaniuk, & Blake, 2002).

Several critical parameters of motion have been identified. First-order motion (also known as Fourier motion) results from an object that differs in light energy (luminance) from its background, for example, a bird flying across a blue sky or the light from a plane moving against the night sky. Second-order (non-Fourier) motion results from a moving contour that does not differ in luminance from the background but does differ in texture, color, or some other nonluminant property, for example, two pieces of different fabrics or a camouflaged animal in the undergrowth. These two kinds of motion are thought to be processed by separate pathways. Our ability to detect motion (i.e., judging its absolute presence) is influenced by the duration, size, speed, and luminance of the moving target. It is improved by cues that allow the target to be segregated (e.g., color) and when other objects move in different directions from the target we are tracking, also known as relative motion. This is perhaps not surprising given that visual system might exploit the fact that real-world objects typically move against a background. Our ability to discriminate motion (i.e., judging presence as well as some other quality such as speed or direction) is improved by longer durations, is robust in the presence of noise, and can discriminate global and local differences in direction at the same time.

Discrimination of speed is influenced by the spatial frequency and contrast of moving elements. Both detection and discrimination are influenced by fatigue, attention, and learning (practice). Perhaps the most famous phenomena in motion perception is the Motion Aftereffect (MAE) that is produced when one stares at one direction of motion for a long time (around 30 seconds, also known as adaptation), for example, a waterfall. If a static surface is then observed, it appears to move in the opposite direction. Current theories propose that mutual inhibition builds up between directionally selective neurons during adaptation; this inhibition remains once the stimulus is removed, so the balance of neural processing is disrupted and the stationary stimulus appears to move in opposition to the preferred direction of the inhibited neurons (Barlow, 1990).

In order to perceive motion correctly the visual system has adopted solutions that work very well under most natural ecologically plausible conditions but, importantly, fail under sensory laboratory or nonecological settings. These failures are informative because they uncover the prior assumptions of the visual system and its solutions to particular problems. For example, a simple strategy for identifying direction of motion is to sample the presence of the stimulus across spatially adjacent locations, such that it is present at one location before the other, and then integrate these samples at a second level. This two-step local-to-global process is intuitively appealing and generally works well but faces several difficulties in the laboratory. For example, it does not differentiate between a real moving stimulus and two individual static stimuli that appear separately—but with correct timing—in two sampled locations. This leads to "illusory apparent motion" when there was no physical motion. It appears that this is a good approximation of what happens during motion perception, as it allows successive static stimuli to display apparent motion when the delay between the two stimuli is proportionate to the distance and expected speed (e.g., film, animation, or computer displays).

The aperture problem is also a product of local-global sampling and integration. At the earliest stages of processing, the neurons in the visual system have small receptive fields, similar to looking through a port-hole or airplane window (i.e., an aperture). If an object is wider than the aperture, its axial motion is ambiguous. That is, if you looked out a small round window and saw a tall post moving from left to right, that post could only be moving from left to right, or it could be moving from left to right as well as up or down and you wouldn't know (until the top or bottom of the post appeared). The aperture problem demonstrates the hierarchical nature of motion processing in the visual system. In order to overcome this problem, integration of the local signals is informed and constrained by unambiguous information arriving from special features of the visual stimulus, such as intersections and borders, in order to eventually construct global registration speed and direction in a reference frame that distinguishes coherent objects from the background (Sekuler, Watamaniuk, & Blake, 2002).

Another problem is the so-called "correspondence problem" that occurs because a pattern of light on the retina could correspond to an indefinite number of real world stimuli; motion involves changes in space as well as time, so it adds further complexities in matching. A clear demonstration of this problem is the Wagon Wheel Effect: under stroboscopic light or in cinema—both unlikely ecological situations—a spoked wheel sometimes appears to rotate backward. This is a side effect of the visual system's attempt to solve the correspondence problem by exploiting various regularities in the physical world, such as the similarity between successive stimuli and the tendency for surfaces and objects to be constant (rather than abruptly ceasing to exist).

Finally, a number of brain regions are implicated in motion processing. In the primate brain, primary visual cortex (VI) and middle temporal (V5/MT) and global (V5/MT) stages of processing are described above. Neurons in area V5/MT of a monkey's brain shows direction selectivity, responses to depth, adaptation to motion, modulation from attention, and correlations with behavioral decisions about motion. Other brain regions are also involved in motion processing: the Superior Temporal Sulcus, Intra-Parietal Sulcus, Frontal Eye Fields, and the Kinetic Occipital Area (Orban & Vanduffel, 2004; Blake, Sekuler, & Grossman, 2003; Britten, 2004). A dramatic demonstration of the necessity of the occipto-parietal region in motion processing comes from rare instances of akinotopsia, or "motion blindness." Patients with this condition (with cortical damage that encompasses human area MT) cannot see movement; as a result, moving objects change location abruptly rather than smoothly. However, auditory and tactile cues to motion can be used to compensate (Zihl, von Cramon, & Mai, 1983; Blake, Sekuler, & Grossman, 2003).

REFERENCES

Barlow, H. B. (1990). A theory about the functional role and synaptic mechanism of visual aftereffects. In C. Blakemore (Ed.), *Coding and efficiency* (pp. 363–375). Cambridge: Cambridge University Press.

Britten, K. H. (2004). The middle temporal area: Motion processing and the link to perception. In L. M. Weiss & J. S. Werner (Eds.), *The visual neurosciences* (Vol. 1). London: MIT Press.

Blake, R., Sekuler, R., & Grossman, E. (2003). Motion processing in human visual cortex. In J. H. Weiss & C. E. Weiss (Eds.), *The primate visual system*. Boca Raton, FL: CRC Press.

Sekuler, R., Watamaniuk, S. N. J., & Blake, R. (2002). Visual motion perception. In H. Pashler (Series Ed.) & S. Yantis (Vol. Ed.), *Stevens' handbook of experimental Psychology: Vol. 1. Sensation and perception* (3rd ed.). New York: John Wiley & Sons.

Orban, G. A., & Vanduffel, W. (2004). Functional mapping of motion regions. In L. M. Weiss & J. S. Werner (Eds.), *The visual neurosciences* (Vol. 1). London: MIT Press.

Warren, W. H. (2004). Optic flow. In L. M. Weiss & J. S. Werner (Eds.), *The visual neurosciences* (Vol. 1). London: MIT Press.

Zihl, J., von Cramon, D., & Mai, N. (1983). Selective disturbance of movement vision after bilateral brain damage. *Brain, 106,* 313–340.

SUGGESTED READINGS

Blake, R., Sekuler, R., & Grossman, E. (2003). Motion processing in human visual cortex. In J. H. Kaas & C. E. Collins (Eds.), *The primate visual system.* Boca Raton, FL: CRC Press.

Sekuler, R., Watamaniuk, S. N. J., & Blake, R. (2002). Visual motion perception. In H. Pashler (Series Ed.) & S. Yantis (Vol. Ed.), *Stevens' handbook of experimental psychology: Vol. 1. Sensation and perception* (3rd edition). New York: John Wiley & Sons.

LOTTE METEYARD
BAHADOR BAHRAMI
University College, London

See also: **Motion Parallax and Structure from Motion; Perception**

MOTIVATION

Motivation leads to the instigation, persistence, energizing, and directing of behavior. Motivation refers to the energizing and directive states of animals and humans. The term *arousal* is used to describe the energizing aspect of motivation. The directing or steering aspect is related to goals. Thirsty animals look for water, or a person in a stressful job tries to escape from an unpleasant work situation. For humans, motivation largely involves complex, learned, social states. These states, like the beliefs associated with them, are continuously modified through many experiences.

Motivation in Humans and Nonhuman Animals

Motivation as a state is changeable, with high and low intensity at different times and with many kinds of motivations occurring either simultaneously or in rapid succession. Motivational disposition also occurs. Because it is in the nature of a trait, the distinction is made between the situational variable of a motivational *state* and the dispositional variable of a motivational *trait*. Trait motivations can be seen, for example, in the fact that within a species (human or non-human), some individuals are far more fearful than others.

Complex social motivations occur not only in people but also in nonhuman primates (like rhesus monkeys and

gorillas). Many social motivations result from complex experiences in group living (de Waal, 2008). Nonhuman primates have motivations that have similarities with human motivations, and all animals have strong motivations linked to survival. Species-specific characteristics occur with regard to motivation, and new research continues to provide clarity on what these characteristics are.

Motivation involves cues (stimuli that provide information) and goals. In humans, goals are often implicit, that is, outside of awareness (Locke & Latham, 2002). Motivation typically involves approach (such as seeking approval or task success) or avoidance (prevention of censure or of task failure). Motivational disposition differs from actual motivation, in that one may be inclined to be fearful (disposition) but in any given situation one is not afraid as an aroused motivational state.

States of motivation, like hunger and fear, are experienced by species other than humans, but some motivations appear to be uniquely human, such as the striving for excellence in achievement. Motivation also plays a major role in psychodynamic theories of personality, such as those of Alfred Adler and Sigmund Freud. The literature that deals with psychological disorders addresses various disturbances in motivation, such as depression and anxiety.

Positive motivation is prominent in the theory of Adler, who posited that all human beings have a fundamental "need to belong" (Ferguson, 1989), which in healthy individuals directs them to strive to contribute to the wellbeing of the group. The need to belong can lead to constructive and prosocial actions but, when the person believes he or she does not belong, it can lead to destructive and disturbing behavior (Dreikurs & Soltz, 2007).

Many internal variables, such as emotion, learning, and information processing, are closely related to motivation. For example, emotion, mood, and motivation are often linked (Ferguson, 2000). Although related, they are independently defined and investigated. Motivation involves an active process, which in humans has significant social and cultural meaning. Motivation arises as an outgrowth of cognitions (beliefs about self and others, for example), and it also leads to many kinds of cognitions. A person's self-concept is closely linked to many types of motivations, including states of anxiety. In human adults, family background (Ferguson, Hagaman, Grice, & Peng, 2006) can play a major role regarding values and goals that in turn shape motivation (Ferguson, 2006).

Humans have many cognitive representations that serve as goals, such as seeking new friends or finding a new job. Motivation, although influenced by external factors, refers to processes internal to the individual. Thus, others can set goals for a person (Locke & Latham, 2006), such as when a parent sets a goal for a child's achievement or an employee's supervisor sets goals for work accomplishments. However, such externally set goals may not be motivating because the individual internally does not self-set that goal.

Intensity of Motivation

Motivation differs not only in kind, such as an individual's being thirsty rather than hungry, but also in intensity. One can be more or less thirsty, more or less hungry. Intensity refers to the energizing aspect of motivation. The energizing effect of heightened motivation can be observed by means of physiological measures as well as by overt responses. Measures of brain waves, skin conductance, heart rate, and muscle tension have been used to study the intensity dimension of motivation. Under conditions of drowsiness and low excitation, electroencephalographic recordings generally show slow and large brain waves with a regular pattern, whereas in excited alertness the pattern is one of fast, low, irregular waves. When energized or excited, individuals also tend to show an increase in muscle potential, as measured by electromyographic recordings, and a decrease in skin resistance. Individual differences lead to variations in physiological responses under arousal (excitement).

Animals generally run, turn wheels, and press bars at a faster rate when they have an increased intensity of motivation. For many species, including humans, heightened motivation tends to increase effort, persistence, responsiveness, and alertness. Some theorists (e.g. Steriade, 1996) found increased motivational intensity to be associated with cortical desynchronization, with the firing of specific neurons, and with signs of behavioral arousal. Physiological, neurochemical, and psychological processes are related to changes in motivational intensity. Motivation affects immunological functioning (Cohen & Herbert, 1996). High self-imposed time-pressure motivation can lead to cardiovascular impairment as in strokes and heart disease. In many ways, motivational states have a strong impact on the total health of the individual.

Complex Relationships Exist between Behavior and Motivation

One cannot infer the existence of a motivation merely by the presence of certain behaviors. For example, because someone is aggressive does not presuppose a motivation or drive for aggression. Behavior is due to many factors. This is illustrated with eating disorders like obesity or bulimia, as well as in everyday life when people are not food deprived but nevertheless crave food when bored or anxious. Likewise, individuals can find food to be aversive and abstain from eating even when there is a strong tissue need for nourishment (Capaldi, 1996). People can eat when feeling unloved, and individuals may refrain from eating when motivated to seek social approval, obtain a job, or participate in a political hunger strike. Sexual behavior may occur when individuals seek power, prestige,

or social approval rather than sexual gratification related to sexual arousal. Although physiological needs may be powerful sources of motivation, they are neither necessary nor sufficient as the basis for motivation.

External rewards affect motivation and behavior. When external rewards are motivating, they are called incentives. Incentives are used in many areas of human life, such as by teachers in school, parents at home, and employers in the workplace. There are also reward pathways in the brain that play a crucial role in addiction. When external rewards are used to energize or direct behavior, this is known as extrinsic motivation, and it differs from intrinsic motivation, which is internally generated (Deci, Kostner, & Ryan, 2001). Extrinsic and intrinsic motivation affect behavior in very different ways. Adlerian psychologists have found that children trained with encouragement and self-reliance rather than with praise and rewards are more likely to maintain socially constructive behaviors (Dreikurs, Grunwald, & Pepper, 1999; Dreikurs & Soltz, 2007).

Fear and Anxiety Compared to Achievement Striving and Success Seeking

Learning of all kinds, including early life experiences, shapes the way animals and humans respond to stressful and fear-arousing events. Different situations arouse motivations of fear and anxiety for different species. Individual differences occur within a species in terms of prior experiences. Stimuli associated with pain come to evoke fear. Fear occurs when painful stimulation is anticipated. In humans, painful events are often symbolic and not merely physical, such as "fear of failure." Fear of failure leads people to be defensive. Their behaviors are directed toward preventing failure rather than toward attaining success (Covington, 2000). In contrast, people who have a mind-set (Dweck, 2006) that encompasses growth and new learning are far less likely to be defensively oriented toward failure prevention.

Sigmund Freud postulated that human neurosis has its roots in anxiety. Clinical, field, and laboratory findings have demonstrated that defensive motivations such as fear and anxiety are likely to lead to behaviors that interfere with effective task performance and creative problem solving. Task-oriented anxiety can be beneficial when the individual exerts effort toward task mastery, but self-oriented anxiety is likely to engender thoughts that indicate preoccupation with self-worth or with personal safety, which interfere with problem solving and limit the amount of attention given to task demands. Anxiety can lead to stress-induced illness and lower immune system activity, and it is associated with lowered productive energy (Thayer, 1989). Memory, attentional control, and retrieval efficiency tend to suffer when an individual is anxious.

Anxiety tends not to lead to effective functioning. However, many persons are not aware of how anxious they are. Studies have shown that there are individuals who do not report high anxiety, yet show anxiety behaviorally and physiologically. Such persons show a variety of ways for avoiding conscious experience of anxiety (Derakshan, Eysenck, & Myers, 2007; Eysenck, 2004). Self-awareness and positive self-concepts help to overcome negative beliefs and strategies that lead to the impairing effects of anxiety. Coping strategies improve when people believe that positive outcomes are possible and when they have self-confidence and confidence in others. When a person feels belonging, bonds with others, and contributes to the welfare of others, the individual functions effectively in many spheres of living. Contemporary writers have written about the need to belong, to feel competent, and to be self-determining—ideas that were formulated by Alfred Adler many decades ago (Adler, 1927/1959; Ferguson, 2001).

For humans, self-direction and symbolic processes are fundamental in determining motivation and its effects on behavior. Altruism and prosocial motivation enable humans to establish long-term emotional bonding, to overcome adversity, and to engage in cooperation and creative problem solving. Situational factors as well as intrinsic motivation shape people's cooperative or competitive actions and attitudes. Organismic (individual differences) and species variables are important in studying motivation. Additionally, for humans, societal and personal values, cultural and personal experiences, and many situational variables shape motivation and its effect on behavior.

REFERENCES

Adler, A. (1927/1959). *The practice and theory of individual psychology*. Paterson, NJ: Littlefield, Adams, 1959. (Originally published in 1927.)

Capaldi, E. D. (1996). Introduction. In E. D. Capaldi (Ed.), *Why we eat what we eat: The psychology of eating* (pp. 3–9). Washington, DC: American Psychological Association.

Cohen, S., & Herbert, T. B. (1996) Health psychology: Psychological factors and physical disease from the perspective of human psychoneuroimmunology. *Annual Review of Psychology, 47*, 113–142.

de Waal, F. B. M. (2008). Putting the altruism back into altruism: The evolution of empathy. *Annual Review of Psychology, 59*, 279–300.

Deci, E. L., Kostner, R., & Ryan, R. R. (2001). Extrinsic rewards and intrinsic motivation in education: Reconsidered once again. *Review of Educational Research, 71*, 1–27.

Derakshan, N., Eysenck, M. W., & Myers, L. B. (2007). Emotional information processing in repressors: The vigilance-avoidance theory. *Cognition &Emotion, 21*, 1585–1614.

Dreikurs, R., Grunwald, B. B., & Pepper, F. C. (1999). *Maintaining sanity in the classroom: Classroom management techniques.* (2nd ed.). Philadelphia: Taylor & Francis.

Dreikurs, R., & Soltz, V. (2007). *Children: The challenge.* New York: Penguin.

Eysenck, M. W. (2004). Trait anxiety, repressors, and cognitive biases. In J. Yiend (Ed.), *Cognition, emotion and psychopathology: Theoretical, empirical, and clinical directions.* Cambridge, UK: Cambridge University Press.

Ferguson, E. D. (1989). Adler's motivational theory: An historical perspective on belonging and the fundamental human striving. *Individual Psychology: Journal of Adlerian Theory, Research &Practice, 45*, 354–361.

Ferguson, E. D. (2000). *Motivation: A biosocial and cognitive integration of motivation and emotion.* New York: Oxford University Press.

Ferguson, E. D. (2001). Adler and Dreikurs: Cognitive-social dynamic innovators. *Journal of Individual Psychology, 57*, 324–341.

Ferguson, E. D. (2006). *Adlerian theory: An introduction.* Chicago: Adler School of Professional Psychology.

Ferguson, E. D., Hagaman, J., Grice, J. W., & Peng, K. (2006). From leadership to parenthood: The applicability of leadership styles to parenting styles. *Group Dynamics: Theory, Research, and Practice, 10*, 43–56.

Locke, E. A., & Latham, G. P. (2002). Building a practically useful theory of goal setting and task motivation: A 35-year odyssey. *American Psychologist, 57*, 705–717.

Locke, E. A., & Latham, G. P. (2006). New directions in goal-setting theory. *Current Directions in Psychological Science, 15*, 265–268.

Steriade, M. (1996). Arousal: Revisiting the reticular activating system. *Science, 272*, 12 April, Nu. 5259, 225–226.

Thayer, R. E. (1989). The biopsychology of mood and arousal. New York: Oxford University Press.

EVA DREIKURS FERGUSON
Southern Illinois University Edwardsville

See also: Intrinsic Motivation

MOTIVATIONAL INTERVIEWING

Motivational interviewing (MI; Miller & Rollnick, 2002) is a client-centered, goal-directed, brief treatment approach for helping people prepare for behavior change by building their intrinsic motivation and strengthening their commitment to a change process. It is one of the most well defined and rigorously studied psychotherapeutic interventions for substance use disorders, with a growing empirical base for its application in a variety of other behavioral areas. Four key principles and a style of interaction called the "MI spirit" guide the strategic application of two sets of techniques: (1) fundamental client-centered counseling strategies for developing a highly empathic environment in which clients may discuss their behavioral problems; and (2) direct methods for eliciting client statements that support behavior change (referred to as "change talk"). Many resources and training methods exist for teaching therapists how to practice MI. This article covers each of these areas in detail.

Empirical Support

MI has substantial empirical support across single and multisite clinical trials for enhancing treatment engagement and reducing substance use among clients abusing or dependent on alcohol or drugs. Meta-analytic reviews of MI (Burke, Arkowitz, & Menchola, 2003; Hettema, Steele, & Miller, 2005) indicate moderate treatment effect sizes, roughly equivalent to other evidence-based treatment approaches, across substance use outcomes at one- to three-month follow-up points. Typically, these effects decline over time, unless MI is delivered at the beginning of a standard treatment program wherein the positive MI treatment effects are maintained.

Overall, the most consistent treatment improvements have been found in studies in which participants primarily abuse alcohol rather than drugs and are adults rather than adolescents. MI also has been applied in health care, being moderately effective in the management of cardiovascular disease, diabetes, diet, and hypertension, though not with HIV-risk behaviors (Burke et al., 2003; Hettema et al., 2005). More recently, MI has been integrated into treatments for psychological problems such as depression, anxiety, eating disorders, and psychosis. These approaches are promising, but await further systematic evaluation before they can be deemed evidence-based.

Principles and MI Spirit

Miller and Rollnick (2002) delineate four key principles of MI that guide the use of specific interventions. MI is more of a style or way of being with people based on these principles rather than a mere application of techniques. Each principle is described next.

Express Empathy

Empathy involves therapists' attempt to accurately understand their clients' perspectives without judgment or criticism. Being able to listen carefully to what clients mean is a critical skill in MI because the nuances of how clients talk about their behaviors often reveals their motivations for changing or remaining the same.

Develop Discrepancy

Motivation for behavior change often depends on the existence of a discrepancy between the client's current behavior and important values or goals. Becoming aware of these discrepancies may serve as an impetus for change in that changed behavior might help clients feel they are acting in ways consistent with their preferred self-perceptions. For example, a teacher who prides herself in being a positive role model for her students might stop smoking marijuana if she believes this behavior is discrepant with what she would want her students to know about her. Therapists listen carefully for discrepancies and attempt to develop an understanding of them in clients, who presumably may have some ambivalence about potentially detrimental behaviors.

Roll with Resistance

Resistance in MI refers to those issues that support maintaining behaviors. Clients often express this resistance directly by telling therapists why a behavior is beneficial or not problematic. They also may state how they cannot change given their limited skills or resources. Sometimes, clients may be argumentative, negating, or dismissive in style while still expressing reasons for change. MI therapists focus on what is said rather than being blinded by how it is communicated so that they do not mistake a style of interaction for an indicator of low motivation. Furthermore, therapists view client resistance as an opportunity to understand the difficulties or obstacles to change rather than seeing it as an impediment to change. MI therapists avoid adopting a confrontational or authoritative therapeutic style that might engender more client resistance.

Support Self-Efficacy

Clients typically become more motivated when they believe they can change their behaviors. When clients lack confidence, they often shy away from behavior change. Therapists look for opportunities to support the clients' self-efficacy by helping them recognize their personal strengths and available resources. Likewise, they pay particular attention to the clients' past successful change efforts that might inform how they might approach their current behavioral problems.

By embracing these principles, therapists adopt a style of interaction that is (1) collaborative, by demonstrating respect for the clients' ideas and goals and "meeting them where they are at" motivationally; (2) evocative, by eliciting clients' change talk; and (3) supportive of the clients' autonomy to make decisions about behavior change. These three components embody the spirit of how therapists interact with clients and are a hallmark of MI.

Techniques

Therapists use both fundamental skills (open questions, affirmations, reflections, and summaries) and direct methods for evoking change talk, in both instances avoiding strategies inconsistent with the approach (such as unsolicited advice or direct confrontation) to increase client motivation for change during the session (Miller & Rollnick, 2002). Therapists attend to the balance of client statements supporting behavior change or inaction to gauge client motivation and to adjust their use of MI strategies accordingly. Therapists' capacity to elicit change-oriented client statements and reduce resistant ones, with the aim of strengthening clients' commitment to change, is seen as a necessary element in MI (Amhrein et al., 2003).

Fundamental Skills

Open questions, affirmations, reflections, and summaries (OARS) are the mainstay of all MI sessions. In particular, MI relies heavily on skilled use of reflective listening, in which therapists restate or paraphrase their understanding of what a client has said in order to express empathy as well as to bring attention to ambivalence, highlight change talk, and explore and lessen resistance. Open questions encourage client elaboration and may draw out motivations for change (e.g., "How could you apply your past success to your current situation?"). Affirmations (i.e., reflection of clients' strengths and past change efforts) build collaboration between therapists and clients and promote self-efficacy. Summaries provide opportunities for therapists to demonstrate fuller understanding of the clients' experiences, collect change talk to tip the balance toward change, link discrepant statements that capture the clients' ambivalence, and shift focus to other behavioral areas (e.g., move from discussing alcohol to anxiety symptoms). In general, therapists are encouraged to reflect more than question, use more open than closed questions, and to genuinely affirm clients in each session.

Direct Methods

Direct methods for evoking client change talk hinge on the capacity of therapists to recognize how clients talk about change. Motivations are revealed in change talk in terms of *desire, ability, reason, need,* and/or *commitment* (DARN-C). These can be described as: desire ("I want to stop drinking"), ability ("I can stop drinking"), reason ("If I stop drinking, I might not lose my job"), need ("I will die if I continue to drink"), or commitment ("I will stop drinking") to change (Amhrein et al., 2003). Therapists identify the extent to which clients express motivation in each of these areas, use their fundamental skills to support change talk revealed by the client, and then in a goal-oriented fashion directly attempt to draw out from the client the area of motivation that may be absent in the conversation. For example, clients who have expressed the benefits of drug use might be asked about the benefits of drug abstinence and the costs of continued use. Alternatively, these clients might be asked to look to the future at some time interval (e.g., one year from now) and consider where their lives are headed with continued drug use compared with if they were to stop using drugs. MI has a host of techniques designed to elicit these kinds of change-promoting statements, with the aim of garnering a commitment to change once clients have sufficiently developed their motivation for change. The strength of a client's commitment to change a behavior has been found to be a significant positive predictor of the likelihood that the client will actually make this change (Amhrein et al., 2003).

Learning Motivational Interviewing

A variety of training resources exist to learn MI. These resources include textbooks, treatment manuals, training videotapes, a supervision manual, and an international training group called the Motivational Interviewing Network of Trainers. Many of these resources are accessible at http://www.motivationinterview.org. In addition, Miller and colleagues (2004) have shown that therapist participation in intensive MI workshops, plus post-workshop expert individual supervision based on direct observation (via recorded sessions) with performance feedback and individualized coaching, results in substantial increases in therapists' MI skills and in the frequency of clients' change talk. Feedback and coaching interventions typically rely on MI performance rating scales. Workshops alone have not been found to produce these types of positive therapist training effects, underscoring the importance of clinical supervision and ongoing practice to develop MI skills.

MI is an empirically supported substance abuse treatment with growing application in a variety of behavioral health and psychological areas. It has a clear set of principles and techniques that guide implementation and substantial training resources to prepare therapists to conduct MI proficiently. Several critical areas challenge the future development of MI. These challenges include gaining a better understanding of how MI works (e.g., the relative importance of fundamental skills and direct methods), developing innovative ways to deliver MI to clients (e.g., computer-based intervention) and to teach therapists the approach (e.g., interactive CDs and simulated trainings), determining the effectiveness of MI when delivered in real-world clinical settings, and promoting the dissemination of MI in a way such that those who claim to use this intervention do so with adequate skill to achieve the improved client outcomes that are the promise of MI.

REFERENCES

Amhreim, P., Miller, W. R., Yahne, C. E., Palmer, M., & Fulcher, L. (2003). Client commitment language during motivational interviewing. *Journal of Consulting and Clinical Psychology, 71,* 862–878.

Burke, B. L., Arkowitz, H., & Menchola, M. (2003). The efficacy motivational interviewing: A meta-analysis of controlled trials. *Journal of Consulting and Clinical Psychology, 71,* 843–861.

Hettema, J., Steele, J., & Miller, W. R. (2005). Motivational interviewing. *Annual Review of Clinical Psychology, 1,* 91–111.

Miller, W. R., & Rollnick, S. (2002). *Motivational interviewing: Preparing people for change* (2nd ed.). New York: Guilford Press.

Miller, W. R., Yahne, C. E., Moyers, T. B., Martinez, J., & Pirritano, M. (2004). A randomized trial of methods to help clinicians learn motivational interviewing. *Journal of Consulting and Clinical Psychology, 72,* 1052–1062.

SUGGESTED READINGS

Arkowitz, H., Westra, H. A., Miller, W. R., & Rollnick, S. (2008). *Motivational interviewing in the treatment of psychological problems.* New York: Guilford Press.

Rollnick S., Miller, R. W., & Butler, C. C. (2008). *Motivational interviewing in health care: Helping patients change behavior.* New York: Guilford Press.

STEVE MARTINO
Yale University School of Medicine

See also: Client-Centered Therapy; Interview Assessment; Structured and Semistructured Interviews

MOTOR CONTROL

Everyday actions such as reaching for an object, opening a bottle, or driving a car are rarely experienced as a problem. However, a brief consideration of how voluntary movements come about helps to appreciate the complexity of motor control. Movements are the result of actively modulated muscle forces, but only to some extent. Once a limb is set into motion, it exerts forces on other parts of the body. In addition there are external forces, gravity in particular. Thus, although initiated actively, the further course of a movement is shaped by nonmuscular forces in addition to muscular ones. The forces acting on a joint are combined in complex ways into torque, and the angular rotations at several joints determine the spatial position of the end effector, e.g., the tip of the finger. All in all, there is a complex transformation from muscle excitation to movement of an end effector, which can be broken down into partial transformations: from muscle excitations to muscle forces, from muscle forces to joint torques, from joint torques to joint rotations, from joint rotations to movement of the end effector.

When we use a tool, for example, a computer mouse to control the position of a cursor on a monitor, extrinsic transformations are added to the intrinsic ones. The very simple task of moving the cursor to an icon requires that intrinsic and extrinsic transformations are mastered. From an intended movement of the cursor, the pattern of muscle excitations has to be derived that will result in a movement that matches the intention.

Consider the simple extrinsic transformation of the hand movement into the motion of the cursor on a monitor. The intended output is a straight path of the cursor from its current position to an icon. One way to approximate this path is by means of closed-loop control. The position of the cursor is continuously monitored, and whenever it deviates from the straight path, the movement of the hand is changed to correct the error. The position of the cursor, that is, the output of the transformation, is used as visual feedback for the continuous modulation of the input of the transformation, the position of the hand. Thus there is a closed loop from input to output and back to input. To the extent that closed-loop control is accurate, the output of the transformation approximates the desired output.

The cursor on the monitor can also be moved, though less accurately, when the eyes are closed before the movement is started. In this case the loop is not closed, but control is open-loop. Accuracy depends critically on how well the extrinsic transformation has been learned. The product of such learning is generally referred to as an internal model of the transformation. Internal models can be quite accurate for simple transformations, but for more complex transformations open-loop control becomes inaccurate.

Humans combine closed-loop and open-loop control in principle. However, control can rely more on the one or on the other type of process, depending on the nature of the task. Closed-loop control is plagued with temporal delays and the risk of instability (or control loss). The minimization of this risk requires slow movements. Rapid movements become possible only when open-loop control is added. By this the demands on closed-loop control are reduced. It mainly serves to compensate for the remaining inaccuracies that are inherent to internal models of transformations.

In the majority of cases the intended movement of the end effector is only incompletely specified by the task requirements, for example, when only start and target locations are given. This fact is often referred to as motor equivalence, in that the task can be performed in several different and equivalent ways, or as the degrees-of-freedom problem, in that the task does not fully constrain the degrees of freedom in movement production. Specification of a unique movement requires that additional constraints are taken into account. There are several such constraints that are likely to play a role, such as smoothness of the movement or minimal energy consumption. Among these constraints are also future motor requirements. Movement characteristics are specified in an anticipatory manner, that is, from their very start movements depend on what will happen toward their end or thereafter. The anticipatory effects strongly suggest that an internal representation of a movement is developed before its start and is used for open-loop control once the movement has been initiated.

The anticipatory nature of motor control can be illustrated by several findings. For example, movements to small targets tend to be initiated with a smaller velocity than movements to large targets. Similarly, movements to distant targets are initiated with a higher velocity than movements to near targets. With respect to movement duration, this is roughly constant for a constant ratio of amplitude and target width, and when this ratio is varied, movement time is linearly related to its logarithm. This is one of the most robust relationships in the field of motor control, called Fitts's law. Initial velocity does also depend on whether an object to be grasped at the end of a reach can be broken or not, has to be displaced gently or to be thrown forcefully, etc. In sequential movements, such as sequences of key presses, the latency of the first element in the sequence does not only depend on the characteristics of this element, but also on the number of subsequent elements. Initial postures, such as of the hand in grasping an object, do also depend on the posture at the end of the movement. More specifically, initial comfort tends to be compromised for end-state comfort. Thus in general the characteristics of a particular movement depend not only on present and past, but also on the future.

The anticipatory nature of motor control becomes evident not only in voluntary movements themselves, but also at more remote sites of the body. For example, when an arm is lifted voluntarily to reach for an object, this changes the location of the center of mass and represents a potential threat to balance. To counter the threat, the movement of the arm is preceded by excitations of postural muscles in the legs. Anticipatory postural adjustments are a fairly general accompaniment of voluntary movements, and they reveal an astonishing flexibility even when unusual postures are taken before a limb is moved voluntarily.

Neither intrinsic nor extrinsic transformations are constant. Intrinsic transformations are modulated slowly as children grow up and as muscle strength increases and declines across the lifespan. On a faster time scale, muscles fatigue so that with a constant level of excitation they produce less force. Extrinsic transformations, of course, can be quite variable. We use different tools, and we move in different directions relative to gravity. From such considerations it follows that motor control must be highly flexible and adaptive, and indeed it is.

Adjustments to novel transformations have been studied in different ways. Perhaps the most radical changes of visuomotor transformations can be produced by means of spectacles that turn the visual world upside down or reverse left and right. Normal motor behavior can be re-established within a couple of days even though visual perception never becomes quite normal again. (A classic movie on adaptation to such glasses shows the participant riding on a bike in the streets of Innsbruck/Austria.) Much less dramatic is the effect of wearing wedge prisms that displace the visual world laterally by a few degrees. With a novel visuomotor transformation of this kind adaptation can be achieved within minutes.

Extrinsic visuomotor transformations can easily be implemented by means of a computer monitor and hand movements to control the position of a cursor. Adaptation to a novel visuomotor gain is achieved within a small number of movements. Even when a novel relation between the distance of the cursor on the monitor and the amplitude of a hand movement is experienced with only a single amplitude and direction, the acquired internal model generalizes across all amplitudes and directions. This is quite different for adaptation to a visuomotor rotation, where the relation between the direction of hand movement and of cursor motion is altered. Adaptation here is restricted to the direction experienced during practice and nearby directions. There is evidence that not only the behavioral characteristics of amplitude and direction adaptation are different, but also their neural substrates.

SUGGESTED READINGS

Heuer, H. (2003). Motor control. In A. F. Healey & R. W. Proctor (Eds.), *Handbook of psychology, Vol. 4: Experimental psychology* (pp. 317–354) Hoboken, NJ: John Wiley & Sons.

Schmidt, R. A., & Lee, T. (2005). *Motor control and learning: A behavioral emphasis* (4th ed.). Champaign, IL: Human Kinetics.

HERBERT HEUER
University of Dortmund, Germany

See also: Akathisia; Fitts's Law; Gross Motor Skill Learning

MOTOR SKILL LEARNING (See Gross Motor Skill Learning)

MOURNING (See Grief)

MOWRER, O. HOBART (1907–1982)

O. H. Mowrer was born on a farm in Unionville, Missouri, in 1907. He completed his undergraduate studies at the University of Missouri in 1929 and his Ph.D. at Johns Hopkins in 1932. Although Mowrer suffered from repeated and chronic depression, he had a successful career and made major contributions to psychology. He published a series of 19 papers concerning vestibule-ocular reflexes and spatial orientation that, while not often cited in psychological literature, were well received in otology and sensory physiology. They also served, somewhat paradoxically, to gain him an appointment (1934–1940) at Yale's Institute of Human Relations. There he developed theoretical and research interests in the psychology of learning, language, psychopathology, certain cognitive processes, and interpersonal relations that importantly influenced his subsequent career.

During his tenure at the Harvard Graduate School of Education (1940–1948), Mowrer had a courtesy appointment in the Department of Psychology and was associated with Talcott Parsons, Clyde Kluckhohn, Gordon Allport, and Henry Murray in the establishment of the Department of Social Relations. During the latter part of this period he was editor of the *Harvard Educational Review* and was instrumental in the ultimate transfer of all editorial responsibility to a student board.

In 1948, Mowrer was appointed research professor of psychology at the University of Illinois, a position held until his retirement in 1975. From 1953 to 1954, he was president of the American Psychological Association and served on the editorial panel of several professional journals. His best-known and probably most enduring practical contribution is a means of treating nocturnal enuresis known as the bell-and-pad method. His more substantive contributions are in learning, language, and interpersonal psychology. He is also widely cited for his two-factor theory of learning. Late in his life he developed a form of therapy, confessional in nature, that he labeled Integrity Therapy.

Mowrer's complete bibliography contains some 235 items, a dozen of which are books. His major publications include *Abnormal Reactions or Actions: Learning Theory and Personality Dynamics*, Chapter 11 in *The History of Psychology in Autobiography*, *Learning Theory and Behavior*, *Leaves from Many Seasons*, *Selected Papers*, and *Learning Theory and Symbolic Processes*.

SUGGESTED READINGS

Mowrer, O. H. (1950). *Learning theory and personality dynamics.* Malabar, FL: Krieger.

Mowrer, O. H. (1960). *Learning theory of the symbolic processes.* Washington, DC: APA.

Mowrer, O. H. (1967). *Morality and mental health.* Chicago: Rand McNally.

STAFF

MULTICULTURAL ASSESSMENT

Multicultural assessment focuses on the evaluation of individuals, taking into account their cultural context. Multicultural assessment involves "a continuing and open-ended series of substantive and methodological insertions and adaptations designed to mesh the process of assessment and evaluation with the cultural characteristics of the group [individual] being studied" (Padilla & Borsato, 2008, p. 6). Assessment results influence educational opportunities, diagnosis, and employment. Therefore, culturally appropriate testing practices are critical given the potentially important and long-term consequences for the examinee.

Types of Assessment

Assessment practices take many forms. Most often people think of the tests that they took in school in which there is one correct answer, and a score is derived based on how "well" the person has done on the test. These tests are considered quantitative in nature, given that they yield a numerical indicator of performance. In educational settings, the most frequently used tests are those that yield scores indicating aptitude, achievement, and intelligence. The use of these cognitive tests has been challenged on the basis of differences in scores between racial and ethnic groups. To address these findings, the most widely used cognitive tests, including intelligence tests, are normed and standardized on the basis of nationally representative samples reflecting current census data.

For example, proportional representation of racial and ethnic groups, urban and rural residence, and socioeconomic status is often included. This enables test developers to determine whether differential scoring patterns for particular groups are evident. If so, further research can be conducted to determine the potential sources of the differences. Similarly, information is available with respect to the most widely used quantitative personality tests and differential scoring patterns for various racial and ethnic groups (e.g., the Minnesota Multiphasic Personality Inventory).

Qualitative measures require narrative responses, as in the case of interviews and projective measures. The clinical interview is used to gather information about an individual's background, perceptions of events, attitudes, and the like. Projective measures require the individual to respond to ambiguous stimuli, such as inkblots and pictures. These verbal responses are examined to derive impressions regarding an individual's personality style and inner (unconscious) life.

Both qualitative and quantitative measures have been challenged with respect to diversity issues. Specific interview guides such as the Cultural Assessment Interview Protocol (Greiger, 2008) have been developed to address such concerns. This interview protocol includes specific attention to an individual's racial and cultural identity, acculturation, family structure, immigration issues, and experience with bias and discrimination. Information obtained from the interview can influence the interpretation of test results. For example, many achievement and intelligence tests require familiarity with knowledge taught in the mainstream American educational system. If students have had limited exposure to this material given their educational history, especially among immigrant populations, then this circumstance will affect the meaning of their achievement and intelligence test scores.

Some thematic apperception tests, like the Tell-Me-A-Story test, have been developed to present children from diverse backgrounds with culturally relevant pictures to which to respond. Another example of a culturally based assessment tool is the cultural genogram, which provides a framework for creating a family tree that graphically presents clients' and families' cultural beliefs and practices (Shellenberger et al., 2007).

In addition to qualitative and quantitative assessment, the *Diagnostic and Statistical Manual* (DSM-IV-TR; American Psychiatric Association, 2000), a primary tool used for clinical diagnosis, contains an Outline for Cultural Formulation to assess and evaluate clients' symptoms within a cultural context. Five areas are used in this process, including the cultural identity of the client, a cultural explanation of the individual's illness, cultural factors related to psychosocial environment and levels of functioning, cultural elements of the relationship between the individual and the clinician, and an overall cultural assessment for diagnosis and care.

Cultural Factors

Conducting culturally appropriate evaluations includes consideration of a variety of factors in addition to the actual measures used. Evaluators must be culturally competent. They must be familiar with a wide range of assessment tools and their use with racially and ethnically diverse populations and knowledgeable about the psychometric features (e.g., reliability, validity) of the tests they use in relation to these groups.

Given the lack of information regarding the multicultural use of many tests, clinicians and educators must be able to make informed decisions about the appropriate use of particular tests with groups on which a particular test may not be based. At times, the evaluator may be forced to use translated versions of instruments or an interpreter to assist in the administration of the test. For example, administration of tests in English to language-minority examinees raises serious issues of validity (Padilla & Borsato, 2008). A simple translation to the language of the examinee is also problematic, however, because of the difficulty in ensuring that the items retain their meaningfulness across cultures (construct equivalence). The process of adapting measures cross-culturally is an arduous one. Assessments must be translated or adapted (and subsequently reviewed) by individuals who are fluent in both languages and knowledgeable about both cultures. Any changes recommended by the reviewers should be made, and then the assessment should be pilot-tested and field-tested. Tests may need to be restandardized and renormed for cross-cultural use, and appropriate validity studies conducted.

In addition to item content, multicultural assessment practices include attention to test formats, with respect to whether the response format makes sense within a particular cultural context. For example, is it meaningful to ask the examinee to respond to a Likert-type scale (e.g., strongly agree/agree/strongly disagree) or a true/false format? Some groups may find these response categories confusing. Many tests are now available through computer administration, in which case issues such as computer access and familiarity with technology may affect the obtained results. Some studies suggest that computerized administration is preferable for racial and ethnic minorities, and the question has been raised whether women may fare better with traditional than with computerized forms of administration.

Legal and Ethical Issues

Ethical and legal issues are important to consider when conducting assessments with diverse populations. The *Ethical Principles of Psychologists and Code of Conduct* (American Psychological Association, 2002a) outlines general principles and standards that apply to assessment, and other adopted guidelines note the importance of culture-centered ethical practices for research and assessment (American Psychological Association, 2002b). These documents mandate that assessment be conducted by a culturally competent examiner who utilizes valid testing procedures.

Concerns have arisen regarding the disproportionately high number of African American students who placed in special education classes. Historically, placements have been made largely on the basis of intelligence and achievement test scores. Challenges to the use of intelligence tests for this purpose have led to litigation and limitations being placed on the use of particular instruments in evaluating students from the African American community. Laws have been essential in attempting to create fair testing practices, particularly with respect to individuals with disabilities in educational settings (Rhodes, Ochoa, & Ortiz, 2005).

In addition, the Education for All Handicapped Children Act (EHA) of 1975 put in place nondiscriminatory assessment procedures that include attention to ethnic and cultural minorities. In 1990, amendments were made to the EHA in the form of the Individuals with Disabilities Education Act (IDEA), which placed greater emphasis on timely (e.g., early interventions) and comprehensive multidisciplinary evaluations. The 1997 revision to the IDEA addresses issues of parental consent, native language, parental notice, evaluation procedures, eligibility determination, exclusionary factors, IEP process considerations, and nondiscriminatory assessment procedures.

Process of Assessment

Multicultural issues may affect every step of the assessment process, including determining whether an evaluation should be conducted, selecting appropriate measures, administering the assessment tools, interpreting the results, and making recommendations. Making a decision as to whether an evaluation is indicated rests in part on understanding the context of the individual examinee. For example, in the case of a recent immigrant to the United States, a determination may be made that the testing should be postponed to allow the individual time to adjust to current conditions in the new environments (e.g., home, school, community, workplace). Instrument selection rests on knowing the most current measurement options available and obtaining up-to-date information regarding their use with diverse populations (e.g., the psychometric properties of the instruments).

Administration of the tests requires cultural sensitivity, given that the examinee may be unfamiliar with the testing format and may require more explanation during the assessment process. Interpretation requires that the examiner focus on what will be of greatest benefit to the individual being assessed. Information obtained during the clinical interview should always be integrated into the report to make sense of the results. Recommendations must take into consideration the context of the individual's life, personal strengths and limitations, familial support, and available resources in the community.

Multiple cultural variables must be considered at every step of the assessment process, beginning with the referral process and ending with the interpretation and formulation of recommendations based on the findings of the evaluation. The examiner must be culturally competent and knowledgeable about various measures and their use with diversity populations to ensure appropriate multicultural assessment practices.

REFERENCES

American Psychiatric Association. (2000). *Diagnostic and statistical manual of mental disorders* (4th ed., text rev.). Washington, DC: Author.

American Psychological Association. (2002a). *Ethical principles of psychologists and code of conduct.* Washington, DC: Author.

American Psychological Association. (2002b). *Guidelines on multicultural education, training, research, practice and organizational change for psychologists.* Washington, DC: Author.

Dana, R. H. (2005). *Multicultural assessment: Principles, applications, and examples.* Mahwah, NJ: Lawrence Erlbaum.

Padilla, A. M., & Borsato, G. N. (2008). Issues in culturally appropriate psychoeducational assessment. In L. A. Suzuki & L. G. Ponetrotto, *Handbook of multicultural assessment* (3rd ed., pp. 5–21). San Francisco, CA: Jossey-Bass.

Rhodes, R. L., Ochoa, S. H., & Ortiz, S. O. (2005). *Assessing culturally and linguistically diverse students: A practical guide.* New York: Guilford Press.

Ridley, C. R., Li, L. C., & Hill, C. L. (1998). Multicultural assessment: Reexamination, reconceptualization, and practical application. *The Counseling Psychologist, 26*(6), 827–910.

Shellenberger, S., Dent, M. M., Davis-Smith, M., Seale, J. P., Weintraut, R., & Wright, T. (2007). Cultural genogram: A tool for teaching and practice. *Familes, Systems, and Health, 25*(4), 367–381.

Suzuki, L. A., & Ponterotto, J. G. (Eds.). (2008). *Handbook of multicultural assessment.* San Francisco, CA: Jossey-Bass.

Suzuki, L. A., & Ponterotto J. G. (2008). Multicultural assessment: Trends and future directions. In L. A. Suzuki & L. G. Ponetrotto, *Handbook of multicultural assessment* (3rd ed., pp. 666–671). San Francisco, CA: Jossey-Bass.

LISA A. SUZUKI
New York University

MUNINDER K. AHLUWALIA
Montclair State University

See also: **Cross-Cultural and Cross-National Assessment; Cultural Bias in Psychological Testing; Psychological Measurement, Bias in; Testing Bias**

MULTICULTURAL COUNSELING

Multicultural counseling, sometimes referred to as cross-cultural counseling, is a relatively new discipline within the helping professions. It has been called the fourth theoretical force in counseling after the psychodynamic, cognitive-behavioral, and humanistic approaches to helping (Pedersen, 1991). The discipline of multicultural counseling is the direct result of key historical and social movements in the United States following World War II that continued through the last half of the twentieth century. This can be characterized as a period of great change in American society that was initiated by a fundamental questioning of the nature of social exclusion for many groups of people. Groups that had been historically marginalized and oppressed began to demand, as never before, social, economic, and political inclusion within the mainstream of American life. These demands manifested themselves in large-scale social and political movements that ultimately forced significant changes to the country's landscape. At the vanguard of these movements was the struggle for racial and ethnic equality that served as a major catalyst for the efforts of other traditionally excluded groups to demand access, equity, and social justice (Burnhill, Butler, Hipolito-Delgado, Humphrey, Lee, Muñoz, & Shin, 2009).

Operationally defined, multicultural counseling is a helping interaction between counselor and client that takes the personal dynamics of the counselor and client into consideration alongside the dynamics found in the cultures of the counselor and the client. Multicultural counseling, therefore, underscores the cultural background and individual experiences of diverse clients and how their psychosocial needs might be identified and met through counseling (Lee & Ramsey, 2006; Sue & Sue, 2002). Within this context, counselors and psychotherapists must consider differences in areas such as language, social class, gender, sexual orientation, disability status, race, and ethnicity between therapist and client. These factors may be potential impediments to effective intervention, and counselors need to work to overcome the barriers such variables might produce in the helping process.

Because the recognition of culture is an important part of the counseling relationship, multicultural counseling assumes that counselors will be culturally competent in their interactions with clients from diverse cultural backgrounds. The foundation of counselor cultural competency is developing personal awareness through an examination of one's own cultural heritage, values, and biases and their possible impact on clients from diverse backgrounds. It also involves acquiring knowledge about the history, experiences, and cultural values of diverse client groups. Such awareness and knowledge form the basis for effectively employing counseling skills that are consistent with clients' cultural backgrounds and individual experiences (Sue, Arredondo, & McDavis, 1992).

Culturally competent counselors, therefore, are able to view each client as a unique individual, while at the same time taking into consideration their common experiences as human beings (i.e., the developmental challenges that face all people), as well as the specific experiences that come from their cultural background. Multicultural counselors must do all of this, while constantly being in touch with their own personal and cultural experiences as unique human beings who happen to be a professional counselor.

Culturally competent counseling involves entering a cross-cultural therapeutic relationship that brings with it certain unique challenges and inherent opportunities. Facilitating such a relationship involves entering a challenging area of counseling or psychotherapy. This helping space can be conceptualized as the cross-cultural zone. In much of the multicultural counseling literature, this helping space has been traditionally conceptualized as a white counselor engaging in a helping relationship with a client of color. However, the cultural gaps that exist between counselor and client in the cross-cultural zone may also consist of distinct differences in aspects such as sexual orientation, disability status, religion, language preference, socioeconomic status, gender, or age.

Counseling in the cross-cultural zone can often be a sociopolitical process related to a power differential between counselor and client. This is particularly true if, because of skin color, gender, sexual orientation, language preference, or disability status, a client occupies minority status in society. Such a position is usually characterized by forces of racism, sexism, homophobia, or ableism that impact negatively on academic, career, or personal-social development. Significantly, in many instances, counseling practice has been perceived as a tool of power, oppression, or social control among many groups of people (Lee, 2006).

Similarly, it is important that counselors upon entering the cross cultural zone consider the nature of the cultural privilege they may possess due to the color of their skin, gender, sexual orientation, ability status, language preference, or other social or economic characteristic. Privilege can be conceived along several dimensions. First, it is generally unearned. In most cases individuals are born with it, and their privilege tends to be innate. Second, individuals with privilege generally tend to be unaware of the unearned benefits that accrue from their privileged status. Third, privilege gives the individual who has it distinct cultural, social, and economic advantages. Individuals with privilege are generally seen to be in a position of social or economic dominance when compared with those who lack these advantages (McIntosh, 1989). The dynamics of power and privilege must therefore be factored into the counseling equation in the cross cultural zone. This is particularly the case for those clients whose counseling issues relate to the stress of prejudice, discrimination, or socioeconomic disadvantage (Lee & Diaz, 2009).

Culturally competent counselors must enter the cross-cultural zone with a repertoire of responsive skills. They should be able to use counseling strategies and techniques that are consistent with the life experiences and cultural values of their clients. Culturally competent counselors should include a number of theoretical approaches in their repertoire. It is important for a counselor's style to be sufficiently integrative that he or she can use a variety of helping approaches. These approaches should incorporate diverse worldviews and practices.

REFERENCES

Burnhill, D. A., Butler, A. L., Hipolito-Delgado, C. P., Humphrey, M., Lee, C. C., Muñoz, O., et al. (2009). The evolution of multicultural counseling: An historical overview. In C. C. Lee, D. A. Burnhill, A. L. Butler, C. P. Hipolito-Delgado, M. Humphrey, O. Muñoz, & H. J. Shin (Eds.), *Elements of culture in counseling* (pp. 3–18). Columbus, OH: Pearson.

Lee, C. C. (2006). Entering the cross-cultural zone: Meeting the challenges of culturally responsive counseling. In C. C. Lee (Ed.). *Multicultural issues in counseling: New approaches to diversity* (3rd ed., pp. 13–19). Alexandria, VA: American Counseling Association.

Lee, C. C., & Diaz, J. M. (2009). The cross-cultural zone in counseling. In C. C. Lee, D. A. Burnhill, A. L. Butler, C. P. Hipolito-Delgado, M. Humphrey, O. Muñoz, & H. J. Weiss (Eds.), *Elements of culture in counseling* (pp. 95–104). Columbus, OH: Pearson.

Lee, C. C., & Ramsey, C. J. (2006). Multicultural counseling: A new paradigm for a new century. In C. C. Lee (Ed.), *Multicultural issues in counseling: New approaches to diversity* (3rd ed., pp. 3–11). Alexandria, VA: American Counseling Association.

McIntosh, P. (1989). White privilege: Unpacking the invisible knapsack. *Peace and Freedom, 2*, 10–12.

Pedersen, P. B. (1991). Special Issue: Introduction to the special issue on multiculturalism as a fourth force in counseling. *Journal of Counseling and Development, 70*, 4–5.

Sue, D. W., Arredondo, P., & McDavis, R. J. (1992). Multicultural counseling competencies: A call to the profession. *Journal of Counseling and Development, 70*, 477–486.

Sue, D. W., & Sue, D. (2002). *Counseling the culturally diverse: Theory and practice.* (4th ed.). Indianapolis, IN: John Wiley & Sons.

SUGGESTED READINGS

Lee, C. C., Burnhill, D. A., Butler, A. L., Hipolito-Delgado, C. P., Humphrey, M., Muñoz, O., & Shin, H. J. (Eds.). (2009). *Elements of culture in counseling.* Columbus, OH: Pearson.

Pack-Brown, S. P., & Williams, C. B. (2003). *Ethics in a multicultural context.* Thousand Oaks, CA: Sage.

Roysircar, G., Arredondo, P., Fuertes, J. N., Ponterotto, J. G., & Toporek, R. L. (2003). *Multicultural counseling competencies 2003: Association for Multicultural Counseling and Development.* Alexandria, VA: Association for Multicultural Counseling and Development.

COURTLAND C. LEE
University of Maryland at College Park

See also: **Culture and Psychotherapy; Ethnocultural Psychotherapy**

MULTIPLE CORRELATION

Multiple linear correlation, which is the simplest and most common form of multiple correlation, is usually measured by a coefficient that ranges between zero and one (symbolized as R); it represents the highest possible degree of association between a weighted linear combination of several given predictor variables and a single criterion variable. For any particular case in a dataset, a prediction can be generated by multiplying its values on each of the predictor variables by the optimal weighting coefficients found by the least-squares method and adding a constant. R is then the ordinary Pearson's coefficient of linear correlation (r) between the predicted and actual criterion values.

If each prediction is subtracted from the actual value of the criterion, and these differences (i.e., residuals or errors) are squared and then added, the resulting sum is called the residual (or error) sum of squares, symbolized as $SS_{residual}$ (or SS_{error}). The SS of the criterion values from their own mean is called, in this context, SS_{total}. The amount by which SS_{error} is less than SS_{total} is known as $SS_{regression}$, and the ratio of $SS_{regression}$ to SS_{total} is the *coefficient of multiple determination*, which is also called the "proportion of variance accounted for" by the multiple regression. This proportion bears a simple relation to R; it equals R^2. For example, when R equals .5, one-fourth (.25) of the criterion variance has been accounted for by the combination of predictor variables; the variance of the residuals is therefore 75% of the criterion variance and is considered unaccounted for, or "unexplained."

In psychological research, the goal of a multiple correlation analysis is usually to attain the highest possible R between a criterion of interest (e.g., level of self-esteem) and a relatively small set of fairly independent predictor variables (e.g., number of close friendships; annual income; level of education, and so on). Indeed, a given value for R is more likely to attain statistical significance when it is attained from fewer predictors, and R tends to be higher when the correlations among the predictors are lower. In the ideal case, the linear correlation between any two predictors is zero, and R^2 is equal to the sum of the squared R's of each predictor with the criterion. The levels of any dichotomous predictor are simply coded with two different arbitrary numbers, but categorical predictors with k levels must first be converted to k-1 dichotomous "dummy" variables. When the criterion is dichotomous, procedures other than multiple R (e.g., logistic regression) are recommended.

The significance test for R requires the usual assumptions of parametric inference, plus the existence of a multivariate normal distribution in the population, but the latter is not considered critical for large sample sizes. Unfortunately, the value for R obtained from a sample tends to overestimate the corresponding population R, and this bias increases as the number of predictors (P) increases relative to the sample size (N). Based on R, P, and N, a measure called *adjusted R* yields a more accurate estimate for population R.

SUGGESTED READING

Cohen, J., Cohen P., West, S. G., & Aiken, L. S. (2002). *Applied multiple regression/correlation analysis for the behavioral sciences* (2nd ed.). Hillsdale, NJ: Lawrence Erlbaum.

BARRY H. COHEN
New York University

See also: Multiple Regression; Logistic Regression

MULTIPLE PERSONALITY (See Dissociative Identity Disorder)

MULTIPLE REGRESSION

The simplest and most commonly used form of multiple regression (*MR*) is multiple linear regression. This method uses a linear combination (i.e., a weighted average) of predictor variables to maximize the accuracy with which a criterion variable can be predicted; the end result is a multiple regression equation in which each predictor variable is multiplied by its optimal weight, and a constant (called the *Y*-intercept) is added. The accuracy or lack of accuracy of a regression equation is measured by summing the squared differences between the predicted and actual criterion values for each case in the dataset; this quantity is symbolized as SS_{error} (or $SS_{residual}$). The set of weights, called partial regression slopes, that lead to the smallest value of SS_{error}, is known as the Ordinary Least Squares (*OLS*) regression solution; these same weights produce the largest possible value for R. R^2 equals the proportion of criterion variance that is accounted for by a multiple regression equation, and the increase in R^2 produced by adding a predictor variable is equal to the square of what is called the *semipartial* (or *part*) correlation of that predictor with the criterion, given the other predictors that were already in the equation.

If the goal of a particular *MR* analysis is obtaining accurate predictions, usually some form of stepwise regression is used. Commonly, the predictor with the highest validity (i.e., correlation with the criterion) is added first to the equation, and then the predictor with the highest semipartial correlation is added, provided that a statistically significant amount of explained variance is being added. Adding a third predictor can reduce the semipartial correlation of the second predictor to the point where it is no longer statistically significant and may therefore be deleted from the equation, although it can be tested again for inclusion at a later step. In general, an additional predictor will be helpful if it has at least a moderate validity, but is not highly correlated with the other predictors (i.e., it has a relatively high value for tolerance), or it has a very

low validity but a fairly high correlation with some other predictors (i.e., it acts as a suppressor variable).

If the goal of the *MR* is to test a theoretical model, the order in which variables are added may be determined in advance, leading to a hierarchical regression analysis. In some cases, uninteresting ("nuisance") variables are added regardless of their explained variance, and variables of interest may be added and tested in "blocks" of related predictors. A frequent concern is whether particular types of predictors add significantly to the explained variance, once other predictors have been taken into account. If all of the variables involved in an *MR* analysis are transformed into standardized (*z*) scores, the *Y*-intercept becomes zero, and the predictors are multiplied by standardized partial regression slopes (commonly called "beta weights"), which are no longer influenced by units of measurement, and therefore give some indication of the relative importance of each predictor in the equation.

SUGGESTED READINGS

Cohen, J., Cohen P., West, S. G., & Aiken, L. S. (2002). *Applied multiple regression/correlation analysis for the behavioral sciences* (2nd ed.). Hillsdale, NJ: Lawrence Erlbaum.

Draper, N. R., & Smith, H. (1998). *Applied regression analysis* (3rd ed.). New York: John Wiley & Sons.

BARRY H. COHEN
New York University

See also: Linear Regression; Logistic Regression; Multiple Correlation

MULTIVARIATE METHODS

Multivariate methods provide options for analyzing and understanding the essence of a set of well-chosen variables. Myriad information is potentially available to researchers, policy makers, and practitioners with which to examine group differences, predict outcomes, explore patterns, and investigate models. Statistical methods are needed to make sense of this information and to come to meaningful conclusions that synthesize and simplify the data.

Overview

Multivariate methods offer procedures that illuminate data and allow revealing patterns and relationships to emerge and be verified (Harlow, 2005). It is constructive to organize multivariate methods into different sets of procedures, each focusing on specific kinds of research questions and variables. Below, five sets of multivariate methods are discussed; there could be other methods, limited only by the ingenuity of researchers and the resources at their disposal. For methods discussed, descriptions highlight the main features, and how to apply and evaluate methods. With multivariate methods, results are evaluated with multiple criteria such as significance tests (e.g., F or χ^2), effects sizes (e.g., proportion of shared variance indicated by R^2 or eta-squared), theoretical relevance, and other indices that reveal the statistical story (Abelson, 1995; Kline, 2004).

The first set of methods asks whether there are differences between two or more groups on the mean scores for one or more variables. The second set utilizes prediction models to examine relationships among cogent independent and outcome variables. The third set explores underlying dimensions in a set of variables or objects. The fourth set involves testing well-specified structural equation models of relationships among relevant variables. The fifth set incorporates a longitudinal aspect to understand causal links among variables across multiple time points. Finally, a summary is provided to integrate highlights for each set of methods.

Different Kinds of Multivariate Methods

Group Difference Methods

The first set of methods focuses on group differences (Maxwell & Delaney, 2003; Tabachnick & Fidell, 2007) and addresses the following question: Are there significant differences in means across two or more groups, and how much of a relationship is there between the grouping and outcome variables? Analysis of covariance (ANCOVA) allows examination of group differences on a single outcome after controlling for potentially confounding effects of one or more variables, called covariates. Multivariate analysis of variance (MANOVA) is used to examine group differences with linear combinations of several dependent variables. Multivariate analysis of covariance (MANCOVA) extends ANCOVA and MANOVA when investigating group differences on multiple dependent variables, controlling for one or more covariates. For group difference methods, the focus is on means across groups. For each method, one evaluates whether variation in the means between each group is more salient than variation in scores within each group. If the between-group differences are greater than the random differences among scores within each group, we have evidence that the grouping variable relates to the outcome scores.

For example, suppose one investigates whether two teaching approaches (lecture versus interactive) yield different mean scores on student performance. An investigator would use ANCOVA to control for several potential confounds (e.g., learning style and previous grade average, previous number of courses in content area) before assessing whether performance differed between students in a class that uses lectures versus a class that fosters interactions between the teacher and students. A MANOVA would be used to assess whether lecture versus interactive teaching approaches yields different scores on several student-performance variables (e.g., exams, homework, quizzes, projects). MANCOVA would show whether students had different scores on exams, homework, quizzes and projects depending on whether they had lecture or interactive teaching approaches, after taking into account their scores on learning style, previous grade average and previous number of courses in the content area. For ANCOVA, MANOVA, or MANCOVA, mean differences in teaching methods can be evaluated with multiple criteria. One would expect an F-test to reveal significant mean differences, an eta-squared effect size showing considerable shared variance between the grouping variable (teaching method) and the outcome(s) (student performance); and results to reveal a compelling statistical story consistent with relevant theory.

Prediction Methods

Second, prediction methods focus on the relationship between several predictor variables and one or more outcomes (Cohen, Cohen, West, & Aiken, 2003). The main questions addressed with these methods are (1) How much of an outcome can we know given a set of predictor variables and (2) Is the degree of relationship significantly different from zero? When there are multiple predictors and a single continuous outcome, multiple regression (MR) is preferred. If the emphasis is on exploring relationships among multiple predictors and multiple outcomes, consider using canonical correlation (CC). With multiple predictors and a single categorical outcome, discriminant analysis (DA) is appropriate. Alternatively, logistic regression (LR) may assess the probability of a categorical outcome from a set of categorical or continuous predictors. For prediction methods, the focus is on one or more weighted combinations of variables that reveal relationships among variables, showing how scores increase or decrease in predictable ways. If the pattern of covariance between two sets of scores is almost as large as the average random variance within scores for each variable, there is evidence of an association between predictor and outcome variables.

Building on the previous example, suppose that instead of examining possible mean differences, one wants to understand relationships between student performance and several predictor variables (e.g., learning style, previous grade average, previous number of courses in content area, and number of study hours). One could use MR to predict a single measure of student performance (e.g., course grade) from the predictors. CC would be useful to predict several measures of student performance (e.g., exams, homework, quizzes, projects) from the set of predictors. DA could assess associations between predictors and a categorical performance outcome (e.g., passed versus failed course). LR is an alternative if interest is in finding the likelihood of falling in an outcome reference category (e.g., passing a course) given the set of predictor variables. Each of these prediction methods could be evaluated by multiple criteria, hopefully revealing significant relationships with a meaningful proportion of shared variance among the predictors and outcome(s).

Dimensional Methods

Third, dimensional methods delineate the underlying facets in a large set of variables or individuals (Grimm & Yarnold, 1995, 2000). Principal components analysis (PCA) is useful for explaining a large set of correlated variables with a smaller set of orthogonal components. Factor analysis (FA) can be used to identify a set of theoretical factors that explain the shared common variance in a set of variables. When there is interest in identifying how individuals or objects are similar, multidimensional scaling (MDS) or cluster analysis (CA) are useful methods for revealing underlying dimensions or clusters of similar persons or objects. With these methods, the focus is on correlations or similarities among the variables or objects and the underlying dimensions. If there is sufficiently more inter-correlation or similarity within dimensions than across dimensions, and if each variable or object relates predominantly with just one dimension, there is greater confidence that the dimensions adequately explain variation and covariation among the entities.

In contrast to group difference or prediction methods, the focus is now on descriptively understanding the underlying dimensions in a single set of entities, whether variables or objects. Using the ongoing example, one could use PCA or FA to explore dimensions that explain the relationships among a single set of variables (e.g., learning style, previous grade average, previous number of courses in content area, number of study hours, exam scores, homework scores, quiz scores, and project scores). One might expect to find at least two underlying components or theoretical factors, one related to the first five variables (learning experience) and a second corresponding to the last four variables (student performance). Alternatively, one could use MDS or CA to examine whether there were different dimensions or clusters of students based on the students' scores on several learning and performance variables. With MDS or CA methods, one might qualitatively identify separate dimensions or clusters that provide insight into learning and performance (e.g., interactive learners with moderate previous experience and high performance; lecture-based learners with high experience and moderate performance).

Structural Equation Models

Fourth, structural equation modeling (SEM) is useful for testing complex patterns of hypothesized relationships among a set of variables (Bollen, 2009; Kline, 2005). For SEM, the main focus is finding a close match between a hypothesized theoretical model and the pattern of variation and covariation in the data. Path analysis (PA) is a SEM method useful with a multifaceted predictive model with multiple constructs that are each measured with a single variable. Confirmatory factor analysis (CFA) permits testing a specified pattern of relationships among latent factors and their respective measures as opposed to the exploratory approaches of PCA and FA. Latent variable modeling (LVM) combines both PA and CFA by allowing hypothesized predictions among several theoretical factors, each measured by several variables.

SEM methods can be applied to the student learning example. One could choose PA to test a theoretically-grounded prediction model that is more complex than those analyzed with MR, and includes several predictors (learning style, previous grade average, and previous number of courses in content area), mediators (motivation, number of study hours, and self-efficacy), and performance (exams, homework, quizzes, and projects). CFA could verify links between these three sets of predictor, mediator, and outcome measures, and the underlying latent factors of learning experience, facilitation, and performance. LVM could examine whether a predicted mediational relationship among the three latent factors and their respective measures adequately explains the variation and covariation in the data. With these SEM methods, several evaluation criteria would be examined including chi-square significance tests, effect sizes, theoretical relevance and other fit indices.

Longitudinal Methods

Fifth, longitudinal methods allow examining patterns of change over time (Little, Schnabel, & Baumert, 2000; van Montfort, Oud, & Satorra, 2007). The first three of the following longitudinal methods can also be classified as SEM methods. Cross-lagged design (CLD) allows examination of several constructs over several time points. With CLD, causal evidence for temporal ordering is obtained when a construct consistently serves as a stronger predictor of other constructs measured at subsequent time points, than when it serves as an outcome of other constructs measured at previous time points. Latent growth modeling (LGM) allows investigation of the level and rate of change over time. Multilevel modeling (MLM) is useful in explaining outcomes across time by several levels of data, such as from individuals and institutions.

Time series (TS), dynamic factor analysis (DFA), and latent transition analysis (LTA) are longitudinal methods useful when exploring patterns of change in one or more variables over a number of time points. For these methods, data are collected at regular intervals over a long period of time (e.g., weekly assessments over a one-year period).

To apply these longitudinal methods, one could use CLD to verify a hypothesized causal pattern of learning experience predicting facilitation variables which, in turn, predict performance outcomes by examining the strength of the relationships across the three sets of measures across three or more time points. With LGM, one could examine changes in level and slope for any or all of the three sets of learning, facilitation, and performance variables across three or more time points. To examine effects of both student and teacher variables on student performance, one could use MLM, including several teacher-level variables (e.g., teaching approach and years of teaching experience). I could examine patterns of change across multiple time points for student performance with TS, and for learning, facilitating and performance measures with DFA and LTA. Multiple evaluation criteria (e.g., χ^2, effects sizes, and theoretical relevance) provide evidence of model fit for each longitudinal method.

Several multivariate methods (see Figure 1) have been elucidated to understand relationships among a set of variables in well-constructed research studies. Group difference multivariate methods (ANCOVA, MANOVA, MANCOVA) examine how means vary across two or more groups, on one or more outcomes, sometimes controlling for covariates. Prediction methods (MR, CC, DA, LR) examine how predictors relate to one or more outcome variables. Dimensional methods (PCA, FA, MDS, CA) allow exploration of underlying dimensions among a set of variables, and of the relationships and distinctions among the dimensions. SEM methods (PA, CFA, LVM) allow the testing of complex hypothesized relationships and the assessment of how well a model of these relationships explains the pattern of variation and covariation in a multivariate dataset. Longitudinal methods (CLD, LGM, MLM, TS, DFA, LTA) allude to the causal nature underlying variables measured across multiple time points. Any or all of the methods discussed, as well as others not mentioned, could help clarify multivariate patterns in a set of variables, helping to bring greater understanding and explanation about meaningful issues.

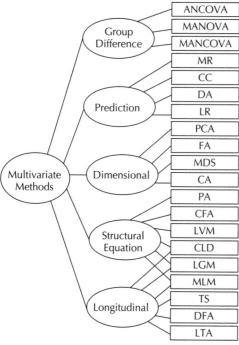

Figure 1. Twenty Multivariate Methods Delineated into Five Sets

Note: ANCOVA = Analysis of Covariance, MANOVA = Multivariate Analysis of Variance, MANCOVA = Multivariate Analysis of Covariance, MR = Multiple Regression, CC = Canonical Correlation, DA = Discriminant Analysis, LR = Logistic Regression, PCA = Principal Component Analysis, FA = Factor Analysis, MDS = Multidimensional Scaling, CA = Cluster Analysis, PA = Path Analysis, CFA = Confirmatory Factor Analysis, LVM = Latent Variable Modeling, CLD = Cross-Lagged Design, LGM = Latent Growth Modeling, MLM = Multilevel Modeling, TS = Time Series, DFA = Dynamic Factor Analysis, and LTA = Latent Transition Analysis.

REFERENCES

Abelson, R. P. (1995). *Statistics as principled argument.* Mahwah, NJ: Lawrence Erlbaum.

Bollen, K. A. (2009). *Structural equations with latent variables* (2nd ed.). Hoboken, NJ: John Wiley & Sons.

Cohen, J., Cohen, P., West, S. G., & Aiken, L. S. (2003). *Applied multiple regression/correlation analysis for behavioral sciences* (3rd ed.). Mahwah, NJ: Lawrence Erlbaum.

Grimm, L. G., & Yarnold, P. R. (1995). *Reading and understanding multivariate statistics.* Washington, DC: American Psychological Association.

Grimm, L. G., & Yarnold, P. R. (2000). *Reading and understanding more multivariate statistics.* Washington, DC: American Psychological Association.

Harlow, L. L. (2005). *The essence of multivariate thinking: Basic themes and methods.* Mahwah, NJ: Lawrence Erlbaum.

Kline, R. B. (2004). *Beyond significance testing: Reforming data analysis methods in behavioral research.* Washington, DC: American Psychological Association.

Kline, R. B. (2005). *Principles and practice of structural equation modeling.* New York: Guilford Press.

Little, T. D., Schnabel, K. U., & Baumert, J. (2000). *Modeling longitudinal and multilevel data: Practical issues, applied approaches and specific examples.* Mahwah, NJ: Lawrence Erlbaum.

Maxwell, S. E., & Delaney, H. D. (2003). *Designing experiments and analyzing data: A model comparison perspective* (2nd ed.). Mahwah, NJ: Lawrence Erlbaum.

Tabachnick, B. G., & Fidell, L. S. (2001). *Using multivariate statistics* (4th ed.). Boston: Allyn & Bacon.

Van Montfort, K., Oud, J., & Satorra, A. (2007). *Longitudinal models in the behavioral and related sciences.* Mahwah, NJ: Lawrence Erlbaum.

Lisa L. Harlow
University of Rhode Island

See also: Analysis of Covariance; Analysis of Variance; Factor Analysis; Multiple Correlation

MUNCHAUSEN SYNDROME (See Factitious Disorder)

MURRAY, HENRY A. (1893–1988)

Henry A. Murray received his B.A. degree from Harvard University and later the M.A. and then the M.D. degree from Columbia University. He completed residency in surgery at Columbia Presbyterian Hospital. During his residency, he had the unusual experience of helping to care for the future president of the United States, Franklin D. Roosevelt. Following this, he spent four years at the Rockefeller Institute studying embryology. In 1927 he received the Ph.D. from Cambridge University in England. While at Cambridge he became acquainted with the writings of Carl Jung, whose *Psychological Types* had recently been translated to English.

This apparently contributed to a change in his interest from the biological sciences to psychology. Upon returning to the United States, he was invited to be Morton Prince's assistant at the newly formed psychological clinic at Harvard University. Over the objections of some, he succeeded Prince as its director. His interests began to turn more toward the Freudian approach to psychology. In 1928 he helped form the Boston Psychoanalytic Association, and in 1933 he became a member of the American Psychoanalytic Association.

His interests continued in the direction of personality. By 1938, he embarked on the research published in *Exploration of Personality*. In this work, he developed his taxonomy of needs and presses that characterize people's directions in their lives and activities. Thus, he developed a systematic and dynamic approach to personality. Out of these studies there developed the Thematic Apperception Test (TAT), a projective technique consisting of semivague pictures in which the subject was asked to tell a story about each. The responses were analyzed in terms of Murray's system.

During World War II, Murray served in the Army Medical Corps. After the war, he returned to Harvard, where he was instrumental in establishing Harvard Interdisciplinary Department of Social Relations. His association with Clyde Kluckhohn resulted in the classic work *Personality in Nature, Society, and Culture*.

In 1961 the American Psychological Association honored him with its Distinguished Contribution Award. He received the Gold Medal Award in 1969 from the American Psychological Foundation for lifelong significant contributions to psychology. Murray hoped to foster a more comprehensive and systematic approach to personality as well as to complete an analysis of the writings of Herman Melville, but failing health prevented the completion of these efforts. He died of pneumonia at the age of 95.

He goes down in history as one of the most important personality theorists of the twentieth century.

SUGGESTED READINGS

Murray, H. A. (1938). *Explorations in personality*. New York: Oxford University Press.

Murray, H. A., Kluckhohn, C., & Schneider, D. M. (1953). *Personality in nature, society, and culture*. New York: Knopf.

Murray, H. A. (1940). What should psychologists do about psychoanalysis? *Journal of Abnormal Psychology and Social Psychology, 35*, 150–175.

RALPH W. LUNDIN
Wheaton, IL

MUSCLE RELAXATION (See Progressive Muscle Relaxation)

MUSIC THERAPY

Music therapy (MT) is an evidence-based behavioral science that elicits beneficial change in an individual or group through unique music techniques. Music therapy treatment uses psychological principles within a standard therapeutic paradigm: identification of a specific problem, assessment, development of a treatment plan incorporating research-based techniques, and evaluation of observable and measurable outcomes. Matching the music stimuli to the music preference of the client is a critical component. Over 83% of music therapists use a behavioral approach to therapy (Silverman, 2007), while a small number utilize psychoanalytic or interpretive techniques (Darrow, 2004). This article focuses on the cognitive-behavioral approaches.

Music has been important in healing for centuries, but most historians trace the beginning of the MT profession to volunteer concerts in veterans' hospitals immediately following World War II. Currently, MT is widely developed in the United States, with over 70 colleges and universities providing degrees at the bachelor's, master's, and doctoral levels. The American Music Therapy Association (AMTA), the professional organization, has over 4,000 members. The Certification Board for Music Therapy is a separate, independent organization with a national certification test. Those who are certified use the professional designation MT-BC, Music Therapist—Board Certified. The *Journal of Music Therapy*, a publication of AMTA, was established in 1964 and is the premier refereed journal in the field.

Music therapy is applied to a variety of clinical problems across the life span, from infancy to old age. Techniques integrate the understanding of perceptual/cognitive responses to music with the sciences of psychology, learning, medicine, and rehabilitation (Darrow, 2004). Music therapy sessions may include the full gamut of human interactions with music: performing, listening, discussing, moving to, and composing or creating music. To be optimally effective for the widest range of people, the music therapists' repertoire includes classical music and popular music from many tastes, cultures, and age ranges. Music is acoustically different from all other sound. As a complex, organized auditory stimulus with multi-layers of pitch, rhythm, harmony, style, and even language, it is uniquely processed and stored by the neurological system. It is a universally positive element of all cultures with cognitive, motor, and emotional learned responses to particular selections and genres.

Music is used in a variety of ways to accomplish therapeutic objectives. Sometimes music functions as a stimulus to initiate a desired response. For instance, a favorite song may be used to elicit awareness from a nonresponsive coma patient. A song from the past may stimulate long-term memories for reminiscence with an Alzheimer's patient or may elicit a strong emotional response from a patient with PTSD who is learning coping strategies.

Continuous music is used to structure desired responses. For example, a patient in physical rehabilitation may walk to music with a definitive beat timed to enhance gait consistency. Additionally, music style, tempo, and volume may be altered across time to move a patient in pain from a hyperalert state to sleep or, alternatively, to energize a withdrawn client from a state of lethargy to a more desirable activity level.

In learning activities, music may convey information for memorization such as the "ABC Song," the "50 Nifty States" (for identifying state capitals), or the multiplication tables set to music. Such techniques are effective for those with learning problems, such as children in special education programs or those with short-term memory loss due to neurological injury.

Music therapy facilitates group therapy interventions and increases attendance at sessions. Research has shown increased benefits when music is added to typical group therapy interventions. Pelletier's meta-analysis (2004) showed that both music activities and music paired with assisted-relaxation procedures significantly decrease measures of stress. Lyric analysis of popular music helps clients focus on value systems and cognitive perceptions. Song writing benefits expression of therapeutic change, motivation, and social concern. Movement to music promotes activity and exercise while elevating mood or facilitating expression. MT is especially effective in short-term acute mental health settings, since patients typically respond quickly and with great interest. It is also especially effective with those adolescents who consider music to be an integral part of their life.

Music is so highly preferred by most people that it functions very effectively as reinforcement. Access to music listening or other musical activities highly valued by the patient is contingent on demonstration of the desired objective. Research has shown that contingent music is probably the single most powerful technique in the therapist's repertoire (Standley, 1996).

Medical music therapy is a rapidly emerging clinical specialty, with programs established nationwide in neonatal intensive care units, pediatric units, cancer settings, and general medical hospitals. A meta-analysis of research in this area showed positive benefits for pain reduction, surgical recovery, anxiety reduction, increased motor/neurological ability, shortened length of labor in childbirth, increased or stabilized respiratory patterns, reduction of depression, and facilitation of adjustment to medical traumas (Standley, 2000). Music therapy is widely used in hospice programs and palliative care to alleviate anxiety and pain, increase physical comfort, and improve quality of life for those with terminal illnesses.

With premature infants MT is effective in stabilizing respiration and improving oxygen saturation levels, in calming behavior state and increasing weight gain, in enhancing maturation and shortening hospital stay, in increasing the immature neurological system's tolerance for stimulation, and in reinforcing non-nutritive sucking to increase feeding rates (Standley, 2002). MT can also facilitate parent training to reduce over-stimulation of premature infants with immature neurological systems.

Music therapy is a continually expanding field, as clinicians demonstrate innovative ways to use music for therapeutic benefit. The profession's emphasis on research provides an expanding evidence-base for clinical application and wellness uses. Music therapists thrive as part of an agency's interdisciplinary team or in private practice. People of all ages consider music therapy to be an integral part of their rehabilitation program. It is a highly cost-effective and beneficial therapeutic intervention.

REFERENCES

Darrow, A. (2004). *Introduction to approaches in music therapy*. Silver Spring, MD: American Music Therapy Association.

Pelletier, C. (2004). The effect of music on decreasing arousal due to stress: A meta-analysis. *Journal of Music Therapy, 41,* 192–214.

Silverman, M. (2007). Evaluating current trends in psychiatric music therapy: A descriptive analysis. *Journal of Music Therapy, 44*(4), 388–414.

Standley, J. (1996). A meta-analysis on the effects of music as reinforcement for education/therapy objectives. *Journal of Research in Music Education, 44,* 105–133.

Standley, J. (2000). Music research in medical treatment. In American Music Therapy Association (Ed.), *Effectiveness of music therapy procedures: Documentation of research and clinical* practice (3rd ed.; pp. 1–64). Silver Spring, MD: American Music Therapy Association.

Standley, J. (2002). A meta-analysis of the efficacy of music therapy for premature infants. *Journal of Pediatric Nursing, 17,* 107–113.

SUGGESTED READINGS

Davis, W., Gfeller, K., & Thaut, M. (2008). *An introduction to music therapy: Theory and practice* (3rd ed.). Silver Spring, MD: American Music Therapy Association.

Standley, J., & Jones, J. (2007). *Music techniques in therapy, counseling, and special education* (3rd ed.). Silver Spring, MD: American Music Therapy Association.

Standley, J., Gregory, D., Whipple, J., Walworth, D., Nguyen, J., Jarred, J., et al. (2005). *Medical music therapy: A model program for clinical practice, education, training, and research.* Silver Spring, MD: American Music Therapy Association.

JAYNE M. STANDLEY
Florida State University

See also: **Art Therapy; Group Therapy**

MYELIN

Myelin is a protein and lipid-rich substance that is produced by oligodendrocytes in the central nervous system and Schwann cells in the peripheral nervous system. Myelin is elaborated into a sheath and wrapped, in a concentric fashion, around an axon. The deposition of myelin in a spiraling pattern around an axon generates two morphological features of the myelin sheath: the major dense line (DL) and the intraperiod line (IL). The DL is formed when the cytoplasm within the myelin process is lost, and the apposing plasma membranes come together. As the myelin sheath spirals around the axon, the outer faces of the plasma membrane of each wrap oppose each other to form the IL. The ensheathment of an axon with myelin is not continuous along its length, but is laid down as segments of myelin (internodes) that are interrupted, at regular intervals, by areas devoid of myelin, which are termed the nodes of Ranvier.

The enrichment of sodium channels at the Ranvier nodes and the insulating properties of the myelin sheath allow impulses to be swiftly funneled by passive spread from one node to the next. This movement of the action potential from node to node is termed saltatory conduction, and it enables myelinated axons with a diameter of 4 μm to convey information at the same speed as unmyelinated axons with a diameter of 500 μm. Therefore, axon myelination provides the means by which the nervous system can convey electrical impulses at high speeds in a confined manner. Conversely, any loss of axon myelination, as seen in demyelinating diseases or nervous system trauma, disrupts action potential propagation, resulting in devastating consequences to normal motor and sensory functions.

Although myelin enhances action potential propagation in a similar fashion for both the peripheral nervous system (PNS) and the central nervous system (CNS), its biochemical composition and its manner of deposition is distinct in these two systems. For example, within the CNS a single oligodendrocyte is capable of ensheathing up to 50 axons with an internode of myelin, whereas in the PNS a single Schwann cell will ensheath only one axon with myelin. Moreover, although the chemical composition of myelin is 70% lipids (in the form of cholesterol, phospholipids, sphingolipids, and phosphatidates) and 30% protein in both the CNS and PNS, the protein composition is distinct for these two systems. For example, the major proteins that make up the CNS myelin include myelin basic protein (MBP), proteolipid protein (PLP), and myelin-associated glycoprotein (MAG), whereas the major proteins for PNS myelin include MBP, the myelin P0 and P2 proteins, and peripheral myelin protein 22 (PMP-22). Both immunohistochemical and transgenic studies have demonstrated that MBP and PLP are important for myelin compaction, whereas MAG is important in the early axonal-glial interactions necessary to elicit myelin ensheathment of the axon. Both the P proteins and PMP-22 function in the formation and stabilization of PNS myelin. Recently, it has been determined that the myelin proteins MAG and NOGO are potent inhibitors to neurite outgrowth. The presence of these myelin proteins in the CNS may account for the limited regenerative capacity of CNS axons following injury.

Diseases that arise as a result of the selective destruction of oligodendrocytes and/or their product, myelin, fall into two main groups: acquired diseases and hereditary metabolic disorders. The most common acquired disease is multiple sclerosis, a suspected autoimmune disease that is characterized by the presence of demyelinated axons (plaques) within CNS fiber tracts. Examples of heredity metabolic disorders are the leukodystrophies, which are degenerative diseases that arise as a result of the absence or malfunctioning of enzymes that control the production or metabolism of myelin proteins.

RAYMOND J. COLELLO
Virginia Commonwealth University

See also: **Central Nervous System; Neurochemistry**

MYERS-BRIGGS TYPE INDICATOR (MBT)

The Myers-Briggs Type Indicator® assesses healthy personality differences by identifying 16 personality types that result from interactions among two pairs of bipolar mental functions and two pairs of bipolar attitudes, as described in C. G. Jung's theory of psychological types (1923/1971) and as interpreted and extended by Katharine C. Briggs and Isabel Briggs Myers. Versions of the instrument have been published since 1943, with three manuals (Myers, 1962; Myers & McCaulley, 1985; Myers, Quenk, & Hammer, 1998). The specified mental functions and attitudes are identified using forced-choice items that elicit preferences for one or the other pole within four pairs of opposites. These four pairs are as follows: (1) opposite ways of perceiving-sensing (S), gathering information through the five senses and trusting facts and details, versus intuition (N), perceiving patterns, interconnections, and inferences and trusting future possibilities; (2) opposite ways of judging—thinking (T), reaching conclusion through logical analysis to arrive at trust, versus feeling (F), reaching conclusions by weighing important values to arrive at harmony; (3) opposite attitudes or orientations of energy—extraversion (E), gaining and using energy primarily in the outer world of activities and people, versus introversion (I), gaining and using energy through the inner world of ideas, concepts, and internal experience; and (4) a judging (J) attitude when functioning in the outer world, using the preferred form of judgment (thinking or feeling) to organize the world and achieve closure, versus a perceiving (P) attitude in the outer world, using the preferred form of perception (sensing or intuition) to stay open as long as possible to incoming information. The judging-perceiving dichotomy was added by Myers and Briggs to Jung's original three dichotomies as a way of identifying the dynamic character of each type.

Determining a Type

Items on each of the four MBTI scales (E-I, S-N, T-F, and J-P) ask the respondent to choose between equally legitimate but opposite ways of being. In the Jung-Myers theory, healthy adaptation requires use of all eight types of elements at least some of the time. Everyone has access to all eight of them but, theoretically, has a preference for one of each pair over its opposite, typically reporting more interest and comfort in using preferred functions and attitudes. Preferences are not the same as skills, and it is possible to use a preference ineptly and a nonpreference effectively. Type specialization is similar to handedness, in that using one's preferred hand seems natural, comfortable, and automatic, whereas use of the other hand feels less awkward and uncomfortable and requires conscious effort. However, both a less-preferred hand and a less-preferred pole of a type of dichotomy can be used when

required or when it is appropriate for a particular task or situation.

The psychometric goal of the instrument is to sort people into preference categories rather than measure amounts of traits. A forced-choice format is therefore necessary since a person is assumed to prefer one pole of a dichotomy over the other; that is, a person is either an extravert or an introvert. Having a preference does not prevent use of the opposite, non-preferred pole, though this may require greater effort. A respondent who prefers thinking rather than feeling is free to use feeling when appropriate. A Preference Clarity Index (formerly preference score) shows how consistently a preference has been reported. Preferences are categorized by a four-letter type; for example an ENFP has preferences for the extraverted attitude, intuitive perception, feeling judgment, and a perceiving attitude toward the outer world (for this type, intuition). The 16 types are seen as qualitatively distinct from one another.

Type Dynamics

Although each type dichotomy has explanatory and predictive power independent of its interaction with the other three, hypothesized dynamic interactions among them are central to the construction and interpretation of the MBTI instrument. The Jung-Myers theory specifies a hierarchical structure with a dominant (favorite) function (either S, N, T, or F) that is used most often and is capable of greater development and effectiveness. This function is used primarily in the preferred attitude of extraversion or introversion. An auxiliary (second favorite) function comes from the other function pair (if S or N is dominant, T or F is auxiliary, and vice versa) is somewhat less comfortable and developed and it tends to be used in the nonpreferred attitude of E or I. An inferior function (opposite in both function and attitude to the dominant) is least used and developed, is typically accessed with great difficulty, and may erupt inappropriately under stress. A tertiary function (opposite to the auxiliary) is relatively undeveloped as well. Although the MBTI instrument does not measure hypothesized type dynamics directly, the hierarchical structure is observable in behavior, thus providing empirical evidence for the hierarchical development of the functions and a typological rather than a trait interpretation of personality. Accurate and effective interpretations of the MBTI, however, requires an understanding of the theory that underlies it.

Research and Applications

More than 50 years of research on the MBTI instrument has established the construct validity of its four dichotomies (CAPT, 2008; Myers & McCaulley, 1985; Myers et al., 1998). Research on the dynamic character of types is increasing with the most recent by Mitchell

(2006). Test-retest and internal consistency reliability of both earlier and current forms are acceptable, with coefficient alphas for Form M of .91 for the E-I and T-F scales and .92 for the S-N and J-P scales (Myers et al., 1998).

Respondents to the MBTI receive their four-letter type, associated preference clarities, and a written type description, available in a booklet or as a computer report. The 93-item Form M is the standard form (Myers, McCaulley, Quenk, & Hammer, 1998). Over 2 million people a year take the instrument, and it has been translated into 21 languages, making the MBTI the most widely used assessment of healthy personality worldwide. There are two advanced forms with associated manuals: the 144-item MBTI® Step II (Quenk, Hammer, & Majors, 2001) that identifies 20 facets of the four dichotomies, and the 222-item MBTI® Step III (Myers, McCaulley, Quenk, Hammer, & Mitchell, in press), which assesses type development. Results for both forms are available as individualized computer reports. MBTI Step I and Step II are commonly applied in education, career development, organizational behavior, group functioning, team development, personal and executive coaching, and psychotherapy with individuals and couples. Step III is used for individual counseling and coaching.

REFERENCES

CAPT. (2008). *MBTI Bibliography*. Retrieved July 11, 2008, from http://www.capt.org/research.

Jung, C. G. (1921/1971). Psychological types. In G. Adler & R. F. C. Hull (Ed. & Trans.), *Collected works, Vol. 6*. Princeton, NJ: Princeton University Press.

Mitchell, Wayne D. (2006). Validation of the full dynamic model of type. *Journal of Psychological Type, 66*(5).

Myers, I. B. (1962). *Manual: The Myers-Briggs Type Indicator*. Princeton. NJ: Educational Testing Service.

Myers, I. B., & McCaulley, M. H. (1985). *Manual: A guide to the development and use of the Myers-Briggs Type Indicator* (2nd ed.) Mountain View, CA: Davies-Black.

Myers, I. B., McCaulley, M. H., Quenk, N. L., & Hammer, A. L. (1998). *MBTI manual: A guide to the development and use of the Myers-Briggs Type Indicator* (3rd ed.). Mountain View, CA: CPP.

Myers, I. B., McCaulley, M. H., Quenk, N. L., Hammer, A. L., & Mitchell, W. D. (In press). *MBTI step III manual: Exploring personality development using the Myers-Briggs Type Indicator® instrument*. Mountain View, CA: CPP.

Quenk, N. L., Hammer, A. L., & Majors, M. S (2001). *MBTI step II manual: Exploring the next level of type with the Myers-Briggs Type Indicator form Q*. Mountain View, CA: CPP.

SUGGESTED READINGS

Myers, I. B. (with Kirby, L. K., & Myers, K. D.). (1998). *Introduction to type®* (6th ed.). Mountain View, CA: CPP.

Myers, K. D., & Kirby, L .K. (1994). *Introduction to type dynamics and development*. Mountain View, CA: Davies-Black.

Quenk, N. L. (In press). *Essentials of Myers-Briggs Type Indicator assessment* (2nd ed.). Hoboken, NJ: John Wiley & Sons.

NAOMI L. QUENK
Analytical Psychology, Ltd., Albuquerque, NM

See also: **Analytical Psychology; Personality Assessment; Self-Report Inventories**

N

NARCISSISM

Narcissism has been conceptualized and studied both as a general personality trait on which individuals exist on a continuum from nonnarcissistic to narcissistic and as a mental disorder (narcissistic personality disorder; NPD) in which there is an emphasis on the maladaptive nature of narcissistic traits. Regardless of the type of conceptualization used, the traits ascribed to narcissism are similar. Narcissistic individuals tend to be grandiose, arrogant, entitled, manipulative, preoccupied with status, and nonempathic. Although narcissism was originally conceptualized within a psychoanalytic or psychodynamic framework, more empirically based work began when NPD was included as an official diagnosis in the third version of the *Diagnostic and Statistical Manual of Mental Disorders* (DSM-III; American Psychiatric Association, 1980). Interestingly, most of this research has been undertaken by social and personality psychologists who have studied narcissism in a dimensional manner using nonclinical samples. Empirical data on NPD are sparse.

One difficulty inherent in the study of narcissism or NPD is the heterogeneity of conceptualizations of the construct. Depending on one's orientation, the psychological make-up of narcissistic individuals is viewed quite differently. A fundamental question in the study of narcissism has been whether narcissistic individuals genuinely like themselves (e.g., have high self-esteem) or whether their grandiosity masks feelings of inferiority. This latter "vulnerability" perspective on narcissism, in which narcissistic individuals are believed to harbor significant doubts about themselves and their abilities, is consistent with the positions taken by prominent theorists (e.g., Kohut, Kernberg) and can be found among the lay public and clinicians alike. This perspective also exists in the current DSM text (DSM-IV-TR; American Psychiatric Association, 2000), in which individuals with NPD are believed to have "vulnerability in self-esteem" that makes them "very sensitive to 'injury' from criticism or defeat." "Although they may not show it outwardly, criticism may haunt these individuals and may leave them feeling humiliated, degraded, hollow, and empty" (APA, 2000, p. 715). The DSM-IV-TR conceptualization of NPD may be closest to the position taken by Morf and Rhodewalt (2001) in which they argue that narcissistic individuals have a "grandiose, yet vulnerable self-concept" (p. 178).

They argue that narcissistic individuals need regular "external self-affirmation" to maintain their grandiose self-image, but this comes at the cost of driving others away because of their insistent need for attention and affirmation and their disinterest in the needs of others.

The notion that narcissistic individuals do not like themselves "deep down," however, is not entirely reconcilable with empirical data. For example, studies that focus on trait narcissism have found that narcissism is related to greater psychological health as reflected in lower daily ratings of anxiety, sadness, and loneliness and higher ratings of well-being (Sedikides, Rudich, Gregg, Kumashiro, & Rusbult, 2004).

So, do narcissistic individuals actually think highly of themselves or is their grandiosity a cover for feelings of insecurity? How can these different conceptualizations of narcissism be reconciled? Should NPD be considered a disorder if it is associated with greater emotional well-being? First, it is possible that individuals with particularly high and maladaptive levels of narcissism (i.e., those with symptoms of NPD) do experience psychological distress. Miller, Campbell, and Pilkonis (2007) found that NPD scores were positively related to anxiety and depression, although the relationship was small. Second, regardless of whether narcissistic individuals experience distress, there is evidence that individuals with NPD symptoms are impaired in a number of domains (e.g., romance and work), thus meeting one aspect of the DSM-IV-TR criteria for a mental disorder, namely, the presence of disability (i.e., impairment). A third issue is that there may be multiple forms of narcissism with potentially different etiological factors and basic underlying traits that are unintentionally comingled. For instance, Wink (1991) factor-analyzed six narcissism measures and found two independent factors that he titled Vulnerability-Sensitivity and Grandiosity-Exhibitionism. Individuals high on either of these factors were rated by spouses as being arrogant, conceited, bossy, opportunistic, demanding, and cruel. However, only individuals rated as being high on grandiose narcissism were rated by spouses as being outspoken, assertive, a show-off, and aggressive. Alternatively, individuals scoring high on vulnerable narcissism were rated by spouses as being high on traits related to anxiety, worrying, complaining, and being defensive.

More recently, Miller and Campbell (2008) suggested that these different conceptualizations of narcissism could be understood through the use of a general trait model of personality, such as the Five-Factor Model. Both grandiose and vulnerable forms of narcissism manifest a substantial negative relationship with the domain of Agreeableness, which measures an individual's tendency to interact with others in a trusting, honest, empathic manner versus a noncompliant, aggressive, immodest, and manipulative style. Where these two forms of narcissism differ primarily is in relation to the domains of Neuroticism (i.e., the tendency to experience negative emotions like depression and anxiety) and Extraversion (i.e., the tendency to be sociable, active, and assertive). Grandiose narcissism is negatively related to Neuroticism (e.g., depression, anxiety, self-consciousness) and positively related to Extraversion (e.g., assertiveness, activity level, excitement seeking). The opposite is true for the vulnerable form of narcissism, as these individuals are prone to negative emotions like depression and anger (i.e., high on Neuroticism) and are less gregarious and assertive (i.e., low on Extraversion). Grandiose and vulnerable narcissism also manifested divergent relations with self-esteem (i.e., grandiose narcissism is positively related to self-esteem; vulnerable narcissism is negatively related), psychological distress (i.e., grandiose narcissism is negatively related; vulnerable narcissism is positively related), and perceptions of received parenting (i.e., vulnerable but not grandiose narcissism was related to negative parenting styles such as being psychologically controlling and cold).

Understanding these different forms of narcissism is critical, because they reflect important differences with regard to basic personality traits, psychological well-being, and etiology. Use of a dimensional model of personality to conceptualize narcissism may allow the greatest flexibility in that one can assess traits underlying grandiose, vulnerable, or combinations of grandiose and vulnerable narcissism. We believe that it is vital that DSM-V include content or a system that allows for the conceptualization and assessment of these various forms of narcissistic personalities.

REFERENCES

American Psychiatric Association (1980). *Diagnostic and statistical manual of mental disorders* (3rd ed.). Washington, DC: Author.

American Psychiatric Association (2000). *Diagnostic and statistical manual of mental disorders* (4th ed., text rev.). Washington, DC: Author.

Miller, J. D., & Campbell, W. K. (2008). Comparing clinical and social-personality conceptualizations of narcissism. *Journal of Personality, 76,* 449–476.

Miller, J. D., Campbell, W. K., & Pilkonis, P. A. (2007). Narcissistic Personality Disorder: Relations with distress and functional impairment. *Comprehensive Psychiatry, 48,* 170–177.

Morf, C. C., & Rhodewalt, F. (2001). Unraveling the paradoxes of narcissism: A dynamic self-regulatory processing model. *Psychological Inquiry, 12,* 177–196.

Sedikides, C., Rudich, E., Gregg, A., Kumashiro, M., & Rusbult, C. (2004). Are normal narcissists psychologically healthy?: Self-esteem matters. *Journal of Personality and Social Psychology, 87,* 400–416.

Wink, P. (1991). Two faces of narcissism. *Journal of Personality and Social Psychology, 61,* 590–597.

SUGGESTED READINGS

Cain, N. M., Pincus, A. L., & Ansell, E. B. (2008). Narcissism at the crossroads: Phenotypic description of pathological narcissism across clinical theory, social/personality psychology, and psychiatric diagnosis. *Clinical Psychology Review, 28,* 638–656.

Miller, J. D., & Campbell, W. K. (2008). Comparing clinical and social-personality conceptualizations of narcissism. *Journal of Personality, 76,* 449–476.

Joshua D. Miller
W. Keith Campbell
University of Georgia

See also: Narcissistic Personality Disorder; Self-Esteem

NARCISSISTIC PERSONALITY DISORDER

Narcissistic personality disorder (NPD) is described in the *Diagnostic and Statistical Manual of Mental Disorders* (DSM IV-TR; American Psychiatric Association, 2000) as "a pervasive pattern of grandiosity, need for admiration, and lack of empathy," and it is identified by nine criteria. People with NPD have a grandiose sense of self-importance and accompanying grandiose fantasies. They believe that they are special and unique, and they have a strong need for admiring attention. Considered to lack empathy, that is, being unwilling or unable to recognize the feelings and needs of others, they come across as arrogant and haughty. They have a sense of entitlement, with expectations of receiving special treatment and exceptions, and tendencies to be exploitive and take advantage of other people. Envy of others is common, or alternatively, they believe that others envy them because of their specialness or talents.

Some narcissistic personalities, called "shy," tend to be sensitive, inhibited, hyperreactive, shame-ridden, and socially withdrawn (Akhtar, 2003). These individuals nevertheless possess the same pathological grandiose self-image and emotional dysregulation. Narcissistic personalities can also present with psychopathic or antisocial characteristics ranging from inconsistent moral standards (moral perfectionism versus moral compromises and dishonesty) to more specific criminal behavior (one-time crimes or specialized recurrent felonies) (Gunderson & Ronningstam, 2001).

Narcissism ranges from healthy and normal to pathological and enduring, with more or less severe forms of character dysfunction. Normal narcissism refers to all aspects of normal self-esteem within a normally functioning self-structure (Stone, in Ronningstam, 1998). This would include not only self-preservation, self-regard, and a positive feeling from the body self (health and attractiveness), but also self-assertiveness, with normal levels of entitlement and competitiveness, and affiliation, with empathy and compassion.

Pathological narcissism is identified by degree of severity, dominance of aggression versus shame, and the extent to which its manifestations are overt or internally hidden. When the level of pathological narcissism is less severe, temporary, situational, or limited to a set of specific character features that interfere to a lesser degree with regular personal, interpersonal, or vocational functioning, it is referred to as a narcissistic trait or disturbance. Pathological narcissism differs from normal narcissism in the sense that self-esteem regulation serves to protect and support a grandiose but fragile self. Affect regulation is compromised by difficulties in processing and modulating feelings, specifically anger, shame, and envy. Interpersonal relationships are used primarily to protect or enhance self-esteem and other self-regulatory functions, at the expense of mutual relativeness and intimacy. People with disordered narcissism or NPD can be high functioning, creative, and successful, since healthy and extraordinary narcissistic capacity may coexist with more pathological dysfunctional traits.

Prevalence and Natural History

NPD is relatively uncommon in the general population and more frequent in specific clinical samples of individuals with personality disorders or certain substance-abuse problems, especially among patients seen in private practice. The DSM-IV-TR states that 50–75% of persons diagnosed with NPD are male. Although narcissistic personality disorder develops in adulthood, narcissistic features can be seen in children and may be frequent among young people in their late teens and early twenties because of transitional developmental challenges. Once formed, narcissistic personality disorders are likely to persist into middle and old age.

Etiology

Studies have suggested a genetic influence in the development of personality disorders, including NPD. Of specific importance are inherited variations in hypersensitivity, strong aggressive drive, low anxiety, limited frustration tolerance, and defects in affect regulation (Schore, 1994). Inconsistent attunement and insufficient attachment in the early parent-child interaction can lead to failure in the development of self-esteem and affect regulation. Paulina

Kernberg (in Ronningstam, 1998) identified children at risk for NPD as those who are assigned roles or functions beyond or inconsistent with their normal developmental tasks and those who are adopted and have therefore been both rejected and chosen. Others have pointed to the caregiver's insensitivity to the child's emotional experiences and tendencies to misread the child's feelings and reactions and to ascribe their own feelings, intentions, and ambitions to the child. Not valued and seen in his or her own right, the child is nevertheless intensively attended to and specially valued as a regulator of the parent's self-esteem. Overindulging and insufficient limit-setting can also contribute to adult NPD (Young, in Ronningstam 1998).

External traumatic experience in adults can overwhelm the self and trigger narcissistic symptoms such as shame, humiliation, and rage, defined as "trauma-associated narcissistic symptoms" or TANS (Simon, 2001). Although underlying vulnerability to such stress can stem from the presence of pathological narcissism or NPD, even people with relatively healthy self-esteem can develop narcissistic symptoms after experiencing a more-or-less severe narcissistic humiliation.

Course and Prognosis

The persistence over time of narcissistic patterns, especially in interpersonal relations, generally leads to guarded or poor prognosis. When denial of problems and factors in the environment that can interfere with grandiose attitudes and pursuits are combined with a compensatory fantasy life and the opportunities for gratifying support of narcissistic functioning, the individual's motivation for treatment is usually low. NPD may worsen over the years, with more severe envy, disillusionment, and contempt. Middle age can be an especially critical period for the development of NPD. The challenge of facing personal and professional limitations, losses, and other challenges to the self-esteem can reinforce specific pathological or defensive narcissistic traits, leading to chronic denial, emptiness, devaluation, guilt, and cynicism. However, in some narcissistic individuals, increased realization and motivation for change in this stage of life can make treatment efforts more favorable and improve prognosis (Kernberg, 1984).

Empirical findings (Ronningstam, Gunderson, & Lyons, 1995) have shown that NPD patients with less severe narcissistically disturbed object relations may have a better prognosis and actually improve over time. Improvements were related to three types of corrective life experiences: (1) corrective achievements; such as graduations, promotions, recognitions, or acceptance to schools, programs, or positions applied for, led to a more realistic and accepted sense of self, with less need for unrealistic grandiose fantasies and exaggerations of talents and personal qualities; (2) corrective relationships, typically long-term, close, and mutual, caused prior interpersonal characteristics such as devaluation, entitlement, exploitive behavior, and arrogance to diminish; and (3) corrective disillusionment, incompatible experiences that challenge the previous grandiose self-experience, brought the view of self into greater congruence with actual talents, abilities, and status. Such experiences may reflect the realization of personal, intellectual, or vocational limitations, failure to achieve life goals or conform to narcissistically determined ideals and standards, or even personal losses or lost opportunities in life. The impact of such experiences must not be too adverse, or else narcissistic pathologies may actually worsen.

Treatment

The often symptom-free narcissistic individual usually seeks treatment for three reasons: acute crises caused by failures or losses; in response to requests or ultimatums from family, employer, or court; or increasing sense of dissatisfaction or meaninglessness in one's life. Comorbid dysthymia, acute depression, bipolar disorder, or substance abuse may also force narcissistic people to treatment. Narcissistic patients' motivation varies greatly, depending upon whether they experience urgency and ultimateness, have capacity for affect tolerance and regulation, or lack outside sources of gratification that support narcissistic functioning. Denial of problems and limitations and perpetuation of self-enhancing behavior amplify the subjective experience of self-sufficiency. Self-aggrandizing and blaming of others for failures are examples of strategies that can undo the patient's ability to attend to and integrate constructive feedback (Morf & Rhodewalt, 2001). Fragile self-esteem, low affect tolerance, and urges to ignore or even destroy what the therapist can offer tend to limit the narcissistic patients' capacity to form and use a therapeutic alliance. The treatment process in itself requires abilities that narcissistic individuals may be lacking, such as a capacity for symbolization, openness to mourning, tolerance of psychic pain, empathic understanding of their own as well as others' feelings and experiences, and capacity for mutual interpersonal relationships.

Psychoanalysis and psychoanalytically oriented psychotherapy have been considered the treatment of choice for patients with pathological narcissism and NPD. In the late 1960s, Otto Kernberg and Heinz Kohut introduced two radically different approaches: an ego-psychological object relations perspective and a self-psychology vantage. The strategy suggested by Kernberg (1975) addresses narcissism as a defensive resistance and relies heavily on reality testing and on confrontation and interpretation of the pathological grandiose self and the negative transference. Kohut (1968) focused on empathic observations and the development and working through of three types of transference—mirroring, idealizing, and twinship or alter-ego transference—as a way of correcting the structural deficits that characterize narcissistic

disorders. Narcissism is here identified as a protection of self-cohesion. More recently, John Fiscalini (1994) introduced a method of interpersonal coparticipant psychoanalytic inquiry, which alternates between confrontational and empathic exploration of the narcissistic transference-countertransference matrix. This strategy focuses on exploring the patient's interpersonal interactions, specifically the difficulties tolerating challenges to own perspectives and self-esteem. Narcissism is seen as a psychological defense by oneself against others and as representing the self-esteem, specifically with respect to self-centeredness, self-inflation, and self-perfection.

Outside the psychonanalytic realm, a schema-focused therapy developed by Jeffrey Young (Young et al., 2003) combines cognitive, behavioral, experiential, and transference-based techniques to change narcissistic schemas and modes. Based on three early maladaptive core schemas for narcissism, entitlement, emotional depravation, and defectiveness, Young identifies three modes that characterize most patients with NPD: the lonely child, the self-aggrandizer, and the detached self-soother. Associated with each schema and mood are coping styles such as overcompensation, dominance, and excessive self-assertion or recognition and status seeking. The goal of the treatment is to construct a healthy adult mode by helping the patient to repair and regulate the significant narcissistic moods. A broad variety of cognitive and behavioral strategies and techniques are used, including confrontation; modeling; limit setting; encouragement; imagery exercises; exploring, negotiating, and adapting the different modes; and homework assignments.

Other treatment modalities include the therapeutic milieu and family, couples, and group therapy (see Ronningstam, 1998). Although there are many accounts of psychodynamic and psychoanalytic treatment of people with NPD, there are presently no empirical studies on treatment course and efficacy for NPD. Treatment planning is guided by clinical evaluation, and the choices of modalities and strategies depend upon the particular complexion of a patient's narcissistic functioning and circumstances. No specific psychopharmacological treatments have proved to be effective for pathological narcissism and NPD. However, when these patients present with a comorbid Axis I disorder, such as bipolar disorder, major depression, or anxiety disorder, psychopharmacological treatment can be beneficial. However, such treatment is often challenging due to the narcissistic patients' reluctance to subordinate themselves to ordinations and their hypersensitivity to side effects, especially those affecting sexual and intellectual functioning.

Comorbid narcissistic personality disorder can have serious implications in the treatment of Axis I disorders. When symptomatology such as substance use, hypomania or mania, or anorexia accentuates grandiosity, internal control, self-sufficiency, or other narcissistic traits, symptom reduction may not be of primary interest for narcissistic patients, leading to low treatment compliance. Treatment of the suicidal narcissistic patient presents specific challenges, because suicide-related thoughts and feelings in these patients can occur in the absence of depression. The fantasy of suicide can support an illusion of mastery and control ("I fear nothing, not even death"). It can shield against anticipated narcissistic threats and injuries ("death before dishonor"). Suicidal impulses may stem from an aggressive, revengeful, and controlling attitude, as in "my way or no way" or "I'll show you." They can also arise from a grandiose delusion of indestructibility or represent the wish to attack or destroy an imperfect, failing, intolerable self (Ronningstam & Maltsberger, 1998). Chronic suicidal preoccupation may be important for the narcissistic patient's self-esteem and internal control, and it may in a paradoxical way support a sense of dignity and autonomy and that it is worth staying alive.

REFERENCES

Akhtar, S. (2003). *New clinical realms: Pushing the envelope of theory and technique*. Northvale, NJ: Jason Aronson.

American Psychiatric Association (2000). *Diagnostic and statistical manual of mental disorders* (4th ed., text rev.). Washington, DC: Author.

Fiscalini, J. (1994). Narcissism and coparticipant inquiry: Explorations in contemporary interpersonal psychoanalysis. *Contemporary Psychoanalysis, 30*(4), 747–776.

Gunderson, J., & Ronningstam, E. (2001). Differentiating antisocial and narcissistic personality disorder. *Journal of Personality Disorders, 15*, 103–109.

Kernberg, O. F. (1975). *Borderline conditions and pathological narcissism*. New York: Jason Aronson.

Kernberg O. F. (1984). *Severe personality disorders*. New Haven: Yale University Press.

Kohut, H. (1968). The psychoanalytic treatment of narcissistic personality disorder. *Psychoanalytic Study of the Child, 23*, 86–113.

Morf, C. C., & Rhodewalt, F. (2001). Unraveling the paradoxes of narcissism: A dynamic self-regulatory processing model. *Psychological Inquiry, 12*, 177–196.

Ronningstam, E. (Ed.). (1998). *Disorders of narcissism: Diagnostic, clinical and empirical implications*. Washington, DC: American Psychiatric Press.

Ronningstam, E., Gunderson, J., & Lyons, M. (1995). Changes in pathological narcissism. *American Journal of Psychiatry, 152*, 253–257.

Ronningstam, E., & Maltsberger, J. (1998). Pathological narcissism and sudden suicide-related collapse. *Suicide and Life-Threatening Behavior, 28*(3): 261–271.

Schore, A. (1994). *Affect regulation and the origin of the self*. Hillsdale, NJ: Lawrence Erlbaum.

Simon, R. I. (2001). Distinguishing trauma-associated narcissistic symptoms from posttraumatic stress disorder: A diagnostic challenge. *Harvard Review of Psychiatry, 10*, 28–36.

SUGGESTED READINGS

Fiscalini, J., & Grey, A. L. (Eds.). (1993). *Narcissism and the interpersonal self*. New York: Columbia University Press.

Masterson, J. F. (1993). *The emerging self. A developmental, self and object relations approach to the treatment of the closet narcissistic disorder of the self*. New York: Brunner/Mazel.

Ronningstam, E. (2005). *Identifying and understanding the narcissistic personality*. Oxford, UK: Oxford University Press.

ELSA RONNINGSTAM
Harvard University Medical School

See also: Narcissism; Personality Disorders; Self-Esteem

NARCOLEPSY

Narcolepsy is a disorder characterized by persistent daytime sleepiness. Despite this daytime sleepiness, narcoleptics often do not sleep well at night. In addition to sleepiness, narcoleptics have REM (Rapid Eye Movement) sleep shortly after they go to sleep, in contrast to the 1–1.5 hours taken by normal individuals before their first REM sleep period. Thus short sleep latency, indicative of sleepiness, plus REM sleep shortly after sleep onset, can be used to diagnose narcolepsy.

In addition to these symptoms, narcoleptics have hypnagogic hallucinations, which are hallucinations at sleep onset that incorporate elements of the environment, such as seeing snakes in the bed or intruders entering the bedroom. However, the most striking symptom of narcolepsy is cataplexy. Cataplexy is a loss of muscle tone without loss of alertness. Cataplexy attacks can last for seconds to minutes, with the patient fully aware of all that is happening during the attack.

Cataplectic attacks are most commonly triggered by laughter, but they can also be triggered by other sudden onset, strong emotions, such as sudden anger. Normal individuals get weak at these times, as in "doubling over with laughter," but in normal persons this weakness is limited by a system that maintains muscle tone. This system is defective in narcoleptics. It should be emphasized that cataplectic attacks are distinct from the sleep attacks that occur in this disorder. A related symptom is sleep paralysis, which most commonly occurs upon awakening. A narcoleptic may awaken fully from a dream and be unable to move for many seconds or minutes. Normal individuals may experience this symptom briefly and rarely, but many narcoleptics have this symptom regularly.

Not all persons with narcolepsy have clinically significant cataplexy, and there is some possibility that narcolepsy with and without cataplexy may represent disorders with differing causes. It has been shown that cataplexy and most likely sleep paralysis as well result from the inappropriate activation of a brain circuit that normally functions to prevent the acting out of dreams in REM sleep. The hypnagogic hallucinations can also be seen as an intrusion of REM sleep dreaming into waking.

Narcolepsy has a prevalence of approximately 1 in 2,000 people. The onset of symptoms typically occurs in the teens or twenties. Sleepiness is usually the initial symptom, followed weeks later, but sometimes as long as 1 or 2 years later, by cataplexy. Narcolepsy is equally common in males and females. After the onset period, symptoms do not greatly change with age. However, cataplexy, both in humans and in canine narcoleptics, does appear to diminish somewhat with age.

Work with narcoleptic dogs (Lin et al., 1999) and in mutant mice (Chemelli et al., 1999) led to the discovery of the cause of most narcolepsy in humans. It was found that narcolepsy is caused by a loss on average of 90% of neurons containing a neurotransmitter called hypocretin and also known as orexin (Thannickal et al., 2000). There is no evidence that any other neuronal cell type is affected. The leading theory is that the loss of hypocretin cells in narcolepsy is caused by an immune system attack. Most persons with narcolepsy (95% of Caucasian narcoleptics) have a particular human leukocyte antigen (HLA) type that is present in only about 25% of non-narcoleptics. HLA molecules help the immune system recognize foreign antigens, and most HLA linked disorders are thought to be autoimmune (Siegel, 2004).

Animal work has unraveled the neuronal activity patterns responsible for cataplexy. Cataplexy is caused by a sudden cessation of activity in brainstem neurons containing the neurotransmitter norepinephrine and the simultaneous activation of other neurons containing the inhibitory neurotransmitters glycine and gamma-aminobutyric acid (GABA). Norepinephrine excites motor neurons and thereby maintains muscle tone. In contrast GABA and glycine inhibit motor neurons and thereby reduce muscle tone. The coordinated inactivation of norepinephrine neurons and activation of neurons containing GABA and glycine is responsible for the suppression of muscle tone in REM sleep and in cataplexy.

It is thought that, during sudden strong emotions, hypocretin normally excites norepinephrine cells, preventing their cessation of activity and blocking the correlated activation of inhibitory cells in the medulla. When hypocretin cells are lost, this excitation of norepinephrine cells does not occur, resulting in cataplexy. Hypocretin cells also activate a number of arousal systems. Therefore the loss of hypocretin cells causes the sleepiness experienced by narcoleptics. Recording from hypocretin neurons in normal rats revealed that these cells are maximally active during pleasurable motor activities and are inactive during sleep (Mileykovskiy et al., 2005).

The sleepiness of narcolepsy can be treated by stimulants, including amphetamines, methylphenidate, and modafinil. These drugs have little effect on cataplexy. Cataplexy can be treated by antidepressant medications that boost the effects of monoamine neurotransmitters, including norepinephrine. Selective serotonin reuptake inhibitors, which have metabolites that act on norepinephrine receptors, are also effective in the treatment of cataplexy. Gamma hydroxybutyrate has some beneficial effects on both cataplexy and daytime sleepiness. However, none of the current treatments are fully effective, and all can have side effects. It is hoped that administration of hypocretin will ultimately be more effective in reversing the symptoms of narcolepsy.

REFERENCES

Chemelli, R. M., Willie, J. T., Sinton, C. M., Elmquist, J. K., Scammell, T., Lee, C., et al. (1999). Narcolepsy in orexin knockout mice: Molecular genetics of sleep regulation. *Cell, 98,* 437–451.

Lin, L., Faraco, J., Kadotani, H., Rogers, W., Lin, X., Qui, X., et al. (1999). The REM sleep disorder canine narcolepsy is caused by a mutation in the hypocretin (orexin) receptor gene. *Cell, 98,* 365–376.

Mileykovskiy, B. Y., Kiyashchenko, L. I., & Siegel, J. M. (2005). Behavioral correlates of activity in identified hypocretin/orexin neurons. *Neuron, 46,* 787–798.

Siegel, J. M. (2004). Hypocretin (orexin): Role in normal behavior and neuropathology. *Annual Review of Psychology, 55,* 125–148.

Thannickal, T. C., Moore, R. Y., Nienhuis, R., Ramanathan, L., Gulyani, S., Aldrich, M., et al. (2000). Reduced number of hypocretin neurons in human narcolepsy. *Neuron, 27,* 469–474.

SUGGESTED READINGS

Siegel, J. M. (2000). Narcolepsy. *Scientific American, 282,* 76–81.

University of California–Los Angeles (UCLA) Psychiatry and Biobehaviorial Sciences, Center for Sleep Research. Retrieved February 24, 2009, from http://www.npi.ucla.edu/sleepresearch.

Jerome Siegel
University of California, Los Angeles

See also: **Neurotransmitters; Rapid Eye Movement Sleep**

NATIONAL ACADEMY OF NEUROPSYCHOLOGY

The National Academy of Neuropsychology (NAN) was founded in 1975 as a membership organization established for individuals interested in the field of neuropsychology, a field within psychology focused on the practice and study of the relationship between the brain and behavior. With over 3,300 members in all states and 24 countries, NAN has developed into an organization that represents the diverse interests of scientist-practitioners, clinicians, and researchers in the field of neuropsychology.

NAN was founded to represent the professional aspects of neuropsychology in the United States. As NAN grew, its mission statement expanded to advance neuropsychology as a science and health profession, to promote human welfare, and to generate and disseminate knowledge of brain-behavior relationships.

The first formal meeting of NAN membership took place during August 1976 with Arthur Canter serving as the first president. In 1979, NAN *Clinical Neuropsychology* was adopted as the official journal, co-edited by Lawrence Hartlag and Charles Golden. This journal evolved into the *International Journal of Clinical Neuropsychology* (IJCN) until 1985 when the *Archives of Clinical Neuropsychology* became the official journal, edited by Raymond Dean. The current editor is Robert J. McCaffrey.

The first annual convention was held in Orlando, Florida, in 1981, with approximately 220 attendees. Every year since, NAN has held an annual meeting during the fall or winter months. Over the years, attendance has grown to approximately 2,000 registrants. Numerous volunteers offer their time for the operation of the executive board, committees, special interest groups, and programs, as well as filling the roles of professional staff at a full-time central office. The NAN executive board and most committees meet several times a year to conduct the business of NAN.

NAN recognizes excellence in the practice of neuropsychology with a series of prestigious awards. Awards are given for the best research paper published in the *Archives of Clinical Neuropsychology* (CAN), distinguished lifetime contributions to neuropsychology, distinguished service, early career and career service, outstanding dissertation, and student poster. NAN has always been in the forefront of supporting investigation and research within the field of clinical neuropsychology. To support this effort, NAN created a Clinical Research Grants Program, which funds projects that are aimed at producing new and clinically relevant topics.

NAN advocates for its membership and for the field of neuropsychology, in general. The Professional Affairs and Information Committee (PAIC) is engaged in a broad spectrum of activities designed to assist with issues related to reimbursement, professional development, and marketing of services. NAN has developed alliances with the American Psychological Association and health organizations that are involved in the science and practice of brain-behavior relationships. NAN panels serve in consulting roles with sports organizations, military leaderships and organizations, a congressional task force, and national political leaders.

NAN offers continuing education programs in connection with its annual conference and through the Distant CE Internet-based program. Courses on neuropsychology and other topics relevant to neuropsychology have been developed, and courses on mild brain injury and psychopharmacology are currently being investigated.

The Policy and Planning Committee has drafted position papers on topics relevant to the practice of neuropsychology including third-party observers, technicians, test security, definition of neuropsychologist, cognitive rehabilitation, informed consent, symptom validity testing, and learning disorders and a variety of other topics. All position papers as well as information about the Academy are posted on the NAN web site: http://www.nanonline.org.

ROBERT W. ELLIOT
Aerospace Health Institute, Los Angeles, CA

CHARLES GOLDEN
Nova Southeastern University, FL

ROBERT MCCAFFREY
State University of New York at Albany, NY

NATIONAL ACADEMY OF SCIENCES

Since its founding in 1863, the United States National Academy of Sciences (NAS) has served as both an honorific association of distinguished American and international scientists and as an autonomous, nonprofit organization providing independent advice on science and technology to government agencies. The NAS has provided such advice from the beginning of its existence and in conformity to the terms of its charter, which states that it will advise the federal government on scientific and technological matters whenever called upon.

Up until the end of the nineteenth century, the Academy's membership centered on the hard science disciplines of physics, mathematics, and the like. The first psychologist elected to the Academy was James McKeen Cattell, who attained membership in 1901. As first organized, the Academy was composed of discipline-based Standing Committees among which the membership was distributed. Cattell's field was experimental psychology, which at the time of his election was new enough that there was no Academy Standing Committee available to represent it. As a result, he joined the Standing Committee on Anthropology, which represented the discipline closest to his own. By 1910 the NAS had three psychologist members, and this factor, along with the rapid growth in scientific disciplines and interdisciplinary work, led the Academy to rethink its organization. A Committee on Anthropology and Psychology was therefore created in 1911. By 1948, though, there were 23 psychologist members (representing approximately 5% of total Academy membership), as opposed to nine anthropologists. Accordingly, psychologists were given a section of their own for representation within the Academy, which they continue to have. At present (May, 2008), the NAS Section of Psychology includes 63 members and foreign associates.

In anticipation of U.S. participation in World War I, the Academy in 1916 established the National Research Council. Originally conceived as a body to help the federal government mobilize science and technology for the war, the Research Council in 1918 became a permanent organization serving as the operating agency of the Academy, in which capacity it conducted and continues to conduct studies to provide advice on science and technology to government agencies. The wartime organization of the Research Council included a Committee on Psychology, which, under the leadership of Robert M. Yerkes (elected to Academy membership in 1923), undertook studies of morale, personnel classification and selection, and intelligence testing of Army recruits.

The 1919 peacetime reorganization of the Research Council saw the creation of a Division of Anthropology and Psychology, which worked on a number of war-related matters during World War II, including the selection and training of pilots. Reorganizations of the Research Council in 1962, 1973, 1982, and 2000 placed psychology in cross-disciplinary units focused on broad policy problems. Currently, Research Council studies with a significant psychological component are undertaken largely under the auspices of the Division on Behavioral and Social Sciences and Education (DBASSE), although other study units, most notably those operating under the Institute of Medicine (IOM), may draw on expertise in psychology as well.

DANIEL BARBIERO
U.S. National Academy of Sciences

NATIONAL INSTITUTE OF CHILD HEALTH AND HUMAN DEVELOPMENT

In the early days of his administration, President John F. Kennedy recognized the need for a federal agency focusing on research in child health and human development. After passage of legislation sponsored by his administration, President Kennedy authorized the creation of the National Institute of Child Health and Human Development (NICHD) of the National Institutes of Health. It was the first NIH institute to investigate human development through the entire life process. The new institute concentrated on understanding developmental

disabilities—including intellectual disability—and on development from conception through infancy and childhood and on into the stages of maturation.

In 2008, Congress renamed the institute the Eunice Kennedy Shriver National Institute of Child Health and Human Development in recognition of Mrs. Shriver's pivotal role in convincing her brother, President Kennedy, of the need for the Institute and for legislators to approve and fund it.

The NICHD is now comprised of four centers and two divisions: the Center for Population Research; the Center for Developmental Biology and Perinatal Medicine; the Center for Research for Mothers and Children; the National Center for Medical Rehabilitation Research; the Division of Epidemiology, Statistics, and Prevention Research (DESPR); and the Division of Intramural and Extramural Research. Intramural research is conducted by scientists at the NIH campus, as well as by DESPR research partners at other institutions. The Extramural Centers support research across the nation and the globe, through funding research grant applications from scientists.

All of these NICHD centers and divisions are devoted to its core mission of ensuring that every person is born healthy and wanted; that women suffer no harmful effects from the reproductive process; that all children have the chance to fulfill their potential to live healthy and productive lives free from disease or disability; and that the health, productivity, independence, and well-being of all people are enhanced through optimal rehabilitation. Behavioral research is an essential part of this mission, with programs devoted to development and behavior in both intra- and extramural arenas. In particular, researchers in several units within the Comparative Ethology Branch investigate behavioral, cognitive, and physiological development in humans and in nonhuman primates. The Division of Epidemiology, Statistics and Prevention Research also conducts research on child and adolescent behavior.

The Extramural Research program includes three branches devoted to behavioral science research: the Demographic and Behavioral Sciences Branch (Center for Population Research); the Child Development and Behavior Branch (Center for Research for Mothers and Children); and the Intellectual and Developmental Disabilities Branch (Center for Developmental Biology and Perinatal Medicine). NICHD-funded scientists have made unparalleled contributions to society, ranging from the development of a vaccine that prevents meningitis caused by *Haemophilus influenzae* type b (Hib,) a leading cause of mental retardation; to developing a screening test for hypothyroidism in newborns; to demonstration of the effectiveness of early intervention programs to reduce the likelihood of cognitive impairment among disadvantaged children.

The Institute is responsible for disseminating these and other findings to outside audiences, including other researchers, health care professionals, and the public. For more information, visit http://www.nichd.nih.gov, or call (phone) 800-370-2943 (TTY) 888-320-6942.

NATIONAL INSTITUTE OF MENTAL HEALTH

The National Institute of Mental Health (NIMH) is one of 27 Institutes and Centers of the National Institutes of Health (NIH). Formally established in 1949, it was one of the first four NIH Institutes. Research and research training at NIMH address a variety of mental disorders, including attention deficit hyperactivity disorder, autism spectrum disorders, anxiety disorders, bipolar disorder, borderline personality disorder, depression, eating disorders, post-traumatic stress disorder, and schizophrenia.

As the lead federal agency for research on mental and behavioral disorders, NIMH aims to transform the understanding and treatment of mental illnesses through basic and clinical research, paving the way for recovery, prevention, and cure.

NIMH advances its mission and priorities through two primary programs: the extramural research program and the intramural research program. Under a rigorous and highly competitive process, the extramural program awards funds through grants and contracts to individual investigators and to public and private research institutions throughout the world. In addition to the Office of the Director, NIMH is comprised of major divisions that cover the realm of mental health disorders research: the Division of Neuroscience and Basic Behavioral Science; the Division of Adult Translational Research and Treatment Development; the Division of Developmental and Translational Research; the Division of AIDS and Health and Behavior Research; and the Division of Services and Intervention Research.

In the intramural research program, noted NIMH researchers conduct basic, translational, and clinical research to advance understanding of the causes, treatment, and prevention of mental disorders. Through these programs, NIMH makes ongoing investments in order to accomplish its major objectives which are to

- Promote discovery in the brain and behavioral sciences to fuel research on the causes of mental disorders
- Chart mental illness trajectories to determine when, where, and how to intervene
- Develop new and better interventions that incorporate the diverse needs and circumstances of people with mental illnesses
- Strengthen the public health impact of NIMH-supported research

NIMH's informational and educational activities include the dissemination of materials on mental illness to health professionals and the public; professional associations; international, national, state, and local officials; and voluntary organizations working in the areas of mental health and mental illness. For more information about NIMH, visit the web site: http://www.nimh.nih.gov.

THOMAS R. INSEL
National Institute of Mental Health

NATIONAL INSTITUTE ON AGING

The National Institute on Aging (NIA), one of 27 institutes and centers of the National Institutes of Health, leads a broad scientific effort to understand the nature of aging and to extend the healthy, active years of life. Congress established the NIA in 1974 to "improve the health and well-being of older Americans through research on aging processes, age-related diseases, and the special problems and needs of the aged." Later legislation designated NIA as the primary federal agency on Alzheimer's Disease (AD) research. NIA conducts intramural research at NIA laboratories in Bethesda and Baltimore, MD, and sponsors extramural research at universities and other research institutions. NIA funds both individual and institutional training and career support at pre- and post-doctoral levels for all stages of careers, and places special emphasis on underrepresented minorities.

Intramural psychological research focuses on topics including individual differences in cognitive and personality processes and traits using experimental, epidemiological, and longitudinal approaches. It has made significant use of the Baltimore Longitudinal Study of Aging cohort.

There are four extramural divisions of NIA: Aging Biology; Geriatrics and Clinical Gerontology; Neuroscience; and Behavioral and Social Research, with psychological research principally located in the latter two. The Division of Neuroscience (DN) focuses on the neurobiology, neuropsychology, and dementias of aging. Emphases include sleep and biological rhythms, sensory processes, and motor functioning. DN supports cognitive neuroscience research using methods ranging from the molecular to the behavioral to address mechanisms of how attention, learning, memory, and language change with age and experience. DN supports basic, population, and clinical research on the etiology, diagnosis, and treatment of AD and other age-related neurodegenerative diseases. DN has supported the development of neuropsychological batteries including the NIH Toolbox. The Alzheimer's Disease Centers Program, which includes 29 centers around the country, supports a range of resources for expanding multidisciplinary research on AD as well as other aspects of age-related cognitive change.

The Division of Behavioral and Social Research (DBSR) supports basic behavioral and social research on the processes of aging at the individual and societal levels, including how people change over the adult life span and the societal impact of population aging. Areas of emphasis include health disparities; aging minds; psychological development; increasing health expectancy; health, work, and retirement; interventions and behavior change; the basic science of behavior change; and genetics, behavior, and the social environments. DBSR supports research on biopsychosocial processes linking health and behavior; cognitive functioning including decision making; human factors involved in, for example, driving or work; motivation, social behavior, and emotional function; stress, coping, and allostatic load; behavior genetics; and resilience and well-being though longitudinal studies, experiments, and randomized clinical trials of behavioral interventions. Recent intervention studies include the long-term effects of cognitive training on everyday functional outcomes in older adults and enhancing the quality of life of dementia caregivers. Interdisciplinary integration of behavioral and social science approaches is encouraged in areas such as neuroeconomics, behavioral economics, and social neuroscience, and significant cognitive and psychosocial modules have been incorporated into national longitudinal studies such as the Health and Retirement Study, the MacArthur Midlife Survey, and the English Longitudinal Study on Aging.

NIA's information dissemination includes the Alzheimer's Disease Education and Referral (ADEAR) Center at http://www.nia.nih.gov/Alzheimers/ and 800-438-4380. Additional information about NIA is available at http://www.nia.nih.gov.

RICHARD J. HODES
Director, National Institute on Aging

NATIONAL INSTITUTE ON ALCOHOL ABUSE AND ALCOHOLISM

The National Institute on Alcohol Abuse and Alcoholism (NIAAA) is one of the 27 institutes and centers of the National Institutes of Health (NIH), the largest funding agency of biomedical research, both biological and behavioral, in the United States. NIAAA's name implies a mission focused on alcohol-use disorders (AUDs), consisting of alcohol abuse and alcohol dependence; and a considerable investment is made into understanding the etiology, progression, heterogeneity, prevention, and treatment of these disorders. The mission of the Institute, however, is much broader than the name suggests and includes research on alcohol use as it relates to health across the lifespan of the individual.

Alcohol has a broad range of effects on the human body, depending on the age of the individual and the level and duration of exposure to alcohol, as well as on individual genetic factors. Utilizing a lifespan perspective, NIAAA focuses on the alcohol-related issues most salient to specific life periods. Because the embryo/fetus is particularly vulnerable to adverse effects of alcohol, NIAAA has a significant research portfolio on fetal alcohol spectrum disorders (FASD), the continuum of birth defects that result from *in utero* alcohol exposure. The most severe of these is fetal alcohol syndrome (FAS), which is characterized by a constellation of effects that may include mental retardation.

Children who drink are at high risk for a number of short- and long-term adverse consequences; therefore, NIAAA is developing guidance for health care providers for screening for early alcohol use and risk for early use. For adolescents, research is focused on why alcohol is appealing to so many young people and on the consequences of adolescent alcohol use, including the association between early use, especially binge drinking, and later alcohol dependence. For older adolescents and young adults, NIAAA seeks to understand why the highest prevalence of alcohol dependence occurs in 18- to 24-year-olds, and how and why many individuals age out of harmful drinking behaviors, while others progress to chronic relapsing dependence. For adults, moderate use of alcohol appears to have certain health benefits for some individuals. Conversely, midlife is also the period when cumulative effects of heavy drinking often manifest as tissue and organ damage. For all ages, the existence of other substance abuse and/or mental disorders may complicate the etiology and treatment of AUDs.

Across NIH, there is increasing attention to the intersection of behavior and biology, especially because three of the leading causes of morbidity and mortality in developed countries—poor diet and lack of exercise, tobacco, and alcohol—have a large behavioral component. With advances in science and technology, the age-old debate about the role of nature versus nurture has evolved into a much more complex analysis of the interplay between genes and environment and their reciprocal influences. NIAAA plays an important role in supporting research in this area. Specifically, susceptibility to alcohol dependence has a significant genetic component (approximately 50%). Ongoing studies are identifying genes that underlie this susceptibility and investigating how the environment influences gene expression and subsequent health and behavioral outcomes. For example, research in epigenetics (i.e., changes that affect expression of genes, but do not change the DNA sequence) is providing insights into how the environment is able to imprint experience onto the genetic code, and into understanding how resulting changes in gene expression influence behavior as well as contribute to cell and tissue damage.

Although researchers are not able to fully model human behavior in rats or even non-human primates, animal models have been central to progress in identifying genes and neural circuits involved in various aspects of alcohol dependence, such as reward, motivation, and tolerance. Animal studies have shown how variations in genetic background can alter the influence of environmental factors and established links between anxiety and alcohol use. In addition, it has been possible to determine the effects of heavy doses of alcohol on the brains of adolescent animals and how they differ from adults, studies that are not ethical in humans. To fully understand human behavior, however, human studies are essential. NIAAA supports a range of human studies investigating motivation and reward, the neuroeconomics of alcohol use, behaviors associated with alcohol misuse, and prevention and treatment interventions. For example NIAAA has recently focused attention on identifying mechanisms of behavior change that can be used to identify opportunities for intervention.

Alcohol research lies at the crossroads of many areas of scientific research. Alcohol is a simple chemical substance that has a variety of biological effects on a number of different organs and tissues and may produce different consequences in different individuals, and its use both affects and is affected by behavior. Alcohol research encompasses the fields of epidemiology, neuroscience, genetics, epigenetics, pharmacology, physiology, behavioral and social science, prevention, and treatment. To move alcohol research forward, and to help the approximately 18 million Americans who suffer from alcohol abuse or dependence, will require cooperation across disciplines and the integration of knowledge from multiple scientific fields. Understanding how biology and behavior reciprocally influence each other holds tremendous promise for preventing and treating alcohol-related problems. For more information about NIAAA, please visit the web site at: http://www.niaaa.nih.gov.

TING-KAI LI
National Institute on Alcohol Abuse and Alcoholism, NIH, Bethesda, MD

NATIONAL INSTITUTE ON DRUG ABUSE

The National Institute on Drug Abuse (NIDA; http://www.nida.nih.gov) is a component of the National Institutes of Health. Its mission is to lead the nation in bringing the power of science to bear on drug abuse and addiction. NIDA's work involves (1) supporting and conducting basic, clinical, and applied research across a broad range of disciplines ranging from genetics and neurobiology to behavioral and social science and (2) ensuring rapid and effective dissemination and use of research results to improve prevention and treatment and inform policy.

Addiction is defined as the compulsive, at times uncontrollable, drug craving, seeking, and use that persist even in the face of extremely negative consequences. In order to avoid confusion with physical dependence, NIDA uses the term addiction rather than drug dependence, which is the clinical term favored by the *Diagnostic and Statistical Manual of Mental Disorders* (DSM-IV-TR; American Psychiatric Association, 2000). The burden of this disease to society is enormous, with an estimated annual economic impact in the United States of more than half a trillion dollars arising from medical consequences, loss of productivity, accidents, and crime (Volkow & Li, 2005). Of particular concern is the impact of drugs and alcohol on young people, as early substance use elevates the odds of substance use disorders later in life. For example, the abuse of marijuana (Grant & Dawson, 1997) or prescription drugs (McCabe, West, Morales, Cranford, & Boyd, 2007) at a young age constitute significant risk factors for the subsequent development of addiction.

Although recent scientific advances confirm that addiction is a brain disease characterized by long-lasting and distinct physiological and molecular changes, many unanswered questions remain related to its biological causes and to the best approaches for their prevention and treatment. Some of the questions currently being investigated by NIDA-funded researchers include the following.

Why Do Some People Become Addicted and Others Do Not?

Addiction has a significant genetic component. In fact, it is estimated that 40–60% of the vulnerability to addiction can be attributed to heritable factors (Goldman, Oroszi, & Ducci, 2005). This estimate includes the contribution of the genes themselves as well as that resulting from gene-environment interactions. Genetic vulnerability for addiction is thought to reflect variability in how people metabolize the drug, their sensitivity to its reinforcing effects, and the drug-induced neuroplastic changes in reward, memory, and executive control circuits (Crabbe, 2002). However, vulnerability or resistance to addiction may also reflect sensitivity to the various stressors and alternative reinforcers in an individual's environment (Rinaldi, Bauco, McCormick, Cools, & Wise, 2001). As we increase our knowledge of the individual differences in genes and gene-environment interactions that make a person more vulnerable to addiction, we will enjoy a growing ability to tailor interventions for those at high risk.

Why Does Addiction Begin Most Frequently during Adolescence?

The tendency of young people to experiment with drugs could reflect behaviors that are normally wired into the adolescent brain (risk-taking, novelty-seeking, response to peer pressure), and could also reflect the incomplete development of brain regions involved in executive control and motivation (Sowell, Thompson, & Toga, 2004). Furthermore, preclinical studies indicate that the neuroadaptations that occur in adolescents exposed to certain drugs, such as nicotine or cannabinoids, are different from those that occur during adulthood (Adriani & Laviola, 2004). Much research is currently focused on finding out whether the sensitivity to neuroadaptations during adolescence extends to other drugs and whether this phenomenon could underlie the heightened addiction vulnerability in those who start using alcohol, nicotine, and marijuana early in life (Baumeister & Tossmann, 2005). Better knowledge of the adolescent brain, its normal functioning, and how it responds to social stressors and reinforcers will spur better strategies to engage adolescents in productive and creative ways that will deter them from experimenting with drugs.

Why Do Addicted People Often Have Other Mental Illnesses?

Individuals suffering from a variety of different disorders (such as depression, anxiety disorder, ADHD, conduct disorder, and schizophrenia) are at a much higher risk of abusing drugs. Similarly, substance abusers and addicted individuals have a higher prevalence of mental disorders than the rest of the population. This phenomenon is likely the result of overlapping environmental, genetic, and neurobiological factors that influence substance abuse and mental illness. Such comorbidities may emerge when individuals with a mental disorder attempt to self-medicate (use of nicotine by individuals with depression or schizophrenia, for example). A more controversial interpretation, requiring additional confirmatory evidence, is the possibility that early exposure to certain drugs of abuse may increase vulnerability to other mental disorders, particularly in people whose genotypes confer increased susceptibility (the greater risk of nicotine abusers developing an anxiety disorder, for example).

What are the Neural Consequences of Environmental Risks?

Drug availability is the most obvious environmental factor that influences addiction. In fact, increased availability of cocaine and methamphetamine has contributed to the recent epidemics of addiction to these drugs. Low socioeconomic class and poor parental support are two additional factors consistently associated with a propensity to self-administer drugs, and that share stress as a potential common feature (Breese, Chu, Dayas, et al., 2005). Additional preclinical studies have provided insights into how environmental factors affect the brain and the consequent behavioral responses to drugs of abuse. Understanding the neurobiological consequences underlying the adverse environmental factors that increase the risks for drug use and addiction will lead to interventions to counteract these changes.

How Can We Repair the Brain Circuits Disrupted by Drugs?

The adaptations in the brain from chronic drug exposure seem to be long-lasting and to involve multiple brain circuits (reward, motivation, learning, inhibitory control / executive function, interoception, and mood). This suggests that new interventions for drug addiction should include strategies that enhance the saliency value of natural reinforcers (including social support), strengthen inhibitory control and executive function, decrease conditioned responses, and improve mood and interoception, if disrupted. An interesting approach is the development of medications that act synergistically with scientifically validated behavioral interventions.

What Is Volition and How Do Drugs Disrupt It?

We have finally gained important insight into how some drugs and alcohol manage to disrupt volitional mechanisms by hijacking the brain circuitry involved both in seeking natural reinforcement and in inhibiting self-control (Volkow & Fowler, 2000). This new knowledge is helping us understand why the addicted person relapses in spite of dire consequences such as loss of child custody or incarceration. Despite such advances, however, addicted individuals continue to be stigmatized by the pernicious yet enduring popular belief that their affliction stems from voluntary behavior. The loss of behavioral control in the addicted person should stimulate a renewed discussion of what constitutes volition, challenge us to further characterize and understand the neurobiological substrates disrupted by drugs, and influence our evolving strategies to optimize the return on our efforts to prevent and treat substance abuse and addiction more effectively.

REFERENCES

American Psychiatric Association. *Diagnostic and statistical manual of mental disorders* (4th ed., text rev.). Washington, DC: Author.

Baumeister, S. E., & Tossmann, P. (2005). Association between early onset of cigarette, alcohol, and cannabis use and later drug-use patterns: An analysis of a survey in European metropolises. *European Addiction Research, 11,* 92–98.

Breese, G. R., Chu, K., Dayas, C. V., et al. (2005). Stress enhancement of craving during sobriety: A risk for relapse. *Alcoholism: Clinical and Experimental Research, 29,* 185–195.

Crabbe, J. C. (2002). Genetic contributions to addiction. *Annual Review of Psychology, 53,* 435–462.

Goldman, D., Oroszi, G. & Ducci, F. (2005). The genetics of addictions: Uncovering the genes. *Nature Reviews Genetics, 6*, 521–532.

Grant, B. F., & Dawson, D. A. (1997). Age at onset of alcohol use and its association with DSM-IV alcohol abuse and dependence: Results from the National Longitudinal Alcohol Epidemiologic Survey. *Journal of Substance Abuse, 9*, 103–110.

McCabe, S. E., West, B. T., Morales, M., Cranford, J. A., & Boyd, C. J. (2007). Does early onset of non-medical use of prescription drugs predict subsequent prescription drug abuse and dependence? Results from a national study. *Addiction, 102*, 1920–1930.

Ranaldi, R., Bauco, P., McCormick, S., Cools, A. R., & Wise, R. A. (2001). Equal sensitivity to cocaine reward in addiction-prone and addiction-resistant rat genotypes. *Behavioral Pharmacology, 12*, 527–534.

Sowell, E. R., Thompson, P. M. & Toga, A. W. (2004) Mapping changes in the human cortex throughout the span of life, *Neuroscientist*, 10, 372–392.

Volkow, N. D., & Fowler, J. S. (2000). Addiction, a disease of compulsion and drive: Involvement of the orbitofrontal cortex. *Cerebral Cortex, 10*, 318–325.

Volkow, N. D., & Li, T. K. (2005). Drugs and alcohol: Treating and preventing abuse, addiction, and their medical consequences. *Pharmacology and Therapeutics, 108*, 3–17.

NORA D. VOLKOW
National Institute on Drug Abuse

See also: **Drug Addiction**

NATIONAL INSTITUTES OF HEALTH

The National Institutes of Health (NIH), the nation's medical research agency, is the primary federal agency for supporting and conducting medical research, including basic, clinical, and translational research. Leading the way to important medical discoveries that improve health and save lives, NIH scientists investigate ways to prevent disease as well as to discover the causes, treatments, and cures for both common diseases and the more than 6,000 rare diseases that affect our nation's citizenry. NIH also contributes knowledge about disease to the global community and collaborates on international health threats. For more than a century, NIH has played a key role in improving the health of the nation.

Composed of 27 institutes and centers (http://www.nih.gov/icd/index.html), the NIH provides leadership and financial support to more than 3,000 institutions in all 50 states, the territories, and in more than 90 countries worldwide. Some 83% of the NIH's more than $29 billion budget supports 325,000 scientists and their work across the country and around the world. Some

of the results of the discoveries supported by NIH have resulted in increased life expectancy, improved quality of life, and reduction in death from stroke, heart attack, and SIDS. The number of AIDS-related deaths fell about 70% in recent years. Infectious diseases, such as rubella, whooping cough, and pneumococcal pneumonia, that once killed and disabled millions of people, are now prevented by vaccines. The quality of life for 19 million Americans suffering with depression has improved as a result of more effective psychotherapy and medication.

Ongoing research includes applying what was learned from the sequencing of the human genome and setting a new course for developing ways to diagnose and treat such diseases such as cancer, Parkinson's disease, and Alzheimer's disease, as well as rare diseases that often contribute insights into more known diseases. Epigenetic mechanisms, affected by development (*in utero*, childhood), environmental chemicals, drugs/pharmaceuticals, aging, and diet will yield better understanding of mental disorders, cancer, autoimmune disease, and diabetes. New and more precise ways to treat cancer are emerging, such as drugs that zero in on abnormal proteins in cancer. Prevention strategies for diabetes and imaging techniques have improved our pathways to understanding disease.

NIH is home to the world's largest clinical research hospital. Through clinical research, scientific discoveries are brought from the laboratory to people who need them via better treatments. More than 350,000 volunteers from across the country and around the world have participated in the program at the NIH Bethesda campus. Off-campus people volunteer everyday to research programs that NIH supports. To learn about the kinds of trials that are underway, visit http://www.clinicaltrials.gov.

The NIH has its own 6,000 scientists, supported by approximately 10% of the budget, who conduct research in the agency's laboratories, most of which are on the Bethesda, Maryland, campus. The NIH is also training the current and next generation of researchers to ensure that the capability to advance medical science remains strong. Many of these scientists-in-training will become leading medical researchers and educators at universities; medical, dental, nursing, and pharmacy schools; schools of public health; nonprofit health research foundations; and private medical research laboratories around the country. NIH has developed strategic programs to bridge the careers of those entering science and support them to independence. NIH is also committed to a diverse workforce and has developed programs to ensure that workforce.

NIH is working toward a future in medicine that is preemptive, predictive, personalized, and participatory. Through new predictive strategies, NIH-supported scientists hope to begin to conquer disease before the first symptoms appear. Additionally, medicines and therapies must truly fit the medical needs of the individual. NIH has focused on partnering with clinical trials participants and seeking public input to the work of the agency. NIH creates many opportunities for the public to obtain information that is science-based, accurate, and timely with the greatest ease. Special programs address the special access needs of a variety of publics.

Some 122 individuals supported by NIH have been awarded the Nobel Prize for the excellence and innovation of their research. For NIH research results, health information resources, or breaking science, visit http://www.nih.gov.

ELIAS A. ZERHOUNI
National Institutes of Health

NATIONAL REGISTER OF HEALTH SERVICE PROVIDERS IN PSYCHOLOGY

The National Register of Health Service Providers in Psychology (National Register) was established in 1974 by the American Board of Professional Psychology (ABPP) at the request of the American Psychological Association (APA) Board of Directors. The impetus for the National Register's establishment was a movement towards national health insurance; the National Register was created as a mechanism to identify licensed psychologists who would qualify for reimbursement as providers of behavioral healthcare services.

Immediately the National Register attracted great interest. APA President Albert Bandura and National Register President Carl Zimet sent a letter in 1975 to licensed psychologists inviting them to apply for the National Register credential. By the end of 1975, 6,900 psychologists were credentialed and by the end of 1978 the number grew to 11,000 (Wellner & Zimet, 1983). Although national health insurance never emerged, the National Register quickly grew into the largest credentialing organization for psychologists, and remains so today.

To qualify for the National Register Health Service Provider in Psychology credential, licensed psychologists are required to demonstrate completion of an approved doctoral program in psychology, as well as a year of internship and a year of postdoctoral experience, both in health service delivery. Throughout the 1970s and 1980s, the National Register's primary function was to identify qualified health service providers to insurers and healthcare organizations.

The exponential growth of the managed care industry in the 1990s shifted the emphasis from the distinctive qualifications of providers to those who would provide services at the lowest cost. This led the National Register to a shift in its core function. A notable example of this shift occurred in the late 1990s. Responding to calls for flexibility in licensing statutes in order to meet healthcare

demands in underserved areas around the country, the National Register initiated a program to enhance licensure mobility. Working with state licensing boards and state psychological associations, the National Register negotiated agreements with licensing boards so that psychologists who possessed the National Register credential could qualify for expedited licensure. This has proved to be extremely successful in serving jurisdictions and individual psychologists (43 jurisdictions in the United States and Canada use the National Register to expedite mobility; more than 750 credentialed psychologists have benefited).

Recognizing that the need to document coursework and experience for a license before receipt of the doctoral degree, the National Register in 1999 instituted a credentials review program for doctoral students, the National Psychology Training Register. To assist doctoral students and early career professionals, the National Register made credentialing scholarships available to ease the financial burden.

The National Register's commitment to consumers led it to launch in 2006 the consumer web site http://www.findapsychologist.org, allowing consumers to conduct free, confidential searches of approximately 12,000 registrants by location, areas of expertise, language spoken, and other characteristics, and to contact the psychologist via confidential information. This site also serves as a consumer resource for psychological information.

Although healthcare organizations continue to use the National Register to verify the credentials of psychologists, the National Register's role has evolved and broadened. These changes are reflected in a new mission statement adopted in 2005.

> The National Register of Health Service Providers in Psychology credentials licensed psychologists, promotes credentialed psychologists to consumers, provides distinction and value to its Registrants, guides psychology students toward credentialing, and enhances psychologists' contributions to integrated health care.

JUDY E. HALL
MORGAN T. SAMMONS
National Register of Health Service Providers in Psychology

NATURE-NURTURE CONTROVERSY

The so-called nature-nurture controversy is a family of controversies about the relative roles of heredity (nature) and environment (nurture) in shaping human characteristics. These controversies exist not so much because the scientific questions involved are difficult—although many are—but because the proposed alternative solutions are perceived as having profound implications for cherished beliefs concerning human equality, social justice, and individual responsibility.

Although precursors of the nature-nurture controversy may be found in the writings of the ancient Greeks, its modern form can be traced back fairly directly to the philosopher John Locke (1632–1704) on the one hand and the naturalist Charles Darwin (1809–1882) on the other.

Locke may be considered the chief ideological father of the nurture side of the controversy. In "An Essay Concerning Human Understanding," he invoked the metaphor of the mind as a blank sheet of paper on which knowledge is written by the hand of experience. His political view that all men are by nature equal and independent had a strong influence on the theorists of the American and French revolutions. In Locke's own view, human political equality was not inconsistent with an inborn diversity of human tendencies and capabilities. In *Some Thoughts Concerning Education* (1934/1683) he wrote: "Some men by the unalterable frame of their constitutions are stout, others timorous, some confident, others modest, tractable, or obstinate, curious, or careless, quick or slow. There are not more differences in men's faces, and the outward lineaments of their bodies, than there are in the makes and tempers of their minds" (§101). Nevertheless, Locke judged the bulk of human variation to be the result of differences in experience: "I think I may say, that of all the men we meet with, nine parts of ten are what they are, good or evil, useful or not, by their education" (§1).

Darwin gave the nature side of the controversy its modern form by placing the human mind solidly in the framework of biological evolution. In books such as *The Descent of Man* and *The Expression of the Emotions in Man and Animals,* Darwin made it clear that human behavior shared common ancestry with the behavior of other animal forms, and that behavioral as well as physical characters were subject to the basic evolutionary mechanism of genetic variation, followed by natural selection of the variants most successful in their environments. Darwin's younger cousin Sir Francis Galton enthusiastically brought Darwin's ideas to the interpretation of human differences. Galton invented mental testing, and he also founded the eugenics movement, which aimed to improve humanity by encouraging the more able to have larger families and the less able to have smaller ones.

Another aspect of the Darwinian continuity of humans with other animals was emphasized by the psychologist William McDougall in the early part of the twentieth century. McDougall developed a social psychology around the doctrine of instincts, the idea that "the human mind has certain innate or inherited tendencies which are the essential springs or motive powers of all thought and action" (1926/1908, p. 20). Examples of such inherited tendencies cited by McDougall were the instincts of gregariousness, self-assertion, curiosity, flight, repulsion, pugnacity, acquisition, construction, parental care, and reproduction.

Both McDougall's instinct doctrine and the Galtonian notion of inherited individual differences in capacities were vigorously rejected in the radical behaviorism of the psychologist John B. Watson, who in 1925 issued a famous challenge: "Give me a dozen healthy infants, well-formed, and my own specified world to bring them up in and I'll guarantee to take any one at random and train him to become any type of specialist I might select … regardless of his talents, penchants, tendencies, abilities, vocations, and race of his ancestors" (1958/1925, p. 82).

The next few decades of the nature-nurture debate were marked by an increasing emphasis on empirical research, involving identical and fraternal twins, adoptive families, and other informative groups. In 1959 lectures (published in 1962 as *Mankind Evolving*), the geneticist Theodosius Dobzhansky elegantly integrated Darwinian concepts with an appreciation of the role of culture in human evolution and Lockean democratic ideals. By 1960, with the publication of the textbook *Behavior Genetics* by J. L. Fuller, a biologist, and W. R. Thompson, a psychologist, it appeared that the nature-nurture controversy might at last be accepted as ordinary science.

The calm was illusory. In 1969 the educational psychologist Arthur R. Jensen published a long article in the *Harvard Educational Review* entitled "How much can we boost IQ and scholastic achievement?" Jensen took a fairly strong hereditarian position, estimating that about 80% of individual variation in IQ was genetic. To make matters worse, he conjectured that at least part of the persistent disadvantage of U.S. blacks in IQ test performance was also genetic in origin.

In 1974, the psychologist Leon Kamin in *The Science and Politics of IQ.* launched an assault on human behavior genetics and its political uses. A more moderate critique was that of the sociologist Christopher Jencks and his colleagues in *Inequality* (1972). Then in 1975, a new front opened up with the publication by the zoologist Edward O. Wilson of *Sociobiology,* which outlined a modern population-genetic basis for the notion that biological instincts might play a central role in human affairs. Not all of the action inspired by these controversies was genteel academic debate—tires were slashed and speakers assaulted. In 1994, a new round of controversy was touched off by R. J. Herrnstein and C. Murray's book *The Bell Curve,* which examined the role of intelligence in American life.

Early in the twenty-first century, with cloning and the sequencing of the human genome in the news, and Nobel prizewinners and Harvard presidents resigning under fire for comments about possible genetic contributions to group differences, it appears that nature-nurture controversies are far from having run their course. It would not do to conclude, however, that no progress has been made since the days of Locke and Darwin. Modern views of biological evolution, while deriving from Darwin, are more complex, differentiated, and mathematical than his and incorporate a much advanced genetics. Modern psychology takes—in its better moments—a vastly more sophisticated view of the organism-environment interplay than the instinct lists of McDougall or the behavioristic battle cries of Watson. Finally, nature-nurture controversialists must accommodate their prejudices to a much larger body of relevant evidence nowadays. Even though nature-nurture controversies continue, they themselves also evolve.

REFERENCES

Fuller, J. L., & Thompson, W. R. (1960). *Behavior genetics*. New York: John Wiley & Sons.

Herrnstein, R. J., & Murray, C. (1994). *The bell curve: Intelligence and class structure in American life*. New York: Free Press.

Jencks, C., Smith, M., Acland, H., Bane, M. J., Cohen, D., Gintis, H., et al. (1972). *Inequality: A reassessment of the effects of family and schooling in America*. New York: Basic Books.

Jensen, A. R. (1969). How much can we boost IQ and scholastic achievement? *Harvard Educational Review, 39*, 1–123.

Kamin, L. J. (1974). *The science and politics of IQ*. Hillsdale, N.J.: Lawrence Erlbaum.

Locke, J. (1934/1683). *Some thoughts concerning education*. Cambridge, UK: Cambridge University Press.

McDougall, W. (1926/1908). *An introduction to social psychology*. Boston: Luce.

Watson, J. B. (1958/1925). *Behaviorism*. New York: Norton.

Wilson, E. O. (1975). *Sociobiology: The new synthesis*. Cambridge, MA: Harvard University Press.

SUGGESTED READINGS

Dobzhansky, T. (1962). *Mankind evolving: The evolution of the human species*. New Haven, CT: Yale University Press.

Hunt, M. (1999). *The new know-nothings: The political foes of the scientific study of human behavior*. New Brunswick, NJ: Transaction Press.

Plomin, R., DeFries, J. C., McClearn, G. E., & Rutter, M. (2001). *Behavioral genetics* (4th ed.). New York: Worth.

JOHN C. LOEHLIN
University of Texas at Austin

See also: **Evolutionary Psychology; Genetics and General Intelligence**

NEAR-DEATH EXPERIENCES

Near-death experiences are profound psychological events occurring to individuals close to death or facing intense physical or emotional danger. Although the term *near-death experience* and its acronym NDE were not coined until 1975, accounts of similar events can be found in the folklore and writings of most cultures. The phenomenon was first described as a clinical syndrome by Heim in 1892, although isolated cases appeared in medical journals throughout the 19th century. Once thought to be rare, NDEs have been documented to occur in 10% to 20% of cardiac arrest survivors.

Moody (1975), who coined the term *near-death experience*, used it to refer to an ineffable experience on the threshold of death that may include hearing oneself pronounced dead, feelings of peace, unusual noises, a sense of movement through a dark tunnel, a sense of being out of the physical body, meeting other spiritual beings, meeting a being of light, a life review, a border or point of no return, and a return to the physical body, followed by profound changes in attitudes and values and elimination of one's fear of death. Noyes and Slymen (1979) factor analyzed the features reported by near-death experiencers into (1) depersonalization elements, such as loss of emotion, separation from the body, and feeling strange or unreal; (2) hyperalertness elements, such as vivid and rapid thoughts and sharper vision and hearing; and (3) mystical elements, such as a feeling of great understanding, vivid images, and revival of memories. Ring (1980) proposed a model of NDEs unfolding in sequential stages of peace and contentment, detachment from the physical body, entering a darkness, seeing a brilliant light, and entering a supernal realm of existence.

Some investigators have identified different types of NDE. Sabom (1982) categorized NDEs as autoscopic, involving an apparent out-of-body experience; as transcendental, involving an apparent passage of consciousness into another dimension; or as combined, involving features of both types. Greyson (1985) classified NDEs as cognitive, dominated by altered thought processes; as affective, dominated by changes in emotional state; as paranormal, involving purported psychic elements; or as transcendental, characterized by apparently mystical or otherworldly features.

How one comes close to death may influence the type of NDE. NDEs dominated by cognitive features, such as temporal distortions, accelerated thoughts, and a life review, are more common in near-death events that are sudden and unexpected than in those that may have been anticipated. NDEs associated with cardiac arrest resemble out-of-body experiences, whereas those without cardiac arrest are more similar to depersonalization, in which one feels oneself or one's body to be unreal. NDEs experienced by intoxicated persons tend to be bizarre and confused, like hallucinations. Although all elements of the NDE can be reported by individuals who merely perceive themselves to be near death, encounters with a brilliant light, enhanced cognitive function, and positive emotions are more common among individuals whose closeness to death can be corroborated by medical records (Kelly, Greyson, & Kelly, 2006).

Retrospective studies of near-death experiencers show them to be psychologically healthy individuals who do not differ from comparison groups in age, gender, race, religion, religiosity, mental illness, intelligence, neuroticism, extroversion, trait and state anxiety, or relevant Rorschach measures. Some studies suggest that the experiencers are good hypnotic subjects, remember their dreams more often, are adept at mental imagery, and tend to acknowledge more childhood trauma and resultant dissociative tendencies than nonexperiencers. It is not known whether these personal traits and recall of prior experiences are the results of an NDE or premorbid characteristics that predispose people to have NDEs when they come close to death.

Several physiological and psychological models have been proposed to explain NDEs, although there has been almost no research testing etiological hypotheses. A plausible psychological explanation suggests that NDEs are products of the imagination, constructed from personal and cultural expectations to protect us from facing the threat of death. However, individuals often report experiences that conflict with their specific religious and personal expectations of death. Although there are some cross-cultural variations in the content of NDEs, these may reflect simply the experiencers' difficulty processing and expressing an experience that is largely ineffable. Specific knowledge individuals had about NDEs previously does not influence the details of their own experiences; people who have never heard or read of NDEs describe the same kinds of experiences as do people who are quite familiar with the phenomenon. Furthermore, children too young to have received substantial cultural and religious conditioning about death report the same kinds of NDEs as do adults; some cases have been reported to have occurred before the child could have acquired any language skills.

Several neurobiological models have been proposed for the near-death experience, invoking the role of endorphins or various neurotransmitters and linking the NDE to specific sites in the brain. At this point, such models are speculative, and none has been tested. A plausible assumption is that NDEs are hallucinations produced either by drugs given to dying patients or by metabolic disturbances or brain malfunctions as a person approaches death. However, many NDEs are recounted by individuals who had no metabolic or organic conditions known to cause hallucinations. Organic brain malfunctions generally produce clouded thinking, irritability, fear, belligerence, and idiosyncratic visions, which are quite incompatible with the exceptionally clear thinking, peacefulness, calmness, and predictable content that typify near-death experiences. Visions in patients with delirium are generally of living persons, whereas those in NDEs are almost invariably of deceased persons. Furthermore, patients who are febrile, anoxic, or given drugs when near death report fewer and less elaborate NDEs than do patients who remain drug-free. That finding may suggest that drug- or metabolically-induced delirium, rather than causing NDEs, in fact inhibits them from occurring, or

alternatively that delirious patients tend not to recall their experiences upon recovery (Kelly, Greyson, & Kelly, 2006).

Behind most physiological theories of NDEs is the belief that abnormal activity of the limbic system or the temporal lobes produces NDE-like experiences. Most of the experiences induced by electrical stimulation of these areas consist of hearing bits of music or singing, seeing isolated and repetitive scenes that seemed familiar, hearing voices, experiencing fear or other negative emotions, or seeing bizarre imagery that is often described as dreamlike. Subsequent researchers have found similar experiential phenomena associated with temporal lobe activity, especially fear and fragmented, distorted experiences quite unlike NDEs.

The major features associated with NDEs can occur in a wide variety of conditions in which the person is clearly not near death. However, despite the wide variety of physiological and psychological conditions under which NDEs occur, many such experiences clearly do occur when the brain is severely impaired. The challenge for explanatory models for NDEs is to take into account the vivid and complex thinking, sensations, and memory formation under conditions in which current neuroscientific models of the mind deem them impossible, such as under general anesthesia and in cardiac arrest. Some have argued that, even in the presence of a flat EEG, some residual brain activity may persist that could account for mental activity typical of NDEs. However, the issue is not whether there is any brain activity, but whether there is the type of brain activity that is necessary for conscious experience. Such activity is detectable by EEG, and it is abolished both by anesthesia and by cardiac arrest, two conditions in which NDEs frequently occur. In cardiac arrest, even neuronal action-potentials, the ultimate physical basis for coordination of neural activity between widely separated brain regions, are rapidly abolished. Moreover, cells in the hippocampus, essential for memory formation, are especially vulnerable to the effects of anoxia. Thus it is not plausible that NDEs under anesthesia or in cardiac arrest can be accounted for by a hypothetical residual capacity of the brain to process and store complex information under those conditions

Regardless of their cause, NDEs may permanently and dramatically alter the individual experiencer's attitudes, beliefs, and values. Aftereffects most often reported and corroborated in long-term follow-up studies, including interviews with near-death experiencers' significant others, include increased spirituality, compassion and concern for others, appreciation of life, belief in postmortem existence, sense of purpose, and confidence and flexibility in coping with life's vicissitudes; and decreased fear of death, interest in materialism, and competitiveness. Although decreased fear of death has been associated with increased suicidal risk, near-death experiencers paradoxically express stronger objections to suicide than do comparison samples, primarily on the basis of increased transcendental beliefs (Kelly, Greyson, & Kelly, 2006; Ring, 1980; Sabom, 1982).

REFERENCES

Greyson, B. (1985). A typology of near-death experiences. *American Journal of Psychiatry, 142*, 967–969.

Heim, A. (1892). Notizen über den Tod durch Absturz. *Jahrbuch der Schweitzerischen Alpclub, 27*, 327–337.

Kelly, E. W., Greyson, B., & Kelly, E. F. (2006). Unusual experiences near death and related phenomena. In E. F. Kelly, E. W. Kelly, A. Crabtree, A. Gauld, M. Grosso, & B. Greyson (Eds.), *Irreducible mind: Toward a psychology for the 21st century* (pp. 367–421). Lanham, MD: Rowman & Littlefield.

Moody, R. A. (1975). *Life after life*. Covington, GA: Mockingbird Books.

Noyes, R., & Slymen, D. J. (1979). The subjective response to life-threatening danger. *Omega, 9*, 313–321.

Ring, K. (1980). *Life at death: A scientific investigation of the near-death experience*. New York: Coward, McCann and Geoghegan.

Sabom, M. (1982). *Recollections of death: A medical investigation*. New York: Harper & Row.

SUGGESTED READINGS

Fox, M. (2003). *Religion, spirituality and the near-death experience*. London: Routledge.

Greyson, B. (2000). Near-death experience. In E. Cardeña, S. Lynn, & S. Krippner (Eds.), *Varieties of anomalous experience: Examining the scientific evidence* (pp. 315–352). Washington, DC: American Psychological Association.

Woerlee, G. M. (2004). *Mortal minds: A biology of the soul and the dying experience*. Utrecht, The Netherlands: de Tijdstrom.

BRUCE GREYSON
University of Virginia Health System

See also: Hallucinations; Stress Consequences

NEED FOR ACHIEVEMENT (See Achievement Need)

NEED FOR AFFILIATION (See Affiliation Need)

NEO PERSONALITY INVENTORY (NEO-PI-R)

The NEO Personality Inventory-Revised (NEO PI-R; Costa & McCrae, 1992) is the updated version of the NEO PI (Costa & McCrae, 1985). The NEO PI-R is a widely used measure of the Five Factor Model (FFM) of adult personality, covering the domains of Neuroticism, Openness to Experience, Extraversion, Agreeableness, and Conscientiousness. The FFM is a robust model of normal personality, with a factor structure that has been replicated across many languages and cultures (McCrae et al., 2005). Information on these factors can be useful for understanding emotional, interpersonal, attitudinal, and motivational characteristics that are important for a variety of applications, including psychotherapy, counseling, and employment decisions. The NEO PI-R has also become a major research tool for examining the relationship between personality and behavioral, physical, and mental health variables. It is not intended, however, to assess overt or severe psychopathology, and it is not necessarily diagnostic of any specific psychiatric disorder found in the *Diagnostic and Statistical Manual of Mental Disorders* (DSM; American Psychiatric Association, 2000).

The NEO grew out of the tradition spawned by the Lexical Hypothesis (LH) of personality: The most important individual differences in personality will be encoded in the natural language as single terms. Development of the original NEO began in the 1970s, when Costa and McCrae were studying personality factors important in aging. The instrument was initially confined to the domains of Neuroticism, Extraversion, and Openness. This was followed by the NEO PI, which added narrower, eight-item "facet scales" to the original three domains as well as broad measures of two new domains, Agreeableness and Conscientiousness. The final NEO PI-R added facet scales to the Agreeableness and Conscientiousness domains, bringing the total number of these focused indices to 30. Information provided by the instrument is said to capture the majority of relevant variance in normal personality characteristics (Costa & McCrae, 1992).

The NEO PI-R is appropriate for individuals 17 years of age and older with at least a sixth-grade reading level. Two full-length forms exist—Observer (R) and Self (S)—consisting of 240 items answered on a 5-point Likert scale ranging from "strongly disagree" to "strongly agree." The Observer report form is a particular strength of the instrument, as no other popular alternatives include this standardized format. Individual or group administrations may be used, and time to completion is typically between 35 and 45 minutes. Gender-based norms are available for both college students and adults. Sixty-item short forms exist (NEO FFI, NEO FFI-R, and NEO-60), as well as a revision for adolescents (the NEO PI-3; McCrae, Costa, & Martin, 2005). The test has been translated into multiple languages (McCrae et al., 2005), and computerized scoring programs and reports are available from the publisher.

Assessing Protocol Validity

In cases where individuals may not fully attend to the questions or may attempt to portray themselves in an inaccurate manner (e.g., by exaggerating or minimizing certain characteristics), it is helpful to have means of assessing response integrity. The NEO PI-R includes three final questions addressing validity issues. These items inquire about item completion, response honesty, and response accuracy. However, the transparency of these questions probably precludes them from being useful in cases in which evaluees have strong motivation to deny misrepresentation, such as forensic evaluations. In these cases, ratings on the Observer form by a disinterested party who knows the subject well may offer a form of validity check. However, the NEO PI-R was not intended for use in samples in which response distortion is common (e.g., forensic assessments), and it should thus not be administered in such settings without an accompanying validated, independent check of response validity.

Because the NEO PI-R is frequently used in research settings where individuals may not be fully invested, and because questions of response accuracy may arise after assessment with the NEO PI-R in clinical settings, interest in developing supplemental validity scales grew after the test's publication. Schinka, Kinder, and Kremer (1997) first proposed positive presentation management, negative presentation management, and inconsistency indices, which have been cross-validated primarily in simulation studies. Respectably high effect sizes separating simulators and psychopathological respondents have been demonstrated (Berry, Bagby, Smerz, Rinaldo, Caldwell-Andrews, & Baer, 2001). Additionally, strong sensitivity and specificity values have been reported in known groups of positive and negative impression-managing evaluees (Morasco, Gfeller, & Elder, 2007). However, insufficient research exists to date to provide consistent cutting scores on these scales for clinical or forensic use.

Personality Domains and Facets

Neuroticism

The Neuroticism domain most closely relates to general psychological distress, although, as previously noted, it is not intended to diagnose any specific psychiatric disorder. Rather, it measures the tendency to experience negative affect as well as difficulty coping with distress. Individuals with high scores on this domain may or may not qualify for a psychiatric diagnosis. Individuals low on Neuroticism are likely calm, even-tempered, and able to handle stressful situations effectively. The facets measured as part of the Neuroticism domain include Anxiety (N1), Angry Hostility (N2), Depression (N3), Self-Consciousness (N4), Impulsiveness (N5), and Vulnerability (N6).

Extraversion

The Extraversion domain on the NEO PI-R measures the extent to which an individual prefers social interaction, large groups, and excitement, in contrast to individuals who may be more reserved, less active, and more likely to avoid social situations. This domain is sometimes conceptualized as the tendency to experience positive emotions. Individuals scoring low on the Extraversion domain are not necessarily socially anxious or unhappy, but rather typically prefer smaller groups or time alone. The facets of the Extraversion domain include Warmth (E1), Gregariousness (E2), Assertiveness (E3), Activity (E4), Excitement-Seeking (E5), and Positive Emotions (E6).

Openness to Experience

Individuals high on the Openness to Experience domain tend to have strong aesthetic appreciation, intellectual curiosity, and emotional sensitivity. They are likely to be in tune with their feelings and enjoy abstract theories or challenges. In contrast, low scorers on this domain may be more conventional, conservative, and appreciative of familiarity. As with the other domains, low scorers on O are not necessarily less psychologically healthy, but rather typically appreciate more structured, predictable environments. The facets of Openness to Experience are Fantasy (O1), Aesthetics (O2), Feelings (O3), Actions (O4), Ideas (O5), and Values (O6).

Agreeableness

The domain of Agreeableness measures the extent to which an individual is inherently altruistic, trusting, cooperative, and sympathetic to others. As with the other domains, neither high nor low scores are viewed as inherently healthier, but rather need to be considered in terms of how adaptive they are in the individual's environment. The Agreeableness facets include Trust (A1), Straightforwardness (A2), Altruism (A3), Compliance (A4), Modesty (A5), and Tender-Mindedness (A6).

Conscientiousness

Conscientiousness, as measured by the NEO PI-R, is comprised of such qualities as organization, planning, reliability, and achievement striving. High-scoring individuals are reliable and pay close attention to detail, while individuals low on this domain may show less motivation for perfection or high achievement, and are often less organized and punctual. Extreme scores on either pole can be problematic, although not necessarily pathological, and the importance of such traits is highly environmentally dependent. The facets of Conscientiousness are Competence (C1), Order (C2), Dutifulness (C3), Achievement Striving (C4), Self-Discipline (C5), and Deliberation (C6).

Reliability and Validity

Reports on the reliability and validity of the NEO PI-R have been quite positive. Internal consistency values range from .87 on the Openness to Experience domain to .92 on the Neuroticism domain. Similarly, internal consistency values for the facets are acceptable for such short scales, ranging from .56 to .81. Three-month test-retest reliabilities are good—.79 for N, .79 for E, .80 for O, .75 for A, and .83 for C—and multi-year reliabilities are comparably strong (Costa & McCrae, 1992). Regarding validity, the five-factor structure measured by the NEO PI-R has, as previously noted, been replicated repeatedly across multiple languages and cultures (McCrae et al., 2005) Further, convergent and discriminant validity of the factors and facets have been supported by dozens of studies, and correlations of self and observer ratings have been moderately high (Costa & McCrae, 1992).

Special Considerations and Applications

Although the NEO PI-R is not intended to be a diagnostic instrument, given that DSM-IV-TR Axis II personality disorders may be considered as maladaptive variants of normal personality characteristics, much recent research has focused on the potential utility of the NEO PI-R for conceptualizing and studying these conditions. Widiger and Lowe (2007) outlined several methods for applying the NEO PI-R and other instruments that assess the FFM to describing personality disorders. They conclude that, given the apparent limitations in understanding personality disorders as categorical variables, as well as the growing evidence for the effectiveness of the dimensional FFM in assessing these conditions, the NEO PI-R is a potentially useful instrument for studying personality disorders.

REFERENCES

American Psychiatric Association. (2000). *Diagnostic and statistical manual of mental disorders* (4th ed., text rev.). Washington, D.C. Author.

Berry, D. T. R., Bagby, R. M., Smerz, J., Rinaldo, J. C., Caldwell-Andrews, A., & Baer, R. A. (2001). Effectiveness of NEO-PI-R research validity scales for discriminating analog malingering and genuine psychopathology. *Journal of Personality Assessment, 76,* 496–516.

Costa, P. T., & McCrae, R. R. (1992). *Revised NEO Personality Inventory (NEO-PI-R) and NEO Five-Factor Inventory (NEO-FFI) professional manual.* Lutz, FL: Psychological Assessment Resources.

Costa, P. T., & McCrae, R. R. (1999). *Inventario NEO reducido de cinco factores (NEO-FFI) manual professional.* Madrid: TEA Ediciones.

McCrae, R. R., Costa, P. T., & Martin, T. A. (2005). The NEO-PI-3: A more readable Revised NEO Personality Inventory. *Journal of Personality Assessment, 84,* 261–270.

McCrae, R. R., Terracciano, A., & 78 Members of the Personality Profiles of Cultures Project. (2005). Universal features of personality traits from the observer's perspective: Data from 50 cultures. *Journal of Personality and Social Psychology, 88,* 547–561.

Morasco, B. J., Gfeller, J. D., & Elder, K. A. (2007). The utility of the NEO-PI-R validity scales to detect response distortion: A comparison with the MMPI-2. *Journal of Personality Assessment, 88,* 276–283.

Schinka, J. A., Kinder, B. N., & Kremer, T. (1997). Research validity scales for the NEO-PI-R: Development and initial validation. *Journal of Personality Assessment, 68,* 127–138.

Widiger, T. A. & Lowe, J. R. (2007). Five-Factor Model assessment of Personality Disorder. *Journal of Personality Assessment, 89,* 16–29.

SUGGESTED READINGS

Malouff, J. M., Thorsteinsson, E. B., & Schutte, N. S. (2005). The relationship between the Five-Factor Model of Personality and Symptoms of Clinical Disorders: A meta-analysis. *Journal of Psychopathology and Behavioral Assessment, 27,* 101–114.

McCrae, R. R. (2002). NEO-PI-R data from 36 cultures: Further intercultural comparisons. In J. Allik & R. R. McCrae (Eds.), *The Five-Factor model of personality across cultures* (pp. 105–125). New York: Kluwer Academic/Plenum.

Sanderson, C., & Clarkin, J. F. (2002). Further use of the NEO-PI-R personality dimensions in differential treatment planning. In T. A. Widiger & P. T. Costa (Eds.), *Personality disorders and the five-factor model of personality* (2nd ed.) (pp. 351–375). Washington, D.C.: American Psychiatric Association.

LINDSEY J. SCHIPPER
MYRIAM J. SOLLMAN
DAVID T. R. BERRY
University of Kentucky

See also: Five-Factor Model of Personality; Personality Assessment; Self-Report Inventories

NEOCORTEX

Two cerebral hemispheres comprise the most anterior and visible portion of the mammalian brain. In humans, most of the surface of these hemispheres is covered by highly convoluted neocortex ("cortex," derived from Greek, meaning bark or covering). Neocortex is found only in mammals and is differentiated from more primitive types of cortex by a complex morphology and lamination pattern. This tissue may be considered the "crown jewel" of mammalian evolution, having expanded more than any other brain region during our evolutionary history. The characteristic convolutions of the cortical surface represent a clever geometric solution to the challenge of fitting more of the two-dimensional neocortical sheet into a braincase without unduly increasing the size of the head. In humans, the neocortex occupies about 80% of the brain mass and is essential for cognitive functions such as rational thought, language, perception, and goal directed behavior.

The neocortex is approximately 2 mm thick and consists of some 12 billion neurons. About 70% of these are large pyramidal shaped cells, and the remainder are smaller stellate shaped cells. Functionally, cortical neurons may be classified based on whether they excite or inhibit their synaptic targets. Whereas pyramidal neurons are excitatory, different types of stellate neurons may be either excitatory or inhibitory. An imbalance of excitation and inhibition can lead to pathological states such as epileptic seizure activity.

Most of the neocortex is made up of six distinct layers of cell bodies and processes. These layers differ from one another in the size and density of their cell bodies and in the relative proportion of neurons of different types. The functional operations of the neocortex may divided into three general components: (1) reception of neural information from sub-cortical and cortical brain regions (via synaptic inputs), (2) integration of this information, and (3) organization of output signals that are projected to the many targets of the neocortex. The cortical layering pattern is related to these basic functions. For example, layer IV of sensory neocortex receives information from lower sensory structures. This information is integrated, and synaptic excitation flows upward and downward to superficial and deeper layers of the cortex.

Finally, pyramidal neurons within these various layers further integrate this information and project the results of this processing (in the form of trains of action potentials) to both subcortical and cortical targets. This vertical spread of activation reflects the organization of the cortex into functional columns or modules, which have been found in many cortical regions. Thus, the cortical column represents a basic functional processing unit, consisting of thousands of neurons spanning the six cortical layers. The entire neocortex is thought to contain hundreds of thousands of such functional columns. The power of the mammalian neocortex as an engine of information processing is thought to derive, in part, from the simultaneous, parallel operation of thousands of such cortical columns.

Functionally, neocortex can be divided into sensory, motor, and association areas. Each sensory modality has multiple cortical representations that are organized in a hierarchical manner. For example, the primary visual cortex, which is in the occipital lobe, performs the initial cortical processing of visual information. Higher visual cortical areas are specialized in analyzing color, motion, and other functional aspects of vision. These areas communicate their analyses to the inferotemporal cortex, which is necessary for object recognition. Thus, whereas primary visual cortex is essential for visual sensation, inferotemporal cortex is essential for perception of objects. Other sensory modalities as well as motor-related areas are organized in a similar hierarchical manner. Most of the neocortex (approximately 75%) cannot be divided into sensory or motor areas and is referred to as association cortex. There are many such areas, some of which support the highest cognitive abilities, such as language, foresight, and abstract reasoning.

Each of the two cerebral hemispheres can be divided into frontal, parietal, occipital, and temporal lobes. These cortical regions are related to certain sensory, motor, or cognitive functions. A brief overview of the main functions and clinical syndromes associated with the cortical lobes is as follows.

The occipital lobes are the hindmost cortical lobe and contain regions necessary for vision. The posterior pole of the occipital lobe is known as the primary visual cortex, and lesions here can produce blindness in the contralateral visual field. More specific visual disorders result when brain damage also includes the neighboring temporal or parietal lobe. For example, lesions to occipito-temporal regions can produce visual agnosias, such as a deficit in recognizing objects, colors, or faces, despite otherwise normal vision.

The parietal lobes constitute the dorsal and lateral area of each hemisphere and mediate somatosensory information from the body, including touch, pain, temperature, and limb position. The parietal lobes also play an important role in higher visual processing and in attending and integrating sensory information from different modalities. Parietal lobe lesions can often cause a striking deficit called unilateral neglect, in which a person ignores visual, auditory, and somatosensory information coming from the side of the body contralateral to the brain lesion.

The temporal lobes contain cortical areas involved in auditory and higher visual processing and areas crucial for learning, memory, multimodal integration, and emotion. Lesions to the temporal lobes' primary auditory area can cause partial or complete deafness. Lesions to associated areas can cause more selective hearing deficits. For example, temporal lobe lesions in the left hemisphere are often associated with disorders of speech perception, and lesions to the symmetrical areas in the right hemisphere can produce deficits in music perception. Within the temporal lobes are structures that are part of the limbic system, which is phylogenetically older than the neocortex. These structures are crucial for forming long-term memories and for emotional behavior.

The frontal lobes occupy almost one half of each cerebral hemisphere in humans. The frontal lobes play a major role in motor activity (control of body movements), participate in language functions, and are important for higher integrative functions, personality traits, emotionality, and executive control (the translation of thought into action). Damage to the primary motor area can cause paralysis on the contralateral side of the body. Fluent speech production is associated with a region (Broca's area) in the left frontal lobe. A large portion of frontal lobes called the prefrontal cortex is involved in a variety of functions involving complex cognitive functions such as problem solving, planning action toward a goal, and using information flexibly.

The two cerebral hemispheres are largely symmetrical in both structure and function. However, some important functions are organized primarily within a single hemisphere. The left hemisphere of almost all right-handed and most left-handed people is essential for many language-related functions. Injuries to specific areas of the left hemisphere often result in language related disabilities such as Broca's aphasia (difficulty with speech production), Wernicke's aphasia (difficulty with comprehension), agraphia (inability to write), and alexia (inability to read). In contrast, the right hemisphere is superior for emotional speech intonation (prosody), appreciation of humor, and visuospatial integration such as recognition of objects and faces. A massive fiber bundle, the corpus callosum, is responsible for communication between the two hemispheres and for coordinating their activity. When this pathway is destroyed, the two hemispheres may begin to act independently. The careful study of such "split-brain" patients has led to many remarkable insights into neocortical organization.

Until recently the primary methods for studying higher mental functions of the human cortex have been the electroencephalogram (for measuring large-scale brain activity) and analysis of cortical dysfunction in people with brain injury. With revolutionary, new brain imaging techniques, such as functional magnetic resonance imaging (fMRI) and magnetoencephalography (MEG), higher mental functions can be studied at higher spatial and temporal resolutions, in real time, as they occur, in healthy and intact human brains. Functional MRI reveals detailed information about regional metabolism in the brain and therefore about the level of neural activity that is elicited throughout the brain during different cognitive, sensory, and motor activities. These new methods have provided exciting new insight into the biology of cognitive functions and complex psychological concepts such as emotional responses, empathy, and altruism.

For example, newly discovered, so-called mirror neurons, have been linked to mechanisms by which we understand and imitate the actions and emotional states of other people. Several experiments have used fMRI to analyze areas of brain activity as subjects were observing an emotion in others (e.g., disgust) and while they were experiencing the same emotion. These experiments revealed that the same cortical and limbic areas become highly active when a person is experiencing an emotion (disgust, happiness, pain, etc.) and when this person sees someone else experiencing the same emotions. These findings suggest that humans perceive emotions in others by activating the same emotions in themselves, and they provide insight into the biology of neocortical capacities (such as empathy and altruism) that were previously considered beyond the reach of neurobiological investigations.

REFERENCES

Braitenberg, V., & Schulz, A. (1991). *Anatomy of the cortex: Statistics and geometry*. New York: Springer-Verlag.

Gazzaniga, M. S. (2000). Cerebral specialization and interhemispheric communication: Does the corpus callosum enable the human condition? *Brain, 123*, 1293–1326.

Heilman, K. M., & Valenstein, E. (Eds.). (2003). *Clinical neuropsychology* (4th ed.). New York: Oxford University Press.

Mountcastle, W. B. (1997). The columnar organization of the neocortex. *Brain, 120*, 701–22.

Rizzolatti, G., Fogassi, L., & Gallese, V. (2006). Mirrors of the mind. *Scientific American, 295*(5), 54–61.

White, E. (1989). *Cortical circuits*. Boston: Birkhauser.

Katarina Lukatela
Harvey A. Swadlow
Brown University Medical School

See also: **Brain; Central Nervous System; Primary Motor Cortex**

NETHERLANDS, PSYCHOLOGY IN

The year 1892 is considered as the starting date of the discipline of psychology in The Netherlands. In that year, Gerard Heymans (1857–1930), professor at the University of Groningen, set up the first psychological laboratory in the country. This laboratory was situated in his own house, and the most important subject was his wife, Anthonia, who participated in perceptual and response time experiments. On the one hand, Heymans did empirical research; on the other hand, he was engaged in systematic philosophical work, which resulted in three main books about epistemology, metaphysics, and ethics. This makes clear that psychological issues were studied within the discipline of philosophy in that period, which continued to be the case until World War II.

At the end of the 1930s, there were about 50 psychologists in The Netherlands. In 1938 a group decided to establish the Dutch Association for Practicing Psychologists (*Nederlands Instituut voor Praktizerende Psychologen, NIPP*), comparable to the American Psychological Association. The aims of NIPP were to enhance the quality of professional psychology and promote the interests of the profession. After World War II it became possible to study psychology as a separate discipline at several universities within the Netherlands, and since then there has been a continuous growth in the number of psychologists in the country. Since the 1950s, about 35,000 persons in the Netherlands have graduated with a masters degree, although about only half of them are or were working as psychologists (Van der Molen & Visser, 2008). To our knowledge, The Netherlands, with a population of 16 million people, has one of the highest density of psychologists in the world: one psychologist for every 500 to 600 inhabitants.

Education and Training

The Bologna agreement (made by 12 European ministers of education) stated that before 2009 all involved countries should move toward one system of higher education consisting of bachelor and master programs. Currently 11 universities in The Netherlands offer such programs in psychology: the University of Amsterdam, the Free University of Amsterdam, the University of Groningen, the Open University of The Netherlands in Heerlen, the University of Leiden, University Maastricht, Radboud University Nijmegen, Erasmus University Rotterdam, the University of Utrecht, the University of Tilburg, and University Twente. The length of the typical bachelor program is three years, while the length of the masters program is one year, which is different from the two-year-long masters programs in most other European countries. However, each year's workload in The Netherlands is higher than elsewhere: 42 weeks of 40 hours (1,680 hours) per year. Bachelor programs are open to students who graduated in preparatory scientific education; masters programs in psychology are open to those who finished a bachelor in psychology. There are exceptions: Most universities obtained a permit to start a highly selective two-year research masters with a more international approach (directed towards a follow-up PhD program). The quality of the psychology programs at universities are assessed every six years by a review committee that is formed by the Dutch Flemish Accreditation Organisation (NVAO). The programs are accredited by the Ministry of Education, Arts and Sciences on the basis of a positive assessment. By 2007, all the programs have received a positive evaluation of the review committee (QANU, 2007).

Prominent Lines of Research

Based among others on the work *Methodology* by De Groot (1961), one of the most famous Dutch psychologists of the twentieth century, psychological research in The Netherlands moved from a phenomenological approach to a scientific empirical approach. Since there are hundreds of highly qualified researchers and thousands of studies that they have published, it is not easy to make a selection of the most prominent lines of research. Below we give a somewhat arbitrary selection.

In the field of clinical psychological research there are many Dutch studies showing that cognitive behavioral therapy is the best treatment for different psychological disturbances. In the field of cognitive psychology, Frijda's (1987) work on *Emotions* has attracted a lot of attention. In

the field of personality, Hendriks, Hofstee, and De Raad (1999) has contributed to the theory and measurement of the Big Five personality factors. This is only one example in a long Dutch tradition that pays much attention to the development of reliable and valid test instruments for the field of selection psychology. Finally, for the field of educational psychology we refer the reader to the work of Schmidt on the method of problem based learning (PBL; see Norman & Schmidt, 1992). This PBL method has shown to be very effective in the enhancement of enduring knowledge and has been very influential all over the world, especially in the context of medical education.

Types of Applied Practice

The main field in which Dutch psychologists are working is the field of mental health care psychology, including forensic psychology; about 50% of the members of the NIPP have a job in this area. About 20% of the members of NIPP are working in the field of industrial and organizational psychology and another 20% are working in the field of developmental and educational psychology. The remaining 10% are working in other or more specialized areas, such as teaching psychology at the universities or other institutions for higher education.

There is a legislative registration procedure for psychologists in the field of mental health care that is stated in the Law for Professions in Individual Health Care. After their university graduation and before they receive the title of *health care psychologist*, students must undertake a two-year program during which they work under the supervision of a qualified psychologist and follow specialized courses. For psychologists in other fields, such as industrial and organizational psychology and developmental as well as educational psychology, the NIPP has developed registration requirements and procedures to promote the quality of the profession and to protect clients against quackery.

Future Prospects

As for psychological education, a recent development is that psychology programs are offered by schools for higher professional education. The focus of these programs is on the practical application of psychology, whereas the university programs have a more scientific focus. Nevertheless, almost 90% of the graduates coming from the universities also acquire positions in the professional field, and only about 10% find a position in the field of scientific research. The question remains regarding how the labor market will respond to graduates from the schools for higher vocational education.

As for psychological research, there is a growing interest in the influence of the neurosciences on psychological issues. Modern techniques like fMRI and EEG are used in different kinds of studies, for example, studies on the development of expertise or the development of drug addiction. These developments are based on the general conviction in The Netherlands that psychology is a biopsychosocial science.

REFERENCES

De Groot, A. D. (1969). *Methodology: Foundations of inference and research in the behavioral sciences.* The Hague: Mouton.

Frijda, N. H. (1987). *The emotions: Studies in emotions and social interaction.* Cambridge: Cambridge University Press.

Hendriks, A. A. J., Hofstee, W. K. B., & De Raad, B. (1999). The Five-Factor Personality Inventory (FFPI). *Personality and Individual Differences, 27,* 307–325.

Norman, G. R., & Schmidt, H. G. (1992). Problem-based learning: Does it prepare medical students to become better doctors? *Academic Medicine, 67,* 557–565.

Van der Molen, H. T., & Visser, K. (2008). Accountability of psychology in The Netherlands. In J. Hall & B. Altmaier (Eds.), *International accountability in professional psychology.* Oxford, UK: Oxford University Press.

QANU (2007). Onderwijsvisitatie Psychologie. [Educational Accreditation of university psychology programs]. Utrecht: QANU.

HENK T. VAN DER MOLEN
Erasmus University Rotterdam, The Netherlands

NEUROCHEMISTRY

A chemical approach to understanding the nervous system had its origins in the late nineteenth century. Early neurochemists found that mammalian brains contained large amounts of fatty substances (lipids), many of which were found to be unique to the nervous system. The human brain contains about 10% lipids, 10% protein, and 78% water, with the remaining 2% represented by DNA, RNA, electrolytes, and other small molecules. The gray matter contains mainly neuronal cell bodies and astroglia, generally regarded as support cells that are often interposed between cerebral blood vessels and neurons. White matter contains nerve axons, which are ensheathed in multilayers of lipid-rich membranes (myelin) produced by oligodendroglia (Schwann cells in peripheral nerves). Brain lipids contain long, highly unsaturated fatty acids incorporated into phospholipids, as well as glycolipids, and little or no free cholesterol or triglyceride (conventional dietary fat, also found in adipose tissue).

The human brain weighs about 1,400 grams, or 2% of total body weight. Its pale appearance belies the fact that about 20% of the total cardiac output is required to supply it with glucose and oxygen and to remove metabolic waste, principally carbon dioxide. The brain is efficient in this process and thus accounts for an even greater portion (about 25%) of the total resting basal metabolic rate. Each molecule of glucose requires 6 molecules of oxygen for its oxidation, yielding 6 molecules of carbon dioxide. In the process, chemical energy for the working of the brain is generated in the form of 38 molecules of ATP (adenosine triphosphate).

By injecting carbon-14-labeled 2-deoxyglucose, a non-metabolized glucose analog, it can be demonstrated that brain regions in animals can be selectively activated behaviorally (e.g., by visual stimulation), evidenced by increased glucose utilization. Regional cerebral blood flow (rCBF) is also increased. These approaches have been adapted for noninvasive studies in human subjects, by incorporating positron-emitting tracers such as fluorine-18 into glucose analogs and employing positron emission tomography (PET). Changes in rCBF can also be studied in the absence of radioactivity by means of functional magnetic resonance imaging (fMRI) by the BOLD (blood oxygen level dependent) imaging method.

The brain and spinal cord are separated from the rest of the body by the "blood/brain barrier" (BBB). This term refers to the observation that while most small molecules readily diffuse from the blood into body organs, if they bear an ionic charge or are hydrophilic, they are excluded from the central nervous system unless a special transport system exists, such as is the case for glucose, vitamins, and essential amino and fatty acids. While this exclusion undoubtedly protects the brain, it necessitates molecular legerdemain and ingenuity in designing neuropharmacological agents.

The high energy needs of the adult brain reflect the enormous volume of information it handles at great speed: sensory input, central processing, storage and retrieval, and output of electrically and chemically coded messages. This is all accomplished by neurons in the form of electrical impulses (neural conduction) and chemical messengers (synaptic transmission), whereby brain cells communicate with one another. In neurotransmission, action potentials, originating in dendrites or in the neuronal cell body, generally move as a rapid depolarization wave down the axon to the presynaptic region. The electrical potential is generated by the efflux of neuronal potassium and influx of sodium. Ultimately, the ionically based electrical gradients must be regenerated by neuronal sodium extrusion and potassium influx.

The chemical work to restore the gradient requires the enzyme Na^+K^+ATPase, which cleaves ATP in the process. While the direction of information flow in neurons is unidirectional—from dendrite to cell body to axon—the supply of critical materials within the neuron is centrifugal: from the cell body out to the farthest reaches of its dendrites and axons. This is important because transcription of RNA and translation into proteins take place in the cell body, and cytoskeletal elements (microtubules, neurofilaments, actin, etc.) and organelles (mitochondria, vesicles, etc.) that migrate centrifugally to the cell extremities via anterograde axonal transport, under the influence of "molecular motor" proteins, the kinesins. There is also a centripetal, or retrograde, flow process mediated by motor proteins (dyneins) and thought to transmit messages from the synapse to the nucleus, for example, with instructions to make more neurotransmitter or to initiate the repair of a damaged nerve.

At the synapse, nerves communicate by a rapid chemically mediated process. The arrival of the axonal depolarization wave at the presynaptic nerve ending causes release of neurotransmitter, a chemical messenger molecule unique to a given neuron, which traverses the synaptic cleft and binds to a specific receptor embedded in the outer membrane of a neighboring postsynaptic neuron. Known neurotransmitters include acetylcholine, glutamate, gamma-aminobutyric acid, glycine, norepinephrine, dopamine, and serotonin. They are released in packets, by the fusion of organelles known as synaptic vesicles with the presynaptic membrane in a process of exocytosis, releasing the neurotransmitters into the synaptic cleft. The emptied vesicles reform by a process of endocytosis and can be recycled. The steps leading from the depolarization wave to presynaptic neurotransmitter release involve many specialized proteins. A number of naturally occurring toxic agents, such as black widow spider venom and botulinum toxin, exert their actions by disrupting the presynaptic synaptic vesicle cycle.

The cellular process that completes the process of synaptic transmission is termed signal transduction. The released neurotransmitter serves as a ligand that binds to a highly specific membrane-spanning protein receptor molecule, the conformation of which is altered when its receptor site is occupied, usually by a guanine nucleotide-binding protein (G-protein), which is coupled to the activation or block of an intracellular second messenger system. The most prominent second messenger systems are mediated by the formation of cAMP (adenosine 3', 5'-cyclic monophosphate) or by the cleavage of the lipid phosphatidylinositol bisphosphate into inositol trisphosphate and diacylglycerol.

These various second messenger molecules increase intracellular calcium and activate various kinase cascades and nuclear transcription factors that lead to the final step in the original neuronal signal, such as continuation of the initial presynpatic depolarization signal, hyperpolarization, secretion, contraction, or induction of mRNA formation. It should be noted that the neurotransmitter itself does not enter the postsynaptic cell and must be removed from the synaptic cleft quickly. This removal is the "off" signal in signal transduction and can be accomplished by neurotransmitter metabolism or uptake by astroglia or by presynaptic reuptake. The entire process of synaptic transmission onset and termination can occur in a few milliseconds. The actions of neuroactive drugs, including stimulants, sedatives, anxiolytics, and antipsychotic agents, as well as illicit addictive substances, can be traced to one or more steps in pre- or postsynaptic transmission.

Neurochemical studies on memory formation in a number of invertebrate and vertebrate species have led to the conclusion that long-term, but not short-term, memory formation requires ongoing protein synthesis. Such conclusions, initially based on the effects of antibiotic blocking agents, have been further documented by genetic mutant, transgenic, and "knockout" studies, primarily in fruit flies and in mice. Our improved understanding of neuroscience at the molecular level has led to a better understanding of drug action and the rational design of new ones.

For example, administration of DOPA, a precursor of dopamine that can penetrate the BBB, alleviates the symptoms of Parkinson's disease resulting from a dopamine deficiency. Inhibitors of acetylcholinesterase address a known deficit in acetylcholine in Alzheimer's disease. By blocking the presynaptic reuptake of serotonin, fluoxetine (Prozac) relieves depression. An inborn error that results in mental retardation, phenylketonuria (PKU), stems from the inability of the liver to convert the amino acid phenylalanine to tyrosine. Hundreds of genetic defects have been identified in recent years, and in many instances, the biochemical phenotypes, such as a defective protein, have been identified as well, an important next step in the eventual discovery of effective therapeutic strategies. Thus PKU can be treated successfully by a diet low in phenylalanine in infancy and early years.

The developing human brain *in utero* and in infancy is particularly susceptible to dietary imbalances. Dietary deficiencies in molecular building blocks that we cannot synthesize, termed "essential," include half of the twenty amino acids that constitute the polypeptide chains that comprise the brain's primary protein structure. There are also two groups of essential fatty acids, referred to as the omega-3 and omega-6 families, that are especially prominent in the phospholipids of brain and retinal membranes. While they are present in human breast milk, they must be added to infant formulas. The most beneficial of the omega-3 fatty acids are plentiful in marine fish and fish oils, and thus seem to validate the ancient adage that "fish are good brain food."

REFERENCES

Agranoff, B. W. (In press). *Brain food gastronomica*. Los Angeles: UCLA Press.

Cooper, J. R., Bloom, F. E., & Roth, R. H. (1996). *The biochemical basis of neuropsychopharmacology* (7th ed.). New York/Oxford, UK: Oxford University Press.

Marszalek, J. R, & Lodish, H. F. (2005). Docosahexaenoic acid. Fatty acid-interacting proteins and neural function: Breastmilk and fish are good for you. *Annual Review of Cellular and Developmental Biology, 21*, 633–657.

Siegel, G. J., Albers, R. W., Brady, S. T., & Price, D. L. (Eds). (2006). *Basic neurochemistry* (7th ed.). Burlington, MA: Elsevier Academic Press.

BERNARD W. AGRANOFF
University of Michigan

See also: Brain; Neuroscience

NEUROIMAGING

Neuroimaging is the use of techniques to map the location of structural and functional regions within the living brain. It is used extensively in clinical practice to identify abnormalities, such as testing for brain tumors, stroke, and other neurological conditions. It is also increasingly used as a diagnostic tool on a finer scale for metabolic diseases and lesions, including differentiation of neurological disorders (e.g., Alzheimer's Disease versus frontotemporal dementia). Structural neuroimaging techniques generate anatomic images relating to the volume, position, and shape of a structure, whereas functional neuroimaging produces data relating to activities to the active processing of the brain, either in a "resting" state or a response to external stimulus. Functional imaging is also used to assess chemical composition and neuroreceptor characteristics. Structural neuroimaging is more likely to be used clinically, while functional neuroimaging is primarily associated with research endeavors.

In psychology, these techniques are primarily used to expand our understanding of how brain activity relates to thinking, feeling, and acting in response to external stimuli or changes associated with development. Structural and functional techniques are often used in conjunction with one another, because each technique can provide unique but complementary information. Selection of the specific imaging tool depends on a number of factors, including whether one is engaged in a clinical or research endeavor, ethical issues, accessibility of the tool, cost of the procedure, degree of spatial and/or temporal resolution required, available data analytic expertise, and age and the presence of metal in the individual.

All imaging procedures quantify for a unit of three-dimensional space within the individual. The measures of three-dimensional space acquired via imaging are referred to as *voxels*. Through quantification, the values of the voxels are then arranged in an array to represent their spatial relationship with the living brain. These data are then typically transformed into an image displayed as a plane in two-dimensional space.

Neuroimaging Techniques

Computed Tomography (CT)

Modern brain imaging was revolutionized in the 1970s with the introduction of computerized X-ray tomography. This was one of the first widely practiced neuroimaging techniques that allowed investigation of the living brain. In computed tomography (CT), multiple X-ray beams of radiation are measured by detectors. Intravenous contrast agents may be used with CT to increase its sensitivity in detecting pathology. CT is particularly good at detecting abnormalities in the bone, calcifications, and acute bleeding. Limitations include exposure to radiation, poor differentiation between soft tissue densities, and circumscribed views of the person being scanned.

Magnetic Resonance Imaging (MRI)

In MRI, radio waves immerse a person centered in a magnetic field with the signals absorbed and re-emitted in proportion to the mobile hydrogen ion concentration in the tissue of the person. The absorbed energy is detected by a radio receiver when it is re-emitted. Images are then created of the biological tissue using a series of changing magnetic gradients and pulse sequences, known as oscillating electromagnet fields. MRI is capable of detecting different tissue types such as tumors, bone damage, and gray versus white matter. The technique is noninvasive, does not expose one to radiation, and has minimal risk for subjects who are carefully prescreened to be acceptable for MR imaging. Structural MRI of the brain produces images of brain anatomy, volumetric measures, and cortical thickness. Functional MRI (fMRI) generates indirect measures of brain activity coupled with changes in blood flow and blood oxygenation over time. FMRI uses standard MRI scanners with fast imaging techniques based on the principle that focal changes in neuronal activity tend to be associated with changes in blood flow and volume. The technique has excellent spatial resolution (within millimeters) and good temporal resolution (within seconds). In fMRI, the goal is often to identify a map of brain regions or a network associated with a short-term physiological response to a cognitive or emotional stimulus. In psychology, fMRI may be used to observe developmental changes, brain function associated with psychiatric disorders, learning, memory, emotional states, or pharmacological agents among other common areas of study. FMRI is now the dominant technique used to study brain function due to the wide accessibility of the equipment and noninvasiveness of the technique.

Related techniques include magnetic response spectroscopy (MRS) and diffusion tensor imaging (DTI). MRS is used to detect the concentration and distribution of endogenous metabolites such as N-acetyl aspartate (NAA), choline (Cho), and lactate (Lac). With MRS imaging, it is possible to acquire noninvasive information on a biochemical level of how the brain functions; however, its low spatial and temporal resolution limits its use. In DTI the goal is to map the orientation of white matter tracts. DTI is a promising tool for assessing white matter connectivity in vivo.

Limitations to MRI include occasional claustrophobia, prohibitive use of metal implants in patients, users, or equipment, and sensitivity to motion artifacts. Pediatric fMRI studies with active paradigms in children under seven years of age are also considerably challenging, thus limiting its usefulness to date in studying development issues at very young ages.

Positron Emission Tomography (PET) and Single Photon Emission Computed

Tomography (SPECT or SPET)

Both PET and SPECT require the use of a radioactive tracer injected or inhaled into the blood stream. The tracer is distributed in the brain and emits a photon signal that is detected by the scanner. Both techniques measure the regional distribution of radioactive activity, which, depending on the labeled tracer, can measure glucose metabolism, blood flow, or the distribution or density of a receptor. Blood flow and metabolism are typically coupled and are used as a measure of neural activity. A variety of tracers are available in PET, each measuring different parameters (e.g., regional cerebral blood flow, glucose metabolism, or receptor distribution). PET is increasingly used as an advanced technique to identify pathology (e.g., tumors and neuronal degeneration). Water containing oxygen 15 is considered the optimal and most widely used PET tracer for assessing blood flow in cognitive studies. In psychology, PET studies are still widely used to study receptor binding and pharmacological effects on neural functioning; however, fMRI has eclipsed its use in cognitive and developmental research. Disadvantages of SPECT and PET include weaker temporal and spatial resolution than fMRI, and restrictions on the number of replications of a study that can be done with an individual in order to limit the amount of radiation exposure for that subject.

Electroencephalogram (EEG) and Event-Related Potentials (ERP)

In EEG, electrical potentials in the brain are measured via the surface of the scalp. Clinically, EEG is frequently used to assist in the diagnosis of neurological disorders (e.g., seizure disorders). In ERP studies, voltage fluctuations derived from EEG recordings are time-locked to specific cognitive or emotional responses that are manipulated by a researcher or situation. ERP has excellent temporal resolution, but less than optimal spatial resolution. Combined ERP-fMRI studies have the potential to improve our ability to understand when in the process a specific brain region is activated.

Magnetoencephalography (MEG)

Magnetoencephalography (MEG) is an imaging technique capable of measuring neuronal function with submillisecond temporal resolution, so it has superior temporal resolution to that found in either PET or fMRI. It relies upon the measurement of changes in magnetic fields due to electrical activity in the neuron. The MEG system works with sensors located in a large helmet that surround the subject's head.

The ability to measure change in magnetic flux at the submillisecond level is important for understanding a variety of perceptual processes and the temporal progression of activity within the brain in response to internal or external stimulation. Unfortunately, there are problems related to spatial localization using MEG because it is mathematically impossible to identify the underlying neural sources associated with unique patterns of activity within the brain. This limitation has impeded wider use of the technique, although combining MEG with fMRi is increasingly popular and may address some of the localization issues.

Diffuse Optical Imaging (DOI) or Diffuse Optical Tomography (DOT) and Event-Related Optical Signal (EROS)

DOI, DOT, and EROS are additional noninvasive imaging techniques. They use near–infrared light to measure the optical absorption of hemoglobin to create images. There is a great interest in these techniques, particularly for pediatric populations, because they have the potential to be portable, low-cost, and more forgiving of subject movement. These methods are not widely available as of yet and are limited by how well they can detect activity more than a few centimeters of depth within the brain.

Transcranial Magnetic Stimulation (TMS)

TMS is a method of producing temporary interruption of brain functioning in order to determine if a particular region is involved in a function such as language or cognition. In TMS, an electromagnetic coil is held near the scalp, emitting weak electrical currents from the coil to the brain tissue via the generation of a magnetic field. Repetitive transcranial magnetic stimulation (rTMS) is now being tested and used to produce longer lasting changes. There are a number of neurological and psychiatric conditions in which TMS and rTMS are being tested as a treatment intervention.

SUGGESTED READINGS

Fu, C, H, Y., Senior, C., Russell, T. A., Weinberger, D., & Murray, R. (2003). *Neuroimaging in psychiatry*. New York: Martin Dunitz.

Gillard, J. H., Waldman, A. D., & Barker, P. D. (2005). *Clinical MR neuroimaging: Diffusion, perfusion and spectroscopy*. Cambridge, UK: Cambridge University Press.

Huettel, S. A., Song, A. W., & McCarthy, G. (2003). *Functional magnetic resonance imaging*. Sunderland, MA: Sinauer Associates.

JULIE SCHWEITZER
University of California, Davis School of Medicine

See also: **Cognitive Neuroscience; Electroencephalography; Magnetic Resonance Imaging**

NEUROIMAGING IN PEDIATRIC BIPOLAR DISORDER

Pediatric bipolar disorder (PBD), like the adult counterpart of the disorder, has been characterized by structural and functional abnormalities in the brain regions responsible for emotional regulation, attentional control, and executive functioning. Studies of PBD subjects have revealed that adult and pediatric bipolar disorder may have shared neurological underpinnings. A few key differences between these populations have also been found, which may provide some insight into vulnerability markers for the disorder (Hajek, Carrey, & Alda, 2005), independent of effects of repeated mood episodes and long-term medication use.

Bipolar disorder is characterized by extreme affective fluctuation as well as cognitive deficits in the realms of attention, executive function, short-term memory, and prepotent response inhibition. It has been hypothesized that both cognitive and affective deficits may be accounted for by dysfunction in a highly interactive extended brain network that includes prefrontal regions, medial temporal regions (amygdala and hippocampus), and subcortical regions (striatum and thalamus). The amygdala and striatum are key regions for the processing of emotional stimuli and reward, and they are highly connected to prefrontal regions involved in executive function, attention, modulation of emotion, and reward-based decision making. Emotional dysregulation is thought to arise from impaired inhibitory feedback from prefrontal cortical regions to medial temporal and subcortical structures. Prefrontal and amygdalar connections to the hypothalamus modulate cortisol release, and dysfunction in this system may be responsible for the so-called neurovegetative symptoms of bipolar disorder, including impaired sleep, appetite, and arousal (Adler, Delbello, & Strakowski, 2006).

Individuals who develop bipolar disorder in childhood and adolescence do so in the midst of ongoing significant developmental brain changes. In healthy brain development, late childhood is marked by rapid growth in gray matter in prefrontal cortical areas, followed by a subsequent decrease in early to late adolescence. In fact, recent evidence suggests that functional and structural brain changes continue to occur well into early adulthood (Giedd, 2008). Thus any neuroimaging study in a pediatric population must take into account the varying developmental stages of the subjects. Age-related changes in brain structure and function may be of particular importance in this population, and they may provide valuable information about the long-term effects of bipolar illness onset on brain maturation during this developmentally sensitive period (DelBello, Adler, & Strakowski, 2006).

Structural MRI

Structural magnetic resonance imaging (MRI) provides high-resolution images of brain structures, from which the make-up and volume of various brain regions can be extrapolated. One structural finding that is consistent in both adult and pediatric bipolar brains is the presence of white matter hyperintensities, or areas where the density of myelin, a protective substance which insulates nerve fibers, is particularly high (Delbello et al., 2006). Also, both pediatric and adult bipolar subjects exhibit decreased volumes in prefrontal cortical regions such as the anterior cingulate, orbitofrontal, and dorsolateral prefrontal cortices. Although adult bipolar subjects exhibit increased lateral and third ventricular volumes, this finding has not been replicated in PBD subjects, suggesting it is a byproduct of illness duration. Also in contrast to adults, smaller whole brain and hippocampal volumes, as well as greater temporal lobe volumes, have also been found in child and adolescent bipolar subjects in comparison to healthy peers (Demeter, Townsend, Wilson, & Findling, 2008), though these results are mixed and warrant further investigation.

The amygdala, a key structure in emotional processing, has been found to be decreased in volume in bipolar youths relative to healthy peers; this is in contrast to studies of bipolar adults that report normal or increased amygdala volumes. Decreased amygdala size may be a neurobiological risk factor specific to bipolar disorder. Furthermore, although amygdala volumes decrease with age in healthy adolescents, in bipolar adolescents, the opposite occurs (DelBello et al., 2006). Whether these age-related abnormalities in amygdalar development are precipitants of bipolar illness or secondary to illness duration or to medication exposure is unclear.

Another brain region that exhibits an abnormal developmental trajectory in bipolar patients is the ventral prefrontal cortex (VPFC), an area thought to be involved in modulating emotional processing and physiological responses to emotional stimuli. VPFC volumes decline in all adolescents as they move towards young adulthood; however, there is evidence to suggest that in bipolar youth, this decline proceeds more rapidly, and that decreases in VPFC volume are related to the experience of repeated affective episodes. First episode adolescents and adults exhibited no differences in VPFC volume relative to healthy peers. The rapid-cycling subtype of bipolar has been associated with larger volume deficits in this area (Adler et al., 2007; Blumberg et al., 2006).

Functional MRI

Functional magnetic resonance imaging (fMRI) allows researchers to examine regional brain activation in response to specific neuropsychological tasks or stimuli. Both during mood episodes and euthymic periods, patients with bipolar disorder exhibit deficits in working memory, attention, executive functioning, and labeling of emotional facial expressions (Demeter et al., 2008; McClure-Tone, in press). Results from fMRI studies using emotional processing and attentional tasks in euthymic bipolar adults reveal increased activity in ventral prefrontal cortex, amygdala and subcortical regions and decreased activity in dorsolateral prefrontal cortex relative to healthy controls (Phillips & Vieta, 2007).

In the few fMRI studies in bipolar children and adolescents, results are equivocal. Studies using tasks of sustained attention, working memory, and prepotent inhibition have revealed abnormalities in dorsolateral and ventrolateral prefrontal cortices (DLPFC and VLPFC), temporal areas, and striatum relative to healthy peers. Age-related increases in VPFC activation found in healthy controls during a prepotent response inhibition task were absent in age-matched bipolar adolescents, suggesting abnormal development in this region (DelBello et al., 2006). Studies involving processing of neutral and emotional faces in bipolar adolescents have found increased amygdalar and striatal activity, abnormal VLPFC activity, and decreased activity in posterior face processing circuitry. Amygdala hyperactivity in response to negatively valenced emotional scenes was found to decrease as depressive symptoms decreased in a group of bipolar adolescents treated with lamotrigine (McClure-Tone, in press). Further research controlling for mood state, psychiatric comorbidity, medication effects, and task variability is necessary to clarify the functional deficits present in PBD brains.

Other Techniques

Various emerging neuroimaging techniques provide a more nuanced look at brain structure and function.

Diffusion tensor imaging (DTI) is an imaging technique which measures water diffusion and can provide information about the integrity of white matter tracts (axons) which allow for the efficient transduction of nerve signals throughout the brain. DTI studies in both bipolar adults and adolescents indicate loss of axonal integrity in areas bordering the prefrontal cortex. Magnetic resonance spectroscopy (MRS) allows for the measurement of the concentration of a specific biochemical compound in a localized region of the brain. Preliminary results indicate abnormalities in biomarkers of neuronal metabolism, viability, and second-messenger signaling pathways in prefrontal regions in both pediatric and adult bipolar patients; in some cases this was rectified by treatment with mood stabilizers. Overall, results from MRS studies in bipolar subjects are intriguing but inconclusive, putatively due to variability in medications and mood states (DelBello et al., 2006).

Future Directions

Overall, neuroimaging results in pediatric bipolar disorder mirror those found in bipolar adults; both populations exhibit structural and functional abnormalities in fronto-striatal-thalamic circuits and in medial temporal structures. Regions which are decreased in volume exclusively in PBD subjects and/or which exhibit altered developmental trajectories during bipolar child and adolescent brain maturation, such as the amygdala, hippocampus, and VPFC, may represent neurodevelopmental markers of risk. To further clarify neuroanatomical markers of risk for bipolar disorder, studies of at-risk children (i.e., offspring of bipolar parents) may be particularly useful. Imaging studies of children at risk for bipolar disorder have yielded mixed results (Gogtay et al., 2007; Ladouceur et al., 2008; Singh, DelBello, Adler, Stanford, & Strakowski, 2008). Further study of this population with longitudinal follow-up is necessary.

Results from neuroimaging studies in PBD are confounded by a number of factors. Subjects in these studies are often on a variety of medications, may be in varying mood states, and often exhibit a number of comorbid psychiatric conditions, particularly ADHD. Future neuroimaging studies in this population should attempt to control carefully for the potential effects of these confounds. When clinically feasible, both medicated and unmedicated subjects should be tested and compared (Phillips, Travis, Fagiolini, & Kupfer, 2008).

The validity of the diagnosis of bipolar disorder in pediatric populations is a controversial topic, and there is no true consensus on how and if the adult criteria for the disorder should be adapted for youths. To avoid diagnostically heterogeneous samples, future imaging studies should compare subtypes of PBD. Leibenluft and her colleagues have recently proposed differentiating between "narrow" and "broad" phenotypes of PBD, with the "narrow" subtype continuing to require cardinal symptoms of bipolar disorder such as elated mood and grandiosity, and the "broad" phenotype being an apt category for youths who present with chronic irritability and hyperarousal (Leibenluft, Charney, Towbin, Bhangoo, & Pine, 2003). Neuroimaging studies of individuals who exhibit this "broad" phenotype, also known as severe mood dysregulation, are underway, and may help to illuminate the physiological differences between these subtypes, shedding light on a murky diagnostic picture.

REFERENCES

Adler, C. M., DelBello, M. P., Jarvis, K., Levine, A., Adams, J., & Strakowski, S. M. (2007). Voxel-based study of structural changes in first-episode patients with bipolar disorder. *Biological Psychiatry, 61*, 776–781.

Blumberg, H. P., Krystal, J. H., Bansal, R., Martin, A., Dziura, J., Durkin, K., et al. (2006). Age, rapid-cycling, and pharmacotherapy effects on ventral prefrontal cortex in bipolar disorder: A cross-sectional study. *Biological Psychiatry, 59*, 611–618.

Demeter, C., Townsend, L., Wilson, M., & Findling, R. (2008). Current research in child and adolescent bipolar disorder. *Dialogues in Clinical Neuroscience, 10*, 215–228.

Giedd, J. (2008). The teen brain: Insights from neuroimaging. *Journal of Adolescent Health, 42*, 335–343.

Gogtay, N., Ordonez, A., Herman, D., Hayashi, K., Greenstein, D., & Vaituzis, C. (2007). Dynamic mapping of cortical development before and after the onset of pediatric bipolar illness. *Journal of Child Psychology and Psychiatry, 48*, 852–862.

Hajek, T., Carrey, N., & Alda, M. (2005). Neuroanatomical abnormalities as risk factors for bipolar disorder. *Bipolar Disorder, 7*, 393–403.

Ladouceur, C., Almeida, J., Birmaher, B., Axelson, D., Nau, S., Kalas, C., et al. (2008). Subcortical gray matter volume abnormalities in healthy bipolar offspring: Potential neuroanatomical risk marker for bipolar disorder? *Journal of the American Academy of Child & Adolescent Psychiatry, 47*, 532–539.

Leibenluft, E., Charney, D., Towbin, K., Bhangoo, R., & Pine, D. (2003). Defining clinical phenotypes of juvenile mania. *American Journal of Psychiatry, 160*, 430–437.

McClure-Tone, E. (In press). Social cognition and cognitive flexibility in bipolar disorder. In D. Miklowitz & D. Cicchetti (Eds.), *Bipolar disorder: A developmental psychopathology approach*. New York: Guilford Press.

Phillips, M., Travis, M., Fagiolini, A., & Kupfer, D. (2008). Medication effects in neuroimaging studies of bipolar disorder. *American Journal of Psychiatry, 165*, 313–320.

Phillips, M., & Vieta, E. (2007). Identifying functional neuroimaging biomarkers of bipolar disorder: Towards DSM-V. *Schizophrenia Bulletin, 33*, 893–904.

Singh, M., DelBello, M. P., Adler, C. M., Stanford, K., & Strakowski, S. M. (2008). Neuroanatomical characterization of child offspring of bipolar parents. *Journal of the American Academy of Child & Adolescent Psychiatry, 47*, 526–531.

SUGGESTED READINGS

Adler, C. M., DelBello, M. P., & Strakowski, S. M. (2006). Brain network dysfunction in bipolar disorder. *CNS Spectrums, 11*, 312–320.

DelBello, M. P., Adler, C. M., & Strakowski, S. M. (2006). The neurophysiology of childhood and adolescent bipolar disorder. *CNS Spectrums, 11*, 298–311.

ANJANA MURALIDHARAN
Emory University

See also: Bipolar Disorder; Neuroimaging

NEUROPSYCHOLOGICAL ASSESSMENT (See Neuropsychology)

NEUROPSYCHOLOGICAL DEVELOPMENT

Research in developmental neuropsychology first started because it was believed that children are neurologically simpler than adults and would provide clearer data as to the relationship between brain function and behavior. This turned out to be a somewhat simplistic view, and the study of the developing nervous system quickly raised a number of important new questions, such as "Why does the young brain appear to be so flexible in compensating for injury?" and "How do environmental factors influence the developing brain?" In addressing such questions, we must first provide an overview of the neural developmental process.

Neural Development

The growth of the brain and nervous system occurs as a series of changes that take place in a fixed sequence. It begins with cell migration, during which nerve cells are formed in the inner or ventricular lining of the brain and migrate through the layers that already exist, to eventually form a new outer layer. Thus the cortex actually matures from the inner to the outer surfaces. During this stage, axons (the elongated neural filament that carries information away from the cell body) begin to sprout from migrating cells. Each axon has a specific target it must reach if the neuron is to be functional. The growth of dendrites (fiberlike processes that receive neural information from other nerve cells) is much slower and involves much more branching and elaboration. In early development there appears to be an overabundance of dendritic branches, but unused branches are eventually lost in a process referred to as "pruning."

Synapses (junctions between two nerve cells, where neurochemical processes transmit signals from one cell to the other) begin to form about two months before birth and continue for at least two years after birth in humans. As in the case of dendrites, experience affects the survival of synapses. Only the regularly used synapses survive, with up to 50% disappearing through a process referred to as "shedding."

Axons are surrounded by myelin, a fatty insulating sheath. The degree of myelination is sometimes used as an index of neural maturation, and this index shows that the neocortex matures relatively early during gestation, whereas the sensory and motor areas begin to mature just before birth. Some areas of the cortex involved in higher-level processing continue to mature for four or more months after birth.

It used to be believed that neural development was finished after about two years of age, but in fact it continues well beyond this point. Brain development occurs at irregular intervals that are called "growth spurts" (Banich, 1997). Such spurts occur at around 3–18 months and at 2–4, 6–8, 10–12, and 14–16 years of age. Except for the first spurt, during which brain weight increases by about 30%, each subsequent growth spurt increases brain mass by 5–10%. These growth spurts may be correlated with overt changes in behavior; for example, the first four episodes of rapid brain growth seem to coincide with the four principal stages of cognitive development according to Piaget (Kolb & Wishaw, 2009).

Changes in the neural system continue well beyond adolescence, however, and some of the later changes are associated with cell losses. For instance, the area of the occipital cortex that receives projections from the fovea of the eye contains about 46 million neurons per gram of tissue in a 20-year-old but only 24 million neurons per gram in an 80-year-old. This cell loss is believed to account for some of the loss of visual acuity in older individuals (Coren, Ward, & Enns, 1999). Similar losses in other areas of the brain might be expected to also affect age-related changes in functioning.

Environmental and Experiential Effects

The development of the nervous system is affected by the environment and by the activities of the organism. The general principle that describes the interaction between the environment and the developing nervous system is functional validation. According to this principle, some form of stimulation or neural activity is needed to "validate" the usefulness of sections of the nervous system. In the absence of such validation, these units cease to function and do not continue their growth and maturation. We have already seen this process in action when we noted that unused synapses and dendrites seem to disappear with age.

Even the size and mass of the brain can be affected by experience. Exposure to a stimulus-rich environment increases brain size, especially in the neocortex, presumably by validating the functionality of many additional pathways. Such enriched stimulus exposure seems to increase the number of dendrites and synapses, especially if the enriched experience is given early in life. Animals with such enlarged brains seem to perform better on a number of behavioral tasks, including those involving memory and learning.

Environmental effects, in the form of traumas that affect the developing fetus (which might include the influence of toxic agents, mechanical injury, or chemical imbalances), can cause dramatic disturbances in neural development resulting in major dysfunctions. However, some traumas are not easily detected at the neural level, but only become manifest as behavioral changes (e.g., learning disabilities, reduced intelligence, personality disturbances, motor insufficiencies). Some behavioral indicators of disrupted neuropsychological development are quite subtle and are often referred to as *soft signs*.

Asymmetry and Neuropsychological Development

As an example of how neuropsychological development interacts with behavior, I will use lateral asymmetries in function. The functional differences between the two cerebral hemispheres are well known (e.g., language function is predominantly represented in the left hemisphere and spatial functions in the right hemisphere). It is possible that these differences come about because there is a left-to-right maturational gradient during development (e.g., Gazzaniga, 1998), meaning that the left hemisphere develops earlier than the right. Hence the left hemisphere gains control over language functions, not because it is intrinsically specialized for them, but simply because it is the more developed and dominant hemisphere when language functions are developing. There is enough plasticity for the right hemisphere to take over language function if the left is damaged, but only if this situation occurs early in development; later in development this form of compensation is not possible, because the functional properties of the nervous system become more fixed and specialized over time. Thus if left hemisphere damage occurs before age five, the recovery of speech is usually possible, with the right hemisphere reorganizing to take over most of the functions lost by the left; after that age, however, there is little hope for recovery of function (see Kolb & Wishaw, 2009). Presumably, plasticity is now gone and all of the right hemisphere functions are now set and fixed.

Left-handedness is another soft sign that suggests that there has been some form of damage or disruption in neurological development that cannot be specifically seen in physiological examinations. It has been argued (e.g., Coren, 1992) that all human beings are genetically programmed to be right-handed, and that left-handedness results from early damage to the relevant neural pathways or brain centers or from disrupted maturational processes. This explains why individuals who are born from a difficult pregnancy or a stressed birth are twice as likely to be left-handed, and also why left-handers seem to mature more slowly and are more likely to suffer from a variety of behavioral and physiological problems.

Handedness illustrates the usual sequence of neuropsychological development, starting with an early indication of a bias toward a particular functional pattern and followed with a gradual loss of plasticity and more functional specialization with age (Coren, 1992). Thus at birth there are indications that there is functional asymmetry that is correlated with handedness in the form of a tonic neck reflex and limb extension in infants. For tasks such as reaching, handedness is not reliable before six months of age and gradually becomes more stable and consistent up to about the age of eight years. Attempts to change handedness demonstrate the loss of plasticity of function with increasing age, and they are seldom successful after age nine (Porac, Coren, & Searleman, 1986). This same sequence of stages (initial developmental predisposition, period of environmental vulnerability, period of plasticity, and finally fixed functional properties) commonly appears in neuropsychological development, whether we are looking at neurological structures, complex patterns of cerebral organization, or functional manifestations of behavior.

REFERENCES

Coren, S. (1992). *The left-hander syndrome: The causes and consequences of left-handedness*. New York: Free Press.

Coren, S., Porac, C., & Duncan, P. (1981). Lateral behaviors preference in pre-school children and young adults. *Child Development, 52,* 443–450.

Coren, S., Ward, L. M., & Enns, J. T. (2004). *Sensation and perception* (6th ed). Hoboken, NJ: John Wiley & Sons.

Gazzaniga, M. S. (1998). *The mind's past.* Berkeley, CA: University of California Press.

Kolb, B., & Wishaw, I. Q. (2009). *Fundamentals of neuropsychology.* New York: Worth.

Porac, C., Coren, S., & Searleman, A. (1986) Environmental factors in hand preference: Evidence from attempts to switch the preferred hand. *Behavior Genetics, 16,* 251–261.

SUGGESTED READINGS

Stiles, J. (2008). *The fundamentals of brain development: Integrating nature and nurture.* Cambridge, MA: Harvard University Press.

STANLEY COREN
University of British Columbia, Canada

See also: Brain Injuries; Central Nervous System; Myelin; Neuroscience

NEUROPSYCHOLOGICAL REHABILITATION

Neuropsychological rehabilitation refers to training experiences and learning exercises that attempt to restore higher integrative brain functions following an acquired brain injury (Luria, 1948/1963) and/or teaching patients to compensate for residual higher order brain disturbances in their personal and interpersonal life (Prigatano, 1999). These activities are employed with both adults and children. Neuropsychological rehabilitation with adults attempts to help them deal with the problem of "lost normality" by having them return to a productive lifestyle and find ways of maintaining mutually satisfying interpersonal relationships (i.e., work and love). For children and their parents, the attempt is to help them both deal with the problem of the child "not developing normally." This requires considerable effort at helping the child and parent realistically adjust to whatever permanent changes may be imposed by brain injury, without having children lose their "individuality." That is, in both adults and children, the goal is to help them improve in their higher cerebral functioning and adjust to those functions that cannot get better, but to do so in a manner that still allows them to be true to who they are. The goal is not simply to have them adjust to society at the risk of losing their individuality.

Early efforts at neuropsychological rehabilitation focus primarily on cognitive deficits and their remediation (Newcombe, 2002). Cognition refers to the ability of the brain to process, store, retrieve, and manipulate information to solve problems. Although some clinicians emphasize the importance of this basic form of rehabilitation in neuropsychological interventions (see Stuss, Winocur, & Robertson, in press), neuropsychological rehabilitation includes training efforts that address the cognitive, emotional, and motivational disturbances associated with various forms of brain injury. These disturbances appear to be interconnected, and both have been related to rehabilitation outcome (Prigatano, 1999). Consequently, neuropsychological rehabilitation is based on the application of knowledge derived from the broad field of the neurosciences (which includes neuropsychology) as well as from clinical psychology, psychiatry, psychoanalysis, analytic psychology, sociology, and cultural anthropology. All these areas contribute to the necessary "database" for understanding patients' behavior and planning interventions. Brain injury often affects the patients' subjective experience of themselves. Thus, neuropsychological rehabilitation must be based on a broad knowledge of human behavior and the various forms of conscious disturbances that can occur following neurological, as well as psychiatric, disorders.

The seminal work of Kurt Goldstein (1942), who has been described as the "great precursor" of neuropsychological rehabilitation (Newcomb, 2002), emphasized the importance of dealing with the patients' cognitive deficits, their emotional reactions to those deficits, and placing them in an environment that would facilitate recovery and avoid the "catastrophic reaction." Later work of Ben-Yishay and Diller (1993) emphasized the importance of systematic cognitive retraining activities and the effective management of patients' catastrophic reactions within a therapeutic milieu. Collectively, these observations form the "foundations" of neuropsychological rehabilitation.

Today, neuropsychological rehabilitation includes six major ingredients: cognitive rehabilitation, psychotherapy (or at least psychotherapeutic interventions), the establishment of a therapeutic milieu that facilitates recovery and avoids deterioration, the establishment of protected work trials or an educational setting that allows the patient to be productive, and the active engagement of family members in the rehabilitation process. The sixth and often-neglected ingredient is the professional management of the treating clinicians' positive and negative reactions to patients and their families (Prigatano, 2008). These activities focus on helping the patient at three different levels of intervention.

The first level of intervention is the application of training experiences to reduce the underlying impairment directly caused by a brain injury (e.g., memory impairment). The second level focuses on reducing the disability caused by the impairment (e.g., teaching patients to meaningfully compensate for memory impairments in their daily life). Finally, neuropsychological rehabilitation helps directly deal with the patient's subjective experience (the third level). The focus of this rehabilitation activity is to enhance a patient's functional capacity and to reduce impairments, as well as to increase their personal sense of competency and psychological well-being in the face of residual impairments and disabilities caused by brain dysfunction. To do this requires that the treating clinician must apply scientific principles to patient care while understanding the patient's phenomenological experience and broader issues in adaptation when there are major losses in life.

Recent and exciting cognitive rehabilitation advances center around the application of computer-generated stimuli presented to patients using behavioral principles of reinforcement and shaping (see Prigatano, 2008). It is difficult to identify advances in the psychotherapeutic work with brain-dysfunctional patients or the refinement of the therapeutic milieu model; yet they remain crucial components of this type of work. Protective work trials and educational experiences are also similar to what had earlier been described by Goldstein (1942). Neuropsychological rehabilitation of children has shown, in one randomized control study, the potential value of including family members in the rehabilitation process (see Prigatano, 2008). No studies have appeared that have documented that effective professional management of the therapists' reactions to patients and/or their family members resulted in improved rehabilitation outcome for the patients.

A number of studies have demonstrated, however, the importance of the working alliance between the patient and rehabilitation therapists for treatment outcome, as measured at the time of discharge and several years postdischarge (see Prigatano, in press). The psychological and biological variables responsible for establishing a good working alliance between patient and therapist have not been adequately studied. Research has also demonstrated that impaired self-awareness (ISA) has clearly been related to the process and outcome of neuropsychological rehabilitation (Prigatano, in press). Measuring ISA as a neurologically based disorder and denial of disability as a psychologically based disorder continues to be an area of considerable clinical research interest. Separating these two disorders may help explain why some patients show improvement in apparent awareness as a result of neuropsychological rehabilitation while other patients do not.

Future work will undoubtedly expand the role of cognitive prostheses in the rehabilitation of patients with brain and spinal injuries (Anderson et al., 2004), as well as greater involvement of family in orchestrating environmental changes that will facilitate recovery and adaptation. Long-term studies are still needed to demonstrate the efficacy of this type of rehabilitation as it relates to maintaining employment and maintenance of interpersonal relationships with a decrease in psychiatric morbidity with time. Although clinicians in the field have argued that these changes should be expected, empirical support for these assertions remains limited.

The lack of evidence-based studies in this area, plus the economic realities of diminishing health-care dollars in Western countries, has stunted the growth of neuropsychological rehabilitation. It remains, however, a field of clinical and research endeavors that sustain strong interest by the professional community, as witnessed by a journal with the same name, *Neuropsychological Rehabilitation*, published by Psychology Press.

REFERENCES

Andersen, R. A., Burdick, J. W., Musallam, S., Pesaran, B., & Cham, J. G. (2004). Cognitive neural prosthetics. *Trends in Cognitive Sciences, 8*(11), 486–493.

Ben-Yishay, Y. & Diller, L. (1993). Cognitive remediation in traumatic brain injury: Update and issues. *Archives of Physical Medicine and Rehabilitation, 74*, 204–213.

Goldstein, K. (1942). *Aftereffects of brain injuries in war.* New York: Grune and Stratton.

Luria, A. R. (1948/1963). *Restoration of function after brain trauma* (in Russian). Moscow: Academy of Medical Science. (Originally published by Pergamon, London.)

Newcombe, F. (2002). An overview of neuropsychological rehabilitation: A forgotten past and a challenging future. In W. Brower,

E. van Zomeren, I. Berg, A. Bouma, & E. de Haan (Eds.), *Cognitive rehabilitation: A clinical neuropsychological approach* (pp. 23–51). Amsterdam: Boom.

Prigatano, G. P. (1999). *Principles of neuropsychological rehabilitation.* New York: Oxford University Press.

Prigatano, G. P. (2008). Neuropsychological rehabilitation and psychodynamic psychotherapy. In J. Morgan and J. Ricker (Eds.), *Textbook of clinical neuropsychology* (pp. 985–995). New York: Taylor & Francis.

Prigatano, G. P. (in press). Anosognosia and the process and outcome of neurorehabilitation. In D. T. Stuss, G. Winocur, & I. H. Robertson (Eds.), *Cognitive neurorehabilitation: Evidence and application* (2nd ed.). Cambridge, UK: Cambridge University Press.

Stuss, D. T., Winocur, G., & Robertson, I. H. (in press). *Cognitive neurorehabilitation: Evidence and application* (2nd ed.). Cambridge, UK: Cambridge University Press.

SUGGESTED READINGS

Prigatano, G. P. (1999). *Principles of neuropsychological rehabilitation.* New York: Oxford University Press.

Stuss, D. T., Winocur, G., & Robertson, I. H. (Eds.). (2008). *Cognitive neurorehabilitation: Evidence and application* (2nd ed.). Cambridge, UK: Cambridge University Press.

GEORGE P. PRIGATANO
*St. Joseph's Hospital and Medical Center,
Phoenix, Arizona*

See also: Brain Injuries; Neuropsychological Development; Neuropsychology

NEUROPSYCHOLOGY

Historically, the field of neuropsychology was derived not only from the discipline of psychology, but also from the various related disciplines within the traditional professions of medicine, education, and law (Meier, 1997). The term *neuropsychology* is a combination of the word *neurology*, which is defined as a branch of medicine that deals with the nervous system and its disorders, and *psychology*, which is defined as the study of behavior or the mind (Finger, 1994). One of the first people to combine the words neurology and psychology into neuropsychology was Kurt Goldstein (Frommer & Smith, 1988) in his book *The Organism* (1939). Neuropsychology today is used to describe a field of psychology that principally circumscribes the identification, quantification, and description of changes in behavior that relate to the structural and cognitive integrity of the brain (Golden, Zillmer, & Spiers, 1992). Although neuropsychological techniques and questions have long existed, the clinical side of the field did not start to expand until the late 1970s. Most practitioners in the field have been trained within the last two decades, with the majority of those in the last 10 years. Neuropsychologists are most prominently represented professionally by the National Academy of Neuropsychologists, Division 40 (Clinical Neuropsychology) of the American Psychological Association, and the International Neuropsychological Society (INS).

The Neuropsychologist as a Professional

Most individuals who call themselves neuropsychologists are professionals involved with assessing and treating human patients (i.e., clinical neuropsychology) (Finger, 1994). A majority of neuropsychologists in practice work with either psychiatric or neuropsychological populations in a variety of settings: private practice, university-based medical centers, psychiatric hospitals, general community hospitals, mental health centers, university psychology departments, and prisons (Golden, 1983).

Neuropsychologists are involved in specifying the nature of brain-related disorders and applying this information to rehabilitation and education. In order to achieve this, the Clinical Neuropsychologist is required to establish a comprehensive database of historical and current general medical, surgical, neurological, neuroradiological, pharmacological, developmental, and psychosocial factors underlying the presenting problem (Meier, 1997). Research neuropsychologists study multiple areas, such as the relationships between brain functions and specific neurological disorders, the cognitive and emotional consequences of specific diseases, the role of neurological and genetic disorders in the development of childhood learning and behavioral problems, the relationship of neuropsychological measures and neuroradiological findings, the neurodevelopment of psychiatric disorders, patterns of cognitive impairment associated with specialized areas of the brain, the validity and reliability of neuropsychological tests, linguistic development and disorders, and the progression of specific disorders.

Clinical neuropsychologists are required to be licensed at the state level in the United States but not in all countries outside the United States. Research neuropsychologists may be able to practice without a license in some jurisdictions. Most licensed neuropsychologists are licensed as clinical psychologists because few states have licensure in this specific specialty. Although all licensed psychologists can technically practice neuropsychology, APA and state ethical requirements limit practice to those with adequate training. The most common measure of adequate training in the field is board certification by the American Board of Clinical Neuropsychology (ABCN) or the American Board of Professional Neuropsychology (ABPN).

Diagnosis in Neuropsychology

One of the major questions facing neuropsychologists is the differentiation of brain damage from the major psychiatric disorders (Golden, Zillmer, & Spiers, 1992). The reason for the difficulty in differentiation lies in the fact that the range of psychiatric disorders is broad and involves elements of cognitive impairment commonly seen in brain injury. The area of diagnosis for the neuropsychologist includes three subareas. The first subarea involves the identification of the presence of a brain injury in which a differentiation must be made between disorders caused by emotional problems and those caused by injury to the function of the brain. The second subarea involves the specification of the nature of the deficit caused by brain damage, including localizing the injury to specific areas of the brain. The third subarea includes the identification of the underlying process or underlying cognitive disorder (Golden, 1992).

Neuropsychologists are also active in gerontology, where diagnostic assessments can confirm the presence of dementing disorders and differentiate between various causes of dementia (such as Alzheimer's disease from multi-infarct dementia), as well as identify individuals with early signs of these disorders, which may lead to appropriate interventions medically or psychologically. Pediatric neuropsychology is also an important area with the emphasis on the assessment and identification of such disorders as learning disabilities, hyperactivity, autism, and other related disorders.

Neuropsychological Assessment

The primary goal of assessment in neuropsychology is to address the relevant neurobehavioral aspects of higher psychological functioning that are considered to be central to understanding the cognitive strengths and deficits of the individual (Meier, 1997). In neurodiagnostic settings, there is an emphasis on the search for dysfunctional aspects of an individual's cognition and behavior that aid in diagnosis of the particular lesion, disease, syndrome, or condition (Golden, Zillmer, & Spiers, 1992). In addition, neuropsychological assessments can also serve as a baseline for a patient's abilities so that a course of recovery or decline in a patient can be evaluated (Golden, Zillmer, & Spiers, 1992).

Neuropsychological assessments are typically organized into standardized or flexible batteries. Standardized batteries are those in which patients take all tests in a given battery. Some examples of standardized neuropsychological batteries include the Halstead-Reitan and the Luria Nebraska test batteries. Both batteries are composed of an established set of tests that assess those neurocognitive functions that are susceptible to disruption from neurologic impairment, including those sustained after head injury (Smith, Barth, Diamond, & Giuliano, 1998). Flexible neuropsychological batteries are those in which the neuropsychologist creates a customized battery of specific tests or modifies a basic battery based on individual patient issues and history (Smith et al., 1998). Others may use a combination of these approaches: a standard battery of tests given to all or nearly all clients, augmented by additional tests selected for the client's situation. This latter approach has become increasingly more common.

Treatment Evaluation

Neuropsychologists may use tests to evaluate the effectiveness of interventions with a client after brain injury. Such interventions may include medical treatment (e.g., surgery for chronic epilepsy), speech therapy, occupational therapy, physical therapy, or whether a particular drug makes a patient better or worse in terms of neuropsychological functioning (Golden, 1983). For instance, a study by Goldberg et al. (1982) found significant improvement in memory after drug treatment. These studies aid in documenting and evaluating the effects and value of treatment. Neuropsychologists may also engage in rehabilitation using cognitive retraining (Golden, Zillmer, & Spiers, 1992). However, treatment remains a relatively small part of the activities of the average neuropsychologist.

Rehabilitation

The primary objective of neuropsychological rehabilitation is to improve the quality of life of individuals who have sustained neurological insult that may involve cognitive, behavioral, emotional, and social factors (Hanlon, 1994). Neuropsychological assessment can serve as a first step in developing a rehabilitation program for a patient because it allows the clinician to fully document the details of the patient's strengths and weaknesses. Documentation integrated with an understanding of brain function allows the clinician to understand the behavioral, cognitive, and emotional effects of an injury (Golden, Zillmer, & Spiers, 1992).

Hanlon (1994) described four primary approaches to cognitive rehabilitation that are currently practiced: (1) the direct retraining approach that involves the use of repetitive drills and exercises; (2) the substitution-transfer model, in which visual imagery is used to facilitate verbal retention, verbal mediation, and elaboration to compensate for visual memory dysfunction; (3) the functional compensation and adaptation model, which involves the use of any and all strategies, techniques, devices, and adaptive equipment that enable the patient to perform tasks that can no longer be performed in a conventional manner; and (4) the behavioral approach, which is based on the principles of learning theory and behavior.

A relatively new area of rehabilitation has been in prevention, specifically when dealing with dementing diseases. These techniques and ideas are based on the idea that mental and physical activity (as well as medication) can lead to delays in the development of dementia, an area fueled by the aging of the baby boomer population (Center for Disease Control, 2008).

Future Trends in Neuropsychology

The field of neuropsychology continues to expand. The major changes that have taken place reflect improvement in the sophistication and specificity of the questions asked and the answers to the questions, although many of the diagnostic instruments themselves are similar to those that have been used for the past half century. Kay and Starbuck (1997) have noted that the relatively low cost of personal computers and the potential of having computers perform labor-intensive scoring and test administration procedures may explain the popularity of computer applications in neuropsychological assessment. The impact of computers has slowly been seen, but there has been resistance from researchers, consumers, and test companies who wish to continue to emphasize traditional techniques. Another growing area is the combined use of newer neuroradiological techniques that measure in vivo changes in the brain and concurrent neuropsychological testing to better identify the specific brain areas involved in specific tests and disorders. The use of neuroradiological techniques to better specify the nature and extent of disorders while the client is alive has allowed a continued explosion of knowledge compared to earlier research, which was based on much less accurate techniques or on autopsy after the client's death.

REFERENCES

Centers for Disease Control (2008). *The Healthy brain initiative.* Atlanta, GA: Author.

Finger, S. (1994). History of neuropsychology. In D. W. Zaidel (Ed.), *Neuropsychology* (pp. 1–28). San Diego: Academic Press.

Frommer, G. P., & Smith, A. (1988). Kurt Goldstein and recovery of function. In S. Finger, T. E. LeVere, C. R. Almli, & D. G. Stein (Eds.), *Brain injury and recovery: Theoretical and controversial issues* (pp. 71–88). New York: Plenum Press.

Goldberg, E., Gerstman, L. J., Mattis, S., Hughes, J. E. O., Bilder, R. M., & Sirio, C. A. (1982). Effects of cholinergic treatment of posttraumatic anterograde amnesia. *Archives of Neurology (Chicago), 39,* 581.

Golden, C. J., Zillmer, E., & Spiers, M. (1992). *Neuropsychological assessment and intervention.* Springfield, IL: Charles C. Thomas.

Goldstein, K. (1939). *The organism.* New York: American Book Co.

Hanlon, R.E. (1994). Neuropsychological rehabilitation. In D. Zaidel (Ed.), *Neuropsychology: Handbook of Perception and Cognition* (pp. 317–338). San Diego, CA: Academic Press.

Kay, G. G., & Starbuck, V. N. (1997). Computerized neuropsychological assessment. In M. E. Maruish & J.A. Moses, Jr. (Eds.), *Clinical neuropsychology: Theoretical foundations for practitioners* (pp. 143–161). Mahwah, NJ: Lawrence Erlbaum.

Meier, M. J. (1997). The establishment of clinical neuropsychology as a psychological specialty. In M. E. Maruish & J. A. Moses, Jr. (Eds.), *Clinical neuropsychology: Theoretical foundations for practitioners* (pp. 1–31). Mahwah, NJ: Lawrence Erlbaum.

Smith, R. J., Barth, J. T. Diamond, R., & Giuliano, A. J. (1998). Evaluation of head trauma. In G. Goldstein, P. D. Nussbaum, & S. R. Beers (Eds.), *Neuropsychology* (pp. 136–170). New York: Plenum Press.

SUGGESTED READINGS

Golden, C. J., Espe-Pfeifer, & Wachsler-Felder, J. (2000). *Neuropsychological interpretation of objective psychological tests.* New York: Kluwer.

Horton, A. M. (2003). *Handbook of forensic neuropsychology.* New York: Springer.

Reitan, R. M., & Wolfson, D. (1993). *The Halstead-Reitan neuropsychological battery.* Tucson, AZ: Neuropsychology Press.

CHARLES GOLDEN
Nova Southeastern University

See also: Brain Injuries; Neuropsychological Development; Neuropsychological Rehabilitation

NEUROSCIENCE

One of the primary goals of psychology is to understand the biological, experiential, and social factors that shape and guide behavior. Neuroscientists share this goal, but focus their efforts toward understanding how the central and peripheral nervous systems control behavior.

Neuroscience became identified as an independent and identifiable discipline in the 1960s, and the field has rapidly evolved and grown over the ensuing decades. For example, the Society for Neuroscience (SFN) has grown from 500 members at its founding in 1969 to over 38,000 current members. According to the society's website, SFN is the world's largest organization of scientists and physicians devoted to the advancement of our understanding of the brain and nervous system. In addition to SFN, and reflecting the explosive growth of neuroscientific research, many other neuroscience societies now exist around the world, including the International Behavioral Neuroscience Society (IBNS) and the Federation of European Neuroscience Societies (FENS).

Reflecting its history, neuroscience is multidisciplinary, integrating the fields of psychology, psychiatry, medicine, molecular and cell biology, and computer science, among others. This multidisciplinarity is essential for progress toward a comprehensive understanding of brain-behavior relations. In addition to understanding how the nervous system functions under normal conditions, significant efforts are directed toward understanding diseases and disorders of the nervous system, including autism, Alzheimer's disease, amyotrophic lateral sclerosis (ALS), schizophrenia, and Parkinson's disease. But it is the basic research that provides the foundation upon which the clinical and other applied research domains rely.

Neuroscientists seek to explain how the nervous system develops, how it evolved, and how it contributes to the organization of behavior. Progress in such broad domains of inquiry is made possible by investigating nervous system function at many levels of analysis: from molecules to neurons to systems to social groups. For example, neurophysiologists investigate neuronal communication in individual cells as well as the interactions among populations of cells in large neural networks. Neuropharmacologists investigate the chemical basis of neural communication and the effects of drugs on nervous system function. Neuroanatomists investigate the gross structure of the nervous system, including the fiber tracts that connect neural structures to each other and to the muscles that make behavior possible. Neuroethologists investigate the neural systems that make complex, "natural" behaviors—such as birdsong—possible.

In addition to these older and more established domains of neuroscience research, new domains continue to emerge. For example, cognitive neuroscientists focus primarily on the neural basis of perception and cognition in humans. Computational neuroscientists use modern computing technologies to model nervous system function, thereby providing an alternative method for testing theories and generating new hypotheses. More recently, neuroeconomics has emerged as an independent discipline that aims to understand the neural basis of decision-making. Thus, neuroscience reflects every major domain of inquiry within the biological and psychological sciences, employing a variety of species and technological approaches.

Early Greek philosophers' attempted to provide possible explanations about the brain and its function. As early as 400 B.C.E., many people were intrigued by the complex structure of the brain. Hippocrates considered the brain to be the organ of the senses, knowledge, wisdom, and intelligence. Plato also considered the brain the seat of mental processes, whereas his student, Aristotle, considered the brain merely an organ for cooling the heart, which he believed to be the true center of mind and emotion. Around 200 B.C.E., Galen wrote of the brain and nerves as major systems of the body, and he conducted dissections to explore the anatomy of the central nervous system.

It wasn't until the late nineteenth and early twentieth centuries that the modern foundation for neuroscience was laid. In 1864, John Hughlings Jackson wrote about the loss of speech after brain injury and conducted research on seizures in epileptic patients. About 20 years later, Santiago Ramon y Cajal discovered that nerve cells were independent cellular elements and established the Neuron Doctrine that identified the neuron as the basic structural and functional unit of the nervous system. This was a breakthrough concept because, until then, the Reticular Theory had predominated; this theory stated that the brain is composed of a single mass of connected tubes, similar to the circulatory system. Not long thereafter, Sir Charles Sherrington expanded on Cajal's work through studies of the reflex arc—work that led him to suggest that neurons communicate with each other across discernible gaps that he called "synapses." Around the same time, Ivan Pavlov, a physiologist who had already performed groundbreaking work on the nervous control of digestion, made the serendipitous discovery that salivation can be triggered by stimuli in the environment that reliably predict the delivery of food. This finding would contribute to the emergence of the behaviorist approach to psychology and, decades later, form the basis for one of the most successful domains of inquiry within the field of neuroscience.

Psychology's complex relationship with neuroscience is reflected in the history of those American Psychological Association (APA) journals that have been devoted to animal behavior and its biological bases. Specifically, in 1911, the *Journal of Animal Behavior* was established under the editorship of Robert M. Yerkes. Seven years later, this journal was replaced by *Psychobiology*, a journal formed under the editorship of Knight Dunlap. Then, in 1921, *Psychobiology* was replaced by the *Journal of Comparative Psychology* (JCP), formed under the joint editorship of Dunlap and Yerkes. JCP thrived under the editorship of such prominent psychologists as Harry Harlow, William Estes, and Eliot Stellar until 1947, when it was renamed the *Journal of Comparative and Physiological Psychology* (JCPP). By that time, physiological psychology was an identifiable branch of psychology devoted (among other things) to understanding the nervous system and its control of peripheral organ systems that are central to such basic "motivated" behaviors as eating, drinking, and reproduction. Finally, in 1983, shifting emphases within the field led to the division of JCPP into the *Journal of Comparative Psychology* (again) and *Behavioral Neuroscience,* the latter founded by Richard Thompson. Today, *Behavioral Neuroscience* continues as a leading repository of research devoted to understanding the neural bases of behavior.

Given this history, it should not be surprising that many psychologists have made critical contributions to the field of neuroscience. For example, in the middle of the last century, Donald Hebb inspired what is now referred to as Hebb's Law, which has been pithily summarized as the notion that "neurons that fire together wire together." Today, the notion of a Hebbian synapse captures the idea that correlated activity among neurons plays a critical role in a variety of processes associated with learning and memory, as well as other forms of neural plasticity.

Another prominent psychologist, Karl Lashley, sought to identify the locations within the brain where memories are stored—he called them "engrams"—and published his work on the biological memory in the book, *In Search of the Engram*. The neuropsychologist, neurobiologist, and Nobel laureate, Roger Sperry, conducted research in patients who had undergone a "split-brain" procedure—in which the large fiber bundle that connects the two cerebral hemispheres is disconnected—as a treatment for epilepsy. His work contributed to much of what we currently know about lateralized functions in the brain. Edward Tolman's work on spatial learning in rats is now seen as the critical foundation for our understanding of the hippocampus and its functional role in memory processing and spatial navigation.

Richard F. Thompson, mentioned earlier, was a key figure in the integration of Pavlov's work on conditioned responses with modern neuroscience. In general, the behavioral paradigms developed and refined by psychologists have provided the foundation for all neuroscientists interested in the neural and molecular mechanisms that underlie behavior. With such a rich interconnected history, it is not surprising that today the fields of psychology and neuroscience continue to influence each other. Continued interactions between psychology and neuroscience will be important for shaping the future directions of both. Both fields will continue to be devoted to understanding the biological foundations of behavior and the developmental and evolutionary forces that have shaped the diversity of behavior throughout the animal kingdom—from flies to humans. As with other natural sciences, like physics and chemistry, extensive collaborations will be critical for future progress in understanding brain-behavior relationships in human and non-human animals, and in natural and clinical populations.

SUGGESTED READINGS

Hebb, D. O. (1949). *The organization of behavior: A neuropsychological theory*. New York: John Wiley & Sons.

Kandel, E. R., Schwartz, J. H., & Jessell, T. M. (2000). *Principles of neural science* (4th ed.). New York: McGraw-Hill Medical.

Lashley, K. S. (1950). In search of the engram. *Symposia of the Society for Experimental Biology, 4*, 454–482.

Pavlov, I. P. (1927). *Conditioned reflexes: An investigation of the physiological activity of the cerebral cortex* (G. V. Anrep, Trans.). London: Humphrey Milford/Oxford University Press.

Sherrington, C. S. (1906). *The integrative action of the nervous system*. New Haven, CT: Yale University Press.

Squire, L. R., Bloom, F. E., & Spitzer, N. C. (2008). *Fundamental Neuroscience* (3rd ed.). New York: Academic Press.

Thompson, R. F. (1994). Behaviorism and neuroscience. *Behavioral Neuroscience, 101*, 259–265.

Tolman, E. D. (1948). Cognitive maps in rats and men. *Psychological Review, 55*, 189–208.

AMY JO MARCANO-REIK
MARK S. BLUMBERG
University of Iowa

See also: **Cognitive Neuroscience; Neuropsychological Development; Neuropsychology; Social Neuroscience**

NEUROSIS

Although the concept of neurosis dates to 1769 in Cullen's *Synopses and Nosology*, it awaited Freud's early attempts to explain and treat a host of neurotic symptoms, most notably hysterical ones, to establish its nosological prominence. In fact, the focus on the concept and the importance attributed to it as a unique psychopathological condition parallel the prominence and importance of psychoanalysis within the discipline of psychiatry. The general diagnosis of neurosis and many subtypes were included in the first and second editions of the *Diagnostic and Statistical Manual* (DSM) of the American Psychiatric Association, which is that organization's attempt to construct a nosological schema of psychopathology. These manuals were used by generations of psychiatrists and clinical psychologists trained in the heyday of psychoanalysis in the United States. Psychoanalysts maintained prominent administrative and teaching positions in the most prestigious psychiatry departments, clinical psychology doctoral programs, and psychology internships in the post–World War II years. Fenichel's (1945) tome, *The Psychoanalytic Theory of Neurosis*, was requisite reading for clinicians going through these training programs.

The political climate changed in the 1980s when DSM III was introduced. This new version was developed by a group of psychiatric researchers who decided to keep an etiological theory out of their attempt to classify psychopathology. They wanted to develop instead a descriptive nosological system and hoped that classifying psychopathology on the basis of manifest symptoms would increase interrater reliability in making diagnostic distinctions and researching psychopathology. They regarded the psychoanalytic emphasis on underlying etiology and meaning as a way of classifying disorders to be unproved and too vague to promote adequate interrater reliability. This striking shift in nosological approach was hotly contested by many clinicians who found the psychoanalytic emphasis more useful. Nonetheless, the researchers prevailed. Neurosis became collateral damage in this paradigmatic shift, first being included parenthetically in DSM III, and then being excluded from DSM IV.

Psychoanalytic History of Neurosis

Interestingly, however, a similar pattern occurred within psychoanalysis: That is, the concept of neurosis virtually disappeared from both the psychoanalytic literature and psychoanalytic scientific meetings (Sugarman, 2007). It appears that what is referred to as the "widening scope of psychoanalysis" to include the treatment of more disturbed patients, a trend that began in the late 1960s with Otto Kernberg's description of the borderline personality and Heinz Kohut's delineation of the narcissistic personality, led to a de-emphasis on the type of psychopathology that for many decades was the bread and butter of the practicing psychoanalyst. But there are also other more substantive reasons for neurosis fading into obscurity, reasons that have to do with how the concept was defined and understood.

Definitional Problems

The traditional psychoanalytic definition of neurosis involved various types of symptom pictures, dating to Freud's original interest in hysterical symptoms. Fenichel's (1945) textbook, for example, included anxiety neurosis, conversion neurosis, organ neurosis, obsessive-compulsive neurosis, impulse neurosis, and depressive neurosis. But other analysts soon expanded the definition of neurosis beyond symptomatic conditions to include problems of character or personality. Hence, Waelder (1958) coined the term *character neurosis*. Diagnoses of masochistic character, neurasthenic hypochondriac character (Schilder, 1979), anal character, and others soon appeared in the psychoanalytic literature. Although this expansion of the concept to include neurotic character traits seemed clinically valid, it proved theoretically confusing. Some saw the concept of character neurosis as paralleling symptom neurosis, the only differentiating factor being whether the trait in question was ego syntonic (hence characterological) or ego alien (hence symptomatic). Some, however, viewed character neuroses as more pathological than symptom neuroses, while others preferred the psychiatric term, *personality disorder,* which they differentiated from the neuroses. Consequently the definition of neurosis became confused. As its phenomenological referents became unclear, its popularity waned.

A Developmental Lag in Theory

The most serious reason for the virtual disappearance of the concept of neurosis from the psychoanalytic literature is the slowness to integrate Freud's structural theory with clinical practice. Two American psychoanalysts, Fred Busch (1995) and Paul Gray (1994), have noted this "developmental lag" with regard to analytic technique. The same holds true for psychoanalytic nosology (Sugarman, 2007). Freud's original diagnostic categories, including neurosis, were differentiated on the basis of the unconscious sexual drive derivatives thought to be causing the symptom in question. He thought that the patient's inability to allow sexual ideation or feelings into conscious awareness dammed up their sexual energy or libido and created symptoms; others extended this model to character traits. Neurotic symptoms or character traits were considered to be caused by unconscious phallic-oedipal derivatives, whereas more severe psychopathology was considered caused by developmentally more primitive oral or anal drive derivatives.

This sort of thinking, characteristic of Freud's earlier topographic model, was replaced in 1923 by the structural model in his book, *The Ego and the Id.* Freud never attempted to revisit nosology after this theoretical revision, even though the structural concepts of the ego and the superego both require and allow for a far more sophisticated approach to diagnosis. Furthermore, the emphasis on unconscious drive derivatives as ways to distinguish psychopathology proved to be inaccurate. Many clinicians noted that some neurotic patients show primarily oral or anal drive derivatives, and that some more disturbed patients demonstrate significant oedipal thoughts and fantasies. This failure of the etiological model to adequately differentiate neurosis from more serious psychopathology led to a de-emphasis of neurosis instead of a revision of the explanatory model.

A Structural Definition of Neurosis

Only recently (Sugarman, 2007) has it been suggested that the concept of neurosis retains clinical value in guiding psychoanalytic technique so long as it is redefined along structural grounds. This redefinition proposes that symptoms or character traits should be defined as neurotic if they occur in a mind that is neurotically structured. That is, if they occur in a patient with sufficient mental structure to be deemed neurotic, they should be considered a symptom or character neurosis. To date, four major structural criteria for designating a mind as neurotically organized have been suggested, although it is expected that others will be proposed as this diagnostic revision is discussed and studied. These four criteria are (1) the capacity for self-reflection or mentalization; (2) the capacity for affect regulation; (3) the capacity for narcissistic regulation; and (4) the precedence of intrapsychic conflict over developmental arrest. Understanding neuroses in terms of these underlying mental structures will allow clinicians to once again use that diagnosis to determine differential treatment strategies.

REFERENCES

Busch, F. (1995). *The ego at the center of clinical technique*. Northvale, NJ: Jason Aronson.

Fenichel, O. (1945). *The psychoanalytic theory of neurosis*. New York: Norton.

Gray, P. (1994). *The ego and the analysis of defense*. Northvale, NJ: Jason Aronson.

Schilder, P. (1979). *On neuroses*. New York: International Universities Press.

Sugarman, A. (2007). Whatever happened to neurosis? Who are we analyzing? And how? *Psychoanalytic Psychology, 24*, 409–428.

Waelder, R. (1958). Neurotic ego distortion. *International Journal of Psychoanalysis, 39*, 243–244.

SUGGESTED READINGS

Howells, J. G. (1989). *Modern perspectives in the psychiatry of the neuroses*. New York: Brunner/Mazel.

Tyson, P. (1996). Neurosis in childhood and in psychoanalysis: A developmental reformulation. *Journal of the American Psychoanalytic Association, 44*, 143–165.

Alan Sugarman
University of California, San Diego

See also: **Anxiety Disorders**

NEUROTRANSMITTERS

A neurotransmitter is a chemical substance that carries a "message" from the terminal bouton (button) of one nerve cell or neuron across a tiny gap (synapse) to receptor sites on another neuron. Neurotransmitters are, in general, synthesized in the neuron's cell body and stored in tiny sacs called synaptic vesicles.

Nobel Prize winner Otto Loewi is credited with demonstrating synaptic transmission's chemical nature in 1920. Loewi isolated a frog heart with an attached vagus nerve. Stimulating the nerve caused the heart's rate to decrease, and when Loewi extracted some of the fluid around the heart and applied it to an unstimulated second heart, the second heart's rate slowed as well. Loewi concluded that stimulating the nerve to the first heart had released a chemical at the synapse between the vagus nerve and the heart, and this chemical had transported the message to the heart to slow down. Because he had stimulated the vagus nerve, Loewi called the mysterious chemical *Vagusstoff*, which was later found to be acetylcholine (ACh).

When a neurotransmitter such as ACh diffuses across the synapse, it binds to specific postsynaptic receptors to produce either a local excitatory effect or an inhibitory effect. Whether the postsynaptic neuron passes on the message by producing an action potential depends on the sum of the influences it receives from presynaptic neurons.

A neurotransmitter that remained in the synapse for any length of time would limit the number of messages passed from one neuron to another. Thus, the neurotransmitter is rapidly inactivated almost from the moment of its release. One common method of inactivation is called *reuptake*, a process through which the neurotransmitter is taken back into the presynaptic neuron from which it was released.

The second major inactivation mechanism is used on ACh and on neuropeptide neurotransmitters and is called *enzymatic degradation*. In the case of ACh, acetylcholinesterase (AChE) breaks the ACh molecule into two parts, neither of which produces the effect of ACh. Neuropeptides, once released, are degraded by peptidase. *Diffusion*, the drifting away of neurotransmitter molecules from the synapse, is another inactivation method that occurs with all the neurotransmitters.

The brain uses as many as 100 neurotransmitters. For many years, it was believed that each neuron released only one particular neurotransmitter from all its nerve terminals. We now know that many if not most neurons release two or three transmitters, and some may release as many as five or six.

Neurotransmitters can be classified into two major categories: *small molecule* and *large molecule*. The small-molecule neurotransmitters include the *amino acids* (e.g., GABA, glutamate), the *monoamines* (e.g., norepinephrine, dopamine, serotonin), the *soluble gases* (e.g., nitric oxide), and acetylcholine. The large-molecule neurotransmitters include the *endogenous opioids*, substance P, oxytocin, antidiuretic hormone (ADH), and cholecystokinin (CCK).

Small-Molecule Neurotransmitters

Gamma-aminobutyric acid (GABA) is an example of an amino acid neurotransmitter. GABA is the most common inhibitory neurotransmitter in the brain, and the destruction of GABA neurons in a major motor system (the basal ganglia) occurs in Huntington's disease. Symptoms of Huntington's disease include involuntary movements. Antianxiety drugs such as diazepam (Valium) and alprazolam (Xanax) act by stimulating GABA receptors. Other amino acid neurotransmitters include glutamate (the most common excitatory neurotransmitter in the brain), glycine, and aspartate.

The monoamines are further divided into the *catecholamines* (dopamine, epinephrine, norepinephrine) and the *indoleamines* (serotonin, melatonin). Dopamine is importantly implicated in two major brain disorders: schizophrenia and Parkinson's disease. In Parkinson's disease, cells die in a brain area called the substantia nigra (Latin for "black substance"). In the course of the disease, the "black substance" actually becomes white because of the loss of dopamine-producing cells. Nigral cells normally project dopamine to the basal ganglia. Without the neurotransmitter, the afflicted individual begins to develop characteristic symptoms such as tremor at rest, rigidity, and slowed movement. Replacement therapy—supplying drugs to increase the amount of dopamine in the brain (for example, L-dopa)—may work temporarily, but unfortunately, the disease is progressive.

Schizophrenia is also associated with defects in the dopamine system, in this case by increased activity. Major antipsychotic drugs, both typical—such as chlorpromazine (Thorazine)—and atypical—such as risperidone (Risperdal)—block subtypes of dopamine receptors.

Norepinephrine (also called noradrenalin) is the neurotransmitter in the postganglionic sympathetic nervous system and is also found in the brain. Decreased norepinephrine and/or serotonin activity in the brain are thought to contribute to depression. Most drugs used to treat depression increase the release of norepinephrine, serotonin, or both.

Melatonin is manufactured in and secreted by the pineal gland in response to the ambient level of light. It is importantly involved in the body's biological clock, and low doses have been used to treat insomnia and the effects of jet lag.

The soluble gases appear to break all the "rules" governing the actions of neurotransmitters. They are made in all parts of neurons, are released as soon as they are manufactured, and do not affect postsynaptic receptors. The soluble gases identified at this time are nitric oxide and carbon monoxide. Nitric oxide is apparently involved in such disparate functions as penile erection, dilation of blood vessels in areas of the brain that are metabolically active, and learning. Popular drugs used to treat erectile dysfunction, such as sildenafil (Viagra), work by enhancing the effects of nitric oxide.

The remaining small-molecule neurotransmitter, acetylcholine (ACh), is found in the brain and spinal cord, and it is also the chemical that carries messages from the motor nerves to the skeletal muscles. In this latter role, ACh is involved in movement disorders such as myasthenia gravis, which is characterized by severe muscle weakness, particularly after exercise, with recovery after a period of rest. The acute symptoms of the disorder can be treated by the injection of a drug that inhibits the breakdown of ACh in the synapse, which results in more ACh available to stimulate the skeletal muscles.

Large-Molecule Neurotransmitters

The endogenous opioids, also called the "endorphins," or "endogenous morphine-like substances," are some of the most important of the large-molecule neurotransmitters. Because opiates such as morphine and heroin are so addictive, brain researchers suspected that there were receptors for the opiates in the brain. In 1973, such receptors were found, which led to the further discovery of naturally occurring neurotransmitters with opiate-like properties, such as the induction of analgesia and euphoria. Some functions in which the endogenous opiates have been implicated include the placebo effect, runner's high, and pain relief from acupuncture (but not from hypnotically induced analgesia).

Other large-molecule neurotransmitters include substance P (involved in pain perception), oxytocin (responsible for labor pains), and cholecystokinin (involved in hunger satiety). Like oxytocin, antidiuretic hormone (ADH) is released from the posterior lobe of the pituitary gland. ADH acts on the kidneys to conserve the body's water supply; lack of it results in diabetes insipidus, which is characterized by extreme thirst, copious drinking, and frequent urination.

SUGGESTED READINGS

Cooper, J. R., Bloom, F. E., & Roth, R. H. (1996). *The biochemical basis of neuropharmacology* (7th ed.). New York: Oxford University Press.

Kandel, E. R., Schwartz, J. H., & Jessell, T. M. (2000). *Principles of neural science* (4th ed.). New York: McGraw-Hill.

Klein, S. B., & Thorne, B. M. (2007). *Biological psychology*. New York: Worth.

B. MICHAEL THORNE
Mississippi State University

See also: GABA Receptors

NEW ZEALAND, PSYCHOLOGY IN

To describe psychology in any country an author must touch on three facets of the discipline: knowledge, practice, and practitioners. In this overview of psychology in Aotearoa/New Zealand, we outline the workforce, describe the current practice regime, and discuss the most significant issue for psychological knowledge.

Psychology Workforce

In 2006, 2,000 registered psychologists held a current Annual Practicing Certificate (APC), meaning that there could be about 3,000 psychologists in this country. Some 90% of the practitioners self-identify as Pākehā (New Zealander of European descent) or "Other European" ethnicity, and over 60% are female. Psychological services are represented predominantly by clinical, educational, and counseling psychology, along with teaching and research.

However, there have long been concerns that psychologists practicing in health, education, youth, and criminal justice settings do not provide appropriate services to the indigenous Māori and Pacific Island people (Abbott & Durie, 1987). As part of the effort to address that concern, the New Zealand Psychologists Board expects practitioners to ensure that they have the awareness, knowledge, and skill necessary to deliver psychological services to people of diverse worldviews and cultures in ways that are adjudged culturally safe by the clients. That cultural competence is to be centered on the practitioner's understanding that they are a culture bearer, together with an informed appreciation of the cultural basis of psychological knowledge.

Regulation of Practice

In Aotearoa/New Zealand psychological practice is guided by the New Zealand Psychological Society *Code of Ethics for Psychologists Working in Aotearoa/New Zealand* (2002) and the Health Practitioners Competency Assurance Act. The intent of the act is to ensure the health and safety of members of the public, and only psychologists who are registered with the Psychologists Board and have a current APC can legally practice or claim to be practicing psychology. This regulatory regime owes much to the medical model of practitioner and patient and sits awkwardly with domains of psychological practice such as industrial/organizational, community, and educational. Teachers of psychology are only required to be registered if they are responsible for training of practitioners, so the majority of psychologists in universities are not registered. The New Zealand Psychological Society is the premier professional association for psychologists in New Zealand supporting its members in safe, effective, and ethical practice.

Cultural Basis of Psychological Knowledge

Psychology was introduced into New Zealand from the United States and United Kingdom (Herbert & Morrison, 2007), and New Zealand graduates consequently fit relatively easily into overseas institutions and practice regimes. Until relatively recently there has been only sporadic interest in identifying and discussing the epistemological foundations of psychology, although there is agreement that psychology has been focused on the scientific analysis of the behavior of (biologically) individual humans (Black & Huygens, 2007). This analysis has provided a substantial body of information about people's behavior, but it has not enabled the discipline to engage effectively and appropriately with peoples with differing worldviews. To make that observation less abstract, we offer brief discussions of three areas important to clients and practitioners: first, the connection between knowledge and relationships; second, the centrality of culture for

people; and finally, the place of spirituality in human life, utilizing contributions to a recently published handbook of professional practice (Evans, Rucklidge, & O'Driscoll, 2007).

Mainstream psychology valorizes disinterested or objective knowledge that can be conveyed in words, tables, and figures whereas, in many cultures, knowledge is embedded within and is inseparable from relationships. To gain valid knowledge from or about a person in the Maori world requires establishing a relationship between the investigator and the subject (Gavala & Taitimu, 2007). In Pacific thought, *vā*—which are relationships between the three elements of *Atua* (God), *Tagata* (people) and *Laufanua* (environment)—sustain valid knowledge (Kingi-'Ulu'ave, Faleafa, & Brown, 2007, p. 72). As psychology needs to provide recognizably valid knowledge and practice must be culturally safe, there is an ongoing reappraisal of current epistemology and the self-contained individualism it sustains (Love & Waiktoki, 2007). Māori models of human well-being, such as *Whare Tapa Whā* (the four-sided house), provide significant resources for that project (Gavala & Taitimu, 2007).

People's culture provides the framework within which they understand their world, give meaning to events, interpret their own and others' actions, and relate to those around them. Consequently, many indigenous models or theories of health and well being assert that being in the world is always being within the cultural world. A key response to this issue is to discuss the culture of psychology (Black & Huygens, 2007; Williams & Cleland, 2007). Recognition that the discipline has its own culture that is largely consistent with the dominant Western individualism has to be addressed in relation to therapeutic practice (Taylor & Dickinson, 2007) and research (Chamberlain, 2007). Concurrently, there is a growing recognition that mainstream psychology, because it has routinely marginalized culture, has been incapable of understanding the nature and role of people's interpretations in shaping how they respond to their world.

The sharpest challenge to the simple realist empiricism of mainstream psychology has been around the place of spirit and spirituality in healthy human life. As a secular science born in the Enlightenment, psychology has eschewed religion. That commitment undermines psychologists' attempts to address the impacts of colonization on peoples and their communities, as the discipline has no theories or procedures for understanding why seizure of a people's land should lead to fragmentation of identity and a loss of spirit. In contrast, Maori theorizing of health and well-being asserts the necessity of a balanced interdependence between four facets of the person: *wairua* (spirit), *hinengaro* (cognition and emotion), *tinana* (physical being), and *whanau* (family and social relationships) (Gavala & Taitimu, 2007). That balanced interdependence is symbolized as a house of four walls (*Whare Tapa Whā*) that stands on the *Whenua* (ancestral lands). That representation not only helps capture the impact of land alienation and other colonial processes, but also offers a basis for psychologists to provide assistance, provided they acknowledge the role of *wairua*. (Love & Waitoki, 2007).

In conclusion, psychology in Aotearoa/New Zealand is evolving as it seeks to recognize, understand, and respond to cultural differences, so that all persons and peoples are able to access services that relate to and meet their needs.

REFERENCES

Abbott, M. H., & Durie, M. H. (1987). A whiter shade of pale. *New Zealand Journal of Psychology, 16*, 58–71.

Black, R., & Huygens, I. (2007). Pākehā culture and psychology. In I. M. Evans, J. J. Rucklidge, & M. O'Driscoll (Eds.), *Professional practice of psychology in Aotearoa New Zealand* (pp. 49–66). Wellington: New Zealand Psychological Society.

Chamberlain, K. (2007). Research ethics and the protection of human participants. In I. M. Evans, J. J. Rucklidge, & M. O'Driscoll (Eds.), *Professional practice of psychology in Aotearoa New Zealand* (pp. 163–179). Wellington: New Zealand Psychological Society.

Evans, I. M., Rucklidge, J. J., & O'Driscoll, M. (Eds.). (2007). *Professional practice of psychology in Aotearoa New Zealand*. Wellington: New Zealand Psychological Society.

Gavala, J., & Taitimu, M. (2007). Training and supporting a Māori workforce. In I. M. Evans, J. J. Rucklidge, & M. O'Driscoll (Eds.), *Professional practice of psychology in Aotearoa New Zealand* (pp. 229–244). Wellington: New Zealand Psychological Society.

Herbert, A. M. L., & Morrison, L. (2007). Practice of psychology in Aotearoa: A Maori perspective. In I. M. Evans, J. J. Rucklidge, & M. O'Driscoll (Eds.), *Professional practice of psychology in Aotearoa New Zealand* (pp. 35–47). Wellington: New Zealand Psychological Society.

Kingi-'Ulu'ave, D., Faleafa, M., & Brown, T. (2007). A Pasifika perspective of psychology in Aotearoa. In I. M. Evans, J. J. Rucklidge, & M. O'Driscoll (Eds.), *Professional practice of psychology in Aotearoa New Zealand* (pp. 67–83). Wellington: New Zealand Psychological Society.

Love, C., & Waitoki, W. (2007). Multicultural competence in bicultural Aotearoa. In I. M. Evans, J. J. Rucklidge, & M. O'Driscoll (Eds.), *Professional practice of psychology in Aotearoa New Zealand* (pp. 265–280). Wellington: New Zealand Psychological Society.

Taylor, J. E., & Dickson, J. A. (2007). Confidentiality and privacy. In I. M. Evans, J. J. Rucklidge, & M. O'Driscoll (Eds.), *Professional practice of psychology in Aotearoa New Zealand* (pp. 131–146). Wellington: New Zealand Psychological Society.

Williams, M. W., & Cleland, A. M. M. M. T. (2007). Asian peoples in New Zealand: Implications for psychological practice. In I. M. Evans, J. J. Rucklidge, & M. O'Driscoll (Eds.), *Professional practice of psychology in Aotearoa New Zealand* (pp. 85–102). Wellington: New Zealand Psychological Society.

RAYMOND NAIRN
PAMELA HYDE
New Zealand Psychological Society

NICOTINE-RELATED DISORDERS

Nicotine is a pale yellow, toxic liquid found in the leaves of 66 different species of plants. Nicotine is generally extracted from dried *Nicotiana tabacum* leaves, for the production of tobacco products and insecticide (nicotine sulfate). Nicotine falls within the category of chemical compounds called alkaloids, organic substances whose bitter taste (and often poisonous properties) discourage animals from eating the plants that contain them. Nicotine's first use dates back centuries (as early as the 1500s), during which nicotine was consumed for its stimulant and hunger-reducing properties. However, nicotine is extremely poisonous and can cause respiratory failure, convulsions, nervous system paralysis, and death if a single dose of 50 mg or more is consumed.

Several types of tobacco products contain nicotine, including cigarettes, cigars, pipes, bidis (small, thin hand-rolled cigarettes from Southeast Asia), kreteks (clove cigarettes), and smokeless tobacco (including snuff, chew, gutka). The amount of nicotine contained in tobacco products varies widely, both by and within product category. Specifically, the amount of nicotine found in snuff varies from 0.23% to 68.14%. Across American cigarettes, the amount of inhaled nicotine has been on the rise, and currently ranges from 1.73–2.42 milligrams by cigarette. One cigarette delivers approximately 2.0 milligrams of nicotine, along with 4,000 other chemicals, to the lungs, nose and mouth within 10 seconds of inhalation.

Smoking quickly transports nicotine to the brain, affecting multiple brain systems. Specifically, smoking affects the mesolimbic system, the pleasure center of the brain, by increasing levels of dopamine, a neurotransmitter essential to the functioning of the central nervous system and emotion regulation. Dopamine elicits feelings of euphoria and has been implicated in the addictive process of nicotine and other substances of abuse. In terms of the craving associated with tobacco use, nicotine influences the brain systems associated with emotion and reward, including the insula, orbitofrontal cortex, anterior cingulated cortex, and areas that have a high density of nicotinic receptors, including the thalamus and midbrain.

Due to nicotine's addictive and toxic properties, it has serious and fatal health consequences. Throughout the world, smoking has contributed to 5.4 million deaths annually. Smoking has been linked to cancer (particularly lung cancer), cardiovascular disease (including coronary heart disease), pulmonary disease, and reproductive health problems (such as stillbirth and sudden infant death syndrome; SIDS). Secondhand smoke is also a major health concern, causing a number of health problems in non-smokers including severe asthma, heart disease, and lung problems.

Quitting smoking can reduce health hazards. In the order of most to least effective, smoking cessation programs include pharmacological approaches, behavioral modification programs, and self-help approaches. A combination of behavioral and pharmacological approaches has been found to result in the highest success in achieving long-term smoking cessation. The most popular pharmacological approach to smoking cessation includes nicotine replacement therapies (NRTs), which frequently take the form of patches, gum, and nasal spray. Other pharmacological approaches include non-nicotine replacement therapies, such as the antidepressant, buproprion (Zyban), and the nicotinic receptor partial agonist, varenicline (Chantix). With the variety of smoking-cessation treatments available, a primary care physician can help individuals determine which approach may best fit their needs.

SUGGESTED READINGS

Centers for Disease Control and Prevention. (1999). Determination of nicotine, pH, and moisture content of six U.S. commercial moist snuff products—Florida. *Morbidity and Mortality Weekly Reports, 48*(19).

McClernon, F. J., & Gilbert, D. G. (2004). Human functional imaging in nicotine and tobacco research: Basics, background, and beyond. *Nicotine & Tobacco Research, 6*(6), 941–959.

U.S. Department of Health and Human Services (2006). *The Health consequences of involuntary exposure to tobacco smoke: A report of the Surgeon General*. Atlanta, GA: U.S. Department of Health and Human Services, Centers for Disease Control and Prevention, Coordinating Center for Health Promotion, National Center for Chronic Disease Prevention and Health Promotion, Office on Smoking and Health.

World Health Organization (2007). *The scientific basis of tobacco product regulation*. Report of a WHO study group, WHO Technical Report Series, World Health Organization, Switzerland.

SARAH W. FELDSTEIN EWING
KENT HUTCHISON
University of New Mexico

See also: **Smoking Behavior**

NIGERIA, PSYCHOLOGY IN

Psychology is relatively new to Nigeria. Its origins can be traced to the offering of courses in counseling and educational psychology in departments of education at the few universities in the country at that time. As an academic discipline, psychology is said to have started in 1964 when the first department of psychology was established at the University of Nigeria, Nsukka, with 16 students and two lecturers (Olomolaiye, 1985). Psychology's identity in Nigeria has been that of a social-science discipline (Obot & Gire, 1995).

There are very few psychologists in Nigeria. Obot (1996) put the number of psychologists in active practice in Nigeria at "several hundred." A more recent estimate by Gire (2004) places the number around 7,000, an optimistic but still small number in a country with an estimated population of 140 million people. This means that there are fewer than 50 psychologists per 100,000 citizens, a vast majority of whom work in major urban centers. Two main factors account for the difficulty in estimating the number of psychologists in Nigeria. First, it is difficult to define who qualifies to hold the title of psychologist. Second, there is no statutory body responsible for regulating psychology as a profession.

The Nigerian Psychological Association (NPA), founded in 1984, is the body that represents the professional interests of psychologists. Full membership in the NPA is now open only to those "with at least a master's degree or equivalent from recognized universities" (Nigerian Psychological Association, 1984, p. 4).

Psychologists work in concert with a number of other professionals, particularly physicians and psychiatrists, because outside of academic settings, psychologists in Nigeria are most likely to be found in the psychiatric departments of major federal and state hospitals and teaching hospitals. There are many more physicians than psychologists in Nigeria. Given the small number of psychologists and the fact that psychology has yet to establish a foot-hold as a viable profession, the spread across many domains reduces their visibility and actually minimizes the impact that psychologists are capable of making.

Scope of Psychological Practice

At present, the scope of psychological practice in Nigeria remains limited. At a superficial level, the low impact of psychology is due to the scarcity of professional psychologists and, hence, the lack of available psychological services. However, the problem is much more fundamental and may be the result of the perceived irrelevance of psychology by the general population.

One of the important areas in which Nigerian psychologists are providing professional services is in health care. Two health-related areas in which psychologists are involved heavily are in the training of medical students and the provision of mental-health services. Although a few psychologists are involved in medical education, these individuals have not yet attained equality with their physician colleagues. The two main problems reported by psychologists were perceived inequality with their medical colleagues and a belief that medical administrators were not interested in or appreciative of their work (Obot, 1988).

A few psychologists can be found in industrial settings, such as personnel offices. There are also psychologists working in research centers engaged in research on a diverse array of issues (Obot, 1996). A few psychologists can also be found in the armed forces (including the

Nigerian Defense Academy), in schools, and in prisons (Gire, 2004).

There appear to be two main impediments to the practice of psychology in Nigeria. The first problem is the absence of clear and established ethical guidelines that would regulate the activities of psychologists. The other problem is the dearth of locally developed theories that would guide both research and practice. Failing that, the "imported" theories available ought to at least have been validated and deemed appropriate for the Nigerian context. Unfortunately, this has not been done. This issue should be of concern to both Nigerian and other psychologists in the developing world.

Challenges and Prospects

The future looks bright for psychology in Nigeria. This view is based on a number of factors, three of the most pertinent of which are societal need, a growing acceptance and positive view of psychology, and advances in information technology. Although Nigeria as noted has an estimated population of 140 million, the number of practicing psychologists in Nigeria is grossly inadequate. Areas in which psychologists are poised to make an impact include the legal system, including prisons; community development; business organizations; and responding to individual needs through private practice.

The other opportunity that Nigerian psychologists must capitalize on is the public's image of psychology. Obot (1993) found that respondents generally viewed psychology positively. Although some myths, such as the ability to read minds, need to be dispelled, the acceptance that psychologists provide solutions to problems of living suggests that the public might respond positively to psychological services if they became available. Another opportunity for the growth of psychology involves the enormous possibilities brought about by advances in technology generally, but especially the Internet, to enhance the acquisition of knowledge, the exchange of ideas, mentoring, and interaction with a vast network of colleagues from across the globe.

Despite these prospects, psychologists must contend with enormous challenges in order for this potential to be realized. One of the most important challenges is the availability of personnel. Harsh economic and political conditions have led many highly qualified psychologists to leave Nigeria for better opportunities abroad, a phenomenon popularly referred to as "brain drain." Also, psychologists sorely need to make a strong case for the value and role of psychology in the everyday experience and well-being of citizens and to create a career structure and job classification for psychologists.

Another challenge for Nigerian psychology is the need for a culturally relevant body of knowledge. Uzoka (1989) considers the lack of guiding philosophies or theories in research as the most serious indictment of psychology in Nigeria. He argues that Nigerian psychology has been too dependent on Western models. Thus, for psychologists to fulfill the enormous potential that lies ahead, commitment to and support for research is critical. Clearly, psychology has many contributions to make to Nigerian society. To do so, psychologists need to increase the number and quality of professionals, collaborate with their counterparts in other parts of the world, advocate for a career structure, and become ardent advocates of the potential that psychology holds for Nigeria.

REFERENCES

Gire, J. T. (2004). Psychology in Nigeria: Origins, current status and future. In M. J. Stevens & D. Wedding (Eds.), *Handbook of international psychology* (pp. 43–58). New York: Brunner-Routledge.

Nigerian Psychological Association (1984). *The constitution of the Nigerian Psychological Association*. Lagos: Author.

Obot, I. S. (1988). Social science and medical education in Nigeria. *Social Science and Medicine, 26,* 1191–1196.

Obot, I. S. (1993). What do they think of us? The public image of psychology and psychologists in Nigeria. *Nigerian Journal of Basic and Applied Psychology, 3,* 1–9.

Obot, I. S. (1996). Country profile: Nigeria. *Psychology International, 7,* 4–5.

Obot, I. S., & Gire, J. T. (1995). Psychology and national development. *Nigerian Journal of Basic and Applied Psychology, 4,* 20–31.

Olomolaiye, F. (1985). What psychology has to offer Nigeria now. In E. Okpara (Ed.), *Psychological strategies for development* (pp. 341–351). Enugu: Nigerian Psychological Association.

Uzoka, A. F. (1989). Twenty-five years of professional psychology in Nigeria. *Journal of Basic and Applied Psychology, 2,* 93–115.

JAMES T. GIRE
Virginia Military Institute

NIGHTMARES

Nightmares are defined as disturbing dreams associated with anxiety or fear that result in an awakening from sleep. The subject usually is readily aroused to full alertness and is able to recall much of the content of the dream. This distinguishes nightmares from night terrors, which are associated with a prolonged transition to wakefulness and scant recall of dream narrative. Although nightmares are featured prominently in literature and descriptive psychoanalytic writings, there is limited empirical research on this phenomenon. This fact is driven in part by pragmatic scientific limitations that make it difficult to observe neurocognitive events during the actual dream. Dreams can only be recalled following an awakening, and the fidelity of recall is not known. For example, it is possible that dream recall is limited to dream events occurring in the immediate period just prior to arousal. Further, dream recall is subject to retrieval biases in which the subject imposes order on what has been a chaotic mental experience.

Nightmares are generally thought to be associated with Rapid Eye Movement (REM) sleep. However, nightmares have also been observed in subjects during lighter stages of non-REM sleep. Nightmares typically occur in the last hours of sleep, when the sufferer is more easily aroused. Studies that involve awakening subjects at various points in time across the sleep cycle have found that the extent of dream recall increases as a function of time elapsed since sleep onset, irrespective of sleep stage (Rosenlicht et al., 1994). Thus, nightmares experienced at the end of the sleep cycle are associated with better recall than those occurring early in the sleep cycle. Despite a large number of polysomnographic studies in subjects with posttraumatic nightmares, there have been very few nightmares captured during laboratory studies (Woodward et al., 2000).

Nightmares are often confused with night terrors, which represent a clinically distinct parasomnia. Night terrors involve an incomplete awakening from slow wave sleep (non-Rapid Eye Movement sleep with predominant slow frequency brain activity) and are associated with disorientation, severe distress, and prominent autonomic arousal. During the night terror, the sufferer, typically a young child, is difficult to awaken and sooth. After a prolonged transition to full waking, the sufferer usually has no or only vague recall of dream content. Night terrors usually occur in the first hours of sleep, when slow wave sleep stages are prominent. Factors that increase slow wave sleep pressure, such as sleep loss, can increase the risk for night terrors.

Whereas nightmares are experienced universally at one time or another, the experience of frequent nightmares is considerably less common. The *Diagnostic and Statistical Manual Mental Disorders* (DSM-IV; American Psychiatric Association, 2000) includes the diagnosis of Nightmare Disorder, which was formerly referred to as Dream Anxiety Disorder. The criteria for this disorder include repeated awakenings from sleep with recall of frightening dreams that lead to significant distress. Although the precise epidemiology of this disorder is yet to be determined, the available data suggest that it occurs in 10–50% of children, with a peak incidence between the ages of three and six and a decline in frequency with age. Nightmares occur with less frequency in adults and can be associated with alcohol withdrawal, dopamine stimulating medications, beta blockers, or withdrawal of REM suppressing medication. Among persons with insomnia, nightmares are reported in approximately of 18% of those surveyed (Ohayon et al., 1997). These and other surveys have reported a higher prevalence of frightening dreams in women than in men. Unfortunately, survey data are limited by the fact that respondents are often confused about the difference between night terrors and nightmares.

There has long been an interest in the relationship between trauma exposure and nightmares. Nightmares appear to be the primary domain of sleep disturbance related to exposure to traumatic stress. Classically, the nightmare involves the mulitisensory recall of an actual traumatic experience. During the dream, people may feel as if they are re-experiencing in vivid detail various aspects of the trauma, including intense feelings of fear or horror. When nightmares occur in REM sleep, during which skeletal muscles are atonic, the sufferer may experience a sense of paralysis and an inability to escape. The associated feelings of helplessness may account for the observation that nightmare experience, in contrast to cognitive behavior therapy, may involve an exposure to trauma memories that is nontherapeutic.

At present there are few data to validate the diagnosis of nightmare disorder as a separate nosological entity from PTSD. Several studies have examined sleep polysomnography in idiopathic nightmare subjects and have found less evidence for sleep fragmentation than subjects with posttraumatic nightmares. One large study of combat veterans found that frequent nightmares were virtually specific for those diagnosed with PTSD at the time of the survey (Neylan et al., 1998). In this study, combat exposure was highly associated with nightmares, moderately associated with sleep onset insomnia, and only weakly related to sleep maintenance insomnia. These relationships are consistent with the results of a combat veteran twin study (True et al., 1993) showing that combat exposure was highly correlated with reports of dreams and nightmares and only weakly associated with sleep maintenance insomnia. These observations are also consistent with several other studies showing a low to moderate correlation between nightmares and other domains of sleep disturbance.

There is no standardized treatment for frequent nightmares. There are a number of small-scale open-label trials using sedating antidepressants, cyproheptadine, benzodiazepine, and antihistamines. Randomized controlled studies of the alpha 2 receptor agonist, guanfacine, did not show efficacy for nightmares or sleep disturbances (Neylan et al., 2006). However, there are emerging data from controlled trials that the alpha 1 antagonist, prazosin, is effective for nightmares in PTSD patients (Raskind et al., 2007). One novel treatment for repetitive nightmares is dream rehearsal therapy. Nightmare sufferers describe their nightmares in the context of group psychotherapy. They then repetitively rehearse an alternate and nontraumatic outcome to their nightmare narrative. This technique has been found to reduce the frequency and intensity of recurrent nightmares (Krakow et al., 2001). Imagery rehearsal therapy best suited a subgroup of patients with stereotypic repetitive nightmares. Although effective, imagery rehearsal therapy is not always tolerated by all patients and requires expertise and sensitivity to trauma experiences generally found only in PTSD specialty clinics.

REFERENCES

American Psychiatric Association. (2000). *Diagnostic and statistical manual of mental disorders* (4th ed., text rev.). Washington, DC: Author.

Krakow, B., Johnston, L., Melendrez, D., et al. (2001). An open-label trial of evidence-based cognitive behavior therapy for nightmares and insomnia in crime victims with PTSD. *American Journal of Psychiatry, 158*, 2043–2047.

Neylan, T. C., Lenoci, M., Samuelson, K. W., et al. (2006). No improvement of posttraumatic stress disorder symptoms with guanfacine treatment. *American Journal of Psychiatry, 163*, 2186–2188.

Neylan, T. C., Marmar, C. R., Metzler, T. J., et al. (1998). Sleep disturbances in the Vietnam generation: Findings from a nationally representative sample of male Vietnam veterans. *American Journal of Psychiatry, 155*, 929–933.

Ohayon, M. M., Morselli, P. L., & Guilleminault, C. (1997). Prevalence of nightmares and their relationship to psychopathology and daytime functioning in insomnia subjects. *Sleep, 20*, 340–348.

Raskind, M. A., Peskind, E. R., Hoff, D. J., et al. (2007). A parallel group placebo controlled study of prazosin for trauma nightmares and sleep disturbance in combat veterans with post-traumatic stress disorder. *Biological Psychiatry, 61*, 928–34.

Rosenlicht, N., Maloney, T., & Feinberg, I. (1994): Dream report length is more dependent on arousal level than prior REM duration. *Brain Research Bulletin, 34*, 99–101.

True, W. R., Rice, J., Eisen, S. A., Heath, A. C., et al. (1993). A twin study of genetic and environmental contributions to liability for posttraumatic stress symptoms. *Archives of General Psychiatry, 50*, 257–264.

Woodward, S. H., Arsenault, N. J., Murray, C., Bliwise, D. L. (2000). Laboratory sleep correlates of nightmare complaint in PTSD inpatients. *Biological Psychiatry, 48*, 1081–1087.

THOMAS C. NEYLAN
University of California, San Francisco

See also: **Posttraumatic Stress Disorder; Stress Consequences**

NOISE POLLUTION

Noise and sound do indeed differ in that noise is unwanted, intrusive, and bothersome sound that has been judged at a higher cognitive level. Some sounds may be deemed pleasant by some listeners while the same sounds are judged as intrusive and annoying by other listeners; yet at other times, the same sounds once judged pleasant can become disturbing in another context. As a result, the oft-heard expression "Music to some people; noise to others" has been quoted to argue that little can be done to abate noise. However, in trying to curb noise, ordinances and laws have been passed based on the concept of the "reasonable person" standard. In other words, would a person of reasonable sensitivities deem this particular sound to be noise? These ordinances and laws have been passed because noise pollution has grown immensely in the past century, due in large part to advances in noise-producing and noise-related technology. Additionally, a growing body of research has demonstrated that noise can no longer be viewed as "simply annoying;" rather, noise is a serious mental and physical health hazard.

Sound that is too loud (e.g., very loud music), even when enjoyed by the listener, can harm the hair cells of the ears. Individuals exposed to these very loud sounds over time may experience a loss in hearing. Very loud, intense sounds heard once, such as an extremely loud gunshot going off near the ear, may also harm hearing. The evidence that noise can result in a loss of hearing has been well established.

Unwanted, uncontrollable, and unpredictable sounds that intrude upon us, identified as noise, do not have to be loud to bring about physiological damage. A dripping faucet or passing overhead jets can be bothersome, and the stress brought about by these disturbing noises can result in higher blood pressure, heart-rate increases, or the loss of needed sleep. Studies on individuals who work in noisy occupations or who live in noisy communities have reported that sustained exposure to noise and the concomitant sustained stress can result in cardiovascular and circulatory ailments. Sleep disturbances and consequent feelings of fatigue have also been reported. Relationships to other physiological ailments (e.g., gastrointestinal disorders and hormonal changes) are still under investigation. The potential physiological harm of noise, especially in the cardiovascular area, has led the World Health Organization to caution people about the health hazards of noise.

Parents and educators should pay heed to the research that has strongly demonstrated that noise may impair cognitive development in very young children, as well as learning and reading skills. Noise has been found to impede the language and cognitive development of children living in noisy households. Children attending schools exposed to highway, rail, or aircraft noise do more poorly in reading and learning tests. Studies have also found that school reading scores will improve when the noise source is removed.

Noise can also take a toll on our mental health in that there are many studies that report that noise annoys, angers, and irritates people. Some people find themselves becoming aggressive in response to a noisy neighbor's loud parties or loud-music listening habits. In New York City, noise complaints to the city's complaint hotline led the list of complaints with over 350,000 complaints in fiscal 2007. Urban residents are not the only ones complaining that noise has diminished their quality of life; many small town residents report the same. Individuals who leave noisier urban centers may discover that the "noise has followed them." One person's quiet in a small town was disturbed by a noisy windmill that his neighbor installed to save energy. Another person found out that a dog pound was being planned for the vacant lot across her backyard, and still another neighbor learned that the very small, infrequently used airport was going to expand. It should be noted that noise need not lead to observable physiological symptoms; a diminished quality of life should be sufficient to speak to the psychological harm brought about by noise.

With the advent of loud automobile stereo systems and cell phones, there has been a growth of another source of noise, namely the lack of respect displayed by people toward others as they zoom by homes with their so called "boomcars" or speak loudly on their cell phones in restaurants or on buses. Disrespect toward others is also shown when residents play their home television sets loudly or refuse to put soft coverings on their floors when they live above others. Individuals believe they have inherent rights, but these rights do not include disturbing others. Rather than just speaking of rights, people should also focus on responsibilities, because a civilized society depends on both rights and responsibilities.

In 1972, Congress passed the Noise Control Act, which entitled people to be free from noises that could jeopardize their health and well-being. The Office of Noise Abatement and Control (ONAC) within the Environmental Protection Agency (EPA) was charged with carrying out the act. Noise limits were set for trains, trucks, and machinery, and there was talk of putting labels on noisy consumer products such as vacuum cleaners. Under the Quiet Communities Act of 1978, EPA was asked to assist states with their noise control programs. ONAC also published educational materials to teach people about the dangers of noise and how to protect themselves from noise. During the early 1980s, however, funding for ONAC essentially ceased, and there is currently only a skeleton office with minimal noise-control activity.

Today cities are passing noise control ordinances (e.g., to curb motorcycle noise and loud car stereos) and in 2007, the city of New York revised its 25-year-old Noise Code. The European Union has charged its member countries to devise noise maps for the major cities and to develop noise strategies after these noise maps are in place. Anti-noise groups can be contacted on the Internet so that all people can learn about what they can do to lessen the din. Less noise means a quieter, healthier environment for all of us.

SUGGESTED READING

Bronzaft, A. L. (2002). Noise pollution: A hazard to physical and mental well-being. In R. B. Bechtel & A. Churchman (Eds.), *A handbook of environmental psychology* (pp. 499–510). New York: John Wiley & Sons.

ARLINE L. BRONZAFT
City University of New York

NONDIRECTIVE THERAPY (See Client-Centered Therapy)

NONPARAMETRIC STATISTICAL TESTS

Statistical tests in the ANOVA and correlation families (e.g., *t*-test, Pearson's correlation, multiple regression, path analysis) require the distribution underlying the dependent variables to be normally distributed. Because the normal curve is defined by two parameters (the mean and standard deviation), such tests are referred to *parametric*. Another class of tests is called *nonparametric*, or more properly, *distribution-free*, because they do not make any assumptions about the parameters of the population from which the sample(s) are drawn. However, while they are distribution-free, they are not assumption-free. Many of the nonparametric tests have the same assumptions as parametric ones, such as that the observations are independent; that they are at a certain level of measurement (e.g., nominal or ordinal); and with some, that the distributions are similar across groups (i.e., if they are skewed, then they are skewed in the same direction for all groups).

Nonparametric tests can be classified in two ways: by what the researcher wants to know, and by the type of data that can be analyzed. As with parametric tests, nonparametric tests can be used either to show the strength of the relationship between variables or to indicate whether differences between groups (or times) are significantly different from one another. In terms of the types of data, there are some nonparametric tests that are used with nominal data (counts of the number of people in various groups) and others that are used with ranked data.

Nominal Data/Differences

When the interest is whether two or more groups differ with respect to the number or proportion of people with different attributes (e.g., do more people improve with behavior therapy or with medication), the test that is used is chi-squared (χ^2). The null hypothesis is that the two variables are independent; if 40% of the patients were in the behavior therapy group, then 40% of the improved patients should have been in this condition. The degree to which there are more (or fewer) than the expected number of people in this group shows that improvement is not independent of treatment condition. There can any number of categories for either variable, although the more categories there are, the smaller the frequencies in each cell. When the expected frequency in any of the cells is less than five, then it is better to use Fisher's exact test. Before the days of desktop computers, this situation was handled by using the Yates's correction; however, this produces results that are too conservative, and there is now no need to use it. For related data (e.g., if we are comparing a control group that has been matched to a group of people with a disorder; or looking at two binary variables from the same person), McNemar's χ^2 is used when there are two groups, and Cochran's Q test when there are more than two.

Nominal Data/Strength of Relationship

The contingency coefficient, C, is derived from the χ^2 test; it is the square root of $[\chi^2/(\chi^2 + N)]$. Unfortunately, C has a major limitation: Its upper limit is less than 1 and depends on the number of categories for each of the variables. This means that two different values of C cannot be compared with one another unless they derive from tables of the same size. When there are two or more "predictor" variables and a dichotomous outcome, a logistic regression should be used rather than the parametric least-squares regression. Discriminant function analysis can also be used, but it makes more assumptions about multivariate normality of the predictor than does logistic regression, and it is slowly being replaced.

Ranked Data/Differences

Most parametric tests in the ANOVA family have nonparametric counterparts. The nonparametric equivalent of the t-test for independent means is the Mann-Whitney U test, which is basically the same as the Wilcoxon Rank-Sum Test. The Wilcoxon Signed-Ranked Test is the nonparametric analog of the paired t-test. For three or more groups, the one-way ANOVA is replaced by the Kruskal-Wallis test, and the repeated measures ANOVA is replaced by the Friedman two-way ANOVA. Unfortunately, there are no nonparametric equivalents of ANOVA. If parametric tests were used with the raw data instead of first transforming the scores into ranks, then the resulting p levels cannot be trusted. Further, these tests should not be used when the sample size in any group is less than five, because again the p level would be inaccurate.

Ranked Data/Strength of Relationship

The bad news is that there are a number of nonparametric correlation coefficients to choose from: Spearman's ρ (rho) and three variants of Kendall's τ (tau), called A, B, and C. The good news is that they are rarely needed. Spearman's ρ is merely a computational simplification of Pearson's Product-Moment correlation, r, dating back to the days before computers made such simplifications unnecessary. The two correlations, r and ρ, will give identical values for the coefficient. The different versions of Kendall's τ depend on whether there are tied values (in which case B is used instead of A), and whether the data table is square (use τB) or rectangular (τC). It yields a lower value for the coefficient than r (or ρ) because it is based on a different underlying distribution, but if r is significant, ρ will also be significant.

Permutation Tests

Although the nonparametric tests do not assume a normal distribution, the p levels for them are obtained from theoretical probability functions, such as for the χ^2 and the Mann-Whitney U tests. Permutation tests can be used when the probability function is unknown. The most well-known version of a permutation test is Fisher's exact test, which is used when the χ^2 distribution is inexact because sample sizes are small. The procedure consists of computing all possible rearrangements of the data. That is, the data from both groups are pooled, and then the subjects are assigned to groups in every possible way. For example, assume the obtained data consist of three people who end up in either of two groups: those who improved during therapy (Group 1) and those who did not (Group 2). We will label the people in Group 1 as A, B, and C and call those in Group 2 X, Y, and Z. One re-arrangement of the data would be (A, B, X) and (C, Y, Z); another would be (A, B, Y) and (C, X, Z); and so on. From this, we can determine the exact probability of the data having come out in the pattern (A, B, C) and (X, Y, Z). Needless to say, this is a computationally intensive technique and was impractical before the days of computers. In fact, Fisher, who developed this approach, lost interest in it when he could not do the necessary calculations by hand. Now, permutation tests are becoming more common, because they (1) yield exact probabilities; (2) make no assumptions about the underlying distributions; and (3) can handle situations for which no test exists, such as unbalanced designs.

Power

Many textbooks state that parametric statistics should be used whenever possible, because they are more powerful than the nonparametric ones, where "powerful" means that the test is able to detect a difference or a relationship when one is actually present. This assertion is only partially true. Nonparametric statistics for nominal data (e.g., χ^2, C) do in fact have relatively low power. However, the loss of power with tests for ranked data is actually quite small and derives mainly from the transformation of actual values into ranks, which results in a loss of information. However, when the underlying distribution is highly skewed, has many outliers, or does not meet the assumptions of parametric tests in other ways, the nonparametric tests may in fact be more powerful than their parametric counterparts.

Limitations

In addition to the loss of power, nonparametric statistics have other limitations. They tend to be less flexible than parametric ones, and they do not allow certain hypotheses to be tested. For example, as noted above, there is no nonparametric equivalent of covariance adjustments. Also, except for very limited cases, it is not possible to test for interactions in two-way ANOVAs. Finally, the nonparametric tests do not always test the same null hypotheses as their parametric equivalents. If the distributions of scores are *not* the same across groups, then a significant non-parametric test may reflect differences in location, and/or shape, and/or dispersion, and we won't know which is responsible for the significance. If the distributions are the same across groups, then statistical significance implies a difference in location (as with parametric tests), but the location parameter being tested is the median, not the mean, of the scores.

SUGGESTED READINGS

Norman, G. R., & Streiner, D. L. (2008). *Biostatistics: The bare essentials* (3rd ed.). Toronto: B. C. Decker.

Siegel, S., & Castellan, N. J. (1988). *Nonparametric statistics for the behavioral sciences* (2nd ed.). New York: McGraw-Hill.

DAVID L. STREINER
University of Toronto

See also: Chi-square Test; Kruskal-Wallis Test;
Mann-Whitney U Test

NONSUICIDAL SELF-INJURY

Nonsuicidal self-injury (NSSI) refers to the deliberate destruction of one's own body tissue without suicidal intent and for purposes not socially sanctioned. Although terms such as self-mutilation and deliberate self-harm have also been used for this behavior, NSSI has increasingly become the term of choice. Common examples of NSSI include skin-cutting, burning, scratching, needle-sticking, rubbing against rough surfaces, hitting or banging body parts, and interfering with wound healing. In general, behaviors associated with eating disorders (e.g., binging or purging) and substance disorders (e.g., alcohol or drug use) are not considered NSSI, because they are not accompanied by specific intent to physically damage one's body tissue. Similarly, most cases of tattooing and body piercing are not considered NSSI, because they are socially sanctioned forms of body decoration or artistic expression. Importantly, NSSI can be distinguished from suicidal behavior. Unlike suicide attempts, NSSI is not performed with the intent to die, and the injuries caused by NSSI are rarely life-threatening or medically severe (Klonksy & Muehlenkamp, 2007).

Prevalence of Demographics

Approximately 4% of adults in the general population report a history of NSSI (Briere & Gil, 1998; Klonsky, Oltmanns, & Turkheimer, 2003). Rates of NSSI are similar for men and women, although women may be more inclined to cut and men more inclined to burn or bang body parts (Klonsky & Muehlenkamp, 2007). NSSI may be more common among Caucasians than non-Caucasians (e.g., African Americans, Asians, Hispanics), although not all studies confirm this (Jacobson & Gould, 2007; Klonksy & Muehlenkamp, 2007). Recent studies have found disproportionately high lifetime rates of NSSI—between 13% and 23%—among adolescents and young adults (Jacobson & Gould, 2007). When compared to estimates of 4% among adults, these rates may indicate that the prevalence of NSSI has increased in recent years. Not surprisingly, rates of NSSI are highest among psychiatric patients. Approximately 20% of adults and 40–80% of adolescent psychiatric patients report a history of NSSI (Klonsky & Muehlenkamap, 2007; Nock, Joiner, Gordon, Lloyd-Richardson, & Prinstein, 2006).

Descriptive Characteristics

Age of onset is typically between ages 12 and 14 (Jacobson & Gould, 2007), although it is not uncommon for NSSI to begin after age 17. Cutting, scratching, banging, hitting, and burning are among the most common NSSI behaviors, and most people who self-injure have used multiple methods (Klonsky & Muehlenkamp, 2007). Perhaps surprisingly, most individuals who self-injure only do so once or a few times, and only a minority go on to self-injure frequently. Chronic self-injurers typically experience frequent urges to self-injure and make many efforts to resist those urges (Klonsky & Glenn, 2008a).

Psychological Characteristics

On average, individuals who self-injure display particular psychological characteristics. First and foremost, most self-injurers experience frequent and intense negative emotions accompanied by difficulty regulating these emotions (Klonsky & Muehlenkamp, 2007; Klonsky et al., 2003). In addition, self-injurers tend to be self-critical and experience intense self-directed anger (Klonsky et al., 2003; Klonsky & Muehlenkamp, 2007).

The presence of NSSI does not indicate the presence of any particular psychiatric diagnosis. Individuals who self-injure can exhibit a variety of psychiatric symptoms, and some do not meet criteria for a psychiatric disorder (Klonsky & Olino, 2008; Nock et al., 2006). The *Diagnostic and Statistical Manual of Mental Disorders* (American Psychiatric Association, 2000) lists NSSI as a symptom of borderline personality disorder (BPD). NSSI exhibits a robust correlation to BPD, but it is also associated with many other personality disorders including the schizotypal, avoidant, and dependent personality disorders (Klonsky et al., 2003). In addition, studies have reported relationships between NSSI and depression, anxiety, eating disorders, and substance disorders (Klonsky & Muehlenkamp, 2007).

Although NSSI can be distinguished from suicide attempts on the basis of intent and medical severity, individuals who self-injure are more likely to consider and attempt suicide (Jacobson & Gould, 2007; Klonsky & Muehlenkamp, 2007). Certain characteristics of NSSI appear to be indicative of heightened suicide risk. For example, those who utilize multiple NSSI methods and those who self-injure to cope with overwhelming negative emotions or express self-directed anger are more likely to attempt suicide (Klonsky & Olino, 2008; Nock & Prinstein, 2005; Nock et al., 2006).

Childhood Environment

Much theory has emphasized the role of childhood adversities in the development of NSSI. Although many studies find a relationship between NSSI and emotional or physical neglect during childhood, other studies fail to confirm this relationship (Klonsky & Glenn, 2008b). A meta-analysis of 43 studies found that the relationship of NSSI to childhood sexual abuse is relatively modest (Klonsky & Moyer, 2008). In general, many studies report links between NSSI and childhood sexual or physical abuse, but other studies find small or no associations (Jacobson & Gould, 2007; Klonsky & Moyer, 2008). Therefore, whereas histories of neglect or abuse may be more common in those who self-injure, such histories are neither necessary nor sufficient for the development of NSSI.

Motivations

To those unfamiliar with NSSI, the behavior can be difficult to understand. Obtaining benefit from self-inflicted pain and injury is counterintuitive. However, a large body of evidence has helped identify the most common motivations for NSSI.

The most common motivation for NSSI is a desire to regulate affect or emotion (Klonsky, 2007). In short, NSSI is most often performed to alleviate intense and overwhelming negative emotions. Reasons commonly identified for engaging in NSSI include: "to release emotional pressure that builds up inside of me," "to control how I am feeling," and "to get rid of intolerable emotions" (Klonsky, in press). Feelings such as anger, anxiety, fear, sadness, shame, and frustration tend to precede episodes of NSSI, whereas people often feel more calm, relaxed, and relieved after engaging in NSSI, although feelings of shame and guilt are also relatively common afterwards (Briere & Gil, 1998; Klonsky, in press). There is evidence that those who self-injure most often are those who experience the greatest reduction in negative emotions following NSSI (Klonsky, in press). Aggregating across more than a dozen studies, it appears that as many as 95% of self-injurers engage in NSSI to obtain relief from intense negative emotions. Many psychological (e.g., distraction) and biological (e.g., release of endorphins) hypotheses have been offered regarding *how* NSSI reduces negative emotions, but more research is needed (Klonsky, 2007).

Another common motivation for NSSI is self-punishment or self-directed anger. For example, some report that they engage in NSSI "to punish myself" or "to express anger at myself". Aggregating across more than a dozen studies, it appears that approximately half of self-injuries report this motivation (Klonsky, 2007; Klonsky, in press).

Other motivations for NSSI are also apparent, but tend only to be relevant for a minority of self-injurers. These include engaging in NSSI to influence others, interrupt episodes of depersonalizations or derealizations, cope with suicidal thoughts, bond with friends, and generate excitement. It is important to note that different motivations are not mutually exclusive; rather, different motivations often co-occur and some are conceptually related.

Recent research suggests that different motivations may fall within superordinate categories. For example, motivations related to regulating negative emotions, punishing oneself, coping with suicidal thoughts, and halting dissociative episodes tend to be more self-focused and cluster together into an intrapersonal category (Klonsky & Glenn, in press; Nock & Prinstein, 2005). In contrast, motivations related to influencing others, bonding with peers, or excitement seeking tend to occur in more social contexts and cluster together into an interpersonal category (Klonsky & Glenn, in press; Nock & Prinstein, 2005). In general, self-injurers who endorse more motivations report more symptoms of depression, anxiety, and suicidality; however, endorsement of intrapersonal functions (e.g., emotion-regulation, self-punishment) is particularly predictive of a more severe clinical presentation (Klonsky & Glenn, in press; Nock & Prinstein, 2005).

Treatment

There have been no published studies examining the efficacy or effectiveness of treatments designed specifically to treat NSSI. Similarly, the field lacks evidence regarding the effectiveness of psychotropic medications for treating NSSI. Psychotherapies utilized to treat NSSI were typically developed to treat disorders in which NSSI is common (e.g., mood disorders and borderline personality disorder). In theory, because NSSI is most often performed to cope with intense and overwhelming negative emotions, psychotherapies and medications that reduce the frequency and intensity of negative emotions should reduce the need for, and thereby occurrence of, NSSI. Similarly, psychotherapies that improve skills for regulating emotions should theoretically reduce the need for and occurrence of NSSI.

In general, research suggests that psychotherapies emphasizing functional assessment, emotion regulation, and problem solving are most effective for reducing NSSI (for a brief review, see Klonsky & Muehlenkamp, 2007). In addition, there is emerging evidence that physical exercise can help self-injurers resist self-injurious urges and may be a useful supplement to treatment (Klonsky & Glenn, 2008a). While there are many viable options for treating NSSI, more research is needed to identify the existing approaches that are most effective and to develop new interventions optimized for individuals who self-injure.

REFERENCES

American Psychiatric Association. (2000). *Diagnostic and statistical manual of mental disorders* (4th ed., text rev). Washington, DC: Author.

Briere, J., & Gil, E. (1998). Self-mutilation in clinical and general population samples: Prevalence, correlates, and functions. *American Journal of Orthopsychiatry, 68,* 609–620.

Jacobson, C. M., & Gould, M. (2007). The epidemiology and phenomenology of nonsuicidal self-injurious behavior among adolescents: A critical review of literature. *Archives of Suicide Research, 11,* 129–147.

Klonsky, E. D. (in press). The functions of self-injury in young adults who cut themselves: Clarifying the evidence for affect-regulation. *Psychiatry Research.* Retrieved March 10, 2009, from http://www.sciencedirect.com/science.

Klonsky, E. D., & Glenn, C. R. (in press). Assessing the functions of nonsuicidal self-injury: Psychometric properties of the Inventory of Statements about Self-Injury (ISAS). *Journal of Psychopathology and Behavioral Assessment.*

Klonsky, E. D., & Glenn, C. R. (2008a). Resisting urges to self-injure. *Behavioural and Cognitive Psychotherapy, 36,* 211–220.

Klonsky, E. D., & Glenn, C. R. (2008b). Psychosocial risk and protective factors for self-injury. In M. K. Nixon & N. Heath (Eds.), *Self-injury in youth: The essential guide to assessment and intervention.* New York: Routledge.

Klonsky, E. D., & Moyer, A. (2008). Childhood sexual abuse and non-suicidal self-injury: Meta-analysis. *British Journal of Psychiatry, 192,* 166–170.

Klonsky, E. D., & Olin, T. M. (2008). Identifying clinically distinct subgroups of self-injurers among young adults: A latent class analysis. *Journal of Consulting and Clinical Psychology, 76,* 22–27.

Klonsky, E. D., Oltmanns, T. F., & Turkheimer, E. (2003). Deliberate self-harm in a nonclinical population: Prevalence and psychological correlates. *American Journal of Psychiatry, 160,* 1501–1508.

Nock, M. K., Joiner, T. E., Gordon, K. H., Lloyd-Richardson, E., & Prinstein, M. J. (2006). Nonsuicidal self-injury among adolescents: Diagnostic correlates and relation to suicide attempts. *Psychiatry Research, 144,* 65–72.

Nock, M. K., & Prinstein, M. J. (2005). Contextual features and behavioral functions of self-mutilation among adolescents. *Journal of Abnormal Psychology, 114,* 140–146.

SUGGESTED READINGS

Klonsky, E. D. (2007). The functions of deliberate self-injury: A review of the evidence. *Clinical Psychology Review, 27,* 226–239.

Klonsky, E. D., & Muehlenkamp, J. J. (2007). Self-injury: A research review for the practitioner. *Journal of Clinical Psychology: In Session, 63,* 1045–1056.

Nock, M. K. (in press). *Understanding nonsuicidal self-injury: Origins, assessment, and treatment.* Washington, DC: American Psychological Association.

E. David Klonsky
Stony Brook University

See also: Suicidal Behavior among Youth; Suicidality

NONVERBAL COMMUNICATION

Although language is obviously important in interactions, the nonverbal side of communication usually has a greater impact on how we think about others and relate to them. Nonverbal communication may be defined as the sending and/or receiving of information and influence through one's immediate environment, appearance, and nonverbal behavior (Patterson, 2002). Unlike verbal communication, nonverbal communication is always "on" in social settings, with the sending and receiving sides operating simultaneously. That is, even in the absence of conversation, we are continually sending and receiving nonverbal signals. Although verbal communication requires some attention and deliberation, nonverbal communication often operates automatically and outside of awareness. In turn, this leads to another characteristic—cognitive efficiency. Thus, the nonverbal system typically runs with minimal effort, freeing cognitive resources for more demanding activities.

Component Elements

A number of loosely related cues and behaviors comprise the nonverbal system of communication. First, the immediate physical environment for interactions may often be selected, or even manipulated, to affect the course of interaction. Room size, the design and arrangement of furniture, and the quality of furnishings also reflect status and reinforce power differences, especially in the workplace. Appearance cues quickly signal gender, race, age, attractiveness, and other characteristics affecting expectancies about others and how we interact with them. Next, distance and arrangement are important in overall involvement between people and constrain other components in nonverbal communication. The visual channel is the primary means of gathering information about others, and sustained mutual gaze increases the intensity of interactions.

Facial expressions are not only signs of emotions, but also of intentions, that is, they indicate how people are likely to act (Fridlund, 1994). For example, an "angry" face is not simply an indicator of underlying anger but, more importantly, a threat. Posture and movement reflect mood, interest, and openness to interaction. Gestures are a specific form of movement that typically accompany speech, qualify its meaning, and facilitate fluid speaking. Touch is an intimate behavior that can signal affection, support, comfort, and power. Vocal cues are characteristics of speech, such as pitch, loudness, tempo, and intonation that modify the meaning of verbal comments and indicate speakers' feelings. Finally, olfactory cues, including naturally occurring scents called pheromones, have powerful effects on our judgments and behavior. Although it is convenient to focus on these components in isolation, they are sent and received in a holistic fashion as relatively coordinated patterns. Thus, the meaning and impact of any single component is always qualified by the larger pattern of components.

Determinants

Several factors contribute to habitual tendencies in sending and receiving nonverbal communication. First, over the course of evolution, biology has shaped how we communicate with one another. Hardwired preferences for specific characteristics in mate selection, attention to and nurturing behavior with offspring, and sensitivity to expressive behavior have been selected over the course of evolution because they are adaptive. Culture provides another level of influence, learned over time, promoting a common, beneficial pattern of communicating within a particular society. For example, people in Eastern cultures that are more collectivistic in orientation tend to be less expressive in public settings than are people in Western, more individualistic cultures.

Next, biology and culture combine in determining gender differences in communication styles and nonverbal sensitivity. In general, females are more expressive and better judges of nonverbal communication than are males. Finally, individual differences in personality shape habitual patterns in sending and receiving nonverbal behavior. For example, compared to nonanxious people, socially anxious individuals typically avoid high levels of nonverbal involvement (e.g., close approaches, more gaze, and increased expressiveness) and are less accurate in judging others' nonverbal behavior. The combination of these determinants shapes habitual patterns of nonverbal communication. Nevertheless, patterns of nonverbal communication are also affected by the immediate setting, interpersonal goals, and our interaction partners.

Functions of Nonverbal Communication

A first function of nonverbal communication is providing information. Through our immediate physical environment, appearance, and nonverbal behavior, we signal basic information about emotions, intentions, and attitudes. In fact, "thin slices" of behavior lasting from just a few seconds to a few minutes are sufficient for making relatively accurate and adaptive judgments about personality and motivation (Ambady & Rosenthal, 1992). These rapid and often automatic judgments help us anticipate how others are likely to act and adjust our behavior appropriately.

Next, regulating interaction refers to the role of nonverbal behavior in facilitating the routine give-and-take between people in social settings. Subtle, often automatic, behavioral changes help to coordinate the give-and-take of conversations without intruding on the verbal content. For example, speakers ending a conversational turn cease gesturing, pause longer, change vocal cues, and usually look at the listener. In a complementary fashion, listeners about to take a speaking turn typically take an audible inhalation, adjust their posture, and start a gesture. Nonverbal behaviors are at the core of our unspoken interactions with strangers. In choosing a seat in a waiting room or simply passing a stranger on the sidewalk, adjustments in spacing, gaze, and facial expression regulate privacy or signal openness to others (Patterson et al., 2007).

Expressing intimacy identifies the affect-driven function at the core of relationships. In general, people in more intimate relationships are more comfortable with closer distances, higher levels of gaze, greater expressiveness, and more frequent touch. Close approaches, eye contact, and touch may also be employed in exercising influence. That is, nonverbal communication may be used to achieve specific interpersonal goals. A smile and a pat on the back may reinforce someone for a desirable behavior. In contrast, a close approach and a stare may be a threat. Nonverbal behavior is also an important part of successful deception. Finally, nonverbal communication is critical in managing impressions. In employment interviews, on first dates, or when meeting someone important, people make deliberate decisions about what to wear and carefully monitor their behavior to create a positive impression. Sometimes collaborative nonverbal displays are coordinated to create or reinforce particular images. For example, a feuding husband and wife may hold hands and smile in front of family members to cover their conflict.

In summary, the nonverbal system is an adaptive means of communication that typically operates automatically and often outside of awareness. There are a variety of identifiable components in the nonverbal system, but their impact and meaning is a product of how the elements are coordinated in holistic patterns. Biology, culture, gender, and personality are the primary determinants shaping the patterns of nonverbal communication. Finally, the adaptive nature of nonverbal communication is evident in several functions including providing information, regulating interaction, expressing intimacy, exercising influence, and managing impressions.

REFERENCES

Ambady, N., & Rosenthal, R. (2002). Thin slices of expressive behavior as predictors of interpersonal consequences: A meta-analysis. *Psychological Bulletin, 111,* 256–274.

Fridlund, A. J. (1994). *Human facial expression: An evolutionary view.* San Diego, CA: Academic Press.

Patterson, M. L. (2002). Psychology of nonverbal communication and social interaction. In the *Encyclopedia of life support systems (EOLSS), Psychology.* Oxford, UK: http://www.eolss.net.

Patterson, M. L., Iizuka, I., Tubbs, M., Ansel, J., Tsutsumi, M., & Anson, J. (2007). Passing encounters East and West: Comparing Japanese and American pedestrian interactions. *Journal of Nonverbal Behavior, 31,* 155–166.

SUGGESTED READINGS

Bargh, J. A., & Williams, E. L. (2006). The automaticity of social life. *Current Directions in Psychological Science, 15,* 1–4.

Manusov, V., & Patterson, M. L. (Eds.). (2006). *The Sage handbook of nonverbal communication.* Thousand Oaks, CA: Sage.

MILES L. PATTERSON
University of Missouri-St. Louis

See also: **Interpersonal Relationships**

NORM-REFERENCED TESTING

A norm-referenced test (NRT) refers to a test on which the score of an examinee is reported in comparison to a distribution of scores of other examinees in a reference group. The standards for comparisons are called norms, and the group in which the norms are obtained is called a norm group. Norm-referenced testing differs from criterion-referenced testing (CRT), in that the primary purpose of CRTs is to determine how examinees perform in comparison to a predetermined performance level or outcome. NRTs provide information on how well an examinee performs in comparison to other examinees, whereas CRTs provide information on what an examinee knows and can do. A mathematical test used to determine an examinee's performance against specific curriculum outcomes is an example of CRT. By comparison, when assessing mathematical aptitude of examinees, the reference point becomes a specific comparison group.

Uses and Applications

When there are no universally acceptable criteria against which to compare scores, NRTs provide useful information to enhance decisions made by psychologists and other practitioners. As Rodriquez (1997) notes, NRTs provide objective data that can be used along with subjective impressions to make better decisions. In practice, NRTs are used to rank examinees in order to highlight similarities or differences among and between examinees across a continuum for a specific construct, thus providing additional information to better understand the performance of a specific examinee in relation to his/her peers. Typically, most aptitude, interest, and personality inventories are norm-referenced.

Comparisons in performance among examinees are made using norm tables that provide a frame of reference for interpreting the scores of examinees. Some of the most common norm tables used by psychologists include percentile ranks, normalized standard scores, and developmental scales (Murphy & Davidshofer, 2005). Percentile ranks indicate the percentage of examinees from the norm group that falls at or below a specific score. For example, a score on the 70th percentile indicates that the examinee performed as well or better than 70% of the norm group. Normalized standard scores are raw scores from a norm group that have been transformed via a non-linear transformation to approximate a normal distribution; these standardized scores include z-scores (mean 0 and standard deviation 1) and T-scores (mean of 50 and standard deviation 10). For example, the performance of an examinee with a normalized z-score of 2 (T-score of 70) is similar in performance to the top 3% of the norm group. Developmental scales compare an individual to that of the average person in the norm group at a similar level, for example, age or grade level norms. Thus, a raw score of 52 that corresponds to a grade-equivalent score of 6.0 indicates that the examinee performs at the level of a student beginning the sixth grade.

The construction of norm tables, called norming, is a complex, costly, and time-consuming process. Depending on the purpose of testing, norm tables can be developed at different levels (e.g., national or local) and for different samples of the population (e.g., males or college students). However, the usefulness of any set of norms depends on a number of factors. These include the composition of the sample on which the norms are based, the relevance of the examinee population to the instrument for which norms are developed, and the recency of the norms being used. Typically, norms are updated every 5 to 8 years, depending on the purpose and use of the test. Crocker and Algina (1986) provide a comprehensive nine-step process for conducting a norming study that includes the identification of the population of interest, selection of the sample, analysis of data collected, reporting of scores, and documentation of the process.

Advantages and Limitations

The advantages and limitations of any testing process must be considered in the context for which the testing is conducted. The advantage of NRTs is that these tests provide information about the performance of examinees when there are no fixed criteria or performance standards to compare against. The disadvantage of NRTs, however, is that they cannot provide information to measure progress of the examinee or group; they provide information only concerning where specific examinees or groups fall within the whole. However, with the emphasis on diversity in psychology, it should be noted that the debate regarding how and when normative comparisons are considered valid is still ongoing.

Norm reference testing is one of the most widely used forms of testing in psychology. Used effectively, NRTs provide a vital source of information for enhancing the diagnosis of problems and needs as well as in the determination of appropriate interventions for assisting clients and patients. Specifically, norm reference testing takes on an added significance in a discipline dominated by key concepts and critical behaviors that are often difficult to interpret, and where definitions and meaning depend on the specific circumstances and on the people making the interpretations. In this context, NRTs are useful tools for making comparisons to enhance our understanding of human behavior.

REFERENCES

Crocker, L, & Algina, J. (1986). *Introduction to classical and modern test theory*. New York: Holt, Rinehart and Winston.

Gregory, R. J. (2004). *Psychological testing: History, principles, and applications* (5th ed.). Boston: Pearson/Allyn & Bacon.

Murphy, K. R., & Davidshofer, C. O. (2005). *Psychological testing: Principles and applications* (6th ed.). Upper Saddle River, NJ: Pearson Education.

Rodriguez, M. (1997). Norming and norm reference test scores. Paper presented at the annual Meeting of the Southwest Educational Research Association, January 23–25.

ANIL KANJEE
Human Sciences Research Council, South Africa

See also: **Psychological Assessment**

NORMALITY (See Abnormality; Psychological Health)

NULL HYPOTHESIS SIGNIFICANCE TESTING

Null hypothesis significance testing (NHST) is an inferential statistical method for deciding whether a well-specified hypothesis, identified as the *null hypothesis*, is to be regarded as true for a population from which a given set of data has been obtained by random sampling.

In the usual procedure the data from a particular dependent (i.e., measured) variable are first summarized by a single number called a *test statistic*. Usually, some assumptions must then be made in order to find the relative likelihoods of all possible values of that test statistic when the null hypothesis is true, and thus to find the null hypothesis distribution (NHD). The next step is to calculate the probability of obtaining one's actual test statistic from the NHD, or one that is even further from the mean of the NHD. From what is called the "frequentist" point of view, that probability, called a *p value*, tells us the proportion of times that the NHD would yield a test statistic at least as inconsistent with the null hypothesis as the one you obtained, over many exact replications of your study. In the accept-support (AS) form of NHST, researchers actually want to obtain a *p* value that is close to its maximum of 1.0, because the null hypothesis being tested is consistent with the theory that motivated the study.

The far more common (and controversial) form of NHST is the reject-support (RS) form, in which the null hypothesis usually represents a total lack of any deterministic effect in the population (the so-called *nil* hypothesis), so that the NHD represents the effects of chance factors alone. In this case, researchers are hoping for a small *p* value, in order to reject the null hypothesis (symbolized as H_0) as implausible, and to thus offer support for the alternative hypothesis (H_A, the complement of H_0), which is more consistent with the researcher's theory. The probability level below which a *p* value leads to the rejection of H_0 is called the *alpha* (α) *level*, and it should be determined for a study before the data are analyzed. Note that whenever a study produces a *p* less than (α), the results are declared to be statistically significant (i.e., not suspected of occurring entirely by chance); however, there are actually two possibilities: (1) H_0 happens to be true, and the result is a relatively rare occurrence; rejecting H_0 in this case is a mistake, called a *Type I error*; or (2) H_0 is not true, in which case rejecting it is correct.

The modern use of NHST to control Type I errors stems directly from the work that Sir Ronald Fisher (1925) first published in the 1920s. It is Fisher who settled on .05 as the most reasonable value for alpha (Cowles, 2000), and to this day, the .05 level is still considered the default alpha for psychological research. If a "null study" is one for which H_0 is really true, then the value set for alpha is the proportion of null studies that will result in Type I errors. Note that because there is no way to know how often null studies are conducted (if ever), we cannot know how often Type I errors occur overall. Nonetheless, the reader may wonder why we allow as many as 5% of all null studies to be erroneously declared significant. The short answer is that requiring an even smaller *p* value for significance means that a larger percentage of non-null studies would fail the significance test, and be unnecessarily viewed with suspicion.

Fisher felt strongly that failing to attain significance should never lead to a decision to accept H_0, but only to a state of reserved judgment. However, over Fisher's objections, Neyman and Pearson (1933) presented an alternative, decision-based version of NHST, in which failing to reject the null hypothesis led to two additional possibilities: (1) H_0 happens to be true, in which case the decision is correct; or (2) H_0 is not true, in which case failing to reject it is a mistake called a *Type II error*. The proportion of non-null studies that do *not* attain significance is symbolized as *beta* (β), and the proportion that do is called the *power* of the test. Power depends on just how "non-null" the study is (i.e., the population *effect size*), how large the samples are, and how large a value is set for alpha. The current practice of NHST is a practical (some would argue, haphazard) mixture of elements from both Fisher's and the Neyman-Pearson systems. For example, psychologists report *p* values variously as only less than or greater than a single alpha level (usually .05), less than the lowest potential alpha level separately for each test (e.g., $p < .01$; $p < .005$), or exactly as obtained from statistical software (e.g., $p = .003$; $p = .087$).

NHST has been sharply criticized since its inception for being illogical, misleading, and misused (e.g., Berkson, 1938; Rozeboom, 1960), and the number of articles critical of NHST has increased dramatically in recent years. One of the most serious criticisms is that the use of NHST almost inevitably leads researchers to a number of mistaken beliefs, such as that (1) a small *p* value tells us that H_0 is unlikely given the data, when in fact it tells us only that the data are unlikely given that H_0 is true; (2) a small *p* implies that the effect size being tested is large, or of practical importance; and (3) a large *p* implies that H_0 is true, or that we can act as though it is true. Nonetheless, NHST is currently used in roughly 94% of empirical articles published in prominent psychological journals (Hubbard & Ryan, 2000). The saving grace of NHST may be that most psychological studies do not deal with very small effect sizes, and when they do they have little power to detect them, so that statistically significant results are most often associated with reasonably large effect sizes. This is not to say, however, that the psychological literature could not benefit greatly from the increased reporting and interpretation of effect size estimates, and/or confidence intervals.

REFERENCES

Berkson, J. (1938). Some difficulties of interpretation encountered in the application of the chi-square test. *Journal of the American Statistical Association, 33*, 526–542.

Cowles, M. (2000). *Statistics in psychology: An historical perspective* (2nd ed.). Mahwah, NJ: Lawrence Erlbaum.

Fisher, R. A. (1925). *Statistical methods for research workers*. Edinburgh: Oliver & Boyd.

Hubbard, R., & Ryan, P. A. (2000). The historical growth of statistical significance testing in psychology—and its future prospects. *Education and Psychological Measurement, 60*, 661–681.

Neyman, J., & Pearson, E. S. (1933). The testing of statistical hypotheses in relation to probabilities a priori. *Proceedings of the Cambridge Philosophical Society, 29*, 492–510.

Rozeboom, W. W. (1960). The fallacy of the null hypothesis significance test. *Psychological Bulletin, 57*, 416–428.

SUGGESTED READINGS

Harlow, L. L., Mulaik, S. A., & Steiger, J. H. (Eds.). (1997). *What if there were no significance tests?* Mahwah, NJ: Lawrence Erlbaum.

Kline, R. B. (2004). *Beyond significance testing: Reforming data analysis methods in behavioral research*. Washington, DC: American Psychological Association.

Nickerson, R. S. (2000). Null hypothesis significance testing: A review of an old and continuing controversy. *Psychological Methods, 5*, 241–301.

BARRY H. COHEN
New York University

See also: **Effect Size; Errors, Type I and Type II; Significance Testing**

O

OBESITY

Over the past three decades, the prevalence of obesity in the United States has increased at an alarming rate: almost one-third of the adult population is now obese. The seriousness of this phenomenon is highlighted by the fact that in the United States 5 of the 10 leading causes of death are directly linked to obesity. Excess body weight increases morbidity, decreases life expectancy, and diminishes quality of life. We summarize the scope and seriousness of the obesity epidemic, and we describe the effectiveness of behavioral and pharmacological interventions for the management of obesity.

Scope and Seriousness of Obesity

Data from national surveys (Ogden et al., 2006) indicate that the prevalence of adult obesity (defined as Body Mass Index ≥ 30; BMI is calculated as weight in kilograms divided by height in meters squared) doubled between 1980 and 2002. Currently, 32.2% of the adult population is obese, and an additional 34.1% is considered "overweight" (i.e., BMI between 25 and 30). A combination of environmental factors appears to be responsible for this sharp rise in the prevalence of obesity, including: decreased physical activity related to greater mechanization at work and home; increased availability of low-cost, palatable foods; higher energy intakes due to larger portion sizes; and the increased consumption of energy-dense foods (Hill & Peters, 1998).

Evidence documenting the deleterious impact of excess weight on health and longevity continues to accumulate (Mokdad, Marks, Stroup, & Gerberding, 2004). Obesity is directly associated with an array of health complications, including cardiovascular disease (CVD), diabetes, hypertension, hyperlipidemia, asthma, osteoarthritis, and breast, prostate, and pancreatic cancers. A higher BMI predicts premature death, disability, and reduced quality of life. For persons with BMI greater than 30, mortality rates from all causes, but particularly from CVD, are increased by 50–100% when compared to those with BMIs of 20–25. Conservative estimates put the number of obesity-related deaths per year at 111,000, while other data suggest the number may be as high as 400,000 (Mokdad et al., 2004). Some argue that the increased prevalence

of obesity may trigger a decline in life expectancy in the United States within the current century.

Obesity exacts not only a toll in terms of morbidity and mortality, but it also has substantial economic and psychosocial effects. Obesity accounts for 9.1% of the nation's health expenditures, an amount in excess of 78 billion dollars (Finkelstein, Fiebelkorn, & Wang, 2003). Recent data indicate that the health costs associated with obesity now exceed those caused by smoking and problem drinking. In addition, the social and psychological effects of obesity are profound and include social discrimination, personal distress, and decreased emotional well-being.

Treatment of Obesity

The rationale for treating obesity stems from a body of research demonstrating that weight loss can reverse many of the adverse effects associated with obesity. Reductions in body weight, even if modest (e.g., 5–10%), produce beneficial effects on hypertension, glucose intolerance, and hyperlipidemia. The results from the Diabetes Prevention Program (DPP; Diabetes Prevention Program Research Group, 2002) dramatically illustrate the ability of weight-loss to prevent disease onset. Over the course of 2.8 years, the DPP intervention reduced the incidence of diabetes by 58% as compared with a placebo control group. The efficacy of weight-loss treatment in preventing hypertension and the progression of heart disease has also been well-documented. Thus, the ability of weight-loss treatments to produce clinically meaningful outcomes has been clearly established.

Lifestyle Modification

"Lifestyle: (i.e., behavioral) interventions represent the first line of professional treatment for the management of obesity" (National Heart, Lung, and Blood Institute, 1998). Participants are taught to modify their eating and physical activity patterns to produce a negative energy balance and thereby lose weight. Cognitive-behavioral strategies are used to assist the participant in modifying eating and exercise habits. These procedures typically include self-monitoring, goal setting, performance feedback, reinforcement, stimulus control, cognitive reframing, and problem solving. The targeted goals usually entail a low-calorie eating pattern (i.e., a deficit of 500 to 1000 kcal/day below steady state) coupled with increases in moderate intensity level of physical activity (e.g., walking for 30 min/day on most days of the week).

The theoretical basis for the current lifestyle interventions is derived largely from cognitive behavioral models, particularly social cognitive theory (SCT; Bandura, 1997). SCT describes how personal factors (i.e., cognitions, emotions) and aspects of the social and physical environment influence how behavior and how a person's behavior in turn may have a reciprocal influence on these personal and environmental factors. From a SCT perspective, the initiation and maintenance of behavioral changes involve four sets of constructs.

1. *Health knowledge.* The individual's awareness of how a specific behavior affects health.
2. *Beliefs regarding self-efficacy and outcome expectancies.* The individual's belief in his or her ability to perform a specific behavior in a particular situation and the individual's belief that performing a specific behavior will have a particular outcome.
3. *Self-regulatory skills.* The ability of the individual to exert control over his or her behavior, cognitions, and environment. This process entails several subcomponents: (1) performance standards—the goals by which the individual judges his or her behavior; (2) self-observation—the awareness of internal and external influences on one's behavior; (3) self-judgment—the comparison of one's behavior to a performance standard; and (4) self-reaction—one's cognitive, behavioral, or environmental response to self-observation and self-judgments.
4. *Barriers to change.* Perceived personal or environmental impediments to performing a specific behavior.

Lifestyle interventions target the key constructs of SCT in the following ways: (1) by increasing health knowledge regarding the influence of diet and physical activity on weight and risk for disease; (2) by enhancing self-efficacy and positive outcome expectancies through the promotion of a series of successful experiences in changing eating and exercise behavior; (3) by improving self-regulatory skills through the use of goal setting, written self-monitoring, self-reinforcement, stimulus control, and cognitive restructuring strategies; and (4) by overcoming impediments to change through problem solving of barriers to the initiation or maintenance of change.

More than 150 studies have evaluated the efficacy of lifestyle interventions. Reviews (e.g., Wadden, Crerand, & Brock, 2005) of randomized trials show that lifestyle interventions, typically delivered in 15 to 24 weekly group sessions, produce average weight losses of 5 to 10 kg. This amount of weight loss is usually associated with significant improvements in selected risk factors for disease (e.g., blood pressure, blood glucose) as well as in psychological well-being

The clinical significance of weight reductions achieved in lifestyle interventions is determined by two factors: the magnitude of the weight loss and whether or not the weight loss is maintained over the long run. In obese individuals with BMIs in the range of 30–40 lifestyle interventions commonly produce weight losses of approximately 0.4 kg per week of treatment, and the longer the initial length of treatment, the greater the weight reduction.

Because initial weight loss is highly correlated with long-term weight change, the length of initial treatment plays a crucial role in determining whether a clinically significant long-term change in body weight is achieved. With increased length of treatment, the magnitude of initial weight loss increases. Although some have been concerned that larger initial losses would be more difficult to maintain, research findings demonstrate that the magnitude of initial weight loss has a high positive association with the long-term weight reduction.

Although extending the initial length of lifestyle treatment increases overall weight loss, the rate of weight loss slows after 20 weeks and tends to plateau thereafter, reaching an asymptote after 6–8 months of treatment. In most lifestyle intervention studies, treatment has ended after 4–6 months, and participants are then followed for an additional period. By 18 months following study entry, participants regain approximately one-half to one-third of their initial weight losses. Moreover, longer-term follow-ups generally show a gradual but reliable return toward pretreatment weights.

A complex interaction of physiological, psychological, and environmental variables appears responsible for the difficulty in maintaining treatment-induced weight losses. Physiological factors, such as decreased energy needs and a decrease in metabolic rate, prime the obese person for a regaining of lost weight. Continuous exposure to an environment conducive to sedentary lifestyle and rich in fattening foods, combined with a dieting-induced heightened sensitivity to palatable foods, further disposes the individual to setbacks in dietary control. Most obese persons cannot sustain on their own the substantial degree of psychological control needed to cope effectively with this unfriendly combination of biology and environment.

A number of researchers (e.g., Perri, Nezu, & Viegener, 1992) have argued for the conceptualization of obesity as a chronic condition requiring extended follow-up care (akin to the models of ongoing care for the management of diabetes or hypertension). Long-term success may be more likely to occur when obese participants are provided with treatment regimens that incorporate extended care sessions, specifically designed to enhance long-term progress (Perri et al., 2008). Indeed, evidence now exists indicating that continuing contact beyond the usual 4–6 month treatment period improves longer-term outcome in weight management. Several randomized, controlled trials of lifestyle interventions (e.g., Svetkey et al., 2008) have incorporated a "continuous care" approach to weight management and have enabled participants to achieve and maintain substantial amounts of weight loss for several years. Thus, the longer obese persons are under professional care for weight management, the more likely they are to sustain reductions in body weight.

Pharmacological Treatment of Obesity

The use of medication for weight loss is typically reserved for obese persons who have been unsuccessful in behavioral treatment. Two drugs are currently approved for long-term use in weight management. Sibutramine (Meridia®), a monoamine-reuptake inhibitor, enhances satiety and also produces a minor increase in basic metabolic rate. Sibutramine (15mg/day) produces an average decrease in body weight of 5% beyond what is accomplished with placebo and brief dietary instruction (Padwal & Majumdar, 2007). However, the use of sibutramine is associated with a number of significant side effects, including insomnia, nausea, and constipation, and in some people, a significant increase in blood pressure. Because obesity and high blood pressure are often linked, sibutramine is not a viable treatment option for patients with hypertension.

Orlistat (Xenical®) acts as a gastric and pancreatic lipase inhibitor that prevents the absorption of up to 30% of dietary fat. Orlistat produces mean (placebo-subtracted) weight reductions of approximately 3% (Padwal & Majumdar, 2007). The use of orlistat is associated with reductions in blood pressure, total cholesterol, and fasting glucose in diabetic patients. Common side effects (associated with excessive dietary fat intake) include abdominal pain, fecal urgency, and fecal soiling. Because of these unpleasant side effects, many obese patients refuse orlistat as a treatment option.

Although both sibutramine and orlistat are successful in producing moderate amounts of weight loss, these agents appear to be more effective when combined with lifestyle treatment than when used alone. In a recent study (Wadden et al., 2005), the combination of lifestyle treatment plus pharmacotherapy produced weight losses twice the magnitude of medication alone.

The recent epidemiclike increase in the prevalence of obesity has highlighted awareness of the serious adverse consequences that obesity exerts on health and well-being. However, reductions in body weight, even when modest, can reverse many of the negative consequences associated with obesity. Lifestyle modification programs, based on social cognitive theory, represent the first line of professionally delivered treatments for obesity. Lifestyle treatments, delivered in weekly group sessions over the course of 4–6 months, produce weight reductions of 5–10%. Combining lifestyle modification with pharmacotherapy increases the effectiveness of initial treatment, and providing a program of extended follow-up care increase success in the long-term management of obesity.

REFERENCES

Bandura, A. (1997). *Self-efficacy: The exercise of control*. New York: W. H. Freeman and Co.

Diabetes Prevention Program Research Group. (2002). Reduction in the incidence of type 2 diabetes with lifestyle intervention or metformin. *New England Journal of Medicine, 346*, 393–403.

Finkelstein, E. A., Fiebelkorn, I. C., & Wang, G. (2003). National medical spending attributable to overweight and obesity: How much, and who's paying? *Health Affairs, W3*, 219–226.

Hill, J. O., & Peters, J. C. (1998). Environmental contributors to the obesity epidemic. *Science, 280*, 1371–1374.

Mokdad, A. H., Marks, J. S., Stroup, D. F., & Gerberding, J. L. (2004). Actual causes of death in the United States, 2000. *Journal of the American Medical Association, 291*, 1238–1245.

National Heart, Lung, and Blood Institute. (1998). Clinical guidelines on the identification, evaluation, and treatment of overweight and obesity in adults: The evidence report. *Obesity Research, 6*, 51S–209S.

Ogden, C. L., Carroll, M. D., Curtin, L. R., McDowell, M. A., Tabak, C. J., & Flegal, K. M. (2006). Prevalence of overweight and obesity in the United States, 1999–2004. *Journal of the American Medical Association, 295*, 1549–1555.

Padwal, R., & Majumdar, S. (2007). Drug treatments for obesity: Orlistat, sibutramine, and rimonabant. *The Lancet, 369*, 71–77.

Perri, M. G., Limacher, M. C., Durning, P. E., Janicke, D. M., Lutes, L. D., Bobroff, L. B., et al. (2008). Treatment of obesity in underserved rural settings (TOURS): A randomized trial of extended-care programs for weight management. *Archives of Internal Medicine*.

Perri, M. G., Nezu, A. M., & Viegener, B. J. (1992). *Improving the long-term management of obesity: Theory, research, and clinical guidelines*. New York: John Wiley & Sons.

Svetkey, L. P., Stevens, V. J., Brantley, P. J., Appel, L. J., Hollis, J. F., Loria, C. M., et al. (2008). Comparison of strategies for sustaining weight loss. *Journal of the American Medical Association, 299*, 1139–1148.

Wadden, T. A., Berkowitz, R. I., Womble, L. G., Sarwer, D. B., Phelan, S., Cato, R. K., et al. (2005). Randomized trial of lifestyle modification and pharmacotherapy for obesity. *New England Journal of Medicine, 353*, 2111–2120.

Wadden, T. A., Crerand, C. E., & Brock, J. (2005). Behavioral treatment of obesity. *Psychiatric Clinics of North America, 28*, 151–170.

Michael G. Perri
Lisa M. Nackers
University of Florida

See also: **Food Addiction; Weight Control**

OBJECT RELATIONS THEORY

Object relations theory is a psychoanalytic contribution that emphasizes the role of the object in psychological processes, that is, the role of other persons or elements of others, most notably an individual's parents or a primary caregiver. More specifically, object relations refer to a theory of intrapsychic activity based on the internalization of functional aspects of the experience of others and how they relate to one another in an individual's mind. There are many conceptual nuances to this generic theory that are derived from several historical traditions comprising the evolution of psychoanalytic thought. According to Freud, an object is the most variable aspect of drive activity and can be the source of pleasure, pain, anxiety, and wish and fantasy formation, whether real or imagined, and it is necessary for psychic development.

An object can be a person or an aspect of a person that is internalized by an individual, whether animate or inanimate, abstract or concrete, whole or in part, or congruent or fractured in composition, element, and form. An object can be a fantasized relation based on wish and defense and a source of both discomfort and gratification, depending on the motives and anxieties that it generates. In psychoanalytic discourse, the mother is usually considered the primary object, but the father also plays an irrevocable role, as does any other significant person whom individuals experientially encounter in the course of their psychological development. An object can further be an event or series of events imposed by an external source, whether discrete, acute, or cumulative, such as societal influence, the forces of nature, and cultural institutions that are imposed on the people by virtue of their ontological context.

The role of the object revolutionized psychoanalytic theory and is incorporated in every school of psychoanalytic thought. An object may be sentient, affective, perceptual, imagistic, or conceptual, such as an *object representation*, which may also be referred to as an *internal object* and which is often the contents, attributes, and functional properties of others who are incorporated into the psychic structure. Object representations are the re-presentations of the contents and form of what the person internalizes, as well as the conceptual constructs that are conceived in relation to such experiential objects. Internal objects are therefore the qualities, traits, and individual elements of others that often serve various intrapsychic purposes or functions. These elements are encoded and filtered through the psychic registers that constitute the structural organization of mind, and they are subjected to bodily and emotive reverberations, as well as fantasy relations, and semiotically arranged within the unconscious abyss of the experiential subject. Objects may also be deliberately preferred, selected, or intentionally desired, which is a process commonly referred to as *object choice*. Potentially a whole matrix of interrelations can be established between external objects and their internal representations, unconscious resonance states, conceptual signifiers, and derived meaning systems.

Objects and their relations occur on the level of personality formation and lend order to an organizational structure that affects communication between people (hence the term *object relationships*) and within interrelationships with a whole host of others, as well as such external systems as social institutions. Object relations are also causally determinate and correlated with various forms of psychopathology and human suffering. Within the psychoanalytic literature, objects are deemed good and bad, loved and hated, analytic and narcissistic in aim, coveted and attained, lost and recovered, denied or forsaken, repressed or dissociated, libidinal and aggressive in nature, and invested with mental energy (as in *object cathexis*), as well as de-invested, relinquished, and given up. Objects may also be fixated or mourned, variable or constant (as in object constancy), permanent or transitory (as in transitional objects, whereby evoked mental representations of others are infused or attached to inanimate things for soothing purposes, such as a stuffed animal, blanket, or pacifier).

There are several theorists in the history of the psychoanalytic movement who emphasize the role of the object and have therefore developed specified accounts of the impact of others on mental functioning. Object relations theory was initiated by Freud after he designated the object as the aim of a drive in its procurement of satisfaction and made the mother the primary object of early psychic investment. Within Freud's lifetime, proponents of object relations theory started to give greater weight to the role of the object, in contrast to the primacy of the unconscious and, concurrently, that of ego development. This led to radical preferences given to the significance of the object versus the ego versus unconscious mentation and was the impetus behind the development of the British school of object relations championed by diverse theorists such as Klein, Fairbairn, Winnicott, Bion, Balint, Sandler, and lesser-known others, such as Ian Suttie. Simultaneously, the focus on the role of the object was broadened significantly by Bowlby in the fields of pediatrics, attachment, and child development.

As ego psychology gained prominence in America, there also arose the interpersonal school of psychoanalysis, often attributed to Sullivan, and with contemporary object-relations approaches introduced by Mahler and Kernberg. Within the French school initiated by Lacan, the role of the object was attributed to both parents, society at large, and the symbolic functions of language that operate unconsciously within culture, whether this refers to the desire of the other or the symbolic order that defines the other, hence the formal parameters of signification and culture that are superimposed on the person, in whom it becomes socially subsumed and determined.

The British school and the American interpersonal movement have figured prominently in Kohut's self-psychological theory, in which the status of the object and its functions are absorbed under the general category of self-organization, regulation, and transformation attributed to the enlistment of self-objects, which are the evoking-responding-sustaining experiential nexus of the internalized functionality of objects that affect the structural cohesiveness of the self. This theoretical framework in the history of psychoanalysis, along with the focus on the interpersonal relationship that is established during the therapeutic encounter, is the precursor for the current focus on intersubjectivity, which emphasizes the relational dyad, mutuality, and the conceptual shift from a one-person to a two-person psychology. The historical modifications in object relations theory that led to the pivotal reappropriation of the object in self-psychology have unequivocally served as a platform for intersubjectivity theory, relational psychoanalysis, and contemporary attachment theory. Object relations theory may be said to be a proper predecessor to many areas of interest within the empirical behavioral sciences—including developmental psychology, theories of motivation, understanding personality, psychopathology studies, and psychotherapy research—and it arguably provides an interactive bridge to resolving the nature-nurture debate.

SUGGESTED READINGS

Bacal, H. A., & Newman, K. M. (1990). *Theories of object relations: Bridges to self-psychology.* New York: Columbia University Press.

Bowlby, J. (1969). *Attachment and loss: Vol. 1. Attachment.* New York: Basic Books.

Fairbairn, W. R. D. (1994). *From instinct to self: Selected papers of W. R. D. Fairbairn: Vols. I & II.* Northvale, NJ: Jason Aronson.

Freud, S. (1915). Instincts and their vicissitudes. In J. Strachey (Ed. & Trans.), *The standard edition of the complete psychological works of Sigmund Freud: Vol. 14* (pp. 117–140). London: Hogarth Press.

Greenberg, J., & Mitchell, S. A. (1983). *Theories of object relations.* Cambridge, MA: Harvard University Press.

Klein, M. (1975) *Envy and gratitude and other works, 1946–1963.* London: Virago Press.

Kohut, H. (1971). *The analysis of the self.* New York: International Universities Press.

Lacan, J. (2006). *Écrits* (B. Fink, Trans.). New York: Norton.

Sullivan, H. S. (1953). *The interpersonal theory of psychiatry.* New York: Norton.

Winnicott, D. W. (1958). *Collected papers.* New York: Basic Books.

JON MILLS
International Federation for Psychoanalytic Education

See also: **Personality, Interpersonal Theories of; Personality, Psychodynamic Models of; Psychoanalytic Theories**

OBJECT SPLITTING

Intense, over-reactive, extreme—these are a few of the adjectives used by therapists to describe individuals whose reactions are governed by defensive splitting. Splitting is a psychological defense mechanism that affects the way current and past events are experienced or remembered. Under the influence of splitting, the world is evaluated in extremes of "all good" or "all bad." Life is precarious, as relatively minor events have the power to trigger episodes of intense despair or rage. Splitting creates rapid reversals in well-being and wreaks havoc on interpersonal relationships.

Analytic and Object Relations Approaches to Splitting

The process of mental splitting was originally suggested by Freud, who observed that certain patients had two separate and contradictory versions of reality that co-existed. In different therapy sessions, and sometimes even within the same session, these patients would evaluate events or people in completely different ways. Although this dynamic was first observed in adults who suffered from fetishes, child analysts noted a similar mental process in their young patients and speculated that the polarized extremes created by splitting allowed for normal psychic development. Although there are differences in the ways that British and American object relations theorists view the specific mechanics of splitting, both recognize its role in helping the developing child protect soothing or affirming psychic resources from aggression and disillusionment.

Psychoanalysts also believe that, by middle childhood, a healthy psychic structure matures in ways that allow splitting to recede. As that happens, the individual is able to accept aspects of self and others as less than perfect but "good enough." At the end of this process, known in the analytic realm as rapprochement, the perfect and dreadful elements can be held in awareness at the same moment in time, allowing the good to offset the full experience of the bad.

Children who lack sufficient positive intrapsychic resources or who have excessively hostile intrapsychic worlds retain a psychic structure that is defined by extreme poles. Splitting then becomes maladaptive, in that it obstructs the integration process that is essential to optimal mental health. Children who are victims or observers of ongoing trauma, or who have been emotionally neglected, may be at high risk for maladaptive splitting.

Splitting compromises an adult's ability to function well in several ways. In order to maintain a view of oneself or one's world that is either completely "all good" or "all bad," contradictory aspects of reality must be denied. Individuals who split also have a tendency to idealize certain people or situations and to devalue others. The internal experience of extreme self-devaluation is overwhelming, and it often can be resolved only by assigning the worst attributes to others. These individuals are then blamed or viewed in ways that justify a release of rage or other intense feelings. To summarize this process, the primitive defenses that are necessary to support splitting (denial, idealization/devaluation, and projective identification) lead to impaired judgment and intense, unstable relationships. Often, adults who present with this constellation of defense mechanisms are diagnosed with narcissistic or borderline personality disorders.

Splitting in Couples and Families

When family members use splitting as a core defense mechanism, predictable problems arise. The couple or family suffers from episodes of rapid and intense reversal in well-being in ways that resemble a roller-coaster. Family members frequently describe themselves as "walking on eggshells," as they are never sure what behaviors might prove to be offensive and trigger disharmony. In good times, problems are ignored or minimized in order to keep the fragile peace. Joint problem-solving skills are rarely developed, as collaboration is hampered when requests for change are experienced as criticism, rejection, or devaluation. Marital dynamics are prone to episodes of hopelessness and despair, as awareness of one problem triggers memories of similar, unresolved episodes that compound and exacerbate the problem at hand. Splitting dynamics may extend into the larger family unit, with different family members being idealized or devalued. Overall, splitting creates relationship instability, poor communication, and inadequate problem-solving abilities.

REFERENCES

Siegel, J. P. (1992). *Repairing intimacy: An object relations approach to couples therapy.* Northvale, NJ: Jason Aronson.

Stone, M. H. (Ed.). (1986). *Essential papers on borderline disorders.* New York: New York University Press.

Volkan, V. (1976). *Primitive internalized object relations.* New York: International Universities Press.

JUDITH P. SIEGEL
*Silver School of Social Work
at New York University*

See also: Object Relations Theory; Splitting

OBSERVATIONAL METHODS (See Behavioral Observation)

OBSESSIONS

Obsessions are described in the *Diagnostic and Statistical Manual of Mental Disorders, Fourth Edition, Text Revision* (American Psychiatric Association, 2000) as recurrent intrusive thoughts, impulses, or images that produce marked anxiety or discomfort. The content of obsessions is ego-dystonic, meaning that they are experienced as intrusive, unwanted, and generally inconsistent with one's self-image, values, beliefs, and behaviors. Obsessions differ from ego-syntonic thoughts about everyday problems (e.g., recurrent thoughts or worries about finances, occupation, relationships, and the like) and should be distinguished from the "brooding" ruminations that are common in depression. Typical obsessions include doubts about whether one did something adequately (e.g., turned off the stove); intrusive sexual, aggressive, or religious thoughts or images (e.g., horrific image of stabbing a friend); thoughts about contamination; and excessive concerns about symmetry or exactness. Individuals with Obsessive-Compulsive Disorder (OCD) experience frequent obsessions that are severe enough to cause significant functioning impairment and try to suppress or neutralize their obsessions with other thoughts or compulsive actions. Unlike individuals with psychotic or delusional disorders, individuals with OCD generally recognize their obsessions as senseless and know that the obsessions originate in their own minds.

Although pure obsessions (i.e., obsessions without overt compulsions) were traditionally assumed to be infrequent, treatment centers worldwide have reported between 1.5% and 44% of OCD patients report no overt compulsions (median = 20%; see Freeston & Ladouceur, 1997). Moreover, epidemiologic studies have found that, in the community, the percentage of individuals with OCD suffering from pure obsessions may be as high as 60%.

Several theories have attempted to explain the development of obsessional problems and related compulsions. A behavioral theory of OCD was offered by Mowrer (1960), who described a two-stage theory in which a fear of specific stimuli is first learned through classical conditioning (stage 1, e.g., the patient feels anxious after thinking a blasphemous thought) and then maintained by operant conditioning (stage 2), as the individual learns to engage in ritualistic behavior to decrease anxiety (e.g., the patient prays compulsively). Thus, rituals are preserved by reinforcing properties of anxiety reduction. Because reinforced behaviors will occur more often in the future, the frequency of rituals increases. Rituals or avoidance behavior maintain the fear response because the sufferer does not stay in contact with the stimulus long enough for the anxiety to extinguish on its own. Hence exposure and response prevention is an effective behavioral treatment for OCD (Foa et al., 2005).

Rachman and DeSilva (1978) found that intrusive thoughts were reported by almost 90% of a nonclinical sample. The content of obsessions is not always distinguishable from that of nonobsessional intrusions (Rachman & DeSilva, 1978; Rassin & Muris, 2007). Hence, cognitive models of OCD characterize intrusive thoughts as normal events that most people experience. Cognitive theorists suggest that intrusive thoughts may develop into obsessions, not because of their content per se, but because of the meaning individuals with OCD attribute to them (for a review of cognitive theory and treatment, see Fama & Wilhelm, 2005). People who appraise intrusions as significant and important can experience negative emotions (e.g., guilt, anxiety) related to a fear of negative consequences. In efforts to reduce discomfort, these individuals often engage in neutralizing strategies such as overt compulsions, mental rituals, avoidance behaviors, and attempts to suppress thoughts. However, suppression experiments suggest that efforts to suppress specific thoughts result in an increase rather than a decrease in their frequency (Wegner, 1989).

Anxiety-provoking appraisals of intrusions may originate from underlying beliefs or assumptions acquired in a religious, cultural, family, or other context(s). For example, the Obsessive Compulsive Cognitions Working Group (e.g., OCCWG, 2005) has suggested that obsessions may develop or persist as a result of appraisals related to beliefs about the overimportance of, and need to control, intrusive thoughts—particularly beliefs related to overestimations of the likelihood of threat and the extent of one's personal responsibility for negative outcomes, and beliefs related to the need to achieve perfectionism and certainty. Research suggests that individuals with OCD and other anxiety disorders are more likely to endorse these types of beliefs than are individuals without OCD. For example, individuals with OCD often overestimate both the probability of negative outcomes and their personal responsibility for preventing them. As a result, they are more likely to interpret intrusions as signs of danger that they must anticipate and avert. Cognitive therapy that addresses these beliefs can effectively reduce OCD symptoms (see Fama & Wilhelm, 2005).

Neuropsychological and information processing research suggests that obsessional problems may result from irregularities in the way individuals with OCD attend to process and organize information (see Chamberlain, Blackwell, Fineberg, Robbins, & Sahakian, 2005). For example, cognitive deficits in the ability to inhibit irrelevant versus relevant stimuli may result in decreased ability to turn one's attention away from intrusive thoughts or images. Similarly, deficits in the ability to inhibit motor responses may lead to an inability to suppress compulsive, ritualistic behaviors. Deficits identified in neuropsychological research are generally consistent with biological models of OCD.

Genetic and neurobiological research on OCD has advanced significantly over the past few decades (see Dougherty & Jenike, 2008). Family and twin studies suggest that at least some forms of OCD are genetically inherited. Results from structural and functional neuroimaging studies suggest that OCD is associated with dysfunction of the cortico-stratial-thalamic circuit, including the orbitofrontal cortex, anterior cingulate, thalamus, and caudate nucleus. These results are consistent with serotonergic and dopaminergic dysfunction, also implicated in OCD. The most common biological treatment for OCD is the use of serotonin reuptake inhibitors (SRIs), although other psychopharmacological agents may be used in addition to or instead of SRIs. Psychosurgery may be indicated for individuals with extreme obsessional problems that are unresponsive to other forms of treatment.

In summary, behavioral, cognitive, neuropsychological, and biological theories have been introduced to explain the development of obsessional problems. A better understanding of obsessional problems may result from an integration of these different areas of research.

REFERENCES

American Psychiatric Association (2000). *Diagnostic and statistical manual of mental disorders* (4th ed., text rev.). Washington, DC: Author.

Chamberlain, S. R., Blackwell, A. D., Fineberg, N. A., Robbins, T. W., & Sahakian, B. J. (2005). The neuropsychology of obsessive compulsive disorder: The importance of failures in cognitive and behavioural inhibition as candidate endophenotypic markers. *Neuroscience & Biobehavioral Reviews, 29*, 399–419.

Dougherty, D. D., & Jenike, M. A. (2008). Obsessive-compulsive disorders. In S. A. Waldman & A. Terzic (Eds.), *Pharmacology and therapeutics. Principles to practice.* Philadelphia, PA: Elsevier/Saunders.

Fama, J. M., & Wilhelm, S. (2005). Formal cognitive therapy: A new treatment for OCD. In J. S. Abramowitz & A. C. Houts (Eds.), *Concepts and controversies in obsessive compulsive disorder.* New York: Springer.

Foa, E. B., Liebowitz, M. R., Kozak, M. J., Davies, S., Campeas, R., Franklin, M. E. et al. (2005). Randomized, placebo-controlled trial of exposure and ritual prevention, clomipramine, and their combination in the treatment of obsessive-compulsive disorder. *American Journal of Psychiatry, 162*(1), 151–161.

Freeston, M. H. & Ladouceur, R. (1997). The cognitive behavioral treatment of obsessions: A treatment manual. Unpublished manuscript.

Mowrer, O.H. (1960). *Learning theory and behavior.* New York: John Wiley & Sons.

Obsessive Compulsive Cognitions Working Group. (2005). Psychometric validation of the obsessive belief questionnaire and interpretations of intrusions inventory-part 2: Factor analyses and testing of a brief version. *Behaviour Research and Therapy, 43*, 1527–1542.

Rachman, S., & DeSilva, P. (1978). Abnormal and normal obsessions. *Behaviour Research and Therapy, 16*, 233–248.

Rassin, E., & Muris, P. (2007). Abnormal and normal obsessions: A reconsideration. *Behaviour Research and Therapy, 45*, 1065–1070.

Wegner, D. M. (1989). *White bears and other unwanted thoughts.* New York: Viking.

JEANNE M. FAMA
SABINE WILHELM
Harvard University Medical School

See also: **Compulsions; Obsessive-Compulsive Disorder**

OBSESSIVE-COMPULSIVE DISORDER

Obsessive-compulsive disorder (OCD) is an anxiety disorder that involves two primary symptoms: *obsessions* and *compulsions*. *Obsessions* are thoughts, ideas, images, impulses, or doubts that are experienced as senseless, unwanted, and distressing. Although people with OCD recognize the thoughts as irrational, these thoughts often evoke anxiety about dreaded consequences. Common themes of obsessions include contamination; responsibility for causing terrible harm (e.g., by making mistakes); violent, sexual, or blasphemous thoughts; or thoughts about things not being just right. Beyond these common themes, some individuals may exhibit unusual obsessions, such as a fear of having an extramarital affair with a stranger by mistake.

Compulsions are urges to perform purposeful behavioral or mental rituals that serve to neutralize the anxiety and doubt evoked by obsessional thoughts. Examples include handwashing, checking, asking for reassurance, ordering and arranging, repeating routine activities, counting, and mentally praying or thinking a "good" thought. As with obsessions, some individuals with compulsions may have unusual rituals, such as having to mentally rearrange words in sentences to form comforting messages. Obsessions and compulsions both tend to be highly specific to the individual and can vary a great deal in content across individuals.

Obsessions and compulsions are phenomenologically related. For example, people with obsessional thoughts concerning contamination from "floor germs" may spend hours washing their hands or other objects thought to be contaminated. Someone with unwanted blasphemous thoughts might repeat prayers until the thought has disappeared. Similarly, a person with fears of causing a house fire may check that appliances are unplugged. Compulsive rituals sometimes take the form of mental acts like repeating phrases to *neutralize* "bad" thoughts, attempting to suppress a thought, or mentally reviewing to gain reassurance that a mistake was not made.

Individuals with OCD may vary in the degree of insight they have about the meaninglessness of their obsessions and compulsions. Although some people recognize the irrationality of their obsessions and the pointlessness of their compulsions, others firmly believe that their obsessions and compulsions are justified. In some cases this belief may approach a delusional intensity. In such cases, "with poor insight" is generally added as a diagnostic specification.

Prevalence and Course

The lifetime prevalence of OCD is about 2–3% in the adult population and 1–2% in children (Karno, Golding, Sorenson, & Burnam, 1988). Although it may begin as early as the preschool years, the average age of onset is in the late teens to early twenties. Males tend to develop OCD at a younger age than females. The onset of OC symptoms is generally gradual. However, as an exception in this regard, some individuals may abruptly develop symptoms following childbirth. Although the severity of obsessions and compulsions may wax and wane, depending on the amount of stress in a person's life, OCD is a persistent condition with a low rate of spontaneous remission. Without effective treatment, a chronic and deteriorating course can be expected.

Comorbidities

Comorbid Axis I diagnoses are more common in individuals with OCD than in individuals with other types of anxiety disorders. Depression is the most frequent comorbid diagnosis, with approximately 50% of individuals with OCD reporting a major depressive episode or dysthymia in their lifetime. Most commonly, the onset of OCD precedes the onset of depression. This most likely indicates that depression occurs as a result of functional impairment and general distress associated with OCD. Generalized anxiety disorder, panic disorder, and social anxiety also tend to co-occur with OCD in as many as 30% to 45% of individuals (Crino & Andrews, 1996). Axis II personality disorders may also occur along with OCD. However, the prevalence rates reported in this domain have not been consistent in the literature.

Differential Diagnosis

It can often be difficult to discriminate between OCD and a number of disorders with similar symptoms. In particular, generalized anxiety disorder, depression, Tourette's syndrome, delusional disorders, hypochondriasis, and body dysmorphic disorder often present with symptoms similar to those associated with OCD. Individuals with these disorders often appear to have obsessions or compulsions; however, the thoughts and behaviors of such individuals have meanings or functions that are inconsistent with the clinical definitions of these terms. OCD must also be distinguished from Obsessive Compulsive Personality Disorder (OCPD). The most notable distinction between OCD and OCPD relates to the degree of congruency between the individual's symptoms and their self-perception. People with OCPD display traits (such as inflexibility and meticulousness) that they find consistent with their world view. Conversely, people with OCD find that their symptoms conflict with their world view. Therefore, OCD tends to be associated with greater subjective distress than OCPD.

Etiological Theories

The causes of OCD are largely unknown, yet its development most likely involves a biological vulnerability to anxiety in combination with psychosocial factors. There is no evidence to support psychoanalytic theories of OCD that propose an interplay of unresolved childhood conflicts as contributing to the development of obsessions and compulsions. The current leading theories of OCD include biological, behavioral, and cognitive-behavioral explanations.

Biological

First, the most widely accepted neurochemical theories of OCD propose that the underlying pathophysiology of this disorder is abnormal serotonin functioning (Gross, Sasson, Chorpa, & Zohar, 1998). In particular, individuals with OCD are thought to have a hypersensitivity in postsynaptic serotonin receptors. Indeed, studies have found evidence for elevated serotonin levels among OCD patients. Moreover, serotonin reuptake inhibitor (SRI) medication is more effective than other forms of pharmacotherapy in the treatment of OCD. It is important to note, however, that whereas some study results support the serotonin hypothesis of OCD, others do not support this model. Moreover, a specific mechanism by which serotonin function may be related to OCD symptoms has not been proposed.

Second, neuroanatomical theories posit that structural and or functional abnormalities of the orbitofrontal-subcortical circuits result in obsessions and compulsive behaviors (Saxena, Bota, & Brody, 2001). The orbitofrontal-subcortical circuits are believed to link the areas of the brain involved in information processing to the areas involved in the initiation of some behavioral responses. More specifically, hyperactivation of these circuits is thought to play a crucial role in OCD. Although it is evident that there is some relationship between these types of brain abnormalities and OCD, the direction of causality remains unclear.

Behavioral

Classical behavioral theories suggest a two-stage process by which OCD develops and is maintained. In the first stage, fear acquisition, a natural event becomes associated with fear by being immediately paired with an aversive stimulus that evokes anxiety. For example, a knife may acquire the ability to elicit anxiety by being paired with a traumatic experience. In the second stage, maintenance, avoidance and compulsive rituals are negatively reinforced because they result in a reduction in anxiety. For example, if checking that the drawers are locked relieves distress evoked by thoughts of knives, this kind of checking is likely to be repeated whenever thoughts of knives occur. In essence, classical conditioning is believed to underlie the development of obsessions and operant conditioning is thought to maintain compulsions (Mowrer, 1960). Although there is evidence that compulsive rituals maintain anxiety via operant conditioning, research does not support the supposition that obsessions simply result from classical conditioning. Therefore, the behavioral model of OCD appears insufficient to explain OCD in its entirety.

Cognitive-Behavioral

The inadequacy of classical behavioral theories of OCD led to the development of a cognitive-behavioral model that considers the way in which individuals with OCD interpret normally occurring intrusive thoughts. This model recognizes that most people have senseless thoughts now and then (e.g., *what if I stabbed someone I care about*) and suggests that a critical component in the development of OCD is how one interprets these thoughts. OCD is thought to develop when an individual has specific types of maladaptive beliefs in which the importance and threat of such intrusive thoughts is unrealistically inflated (Shafran, 2005). Habitually appraising intrusive thoughts in such a biased manner causes one to feel overly responsible for and threatened by their thoughts (e.g., *I'm an immoral person for thinking this,* or *my thoughts are equivalent to actions*). This results in preoccupation with the thought (obsessions) and increasingly anxious mood.

The fear and exaggerated sense of responsibility evoked by obsessional thoughts motivates the person with OCD to engage in compulsive rituals to reduce the probability of feared catastrophes. Rituals and avoidance are, however, excessive responses to stimuli and thoughts that are not actually dangerous. According to this theory, such responses maintain obsessive anxiety because they (1) result in a short-term reduction in obsessional anxiety and (2) prevent the person from realizing that their fears were unrealistic in the first place.

Treatment

Two treatments are effective for OCD: SRI pharmacotherapy and cognitive-behavioral therapy (CBT).

Pharmacotherapy

SRIs (clomipramine, fluoxetine, sertraline, paroxetine, fluvoxamine, and citalopram) are the most effective pharmacological treatment for OCD. These medications block the reuptake of serotonin, which is suspected to be related to OCD symptoms. On average, rates of improvement with adequate trials of SRIs (at least 12 weeks) range from 20% to 40%. However, response varies widely from patient to patient, and side effects such as nausea, sleep disturbances, or decreased sex drive are common. Importantly, once pharmacotherapy is stopped, OCD symptoms return in 85% of patients.

Cognitive-Behavioral Therapy

CBT is based on the behavioral and cognitive-behavioral models of OCD and is the most effective treatment for this disorder. Patients treated with CBT often achieve up to 65% reduction in their OCD symptoms. The two main CBT procedures are (1) exposure with response prevention (EX/RP) and (2) cognitive therapy. Exposure involves prolonged and repeated confrontation with situations that evoke obsessional fears, while response prevention entails refraining from carrying out compulsive rituals. For example, patients with obsessive fears about contamination might be asked to touch a toilet seat and then refrain from washing their hands for the next several hours. EX/RP is thought to work by demonstrating that obsessional fears are unrealistic and that rituals are unnecessary to prevent feared catastrophes. Cognitive therapy involves using rational discourse to help patients recognize and correct faulty appraisals of intrusive thoughts. It is often used in conjunction with EX/RP. Cognitive-behavioral therapy is typically accomplished in a short time span (approximately 15–20 sessions) and generally results in significant improvements that continue to endure after the discontinuation of therapy.

REFERENCES

Crino, R. D., & Andrews, G. (1996). Obsessive compulsive disorder and Axis I comorbidity. *Journal of Anxiety Disorders*, *10*(1), 37–46.

Gross, R. C., Sasson, Y., Chorpa, M., & Zohar, J. (1998). Biological models of obsessive compulsive disorder: The serotonin hypothesis. In R. P. Swinson, M. Anthony, S. Rachman, & M. Richter (Eds.), *Obsessive-compulsive disorder: Theory, research, and treatment* (pp. 141–153). New York: Guilford Press.

Karno, M., Golding, J., Sorenson, S., & Burnam, A. (1988). The epidemiology of obsessive-compulsive disorder in five U.S. communities. *Archives of General Psychiatry*, *45*, 1094–1099.

Mowrer, O. (1960). *Learning theory and behavior.* New York: John Wiley & Sons.

Saxena, S., Bota, R. G., & Brody, A. L. (2001). Brain-behavior relationships in obsessive-compulsive disorder. *Seminars in Clinical Neuropsychiatry*, *6*, 82–101.

Shafran, R. (2005). Cognitive behavioral models of OCD. In J. S. Abramowitz, & A. C. Houts (Eds.), *Concepts and controversies in obsessive-compulsive disorder.* New York: Springer.

Jonathan S. Abramowitz
Brittain L. Mahaffey
Michael G. Wheaton
University of North Carolina at Chapel Hill

OBSESSIVE-COMPULSIVE PERSONALITY DISORDER

Obsessive-compulsive personality disorder (OCPD) is a personality disorder characterized by excessive perfectionism, inflexibility, and need for control that negatively impacts interpersonal relationships, occupational functioning, or other important domains of an individual's life. Individuals with this condition often maintain strict principles and are intolerant of others who do not conform to their standards.

Because of its nomenclature and historical clinical definition, OCPD is often confused with obsessive-compulsive disorder (OCD), but the empirical literature suggests that the key features of these conditions are disparate and has not supported a precursory relationship between OCPD and the development of OCD. Rather, as elaborated in this article, OCPD is a qualitatively distinct condition typified not by "ego-dystonic" anxiety-producing thoughts, but by "ego-syntonic" internal rules governing behavior that cause significant distress when violated. Individuals with OCPD often lack insight into their role in occupational and social impairments and are likely to seek treatment at the behest of family members (as opposed to being self-motivated) or to present for treatment primarily for a comorbid anxiety or depressive disorder. The following text provides an introduction to the core features of this syndrome, its theoretical conceptualizations, and its implications for treatment.

Definition and Prevalence

The defining features of OCPD have undergone several revisions over time. The DSM-I included the description of "compulsive personality" based mainly on Freud's anal character, which he described as orderly, parsimonious, and obstinate. The DSM-II first included OCPD, defined by excessive concern with conformity and adherence to moral standards (Dowson & Grounds, 1995). Subsequent revisions of the DSM expanded the criteria associated with the condition. The DSM-III-R included nine criteria, of which five were required for official diagnosis. However, increasing the number of diagnostic criteria produced greater variability in the syndrome and was estimated to have doubled the proportion of the population who would qualify for official diagnosis compared to earlier criteria (Pfohl & Blum, 1991).

The DSM-IV omitted two of these criteria (restricted expression of affect and indecisiveness) in order to focus on the central features of the syndrome. The current diagnostic standard for OCPD defines the condition as a pervasive pattern of preoccupation with orderliness, perfectionism, and mental and interpersonal control as indicated by four (or more) of the following eight criteria: (1) preoccupation with details, (2) perfectionism, (3) excessive devotion to work, (4) excessive conscientiousness, (5) difficulty discarding worn or useless items, (6) inability to delegate tasks, (7) miserliness, and (8) rigidity and stubbornness (American Psychiatric Association, 2000). McGlashan et al. (2005) monitored the stability of these criteria over a two-year period and found that rigidity and problems delegating were the most prevalent and least changeable criteria, whereas miserliness and strict moral behaviors were less stable.

Using DSM-IV criteria, it is estimated that the prevalence of OCPD is about 1 percent in community samples and 3–10% in clinical settings (American Psychiatric Association, 2000). Early reports suggested similar incidence of the disorder cross-culturally, but a study of the U.S. population reported that OCPD is significantly less common in Asians and Hispanics relative to Caucasians and African Americans (Grant et al., 2004). Reports of the gender distribution of OCPD have also been mixed. The APA has suggested that the condition is twice as common in men, but the Grant et al. (2004) study found no gender difference in prevalence rate.

Overlap with OCD

Historical clinical opinion has proposed a special relationship between OCPD and OCD, which can be traced back to Freud's anecdotal description of the "Rat Man," who was described as having both conditions. Obsessive-compulsive personality traits have been considered to be prodromal precursors to the development of OCD. For example, Pierre Janet described the "psychasthenic state," which included perfectionism, indecisiveness, and emotional detachment, as a condition that preceded the onset of true obsessions and compulsions (Eisen et al., 2008).

There are some similarities in the symptoms of both disorders. For example, excessive list making and hoarding have been noted in both conditions, though the status of hoarding as a symptom of OCD has recently been questioned. However, the functional roles of these symptoms are notably distinct in each disorder. The obsessive thoughts experienced by individuals with OCD are "ego-dystonic" in that they are experienced as unwanted, upsetting, and personally repugnant. In contrast, the experience of individuals with OCPD is "ego-syntonic" in that they consider their opinions and ways of doing things rational and appropriate. Persons with OCD obsessions about doing harm may feel compelled to write down everything they have done during a day in order to reassure themselves that they have not caused a catastrophe, while individuals with OCPD may believe that making lists of daily activities maximizes efficiency and ensures that no details are overlooked.

Although they are distinct conditions, OCD and OCPD do occasionally co-occur. Comorbidity estimates have suggested that between 23–32% of OCD patients also meet criteria for OCPD, and some studies have suggested that comorbid OCPD is associated with poorer treatment outcome for OCD (Eisen et al., 2008). However, OCPD has also been found to co-occur with a variety of other anxiety disorders and with depression as well (Dowson & Grounds, 1995). In addition, other personality disorders, such as avoidant and dependent personality disorder, have been estimated to co-occur with OCD at least as frequently as OCPD, if not more so (Pfohl & Blum, 1991), which further suggests the lack of a unique relationship between OCD and OCPD.

Theoretical Conceptualizations

Psychodynamic Formulation

The obsessive-compulsive personality was one of the foremost areas of interest for psychoanalysts. Early psychoanalytic writers conceptualized the disorder as a fixation at the anal phase of development caused by inappropriate toilet training. According to this view, power struggles with parental figures could result in an overdeveloped and punitive superego, which would lead an individual to employ defense mechanisms such as regression, reaction formation, isolation of affect, and undoing in order to ward off feelings of guilt, shame, and insecurity (Sperry, 2003). Later writers broadened the formulation and implicated certain parenting styles and home environments in the development of the disorder, especially those that shunned spontaneous expression of affection and included high levels of latent hostility and anger. Salzman (1973) suggested that children growing up in these environments develop overwhelming doubt and low self-esteem, which they compensate for by keeping strict control over themselves and their environment. Although much has been written on OCPD from the psychodynamic viewpoint, these theories have little empirical support.

Cognitive-Behavioral Formulation

Early cognitive theories posited that OCPD was associated with a core feeling of "I should." As a result, individuals with OCPD were likely to have three characteristics: a rigid and stimulus-bound style of thinking; a loss of volition, in that all choices are based on what should be done; and a lack of certainty in wants and feelings when the objectively right answer is not clear. Beck et al. (2004) later elaborated a more extensive cognitive-behavioral conceptualization of the disorder. According to his view, OCPD results from faulty assumptions and schemas that cause maladaptive automatic thoughts. Schemas are stable structures comprised of underlying beliefs that drive cognitive, affective, and motivational processes. The schemas underlying OCPD have characteristic distortions, such as dichotomous thinking ("anything that is not 100% right is wrong"), intolerance of mistakes and errors ("I must avoid mistakes at all costs"), and the need to be in control ("others will not be as careful"). These styles of thinking lead to hypermorality, perfectionism, and officiousness. In contrast to psychodynamic models, cognitive-behavioral models are supported by an emerging body of research (Beck et al., 2004).

Biopsychosocial Formulation

Evolutionary theories of personality suggest that behavioral predispositions for attitudes, feelings, and behaviors that are ethologically adaptive will be selected through natural selection. These evolutionary-derived patterns of relating to others may then become problematic in our present highly individualized and technological society and lead to disorders. Millon and colleagues (2000) have written about OCPD from this perspective and noted that many of the features of OCPD are adaptive up to a certain point. For example, attention to detail and vigilance for errors are beneficial in moderation. In addition, there is some evidence to suggest a possible genetic role in obsessive-compulsive traits, such as a higher concordance of these traits in monozygotic compared to dizygotic twins (Clifford, Murray, & Fulker, 1984). However, specific genes have not yet been implicated, and more thorough genetic investigations are needed.

Style versus Disorder

According to the dimensional model of normal personality traits, individuals with personality disorders represent extremes in a range of normal personality traits. Hence, obsessive-compulsive personality traits can be thought of as spanning a continuum from healthy to pathological. Using the five-factor model of personality traits, Lynam and Widiger (2001) found that individuals with OCPD had elevated scores on the conscientiousness factor, which includes concerns related to order, dutifulness, self-discipline, competence, and deliberation. Building on this approach, a hybrid model of personality disorders has been proposed in which it is suggested that disorders result from a combination of stable traits and less stable symptomatic behaviors (McGlashan et al., 2005).

Treatment

The interpersonal features associated with OCPD have unique implications for treatment, but surprisingly few investigations have been made of treatment outcome for individuals with this disorder. Patients with OCPD are often unmotivated to seek treatment, because their behaviors are subjectively agreeable. In addition, patients often attribute social and occupational problems to the failure of others to conform to their personal standards and do not appreciate the role that their personality traits play in these conflicts. OCPD patients' tendency to be rigid, stubborn, and preoccupied with details can make establishing rapport with them difficult. In general, individuals with OCPD prefer therapeutic approaches that are more structured and problem-focused compared to those based on forming emotional connections (Beck et al., 2004).

Several different treatment strategies have been described for OCPD. Psychodynamic therapy for individuals with OCDP focuses on revealing how individuals' symptoms function as a defense against internal feelings of insecurity and uncertainty. Patients then learn to give up their rigid inflexible patterns and demands of perfection in favor of a more reasonable self-view, with room for human fallibility. One small study suggests that supportive-expressive psychodynamic therapy is effective for treating patients with personality disorders, including OCPD (Barber et al., 2002). This study included 24 OCPD patients in a 52-session treatment and found significant improvement, but did not include a control group.

Several cognitive-behavioral treatments have also been described for this disorder (Beck et al., 2004). The general cognitive approach involves identifying and restructuring the dysfunctional thoughts underlying maladaptive behaviors. Some approaches have suggested the importance of interventions addressing specific skill deficits, such as social skills training, while others encourage schema therapy to address maladaptive schemas, such as unrelenting standards and emotional inhibition (Sperry, 2003). However, to date there are no empirical data to show the effectiveness of these interventions.

Couples and family therapy have also been encouraged, in light of the fact that many individuals with OCPD pursue treatment because of relationship problems. Relationship and family conflicts often result from the controlling and perfectionist demands put on the family system by individuals with OCPD. However, no controlled research studies have been published on the effectiveness of such approaches.

Selective serotonin reuptake inhibitors (SSRIs) are often used to treat the Axis I disorders that co-occur with OCPD. However, to date no pharmacological trials testing the efficacy of medication for the treatment of OCPD have been reported, and psychotherapy is recommended as the treatment of choice (Sperry, 2003).

In summary, OCPD is characterized by perfectionism, orderliness, and excessive need for control. These features have been a longstanding topic of interest for the psychological community, but relatively few empirical findings have been reported concerning the etiology and treatment of this disorder. Early psychodynamic theories implicating deficient toilet training in the pathogenesis of the disorder are unfounded. Cognitive-behavioral theories, which have initial empirical support, have suggested the importance of maladaptive schemas and dysfunctional thoughts. Unlike the clinical obsessions seen in OCD, the symptoms of OCPD seem reasonable and acceptable to the individual. People with this condition are often unmotivated to change themselves, yet might seek treatment because of interpersonal or occupational problems that arise as secondary to their personality traits. Case studies and small open trials have suggested that both psychodynamic and cognitive-behavioral interventions can effectively treat individuals with OCPD, although no treatment has yet been empirically validated in large controlled trials. Much more research on this condition is needed.

REFERENCES

American Psychiatric Association. (2000). *Diagnostic and statistical manual of mental disorders* (4th ed., text rev.). Washington, DC: Author.

Barber, J., Morse, J., Kakauer, I., et al., (2002). Change in obsessive-compulsive and avoidant personality disorder following time-limited supportive-expressive therapy. *Psychotherapy, 34,* 133–143.

Beck, A. T., Freeman, A., Davis, D., & Associates. (2004). *Cognitive therapy of personality disorders* (2nd ed.). New York: Guilford Press.

Clifford, C. A., Murray, R. M., & Fulkner, D. W. (1984). Genetic and environmental influences on obsessional traits and symptoms. *Psychological Medicine, 14*(4), 791–800.

Dowson, J. H., & Grounds, A. T. (1995). *Personality disorders: Recognition and clinical management.* Cambridge, UK: Cambridge University Press.

Eisen, J. L., Mancebo, M. C, Chiappone, K. L., Pinto, A., & Rassmussen, S. A. (2008). Obsessive-compulsive personality disorder. In J. A. Abramowitz, D. McKay, & S. Taylor (Eds.), *Clinical handbook of obsessive-compulsive disorder and related problems.* Baltimore: Johns Hopkins University Press.

Grant, B. F., Hasin, D. S., Stinson, F. S., Dawson, D. A., Chou, S. P., Ruan, W. J., et al. (2004). Prevalence, correlates, and disability of personality disorders in the United States: Results from the national epidemiologic survey on alcohol and related conditions. *Journal of Clinical Psychiatry, 65*(7), 948–958.

Lynam, D. R., & Widiger, T. A. (2001). Using the five-factor model to represent the DSM-IV personality disorders: An expert consensus approach. *Journal of Abnormal Psychology, 110*(3), 401–412.

McGlashan, T. H., Grilo, C. M., Sanislow, C. A., et al. (2005). Two-year prevalence and stability of individual DSM-IV criteria for schizotypal, borderline, avoidant, and obsessive-compulsive personality disorders: Toward a hybrid model of Axis II disorders. *American Journal of Psychiatry, 165,* 883–889.

Millon, T., Davis, R., Millon, C., Escovar, L., & Meagher, S. (2000). *Personality disorders in modern life.* New York: John Wiley & Sons.

Pfohl, B., & Blum, N. (1991). Obsessive-compulsive personality disorder: A review of available data and recommendations for DSM-IV. *Journal of Personality Disorders, 5,* 363–375.

Salzman, L. (1973). *The obsessive personality.* New York: Jason Aronson.

Sperry, L. (2003). *Handbook of diagnosis and treatment of DSM-IV-TR personality disorders* (2nd ed.). New York: Brunner-Routledge.

SUGGESTED READING

Sperry, L. (2006). *Cognitive behavior therapy of DSM-IV-TR personality disorders* (2nd ed.). New York: Routledge.

Jonathan S. Abramowitz
Michael G. Wheaton
Brittain L. Mahaffey
University of North Carolina at Chapel Hill

OCCUPATIONAL HEALTH PSYCHOLOGY

Occupational health psychology (OHP) is an interdisciplinary specialty at the crossroads of psychology and public health within the organizational context of work environments. The Occupational Safety and Health Act of 1974 established that employees in the United States should have a safe and healthy work environment. Similar legislation has been enacted in The Netherlands, Sweden, and the European Union. OHP applies several specialties within psychology to organizational settings for the improvement of the quality of work life, the protection and safety of workers, and promotion of healthy work environments.

Healthy work environments are ones in which people feel good, achieve high performance, and have high levels of well-being. One of the earliest American psychologists concerned with health in industrial contexts was Donald Laird, Director of the Colgate Psychological Laboratory who garnered support from the Central New York Section of the Taylor Society. In Europe, Levi's (2000) lifelong research in Europe focused on integrating psychosocial factors into preventive medicine, as reflected in his contribution to the U.S. Surgeon General's report in 1979. In the United States, Sauter, Murphy, and Hurrell (1990) focused attention on the psychological hazards of workplaces.

Ecological Dimensions of OHP

As early as 1961, Abraham Maslow was calling for the definition and creation of healthy work environments. Healthy work environments may be characterized by high productivity, high employee satisfaction, good safety records, low frequencies of disability claims and union grievances, low absenteeism, low turnover, and the absence of violence. The ecological dimensions of OHP are: the work environment, the individual, and the work-family interface.

The Work Environment

The health of a work environment may be influenced by a broad range of occupational, psychological, organizational, and work design demands or stressors. Adkins (1999) brings attention to the more contextual notion of organizational health as the evolving practice of OHP in specific organizational settings. Levi (2000) has maintained a career-long focus on the health of the work environment and as a Member of Parliament in Sweden from 2006 has aimed to translate the best research into public policy.

The Individual

A broad range of individual characteristics similarly influences the health of a work environment. These characteristics include career stage, age, coping style, negative affectivity, self-esteem, health-status, and self-reliance. Beyond designing work environments that are person-oriented and healthy, OHP is concerned with individuals in their own right (Quick, 1999). Some of the specific concepts related to individual behavior important to OHP include emotion, anger, workaholism, and gender difference predispositions. Gender, one important diversity difference in organizations, is an individual characteristic that has important implications for OHP.

The Work-Family Interface

People live in multiple life arenas and work environment demands are not the only ones that impact their health. Work-family conflict can result in a greater prevalence of physical health symptoms, hypertension, substance abuse, anxiety, and depression (Eby, Casper, Lockwood, Bordeaux, & Brinley, 2005). Employees with work-family conflict also have lower organizational commitment, job satisfaction and intentions to remain with their firms (Eby et al., 2005). OHP seeks to identify the supports organizations can provide to reduce this conflict such as dependent-care assistance (e.g., on-site child care, eldercare resource and referral programs), alternative work schedules (e.g., flextime, compressed work weeks, part-time work), alternative work locations (e.g., telecommuting, mobile office platforms), family-leave benefits (e.g., maternity and paternity leave), family-related relocation assistance (spouse job-finding assistance), and employee assistance programs. Although these programs can reduce work-family conflict, informal support (from supervisors, coworkers) for work-family issues is equally important. In fact, if informal organizational support is lacking, work-family programs are likely to be underutilized and unable to exhibit their potential beneficial effects (Eby et al., 2005).

Recent models of the work-family interface suggest that multiple roles can also be health-enhancing; This phenomenon has been labeled work-family facilitation or work-family enhancement. This perspective argues that positive affective experiences that occur or skills developed in one domain (e.g. family) can have beneficial effect on the other domain through positive affective spillover or skill transfer. As future research develops, we will have a better idea of some of the positive outcomes associated with this phenomenon.

Preventive Stress Management and OHP

The public health model classifies interventions into three categories: primary interventions, secondary interventions, and tertiary interventions. Primary prevention aims to intervene with the health risk or stress. Secondary prevention aims to intervene with the stress response or asymptomatic disorders. Tertiary prevention aims to intervene with distress and symptomatic disorders. Klunder (2008), as an organizational clinical psychologist, employed the theory of preventive stress management

in an OHP context over a six-year period to design and implement primary, secondary, and tertiary interventions for over 10,000 personnel in a major industrial restructuring and closure process. In this high-risk work environment with dramatic daily change, there was concern that serious problems, such as suicide and workplace violence, might become overtly manifest. This was a particular concern for the at-risk employee population. The at-risk employee population presented with very complicated personal and family problems, and with little or no identified plan of action to resolve them. Troubled employees with chronic performance problems were facing layoffs without a realistic transition plan. Many workers developed or experienced exacerbation of existing physical problems. The occupational medicine clinic estimated that over 30% of the workforce had no medical insurance.

Suicides and Workplace Violence

Suicides and workplace violence were two key outcome concerns over the six-year closure. The results affirmed the comprehensive OHP strategy for the health of this working population. While there was a degree of reported suicidal ideation and intent, swift and direct intervention resulted in several saved lives. No completed suicides occurred related to the closure process. During much of this period, the Centers for Disease Control and Prevention reported suicide rates varying from 16 per 100,000 to 2.2 per 100,000. While there was some angry language at times and heated emotions, with very minor pushing and shoving on occasion, there was never a serious physical altercation throughout the six-year period.

Labor Grievances and Complaints

The OHP interventions resulted in significant cost avoidance. The Equal Employment Opportunity (EEO) Office indicated that overall approximately 40% of initial complaints move to formal status. The minimum administrative and investigative costs associated with a formal complaint are $80,000 regardless of whether it is validated. Based on the highest risk and highest/severe risk complaints, EEO projections attributed an administrative saving between $23.9M and $33.7M. These are processing costs and do not include an undetermined amount of potential outcome costs that may have been awarded to complainants.

Other Important Occupational Health Issues
Safety Climate

Another important issue in OHP is the prevention of occupational accidents. One factor that is important to accident prevention is the safety climate of an organization. Organizational safety climate is defined as the shared perceptions of organizational members with respect to safety policies, procedures, and practices (Zohar, 2003). Such a safety climate should relate to occupational health behaviors that workers engage in and this, in turn, influences accidents at work. Understanding the features of the work environment that encourage safe behavior at work has real implications for accident reduction and prevention.

Other Workplace Health Concerns

In addition to the health-delineated concerns above, OHP concerns itself with various other worker-health concerns. These include tobacco use, drug and alcohol abuse, and HIV/AIDS because they have been recognized as critical problems by the International Labour Organization (ILO). These employee health issues influence not only employees but their organizations as well. Moreover, job stress may contribute to these problems, as it may lead to poor decision-making regarding use of tobacco, alcohol, and drugs, or behaviors that put workers at risk for HIV infection. To address these and related health concerns, the ILO has developed the SOLVE intervention program. SOLVE is a multilevel longitudinal training program that trains managers and front-line workers about five distinct occupational health problems: job stress, workplace violence, tobacco use, drug and alcohol abuse, and HIV/AIDS. Preliminary evidence suggests that SOLVE, implemented in dozens of countries around the world, leads to learning about important health issues (Probst, Gould, & Caborn, 2008). The intent is that the knowledge gained via SOLVE will also aid in the global reduction of these various health concerns.

Training in Occupational Health Psychology

Formal training in OHP is equally interdisciplinary. As of 2001, examples of universities that have incorporated courses in OHP and/or minors at the doctoral level include Bowling Green State University, Kansas State University, University of Minnesota, University of Houston, Tulane University, Clemson University, Portland State University, and University of California—Los Angeles. Schneider, Camara, Tetrick, and Stenberg (1999) discuss the role of post-doctoral educational, for example as funded for several years through the APA/NIOSH post-doctoral fellowships, and the U.S. Air Force funded a post-doctoral OHP fellowship at Harvard Medical School in 1998–1999. Finally, there is now a European Academy of Occupational Health Psychology.

REFERENCES

Adkins, J. A. (1999). Promoting organizational health: The evolving practice of occupational health psychology. *Professional Psychology: Research and Practice, 30*, 129–37.

Eby, L. T., Casper, W. J., Lockwood, A., Bordeaux, C., & Brinley, A. (2005). A twenty-year retrospective on work and family research in IO/OB: A review of the literature. *Journal of Vocational Behavior, 66*, 124–197. [Monograph]

Klunder, C.S. (2008). Preventive stress management at work: The case of the San Antonio Air Logistics Center, Air Force Materiel Command (AFMC). Paper presented at Society of Psychologists in Management Conference and Institutes, San Antonio, 29 February.

Levi, L. (2000). *Guidance on work-related stress: Spice of life or kiss of death* (100 pages).

Luxembourg: European Commission, Directorate-General for Employment and Social Affairs, Health & Safety at Work.

Probst, T. M., Gold, D., & Caborn, J. (2008). A preliminary evaluation of SOLVE: Addressing psychosocial problems at work. *Journal of Occupational Health Psychology, 13*, 32–42.

Quick, J. C. (1999). Occupational health psychology: Historical roots and future directions. *Health Psychology, 18*, 82–88.

Quick, J. C. & Tetrick, L. (2003). *Handbook of occupational health psychology*. Washington, DC: American Psychological Association.

Sauter, S. L., Murphy, L. R., & Hurrell, J. J. (1990). Prevention of work-related psychological distress: A national strategy proposed by the National Institute of Occupational Safety and Health. *American Psychologist, 45*, 1146–1158.

Zohar, D. (2003). Safety climate: Conceptual and measurement issues. In J. C. Quick & L. E. Tetrick (Eds.), *Handbook of occupational health psychology*. Washington, DC: American Psychological Association.

SUGGESTED READING

Macik-Frey, M., Quick, J. C., & Nelson, D. L. (2007). Advances in occupational health: From a stressful beginning to a positive future. Journal of Management, 33, 189–205.

James Campbell Quick
Wendy J. Casper
University of Texas at Arlington

See also: Health Psychology; Occupational Stress

OCCUPATIONAL INTERESTS

The literature on interests offers many definitions of the term. Interests may be defined, for example, as activities or stimuli that engage one's attention and curiosity. Edward K. Strong, one of the most influential authorities on interests, proposed that interests involve enduring attention, positive feeling, and action directed toward the object of interest, as well as preference for that object over another. Occupational interests in particular may be understood as "patterns of likes, dislikes, and indifferences regarding career-relevant activities and occupations." Notably, interests only relay information about the likelihood that an activity will be initiated and continued; interest in the activity does not guarantee that the activity will be carried out successfully. For career interests this means that an individual's interest in a career does not carry the promise of his or her high performance in it. Additional factors, such as abilities, bridge the gap between interest and performance.

Origin of Interests

Heredity, environment, social factors, ability, and personality are several potential sources of vocational interests. Heredity may indirectly predispose an individual to develop particular interests by influencing disposition, ability, and physical characteristics. Importantly, an individual's genetic makeup limits one's potential within various domains (e.g., sports).

The environment may influence vocational interests via role models, socialization, reinforcement, and social roles. Children and adolescents find role models to observe and emulate. The activities and interests of the role model are tried out, and those that are in line with the young individual's character and abilities become part of his or her self-concept. Further, when an individual's performance of a certain activity is recognized or rewarded (i.e., reinforced), the interest in that activity tends to become stronger. Parents play an important role both as role models and as agents of socialization who provide reinforcement. This dual role may partly explain the high correlation found between the interests of parents and children. Notably, occupational interests may also be influenced by social factors. Sex roles and occupational prestige may provide a framework of socially appropriate interests from which an individual may select interests to pursue.

Psychologists generally agree that actual ability and interests are weakly, if at all, related. The former influences success at an activity, while the latter influences willingness to perform the activity repeatedly. Self-estimated ability, rather than true ability, is believed to influence the development of interests. Individuals tend to maintain interest in activities that they believe they perform well, that are satisfying, and for which they expect to receive positive reinforcement. Individual differences in personality partly account for the interests that develop. Depending on an individual's disposition, particular types of stimuli will grab his or her attention and stir his or her curiosity.

Influences on interests appear to play out mostly during an individual's youth, as individuals in their late teens or early 20s exhibit interests that are relatively stable. Although it is less common, interests can also emerge or fade in adulthood.

Categories of Interests

Donald Super distinguished four categories of interest: expressed interests, manifest or evidenced interests,

tested interests, and inventoried interests. Expressed interests are those that an individual is able to describe without the aid of a list. These interests are subjective in that they are related to individuals' evaluation of their own internal state. Manifest or evidenced interests are those that individuals exhibit when they participate in certain activities, particularly during their free time. Tested interests can be evaluated by checking how much a person knows about a particular subject. Finally, inventoried interests, as the name suggests, are based on self-reports on interest inventories. Interest inventories are described in the next section.

Interest Inventories

Interest inventories are tests that assess an individual's preference for particular activities or occupations. Respondents choose activities they would enjoy taking part in from a checklist and use rating scales to indicate the strength of their interest in these activities. Interest inventories are very commonly utilized due to their ease of interpretation and relatively low cost of use. One major advantage of interest inventories, beyond just asking individuals about their interest, is that many of them are normed and provide a comparison of a tested individual's level of interest against various norm groups.

Interest inventories created by Edward K. Strong, Frederic Kuder, and John L. Holland have been dubbed the "Big Three." The Strong Interest Inventory (SII), the longest continuously published interest inventory, was constructed via the empirical method of contrast groups. In this method, preferences that predict group membership are determined, consistency of the test taker's preferences with those of a particular group is evaluated, and a score predicting group membership is computed. The SII asks individuals to indicate their degree of like or dislike for 291 items. The SII profile created for the respondent is organized into four sets of scales: general occupational themes, basic interest scales, occupational scales, and personal styles scales. The general occupational themes give information about the respondent's work personality and are based on Holland's model. The basic interest scales break down the general occupational themes into work, school, and leisure-related activities. The occupational scales direct respondents toward the occupations for which they received the highest scores and are likely to find most appealing. The personal styles scales give information about a respondent's style in the domains of work, learning, risk-taking, leadership, and team participation. More recently, based on career-related self-efficacy research, a Confidence component (self-estimated ability) has been added to the Strong Interest Inventory.

The Kuder Career Search (KCS) was constructed via a clustering technique whereby the interests of people in various occupations were reduced down to basic, underlying dimensions of interests. The KCS presents individuals with 60 sets of three activities and asks them to select from each group the most and least appealing activities. The KCS has two scales: the Kuder Career Clusters and Person Matches. The Kuder Career Clusters compares respondents' likes and dislikes to members of particular sets of occupations. The Person Matches find individuals within a large pool of data who best match the respondent in interests. Respondents are provided with detailed job descriptions of these individuals.

The Holland Self-Directed Search (SDS) was created using the rational method of scale construction whereby items are grouped according to a particular theory. The theory at the root of the SDS is that interests can be organized into six types: Realistic, Investigative, Artistic, Social, Enterprising, and Conventional. This is often referred to as the RIASEC model. Respondents are presented with 228 items organized into five sections: activities, competencies, occupational preferences, and two self-rating of abilities sections. Individuals are asked to indicate which activities they would like and which they would dislike, which activities they feel competent in and which they do not feel competent in, and which occupations they are interested in and which they are not interested in, and they are asked to rate their skills and abilities in relation to the general population. The SDS profile provides a 3-letter Holland code that individuals can use to find the careers that are most appropriate for their interests and competencies. A list of occupations is provided. Notably, the Strong Interest Inventory as noted earlier uses Holland's typology in its occupational themes. Over time, many of the interest inventories also incorporated Holland's model into their measure, given extensive research that has been generated in support of that model.

Other interest inventories include the Campbell Interest and Skill Survey (CISS), which is notable for its extra feature of skill scales that indicate how confident respondents are in their ability to carry out a range of occupational activities; the Career Assessment Inventory (CAI), which was created especially for the use of individuals who were not going to college; and the Jackson Vocational Interest Survey (JVIS), which is distinct for its innovative qualities. The JVIS attempts to alleviate problems of response bias by using forced-choice formats and special item selection techniques. This instrument is also unique in its emphasis on work styles instead of interests, its attempted suitability for research purposes, and its use of complex statistical techniques in scale and occupational cluster-building.

Interest Assessment Innovation

In the last 25 years, interest inventories have been extensively revised to address considerations of bias and to include an increased number of occupations. The computer has spurred additional innovations in the assessment of interest, creating a movement away from paper-and-pencil assessment toward automated administration and scoring. At the same time, the availability of a myriad of career interest measures on the Internet has also created the danger of limited quality control, particularly with respect to users not being informed about the psychometric qualities of poorly developed measures.

Practical Advice for Discovering Career Interests

Individuals who are in the process of figuring out their occupational interests can do several things to tap their likes and dislikes. It is a good idea to complete a number of inventories, making an effort to be as honest as possible in the responses, and to carefully review the results. Inventories can underscore things about individuals that they that did not realize about themselves and propose appropriate career fields for a person with their constellation of interests. Individuals should take a good look inward and honestly consider how their abilities, interests, and shortcomings match up with the features of various occupations. Those who have not had enough experience with various areas to know where their interests may lie should explore hobbies and careers. Trying out activities refers to the attempt to participate in a variety of things in order to discover one's interests. Experience serves to bring interests into awareness. Such career exploration activities are a key to identifying one's interests.

REFERENCES

Borgen, F. H. (1986). New approaches to the assessment of interests. In W. B. Walsh & S. H. Osipow (Eds.), *Advances in vocational psychology: Vol. 1. The assessment of interests* (pp. 83–125). Hillsdale, NJ: Lawrence Erlbaum.

Hansen, J. C., & Bubany, S. T. (2008). Expressed, manifest, tested, and inventoried interests. In *Encyclopedia of counseling* (Vol. 4, pp. 1537–1539). Thousand Oaks, CA: Sage.

Savickas, M. L. (1999). The psychology of interests. In M. L. Savickas & A. R. Spokane (Eds.), *Vocational interests: Their meaning, measurement, and counseling use* (pp. 19–56). Palo Alto, CA: Davies-Black.

SUGGESTED READINGS

Holland, J. L. (1997). *Making vocational choices: A theory of vocational personalities and work environments* (3rd ed.). Odessa, FL: Psychological Assessment Resources.

Parsons, F. (1909). Choosing a vocation. Boston: Houghton Mifflin.

Super, D. E. (1957). *The psychology of careers: An introduction to vocational development.* New York: Harper & Brothers.

FREDERICK T. L. LEONG
JULIYA GOLUBOVICH
Michigan State University

See also: Interests; Strong Interest Inventory; Vocational Testing

OCCUPATIONAL STRESS

Occupational stress poses a significant threat to the health and well-being of employees as well as potential costs to organizations. Occupational stressors are stress-producing events or conditions in an organization and can include factors associated with one's work role (e.g., role ambiguity, overload, work-family conflict, and interpersonal conflict), the social context of the work environment (e.g., workplace aggression, injustice, sexual harassment), and the physical work environment (e.g., safety, spatial organization, ambient environment).

Although stressors external to the organization (e.g., weather) may also cause employees to experience stress, this entry is concerned with organizational stressors. In addition, Although some challenge-related stressors may produce positive effects known as *eustress*, we focus only on stressors that produce negative outcomes, known as *distress*. Employees who are unable to remove or cope with stress-producing events may experience a range of strains. We outline three theories of occupational stress: role theory, the job demands-control model, and the model of work frustration-aggression. Although each takes a unique perspective, together they offer a more complete understanding of the relationship between stressors and strain in the workplace.

Role Theory

A role refers to the function an employee fulfills in his or her work environment. Individuals learn about the expectations of their roles through communication and interaction with other employees, in addition to observing colleagues within the work context (Kahn, Wolfe, Quinn, Snoek, & Rosenthal, 1964). Role theory posits that a "sender" communicates information or places demands on a "receiver," who sometimes perceives the communication as demanding, ambiguous, or too difficult to complete (Beehr, 1985). These demanding, ambiguous, or confusing messages can then cause employees to experience job-related strains.

The three main types of role stressors that are generally considered in role theory include role ambiguity, role conflict, and role overload. Role ambiguity takes place when employees are unclear about their work duties, job goals, or day-to-day responsibilities (Jex, 1998). Role ambiguity occurs when there is insufficient or misleading information about one's job role leading to uncertainty about colleagues' or supervisors' expectations. Related to role ambiguity is role conflict, which refers to competing and incompatible demands from two or more sources in the work environment (Kahn et al., 1964). Role conflict can affect role ambiguity because the senders present mixed messages to a receiver, who then becomes uncertain about which sender to attend to and what exactly his or her role entails. Role conflict and ambiguity may also be associated with role overload or an employee's perception that he or she is facing excessive quantitative (i.e., too much work in too little time) or qualitative (i.e., insufficient skill-base) demands.

Role theory posits that role-related stressors are associated with individual and organizational strains. These strains may include employee attitudes (e.g., job satisfaction, organizational commitment, intentions to quit), employee well-being (e.g., mental and physical health), and employee behaviors (e.g., job withdrawal, absenteeism) (Beehr & Glazer, 2005). These individual strains, in turn, have negative implications for the organization in terms of higher turnover, productivity, and withdrawal costs.

Job Demands-Control Model

Whereas role theory specifies that stressors arising from role-related communication are associated with higher levels of strain, Karasek's (1979) job demands-control (JD-C) model posits an interaction between work demands and job control. JD-C suggests that high work demands in the face of low job control will adversely affect employee health. Job demands refer to the physical, psychological, or social aspects of work that require continual physical, emotional, or cognitive effort. In the face of high demands, employees who do not have the autonomy to re-organize or re-prioritize their work to properly manage their demands (i.e., job control) will experience higher levels of strain. In contrast, when employees do have autonomy over their work, this control will mitigate the adverse health effects of high job demands and stimulate active learning.

Although research has generally supported the additive effect of the model (i.e., high demands and low autonomy are independently associated with higher levels of strain), the interactive effects have been equivocal. Karasek and Theorell (1990) later expanded the JD-C model to include social support as a third component, arguing that the highest levels of strain occur when job demands are high but control and support are low. They defined support as the level of helpful interaction an employee receives from his or her co-workers or supervisors. Demerouti, Bakker, Nachreiner, and Schaufeli (2001) broadened the JD-C and support model to suggest that other resources, in addition to or instead of job control and support, may buffer the adverse effects of high demands. Specifically, Demerouti and colleagues proposed the inclusion of other job resources, which may include the physical, social, or psychological aspects of a job that help employees achieve work goals, reduce demands, or stimulate personal growth. In addition to job control, their job demands and resources (JD-R) model allows for not only the possibility that other resources (e.g., growth opportunities) will buffer the adverse effects of job demands, but also that such resources may lead to positive outcomes. For instance, the JD-R model suggests that in the face of high social support, high job demands will be associated with higher levels of job commitment, whereas low social support will result in higher levels of employee burnout.

Model of Work Frustration-Aggression

Whereas the JD-C and role theories largely focus on the direct link between organizational stressors, such as job- and role-related demands and job strain, Spector's (1997) organizational frustration model considers the cognitive and affective mediators that explain why stressors are linked to these adverse outcomes. Spector argued that factors that thwart individual goals (i.e., stressors) will lead to cognitive appraisals about the situation. He posited that employees will engage in cognitive activity to evaluate factors such as the importance of the goal and the number and severity of stressors. Within this cognitive process, if employees evaluate the stressor to be significant (e.g., the stressor thwarts a valued goal), they will experience frustration that will provoke a negative behavioral reaction such as counterproductive or aggressive work behaviors. However, he posited that aggressive outcomes will only ensue under certain conditions. For instance, if employees fear being caught or are able to exercise self-control, they may not react aggressively. In contrast, impulsive individuals or those who feel alienated or hostile towards their organization's regulations will be more likely to react in a counterproductive or aggressive manner. Building on this model of frustration and aggression, Fox and Spector (1999) considered the affective mediators of stressors and their outcomes. They posited and found that when frustrating events are followed by a negative emotional response, individuals are more likely to engage in counterproductive or aggressive behaviors.

Whereas prior stress models focused largely on the health-related outcomes of employees, the organization frustration model explicitly considered the behavioral outcomes. Spector and colleagues argued that the experience of frustration will be associated with aggressive reactions such as counterproductive work behaviors. They define counterproductive work behaviors as behaviors that interfere with the performance or effectiveness of organizations. Such behaviors may include hostility directed at other employees (e.g., gossiping and other rude behaviors) and hostility directed at the organization (e.g., withdrawing from work, taking longer breaks, damaging organizational property). Frustrating events may include any stressor that thwarts employee objectives, such as job constraints, interpersonal conflict with other employees, or any of the role- or job-related stressors discussed at the outset of this entry or in prior theories.

In summary, the three theories presented herein together represent a selection of three key theories that explain the effects of stressors on strains. Role theory focuses on the direct relationship between role-related stressors and job strains. JD-C and JD-R both expand the possible stressors associated with strains, and consider moderating factors that mitigate or exacerbate these strains. Finally, the model of work frustration provides an understanding of the cognitive and affective mediators of stressors on strains. This set of models helps to explain when, why, and how a range of stressors relate to a variety of possible strains.

REFERENCES

Beehr T. A. (1985). Organizational stress and employee effectiveness: A job characteristics approach. In T. A. Beehr & R. S. Bhagat (Eds.), *Human stress and cognition in organizations* (pp. 57–81). New York: John Wiley & Sons.

Beehr, T. A., & Glazer, S. (2005). Organizational role stress. In J. Barling, E. K. Kelloway, & M. R. Frone (Eds.), Handbook of work stress (pp. 7–33). Thousand Oaks, CA: Sage.

Demerouti, E., Bakker, A. B., Nachreiner, F., & Schaufeli, W. B. (2001). The job demands-resources model of burnout. *Journal of Applied Psychology, 86,* 499–512.

Fox, S., & Spector, P. E. (1999) A model of work frustration-aggression. *Journal of Organizational Behavior, 20,* 915–931.

Jex, S. M. (1998). *Stress and job performance: Theory, research, and implications for managerial practice.* Thousand Oaks, CA: Sage.

Kahn, R. L., Wolfe, D. M., Quinn, R. P., Snoek, J. D., & Rosenthal, R. A. (1964). *Organizational stress: Studies in role conflict and ambiguity.* New York: John Wiley & Sons.

Karasek, R. (1979). Job decision latitude, job demands and mental strain: Implications for job redesign. *Administrative Science Quarterly, 24,* 285–308.

Karasek, R., & Theorell, T. (1990). *Healthy work: Stress, productivity and the reconstruction of working life.* New York: Basic Books.

Spector, P. E. (1997). The role of frustration in antisocial behavior. In R. A. Giacalone & J. Greenberg (Eds.), *Antisocial behavior in organizations* (pp. 1–17). Thousand Oaks, CA: Sage.

M. SANDY HERSHCOVIS
TARA C. REICH
University of Manitoba, Canada

See also: Job Stress Survey; Occupational Health Psychology

OEDIPUS COMPLEX

The Oedipus complex is a psychoanalytic concept that refers to psychological conflicts experienced by every individual. The complex was named by Sigmund Freud in 1910 after the Greek tragedy of King Oedipus (Freud, 1910/1957). As a baby, Oedipus narrowly escaped being killed by his father. Later he unknowingly killed his father and inadvertently married his mother. When he came to realize what he had done—that the man he had killed was his father, and that the woman he was having sex with was his mother—he was so horrified that he blinded himself and gave up his kingdom. The story suggests how there may be aggressive competition between fathers and sons. It also shows how powerful is the taboo against incest, and how incestuous feelings may cause intense guilt. Freud held that every boy struggles with such feelings. Later he extended this theory to girls, because they have feelings of rivalry toward their mother figures as a consequence of harboring secret erotic feelings toward their father figures (Freud, 1933/1964). Psychoanalysts view these conflicts as entirely normal, although they are often the source of conflicts in later life (Young, 2001).

As psychoanalysts developed Freud's ideas, this complex has come to have several interrelated meanings. Three main processes are involved. First, the Oedipus complex refers to the fact that children's earliest sensual feelings are directed toward a person, usually a parent, with whom a sexual relationship would be incestuous. In order to disavow incestuous feelings, children have to learn to redirect their erotic interests toward a non-familial person. Incestuous feelings are so powerful and forbidden that we repress them from consciousness; this is one major way in which the unconscious mind develops and then influences us throughout our lives.

Second, the Oedipus complex may refer to all of the triangular rivalries that originate in early childhood. For example, a boy wishing to get closer to his mother may treat his father as a rival; when he wishes to get closer to his father, his mother becomes a rival. A girl wishing to get closer to her mother may treat her father as a rival; when she wishes to get closer to her father, her mother becomes a rival. These conflicts do not necessarily involve the persons who are literally the child's mother and father; they may involve a variety of mother-figures or fatherfigures, as well as siblings or other family members. Difficulties with situations in which three persons are in a relationship are very common throughout life. Many of us struggle with feelings of being left out, of comparison and competitiveness (rivalry and jealousy), and the like. These difficulties occur with particular intensity in sexual situations.

Third, the Oedipus complex refers to the way in which children and adolescents mature into their adult identity, especially around sexuality. In one "pre-Oedipal" type of identification process, we become attached to a person and consequently become like that person (in which case we identify with that person because we like, admire, or even fear the person), or we become attached to a person and consequently become someone that person would like us to be (in which case our identity is formed by our need to have that person become attached to us).

However, Oedipal processes of identification are more complicated than this pre-Oedipal type. For example, a boy may identify with a man's sexual personality, not just because that is his gender, but also because he is attached to his mother (or mother-figures) and knows that she is erotically interested in men. Alternatively, a boy may

identify with a woman's sexual personality because he is attached to his father (or father-figures) and knows that he is erotically interested in women. A girl may identify with a woman's sexual personality, not just because that is her gender, but also because she becomes attached to her father (or father-figures) and knows that he is erotically interested in women. Alternatively, a girl may identify with a man's sexual personality because she is attached to her mother (or mother-figures) and knows that she is erotically interested in men.

These are complicated processes that normally occur outside of our conscious awareness. According to classical psychoanalytic theory, every boy and girl struggles with these feelings and identification processes in the course of psychological maturation. These feelings are not only those of sensuality and love (as well as the forbidden eroticism of incestuous fantasies and desires), but also of competition, resentment, and hostility. Thus, the particular details of an individual's Oedipus complex are believed to have a major influence on the formation of personality, which includes one's gender identity, pattern of adult eroticism, and sexual orientation—including how bisexual feelings within the person's makeup are addressed (Barratt, 2005).

In most versions of psychoanalytic theory, the Oedipus complex is believed to be triggered by the young child's ability to recognize that there is a special relationship—notably, the sexual relationship—that occurs between adult women and men (mothers and fathers) and from which the child is excluded. This recognition occurs in what psychoanalysts call the "primal scene" (which sometimes literally refers to the child's awareness that his or her parents have intercourse). Most psychoanalysts believe that this becomes possible with language acquisition and the cognitive developments that occur around age three or four, although there are some different opinions as to when this complex begins (Britton, 1990). Typically, the Oedipus complex is intense around age five, settles down temporarily in middle childhood, and is re-activated in adolescence, when teenagers struggle with issues of sexuality, maturation, and identity. However, psychoanalysts generally agree that the conflicts associated with the Oedipus complex continue throughout our lives and can be a source of much unhappiness and unnecessary suffering.

Although some aspects of this theory are controversial, the Oedipus complex is an important way of understanding many aspects of an individual's emotional, relational, and sexual development, as well as the origins of adult character and conflicts (Covitz, 1998; Hartocollis, 1999). It has also been used to explain many features of religious belief as well as other aspects of social and cultural phenomena.

REFERENCES

Barratt, B. B. (2005). *Sexual health and erotic freedom*. Philadelphia, PA: Xlibris.

Britton, R. (1990). *The Oedipus complex today: Clinical implications.* London: Karnac.

Covitz, H. H. (1998). *Oedipal paradigms in collision: A centennial emendation of a piece of Freudian canon (1897–1997).* New York: Peter Lang.

Freud, S. (1957). Five lectures on psychoanalysis. In J. Strachey (Ed.), *The standard edition of the complete psychological works of Sigmund Freud: Vol. 11* (pp. 9–56). London: Hogarth Press. (Original work published in 1910)

Freud, S. (1964). New introductory lectures on psychoanalysis. In J. Strachey (Ed.), *The standard edition of the complete psychological works of Sigmund Freud: Vol. 22* (pp. 5–182). London: Hogarth Press. (Original work published in 1933)

Hartocollis, P. (Ed., 1999). *Mankind's Oedipal destiny: Libidinal and aggressive aspects of sexuality.* New York: International Universities Press.

Young, R. (2001). *The Oedipus complex: Ideas in psychoanalysis.* London: Totem Books.

BARNABY B. BARRATT
Prescott, AZ

See also: **Family Development, Theories of**

OPERANT CONDITIONING

Operant conditioning, a term coined by B. F. Skinner (1937), has several shades of meaning. It is both an experimental procedure and a behavioral process. In the latter sense, it is a biological adaptation with a plausible evolutionary interpretation and can be observed in the environment-behavior relations of any species with a complex nervous system. The study of operant conditioning and related phenomena comprises a substantial research paradigm within psychology in both laboratory and applied settings. This paradigm endorses tightly controlled experiments to discover behavioral principles; the direct extension of those principles to behavior therapy, education, organizational behavior, and other applications; and the use of the principles as interpretive tools for understanding complex human behavior such as language, memory, and problem solving.

The Operant Conditioning Procedure

In an operant conditioning procedure, a consequence is explicitly arranged to follow a particular class of behavior; specifically, the experimenter arranges a contingency in which a stimulus is presented if and only if a target behavior has just occurred. For example, an apparatus might be designed so that, whenever a rat presses a lever, a drop of water drips into a dish from which the rat can drink. If the rat has recently been denied access to water,

the strength of the target behavior will change; among other effects, the rate of pressing the lever will increase in that setting and in similar settings. If replications and suitable control conditions demonstrate that this change in strength is in fact due to the contingency, and is not a coincidence, the procedure is an instance of positive reinforcement, and water is called a reinforcing stimulus.

If the rat has not been deprived of water, the procedure might have no demonstrable effect on behavior. Under these conditions, if the rat were forced to drink by squirting water in its mouth, for example, we would expect the rate of lever-pressing to decrease relative to a baseline condition. We then speak of a punishment contingency and of water as a punishing stimulus. Thus both reinforcement and punishment are defined, not by procedures or by the nature of particular stimuli, but by their effects on the probability of behavior under given conditions.

Thorndike (1898) was the first researcher to study operant conditioning systematically, but Skinner is recognized for developing the framework and much of the experimental foundation for modern operant theory. He designed most of his own apparatus, including the now-standard experimental chamber that bears his name. Skinner was the first to discover that the rate of behavior in freely moving organisms was highly sensitive to a wide variety of independent variables. In experiments using Skinner's methodology, the demonstration of operant principles has been found to be highly reliable in many species. Single-subject designs are preferred, since the behavioral principles of interest are revealed in the detailed interactions of organism and environment and may be obscured by averaging cases. Skinner recognized that appropriate units of analysis in psychology should not be defined in advance by the experimenter, but should be determined empirically, by looking for orderly relationships between the organism and its environment. The units that emerge from such an analysis are three-term contingencies of environment, behavior, and consequence, and no one term can be understood in isolation.

Operant Conditioning as a Behavioral Process

Operant conditioning procedures have revealed that behavior changes in strength or probability when it is followed by biologically important consequences such as access to food, water, sexual activity, or escape from painful stimuli, cold, or excessive heat. Activities that tend to promote survival and reproduction become more frequent, while those that bring harm are reduced or eliminated. Operant conditioning is thus an important evolutionary advance enabling an organism to adapt to unpredictable environments where nourishment, comfort, potential mates, and danger are not ubiquitous but must be searched out, fought for, or avoided.

Food, water, and sexual contact are all examples of unconditioned reinforcers, stimuli that are innately reinforcing under relevant motivating conditions, presumably because organisms for whom they functioned as such were more likely to have offspring than those for whom they did not function in this way. However, neutral stimuli can acquire a reinforcing function if they are frequently paired with unconditioned reinforcers. Thus we learn to respond to the dinner bell, to hunt for a water bubbler, and to approach a member of the opposite sex who smiles at us. In humans, money, fame, and prestige are typically effective conditioned reinforcers only indirectly related to survival and differential reproduction. However, propaganda, education, or indoctrination can sometimes establish biologically maladaptive consequences as effective reinforcers: Soldiers charge into a hail of bullets, monks take vows of lifelong celibacy, anorexic teenagers turn away their meals, and young militants blow themselves up in Baghdad and elsewhere.

The strengthening of adaptive behavior and the weakening of ineffective behavior is a selection process, analogous in many respects to natural selection. Behavior is variable; even a highly practiced behavior will vary somewhat from one instance to the next. By differentially reinforcing responses with some property, such as relatively forceful lever presses, for example, an experimenter can effect a change in the distribution of responses. More and more forceful lever presses occur to the point that the typical response is wholly unrepresentative of the original distribution of behavior. When organisms are exposed to such programs of gradually changing contingencies—a process called shaping—behavior can evolve and become highly differentiated over the lifetime of the individual, much as the morphology of organisms changes over evolutionary time. The repertoires of the skillful juggler, rock climber, and gymnast have presumably been shaped mainly by programs of intrinsic contingencies, but the repertoires of the seeing-eye dog, the race horse, the mathematician, the engineer, and the historian are likely to have been shaped mainly by programs of contingencies explicitly arranged by trainers or educators.

The Domain of Operant Conditioning

Some response systems, such as respiration, circulation, and digestion, serve a narrow function in the economy of the organism, and for them to vary substantially with arbitrary contingencies of reinforcement would not be adaptive. In contrast, the orientation of receptors and responses mediated by skeletal muscles, such as the vocal apparatus, limbs, digits, and other effectors, can be recruited for a wide variety of functions, with some variability from one species to another. Operant conditioning can most easily be demonstrated in the latter class of response systems.

It is characteristic of students of operant conditioning to confine their experimental analyses to objective, measurable variables. However, in any experiment some part of the behavior of an organism is always below the threshold of observability. Since this threshold depends on the tools of the investigator and is not an intrinsic property of behavior, it must be assumed that the principles of operant conditioning apply not only to behavior that can be observed, but also to covert behavior as well.

The psychologist's understanding of covert behavior is necessarily interpretive rather than experimental. The principle of reinforcement has been useful in such interpretations, because the terms of the analysis have been well established in single subjects under analogous conditions in the laboratory. However, the extent to which operant conditioning and other principles of learning provide a sufficient foundation for an interpretation of such phenomena as language, recall, covert problem solving, imagery, and perception remains controversial. In most adult humans, verbal rules (e.g., "Turn right at the second traffic light") can have effects on behavior comparable to those of direct exposure to relevant operant conditioning procedures. Behaviorists argue that such examples of rule-governed behavior do not require appeals to new principles but can be derived from established principles of learning. From this perspective, operant conditioning is the primary principle underlying all adaptive complexity in behavior.

REFERENCES

Skinner, B. F. (1937). Two types of conditioned reflex: A reply to Konorski and Miller. *Journal of General Psychology, 16,* 272–279.

Thorndike, E. L. (1898). *Animal intelligence: An experimental study of the associative processes in animals.* Psychological Review Monograph Supplements, 2 (4, whole No. 8).

SUGGESTED READINGS

Catania, A. C. (2007). *Learning.* Cornwall-on-Hudson, NY: Sloan.

Donahoe, J. W., & Palmer, D. C. (2004). *Learning and complex behavior.* Richmond, MA: Ledgetop Publishing. (Original work published 1994)

Skinner, B. F. (1938). *The behavior of organisms: An experimental analysis.* New York: Appleton-Century-Crofts.

Skinner, B. F. (1953). *Science and human behavior.* New York: Macmillan.

DAVID C. PALMER
Smith College

See also: **Autoshaping; Instrumental Conditioning; Pavlovian Conditioning**

OPERATIONAL DEFINITION

Few topics in the area of scientific communication have been as troublesome as that of operational definition. Psychologists have done their share both to clarify and to muddy the waters regarding this problem, and the following outlines some of the principal facets to be considered.

Operationism

Operationism was initiated by Harvard University physicist P. W. Bridgman, who had reviewed the history of definitions of fundamental physical concepts such as length, space, and time as they were used before Einstein to discover why they required such drastic revisions in Einstein's revolutionary theorizing. Bridgman concluded that the traditional Newtonian definitions had contained substantial amounts of meaning not related to their actual physical measurements (e.g., the assumption of an absolute scale for time); it was this kind of excess meaning that was responsible for Einstein's need to make radical reformulations in these concepts.

Bridgman suggested that to avoid similar roadblocks in the development of physical theory it would be necessary to impose more stringent requirements on the making of definitions. His proposal was that concepts should be defined strictly in terms of the operations used to measure them. As he puts it, "The concept is synonymous with the corresponding set of operations."

Bridgman found that nothing was quite as simple and straightforward as it had seemed at first. He subsequently made some strategic retreats from his initially monolithic position, such as acknowledging at least the temporary admissibility of paper-and-pencil operations and accepting the usefulness of abstract concepts.

The idea that the meaning of all concepts should be restricted to the necessary operations underlying them had an immediate appeal for psychologists. Operationism was promulgated early in the field of psychology by S. S. Stevens. Stevens was careful to point out that the operational-definition movement was simply a formalization of the methodology that had always been used by effective scientists, including psychologists.

Unfortunately, the balanced position advanced by Stevens did not quite prove to be the norm. Probably the single most important negative factor was the overselling of the operational ideal, especially as applied to situations in which perfectly operational definitions of psychological concepts were clearly not even approximately feasible. Also, there was the continuing persistence of the more grandly conceived operationism, and the consequent overloading of what should have been merely a fundamental methodological principle with essentially fewer relevant substantive issues of one kind or another. The net result has been that far too little attention has been paid to the central principle.

A good example of the communication difficulties that await the unwary user or reader is afforded by the word *frustration*. Quite apart from the further complications of theoretical nuances, this word is used in at least three distinct ways, which are usually but by no means always kept clearly separated: (1) as a kind of blocking operation that prevents a motivated organism from obtaining a goal or persisting in goal-directed behavior; (2) as the kind of behavior that appears when such a goal-oriented organism is thus blocked; and (3) as some hypothetical inner process that is assumed to be responsible for the overt behavioral responses to the blocking operation.

None of the secondary and tertiary disputes over operationism can eliminate the fact that psychologists all too often simply fail to communicate adequately with each other because they continue to use key terms in a variety of loosely defined and highly ambiguous ways. Some basic considerations need to be emphasized. First, operational definitions are not all-or-none achievements; rather, there is a continuum of operational clarity in definitions, that is, in the degree to which ambiguity and excess meaning have been eliminated.

Second, full operational clarity needs to be an objective to be kept clearly in mind throughout all phases of theoretical and empirical research; acceptance of ambiguity must be regarded in many situations as a necessary but, it is hoped, not a permanent condition, and it is important that scientific communicators explicitly recognize this state of affairs rather than gloss over the problem.

Third, substantive issues involving defined concepts must be allowed to intrude on and confuse the primarily methodological criteria associated with operational definitions.

Fourth, it is hoped that recognition of the importance of these considerations serves as a spur to improve definitional clarity and ultimately to help make improvements in theoretical development. Taking this kind of positive approach to the definitional problem should also serve to help free psychologists from the semantic quagmires in which so many key concepts are still entangled.

MELVIN H. MARX
N. Hutchinson Island, FL

OPPOSITIONAL DEFIANT DISORDER

Oppositional defiant disorder (ODD) is a recurrent pattern of negativistic, disobedient, and hostile behavior by young people toward authority figures. A diagnosis of ODD requires that four or more of the following eight symptoms have been present over the course of at least 6 months: (1) losing one's temper, (2) arguing with adults, (3) actively defying adults' requests or rules, (4) deliberately annoying others, (5) blaming others for mistakes, (6) being easily annoyed, (7) being angry and resentful, and (8) being spiteful or vindictive (American Psychiatric Association, 2000). Those receiving a diagnosis of ODD exhibit such behaviors at a frequency above what is considered to be developmentally appropriate, and such behaviors lead to significant impairment in social or academic functioning. These symptoms need only be present in one setting to warrant a diagnosis, and children sometimes exhibit symptoms in the home setting without concurrent problems at school or in the community. Likewise, teachers may identify ODD symptoms among students who do not show the same severity of problems in nonacademic settings (Drabick, Gadow, & Loney, 2007).

Estimated rates of ODD in the general population range as high as 16%, depending on the sample (American Psychiatric Association, 2000), with an average of 6 to 10% in different samples. Oppositional behavior and associated aggressiveness are among the most common reasons for referral to child mental health professionals (Steiner & Remsing, 2007). A diagnosis of ODD is more common in males than in females, with gender differences more pronounced in children than in adolescents (American Psychiatric Association, 2000). Although the manifestation of the symptoms are the same for girls and boys, there are some notable gender differences; for example, ODD is a strong risk factor for conduct disorder (CD) in boys only.

Although children with ODD have a broad tendency to respond angrily and are often verbally aggressive, they do not display the frequent physically aggressive behaviors observed in CD. These two diagnoses are, in fact, mutually exclusive; to be diagnosed with ODD, a child cannot also meet criteria for CD (American Psychiatric Association, 2000). However, Loeber (1990) has hypothesized that aggressive behavior in the elementary school years, including verbal aggression, is part of a developmental trajectory that can lead to CD and to adolescent delinquency. Indeed, a subset of children with ODD will proceed to develop CD, whereas some children will develop CD without ever meeting diagnostic criteria for ODD (American Psychiatric Association, 2000). Those children who show diverse behavioral problems across multiple settings are at most risk for continued behavioral problems. Likewise, certain environmental risk factors, such as a dysfunctional family setting, inconsistent or harsh parenting practices, socioeconomic disadvantage, or a violence-ridden neighborhood, can play a role in moving children along this developmental pathway (e.g., McGee & Williams, 1999).

Oppositional defiant disorder may start very early among inflexible infants with irritable temperaments (Loeber, 1990), thus demonstrating possible biologically based precursors. Furthermore, exacerbation of such early behavioral problems such as impulsivity, overactivity, and mild aggression may lead to more serious forms of disruptive behaviors later on, including ODD. Children with difficult temperaments and early emerging behavioral problems are at an elevated risk for failing to develop positive attachments with caregivers and for becoming involved in increasingly coercive interchanges with parents, teachers, and other adults.

Loeber (1990) has hypothesized that children begin to generalize their use of coercive behaviors to other social interactions, leading to increasingly oppositional and disruptive behavior with peers and adults and to dysfunctional social-cognitive processes. These dysfunctional processes serve, in turn, to maintain problem behavior sequences. Children with ODD have been shown to use problem-solving strategies that rely on aggressive solutions, to have difficulties encoding social information accurately, and to expect that aggressive solutions to problems will work (Crick & Dodge, 2000). Such difficulties have been documented as early as the preschool years and are not accounted for by comorbidity with other disruptive behavior problems, such as attention-deficit/hyperactivity disorder. Notably, children with ODD lack insight into their defiant behavior and usually justify their behavior as a reaction to unfair demands (American Psychiatric Association, 2000).

Historically, psychosocial treatment of oppositional, conduct-disordered children has been perceived to be difficult and not very productive. However, in recent years, randomized clinical research trials have identified empirically supported treatments for ODD and CD, with cognitive-behavioral interventions comprising the majority of the theoretical orientations investigated. Brestan and Eyberg (1998) have identified two parent training intervention programs with well-established positive effects and 10 other programs as probably efficacious for treating disruptive behavior disorders, such as ODD. Treatment strategies aimed at parents (e.g., improving parental monitoring, improving consistency in discipline), as well as cognitive-behavioral treatments targeting children (e.g., problem-solving skills training, anger management, impulse control), have led to a reduction in behavioral problems and externalizing symptomatology in children, including those with ODD (see Brestan & Eyberg, 1998).

Treatment outcome research indicates that a combination of interventions for both parents and children may be the most efficacious approach in treating ODD. For example, almost half of the treatments reviewed by Brestan and Eyberg (1998) included parent participants. However, behavioral parent training programs for parents of children with ODD are most effective when they are provided in combination with a child-focused problem-solving skills training component (Behan & Carr, 2000). Group intervention programs, which are time- and cost-efficient, are usually as clinically effective as individually based programs in treating ODD (Behan & Carr, 2000), and group programs accounted for more than half of the outcome studies reviewed by Brestan and Eyberg (1998). Intensive, comprehensive prevention programs have been developed and implemented with high-risk children, starting as early as first grade. Evaluation of these preventive programs has indicated that aggressive behavior and other symptoms associated with ODD and CD can be reduced through early intervention (e.g., Bierman et al., 2007), which underscores the importance of early assessment, identification, and treatment.

REFERENCES

American Psychiatric Association. (2000). *Diagnostic and statistical manual of mental disorders* (4th ed., text rev.). Washington, DC: Author.

Behan, J., & Carr, A. (2000). Oppositional defiant disorder. In A. Carr (Ed.), *What works with children and adolescents? A critical review of psychological interventions with children, adolescents, and their families* (pp. 102–130). New York: Brunner-Routledge.

Bierman, K. L., Coie, J. D., Dodge, K. A., Foster, E. M., Greenberg, M. T., Lochman, J. E., et al. (2007). Fast track randomized controlled trial to prevent externalizing psychiatric disorders: Findings from grades 3 to 9. *Journal of the American Academy of Child and Adolescent Psychiatry, 46,* 1250–1262.

Brestan, E. V., & Eyberg, S. M. (1998). Effective psychosocial treatments of conduct-disordered children and adolescents: 29 years, 82 studies, and 5,272 kids. *Journal of Clinical Child Psychology, 27,* 180–189.

Crick, N. R., & Dodge, K. A. (1994). A review and reformulation of social information-processing mechanisms in children's social adjustment. *Psychological Bulletin, 115,* 74–101.

Drabick, D. A. G., Gadow, K. D., & Loney, J. (2007). Source-specific oppositional defiant disorder: Comorbidity and risk factors in referred elementary schoolboys. *Journal of the American Academy of Child and Adolescent Psychiatry, 46,* 92–101.

Loeber, R. (1990). Development and risk factors of juvenile antisocial behavior and delinquency. *Clinical Psychology Review, 10,* 1–42.

McGee, R., & Williams, S. (1999). Environmental risk factors in oppositional defiant disorder and conduct disorder. In H. C. Quay & A. E. Hogan (Eds.), *Handbook of disruptive behavior disorders* (pp. 419–440). New York: Kluwer Academic/Plenum.

Steiner, H., & Remsing, L. (2007). Practice parameter for the assessment and treatment of children and adolescents with oppositional defiant disorder. *Journal of the American Academy of Child and Adolescent Psychiatry, 46,* 126–141.

SUGGESTED READINGS

Frick, P. J., & Muñoz, L. (2006). Oppositional defiant disorder and conduct disorder. In C. Essau (Ed.), *Child and adolescent psychopathology: Theoretical and clinical implications* (pp. 26–51). New York: Routledge/Taylor & Francis Group.

Nock, M. K., Kazdin, A. E., Hiripi, E., & Kessler, R. C. (2007). Lifetime prevalence, correlates, and persistence of oppositional defiant disorder: Results from the National Comorbidity Survey Replication. *Journal of Child Psychology and Psychiatry, 48,* 703–713.

TAMMY D. BARRY
University of Southern Mississippi

JOHN E. LOCHMAN
University of Alabama

See also: **Conduct Disorder; Juvenile Delinquency**

OPTIMAL FUNCTIONING

The area of optimal functioning was introduced into modern scientific psychology by Marie Jahoda. Those contributing most heavily to the area or optimal functioning were originally humanistic psychologists, who see optimal functioning as qualitatively different from normality or lack of pathology. More recently, the mantle of optimal functioning has been taken up by those in the fields of positive psychology and athletic performance.

Simply stated, this area of psychology is a scientific investigation of what the person is capable of becoming, of the best the person can be, and of the way the person can realize any number of personal potentials. That some people are exceptional in the ways they have developed their lives and have promoted the development of those around them, and that we all have particular times when we function extraordinarily well, has long been recognized in psychology. It has been the task of workers in this area to examine these phenomena in systematic and scientific ways.

Historical Traditions

Self-Actualization

Abraham Maslow's (1971) investigation of optimal functioning asserts that there are two basic realms of human need. One, called the D or deficiency realm, is composed of the things we need in order to be functioning persons or minimally adequate as human beings. These include the physiological needs for food, water, and other biological requirements; the safety needs to be protected from chaos; the love and belongingness needs to be included in a family or friendship group to protect us from loneliness; and our esteem needs for self-respect, self-esteem, and for a sense of accomplishment and worth.

The B needs represent the needs that enable us to be self-actualizing human beings—our needs for self-actualization and our aesthetic needs. Maslow posited that these B-level needs, or meta-needs, are just as necessary as the D-level needs. If D needs are not met, one becomes ill physiologically and psychologically. If the B-level need is not met, one develops meta-pathologies. For Maslow, self-actualized persons are aided in their development by intense moments of ecstasy, joy, and insight called peak experiences. These are moments of transcendence that take a person beyond self-actualization to what Maslow called the Z realm, a realm beyond the self that transcends both space and time.

Beautiful and Noble Person

Working within the tradition of Maslow's approach, Landsman (1974) developed a system for investigating the optimally functioning person, "the Beautiful and Noble

Person." Landsman describes his Beautiful and Noble Person as a self that proceeds from (1) the passionate self, a self-expressive, self-enjoying state; to (2) the environment-loving self, where the person cares deeply for the physical environment and the tasks to be accomplished in the world; and finally to (3) the compassionate self, which enables the person to be loving and caring towards other persons.

Fully Functioning Person

Rogers (1980) described what he considered to be the optimally functioning or, in his terms, the "fully functioning" person. In contrast to Maslow's approach, Rogers emphasized the process of being fully functioning as it occurs moment by moment in every person's life, rather than being primarily concerned with describing characteristics of persons. Rogers' emphasis is on process, rather than structural components of the optimally functioning person. His work has been of the greatest influence in the field of psychotherapy, with less attention being devoted to formal research investigation of healthy persons outside the therapeutic situation.

Rogers starts with the assumption that every person has the capacity to actualize or complete his or her own inner nature. The key to this is for the person to remain in contact with his or her deepest feelings, which Rogers called organismic experiences. These deeper feelings can be symbolized accurately in the person's awareness or they can be distorted. Optimal functioning is promoted when the person is able to know in awareness exactly what is happening at this deeper, organismic level. The person must be able to develop the kind of self or self-structure that is able to be congruent or in harmony with the person's own deep feelings or experiences.

Psychology of Optimal Persons

Another formulation of optimal functioning centering on the concept of process, which emphasizes constant change, is Kelly's (1980) formulation of the psychology of an optimal person. The unit of analysis here is the personal construct, a meaning dimension a person might hold, such as seeing people as loving versus rejecting. The personality of the individual is made up of a number of these personal constructs dimensions. Kelly's system of optimal functioning requires that each individual use his or her system of personal meaning in order to complete what he termed "full cycles of experiences," in which each individual creates his or her own conceptions of the world in such a way that these conceptions are continually tested and re-evaluated. The goal of a full cycle of experience is that the total system of personal constructs will continue to change and develop so that a person can keep pace with an ever-changing world. The work within this framework has centered on ways to evaluate each of the

steps and to promote a progression through these steps as elaborated by Epting and Amerikaner (1980). The concern in construct theory is more with the way in which people invent or create themselves than with their uncovering or discerning an inner self.

Optimal Personality Traits

Coan (1977) undertook a multivariate study of optimal functioning persons, later elaborating the theoretical implications of this work. In this empirical approach, Coan employed a battery of tests that took university students six hours to complete and included measures pertaining to various aspects of cognitive capacities, attitudes, awareness, personality, beliefs, and adjustments. His factor analysis yielded 19 obliquely rotated factors, with no single general factor accurately representing a global personality trait of self-actualization. Coan suggests, from his own work and from his reading of Eastern and Western theories of optimal functioning, that five basic characteristics can be isolated that characterize the ideal human condition: efficacy, creativity, inner harmony, relatedness, and transcendence.

Recent Advances

Sports Psychology and Athletic Performance

The fields of sports psychology and athletic performance have, over the past three decades, focused significant attention on the area of optimal functioning. This has led to a substantial amount of research focused on an area of optimal functioning as it is applied to specific tasks, often referred to as peak performance. In this vein, Yuri Hanin (1997) has proposed a model of individual zones of optimal functioning (IZOF). This model is both phenomenological and idiographic in nature, and focuses on the nature of emotions on sports performance. Hanin's model attends to the nature of emotional experience, the connections between the repetitive nature of athletic activities, and how the interplay of the two often result in relatively stable patterns of emotion. More specifically, it addresses the effect of reflected emotional experience on performance, with distinctions made between positive and negative as well as optimal and dysfunctional emotional dimensions.

Positive Psychology

Another burgeoning area of psychology that has recently entered the realm of optimal functioning is the field of *positive psychology*. Seligman and Csikzentmihalyi (2000), among others, describe positive psychology as the scientific investigation of common human strengths and qualities. Moreover, positive psychology approaches human capabilities and potentials from a more optimistic and favorable standpoint than most psychological approaches; the emphasis is not on pathology, but rather on the strengths that humans demonstrate in various arenas, how people can endure and thrive in adverse situations, and how people's lives can be richer, more complete, and worth living.

Optimal Functioning and Issues of Diversity

Though the concept of optimal functioning has existed for decades, cultural considerations regarding optimal functioning have been largely overlooked. Constantine and Sue (2006) assert that characterizations of optimal functioning are bound by the culture and society in which a person lives. They contend that culture is a principal force in not only the definition of optimal functioning, but also in the identification and recognition of human strengths and the ability to persevere in the face of adversity. Further, they emphasize that a person's culture is not a unitary construct, and the interaction between a person's experience and the meaning of optimal functioning derived from the dominant culture yields a myriad of potential interpretations.

Other Significant Contributions

For the serious student of optimal functioning, special attention should be given to a number of other important systems of thought. These include Csikszentmihalyi's concept of "flow," Shostrum's work on developing the Personal Orientation Inventory and Personal Orientation Dimension, Jung's concept of individuation, Fromm's productive character, Allport's conception of propriate functioning, Erikson's conception of maturity, Adler's formation of social interest, Horney's sense of a real self and self-alienation, Reich's notion of the genital character with self-regulation, Jourard's concept of self-disclosure, White's concern with competence, and Ziller's notion of the transcendent personality.

REFERENCES

Coan, R. W. (1977). *Hero, artist, sage, or saint.* New York: Columbia University Press.

Constantine, M. G., & Sue, D. W. (2006). Factors contributing to optimal functioning in people of color in the United States. *The Counseling Psychologist, 34*(2), 228–244.

Epting, F., & Amerikaner, M. (1980). Optimal functioning: A personal construct approach. In A. W. Landfield & L. M. Leitner (Eds.), *Personal construct psychology: Psychotherapy and personality.* New York: John Wiley & Sons.

Hanin, Y. L. (1997). Emotions and athletic performance: Individual zones of optimal functioning model. *European Yearbook of Sport Psychology, 1,* 29–72.

Kelly, G. A. (1980). A psychology of the optimal man. In A. W. Landfield & L. M. Leitner (Eds.), *Personal construct psychology: Psychotherapy and personality.* New York: John Wiley & Sons.

Landsman, T. (1974). The humanizer. *American Journal of Orthopsychiatry, 44,* 345–352.

Maslow, A. H. (1971). *The farther reaches of human nature.* New York: Viking Press.

Rogers, C. A. (1980). *A way of being.* Boston: Houghton Mifflin.

Seligman, M. E. P., & Csikszentmihalyi, M. (2006). Positive psychology: An introduction. *American Psychologist, 55,* 5–14.

SUGGESTED READINGS

Csikszentmihalyi, M. (1990). *Flow: The psychology of optimal experience.* New York: Harper & Row.

Mittleman, W. (1991). Maslow's study of self-actualization: A reinterpretation. *Journal of Humanistic Psychology, 31*(1), 114–135.

Seligman, M. E. P. (2002). *Authentic happiness: Using the new positive psychology to realize your potential for lasting fulfillment.* New York: Free Press.

DANIEL PHILIP
University of North Florida

FRANZ R. EPTING
University of Florida

ROM BRAFMAN
Palo Alto, CA

ORAL STAGE (See Psychosexual Stages)

ORGANIZATIONAL PSYCHOLOGY (See Industrial-Organizational Psychology)

OSGOOD, CHARLES EGERTON (1916–1991)

Charles Osgood received the BA degree from Dartmouth College (1939) and the PhD degree from Yale in 1945. He then served as research associate for the U.S. Office of Scientific Research and Development, where he worked on the training of B-29 gunners. He was an Assistant Professor of Psychology at the University of Connecticut from 1946–1949, and then moved to the University of Illinois at Urbana-Champaign where he remained throughout his career. He became Professor of Psychology and Director of the Institute of Communication Research. In 1960 he received the Distinguished Scientific Contribution Award from the American Psychological Association. He was elected President of the American Psychological Association in 1963. He was a member of the American Academy of Arts and Sciences and elected to the National Academy of Sciences.

Osgood's experimental research centered around the role of meaning within the context of learning theory. To do so, he developed the Semantic Differential Method, which has been applied to the analysis of attitudes, attitude change, personality structure, clinical diagnosis, vocational choice, consumer reactions to products and brands, and the role of meaning within different cultures. The technique was described in *The Measurement of Meaning*. The Semantic Differential consists of a quantitative procedure for measuring connotations of any given concept—it involves ratings and a variety of statistical techniques involving factor analysis. All societies studied revealed that humans can be thought of on three dimensions: good–bad (evaluation); strong–weak (potency); and active–passive (activity).

Many psychologists believe that Osgood's technique is a useful tool for exploring many of the higher mental processes in human beings. He published *A Method and Theory in Experimental Psychology* in 1953.

SUGGESTED READINGS

Osgood, C. E. (1953). *A method and theory in experimental psychology.* New York: Oxford University Press.

Osgood, C. E. (1979). *Focus on meaning: Explorations on semantic space.* The Hague: Mouton.

Osgood, C. E. (1988). *Psycholinguistics, cross-cultural universals, and prospects for mankind.* New York: Praeger.

Osgood, C. E., Suci, G., & Tannenbaum, P. (1957). *The measurement of meaning.* Urbana, IL: University of Illinois Press.

STAFF

OXYTOCIN

Oxytocin is a nonapeptide hormone and neuromodulator with a range of physiological and psychological effects related to reproduction, social cognition, and behavior (Burbach et al., 2006). Oxytocin is produced predominantly in the hypothalamus and is projected to the posterior pituitary for release into circulation, where it acts as a hormone. Oxytocin released into circulation plays important roles in regulating both lactation and the progression of labor. Oxytocin is the most uterotonic substance known, and pitocin, a synthetic oxytocin, is widely used by physicians to stimulate the progression of labor. Nipple stimulation during nursing stimulates synchronous firing of hypothalamic neurons via a reflex arch, resulting in the pulsatile release of oxytocin from the mother's pituitary gland. This elevation in oxytocin stimulates milk ejection by causing myoepithelial cells in the mammary gland to contract.

Oxytocin is also projected to sites within the central nervous system where it acts as a neuromodulator to affect emotionality and behavior. Oxytocin receptors are found in discrete limbic brain areas known to regulate behavior. Most of our understanding of the role of central oxytocin is derived from animal studies. However, there are increasing numbers of studies suggesting that oxytocin regulates social cognition in humans as well.

Anxiety and Emotionality

Oxytocin reduces the physiological reaction to stressful situations and is considered to be anxiolytic. Lactating animals and humans exhibit a clearly decreased response to stressors. Lactating rats show an attenuated elevation in stress hormone in response to white noise, compared to virgins. Infusion of oxytocin in virgin rats also dampens the elevation of stress hormones in response to stress, suggesting that the increased oxytocin released during lactation may be acting to buffer the individual from environmental stressors. Oxytocin also has anxiolytic effects in behavioral assays of anxiety, such as the elevated plus maze.

In male rats, oxytocin mediates the decreased anxiety-like behavior and increased risk-taking behavior following mating, suggesting that OT may mediate the sedation and calmness anecdotally reported in the postcoital period in humans. In humans, intranasal oxytocin infusion enhances the effects of social support in the suppression of cortisol secretion and subjective responses to psychosocial stress (Heinrichs et al., 2003). Moreover, functional magnetic resonance imaging studies have shown that oxytocin decreases amygdala activation following the viewing of fear-inducing visual stimuli.

Reproductive Behavior

In animal models, central oxytocin facilitates female sexual behavior, or receptivity (Burbach et al., 2006). Receptivity in rodents is regulated primarily by the sequential actions of ovarian estrogen and progesterone. Estrogen increases both oxytocin synthesis and the density of oxytocin receptors in regions of the hypothalamus involved in the regulation of sexual behavior. Oxytocin injections into the hypothalamus of estrogen-primed female rats facilitate female sexual behavior, while oxytocin antagonists block this behavior. Once mating occurs, vaginocervical stimulation results in a release of oxytocin into the plasma as well as into the cerebrospinal fluid. Oxytocin may also play a role in sexual performance in males. For example, oxytocin levels in the cerebrospinal fluid are elevated after ejaculation in male rats, and oxytocin injections decrease the latency to ejaculation. Oxytocin also stimulates the occurrence of spontaneous, noncontact penile erections in male rats. The role of oxytocin in human sexuality is unclear; however, plasma oxytocin levels increase during sexual arousal and peak at orgasm in both men and women.

Social Memory

Animals living in social groups must be able to recognize familiar individuals. Several studies have suggested a role for oxytocin in the formation or expression of social memory (Ferguson et al., 2002). In rodents, social memory is based primarily on olfactory cues and can be quantified by measuring the decrease in olfactory investigation after repeated exposure to the same individual. Low doses of oxytocin enhance the formation of social memory in rats. Higher doses of oxytocin result in an amnesiac effect. Mice lacking a functional oxytocin gene fail to recognize individuals even after repeated exposure, but display normal social memory after a single injection of oxytocin.

Maternal Behavior and Mother-Infant Bonding

Oxytocin plays an important role in initiating maternal nurturing behavior and mother-infant bonding in animal models (Lim & Young, 2006). In many species, virgin females fail to display nurturing behavior toward infants of others, but females display extensive maternal care for their own offspring beginning moments after giving birth. Virgin rats receiving oxytocin injections into the brain display nurturing behavior toward pups, while interfering with oxytocin transmission interferes with the normal onset of maternal care in parturient dams. Once initiated, blocking oxytocin transmission does not interfere with maternal behavior, suggesting that oxytocin is important for the initiation, but not the maintenance, of maternal behavior. Mutant mice that lack functional oxytocin receptors or disrupted oxytocin release display severe deficits in maternal responsiveness.

In sheep, oxytocin is released in the brain within 15 minutes of delivery of the lamb and is thought to mediate the selective bond between the mother and her lamb. Infusion of oxytocin into the brain of an estrogen-primed ewe elicits full maternal responsiveness within 30 seconds. Furthermore, vaginocervical stimulation in an estrogen-primed ewe, which causes the central release of oxytocin, also elicits full maternal responsiveness. Typically, postpartum ewes will allow their own lamb to suckle while rejecting other lambs. Stimulating oxytocin release during exposure to an unfamiliar lamb stimulates the ewe to bond with that lamb even if she has previously bonded with her own lamb.

It is unclear whether oxytocin significantly influences the mother-infant bond in humans, although correlational studies suggest that endogenous oxytocin does influence personality traits in postpartum women. For example, women who give birth by cesarean section have fewer oxytocin pulses during breast-feeding than those who give birth vaginally, and are less likely to describe themselves during the postpartum period as exhibiting a calm personality or high levels of sociality. In mothers delivering by cesarean section, oxytocin levels are correlated with the degree of openness to social interactions and with calmness.

Pair Bonding in Monogamous Species

Like the bond between a mother and infant, strong social attachments are formed between mates in monogamous species. Prairie voles are a socially monogamous species of rodent and have been extensively studied as a model for understanding the neural basis of monogamy (Young & Wang, 2004). In the prairie vole, oxytocin plays a role in formation of the bond of the female for the male, and may play a role in both sexes. Oxytocin is released in the brain during mating, and perhaps also during other affiliative interactions. Infusion of oxytocin into the brain of a female prairie vole even in the absence of mating results in the formation of a pair bond. Oxytocin facilitates the formation of a social bonding in part through its interactions with the dopamine system in the nucleus accumbens. Interestingly, nonmonogamous vole species have little or no oxytocin receptors in the nucleus accumbens, suggesting that variation in oxytocin receptor expression may contribute to variation in the ability to form social bonds.

The role of oxytocin in human social relationships remains to be determined. Sex in humans may play a role in strengthening the emotional attachments between partners, and vaginocervical stimulation, nipple stimulation, and orgasm, each components of human sexuality, facilitate oxytocin release.

Social Cognition in Humans

There is growing evidence that oxytocin may influence social cognition and behavior in humans. Many of these studies have used intranasal delivery of oxytocin, which is presumed to penetrate the blood-brain barrier, although this has never been documented. Therefore, care must be taken in the interpretation of these data. Nevertheless, the findings from these human studies are quite intriguing. For example, intranasal oxytocin infusions enhance interpersonal "trust" as assessed using economic-based games (Kosfeld et al., 2005). Intranasal oxytocin infusions decrease amygdala activity in response to socially relevant visual stimuli, providing a potential mechanism for increasing interpersonal trust. The ability to infer the emotional states of others based on subtle facial expression, referred to as "mind reading," is also enhanced by intranasal oxytocin. Oxytocin treatment increases the time spent gazing at the eye region of human faces and enhances memory of facial identity, an effect reminiscent of its role in social recognition in rodents.

Autism

Given its modulatory effects on social cognition in animals and humans, there has been increasing speculation that oxytocin systems may contribute to the disruption of social cognitive processes in autism spectrum disorder (ASD) and schizophrenia (Bartz & Hollander, 2006).

Indeed, a single study reports that autistic individuals have lower circulating plasma levels of oxytocin than healthy subjects, although this has yet to be replicated. Several genetic studies have also suggested an association between polymorphisms in the oxytocin receptor gene and autism. These observations have led to speculation that oxytocin should be considered as a potential treatment for reducing the social cognitive disruptions in ASD. In fact, intranasal oxytocin enhances retention of social information in autistic patients in certain tasks (Hollander et al., 2007). More comprehensive studies of the effects of oxytocin on social cognition and function in ASD are needed to critically interpret these findings, however.

REFERENCES

Bartz, J., & Hollander, E. (2006). The neuroscience of affiliation: Forging links between basic and clinical research on neuropeptides and social behavior. *Hormones and Behavior, 50,* 518–528.

Burbach, P., Young, L. J., & Russell, J. (2006) Oxytocin: Synthesis, secretion and reproductive functions. In J. D. Neill (Ed.), *Knobil and Neill's physiology of reproduction* (3rd ed.) (pp. 3055–3127). Amsterdam, the Netherlands: Elsevier.

Ferguson, J. N., Young, L. J., & Insel, T. R. (2002). The neuroendocrine basis of social recognition. *Frontiers in Neuroendocrinology, 23,* 200–224.

Heinrichs, M., Baumgartner, T., Kirschbaum, C., & Ehlert, U. (2003). Social support and oxytocin interact to suppress cortisol and subjective responses to psychosocial stress. *Biological Psychiatry, 54,* 1389–1398.

Hollander, E., Bartz, J., Chaplin, W., Phillips, A., Sumner, J., Soorya, L., Anagnostou, E., & Wasserman, S. (2007). Oxytocin increases retention of social cognition in autism. *Biological Psychiatry, 61,* 498–503.

Kosfeld, M., Heinrichs, M., Zak, P. J., Fischbacher, U., & Fehr, E. (2005). Oxytocin increases trust in humans. *Nature, 435,* 673–676.

Lim, M. M., & Young, L. J. (2006). Neuropeptidergic regulation of affiliative behavior and social bonding in animals. *Hormones & Behavior, 50,* 506–517. (Erratum appears in [2007] *Hormones and Behavior, 51*(2), pp. 292–293.)

Young, L. J., & Wang, Z. (2004). The neurobiology of the pair bond. *Nature Neuroscience, 7,* 1048–1054.

SUGGESTED READINGS

Hammock, A. E. D., & Young, L. J. (2006). Oxytocin, vasopressin, and pair bonding: Implications for autism. *Philosophical Transactions of the Royal Society: Biological Sciences, 361,* 2187–2198.

Marazziti, D., & Catena Dell'Osso, M. (2008). The role of oxytocin and neuropsychiatric disorders. *Current Medicinal Chemistry, 15,* 698–704.

LARRY J. YOUNG
Emory University School of Medicine

P

PAIN DISORDER

Medical illness in no way excludes the possibility of psychiatric illness. Medically ill patients are, in fact, much more likely to have psychiatric illness than patients without medical illness. Psychiatric illness in no way precludes the possibility of medical illness. Psychiatric illness is, in fact, associated with health behaviors and psychophysiological changes known to promote medical illness.

Any discussion of psychiatric disorders in people with chronic pain is haunted by the concept of psychogenic pain. We are drawn to the concept of psychogenic pain because it fills the gaps left when we fail in our attempts to explain clinical pain exclusively in terms of tissue pathology. Psychogenic pain, however, is an empty concept. Positive criteria for the identification of psychogenic pain, mechanisms for the production of psychogenic pain, and specific therapies for psychogenic pain are lacking. The diagnosis of psychogenic pain too often only serves to stigmatize further the patient who experiences chronic pain.

Somatoform Disorders, Illness Behavior, and the Sick Role

Sickness is a complicated psychological and social state that can be understood from a variety of perspectives. The concept of the sick role was first introduced by Parsons (1951). The sick role is granted to individuals provided that they regard their condition as undesirable and are not held responsible for it (i.e., under their control). If granted, individuals are allowed exemption from their usual obligations to a greater or lesser extent and are considered to be deserving of attention. Obligations to seek the advice and assistance of a person regarded as competent to diagnose and treat the condition and to cooperate with that person are associated with the sick role.

The concept of illness behavior was introduced by Mechanic (1962) as a complement to the sick role, delineating the contribution of the patient to the role-granting process. Illness behavior is described as "the ways in which individuals experience, perceive, evaluate, and respond to their own health status." This definition recognizes the possibility that a person may be concerned about illness in the absence of symptoms.

Illness behavior is a concept more easily applied to individual patients than "sick role" and has therefore seen

more use in clinical settings. However, it is dependent on social definitions of what constitutes legitimate illness. Though medical science determines what will qualify as disease based on objective changes in anatomy and physiology, society determines what will qualify as illness. These often follow each other quite closely, but there can be interesting discrepancies. Essential hypertension is a disease usually without symptoms. It has taken a concerted educational effort on the part of the medical profession to convince the public that it is an illness that should be monitored and treated. Fibromyalgia is an illness increasingly accepted. Because the medical profession has not been able to identify objective changes in physiology with this illness, many physicians question whether it qualifies as a legitimate disease. Physicians, insurance companies, and compensation systems can find themselves in disagreement with patients who have chronic pain about whether a legitimate disease or illness is causing the symptoms.

Pilowsky (1971) introduced the concept of abnormal illness behavior for those situations where physician and patient disagree about the applicability of the sick role to the patient's condition. He contended that patients with truly abnormal illness behavior have extreme difficulty accepting the advice of any physician if it does not agree with their own appraisal of their health status. He cautioned that misdiagnoses of abnormal illness behavior can occur when physician and patient do not share a common culture. When diagnosing the patient's disagreement with his or her physician as pathological, it is also important to keep in mind the limitations of current diagnostic tests and disease criteria.

Pain Disorder

In many prevalent pain syndromes (e.g., low back pain, headache, fibromyalgia), it is difficult to identify the tissue pathology giving rise to symptoms. When a somatic cause for pain cannot be identified, many clinicians begin to seek psychological causes, that is, psychogenic pain, and some have suggested that certain personality styles predispose people to develop chronic pain: pain prone personality (Engel, 1959; Blumer & Heilbronn, 1982). Pain Disorder is the current psychiatric diagnosis that most closely corresponds to the diagnosis of psychogenic pain (Hiller, Heuser, & Fichter, 2000).

Diagnosis

Since pain disorder is an important but problematic concept at the interface of pain medicine and psychiatry, it is essential to understand some of the history of the concept. In *DSM-II* (American Psychiatric Association [APA], 1968), there was no specific diagnosis pertaining to pain. Painful conditions caused by emotional factors were considered part of the psychophysiological disorders. In 1980, *DSM-III* introduced a new diagnostic category for pain problems, Psychogenic Pain Disorder (APA, 1980). To qualify, a patient needed to have (1) severe and prolonged pain that was (2) inconsistent with neuroanatomical distribution of pain receptors, without detectable organic etiology or pathophysiologic mechanism. Related organic pathology was allowed, but the pain had to be "grossly in excess" of what was expected on the basis of physical exam. Accepted indications that psychological factors were involved in the production of the pain were (1) a temporal relationship between pain onset and an environmental event producing psychological conflict, (2) pain appears to allow avoidance of some noxious event or responsibility, and (3) pain promotes emotional support or attention the individual would not have otherwise received. However, this kind of evidence never proves that psychological factors have caused a pain report.

Difficulties in establishing that pain was psychogenic led to changes in the diagnosis for *DSM-III-R* (Stoudemire & Sandu, 1987). In *DSM-III-R* (APA, 1987), the diagnosis was renamed Somatoform Pain Disorder, and three major changes were made to the diagnostic criteria. The requirements for etiologic psychological factors and lack of other contributing mental disorders were eliminated, and a requirement for "preoccupation with pain for at least six months" was added. In *DSM-III-R*, Somatoform Pain Disorder becomes a diagnosis of exclusion. The diagnosis is made when medical disorders are excluded in a patient preoccupied with pain.

Somatoform Pain Disorder was rarely used, for a number of reasons: (1) The meaning of "preoccupation with pain" was unclear, (2) whether pain exceeds that expected is difficult to determine, (3) the diagnosis does not apply to many patients disabled by pain where a medical condition is contributory, (4) the term "somatoform pain disorder" implies that this pain is somehow different from organic pain, and (5) acute pain of less than 6 months' duration was excluded (King & Strain, 1992). As a consequence, the *DSM-IV* category of Pain Disorder was proposed, with two subtypes based on whether the symptoms were not (code 307.80) or were (307.89) accompanied by a general medical disease.

For a diagnosis of Pain Disorder Associated with Psychological Factors, (1) pain must be present in one or more anatomical sites; (2) be the predominant focus of the clinical presentation; (3) be of sufficient severity to warrant clinical attention; (4) the pain causes significant distress or impairment in important areas of functioning; and (5) psychological factors must be judged to have the major role in the onset, severity, exacerbation, or maintenance of the pain. In addition, the symptoms must not be intentionally produced, and they cannot be accounted for by some other psychiatric diagnosis. If there is no medical condition accompanying the symptoms, the diagnosis is coded 307.80. If, however, both psychological factors and a general medical condition are judged to play important roles, the diagnosis is Pain Disorder Associated with Both Psychological Factors and a Medical Condition (307.89). If a medical condition is present, then the associated general medical condition or anatomical site of the pain is coded on Axis III. Both codes are specified as being acute or chronic, depending on duration, with 6 months being the cut differentiating acute from chronic symptoms (APA, 1994).

To facilitate differential diagnosis, the *DSM* includes a category but not a formal diagnosis of Pain Disorder Associated with a General Medical Condition. This category is used when a general medical condition is judged to have a major role in the onset, severity, exacerbation, or maintenance of the pain, and if psychological factors are present, they are not judged to have a major role. The diagnostic code for the pain is selected based on the associated general medical condition, if one has been established, or on the anatomical location of the pain, if the underlying general medical condition is not yet clearly established (e.g., low back [724.2] and headache [784.0]).

No guidance is given in determining when psychological factors have a major role in pain or are considered important enough in the presence of a painful medical disorder to be coded as a separate mental disorder. Given the high rates of mood and anxiety disorders among disabled chronic pain patients, many patients most appropriate for the diagnosis would be excluded. The diagnosis thus continues covertly as a diagnosis of exclusion with no clear implications for therapy.

Treatment

Because chronic pain often has multiple causes or contributing factors, it often does not respond to either purely somatic *or* purely psychological treatments. Persistent pain can set into motion a vicious circle of reinforcing features that then becomes a self-perpetuating problem independent of the initiating illness or injury. Deactivation, depression, disuse, medication misuse, and vocational dysfunction are common contributing factors to the suffering and disability associated with chronic pain. Although simpler cases of chronic pain may respond to an approach based on the biomedical model, this is not true for the extremely disabled or prolonged cases likely to be referred to psychiatrists or psychologists.

Patients with disabling chronic pain are prone to doctor shopping, where they obtain medications and procedures from a number of physicians unknown to each other. It is not possible to successfully treat a patient with chronic pain who has not formed a solid and honest therapeutic alliance with his or her treating physician.

The needs of patients with disabling chronic pain often outstrip the resources of many primary care physicians. These patients are most appropriately treated by a multidisciplinary team, including physicians, psychologist, physical therapist, occupational therapist, and nurse, who are experienced in the treatment of chronic pain. The treatment of chronic pain is in many ways counterintuitive to both the clinician and the patient. Many medications used for acute pain are contraindicated. Relief from pain must often be secondary to reduction in disability and deactivation. Clinical phenomena that seem clearly caused by the pain (e.g., depression) must be addressed before pain relief is possible.

Most important, *pain is not itself a psychiatric disorder.* Chronic pain is frequently complicated by psychiatric disorders, however. The most common of these is depression. Psychiatric treatment of these disorders has an important role to play in the rehabilitation of the chronic pain patient.

A Biopsychosocial Model of Pain and Suffering

Psychiatric diagnosis and psychological treatment can add an essential and often neglected component to the conceptualization and treatment of chronic pain. However, it is critical to avoid a dualistic model that postulates that pain is either physical or mental in origin. This model alienates patients who feel blamed for their pain. It also is inconsistent with modern models of pain causation. Multiple lines of evidence suggest that pain is a product of efferent as well as afferent activity in the nervous system. Tissue damage and nociception are neither necessary nor sufficient for pain. Indeed, it is now widely recognized that the relationship between pain and nociception is highly complex and must be understood in terms of the situation of the organism as a whole.

Pain usually, but not always, produces suffering. Traditionally, this suffering has been understood as arising from a form of pathology intrinsic to the individual, hence the traditional view that pain is either due to tissue pathology (nociception) or due to psychopathology (psychogenic). An alternative model that allows us to escape this dualism is to think of pain as a biopsychosocial process involving psychological and social components as well as physical ones (Turk & Monarch, 2002). The implication is that successful treatment must address all of these contributions to the experience of pain and related disability.

REFERENCES

American Psychiatric Association. (1968). *Diagnostic and statistical manual of mental disorders* (2nd ed.). Washington, DC: Author.

American Psychiatric Association. (1980). *Diagnostic and statistical manual of mental disorders* (3rd ed.). Washington, DC: Author.

American Psychiatric Association. (1987). *Diagnostic and statistical manual of mental disorders* (3rd ed. revised). Washington, DC: Author.

American Psychiatric Association. (1994). *Diagnostic and statistical manual of mental disorders* (4th ed.). Washington, DC: Author.

Blumer, D., & Heilbronn, M. (1982). Chronic pain as a variant of depressive disease: The pain-prone disorder. *Journal of Nervous and Mental Disease, 170,* 381–406.

Engel, G. L. (1959). Psychogenic pain and the pain-prone patient. *American Journal of Medicine, 26,* 899–918.

Hiller, W., Heuser, J., & Fichter, M. M. (2000). The DSM-IV nosology of chronic pain: A comparison of pain disorder and multiple somatization syndrome. *European Journal of Pain, 4,* 45–55.

King, S. A., & Strain, J. J. (1992). Revising the category of somatoform pain disorder. *Hospital and Community Psychiatry, 43,* 217–219.

Mechanic, D. (1962). The concept of illness behavior. *Journal of Chronic Disease, 15,* 189–194.

Parsons, T. (1951). *Social systems.* London: Routledge and Kegan Paul.

Pilowsky, I. (1971). The diagnosis of abnormal illness behavior. *New Zealand Journal of Psychiatry, 5,* 136–141.

Stoudemire, A., & Sandu, J. (1987). Psychogenic/idiopathic pain syndromes. *General Hospital Psychiatry, 9,* 79–86.

Turk, D. C., & Monarch, E. S. (2002). Biopsychosocial perspective on chronic pain. In D. C. Turk & R. J. Gatchel (Eds.), *Psychological approaches to pain management: A practitioner's handbook* (pp. 1–29). New York: Guilford Press.

DENNIS C. TURK
University of Washington

See also: **Chronic Pain, Psychological Factors in**

PAIN THEORIES

The traditional theory of pain, which evolved during the early twentieth century, holds that pain is a specific sensation produced by a direct-line pain pathway from pain receptors in the body to a pain center in the brain. Research based on this theory focuses on acute pain evoked by noxious stimulation and has investigated physiological mechanisms at every level of the pathway from receptors to cerebral cortex (Dostrovsky & Craig, 2006). Although acute pain due to injury or surgery is now generally well controlled by a variety of drugs, the direct-line theory of pain has failed to reveal new therapies to control chronic pain such as the neuralgias and fibromyalgia.

The gate control theory of pain, proposed by Melzack and Wall in 1965, focused on chronic pain, and it postulated that neural gates in the spinal cord can be opened or closed by signals descending from the brain, as well as by sensory information ascending from the body. The theory also highlighted the psychological functions of the brain and produced an explosive growth of knowledge related to pain. Brain research, which includes cognitive neuroscience, has led to two major classes of drugs and several psychological techniques to relieve pain. Moreover, it connects the field of pain to the exciting research on the neural mechanisms of consciousness that generate the experience of pain.

The gate control theory stimulated a shift away from the traditional direct-line pain pathway to the concept of parallel neural networks in the brain associated with the sensory, affective, and cognitive dimensions of subjective pain experience (Melzack & Casey, 1968). Furthermore, research on the language of pain—the words we use to describe the sensory, affective, and cognitive qualities of our pains—has produced questionnaires that allow us to comprehend one another's subjective pain experience. The translations of the Short-Form McGill Pain Questionnaire (Melzack, 1975) into more than 50 languages provide a universal communication system to study pain in humans.

Toward a New Theory

Phantom limb pain, which occurs after the amputation of a limb, reveals the powerful role of the brain in pain perception. A high-level cordectomy—total removal of several segments of spinal cord so that sensory information from the pelvis and legs is unable to arrive at the brain—does not stop intense pain in the phantom half of the body.

The extraordinary reality of painful phantom limbs indicates that the brain does more than detect and analyze

sensory inputs; it generates perceptual experience even in the absence of external inputs (Melzack, 1989). We do not need a body to feel a body, or a physical injury to feel pain. The brain can generate both experiences.

The subjective experience of pain has served as a guide to the search for the brain mechanisms that generate it (see McMahon & Koltzenburg, 2006). Beginning in 1972, drugs that were prescribed to control depression were unexpectedly found to produce significant relief of several forms of chronic pain. Similarly, drugs developed to control epilepsy were found to relieve severe chronic pains associated with diseases of nerves. Recently developed variants of both classes of drugs are more effective and have fewer side effects. These drugs, which evolved from the top-down approach based on patients' subjective descriptions of their pain, have produced a new pharmacology of chronic pain focused on the brain. Both classes of drugs are now major sources of relief for many severe, previously intractable chronic pains.

The recognition that pain is a multidimensional experience determined by psychological as well as physical factors has broadened the scope of pain therapies. Psychological therapies, which were once used only as a last resort when drugs or neurosurgery failed to control pain, are now an integral part of all pain-management strategies. The concept that pain is the result of multiple contributions gave rise to a variety of psychological approaches, such as relaxation, hypnosis, and several cognitive therapies (Keefe, Dixon, & Pryor, 2005).

The field of pain continues to evolve, and there are reasons to be optimistic about its future. First, imaging techniques are increasingly being used to study physiological events in the brains of human beings while they simultaneously report their subjective pain experiences

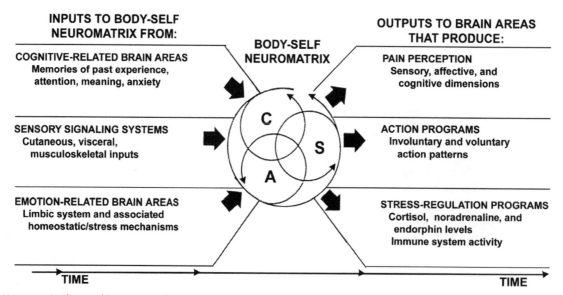

Figure 1. Neuromatrix Theory of Pain Factors that contribute to the patterns of activity generated by the body-self neuromatrix, which is comprised of sensory (S), affective (A), and cognitive (C) neuromodules. The output patterns from the neuromatrix produce the multiple dimensions of pain experience, as well as concurrent homeostatic and behavioral responses.

(Bushnell & Apkarian, 2006). These techniques have confirmed pain-related activity in widely distributed, highly interconnected areas and support the concept that pain is generated by a complex neural network—the body-self neuromatrix—which has multiple inputs and outputs, as shown in Figure 1 (Melzack, 2005). Second, the detailed knowledge and technical skills developed for research on the spinal cord can be used to explore brain mechanisms in humans and animals. The shift to a top-down strategy that begins with brain function and conscious experience will expand the field of pain by incorporating the rapidly growing knowledge of cognitive neuroscience and the evolution of the brain. The potential of this hybrid vigor is a direct attack on pain and suffering in the structures that generate them. Third, our knowledge of the genetic basis of the development of the brain is growing rapidly. At the same time, a large number of genes related to pain have been identified (Mogil, 2004). The study of pain, therefore, has broadened and now incorporates research in epidemiology and medical genetics as well as sociological and cultural studies (see McMahon & Koltzenburg, 2006). The inevitable convergence of these three approaches to reveal the functions of the brain will hopefully lead to the relief of the pain and suffering now endured by millions of people.

REFERENCES

Bushnell, M. C., & Apkarian, A. V. (2006). Representation of pain in the brain. In S. B. McMahon and M. Koltzenburg (Eds.), *Wall and Melzack's textbook of pain* (5th ed., pp. 291–304). Edinburgh: Elsevier/Churchill Livingston.

Dostrovsky, J. O., & Craig, A. D. (2006). Ascending projection systems. In S. B. McMahon & M. Koltzenburg (Eds.), *Wall and Melzack's textbook of pain* (5th ed., pp. 187–204). Edinburgh: Elsevier/Churchill Livingston.

Keefe, F. J., Dixon, K. E., & Pryor, R. W. (2005). Psychological contributions to the understanding and treatment of pain. In H. Merskey, J. D. Loeser, & R. Dubner (Eds.), *The paths of pain: 1975–2005* (pp. 403–420). Seattle: IASP Press.

McMahon, S. B., & Koltzenburg, M. (Eds.). (2006). *Wall and Melzack's textbook of pain* (5th ed.). Edinburgh: Elsevier/Churchill Livingston.

Melzack, R. (1975). The McGill Pain Questionnaire: Major properties and scoring methods. *Pain, 1,* 277–299.

Melzack, R. (1989). Phantom limbs, the self and the brain (The D. O. Hebb Memorial Lecture). *Canadian Psychology, 30,* 1–14.

Melzack, R. (2005). Evolution of the neuromatrix theory of pain. The Prithvi Raj Lecture. *Pain Practice, 5,* 85–94.

Melzack, R., & Casey, K. L. (1968). Sensory, motivational, and central control determinants of pain: A new conceptual model. In D. Kenshalo (Ed.), *The skin senses* (pp. 423–443). Springfield, IL: Charles C. Thomas.

Melzack, R., & Wall, P. D. (1965). Pain mechanisms: A new theory. *Science, 150,* 971–979.

Mogil, J. (Ed.). (2004). *The genetics of pain.* Seattle: IASP Press.

SUGGESTED READINGS

McMahon, S. E., & Koltzenburg, M. (Eds.). (2006). *Wall and Melzack's textbook of pain* (5th ed.). Edinburgh: Elsevier/Churchill Livingston.

Melzack, R., & Wall, P. D. (1996; reprinted 2008). *The challenge of pain.* London: Penguin.

Merskey, J., Loeser, J. D., & Dubner, R. (Eds.). (2005). *The paths of pain: 1975–2005.* Seattle: IASP Press.

RONALD MELZACK
McGill University

See also: **Phantom Limb Pain**

PAIRED COMPARISONS

Psychologists are interested in quantifying psychological responses to physical stimuli. In this domain, called psychophysics, researchers have developed several useful approaches, including the method of paired comparisons.

A simple approach to assessing the magnitude of a psychological response to different stimuli would involve ranking stimuli from low to high on a dimension that does not have a direct physical manifestation, such as loudness, attractiveness, or desirability. Unfortunately, ranking produces ordinal data, which means that the researcher can assess the relative, but not the actual, magnitude of the difference between elements of the pair. That is, one knows that a given stimulus leads to a larger response than another stimulus, but not how much larger.

To remedy this problem, psychologists use the method of paired comparisons. In the standard form of this procedure, researchers present stimuli in pairs, and observers identify which stimulus produces the greater response. Stimuli are paired exhaustively with every other stimulus; with statistical modeling, one can develop an interval-scale metric. Such a metric creates a continuum such that if two pairs of stimuli are at the same distance from one another on the continuum, there is an equal difference in the magnitude of the psychological response.

L. L. Thurstone (1927) developed the method and its mathematical derivation. He assumed that presentation of each stimulus resulted in an average response but that there was normally distributed variability in responses to that stimulus. Based on the average and the variability of responses, he could construct an interval-scale continuum that reflected how far apart any two stimuli are with respect to the psychological magnitude of the response. As such, one can assess not only relative magnitude, as with simple ranks, but also actual numerical differences between the stimuli.

Since the development of the original method of paired comparisons, psychologists have created more sophisticated models of the underlying psychological process. A recent approach links paired comparisons to structural equation modeling, which permits testing multidimensional models of psychological responses (Maydeu-Olivares & Böckenholt, 2005).

In addition, psychologists have documented the reliability associated with using fewer observations than are traditionally employed and with using a subset of comparisons rather than all possible pairs, a number that grows large very quickly as the number of elements in a set increases.

One particular advantage of the new models is that they can handle intransitivities. That is, in comparing the set A, B, and C, if A is experienced as larger than B, and B larger than C, then one would expect A to be seen as larger than C. Because choices may be very difficult and because participants normally show variability in responses, however, a participant may respond that C is larger than A, reflecting an intransitivity. The new statistical approaches, facilitated by power computers, can partial out variability due to factors other than the dimension of interest.

REFERENCES

Maydeu-Olivares, A., & Böckenholt, U. (2005). Structural equation modeling of paired-comparison and ranking data. *Psychological Methods, 10*, 285–304.

Thurstone, L. L. (1994). A law of comparative judgment. *Psychological Review Special Issue: The centennial issue of the Psychological Review, 101*, 266–270.

SUGGESTED READING

David, H. A. (1988). *The method of paired comparisons*. London: Griffin.

BERNARD C. BEINS
Ithaca College

PAKISTAN, PSYCHOLOGY IN

Pakistan came into existence on August 14, 1947, after the division of British India into East and West Pakistan. At this time psychology was being taught as a branch of philosophy, but the history of psychology in Pakistan dates back to the 1920s. This history began with three departments of philosophy in the city of Lahore in West Pakistan that offered a master's program in both philosophy and psychology. Today there are more than 28 independent departments of psychology. In East Pakistan, a master's program in psychology was offered at two universities: Dacca and Rajshahi. These universities also offered MPhil and PhD degrees without a formal coursework. In 1971, East Pakistan was split away and became Bangladesh, and until the early 1980s there was no post–master's training offered in clinical psychology in Pakistan. Most of the clinical psychologists practicing in Pakistan at that time were qualified from abroad. Then two institutes were established to provide post–master's degrees, one at Karachi University in 1983 and the other at Punjab University in 1984.

Organization of Psychology

The oldest and largest psychological organization is the Pakistan Psychological Association (PPA), which was established in 1968 at Dacca in the former East Pakistan. The second oldest organization is the Pakistan Association of Clinical Psychologists (PACP), which was established in 1988 and promotes the mental health role of clinical psychologists in Pakistan. The Society for the Advancement of Muslim Psychology was also established in 1988 through the efforts of Mohammad Ajmal and Azhar Ali Rizvi. The aim of this society is to develop an indigenous therapeutic modality based on the works of renowned Muslim Scholars such as Ibn-e-Sina, Ghazali, Razi, and Ashraf Ali Thanvi.

Patterns of Education and Training

At the undergraduate level, the primary criterion for admission to most universities in Pakistan is prior academic performance. It includes 10 years of secondary school, culminating in the secondary school certificate (matriculation) and two years of college, after which the intermediate certificate is awarded. Students attain a bachelor's degree in arts or sciences on completion of two additional years of undergraduate study following the intermediate certificate. Of late, many colleges and universities have started four-year BS (honors) programs in applied psychology and clinical psychology (equivalent to a master's degree) and MS programs in applied psychology and clinical psychology (equivalent to an MPhil degree). English is the medium of instruction. The majority of the prescribed readings are written by Western authors. Post–master's programs including both MPhil and PhD are being offered at Karachi University, Peshawar University, Punjab University, and Quaid-i-Azam University, and at the Institutes of Clinical Psychology in Karachi and Lahore. In addition, the two institutes also offer a post–master's diploma program of 12 months' duration in clinical psychology. The method of instruction at the undergraduate and graduate level is primarily lecture-based. Seminars and group discussions are often adjunctive methods used in graduate instruction.

Prominent Lines of Research

The main focus remains on quantitative research, but mixed design research is also conducted. Beside adaptations of tests developed in the West, there are also a few indigenous psychological tests that have been developed in Pakistan. Rahman and Sitwat (1997) developed an indigenous Symptom Checklist in Urdu as a screening device for psychopathology (i.e., for anxiety, depression, obsessive compulsive, somatization, schizophrenia, and level of frustration tolerance), which was later revised on both clinical and nonclinical groups. Recently, Dawood (2008) developed an Indigenous Scale of Emotional Intelligence based on Goleman's model. Ansari (2001) examined studies in Pakistani journals and found that the theoretical and philosophical treatment of psychological issues, which had previously commanded a central place, has declined sharply from previous times, while topics in developmental and educational psychology showed a marked increase.

Types of Applied Practice

At present, the primary occupations available to Pakistani psychologists include teaching at the undergraduate (60%) and graduate (15%) level, conducting psychological assessment for personnel selection (7%) in the civil service and armed forces, delivering psychotherapy services in various clinical settings (7%), working in research centers and special education institutions (4%), and the remainder (7%) in other categories (Ansari, 2001).

Many clinical psychologists practice Western modalities. However, there is an indigenous model of therapy based on the meditations practiced by Sufis (mystics) and practiced throughout the Muslim world. This practice is known as "Zikr Allah," which means "Remembering God" (Awan, 2003). This method practices the cleansing of the heart so as to attain nearness to Allah, as it is believed that Allah emanates peace.

Future Prospects and Directions

As a developing country presently with inflation as high as 25% and a population of 165 million with high unemployment and severe political unrest, Pakistan is passing through a very difficult period. Its manifold psychosocial problems include (1) post–9/11, Muslims around the globe feel marginalized and stereotyped as "terrorists," which is resulting in widespread anxiety and a feeling of helplessness at not being able to defend themselves against anti-Islamic bias in the media; (2) with respect to suicide bombing, a new phenomenon around the globe that emerged after 9/11, a recent survey conducted by Yousafzai and Siddiqi (2007) in the tribal areas of Pakistan revealed that, despite the strong inclination toward religion in that area and belief in "jihad" as a religious obligation, the majority (90%) of people condemn suicide bombing completely; (3) Pakistani women are still marginalized, and most are forced to stay at home and assume sole responsibility for all domestic tasks; (4) according to the National Assessment Report of 2006 on Problem Drug Use in Pakistan, there are 630,000 opiate users in Pakistan (UN Office on Drugs & Crime, World Drug Report, 2008); (5) there is a concentrated epidemic of HIV/AIDS among the injecting drug users in Pakistan, and (6) the recent surge in inflation, with high unemployment and frequent load shedding of electricity is resulting in innumerable emotional problems.

Keeping in focus the above mentioned issues presently confronting Pakistan, it is extremely important to establish immediately more master's and doctoral programs in clinical psychology in Pakistan, in order to correct the presently very low ratio of one clinical psychologist to 165,000 people. Furthermore, there is a great need for cross-cultural research that will foster communication and understanding of different lifestyles, values, and perceptions. Well-known psychologists and heads of psychology departments were interviewed in the course of writing this article, and the majority are optimistic about the future of psychology in Pakistan, provided that a concerted effort is made to produce professionals in all specialties of psychology and that the PPA can educate the government, the private sector, and the general public to appreciate the potential contribution of psychology to individual and communal life in Pakistan.

REFERENCES

Ansari, Z. A. (2001). Development of psychology in Pakistan. In S. H. Hashmi (Ed.), *The state of social sciences in Pakistan* (pp. 97–108). Islamabad: Allama Iqbal Open University.

Awan, M. A. (2003). Treatment of mental illnesses through Zikr Allah. *Al Murshad [The Spiritual Teacher]*, 24, 4–6.

Dawood, S. (2008). *Development of an indigenous scale for emotional intelligence*. Unpublished doctoral dissertation, Centre for Clinical Psychology, University of the Punjab, Lahore.

Rahman, N. K., & Sitwat, A. (1997, February). *Factor analysis of Symptom Checklist developed at the Center for Clinical Psychology, Punjab University, Lahore*. Paper presented at 11th International Psychiatric Conference, Karachi.

United Nations Office for Drug Control and Crime. (2008). *World Drug Report*. New York: United Nations Publications.

Yousafzai, A. W., et al. (2007). *Attitudes and perceptions of people towards suicide bombing: A questionnaire survey in Tribal Areas of Pakistan*. Paper presented at the International Conference on Impact of Global Violence on Mental Health: A Challenge for Mental Health Professionals. Lahore: Centre for Clinical Psychology, University of the Punjab.

NOSHEEN K. RAHMAN
Punjab University, Lahore, Pakistan

PANIC DISORDER

Panic disorder (PD) (with and without agoraphobia) is a debilitating condition with a lifetime prevalence of approximately 1.5% (American Psychiatric Association, 2000). Studies have demonstrated that this prevalence rate is relatively consistent throughout the world. Approximately twice as many women as men suffer from PD. Although PD typically first strikes between late adolescence and the mid-30s, it can also begin in childhood or in later life. Although data on the course of PD are lacking, it appears to be a chronic condition that waxes and wanes in severity. Consequences of PD include feelings of poor physical and emotional health, impaired social functioning, financial dependency, and increased use of health and hospital emergency services.

Description of PD

As defined in the fourth edition text revision of the *Diagnostic and Statistical Manual of Mental Disorders* (American Psychiatric Association, 2000), the essential feature of PD is the experience of recurrent, unexpected panic attacks. A panic attack is defined as a discrete period of intense fear or discomfort that develops abruptly, reaches a peak within 10 minutes, and is accompanied by at least 4 of the following 13 symptoms: shortness of breath, dizziness, palpitations, trembling, sweating, choking sensations, nausea/abdominal distress, depersonalization, paresthesias (numbness/tingling), flushes/chills, chest pain, fear of dying, and fear of going crazy or doing something uncontrolled. To warrant the diagnosis of PD, an individual must experience at least two unexpected panic attacks, followed by at least 1 month of concern about having another panic attack. The frequency of attacks varies widely, from several attacks each day to only a handful of attacks per year.

The vast majority of PD patients seeking treatment present with agoraphobia. Agoraphobia is the experience of anxiety in situations where escape might be difficult or where help may not be immediately available should a panic attack occur. Common agoraphobic situations include airplanes, buses, trains, elevators, being alone, or being in a crowd. As a result of the anxiety experienced in these situations, individuals often develop phobic avoidance resulting in a constricted lifestyle. The severity of agoraphobia ranges from mild to severe.

Causes of PD

Following is a brief review of some of the most promising theories about the causes of PD.

Genetic Theories of PD

One line of evidence for a biological etiology of PD comes from studies that demonstrate that panic tends to run in families. These studies have found that approximately half of all PD patients have at least one relative with PD, that first-degree relatives of PD patients are approximately five times more likely to develop PD than first-degree relatives of normal controls, and that PD and agoraphobia with panic attacks are more than five times as frequent in monozygotic twins than in dizygotic twins of patients with PD (Woodman & Crowe, 1995).

Neurotransmitter Theories of PD

Biological theorists attempt to provide an indirect link between PD and specific neurotransmitter systems by assessing the effects of drugs on these neurotransmitter systems. Specifically, they attempt to demonstrate that drugs used to treat panic increase the availability of a specific neurotransmitter or its metabolite, whereas drugs that induce panic decrease the availability of the same neurotransmitter. An association may also be established by demonstrating that antipanic drugs decrease the availability of a specific neurotransmitter whereas panic-provoking drugs increase the availability of the same neurotransmitter. Neurotransmitters commonly implicated in the etiology of PD include norepinephrine, serotonin, and gamma-aminobutyric acid (GABA; Papp, Coplan, & Gorman, 1992).

Psychological Theories of PD

Several proposed psychological theories of PD are well supported by empirical data suggesting that psychological factors are central to the etiology and maintenance of PD. The cognitive model of PD proposes that panic attacks occur when individuals perceive certain somatic sensations as dangerous and interpret them to mean that they are about to experience sudden, imminent disaster (Clark, 1986). For example, individuals may develop a panic attack if they misinterpret heart palpitations as signaling an impending heart attack. The vicious cycle culminating in a panic attack begins when a stimulus perceived as threatening creates feelings of apprehension. If the somatic sensations that accompany this state of apprehension are catastrophically misinterpreted, the individual experiences a further increase in apprehension, elevated somatic sensations, and so on, until a full-blown panic attack occurs.

Pure behavioral models focus on the fact that panic attacks and agoraphobia are maintained by negative reinforcement. That is, individuals prone to panic attacks and agoraphobia avoid anxiety sensations and situations that may provoke anxiety. This leads to increased sensitization to anxiety symptoms and fuels further avoidance. Support for this model comes from learning theory and animal studies, as well as from treatment studies demonstrating that exposure-based treatments, in which patients confront sensations and situations that they previously avoided, lead to improvement (Barlow, 2001).

Assessment of PD

An in-depth clinical interview that captures the frequency, intensity, and duration of panic attacks and the nature of avoidance behaviors (agoraphobia) is essential in diagnosing panic disorder. Because panic disorder symptoms mimic those of several medical conditions, a medical evaluation is also recommended to rule out these conditions. Self-report inventories are available that facilitate treatment planning and are indicators of clinical progress. A self-administered questionnaire for PD is available online through the Anxiety Disorders Association of America Web site (http://www.adaa.org/GettingHelp/SelfHelpTests/selftest_Panic.asp). Actual diagnosis should be made only by a mental health professional or physician.

Treatment of PD

Psychotherapy, specifically cognitive-behavioral therapy (CBT), and pharmacotherapy have both been shown to be effective treatments for PD (Wolfe & Maser, 1994). CBT treatment elements include psychoeducation, cognitive restructuring, anxiety management skills training, and in vivo and interoceptive exposure. The psychoeducation component teaches the distinction between anxiety and fear/panic, the cause and nature of panic, and how the cycles of panic and anxiety are maintained. A main goal of psychoeducation is to elucidate the usefulness of anxiety and panic for survival and to correct misinterpretations of anxiety symptoms (e.g., panic attacks are dangerous) that contribute to the cycle of panic. Patients are also encouraged to self-monitor their panic symptoms.

Cognitive restructuring aims to change distorted thinking patterns that may feed anxiety and panic. At first, the patient is oriented to the importance of thoughts as potential emotional triggers (e.g., "increased heart rate is a sign that I'm having a heart attack!"). Thoughts are then carefully examined, questioned, and empirically challenged in light of any evidence that may or may not be available to support them. Thoughts are not accepted as fact. Common thinking errors are identified, such as heightened risk perception and catastrophizing, and alternative evidence-based hypotheses are developed.

Anxiety management skills, such as breathing control and progressive muscle relaxation, are also used in treatment; their primary aim is to decrease the physical aspects of panic. Because the breathing retraining treatment component can be conceptualized as a way to avoid panic, and thus as a safety behavior, it ought to be used carefully (Barlow & Craske, 2008). For it to remain a helpful technique, patients should not use breathing retraining as an avoidance strategy. With applied relaxation, patients are taught progressive muscle relaxation to lower their physical arousal, and once this skill is learned, it is applied in anxiety- and panic-provoking situations.

The exposure phase of treatment is in vivo exposure and interoceptive exposure. In vivo exposure is an essential treatment component that aims to help patients systematically confront feared external stimuli, particularly those associated with agoraphobia, so as to extinguish the conditioned emotional responses to these cues. Hierarchies are constructed to guide this phase of treatment, beginning with situations least feared and working up to those that are most feared (e.g., driving 1 mile on a highway up to driving 20 miles on a highway). Patients are instructed to gradually confront each situation and wait for the anxiety to subside rather than use escape or avoidance of the situation to decrease the anxiety. With interoceptive exposure, patients are systematically exposed to feared bodily sensations that resemble panic attacks and that, as a result, they have come to fear and avoid. Hierarchies are also constructed, starting with minimally distressing physical exercises and escalating to increasingly anxiety-provoking physical symptoms (e.g., walking up stairs to get one's heart rate going 100 beats per minute for 2 minutes up to getting one's heart rate up to 150 beats per minute for 5 minutes). The goal here is for the patient to learn through direct experience that although uncomfortable, the physical sensations are not dangerous and can be tolerated. Support for the efficacy of CBT for PD treatment is provided by extensive studies yielding high-quality data (see Barlow & Craske, 2008).

Four classes of medication have been shown to be effective in the treatment of PD: selective serotonin reuptake inhibitors, serotonin and norepinephrine reuptake inhibitors, benzodiazepines, and monoamine oxidase inhibitors. Studies demonstrate that medications from all four classes have similar efficacy. The choice of medication for a patient depends on a consideration of possible side effects, medication cost, and other clinical circumstances (e.g., the existence of comorbid disorders such as depression).

Studies that compare the effectiveness of combining CBT and antipanic medication with the effectiveness of each modality separately have thus far been inconclusive. However, conventional clinical wisdom suggests that a combination is at least equivalent to either modality alone and is likely to offer increased benefit.

Case Example

James is a 31-year-old European American man. He lives with his wife, Maggie, who is currently pregnant, and their 2-year-old son, Keith. Ever since Maggie gave birth 2 years ago, James has been extremely anxious and panicky. His panic attacks have worsened over this 2-year period, increasing in frequency and intensity. James describes the first time he felt what he now knows to be a panic attack. On the eve of Keith's birth, as James rushed Maggie to the hospital, he noticed odd physical sensations while wheeling Maggie into the maternity wing. James recalls shortness of breath, dizziness, and a racing heart. James also remembers feeling detached from reality, as if the hospital halls and all of the doctors and nurses were unreal. Conversations in the hallway and all other sights and sounds around him seemed to move in slow motion, almost at a standstill. Once Maggie arrived safely in a hospital room and was taken care of by the staff, James's symptoms went away. However, since that instance, James has experienced similar symptoms often, in a variety of usually stress-free situations: driving down local side streets, shopping in the supermarket, and watching television at home. James is hyperaware of his body and thus alert to uncomfortable physical sensations. He often believes that soon after his heart begins to race and his breathing quickens, he will have a heart attack and die. James refuses to drink coffee or go to the gym as he used to, and he prefers to stay close to home for fear of experiencing panic in a place where he can't get help or flee. James always carries alprazolam (a tranquilizing medication) in his pocket, in case he experiences terrifying panic symptoms in public. This is one of James's safety behaviors, a way for him to control his fear. Currently, James has difficulty sleeping and eating. He has lost 9 pounds in the past 6 months and is starting to feel depressed.

REFERENCES

American Psychiatric Association. (2000). *Diagnostic and statistical manual of mental disorders* (4th ed., text rev.). Washington, DC: Author.

Barlow, D. H. (2001). *Anxiety and its disorders* (2nd ed.). New York: Guilford Press.

Barlow, D. H., & Craske, M. G. (2008). Panic disorder and agoraphobia. In D. H. Barlow (Ed.), *Clinical handbook of psychological disorders: A step-by-step treatment manual* (pp. 1–64). New York: Guilford Press.

Barlow, D. H., Gorman, J. M., Shear, M. K., & Woods, S. W. (2000). Cognitive-behavioral therapy, imipramine, or their combination for panic disorder: A randomized controlled trial. *Journal of the American Medical Association, 283*(19), 2529–2536.

Clark, D. M. (1986). A cognitive approach to panic. *Behaviour Research and Therapy, 24*, 461–471.

Mayo Foundation for Medical Education and Research. (n.d.). *Panic attacks and panic disorder.* Retrieved March 10, 2008, from http://www.mayoclinic.com/health/panic-attacks/DS00338.

Papp, L. A., Coplan, J., & Gorman, J. M. (1992). Neurobiology of anxiety. In A. Tasman & M. B. Riba (Eds.), *Review of psychiatry* (Vol. 11, pp. 307–322). Washington, DC: American Psychiatric Association Press.

Wolfe, B. E., & Maser, J. D. (Eds.). (1994). *Treatment of panic disorder: A consensus development conference.* Washington, DC: American Psychiatric Association Press.

Woodman, C. L., & Crowe, R. R. (1995). The genetics of panic disorder. In G. Asnis & H. M. van Praag (Eds.), *Panic disorder: Clinical, biological, and treatment aspects* (pp. 66–79). New York: John Wiley & Sons.

SUGGESTED READINGS

http://www.anxieties.com

http://www.nimh.nih.gov/health/topics/panic-disorder/index.shtml

WILLIAM C. SANDERSON
RANDI A. DUBLIN
Hofstra University

PARADOXICAL INTERVENTION

Paradoxical interventions are psychotherapeutic tactics that seem to contradict the goals they are designed to achieve. For example, a therapist may prescribe that clients deliberately have an unwanted symptom or restrain them from changing. In the classic definition of a therapeutic double-bind or paradox, "an injunction is so structured that it (1) reinforces the behavior the patient expects to be changed, (2) implies that this reinforcement is the vehicle of change, and (3) thereby creates a paradox because the patient is told to change by remaining unchanged" (Watzlawick, Beavin, & Jackson, 1967, p. 241).

References to resolving problems with paradoxical interventions appear as early as the eighteenth century. In the twentieth century, Dunlap applied the technique of negative practice to problems such as stammering and enuresis. Rosen, through direct psychoanalysis, encouraged psychiatric patients to engage in aspects of their psychosis in order to prevent relapse. Frankl used paradoxical intention to help his patients revise the meaning of their symptoms. The most influential literature on therapeutic paradox, however, derives from Bateson's 1952–1962 project on communication. Bateson, Jackson, Haley, Weakland, and others explored the role of paradoxical double-bind communications in resolving as well as creating problems. Influenced by systemic/cybernetics ideas and by the work of master hypnotist Milton Erickson, descendants of the Bateson project such as Haley, Weakland, Watzlawick, Fisch, and Selvini-Palazzoli went on in the 1970s to develop family therapy models with paradox as a central feature. Around the same time, Frankl's paradoxical intention technique was adopted by behavior therapists, who demonstrated its usefulness with specific symptoms such as insomnia, anxiety, urinary retention, and obsessions.

Although paradoxical interventions have been historically associated with particular theoretical frameworks, the current literature tends to treat them as techniques that can be applied and explained apart from the models in which they were developed. Indeed, paradoxical interventions cut across theoretical boundaries, and paradoxical elements can be found in virtually all schools of psychotherapy (Seltzer, 1978). Nevertheless, there are striking differences in how therapists of different theoretical orientations use paradoxical interventions. In comparing cognitive-behavioral and strategic-systemic approaches—the two frameworks most akin to therapeutic paradox—one finds that behavior therapists use paradoxical intention to interrupt within-person exacerbation cycles, while strategic-systems therapists use a wider variety of paradoxical interventions and more often focus on between-person (family) interactions. Another difference is that behavior therapists make their rationale explicit, and strategic therapists typically do not. Thus, a behavior therapist aiming to reduce performance anxiety by adopting a paradoxical attitude would typically explain how the client's intention to force sleep is actually exacerbating the problem and why a paradoxical intention to stay awake might make sleep come easier. The *intention* in this example is clearly the client's, not the therapist's, and the client is expected to do (or at least try to do) what he or she is told. In strategic applications, however, the therapist sometimes expects a patient or family to do the opposite of what is proposed, and in this sense, the therapist's intention is paradoxical. In contrast to the openly shared, educational rationale of a behavior therapist, strategic therapists attempt to maximize compliance (or defiance) by framing suggestions in a manner consistent (or deliberately inconsistent) with the client's own idiosyncratic worldview (Fisch, Weakland, & Segal, 1982).

Types of Applications

Several schemes for classifying paradoxical interventions have been offered (cf. Seltzer, 1986). Of the many types, the most commonly used are symptom prescription and restraint from change. Variations of these two techniques—asking clients to engage in the behavior they wish to eliminate and restraining them from changing—have been applied in both individual and family therapy. However, nearly all controlled studies of therapeutic paradox have involved symptom prescription with individuals. Based on an early meta-analysis of these studies, Shoham-Salomon and Rosenthal (1987) proposed that the outcome may depend largely on how these interventions are administered.

Most paradoxical interventions involve some combination of prescribing, reframing, and positioning. *Prescribing* means telling people what to do (giving tasks, suggestions, and so on) either directly or indirectly. For example, a therapist might ask a patient to deliberately have a panic attack or prescribe that an overinvolved grandmother take full responsibility for a misbehaving child, expecting that she will back off and let the mother take charge. *Reframing* involves redefining the meaning of events or behavior in a way that makes change more possible. Although reframing resembles interpretation, its goal is to provoke change rather than provide insight; the accuracy of redefinition is less important than its impact. Thus, Haley described a case in which a wife becomes more sexually responsive after her low sex drive was reframed as a way of protecting the husband from the full force of her sexuality, and Selvini-Palazzoli, Cecchin, Prata, and Boscolo (1978) pioneered the use of positive connotation, a technique for changing dysfunctional family patterns by ascribing noble intentions to both the identified patient's symptom and the behaviors of family members that support it. *Positioning* is a term for altering the therapist's own role, or potential role, in a problem-maintaining system. Prescribing, reframing, and positioning are interwoven, with each at least implicit in any paradoxical strategy or intervention. Thus, prescribing that someone be deliberately anxious reframes an involuntary symptom as controllable, reframing problem behavior as a protective sacrifice carries an implicit (paradoxical) prescription not to change, and warning against the dangers of improvement sometimes helps reverse or neutralize a therapist's role in a problem cycle.

Applications of paradox tend to be most varied and complex in marital and family therapy. In one case, where the focus was on reversing family members' well-intentioned but self-defeating attempts to solve a problem, a therapy team coached the relatives of a depressed stroke victim to encourage him by discouraging him (Fisch et al., 1982). In another case, a therapist asked a depressed husband to pretend to be depressed and asked his wife to try to find out if he was really that way. For extreme marital stuckness, a therapist may recommend paradoxical interventions such as prescribing indecision about whether a couple should separate. The most dramatic examples of paradox with families come from the early work of the Milan team (Selvini-Palazzoli and colleagues). After complimenting a severely obsessive young woman and her parents for protecting each other from the sadness associated with the death of a family member several years earlier, the team prescribed that the family meet each night to discuss their loss and suggested that the young woman behave symptomatically whenever her parents appeared distraught.

Clinical reports describe successful applications of paradoxical intervention with a wide variety of problems, including anxiety, depression, phobia, insomnia, obsessive-compulsive disorder, headaches, asthma, encopresis, enuresis, blushing, tics, psychosomatic symptoms, procrastination, eating disorders, child and adolescent conduct problems, marital and family problems, pain, and psychotic behavior (Seltzer, 1978). Paradoxical strategies appear least applicable in situations of crisis or extreme instability, such as acute decompensation, grief reactions, domestic violence, suicide attempts, or loss of a job, but there have been too few controlled studies to list indications and contraindications with any degree of certainty.

Although some authors advocate reserving paradoxical approaches for difficult situations where more straightforward methods have not succeeded or are unlikely to succeed, paradoxical strategies are too diverse for this to make sense as a blanket rule. For example, paradoxical symptom prescription could reasonably be a first line of approach for involuntary symptoms like insomnia that, to some extent, are maintained by attempts to stave them off.

Change Process

Explanations of how and why paradoxical interventions work are as diverse as the interventions themselves. Behavioral, cognitive, and motivational processes—alone and in combination—have been proposed to explain change in both individuals and families. At the individual level, a behavioral account of why symptom prescription helps involuntary problems such as insomnia, anxiety, and obsessive thinking is that, by attempting to have the problem, patients cannot continue their usual ways of trying to prevent it, thereby breaking an exacerbation cycle. Cognitive explanations of the same phenomena emphasize that symptom prescription redefines the uncontrollable as controllable, reduces fear of fear (or recursive anxiety), and in a fundamental way, alters the symptom's meaning. A third, rather different change mechanism has been suggested for situations where clients appear to defy or oppose a therapist's directive: The client presumably rebels to reduce psychological reactance, a motive state hypothesized by Brehm to be aroused by threats to perceived behavioral freedom.

Not surprisingly, explanations of how paradoxical interventions promote change at the family-systems level are more diverse and more abstract. Some paradoxical interventions are assumed to interrupt problem-maintaining interaction cycles between people (Fisch et al., 1982), and some, like positive connotation, presumably operate by introducing new information into the system or by changing the meaning of the symptom and the family interaction that supports it (Selvini-Palazzoli et al., 1986). Motivational explanations of systems-level change suggest that paradoxical interventions work by activating relational dynamics such as compression and recoil (Stanton, 1984) or by creating disequilibrium among systemic forces aligned for and against change (Hoffman, 1990).

Some theories of paradoxical intervention attempt to combine or integrate various change processes. Rohrbaugh, Tennen, Press, and White (1981) proposed a compliance-defiance model distinguishing two types of paradoxical interventions. Compliance-based symptom prescription is indicated (1) when an unfree (involuntary) symptom like insomnia is maintained by attempts to stave it off and (2) when the potential for reactance is low (i.e., when clients are unlikely to react against attempts

to influence them). Defiance-based interventions, on the other hand, work because people change by rebelling. These are indicated when clients view the target behavior as relatively free (voluntary) and when the potential for reactance is high.

Findings from several experimental studies support this compliance-defiance model. For example, Broomfield and Espie (2003) found that, following paradoxical instructions to stay awake, patients with involuntary sleep-onset insomnia reported reduced sleep efforts, less performance anxiety, and lower sleep latencies than control patients receiving nonparadoxical intervention. Similarly, Ascher and Schotte (1999) found that symptom prescription for performance anxiety worked best for patients high on "fear of fear," apparently because the intervention interrupted a strongly recursive problem-maintaining process. By contrast, symptom prescription, targeting the more voluntary (free) behavior of procrastination, appears to work better than straightforward self-control interventions for clients high in reactance potential, regardless of whether reactance potential is assessed or manipulated (Shoham-Salomon, Avner, & Neeman, 1989).

Another model of therapeutic paradox originally proposed by Watzlawick and colleagues (1967) incorporates behavioral and cognitive explanations of change. The therapeutic double-bind—a directive to deliberately engage in involuntary symptomatic behavior—is a mirror image of the pathogenic "be spontaneous" paradox. The only way to obey such a directive is by disobeying it. According to Watzlawick and colleagues (1967), two possible consequences follow: If the client is not able to produce the symptom on demand, he or she will show less of the problem; if the client does produce the symptom, it will be with a greater sense of mastery and control. In this way, clients are "changed if they do and changed if they don't." If the symptomatic behavior itself does not change, at least the client's perception of it changes—and as Raskin and Klein put it, behaviors over which one has control might be sins, but they are not neurotic complaints. Studies by Shoham and colleagues provide some empirical support for this "two paths to change" model.

Efficacy

When paradoxical interventions are part of a broader therapeutic strategy, their specific contribution to clinical outcome is difficult to evaluate. Nevertheless, dramatic and seemingly enduring effects on individuals and families have been documented in numerous clinical reports, case studies, and qualitative literature reviews (Seltzer, 1986).

Controlled experimental studies of paradoxical interventions with individual clients have yielded mixed results. Two independent meta-analytic reviews (Hill, 1987; Shoham-Salomon & Rosenthal, 1987) indicate that paradoxical interventions compared favorably to no-treatment control conditions, but comparisons with nonparadoxical treatments have been equivocal. Whereas Hill's meta-analysis found paradox to be superior, Shoham-Salomon and Rosenthal found that the overall effect of paradoxical interventions was as large (but no larger than) the average effect size of psychotherapy in general. In terms of applicability to specific problems, the best evidence for efficacy seems to involve paradoxical intention treatments for insomnia (Morin et al., 1999).

Research also suggests that some forms of paradoxical intervention may be more effective than others. In Shoham-Salomon and Rosenthal's (1987) meta-analysis, the effect sizes of two types of positively connoted symptom prescriptions were significantly greater than those of other, nonparadoxical treatments or of symptom prescriptions that did not include a positive frame. Paradoxical interventions were most effective when the therapist either reframed the symptom positively before prescribing it (for example, praising a depressed client's tolerance for solitude or willingness to sacrifice for the good of others) or explained the paradoxical intentions (exacerbation-cycle) rationale in a way that defined the client as not sick but stuck. Finally, in a study directly testing the importance of positive connotation, Akillas and Efran (1995) found that socially anxious men improve more when a prescription to be anxious was presented with a positive frame (rationale) than when it was not. This supports the view that symptom prescriptions work best when they aim to alter the meaning a client attributes to the symptom.

Research on paradoxical interventions is not without limitations. For example, meta-analytic results must be interpreted cautiously because stringent inclusion criteria may compromise the clinical or ecological validity of conclusions. Moreover, as noted previously, research in this area has focused almost exclusively on symptom prescription with individuals. There have been too few controlled studies to summarize the efficacy of other forms of therapeutic paradox (e.g., restraint from change) or of applications with interactional systems and families.

Ethical Issues

As the popularity of paradoxical therapy increased during the 1980s, concern also grew about ways in which these techniques can be misused. Strategic applications in which therapists do not make their rationale for particular interventions explicit to clients have been criticized as manipulative and potentially harmful to the client–therapist relationship.

Defenders of strategic therapy, on the other hand, argue that good therapy is inherently manipulative and that therapeutic truth telling can be not only naive but also discourteous. Responsible therapists of all persuasions agree that paradox should not be used for the shock value or power it promises. Encouraging a symptom or restraining people from changing can be disastrous if done sarcastically or from a sense of frustration ("There's

the window, go ahead and jump!"). It is also significant that therapists like Haley, Weakland, Palazzoli, and Hoffman, who pioneered the use of paradoxical methods, now give them less emphasis; even therapists well versed in strategic methods find the term *paradoxical* confusing, inaccurate, and overly loaded with negative connotations. Of particular concern is that the term *paradoxical intervention*, cut loose from its theoretical and clinical moorings, is too easily seen as a quick fix or a gimmick.

Three guidelines may decrease the potential for misusing paradoxical interventions: First, define behavior positively. When prescribing a symptom or restraining change, avoid attributing unseemly motives to people (like needing control and trying to resist or defeat another); ascribe noble intentions not only to the symptom but also to what other people are doing to support it. Second, be especially cautious with challenging or provocative interventions. When restraining clients from change, for example, it is safer to suggest that change may not be advisable than to predict it will not be possible. Third, have a clear theoretical formulation of how the problem is being maintained and how a paradoxical intervention may help to change that. The most important guideline for paradoxical (or any other) intervention is having a coherent rationale for using it.

REFERENCES

Akillas, E., & Efran, J. S. (1995). Symptom prescription and reframing: Should they be combined? *Cognitive Therapy and Research, 19,* 263–279.

Ascher, L. M., & Schotte, D. E. (1999). Paradoxical intention and recursive anxiety. *Journal of Behavior Therapy and Experimental Psychiatry, 30,* 71–79.

Broomfield, N. M., & Espie, C. A. (2003). Initial insomnia and paradoxical intention: An experimental investigation of putative mechanisms using subjective and actigraphic measurement of sleep. *Behavioural and Cognitive Psychotherapy, 31,* 313–324.

Fisch, R., Weakland, J. H., & Segal, L. (1982). *The tactics of change.* San Francisco: Jossey-Bass.

Hill, K. A. (1987). Meta analysis of paradoxical interventions. *Psychotherapy, 24,* 266–270.

Hoffman, L. (1990). Constructing realities: An art of lenses. *Family Process, 29,* 1–12.

Morin, C. M., Hauri, P. J., Espie, C., Spielman, A., Buuysse, D. J., & Bootzin, R. R. (1999). Nonpharmacologic treatment of chronic insomnia. *Sleep, 22,* 1–25.

Rohrbaugh, M., Tennen, H., Press, S., & White, L. (1981). Compliance, defiance, and therapeutic paradox: Guidelines for strategic use of paradoxical interventions. *American Journal of Orthopsychiatry, 51,* 454–497.

Seltzer, L. F. (1986). *Paradoxical strategies in psychotherapy: A comprehensive overview and guide book.* New York: John Wiley & Sons.

Selvini-Palazzoli, M., Cecchin, G., Prata, G., & Boscolo, l. (1978). *Paradox and counterparadox.* New York: Aronson.

Shoham-Salomon, V., Avner, R., & Neeman, R. (1989). You are changed if you do and changed if you don't: Mechanisms underlying paradoxical interventions. *Journal of Consulting and Clinical Psychology, 57,* 590–598.

Shoham-Salomon, V., & Rosenthal, R. (1987). Paradoxical interventions. A meta-analysis. *Journal of Consulting and Clinical Psychology, 55,* 22–28.

Stanton, M. D. (1984). Fusion, compression, diversion, and the workings of paradox: A theory of therapeutic/systemic change. *Family Process, 23,* 135–167.

Watzlawick, P., Beavin, J., & Jackson, D. D. (1967). *Pragmatics of human communication.* New York: Norton.

SUGGESTED READING

Shoham, V., & Rohrbaugh, M. (1997). Interrupting ironic processes. *Psychological Science, 8,* 151–153.

VARDA SHOHAM
MICHAEL J. ROHRBAUGH
University of Arizona

See also: Cognitive Therapy

PARADOXICAL SLEEP

Paradoxical sleep is a sleep stage characterized physiologically by a lack of muscle tone; rapid eye movements (REMs), which are not always rapid; and an awake cortical electroencephalographic (EEG) pattern. The paradox refers to the disparity between the alert EEG pattern, implying that the person is awake or nearly so, and the indications that the person is actually more deeply asleep than at other times (difficulty in arousing, reduced muscle tone). The lack of muscle tone prevents the sleeper from performing the activities reflected in the alert EEG pattern. *REM without atonia* or *REM behavior disorder* is a sleep disorder in which the atonia fails to occur, with the result that the sleeper may actually perform his or her REM sleep actions.

The term *paradoxical sleep* was introduced in French researcher Michel Jouvet's 1967 *Scientific American* article on the states of sleep. Jouvet used the term to describe a period of apparent sleep in cats in which they exhibited high levels of neural activity with completely relaxed neck muscles. In humans, such periods are also characterized by eye movements, at least some of which are rapid. Sleep researchers use the term *REM sleep* with human subjects but *paradoxical sleep* with animals, because many species do not exhibit eye movements.

REM or paradoxical sleep is just one of several stages that a sleeping organism passes through during a sleep bout. One way to categorize the stages is into REM sleep and non-REM (NREM) sleep. Four stages are usually distinguished in NREM sleep, labeled appropriately Stages 1–4, with the stages representing progressively deeper sleep. Stages 3 and 4 are collectively called *slow-wave sleep* (SWS), because the EEG waves are slower than in Stages 1 and 2.

REM sleep is associated with erections in males and vaginal moistening in females, as well as with reports of dreaming. In males at least, the genital changes are not necessarily associated with sex-related dreaming. Dreams also have been reported in SWS, but they are more frequent in REM sleep and generally more elaborate.

Studies of people awakened from REM sleep have answered several questions about dreaming. For example, apparently all normal humans dream, even though many people claim that they do not. When the nondreamers are awakened during REM sleep, they usually report dreams, although their dreams may be less vivid than those of people who usually remember their dreams upon awakening. Another observation is that dreams last about as long as they seem to.

A number of studies have attempted to determine the function of REM sleep by depriving volunteers of it. In general, subjects awakened during each REM stage and kept awake for several minutes increase their attempts at REM sleep and develop mild, temporary personality changes. Studies of paradoxical sleep deprivation in animals reveal similar increased attempts at REM sleep and some general disturbances, none of which solves the mystery of REM sleep's function.

According to one explanation, sleep is an adaptive mechanism developed to conserve energy at night, when food gathering would be difficult for an animal active in the daytime. However, the evolution of many animals has resulted in regular patterns of locomotor activity, thought to occur approximately every 2 hours, during which food gathering and other activities related to survival might occur. If this 2-hour cycle continued around the clock, the animal would have its sleep periodically interrupted. Thus, to get a full night's sleep *and* continue with the 2-hour activity cycle, the animal enters a period of paradoxical sleep in which only the brain awakens.

Another possibility is that REM or paradoxical sleep is important for strengthening memories. Studies have shown that humans and other mammals increase REM sleep periods following a new learning experience, and without this increase, memory deficits result. However, some researchers have noted that clinical evidence in humans suggests that REM sleep can be reduced dramatically with little or no effect on learning and memory. Yet another possibility is that infants spend an inordinate amount of time in REM sleep because such sleep is associated with the development of the brain. Obviously, the number of disparate explanations suggests that we do not at this time have the final answer on the functions of paradoxical sleep.

SUGGESTED READINGS

Hobson, J. A. (1995). *Sleep*. New York: Scientific American Library.

Hobson, J. A., Pace-Schott, E. F., & Stickgold, R. (2000). Dreaming and the brain: Toward a cognitive neuroscience of conscious states. *Behavioral and Brain Sciences, 23,* 793–1121.

Rock, A. (2004). *The mind at night: The new science of how and why we dream.* New York: Basic Books.

B. MICHAEL THORNE
Mississippi State University

See also: Sleep Cycle; Sleep Disorders

PARAMETRIC STATISTICAL TESTS

Parametric statistical tests, as opposed to nonparametric or distribution-free tests, are based on various assumptions regarding the characteristics, properties, and forms of the distributions of populations from which the data are drawn. A large number of statistical tests are included among the parametric tests, primarily hypothesis testing procedures derived from the general linear model. These include both univariate and multivariate statistical tests: the *t* test, univariate and multivariate analysis of variance (ANOVA) and covariance (including repeated measures), Pearson product-moment correlation, simple and multiple regression (and variants including logistic regression), Hotelling's T^2, discriminant function analysis, canonical correlation, and multivariate set correlation.

When their underlying assumptions are met, parametric statistical tests are generally considered more powerful than their nonparametric alternatives. However, it is more for their versatility than for their statistical power that parametric tests have become the most common tools in behavioral research. Parametric procedures are widely available and easily implemented using readily available statistical software packages. In addition, many parametric tests can be supplemented with a wide array of follow-up procedures that help explicate the results. Similar follow-up procedures are usually not available for nonparametric statistical tests. For example, a researcher who obtains a statistically significant ANOVA *F* test is able to choose from a number of different post hoc means comparisons procedures more or less tailored to suit different situations (e.g., the Bonferroni test, Dunnett's test, Scheffé's test, trend analysis, Tukey's HSD test, etc.). An especially important development is that the interpretation of parametric test results no longer needs to be limited to significance test *p*-values. Many measures of magnitude of effect ("effect size") are readily available, easy to calculate, and easy to interpret for most, if not all, parametric statistical procedures. Effect size measures in common use for parametric tests include Cohen's *d*, Cohen's *f*, η^2, ω^2, r^2, and multiple R^2.

The principal assumptions on which parametric tests are based include independence of the observations, normality of the underlying population distributions, and homogeneity of the population variances across groups (for multiple group procedures). Additional assumptions may be required for some parametric procedures, such as linearity of regression (Pearson product-moment correlation), homoscedasticity (simple and multiple regression), homogeneity of regression slopes (univariate and multivariate analysis of covariance), and sphericity/compound symmetry and homogeneity of treatment-difference variances (univariate and multivariate repeated measures). The principal assumptions for multivariate statistics include independence of the observations, multivariate normal distributions for all dependent variables, and homogeneity of the variance-covariance (dispersion) matrices across groups.

The primary concern when assumptions are violated is that the significance level (*p* value) associated with a statistical test result may be seriously in error, increasing either Type I or Type II error rates. Fortunately, under many circumstances, univariate statistics seem to be robust despite violations of assumptions. One exception is the violation of the assumption of independence, which is always serious. Even a small degree of departure from statistical independence in the observed scores can result in substantial increases in Type I error rates. Robustness may also be compromised under certain conditions, such as when two or more assumptions are violated simultaneously, when group sample sizes are very small (e.g., <5), when sample sizes are unequal, or when one-tailed significance tests are used.

Equal or very nearly equal group sample sizes can alleviate most concerns about violation of assumptions except for the assumption of independence. When violation of assumptions is a concern, various remedial techniques can be employed, including data transformations (e.g., square root, arcsine, log) or the use of alternative, specialized analytical procedures (e.g., jackknifing, bootstrapping, Welch's *t*-test, randomization tests, generalized estimating equations, nonparametric statistics, and other distribution-free methods). The assumptions underlying repeated measures procedures appear to be more restrictive than for univariate tests. Consequently, repeated measures procedures may not be as robust as univariate tests. Although not as much research has been conducted as for univariate procedures, multivariate statistical tests appear to be robust to violation of assumptions under many commonly occurring circumstances.

SUGGESTED READINGS

Agresti, A., & Finlay, B. (2009). *Statistical methods for the social sciences* (4th ed.). Upper Saddle River, NJ: Pearson Prentice-Hall.

Grissom, R. J., & Kim, J. J. (2005). *Effect sizes for research: A broad practical approach.* Hillsdale, NJ: Lawrence Erlbaum.

Maxwell, S. E., & Delaney, H. D. (2004). *Designing experiments and analyzing data: A model comparison perspective* (2nd ed). Mahwah, NJ: Lawrence Erlbaum.

Meyers, J. L., & Well, A. D. (2003). *Research design and statistical analysis* (2nd ed.). Mahwah, NJ: Lawrence Erlbaum.

Tabachnick, B. G., & Fidell, L. S. (2007). *Using multivariate statistics* (5th ed.). Boston: Pearson Education, Inc.

JOSEPH S. ROSSI
University of Rhode Island

PARANOIA (See Delusional Disorder)

PARANOID PERSONALITY DISORDER

Most people recognize the term *paranoid* as unwarranted suspiciousness or mistrust of others' actions or intentions due to belief that others are seeking harm or harboring ill will toward them. Anyone can have such concerns for a time, but when it becomes a pervasive and enduring feature of one's way of dealing with the world, then this can constitute a paranoid personality disorder. Among mental health disciplines, there is consensual agreement reflected in the American Psychiatric Association's (APA) *Diagnostic and Statistical Manual* (*DSM;* the gold standard for diagnosis of psychiatric disorders) that a personality disorder is an enduring, inflexible pattern of behavior across a broad range of functional contexts that produces either clinically significant personal distress or disruption and impairment in a person's social, occupational, or "other important areas of functioning" (APA, 2000). The prevalence of paranoid personality disorder (PPD) has been estimated to range from 0.5–2.5% in the general population, to be four times more prevalent in outpatient psychiatric settings, and to occur 10–30% in inpatient psychiatric facilities (APA, 2000). It is also thought to be more prevalent among males. Though it is a comparatively uncommon condition, its impact can be pervasive. Many would agree that dramatic examples in history of paranoid personalities include Joseph Stalin and perhaps Saddam Hussein.

More specifically, the *DSM-IV* describes PPD as including a pervasive distrust and suspiciousness of others whose motives are perceived as malevolent. This must represent a generalized concern occurring in many situations. Four or more of the following features must be present to make the diagnosis: (1) unjustified suspicions of being harmed, exploited, or deceived; (2) unwarranted doubts concerning the loyalty and fidelity of friends or trusted associates; (3) unwillingness to confide in others due to fear that any disclosures will be used against them; (4) perception of threats or derogation in innocuous events or communications; (5) a persistent grudging, unforgiving orientation toward perceived attacks and injuries; (6) a hostile, counterattacking response to imagined attacks on one's reputation; and (7) recurring unwarranted doubts or suspicions about the sexual loyalty of one's partner. Bernstein and Useda (2007) have suggested, however, that *DSM-IV* criteria tend to overemphasize the cognitive features of mistrust and suspiciousness and give lesser consideration to behavioral, affective, and interpersonal features involving the antagonistic, aggressive nature, hypervigilance, and rigidity in the attitudes and behavior of people with PPD. People with PPD may often be rather reclusive and not stand out in public, as they hide their irrational concerns and beliefs. But once any kind of relationship involving intimacy is established, these characteristics inevitably emerge.

Paranoid behavior also can be present in other conditions that must be distinguished in a differential diagnosis, which can be important in making treatment decisions. People with paranoid schizophrenia may behave in a similar fashion, but their thinking is fundamentally disordered and usually must be treated with medications. A delusional disorder is classified as a separate psychotic condition that generally may be confined to a specific concern that is intractable but not necessarily bizarre or psychotic, such as infidelity of a partner, that one is being followed, or that one has been singled out for persecution. There are also central nervous system diseases or organic delusions, typically in the elderly, that are related to cognitive decline or dementias. These can be quite unsettling, such as a loved one suddenly not recognizing one's spouse, who is perceived as a stranger.

In addition, other personality disorders can have paranoid features. Individuals with schizotypal personality disorder are not psychotic but rather are odd in their behavior and thinking. They can entertain unwarranted suspicions, but these are secondary features of their more general eccentricities. Individuals with schizoid personality disorder are aloof, cold, and withdrawn; however, these characteristics are not out of a self-protective need or out of suspicion of others, but simply out of a preference for being alone. Stress in borderline personalities, often stemming from tumultuous relationship issues, can produce very paranoid, suspicious, and counterattacking behavior, as can personal slights to individuals who suffer from narcissistic personality disorder; they can be ruthlessly vindictive when their omnipotence is challenged. Individuals with avoidant personality disorder may fear others, but this is because of their concern about rejection for their perceived inadequacies rather than unwarranted malice on the part of others.

An alternative approach to distinguishing or differentiating PPD from other conditions is to recognize the diagnostic comorbidity of different personality disorder types. In fact, a mixed personality disorder involving a variety of different personality features is actually the most common diagnosis made by practitioners. It has been estimated that three fourths of those diagnosed with PPD have other personality disorders, particularly borderline, narcissistic, schizoid, schizotypal, and avoidant types (Widiger & Trull, 1998). Observations about such diagnostic overlap have led many to consider that PPD might better be considered as a *dimension* of functioning that cuts across human adjustment, rather than a discrete category. That view would allow paranoid thinking to represent one end of a mistrust–trust continuum that could characterize normal and abnormal functioning in relationships.

Another consideration is that PPD represents not an extreme of normal variation present in all individuals but is part of a distinct and uncommon spectrum disorder, joining schizotypal personality on the schizophrenia disease spectrum. It has also been considered that PPD could be a delusional spectrum disorder. However, in their authoritative review, Bernstein and Useda (2007) concluded that empirical findings for either possibility have been only partially supported at best and must be regarded as inconclusive.

To date, there is no universally accepted or empirically supported theory of PPD. Psychoanalytic theory would consider the primacy of the defense mechanism of projection of hostile feelings onto others, who in turn are viewed as being malevolent and harmful (Vaillant, 1994). Cognitive theorists have focused on the process in which misattribution of social cues and attentional biases produces the hypervigilance that is exhibited by social phobics (Bögels & Mansell, 2004). Beck and colleagues (1990) construe PPD as harboring deeply ingrained cognitive schemas involving a sense of inadequacy that is externalized so that others are seen as the source for these painful feelings.

Perhaps the most encompassing analysis of PPD is provided by Millon's integrated theory of personality (Millon, 1999; Millon & Davis, 1996). In Millon's view, persons with PPD are preoccupied with matters of adequacy, power, and prestige. They tend to view themselves as superior to others and are often aggrieved about perceived conspiracies and enemies that deny them due recognition. They experience a general and unjustified suspiciousness, hypersensitivity to hostility and deception, and a self-isolating and constricted emotional life. The success of others relative to the efforts of individuals with PPD is attributed not to competitors' greater ability but rather to malevolent forces preventing them from enjoying similar success. These rigid schemas are tightly maintained. Individuals with PPD select isolated experiences as data supportive of their convictions while discarding contradictory events or experiences. Their extensive tendency

to project feelings of envy, resentment, and anger maintains their view that others are harboring ill will toward them. With their considerable social isolation, there is little opportunity for challenge of their inflated self-esteem or grandiose fantasies.

Although maintenance of superiority, rather than avoidance of inadequacy, would seem emphasized by this view, Millon notes that such individuals' core representations of relationships actually derive from an early history of being mistreated, dominated, and betrayed by punishing or sadistic parent figures or primary caretakers. These internalized prototypical objects are immutable, and their influence pervasive. Their malevolent nature and untrustworthy character are projected onto all other relationships these individuals may encounter. Thus, even contradictory decent, kind, or caring behavior may elicit suspicion rather than trust.

Intrapsychically, the primary psychological defense mechanism employed with PPD is projection. Their own feelings of anger, covetousness, and envy that may stem from their own inherent weaknesses and fallibilities are externalized onto others, who are viewed as resenting them. In doing so, such an individual achieves a consistency in sustaining a sense of persecution and righteous indignation for the unfairness he or she must face. Above all, the organization of PPD is predominated by an inflexibility and rigidity that effectively prevents corrective experiences that individuals with other disorders can encounter. Whether predisposed biologically or as a result of early learning experiences, these individuals appear lacking in a capacity for empathy or tenderness, feeling states that are viewed as weaknesses or to be abhorred. Their aversion to intimacy or to reliance upon others guarantees that external influences and opportunities for social reality testing are effectively prevented. Determined to go it alone, people with PPD have learned to reject empathy and kindness, whether it is given or received. This, in turn, heightens the likelihood that others will eventually seek distance from them and act in a restrained or guarded manner in response to such treatment. When the irrational nature of such beliefs or behavior is irrefutably and humiliatingly exposed, individuals with PPD rewrite history concerning what publicly occurred, even if it involves creation of delusional beliefs to maintain their equilibrium.

Treatment of the patient with PPD must take these considerations into account or court almost immediate failure. Establishment of trust and confidence in the therapeutic relationship will come from increases in the individuals' sense of competence in managing threats to their self-esteem. This is a fundamental and critical objective that must be considered, irrespective of the particular theoretical orientation of the practitioner. Behavioral technique, for example, cannot emphasize external contingencies, as control from outside is what people with PPD most fear. Emphasis on self-efficacy and effectiveness in controlling the environment will have greater appeal. Social skills training to interpret or consider interpersonal interactions in a less threatening way can promote a less defensive or counterattacking response. This can be helpful if the patient with PPD can come to feel this will increase her or his effectiveness and sense of control. Pharmacotherapy can be beneficial to address any anxiety or depression associated with defensive failures experienced by such patients. This may be especially important if they become upset as the result of their having taken chances in treatment. Antipsychotics, of course, are the last line of defense against full-blown decompensation. Given that these medications are external agents, they may be resisted initially in treatment, and judicious timing may be required if medications are to be accepted.

An essential starting point of treatment in managing PPD recognizes that a sense of autonomy is a matter of psychological survival. No matter how arrogant, intimidating, or obnoxious their presentation may be, the practitioner must retain a sense of patience combined with firmness and a nonjudgmental authority to gain the respect of these individuals; this is a preliminary step to establishing a trusting relationship. Empathy must be carefully expressed to be perceived as both credible and sincere and not a message of pity that conveys superiority. Confrontation of delusional systems is likely to result only in greater distortion or defensive maneuvers, since they represent crucial aspects of efforts to maintain the patient's sense of self-esteem and autonomy. Though fundamental change in personality functioning may be unrealistic in most cases, the benefits of a less alienated and more productive life may still be attainable for many in the hands of a skillful therapist.

REFERENCES

American Psychiatric Association. (2000). *Diagnostic and statistical manual of mental disorders* (4th ed., text rev.). Washington, DC: Author.

Beck, A. T., Treeman, A. T., & Associates. (1990). *Cognitive therapy of personality disorder*. New York: Guilford.

Bernstein, D. P., & Useda, J. D. (2007). Paranoid personality disorder. In W. T. O'Donohue, K. A. Fowler, & S. O. Lilenfeld (Eds.), *Personality disorders: Toward the DSM-V* (pp. 41–62). Thousand Oaks, CA: Sage.

Bögels, S. M., & Mansell, W. (2004). Attention processes in the maintenance and treatment of social phobia: Hypervigilance, avoidance, and self-focused attention. *Clinical Psychology Review, 24*, 827–856.

Millon T. (1999). *Personality-guided therapy*. New York: John Wiley & Sons.

Millon, T., & Davis, R. (1996). *Disorders of personality: DSM-IV and beyond*. New York: John Wiley & Sons.

Vaillant, G. E. (1994). Ego mechanisms of defense and personality psychopathology. *Journal of Abnormal Psychology, 103*, 44–50.

Widiger, T. A., & Trull, T. J. (1998). Performance characteristics of the DSM-III-R personality disorder criteria set. In T. A. Widiger, A. J. Frances, H. A. Pincus, T. Ross, M. B. First, W. W. Davis, et al. (Eds.), *DSM-IV sourcebook I* (vol. 4, pp. 357–373). Washington, DC: American Psychiatric Association.

ROBERT G. HARPER
Baylor College of Medicine

See also: **Irrational Beliefs; Personality Disorders**

PARAPHILIAS (See Sexual Deviations)

PARASYMPATHETIC NERVOUS SYSTEM

The parasympathetic nervous system (PNS) is one of the divisions of the autonomic nervous system that controls the function of organs and glands in the body (the efferent portion), and the PNS senses changes in these visceral systems (the afferent portion); the other autonomic division is the sympathetic nervous system (SNS). The neurons that comprise the efferent PNS (also called the craniosacral system) arise from either the cranial nerves, which exit from the brain stem and spinal cord, or from the sacral portion of the spinal cord. Cranial nerve parasympathetic fibers innervate the viscera of the head, neck, chest, and upper abdomen, including the upper portions of the gastrointestinal (GI) tract. Sacral parasympathetic fibers innervate the lower GI tract and other organs of the pelvis.

The anatomy of the efferent autonomic innervation of each organ or gland includes preganglionic neurons that exit the brain or spinal cord and postganglionic neurons that directly innervate the target organ. Preganglionic and postganglionic neurons communicate at a ganglion (plural is *ganglia*) that is comprised of the cell bodies of the postganglionic neurons. In the PNS, the preganglionic fibers exiting the brain or spinal cord extend across relatively long distances in the body before reaching the ganglion. Typically, ganglia are found very near or even in the wall of the target organ or gland. Thus, the postganglionic neurons are very short because they extend only from the ganglion to the target. The neurotransmitter released by the axon terminals of the preganglionic neurons is acetylcholine. Acetylcholine acts on nicotinic cholinergic receptors, which are found on the postganglionic neurons. The neurotransmitter released by the postganglionic neuron onto the target organ or gland is acetylcholine, which activates muscarinic-type cholinergic receptors. Afferent autonomic fibers reaching the central nervous system run within the same nerves carrying efferent autonomic fibers. The visceral afferents comprise more than 50% of fibers in the parasympathetic nerves. Afferent autonomic fibers provide sensory information about the state of an organ, such as distension of the bladder, and also relay pain and other signals such as changes in hormones, local tissue metabolic state, and immune function from the periphery.

The organs and glands controlled by the efferent PNS typically receive input from both divisions of the autonomic nervous system (i.e., dual innervation), and in such organs, the activity in the two divisions often produces opposite effects on the organ. For example, heart rate is controlled by both autonomic divisions. Increased activity in the PNS or decreased activity in the SNS decreases heart rate, and decreased activity in the PNS or increased activity in the SNS increases heart rate. Thus, each of the two divisions is capable of bidirectionally influencing the heart rate.

When the body is at rest, many of the organs are conserving or actively storing metabolic resources for later use, a process known as anabolism. Often during such states, activity in the parasympathetic system is high, relative to periods when the organism is mobile, challenged, and/or under stress. For example, during rest or relatively low levels of bodily activity, digestion of food is a priority. Increased parasympathetic activation enhances digestion by producing increased motility and blood flow and through secretion of digestive fluids such as acid and enzymes into the GI tract. When an organism requires metabolic energy to maintain activity above resting levels (e.g., in response to a stressor or with physical exertion), activity in the parasympathetic system tends to decrease at the same time that activity in the sympathetic system tends to increase. At very high levels of metabolic need, parasympathetic activation of some organs may cease altogether. In general, humans operate somewhere between the two extremes of inactivity and high energy mobilization during which parasympathetic effects on the organs and glands will be intermediate and tuned to the specific needs of each organ system.

In addition to the tendency for the two autonomic branches to operate in a reciprocal fashion under extremes of activity or inactivity, the two divisions can operate nonreciprocally and independently. Thus, although a common pattern of autonomic control consists of the reciprocal activation of one autonomic division accompanied by a decrease in activity in the other division, this is not the only pattern of response that can occur. The two divisions can have uncoupled effects on a target organ, with increased or decreased activity in one division and the absence of any change in the other. Alternatively, the two branches can exert coactivational effects with simultaneous increases or decreases in activity in both divisions. Thus, one cannot measure function in one division and, on that basis alone, infer the activation level in the other.

Human studies utilizing noninvasive estimates of parasympathetic function have become commonplace. These include several metrics reflecting variations in heart rate that occur at the respiratory frequency, called respiratory sinus arrhythmia (RSA) or high-frequency heart rate variability. These estimates of vagal activity at the heart, along with respiratory parameters, can reveal important alterations in cardiorespiratory function. Altered RSA in individuals has been linked to physical as well as mental health problems and poor emotion regulation capabilities. Considerable psychological and physiological theory has been and continues to be generated concerning how RSA and other metrics reflecting cardiac vagal activity may be related to poor physical (e.g., cardiovascular disease, diabetes) and mental (e.g., depression) health.

Recent advances have also been made in understanding the integration of afferent and efferent parasympathetic and sympathetic activity within the central nervous system. Functional magnetic resonance imaging (fMRI) studies in humans have implicated the dorsal anterior cingulate cortex and the amygdala in integrated central control over autonomic effector responses to behaviorally relevant events. Right insular and orbitofrontal cortices, in addition to the amygdala, are involved in central integration of afferent autonomic activity in behavioral contexts. Models of the integration of the central nervous system with autonomic and other peripheral neural functions will provide new insights into the important role of the autonomic nervous system in human functioning within behavioral contexts.

SUGGESTED READINGS

Berntson, G. G., Cacioppo, J. T., & Grossman, P. (2007). Whither vagal tone. *Biological Psychology, 74*, 295–300.

Berntson, G. G., Cacioppo, J. T., & Quigley, K. S. (1991). Autonomic determinism: The modes of autonomic control, the doctrine of autonomic space, and the laws of autonomic constraint. *Psychological Review, 98*, 459–487.

Brading, A. (1999). *The autonomic nervous system and its effectors.* Oxford: Blackwell Science.

Chambers, A. S., & Allen, J. J. B. (2007). Introduction to special issue on cardiac vagal control, emotion, psychopathology, and health. *Biological Psychology, 74*, 113–115.

Critchley, H. D. (2005). Neural mechanisms of autonomic, affective, and cognitive integration. *Journal of Comparative Neurology, 493*, 154–166.

Loewy, A. D., & Spyer, K. M. (1990). *Central regulation of autonomic function.* New York: Oxford.

KAREN S. QUIGLEY
Department of Veterans Affairs New Jersey Healthcare System, East Orange, NJ, and New Jersey Medical School, University of Medicine and Dentistry of New Jersey

See also: Central Nervous System; Sympathetic Nervous System

PARENT MANAGEMENT TRAINING

Parent management training (PMT) employs a therapist as a consultant who works directly with a parent (mediator) to alleviate the problem behavior of a child (target). The basic PMT format consists primarily of instruction by the therapist in parenting techniques, structured modeling, role plays and practice sessions, and homework assignments for the parent to practice skills with the child (see McMahon & Forehand, 2003; Patterson & Forgatch, 2005). This format is based on the assumption that the interactions between parent and child contribute to the development and/or maintenance of child problem behaviors; PMT targets problematic parenting strategies and replaces them with a repertoire of skills that effectively manage, and eventually improve, the child's behavior, as well as improve broader parent–child interactional patterns.

Although PMT has been applied to a wide range of child problems such as pervasive developmental disorders, attention deficit/hyperactivity disorder (ADHD), and enuresis, it has been utilized as a therapeutic intervention primarily for disruptive or acting-out behavior (e.g., aggression, noncompliance, destructiveness) of children. This type of behavior is one of the most frequent causes of referrals for child mental health treatment. Disruptive, aggressive, or delinquent behavior of children and adolescents is a significant problem for society, not only as a direct result of the difficulties caused by such behaviors themselves but also because such behavioral patterns often persist, or worsen, into adulthood, when their consequences are much greater.

Because the emotional and financial costs associated with disruptive behaviors can be so significant for families and society, clinical researchers have devoted substantial energy to understanding the causes of this behavior and determining ways of treating and preventing it in youth. Countless studies have shown that the family is one of the most consistent areas of a child's life in contributing to both the development and the treatment of disruptive behavior. Positive parenting practices, such as a supportive parent–child relationship, authoritative discipline methods, and close supervision, are major protective factors against the development of disruptive behavior. In contrast, negative or coercive parenting practices, such as harsh punishment, guilt induction, and critical comments to the child, contribute to the development of child and adolescent problem behavior. As such, PMT, which promotes positive parenting and reduces negative parenting, has become the intervention of choice for treating and preventing disruptive behavior problems of children and adolescents. Empirical studies, meta-analyses, reviews, and task force conclusions all provide substantial support for PMT as one of the most effective therapeutic interventions for the disruptive or acting-out behavior of children.

Several variations of PMT have been developed and empirically evaluated, and although each has a slightly different emphasis or format, all PMT programs share several common or core elements, including (1) focusing more on parents than the child; (2) teaching parents to identify, define, and record child behavior; (3) instructing parents in social learning principles (e.g., reinforcement of prosocial behavior, withdrawal of attention for misbehavior through the use of ignoring or time-out); (4) teaching new parenting skills via didactic instruction, modeling, role playing, and practicing with the child in the clinic and at home; (5) discussing ways to maximize generalization of skills from the clinic to the home; and when necessary (6) addressing contextual issues affecting parents (e.g., depressive symptoms), the family (e.g., marital conflict), and the community (e.g., neighborhood violence) that may interfere with the acquisition or maintenance of new parenting skills and the promotion of adaptive child behavior.

The development of PMT as an empirically validated practice has occurred in three distinct stages: establishment, generalization, and enhancement. The first stage (from 1960 to 1975) involved the establishment of the parent training format and tests of its efficacy as a treatment for child problem behaviors. Early studies, which included a large number of descriptive studies and single-case designs, found support for the short-term efficacy of the parent training model in reducing disruptive child behaviors and improving parenting practices.

The second stage of research was conducted between approximately 1975 and 1985 and focused on the long-term effects and generalization of PMT. Such generalization has been shown to occur in at least four areas: setting (transfer of behavior changes from the clinic to home or school), temporal (maintenance for behavior change over time), sibling (application of new parenting skills with nontargeted children), and behavioral (concomitant improvements in nontargeted behaviors).

The third stage of PMT research, which began in 1986 and continues today, examines ways to expand and enhance the PMT curriculum. This line of research has considered a wide range of factors that can impact the implementation and outcome of parent training. For example, the role of developmental variables (e.g., the child's age) has been emphasized in developing and tailoring PMT interventions. PMT has been found to be more effective with younger than older children, and their families are less likely to drop out of treatment. With older children, particularly adolescents, PMT interventions may not only be less effective but also be more difficult to implement.

As another example of the findings from this stage of PMT research, several researchers have considered the contextual factors that can affect PMT, thus broadening the perspectives for treating child disruptive behavior. For example, in addition to the traditional teaching of parenting skills, the PMT paradigm may be modified to include multiple areas of family functioning as targets for intervention (e.g., parental depressive symptoms and/or marital adjustment). More recently, interventions have been designed to involve and coordinate multiple levels of the child's environment, including the home, school, clinic, and community (The Conduct Problems Prevention Research Group, 2002).

Finally, emphasis has shifted toward the public dissemination and real-world sustainability of PMT interventions (Sanders, Turner, & Markie-Dadds, 2002; Schoenwald & Hoagwood, 2001). This shift has highlighted that the development and evaluation of PMT, like many evidence-based practices, has paid little attention to cultural and economic diversity among clients (Forehand & Kotchick, 1996). PMT, and the conceptual models of parenting on which it is based, were developed with mostly middle-class families of European-American descent. Because culture has such an important influence on parenting, it seems logical, if not essential, that cultural factors be considered when designing and implementing parenting interventions. Empirical investigation into the development and efficacy of culturally relevant PMT interventions is sorely needed. Until such data are available, clinicians employing PMT are encouraged to assess and address the influence of cultural norms and socioeconomic context on parenting with their clients so that the intervention may be maximally sensitive and effective.

REFERENCES

Forehand, R., & Kotchick, B. A. (1996). Cultural diversity: A wake-up call for parent training. *Behavior Therapy, 27,* 187–206.

McMahon, R. R., & Forehand, R. L. (2003). *Helping the noncompliant child* (2nd ed.). New York: Guilford.

Patterson, G. R., & Forgatch, M. S. (2005). *Parents and adolescents living together: Part 1: The basics.* Champaign, IL: Research Press.

Sanders, M. R., Turner, K. M. T., & Markie-Dadds, C. (2002). The development and dissemination of the triple P—positive parenting program: A multilevel, evidence-based system of parenting and family support. *Prevention Science, 3,* 173–189.

Schoenwald, S. K., & Hoagwood, K. (2001). Effectiveness, transportability, and dissemination of interventions: What matters when? *Psychiatric Services, 52,* 1190–1197.

The Conduct Problems Prevention Research Group. (2002). The implementation of the fast track program: An example of a large-scale prevention science efficacy trial. *Journal of Abnormal Child Psychology, 30,* 1–17.

SUGGESTED READINGS

Forehand, R., & Long, N. (2002). *Parenting the strong-willed child.* Chicago: Contemporary Books.

Kazdin, A. (2005). *Treatment for oppositional, aggressive, and antisocial behavior in children and adolescents.* New York: Oxford University Press.

McMahon, R. J., Wells, K. C., & Kotler, J. S. (2006). Conduct problems. In E. J. Mash & R. A. Barkley (Eds.), *Treatment of childhood disorders* (pp. 137–268). New York: Guilford.

REX FOREHAND
University of Vermont

BETH A. KOTCHICK
Loyola College in Maryland

ANNE SHAFFER
University of Minnesota

LAURA GALE MCKEE
University of Vermont

See also: Parental Approaches

PARENTAL ALIENATION SYNDROME

Richard Gardner (1985) first defined parental alienation syndrome (PAS) as a conscious effort on the part of one parent to purposely disrupt and destroy his or her child's relationship with the other biological parent. This process is related to divorce, and Gardner suggested that it was an effort on the part of one parent (according to Gardner, the biological mother in the vast majority of cases) to denigrate the other parent in a way that the child would no longer wish to maintain a relationship with the denigrated parent.

Gardner defined eight characteristics as the identifying features of PAS. As Gardner defined them, the first of these features was negative statements made by the child about the denigrated parent, statements that would be said in front of anyone. Gardner suggested that these negative statements indicated that the child was repeating things the other parent had said and thus was internalizing these negative feelings.

A second PAS characteristic identified by Gardner was the child's giving weak rationalizations in justifying the negative statements concerning the denigrated parent. A related third characteristic was an inability to identify any positive traits or experiences related to the denigrated parent, and even a lack of ambivalent feelings toward this parent. A fourth feature was the contention by one parent that the decision to reject the other parent was the child's decision, regardless of the child's age or developmental level.

A fifth PAS characteristic proposed by Gardner was automatic support for the parent who is loved. This support would be so strong that the loved parent could do no wrong in the eyes of the child. Correspondingly, the sixth feature was an absence of guilt regarding the denigrated parent, suggesting that the child viewed the alienated parent as doing no good and consequently had no reason to feel guilty or bad about refusing or not wanting to spend time with the alienated parent.

The seventh of Gardner's features was the attribute of seeming to mimic phrases of the loved parent. In other words, the child used language that was atypical for someone his or her age. The last and eighth characteristic in Gardner's definition of PAS was negative feelings associated with the denigrated parent's extended family. Because of the spread of negative feelings to other members of that family, the child would have little or no interest in maintaining a relationship with anyone associated with the denigrated parent.

When Gardner initially developed his notion of PAS, there appeared to be some positive response to the concept within the field of psychology. Cartwright (1993) discussed the concept as though it had readily been accepted within psychology, even though the majority of the citations in Cartwright's article related to Gardner's own work. Cartwright further suggested that the judicial system needed to take quick and forceful judgment against alienating parents and that, without this type of judgment, children would be at risk for developing severe psychological disorders. At the same time, however, he stated that there was a lack of empirical evidence that such disorders would occur and that there was no longitudinal research available on PAS. Even while acknowledging this lack of empirical evidence or research, however, Cartwright asserted that the problem of PAS was much more serious than had been previously recognized.

A more recent article that Cartwright coauthored (Vassiliou & Cartwright, 2001) purports to discuss PAS from the alienated parent's viewpoint. It is important to note that the publications cited in this article date from almost 10 years prior to the previous Cartwright (1993) article. No empirical evidence is cited that acknowledges the existence of PAS or speaks to its effects on children. In this article, Vassiliou and Cartwright claim to be studying the effects of PAS on parents, but they acknowledge that all of their only six participants were self-identified as victims of PAS. In other words, no outside criteria are offered as to the existence of the syndrome, other than the belief of the participants in it.

One other researcher who appears to find some credence in PAS is Richard Warshak (2002). Warshak acknowledges the controversial nature of the PAS concept by discussing some of the criticisms related to such issues as its validity and reliability, as well as problems related to expert testimony that is given in courts of law. While acknowledging that PAS has not been openly accepted within psychology, some testifying experts still argue that PAS exists. Once again, no empirical research or data are offered; instead, the arguments in the courtroom tend to be mostly theoretical and based on reports by a small number of individuals who believe the syndrome is valid.

Warshak (2002) contends that PAS exists and that the controversy regarding it is related to the misdiagnosis of PAS, when in fact in certain cases alienation is due to some other cause. One of the important issues raised by Warshak is that PAS is often used as a legal means or weapon in divorce cases, in an effort to gain sole custody of children. Warshak also recognizes that there are reasons for alienation that may have to do with the alienated parent. Thus there may be instances when there are legitimate reasons why a child does not want to spend time with a parent and when this preference is not related to any purposeful denigration on the part of the other parent.

The lack of any empirical evidence has not kept some within the legal community from embracing PAS. Turkat (2002), while acknowledging that there is no empirical research verifying the existence of PAS, uses the writings and work of Gardner, whom he says has "a wealth of experience" (p. 45), to justify the inclusion of more than one chapter on PAS in a text written for the legal community. What appears to have occurred, at least to some extent, is an accepted belief in much of the legal community in a psychological syndrome for which there is no empirical research suggesting that it exists.

Kelly and Johnston (2001) also recognize that alienation may occur in some divorce cases, but they express doubt that a true parental alienation syndrome exists. They argue that there are many valid reasons why a child may refuse or resist contact with a parent, and that to assume that this is almost always due to the other parent purposely denigrating the alienated parent is unwarranted. Instead, Kelly and Johnston suggest a different perspective on alienation, one that focuses on the child instead of the parents. In their view, alienation should be seen as a break in attachment between one parent and the child. When this occurs, the key is to examine the factors that led to this change in attachment.

Rueda (2004), in an attempt to demonstrate reliability of the assessment of PAS, encountered a high level of apathy from therapists, who were often unwilling to be involved in research on this controversial issue. The major flaw in Rueda's research is the acceptance of a concept with no empirical evidence. Rueda's research was based almost completely on Gardner's work, including the use of an assessment tool developed by Gardner that does not meet minimal standards of validity or reliability.

Faller (1998) has not been able to find any scientific foundation to support either the validity or reliability of PAS. Yet Gardner's unsubstantiated theory has been used in many custody disputes, often when children express a desire not to see their father. Faller suggests that this theory's use within the legal system has had serious negative consequences for many children whose custody has been changed on the basis of an invalid theory. Dallam (1999), another critic of Gardner's theory, points out that PAS is not validated by any empirical studies, that Gardner's work was often self-published and not subject to peer review, and that Gardner's theory is grounded in gender bias, since the theory claims that 90% of alienators are mothers. On the other hand, although Gardner claimed that 10% of cases involved alienation by men, Wood (1994) was unable to find a single reported case in which PAS testimony was introduced on behalf of the mother.

Despite there being no empirical evidence that PAS exists, it continues to affect countless numbers of lives through the legal process. King and Kaganas (1998) offer a coherent argument that recommends changes in the legal system regarding what can be considered expert testimony. In particular, King expresses reservations about expert witnesses predicting the future. Although divorce cases often lead to contentious relationships between ex-spouses, it is impossible to predict that this contention will lead to future difficulties in parental-child relationships, even though some expert witnesses make this claim. Most disturbing is the fact that some psychologists and lawyers continue to write about PAS as though it were real. PAS appears to have become a legal means for men to gain custody of children. While there is some indication that the judicial system is beginning to disallow PAS as evidence or testimony, the field of psychology could assist through greater efforts to discount what appears to be pseudoscience (at best) disguised as science.

REFERENCES

Cartwright, G. F. (1993). Expanding the parameters of Parental Alienation Syndrome. *The American Journal of Family Therapy*, *21*, 205–215.

Dallam, S. (1999). The Parental Alienation Syndrome: Is it scientific? In E. T. Charles & L. Crook (Eds.), *Exposé: The failure of family courts to protect children from abuse in custody disputes* (pp. 67–93). Los Gatos, CA: Our Children Our Future Charitable Foundation.

Faller, K. C. (1998). The Parental Alienation Syndrome: "What is it and what data support it?": Reply. *Child Maltreatment: Journal of the American Professional Society on the Abuse of Children*, *3*, 312–313.

Gardner, R. (1985). Recent trends in divorce and custody litigation. *Academy Forum*, *29*, 3–7.

Gardner, R. (1999). Guidelines of assessing parental preference in child-custody disputes. *Journal of Divorce and Remarriage*, *30*, 1–9.

Kelly, J. B., & Johnston, J. R. (2001). The alienated child: A reformulation of parental syndrome. *Family Court Review*, *39*, 249–266.

King, M., & Kaganas, F. (1998). The risks and dangers of experts in court. *Current Legal Issues*, *1*: 221–242.

Rueda, C. A. (2004). An inter-rater reliability study of Parental Alienation Syndrome. *American Journal of Family Therapy*, *32*(5), 391–403.

Turkat, I. R. (2002). *Child visitation interference in family law litigation*. Future 1st Global.

Vassiliou, D., & Cartwright, G. F. (2001). The lost parents' perspective on Parental Alienation Syndrome. *The American Journal of Family Therapy*, *29*, 181–191.

Warshak, R. (2002). Misdiagnosis of Parental Alienation Syndrome. *American Journal of Forensic Psychology*, *20*, 31–52.

Wood, C. L. (1994). The Parental Alienation Syndrome: A dangerous aura of reliability. *Loyola of Los Angeles Law Review*, *27*, 1367–1415.

BETH A. VENZKE
Concordia University-Chicago

PARENTAL APPROACHES

Parents have a legal and moral duty to rear their children. This includes providing for their sustenance and well-being, as well as their social, ethical, and personal development. In order to fulfill this responsibility, parents have to find ways to convey their principles, expectations, and regulations. Therefore, parents should aspire to raise confident and satisfied children who ultimately develop into adults who can function independently and contribute to the welfare of society.

Historically, in patriarchic societies, children were considered property of the father. Fathers had the supreme right to command blind obedience. In addition, religious doctrine mandated parents to make their children God-fearing subjects by requiring them to submit to religious commandments "to honor thy mother and father." Agrarian societies in the past needed children to provide the labor to tend to the farm. Thus, up until this past century, the majority perspective of the social culture advocated an authoritarian approach to parenting as the optimal method for transferring the philosophy and practices of the parents to the children.

The popularization of Freud's writings in the twentieth century drew consideration to the value of children's instinctive needs. Autocratic child-rearing practices were seen as contributing to the anxiety of children by forcing them to fit into the mold of the sexually repressed Victorian culture. Instead, psychoanalytic writers promoted a philosophy of parental permissiveness as the optimal method to help children more fully develop their relationship with their instinctual needs by privileging the wisdom of the unconscious. Thus, parents were encouraged to indulge children's psychosexual development by practicing a laissez-faire, nonintrusive approach with their children.

Alfred Adler, a contemporary of Freud, advocated the inclusion of social development and responsibility as mediating principles into Freud's position of the primacy of psychosexual development. Dreikurs and Grey (1968), students of Adler, developed a democratic position of parenting that forged a middle ground of parental authority. Their both-and approach stressed that children should be encouraged to balance freedom with responsibility. The combination of teaching children both freedom and responsibility placed new challenges on parenting. Parents no longer had an either/or solution of tyranny or indulgence but needed to creatively encourage children through natural and logical consequences.

Benefits of Authoritative Parenting

Diana Baumrind's research of more than 30 years supported the benefits of a rational approach to parenting that fostered child development through an artful balance of control with responsiveness. Baumrind (1971) initially articulated three parental approaches to handling authority as *authoritative, authoritarian,* and *permissive.* Later, she added a fourth category called rejecting-neglecting, or parents who were *unengaged.*

In cluster and factor analyses, Baumrind (1989) identified *demandingness* and *responsiveness* as the two major modalities in the parenting process. Demandingness correlates with parental attributes that provide appropriate direction and control. Demanding parents can be *confrontive,* even if such a position results in open conflict. Confrontation is contrasted with coercive approaches that demand power without reason. Confrontation of the problem behavior (versus intimidating the child) can result in resolution and negotiation of conflict, which enhances the child's internal decision making, self-esteem, and communication skills. Parents who insist children embrace individually appropriate levels of responsibility, or *high maturity demands,* promote higher levels of prosocial behaviors and academic competence. Appropriate parental *monitoring* is preferable to an overly intrusive and constrictive approach, which diminishes an appropriate level of exploration and autonomy. Reinforcement, logical consequences, negotiation, and rational punishment are methods that can teach children desirable values, attitudes, and behaviors.

The preceding demanding attributes of parental authority, alone, are insufficient to raise healthy, confident, and competent children. Parents who demonstrate *responsiveness* establish a loving environment that is sensitive to and accommodative of the child's needs (Bowlby, 1969). Children who experience *affective warmth* from parents develop feelings of object permanence and feel securely *attached and bonded* to their environment. These children become attuned to parental demands and are more prone to be cooperative than children with a cold or uninvolved parent. *Reciprocity* is the extent that parents listen and respond to the needs and feelings of the child. Parents *sensitively attuned* to the child's motivational system can use reciprocity to uncover win–win solutions in the intergenerational dialogue. Responsive parents model prosocial communications to the child and produce children who authentically desire harmony with their

parents. These children learn how to negotiate and balance their needs within the context of responsibility for the good of the welfare of the environment.

Authoritative parents, who are high in both responsiveness and demandingness, remain receptive to the needs of the child for attachment and autonomy but take responsibility for firmly guiding the actions of the child. Authoritarian (autocratic) parents are high in demandingness but low in responsiveness. They set absolute standards for their children and require unquestioned obedience and submission to their authority. Permissive (indulgent) parents are high in indulgence but low in control. These parents put few demands on their children, usually accept their children's impulses, and for the most part, avoid conflict. Unengaged (neglectful-rejecting) parents are low in both authority and nurture. Out of all parental styles, they produce children with the most severe problems because their children are forced to fend for themselves or depend too much on their peer group for support (see Table 1).

Cultural Considerations

Baumrind's early research (1971) began by measuring mostly middle-class, Caucasian children who were being raised by one or both parents. Nonetheless, much of the research holds that authoritative parenting works best across cultural, racial, gender, and socioeconomic factors and family structure. Therefore, authoritative caregiving can be effective for child rearing despite the relationship between caregiver and child. However, Baumrind (1995) cautioned that the blend of demandingness and responsiveness is dependent upon the social and cultural context of the child.

Brofenbrenner (1982/1979) agreed that the optimal balance of freedom and control depends upon the level of stability of the larger society. On account of the massive change of the family's ecology, he suggested that there is a greater need for structure in the modern family. More specifically, Kohn (1977) stated that African American parents often used authoritarian methods to instill obedience in their children to help them adapt to a bicultural reality of minority status in the American culture. Parenting does not occur in isolation from the context.

Similarly, there have been different gender implications of parenting styles. The authoritarian approach emanates from a masculine manner of handling authority, whereas authoritative parenting is much more compatible

Table 1. Parental Styles

Demandingness	Responsiveness	
	High	Low
High	Authoritative	Authoritarian
Low	Permissive	Unengaged

with female development and feminine use of authority. Gilligan's (1982) research proved that girls respond much more to a consensually based approach so that they can discover their own voice.

Research on parental approaches strongly supports an authoritative approach, which blends a flexible balance of demandingness and responsiveness through the child's developmental process. This approach provides the nurture, safety, protection, respect, and limits (Pesso, 1973) that children need to optimally realize their potential as healthy, confident, and vital members of society. However, parents need to adapt their mixture of demandingness and responsiveness to the idiosyncrasies of the child, culture, and context.

REFERENCES

Baumrind, D. (1971). Current patterns of parental authority. *Developmental Psychology Monographs, 4* (1, Pt. 2).

Baumrind, D. (1989). Rearing competent children. In W. Damon (Ed.), *Child development today and tomorrow* (pp. 349–378). San Francisco: Jossey-Bass.

Baumrind, D. (1995). *Child maltreatment and optimal caregiving in social contexts.* New York: Garland.

Bowlby, J. (1969). *Attachment and loss: Vol. 1. Attachment.* New York: Basic Books.

Brofenbrenner, U. (1982/1979). *The ecology of human development.* Cambridge, MA: Harvard University Press.

Dreikurs, R., & Grey, L. (1968). *Logical consequence: A new approach to discipline.* New York: Meredith.

Gilligan, C. (1982). *In a different voice: Psychological theory and women's development.* Cambridge, MA: Harvard University Press.

Kohn, M. L. (1977). *Class and conformity: A study in values* (2nd ed.). Chicago: University of Chicago Press.

Pesso, A. (1973). *Experience in Action.* New York: New York University Press.

SUGGESTED READINGS

Dreikers, R., & Soltz, V. (1968). *Children: The challenge.* New York: Meredith.

Gottman, J. (1997). *The heart of parenting: Raising an emotionally intelligent child.* New York: Simon and Schuster.

RUSSELL HABER
University of South Carolina

See also: **Parent Management Training**

PARTICIPANT OBSERVATION

Participant observation is a qualitative research method for collecting data that depends on direct, firsthand sensory experience of human events, activities, and interactions. Researchers record and interpret what they see, hear, smell, touch, and taste in the course of watching, listening, and often, but not always, asking about what is occurring. Participant observation is often equated with sociological field research or field study and with anthropological ethnography, because methodologists in these two disciplines are most associated with the method's development and articulation. Field sociologists and sociocultural anthropologists pioneered methods of participant observation for several purposes. First, early-twentieth-century social scientists wanted to document the ways of living of non-Western societies before modernization changed them. Second, scholars in industrialized nations studied people and groups in their own nations about which little was publicly known. Some of this work focused on representing people's lives in particular times and places as they themselves experienced and understood it. Other work aimed to use the material to develop universals, abstractions, and generalizations about humans and their societies. Research also was formulated around social problems, such as how to improve the lives of the urban poor.

Participant observation differs from ordinary involvement in daily affairs by being more reflexive, systematic, and focused. Focus is the deliberate choice of what to record and may be directed by questions and topical areas; topics and questions are often developed from theoretical and conceptual interests. How researchers develop their systems or routines for participant observation likewise varies, depending on the epistemological framework guiding the research. Finally, researchers observe and record *themselves* observing and recording *others*, their research subjects or participants, so as to reflexively account for the influence of their own presence on what is happening.

Participant observation approaches vary by how much the researcher is simultaneously observing and participating. Typically, minimal participation permits maximum observation, and the more engaged researchers are with participating, the less attention they can give to observing. However, some human experiences can be represented only from an account of participation, so the minimal participation position is not always ideal.

Four participant observation roles were formulated by sociologist Buford Junker and elaborated by his colleague Raymond Gold (1958). The *complete participant* interacts as a member of a group whose other members are unaware of the research; the research is covert. The *participant-as-observer* is known to be a researcher to the members of the group studied and depends on the researcher role to prevent overidentifying with the participant position. The *observer-as-participant* is known as a researcher to those studied, but interactions with them are brief and circumscribed, such as a researcher who engages with respondents in 1-hour interviews. The *complete observer* is likewise covert but operates from a distance and has no direct contact with whoever is being studied; complete observers may eavesdrop but never ask. Gold acknowledges that researchers may slip in and out of these various roles in the course of a single investigation.

An early classic of participant observation in psychology is the social psychologist John Dollard's study of the socialization and maturation of African Americans in a small town in the southern United States. Framed with his psychoanalytic and sociological preparation, Dollard combined participant observation with life history interviewing to examine "the social situation as a means of patterning the affects of white and Negro people, as a mold for love, hatred, jealousy, deference, submissiveness, and fear" (1957, p. 2).

What is remarkable about Dollard's study, first published in 1937, is his candid discussion of the limitations and issues of the method of participant observation. Because the instrument of data collection is the human researcher, it is vulnerable to the limitations of that individual's biases, and Dollard discusses how his upbringing, personal proclivities, and disciplinary perspectives both informed and biased his observations and interpretations. He also points out limitations due to what an observer may be permitted to see or experience in a social setting, as well as to how participants may attempt to perform their ideal lives for researchers while hiding their realities. Dollard suggests that researchers can address both observer bias and participant manipulation with reflexivity and an acute, focused attention.

More recent criticisms by feminist and postmodernist scholars (e.g., Wolf, 1992) point out other limitations of participant observation. The events and activities accessible to observers depend on what participants are willing to share; men and women researchers, for example, may be permitted access to different cultural scenes and social situations. Equally as problematic is how the participant observer's experiences are rendered in an account of others' lives; all accounts are fabrications of some kind, and such representations limit what others can learn about participants from such accounts.

In addition to its occasional applications in social psychology, participant observation has been applied in ecological and naturalistic psychology. It has been advocated more recently by scholars interested in developing feminist, cultural, interpretive, narrative, hermeneutic, and phenomenological approaches to psychology. Among those whose participant observation research has arguably been most exemplary is Michelle Fine (1991, 1992), who has studied the experiences of marginalized youth in a variety of situations.

REFERENCES

Dollard, J. (1957). *Caste and class in a southern town* (3rd ed.). Garden City, NY: Doubleday Anchor.

Fine, M. (1991). *Framing dropouts: Notes on the politics of an urban public high school*. Albany, NY: State University of New York Press.

Fine, M. (1992). *Disruptive voices: The possibilities of feminist research*. Ann Arbor: University of Michigan Press.

Gold, R. (1958). Roles in sociological field observations. *Social Forces, 36*, 217–223.

Wolf, M. (1992). *A thrice told tale: Feminism, postmodernism, and ethnographic responsibility*. Stanford, CA: Stanford University Press.

SUGGESTED READINGS

DeWalt, K. M., & DeWalt, B. R. (2002). *Participant observation: A guide for fieldworkers*. Walnut Creek, CA: Altamira.

Emerson, R. M., Fretz, R. I, & Shaw, L. L. (1995). *Writing ethnographic fieldnotes*. Chicago: University of Chicago Press.

Spradley, J. P. (1980). *Participant observation*. New York: Holt, Rinehart & Winston.

JUDITH PREISSLE
University of Georgia

See also: **Qualitative Research Methods**

PARTNER ABUSE

Partner abuse is variously referred to as domestic violence, battering, wife beating, spouse abuse, spousal assault, partner aggression, and intimate partner violence. Partner abuse is a very broad term, most typically referring to three distinct types of abusive behaviors that occur within the context of an intimate relationship: physical, psychological, and sexual. Physical abuse includes behaviors ranging in severity from those that are unlikely to result in injury, such as pushing and grabbing, to those that can be life-threatening, such as choking, kicking, beating, and using a weapon against a partner. The definition of psychological abuse is broad, encompassing behaviors that range from insulting or swearing at a partner, to threatening a partner, to engaging in jealous behaviors, to isolating a partner from friends and family. Sexual abuse refers to any undesired sexual contact that is psychologically or physically coerced and includes behaviors such as insisting a partner have sexual intercourse without a condom and using physical force or threat of force to obtain oral, anal, or vaginal intercourse. Because of the greater research emphasis on physical abuse than on psychological and sexual abuse, physical partner abuse is our focus here.

Physical partner abuse can occur in any type of intimate relationship, including marital relationships, dating relationships, heterosexual relationships, and gay or lesbian relationships. Partner abuse may also occur after an intimate relationship has ended via divorce, separation, or breakup. Partner abuse behaviors can occur in different patterns in relationships. Sometimes one partner (male or female) engages in abusive behaviors, and the other does not. In other relationships, both partners engage in abusive behaviors. In some relationships, physically abusive behaviors occur infrequently when arguments or disagreements get heated and rarely result in severe assaults, serious injuries, or one partner feeling very afraid of the other. This pattern has been called "common couple violence," because it seems to be the most widespread form of partner abuse. Common couple violence can be contrasted to a pattern of partner abuse behaviors that escalates in severity and frequency over time. This type of partner abuse is often called battering or wife beating, and the abusive behaviors are used by one partner to control, intimidate, and instill fear in the other partner.

Prevalence

Partner abuse is one of the most common forms of violence in our society. The 1975 and 1985 National Family Violence Surveys (Straus & Gelles, 1990) revealed that approximately 12% of married or cohabiting men and women in the United States engage in physical aggression against a partner each year. The lifetime prevalence of such aggression is approximately 28%. Further, approximately 3–5% of married or cohabiting men and women engage in severe physical aggression (e.g., choking, kicking, beating up) each year. Another epidemiological survey of intimate partner violence produced roughly similar lifetime prevalence estimates (Schafer, Caetano, & Clark, 1998), and the National Violence against Women Survey found that women were more likely to report physical and sexual victimization, and men were more likely to report having experienced only psychological victimization by a partner (Coker et al., 2002).

The prevalence of physical partner abuse is often higher in samples of adolescent and young adult heterosexual dating relationships; approximately 30–50% of adolescents and young adults report experiencing one or more acts of physical aggression in their dating relationships (O'Leary, Slep, Avery-Leaf, & Cascardi, 2008). Although the reasons for the greater likelihood of physical aggression in dating relationships is not fully understood, as discussed later in the section on risk factors, being younger is associated with a significantly greater risk for engaging in partner abuse behaviors even for men and women who are married or cohabiting. Partner abuse in gay and lesbian relationships has received less research attention, but available evidence suggests a similar prevalence of partner abuse in same-sex relationships (Renzetti, 1997).

Importantly, these prevalence estimates, and the previously described patterns of partner abuse, represent only the scope and nature of partner abuse in the United States. Partner abuse has been addressed as an international problem, and in many countries, the abuse of females is a lifelong issue that begins at conception and includes many forms of abuse other than partner aggression (e.g., female infanticide, sexual trafficking of adolescent girls, clitoridectomies of young women) (Watts & Zimmerman, 2002).

Risk Factors

A variety of characteristics have been associated with increased risk of physical aggression in relationships (Schumacher, Feldbau-Kohn, Slep, & Heyman, 2001). Before we list these risk factors for partner abuse, it is important to note that although these characteristics are associated with increased risk for partner abuse, they may or may not be causes of partner abuse. Although the majority of research on risk factors for partner abuse has focused on male-perpetrated abuse in heterosexual relationships, many of the risk factors for male aggression and female aggression are similar. Much less is known about the factors associated with partner aggression in same-sex relationships.

Although partner abuse can occur in the relationships of individuals of any age or socioeconomic group, certain demographic characteristics have been associated with increased risk for perpetration of partner abuse. Being younger, having less education, having lower income, and having lower occupational attainment are all associated with increased risk for partner abuse. Having certain life experiences is also associated with increased risk for engaging in partner abuse. Experiencing childhood sexual or physical abuse or in childhood witnessing parents engage in partner abuse is associated with increased risk for partner violence in adulthood.

A variety of psychological factors also appear to be associated with increased risk for partner abuse. Those who engage in partner-abusing behaviors may be more likely to have heavy or problem drinking, drug problems, anger, hostility, depression, stress, low self-esteem, assertiveness deficits, personality disorders, and other types of psychological disorders than those who do not engage in partner abuse. There are also relationship characteristics that have been associated with increased risk for partner physical abuse, such as negative communication styles, unhappiness or dissatisfaction with the relationship, and verbal or psychological aggression.

Consequences

The physical and psychological consequences of partner abuse are many and varied (Coker et al., 2002). Men and women who report having been victims of physical partner abuse are more likely to report poor health, symptoms of depression, substance use, injuries, a chronic health condition, and a chronic mental illness. Importantly, and perhaps surprisingly, psychological abuse is even more strongly associated with most of these types of negative consequences than physical abuse. Although women engage in physically aggressive behaviors against a partner at approximately the same rate as men, they are significantly more likely to sustain physical injuries as a result of such abuse. The impact of partner abuse extends beyond those who experience it directly. As a result of partner abuse, society incurs substantial costs related to mental health care, physical health care, criminal justice interventions, child welfare, social services, and lost work productivity.

Interventions

A variety of psychological interventions, particularly psychoeducational and therapy groups for men (and occasionally women) who abuse their partners, are currently utilized (Babcock, Green, & Robie, 2004). Many of these treatment programs serve individuals who have been arrested for partner abuse or have otherwise been identified by the criminal justice system as a perpetrator of partner abuse. The most widely available form of treatment is a group treatment developed by the Duluth Domestic Abuse Project in Minnesota, which is often referred to as Duluth Model treatment. This intervention is designed to help individuals, particularly men, who have engaged in partner abuse to challenge beliefs about their right to exert power and control over their partner and instead to strive for egalitarian, nonviolent relationships.

Another type of intervention for partner abuse, which is gaining popularity, is cognitive behavior therapy or CBT. This intervention is designed to help individuals who have engaged in partner violence identify the pros and cons of changing their behaviors; learn new skills such as communication, assertiveness, and social skills, which individuals who engage in partner abuse often lack; learn strategies to manage anger and relax; and challenge thoughts that encourage violent behavior. Although they are not widely available, for women and men in less severely abusive relationships or in relationships in which both the male and female engage in physically aggressive behaviors, couple or marital therapy-based interventions designed specifically to reduce psychological and physical aggression can be useful (O'Leary, Heyman, & Neidig, 1999). In addition to psychological interventions for perpetrators, various legal interventions, including arrest, prosecution, and restraining orders, are also used to manage this problem. For severely abused women, support groups for women are commonly used, along with legal advocates, shelters, social service agencies, and individual therapeutic interventions.

REFERENCES

Babcock, J. C., Green, C. E., & Robie, C. (2004). Does batterer's treatment work? A meta-analytic review of domestic violence treatment. *Clinical Psychology Review, 23*, 1023–1053.

Coker, A. L., Davis, K. E., Arias, I., Desai, S., Sanderson, M., Brandt, H. M., et al. (2002). Physical and mental health effects of intimate partner violence for men and women. *American Journal of Preventive Medicine, 23*, 260–268.

O'Leary, K. D., Heyman, R. E., & Neidig, P. (1999). Treatment of wife abuse: A comparison of gender-specific approaches. *Behavior Therapy, 30*, 475–505.

O'Leary, K. D., Slep, A. M. S., Avery-Leaf, S., & Cascardi, M. (2008). Gender differences in dating aggression among multiethnic high school students. *Journal of Adolescent Health, 42*, 473–479.

Renzetti, C. M. (1997). Violence and abuse among same-sex couples. In A. P. Cardarelli (Ed.), *Violence between intimate partners: Patterns, causes, and effects* (pp. 70–89). Boston: Allyn & Bacon.

Schafer, J., Caetano, R., & Clark, C. L. (1998). Rates of partner violence in the United States. *American Journal of Public Health, 88*(11), 1702–1704.

Schumacher, J. A., Feldbau-Kohn, S., Slep, A. M. S., & Heyman, R. E. (2001). Risk factors for male-to-female partner physical abuse. *Aggression and Violent Behavior, 6*, 281–352.

Straus, M. A., & Gelles, R. J. (1990). *Physical violence in American families*. New Brunswick, NJ: Transaction.

Watts, C., & Zimmerman, C. (2002). Violence against women: Global scope and magnitude. *Lancet, 359*, 1232–1237.

SUGGESTED READINGS

Johnson, M. P., & Ferraro, K. J. (2000). Research on domestic violence in the 1990s: Making distinctions. *Journal of Marriage and the Family, 62*, 948–963.

Lewis, S. F., & Fremouw, W. (2001). Dating violence: A critical review of the literature. *Clinical Psychology Review, 21*, 105–127.

Stith, S. M., Smith, D. B., Penn, C. E., Ward, D. B., & Tritt, D. (2004). Intimate partner physical abuse perpetration and victimization risk factors: A meta-analytic review. *Aggression and Violent Behavior, 10*, 65–98.

JULIE A. SCHUMACHER
University of Mississippi Medical Center

K. DANIEL O'LEARY
Stony Brook University

PASSIVE-AGGRESSIVE PERSONALITY DISORDER

The concept of Passive-Aggressive Personality Disorder (PAPD) is less controversial than its validity. The disorder used to be known as Negativistic Personality Disorder

(NEGPD) and has undergone several changes in terms of its classification, criteria, and appearance within empirical studies. Its original appearance in the *Diagnostic and Statistical Manual for Mental Disorders* was in 1952 (*DSM-I*; American Psychiatric Association [APA]). Criteria for this disorder centered on dispositional qualities of individuals who would passively resist demands related to everyday routines (Rotenstein et al., 2007). Subsequent versions of the *DSM* would lead to revised criteria by which PAPD was identified within clinical fields. Clinicians responsible for these revisions often related their rationale for doing so because of clients' tendencies to show pervasive oppositional thoughts, feelings, and behaviors that also manifested themselves within interpersonal relationships (Ritzler & Gerevitz-Stern, 2007).

Although PAPD was listed in Appendix B of the *DSM-IV*, it is not officially recognized as a personality disorder within mental health fields (Widiger, 2003). However, many clinicians and researchers believe that passive-aggressive traits are not well represented within more formally recognized personality disorders and continue to study passive-aggressive individuals in order to more adequately understand its features and origins (Rotenstein et al., 2007).

Currently, there are seven criteria associated with PAPD. The *DSM-IV* (APA, 1994) states that a client with Passive Aggressive Personality Disorder (1) passively resists fulfilling routine social and occupational tasks, (2) complains of being misunderstood and unappreciated by others, (3) is sullen and argumentative, (4) unreasonably criticizes and scorns authority, (5) expresses envy and resentment toward those apparently more fortunate, (6) voices exaggerated and persistent complaints of personal misfortune, and (7) alternates between hostile defiance and contrition. Individuals who meet at least four of these criteria can be diagnosed with the disorder.

The *DSM-IV-TR* (APA, 2000) also states that individuals with PAPD display overt ambivalence, engage in intense conflicts between the desire to be self-assertive and the desire to be dependent on others, show a superficial layer of bravado to mask poor levels of self-confidence, and foresee the worst-case scenario in virtually all situations. There are also tendencies for the passive-aggressive individual to procrastinate when it comes to completing tasks, deliberately display inefficiency when work-related demands are made, and deliberately become forgetful when specific requests are made. These characteristics can at times be viewed as signs of major depression or occur simultaneously with periods of dysthymia. The notion of PAPD is often hard for some professionals to diagnose because the criteria for this disorder have changed so much since its original appearance in the *DSM*. For this primary reason, assessing the presence of PAPD is often scientifically difficult (Bradley, Shedler, & Westen, 2006).

In terms of assessing PAPD, several instruments have scales that measure passive-aggressive characteristics.

The Millon Clinical Multiaxial Inventory (MCMI; Millon, 1994) has a passive-aggressive scale that has some scientific validity, and research studies have indicated that clients identified as alcoholic tend to score significantly higher on this particular scale than counterparts (Fernandez-Mantalvo, Landa, Lopez-Goni, Loria, & Zuela, 2002). Although the MCMI cannot specifically assess PAPD, its passive-aggressive scale appears able to detect significant levels of psychopathology (Ritzler & Gerevitz-Stern, 2007).

The Minnesota Multiphasic Personality Inventory (Morey, Waugh, & Blashfield, 1985) also has a passive-aggressive scale that was initially based on *DSM-III* criteria for PAPD. However, research has not been able to establish sound measures of this scale's validity (Ritzler & Gerevitz-Stern, 2007). It is for this reason that projective measures and structured interviews are also used to assess possible PAPD.

Research on projective tests like the Thematic Apperception Test (TAT) and the Rorschach suggest that passive-aggressive themes often exist when diagnosed clients revealed their stories during the course of these examinations (Ritzler & Gerevitz-Stern, 2007). It should be noted that none of these instruments has specifically been used to make clinical diagnoses of PAPD, but the uncovering of passive-aggressive themes from a significant sample of test takers has suggested that these projective measures appear to be useful in further studying the disorder.

The treatment of PAPD is equally as diverse as its criteria. Because of the impact that a client with PAPD features often has on family and social systems, integrative family-system treatment is considered to be one of the more effective approaches (Carlson, Melton, & Snow, 2004). The multifaceted nature of family-system treatment draws from several different theories, including psychodynamic, cognitive-behavioral, and Adlerian. Although it is largely up to the therapist or counselor to determine the best theoretical approach, it is important to recognize that acting-out issues and transference behaviors are likely to occur (Carlson et al., 2004). Dialogue between family members is essential for the treatment process, because individuals with PAPD features are not able to overtly display or process their anger.

In terms of the family system, individuals who engage in therapeutic work with a client who has PAPD features can often develop assertiveness skills that allow them to better manage anxiety and conflict-based situations that may have previously gone unnoticed because of the interpersonal influence the client has had on the system (Carlson et al., 2004). The direct dialogue and feedback that is encouraged in such therapeutic practice on the part of all family members can be considered an asset to therapeutic work that has the potential to improve interpersonal and intrapersonal relationships.

It is for this reason that group therapy is sometimes considered an effective means of treating PAPD features (Long & Long, 2001). Individuals with PAPD features often lack social skills that, through training and role-playing with others in a supportive environment such as group therapy, may provide a necessary opportunity to directly call attention to their interpersonal behaviors that contribute to their passive-aggressive patterns. Group sessions are usually focused on providing direct and concrete feedback to clients as they observe and give in vivo feedback about each other's behavior. Overt dialogue can be considered the main mechanism to elicit change.

By engaging in overt dialogue, individuals are forced to confront anger-related issues that would otherwise become manifest in covert form. Calling attention to nonverbal cues also helps to provide individuals with PAPD features with important feedback about their thoughts, feelings, and behaviors, which can often be viewed in a disorganized fashion (Long & Long, 2001). Direct dialogue about verbal and nonverbal expressions of anger appears to be especially helpful for children and adolescents who present with PAPD features, primarily because of their concrete thinking style (Long & Long, 2001). It should also be noted that therapeutic intervention for PAPD clients can be enhanced via medication.

Similar to the findings of studies with clients who are depressed, medication and therapeutic treatment together appear to be the best regimen for working with clients who have PAPD features (Carlson et al., 2004). This is not to say that one treatment alone would not be able to work but rather that some combination of these two therapeutic venues may be the most effective approach in working with a client with PAPD features. Types of medication to be used will vary according to a client's age and physical condition, and clinicians and counselors are strongly advised to communicate with one another if a client is to be treated with both psychotherapeutic and medicinal approaches.

Although cultural variables may also be related to a client's expression of anger, there is not enough current research to pinpoint particular demographic samples that are likely to present with PAPD features (Rotenstein et al., 2007). Research may one day provide a clearer understanding of populations who tend to manifest PAPD symptoms, but mental health workers are strongly encouraged to assess PAPD features on a case-by-case basis.

REFERENCES

American Psychiatric Association. (1952). *Diagnostic and statistical manual of mental disorders*. Washington, DC: Author.

American Psychiatric Association. (1994). *Diagnostic and statistical manual of mental disorders* (4th ed.). Washington, DC: Author.

American Psychiatric Association. (2000). *Diagnostic and statistical manual of mental disorders* (4th ed., text rev.). Washington, DC: Author.

Bradley, R., Shedler, J., & Westen, D. (2006). Is the appendix a useful appendage? An empirical examination of depressive, passive-aggressive (negativistic), sadistic, and self-defeating personality disorders. *Journal of Personality Disorders, 20,* 524–540.

Carlson, J., Melton, K., & Snow, K. (2004). Family treatment of passive-aggressive (negativistic) personality disorder. In M. MacFarlane (Ed.), *Family treatment of personality disorders: Advances in clinical practice* (pp. 241–272). Binghamton, NY: Haworth.

Fernandez-Mantalvo, J., Lander, N., Lopez-Goni, J., Lorea, I., & Zarzuela, A. (2002). Personality disorder in alcoholics: A descriptive study. *Revista de Psicopathologia y Psicologia Clinica, 7,* 215–225.

Long, N., & Long, J. (2001). *Managing passive-aggressive behavior of children and youth at school and home: The angry smile.* Austin, TX: PRO-ED.

Millon, T. (1994). *Millon clinical multiaxial inventory manual* (3rd ed.). Minneapolis, MN: National Computer Systems.

Morey, L., Waugh, M., & Blashfield, P. (1985). MMPI scales for *DSM-III* personality disorders: Their derivation and correlates. *Journal of Personality Assessment, 49,* 245–251.

Ritzler, B., & Gerevitz-Stern, G. (2007). Rorschach assessment of passive-aggressive personality disorder. In S. Huprich (Ed.), *Rorschach assessment of the personality disorders* (pp. 345–369). Mahwah, NJ: Lawrence Erlbaum.

Rotenstein, O., McDermut, W., Bergman, A., Young, D., Zimmerman, M., & Chelminski, I. (2007). The validity of *DSM-IV* passive-aggressive (negativistic) personality disorder. *Journal of Personality Disorders, 21,* 28–41.

Widiger, T. (2003). Personality disorders and axis I psychopathology: The problematic boundary of axis I and axis II. *Journal of Personality Disorders, 17,* 90–108.

SUGGESTED READINGS

Kantor, M. (2002). *Passive-aggression: A guide for the therapist, the patient and the victim.* Westport, CT: Praeger.

O'Donohue, W., Fowler, K., & Lilienfeld, S. (2007). *Personality disorders: Toward the DSM-V.* Thousand Oaks, CA: Sage.

ADAM ZAGELBAUM
Sonoma State University

JON CARLSON
Governors State University

See also: **Personality Disorders**

PASTORAL COUNSELING

Pastoral counseling (also known as pastoral care) is the provision of psychotherapy by ordained ministers, priests, rabbis, and other religious leaders. Religious communities have turned to clergy in times of crisis for millennia, and pastoral counseling remains today a vital resource for many people dealing with significant emotional, relational, physical, and spiritual concerns.

By virtue of their role as clergy, pastoral counselors have access to people across the life span. Clergy can therefore forge long-term trusting relationships in ways that psychologists ordinarily cannot. Clergy are also an inherent part of people's support systems during critical life transitions such as birth, marriage, illness, and death, when many individuals are vulnerable to psychological problems. Thus, pastoral counseling is often a natural first choice of treatment, as clergy can respond to many individuals in crisis and transition more quickly and efficiently than psychologists and other mental health practitioners. Furthermore, because the professional integration of psychotherapy and spirituality is a relatively new endeavor among psychologists, religious individuals seeking spiritually integrated care are more likely to seek psychotherapy from clergy. For these and other reasons, people turn more often to clergy and their religious communities than to mental health providers when they are experiencing psychological problems (Norris, Kaniasty, & Scher, 1990). Although the current prevalence of pastoral counseling seeking is unknown, in one national survey, 4 of 10 Americans indicated that they had sought counseling from clergy (Veroff, Kulka, & Douvan, 1981).

People bring many common mental health concerns to pastoral counselors and clergy. Pastoral counselors therefore practice psychotherapy for many of the same problems seen by psychologists, including grief, anxiety, marital problems, depression, alcohol and drug problems, domestic violence, severe mental illness, and coping with disease and suicide. There is evidence to suggest that pastoral counseling is effective for some difficulties. In one study of people in a hospital waiting room whose loved ones were undergoing cardiac bypass surgery, those who experienced pastoral support reported more positive mental health outcomes than those who did not (VandeCreek, Pargament, Belavich, Cowell, & Friedel, 1999). Another investigation found pastoral counseling to be as effective as cognitive behavioral therapy in reducing symptoms of depression (Propst , Ostrom, Watkins, Dean, & Mashburn, 1992).

More generally, numerous research studies have underscored the value of religious coping resources that are often encouraged and facilitated by pastoral counseling (Pargament, 1997), such as spiritual support, forgiveness, benevolent religious reappraisals, and religious rituals. Pastoral counseling may also be the most obvious resource for individuals experiencing struggles with their faith, including questions and doubts about spiritual and religious issues, emotional tension in their relationship with God (e.g., anger toward God, feelings of being punished by God), and spiritually based conflicts with other people.

It is important to recognize that the work of pastoral counselors and clergy is itself stressful and requires support. Clergy are commonly called on for both ritual and counseling in life's most difficult moments, including the period before and after the death of loved ones. Pastoral counselors therefore frequently face the daunting task of providing support in the direst of times and helping to make loss, suffering, injustice, and death meaningful in the context of religious beliefs. As a result, clergy are vulnerable to burnout and posttraumatic stress disorder (Spilka, Hood, Hunsberger, & Gorsuch, 2003). Pastoral counselors are also vulnerable to the development of their own spiritual struggles, which pose psychological and physical health risks. Thus, like their mental health counterparts, clergy and pastoral counselors can benefit from psychological support.

Traditionally, religious and psychological professionals have had relatively little contact with each other. There is, however, a growing rapprochement between these two communities. Professional organizations such as the American Association of Pastoral Counselors (AAPC; http://www.aapc.org) have adopted professional standards that incorporate psychological knowledge and principles into the training and work of pastoral counselors. AAPC has further promoted relationships with national mental health organizations. For example, in 2004 the Center for Substance Abuse Treatment, Substance Abuse, and Mental Health Services Administration (commonly known as SAMHSA) funded an intensive clergy-training project in which core knowledge about helping individuals and their families affected by substance use difficulties was imparted to AAPC members. Thus, today's pastoral counselors are receiving training in psychological approaches to treatment. Additionally, psychology researchers and practitioners are becoming more sensitive to the spiritual dimension of psychological problems and solutions (Pargament, 2007), and there is already a considerable body of research on pastoral counseling. Thus, the future is likely to witness the development of stronger alliances and collaborative programs involving pastoral counselors, clergy, and psychologists.

REFERENCES

Norris, F. H., Kaniasty, K. Z., & Scher, D. A. (1990). Use of mental health services among victims of crime: Frequency, correlates, and subsequent recovery. *Journal of Consulting and Clinical Psychology, 58,* 538–547.

Pargament, K. I. (1997). *The psychology of religion and coping: Theory, research, practice.* New York: Guilford Press.

Pargament, K. I. (2007). *Spiritually integrated psychotherapy: Understanding and addressing the sacred.* New York: Guilford Press.

Propst, R. L., Ostrom, R., Watkins, P., Dean, T., & Mashburn, D. (1992). Comparative efficacy of religious and nonreligious cognitive-behavioral therapy for the treatment of clinical depression in religious individuals. *Journal of Consulting and Clinical Psychology, 60*(1), 94–103.

Spilka, B., Hood, R. W., Hunsberger, B., & Gorsuch, R. (2003). *The psychology of religion: An empirical approach* (3rd ed.). New York: Guilford Press.

VandeCreek, L., Pargament, K. I., Belavich, T., Cowell, B., & Friedel, L. (1999). The unique benefits of religious support during cardiac bypass surgery. *Journal of Pastoral Care, 53,* 19–29.

Veroff, J., Kulka, R. A., & Douvan, E. (1981). *Mental health in America: Patterns of help-seeking from 1957 to 1976.* New York: Basic Books.

SUGGESTED READINGS

Chalfant, H. P., Heller, P. L., Roberts, A., Briones, D., Aguirre-Hochbaum, S., & Farr, W. (1990). The clergy as a resource for those encountering psychological distress. *Review of Religious Research, 31*(3), 305–313.

Dittes, J. E. (1999). *Pastoral counseling: The basics.* London: Westminster John Knox Press.

Wicks, R. J., Parsons, R. D., & Capps, D. (Eds.). (2003). *Clinical handbook of pastoral counseling.* Mahwah, NJ: Paulist Press.

Kenneth I. Pargament
David H. Rosmarin
Bowling Green State University

See also: Counseling; Religion and Mental Health; Religion and Psychology

PATIENT ADHERENCE

Patient adherence is defined as the extent to which patients follow prescribed treatment regimens (Haynes et al., 2008). Adherence supports health promotion (e.g., exercise and diet), treatment of disease, symptom management, and efficient health care delivery. The term *adherence* is used rather than *compliance* because its meaning is more consistent with views of patients as active participants in health care rather than passive recipients of services. Although this article is limited to medication adherence, the issues are relevant for adherence to other prescribed regimens.

Adherence involves a complex set of behaviors. It requires that patients take a medication at the prescribed time, in the correct amount, and under indicated conditions (e.g., with meals). Because adherence failures involve errors of omission, commission, or timing, reported adherence rates need to be defined. Patients are sometimes classified as adherent even if they are less than 100% adherent, because optimal adherence depends on the specific medication, treatment goals, and individual factors, including age, disease severity, genetic variations in drug metabolism, and health-related quality of life. Pharmacogenomics will help define optimal adherence for particular medications, given individual genetic profiles (Rodon et al., 2006). Therefore, no single level of adherence is appropriate in all situations. Investigators can look at disease-specific markers to connect optimal adherence to clinical outcomes.

Measurement

Adherence measures should be unobtrusive, objective, and practical. Biological measures (e.g., blood assays) can be obtrusive, whereas microelectronic monitoring is relatively unobtrusive and objective. Although practical, self-reports of adherence and pill counts have been shown to overestimate adherence to medications and therefore may be less desirable than other measures (Guerrero, Rudd, Bryant-Kosling, & Middleton, 1993). A combination of adherence measures may be useful. For example, self-report and electronic monitoring predicted lower viral loads among individuals who were HIV positive (Llabre et al., 2006).

Extent and Consequences of Nonadherence

Estimates of nonadherence are often cited at 50% and range from 0 to more than 100% for a variety of patients, diagnoses, and treatments (Haynes et al., 2008). Nonadherence reduces health outcomes and increases health care costs (Kane & Shaya, 2008).

Theories of Nonadherence

Social-behavioral theories are used to explain nonadherence, including the health belief model (Strecher & Rosenstock, 1997), the common sense model (Leventhal, Brissette, & Leventhal, 2003), and social learning theory (Bandura, 1997). Park and colleagues (1999) integrated the common sense model with cognitive theory, proposing that nonadherence is influenced by illness representation, cognitive function, and external aids. Such multifactor models recognize that patients must understand how to adhere, accept the prescribed regimen, develop an adherence plan that integrates information for all medications, and then implement the plan.

Predictors of Nonadherence

Nonadherence occurs for many reasons. Patients may intentionally not adhere to avoid side effects or because of barriers (e.g., affordability) or inadvertently not adhere because they do not understand or remember how or when to take medication.

Illness and Treatment Variables

Nonadherence increases with regimen complexity (e.g., times of day), and decreasing dosing schedules is demonstrated to improve adherence (see Haynes et al., 2008). Adherence also varies with symptoms, medication side effects, illness representation (Leventhal et al., 2003), perceived benefits of treatment, and severity of illness (Strecher & Rosenstock, 1997).

Patient Variables

There is little evidence that nonadherence varies with gender or ethnic factors, although these factors may be related to others, such as concerns about costs. Nonadherence is associated with education, cognitive ability, and age. Less educated patients tend to have lower health literacy (ability to understand basic medical and services information), leading to poor health outcomes and lower utilization of services (Nielsen-Bohlman, Panzer, & Kindig, 2004). Older adults' nonadherence is a critical problem because they are a growing segment of the population, tend to use more health services, and are more vulnerable to the consequences of nonadherence. Older adults' comprehension of medication information is predicted by education level (Nielsen-Bohlman et al., 2004) and nonadherence by cognitive ability (Insel, Morrow, Brewer, & Figueredo, 2006). Nonadherence may be higher for middle-aged than for young-old adults (age 65–74; Park et al., 1999), perhaps because busy lifestyles increase forgetting.

Provider–Patient Communication

Patient adherence also relates to improved physician communication variables, such as amount of information and partnership building (Aspden, Wolcott, Bootman, & Croenwett, 2007).

Reducing Nonadherence

There are few intervention studies with rigorous designs such as randomized control trials (Haynes et al., 2008). Moreover, interventions targeting adherence alone are not sufficient, because the goal is to improve clinical outcomes (Haynes et al., 2008).The literature suggests the importance of several interventions, although they tend to be complex and difficult to implement. More convenient care (e.g., provision of care at work or home), improved instruction, simplified dosing, reminders, telephone follow-up, self-monitoring, reinforcement, and tailoring the regimen to daily habits are among the successful approaches (Haynes et al., 2008). Interventions often involve cognitive or psychosocial approaches.

Cognitive Approaches

Nonadherence is associated with more complex regimens, suggesting that simplifying regimens by reducing or synchronizing times improves adherence (Haynes et al., 2008). Sensorimotor barriers can be mitigated by simple interventions such as large print on labels and easy-to-open containers (Park & Jones, 1997). Comprehension and memory problems are addressed by improving instructions, including more information, simple language, clear formats, pictures that reinforce text, and organization based on patients' schemas for taking medication (Morrow et al., 2005). Nonadherence is reduced by improved packaging, calendars or aids that help patients organize, pill organizers if they are correctly loaded, and automated telephone messages that support prospective memory and symptom monitoring (Al-Eidan, McElnay, Scott, & McConnell, 2002; Park & Jones, 1997).

Psychosocial Approaches and Patient Education

Educational programs based on psychosocial approaches focus on intentional nonadherence. There is evidence that they improve adherence by targeting belief-based barriers, such as perceived vulnerability to illness and the benefits and costs of treatment (Strecher & Rosenstock, 1997). Benefits may occur for reasons in addition to influencing specific beliefs, such as increased patient knowledge or self-efficacy.

Other Interventions

Several methods attempt to shape adherence behavior, including behavioral contracting, feedback, and financial incentives (Giuffrida & Torgerson, 1997). Nonadherence is reduced by increasing social support, which may reflect the influence of significant others on patients' prospective memory, health beliefs, or self-efficacy (Park & Jones, 1997).

Although there are many adherence studies, few have adequately measured adherence, and nonadherence remains a pervasive health care problem (e.g., Haynes et al., 2008). Challenges for future research include the following: There is a need for intervention research based on comprehensive models that address both intentional and unintentional adherence. A complex, patient-based approach is needed, including profiles of nonadherent patients, so that providers can recommend methods for specific nonadherence conditions. Finally, research should focus on implementing interventions within existing health delivery systems once efficacy has been demonstrated in clinical trials.

REFERENCES

Al-Eidan, F. A., McElnay, J. C., Scott, M. G., & McConnell, J. B. (2002). Management of *Helicobacter pylori* eradication:

The influence of structured counseling and follow-up. *British Journal of Clinical Pharmacology, 53*(2), 163–171.

Aspden, P., Wolcott, J. A., Bootman, J. L., & Croenwett. L. R. (2007). *Preventing medication errors.* Washington, DC: National Academies Press.

Bandura, A. (1997). Self-efficacy and health behaviour. In A. Baum, S. Newman, J. Weinman, R. West, & C. McManus (Eds.), *Cambridge handbook of psychology, health, and medicine* (pp. 160–162). Cambridge, England: Cambridge University Press.

Giuffrida, A., & Torgerson, D. (1997). Should we pay the patient? A review of financial incentives to enhance patient compliance. *British Medical Journal, 3,* 703.

Guerrero, D., Rudd, P., Bryant-Kosling, C., & Middleton, B. (1993). Antihypertensive medication-taking. Investigation of a simple regimen. *Journal of Hypertension, 6,* 586–592.

Haynes, R. B., Yao, S., Degani, A., Kripalani, S., Garg, A., & McDonald, H. P. (2008). Interventions for enhancing medication adherence (Review). *The Cochrane Database of Systematic Reviews, Cochrane Library.* Hoboken, NJ: John Wiley & Sons.

Insel, K., Morrow, D., Brewer, B., & Figueredo, A. (2006). Executive function, working memory and medication adherence among older adults, *Journal of Gerontology: Psychological Sciences, 61B,* 102–107.

Kane, S., & Shaya, F. (2008). Medication non-adherence is associated with increased medical health care costs. *Digestive Diseases and Sciences, 53*(4), 1020–1024.

Leventhal, H., Brissette, I., & Leventhal, E. A. (2003). The common-sense model of self-regulation of health and illness. In L. D. Cameron & H. Leventhal (Eds.), *The self-regulation of health and illness behavior.* London: Routledge.

Llabre, M. M., Weaver, K. E., Duan, R. E., Antoni, M. H., McPherson-Baker, S., & Schneiderman, N. (2006). A measurement model of medication adherence to highly active antiretroviral therapy and its relation to viral load in HIV-positive adults. *AIDS Patient Care and Studies, 20*(10), 701–711.

Morrow, D. G., Weiner, M., Young, J., Steinley, D., Deer, M., & Murray, M. (2005). Improving medication knowledge among older adults with heart failure: A patient-centered approach to instruction design. *Gerontologist, 45,* 545–552.

Nielsen-Bohlman, L., Panzer, A. M., & Kindig, D. A. (2004). *Health literacy: A prescription to end confusion.* Washington, DC: National Academies Press.

Park, D. C., Hertzog, C., Leventhal, H., Morrell, R. W., Leventhal, E., Birchmore, D., et al. (1999). Medication adherence in rheumatoid arthritis patients: Older is wiser. *Journal of the American Geriatrics Society, 47,* 172–183.

Park, D. C., & Jones, T. R. (1997). Medication adherence and aging. In A. D. Fisk & W. A. Rogers (Eds.), *Handbook of human factors and the older adult* (pp. 257–287). San Diego, CA: Academic Press.

Rodon, D. M., Altman, R. B., Benowitz, N. L., Flockhart, D. A., Giacomini, K. M., & Johnson, J. A. (2006). Pharmacogenomics: Challenges and opportunities. *Annals of Internal Medicine, 145,* 749–757.

Strecher, V. J., & Rosenstock, I. M. (1997). The health belief model. In A. Baum, S. Newman, J. Weinman, R. West, & C. McManus (Eds.), *Cambridge handbook of psychology, health, and medicine* (pp. 113–116). Cambridge, England: Cambridge University Press.

SUGGESTED READINGS

Aspden, P., Wolcott, J. A., Bootman, J. L., & Croenwett. L. R. (2007). *Preventing medication errors.* Washington, DC: National Academies Press.

Haynes, R. B., Yao, S., Degani, A., Kripalani, S., Garg, A., & McDonald, H. P. (2008). Interventions for enhancing medication adherence (Review). *The Cochrane Database of Systematic Reviews, Cochrane Library.* Hoboken, NJ: John Wiley & Sons.

Park, D. C., & Jones, T. R. (1997). Medication adherence and aging. In A. D. Fisk & W. A. Rogers (Eds.), *Handbook of human factors and the older adult* (pp. 257–287). San Diego, CA: Academic Press.

DANIEL G. MORROW
University of Illinois at Urbana-Champaign

KATHLEEN C. INSEL
University of Arizona

PAVLOV, IVAN PETROVICH (1849–1936)

Ivan Petrovich Pavlov was the eldest of 11 children. He learned about hard work and responsibility at an early age. In 1860, Pavlov entered a theological seminary, but in 1870 he changed his mind and went to the University of St. Petersburg to study to begin a long career in physiological research. He earned his doctorate in 1883 from the Military Medical Academy. In 1891, he was appointed director of the Department of Physiology at the Institute of Experimental Medicine in St. Petersburg, and in 1897, he became a professor at the university. In 1904, his research work on the primary digestive glands was recognized with the Nobel Prize.

Pavlov's research also concerned nerves of the heart and studies of higher nerve centers of the brain. His methodology for the research, and his greatest scientific achievement, was conditioning, a technique that significantly influenced the development of psychology. Pavlov's research became a model and standard for objectivity and precision. In his controlled experiments, he studied the formation of conditioned responses, reinforcement, extinction, spontaneous recovery, generalization, discrimination, and higher-order conditioning (all applied concepts to learning and association in psychology). Pavlov's most important writings were *The Work of the Digestive Glands* and *Conditioned Reflexes.*

Pavlov's work was a cornerstone for the development of behaviorism, in which the conditioned reflex is important.

John B. Watson took the conditioned reflex as the basic unit of behavior and made it the building block of his program of behaviorism. The conditioned response was used during the 1920s, in the United States, as the foundation for learning theories, thus generating further research and theory.

SUGGESTED READING

Pavlov, I. P. (1927). *Conditioned reflexes*. London: Routledge and Kegan Paul.

N. A. HAYNIE
Honolulu, HI

PAVLOVIAN CONDITIONING

Pavlovian conditioning, also known as classical conditioning, is a reliable training procedure that results in an organism responding to a stimulus that previously did not evoke a response. It involves pairing an initially innocuous stimulus, such as a light or tone, with another stimulus that naturally provokes a response, such as food or an electrical shock. The previously neutral stimulus comes to control responding and typically evokes the same behavior that the biologically significant stimulus provoked, albeit weaker. Once a stimulus acquires behavioral control, it is known as a conditioned stimulus (CS) because it required conditioning, or training, to elicit the behavioral response that the unconditioned stimulus (US) naturally evokes. The innate reaction to the US is called the unconditioned response (UR), and the acquired response to the CS is called a conditioned response (CR).

Conditioned responses often mimic the UR, such as a conditioned eyeblink in response to a tone that has been paired with a puff of air to the eye, but they can also take the form of a compensatory response as if in preparation for the UR. This is most typically seen with select drugs (e.g., opiates); for example, if a habitual heroin user engages in the same preparatory behaviors before injecting heroin, then that person's body will learn to associate those preparatory cues with the effects of the heroin. The drug user's body will eventually learn to emit a conditioned compensatory response whenever the preparatory cues are present in order to combat the effects of the heroin in an effort to maintain homeostasis; this is believed to explain at least a part of drug tolerance (Siegel, 1975). The resultant CR, mimetic or compensatory, is explained as the CS-US pairings producing a mental link called an *association* between representations of the CS and US. There are many theories concerning how these associations are formed (e.g., see Domjan, 2003).

Extinction

Following conditioning, extinction refers to the eventual cessation of conditioned responding to the CS when it is presented multiple times in the absence of the US. Notably, extinction does not result in permanent erasure of the association between the CS and US; it simply involves learning a new CS–no US relationship between them. Recovery of the CR is commonly observed after the passage of time (spontaneous recovery; Pavlov, 1927), if the CS is presented in a context different from that in which extinction occurred (renewal; Bouton & King, 1986), or if the US is presented in isolation (reinstatement; Rescorla & Heth, 1975).

Contiguity and Contingency

Pavlovian conditioning appears to obey the principles of contiguity and contingency. High contiguity refers to close proximity of the CS and US in space and/or time, conditions that favor Pavlovian conditioning. In delay conditioning, in which there is no interval between CS termination and US onset, there is good contiguity, but in trace conditioning, in which a gap is interposed between CS termination and outcome onset, contiguity is weaker, and less conditioned responding is observed. Similarly, there is good spatial contiguity between a food hopper and a light that is located just above it, but poor spatial contiguity if the light is located on the opposite side of the room from the hopper; the former situation results in more rapid conditioning. Associations can be established regardless of whether the CS occurs before or after the US in time, but forward pairings are needed for expression of the CR (e.g., Arcediano & Miller, 2002). Contingency captures the sufficiency and necessity of the CS for the occurrence of the US. It asks whether the US can occur without the CS and whether the presence of the target CS is necessary for delivery of the US. Contingency, and hence conditioned responding, is weakened if either the CS or US occurs without the other. Both contiguity and contingency are more sensitive to recent events than to less recent events (i.e., recency), meaning that the association learned most recently is usually expressed. But long retention intervals decrease the advantage of recency, sometimes leading to responding more consistent with initial contiguity and contingency (i.e., primacy). Associations are most easily established if the stimulus and outcome are always presented together and in close contiguity, but under select circumstances, associations can be formed with contiguity alone or contingency alone. Notably, contiguity between mental representations of CSs and USs are what promote the formation of associations that result in CRs, and thus it is for these mental events that contiguity is critical, not necessarily contiguity between the physical stimuli themselves. For example, sensory preconditioning (CS1 → CS2 followed by CS2 → US) and second-order conditioning (CS2 → US followed by CS1 → CS2) are procedures that establish CRs to CS1 without CS1 ever being paired directly with the US.

Stimulus Competition

Potential CSs trained in compound have been found to compete with each other for control of responding. One classic example of stimulus competition is overshadowing (Pavlov, 1927), in which two cues are trained together. Relative to each cue being trained alone with the US, this results in weaker conditioned responding to each cue when it is tested alone. Critically, stimuli must be trained in compound in order for competition to occur between them. Importantly, there are several demonstrations that strong conditioned responding can be recovered from competitive situations without further training of the target cue. For example, extinguishing one of the two stimuli from overshadowing treatment results in a strong CR to the other stimulus (e.g., Matzel, Schachtman, & Miller, 1985). Thus, it is unclear whether stimulus competition arises from an acquisition deficit or a performance deficit.

Stimulus Interference

Stimulus interference also results in reduced CRs, but unlike stimulus competition, interference occurs when stimuli are trained apart, particularly if the training is phasic. For example, A-C training followed by B-C training weakens behavioral control by A. The decrement in responding observed with interference is generally weaker than with stimulus competition (Vadillo, Castro, Matute, & Wasserman, 2008). In order for interference to be observed, there must be at least one common element between the two phases, such as the same CS or the same US. Interference is stronger when the two training phases are more similar (Amundson & Miller, 2007). Of course, complete similarity would not produce interference, as it would simply amount to more training of the same stimuli.

One explanation offered to account for interference emphasizes the role that contextual cues play in determining which of the two potentially interfering associations will be expressible in that context (Bouton, 1993). According to this theory, the context is defined by both spatial and temporal cues. Bouton suggests that organisms use the context to disambiguate which association should be expressed after it acquires conflicting information. For example, in a typical interference experiment, the CS is paired with the US in Phase 1 and then not reinforced in Phase 2. Since the temporal context at the time of testing is more similar to the one that was present during Phase 2 training, conditioned responding reflects the contingency of Phase 2 (retroactive interference).

Note that this training sequence encompasses acquisition followed by extinction, and recovery from extinction is widely observed. Imposing a retention interval decreases the contextual similarity between the extinction treatment and test contexts, and this appears to cause the organism to revert to the first-learned association, showing a primacy effect (i.e., behavior consistent with the CS-US pairings). This spontaneous recovery effect presumably occurs because the test context is perceived as a new context. Conflicting information such as provided by extinction treatment is context-specific, but first-learned information (i.e., the reinforced association) is context-general and more readily generalizes to new contexts. Despite the many similarities between stimulus competition and stimulus interference, most contemporary theories of learning can account only for competition, not interference.

Conditioned Inhibition

Conditioned inhibition reflects an association in which the CS appears to signal the absence of the US. This is conventionally tested by pairing the CS with another CS that predicts the US to measure how much the conditioned inhibitor decreases responding to the conditioned excitor (i.e., a summation test) and by reinforcing the CS to measure how many pairings it takes for it to come to control excitatory responding (i.e., a retardation test). Using both tests is advocated because it is possible to "pass" either test alone based on factors other than conditioned inhibition (Rescorla, 1969).

There are multiple methods for producing conditioned inhibition. The most common is Pavlov's procedure, in which a conditioned excitor is reinforced when it is presented alone but not reinforced when it is presented in compound with the conditioned inhibitor. Explicitly unpaired inhibition is when the US is systematically presented when the conditioned inhibitor is absent and the inhibitor is presented when the US is absent; notably, explicitly unpaired inhibition requires that the training trials be highly massed. Differential inhibition is when the conditioned excitor with its US and the conditioned inhibitor are explicitly unpaired. Backward inhibition is when the US is presented before the conditioned inhibitor, and inhibition of delay is when a CS is presented for an extended duration and not reinforced until the end. In the latter case, early parts of the CS become a conditioned inhibitor and later parts become more excitatory as it nears termination. Each of these procedures is effective in producing a conditioned inhibitor, but they differ in the amount of training they require and the strength of inhibition they produce.

Pavlovian associations are ubiquitous across different domains of psychology and in life. They represent the most basic building blocks for learning more complex associations. Pavlovian conditioning has been demonstrated across very complex and very simple organisms; it has even been demonstrated in a severed spinal cord (e.g., Joynes, Illich, & Grau, 1997). The associations formed using Pavlovian conditioning arguably are the foundation for all higher-order cognitive processing.

REFERENCES

Amundson, J. C., & Miller, R. R. (2007). Similarity in spatial origin of information facilitates cue competition and interference. *Learning and Motivation, 38*, 155–171.

Arcediano, F., & Miller, R. R. (2002). Some constraints for models of timing: A temporal coding hypothesis. *Learning and Motivation, 33*, 105–123.

Bouton, M. E. (1993). Context, time, and memory retrieval in the interference paradigms of Pavlovian learning. *Psychological Bulletin, 114*, 80–99.

Bouton, M. E., & King, D. A. (1986). Effect of context on performance to conditioned stimuli with mixed histories of reinforcement and nonreinforcement. *Journal of Experimental Psychology: Animal Behavior Processes, 12*, 4–15.

Domjan, M. (2003). *The principles of learning and behavior* (5th ed.). Belmont, CA: Wadsworth.

Joynes, R. L., Illich, P. A., & Grau, J. W. (1997). Evidence for spinal conditioning in intact rats. *Neurobiology of Learning and Memory, 67*, 64–68.

Matzel, L. D., Schachtman, T. R., & Miller, R. R. (1985). Recovery of an overshadowed association achieved by extinction of the overshadowing stimulus. *Learning and Motivation, 16*, 398–412.

Pavlov, I. P. (1927). *Conditioned reflexes.* London: Oxford University Press.

Rescorla, R. A. (1969). Pavlovian conditioned inhibition. *Psychological Bulletin, 72*, 77–94.

Rescorla, R. A., & Heth, C. D. (1975). Reinstatement of fear to an extinguished conditioned stimulus. *Journal of Experimental Psychology: Animal Behavior Processes, 104*, 88–96.

Siegel, S. (1975). Evidence from rats that morphine tolerance is a learned response. *Journal of Comparative and Physiological Psychology, 89*, 498–506.

Vadillo, M. A., Castro, L., Matute, H., & Wasserman, E. A. (2008). Backward blocking: The role of within-compound associations and interference between cues trained apart. *Quarterly Journal of Experimental Psychology, 61*, 185–193.

Bridget L. McConnell
Ralph R. Miller
State University of New York at Binghamton

See also: **Instrumental Conditioning; Operant Conditioning**

PEABODY PICTURE VOCABULARY TEST

The Peabody Picture Vocabulary Test (PPVT) is an individually administered, norm-referenced test of single-word receptive (or hearing) vocabulary. Originally published in 1959, the PPVT has been revised several times and currently exists in its fourth edition (PPVT-4; Dunn & Dunn, 2007). In addition to assessing receptive vocabulary, test authors report that the PPVT-4 may be used as a means of estimating verbal development (Dunn & Dunn, 2007).

Normed with a sample of 3,540 individuals ages $2\frac{1}{2}$ to 90 representative of March 2004 U.S. census data, the PPVT-4 features two parallel forms (Form A and Form B), each consisting of 228 test items. Items consist of two stimuli, a word spoken by the examiner and four pictures on a single card; the examinee selects the picture that best represents the examiner's spoken word. Raw scores may be translated into age-based standard scores (i.e., $M = 100$; $SD = 15$), percentile ranks, stanines, age equivalents, and grade equivalents.

Psychometric support is presented in the test manual, which suggests that the PPVT-4 is reliable and has demonstrated various forms of validity (Dunn & Dunn, 2007). With respect to reliability, internal consistency ($M_{\alpha\ coefficient} = .97$ for Form A and .96 for Form B), test–retest (4-week interval, $M_r = .92$ across age groups), and alternate form ($M_r = .88$ across age groups) reliabilities are satisfactory. Validation studies presented by the test's authors also provide initial support for the PPVT-4. The PPVT-4 shows concurrent validity as evidenced by its strong and positive relationships with various measures of expressive and receptive language, including the PPVT-III ($M_r = .92$ across age groups). Support for the validity of the PPVT-4 also exists in the form of special population studies. For example, children with language delay ($N = 63$; $M = 87.5$), hearing impairments with cochlear implant ($N = 46$; $M = 72.0$), and intellectual disability ($N = 70$; $M = 70.6$) performed significantly below normative means. Adults with language disorders ($N = 45$; $M = 86.4$) also performed below normative expectations. At the other end of the score distribution, children identified as gifted scored significantly above normative expectations ($N = 55$; $M = 118.2$).

At the time of this article, no independent validity studies have been published for the PPVT-4; however, the PPVT-4's most recent predecessor, the PPVT-III, was identified as an empirically supported language assessment instrument for use with pediatric populations (Campbell, Brown, Cavanagh, Vess, & Segall, 2008). For example, the PPVT-III demonstrated adequate construct validity for use with typically developing children, children with cochlear implants, and children with autism. In contrast, however, the PPVT-III demonstrated variable validity for young African American children, as evidenced by lower scores when compared with measures of cognitive ability and achievement (Campbell, Bell, & Keith, 2001). Because of its brevity and its positive relationship with measures of verbal cognitive ability, previous versions of the PPVT have been used as a proxy for cognitive functioning with various pediatric and developmentally delayed populations, such as children with autism, spina bifida, and language delay (Campbell et al., 2008).

REFERENCES

Campbell, J. M., Bell, S. K., & Keith, L. (2001). Concurrent validity of the Peabody Picture Vocabulary Test, Third Edition as an intelligence and achievement screener in a sample of low-SES African-American children. *Assessment, 8*, 85–94.

Campbell, J. M., Brown, R. T., Cavanagh, S. E., Vess, S. F., & Segall, M. J. (2008). Evidence-based assessment of cognitive functioning in pediatric psychology. *Journal of Pediatric Psychology*, doi:10.1093/jpepsy/jsm138.

Dunn, L. M., & Dunn, D. M. (2007). *Peabody Picture Vocabulary Test* (4th ed.). Minneapolis, MN: NCS Pearson.

SUGGESTED READINGS

Condouris, K., Meyer, E., & Tager-Flusberg, H. (2003). The relationship between standardized measures of language and measures of spontaneous speech in children with autism. *American Journal of Speech-Language Pathology, 12*, 349–358.

Restrepo, M. A., Schwanenflugel, P. J., Blake, J., Neuharth-Pritchett, S., Cramer, S. E., & Ruston, H. P. (2006). Performance on the PPVT-III and the EVT: Applicability of the measures with a sample of preschool children from the South. *Language, Speech, and Hearing Services in the Schools, 37*, 17–27.

JONATHAN M. CAMPBELL
AILA K. DOMMESTRUP
University of Georgia

PEDIATRIC PSYCHOLOGY

Pediatric psychology focuses on issues associated with chronic and acute illnesses that confront children, adolescents, and their families. Pediatric psychologists' domains of interest include, but are not limited to, chronic illness, psychosocial adjustment, quality of life, adaptation associated with illness, illness and injury prevention, health services research, and health promotion and public health. The field of pediatric psychology is little more than 35 years old. It grew from clinical and developmental psychology and was influenced by Jerome Kagan, Jonas Salk, Logan Wright, and Donald Routh.

The Society of Pediatric Psychology (SPP) was established as a separate division of the American Psychological Association (APA) in 2001. Prior to 2001, the SPP was part of the Division of the Society of Clinical Psychology; thus its origins were primarily clinical, with the majority of research being clinical research. The society's major publication was a newsletter, *Pediatric Psychology* (now the *Journal of Pediatric Psychology*). The SPP sponsors a biannual national conference as well as regional conferences. It also produces professional texts, including the *Handbook of Pediatric Psychology* (now in its fourth edition), which defines the field regarding research trends and clinical practice. The society also has developed a number of task forces to address major issues confronting children and

their families with chronic illnesses, including the training of professional psychologists to work with chronically ill children (Spirito et al., 2003).

Pediatricians and psychologists have long recognized the value in a collaborative relationship between their respective fields. The relationship between the disciplines began to evolve in an attempt to address issues of disease prevention and the management of chronic illnesses in children and adolescents. Over the past 10 years, the SPP and the American Academy of Pediatrics (AAP) have formalized their relationship by including pediatric psychologists on key AAP committees and task forces.

The field of pediatric psychology has spawned an impressive body of research in the field of chronic illness, which is particularly important given the increasing number of children and adolescents who now survive catastrophic diseases that were previously considered death sentences (e.g., cancer, cystic fibrosis). With advances in medical technology, these children are now surviving well into adulthood, providing pediatric psychologists with important research questions concerning adherence, quality of life, family issues, and later functional outcome.

The field now struggles with national issues such as providing health care to all children. This issue has become a major collaborative endeavor for the SPP and the AAP (Brown & Roberts, 2000). Other areas of recent focus include the integration of psychologists into the primary care medical setting and support for greater behavioral research and training from the National Institutes of Health. Access to psychological care for all children and funding for clinical services remain major issues for pediatric psychologists in the twenty-first century (Brown & Roberts, 2000).

Training in Pediatric Psychology

Pediatric psychologists receive intensive training at the graduate, predoctoral internship, and postdoctoral levels and are exposed to a number of different areas of pediatric health care across an array of settings (e.g., transplantation, pain management, adherence to treatment). Pediatric psychology is interdisciplinary, and education and training in the field include life span developmental psychology and psychopathology, assessment, intervention and empirically validated treatments, research methodology, public policy, and professional training. Pediatric psychologists must have a working knowledge of ethical and legal issues, particularly as these issues affect working with children and adolescents in health care settings (Spirito et al., 2003). Aspiring pediatric psychologists must have a comprehensive understanding of the needs of children, adolescents, and families with regard to physical, cognitive, social, and emotional functioning and development as these areas relate to health, illness, and injury.

Pediatric psychologists receive their training in a variety of health-related environments, including primary care (e.g., ambulatory care pediatric clinics, primary care pediatric practices), tertiary care (e.g., cancer centers, specialty clinics), and schools in order to maximize the trainee's exposure to situations and experiences. Training programs often include special emphasis on (1) prevention and health promotion strategies, (2) family-related challenges associated with adjustment and adaptation to diseases, (3) social issues affecting health care, (4) disease information and disease psychosocial response, (5) collaboration with pediatric health care providers, (6) consultation and liaison roles with specialty and inpatient services, and (7) multicultural awareness and sensitivity, particularly as they relate to the health care setting (La Greca & Hughes, 1999). Recently, greater emphasis has been placed on ethical issues concerning family challenges, child advocacy, conflict of interest in addressing multiple family members and health care workers, and continuing education opportunities for both pediatric psychologists and other health care providers (Spirito et al., 2003).

The training of pediatric psychologists emphasizes learning about both chronic diseases and the patterns of adaptation that occur among children and their families (Spirito et al., 2003). Students are encouraged to attend seminars and lectures and to learn through clinical observation, while gaining clinical experience through practica, internships, and postdoctoral training. Spirito and colleagues (2003) have recommended that trainees refine their clinical skills as practitioners and researchers by addressing important questions in their own research programs. Given the importance of developmental, clinical, and health psychology in the foundation and evolution of pediatric psychology, it is imperative that pediatric psychologists receive solid training in all the fundamental areas of psychology. Moreover, they need to be able to recognize the subsequent impact these specialty areas will have on health-related issues for children and adolescents and their families.

The Roles of a Pediatric Psychologist

Pediatric psychologists traditionally work in outpatient primary care, specialty clinics, emergency departments, and inpatient settings. They perform assessments and consultations, promote health and well-being, often provide training to other medical staff, conduct research (particularly clinical research), and engage in collaborative projects with other health care professionals. In addition, pediatric psychologists may provide services to the communities in which they practice through education and outreach (Drotar, Spirito, & Stancin, 2003).

In primary care settings, pediatric psychologists typically provide screenings for developmental disorders and psychopathology. They may also be involved in primary and secondary prevention programs for particular conditions (e.g., obesity) that place children at significant risk for other diseases. In a primary care setting, pediatric psychologists frequently treat children presenting learning and behavioral problems (e.g., attention-deficit/hyperactivity disorder [ADHD]), somatic conditions (e.g., recurrent headaches, abdominal pain), and eating and bedtime challenges (behavioral pediatrics) (Finney, Riley, & Cataldo, 1991).

Compelling data suggest that pediatricians frequently underidentify mental health issues and underrefer patients for mental health services (Costello, 1986). However, such underidentification can be averted through an integrated approach to primary care involving collaborations between pediatric psychologists and pediatricians. These collaborations will strengthen pediatric psychologists' ability to provide assessment and psychotherapy in the primary care setting. Given the time restraints in pediatric practice, particularly in heavily penetrated managed care environments, psychologists are often welcomed in pediatric ambulatory care settings because they assist with psychosocial issues that often present in such settings.

In inpatient settings, pediatric psychologists often assist children and their families in negotiating the stresses associated with chronic illnesses, injuries, behavioral problems, and pain management. Pediatric psychologists are especially concerned with parental coping and adjustment, treatment adherence, and the management of anxiety in children and caregivers. Pediatric psychologists are responsible for communicating their findings and recommendations to other health care professionals, through either direct communication or multidisciplinary case reviews (Drotar, 1995).

Recently, pediatric psychologists have been challenged with proving their viability within the health care arena and generating reimbursable services from third-party payers. Research activities also must be reimbursed by means of external grant support. Despite these challenges, the integration of clinical care, research, and training has been a significant component of the core values embraced by pediatric psychologists.

Topics of Interest in Pediatric Psychology

The interests of pediatric psychologists include specific illnesses and diseases, developmental and behavioral problems, pain management, adherence to treatment demands, quality of life, stress and coping, and other psychological conditions associated with chronic illnesses, including the cognitive and affective sequelae of diseases. In addition, pediatric psychologists are concerned with both child and family adjustment and adaptation to health challenges. Recently, many researchers have begun to endorse a noncategorical approach to the study of chronic diseases in which particular constructs are examined across diseases and conditions (e.g., coping).

Much of the literature in the field of pediatric psychology has focused on chronic illnesses (e.g., asthma, cancer, cystic fibrosis, sickle cell disease, diabetes, spina bifida). Recently, pediatric psychologists have become interested in public health issues such as access to care, health services research, and injury prevention. As the field of pediatric psychology enters its tertiary stage of development, there has been a search to empirically confirm descriptive and correlational studies by means of experimental paradigms and longitudinal studies. Thus, the research landscape in pediatric psychology has turned from descriptive and correlational studies to randomized clinical trials and longitudinal investigations.

With children now surviving many catastrophic diseases, research has focused on the study of the late effects (e.g., cognitive and psychosocial functioning) on children who have survived cancer into adolescence and adulthood. Moreover, with the improved prognosis of many of these diseases, research programs now focus on issues related to the developmental transition from adolescence to young adulthood. Another area of increasing focus has been obesity, which represents a national epidemic among both children and adolescents. Given the increase in prevalence of chronic illness—due in large part to the survival of children with these once-fatal diseases—the field of pediatric psychology will continue to employ the services of psychologists. Poor access to health care, especially among children from lower socioeconomic groups, also is a major challenge to be addressed over the next decade, particularly as we negotiate the crises associated with health care in this country.

Health Promotion and Injury Prevention

Two emerging and overlapping areas of interest for pediatric psychologists are the promotion of healthy living and the prevention of injuries. Over the past decade, there has been a significant increase in childhood obesity and adolescent substance abuse, as well as a decline in health-promoting behaviors (e.g., physical activity, healthy diets). There has been a recent emphasis on the identification of health-related risks and the implementation of interventions for the purpose of reducing the risks of serious injury or illness (Roberts, Brown, Boles, Mashunkashey, & Mayes, 2003). Many experts agree that it is essential to equip children and adolescents with the knowledge to lead healthy lives to ensure healthy lifestyles throughout adulthood.

Although physicians recognize the importance of emphasizing health promotion and injury prevention, they frequently face considerable time constraints. This provides an important opportunity for pediatric psychologists to assist the pediatric community in understanding the steps they may take to reduce disease and injury.

Pediatric psychologists can provide intervention strategies aimed at promoting a healthier and safer lifestyle for both children and their families.

Overall View of the Field

Over the past three decades, the focus of pediatric psychology has evolved from case studies and basic descriptive research to more sophisticated investigations with a greater emphasis on randomized controlled trials and longitudinal designs (Roberts, Mitchell, & McNeal, 2003). Research has often used a developmental perspective based on the premise that illnesses affect children and adolescents in different ways.

Although the studies conducted on chronic illnesses and psychosocial adjustment and adaptation are informative, this type of explicative research does not always elucidate the clinical applicability or clinical implications of suffering from a chronic disease. Thus, more data are needed to inform pediatric psychologists about assessment, intervention, and prevention. Finally, an ideal research perspective is contingent on the integration of empirical research and application to intervention strategies in ecologically valid settings (Roberts, McNeal, Randall, & Roberts, 1996).

REFERENCES

Brown, K. J., & Roberts, M. C. (2000). Future issues in pediatric psychology: Delphic survey. *Journal of Clinical Psychology in Medical Settings, 7*, 5–15.

Costello, E. J. (1986). Primary care pediatrics and child psychopathology: A review of diagnostic, treatment, and referral practices. *Pediatrics, 78*, 1044–1051.

Drotar, D. (1995). *Consulting with pediatricians: Psychological perspectives.* New York: Plenum Press.

Drotar, D., Spirito, A., & Stancin, T. (2003). Professional roles and practice patterns. In M. C. Roberts (Ed.), *Handbook of pediatric psychology* (pp. 50–66). New York: Guilford Press.

Finney, J. W., Riley, A. W., & Cataldo, M. F. (1991). Psychology in primary care: Effects of brief targeted therapy on children's medical care utilization. *Journal of Pediatric Psychology, 16*, 447–461.

Kazak, A. E. (2002). *Journal of Pediatric Psychology (JPP)*, 1998–2002: Editor's vale dictum. *Journal of Pediatric Psychology, 27*(8), 653–663.

La Greca, A. M. (1997). Reflections and perspectives on pediatric psychology: Editor's vale dictum. *Journal of Pediatric Psychology, 22*(6), 759–770.

La Greca, A. M., & Hughes, J. (1999). United we stand, divided we fall: The education and training needs of clinical child psychologists. *Journal of Clinical Child Psychology, 28*, 435–447.

Roberts, M. C. (1992). Vale dictum: An editor's view of the field of pediatric psychology and its journal. *Journal of Pediatric Psychology, 17*(6), 785–805.

Roberts, M. C., Brown, K. J., Boles, R. E., Mashunkashey, J. O., & Mayes, S. (2003). Prevention of disease and injury in pediatric psychology. In M. C. Roberts (Ed.), *Handbook of pediatric psychology* (pp. 84–98). New York: Guilford Press.

Roberts, M. C., McNeal, R. E., Randall, C. J., & Roberts, J. C. (1996). A necessary reemphasis on integrating explicative research with the pragmatics of pediatric psychology. *Journal of Pediatric Psychology, 21*(1), 107–114.

Roberts, M. C., Mitchell, M. C., & McNeal, R. (2003). The evolving field of pediatric psychology: Critical issues and future challenges. In M. C. Roberts (Ed.), *Handbook of pediatric psychology* (pp. 3–18). New York: Guilford Press.

Spirito, A., Brown, R. T., D'Angelo, E., Delamater, A., Rodrigue, J., et al. (2003). Training pediatric psychologists for the 21st century. In M. C. Roberts (Ed.), *Handbook of pediatric psychology* (pp. 99–118). New York: Guilford Press.

SUGGESTED READING

Roberts, M. C. (Ed.). (2003). *Handbook of pediatric psychology.* New York: Guilford Press.

RONALD T. BROWN
ABBY B. HARVEY
Temple University

PEDOPHILIA

Pedophilia is typically defined as sexual attraction to prepubescent children, reflected in a person's sexual thoughts, fantasies, urges, sexual arousal, or behavior regarding children (American Psychiatric Association, 2000; World Health Organization, 1997). There are two key aspects to emphasize in this definition: first, the sexual interest in children is persistent, and second, the children of interest are prepubescent and thus show few or no signs of secondary sexual development. This means that someone who has expressed a sexual interest in children or who has engaged in sexual behavior involving a child is not necessarily a pedophile. It also means that individuals who are attracted to sexually maturing children or sexually mature adolescents, even if they are below the legally defined age of consent, are unlikely to be pedophiles.

Pedophilia has received a great deal of attention from psychologists, driven by concerns about the intuitive link between pedophilia and sexual offending against children. Pedophilia is an important motivation for sexual offending against children, but the two concepts are not synonymous. Some pedophiles have no known history of sexual contacts with children, and a conservative estimate suggests that only half of sex offenders against legal minors are pedophiles (see Seto, 2008).

Most of the research on pedophilia has been conducted with men who have been recruited from clinical or correctional settings. Much less is known about pedophilia

in women or among individuals who are not involved in clinical services or the criminal justice system. The prevalence of pedophilia in the general population is unknown, as the necessary epidemiological research has not been conducted yet.

Diagnosis

Pedophilia can be diagnosed on the basis of self-report, sexual history, and physiological responses to sexual stimuli presented in a laboratory. Self-report is the simplest and most direct source of information, but this method is often limited because individuals are reluctant to admit that they are sexually interested in children. Thus, other sources of information are helpful. Regarding sexual history, pedophilia is more likely among male sex offenders who have boy victims, multiple child victims, younger child victims, or unrelated child victims, and it is negatively associated with number of adult sexual partners. Regarding physiological responses, men who are diagnosed as pedophilic on the basis of their self-report or sexual behavior involving children can be distinguished from other men in their penile responses when presented with sexual stimuli depicting children or adults in the laboratory. Among male sex offenders, sexual arousal to children as assessed in the laboratory is one of the strongest predictors of who will sexually offend again. Recent research suggests that unobtrusively recorded viewing time can distinguish pedophilic men from other men, such that pedophilic men look relatively longer at images of children.

Etiology and Development

Pedophilia can be described as a sexual preference that is similar to heterosexual or homosexual orientation in the sense that it seems to emerge around the time of puberty and appears to be stable over time. Some pedophiles acknowledge being aware of their sexual interest in children from a very early age, just as other individuals report being aware of their opposite-sex or same-sex attractions early in life.

There is accumulating evidence demonstrating that pedophilia is associated with neurological problems. Pedophilic men score lower than nonpedophilic men on measures of intelligence and other cognitive abilities, such as memory, and they are more likely to have incurred head injuries before the age of 12 (Cantor, Blanchard, Robichaud, & Christensen, 2005). In addition, a recent research study suggests that pedophilic men differ by having less white matter volume in two tracts that are thought to connect areas of the brain involved in the identification of visual stimuli as sexually relevant (Cantor et al., in press).

Pedophilia can co-occur with other paraphilias. For example, studies suggest that approximately 1 in 6 pedophiles have engaged in exhibitionism and approximately 1 in 5 pedophiles have engaged in voyeurism (Abel, Becker, Cunningham-Rathner, Mittelman, & Rouleau, 1988). This comorbidity of pedophilia with other paraphilias has implications for risk assessment and intervention, because having multiple paraphilias is a risk factor for sexual recidivism among sex offenders. Comorbidity of paraphilias also has implications for etiological theories, because it suggests that factors that influence the development of one paraphilia may also influence the development of other paraphilias. It is possible that the nature, location, and timing of disturbances in brain development (e.g., as a result of maternal malnutrition, maternal illness, or fetal exposure to toxins) might influence which paraphilias manifest.

Interventions

The most common approaches to the management of pedophilia involve restricting access to children, the use of conditioning techniques to decrease sexual arousal to children, medications to reduce sex drive by reducing endogenous testosterone levels, and cognitive-behavioral treatments designed to teach individuals how to identify potentially risky situations and how to avoid or cope with these situations in order to refrain from engaging in sexual contacts with children. There is evidence that conditioning can decrease sexual arousal to children in the short term, but long-term follow-ups are needed. There is also evidence that sex-drive-reducing medications can be efficacious, but compliance is a serious problem. Finally, the evidence regarding cognitive-behavioral treatments is weak, as the only randomized clinical trial published to date did not find a significant benefit of treatment in terms of reduced future offending.

Many clinicians and researchers assume that pedophilia is a sexual disorder that can be managed but not changed with current intervention technologies. It is likely that a successful intervention for pedophilia will involve further work on the etiology and development of brain differences associated with pedophilia. Preventing pedophiles from acting upon their sexual interests in children will involve outreach efforts to identify at-risk individuals and sexual abuse prevention programs provided to children and their parents.

REFERENCES

Abel, G. G., Becker, J. V., Cunningham-Rathner, J., Mittelman, M., & Rouleau, J. L. (1988). Multiple paraphilic diagnoses among sex offenders. *Bulletin of the American Academy of Psychiatry and the Law, 16,* 153–168.

American Psychiatric Association. (2000). *Diagnostic and statistical manual of mental disorders* (4th ed., text revision). Washington, DC: Author.

Cantor, J. M., Blanchard, R., Robichaud, L. K., & Christensen, B. K. (2005). Quantitative reanalysis of aggregate data on IQ in sexual offenders. *Psychological Bulletin, 131,* 555–568.

Cantor, J. M., Kabani, N., Christensen, B. K., Zipursky, R. B., Barbaree, H. E., et al. (in press). Cerebral white matter deficiencies in pedophilic men. *Journal of Psychiatric Research.*

Seto, M. C. (2008). *Pedophilia and sexual offending against children: Theory, assessment, and intervention.* Washington, DC: American Psychological Association.

World Health Organization. (1997). *The ICD-10 classification of mental and behavioural disorders: Clinical descriptions and diagnostic guidelines.* Geneva: Author.

SUGGESTED READINGS

Blanchard, R., Klassen, P., Dickey, R., Kuban, M. E., & Blak, T. (2001). Sensitivity and specificity of the phallometric test for pedophilia in nonadmitting sex offenders. *Psychological Assessment, 13,* 118–126.

Quinsey, V. L. (2003). The etiology of anomalous sexual preferences in men. *Annals of the New York Academy of Sciences, 989,* 105–117.

Seto, M. C. (2007). Treatment of pedophilia. In G. O. Gabbard (Ed.), *Gabbard's treatments of psychiatric disorders* (4th ed., pp. 657–669). Washington, DC: American Psychiatric Publishing.

MICHAEL C. SETO
*Centre for Addiction and Mental Health and
University of Toronto*

See also: **Child Sexual Abuse; Sex Offenders; Sexual Deviations**

PEER INFLUENCES

High-quality relationships are important for all aspects of the development and well-being of children and adolescents. Traditionally, the relationships between children and adults have been viewed as the most important vehicle for ensuring effective socialization and development. Child–child relationships are assumed to be, at best, relatively unimportant and, at worst, unhealthy influences. Such views are mistaken. Prominent theorists such as Sigmund Freud, George H. Mead, Jean Piaget, Erik Erikson, and Lawrence Kohlberg have argued that high-quality peer relationships are essential for an individual's development, socialization, and well-being, and hundreds of research studies have validated these views. Young people acquire competencies, attitudes, values, and perspectives in encounters with peers as they strive to occupy a comfortable niche within their peer culture. Compared with interactions with adults, interactions with peers tend to be more frequent, more intense, and more varied. Some of the more important consequences and correlates of peer influences are discussed in this article. Specific research studies supporting the statements to follow may be found in Johnson (1980, 2009), Ladd (1999), and Prinstein and Dodge (2008).

Influences on Values, Attitudes, Perspectives, and Social Competencies

In their interactions with peers, children and adolescents directly learn attitudes, values, competencies, and information unobtainable from adults. The way in which ingroup messages are phrased, the nature of clothing and hairstyles, the music valued, what is enjoyable or distasteful, what competencies need to be practiced and developed, and how to react to adult authority are largely based on peer influences. The socializing importance of peers does not end during adolescence. Friends and colleagues have a critical impact on people's values, attitudes, perspectives, and social competencies throughout their lives.

Prosocial and Antisocial Behavior

Interaction with peers provides support, opportunities, and models for prosocial or antisocial behavior. Peers provide the norms, models, and motivation for engaging in prosocial actions and the opportunity for doing so. If peers promote prosocial actions such as altruism, cooperation, help and assistance, and respect for individuals, people will tend to engage in such behavior. It is while interacting with peers that a person has the opportunity to help, comfort, share with, take care of, and give to others. Without peer interaction, many forms of prosocial values and commitments could not be developed. There is a solid and established link between peer acceptance and prosocial behavior. In addition, peer influence is a useful resource in decreasing violence, aggression, and other antisocial behavior in children and adolescents.

Whether children and adolescents engage in problem or transition behaviors, such as delinquency and the use of illegal drugs, is related to their peers' attitudes toward such behaviors. If individuals perceive their friends as disapproving of such actions, they will tend not to engage in them. Furthermore, the wide-scale rejection of a person by peers tends to promote antisocial actions, including aggressiveness, disruptiveness, and other negatively perceived behavior. Individuals who are high in social anxiety and afraid that their peers will dislike them may be especially vulnerable to peer influences toward antisocial behaviors.

Impulsiveness

Children frequently lack the time perspective needed to tolerate delays in gratification. As they develop and are socialized, however, the focus on their own immediate impulses and needs is replaced with an ability to take longer time perspectives and view their individual desires from the perspectives of others. Peers provide models of—and expectations, directions, and reinforcements for—learning to control one's impulses.

Aggressive impulses provide an example. Whereas instrumental aggression aimed at achieving selfish ends is correlated with peer rejection, aggressive and rough play may have developmental benefits. Peer interaction involving such activities as rough-and-tumble play is important in helping children learn to master aggressive impulses. Rough-and-tumble play promotes the acquisition of a repertoire of effective aggressive behaviors and helps to establish the necessary regulatory mechanisms for modulating aggressive affect. Children and adolescents who are unusually timid in the presence of an attack have often lacked exposure to rough-and-tumble play with peers.

Perspective-Taking Ability

Children learn to view situations and problems from perspectives other than their own through their interaction with their peers. Such perspective taking is a critical competency for cognitive and social development. It has been related to a number of important characteristics, including the abilities to present and comprehend information, resolve conflicts, disclose personal information, help in group problem solving, and display positive attitudes toward others in the same situation. All psychological development may be described as a progressive loss of egocentrism and an increase in the ability to take wider and more complex perspectives. Primarily through interaction with one's peers, egocentrism is lost and increased perspective-taking ability is gained.

Autonomy

Autonomy is the ability to understand what others expect in any given situation and to be free to choose whether to meet their expectations. In making decisions concerning what behavior is appropriate, autonomous people tend to consider both their internal values and the expectations of other people and then to respond in flexible and appropriate ways. Autonomy results from the internalization of values derived from caring and supportive relationships and the acquisition of social sensitivity. Peer relationships have a powerful influence on these variables. Children and adolescents with a history of isolation from or rejection by peers often are inappropriately other-directed. They conform to group pressures even when they believe the recommended actions are wrong or inappropriate.

Loneliness

Children and adolescents need peer relationships to avoid the pain of loneliness. Although adults can provide certain forms of companionship, children need close and intimate relationships with peers with whom they can share their thoughts and feelings, aspirations and hopes, dreams and fantasies, and joys and pains. Peer rejection and peer victimization predict loneliness and its accompanying emotional distress.

Identity

Throughout infancy, childhood, adolescence, and early adulthood, a person moves through several successive and overlapping identities. The physical changes involved in growth, the increasing number of experiences with other people, one's increasing responsibilities, and one's general cognitive and social development all cause changes in self-definition. The final result is a coherent and integrated identity. In peer relationships, children become aware of the similarities and differences between themselves and others, experiment with a variety of social roles that help them integrate their sense of self, clarify their attitudes and values, and develop a frame of reference for perceiving themselves.

Coalitions

For humans, banding together has survival value against enemies and environmental problems. In childhood, most people make friends and form attachments. Coalitions are formed that provide help and assistance not only during childhood and adolescence but also throughout adulthood. This instinct for coalitions is sometimes formalized through organizations such as fraternities and sororities that bring young adults together for mutual benefit.

Aspiration and Productivity

In both educational and work settings, peers have a strong influence on productivity and aspirations. Supportive relationships with peers are related to using one's abilities in achievement situations and to academic competence. Peer rejection predicts school absenteeism, grade retention, and adjustment difficulties. The more one's peers value academic excellence and the higher their academic aspirations, the more likely one is to achieve and to seek out opportunities for higher education. Positive peer relationships are related to successful problem solving. A recent meta-analysis found that positive relationships among students had a profound and quite significant influence on achievement.

Psychological Health

The ability to maintain interdependent, cooperative relationships is a prime manifestation of psychological health. Poor peer relationships in elementary school predict psychological disturbance and delinquency in high school, and poor peer relationships in high school predict adult pathology. The absence of friendships during childhood and adolescence seems to increase the risk of mental disorder. Peer rejection predicts loneliness and emotional distress, whereas friendships and peer acceptance are related to socioemotional adjustment. Children adapt better to stressful situations when in the presence of friends or familiar peers. Both being a bully and being a victim are linked with a number of adjustment difficulties during childhood, including anxiety, loneliness, depression, and school maladaptation, and many of these adjustment difficulties extend into adulthood.

Promoting Positive Peer Relationships

Contemporary children tend to have fewer occasions for peer interaction than did previous generations. Fostering constructive peer relationships may be one of the most important challenges facing parents, educators, and other adults who wish to promote children and adolescents' healthy development and effective socialization. To promote positive peer relationships, children should first have continuous opportunities to cooperate with peers and occasionally engage in competitions. Second, children should receive specific training in the skills needed to build and maintain positive relationships. Being skilled in resolving conflicts may be especially important for constructive peer relationships. Third, prosocial norms such as caring, support, encouragement, assistance, and reciprocity should be established. The rights and responsibilities of collaborators and friends should be clear. Fourth, civic values need to be instilled. Those values include respect for the efforts of others and for them as people, behaving with integrity, caring for others, compassion when others are in need, and commitment to the well-being of others and the common good.

REFERENCES

Johnson, D. W. (1980). Importance of peer relationships. *Children in Contemporary Society, 13*, 121–123.

Johnson, D. W. (2009). *Reaching out: Interpersonal effectiveness and self-actualization* (9th ed.). Boston: Allyn & Bacon.

Ladd, G. (1999). Peer relationships and social competence during early and middle childhood. *Annual review of psychology* (Vol. 50, pp. 333–359). Palo Alto, CA: Annual Reviews.

Prinstein, M. J., & Dodge, K. A. (Eds.). (2008). *Understanding peer influence in children and adolescents.* New York: Guilford Press.

DAVID W. JOHNSON
ROGER T. JOHNSON
University of Minnesota

See also: **Conformity; Friendships; Interpersonal Relationships**

PEER STATUS

Within the first few years of life, children establish relatively stable social positions among their peers. Research has demonstrated longitudinal associations between peer status and a variety of developmental outcomes. However, the correlational nature of this research leaves open the question of whether peer status exerts a unique, causal impact on psychological adjustment. Presented here is a brief synthesis of existing research in the field of peer status, including current definitions of the constructs of peer status and a review of key developmental outcomes often associated with peer status.

Defining and Measuring Peer Status

The construct of peer status has been conceptualized in two distinct ways, each associated with a unique set of developmental outcomes. Traditionally, a preference-based measure of peer status referred to as "sociometric status" has been used (see Coie & Dodge, 1983). This measure involves assessing the degree to which a youth is liked or disliked by same-grade peers by using a peer nomination procedure. The term *social preference* is typically used to refer to a child's relative frequency of positive nominations, whereas *social impact* typically refers to the total frequency of nominations, either positive or negative. Peer nominations may be converted into standardized scores to identify children with relatively extreme acceptance, rejection, social preference, and/or social impact scores. These standard scores may then be used to establish several categories of sociometric peer status. Sociometrically popular youth are strongly liked and rarely disliked. Conversely, rejected status is indicative of few nominations of likability and many nominations of dislikability. Youth who are rarely nominated as either likable or dislikable (i.e., low social impact) are referred to as neglected, whereas youth who are nominated by peers as both likable and dislikable (i.e., high social impact) are assigned a sociometric status of controversial. Approximately half of youth do not qualify for one of these four extreme status groups, and they are referred to as average (Coie & Dodge, 1983).

A second conceptualization of peer status has emerged out of studies of peer status in middle childhood and adolescence, as well as past research in sociology and human ethology. Several such studies have revealed that as youth develop, they are increasingly capable of distinguishing between their own personal preferences and their peers' global reputations of popularity among others. This second, reputation-based construct has been referred to as "peer-perceived popularity" (e.g., LaFontana & Cillessen, 1999; Parkhurst & Hopmeyer, 1998) and typically is assessed by asking youth to nominate peers who are "most popular" and "least popular." Of note, youth with high levels of reputation-based popularity include both those who are sociometrically popular and those who are sociometrically controversial.

Associations between Peer Status and Psychological Adjustment

Substantial research has documented longitudinal associations between peer status and a variety of important developmental outcomes. This research has focused almost exclusively on preference-based status as a predictor; relatively little work has examined long-term outcomes of peer-perceived popularity. For instance, past studies have found that children who are strongly disliked by peers (i.e., sociometrically rejected) are less likely to complete their secondary education, develop long-term romantic relationships, or demonstrate vocational competence as adults. Additionally, there is increasingly strong evidence supporting a longitudinal relationship between peer status and a variety of mental health outcomes, including externalizing symptoms (e.g., aggression, delinquency, behavior disorders), internalizing symptoms (e.g., depression, anxiety), and health risk behaviors (e.g., smoking, drinking, unsafe sex). A brief review of each of these three categories of psychological symptoms follows.

Peer Status and Externalizing Behavior

The overwhelming majority of studies examining peer status as a predictor of externalizing symptoms have offered evidence that children who are rejected by peers are at risk for later aggressive, delinquent, oppositional, and illegal behavior. This finding appears to be consistent across ethnic groups and also across different stages of development. A similar pattern of findings is evident in studies that use children's, parents', or teachers' reports of externalizing symptoms, with some evidence to suggest that peer status predicts externalizing symptoms more than 10 years later.

Recent work has offered intriguing directions for further understanding the nature of the association between peer rejection and externalizing symptoms. Some work has indicated that a subgroup of rejected children (i.e., those who are also aggressive toward peers) are more likely to be at risk for later externalizing symptoms than nonaggressive rejected youth. Other work has suggested that aggressive behavior is a primary determinant of peer rejection, implying a reciprocal, longitudinal association between peer rejection and peer aggression (i.e., a cycle) that ultimately contributes to externalizing symptoms. These reciprocal transactions between aggressive behavior and rejection by peers are thought to influence children's development of specific social-cognitive skill deficits (i.e., maladaptive social information processing of social cues within the environment) and the development of deviant peer group affiliations. Both social information processing deficits and deviant peer group affiliations might explain the long-term risks of childhood rejection and aggression on later externalizing symptoms.

Peer Status and Health Risk Behaviors

Several studies have suggested that peer status also may be associated with behaviors that can increase the risk of physical health problems, substance use, sexual risk behaviors, and weight-management behaviors. The majority of research in this area has examined the prediction of substance use. Studies from longitudinal investigations indicate that childhood peer rejection is associated with later substance use, regardless of when peer rejection is measured in the developmental process. However, there also has been some research supporting a possible link between positive measures of peer status (i.e., high social preference) and increased risk for substance use (Allen, Porter, McFarland, Marsh, & McElhaney, 2005). Recent research has begun to resolve these seemingly discrepant findings by also examining peer-perceived popularity as a predictor of health risk behaviors. Unlike results on sociometric peer status, there is consistent evidence suggesting that high levels of peer-perceived popularity are associated with high levels of health risk behaviors that are considered normative and acceptable among peers (e.g., alcohol use, maladaptive weigh-management behaviors among girls). In other words, although youth may not like peers who are engaged in health risk behaviors, they do regard these peers to be of high social status within the peer context.

Peer Status and Internalizing Symptoms

Studies examining associations between peer status and internalizing symptoms have offered mixed results, probably because of variability in the types of outcomes assessed and the method used to measure internalizing symptoms. The vast majority of studies in this area have examined sociometric status as a predictor of internalizing outcomes. Studies that have examined the prediction of internalizing symptoms as a broad domain of psychopathology (e.g., from an overall symptom checklist) generally report that peer rejection is associated with later internalizing symptoms. In some instances, a combination of peer rejection and aggression or a combination of peer rejection and withdrawal has been associated with increases in internalizing symptoms over time. There also has been evidence to suggest that chronically rejected boys may be especially susceptible to internalizing difficulties (Burks, Dodge, & Price, 1995).

Results pertaining to the link between peer rejection and depressive symptoms are mixed. Several studies have revealed that peer rejection is associated longitudinally with increasing levels of depressive symptoms, while other studies have failed to find an association between peer rejection and depressive symptoms (e.g., Woodward & Fergusson, 1999). Cognitive theories, which have been especially fruitful in understanding the development of depressive symptoms, may help to account for variability in the link between peer status and internalizing symptoms. For example, it seems that variability exists in rejected youths' perceptions of their peer status and that the discrepancy between youths' actual and perceived peer status may be predictive of increases in depression. Alternatively, diathesis-stress models of depression suggest that the predisposition to interpret stressful events in a certain manner (i.e., "depressogenic attributional style") may increase depression risk for those who experience negative life stressors (Abramson, Metalsky, & Alloy, 1989). Peer rejection may be seen as a relevant stressful experience that elicits these negative cognitive interpretations in vulnerable youth. Research has confirmed that the interaction between a depressogenic cognitive style and sociometric peer rejection is longitudinally associated with increases in depressive symptoms (e.g., Prinstein & Aikins, 2004).

In sum, there is substantial evidence to suggest that peer status is associated with a range of psychological symptoms and health risk behaviors. In particular, much research suggests that peer rejection may exert a direct effect on later psychological adjustment or may interact with other behavioral difficulties (e.g., aggression, withdrawal) to produce risk for psychopathology.

REFERENCES

Abramson, L. Y., Metalsky, G. I., & Alloy, L. B. (1989). Hopelessness depression: A theory-based subtype of depression. *Psychological Review, 96*, 358–372.

Allen, J. P., Porter, M. R., McFarland, F. C., Marsh, P., & McElhaney, K. B. (2005). The two faces of adolescents' success with peers: Adolescent popularity, social adaptation, and deviant behavior. *Child Development, 3*, 747–760.

Burks, V. S., Dodge, K. A., & Price, J. M. (1995). Models of internalizing outcomes of early rejection. *Development and Psychopathology, 7*, 683–695.

Coie, J. D., & Dodge, K. A. (1983). Continuities and changes in children's social status: A five-year longitudinal study. *Merrill-Palmer Quarterly, 29*(3), 261–282.

LaFontana, K. M., & Cillessen, A. H. N. (1999). Children's interpersonal perceptions as a function of sociometric and peer-perceived popularity. *Journal of Genetic Psychology, 160*(2), 225–242.

Parkhurst, J. T., & Hopmeyer, A. (1998). Sociometric popularity and peer-perceived popularity: Two distinct dimensions of peer status. *Journal of Early Adolescence, 18*(2), 125–144.

Prinstein, M. J., & Aikins, J. W. (2004). Cognitive moderators of the longitudinal association between peer rejection and adolescent depressive symptoms. *Journal of Abnormal Child Psychology, 32*, 147–158.

Woodward, L. J., & Fergusson, D. M. (1999). Childhood peer relationship problems and psychosocial adjustment in late adolescence. *Journal of Abnormal Psychology, 27*, 87–104.

SUGGESTED READINGS

LaFontana, K. M., & Cillessen, A. H. N. (2002). Children's perceptions of popular and unpopular peers: A multimethod assessment. *Developmental Psychology, 38*(5), 635–647.

Prinstein, M. J., Rancourt, D., Guerry, J. D., & Browne, C. B. (2009). Peer reputations and psychological adjustment. In K. H. Rubin, W. M. Bukowski, & B. Laursen (Eds.), *Handbook of peer interactions, relationships, and groups*. New York: Guilford Press.

CAROLINE B. BROWNE
MITCHELL J. PRINSTEIN
NICOLE HEILBRON
University of North Carolina at Chapel Hill

See also: Adolescent Development; Child Psychology; Interpersonal Relationships

PEER TUTORING

Peer tutoring is an instructional strategy that employs peer interaction for the purpose of teaching and learning. Peers are defined as individuals of comparable stature, such as school-age children.

Benefits

The benefits of peer tutoring include (1) superiority to traditional models, (2) effectiveness in promoting both academic and affective outcomes, (3) effectiveness with vulnerable student populations, and (4) versatility and cost-effectiveness. In a recent meta-analysis of 81 studies of peer assisted learning strategies (PAL) applied to elementary students, PAL strategies outperformed traditional methods, with a large effect size of .59 for academic outcomes. In this research synthesis there were no differences in effects between peer tutoring and small group procedures such as cooperative learning, with both yielding comparable positive results (Rohrbeck, Ginsburg-Block, Fantuzzo, & Miller, 2003).

In addition to academic benefits, peer tutoring results in significant nonacademic outcomes, including enhancements in social skills, self-concept, behavior, and academic motivation (Ginsburg-Block, Rohrbeck, & Fantuzzo, 2006; Ginsburg-Block, Rohrbeck, Lavigne, & Fantuzzo, 2008). Studies have shown peer tutoring strategies to be effective for vulnerable groups of students including low-income, minority, urban, English language learners, and students with disabilities. Finally, peer tutoring has been shown to be a cost effective and versatile strategy considering its significant effects, relatively low costs, and multiple uses.

Underlying Mechanisms

Changes in cognition, behavior, and motivation associated with social learning opportunities are theorized to produce the learning outcomes observed in peer tutoring participants. Although the specific procedures employed in peer tutoring vary according to the peer tutoring model being implemented, a body of research has identified several effective components of peer tutoring. Peer tutoring strategies that enable tasks and evaluation standards to be individualized according to student performance, provide opportunities for student autonomy, establish a structure for peer interactions, and use interdependent group reward contingencies have yielded significantly better results than strategies lacking these components (Ginsburg-Block et al., 2006; Rohrbeck et al., 2003).

Evidence-Based Models

The effectiveness of several peer tutoring models has been established through multiple well-controlled experimental research studies. Examples of these evidence-based models include Classwide Peer Tutoring (CWPT), Peer Assisted Learning Strategies (PALS), and Reciprocal Peer Tutoring (RPT). CWPT was developed by researchers at the University of Kansas to enable students with disabilities to succeed in regular education classrooms. The key components of CWPT are reciprocal roles for student dyads, frequent opportunities for practice and feedback, weekly evaluation of performance, opportunities for students to monitor their own performance, individual and group contingencies, and public posting of performance outcomes.

PALS was developed by researchers at the Peabody College of Vanderbilt University as an enhancement to CWPT. PALS incorporates CWPT with computerized curriculum-based measurement procedures that are used to closely monitor student progress. RPT was developed for low-achieving students and involves pairing students of comparable ability together to reduce competition and increase collaboration among participants who may initially be reluctant to collaborate. In common with other peer tutoring models, the key components of RPT include structured reciprocal peer interactions and an interdependent group-reward contingency. Taken together these models have been successfully applied across content areas, grade levels, and learners with diverse characteristics (Ginsburg-Block, Rohrbeck, Fantuzzo, & Lavigne, 2006).

REFERENCES

Ginsburg-Block, M., Rohrbeck, C., & Fantuzzo, J. W. (2006). A meta-analytic review of the social, emotional, and behavioral outcomes of peer assisted learning. *Journal of Educational Psychology, 98*(4), 732–749.

Ginsburg-Block, M., Rohrbeck, C., Fantuzzo, J. W., & Lavigne, N. C. (2006). Peer assisted learning strategies. In G. Bear & K. Minke (Eds.), *Children's needs III: Understanding and addressing the developmental needs of children* (pp. 631–645). Bethesda, MD: National Association of School Psychologists.

Ginsburg-Block, M., Rohrbeck, C., & Lavigne, N., & Fantuzzo, J. W. (2008). Peer Assisted Learning: An academic strategy for enhancing motivation among diverse students. In A. E. Gottfried & C. Hudley (Eds.), *Academic motivation and the culture of school in childhood and adolescence* (pp. 247–273). New York: Oxford University Press.

Rohrbeck, C., Ginsburg-Block, M., Fantuzzo, J., & Miller, T. (2003). Peer assisted learning interventions with elementary school students: A meta-analytic review. *Journal of Educational Psychology, 95*(2), 240–257.

MARIKA GINSBURG-BLOCK
University of Delaware

PERCEPTION

Perception refers to the experience of obtaining sensory information about the world of people, things, and events and the underlying processes.

The Classical Theory: 1. The Elementary Sensations

Successive British philosophers from Hobbes to Berkeley to Mill, being empiricist epistemologists, considered perceptions as learned assemblies of more elementary experiences. Scientific study began in 1838, when J. Müller identified the separable sensory modalities; to H. von Helmholtz (Müller's student), a modality provides elementary sensations from specific receptors, each sensitive to some physical stimulation. Thus, the eye's retina contains cones sensitive to long, middle, or short wavelengths (L, M, S), providing red, green, or blue points of color sensation, respectively. (Graphic artists had long used arrays of a few kinds of dots to portray all colors.)

The Classical Theory: 2. Objects, Depth, Constancies, Illusions

Since light at the eye is two-dimensional (Figure 1A), depth cannot be directly sensed in this approach. Fortunately, normal environments offer depth cues (Figures 1C and 1D are simple examples), well studied by fifteenth-century artists. To classical theory, depth perception derives from memory *associations* between such cues and accompanying actions (reaching, eye movements, etc.). Cues, as dissected by receptors (symbolized in Figure 1E), plus learned unconscious rules relating objects to their retinal images, let perceivers unconsciously infer various object attributes. Thus, although the size, shape, and brightness of an object's retinal image change with distance, viewpoint, and illumination, and although saccades (glances) fracture what lies before us, the correct use of the cues (including eye-movement commands) provides size constancy, shape constancy, color constancy, transsaccadic constancy, and so forth. Misperceptions, or illusions, are presumably erroneous unconscious inferences (e.g., perceiving something as larger because of misperceiving it as farther).

Perceptions should therefore be predictable from a pointwise analysis of the sensory pattern, plus from a list of the probabilities of that pattern's alternative sources in the perceiver's past environmental encounters. (Most displays do indeed reflect such probabilistic or *Bayesian* principles; see Geisler [2008] for a recent review.)

However, the classical theory has since expired, epistemologically because some animal species respond to depth without prior visuomotor experience, and scientifically because the supposedly independent receptors are actually interconnected, not independent. Before facing that critical issue, however, the theory faced recent consequential competitors.

Organization, Figure-Ground, and the Gestaltist Argument

To Gestalt theorists (notably M. Wertheimer, W. Köhler, and K. Koffka), visual systems respond directly to an overall configuration (or *Gestalt*) of sensory stimulation, not by pointwise analysis. The primary visual units are shaped regions, as in Figure 2A (Rubin's figure-ground phenomenon): there, only one region (urn or pair of faces) is shaped *figure* at any time, the other being shape-free *ground*, so laws of figure-ground organization determine what we perceive. By the law of good continuation, for example, a familiar number is concealed and revealed in Figures 2B and 2C, respectively, and the apparent cube in Figure 2E is compellingly flat in Figure 2D. Such phenomena were offered as evidence for isomorphic (same-shaped) configured current-flow cortical processes, as opposed to associative learning.

However, Gestalt theory has not made its case on isomorphism; its belief that figural organization must precede any effects of familiarity is contradicted by Figures 2I and J, which are examples of denotative shapes established by M. Peterson and B. Gibson; moreover, so-called organizational laws themselves may simply reflect learned environmental likelihoods, as E. Brunswik proposed, and as animals' protective coloration (Figure 2F) suggests. The Gestalt phenomena themselves remain important in making visual displays (Z. Pylyshyn), in improving search procedures in airports and x-ray clinics (J. Wolfe), and in learning how our perceptual systems work, so quantifying organizational laws continues (e.g., J. Pomerantz, M. Kubovy).

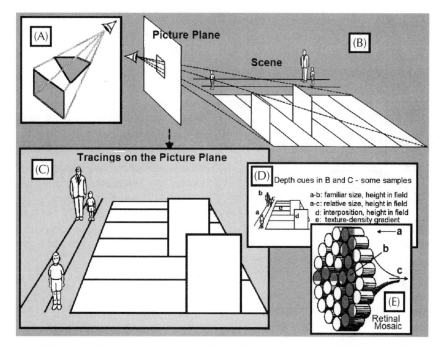

Figure 1. Vision, in the classical theory. A. Because eyes receive only two-dimensional arrays of light, layout B and plane C can provide the same image. At D, some characteristic depth cues. E, a schematic sketch of the retina, with independent light-sensitive cells at a, receiving the interposition cue (d from previous figure, D) at b, and a cable c of independent nerve fibers carrying the receptor information toward the brain.

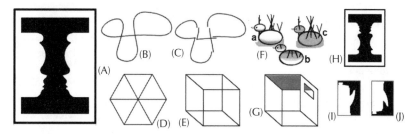

Figure 2. Gestalt theory and some limits. A. Figure and ground: Only one region at a time has shape. B, C. By the law of good continuation, the "4" at C is concealed at B. Because D is simpler as a bidimensional shape than E, E looks more reversibly tridimensional. F. The bird at a is highly visible against its natural background; with protective coloration as at b, it is much less so, as at c. G. Although its orientation is fixed at upper right, this "killer cube" seems free to reverse at lower left, showing that perceived objects are *not* wholes (Gestalten). H. Is the black urn easier to see as figure here than at A? I, J. Figural emergence does not precede any effects of familiarity, as believed; see text.

More broadly, different Gestaltist-like efforts toward a quantifiable principle, assuming that we perceive the simplest structure that fits each stimulus pattern (cf. Figures 2D and E), were attempted separately by F. Attneave, by the present author (with E. McAlister), by E. Leeuwenberg (1960) and colleagues, and most recently by Z. Pylyshyn (2008).

However, a simplicity principle cannot be simple, for reasons discussed here after noting the classical theory's other major opponent.

Direct Perception versus Inference and Isomorphism

Opposing both Helmholtzian and Gestaltist approaches, J. J. Gibson argued that natural environments provide invariants of stimulus information (notably, the optical expansion pattern of an approaching surface varies with its slant, approach rate, etc.). Such invariants could enable direct perception of objects and layouts, making the classical inferences from depth cues and the Gestaltists' organizational isomorphism unnecessary. This approach has generated sophisticated analyses of visual information (e.g., J. Todd) but ignores the Helmholtzian and Gestalt phenomena: Depth cues and organizational factors certainly do appear to work, at least in pictures and movies (for which Gibson's proposed invariants simply fail to apply; see Cutting, 1987).

Moreover, like Gestalt theory, direct perception theory fails to use what we now know about eye and brain.

Modern Neurophysiology, Cell Assemblies, and Phase Sequences

As noted earlier, Helmholtz's assumptions about independent receptor neurons were elegant but wrong. D. Hubel

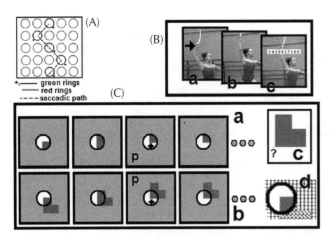

Figure 3. Purposeful perceptual inquiry: separating its components. A. When the eye follows a memorized path, attention (measured by probes) mostly remains one glance ahead; when the eye follows a marked path (as here), attention is widely distributable (Gersch, Kowler, Schintzer, & Dosher, in press). B. Aimed at fixating familiarly moving targets (a) in short movie sequences, glances can both anticipate the target's path and allow for their own shifting time (Hochberg, in press). C. To examine how peripheral landmarks help in combining successive foveal views, moving objects are shown piecemeal through stationary apertures (three versions are shown in a, b, and d); the viewer reports where the probe p had been shown on each object (as at c). See text.

and T. Wiesel, using microelectrodes in 1960, found individual cells with receptive fields selectively sensitive to local shapes and motions. Moreover, the retina and several levels of its cortical projections are mutually connected *in both directions,* providing top-down effects on sensory input (see Wandell Dumoulin & Brewer, 2007 for recent review).

Well before such research actually changed our view of the nervous system, D. Hebb had argued persuasively that neurons that are coactive produce *cell assemblies* and act as pattern-sensitive units, and that repeated serial activities yield *phase sequences* that unfold over time. Given such forward-aiming pattern-sensitive actions and the top-down interactions now amply verified, perceiving is not a passive registration process; it is a multilevel mix of purposeful attentional behaviors.

Attention, the Questing Eye, and Its Schematic Map

Only the retina's tiny central region, the fovea, resolves fine detail. To see more, the viewer executes rapid *intentional* eye movements (saccades), with sequences of about 5 per second, following preselected routes. After such a brief moment of high detail, the region just looked at remains only as a simplified encoded memory (and/or as part of the impoverished peripheral surrounding). Detail not deliberately stored in working memory, as G. Sperling showed in 1960; it is usually lost with that glance. And it is the viewer's brain that elects what to look or listen for next, and then what to encode first in the next glance: So perception starts with motivated attentional processes, not with the retinal mosaic of Figure 1. And limited central selection, peripheral paucity, and sparse transfer across

glances may provide a multistage simplicity principle that accommodates the likes of Figure 2G.

Research now explores how attentional and saccadic routes are each programmed and with what consequences (see Figure 3A); it explores how looking behaviors are shaped both by the viewer's anticipations about the events being attended and about the looking behavior itself (as in Figure 3B) and examines how fovea and periphery contribute to successive integration (Figure 3C). Perception is a purposeful sequential activity, and such research should accompany brain imaging in order to help the latter tell us how our systems work.

REFERENCES[*]

*NOTE: Authors who are cited in the foregoing text and are not listed here are given in Hochberg, 1998, Chs. 1, 11.

Cutting, J. (1987). Rigidity in cinema seen from the front row, side aisle. *Journal of Experimental Psychology: Human Perception and Performance, 13,* 323–334.

Geisler, W. S. (2008). Visual perception and the statistical properties of natural scenes. *Annual Review of Psychology, 59,* 10.1–10.26.

Gersch, T. M., Kowler, E., Schintzer, B. S., & Dosher, B. S. (in press). Attention during sequences of saccades along marked and memorized paths. *Vision Research.*

Hochberg, J. (in press). Perceptual prosody and perceived personality: Physiognomics precede perspective. In Morsella, E. (Ed.), *Expressing oneself/expressing one's self: Communication, language, cognition and identity: A festschrift in honor of Robert M. Krauss.* London: Taylor & Francis.

Hyönä, J., Munoz, D. P., Heide, W., & Radach, R. (Eds.). (2003). *The brain's eye: Neurobiological and clinical aspects of oculomotor research.* Oxford: Elsevier Press.

Peterson, M. A. (1994). Shape recognition can and does occur before figure-ground organization. *Current Directions in Psychological Science, 3,* 105–111.

Todd, J. (2004). The visual perception of 3D shape. *Trends in Cognitive Sciences, 8,* 115–121.

Wandell, B. A., Dumoulin, S. O., & Brewer, A. A. (2007). Visual field maps in human cortex. *Neuron, 56,* 366–383.

Wolfe, J. (2003). Moving towards solutions to some enduring controversies in visual search. *Trends in Cognitive Sciences, 7,* 70–76.

SUGGESTED READINGS

Enns, J. T. (2004). *The thinking eye, the seeing brain.* New York: W. W. Norton.

Hochberg, J. (1998). *Perception and cognition at century's end.* San Diego, CA: Academic Press.

Pizlo, Z. (2008) *3D shape: Its unique place in visual perception.* Cambridge, MA: MIT Press.

JULIAN HOCHBERG
Columbia University

***See also:* Visual Illusions**

PERCEPTUAL CONTROL THEORY

Perceptual control theory (PCT) is a theory of mind that was developed by William T. Powers and his colleagues to explain the purposeful behavior of living organisms (Powers, Clark, & McFarland, 1960). Purposeful behavior is seen in the ability of organisms to produce preselected results in a disturbance-prone world, as in the human ability to drive to a preselected destination despite unpredictable disturbances like road closures and car problems. Powers's use of control theory to explain purposeful behavior was based on his experience as a control engineer, which gave him the opportunity to see that the controlling done by artificial control systems, such as a thermostat, is equivalent to the purposeful behavior carried out by living systems, such as a driver. In both cases, systems are producing preselected results in the face of unpredictable disturbances. PCT is a theory of how systems, living and artificial, produce results on purpose, that is, how they exert control.

Powers was not the first to see the resemblance between controlling and purposeful behavior; that honor probably belongs to the developers of cybernetics, the science of control (and communication) in animals and machines (Wiener, 1948). But Powers went well beyond the cyberneticists and others who had applied control theory to behavior (e.g., Jagacinski & Flach, 2002) by recognizing a truly revolutionary fact about the behavior of control systems, which is that they act to control their perceptual input, not their motor output. Purposeful behavior, according to PCT, is the control of perception, a fact that is captured by the title of Powers's first monograph describing his control theory model of behavior: *Behavior: The Control of Perception* (Powers, 1973).

The idea that behavior is the control of perception is revolutionary because virtually all other theories of behavior, including those that are based on control theory, view behavior as controlled *by* perception. The small difference in the preposition used to describe the theory—control *of* rather than *by* perception—makes all the difference. The idea that behavior is the control *of* perception is so revolutionary that, to this day, people read the title of Powers's 1973 book and conclude that it is about how behavior is controlled *by* perception. Because control of perception is fundamental to Powers's control theory model of purposeful behavior, the theory has come to be called perceptual control theory to distinguish it from other applications of control theory that still view behavior as controlled by perception.

Perceptual control theory views the organism as a collection of closed-loop negative feedback systems, each controlling a different perceptual aspect of the organism's environment. The input to each system is a perceptual function that converts a variable aspect of the environment into a quantitative variable, the perceptual signal. The system compares this perceptual signal with a reference signal that specifies the desired magnitude of the perceptual signal. The comparison is done by subtracting the perceptual from the reference signal. The result is a measure of discrepancy called the error signal, which is converted by an output function into actions that have physical effects on the aspect of the environment that is represented by the perceptual signal. This completes a causal loop that starts and ends with the perceptual signal. If the control system is set up so that the error signal produces actions that move the perceptual signal toward the reference signal, thus reducing the error that caused the actions in the first place, the feedback in the loop is negative, and the system acts to control its perceptual signal, keeping it matching the reference signal.

A well-designed control system will keep its perceptual signal matching a fixed or varying reference signal. For example, a human controller can keep the perception of where a finger is pointing in a fixed reference state, as when one points at a stationary target, or varying reference state, as when one traces out a circle around the target. Moreover, a control system can keep its perceptual signal matching the reference signal while acting to counter disturbances that would push the perceptual signal away from the reference if the system did nothing. So one can keep a finger pointing at a target even while changing one's posture in a way that would push the finger off target if one did not compensate appropriately, and one can keep the finger circling the target even if the target starts moving.

Scientific psychology has been built on the assumption that environmental inputs to the organism are the ultimate cause of behavioral output. This assumption is based on the fact that environmental stimuli often do appear to be the cause of behavioral responses. A simple example is the salivary reflex: Putting food powder into a dog's mouth (the stimulus) results in the secretion of saliva (the response). PCT shows that the apparent causal link from stimulus to response is an illusion (Powers, 1978). The observed relationship between stimulus and response in a control system actually represents the opposing effects of disturbance (stimulus) and action (response) on a controlled perceptual variable. In the salivary reflex, the food powder (stimulus) is a disturbance to a perception being controlled (such as the moistness of the mouth), the effects of which (drying of the mouth) are resisted by the salivation (response). The stimulus–response relationship exists only because the system is controlling a particular perception.

The central concept in PCT is the *controlled variable* (Marken, 2001), which is the environmental correlate of the perceptual signal that a control system controls. According to PCT, organisms act only in order to keep their perceptual signals—and, thus, the corresponding controlled variables—in states specified by their reference signals. Research based on PCT is aimed at determining the variables that organisms control: controlled variables. The basic method used to achieve this goal is called the test for the controlled variable (TCV; Runkel, 1990).

The TCV is an iterative approach to determining whether a particular aspect of the environment is being controlled by an organism. It begins with a hypothesis about the variable the organism might be controlling. The experimenter monitors the hypothetical controlled variable—the dependent variable (DV) in the experiment—while applying disturbances—the independent variable (IV)—that have predictable effects on the DV if it is not under control. The process continues until one finds a definition of the controlled variable that is not affected by all disturbances that would affect it if it were not controlled.

Note that the focus of the TCV differs considerably from that of the conventional psychology experiment. In the latter, the focus is on finding an effect of an IV on the DV, indicating that the IV is the cause of behavior. In the former, the focus is on finding lack of effect of the IV on the DV, indicating that the DV is under control.

Research based on PCT involves both experimentation using the TCV and modeling, typically in the form of computer simulations of control behavior. For example, based on tests to determine the perceptual variables a person controls when catching a fly ball, computer simulations that control these variables have been shown to behave very much like the real person. A computer demonstration of a fly ball catch simulation can be seen online (http://www.mindreadings.com/ControlDemo/CatchXY.html). Other examples of research based on PCT can be found on the Internet (http://www.mindreadings.com) and in a collection of papers by Marken (2002).

PCT has also had considerable influence in the field of counseling psychology (Carey, 2006). This may be because PCT provides a clear, quantitative explanation of internal conflict, which is probably the main reason people seek help in counseling. Conflict occurs when two control systems within the same person, in order to achieve their purposes, require that the same variable be in two different states at the same time, a physical impossibility. For example, conflict occurs when a system with the purpose of staying thin and another with the purpose of eating require that the amount of food consumed be both none and some. Since it is impossible to both eat and not eat, the only way to solve this conflict is for the person to revise the purposes that are the cause of the conflict. A counseling technique, called the method of levels, which is based on the PCT analysis of conflict, has been successfully used to help patients help themselves solve their own conflicts.

Control theory, which was originally developed by electrical engineers, now provides the basic organizational structure of the PCT model of purposeful behavior: the closed negative feedback loop. On that structure, Powers has built a model that accounts for all aspects of the complex phenomenon that is purposeful behavior, including learning, memory, imagination, emotion, language, social interaction, and consciousness. Research has begun in some of these areas, but there is a great deal still to be done. PCT represents a new and unfamiliar approach to understanding behavior. The field is wide open for the adventurous researcher who is interested in understanding the nature of purposeful behavior.

REFERENCES

Carey, T. (2006). *The method of levels: How to do psychotherapy without getting in the way.* Hayward, CA: Living Control System.

Jagacinski, R., & Flach, J. (2002). *Control theory for humans: Quantitative approaches to modeling performance.* Mahwah, NJ: Lawrence Erlbaum.

Marken, R. S. (2001). Controlled variables: Psychology as the center fielder views it. *American Journal of Psychology, 114*(2), 259–282.

Marken, R. S. (2002). *More mind readings: Methods and models in the study of purpose.* St. Louis, MO: Newview.

Powers, W. T. (1978). Quantitative analysis of purposive systems: Some spadework at the foundations of experimental psychology. *Psychological Review, 85,* 417–435.

Powers, W. T. (2005). *Behavior: The control of perception* (2nd ed.). New Canaan, CT: Benchmark. (Original work published 1973.)

Powers, W. T., Clark, R. K, & McFarland, R. L. (1960). A general feedback theory of human behavior, Parts I and II. *Perceptual and Motor Skills, 11,* 71–323.

Runkel, P. J. (1990). *Casting nets and testing specimens: Two grand methods of psychology.* New York: Praeger.

Wiener, N. (1948). *Cybernetics: Or the control and communication in the animal and the machine.* Cambridge, MA: MIT Press.

SUGGESTED READINGS

Cziko, G. (2000). *The things we do: Using the lessons of Bernard and Darwin to understand the what, how and why of our behavior.* Cambridge, MA: MIT Press.

Marken, R. S. (1992). *Mind readings: Experimental studies of purpose.* Gravel Switch, KY: CSG Press.

Runkel, P. J. (2003). *People as living things: The psychology of perceptual control.* Hayward, CA: Living Control Systems.

RICHARD S. MARKEN
University of California at Los Angeles

See also: **Behavioral Modeling; Control Therapy; Homeostasis**

PERCEPTUAL DEVELOPMENT

Parents, educators, and researchers alike often question how infants and children learn to organize and interpret things they see, hear, smell, taste, and touch. The study of perceptual development examines how the use of the five senses changes over time as well as how information perceived in the environment shapes later perceptual abilities. There are several present-day theories of perceptual development that differ in their views of the nature of the information available to infants' sensory systems (see Gibson & Pick, 2000, for a review). For example, some view sensory information as crude and insufficient for perception, and they suggest that the first step is to actively construct a representation of the external world. Another view, the ecological approach, considers sensory information as rich and well organized, in addition to assuming reciprocal interaction between the environment and the perceiver. The present review highlights the fundamentals of perceptual development, and it suggests that this development is best viewed as a bidirectional interaction between maturational factors and experience.

The Development of Visual Perception

Visual perception is dependent on the development of visual acuity, contrast sensitivity, color perception, motion detection, and depth perception. Visual acuity is a measure of how clearly infants see fine details. At birth, cells in the retina of the eye, the connections of these cells to the brain, and the muscles that control eye movements are all relatively immature, which leads to poor control of the movement of the eyes and poor visual acuity. In infants, grating acuity, or the ability to resolve black and white stripes of different widths, is the most commonly studied type of acuity. Research suggests that newborns have approximately 20/3,000 to 20/120 vision that improves to close to adult levels (20/30) by age 8 months (Kellman & Arterberry, 2006).

Images with high-contrast edges and patterns are the most visible and attractive to infants. However, contrast sensitivity, or the ability to distinguish between shades, also improves from about 10 times less than adults at birth to adult levels by age 2 months. Infants are also able to detect and differentiate highly saturated reds and greens as early as age 4 weeks. However, their ability to distinguish subtler colors, such as pastels, is not like that of adults until age 4 months (Kellmann & Arterberry, 2006).

Motion of objects and motion of observation of objects lead to an increased understanding of the visual world. Research has examined the development of many different types of motion. This research has found that motion is better detected by moving versus stationary infants as young as 8 weeks of age (Kellmann & Arterberry, 2006).

Depth perception is relatively poor in the newborn and requires the development of both the muscles involved in coordinating eye movements and cells in the eye, as well as visual experience. By about 4 months of age, infants are able to make use of binocular visual information and perceive depth (Gibson & Pick, 2000).

The Development of Face and Object Perception

Infants' perception of objects requires the knowledge that objects remain the same size and shape with changes in distance and orientation (perceptual constancy) and that objects can be separated from other objects in an array or scene (object segregation). Object constancy appears to be mature at birth. Infants are capable of object segregation by using motion as a cue by age 4 months and even earlier if there are apparent visual gaps between objects.

Studies of the development of face perception suggests that newborns prefer to look at facelike stimuli rather than types of patterns and objects. It was long thought that faces themselves captured the attention of infants and represented an inborn face preference. However, Cassia, Turati, and Simion (2004) have recently argued against this account by showing that the preference for faces can be accounted for by a consistent preference for any stimulus with more elements in the upper half than in the lower half. Regardless of the origins of these face preferences, infants who are only hours old rapidly learn from the environment around them, and they are able to discriminate their mothers from strangers. By the end of the first year of life, infants can categorize gender and race and recognize emotional expressions (Kellman & Arterberry, 2006).

The Development of Auditory Perception

Newborns are able to discriminate among different sound frequencies and intensities and prefer to listen to speech and music rather than noise. Newborns also prefer to listen to their mother's voice, and they show a preference for a story read to them in the womb by their mother over a new version of the same story (DeCasper & Spence, 1986).

Infants are very skilled perceivers of speech sounds. Young infants selectively prefer to listen to sounds within the range of human speech. They are able to discriminate among basic units of sounds (phonemes) across languages. By the end of their first year, infants prefer their native language and are better at discriminating phonemes within their native language than in other languages (Saffran, Werker, & Werner, 2006).

The Development of Touch and Action Perception

Throughout development, perception and action are linked. Infants learn about the environment through touching or mouthing surrounding objects. Oral exploration of objects is dominant until about 4 months of age, when infants begin to gain control of the movements of their limbs. These movements may be crucial to infants in learning to perceive aspects of the world, such as depth and movement, and to infants' improved acuity. This bidirectional influence has been substantiated through research on infants' guided action and reaching behaviors (e.g., Keen, Carrico, Sylvia, & Berthier, 2003), which suggests that perceptual development helps guide actions and thus, in turn, supports further perceptual development.

The Development of Intersensory Perception

Infants typically experience the surrounding world through the simultaneous activation of multiple senses. The study of intersensory perception investigates how infants combine information across modalities. Traditional views of intersensory perception can be divided into two categories: the integration view and the differentiation view (see Lickliter & Bahrick, 2000). The integration view posits that sensory systems are unimodal at birth and, through experience, begin to work together to provide multimodal sensory information. The differentiation view describes an opposite process whereby the senses are integrated early and, through experience, become more differential in their functioning. Although the timing is debated, intermodal perception between vision and sound appears to occur, with little experience, in newborns, and intermodal perception between vision and touch occurs by at least age 1 month.

Common Patterns of Development across Domains of Perception

A question that permeates the study of perceptual development is whether there are domain-general principles that scaffold development across domains. Much of this review reported what we know about perceptual development within sensory systems. However, it is important to consider theorists who suggest that perceptual development is guided by general learning mechanisms. Two of these theories are statistical learning and perceptual narrowing.

Statistical learning is a rapidly occurring, experience-dependent form of perceptual associative learning that is thought to underlie much of perceptual development (Fiser & Aslin, 2002). This type of learning occurs in infants as young as 2 months of age and has been defined as the computation of the probability that a single feature (whether it be a sound or an image) is associated with a second (or additional) feature. This type of learning may serve as the building block for higher-order perceptual processing and has been found in both visual (Fiser & Aslin, 2002) and auditory (see Saffran, Werker, & Werner, 2006) perceptual systems.

Another domain-generated theory of perceptual development posits that the infants' ability to perceptually discriminate within-category stimuli is tuned to the demands of their environment. This results in a decline, from about 6–12 months of age, in the ease of differentiating less frequently encountered types of stimuli and maintenance (or possibly facilitation) of the ability to differentiate frequently encountered stimuli. Perceptual narrowing has

been shown in the development of speech perception, face perception, intersensory perception, and the perception of musical rhythms. Within the area of face perception, research has shown a decline, dependent on experience, in the ability to differentiate less frequently encountered types of faces (such as two other-race faces or two other-species faces). One hypothesized outcome of this developmental process is that adults have more difficulty differentiating and remembering other-race faces as compared with own-race faces (see Scott, Pascalis, & Nelson, 2007).

This review has only highlighted the fundamentals of perceptual development, much of which occurs during the first year of life. During this first year, the primary sensory organs, the body, and the brain all undergo dramatic physical changes. These physical changes interact reciprocally with the surrounding environment in order to build perceptual representations of objects, people, sounds, language, music, and their combination. Across all of these areas, experience with the external world appears to play a prominent role in shaping and defining mature perceptual systems.

REFERENCES

Cassia, V. M., Turati, C., & Simion, F. (2004). Can a nonspecific bias toward top-heavy patterns explain newborns' face preference? *Psychological Science, 15,* 379–383.

DeCasper, A. J., & Spence, M. J. (1986). Prenatal maternal speech influences newborns' perception of speech sounds. *Infant Behavior and Development, 9,* 133–150.

Fiser, J., & Aslin, R. N. (2002). Statistical learning of new visual feature combinations by infants. *Proceedings of the National Academy of Sciences, 99,* 15822–15826.

Gibson, E. J., & Pick, A. D. (2000). *An ecological approach to perceptual learning and development.* New York: Oxford University Press.

Keen, R., Carrico, R. L., Sylvia, M. R., & Berthier, N. E. (2003). How infants use perceptual information to guide action. *Developmental Science, 6*(2), 221–231.

Kellman, P. J., & Arterberry, M. A. (2006). Infant visual perception. In R. Siegler & D. Kuhn (Eds.), *Handbook of child psychology* (6th ed.): *Vol. 2. Cognition, perception, and language.* Hoboken, NJ: John Wiley & Sons.

Lickliter, R., & Bahrick, L. E. (2000). The development of infant intersensory perception: Advantages of a comparative convergent-operations approach. *Psychological Bulletin, 126,* 260–280.

Saffran, J. R., Werker, J. F., & Werner, L. A. (2006). The infant's auditory world: Hearing, speech, and the beginnings of language. In R. Siegler and D. Kuhn (Eds.), *Handbook of child psychology* (6th ed.): *Vol. 2. Cognition, perception, and language.* Hoboken, NJ: John Wiley & Sons.

Scott, L. S., Pascalis, O., & Nelson, C. A. (2007). A domain-general theory of the development of perceptual discrimination. *Current Directions in Psychological Science, 16,* 197–201.

ALEXANDRA MONESSON
LISA S. SCOTT
University of Massachusetts, Amherst

PERFECTIONISM

Perfectionism is a broad and multifaceted personality construct that involves the requirement of perfection or the appearance of perfection for the self or for others. This personality style is thought to incorporate both trait components that reflect a stable and enduring need for the self or others to be perfect and self-presentational facets that reflect the interpersonal expression of perfection or the need to appear perfect (Hewitt & Flett, 1991; Hewitt et al., 2003). It is generally thought that perfectionism is composed of motivational, interpersonal, behavioral, and cognitive processing features (Flett & Hewitt, 2002). At the same time, it is important to clarify what perfectionism is not: it is not obsessiveness, orderliness, rigidity, conscientiousness, or achievement motivation. Although some of these features can at times coexist with perfectionism, they do not constitute perfectionism.

Although the concept of perfectionism has been discussed as a relevant clinical variable over the past 70 years (e.g., Horney, 1950/1991), it has only received research attention for the past 20 years. Several multidimensional conceptualizations have received the most attention in the literature. A model described by Frost, Marten, Lahart, and Rosenblate (1990) proposed that perfectionism involves both self-related dimensions, such as holding unrealistic expectations, critical self-evaluations and concern over errors, doubting one's actions, and interpersonal dimensions reflecting unrealistic parental expectations and parental criticisms. A second conceptualization focuses on the trait and self-presentational dimensions of perfectionism (Hewitt & Flett, 1991; Hewitt et al., 2003). For example, with respect to trait dimensions, self-oriented perfectionism is the requirement for the self to be perfect. It is what we usually think of when we use the term perfectionism.

By contrast, other-oriented perfectionism is the requirement that other people (e.g., spouse, children, subordinates, people in general) should be perfect. As a final variation, socially prescribed perfectionism is the perception that others (e.g., one's parents, boss, people in general) require oneself to be perfect. More recently, an additional component to this conceptualization was proposed that focuses on the need for certain perfectionists to project an image of being perfect, either by emphasizing "to-be-admired" qualities (perfectionistic self-promotion), or by concealing demonstrations of negative qualities or imperfections or refusing to disclose imperfections to other people. Whereas some people rebel against or crumble from social pressures to be perfect, perfectionistic self-presenters need to be seen and recognized by other people as perfectly flawless.

It is clear on the basis of developmental research that this personality style is evident across the age span, and research with children, adolescents, adults, and seniors indicates that it is a relevant personality style to study and understand. There have been several models proposed regarding the development of perfectionistic behavior. Collectively, these models suggest that such behavior can be modeled or imitated by children or learned as a result of contingent parental approval, of reactions to a harsh family environment, or of disrupted relationships with parental figures whereby children learn that, if they appear to be perfect, acceptance and caring will be forthcoming and rejection and abandonment will be forestalled. Although research has begun to address some of these issues, it is difficult at this point to be certain whether there is one pathway or several pathways to the development of perfectionism.

Perfectionism has not been viewed as a personality or psychological disorder per se, but rather as a reflection of what has been termed a core vulnerability factor or a neurotic style that produces a variety of problems for adults, adolescents, and children. The extant research suggests that various dimensions of perfectionism are associated with psychological, physical, relationship, and achievement-related problems. In fact, it has been shown that each of the trait dimensions of perfectionism is associated with certain kinds of clinical disorders and other severe problems. For example, self-oriented perfectionism appears to be associated with unipolar depression, especially in the presence of achievement-related (e.g., job or school shortfalls) stressors. When self-oriented perfectionists experience these kinds of stressful occurrences, they show increased susceptibility to severe and chronic depression symptoms. Furthermore, self-oriented perfectionism has also been associated with anorexia nervosa; in fact, it is this clinical group that has the highest levels of self-oriented perfectionism of any clinical group tested thus far.

Other-oriented perfectionism has been associated with relationship problems, such as general marital dissatisfaction, sexual dissatisfaction, and anger and hostility in the target of the perfectionism. Socially prescribed perfectionism has been associated with a variety of disorders and symptoms patterns, including anxiety disorders, unipolar and bipolar depression, eating disorder symptoms, and general distress. Perhaps most importantly, this dimension of perfectionism has been found to predict not only suicide thoughts in adults and adolescents, but also serious suicide attempts. In fact, it is clear from numerous studies that socially prescribed perfectionism can predict suicidal behavior beyond depression and hopelessness, which are two of the best psychological predictors of such behavior.

Furthermore, there are a variety of achievement-related problems that arise from this type of perfectionism, such as procrastination and task avoidance. Finally, perfectionistic self-presentation has been found to be associated with a variety of indices of eating disorder symptoms as well as difficulties such as precluding one from seeking appropriate help (either from social networks or from professionals) for difficulties and not benefiting fully from treatment due to great difficulty in revealing personal information.

One controversy within the literature is whether perfectionism is or can be adaptive or a healthy personality style (e.g., Greenspan, 2000; Pacht, 1984; Stroeber & Otto, 2006). Some research groups suggest that it can be adaptive for some individuals, whereas other groups suggest that it can only be maladaptive. For example, several researchers suggest that having high standards or expectations that are difficult to attain can be helpful and adaptive in a variety of circumstances. These researchers argue that what some researchers have termed adaptive or healthy perfectionism is actually conscientiousness or need for achievement and not perfectionism. They suggest that, because perfectionism can sometimes be confused with high achievement striving or conscientiousness, it is important to clarify the following distinction: Whereas achievement striving and conscientious involves appropriate and tangible expectations (often very difficult but attainable goals) and produces a sense of satisfaction and rewards, perfectionism involves unrealistic levels of expectations, intangible goals (i.e., perfection), and a constant lack of satisfaction, irrespective of performance.

There are several ways in which perfectionism can lead to psychological difficulties. For example, a diathesis-stress perfectionism model suggests that, when the highly perfectionistic individuals experience failures or setbacks, various forms of distress, symptoms, or disorders develop. Perfectionism is seen to interact with stressful events and enhance the negative impact of stressful failures. Another model suggests that perfectionistic individuals, especially those high levels of interpersonal dimensions of perfectionism, appear to actually create or generate distressing failures experiences. One particularly noxious stressful failure that perfectionists may create involves social alienation and interpersonal disconnection that can result in a variety of serious outcomes.

Because perfectionism is a maladaptive personality style, there have been attempts to develop effective treatments from a variety of theoretical perspectives. There are numerous researchers and clinicians who suggest that, due to perfectionism being an ingrained component of an individual's personality, its effective treatment must be intensive and long-term. Several research reports have indicated that it takes an intensive and a fairly lengthy

course of psychotherapy to change perfectionistic behavior and its attendant adjustment problems (see Blatt, & Zuroff, 2002). On the other hand, there are self-help books available for attempting to deal with perfectionism, although it is not clear whether these books are helpful and whether they truly change perfectionistic behavior.

REFERENCES

Blatt, S. J., & Zuroff, D. C. (2002). Perfectionism in the therapeutic process. In G. L. Flett & P. L. Hewitt (Eds.), *Perfectionism: Theory, research, and treatment* (pp. 393–406). Washington, DC: American Psychological Association.

Flett, G. L., & Hewitt, P. L. (2002). *Perfectionism: Theory, research, and treatment*. Washington, DC: American Psychological Association.

Frost, R. O., Marten, P., Lahart, C., & Rosenblate, R. (1990). The dimensions of perfectionism. *Cognitive Therapy and Research, 14,* 449–468.

Greenspan, T. S. (2000). Healthy perfectionism is an oxymoron. *Journal of Secondary Gifted Education, 11,* 197–209.

Hewitt, P. L., & Flett, G. L. (1991). Perfectionism in the self and social contexts: Conceptualization, assessment, and association with psycho-pathology. *Journal of Personality and Social Psychology, 60,* 456–470.

Hewitt, P. L., Flett, G. L., Sherry, S. B., Habke, M., Parkin, M., Lam, R. W., et al. (2003). The interpersonal expression of perfectionism: Perfectionistic self-presentation and psychological distress. *Journal of Personality and Social Psychology, 84,* 1303–1325.

Horney, K. (1991). *Neurosis and human growth: The struggle towards self-realization*. New York: Norton. (Original work published 1950)

Pacht, A. R. (1984). Reflections on perfection. *American Psychologist, 39,* 386–390.

Stroeber, J., & Otto, K. (2006). Positive conceptions of perfectionism: Approaches, evidence, challenges. *Personality and Social Psychology Review, 10,* 295–319.

SUGGESTED READING

Blatt, S. J. (1995). The destructiveness of perfectionism: Implications for the treatment of depression. *American Psychologist, 50*(12), 1003–1020.

PAUL L. HEWITT
University of British Columbia, Canada

GORDON L. FLETT
York University, Canada

PERFORMANCE-BASED PERSONALITY MEASURES

Performance-based personality measures are assessment techniques that require the respondent to perform a task and that are designed to uncover or elicit information or insight into the personality in action. These tasks might, for example, involve completing a sentence, telling a story, or characterizing an emotion or verbalizing a statement in response to a depicted situation. Performance tests bring aspects of relevant behavior, associations, perceptions, organizations, emotions, and interpersonal attitudes and styles into the consulting room to be observed (Levy, 1963). The task itself is typically incomplete, contradictory, or ambiguous. With little external structure, direction, or guidance provided, respondents must rely on themselves in formulating a solution, which maximizes the effects of individuals' interpretation, processing, and personality on their performance.

Instead of then reporting a trait or characteristic, as they would on a self-report measure, respondents actually demonstrate the trait or characteristic by doing something, while the test administrator observes what they do and draws relevant inferences about their personality makeup. Thus, the interpretive trait or dimension is implicit in the respondent's behavior, whether it is a story, a sentence completion, an early memory, a description, or some other type of production. By examining complex behaviors and inferring covert mental processes, performance-assessment techniques yield rich information about an individual. Understandably, then, these tests are thought to access what makes an individual unique.

Performance measure methodologies vary greatly and induce disparate response processes. For example, early assessment instruments of this kind included indistinct speech interpretation, word association, cloud perception, hand positioning perception, inkblot description, comic strip completion, musical interpretation, and reaction tests. Currently prominent performance-based personality measures include the Rorschach Inkblot Method, the Thematic Apperception Test and other storytelling techniques, sentence completion tests, early memories recall, the Hand Test, and various drawing techniques. Overall, performance measures constitute a class of more or less unrelated methods or techniques, rather than any single way of eliciting and tapping relevant personality information. Indeed, the basic performance measures of personality measure personality in a multimodal, complex, and integrated fashion.

Performance measures of personality emerged in the 1920s and 1930s, when clinicians concluded that the individual was lost in measurements with the techniques of the "mental testers" of the time. Later, these diverse performance-based techniques were linked under the rubric of projective tests. By projection, it is meant that respondents, often unwittingly, project or attribute their own needs, interests, concerns, and desires into the task stimulus by including them in the formulation of their responses.

For numerous reasons, the descriptor *projective* has been subjected to considerable criticism (e.g., Viglione & Rivera, 2001) and largely abandoned in favor of the term *performance* or *performance-based* (Meyer & Kurtz, 2006). The term *performance* was borrowed from tests of ability, such as intellectual or neuropsychological performance tests, in which people actually undertake or perform some type of cognitive task and thereby give these tests considerable content or behavioral validity.

In the past, projective measures were typically juxtaposed against objective measures, a term commonly applied to self-report techniques. This usage suggested undesirable subjectivity and a lack of psychometric rigor in what we now call performance-based personality measures. However, research has demonstrated that these performance measures can be quantified and standardized as a psychological test, as exemplified by the Rorschach Comprehensive System, the Roberts Apperception Test, the Washington University Sentence Completion Test, and various scoring systems for the Thematic Apperception Test. Performance measures may also be used to augment or develop inferences as a method rather than as test. Used as method, a performance measure, whether scored as a test or not, generates relevant information and observations that assist in formulating assessment hypotheses. Such an application of performance tests has been ridiculed by some as unscientific; nevertheless, unexpected tearfulness at a particular point in an early memory procedure or a seemingly sadistic chuckle with "a pelt, it's roadkill" can provide pivotal and otherwise unattainable clues to an individual's underlying concerns and attitudes.

Projection is part of the response process in performance-based personality assessment, but not all of it. It is incorporated in one of the two components found in all performance tests: self-expressive components and organizational components. With regard to self-expression, the test stimulus or task is seen as a stimulus to fantasy, from which we learn about the private life of the individual. This feature has led to the research finding that performance tests are an efficient way of developing hypotheses about what an individual may be unable or unwilling to tell us, because performance measures are less affected than self-report measures by response manipulation and efforts to present the self favorably or unfavorably (Weiner, 2005). The organizational component involves the formal or structural features of the response: how the individual answers the questions, solves the task, structures the response, and makes decisions. Performance measures all pose problems to solve; the adequacy, style, and structure of the solutions to the problems are encompassed by the organizational component.

In emphasizing the projective components, some performance measures have been closely tied to psychoanalytic theory. Research on these measures has supported psychoanalytic concepts related to ego development and impairment, object representations, and orality/dependency, among others. However, there is no reason to associate performance measures with psychoanalytic theory to the exclusion of other theories of covert processes. From a behavioral assessment perspective, a performance test's responses are behavior samples collected under controlled conditions and subject to behavioral laws. We then ascertain the degree to which the test behavior resembles the nontest behavioral target characteristic (e.g., an aggressive attribution to a person in a picture is similar to an aggressive attribution in real life). From comparisons between the overt stimuli and the response, the interpreter infers the covert personality process.

The stimulus in an individually administered projective technique is more than the concrete stimulus itself, that is, more than merely a picture, a sentence stem, a Rorschach plate, or an invitation to remember. The stimulus situation involves an interpersonal relationship and communication, and it invokes a great deal of personality processing, thereby eliciting rich individualistic responses from which much can be learned. The open-ended, free, unstructured format typical of performance tests allows respondents, on the basis of their own personality, to influence a considerable amount of the variance in response content and structure. Accordingly, performance measures induce an individualistic, synthetic, configurational, and constructivist approach to interpretation that brings to light an individual's nature and complexities.

REFERENCES

Levy, L. H. (1963). *Psychological interpretation.* New York: Holt, Rinehart and Winston.

Meyer, G. J., & Kurtz, J. E. (2006). Advancing personality assessment terminology: Time to retire "objective" and "projective" as personality test descriptors. *Journal of Personality Assessment, 87,* 223–225.

Viglione, D. J., & Rivera, B. (2003). Assessing personality and psychopathology with projective tests. In I. B. Weiner, J. R. Graham, & J. A. Naglieri (Eds.), *Handbook of psychology: Assessment psychology* (Vol. 10, pp. 531–553). Hoboken, NJ: John Wiley & Sons.

Weiner, I. B. (2005). Integrative personality assessment with self-report and performance-based measures. In S. Strack (Ed.), *Handbook of personology and psychopathology* (pp. 317–331). Hoboken, NJ: John Wiley & Sons.

SUGGESTED READINGS

Archer, R. P., & Smith, S. R. (2008). *A guide to personality assessment: Evaluation, application, and integration* (pp. 281–336). New York: Routledge.

Groth-Marnat, G. (2003). *Handbook of psychological assessment* (4th ed.). Hoboken, NJ: John Wiley & Sons.

Weiner, I. B., & Greene, R. L. (2008). *Handbook of personality assessment.* Hoboken, NJ: John Wiley & Sons.

DONALD J. VIGLIONE
Alliant International University, San Diego, California

See also: **Figure Drawings; Rorschach Inkblot Method; Sentence Completion Tests; Thematic Apperception Test**

PERSON-CENTERED THERAPY (See Client-Centered Therapy)

PERSON PERCEPTION (See Interpersonal Perception)

PERSONAL CONSTRUCT THEORY

Personal construct theory (PCT) represents a coherent, comprehensive psychology of personality that has special relevance for psychotherapy. Originally drafted by the American psychologist George Kelly in 1955, PCT has been extended to a variety of domains, including organizational development, education, business and marketing, and cognitive science. However, its predominant focus remains the study of individuals, families, and social groups, with particular emphasis on how people organize and change their views of self and world in the counseling context.

At the base of Kelly's theory is the image of the *person-as-scientist,* a view that emphasizes the human capacity for meaning making, agency, and ongoing revision of personal systems of knowing across time. Thus, individuals, like incipient scientists, are seen as creatively formulating *constructs,* or hypotheses about the apparent regularities of their lives, in an attempt to make them understandable and, to some extent, predictable. However, predictability is not pursued for its own sake but is instead sought as a guide to practical action in concrete contexts and relationships. This implies that people engage in continuous extension, refinement, and revision of their systems of meaning as they meet with events that challenge or invalidate their assumptions, prompting their personal theories toward greater adequacy. As it has evolved, construct theory has also imported the model of the person-as-narrator from related meaning-oriented perspectives in psychology, emphasizing the way people seek to use their constructs as themes to impart order to life events and to construct a sense of identity for themselves in the process.

Kelly formally developed his theory through a series of corollaries, which can be broadly grouped into those concerned with the process of construing, the structure of personal knowledge, and the social embeddedness of our construing efforts. At the level of process, PCT envisions people as actively organizing their perceptions of events on the basis of recurring themes, meanings attributed to the "booming, buzzing confusion" of life in an attempt to render it interpretable. By punctuating the unending flow of experience into coherent units, people are able to discern similarities and differences of events in terms that are both personally significant and shared by relevant others. Many personal construct methods, such as repertory grid methods and laddering, explore the personal themes that people use to organize their perceptions of themselves, others, and important life events.

At the level of structure, PCT suggests that meaning is a matter of contrast—an individual attributes significance to an event not only by construing what it is but also by differentiating it from what it is not. For example, a given person's unique description of some acquaintances as laid back can be fully understood only in the context of its personal contrast—say, ambitious or, alternatively, uptight. At a broader level, individuals, social groups, and whole cultures orient themselves according to (partially) shared constructs such as liberal versus conservative, pro-life versus pro-choice, and democratic versus totalitarian, which provide a basis for self-definition and social interaction. Especially important in this regard are *core constructs,* frequently unverbalized meanings that play critical organizing roles for the entirety of our construct systems, ultimately embodying our most basic values and sense of self. Research suggests that these core dimensions of meaning have greater subjective importance than other constructs in people's systems and tend to bear on central existential issues and values.

Finally, at the level of the social embeddedness of our construing, PCT stresses both the importance of private, idiosyncratic meanings and the way in which these arise and find validation within relational, family, and cultural contexts. Studies of successful relationships document the high level of shared constructs between friends and satisfied romantic partners, whereas low levels of similarity in construct content and structure are associated with relationship deterioration.

To a greater extent than other cognitively oriented theories of personality and psychotherapy, PCT places a strong emphasis on emotional experiences, understood as signals of actual or impending transitions in one's fundamental constructs for anticipating the world. For example, individuals might experience threat when faced with the prospect of imminent and comprehensive change in their core structures of identity (e.g., when facing dismissal from a valued career, or betrayal by a partner they counted on to validate a familiar image of themselves). Alternatively, people might experience anxiety when confronted with events that seem almost completely alien and uninterpretable within their previous construct system.

This attention to the delicate interweaving of meaning and affect has made PCT an attractive framework for contemporary researchers and clinicians concerned with such topics as death, trauma, and loss, all of which can fundamentally undercut one's assumptive world and trigger a host of significant emotional and behavioral responses. Research suggests that people who construe their own deaths in contradiction to the basic meanings of their lives report higher levels of death anxiety, but this degree of death threat appears to be mitigated by interventions that make the end of life less alien and frightening, such as hospice care.

As an approach to psychotherapy, PCT stresses the importance of the therapist making a concerted effort to enter the client's world of meaning and understand it from the inside out as a precondition to assisting with its revision. In this way, the therapist does not assume to be an expert who guides clients toward a more rational or objectively true way of thinking. Instead, he or she works to help clients recognize the coherence in their own ways of construing experience, as well as their personal agency in making modifications in these constructions when necessary.

At times, the therapist prompts the client's self-reflection by making use of various interviewing strategies, such as the laddering technique, to help articulate core constructs or uses narrative exercises, such as self-characterization methods, as a precursor to experimenting with new ways of construing self and others. Such changes may be further fostered by the creative use of in-session enactment, fixed role therapy (in which clients try out new identities in the course of daily life), and other techniques. Research on personal construct therapy documents its effectiveness, though it seems more useful in addressing presenting problems characterized by anxiety (such as social anxiety or phobia) and less helpful in addressing the concerns associated with serious mental illness (such as schizophrenia or paranoia).

A unique feature of PCT is its extensive program of empirical research, conducted by hundreds of social scientists around the world. Most of this research has drawn on repertory grids, a flexible set of tools for assessing systems of personal meanings that have been used in literally thousands of studies since Kelly first proposed them. By providing visual and semantic maps of an individual's construct system and how it applies to important facets of one's life (e.g., relationships with friends, partners, and family members), grids have proven useful in both applied and research settings. Among the many topics investigated with this method are the body images of patients with anorexia or cancer, the ability of family members or participants in group therapy to understand one another's outlooks, children's reliance on concrete versus abstract construing of people, and the degree of commonality of work team members in their construing of common projects.

Finally, it is worth emphasizing that PCT, despite its status as the original clinical constructivist theory, remains a living tradition that continues to attract scholars, researchers, and practitioners from a broad range of disciplines. More than many theories, it has established a reliable following and annual conferences outside North America, with vigorous programs of training, research, and practice in countries as diverse as Australia, Germany, Spain, Italy, and the United Kingdom. As it has grown in influence, it has also begun to articulate with other postmodern traditions of scholarship, including social constructionist, feminist, and narrative therapy approaches. Although these various perspectives differ in some respects, each draws attention to how personal identity is constructed and transformed in a social context. Likewise, each focuses on the role of language in defining reality, and each suggests a collaborative role for the psychotherapist who is attempting to assist clients with the problems of living.

SUGGESTED READINGS

Butt, T., & Burr, V. (2005). *An invitation to personal construct psychology.* London: Whurr.

Fransella, F. (2005). *The essential practitioner's handbook of personal construct psychology.* London: John Wiley & Sons.

Journal of Constructivist Psychology. Philadelphia & London: Taylor & Francis.

Kelly, G. A. (1955). *The psychology of personal constructs.* New York: Norton.

Neimeyer, R. A., & Neimeyer, G. J. (Eds.). (2002). *Advances in personal construct psychology.* New York: Praeger.

Neimeyer, R. A., & Raskin, J. (Eds.). (2001). *Constructions of disorder: Meaning making frameworks in psychotherapy.* Washington, DC: American Psychological Association.

Raskin, J. D., & Bridges, S. K. (Eds.). (2002–2006). *Studies in meaning* (Vols. 1–3). New York: Pace University Press.

Winter, D. A., & Viney, L. L. (2005). *Personal construct psychotherapy.* London: John Wiley & Sons.

Robert A. Neimeyer
Sara K. Bridges
University of Memphis

See also: **Repertory Grid Methods**

PERSONALITY AND ILLNESS

The belief that some personalities may predispose persons to illness has had a long history. Hippocrates, the father of modern medicine, wrote around 400 B.C., "There is no illness apart from the mind." Perhaps with a bit of exaggeration, the ancient English physician, Parry of Bath, wrote: "It is more important to know what sort of person has a disease than what sort of disease a person has." In 1917, Alfred Adler, a contemporary of Sigmund Freud, maintained that one's lifestyle—that is, an organized set of beliefs about oneself and the world—determines both the onset and severity of certain physical illnesses or disabilities.

Although definitions of personality differ, they largely refer to a set of enduring beliefs, dispositional tendencies, and behavior patterns that distinguish one person from another. This unique complex of characteristics is believed to significantly impact both one's mental and physical health. Although these enduring personality dispositions may not be easily recognized, there is considerable evidence that they may strengthen the relationship between stressful events and illness.

The impact of personality traits on stress, coping, and illness has received considerable attention. For example, neuroticism has been associated with a wide range of negative outcomes, including depression (Bagby, Quilty, & Ryder, 2008), posttraumatic stress disorder and panic attacks (Engelhard & van den Hout, 2007), Alzheimer's disease (Duchek, Balota, Storandt, & Larsen, 2007), poor health, and several end-of-life distressors (Chochinov et al., 2006). Conversely, optimism has been associated with better health, improved quality of living, and greater longevity.

Certain configurations of traits have been used to distinguish personality types. For example, the typologies listed in the *Diagnostic and Statistical Manual of Mental Disorders* (American Psychiatric Association, 2000) include paranoid, schizoid, schizotypal, antisocial, borderline, histrionic, narcissistic, avoidant, dependent, obsessive-compulsive, and a not-otherwise-specified type. This typological system was constructed to help with the identification of mental disorders. Other researchers focusing on different human functions or conditions have constructed different personality typologies. A few examples of these types are discussed in what follows.

The Impact of Personality on Illness

There has been a great deal written about illness-prone personalities. The general assumption is that the beliefs and emotions typifying certain personalities predispose them to illness. Perhaps the tightest link between these characteristics and illness is through their impact on stress, as certain personality characteristics seem to predispose persons to react more intensely to stressful situations.

The illness-prone personality with considerable research support is the Type A, or coronary-prone, personality (Friedman & Rosenman, 1974). The criteria used in identifying this personality include a behavioral syndrome, referred to as the Type A behavior pattern, and certain beliefs regarding one's self-worth. Coronary-prone individuals believe that their worth is derived solely from their accomplishments and that their success results from being able to do more, and to do it faster, than the next person. Consequently, these individuals are said to be suffering from "hurry sickness." Because they are driven to produce, they grow impatient with tasks that require delayed responses, and because they frequently engage in multitasking, they are more likely to experience frustration and hostility from encountered barriers to success.

These Type A personality characteristics are associated with a significant increase in mortality across all diseases, not just coronary artery disease. The physiological mediator of the relationship between this personality type and mortality seems to be a chronic state of sympathetic nervous system arousal that triggers the release of emergency-related biochemicals such as adrenalin, thyroxin, cortisol, and excitatory neurotransmitters. Sustained high levels of these biochemicals are related to the development and course of a broad spectrum of disease conditions, such as atherosclerosis and cardiac disease, stomach and duodenal ulcers, and irritable bowel disorders. Recent research conducted independently at three universities presents a more complex picture. Accordingly, the increased risk for heart attacks and other illnesses occurs only when Type A characteristics are accompanied by a cynical distrust of others and a tendency to inhibit hostile feelings. Attempts to identify a cancer-prone or arthritis-prone personality have been less successful.

In a meta-analytic review of 101 research studies examining the relationship between specific emotions and psychosomatic illnesses, Friedman and Booth-Kewley (1987) found only weak support for the idea that a specific emotion predisposes a person to a specific disease, but they found stronger support for a generic disease-prone personality. This generic disease-prone personality was associated with the failure to deal properly with depression, anger, hostility, and anxiety. Accordingly, the results seemed to suggest that when powerful emotions are mishandled, they may incline the person toward illness in general. Once this general vulnerability is in place, the particular disease that develops may be a function of either hereditary predispositions, environmental conditions, or an interaction of these influences.

The Impact of Personality on Personal Injury

Other typologies have focused on characteristics that predispose persons to physical injury. Farley (1986) examined differences between personalities who seek thrills (uppercase Ts) and those who tend to avoid them (lowercase ts). Perhaps the accelerating pace of change of modern life is ideally tailored to Type Ts, but it may be overwhelming to type ts. Many thrill-seeking personalities are said to disregard danger in searching for an emotional high. Farley

(1986) suggested that the United States may be a nation of Type Ts. Immigrants settling in America probably had more risk-taking attitudes than citizens remaining in their native countries. Consequently, we often view professional athletes, successful entrepreneurs, or charismatic leaders who take great risks to achieve individual glory as role models. Farley pointed out, however, that although many Type Ts accomplish positive things, other Type Ts engage in antisocial and destructive behavior.

Zuckerman, Buchsbaum, and Murphy (1980) searched for biological causes for a sensation-seeking personality type. Sensation seekers were said to crave novel, complex, and intense sensations and experiences. These researchers found sensation seekers to differ in regard to the brain's potential for responding to stimuli. In contrast to the brains of others, the brains of sensation seekers tend to increase autonomic activity and the potential for responding. This potential for responding, called the initial orienting reflex, includes changes in brain and muscle activity that affect the gonadal hormones, androgen and estrogen. College students who scored high on sensation seeking were more likely to use illegal drugs and cigarettes, to volunteer for unusual kinds of experiments such as sensory deprivation or hypnosis, and to engage in physically dangerous activities such as parachuting or motorcycle riding.

Girdano, Everly, and Dusek (1997) described a personality type, the anxious-reactive personality, who is prone to stress and illness. This personality type was described as taking an abnormally long time to recover from stressful arousal. This lengthy recovery period renders them prone to chronic psychosomatic disorders. Awareness of their stressful symptoms becomes a stimulus for a further heightening of their arousal. The awareness of sensations triggered by the stress response triggers more stress. The person becomes stressed over becoming stressed! The dynamics seem to involve a positive feedback system; this feedback system creates a self-perpetuating reaction that keeps the stress alive long after the stressor is gone. This hypersensitivity to their own symptoms is compounded by the tendency to process harmful or potentially harmful situations repeatedly.

Differences in patterns of perception characterizing certain personality types have received considerable attention. Richard Lazarus and his colleagues have emphasized the critical role of cognitive appraisals in creating chronic emotional states. People make automatic, often unconscious, assessments of what is happening and what it may mean for them or for those they care about. Over time, relatively consistent patterns of perception may develop. Thus, persons with personalities organized to defend against threat will be predisposed to chronic sympathetic nervous system arousal that may lead to illness. Other research has examined the effects of differences in ways of viewing potentially harmful situations. Persons who scan the environment constantly for threat or harm, and those who constantly rehearse or ruminate over past unpleasant situations, seem to suffer greater damage than persons who blunt the effect by distraction or dismissal.

There is considerable evidence for the effects of certain personality traits on health. The crunching of these traits into personality types has been useful in understanding the puzzling dynamics of illness-promoting behavior; however, their use often requires a good deal of force-feeding, that is, ignoring certain characteristics and overemphasizing others. The quest to discover personality types that may prove helpful in predicting future illness or injury is appealing indeed. Consequently, efforts to identify and use these types are likely to continue to enlist the efforts of researchers for some time.

REFERENCES

American Psychiatric Association. (2000). *Diagnostic and statistical manual of mental disorders* (4th ed., text rev.). Washington, DC: Author.

Bagby, R. M, Quilty, L. C., & Ryder, A. C. (2008). Personality and depression. *Canadian Journal of Psychiatry, 53*(1), 14–25.

Chochinov, H. M., Kristjanson, L. J., Hack, T. F., Hassard, T., McClement, S., & Harlos, M. (2006). Personality, neuroticism, and coping towards the end of life. *Journal of Pain and Symptom Management, 32*(4), 332–341.

Duchek, J. M., Balota, D. A., Storandt, M., & Larsen, R. (2007). The power of personality in discriminating between healthy aging and early-stage Alzheimer's disease. *Journals of Gerontology, Series B Psychological Sciences and Social Sciences, 62*(6), 353–361.

Engelhard, I. M., & van den Hout, M. A. (2007). Preexisting neuroticism, subjective stressor severity, and posttraumatic stress in soldiers deployed to Iraq. *Canadian Journal of Psychiatry, 52*(8), 505–509.

Farley, F. (1986, April). The big T in personality. *Psychology Today,* pp. 44–52.

Friedman, H. S., & Booth-Kewley, S. (1987). The "disease-prone personality": A meta-analytic view of the construct. *American Psychologist, 42*(6), 539–555.

Friedman, M., & Rosenman, R. H. (1974). *The type A personality and your heart.* Greenwich, CT: Fawcett.

Girdano, D. A., Everly, G. S., & Dusek, D. E. (1997). *Controlling stress and tension* (5th ed.). Boston: Allyn & Bacon.

Zuckerman, M., Buchsbaum, M. S., & Murphy, D. L. (1980). Sensation seeking and its biological correlates. *Psychological Bulletin, 88,* 187–214.

SUGGESTED READINGS

Karren, K. J., Hafen, B. Q., Smith, N. L., & Frandsen K. J. (2006). *Mind/body health: The effects of attitudes, emotions, and relationships* (3rd ed.). New York: Pearson, Benjamin Cummings.

Goodwin, R. D., & Friedman, H. S. (2006). Health status and the five-factor personality traits in a nationally representative sample. *Journal of Health Psychology, 11*(5), 643–654.

Smith, T. W., & MacKenzie, J. (2006). Personality and risk of physical illness. *Annual Review of Clinical Psychology, 2,* 435–467.

KENNETH B. MATHENY
Georgia State University

ROY M. KERN
Vytautus Magnus University, Lithuania

See also: Somatoform Disorders; Stress Consequences

PERSONALITY ASSESSMENT

Personality assessment is the use of psychological assessment procedures to identify personality characteristics of individuals. These personality characteristics consist of various traits and states. Personality traits are abiding dispositions of people to think, feel, and act in certain ways, to deal with situations in a fairly consistent and predictable manner, and to conduct themselves in a distinctive fashion. When people are asked to describe someone (as in "What is this person like?"), the words they use (e.g., friendly, quiet, self-centered, generous, grouchy) typically identify personality traits. Personality states consist of what people are thinking and the mood they are in at the moment, as in paying close or little attention, being worried or unconcerned, feeling happy or sad, or being anxious, angry, fearful, relaxed, bored, or enthusiastic.

As a method of identifying personality traits and states, personality assessment provides information about how people tend to look at and perceive what is going on around them (e.g., whether accurately or not); how they think about relationships between events (e.g., whether logically or not); how they manage stress (e.g., whether adequately or not), how they experience and express their emotions (e.g., whether in a relatively reserved or relatively intense manner); and the attitudes they have toward themselves, other people, and social interactions (e.g., whether generally positive or negative). Adequately conducted personality assessment of persons who cooperate with the assessment procedures can usually identify both thoughts and feelings of which they are aware and underlying needs, attitudes, and concerns of which they may not be fully aware.

Like psychological assessment in general, personality assessment draws on multiple sources of information. These sources include data obtained from interviewing a person; from talking with other people who know the individual well; from reviewing health, school, military, and other relevant records; from observing the person in certain kinds of natural or contrived situations; and from administering to the person a battery of personality tests. The tests used in personality assessment are of two kinds: self-report inventories and performance-based measures. Self-report inventories ask people fairly directly about their thoughts, feelings, behavior patterns, and life experiences. Such inventories provide a large amount of generally dependable information about an individual's personality characteristics; however, this information is limited to what people are able and willing to say about themselves.

Performance-based measures are based not on what people say about themselves when asked directly, but on inferences assessors draw from how people perform on various tasks, such as making up stories about a series of pictures. These indirect methods can yield information about personality characteristics that individuals may not recognize in themselves or that they might deny if asked about them directly. However, inferences from performance-based measures are often more speculative than conclusions based on self-report inventories, and they are more likely to involve some alternative possibilities as well as some fairly definite certainties. Given their particular strengths and weaknesses, these two types of tests serve their purposes most effectively when they are used in combination as part of a psychological test battery.

Because of its utility in identifying personality states and traits, personality assessment can facilitate decision-making whenever personality characteristics have a bearing on a decision to be made. Two examples of important decisions that depend in part on personality characteristics are deciding on the kind of disorder a psychologically troubled person has and deciding on the type of treatment that is likely to benefit this person. Other examples of decisions in which personality characteristics are relevant include deciding whether a criminal defendant is competent to stand trial, whether a physically ill person can tolerate a surgical procedure, and whether a candidate for a responsible position has certain personal qualities deemed essential to filling the position capably. Such contributions to decision-making account for widespread use of personality assessment in clinical, forensic, health care, and organizational settings.

In using measures of personality characteristics to assist in predicting future behavior, however, assessors must always attend to the constraints of cultural relativism and nonpersonality variance. With respect to cultural relativism, we know that personality is a universal phenomenon. Everywhere in the world, in all groups of people, some individuals will be notable for their kindness and others for their callousness, some for being socially outgoing and some for being socially averse, some for their independent spirit and others for their dependent nature, some for being even-tempered and others for being moody or excitable, and so on, across a broad range of personality characteristics that define what people are like. Similarly, personality assessment methods can be used effectively to

identify personality characteristics with any individual, anywhere, as long as the person is able and willing to be interviewed and tested.

On the other hand, the implications of an individual's personality characteristics for his or her psychological adjustment and sense of well-being are decidedly not universal. Instead, these implications depend without exception on the person's cultural context, defined as whatever national, ethnic, religious, neighborhood, family, or other group values have an impact on this person. For example, someone with an independent spirit is more likely to feel good and fare well in a cultural surround that encourages and admires individualism and self-reliance than in a surround that emphasizes and rewards conformity and group decision-making; someone with a dependent nature, by contrast, would be more likely to adapt successfully in a group-oriented than in an individualistic cultural setting. The use of personality descriptions as a basis for estimating how people will respond to and deal with events in their lives life requires keen awareness of the culturally-based values and expectations that have a bearing on these events.

As for nonpersonality variance, personality assessment findings are more dependable in indicating what people are like than in predicting how they are likely to behave. This fact derives from one of the classic equations in psychology, Kurt Lewin's $B = f(P,E)$ (Behavior is a function of the Person and the person's Environment). Environment in this sense includes in addition to a person's cultural context any other circumstances or situational factors that may influence the person's behavior at a particular point in time. Hence the E in Lewin's equation signifies the nonpersonality variance in a piece of behavior. The less the nonpersonality variance in a piece of behavior, the more fully the behavior can be explained solely on the basis of personality factors, and the more accurately personality assessment can predict or account for this behavior. Conversely, the larger the proportion of nonpersonality variance in some type of behavior, the more limited personality assessment will be in attempting to predict it.

SUGGESTED READINGS

Beutler, L. E., & Groth-Marnat, G. (2003). *Integrative assessment of adult personality* (2nd ed.). New York: Guilford Press.

Dana, R. H. (Ed.) (2000). *Handbook of cross-cultural and multicultural personality assessment*. Mahwah, NJ: Lawrence Erlbaum.

Handler, L., & Hilsenroth, M. J. (Eds.). (1998). *Teaching and learning personality assessment*. Mahwah, NJ: Lawrence Erlbaum.

Hilsenroth, M. J., & Segal, D. L. (Eds.). (2004). *Personality assessment*. Vol. 2 in M. Hersen (Ed.-in-Chief), *Comprehensive handbook of psychological assessment*. Hoboken, NJ: John Wiley & Sons.

Weiner, I. B., & Greene, R. L. (2008). *Handbook of personality assessment*. Hoboken, NJ: John Wiley & Sons.

Wiggins, J. S. (2003). *Paradigms of personality assessment.* New York: Guilford Press.

IRVING B. WEINER
University of South Florida

See also: **Multicultural Assessment; Performance-Based Personality Measures; Self-Report Inventories**

PERSONALITY ASSESSMENT INVENTORY

The Personality Assessment Inventory (PAI; Morey, 1991) is a 344-item self-report inventory that assesses various domains of personality and psychopathology among adults and was designed for use in professional and research settings. Items are answered on a 4-point Likert-type scale according to the extent to which they reflect true descriptions of client experiences. These items are then combined into 22 nonoverlapping full scales, including 4 validity scales, 11 clinical scales, 5 treatment consideration scales, and 2 interpersonal scales (see Table 1). As shown in Table 1, 10 of the full scales contain conceptually derived subscales that were designed to facilitate interpretation and coverage of the clinical constructs. Administration of the inventory takes approximately 50–60 minutes, and test takers should have a reading ability at the fourth-grade level.

Development

The PAI was developed within a construct validation framework that emphasized theoretical articulation of constructs relevant to personality and psychopathology, as well as rigorous psychometric and empirical analyses of item and scale properties. Two criteria were used in the selection of constructs measured by the PAI: the stability of the syndromes' importance within the conceptualization of psychological disorders and the significance of the syndromes in contemporary professional practice. The literature was then reviewed to identify the components that were most fundamental to understanding the constructs, and test items were constructed to assess these individual components.

Two facets of construct validity that were particularly important in the development of the PAI were *content validity,* the adequacy of sampling of content across the construct of interest, and *discriminant validity,* the specificity to the construct of interest. With regard to content validity, the construction of the PAI sought to assure both breadth and depth of content coverage for included constructs. With respect to breadth of coverage, items were selected to provide a balanced sampling of the most important elements of the constructs being measured, often using lower-order subscales to reflect the heterogeneity of content characterizing higher-order full scales. The structure of these subscales was determined by existing empirical and theoretical literature. For example, to measure the breadth of content coverage in assessing depression, the PAI included items to assess physiological, cognitive, and affective symptoms of depression.

The depth of content coverage refers to the need to sample across the full range of construct severity. Several methods were used to ensure that PAI scales include items characteristic of a range of severity levels. For example, the use of graded response item scoring permits respondents to describe the severity of each facet of measured constructs and allows a scale to capture more true variance per item, thus facilitating scale reliability. In addition to differences in depth of severity reflected in response options, item characteristic curves were examined to facilitate the selection of final items that provided information across the full range of syndrome severity, which varies across different constructs. For example, cognitive aspects of anxiety can vary from mild rumination to severe despair and panic, and suicidal ideation can range from vague and poorly articulated thoughts to immediate plans for self-harm. Thus, PAI items were selected to provide an assessment across the severity range of the selected constructs.

Discriminant validity, or the ability of a scale to measure a construct that is specific and free from the influence of other constructs, also played a significant role in the development of the PAI. An important threat to discriminability lies in test bias, as tests designed to assess psychological constructs should not measure demographic variables such as gender, racial/ethnic background, or age. Several steps were taken to avoid test bias in the construction of the PAI. First, all test items were reviewed by a bias panel of lay and professional individuals from various backgrounds. These individuals were asked to identify any items that may inadvertently measure external factors, such as sociocultural background, rather than the intended emotional and behavioral problems, and identified items were removed from the test. Next, differential item functioning was used to eliminate items that seemed to have variation in their validity across demographic groups.

Discriminant validity is also important in facilitating clinical interpretation. A common problem in the field of psychological assessment is that measures designed to assess a particular construct may be highly related to several other constructs, thus making the test results difficult to interpret. To address this, PAI items were selected that had maximal associations with indicators of the construct of interest and minimal associations with indicators of other constructs. The resulting scale intercorrelations reflect the natural comorbidity of scales rather than artifacts of test construction, such as item overlap across scales or nonspecific items. Therefore, the relative

Table 1. PAI Scales and Subscales

Scale		Correlates of High Scores
Validity Scales		
ICN	Inconsistency	Poor concentration or inattention
INF	Infrequency	Idiosyncratic or random response set
NIM	Negative Impression Management	Negative response set due to negative worldview and/or intentional dissimulation
PIM	Positive Impression Management	Positive response set due to repression or intentional dissimulation
Clinical Scales		
SOM	Somatic Complaints	
SOM-C	Conversion	Rare sensorimotor symptoms
SOM-S	Somatization	Frequent, common physical symptoms or vague health complaints
SOM-H	Health Concerns	Preoccupation with physical functioning
ANX	Anxiety	
ANX-C	Cognitive	Ruminative worry
ANX-A	Affective	Nervousness, apprehension
ANX-P	Physiological	Physical signs of anxiety
ARD	Anxiety-Related Disorders	
ARD-O	Obsessive-Compulsive	Intrusive thoughts, rigidity, affective constriction
ARD-P	Phobias	Fears of social situation, public or enclosed places; low scores suggest fearlessness
ARD-T	Traumatic Stress	History of trauma that continues to cause distress
DEP	Depression	
DEP-C	Cognitive	Hopelessness, helplessness, indecisiveness
DEP-A	Affective	Feelings of sadness, anhedonia
DEP-P	Physiological	Disruptions in activity, drive, sleep, and diet patterns
MAN	Mania	
MAN-A	Activity Level	Disorganized overinvolvement
MAN-G	Grandiosity	Inflated self-worth, expansiveness
MAN-I	Irritability	Frustration intolerance, impatience
PAR	Paranoia	
PAR-H	Hypervigilance	Suspiciousness
PAR-P	Persecution	Paranoid beliefs
PAR-R	Resentment	Bitterness, cynicism
SCZ	Schizophrenia	
SCZ-P	Psychotic Experiences	Unusual perceptions or beliefs
SXZ-S	Social Detachment	Social isolation, discomfort, and awkwardness
SCZ-T	Thought Disorder	Confusion, concentration difficulties, disorganization
BOR	Borderline Features	
BOR-A	Affective Instability	Poor emotional modulation
BOR-I	Identity Problems	Feelings of emptiness, lack of purpose
BOR-N	Negative Relationships	Intense, ambivalent relationships
BOR-S	Self-Harm	Impulsivity, self-destructiveness
ANT	Antisocial Features	
ANT-A	Antisocial Behaviors	History of antisocial behavior
ANT-E	Egocentricity	Lack of empathy
ANT-S	Stimulus-Seeking	Cravings for excitement, low boredom tolerance
ALC	Alcohol Problems	Use of and problems with alcohol
DRG	Drug Problems	Use of and problems with drugs
Treatment Consideration Scales		
AGG	Aggression	
AGG-A	Aggressive Attitude	Hostility, poor anger control
AGG-V	Verbal Aggression	Assertiveness, overt anger expression
AGG-P	Physical Aggression	Tendency to physical aggression
SUI	Suicidal Ideation	Frequency and intensity of suicidal thoughts
STR	Stress	Perception of an unpredictable or difficult environment
NON	Nonsupport	Perception that others are unsupportive
RXR	Treatment Rejection	Low motivation for treatment
Interpersonal Scales		
DOM	Dominance	Desire for control in relationships
WRM	Warmth	Interest and comfort with close relationships

specificity of the scales as measures of the constructs of interest facilitates a straightforward interpretation of the PAI results.

Scoring and Interpretation

The PAI was developed and standardized for use in the clinical assessment of individuals in the age range of 18 years through adulthood. A parallel version of the instrument, the Personality Assessment Inventory-Adolescent (PAI-A; Morey, 2007a) is designed for adolescents age 12 to 18. PAI scale and subscale raw scores are transformed to *T*-scores with a mean of 50 and a standard deviation of 10 to provide interpretation relative to a standardization sample of 1,000 community-dwelling adults. This sample was selected to match 1995 U.S. census projections on the basis of gender, race, and age.

As *T*-scores are from a community sample, they offer a useful way to determine if certain problems are clinically significant, because relatively few normal adults will obtain markedly elevated scale scores. To facilitate comparisons and clinical decision making, the PAI manual also provides *T*-score transformations referenced against a representative clinical sample of 1,246 patients selected from a wide variety of professional settings. Additional normative data are also provided for a large sample of college students, as well as for various demographic subgroups of the community standardization sample (i.e., men, women, African-Americans, and individuals over the age of 60 years). In addition, subsequent research has established norms for specific applications and settings, such as public safety applicants, correctional settings, and chronic pain treatment settings.

Reliability and Validity

The second edition of the PAI professional manual (Morey, 2007b) reviews over 500 studies examining the reliability and validity of the PAI in a variety of contexts and populations. Test–retest and internal consistency estimates for the PAI across various studies typically indicate adequate reliability, with most estimates for full scales and subscales typically coefficients in the .80s and .70s, respectively. These estimates have been established across a range of settings and populations.

To assess the validity of the PAI, a number of the best available clinical indicators were initially administered concurrently with various samples to determine their convergence with corresponding PAI scales (Morey, 1991). In addition, hypothesized relations between clinical judgments, such as diagnoses, and their PAI correlates were also evaluated. Numerous simulation studies have also been performed to determine the efficacy of the PAI validity scales in identifying response sets. A comprehensive review of available validity evidence is available in the PAI manual (Morey, 2007b); however, the following

paragraphs provide representative studies from each of the four PAI domains.

The validity scales of the PAI were developed to provide an assessment of the potential influence of systematic and unsystematic response tendencies on PAI test performance. For example, the Negative Impression Management (NIM) scale reflects the degree to which the PAI profile is likely to be distorted in a pathological direction, and numerous studies of feigning and malingering support the efficiency of NIM for identifying these response sets, although factors such as coaching or the nature of the disorder simulated can affect its efficiency. As an example, Rogers, Sewell, Morey, and Ustad (1996) investigated the effectiveness of NIM in identifying naive and sophisticated simulators given a financial incentive to avoid detection while attempting to feign specific disorders. Results suggested that NIM was most effective in identifying the malingering of severe mental disorders for the sophisticated feigners; naive feigners tended to be successfully identified with NIM regardless of the disorder being feigned.

The clinical scales of the PAI provide information about the critical diagnostic features of 11 clinical constructs. For example, the Somatic Complaints scale reflects the nature of the psychological reaction to complaints and concerns about physical functioning and health matters. In a criterion group study distinguishing between individuals with true epileptic seizures and seizures of psychological origin, Wagner, Wymer, Topping, and Pritchard (2005) found that the configuration of the Somatic Complaints subscales was particularly effective in identifying the group with nonepileptic seizures.

The treatment consideration scales of the PAI were designed to provide indicators of potential treatment complications that may not be apparent from diagnostic information. For example, the Aggression scale has been found to be predictive of future risk of aggressive behaviors in a variety of settings. In one such study examining the utility of this scale, Salekin, Rogers, Ustad, and Sewell (1998) found that Aggression scores in correctional inmates were significantly related to criminal recidivism at 1 year following release into the community.

Finally, the interpersonal scales of the PAI assess the interpersonal style of individuals along two dimensions of affiliation: warmth and dominance (control). These scales provide insight into normal variability in interpersonal style, but they have also been found to be related to pathological interpersonal presentations as well. For example, Laulik, Allam, and Sheridan (2007) found that Internet sexual predators demonstrated high scores on Dominance relative to community norms.

Applications

The PAI has received many positive reviews within the assessment discipline (e.g., Helmes, 1993). Moreover, survey data have demonstrated that the PAI ranks among the most frequently used personality instruments in clinical training and practice (Piotrowski, 2000), internship programs (Piotrowski & Belter, 1999), emotional injury cases (Boccaccini & Brodsky, 1999), and assessment of mental status, behavioral risk, and legal competence (Lally, 2003). The test has also generated a substantial amount of research in a variety of mental health, medical, and legal settings, with particular interest in forensic and correctional settings (see review by Edens, Cruise, & Buffington-Vollum, 2001).

REFERENCES

Boccaccini, M. T., & Brodsky, S. L. (1999). Diagnostic test usage by forensic psychologists in emotional injury cases. *Professional Psychology: Research and Practice, 30*, 253–259.

Edens, J. F., Cruise, K. R., & Buffington-Vollum, J. K. (2001). Forensic and correctional applications of the Personality Assessment Inventory. *Behavioral Sciences and the Law, 19*, 519–543.

Helmes, E. (1993). A modern instrument for evaluating psychopathology: The Personality Assessment Inventory professional manual. *Journal of Personality Assessment, 61*, 414–417.

Lally, S. J. (2003). What tests are acceptable for use in forensic evaluations? A survey of experts. *Professional Psychology: Research and Practice, 34*(5), 491–498.

Laulik, S., Allam, J., & Sheridan, L. (2007). An investigation into maladaptive personality functioning in Internet sex offenders. *Psychology, Crime & Law, 13*, 523–535.

Morey, L. C. (1991). *Personality Assessment Inventory professional manual*. Odessa, FL: Psychological Assessment Resources.

Morey, L. C. (2007a). *Personality Assessment Inventory-Adolescent professional manual*. Lutz, FL: Psychological Assessment Resources.

Morey, L. C. (2007b). *Personality Assessment Inventory professional manual* (2nd ed.). Lutz, FL: Psychological Assessment Resources.

Piotrowski, C. (2000). How popular is the Personality Assessment Inventory in practice and training? *Psychological Reports, 86*, 65–66.

Piotrowski, C., & Belter, R. W. (1999). Internship training in psychological assessment: Has managed care had an impact? *Assessment, 6*, 381–389.

Rogers, R., Sewell, K. W., Morey, L. C., & Ustad, K. L. (1996). Detection of feigned mental disorders on the Personality Assessment Inventory: A discriminant analysis. *Journal of Personality Assessment, 67*, 629–640.

Salekin, R. T., Rogers, R., Ustad, K. L., & Sewell, K. W. (1998). Psychopathy and recidivism among female inmates. *Law & Human Behavior, 22*, 109–128.

Wagner, M. T., Wymer, J. H., Topping, K. B., & Pritchard, P. B. (2005). Use of the Personality Assessment Inventory as an efficacious and cost-effective diagnostic tool for nonepileptic seizures. *Epilepsy & Behavior, 7*, 301–304.

SUGGESTED READING

Morey, L. C. (2003). *Essentials of PAI assessment*. New York: John Wiley & Sons.

LESLIE C. MOREY
SARA E. LOWMASTER
Texas A&M University

See also: **Personality Assessment; Self-Report Inventories**

PERSONALITY, BIOLOGICAL BASES OF

The topic of the biological bases of personality was largely theoretical in the first half of the twentieth century because of the primitive stage of the science of neuropsychology, particularly in regard to the brain. Gardner Murphy's 1947 book on personality was subtitled "a biosocial approach," but there was little on biology as a source of personality differences, just some discussion of body types and speculations about the potential role of endocrine hormones and other peripheral physiological variants.

Twenty years later, Hans Eysenck (1967), in his *The Biological Basis of Personality,* described a new approach combining learning theory with the idea of basic personality trait differences rooted in biological differences. Chapters covered heredity, arousal, drugs, and brain damage. Conditionability, based on differences in cortical brain arousal, was postulated as the basis of extraversion, whereas limbic system arousability was suggested to underlie neuroticism. Heredity was the source of differences in biological substrates. Although the focus of attention had shifted from peripheral systems, like the endocrine and autonomic systems, to brain physiology, identification of specific brain loci and pathways was absent.

Whereas Eysenck approached personality from the top (personality traits) down to the bottom (neurobiology of animal behavior), Jeffrey Gray worked from the bottom up, using the experimental study of brain and behavior in the rat to extrapolate the basis of personality in humans according to Eysenck's system of personality dimensions. In his 1971 book, *The Psychology of Fear and Stress,* he outlined a theory of personality based on brain systems involved in sensitivity to signals of punishment and reward. The evidence of brain–behavior relationships was based on experiments with nonhuman species and psychopharmacological research on the treatment of anxiety disorders in humans.

In a subsequent book, *The Neuropsychology of Anxiety,* Gray (1982) developed the theory and cited a vast amount of literature on psychopharmacology and neuropsychology to support his paradigm for personality. His motivational theory, based largely on studies of other species, has been increasingly popular since the development of questionnaire measures of individual differences in reinforcement sensitivities as mediating basic personality traits in humans. Gray's reinforcement sensitivity theory (Corr, in press) proposes that the basic personality traits of extraversion and neuroticism are based on sensitivities to conditioned signals of reward and punishment rather than on conditionability in general, as proposed by Eysenck.

Zuckerman (1994, 2007) outlined a biosocial theory of the trait of sensation seeking. This trait was incorporated into a five-factor system of personality based on genetic, neurological, biochemical, physiological, and conditioning phenomena underlying behavioral and, ultimately, personality traits (Zuckerman, (1991, 2005). The factors are sociability, neuroticism-anxiety, impulsive sensation seeking, aggression-hostility, and activity. The first four of these are strongly related to factors among the Big Five: extraversion, neuroticism, conscientiousness, and agreeableness, respectively.

Extraversion is a major factor in most personality theories, from Eysenck onward. Sociability is a major component of this trait. Extraversion and impulsive sensation seeking both represent different aspects of a general approach mechanism, the former directed toward other persons and the latter toward all stimuli and experiences that have properties of novelty, intensity, variety, and complexity.

In regard to Eysenck's hypothesis that extraversion is based on underarousal of the cortical brain, EEG studies of arousal have yielded mixed results. Brain-imaging studies have found some support for the underarousal theory of extraversion, but the relationship is not limited to the cortex; it has been found in limbic brain (putamen and caudate) areas as well. These are dopamine-rich areas of the brain. Depue and Collins (1999) proposed that dopamine brain pathways are involved in extraversion, particularly the impulsive, agentic type of extraversion rather than impulsive, sensation-seeking type. Zuckerman (2005) maintains that dopamine, particularly in the medial forebrain bundle, underlies both types of approach motivation. Other common correlates of extraversion include the hormone testosterone and the enzyme monoamine oxidase (MAO). Testosterone is high and MAO is low in extraverts, particularly those of more dominant and impulsive natures, and in high sensation seekers. MAO type B is a neuroregulator, preferentially related to dopamine among the monoamines. MAO-B levels are also low in a variety of disorders characterized by impulsive sensation-seeking behavior, including borderline and antisocial personality, alcoholism, and bipolar disorders.

Impulsive sensation seeking shares some of the same biological correlates as extraversion of the agentic type, including testosterone and MAO, but in addition to some evidence for sensitivity of dopamine receptors, there is also evidence of a blunted serotonergic reactivity in pathways mediating behavioral inhibition and control.

Zuckerman (1995) proposed that the mesolimbic dopamine system mediates approach and the serotonergic system, antagonistic to dopamine, underlies the strength of the inhibition mechanism. The ratio of HVA (dopamine metabolite) to 5-HIAA (serotonin metabolite) in the cerebrospinal fluid is highly correlated with degree of rated psychopathy in violent offenders. Arousal of the brain norepinephrine system is also suggested to be blunted in impulsive sensation seeking leading to underarousal of a fear system in the high sensation seeker. Recent findings of negative correlations between glutamate (an excitatory neurotransmitter) in the anterior cingulate cortex (ACC) and sensation seeking also support the idea of weak inhibitory and arousal mechanisms in sensation seeking. The ACC is involved in executive functions, emotional arousal, and control of social and sexual behavior.

Neuroticism is the one personality trait that is predictive of the development of later anxiety and depressive disorders (Zuckerman, 1999). Although peripheral indicators of autonomic arousal are found in these disorders, they are not correlated with the trait in nonclinical subjects, with one exception. Neuroticism is related to the magnitude of the fear-potentiated startle reflex (FPSR). The central nucleus of the amygdala has been identified as the locus of the organization of the fear system in the brain, and the FPSR is a measure of arousal of this system.

Neuroticism is associated with high activation, assessed by EEG, at the right-frontal cortical areas. Negative emotions in general are associated with the right prefrontal cortex, which modifies reactions in the amygdala during stimulation with fear-provoking stimuli.

Activation of the noradrenergic (NA) brain system originating in the locus coeruleus has been related to panic and fear reactions in patients, and there is evidence of a dysregulation of NA in receptors designed to regulate it. Drugs that increase the availability of serotonin are effective in the treatment of panic disorders and depression. But low levels of serotonergic activity are more related to anger and hostility than to anxiety.

Aggression illustrates an interesting gene–environment interaction. A gene associated with MAO type A in mice and humans is related to violent criminality but only in those criminals with a history of childhood maltreatment. A serotonin transporter gene has a role in the expression of anger in men and monkeys. Low levels of a serotonin metabolite are found in impulsive aggressive humans and other primates. Low activity of the autonomic/sympathetic nervous system in children, indicated by low basal heart rate and electrodermal activity, is predictive of criminal aggressive behavior in later adolescent and adult life.

Brain-imaging studies show that lower brain activity in frontal and temporal lobes is associated with criminal aggressive activity, including murder. Hypofrontal brain activity suggests lack of inhibitory control in the brain's executive function. Other brain areas in the hypothalamus and amygdala are direct sources of aggressive behavior but are regulated by activity in the prefrontal cortex. Testosterone is correlated with assertiveness, competitiveness, and sex drive in normal individuals, but it is elevated in persons with histories of violent crimes.

Personality traits represent a balance between approach mechanisms toward people (sociability), against people (aggression), or novel sensations or experiences (sensation seeking), and inhibitory mechanisms (impulsivity vs. control). Neuroticism represents an excessively high level of inhibition with high arousal of negative affect. The biological mechanisms underlying the behavioral ones are shared across several traits. Testosterone, for instance, shares a role in extraversion, sensation seeking, and aggression. Dopamine may also be involved in all three approach traits, whereas serotonin may mediate inhibition of any of them. Evolution did not select for personality traits but for the adaptive advantage of behavioral traits and the particular combination of biological traits underlying them.

REFERENCES

Corr, P. J. (Ed.). (in press). *The reinforcement sensitivity theory of personality*. New York: Cambridge University Press.

Depue, R. A., & Collins, P. F. (1999). Neurobiology of the structure of personality: Dopamine facilitation of incentive motivation and extraversion. *Behavioral and Brain Sciences, 22*, 491–569.

Eysenck, H. J. (1967). *The biological basis of personality*. Springfield, IL: Charles C. Thomas.

Gray, J. A. (1971). *The psychology of fear and stress*. New York: McGraw Hill.

Gray, J. A. (1982). *The neuropsychology of anxiety: An enquiry into the function of the septohippocampal system*. New York: Oxford University Press.

Murphy, G. (1947). *Personality: A biosocial approach to origins and structure*. New York: Harper & Brothers.

Zuckerman, M. (1991) *Psychobiology of personality*. Cambridge, UK: Cambridge University Press.

Zuckerman, M. (1994). *Behavioral expressions and biosocial bases of sensation seeking*. New York: Cambridge University Press.

Zuckerman, M. (1995) Good and bad humors: Biochemical bases of personality and its disorders. *Psychological Science, 6*, 325–332.

Zuckerman, M. (1999). *Vulnerability to psychopathology*. Washington, DC: American Psychological Association.

Zuckerman, M. (2005) *Psychobiology of personality* (2nd ed., revised and updated). New York: Cambridge University Press.

Zuckerman, M. (2007). *Sensation seeking and risky behavior*. Washington, DC: American Psychological Association.

Marvin Zuckerman
University of Delaware

See also: **Personality, Genetic Bases of**

PERSONALITY DEVELOPMENT

Personality refers to an individual's stable tendencies to think, feel, and act in particular ways. The field of personality development focuses on the age at which these tendencies first emerge in childhood, the role of nature (genes) and nurture (environment) in their development, and their patterns of consistency and change across the life span. In this entry, we summarize the most recent findings and conclusions emerging from the field.

Early Emergence of Personality: Child Temperament

During the first year of life, infants show increasingly complex and differentiated emotional and social responses. Sometime in early childhood, these responses cohere into relatively stable individual differences in the way infants interact with strangers, form bonds with caregivers, explore and manipulate their environment, regulate their needs, respond to reinforcements and other environmental contingencies, and express their distress. These early personality tendencies are commonly referred to as temperamental traits to distinguish them from adult personality traits. Temperament dimensions are assumed to be early emerging, biologically based, moderately stable over time, and profoundly influential for the adaptive development of the child. A large body of research supports each of these assumptions (Rothbart & Bates, 2006). Although researchers have discussed slightly different sets of temperament dimensions, most researchers agree on a basic set that includes activity level, attention regulation (vs. distractibility), affiliation-sociability, inhibition, positive emotionality (happy, smiling, laughing), and negative emotionality (irritable, fearful, difficult to soothe).

Child temperament serves as the foundation for adult personality. Studies of personality development have shown that the core temperament dimensions are related to the primary dimensions of adult personality, specifically, the Big Five domains of extraversion-introversion, agreeableness-antagonism, conscientiousness, neuroticism (or emotional stability), and openness to experience (John, Naumann, & Soto, 2008; Putnam, Ellis, &

Rothbart, 2001). More generally, there is compelling evidence that the fundamental features of the Big Five are rooted in neurobiological systems that seem to be present in rudimentary forms in young children. The integration of the dimensions of childhood temperament with the adult Big Five has enabled the field to focus on a core set of trait domains that are broadly relevant for adapting to the challenges that individuals face from childhood through old age.

Role of Nature and Nurture in Personality Development

One important question in the field of personality development concerns the role of nature and nurture in shaping an individual's personality tendencies. That is, why are some individuals shy and others sociable, some friendly and others disagreeable, and some hardworking and others lazy? Decades of research have now demonstrated that these tendencies cannot be attributed exclusively to either nature and biological factors (e.g., genes, hormones, neurotransmitters) or nurture and environmental factors (e.g., parenting, peers, neighborhoods, in utero environment). Instead, nature and nurture each play an important role, individually and in interaction with each other.

Research examining genetic influences on personality—including studies of adopted versus nonadopted siblings and twins reared together versus apart—has reached four broad conclusions. First, all personality traits show at least some degree of heritability. Typically, genetic factors account for about 40–50% of the variability in personality across people. Although researchers are starting to identify specific genes that underlie specific personality traits, this line of research is still in its infancy.

Second, growing up in the same family does not appear to make siblings similar in terms of their personalities (above and beyond genetic similarity). For example, two genetically unrelated (e.g., adopted) siblings raised in the same family tend to be much less similar, on average, than identical twins who were separated at birth and raised in different families.

Third, approximately half the variability in personality across people can be attributed to idiosyncratic experiences that seem to be unique to each sibling, including differential parental treatment, childhood illness or injury, distinctive peer relations (e.g., being bullied), and interactions with an influential teacher or mentor. Thus, both genetic and environmental factors are important influences on personality.

Fourth, genetic and environmental influences are not entirely independent. People select, modify, construct, and reconstruct their experiences in part on the basis of their genetic propensities. For example, children who have trouble with impulse control seem to evoke harsher parenting than those with easier temperaments.

Individuals are not blank slates on which environmental experiences inscribe our personalities. Rather, we all come into the world with a set of innate mechanisms and personal proclivities that come to define our personality through complex interactions with environmental experiences.

Stability and Change in Personality across the Life Span

How stable is personality over time? Do shy children become shy adults? Do ill-tempered adolescents become ill-tempered adults? There is no simple answer to these types of questions, because there are different ways of conceptualizing and measuring stability and change. Researchers studying personality development generally focus on three forms of stability: (1) absolute stability, (2) differential stability, and (3) heterotypic stability. Next we define each form of stability and summarize the most important findings from the research literature.

Absolute Stability

Absolute stability refers to aggregate or sample-level changes (increases or decreases) in the amount, degree, or intensity of a given trait. Absolute stability can be examined longitudinally, by following the same sample of individuals over time, or cross-sectionally, by comparing mean levels of traits across different age groups. Research on age differences in mean levels are often considered investigations of normative personality differences because they provide information about the personality characteristics of the so-called typical person at different ages.

Using the Big Five domains as an organizing framework, researchers have identified several normative changes in personality across the life span (Donnellan & Lucas, in press; Roberts, Walton, & Viechtbauer, 2006; Terracciano, McCrae, Brant, & Costa, 2005). First, on average, people tend to gradually decline in extraversion and neuroticism, gradually increase in agreeableness and conscientiousness, and gradually increase in openness from adolescence to young adulthood, remain stable during adulthood, and then decline in late midlife and old age. These trends generally replicate across both longitudinal and cross-sectional studies.

Although generally small in magnitude, these normative age changes in the Big Five correspond to age-graded changes in social roles and expectations (Helson, Jones, & Kwan, 2002). That is, people tend to increase on personality characteristics that facilitate fulfillment of important adult roles (Roberts, Wood, & Caspi, 2008). Not surprisingly, then, the most profound absolute personality changes occur in young adulthood, when individuals first assume the roles of worker, committed romantic partner, and parent (Rindfuss, 1991). It is easy to see how increasing levels of agreeableness, conscientiousness, and openness to experience, combined with decreasing levels of neuroticism, can facilitate the successful enactment of these roles.

There are two dominant explanations for absolute changes in the Big Five. The intrinsic maturational position holds that normative changes in personality are driven by biological processes, whereas the life course position posits that changes stem from involvement in particular social roles and the life experiences that accompany them. The bulk of the existing evidence is broadly consistent with some version of the life course perspective. Although some age-related changes in personality traits are likely to be rooted in biological changes, an invariant maturational unfolding of personality is unlikely to be the primary reason that traits change during adulthood.

Indeed, the life course perspective is supported by an emerging body of work linking life experiences to personality changes. For example, Robins, Caspi, and Moffitt (2002) found that individuals who were involved in distressed romantic relationships in their early 20s demonstrated increases in neuroticism compared with those in relatively satisfying relationships. Likewise, Roberts, Caspi, and Moffitt (2003) found that work experiences were tied to a variety of changes in basic personality traits, including the finding that greater autonomy at work was tied to increases in the social dominance aspects of extraversion.

Differential Stability

Differential stability concerns the degree to which people who are high (vs. low) on a trait at one point in time maintain their relative ordering over time, regardless of whether the entire sample has increased or decreased over the same period. Differential stability is typically investigated by calculating the correlation between the same personality measures administered across an interval of a sufficient length to be interesting (e.g., years in adulthood, perhaps months in childhood).

A meta-analysis of longitudinal studies showed that the Big Five become increasingly stable from childhood to old age (Roberts & DelVecchio, 2000). This pattern counters William James's famous claim that personality is "set like plaster" by the age of 30. Instead, personality characteristics become increasingly stable after age 30, but people never reach the point where change no longer occurs.

Why does differential stability increase across the life span? Lower differential stability is expected when the individual experiences dramatic environmental and/or maturational changes. As individuals transition into adulthood, maturational changes are reduced, social roles begin to stabilize, environmental changes are increasingly subject to individual control, and a more stable sense of self is formed. These factors tend to increase stability coefficients.

Heterotypic Stability

Heterotypic stability refers to the degree of coherence in the manifestations of a personality trait across development. For example, a highly aggressive toddler might bite and throw toys, whereas a highly aggressive adult might use guns and knives to rob and steal, yet both sets of behavior are assumed to reflect the same underlying trait.

Longitudinal studies spanning many years provide important evidence of heterotypic stability. For example, Caspi, Moffitt, Newman, and Silva (1996) found that children who were rated as being irritable and impulsive by clinical examiners at age 3 were more likely to be violent criminals and dependent on alcohol by age 21. The fact that there is an association between the impressions that preschoolers create on adult interviewers and problems with criminality and alcohol during early adulthood provides strong evidence for the coherence of traits related to antisocial behavior. Similarly, Mischel, Shoda, and Peake (1988) found that the amount of time preschoolers could delay gratification in a laboratory task predicted their academic and social competence as adolescents. Thus, although the manifestations of self-control are quite different in preschoolers and adolescents, the underlying psychological characteristic of being able to forgo immediate impulses to obtain desired long-term outcomes seems to have an appreciable degree of consistency across development.

Taken together, then, available research suggests that personality traits show both consistency and change across the life span. Shy or irritable children are more likely to be shy or irritable adults, but the continuity of these traits over time is far from perfect, and it depends on whether continuity is gauged in absolute or relative terms and whether it is indexed by the exact same or conceptually related behaviors.

Processes Responsible for Personality Stability and Change

What accounts for the stability of personality over time, and conversely, what accounts for change? Several potentially complementary mechanisms seem to promote personality stability. First, personality traits draw out or elicit particular responses from the social environment that can promote personality continuity. For example, individuals who are friendly may evoke more supportive responses from their peers, and this may contribute to more positive social interactions, which in turn reinforces the disposition to be friendly. Second, personality traits shape how people construe social situations. The same objective environment, such as a cocktail party, may mean something quite different to an extravert as opposed to an introvert. Moreover, the different expectancies of the extravert and introvert may generate self-fulfilling prophecies.

Third, individuals play an active role in selecting and manipulating their own social experiences. Individuals will seek out, modify, and even create environments that are consistent with their individual characteristics. For example, individuals who are outgoing and sociable may choose careers that fit well with these tendencies and shun solitary occupations with limited potential for social interaction. Together, these three processes promote a matching between personality traits and characteristics of the situation. Consequently, many life experiences accentuate and reinforce the personality characteristics that were partially responsible for the particular experiences in the first place.

A different set of mechanisms may explain personality changes. First, individuals are responsive to the rewards and punishments of a given setting, and it is possible that long-term exposure to specific contingencies may produce lasting personality changes. In particular, events such as marriage, parenthood, or military service may launch individuals into new environments with different and salient reward structures that produce enduring changes in personality. Second, self-reflection may lead to personality changes. Indeed, a belief in the power of self-reflection to promote change is the essence of insight-oriented psychotherapy. Third, observing others might serve as the catalyst for personality changes, according to social learning principles. For example, watching a coworker receive a large raise because of fastidious work habits may promote imitation of those work behaviors to obtain a similar reward. Finally, feedback from others may create personality changes. Having important close others such as a romantic partner see a somewhat disagreeable individual as responsible and caring may motivate personality changes in that direction.

In conclusion, the personality traits studied in adults and many of the dimensions of temperament studied in children are conceptually similar and can be integrated by using the Big Five structural model. This synthesis enables researchers to study the development of personality across the life span. Genetic factors provide constraints on the way a child develops and account for about half of the variability in personality. Identical twins separated at birth tend to develop similar personalities, despite vastly different upbringings. Personality development (both stability and change) results from the dynamic interplay between individuals and their environments. As people age, they show changes in personality that suggest increasing psychological maturity and an increasing capacity to fulfill important adult roles. Personality tends to become more stable with age, but it never reaches the point of perfect stability. Change continues to occur throughout the life span.

REFERENCES

Caspi, A., Moffitt, T. E., Newman, D. L., & Silva, P. A. (1996). Behavioral observations at age 3 years predict adult psychiatric disorders. *Archives of General Psychiatry, 53*, 1033–1039.

Caspi, A., & Roberts, B. W. (2001). Personality development across the life course: The argument for change and continuity. *Psychological Inquiry, 12*, 49–66.

Costa, P. T., Jr., & McCrae, R. R. (2006). Age changes in personality and their origins: Comment on Roberts, Walton, and Viechtbauer (2006). *Psychological Bulletin, 132*, 26–28.

Donnellan, M. B., & Lucas, R. E. (in press). Age differences in the Big Five across the life span: Evidence from two nationally representative samples. *Psychology and Aging*.

Helson, R., Jones, C., & Kwan, V. S. Y. (2002). Personality change over 40 years of adulthood: Hierarchical linear modeling analysis of two longitudinal samples. *Journal of Personality and Social Psychology, 83*, 752–766.

John, O. P., Naumann, L. P., & Soto, C. J. (2008). Paradigm shift to the integrative Big Five trait taxonomy: History, measurement, and conceptual issues. In O. P. John, R. W. Robins, & L. A. Pervin (Eds.), *Handbook of personality: Theory and research* (3rd ed.). New York: Guilford Press.

Laub, J. H., & Sampson, R. J. (2003). *Shared beginnings, divergent lives: Delinquent boys to age 70*. Cambridge, MA: Harvard University Press.

Mischel, W., Shoda, Y., & Peake, P. K. (1988). The nature of adolescent competencies predicted by preschool delay of gratification. *Journal of Personality and Social Psychology, 54*, 687–696.

Putnam, S. P., Ellis, L. K., & Rothbart, M. K. (2001). The structure of temperament from infancy through adolescence. In A. Eliasz & A. Angleneiter (Eds.), *Advances in research on temperament* (pp. 165–182). Miami, FL: Pabst Science Publishers.

Rindfuss, R. R. (1991). The young adult years: Diversity, structural change, and fertility. *Demography, 28*, 493–512.

Roberts, B. W., Caspi, A., & Moffitt, T. E. (2003). Work experiences and personality development in young adulthood. *Journal of Personality and Social Psychology, 84*, 582–593.

Roberts, B. W., & DelVecchio, W. F. (2000). The rank-order consistency of personality from childhood to old age: A quantitative review of longitudinal studies. *Psychological Bulletin, 126*, 3–25.

Roberts, B. W., Walton, K. E., & Viechtbauer, W. (2006). Patterns of mean-level change in personality traits across the lifespan: A meta-analysis of longitudinal studies. *Psychological Bulletin, 132*, 1–25.

Roberts, B. W., Wood, D., & Caspi, A. (2008). The development of personality traits in adulthood. In O. P. John, R. W. Robins, & L. A. Pervin (Eds.), *Handbook of personality: Theory and research* (3rd ed.). New York: Guilford Press.

Robins, R. W., Caspi, A., & Moffitt, T. E. (2002). It's not just who you're with, it's who you are: Personality and relationship experiences across multiple relationships. *Journal of Personality, 70*, 925–964.

Rothbart, M. K., & Bates, J. E. (2006). Temperament. In W. Damon & R. M. Lerner (Series Eds.). & N. Eisenberg (Vol. Ed.), *Handbook of child psychology: Vol. 3. Social, emotional, and personality development* (6th ed., pp. 99–166). Hoboken, NJ: John Wiley & Sons.

Terracciano, A., McCrae, R. R., Brant, L. J., & Costa, P. T., Jr. (2005). Hierarchical linear modeling analyses of the NEO-PI-R scales in the Baltimore Longitudinal Study of Aging. *Psychology and Aging, 20*, 493–506.

SUGGESTED READINGS

Caspi, A., Roberts, B. W., & Shiner, R. L. (2005). Personality development: Stability and change. *Annual Review of Psychology, 56*, 453–484.

Mroczek, D. K., & Little, T. D. (Eds.). (2006). *Handbook of personality development.* Mahwah, NJ: Lawrence Erlbaum.

RICHARD W. ROBINS
University of California, Davis

M. BRENT DONNELLAN
Michigan State University

See also: Developmental Psychology; Human Development; Personality Psychology

PERSONALITY DISORDERS

Personality disorders represent a clinical condition encompassing various patterns of behaving, feeling, perceiving, managing impulses, and relating to others that are ingrained and habitual. *Personality* is a term used by psychologists to organize a set of characteristics that distinguish one individual from another (Magnavita, 2002). Although each person is unique, there are certain personality adaptations or styles that psychological scientists use to classify people, and research has shown through factor analysis that most people can be categorized on the basis of just three to five different dimensions.

When an individual's personality is chronically dysfunctional, a personality disorder is likely to result. Personality can be considered an emotional immune system that, when functioning adaptively, wards off stress and optimizes health (Millon & Davis, 1996). There are various systems for classifying and diagnosing personality disorders, including categorical, structural, protypal, and relational approaches to classification. The most widely used of these is a categorical diagnostic system developed by a team of clinical scientists in the 1980s and codified in the *Diagnostic and Statistical Manual of Mental Disorders* (*DSM*) of the American Psychiatric Association (2000), of which there have been various editions and changes as research in this area has accumulated.

The *DSM* has been influential in stimulating renewed interest in personality disorders and in spawning research on the epidemiology and clinical treatment of personality disorders. This categorical system refers to discrete personality disorders, of which there are 10 specific ones divided into three clusters: Cluster A, which is considered the *eccentric* cluster and includes paranoid, schizoid, and schizotypal personality disorders; Cluster B, which is

considered the *erratic* cluster and includes antisocial, borderline, histrionic, and narcissistic personality disorders; and Cluster C, which is considered the *anxious* cluster and includes avoidant, dependent, and obsessive-compulsive personality disorders. There is controversy about this part of the *DSM* system, in that many theoreticians and researchers believe that these personality disorders are not discrete categories but rather that there exists a continuum of traits from normal to abnormal. Much research has demonstrated that there is, in fact, significant overlap among these categories, and it is also a fact that in clinical practice multiple personality disorder diagnoses are often given to the same individual.

Historically, personality disorders were originally termed character disorders, and various types of character disorders were identified by early psychoanalytic writers on the basis of presumed points of fixation in an individual's psychosexual development. Although this psychoanalytic formulation has not been scientifically verified, many of the major character types inferred by psychoanalysts from their clinical observations are represented in contemporary systems of classification.

Recently, a new diagnostic system embracing psychodynamic principles has been developed. This system, published in the *Psychodynamic Diagnostic Manual* and referred to as the *PDM*, contributes to conceptualizing and classifying personality disorders more precisely than the *DSM* and has a substantial evidence base (*PDM*, 2006). The *PDM*, which was designed to serve as a companion to the *DSM*, is based on the assumption that personality exists in three basic structures or organizations: neurotic, borderline, psychotic. Each organization has certain functional deficits or weaknesses and can shape the development and manifestation of such traits as being passive, dependent, obsessive, or avoidant.

The study of personality disorders is critical for mental health professionals, because many people who come into treatment for anxiety, depression, substance abuse, and other symptomatic disorders are also diagnosed with a comorbid or co-occurring personality disorder. Hence the treatment of persons with clinical syndromes is often complicated by their having a personality disorder, which often includes a tendency toward self-sabotage and self-defeating patterns of behavior. The treatment of personality disorders has advanced rapidly over the past two decades, which have seen the development of specialized treatments that are well suited for benefiting individuals with personality disorders. Approaches for which there has been an accumulating database to demonstrate their effectiveness include a variety of cognitive-behavioral, schema-focused, psychodynamic, and integrative treatments of these disorders.

The etiology or cause of personality disorders is considered multifactorial and includes genetic predispositions, temperamental variation, parental influence, and sociocultural factors like racism and poverty (Magnavita, 2004). Substantial research and clinical evidence also suggest that, for such severe personality disorders as borderline personality disorder, there is a high (about 60%) probability of the individual having been traumatized by childhood experiences of sexual, physical, or emotional abuse. One ongoing controversy concerns whether borderline or other personality disorders should be diagnosed in children. Those who believe that these conditions should be diagnosed in children cite the need for early identification and prevention, whereas those who oppose doing so consider the diagnosis of a personality disorder is overly stigmatizing and inappropriate for anyone under age 18.

As an even broader issue, some mental health professionals regard the whole concept of personality disorders as unnecessarily stigmatizing, even for adults, and regard diagnosing these disorders as society's way of ignoring ways in which people, especially children and women, have been victimized by their life experiences. However, in order to develop as a science, psychology must have ways of organizing and characterizing maladaptive forms of behavior, for them to be researched and for clinical scientists to have a language for communicating with one another. Personality theory and theories of personality disorders are constantly evolving, and emerging evidence from related disciplines like neuroscience is illuminating the personality system. Newer approaches are also emphasizing personality systematics, which involves attempting to understand the processes that interrelate at all levels of the total ecological system. In this approach, personality is seen as broadly contextualized and influenced by a number of interacting domains, including neurobiological, intrapsychic, interpersonal, family, cultural, and political. As we increasingly become a global village, the concept of personality disorder must take into consideration the array of domains and forces that are exerted on human adaptation and evolution.

REFERENCES

American Psychiatric Association. (2000). *Diagnostic and statistical manual of mental disorders* (4th ed., text rev.). Washington, DC: Author.

Magnavita, J. J. (2002). *Theories of personality: Contemporary approaches to the science of personality*. Hoboken, NJ: John Wiley & Sons.

Magnavita, J. J. (Ed.). (2004). *Handbook of personality disorders: Theory and practice*. Hoboken, NJ: John Wiley & Sons.

Millon, T., & Davis, R. D. (1996). *Disorders of personality: DSM-IV and beyond*. Hoboken, NJ: John Wiley & Sons

Psychodynamic Diagnostic Manual Task Force (PDM). (2006). *Psychodynamic diagnostic manual (PDM)*. Silver Springs, MD: Alliance of Psychoanalytic Organizations.

JEFFREY J. MAGNAVITA
University of Hartford

See also: Antisocial Personality Disorder; Avoidant Personality Disorder; Borderline Personality Disorder; Dependent Personality Disorder; Histrionic Personality Disorder; Narcissistic Personality Disorder; Obsessive-Compulsive Personality Disorder; Paranoid Personality Disorder; Schizoid Personality Disorder; Schizotypal Personality Disorder

PERSONALITY, GENETIC BASES OF

Personality is influenced by genetic and environmental factors. This statement may seem self-evident, but in fact, demonstrating genetic influence on variation across major domains of personality was an important breakthrough, as many twentieth-century models of human behavior attributed personality solely to environmental influences. Even more recently, biometric approaches (approaches to modeling genetic and environmental influences on human behavior) have gone beyond simple estimates of heritability (the magnitude of genetic influence) to examine the different forms of gene-environment interplay—that is, how genetic and environmental factors interact and correlate—on the etiology of personality. Findings from biometric modeling of gene-environment interplay have also stimulated new work in molecular genetics, which has to date struggled to find replicable results linking measured genes to personality domains. We first briefly review biometric models, particularly using twin sample methodology, and the results from decades of research into behavior genetic studies of personality. We then present more recent work into the molecular basis of personality.

Behavior Genetic Studies of Personality

Behavior genetic studies of personality have primarily relied on biometric modeling using twin studies. Twins are a unique natural experiment, and their study provides a way of disentangling the relative influence of genes and the environment. Twins can be either identical (monozygotic, MZ), in which the twins share all of their genes, or fraternal (dizygotic, DZ), in which twins share on average half of their segregating genes. Biometric modeling takes advantage of the fact that, by comparing the similarity within MZ and DZ twin pairs on a phenotype of interest (an observed difference among people, such as a personality trait), it is possible to separate the variance in the phenotype into three sources that, taken together, can be summed to account for the total variance of the phenotype: (1) heritability, the proportion of variance that can be accounted for by genetics; (2) the shared or common environment, the extent to which twins are similar because they grew up in the same household; and (3) the unique or nonshared environment, the extent to which twins are different despite sharing the same household and genes.

Decades of research using biometric modeling is fairly consistent across different samples, personality measures, and personality domains—for almost any normal personality trait, the heritability is around 50%, while the rest of the variance comes from unique environmental influences (Krueger & Johnson, 2008). Almost none of the variation in personality is due to the effects of the rearing family environment, beyond the contribution of shared genetics. These findings replicate across multiple different methods of personality assessment, including self-report, peer-report, and behavioral observation, across gender, such that similar heritability estimates are found for men and women, and across development, from children to adults.

The consistency of this finding is notable for several reasons. First, it is remarkable that different personality traits all share the same relative genetic influence. Each of the "Big Five" factors of personality (i.e., Extraversion, Openness, Agreeableness, Conscientiousness, and Neuroticism), has a heritability coefficient around .4 to .5 (Bouchard & Loehlin, 2001), even though they differ widely in the aspects of human behavior to which they are related. Further, moderate to sizeable estimates of genetic influence have also been found for personality disorders and dimensional measures of pathological personality (Livesley & Jang, 2008). Second, with the exception of a few traits (e.g., altruism; see Krueger, Hicks, & McGue, 2001), the finding of almost nonexistent estimates of shared environment suggest that family-level influences that act to make people similar within families have little or no bearing on personality. It is important to consider what this finding really means. It does not mean that a person's family has little if any influence on his or her personality, but that family influences, independent of genetic effects, play little role in personality similarities within families. This does not rule out the possibility that the family acts in an interactive manner on personality, as opposed to having a main effect (e.g., family-level factors act to enhance or suppress genetic effects on personality). Finally, even though unique environmental effects are important in the etiology of personality, it has been extremely difficult to link personality variation to a specific environmental effect (Turkheimer & Waldron, 2000), a topic we return to later.

Behavior genetics has also been important in examining the etiological structure and stability of personality. In much the same way that factor analysis of measured personality traits can reveal a hierarchical structure to multiple personality traits, structural modeling can also explore whether the genetic and environmental influences on personality are organized in a similar manner (see Krueger & Johnson, 2008, for a review). This type of work has generally shown that the genetic structure of personality (i.e., higher-order trait domains, such as the Big Five) parallels the phenotypic structure; however, there also appear to be genetic influences on more specific personality traits subsumed under the broad domains (e.g., impulsivity) not accounted for by the higher-order genetic factors. One application of this work is important for molecular genetics; there may be different genetic polymorphisms that operate at different levels of a personality hierarchy.

Genetic influences also appear to promote stability of personality over time, while the nonshared environment works to effect change. It is important, however, to note that as people age they tend to select into environments in a way that is not possible earlier in life; as they move into these niches, unique environmental effects may actually work to enhance the stability of personality features over time.

The great challenge of behavior genetic studies of personality has been to elucidate those unique environmental effects that impact the etiology of personality, given that nonshared environment is at least as important in personality variation as genetic influences. One theory that has been put forth is that individual members within a family can experience the same family-level event in their own, unique way; as a result, family-level influences are actually captured under the nonshared environmental estimates in typical biometric models (Krueger & Johnson, 2008). Another possibility is that environments do not have a "main effect" on the etiology of personality, but rather that different environments can moderate the genetic and environmental influences on personality. Put another way—in typical biometric moderation, heritability is estimated across the entire sample, averaging over any differences within the sample. New biometric moderation models allow for estimates of heritability at different levels of an environmental moderator variable. For instance, Krueger, South, Johnson, and Iacono (2008) demonstrated that the heritability of broad personality factors (positive and negative emotionality) in a sample of adolescents varied as a function of parent-adolescent relationship quality.

Molecular Genetic Studies of Personality

Give the consistent and reliable finding of moderately strong genetic influences on personality, it was hoped that a molecular genetic approach would quickly result in identifying measured genes for personality. The first study reporting a significant effect of a measured gene (DRD4, a dopamine receptor gene) on a personality trait (novelty seeking) appeared with great excitement (as recently reviewed by Ebstein, 2006), and it was assumed that the genes for many broad domains of personality would quickly be found. Unfortunately, it has been exceedingly difficult to link personality traits and dimensions with specific genes in a replicable manner, a problem that is shared by research into the genetic basis of psychopathology and physical illness (see South & Krueger, 2008, for a recent review). It has been frustrating for researchers to know that genetic influences account for 50% of the variation in personality, but fail to find specific genes for personality, even as technology continues to improve.

Most researchers examining the molecular genetic basis of personality have rejected a Mendelian (one gene) view of inheritance, instead acknowledging that personality traits as they are currently conceptualized are most likely influenced by many genes, each accounting for a small percentage of the variance (South & Krueger, 2008). The attempt to determine how much variance in personality is accounted for by genetic markers is called quantitative trait loci (QTL) analysis, and the most popular methodology for QTL research is association analysis, in which researchers measure the association between a personality trait and a polymorphism or variant of the gene (called an allele). Unfortunately, meta-analyses have disconfirmed some of the earliest, and it was thought strongest, gene-personality associations.

As suggested for the study of behavior genetics of personality, it may be that the future of molecular genetic approaches to personality lies in incorporating more nuanced conceptualizations of gene-environment interplay. Specifically, just as measured environments may moderate the susceptibility to genetic influences measured by twin methodology, the impact of measured genes on personality may be contingent on environmental influences. For instance, Lahti and colleagues (2005) found an interaction between parental alcohol use during childhood, the DRD4 receptor gene polymorphism, and the personality trait of novelty-seeking in adulthood. Participants with a father who reported greater frequency of alcohol consumption were more likely to have high novelty-seeking scores only if they also had the 2- or 5-repeat alleles of the DRD4 gene. Thus, providing for possible contingencies between measured genes and measured environments may explain, at least in part, the failure to find replicable main effects linking genes and personality traits.

Decades of behavioral genetic research are consistent in demonstrating moderately strong estimates of genetic and unique environmental influences on personality. However, it has been difficult to identify the specific environmental contexts, and the measured genes (from a molecular genetic approach) that are the driving forces behind personality variation. Future research into the genetics of personality would do well to incorporate gene-environment interplay, particularly gene-environment interactions, in developing hypothesis that link specific genetic polymorphisms to personality.

REFERENCES

Bouchard, T. J., Jr., & Loehlin, J. C. (2001). Genes, evolution, and personality. *Behavior Genetics, 31*, 243–273.

Ebstein, R. P. (2006). The molecular genetic architecture of human personality: Beyond self-report questionnaires. *Molecular Psychiatry, 11*, 427–445

Krueger, R. F., Hicks, B. M., & McGue, M. (2001). Altruism and antisocial behavior: Independent tendencies, unique personality correlates, distinct etiologies. *Psychological Science, 12*, 397–402.

Krueger, R. F., & Johnson, W. (2008). Behavioral genetics and personality: A new look at the integration of nature and nurture. In O. P. John, R. W. Robins, & L. A. Pervin (Eds.), *Handbook of personality: Theory and research* (3rd ed., pp. 287–310). New York: Guilford Press.

Krueger, R. F., South, S. C., Johnson, W., & Iacono, W. (2008). The heritability of personality is not always 50%: Gene-environment interactions and correlations between personality and parenting. *Journal of Personality, 76*, 1485–1522.

Lahti, J., Raikkonen, K., Ekelund, J., Peltonen, L., Raitakari, O. T., & Keltikangas-Jarvinen, L. (2005). Novelty seeking: Interaction between parental alcohol use and dopamine D4 receptor gene exon III polymorphism over 17 years. *Psychiatric Genetics, 15*, 133–139.

Livesley, W. J., & Jang, K. L. (2008). The behavioral genetics of personality disorder. *Annual Review of Clinical Psychology, 4*, 247–274.

South, S. C., & Krueger, R. F. (2008). An interactionist perspective on genetic and environmental contributions to personality. *Social and Personality Psychology Compass, 2*, 929–948.

Turkheimer, E., & Waldron, M. (2000). Nonshared environment: A theoretical, methodological, and quantitative review. *Psychological Bulletin, 126*(1), 78–108.

SUGGESTED READINGS

Ebstein, R. P. (2006). The molecular genetic architecture of human personality: Beyond self-report questionnaires. *Molecular Psychiatry, 11*, 427–445.

Krueger, R. F., & Johnson, W. (in press). Behavioral genetics and personality: A new look at the integration of nature and nurture. In L. A. Pervin, O. P. John, & R. W. Robins (Eds.), *Handbook of personality: Theory and research* (3rd ed.). New York: Guilford Press.

SUSAN C. SOUTH
Purdue University

ROBERT F. KRUEGER
Washington University in St. Louis

PERSONALITY, INTERPERSONAL THEORIES OF

The origins of the interpersonal tradition in personality and clinical psychology are found in Harry Sullivan's highly generative interpersonal theory of psychiatry, which considered interpersonal relations and their impact on the self-concept to be core emphases in understanding personality, psychopathology, and psychotherapy. The interpersonal legacy that emerged from Sullivan's work is now in its fourth generation and has dramatically evolved over a nearly 60-year history, increasing in level of theoretical integration, methodological sophistication, and scope. Throughout this history, interpersonal theories of personality have had a reciprocally influential history with research programs that have culminated in well-validated, empirically derived, circular (or circumplex) models and methods that are used to describe individual differences in interpersonal motives, dispositions, and behaviors. The integration of interpersonal theory and the interpersonal circle provides a coherent nomological net for the integrative study of personality, personality assessment, psychopathology, psychotherapy, health psychology, and behavioral medicine (Pincus & Cain, 2008; Pincus, Lukowitsky, & Wright, in press). Thus interpersonal theories of personality (IPC) include multiple methods to assess the interpersonal constructs associated with circumplex structural models, and they tie operational definitions of reciprocal interpersonal processes and patterns of validity in interpersonal behavior directly to these models. Figure 1 presents a contemporary version of the interpersonal circumplex model.

The contemporary interpersonal approach is an exceptionally synthetic framework that includes explicit efforts toward integration of cognitive, attachment, psychodynamic, and evolutionary theories and has even identified psychophysiological and neurobiological substrates. This integrative nature was best described by Horowitz and colleagues, who stated the following: "Because the interpersonal approach harmonizes so well with all of these theoretical approaches, it is integrative: It draws from the wisdom of all major approaches to systematize our understanding of interpersonal phenomena. Although it is integrative, however, it is also unique, posing characteristic questions of its own" (Horowitz et al., 2006, p. 82). Virtually all personality theories touch upon interpersonal functioning, whereas contemporary interpersonal theories simply assert that when we look at a domain of personality or its substrates, our best bet may be to look at it in relation to interpersonal functioning. Thus, contemporary interpersonal theory is also a nexus for bringing together elements from across the theoretical spectrum.

Contemporary Assumptions

Contemporary interpersonal theories (Benjamin, 2003; Horowitz, 2004; Pincus, 2005) share four broad assumptions: First, the most important expressions of personality and psychopathology occur in phenomena involving more than one person (i.e., interpersonal situations). An interpersonal situation can be defined as the experience of a pattern of relating self with other associated individuals with varying levels of anxiety (or security) in which learning takes place. This learning influences the development of self-concept and social behavior. According to Sullivan, interpersonal learning of self-concept and social behavior is based on an anxiety gradient associated with interpersonal situations. All interpersonal situations range from rewarding (highly secure, self-esteem promoting), to various degrees of anxiety (insecurity, low self-esteem), and ending in a class of situations associated with anxiety that is so severe that it results in dissociation from experiences. The interpersonal situation underlies genesis, development, maintenance, and mutability of personality and psychopathology through continuous patterning and repatterning of interpersonal experience in an effort to increase security and self-esteem (positively reinforcing) while avoiding anxiety (negatively reinforcing). Over time, this patterning gives rise to social-cognitive schemas of self and others, as well as enduring patterns of adaptive or disturbed interpersonal relating.

The second assumption of contemporary interpersonal theories is that interpersonal situations occur between proximal interactants and within the minds of those interactants via the capacity for perception, mental representation, memory, fantasy, and expectancy. A potential misinterpretation of the term *interpersonal* is to assume it refers to a limited class of phenomena that can be

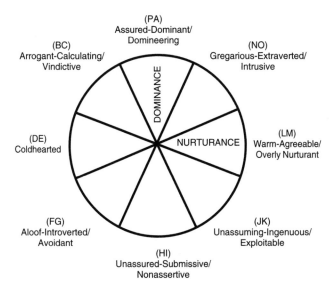

Figure 1. Circumplex model of interpersonal traits and problems

observed only in the immediate interaction between two proximal people. A review of Sullivan's body of work clearly reveals that this dichotomous conception of the interpersonal and the intrapsychic as two sets of distinct phenomena—one residing between people and one residing within a person—is an incorrect interpretation. This contemporary assumption allows contemporary interpersonal theories to incorporate important pantheoretical representational constructs, such as cognitive interpersonal schemas, internalized object relations, and internal working models. Contemporary interpersonal theory does suggest that the most important personality and psychopathological phenomena are relational in nature, but it does not suggest that such phenomena are limited to contemporaneous, observable behavior.

The third assumption of contemporary interpersonal theories is that agency and communion provide an integrative metastructure for conceptualizing interpersonal situations (e.g., Wiggins, 1991). *Agency* refers to the condition of being a differentiated individual, and it is manifested in strivings for power and mastery that can enhance and protect one's differentiation. *Communion* refers to the condition of being part of a larger social or spiritual entity, and it is manifested in strivings for intimacy, union, and solidarity with the larger entity. These metaconcepts form a superordinate structure that can be used to derive explanatory and descriptive concepts at different levels of specificity. At the broadest and most interdisciplinary level, agency and communion serve to classify the interpersonal motives, strivings, and values of human relations (Horowitz, 2004). When motivation is considered in interpersonal situations, we may consider the agentic and communal nature of the individual's personal strivings or current concerns or, alternatively, the more specific agentic and communal goals (e.g., to be in control, to be close) that specific behaviors are enacted to achieve. At more specific levels, the structure provides conceptual coordinates for describing and measuring interpersonal traits and behaviors. The intermediate level of traits includes an evolving set of interpersonal taxonomies of individual differences. Agentic and communal traits imply enduring patterns of perceiving, thinking, feeling, and behaving that are probabilistic in nature, and they describe an individual's interpersonal tendencies aggregated across interpersonal situations. At the most specific level, the structure can be used to classify the nature and intensity of specific interpersonal behaviors. Wiggins's theoretical analysis simultaneously allows for the integration of descriptive levels within the interpersonal tradition as well as expansion of the conceptual scope and meaning of interpersonal functioning. Thus, in addition to assuming that agency and communion are the fundamental metaconcepts of personality, interpersonal theory also asserts

that explicatory systems derived from agency and communion can be used to understand, describe, and measure interpersonal traits and behaviors.

The final assumption of contemporary interpersonal theories asserts that interpersonal behaviors create reciprocal influences on interactants and that patterns of reciprocity can be defined in reference to the interpersonal circumplex (IPC). The most fundamental interpersonal pattern is referred to as interpersonal complementarity, which can be defined by reciprocity for the vertical dimension (i.e., dominance pulls for submission; submission pulls for dominance) and correspondence for the horizontal dimension (friendliness pulls for friendliness; hostility pulls for hostility). Although complementarity is neither the only reciprocal interpersonal pattern that can be describe by the IPC nor proposed as a universal law of interaction, empirical studies consistently find support for its probabilistic predictions. However, complementarity should not be conceived of as behavioral stimulus–response chain of events. Rather, mediating internal psychological processes impact the likelihood of complementary patterns, and thus complementarity is most helpful if it is considered as a common baseline for the field regulatory pulls and invitations of interpersonal behavior associated with healthy socialization. Used this way, chronic deviations from complementary reciprocal patterns may be indicative of pathological functioning, because it suggests impairment in understanding the needs and behavior of others and reduces the likelihood that agentic and communal motives of both persons will be satisfied in the interpersonal situation.

Development and Motivation

Contemporary interpersonal theories agree that the first interpersonal situations are associated with infant attachment: the two fundamental tasks associated with the infant attachment system—staying close and/or connecting to caregivers, separating and exploring—catalyze the internalization of interpersonal behaviors and social learning. These tasks are the first communal and agentic motives, respectively. Over time, emerging developmental achievements (e.g., gender identity) and traumas (e.g., loss of an attachment figure) further catalyze internalization and social learning. Benjamin (2003) proposed three developmental "copy processes" that describe the ways in which early interpersonal experiences are internalized. The first copy process is *identification*, which is strongly identified with early caretakers; there will be a tendency to act toward others in ways that copy how important others have acted toward the developing person. The second copy process is *recapitulation*, which is defined as maintaining a position complementary to an internalized other. This can be described as reacting "as if" the internalized other is still there. The third copy process is *introjection*, which is defined as treating the self as one has been treated. With the inclusion of developmental, motivational, and regulatory processes and mechanisms, contemporary interpersonal theories move beyond description and provide a mature nomological net with applications across psychology, psychiatry, and the social sciences.

REFERENCES

Benjamin, L. S. (2003). *Interpersonal reconstructive therapy.* New York: Guilford Press.

Horowitz, L. M. (2004). *Interpersonal foundations of psychopathology.* Washington, DC: American Psychological Association.

Horowitz, L. M., Wilson, K. R., Turan, B., Zolotsev, P., Constantino, M. J., & Henderson, L. (2006). How interpersonal motives clarify the meaning of interpersonal behavior: A revised circumplex model. *Personality and Social Psychology Review, 10,* 67–86.

Pincus, A. L. (2005). A contemporary integrative interpersonal theory of personality disorders. In M. Lenzenweger & J. Clarkin (Eds.), *Major theories of personality disorder* (2nd ed., pp. 282–331). New York: Guilford Press.

Pincus, A. L., & Cain, N. M. (2008). Interpersonal psychotherapy. In D. C. S. Richard & S. K. Huprich (Eds.), *Clinical psychology: Assessment, treatment, and research* (pp. 213–245). San Diego, CA: Academic Press.

Pincus, A. L., Lukowitsky, M. R., & Wright, A. G. C. (in press). The interpersonal nexus of personality and psychopathology. In T. Millon, R. F. Krueger, & E. Simonsen (Eds.), *Contemporary directions in psychopathology: Toward the* DSM-V *and* ICD-11. New York: Guilford Press.

Wiggins, J. S. (1991). Agency and communion as conceptual coordinates for the understanding and measurement of interpersonal behavior. In W. Grove & D. Cicchetti (Eds.), *Thinking clearly about psychology: Essays in honor of Paul E. Meehl* (Vol. 2, pp. 89–113). Minneapolis: University of Minnesota Press.

SUGGESTED READINGS

Kiesler, D. J. (1996). *Contemporary interpersonal theory and research: Personality, psychopathology, and psychotherapy.* New York: John Wiley & Sons.

Leary, T. (1957). *Interpersonal diagnosis of personality.* New York: Ronald Press.

Pincus, A. L., & Gurtman, M. B. (2006). Interpersonal theory and the interpersonal circumplex: Evolving perspectives on normal and abnormal personality. In S. Strack (Ed.), *Differentiating normal and abnormal personality* (2nd ed., pp. 83–111). New York: Springer.

AARON L. PINCUS
Pennsylvania State University

PERSONALITY, PSYCHODYNAMIC MODELS OF

More than a century after its birth, the psychodynamic model of the mind remains one of the most influential theoretical perspectives in psychology. Although psychodynamic ideas are often criticized within academia, and psychodynamic treatments face numerous challenges in today's managed care environment, the founder of psychoanalysis, Sigmund Freud, remains the most widely cited author in contemporary psychology, both in journal articles and textbooks (Haggbloom et al., 2002). Some psychologists love the psychodynamic model, others hate it, but few ignore it.

The Core Assumptions of Psychoanalysis

Psychodynamic models differ from other models of personality with respect to three key assumptions (see Bornstein, 2003).

Primacy of the Unconscious

A central assumption of psychodynamic theory is that the vast majority of mental processing takes place outside conscious awareness. Moreover, the theory regards unconscious mental processes as primary determinants of personality development and dynamics.

Psychic Causality

According to psychodynamic theory, every event in mental life has an identifiable cause, and there is no such thing as a random thought, urge, or emotion. This has come to be called the principle of *psychic causality*.

Importance of Early Experiences

Most theories attribute particular importance to early experiences in shaping personality, but psychoanalytic theory is unique in viewing the events of infancy and early childhood—including events that occur during the first weeks of life—as having profound (and, to some degree, irreversible) effects on personality development.

Psychodynamic Models of the Mind

Because psychodynamic models of the mind have evolved considerably since Freud's first writings on this topic in the mid-1880s, it is inaccurate (though common) to speak of psychodynamic theory in the singular. There are, in fact, an array of psychodynamic models, each with its own language and emphasis.

Classical Psychoanalytic Theory

Classical psychoanalytic theory includes several theoretical frameworks that were prominent during the first decades of the twentieth century. The first of these was the *drive model*, which conceptualized personality in terms of each person's unique way of coping with and gratifying basic biological drives, including the sex drive. The *topographic model*, described in detail in Freud's (1900/1953) *The Interpretation of Dreams*, conceptualizes personality as reflecting the interplay among conscious, unconscious, and preconscious processes. (Preconscious material is that which exists outside awareness, but unlike unconscious material, which is actively barred from consciousness, preconscious material can be recalled fairly easily.)

During the 1920s, Freud recognized some explanatory limitations of the topographic model and outlined the *structural model*, which conceptualizes personality in terms of the interaction of three psychic structures: the id (the seat of drives and impulses), the ego (the logical, rational, reality-oriented part of the mind), and the superego (the conscience, or moral code). Beyond reality testing and logical thinking, the ego helps manage anxiety through the use of *ego defenses*, self-protective strategies that help minimize anxiety by distorting the individual's perceptions of internal and external events that would otherwise be threatening or upsetting. Among the ego defenses frequently discussed by psychodynamic theorists are repression, denial, projection, and rationalization (see Cramer, 2006).

The most controversial model in classical psychoanalytic theory, the *psychosexual stage model*, contends that beginning in infancy, humans go through an invariant sequence of developmental stages wherein sexual impulses are expressed in different ways; these are commonly identified as the oral, anal, Oedipal (or phallic), latency, and genital stages. If events (either positive or negative) cause a person to become fixated at a particular stage, adult personality will reflect the conflicts and developmental challenges of that stage, and the person will have an oral (dependent), anal (control-oriented), or phallic (competitive) personality (Fisher & Greenberg, 1996).

Object Relations Theory and Self Psychology

As psychoanalysis evolved, theorists paid increasing attention to the ego's role in planning, striving, and aspiring, a view that both complements and extends the traditional Freudian emphasis on the ego as managing anxiety. This perspective, called *ego psychology*, set the stage for two psychodynamic models that emerged from classical psychoanalytic theory, both of which remain influential today.

Object relations theory conceptualizes personality in terms of internalized mental representations of significant figures (sometimes called *introjects*). These include mental representations of parents, siblings, and other important people, as well as mental representations of figures who exist in fantasy rather than reality (e.g., God, a wished-for parent one never had). *Self psychology* shares object relations theory's emphasis on mental representations as the building blocks of personality but focuses primarily on the self representation rather than on mental representations of others (see Kernberg, 1976, and Kohut, 1971, for discussions of these two perspectives).

Contemporary Integrative Models

In recent years, clinicians and researchers have forged connections between psychoanalysis and other theoretical perspectives, in part to enhance the heuristic value of psychodynamic theory and in part to increase the effectiveness of psychodynamic treatment (Bornstein, 2005). Among the more influential contemporary integrative models are those linking psychodynamic principles with ideas and findings from cognitive psychology and cognitive-behavior therapy and those blending psychodynamic constructs with concepts from humanistic and existential psychology.

Converging and Diverging Themes in Different Psychodynamic Perspectives

The common assumptions and contrasting emphases of different psychodynamic models have helped enrich psychologists' understanding of many issues by bringing to these issues the benefit of multiple viewpoints. Among the noteworthy converging and diverging themes in contemporary psychodynamic theory are the following.

Personality Dynamics

All psychodynamic models of the mind concur that unconscious influences play a central role in personality dynamics, but the models differ in how they conceptualize these unconscious influences. For example, classical psychoanalytic theory attributes paramount importance to unconscious conflicts (e.g., regarding sexual attraction to a parent) and to the strategies used to cope with these conflicts. Object relations theory, in contrast, regards unconscious features of internalized mental representations as key in personality (e.g., an unconscious perception of the father as hostile and threatening).

Defense and Coping

Different psychodynamic models agree that some degree of distortion and self-deception is an inescapable by-product of modulating anxiety and coping with external threat. However, the roots of this distortion differ from model to model. Thus, whereas the psychosexual stage model emphasizes the role of early fixation in distorting perceptions of self and others, and the structural model conceptualizes these distortions in terms of ego defenses, self psychology traces these distortions to the internalization of a poorly integrated, permeable self-concept.

Adjustment and Psychopathology

Impaired reality testing and problems with impulse control are cardinal features of psychopathology in all psychodynamic frameworks, but the presumed causes of these difficulties vary across models. Freud's structural model traces impaired reality testing and impulse control problems to poor ego strength (i.e., an imbalance among psychic structures so that too much energy is invested in id or superego, and too little in the ego). Object relations theory views psychopathology in terms of impairments in key introjects, so that one's internalized mental representations are harsh and demanding (in which case feelings of guilt and worthlessness ensue) or weak and unavailable (leading to feelings of helplessness and abandonment).

Evaluating Psychodynamic Models of Personality

No theory of personality is perfect, including the psychodynamic model. Among the key strengths of this perspective is its comprehensiveness: psychodynamic theory is a far-reaching framework with implications for normal and abnormal personality functioning, life span development, social interaction, memory and information processing, and even such distant topics as evolutionary biology, stereotyping, intergroup conflict, sociology, literary criticism, and the psychological origins of culture and religious belief. Among the other strengths of the theory are its clinical utility (aside from its effectiveness as a mode of treatment, psychoanalysis has influenced many other treatment approaches as well) and its heuristic value (psychodynamic theory is rich with ideas regarding the human condition).

Psychodynamic models of the mind have limitations as well, and these include their complexity, their tendency to invoke unobservable theoretical constructs, and some inconsistencies across different psychodynamic frameworks (Bornstein, 2003). Clinicians and researchers also criticize psychodynamic theory for its limited empirical base, although that limitation has been corrected to some degree in recent years with an increased emphasis on the empirical testing of psychodynamic concepts (see Fisher & Greenberg, 1996; Luborsky & Barrett, 2006).

Current Trends in Psychodynamic Theory

More than a century after it was first developed, psychodynamic theory remains strong, and its ideas remain influential within and outside psychology. As to psychoanalysis in its second century, several trends have emerged. First and foremost, clinicians and researchers are actively seeking common ground with cognitive, social, and developmental psychologists, strengthening ties between psychodynamic theory and mainstream psychology. Along somewhat similar lines, studies of the neurological underpinnings of psychodynamic processes have received increasing attention in recent years, an effort bolstered by the development of neuroimaging techniques that allow cortical activity patterns associated with various behaviors and mental processes to be observed directly (Bornstein, 2005).

Other trends characterize psychoanalytic treatment, among the most important of which is an increased interest in developing time-limited psychodynamic interventions for psychological problems (e.g., phobias) that might not require long-term insight-oriented therapy. Along with this effort has come increased attention to conducting controlled empirical studies of the effectiveness of psychodynamic treatment. These investigations have not only documented the effectiveness of psychoanalytic therapy for various psychological disorders but also helped illuminate the kinds of therapist interventions that are (and are not) effective in reducing symptom severity and enhancing overall quality of life.

REFERENCES

Bornstein, R. F. (2003). Psychodynamic models of personality. In T. Millon & M. J. Lerner (Eds.), *Handbook of psychology: Vol. 5. Personality and social psychology* (pp. 117–134). (I. B. Weiner, Editor-in-Chief). Hoboken, NJ: John Wiley & Sons.

Bornstein, R. F. (2005). Reconnecting psychoanalysis to mainstream psychology: Opportunities and challenges. *Psychoanalytic Psychology, 22*, 323–340.

Cramer, P. (2006). *Protecting the self: Defense mechanisms in action.* New York: Guilford Press.

Fisher, S., & Greenberg, R. P. (1996). *Freud scientifically reappraised: Testing the theories and therapy.* New York: John Wiley & Sons.

Freud, S. (1953). The interpretation of dreams. In J. Strachey (Ed. & Trans.), *The standard edition of the complete psychological works of Sigmund Freud* (Vol. IV). London: Hogarth. (Original work published 1900)

Haggbloom, S. J., Warnick, R., Warnick, J. E., Jones, V. K., Yarbough, G. L., Russell, T. M., et al. (2002). The 100 most eminent psychologists of the 20th century. *Review of General Psychology, 6*, 139–152.

Kernberg, O. F. (1976). *Object relations in psychoanalytic theory.* New York: Jason Aronson.

Kohut, H. (1971). *The analysis of the self.* New York: International Universities Press.

Luborsky, L., & Barrett, M. S. (2006). The history and empirical status of key psychoanalytic concepts. *Annual Review of Clinical Psychology, 2,* 1–19.

SUGGESTED READINGS

Bornstein, R. F. (2001). The impending death of psychoanalysis. *Psychoanalytic Psychology, 18,* 3–20.

Brenner, C. (1974). *An elementary textbook of psychoanalysis* (revised ed.). New York: Anchor Doubleday.

Greenberg, J. R., & Mitchell, S. J. (1983). *Object relations in psychoanalytic theory.* Cambridge, MA: Harvard University Press.

ROBERT F. BORNSTEIN
Adelphi University

See also: Ego Psychology; Object Relations Theory; Psychoanalytic Theories

PERSONALITY PSYCHOLOGY

Personality psychology focuses on understanding individual variability in people's thoughts, feelings, and behaviors: why is one person shy and another sociable, one person irritable and another even-tempered, and one person reliable and another irresponsible? One of the hallmarks of the field is that such questions are investigated at multiple levels of analysis, from genes to sociocultural contexts. Consequently, personality researchers use a broad array of methods, including self-report questionnaires, computerized tasks, behavioral observation, brain imaging, and DNA analyses. Individuals trained in personality psychology work at universities, private and federal research institutes, test-publishing companies, organizational consulting firms, and government agencies such as the CIA.

Since its founding as a scientific discipline more than 100 years ago, the study of personality has had a rocky history, rising and falling from prominence within the broader field of psychology. However, recent advances in the understanding of the nature, structure, and development of personality have sparked a renaissance in the field, and personality is now an integral and vibrant part of psychology with close ties to clinical, developmental, and social psychology (John, Robins, & Pervin, 2008).

Although college courses in personality psychology often focus on the grand theories of Freud, Skinner, Rogers, and others, these theories have relatively little direct impact on contemporary research. Instead, most personality psychologists conduct research in one or more of the following areas: (1) personality structure (what are the basic building blocks of personality, and how are they organized?), (2) personality development (what are the developmental origins of personality, and how does it change across the life span?), (3) personality processes (what are the biological, cognitive, emotional, social, and cultural factors that account for personality differences?), and (4) personality applications (what are the real-world consequences of personality for love, work, health, and well-being?). Here we summarize the recent findings and conclusions emerging from each of these areas of research.

Identifying and Organizing the Basic Building Blocks of Personality

The basic building blocks of personality have been conceptualized in a variety of ways by theorists from a wide range of perspectives: as defense mechanisms by psychodynamic theorists, as learned stimulus–response patterns by behaviorists, as information-processing tendencies by cognitively oriented theorists, and as evolved neurologically based systems by biologically oriented theorists. However, most contemporary researchers conceptualize personality in terms of traits. Traits are commonly defined as relatively enduring patterns of thoughts, feelings, and behavior that influence a person's interactions with, and adaptations to, the environment.

One monumental task has been to identify and classify the nearly unlimited number of traits on which individuals differ from each other (John, Naumann, & Soto, 2008). A surprisingly helpful starting point has been language itself. According to the lexical hypothesis, the most important and socially relevant personality characteristics eventually become encoded into the language of all human cultures. Using the logic of the lexical hypothesis, many personality psychologists believe that an empirical analysis of how personality-related attributes (e.g., calm, talkative, dominant, kind) cluster together might provide some insight into the number and nature of the basic units of personality.

Based on extensive analyses by multiple investigators working in the lexical tradition, there is now considerable agreement that five broad domains, known as the Big Five dimensions, capture most of the personality-descriptive terms in the English language. Each domain consists of a cluster of related characteristics: extraversion (talkative, energetic), agreeableness (cooperative, kind), conscientiousness (responsible, dependable), neuroticism (tense, nervous), and openness to experience (traits like curious and artistic). Over the past decade or two, these same five domains have been replicated in many other languages, although in some cases a distinct openness domain fails to emerge, and one or two "culture-specific dimensions" emerge in addition to the Big Five. In general, though, the Big Five dimensions appear to be more or less robust across languages and cultures.

Personality researchers working in different traditions and using other methods also find evidence that the Big

Five dimensions provide a useful taxonomy for the major domains of personality. For instance, the dimensions of extraversion and neuroticism are included in nearly all models of personality trait structure, including biologically based models. Consequently, there is now considerable agreement that the Big Five can serve as a reasonable model of the basic dimensions of adult personality. Moreover, the Big Five traits have proven useful as a way to organize the major dimensions of temperament assessed in children. This downward extension of the Big Five helps to focus attention on a core set of personality dimensions that are broadly relevant for functioning and adaptation across the life span.

Current work on traits is focused on (1) better understanding cross-cultural variability in the Big Five dimensions, (2) developing neurobiologically based theories of the mechanisms underlying each dimension, (3) creating a hierarchical taxonomy by identifying how specific dimensions of personality (e.g., sensation seeking) align with each broad dimension, and (4) investigating novel ways to assess the everyday manifestations of personality traits through the coding of personal spaces, online self-presentation, and interpersonal encounters. Moreover, work continues on further refining the existing personality tests that reliably and validly assess the Big Five dimensions.

Origins of Personality and Its Development across the Life Span

Research on personality development focuses on the age at which individual variability in personality first emerges, the role of nature (genes) and nurture (environment) in shaping personality, and patterns of consistency and change in personality across the life span. Early in development, children show relatively stable individual differences in the way they interact with strangers, form bonds with caregivers, explore and manipulate their environment, regulate their needs, respond to reinforcements and other environmental contingencies, and express their distress. Where do these individual differences come from? Do they reflect nature, nurture, or both?

The eminent psychologist John Watson once famously claimed that he could take any infant at random and train her or him to be anything that he wanted. Researchers now know that Watson was wrong; a voluminous body of research has demonstrated that all psychological attributes reflect the combined influence of both nature and nurture.

Indeed, virtually all personality traits are influenced by genetic factors (Krueger, South, Johnson, & Iacono, 2008), suggesting that they are rooted in neurologically based tendencies that have been shaped by evolution. However, there is no one-to-one correspondence between a person's genetic makeup and her or his personality; personality develops through complex interactions between genetic factors and environmental experiences. An important discovery in this area of research is that genetic and environmental influences are not entirely independent. People select, modify, construct, and reconstruct their experiences, in part based on their genetic propensities. For example, children who have trouble with impulse control seem to evoke harsher parenting than those with easier temperaments. Examples such as this highlight the inappropriateness of the nature-versus-nurture debate and suggest that the critical question is how nature and nurture work together to shape personality development.

Research pointing to a genetic basis for personality does not preclude the possibility that it changes with age or can be affected by life experiences. Researchers investigating these questions often use longitudinal designs, in which the same group of individuals is followed over long periods of time and assessed repeatedly with the same personality measures. Such studies have been used to assess two forms of stability in personality, differential and absolute.

Studies of differential stability evaluate whether individuals maintain the same relative ordering on a trait over time. For example, a researcher might investigate whether individuals who are relatively extraverted compared with their peers in their 20s are also relatively extraverted compared with their peers in their 40s. A summary of the vast number of studies on this topic concluded that the Big Five traits showed increasing differential stability with age (Roberts & DelVecchio, 2000). Specifically, there was a fairly modest amount of differential stability when individuals were followed during their early childhood years, whereas there was a very strong amount of differential stability when individuals were followed in their 50s and older. This pattern of increasing differential stability was basically the same for all Big Five traits and applied to both men and women.

These findings are noteworthy because they confirm that the Big Five traits are relatively enduring characteristics by the time a person reaches adulthood. The current explanation for increasing differential stability with age is that adulthood is a time in the life span when maturational changes are reduced, social roles stabilize, environmental changes are increasingly subject to individual control, and individuals have a more stable sense of self. These conditions tend to promote stability. Even so, such findings also indicate that there is never a time in the life span when personality ceases to change. This seems to contradict a suggestion by William James, who said that personality is "set like plaster" by the age of 30. The Big Five traits do become increasingly stable after age 30; however, there does not appear to be a point when personality is fixed for all people.

Studies about absolute stability examine the degree of stability in the exact amount or level of a personality attribute over time. For example, a researcher might evaluate whether, on average, individuals are more extraverted in their 20s or in their 40s. Both longitudinal and cross-sectional studies suggest that average levels of agreeableness and conscientiousness increase with age, whereas average levels of extraversion, neuroticism, and openness decline. Many of the absolute changes in the Big Five tend to be small and gradual when viewed as year-to-year comparisons. Over decades of life, however, the changes can be quite substantial.

The absolute changes in the Big Five tend to reflect increases in personal qualities that help individuals meet the demands of the adult roles of worker, committed romantic partner, and parent. This trend has been labeled the maturity principle of personality development, because it suggests that personality maturity increases with age. Young adulthood (i.e., the years between the late teens and late 20s) is a time when many absolute changes in personality occur. This is also a time when individuals first assume the roles of worker, partner, and parent. Thus, the average absolute changes in the Big Five seem to match the demands of the life course. This finding raises important, but mostly unanswered, questions about the causal connections between adult roles and personality change.

In summary, research in personality development indicates that personality characteristics are shaped both by intrinsic biological factors and extrinsic life experiences. As people age, they show personality changes that suggest increasing psychological maturity and an increasing capacity to fulfill important adult roles. Personality tends to become more stable with age, but it continues to change throughout the life span. Current work is focused on (1) identifying specific gene–trait linkages that would help to explain the heritability of personality, (2) better understanding the precise features of the environment that interact with genetic dispositions, (3) better understanding how characteristics of temperament in early childhood become elaborated into adult personality characteristics, and (4) better understanding the mediating processes that explain the link between, on the one hand, important life events and roles and, on the other, personality changes.

Personality Processes

Researchers interested in personality processes study why and how a person with particular characteristics acts a certain way. That is, what are the biological, cognitive, affective, social, and cultural processes that account for individual variability in personality? For example, what are the thoughts and feelings that underlie the tendency to be shy, and what are the biological factors (genes, hormones, neurotransmitters, neural activation patterns) that account for those thoughts and feelings?

Recent research has made considerable progress toward identifying the neurobehavioral systems that underlie the basic dimensions of personality (Canli, 2008). Extraversion is associated with the biological system governing incentive motivation and approach behavior, which is linked to the neurotransmitter dopamine. Neuroticism is associated with the biological system governing withdrawal behavior, anxiety, and the detection of threat, which is linked to the neurotransmitter serotonin. Agreeableness is associated with the biological system governing the enjoyment of social bonds and affiliation, which is regulated, at least in part, by the hormone oxytocin. Conscientiousness, particularly effortful control, has been linked to systems associated with executive control involving regions of the prefrontal cortex. Although the biological underpinnings of openness to experience are less well understood, certain facets of this broad domain, such as those related to sensation-seeking and exploratory behavior, are probably connected to the approach system and other biobehavioral systems involved in sensitivity to reward, such as the nucleus accumbens region of the brain and the associated dopaminergic system.

Another active area of research focuses on social cognitive processes implicated in personality differences. Researchers in this tradition examine how expectancies, goals, attributions, and other information-processing tendencies shape the way people perceive situations and their behavior in those situations. These different patterns of thinking can explain why two people interpret the same objective event in often dramatically different ways. For example, according to the social cognitive view of aggression, aggression-prone individuals show a "hostile attribution bias" and perceive ambiguous social cues as threatening and confrontative; as a result, in social interactions, they are relatively likely to feel that they have been insulted, maligned, attacked, or maltreated, even in situations that others might perceive as benign.

Researchers interested in personality processes also study the social-contextual factors that influence how traits are manifested in different situations and life contexts. There is increasing evidence that people are not passively shaped by the environment but instead actively seek out, modify, and even create environments that are consistent with their personalities. These processes, referred to as "person–environment transactions," play out in several ways. First, personality traits draw out or elicit particular responses from the social environment. For example, individuals who are friendly may evoke more supportive responses from their peers, which in turn reinforce their disposition to be friendly. Second, personality traits shape how people construe social situations. The same objective environment, such as a cocktail party, may mean something quite different to an extravert (an opportunity to make friends) as opposed to an introvert (an anxiety-inducing situation). Third, individuals play an active role in selecting and manipulating their own social experiences. Outgoing and sociable individuals may choose careers that fit well with these tendencies and shun solitary occupations with limited potential for social interaction. Together, these three processes promote a match between personality and social contexts. Consequently, many life experiences accentuate and reinforce the personality characteristics that were partially responsible for the particular experiences in the first place.

Finally, with regard to the broader cultural context, recent research suggests that although traits vary somewhat across cultures (e.g., people seem to be more extraverted in some cultures than in others), the structure of personality, the underlying processes that generate personality differences, and the real-world consequences of personality tend to generalize across nations, cultures, and ethnic groups. Despite dramatic differences in cultural customs and practices, people from a wide range of cultures seem to fall in love, hate their neighbors, persist at work, and care for their children in much the same way, and for many of the same reasons, as people in other parts of the world.

With respect to personality processes, then, research identifies the mechanisms through which traits affect behavior and the mechanisms by which factors from genes to cultural contexts influence personality traits and their expression. Current work is focused on (1) developing a better understanding of the neurological systems, brain structures, and specific genes that underlie the broad traits and how these biological substrates interact with life experiences to shape personality differences; (2) more precisely identifying and assessing the cognitive mechanisms underlying personality traits; (3) better understanding how emotion and cognition interact to shape personality differences; and (4) better understanding the underlying dimensions of culture (e.g., individualism vs. collectivism) that account for cross-cultural variability in personality.

Real-World Consequences of Personality

Collectively, personality traits predict many of the outcomes that truly matter in life—health and mortality, academic success, job performance, the capacity to have a successful and lasting romantic relationship, and a wide range of personal and societal problems, including drug abuse and criminality (e.g., Ozer & Benet-Martínez, 2006; Roberts, Kuncel, Shiner, Caspi, & Goldberg, 2007). The precision of these predictions is comparable with that of many biomedical measures that predict diseases, such as electrocardiogram stress tests, ultrasound exams, and screening mammograms.

A life outcome of great importance to individuals and society is health and longevity. Meta-analytic findings suggest that conscientious people live longer than irresponsible and unreliable people (Roberts et al., 2007). The association between conscientiousness and longevity can be explained by the fact that conscientious people tend to engage in behaviors that promote health (e.g., exercise, following doctors' orders) and tend to refrain from behaviors that lead to health problems (e.g., drug and alcohol abuse, risky sexual behavior, unsafe driving, involvement in crime and violence) (Bogg & Roberts, 2004). In addition, but to a lesser extent, individuals who are extraverted, agreeable, and emotionally stable (i.e., low in neuroticism) tend to live longer (Roberts et al., 2007).

Crime and antisocial behavior have enormous consequences to society. Meta-analytic findings suggest that agreeable and conscientious people are less likely to engage in antisocial behavior (Miller & Lynam, 2001). In contrast, individuals who tend to be antagonistic and impulsive are more likely to engage in delinquency and be convicted of a crime.

Close relationships are valued by most adults, and there is consistent evidence linking personality with relationship satisfaction and stability. Meta-analytic findings suggest that low neuroticism is the strongest and most consistent predictor of relationship satisfaction (Heller, Watson, & Ilies, 2004); neurotic individuals tend to be less happy in their relationships and tend to have romantic partners who are themselves less happy. In terms of predictors of divorce, individuals who are neurotic, disagreeable, and lacking in conscientiousness are more likely to get divorced; these three personality effects were each stronger than the association between socioeconomic status and risk for divorce (Roberts et al., 2007).

Meta-analytic findings suggest that conscientiousness is the best personality predictor of both job and school performance (Barrick, Mount, & Judge, 2001; Noftle & Robins, 2007). Importantly, conscientiousness predicts performance in these domains above and beyond the effects of traditional measures of cognitive ability such as IQ tests and SAT scores. Finally, personality influences a person's overall level of happiness and life satisfaction (Heller et al., 2004). Not surprisingly, individuals who are generally free of neuroticism reported having the most satisfying lives. In addition, extraverted, agreeable, and conscientious individuals are generally happier than those who are low on these traits.

Personality is an active area of psychology that intersects with many disciplines. However, personality is also a contentious field, and there are vigorous debates and disagreements, in part because of the complexity of the topic—no other field attempts to explain the whole person. Despite the abundance of unanswered questions and seemingly endless paths for future work, researchers have learned a considerable amount about the structure, development, and consequences of personality over the past 100 years. Using a diverse array of methods, including survey research, computer simulations, brain imaging, and population and molecular genetics, researchers have shown that personality tendencies are highly heritable, replicable across a wide range of cultures, generally stable across the life span, and linked (albeit weakly) to specific genes, hormones, neurotransmitters, and brain activation patterns. This is an exciting and opportune time for personality psychology. The field is well poised to play a significant role in the future of psychology, as it moves toward multilevel, interdisciplinary approaches and an increasing emphasis on individual differences.

REFERENCES

Barrick, M. R., Mount, M. K., & Judge, T. A. (2001). Personality and performance at the beginning of the new millennium: What do we know and where do we go next? *International Journal of Selection and Assessment, 9*, 9–30.

Bogg, T., & Roberts, B. W. (2004). Conscientiousness and health-related behaviors: A meta-analysis of the leading behavioral contributors to mortality. *Psychological Bulletin, 130,* 887–919.

Bouchard, T. J., Jr. (2004). Genetic influences on human psychological traits. *Current Directions in Psychological Science, 13,* 148–151.

Canli, T. (2008). Toward a neurogenetic theory of neuroticism. In D. W. Pfaff & B. L. Kieffer (Eds.), *Molecular and biophysical mechanisms of arousal, alertness, and attention. Annals of the New York Academy of Sciences* (pp. 153–174). Malden, MA: Blackwell Publishing.

Caspi, A., Roberts, B. W., & Shiner, R. L. (2005). Personality development: Stability and change. *Annual Review of Psychology, 56,* 453–484.

Heller, D., Watson, D., & Ilies, R. (2004). The role of the person versus the situation in life satisfaction: A critical examination. *Psychological Bulletin, 130,* 574–600.

John, O. P., Naumann, L. P., & Soto, C. J. (2008). Paradigm shift to the integrative Big Five trait taxonomy: History, measurement, and conceptual issues. In O. P. John, R. W. Robins, and L. A. Pervin (Eds.), *Handbook of personality: Theory and research* (3rd ed., pp. 114–158). New York: Guilford Press.

John, O. P., Robins, R. W., & Pervin, L. A. (Eds.). (2008). *Handbook of personality: Theory and research* (3rd ed.). New York: Guilford Press.

Krueger, R. F., Caspi, A., & Moffitt, T. E. (2000). Epidemiological personology: The unifying role of personality in population-based research on problem behaviors. *Journal of Personality, 68,* 967–998.

Krueger, R. F., South, S., Johnson, W., & Iacono, W. (2008). The heritability of personality is not always 50%: Gene-environment interactions and correlation between personality and parenting. *Journal of Personality, 76,* 1485–1522.

Miller, J. D., & Lynam, D. (2001). Structural models of personality and their relation to antisocial behavior: A meta-analytic review. *Criminology, 39,* 765–798.

Noftle, E. E., & Robins, R. W. (2007). Personality predictors of academic outcomes: Big Five correlates of GPA and SAT scores. *Journal of Personality and Social Psychology, 93,* 116–130.

Ozer, D. J., & Benet-Martínez, V. (2006). Personality and the prediction of consequential outcomes. *Annual Review of Psychology, 57,* 401–421.

Roberts, B. W., & DelVecchio, W. F. (2000). The rank-order consistency of personality from childhood to old age: A quantitative review of longitudinal studies. *Psychological Bulletin, 126,* 3–25.

Roberts, B. W., Kuncel, N. R., Shiner, R., Caspi, A., & Goldberg, L. R. (2007). The power of personality: The comparative validity of personality traits, socio-economic status, and cognitive ability for predicting important life outcomes. *Perspectives on Psychological Science, 2,* 313–345.

Roberts, B. W., Walton, K. E., & Viechtbauer, W. (2006). Patterns of mean-level change in personality traits across the life course: A meta-analysis of longitudinal studies. *Psychological Bulletin, 132,* 1–25.

Roberts, B. W., Wood, D., & Caspi, A. (2008). The development of personality traits in adulthood. In O. P. John, R. W. Robins, & L. A. Pervin (Eds.), *Handbook of personality: Theory and research* (3rd ed., pp. 375–398). New York: Guilford Press.

Robins, R. W., Fraley, R. C., & Krueger, R. F. (Eds.). (2007). *Handbook of research methods in personality psychology.* New York: Guilford Press.

SUGGESTED READINGS

Funder, D. C. (2001). Personality. *Annual Review of Psychology, 52,* 197–221.

Funder, D. C. (2007). *The personality puzzle* (4th ed.). New York: W. W. Norton.

McAdams, D. P. (1995). What do we know when we know a person? *Journal of Personality, 63,* 365–396.

RICHARD W. ROBINS
University of California, Davis

M. BRENT DONNELLAN
Michigan State University

See also: **Personality Assessment; Personality Development; Personality Disorders**

PERSONALITY TESTING (See Personality Assessment)

PERSONALITY, TRAIT THEORIES OF

Personality traits are familiar to laypersons as enduring characteristics of individuals that distinguish them from others. Jane may be exuberant, energetic, and overbearing, whereas Jack is sober, steady, and reserved. Such distinctions are routinely made in everyday life and in literature, and they are facilitated by an enormous vocabulary of trait terms in English and other languages. Trait psychology consists of the scientific study of these characteristics, and trait theories of personality attempt to explain the development and functioning of the person primarily in terms of traits. Personality research is currently dominated by trait approaches, and much has been learned about traits in the past 30 years.

Eye color, verbal intelligence, and musical aptitude are all traits, but they are not usually regarded as personality traits, which deal with the emotional, interpersonal, experiential, attitudinal, and motivational features of the person. McCrae and Costa (2003) defined traits as "dimensions of individual differences in tendencies to show consistent patterns of thoughts, feelings, and actions" (p. 25). People are not automatons that rigidly repeat the same behaviors in every situation and on every occasion, but careful observation of their actions and reactions shows certain patterns that recur and give a sense of coherence. Because these patterns endure for many decades, they have subtle but ultimately very powerful effects on the individual's life.

The Description of Traits

Abundant research has established a number of features of traits. Traits are normally distributed, with a few people scoring very high, a few very low, and most somewhere in the middle. Although it is convenient to talk about introverts and extraverts when we mean those who are below or above average in Extraversion, personality traits are not distinct types but, like most dichotomies, matters of degree.

There is now general agreement that most personality traits can be grouped into five clusters of related traits that define the dimensions of the Five-Factor Model (Digman, 1990). For example, people who are trusting are generally also generous and modest and forgiving; these traits define a factor usually called Agreeableness. Agreeable people may be either high or low on Conscientiousness, which is a factor defined by such traits as self-discipline, caution, and purposefulness. The remaining factors are Extraversion (friendly, active, cheerful), Openness to Experience (imaginative, curious, liberal), and Neuroticism (nervous, glum, irritable). The term *Neuroticism* dates from the middle of the last century, when this constellation of traits was first recognized in patients who were then diagnosed as neurotics (a diagnosis no longer used in psychiatry), but it is a general dimension of personality: everyone has some degree of Neuroticism. A more appealing alternative label that designates the opposite pole is Emotional Stability.

Traits are most commonly measured by questionnaires (e.g., Costa & McCrae, 1992), in which respondents describe themselves or someone they know by responding to a series of questions or statements. For example, someone who strongly agrees with the statement "I really enjoy chatting with people" will be given points for Extraversion. Good measures of personality traits are reliable (reproducible over time and occasions) and valid (related to the kinds of outcomes they should predict). One particularly important test of the validity of trait measures is how well self-reports agree with observer ratings. Most studies show substantial cross-observer agreement for all five factors, provided the observer knows the target well.

Longitudinal research has shown that traits show predictable developmental curves: from adolescence through old age, both men and women tend to become less neurotic, less extraverted, and less open but more agreeable and more conscientious—a pattern usually interpreted as increasing psychological maturity (Roberts, Walton, & Viechtbauer, 2006). The changes are most rapid in the decade of the 20s; after age 30, change is very gradual. At all ages, however, there are individual differences, which tend to be preserved over long periods of time. An outgoing 30-year-old is likely to become an outgoing 80-year-old, and young liberals become old liberals (think of Ted Kennedy).

Traits in Personality Theory

Personality theories are supposed to provide a general account of human nature and an explanation of how individuals develop psychologically and why they function well or poorly. One of the main tasks of personality theory is to explain human development; from a trait perspective, this means explaining how individuals come to show the particular combination of traits they have. Until recently, it was widely assumed that personality was shaped by the environment, especially by child-rearing practices and parent–child relations. Psychoanalytic, behaviorist, and even humanistic psychologies argued that experience shaped personality, and the main disputes concerned which particular features of the environment were crucial. But studies of twins, including identical twins raised in different families, clearly showed that at least half of the variance in adult trait levels is genetically based (Riemann, Angleitner, & Strelau, 1997), and no one can yet account for the other half. Certainly, the lasting influence of parents was greatly exaggerated by classic theories of personality; some contemporary theorists have argued that peer socialization is more important.

Equally surprising were the results of cross-cultural studies. Anthropologists had depicted non-Western cultures as being fundamentally different from those of the West, and they had led most psychologists to assume that traits, if they were found at all, would be very different in the rest of the world. But studies of traits in such diverse societies as Iceland, Malaysia, Korea, Kuwait, and Burkina Faso have consistently found universal patterns (McCrae et al., 2005). In all societies studied, the Five-Factor Model has proven applicable. Age differences are similar in cultures that revere the elderly and those that revile them; gender differences are similar in modern, liberated cultures and in traditional, patriarchal cultures (although, surprisingly, they are more marked in the former; Costa, Terracciano, & McCrae, 2001).

Together, the heritability and universality of personality point to the conclusion that personality traits are biologically based. Many researchers are now looking for genes that influence traits, and some comparative psychologists are assessing personality traits in nonhuman animals. Neuroimaging studies are being used to locate areas of the brain involved in personality processes.

In classical personality theories, traits were considered a relatively minor and peripheral aspect of the individual (compared, for example, with defenses or self-actualization or role-playing). Today, traits have been shown to influence a host of psychological processes, and new personality theories have given traits a central place. In Five-Factor Theory (McCrae & Costa, 2008), traits are depicted as biologically based *basic tendencies* that interact with *external influences* to create *characteristic adaptations* (habits, skills, roles, and so forth). Thus, a person who is by temperament high in Openness to Experience (a basic tendency) and who has the opportunity to study at a university (an external influence) may end up an anthropologist, whose characteristic adaptations include knowledge of kinship patterns, tolerant attitudes toward foreign cultures, and a taste for travel.

In Five-Factor Theory, behavior is seen in this way as the result of the interaction of characteristic adaptations with the demands and opportunities of the moment. Anthropologists will ask questions to try to understand how a new culture functions, but only at times and in places that they have learned are appropriate for questions. Thus, traits have an indirect effect on behavior, and this is why the same traits can be found around the world: In every culture, people learn how to express their traits in a socially appropriate fashion. Conversely, every culture must have developed customs and institutions that allow the expression of Five-Factor Model personality traits. Thus, Five-Factor Theory is, in a sense, also a necessary part of any theory of culture.

Historically, personality theories have often been developed to explain psychopathology. Five-Factor Theory holds that people sometimes develop characteristic maladaptations. These, too, are shaped by both traits and the environment, and if they cause severe distress and impairment of social functioning, they can be considered personality disorders. Five-Factor Theory suggests that psychiatric diagnoses of personality disorders ought to be informed by our knowledge of the Five-Factor Model (Widiger & Trull, 2007), and that these disorders ought to be treated by seeking to develop new adaptations that express the same traits in more benign forms.

Even a perfect understanding of the nature, origin, and operation of traits would not provide a complete theory of personality. It would not explain the individual's sense of identity, the way in which decisions are made on a moment-by-moment basis, or the motivations (like the need for oxygen) that are common to every human being. But traits are so important in the lives of individuals that no complete theory of personality can neglect them or relegate them to the sidelines. Traits are central aspects of human nature, and the body of knowledge so far accumulated about them can form the core of future theories of personality.

REFERENCES

Costa, P. T., Jr., & McCrae, R. R. (1992). *Revised NEO Personality Inventory (NEO-PI-R) and NEO Five-Factor Inventory (NEO-FFI) professional manual*. Odessa, FL: Psychological Assessment Resources.

Costa, P. T., Jr., Terracciano, A., & McCrae, R. R. (2001). Gender differences in personality traits across cultures: Robust and surprising findings. *Journal of Personality and Social Psychology, 81*, 322–331.

Digman, J. M. (1990). Personality structure: Emergence of the Five-Factor Model. *Annual Review of Psychology, 41*, 417–440.

McCrae, R. R., & Costa, P. T., Jr. (2003). *Personality in adulthood: A Five-Factor Theory Perspective* (2nd ed.). New York: Guilford Press.

McCrae, R. R., & Costa, P. T., Jr. (2008). The Five-Factor Theory of personality. In O. P. John, R. W. Robins, & L. A. Pervin (Eds.), *Handbook of personality: Theory and research* (3rd ed., pp. 157–180). New York: Guilford Press.

McCrae, R. R., Terracciano, A., & 78 Members of the Personality Profiles of Cultures Project. (2005). Universal features of personality traits from the observer's perspective: Data from 50 cultures. *Journal of Personality and Social Psychology, 88*, 547–561.

Riemann, R., Angleitner, A., & Strelau, J. (1997). Genetic and environmental influences on personality: A study of twins reared together using the self- and peer report NEO-FFI scales. *Journal of Personality, 65*, 449–475.

Roberts, B. W., Walton, K. E., & Viechtbauer, W. (2006). Patterns of mean-level change in personality traits across the life course: A meta-analysis of longitudinal studies. *Psychological Bulletin, 132*, 3–25.

Widiger, T. A., & Trull, T. J. (2007). Plate tectonics in the classification of personality disorder: Shifting to a dimensional model. *American Psychologist, 62*, 71–83.

SUGGESTED READINGS

Funder, D. C. (1991). Global traits: A Neo-Allportian approach to personality. *Psychological Science, 2*, 31–39.

Ozer, D. J., & Benet-Martínez, V. (2006). Personality and the prediction of consequential outcomes. *Annual Review of Psychology, 57*, 401–421.

ROBERT R. MCCRAE
National Institute on Aging

See also: **Five-Factor Model of Personality; NEO Personality Inventory (NEO-PI-R); Trait Psychology**

PERSONNEL SELECTION

Personnel selection represents an attempt to identify knowledge, skills, abilities, and other characteristics

(KASO) that predict who from among a group of job applicants will perform some job well. Because the objective of personnel selection is to make accurate inferences about some job behavior or outcome, these efforts begin with knowledge and/or theories about job performance.

Job Performance

Most conceptualizations of job performance recognize that there are two major dimensions: task performance and contextual performance (Borman & Motowidlo, 1997). More detailed delineations of performance have been presented and supported by Campbell (1999), but Campbell's dimensions can be aggregated to the simpler task-contextual dimensions. Task performance is generally defined as those aspects of one's job that contribute to the technical core of an organization and that are usually included in an organization's formal description. Contextual performance relates to those tasks that support the technical core but probably are not included in one's job description. They include things such as persisting with enthusiasm and effort, carrying out volunteer activities, and facilitating interpersonal relationships. Recently, Pulakos, Arad, Donovan, and Plamondon (2000) added the notion that adaptive performance (tasks that represent versatility and tolerance for ambiguity in the face of unusual job demands) is another aspect of performance that is required of job incumbents in an increasing number of today's jobs.

Knowledge, Skills, Abilities, and Other Characteristics

The type and level of task, contextual, and adaptive performance must be the basis of decisions about what KASOs are the target of personnel selection efforts designed to fill openings for a particular job. Required performance and the relevant KASOs are determined with the aid of a job analysis, as well as the researcher's knowledge of the literature on job performance and individual differences. At a very basic level, KASOs are categorized into those that specify what an individual can do and what he or she will do. The "can do" elements usually include measures of job knowledge, cognitive ability, and/or physical skills. The "will do" factors usually include measures of personality, interests, or motivation.

These two types of factors can be measured with interviews, paper-and-pencil tests, simulations of job performance, web-based methods, and other procedures. In the remainder of this short description of personnel selection, I describe the nature of some of the KASOs, the ways in which they might be measured, and their relative effectiveness in generating accurate inferences about an applicant's (or person being considered for promotion) future job performance. At the end of this description, I describe the ways in which psychologists validate (i.e., verify) the accuracy of their methods of selection. This application of psychology has been described in detail in several textbooks (e.g., Ployhart, Schneider, & Schmitt, 2006).

Relevant KASOs

The relevance and nature of cognitive ability (usually measured with a paper-and-pencil test or a computerized version of the questions) are best established in the research literature. Cognitive ability tests often have a variety of content, including verbal, numerical, and spatial items, as well as items measuring various aspects of reasoning. Attempts to discern multiple aptitudes have usually concluded that a large general factor typically accounts for the majority of the variance in participant responses. Further, this general factor underlying tests of cognitive ability is especially effective in predicting task performance. Assessments of the validity of these measures indicate that they are valid predictors of task performance across virtually all jobs, but their effectiveness increases with the complexity of the job.

Measures of physical ability are predictive of task performance when the job requires some level of physical ability, as would be true for many construction and maintenance jobs and for police and fire positions, for example. Unlike cognitive ability, however, there appear to be clearly differentiated dimensions of physical ability that are valid predictors if similar abilities (lifting versus running, e.g.) are required for successful job performance (Hogan, 1991). A related, but infrequently studied, domain is that of psychomotor ability, which implies the use of a combination of cognitive, sensory, and muscular activity, as might be the case in the operation of a car or heavy equipment.

Experience in a job is often used to predict performance and can be an indicator of either can do or will do factors. Much of the research on job experience has simply used years in a job, position, or organization as the measure of experience. A more potentially useful and informative way to index experience is to measure an applicant's experience in particular job-relevant tasks or aspects of contextual performance. If that is the case, experience can serve as a proxy for a variety of KASOs.

The will do determinants of performance are predictive of contextual performance and task performance. Will do measures are motivational, and performance in most areas of human endeavor is a combination of motivation and ability. Interest in personality as one determinant of work performance has been spurred by personality theorists' contention that the myriad of available personality measures can be considered measures of one of five major constructs: Agreeableness, Conscientiousness, Emotional Stability, Openness, and Extraversion. In addition, the use of meta-analyses of past research has indicated that at least Conscientiousness measures appear to be usefully valid in predicting performance across a broad range of jobs.

Personality measures also are not highly correlated with measures of cognitive ability and other indices of can do factors; hence, when they are used in combination with those predictors, they often add useful increments to predictive validity. Relationships of personality measures with job performance often tend to be low, and some industrial and organizational psychologists argue that more specific personality constructs (e.g., social skills and achievement motivation) or measures that are more oriented to a specific occupation or job (e.g., customer service orientation) might prove more predictive.

Integrity tests, designed to assess a person's honesty or ethics, also appear to be predictive of various types of counterproductive behavior, including theft or sabotage, as well as a failure to engage in aspects of what I have termed contextual performance. Certainly, one of the most significant hurdles in the use of will do measures is the fact that applicants find it relatively easy to fake these instruments, though the conditions under which they do so and the impact this has on their value in a personnel selection context are still being hotly debated and frequently researched by personnel selection experts.

Researchers are also beginning to evaluate the fit (job, work group, organization) between job applicants and the work situation as a predictor of future organizational success (Kristof-Brown, Zimmerman, & Johnson, 2005).

Methods of Measuring KASOs

The KASOs mentioned earlier can be measured in a variety of ways; perhaps the most frequent approaches have been to use paper-and-pencil measures and interviews. Paper-and-pencil methods (and now computer- or web-based versions of these tests) are very efficient methods of collecting information and can be used to measure a variety of will do and can do constructs. Obviously, such measures require reading comprehension; when the construct measured and the job performance being predicted do not require reading ability, the reading level must be such that it does not bias measurement of the target construct.

Interviews are almost routinely used as part of the selection process in many jobs. Depending on the questions pursued and the skill and training of the interviewer, the interview can be used to assess a variety of factors. Interviews have proven to be valid predictors of subsequent job performance when the interview is structured (that is, questions based on KASOs derived from a job analysis of the target constructs are asked), when the same questions are asked of all interviewees to allow for comparisons of responses, when well-defined rating scales are used by the interviewers to rate responses, and when planned probes are used to pursue ambiguous or incomplete responses.

Biographical data are objectively scored indices of applicants' background and interests. These items can be developed and scored to assess an array of KASOs and are often quite predictive of both task and contextual performance.

Especially for management-level jobs, ratings of performance in simulations of job activities (often called assessment centers) have been popular but expensive ways to collect information. These assessment centers involve observation of performance on a variety of job-relevant factors using several methods (e.g., paper-and-pencil tests, interviews, observations of performance in groups, and performance in handling a sample of administrative tasks) by several trained observers. Assessment centers have proven to be valid across a wide variety of managerial jobs. Also, a frequently used method of assessment of candidates for managerial and high-level executive positions is the individual assessment. This is an in-depth evaluation of candidates, usually by a psychologist who uses multiple methods of collecting data and who provides a written evaluation detailing candidates' strengths and weaknesses. We have relatively little good data on the validity of individual assessments.

The focus in this article has been on making inferences about applicants' future task and contextual performance. Organizations are often also interested in employee withdrawal (regular attendance, turnover), counterproductive work behaviors (sabotage, theft, violence, discrimination, harassment of coworkers), and health and safety outcomes. In these instances, the required KASOs may be somewhat different, but a similar approach using a careful consideration of the outcomes of interest and what this implies for the constructs measured during selection should be followed.

Validating KASOs as Selection Tools

Researchers usually want evidence that the tools they use to make selection decisions actually provide accurate inferences about job behavior. Current and past research findings (Schmidt & Hunter, 1998) provide useful information, and textbooks (Ployhart et al., 2006) and professional guidelines (Society for Industrial and Organizational Psychology, 2003) provide information on the ways in which evidence can be gathered to support the use of selection instruments. In addition to the accuracy of their inferences about performance, researchers must also be cognizant of the impact that their measures have on the selection of minorities and other protected groups; a summary of the difficulties involved in maximizing expected performance and the representation of protected groups is contained in Sackett, Schmitt, Ellingson, and Kabin (2001).

Personnel selection is one of the oldest and most valuable applications of psychology. When selection procedures are based on a carefully developed performance model and are selected or developed to assess KASOs that are relevant to performance, and when those KASOs are measured objectively and reliably, organizations can expect a higher performing workforce, and workers should be placed in situations that maximize their productivity and, hopefully, their satisfaction as well.

REFERENCES

Borman, W. C., & Motowidlo, S. P. (1997). Task performance and contextual performance: The meaning for personnel selection research. *Human Performance, 10*, 99–110.

Campbell, J. P. (1999). The definition and measurement of performance in the new age. In D. R. Ilgen & E. D. Pulakos (Eds.), *The changing nature of performance* (pp. 399–429). San Francisco, CA: Jossey-Bass.

Hogan, J. C. (1991). Physical abilities. In M. D. Dunnette & L. M. Hough (Eds.), *Handbook of industrial and organizational psychology* (vol. 2, pp. 753–831). Palo Alto, CA: Consulting Psychologists Press.

Kristof-Brown, A. L., Zimmerman, R. D., & Johnson, E. C. (2005). Consequences of individuals' fit at work: A meta-analysis of person-job, person-organization, person-group, and person-supervisor fit. *Personnel Psychology, 58*, 281–342.

Ployhart, R. E., Schneider, B., & Schmitt, N. (2006). *Staffing organizations: Contemporary practice and theory.* Mahwah, NJ: Lawrence Erlbaum.

Pulakos, E. D., Arad, S., Donovan, M. A., & Plamondon, K. E. (2000). Adaptability in the workplace: Development of taxonomy of adaptive performance. *Journal of Applied Psychology, 85*, 612–624.

Sackett, P. R., Schmitt, N., Ellingson, J. E., & Kabin, M. B. (2001). High-stakes testing in employment, credentialing, and higher education. *American Psychologist, 56*, 302–318.

Schmidt, F. L., & Hunter, J. E. (1998). The validity and utility of selection methods in personnel psychology: Practical and theoretical implications of 85 years of research findings. *Psychological Bulletin, 124*, 262–274.

Society for Industrial and Organizational Psychology. (2003). *Principles for the validation and use of personnel selection procedures.* Bowling Green, OH: Author.

SUGGESTED READINGS

Guion, R. M., & Highhouse, C. (2006). Essentials of personnel assessment and selection. In R. E. Ployhart, B. Schneider, & N. Schmitt (Eds.), *Staffing organizations: Contemporary practice and theory.* Mahwah, NJ: Lawrence Erlbaum.

Schmitt, N., & Borman, W. C. (Eds.). (1993). *Personnel selection in organizations.* San Francisco, CA: Jossey-Bass.

NEAL SCHMITT
Michigan State University

PERSONOLOGY

The word *personality* is derived from the Latin term *persona,* originally representing the theatrical mask used by ancient dramatic players. As a mask assumed by an actor,

persona suggests a pretense of appearance, that is, the possession of traits other than those that actually characterize the individual behind the mask. In time, the term *persona* lost its connotation of pretense and illusion and began to represent not the mask, but the real person's observable or explicit features. The third meaning that personality acquired delves beneath the surface impression to turn the spotlight on the inner, less often revealed, and hidden psychological qualities of the individual. Thus, through history, the meaning of the term has shifted from external illusion to surface reality to opaque or veiled inner traits. The fourth conception of personality, which is labeled *personology,* comes closest to contemporary use. Today, personality is seen as a complex pattern of deeply embedded psychological characteristics that are expressed automatically in almost every area of psychological functioning; that is, personality is viewed as the patterning of unique characteristics that penetrate the entire matrix of the person.

Henry A. Murray, founder of the personology school of thought, was unusually influential on a large group of brilliant students who worked with him beginning in the early 1930s, when together they published their pioneering text, *Explorations in Personality* (1938). Extraordinarily wide-ranging, influenced early by Jung, but subsequently a founding member of the Freudian-oriented Boston Psychoanalytic Society, Murray was initially trained as a history major at Harvard, as a medical student at Columbia's Physicians and Surgeons, and as neurosurgeon. He later obtained a PhD in biochemistry at Cambridge and had a brief research career in developmental neurobiology at Rockefeller University before turning to psychology, following an invitation at the age of 33 to join Morton Prince at the new Harvard Psychological Clinic in 1926.

Murray was the first to coin the term *personology,* describing it as follows:

> The prevailing custom in psychology is to study one function or one aspect of an episode at a time—perception, emotion, intellection or behaviour—and this is as it must be. The circumscription of attention is dictated by the need for detailed information. But the psychologist who does this should recognize that he is observing merely a part of an operating totality, and this totality, in turn, is but a small temporal segment of a personality. Psychology must construct a scheme of concepts for portraying the entire course of individual development, and thus provide a framework into which any single episode—natural or experimental—may be fitted.
>
> The branch of psychology which principally concerns itself with the study of human lives and the factors that influence their course, which investigates individual differences and types of personality, may be termed "personology" instead of the "psychology of personality," a clumsy and tautological expression. (1938, p. 3)

As a thoroughgoing clinician, Murray believed that a full understanding of behavior called for a complete and detailed study of each individual. Clearly influenced by his friend and colleague Gordon Allport, Murray asserted that efforts must be made to articulate the unique or idiographic features of a person, normal or not.

In what he preferred to call *personalism*, a label borrowed from his friend and early mentor William Stern, Allport (1937) stressed, in a book published a year prior to Murray's *Explorations*, the uniqueness of the individual, stating:

> The outstanding characteristic of a man is his individuality. He is a unique creation of the forces of nature. Separated spatially from all other men, he behaves throughout his own particular span of life, in his own distinctive fashion. (p. 3)
>
> The chief tenet of "personalistic psychology" is that every mental function is embedded in personal life. In no concrete sense is there such a thing as intelligence, space perception, color discrimination, or choice reaction: ... nor can motives ever be studied apart from their personal setting; they represent always the striving of a total organism. (p. 18)

Gardner Murphy, in a 1947 text, contributed another dimension to the triumvirate that brought the concepts of personology to the foreground in the mid-twentieth century. Like Allport and Murray, Murphy was a brilliant and erudite person capable of encompassing all facets of human endeavor, knowledgeable in grand detail of the early Greek philosophers, and thoroughly sophisticated with regard to modern science. A more dazzling and charming threesome would be difficult to find in any review of the history of psychology.

Although few of their numerous doctoral students and collaborators sought to pursue the vast range of topics that this triumvirate studied, many brilliant later associates picked up one or another facet of their work in constructing their own careers. Especially notable in this regard were such mid-century colleagues as Christiana Morgan, L. J. Henderson, Kurt Lewin, Clyde Kluckhohn, Talcott Parsons, David McClelland, James Grier Miller, Saul Rosenzweig, Nevitt Sanford, Donald MacKinnon, Silvan Tomkins, and Robert White. A few paragraphs paraphrasing some of Murray's mid-century propositions for a personologic science may be useful before elaborating a number of contemporary or early twenty-first-century developments.

The person is from the beginning a whole; the whole and its parts are mutually related; the whole being is as essential to an understanding of the parts as the parts are to an understanding of the whole. Theoretically, it should be possible to formulate for any moment the "wholeness" of a person or, in other words, to state in what respect he or she is acting as a unit.

Persons consist of an infinitely complex series of temporarily related activities extending from birth to death. Because of the meaningful connection of sequences, the life cycle of a single individual should be taken as a unit. It is feasible to study the organism during one episode of its existence, but it should be recognized that this is but an arbitrarily selected part of the whole. The history of the person is the person.

What a person knows or believes is, in some measure, a product of formerly encountered situations. Thus, much of what is now inside the person was once outside. For these reasons, the person and its milieu must be considered together, a single creature–environment interaction being a convenient unit for psychology.

Divided it perishes, united it survives. The existence of persons depends on the fact that the vast majority of their actions are adaptive in a Darwinian sense: They serve to restore an equilibrium that has been disturbed, or to avoid an injury, or to attain objects that are of benefit to development. Thus, much of overt behavior is, like the activity of the internal organs, survivalistically purposeful.

Some of the past is always alive in the present. For this reason, the study of infancy is particularly important. The experiences of early life not only constitute in themselves a significant temporal segment of the person's history but also exercise a marked effect on the course of development. To some degree they "explain" succeeding events. ("The child is father to the man.")

Leading developments of personology near the turn of the twenty-first century is the psychologist Theodore Millon (1990; Millon & Davis, 1996). He elaborated the personologic themes of Allport, Murray, and Murphy and asserted that there are common principles that underlie and bind all scientific realms of study. These principles are anchored to the processes and progressions of evolution. Elements of evolutionary theory operate in all aspects of scientific endeavor. Pathological forms of personality functioning are seen as disruptions or imbalances in those evolutionary principles that foster the functions of survival and ecologic adaptation (Millon, 1990).

Personality maladaptations cannot be fully understood by limiting attention to solely one or another facet of functioning, such as cognitive preconceptions, unconscious repetition compulsions, or neurochemical dysfunctions. Rather, each of them represents partial expressions of evolutionary functions that have gone awry. Cognitions, unconscious structures, interpersonal styles, and neuro-hormonal dynamics are viewed, in Millon's formulation, as different forms in which fundamental evolutionary processes are expressed. Evolution is therefore important, in that it can help to identify the clinical domains in which pathology manifests itself. An ontogenetic theory of neuropsychological development stages is presented in Millon's 1969 book; it parallels his theoretical formulations of evolutionary phylogenesis and thereby adds specific substantive hypotheses to the more abstract concepts proposed earlier by Murray.

Millon asserted that psychologists in the twenty-first century should aspire to reintegrate their clinical science. Just as each person is an intrinsic unity, each component of a clinical science should not remain a separate element of a potpourri of unconnected parts. Each component should be integrated into an overall gestalt, a coupled and synergistic unity in which the whole of the science becomes more cohesive, informative, and useful than its individual parts. As Millon wrote:

What better sphere is there within the psychological sciences to undertake such syntheses than with the subject matter of personology. Persons are the only organically integrated system in the psychological domain, evolved through the millennia and inherently created from birth as natural entities, rather than culture-bound and experience-derived gestalts. The intrinsic cohesion of persons is not merely a rhetorical construction, but an authentic substantive unity. Personologic features may often be dissonant, and may be partitioned conceptually for pragmatic or scientific purposes, but they are segments of an inseparable biopsychosocial entity, as well as a natural outgrowth of evolution's progression. (1990, p. 11)

He went on to argue that the separate elements that comprise the science of personology should embody five explicit components:

(1) Universal scientific principles that are grounded in the ubiquitous laws of evolution; despite their varied forms of expression, its principles will provide an undergirding framework for guiding subject-oriented theories. (2) Subject-oriented theories, or explanatory and heuristic conceptual schemas that enable reasonably accurate propositions concerning clinical conditions to be both deduced and understood, encouraging thereby the development of a formal classification system. (3) Classification of personality styles and pathological syndromes, or a taxonomic schema that is derived logically from the theory. It should provide a cohesive organization within which dimensions and categories can be grouped and differentiated, permitting thereby the development of coordinated assessment instruments. (4) Personologic assessments, that is, instruments that are empirically grounded and sufficiently sensitive quantitatively to enable the theory's propositions and hypotheses to be adequately investigated and evaluated, enabling clinicians to specify target areas for interventions. (5) Personalized therapeutic interventions, or coordinated strategies and focused modalities of treatment. Expanding the scope of personology to encompass this final therapeutic component stems from pragmatic questions such as:
Would it not be a great step forward in our field if diagnosis or psychological assessment, following a series of interviews, self-report questionnaires, and projective performance measures, actually pointed clearly to what a clinician should do in therapy? Is it not time for clinicians to expect that diagnosis can lead directly to the course of therapy?

Millon has termed this final component of personology *personalized psychotherapy*. This should not be seen as a vague concept or a platitudinous buzzword, but as an explicit commitment to focus first and foremost on the unique composite of a patient's psychological makeup, followed by a precise formulation and specification of therapeutic rationales and techniques suitable to remedying those personal attributes that are assessed as problematic. Personologic therapists take cognizance of the person from the start, for the psychic parts and environmental contexts take on different meanings and call for different interventions in terms of the specific person to whom they are anchored. To focus on one social environment or one psychological realm of expression, without understanding its undergirding or reference base, is to engage in potentially misguided, if not random, therapeutic techniques.

Fledgling personologic therapists will recognize that the symptoms and disorders that are "diagnosed" represent but one or another segment of a complex of organically interwoven psychological elements. The significance of each clinical feature is best be grasped by reviewing a patient's unique psychological experiences and his or her overall psychic pattern of configurational dynamics, of which any one sphere of expression is but a single part.

REFERENCES

Allport, G. (1937). *Personality: A psychological interpretation*. New York: Holt.

Millon, T. (1969). *Modern psychopathology: A biosocial approach to maladaptive learning and functioning*. Philadelphia: Saunders.

Millon, T. (1990). *Toward a new personology: An evolutionary model*. New York: John Wiley & Sons.

Millon, T., & Davis, R. D. (1996). *Disorders of personality: DSM-IV and beyond*. New York: John Wiley & Sons.

Murphy, G. (1947). *Personality: A biosocial approach to origins and structures*. New York: Harper.

Murray, H. A. (1938). *Explorations in personality*. New York: Oxford University Press.

SUGGESTED READING

Millon, T., & Grossman, S. (2007). Resolving difficult clinical syndromes: A personalized psychotherapy approach. New York: John Wiley & Sons.

THEODORE MILLON
Institute for Advanced Studies in Personology and Psychopathology, Port Jervis, NY

See also: Evolutionary Psychology; Personality Psychology

PERVASIVE DEVELOPMENTAL DISORDERS (See Asperger Syndrome; Autistic Disorder)

PHALLIC STAGE (See Psychosexual Stages)

PHANTOM LIMB PAIN

Phantom limb sensation refers to the perception of a variety of physical feelings in a part of the body that has been removed. Although this is generally associated with limb amputation, phantom sensations have also been reported in women following mastectomy and in certain spinal cord injuries. Phantom limb sensations can include an "awareness" of the missing limb in its usual position or a sense that the affected limb is an unusual size (either too large or too small), is moving, is in an unusual position, is wrapped in cotton, or is wet. Phantom pain, or phantom limb pain, is a subtype of phantom limb sensation in which these perceptions are perceived as noxious. Although there are numerous historical examples of phantom limb pain, the term itself is generally credited to the U.S. Army physician Silas Weir Mitchell, who in 1872 described that "thousands of spirit limbs were haunting as many good soldiers, every now and then tormenting them."

Phantom limb pain may range from the sensation of mild electrical shocks to the excruciating feeling that one's limb is being cramped, twisted, burned, or crushed. Phantom limb pain should be also distinguished from stump pain, which results from postoperative swelling and inflammation or later irritation of the stump by a prosthesis. Phantom limb pain is a prevalent problem following amputation, with as many as 74% of patients reporting some phantom pain, and a notable subset (~30%) reporting an average pain level above 7 (i.e., severe) on a 0–10 scale. The sensation of phantom limb pain typically does not decrease naturally over time, and in many cases, it is thought to increase in intensity.

Although phantom limb pain was once believed to be a psychological reaction to violation of body integrity, modern work suggests that the experience of phantom limb pain results from a combination of neurological factors. Current theories recognize that phantom limb pain may result from changes in the nerve periphery, at the level of the spinal cord, and centrally (i.e., in the somatosensory cortex of the brain). Peripherally, it has been hypothesized that, as a consequence of injury, severed axons sprout regeneratively, forming neuromas (tangled masses that form when axons cannot reconnect) in the residual limb. These neuromas display abnormal evoked activity to mechanical stimuli. Ectopic discharges from these stump neuromas are a source of abnormal afferent input to the spinal cord and may therefore result in the sensation of pain in the absence of stimulus.

At the spinal level, the loss of normal afferent input from an amputated limb appears to result in enduring changes in the synaptic responsiveness of neurons in the dorsal horn, leading to hyperexcitability of pain neurons. The loss of normal signals to the spinal cord is also associated with lasting changes in neurotransmitter levels associated with pain control, including death of GABA interneurons and downregulation of opioid receptors. Finally, a number of changes appear to occur at the brain level, including changes in the structural architecture of the primary somatosensory cortex in which adjacent areas "invade" into the zone representing the missing limb. Phantom limb pain appears to be a complex neurological phenomenon involving changes in all areas, and experimentally, it cannot be explained by activity at a single site.

Although standard pharmacological treatment for phantom limb pain typically involves opioid analgesics, anticonvulsants, and certain antidepressants, efficacy rates are quite poor and in many cases are little higher than would be expected from a placebo. Various complementary and alternative medicine approaches have also been tested for phantom limb pain, including hypnosis, mirror box therapy, reflexology, and virtual reality. Generally speaking, treatments that involve attention focusing, distraction, or manipulation of a visual representation of the missing limb (either through mental imagery or a mirror image of an intact limb) appear to be as effective as pharmacological interventions, although the mechanisms of the effect remain to be demonstrated.

SUGGESTED READINGS

Flor, H., Nikolajsen, L., & Jensen, T. S. (2006). Phantom limb pain: A case of maladaptive CNS plasticity? *Nature Reviews, 7,* 873–881.

MacIver, K., Lloyd, D., Kelly, S., Roberts, N., & Nurmikko, T. (2008). Phantom limb pain, cortical reorganization and the therapeutic effect of mental imagery. *Brain, 131,* 2181–2191.

Mishra, S., Bhatnagar, S., Gupta, D., & Diwedi, A. (2008). Incidence and management of phantom limb pain according to World Health Organization analgesic ladder in amputees of malignant origin. *American Journal of Hospice and Palliative Medicine, 24,* 455–462.

IVAN MOLTON
University of Washington

See also: Pain Theories

PHARMACOTHERAPY (See Psychotropic Medication)

PHENOTHIAZINES (See Antipsychotic Medications)

PHENYLKETONURIA

Phenylketonuria (PKU) is a rare genetic disorder characterized by an inability to metabolize phenylalanine, a common amino acid. Although its incidence and prevalence may vary based on geographical area, PKU occurs in approximately one in 15,000 individuals. The most common variation of PKU (often termed "classic" PKU) is an autosomal recessive condition with a locus on chromosome 12q.

In typical non-PKU individuals, phenylalanine is metabolized into tyrosine, a precursor for dopamine and other neurotransmitters. This process involves a number of substances, most notably oxygen, phenylalanine hydroxylase, and tetrahydrobiopterin (BH_4). For individuals with classic PKU, the aforementioned genetic anomaly results in absence or mutation of the phenylalanine hydroxylase molecule, thus disrupting the metabolic cascade. Other rarer variations of PKU may affect additional components (e.g., BH_4) to this process. For a more extensive review of PKU and genetics, see Blau (2006).

PKU was first discovered by Asbjørn Følling in 1934, following his examination of two young siblings (Dag & Liv Egeland) who presented with severe neurological and cognitive impairment despite the absence of any apparent causes. Subsequent research by Følling and others documented the autosomal recessive nature of the condition and confirmed the link between PKU and disruption of phenylalanine metabolism. Work by researchers such as Robert Guthrie led to the later development of effective tests for identifying individuals with PKU, via the measurement of levels of phenylpyruvic acid and blood phenylanine in urine and blood samples, respectively. For a historical review of PKU, see Christ (2003).

Individuals with PKU are identified at birth and immediately placed on a phenylalanine-restricted diet. Failure to do so results in severe irreversible injury to the developing nervous system and leads to significant neurological and intellectual impairment. Within this context, past studies have documented significant abnormalities in neurophysiology, neuroanatomy, and cognitive functioning in untreated individuals with PKU (Paine, 1957). For example, untreated PKU is linked to decreased levels of dopamine and related neural substances in both the brain tissue (postmortem study) and cerebral spinal fluid (CSF). Neuroanatomical studies have reported an increased incidence of microcephaly (abnormal smallness of the head) and decreased brain volume in untreated PKU individuals as compared to non-PKU individuals.

Another major neuroanatomical sequel of untreated PKU is the disruption of neural connectivity and communication in the brain. Evidence of myelin abnormalities comes from postmortem human studies as well as animal models involving rats with induced hyperphenylalaninemia. In individuals with untreated PKU, posterior periventricular brain areas appear to be most significantly affected, with damage extending into more anterior regions with increased disease severity. On a more micro level, untreated PKU is associated with decreased dendritic branching of pyramidal neurons. Lastly, electrophysiological studies have documented abnormal EEGs, characterized by focal paroxysmal discharges, in individuals with untreated PKU.

With regard to cognitive development, untreated PKU is characterized by significant delays in developmental milestones (e.g., crawling, walking, talking) as well as severe intellectual impairment. Approximately 98% of these individuals fall within the mental retardation range of intellectual functioning. The incidence of secondary comorbid disorders (e.g., epilepsy, autism) is also elevated in individuals with untreated PKU.

The mechanism of injury in PKU appears to be a two-fold process: (1) disruption of phenylalanine metabolism leads to a deficiency in tyrosine and downstream neurotransmitters (e.g., dopamine) that are important for neurological development, and (2) excessive phenylalanine competes with tyrosine and other neural substances to cross the blood-barrier, thus resulting in additional decrement in the levels of tyrosine within the central nervous system (CNS). It has additionally been suggested that, in some uncommon cases, blood phenylalanine levels may reach such extremely high levels so as to be directly toxic to the system.

Whereas individuals with PKU who are identified early and maintained on a phenylalanine-restricted diet are spared the severe consequences of their untreated peers, they do experience more subtle injury and dysfunction. The persistent finding of impairment despite intervention is believed to be related to the fact that phenylalanine is very prevalent in food and is consequently very difficult (if not impossible) to completely eliminate it from one's diet.

Utilizing advanced neuroimaging techniques (e.g., high-resolution magnetic resonance imaging, diffusion tensor imaging), recent studies have documented subtle but consistent gray- and white-matter abnormalities in the brains of individuals with early-treated PKU. From a cognitive standpoint, early-treated PKU is associated with a slight decrease in overall intellectual functioning (mean IQ = 95–97), coupled with circumscribed impairment in a handful of cognitive domains. Most notably, individuals with early-treated PKU have particular difficulties with such higher-order cognitive skills (often termed "executive abilities") as working memory, inhibitory control, cognitive flexibility, planning, and strategy use.

Evidence from neuroimaging, patient, animal, and development studies confirm that the prefrontal cortex (PFC) of the brain plays an integral role in executive abilities. In addition, as noted earlier, tyrosine is a precursor to dopamine, an important neurotransmitter. Whereas dopamine is utilized throughout the brain, it appears that the developing PFC is particularly susceptible to decreases in this crucial neurotransmitter. Within this context, researchers have suggested that early-treated PKU may be best conceptualized as a disorder of prefrontal dysfunction (e.g., Diamond, Prevor, Callendar, & Druin, 1997; Welsh, Pennington, Ozonoff, Rouse, & McCabe, 1990).

Substantial advances in genetics, neuroscience, and psychology over the past 70 years have contributed to our understanding of PKU. Further research is necessary, however, to fully understand this complex genetic disorder. Possible future avenues include the utilization of neuroimaging techniques to further elucidate and characterize the nature of the brain dysfunction experienced by individuals with PKU, the exploration of possible links between PKU and other neurodevelopmental disorders (e.g., autism), and the ongoing search for potential alternate or supplementary treatments (e.g., pharmaceutical intervention).

REFERENCES

Blau, N. (Ed.). (2006). *PKU and BH4: Advances in phenylketonuria and tetrahydrobiopterin.* Heilbronn, Germany: SPS Publications.

Christ, S. E. (2003). Asbjørn Følling and the discovery of phenylketonuria. *Journal of the History of the Neurosciences, 12,* 44–54.

Diamond, A., Prevor, M., Callendar, G., & Druin, D. P. (1997). Prefrontal cortex cognitive deficits in children treated early and continuously for PKU. *Monographs of the Society for Research in Child Development, 62*(4), 1–208.

Paine, R. S. (1957). The variability in manifestations of untreated patients with phenylketonuria (phenylpyruvic aciduria). *Pediatrics, 20,* 290–331.

Welsh, M. C., Pennington, B. F., Ozonoff, S., Rouse, B., & McCabe, E. R. R. (1990). Neuropsychology of early-treated phenylketonuria: Specific executive function deficits. *Child Development, 61,* 1697–1713.

SHAWN E. CHRIST
University of Missouri-Columbia

PHEROMONES

Forty years ago, Karlson and Lüscher (1959) coined the term *pheromone* to describe chemicals that are "excreted to the outside by an individual and received by a second individual of the same species in which they release a specific reaction." They created this term for bombykol, the first conspecific attractant to be identified in an insect (the silkworm). Since the structure elucidation of this long-chain alcohol, hundreds of pheromones have been identified, and it is now commonly accepted that most animals (with the possible exception of birds and marine mammals)

use chemicals released by conspecifics to mediate various social interactions. Frequently, these conspecific chemicals are found in precise mixtures that are discerned at very low concentrations with great specificity, sometimes exerting subtle effects that seem to go beyond the original definition (e.g., kin recognition). Nevertheless, the term *pheromone* remains in common usage, and it is now used to describe almost any chemical cue that mediates intraspecies communication and to which organisms are predisposed to respond.

Pheromones are typically defined by their actions and may have either behavioral or physiological effects, which need not always be immediate. Pheromones appear to have originated in the earliest life forms and continue to serve as the primary means of communication in many invertebrates, fishes, and mammals with nocturnal habits. Their actions may range from simple to extremely complex, and the ways in which organisms employ pheromones are as diverse as their life histories. Generally, the actions of pheromones are species-specific, although this is not always the case. Pheromones with significant behavioral effects are termed *releasers,* and those with physiological effects are often called *primers.* Releasers are better known and include sex pheromones, aggregation pheromones, territorial pheromones, and alarm pheromones. Sex pheromones are used by many terrestrial, aquatic, and aerial species in locating and selecting mates. Some of these are remarkably potent; for example, male moths may be attracted to the odor of females hundreds of meters away. Similarly, male dogs respond to the scent of bitches in heat nearly a kilometer upwind, and male goldfish detect female sex steroids at concentrations as low as 1 gram in 3 billion liters of water (Stacey & Sorensen, in press).

Aggregation pheromones are also used by many species to bring individuals together from a distance (Hardie & Minks, 1999). Examples include unicellular slime molds forming fruiting bodies, swarming insects, and migrating lampreys locating spawning rivers based on the odor of conspecifics that release sulfated steroids, which are detected at concentrations of 1 gram in 10 billion liters (Sorensen et al., 2005). In contrast, many terrestrial mammals, such as antelopes and badgers, use territorial marks to maintain spacing. Alarm pheromones are also commonly used by both terrestrial and aquatic organisms. For example, when injured, many fish release alarm pheromones ("Schreckstoff") from their skin. Because of their potency and specificity, releaser pheromones are frequently used to manage unwanted nuisance species, insects in particular (Cardé & Minks, 1997).

Priming pheromones are employed by a wide variety of species, and their actions may be dramatic. For example, urinary odors of male mice advance puberty in juvenile females (the Vandenburgh effect), whereas female urinary odors have the opposite effect. Pregnant rodents will abort preimplantation embryos if exposed to the odor of a male that is not the father of their young (the Bruce effect). Male goldfish synchronize their endocrine and reproductive cycles with those of ovulatory females by detecting hormonal sex pheromones released by the latter. Among the honeybees, development of future queens is influenced by pheromonal signals circulating within the hive. Not surprisingly, evolution apparently has favored social organisms that achieve physiological synchrony.

Studies of mammalian pheromones increasingly highlight the roles that conspecific odors (pheromones) have on mediating social awareness (Vandenbergh, 1999). Among rodents, it is now clear that individuals are readily discerned and that kin-related odors are part of this process. These odors mediate maternal bonding, territoriality, and the Bruce effect; some term them "signaler pheromones." Strong evidence suggests that peptides associated with the major histocompatibility complex (MHC) have a role in these complex cues, but small aromatics have also been identified. It has been suggested that "modulator" pheromones affect mood and thought processes in humans, although these have yet to be identified or gain wide acceptance (Brennan & Zufall, 2006).

The biochemical nature of pheromones varies enormously across species (Wyatt, 2003). Although hundreds of insect pheromones have been clearly identified, only about a dozen vertebrate pheromones are well understood. Pheromones frequently appear to comprise molecules (or, more often, sets of molecules) that originally served related functions. Many pheromones are mixtures of relatively common metabolites, and context can be important. A good example of this is the goldfish and its relatives, which use common hormonal products as sex pheromones. However, in most organisms some specialization has occurred, as donors often derive benefit from signal production. Many insects, ungulates, and rodents possess pheromone glands that produce large amounts of molecular blends, the release of which they control. A well-known example of such a system is that of the noctuid moths, whose sex pheromones are precise species-specific mixtures of up to seven fatty acids and related acetates, aldehydes, and alcohols.

Among mammals, only two single-component pheromones have been clearly identified (pig and elephant), and most mammalian pheromones, including those of rodents, appear to be complex mixtures whose actions are subtle. Whether specialized or not, pheromonal signals generally have chemical characteristics that complement the ecological needs of the species in question. Thus, alarm and sex pheromones in terrestrial insects are frequently composed of low-molecular-weight and volatile compounds that spread and fade quickly. Interestingly, elephants use some of the same volatile cues as moths. Fish often use relatively small and highly soluble conjugated steroids as sex pheromones. Hyenas, on the other hand, have evolved to use high-molecular-weight compounds as territorial marks that last for months in

the hot sun. In rodents, marking pheromones appear to be associated with a large, stable protein known as a major urinary protein, which is bound to a smaller ligand and is long-lived.

Biological responses associated with pheromonal exposure are attributable to specializations in the nervous systems of the receiving animals. Many parallels exist between invertebrates and vertebrates (Wyatt, 2003). For instance, peripheral sensitivity to pheromones is often sexually dimorphic in both invertebrates and vertebrates. Also, in both instances, processing of pheromonal information appears to be associated with well-defined components of the olfactory systems, which, in the case of rodents, have multiple anatomical components (see later). Pheromones are detected by olfactory receptor neurons located in a sensory epithelium in the nose or mouth of vertebrates and on sensory hairs located on the antennae of invertebrates. They bind with receptor proteins (which have yet to be fully elucidated) on the surface of these neurons and project to specialized regions of the antennal lobe (invertebrates) or olfactory bulb or related structures (vertebrates).

Single-unit recording has shown that pheromonally sensitive receptor neurons in both insects and vertebrates (fish and rodents) are tuned to a narrow range of pheromone compounds. For example, in male moths, axons from olfactory receptor neurons project to a specialized subset of glomeruli, the macroglomerular complex located in the lobe, where well-defined connections give male moths the remarkable ability to discriminate precise species-specific mixtures. In fish, this mapping appears to occur in medial regions of the olfactory bulb. The situation appears even more complex for terrestrial vertebrates, including mammals, which have a multicomponent olfactory system that comprises the main olfactory epithelium and the vomeronasal system (VNO) and is located in the roof of their mouths. Although both systems may mediate pheromone responses (Brennan & Zufall, 2006), especially in experienced animals (e.g., pigs and rabbits), the VNO appears to be the primary system for discriminating pheromones, and it is required for naive rodents to respond to priming cues. The VNO appears specialized; it possesses only microvillar receptor neurons that project to a specific set of mitral (output) cells of the accessory olfactory bulb (AOB). The AOB then projects subcortically to the hypothalamus, where it excites neurosecretory cells to release reproductive hormones when stimulated by primer pheromones.

Although responsiveness to pheromones is fundamentally instinctual, some chemical signals associated with kin and mate recognition appear to be modified by experience. For example, honeybees learn to recognize surface hydrocarbon mixtures on the bodies of nest mates, which then allow them to enter the nest. Young mice will imprint on the odor type of their parents, which appears to be closely associated with the MHC, and avoid it later in life when choosing mates. Also, adult female mice learn the odor of males during mating and distinguish it from other males in the previously mentioned Bruce effect. The latter phenomenon has proven to be an interesting model system for investigating memory. Although it is probable that many behavioral and physiological aspects of human biology are influenced by pheromones, as yet none of these has been conclusively demonstrated or identified, and it seems doubtful that we have a functioning VNO. We are most confident about the role of pheromones in menstrual synchrony, which occurs among women living in close proximity, although these compounds are not yet clearly identified (McClintock, 2000). There are also suggestions that human mate choice is influenced by the smells associated with the MHC system. Odors are of immense value to most organisms because of the potency, specificity, longevity, and high information content; as our understanding of animal cognition grows, an appreciation of the roles pheromones play in the lives of most animals will probably grow as well.

REFERENCES

Brennan, P. B., & Zufall, F. (2006). Pheromonal communication in vertebrates. *Nature, 444*, 308–315.

Cardé, R., & Minks, K. A. (Eds.). (1997). *Insect pheromone research: New directions.* New York: Chapman and Hall.

Hardie, J., & Minks, K. A. (1999). *Pheromones of non-lepidopteran insects associated with agricultural plants.* Wallingford, England: CAB International.

Karlson, P., & Lüscher, M. (1959). "Pheromones": A new term for a class of biologically active substances. *Nature, 183*, 155–156.

McClintock, M. K. (2000). Human pheromones: Primers, releasers, signalers or modulators? In K. Wallen & J. Schneider (Eds.), *Reproduction in context* (pp. 355–420). Cambridge, MA: MIT Press.

Sorensen, P. W., Fine, J. M., Dvornikovs, V., Jeffrey, C. S., Shao, F., Wang, J., et al. (2005). Mixture of new sulfated steroids functions as a migratory pheromone in the sea lamprey. *Nature Chemical Biology, 1*, 324–328.

Stacey, N. E., & Sorensen, P. W. (in press). Fish hormonal pheromones. In D. W. Pfaff, A. P. Arnold, A. Etgen, S. Fahrbach, & R. Rubin (Eds.), *Hormones, brain and behavior* (2nd ed.). San Diego, CA: Elsevier.

Vandenbergh, J. G. 1999. Pheromones, mammals. In E. Knobil & J. D. Neill (Eds.), *Encyclopedia of reproduction* (Vol. 3, pp. 130–135). New York: Academic Press.

Wyatt, T. D. (2003). *Pheromones and animal behaviour.* Cambridge, England: Cambridge University Press.

PETER W. SORENSEN
University of Minnesota

See also: **Animal Learning and Behavior; Comparative Psychology**

PHI COEFFICIENT

The phi (φ) coefficient was proposed by George Utney Yule in 1912 as an index of association between two dichotomous variables. The φ statistic is particularly useful to many research workers because it is the familiar product-moment correlation when computed for data from a bivariate binomial distribution. When such data are organized in a fourfold table, the coefficient is most easily computed as

$$\varphi = \frac{(n_{11} + n_{22}) - (n_{12} + n_{21})}{\sqrt{n_{1.}n_{2.}n_{.1}n_{.2}}}$$

It is tested for significance by $\chi^2 = n_{..}\varphi^2$, which under the null hypothesis of no association is distributed as chi square with 1 degree of freedom.

Because φ is the customary product-moment correlation, except for binomial data, it has the same utility: It is bounded between -1.0 and $+1.0$, and a coefficient with a large absolute value indicates a strong association between the two variables. Furthermore, because it is the customary correlation (r), useful, or ballpark, confidence limits can be set for φ in the same manner as used for r. However, a more mathematically defensible, and usually wider, confidence interval based on odds ratios is presented by Fleiss (1981).

There is an important caveat associated with proper use of the phi coefficient, and this warning depends on how the data are obtained. If they arise from a cross-sectional random sample, there is no need for this warning. In a random cross-sectional sample, n sampling units are obtained, and the fourfold table devised from two variables measured on each unit. Such would be the case if members of a random sample of students were observed to generate a fourfold table according to their gender and right or left eye dominance. From such a sample, φ would be an estimate of the association parameter of a bivariate distribution. This may not be the case, however, for a phi coefficient computed by using data from purposive sampling.

In purposive sampling, such as case-control studies, two groups are created according to the outcome of one dichotomous variable. Then a random sample is obtained from each group, and the fourfold table generated by measuring the second variable on each unit from each sample. Purposive sampling would occur if there is a random sample of male students and a second random sample of females, and eye dominance is recorded for each male and female. The concern about φ computed from such a study is that it lacks the statistical property of *invariance*; hence there may be no valid basis for comparing, or testing for significant difference, between phi coefficients from two different purposive sampling studies, even if data for both samples come from the same bivariate population. This difficulty is explained with good clarity and greater detail in Fleiss (1981), and Berger (1961) has provided a method for comparing coefficients obtained from two different studies.

REFERENCES

Berger, A. (1961). On comparing intensities of association between two binary characteristics in two different populations. *Journal of the American Statistical Association, 56*, 889–908.

Conover, W. J. (1999). *Practical nonparametric statistics* (3rd ed.). New York: John Wiley & Sons.

Fleiss, J. L. (1981). *Statistical methods for rates and proportions* (2nd ed.). New York: John Wiley & Sons.

Yule, G. U. (1912). On the methods of measuring the association between two attributes. *Royal Statistical Society, 75*, 579–642.

SUGGESTED READING

Daniel, W. W. (2002). *Applied nonparametric statistics* (2nd ed.). New York: Duxbury Press.

STANLEY WEARDEN
West Virginia University

See also: **Rank Order Correlation**

PHILOSOPHY AND PSYCHOLOGY (See Psychology and Philosophy)

PHILOSOPHY OF PSYCHOTHERAPY (See Psychotherapy, Philosophy of)

PHINEAS GAGE

On September 13, 1998, a group of brain scientists, including neurologists, neuropsychologists, and neurosurgeons, gathered in the hamlet of Cavendish, Vermont, to commemorate a bizarre anniversary. It was the 150th anniversary of an accident in which a young man named Phineas Gage suffered a brain injury when an iron bar was shot through the front part of his head. The accident itself was remarkable enough—immediately afterward, despite a gruesome wound to the front of his head and brain, Gage was conscious, alert, and talkative, and it seemed rather a miracle that he had even survived. But what followed over the next few decades, and then over the many years since, is what put Cavendish, Vermont, on the scientific map and became the reason for scientists to travel from around the world that late summer day in 1998 to commemorate the anniversary (see Macmillan, 2000).

On September 13, 1848, Phineas Gage was laboring with coworkers to blast a bed for railroad tracks through the rugged, rocky terrain of southern Vermont. While setting an explosive, Gage prematurely triggered an explosion with his tamping iron. The iron was propelled through the front part of his head, entering his left cheek just under the eye, piercing the frontal lobes of his brain, and exiting through the top front part of his head. In light of the comparatively primitive state of medicine in the middle part of the nineteenth century, Gage's medical recovery was nothing short of astonishing—he survived this massive onslaught with normal intelligence, memory, speech, sensation, and movement. Following this surprising recovery, however, Gage displayed a profound change in personality and social conduct that established him as a landmark case in the history of neuroscience. Before the accident, he had been responsible, socially well adapted, and well liked by peers and supervisors. Afterwards, Gage proved to be irresponsible and untrustworthy, irreverent and capricious, with markedly unreliable behavior and little regard for social convention; in short, he was "no longer Gage."

Gage's physician, John Harlow, speculated (very accurately, as it turned out) that there was a causative relationship between the damage to the front part of Gage's brain and the profound change in his personality and social conduct (Bigelow, 1850; Harlow, 1868). Harlow's observations, although never fully appreciated by his contemporaries, hinted at a conclusion that was both radical and prescient: there are structures in the front part of the human brain that are dedicated to the planning and execution of personally and socially adaptive behavior, and to the aspect of reasoning known as rationality. Case reports published over the first several decades of the twentieth century supported Harlow's contention, and modern investigations have documented that the prefrontal region is crucial for moral reasoning, social conduct, planning, and decision making (Damasio & Anderson, 2003; Tranel, 2002). Moreover, when this region is damaged early in life, the development of social and moral reasoning may be permanently blocked (Anderson et al., 1999).

Using tools of modern neuroscience, scientists have performed a detailed reconstruction of the injury to Gage's brain (Damasio, Grabowski, Frank, Galaburda, & Damasio, 1994). From measurements of Gage's skull and the tamping iron (which are part of the Warren Anatomical Medical Museum at Harvard University), scientists were able to reproduce the precise path the tamping iron traversed through Gage's brain. (The skull and iron, which were on display at the 150th anniversary celebration, are remarkably well preserved to this day.) This reconstruction confirmed that the damage most likely included the left and right prefrontal regions, anterior to structures required for motor behavior and speech, in precisely the location that modern studies have highlighted as the key neural underpinning of social conduct and rational decision making.

The importance of the case of Phineas Gage can be more fully appreciated when one considers just how difficult it has been to unravel the cognitive and behavioral functions that are subserved by the prefrontal region of the human brain. The prefrontal sector, situated anterior to the motor/premotor cortices and superior to the sylvian fissure, comprises an enormous expanse of the brain, forming nearly half of the entire cerebral mantle. In humans in particular, this region has expanded disproportionately. Throughout the history of neuropsychology, the psychological capacities associated with the prefrontal region have remained enigmatic and elusive. With the observations of Phineas Gage, however, the special significance of this region began to be appreciated.

Following on Harlow's prescient writings regarding Gage, other investigators have called attention to the oftentimes bizarre development of abnormal social behavior that can follow prefrontal brain injury (e.g., Damasio, Tranel, & Damasio, 1990; Eslinger & Damasio, 1985; Stuss & Benson, 1986). The patients have a number of features in common (see Damasio & Anderson, 2003): inability to organize future activity and hold gainful employment, diminished capacity to respond to punishment, a tendency to present an unrealistically favorable view of themselves, and a tendency to display inappropriate emotional reactions. Making this profile especially puzzling is the fact that most of these patients, like Gage, retain normal intelligence, language, memory, and perception. Other scientists have called attention to the striking characteristics of patients with prefrontal lobe brain injury, especially damage to the ventral and lower mesial portions of this region (the "ventromedial prefrontal" sector). Ventromedial prefrontal cortex damage has been implicated in changes in decision making due to impairment in evaluating the value of available choices to make the best one (Blair et al., 2006). The affected patients also have difficulty with incorporating feedback to change behavior and lack physiological arousal when making risky choices (Bechara, Damasio, Tranel, & Damasio, 1997). Furthermore, the decision making of these patients is less influenced by emotion associated with taking risks (Shiv, Loewenstein, Bechara, Damasio, & Damasio, 2005), and the patients show reduced experience of regret for poor decisions (Camille et al., 2004), similar to the pattern seen in psychopathy.

Blumer and Benson (1975) noted that patients with ventromedial prefrontal damage displayed a personality profile (which the authors termed "pseudo-psychopathic") with features of puerility, a jocular attitude, sexually disinhibited humor, inappropriate and near-total self-indulgence, and complete lack of concern for others. Stuss and Benson (1986) emphasized that the patients demonstrated a remarkable lack of empathy and general lack of concern about others. The patients showed callous unconcern, boastfulness, and unrestrained and tactless behavior. Other descriptors included impulsiveness, facetiousness, and diminished anxiety and concern for the future.

It is interesting to note that this personality profile is strikingly similar to that characterized in clinical psychology and psychiatry as psychopathic (or sociopathic) (American Psychiatric Association, 1994). In fact, this condition has been dubbed "acquired sociopathy," to emphasize the fact that prefrontally injured patients often have personality manifestations that are quite reminiscent of those associated with sociopathy (Barrash, Tranel, & Anderson, 2000; Tranel, 1994). The qualifier "acquired" signifies that in the brain-damaged patients, the condition follows the onset of brain injury and that it occurs in persons whose personalities and social conduct were previously normal (as in the case of Phineas Gage). Patients with acquired sociopathy have a proclivity to engage in decisions and behaviors that have negative consequences for their well-being. They repeatedly select courses of action that are not in their best interest in the long run, making poor decisions about interpersonal relationships, occupational endeavors, and finances. In short, the patients act as though they have lost the ability to ponder different courses of action and then select the option that promises the best blend of short- and long-term benefit.

As it turned out, the misadventures of Phineas Gage provided crucial early clues about the importance of the prefrontal sector of the brain for social behavior, reasoning and decision making, as well as for what can generally be called "personality." Phineas Gage's accident was bizarre, to be sure, but its important place in scientific history is firmly secure.

REFERENCES

American Psychiatric Association. (1994). *Diagnostic and statistical manual of mental disorders* (4th ed.). Washington, DC: Author.

Anderson, S. W., Bechara, A., Damasio, H., Tranel, D., & Damasio, A. R. (1999). Impairment of social and moral behavior related to early damage in the human prefrontal cortex. *Nature Neuroscience, 2,* 1032–1037.

Barrash, J., Tranel, D., & Anderson, S. W. (2000). Acquired personality disturbances associated with bilateral damage to the ventromedial prefrontal region. *Developmental Neuropsychology, 18,* 355–381.

Bechara, A., Damasio, H., Tranel, D., & Damasio, A. R. (1997). Deciding advantageously before knowing the advantageous strategy. *Science, 275,* 1293–1295.

Bigelow, H. J. (1850). Dr. Harlow's case of recovery from the passage of an iron bar through the head. *American Journal of the Medical Sciences, 39,* 13–22.

Blair, K., Marsh, A. A., Morton, J., Vythilingam, M., Jones, M., Mondillo, K., et al. (2006). Choosing the lesser of two evils, the better of two goods: Specifying the roles of ventromedial prefrontal cortex and dorsal anterior cingulate in object choice. *Journal of Neuroscience, 26,* 11379–11386.

Blumer, D., & Benson, D. F. (1975). Personality changes with frontal and temporal lobe lesions. In D. F. Benson, & D. Blumer (Eds.), *Psychiatric aspects of neurologic disease* (pp 151–169). New York: Grune & Stratton.

Camille, N., Coricelli, G., Sallet, J., Pradat-Diehl, P., Duhamel, J., & Sirigu, A. (2004). The involvement of the orbitofrontal cortex in the experience of regret. *Science, 304*, 1167–1170.

Damasio, A. R., & Anderson, S. W. (2003). The frontal lobes. In K. Heilman & E. Valenstein (Eds.), *Clinical neuropsychology* (4th ed., pp. 404–446). New York: Oxford University Press.

Damasio, A. R., Tranel, D., & Damasio, H. (1990). Individuals with sociopathic behavior caused by frontal damage fail to respond autonomically to social stimuli. *Behavioural Brain Research, 41*, 81–94.

Damasio, H., Grabowski, T., Frank, R., Galaburda, A. M., & Damasio, A. R. (1994). The return of Phineas Gage: Clues about the brain from the skull of a famous patient. *Science, 264*, 1102–1105.

Eslinger, P. J., & Damasio, A. R. (1985). Severe disturbance of higher cognition after bilateral frontal lobe ablation: Patient EVR. *Neurology, 35*, 1731–1741.

Harlow, J. M. (1868). Recovery from the passage of an iron bar through the head. *Publications of the Massachusetts Medical Society, 2*, 327–347.

Macmillan, M. (2000). *An odd kind of fame: Stories of Phineas Gage.* Cambridge, MA: MIT Press.

Shiv, B., Loewenstein, G., Bechara, A., Damasio, H., & Damasio, A. R. (2005). Investment behavior and the negative side of emotion. *Psychological Science, 16*, 435–439.

Stuss, D. T., & Benson, D. F. (1986). *The frontal lobes.* New York: Raven Press.

Tranel, D. (1994). "Acquired sociopathy": The development of sociopathic behavior following focal brain damage. In D. C. Fowles, P. Sutker, & S. H. Goodman (Eds.), *Progress in experimental personality and psychopathology research* (Vol. 17, pp. 285–311). New York: Springer.

Tranel, D. (2002). Emotion, decision-making, and the ventromedial prefrontal cortex. In D. T. Stuss & R. T. Knight (Eds.), *Principles of frontal lobe function.* New York: Oxford University Press.

DANIEL TRANEL
DAVID CORDRY
University of Iowa College of Medicine

PHOBIC DISORDER

Whereas most individuals have some level of fear or anxiety about certain situations, objects, or events, phobias are considered to be more extreme, persistent, and irrational fears that produce a conscious avoidance of the feared stimulus. According to the *DSM-IV,* phobic disorder is diagnosed when the following symptoms are present: a marked and persistent fear of a situation or stimulus, exposure to this feared situation or stimulus almost invariably invokes anxiety or panic attacks, the feared situation or stimulus is avoided or endured with intense anxiety or distress, and the avoidance interferes with the individual's functioning or there is marked distress about the phobia (American Psychiatric Association, 2000). Adults with this disorder realize that the fear is excessive, although children may not have this insight. Whereas phobic disorders share in common features of threat-relevant responding (i.e., anxious apprehension, fear, and avoidance), they differ in the object and breadth of threat.

Phobic disorders are classified as types of anxiety disorders and can be divided into three different subtypes: specific phobias, social phobia, and agoraphobia. Specific phobias (formerly known as simple phobias) are marked and persistent fears of clearly discernible and circumscribed objects or situations and entail a very narrowly defined threat response. Five subtypes of specific phobias are recognized in the *DSM-IV:* animal type (e.g., fear of spiders), natural environment type (e.g., fear of storms), blood-injection-injury type (e.g., fear of needles), situational type (e.g., fear of elevators), and other (e.g., fear of vomiting).

Social phobia (also known as social anxiety disorder) involves an excessive fear of social or performance situations in which embarrassment or negative judgments from others might occur. The number of feared situations varies among individuals with social phobia. Social phobia may be considered generalized when the individual fears most social situations, such as fear of giving presentations, fear of engaging in conversations with others, and fear of dating. Nongeneralized social phobia entails a much narrower threat base and is specified when the fear is circumscribed to only one or two social settings, such as only public speaking.

Finally, individuals with agoraphobia fear places where they may have trouble escaping or getting help in case of any felt emergency. These individuals fear that they will have embarrassing or physically or mentally threatening panic-like symptoms, such as losing control of bodily systems, vomiting, or fainting in public places. If individuals also have a history of unexpected panic attacks, which is seen in more than 95% of agoraphobic patients in clinical settings (American Psychiatric Association, 2000), then they are diagnosed as panic disorder with agoraphobia.

Prevalence

Phobias are the most common type of psychiatric disorder in the United States. The lifetime prevalence varies by the type of phobia, with different prevalence rates for men and women. Of the anxiety disorders, specific phobias are one of the most common types, with lifetime prevalence rates of 12.5% (Kessler et al., 2005). Overall, specific phobias are two times more common in women than in men, although the sex ratio varies according to the type of specific phobia. In adults, blood-injury-injection, animal, and natural environment phobias (with the possible exception of height phobias) usually develop during childhood, compared with a later onset, usually in the 20s, for situational phobias (Öst & Treffers, 2001). Social phobia is another common phobia, with lifetime rates reported at 12.1% (Kessler et al., 2005). Social phobia is about 1.3 times more common in women than in men (Heimberg, Stein, Hiripi, & Kessler, 2000). Unlike specific phobias, which most often start in childhood, social phobia typically begins in adolescence or early adulthood. Agoraphobia onset is usually defined by an initial unexpected panic attack, most typically occurring in the mid-20s (Brown, Campbell, Lehman, Grishman, & Mancill, 2001). Agoraphobia has lifetime prevalence rates of approximately 1.1% with panic disorder (Grant et al., 2006) and 1.4% without panic disorder (Kessler et al., 2005), and it is about two times more common in women than in men.

Etiology

There are several theories for why individuals develop phobias. Behavioral models suggest that individuals develop phobias through classical conditioning in which a neutral stimulus is paired with an aversive event. Phobic individuals then avoid the feared stimulus to reduce their anxiety, thereby negatively reinforcing their fear. The person may pair these associations through direct traumatic conditioning (e.g., a child is attacked by a dog), through vicarious observation (e.g., a child witnesses another person attacked by a dog), or through informational transmission (e.g., a child's parent repeatedly tells her that dogs are dangerous). Further, constitutional factors (e.g., neuroticism and history of experiences), contextual factors at the time of the aversive experience (e.g., intensity, expectancy, and controllability), and events after conditioning (e.g., additional stressors) are circumstances that can increase a person's vulnerability to developing conditioned reactions (Mineka & Zinbarg, 1995), and preparedness explains the propensity to develop certain types of phobias (de Silva, Rachman, & Seligman, 1977).

Cognitive models point to cognitive biases as contributing to the maintenance of phobias. The cognitive biases in phobic individuals include hypervigilance for threat cues and an overestimate of the threat posed by the feared stimulus. Whereas cognitive biases can be conceptualized as an anxious *process* common to all phobias, the *content* of these biases becomes relatively specific (through past history and learning experiences) to stimuli of significance to each disorder. For example, the cognitive model for social phobia suggests that individuals tend to look for socially threatening cues (e.g., counting the number of pauses in a conversation), focus on what they are doing wrong in social situations (e.g., concentrating on how much they are shaking or sweating), and misinterpret neutral events as threatening (e.g., believing that they are boring if only a few people laugh at their joke). Support for the cognitive model of phobic disorders comes from experimental laboratory paradigms utilizing visual search tasks in which anxious individuals have been shown to overly attend to stimuli related to their concerns, whereas nonanxious adults direct attention away from the same stimuli (e.g., Wilson & MacLeod, 2003).

Finally, biological theories have suggested that genetics and temperament play a role in the development of phobias. In one comprehensive review, Hettema, Neale, and Kendler (2001) concluded that there is a significant familial aggregation of phobias, with probands 4.1 times more likely to develop a phobia if they have a first-degree relative with the disorder. Other researchers suggest that it is the vulnerabilities for phobias that are heritable (e.g., temperament) and that environmental exposure to the specific phobia is needed to activate the inherited phobia-proneness (Kendler, Karkowski, & Prescott, 1999). The temperament most associated with all anxiety disorders is neuroticism/emotional stability, which is also termed negative affectivity. Like all anxiety disorders, phobic disorders are thought to load differentially on the dimension of negative affectivity, with more pervasive phobias like agoraphobia loading more heavily than social phobia and specific phobias (Brown, Chorpita, & Barlow, 1998).

Treatment

There are numerous treatments that have been used to treat phobias; however, the ensuing paragraphs will focus on the treatments that have received the most empirical support. Cognitive behavioral therapy (CBT) is the most empirically supported treatment for phobias. Some forms of CBT rely more heavily on the behavioral components, whereas other forms may focus more on the underlying cognitions. In cognitive therapy, the focus is on cognitive restructuring, in which clients are encouraged to identify and monitor their irrational thoughts and learn to challenge their distorted thinking. For example, clients may be asked to test their fearful predictions (e.g., asking individuals with agoraphobia to test the notion that they cannot cope with crowded situations), gather evidence to evaluate whether their thinking is realistic (e.g., assessing the odds of the plane crashing by individuals with a phobia of flying), and consider alternative interpretations (e.g., asking individuals with social phobia to consider if shaking while speaking necessarily means that they are foolish). Although several studies have shown cognitive restructuring to be an important component of successful CBT, some researchers have questioned whether adding the cognitive component is more efficacious than behavioral therapy alone.

Behavioral models typically involve either in vivo (real life) exposure or imaginal exposure to the feared stimulus. Exposure therapy is based on the premise that avoidance maintains fear. In traditional in vivo exposure, the client develops a hierarchy of feared situations and is gradually exposed to more fear-provoking conditions until the anxiety eventually attenuates. These feared situations may include touching a spider for an individual with a specific phobia of spiders, going to crowded malls for an individual with agoraphobia, or going to social events for an individual with social phobia. Whereas in vivo exposure tends to be more effective than imaginal exposure, imaginal exposure is often easier to implement, especially if exposure to the feared stimulus cannot feasibly be approached in therapy (e.g., fear of flying). However, virtual reality exposure, in which a computer program generates a realistic context to simulate the phobic situation, has become more popular in the last few years, especially for the treatment of height and flying phobias. Finally, pharmacotherapy has been used with some individuals with phobic disorders. For example, benzodiazepines and certain types of antidepressants (e.g., selective serotonin reuptake inhibitors [SSRIs]) have been used in individuals with agoraphobia and social phobia. Although pharmacotherapy is not traditionally used for individuals with specific phobias, benzodiazepines and SSRIs may be prescribed in severe cases in which the specific phobia is interfering with the individual's daily functioning.

REFERENCES

American Psychiatric Association. (2000). *Diagnostic and statistical manual of mental disorders* (4th ed. text rev.). Washington, DC: Author.

Brown, T. A., Campbell, L. A., Lehman, C. L., Grishman, J. R., & Mancill, R. B. (2001). Current and lifetime comorbidity of the *DSM-IV* anxiety and mood disorders in a large clinical sample. *Journal of Abnormal Psychology, 110,* 585–599.

Brown, T. A., Chorpita, B. F., & Barlow, D. H. (1998). Structural relationships among dimensions of the *DSM-IV* anxiety and mood disorders and dimensions of negative affect, positive affect, and autonomic arousal. *Journal of Abnormal Psychology, 107,* 179–192.

de Silva, P., Rachman, S., & Seligman, M. E. (1977). Prepared phobias and obsessions: Therapeutic outcome. *Behaviour Research & Therapy, 15,* 65–77.

Grant, B. F., Hasin, D. S., Stinson, F. S., Dawson, D. A., Goldstein, R. B., Smith, S., et al. (2006). The epidemiology of *DSM-IV* panic disorder and agoraphobia in the United States: Results from the National Epidemiologic Survey on Alcohol and Related Conditions. *Journal of Clinical Psychiatry, 67,* 363–374.

Heimberg, R. G., Stein, M. B. Hiripi, E., & Kessler, R. C. (2000). Trends in the prevalence of social phobia in the United States: A synthetic cohort analysis of changes over four decades. *European Psychiatry, 15,* 29–37.

Hettema, J., Prescott, C., & Kendler, K. S. (2001). A population-based twin study of generalized anxiety disorder in men and women. *Journal of Nervous and Mental Disease, 189,* 413–420.

Kendler, K. S., Karkowski, L. M., & Prescott, C. A. (1999). Fears and phobias: Reliability and heritability. *Psychological Medicine, 29,* 539–553.

Kessler, R. C., Berglund, P., Demler, O., Jin, R., Merikangas, K. R., & Walters, E. E. (2005). Lifetime prevalence and age-of-onset distributions of *DSM-IV* disorders in the National Comorbidity Survey replication. *Archives of General Psychiatry, 62,* 593–602.

Mineka, S., & Zinbarg, R. (1995). Conditioning and ethological models of SAD. In R. G. Heimberg & M. R. Liebowitz (Eds.), *SAD: Diagnosis, assessment, and treatment* (pp. 134–162). New York: Guilford Press.

Öst, L.-G., & Treffers, P. D. A. (2001). Onset, course, and outcome for anxiety disorders in children. In W. K. Silverman & P. D. A. Treffers (Eds.), *Anxiety disorders in children and adolescents: Research, assessment and intervention* (pp. 293–312). Cambridge, England: Cambridge University Press.

Wilson, E., & MacLeod, C. (2003). Contrasting two accounts of anxiety-linked attentional bias: Selective attention to varying levels of stimulus threat intensity. *Journal of Abnormal Psychology, 112,* 212–218.

SUGGESTED READINGS

Barlow, D. H. (2002). *Anxiety and its disorders: The nature and treatment of anxiety.* New York: Guilford Press.

Craske, M. G. (2003). *Origins of phobias and anxiety disorders: Why more women than men?* Oxford, England: Elsevier.

Craske, M. G. & Waters, A. M. (2005). Panic disorder, phobias, and generalized anxiety disorder. *Annual Review of Clinical Psychology, 1,* 197–225.

ALYSSA M. EPSTEIN
MICHELLE G. CRASKE
University of California, Los Angeles

PHONEMES

Linguistic analyses have traditionally represented the form of speech in terms of phonemes. The word *cat,* for instance, can be represented by a sequence of three phonemes: /k/, /æ/, and /t/. Changes in the phonemic construction of a word result in different words or nonsense words. For example, reordering the phonemes in *cat* produces other words, such as *act* (/ækt/) and *tack* (/tæk/), whereas replacing the /k/ with a /p/ results in a new word, *pat*. Words like *cat* and *pat* that differ on the identity of a single phoneme are referred to as minimal pairs and provide a useful source of evidence for defining the phonemic inventory of a language. In an alphabetic language such as English, the phonemic nature of speech is made explicit by the close correspondence between letters and the phonemes they represent. Logographic languages (e.g., Chinese) do not share this correspondence; instead, characters are used to represent whole words.

A further division of speech sounds is possible, into subphonemic units called phonetic features. The representation of a phoneme consists of a set of phonetic features that capture the similarities and differences between groups of phonemes. For example, the difference between the phonemes /t/ and /k/ is largely due to the difference in the place of closure created by the tongue touching the roof of the mouth. The same contrast is found between /d/ and /g/ and between /n/ and /N/ (the final phoneme in *ring*). This contrast can be represented by one or more place of articulation features.

Sometimes a subphonemic change generates a variant of a phoneme that does not contrast between words. For example, the phoneme /p/ can have two variants in the English language: an aspirated one and an unaspirated one, whereby the former is accompanied by a slight puff of air, and the latter is not. The unaspirated variant is heard in a word like *spin*, while the aspirated one is heard in *pin*. These two variants, [p] and [p^h], are allophones of /p/. Sounds that are allophonic in one language and so do not produce contrasts between words may be contrastive in other languages. For an English speaker, [p] and [p^h] are variants of the same phoneme, but in Thai, a language that makes use of the aspiration contrast, they are two different phonemes.

The concept of allophony is important because the abstract notion of a phoneme obscures a great deal of variation in speech. The particular allophonic form a phoneme takes depends on the context in which it is uttered, and this results in a wide range of acoustic forms being classed as the same phoneme. Similarly, the discrete sequences of symbols in a phonemic transcription do not properly represent the temporal structure of the speech waveform, in which information about different phonemes is spread across time and overlapping. A critical issue in the psychological study of speech is whether mental representations of speech reflect the diversity and detail of the speech waveform or the abstractness and simplicity of the phonemic transcription.

Phonemes in Speech Perception

Some aspects of the organization of speech sounds in perception clearly correspond to phonemic categories. One can create artificial continua by using recorded speech or a speech synthesizer in which the extremes correspond to normal phonemes. Typically, adults show categorical perception of these continua; that is, they will find it difficult to discriminate between two sounds on a continuum that would be classed as the same phoneme but relatively easy to discriminate between two sounds that cross a phoneme

boundary. Infants as young as one month old show similar discontinuities in their perception of these continua. In fact, it seems that early on in development, infants are able to discriminate between speech sounds that are allophonic in their language but are different phonemes in other languages. This ability is lost in the first year of life, as infants become familiar with the phonemes of their native language (e.g., Werker & Tees, 1984).

A possible conclusion from these studies is that people are born with an innate universal phonemic inventory, from which the contrasts relevant to the child's native language are consolidated. However, species such as chinchillas and macaque monkeys have also shown categorical perception of some phonemic contrasts (e.g., Kuhl & Miller, 1975). What is innate may in fact be more physical aspects of the auditory system, which provide a basis for discrimination between some sounds but not others. By this view, the phonemic systems of languages have developed in order to take advantage of these abilities.

Although categorical perception of phonemes is found from infancy, it is less clear how aware people are of these units. Alphabetic languages lend themselves to a phonemic decomposition of speech by the literate adult. This makes the conscious manipulation and decomposition of speech (such as deciding what the initial phoneme of *spin* might be) a relatively simple task. However, for verbally proficient illiterate adults and speakers of nonalphabetic languages, this is not the case (Morais, Cary, Alegria, & Bertelson, 1979). Literate adults categorize speech into phonemic units automatically during speech perception (Gaskell, Quinlan, Tamminen, & Cleland, in press), but the existence of the phoneme at this conscious level may rely on explicit teaching through learning to read alphabetic scripts. The interaction between reading and speech processing is further complicated by studies showing that people automatically activate the written representation of a word when they hear it (e.g., Perre & Ziegler, 2008).

On the other hand, neuroimaging studies suggest that the brain is sensitive to phoneme categories even when no conscious linguistic manipulation is involved. For example, Näätänen and colleagues (1997) compared the amplitude of the mismatch negativity (MMN; the brain's response to a deviant stimulus in a repetitive sequence of stimuli) in response to speech sounds that do or do not cross a phoneme boundary. Even when the sounds were played in the background and ignored by the listeners, within-boundary deviants elicited smaller MMNs than between-boundary deviants.

The phoneme has been proposed as the initial unit of classification in speech perception at a subconscious level. The assumption is that words are identified by comparison between this representation and stored phonemic representations of words. However, the lack of context-invariant characteristics for many phonemes has weakened this proposal, and other models have been suggested in which speech is mapped onto larger units (e.g., the syllable) or smaller units (e.g., acoustic features) before searching the lexicon for a matching word. The matching process between the speech waveform and the mental lexicon has also proved to be sensitive to a wide range of subtle changes in the form of words, suggesting that very little acoustic detail is discarded during the recognition of spoken words.

For example, research has found that listeners of speech are able to use information contained in the first two phonemes of *captain* to decide whether the word they are in the process of hearing is *cap* or *captain*, despite the fact that at the level of the phoneme, the two word onsets are identical (Davis, Marslen-Wilson, & Gaskell, 2002). The crucial information in this case may be the duration of the first vowel (Salverda et al., 2007). Here listeners distinguish between two allophones of /æ/, differing in duration, and use this distinction to arrive at a decision about a word's identity. Hence the phonemic unit may be too abstract to capture all the relevant information about a spoken word.

Phonemes in Speech Production

There is greater agreement among psycholinguists about the role of the phoneme in speech production (e.g., Levelt, Roelofs, & Meyer, 1999). Most current models assume that words are selected according to the conceptual requirements of the speaker, and then the phonemes making up that word are selected for articulation, possibly with reference to a store of known syllables. Originally, these models relied on data from speech errors in order to define the units involved in production. Errors are not common in natural speech, but when they do occur, many of them involve substitutions, anticipations, or perseverations of phonemes. In the case of spoonerisms, the substitution results in sequences that correspond to real words (e.g., "you have hissed all the mystery lectures" instead of "you have missed all the history lectures").

These phonemic errors will often preserve the syllabic information related to the phonemes involved, such that syllable-initial phonemes are unlikely to end up at the end of another syllable. Phonemic similarity and whether the change would produce a real word are also influential factors in defining the likelihood of a speech error. In the last few years, error data have been augmented by more sophisticated techniques that allow error-free speech production to be studied. These techniques have been particularly useful in mapping out the time course of the various processes in speech production (e.g., Schiller, 2000).

The contrast between the role of the phoneme in the perception and production literatures is striking. The fine-grained subphonemic information highlighted by perception studies must originate in the production of speech, yet the models of speech production do not currently incorporate this type of variation. It remains to be seen how the two approaches will fit together as further data refine theories in the two areas.

REFERENCES

Davis, M. H., Marslen-Wilson, W. D., & Gaskell, M. G. (2002). Leading up the lexical garden-path: Segmentation and ambiguity in spoken word recognition. *Journal of Experimental Psychology: Human Perception and Performance, 28,* 218–244.

Gaskell, M. G., Quinlan, P. T., Tamminen, J., & Cleland, A. A. (in press). The nature of phoneme representation in spoken word recognition. *Journal of Experimental Psychology: General.*

Kuhl, P. K., & Miller, J. D. (1975). Speech perception by the chinchilla: Voiced-voiceless distinction in alveolar plosive consonants. *Science, 190,* 69–72.

Levelt, W. J. M., Roelofs, A., & Meyer, A. S. (1999). A theory of lexical access in speech production. *Behavioral and Brain Sciences, 22,* 1–75.

Morais, J., Cary, L., Alegria, J., & Bertelson, P. (1979). Does awareness of speech as a sequence of phones arise spontaneously? *Cognition, 7,* 323–331.

Näätänen, R., Lehtokoski, A., Lennes, M., Cheour, M., Huotilainen, M., Ilvonen, A., et al. (1997). Language-specific phoneme representations revealed by electric and magnetic brain responses. *Nature, 385,* 432–434.

Perre, L., & Ziegler, J. C. (2008). On-line activation of orthography in spoken word recognition. *Brain Research, 1188,* 132–138.

Salverda, A. P., Dahan, D., Tanenhaus, M. K., Crosswhite, K., Masharov, M., & McDonough, J. (2007). Effects of prosodically modulated sub-phonetic variation on lexical competition. *Cognition, 105,* 466–476.

Schiller, N. O. (2000). Single word production in English: The role of subsyllabic units during phonological encoding. *Journal of Experimental Psychology: Learning Memory and Cognition, 26,* 512–528.

Werker, J. F., & Tees, R. C. (1984). Cross-language speech perception: Evidence for perceptual reorganization during the first year of life. *Infant Behavior and Development, 7,* 49–63.

SUGGESTED READINGS

Clark, J., Yallop, C., & Fletcher, J. (2006). *An introduction to phonetics and phonology.* Oxford, England: Blackwell.

McQueen, J. M., Dahan, D., & Cutler, A. (2003). Continuity and gradedness in speech processing. In N. O. Schiller & A. S. Meyer (Eds.), *Phonetics and phonology in language comprehension and production: Differences and similarities* (pp. 39–78). Berlin: Mouton de Gruyter.

Morais, J., & Kolinsky, R. (1994). Perception and awareness in phonological processing—the case of the phoneme. *Cognition, 50,* 287–297.

GARETH GASKELL
JAKKE TAMMINEN
University of York, United Kingdom

PHYSICAL ATTRACTIVENESS

Physical attractiveness has been defined as "that which represents one's conception of the ideal in appearance; that which gives the greatest degree of pleasure to the senses" (Hatfield & Sprecher, 1986, p. 4).

Artists, philosophers, and scientists have long speculated as to the nature of beauty. In the fifth century B.C., for example, the Greek philosopher Aristotle proposed that the golden mean, a perfect balance, was a universal ideal. In recent years, social and evolutionary psychologists, looking at the world through a Darwinian lens of sexual selection, have attempted to identify cultural universals in attractiveness. They have found that people throughout the world appear to prefer men's and women's faces that are (1) symmetrical, (2) average, and (3) sexually dimorphic.

With respect to symmetrical faces, theorists have argued that facial asymmetries indicate a poor genetic heritage, since they may be caused by genetic mutations, pathogens, toxins, and other stressors. Hence symmetry should signal youth, health, and reproductive fitness. Although some researchers have found that people do prefer symmetrical faces (see Marquardt, 2002), most evolutionary biologists find only weak evidence for such a preference (see Gangestad & Scheyd, 2005).

With respect to average faces, social scientists asking people to compare individual faces with average faces generally find that people prefer the latter. In one study, for example, Langlois and Roggman (1990) assembled photographs of men's and women's faces. Then, using video and computer techniques, they generated a series of composite faces. Inevitably, people found the composites to be more appealing than any individual face.

With respect to sexually dimorphic faces, evolutionary theorists argue that men and women should prefer faces of those who are at the peak of their reproductive fitness. Women, for example, generally prefer men whose faces signal mature power (e.g., they prefer masculine faces with a firm jaw and a broad chin). Men prefer women who possess faces that signal lush, adult sexuality (e.g., they prefer thick hair, dewy skin, large eyes, small noses, small chins, and full sensual lips) (see Gangestad & Scheyd, 2005; Rhodes & Zebrowitz, 2002). Women also prefer men with robust bodies; men prefer women with a low waist-to-hip ratio—a characteristic associated with fertility and health.

Evidence That People Are Biased in Favor of the Physically Attractive

Scientists find that most people, most of the time, are biased in favor of the good-looking. The Greek philosopher Sappho contended that "what is beautiful is good." Today, scientists have come to a fuller understanding of just how, where, when, and why physical appearance is important. There seem to be four steps in the stereotyping process:

1. Most people know that it is not fair to discriminate against the unattractive (they would be incensed if others discriminated against them).
2. Privately, most people take it for granted that attractive and unattractive people are different. Generally, they assume that what is beautiful is good and what is unattractive is bad.
3. Most people treat good-looking and average people better than they treat the unattractive.
4. As a consequence, a self-fulfilling prophecy occurs. The way people are treated shapes the kinds of people they become. (Hatfield & Sprecher, 1986, p. 36)

There is evidence that people do perceive attractive and unattractive people differently. In a classic experiment, social psychologists showed college students yearbook photographs of men and women who varied markedly in appearance and asked them about their first impressions of the people depicted. Young adults assumed that handsome men and beautiful women must possess nearly all the virtues. The good-looking were assumed to be more sociable, outgoing, poised, interesting, exciting, sexually responsive, kind, nurturing, warm, modest, strong, and sensitive than their homely peers. They were also expected to have happier and more fulfilling lives.

Not only do people think that the attractive are special but they also treat them that way. Clinicians spend more time with good-looking clients. Teachers reward more attractive students with better grades. Executives are more likely to hire and promote good-looking men and women and to pay them higher salaries. The good-looking are more likely to receive assistance when they are in trouble. Attractive criminals are less likely than others to get caught, to be reported to the authorities, to be found guilty, or to receive strict sentences.

Society's biases give good-looking men and women a marked advantage in intimate relationships as well. The attractive have an easier time meeting potential dates and mates, attract more appealing dates and mates, and end up with better dating and marital relationships. If, in spite of all these advantages, things go wrong, they find it easier to start anew.

What effect does such stereotyping have on men and women? It turns out that the good-looking and unattractive are not as different as people assume them to be. Self-esteem and self-concept are positively related to how good-looking people think they are but not to actual appearance. In general, the personalities of the attractive and unattractive differ only slightly, if at all.

Attractive and unattractive people do seem to differ in one critical respect, however. The good-looking appear to be more confident in romantic and social situations and to possess more social skills than their peers. People expect the good-looking to be charming, so they treat them as if they are. As a consequence, the good-looking become more socially skilled.

This self-fulfilling aspect of physical attractiveness was demonstrated in a classic study by Snyder, Tanke, and Berscheid (1977). Men and women at the University of Minnesota were recruited for a study on the acquaintance process. First, men were given a Polaroid snapshot and biographical information about their partners. In fact, the snapshot was a fake; it depicted either a beautiful or a homely woman. Men were then asked their first impressions of this "potential date." Those who believed they had been assigned a beautiful partner expected her to be sociable, poised, humorous, and socially skilled. Those who thought they had been assigned an unattractive partner expected her to be unsociable, awkward, serious, and socially inept. Such prejudice is not surprising; it is known that good-looking people make exceptionally good first impressions.

The next set of findings, however, was startling. Men were asked to get acquainted with their partners via a telephone call. Men's expectations had a dramatic impact on the way they talked to their partners. Men who thought they were talking to a beautiful woman were more sociable, sexually warm, interesting, independent, sexually permissive, bold, outgoing, humorous, and socially skilled than were men who thought their partner was homely. The men assigned to an attractive woman were also more comfortable, enjoyed themselves more, liked their partners more, took the initiative more often, and used their voices more effectively. In brief, men who thought they were talking to a beautiful woman tried harder.

Within the space of a telephone conversation, women (regardless of their true appearance) became what men expected them to be. Women who were talked to as if they were beautiful soon began to sound that way. They became unusually animated, confident, and socially skilled. Those who were treated as if they were unattractive became withdrawn, lacked confidence, and seemed awkward. The men's prophecies had been fulfilled.

As a final observation, the evidence makes it clear that the good-looking have an advantage. However, a careful analysis of existing data makes it clear that the relationship between appearance and advantage is not a straightforward one. The extremely attractive have only a small advantage over their more ordinary peers. What is really important is to be at least average. Alas, it is the unattractive and the disfigured who suffer the greatest social costs of prejudice.

REFERENCES

Gangestad, S. W., & Scheyd, G. J. (2005). The evolution of human physical attractiveness. *Annual Review of Anthropology*, 34, 523–548.

Hatfield, E., & Sprecher, S. (1986). *Mirror, mirror: The importance of looks in everyday life*. Albany: State University of New York Press.

Langlois, J. H., & Roggman, L. A. (1990). Attractive faces are only average. *Psychological Science*, 1, 115–121.

Marquardt, S. R. (2002). Marquardt beauty analysis. Retrieved from http://www.beautyanalysis.com.

Rhodes, G., & Zebrowitz, L. A. (Eds.). (2002). *Facial attractiveness: Evolutionary, cognitive, and social perspectives: Vol. 1. Advances in visual cognition*. Westport, CT: Ablex.

Snyder, M., Berscheid, E., & Glick, P. (1985). Focusing on the exterior and the interior: Two investigations of the initiation of personal relationships. *Journal of Personality and Social Psychology*, 48, 1427–1439.

Snyder, M., Tanke, E. D., & Berscheid, E. (1977). Social perception and interpersonal behavior: On the self-fulfilling nature of social stereotypes. *Journal of Personality and Social Psychology*, 35, 656–666.

Thornhill, R., & Gangestad, S. (1993). Human facial beauty: Averageness, symmetry and parasite resistance. *Human Nature*, 4, 237–269.

ELAINE HATFIELD
RICHARD L. RAPSON
University of Hawaii

See also: **Evolutionary Psychology; Pygmalion Effect; Sexual Desire**

PHYSIOLOGICAL PSYCHOLOGY

If psychology is defined as the study of behavior, then physiological psychology (also known as biological psychology) is the study of the physiological bases of behavior. It differs from many disciplines of neuroscience, the study of the nervous system, in its emphasis on behavior. The goal of physiological psychology is to understand how the brain functions to control our learned and unlearned behaviors, as well as our hopes, dreams, emotions, and cognitive processes.

Watsonian behaviorism and Skinnerian experimental analysis of behavior emphasized measurement of stimuli and responses, without reference to intervening physiological variables (Boring, 1950). Not only were concepts such as mind and consciousness abandoned but also there was no reference to independent variables such as hunger (food intake was measured in relation to hours of food deprivation). In contrast, the emphasis in physiological psychology is on the brain as *the* intervening variable in behavior.

The basic unit of the brain is the neuron, a cell specialized for the transduction of information by electrochemical means. There are at least 100 billion neurons in the human brain, and one researcher has estimated that "the number of possible interconnections … is greater than the number of atomic particles that constitute the entire universe" (Thompson, 1967, p. 1). To begin to understand how this complex organ regulates behavior, physiological psychologists must not only be experts in behavioral research methods but also be competent in neuroanatomy, neuropharmacology, neuroendocrinology, and neurophysiology.

Although attempts to explain the relation between brain and behavior can be traced back to Descartes (1596–1650) and Wundt's 1874 textbook, *Foundations of Physiological Psychology* (actually a treatise on psychophysics), physiological psychology had its real beginnings in the early 1900s with the work of Shepherd Franz and his student Karl Lashley, both of whom ablated parts of the brains (brain lesions) of animals in search of "engrams" (localized memory traces). Their work led to the abandonment of the idea that memory was stored in small, localized areas of the brain.

Advances in knowledge with the use of human subjects were limited to studying people with accidental or war-related brain injuries and studies of electrical stimulation of different areas of the cerebral cortex during operations on the brain required for medical reasons. This resulted in the mapping of the cerebral cortex for such things as the somatic sensory area, auditory area, motor area, and speech areas, as well as the finding that the frontal lobes were importantly involved in emotions. However, because the brain is roughly bilaterally symmetrical with regard to gross anatomy (nearly identical neuroanatomical structures are located in both halves of the brain) and accidental injuries never resulted in identical damage to both sides of the brain, until recent times most of our knowledge about brain function and behavior has been achieved with the use of animal subjects.

Below the cerebral cortex, nerve cell bodies cluster together in dense masses called nuclei, and they are connected to one another by nerves (a collection of neuronal fibers). The modern era of physiological psychology began in 1939, when the Horsley-Clarke stereotaxic instrument was adapted for use with rats. The use of an instrument that allowed researchers to place electrodes in precise locations (e.g., nuclei or nerves) on both sides of the brain in an inexpensive laboratory animal resulted in thousands of published studies in the next few decades. Research in the 1940s and 1950s was dominated by lesion studies. If ablation of a nucleus on both sides of the brain eliminated or altered a behavior, it was concluded that the nucleus played a critical role in that behavior (assuming that the effects were not due to elimination of sensory input or motor control). Early hypotheses of brain function followed from this rather crude technique. Motivated behaviors such as hunger were believed to be controlled by localized excitatory and inhibitory brain "centers" (Stellar, 1954; note the similarity to early ideas of how memory was stored). With regard to food intake, for example, feeding behavior in rats stopped when small bilateral

lesions were placed in certain nuclei (the "excitatory center") within an area of the brain called the hypothalamus, whereas overeating and eventual obesity were observed when lesions were made in immediately adjacent medial hypothalamic nuclei (the "inhibitory center").

Electrical stimulation studies of deep nuclei became more common in the 1950s, and in 1960 the first study was published in which behavioral changes (feeding behavior) were observed after neurotransmitter agonists and antagonists were placed directly in hypothalamic nuclei via cannulae (Grossman, 1960). Stereotaxically placed knives that allowed transection of nerves without damage to nuclei were added to the physiological psychologist's research arsenal in the 1970s. With the use of microelectrodes, researchers were able to record the activity of single cells when various stimuli were introduced. The end result of years of research with these different invasive techniques was the abandonment of the centers hypothesis in favor of the idea that motivated behaviors were regulated by circuits within the brain (involving a variety of nuclei and neurotransmitter substances).

The goal of physiological studies with animals is that we might learn something about human brain functions. For deeper (phylogenetically older) brain nuclei involved in food and water intake and sexual behavior, this may be true in at least a general sense. For example, lesions of the medial hypothalamic nuclei that result in overeating in rats also produce overeating and obesity in cats, dogs, primates, and birds, and tumors in this area of the brain in humans have similar effects (King, 2006). However, not only do rats lack the cerebral cortex and frontal lobes that humans have but also brain studies of learning behavior in animals were generally limited to simple classical (Pavlovian), operant, and maze tasks. Thus, particularly for higher-order processes such as learning behavior and problem solving, it is often unclear to what extent it is possible to generalize to human brain functioning. The findings from studies investigating the brains of animal species supported only conjecture about what might also be true of humans, because research investigators lacked noninvasive techniques to study the brain in human subjects.

The implementation of invasive experimental techniques is, for obvious reasons, not a viable option in studying the human brain and behavior. Thus, it is not surprising that attempts to search for and develop alternative, noninvasive techniques suitable for studies with human subjects appeared relatively early during the history of physiological psychology. Perhaps the most notable example of an early noninvasive technique is electroencephalography (EEG), that is, the recording of electrical activity produced by the brain and detected by electrodes placed on the scalp of the subject; it is still widely employed. Besides its classical implementation since the 1930s–1940s as a diagnostic tool for neurological conditions like seizure disorders (Kandel, Schwartz, & Jessell, 2000), EEG has been more recently used in physiological psychology research to uncover some of the finer temporal aspects of overall brain activity changes underlying basic perceptual and even higher-order cognitive processes (such as attention and decision making).

Despite their exquisite temporal resolution to rapid changes in overall brain activity patterns, EEG techniques fall short when it comes to providing adequately detailed information on the spatial localization and size of brain regions that are contributing to the EEG signal. It was not until the 1980s and 1990s that new, powerful, noninvasive technologies affording a higher degree of spatial resolution became available; these included positron emission tomography (PET) and functional magnetic resonance imaging (fMRI). These functional imaging technologies allow researchers to study the activity of different regions of the brain indirectly by measuring physiological changes believed to be related to the activity of neurons in those regions. Over the past 15 years, the implementation of MRI-based techniques has resulted in a wealth of published studies on the human brain activity underlying a wide spectrum of cognitive and behavioral processes, such as perception, motor control, emotion, motivation, language, learning, memory, and decision making, to name a few.

For example, recent PET and MRI-based studies have shed new light on the network of regions of the human brain that are crucially involved in linguistic processes (Posner & Raichle, 1994). Overall, these studies have (1) confirmed earlier clinical findings that showed that certain cortical regions of the left side of the brain are more involved in language than corresponding regions on the right side of the brain and (2) identified other regions of the brain (such as the insular cortex and cerebellum) that appear to be important pieces of the language puzzle that had been previously overlooked. Interestingly, recent MRI studies with our closest relatives, the chimpanzees, indicate some similarity in the asymmetry of the so-called language areas of the brain, when comparing the human and chimpanzee brains (Cantalupo & Hopkins, 2001). These studies support the notion that precursors of linguistic abilities might have been present in our pre-human ancestors and that language might have evolved from manual gestures (Corballis, 2003). Similarly, recent neuroimaging studies in humans have not only verified the role of hypothalamic nuclei in feeding behavior (as previously identified in rat studies) but also identified a network of other nuclei that work with the hypothalamic nuclei to control our daily food intake and body weight (e.g., Liu, Gao, Liu, & Fox, 2000; Tataranni et al., 1999).

The higher spatial resolution of functional imaging techniques, compared with EEG, has allowed researchers to gain much greater insight into the localization and even the interconnectivity in networks of regions of the live human brain involved in particular processes (e.g., language). Nonetheless, current functional imaging technologies are hampered by their relatively poor temporal resolution, which does not allow researchers to grasp in sufficient detail the rapidly changing patterns of regional brain activations over time during cognitive tasks. Because EEG and functional imaging techniques like fMRI show strengths and weaknesses that are somewhat complementary to each other (EEG = high temporal resolution; fMRI = high spatial resolution), the merging of these techniques has the potential to provide yet another very powerful tool for future research endeavors into the inner workings of the human brain.

Another noninvasive technique that has recently been adopted by a number of physiological psychologists is transcranial magnetic stimulation (TMS), which is the localized stimulation of a relatively small area (down to about 1 cm^2) of the surface of the brain by application of strong and rapidly changing magnetic fields (Robertson, Théoret, & Pascual-Leone, 2003). Perhaps the most appealing aspect of TMS is that it allows researchers to induce short-lived "virtual lesions" that temporarily interfere with the electrical activity of a localized region of the cortex of the human brain in a noninvasive fashion. This way, physiological psychologists have been able to map the involvement of different cortical brain regions in a variety of functions, including language and memory, mood and emotion, and neuroplasticity.

Because of its complexity, the brain is the least understood organ of our bodies. Everything that you are doing right now (e.g., holding this book, reading this article, integrating the information with the knowledge that you already have, listening to background music) is controlled by your brain. Yet, despite all of our advances in methodology, our cumulative knowledge only begins to scratch the surface for understanding how the brain works. Physiological psychologists have made progress, but after more than a century of research, we still lack an adequate answer to basic questions such as how information is stored in the brain and how organisms regulate their caloric intake. Given the complexity of the brain, it will probably take new breakthroughs in technology, coupled with concerted efforts by researchers from many different areas of science, before we will be able to claim to have finally solved the puzzle of how the brain regulates behavior.

REFERENCES

Boring, E. G. (1950). *A history of experimental psychology* (2nd ed.). New York: Appleton-Century-Crofts.

Cantalupo, C., & Hopkins, W. D. (2001). Asymmetric Broca's area in great apes. *Nature, 414,* 505 .

Corballis, M. C. (2003). From mouth to hand: Gesture, speech, and the evolution of right-handedness. *Behavioral and Brain Sciences, 26,* 199–260.

Grossman, S. P. (1960). Eating or drinking elicited by direct adrenergic or cholinergic stimulation of hypothalamus. *Science, 132,* 301–302.

Kandel, E. R., Schwartz, J. H., & Jessell, T. M. (2000). *Principles of neural science*. New York: McGraw-Hill.

King, B. M. (2006). The rise, fall, and resurrection of the ventromedial hypothalamus in the regulation of feeding behavior and body weight. *Physiology & Behavior, 87*, 221–244.

Liu, Y., Gao, J. H., Liu, H. L., & Fox, P. T. (2000). The temporal response of the brain after eating revealed by functional MRI. *Nature, 405*, 1058–1062.

Posner, M. I., & Raichle, M. E. (1994). *Images of mind*. New York: Scientific American Library.

Robertson, E. M., Théoret, H., & Pascual-Leone, A. (2003). Studies in cognition: The problems solved and created by transcranial magnetic stimulation. *Journal of Cognitive Neuroscience, 15*, 948–960.

Stellar, E. (1954). The physiology of motivation. *Psychological Review, 61*, 5–22.

Tataranni, P. A., Gautier, J. F., Chen, K., Uecker, A., Bandy, D., Salbe, A. D., et al. (1999). Neuroanatomical correlates of hunger and satiation in humans using positron emission tomography. *Proceedings of the National Academy Sciences, USA, 96*, 4569–4574.

Thompson, R. F. (1967). *Foundations of physiological psychology*. New York: Harper & Row.

SUGGESTED READINGS

Breedlove, S. M., Rosenzweig, M. R., & Watson, N. V. (2007). *Biological psychology* (5th ed.). Sunderland, MA: Sinauer Associates.

Carlson, N. R. (2007). *Foundations of physiological psychology* (6th ed.). Boston: Pearson.

Kalat, J. W. (2007). *Biological psychology* (9th ed.). Belmont, CA: Thomson Wadsworth.

BRUCE M. KING
CLAUDIO CANTALUPO
Clemson University

See also: Brain; Neuroimaging; Neuroscience

PIAGET, JEAN (1896–1980)

Piaget published his first scientific paper at the age of 10 and received his doctorate in 1917, at the age of 21, from the University of Neuchatel, for his research studies on mollusks. After working in a psychology laboratory in Zurich, he went to Paris and to Geneva, where he studied the psychology of thought and was appointed Professor of Psychology in 1940. In 1952, he was named Professor of child psychology at the Sorbonne in Paris. He was actively involved in UNESCO and in educational activities in Switzerland.

Piaget's major interest was in intellectual or cognitive behavior throughout childhood and adolescence. His field was genetic epistemology—the examination of the formation of knowledge itself, that is, of the cognitive relations between subject and objects. Piaget studied the relationships that are formed between the individual known as knower and the world he or she endeavors to know.

The two most important concepts of genetic epistemology are *functional invariants* and *structures*. Functional invariants are cognitive processes that are inborn, universal, and independent of age: accommodations, assimilation, and organization. Structures are defined as intellectual processes that change with age. Piaget's structures are identified in the developmental stages of the period of sensorimotor intelligence, the period of preoperational thought, the period of concrete operations, and the period of formal operations.

The structure of the sensorimotor period (birth to 2 years of age) is circular reaction, a simple sensorimotor adaptive response to a specific stimulus, repeated a number of times. The principal structures of preoperational thought (age 2 years to 6 years) are egocentrism (sees only his or her own point of view), centration (attention to only one feature of a situation), and irreversibility (inability to reverse direction of thinking once started). During the period of concrete operations (ages 6 to 11 years), the main structural concept is grouping, a system of classification. It is a coherent and organized symbolic system of thinking with assimilation and accommodation in balance; intellectual adaptation takes place. In formal operations (ages 11 to 15), a lattice-group structure performs scientific reasoning with hypothesis, predictions, and the testing of these. It is a network of ideas in which everything is related to everything else. The balancing of cognitive growth patterns is called the equilibration process; it is the assimilation of new cognitive structures without destroying the existing structure.

Piaget's early books were based on observations and the experiments conducted with his two daughters. Four volumes appeared between 1926 and 1930 on thought processes and conceptualizations in children. In the 1950s, he published *The Psychology of Intelligence* and *The Origins of Intelligence in the Child*.

SUGGESTED READINGS

Piaget, J. (1936). *Origins of intelligence in the child*. London: Routledge and Kegan Paul.

Piaget, J. (1945). *Play, dreams, and imitation in childhood*. London: Routledge and Kegan Paul.

Piaget, J. (1970). *Main trends in psychology*. London: George Allen & Unwin.

Piaget, J. (1972). *The psychology of intelligence*. Totowa, NJ: Littlefield, Adams.

N. A. HAYNIE
Honolulu, Hawaii

PIAGET'S THEORY

Over the course of some 60 years, Jean Piaget (1896–1980), a Swiss biologist and philosopher, formulated a theory of the development of intellectual competence that continues to influence contemporary theories in this domain. Piaget maintained that logical thought depended on learning, social cooperation, biological maturation, and development, by which he meant a series of fundamental changes such that the later ways of thinking are dependent on, yet qualitatively distinct from, the earlier ones, always moving in the direction of greater logical consistency and coherence. He formulated subsidiary theories of the development of moral judgment and reasoning, perception, images, and memory, but always from the perspective of how each was constrained by various levels of intellectual competence.

Genetic Epistemology

Piaget sought to make a contribution to genetic epistemology, a discipline that was initiated by the American psychologist James Mark Baldwin; that draws on philosophy, psychology, logic, biology, cybernetics, and structuralism; and that treats all aspects of such questions as "What is knowing?" "From whence does it come?" and "What conditions make it possible?" Genetic epistemology, as formulated by Piaget, attributed the development of knowledge and intelligence within the individual and within Western scientific cultures to coordinated twin mechanisms that simultaneously sought to preserve (assimilation) and modify (accommodation) the underlying structure of the mind and the culture.

Piaget held that the fundamental structures of our minds are not given a priori but are constructed through evolving systems by which we act on and transform the environment and our own minds. The succeeding levels or stages of the mind are always reformulations or reconstructions of the preceding ways of acting on the world and validating knowledge. They always afford more consistent ways of acting on the world, and they are always more coherent than the preceding ways.

The Epistemic Subject

Piaget's theory of intellectual development is about an idealized person, a person who probably does not exist but who could exist. The person is the epistemic subject, the pure knower who has no individual characteristics—no personality, gender, motivation (other than to know), culture, or nationality—and the theory is about that person. Although Piaget's description of the child's competence to do logical problem solving does not fully account for what the child will in fact do in a problem situation, it does account for what the child can do if no other factors are present to mitigate the performance. Whereas the epistemic subject merely understands and knows events, the ordinary person succeeds in any number of tasks, and often without any understanding of this success. In fact, this lag between success on a task and understanding the task was a topic that Piaget also addressed.

The epistemic subject knows those truths that are necessarily true as opposed to those that are merely true. For example, when A = B and B = C, not only is it true empirically that A = C but also it is necessarily true and must be true; it could not possibly be otherwise, and there is no need to directly examine A and C in any way to know that A equals C and must equal C. At its core, Piaget's theory is about the development of truths that have to be as they are and could not conceivably be different from what they are.

The Clinical Method

In virtually all of Piaget's psychological research, children are seen individually, given some materials or an apparatus to manipulate, and asked questions tailored to children's responses about what they did. What the child says or believes about what was done is important, but greater emphasis is placed on what the child actually does, how the problem is tackled, what errors the child makes, and so forth. Invariably, the child is asked to think about a common childhood event, such as flattening a clay ball or playing marbles, in a new way, or to consider a new possibility in an ordinary childlike task such as lining up sticks in order by their lengths.

The tasks or problems set for the children were usually designed to reveal the structure of the child's reasoning about some epistemological question, like the nature of causality, necessity, implication, time or space, and so forth. They were designed, unlike many contemporary educational assessments, to uncover what the child knows and can do, and not what the child does not know and cannot do.

The Stages of Intellectual Development

All Piaget claimed in his 53 books and 523 articles was that he had developed a general outline or skeleton of a theory, with gaps to be filled in by others. Even with respect to the number of stages of intellectual development, there was some variation in his work from time to time, but most accounts set forth four main stages: the sensorimotor stage (0–2 years), with six substages; the preoperational stage (2–7 years), with two substages; the concrete operational stage (7–12 years), with two substages; and the formal operational stage (12 years and up). Within each stage and substage, Piaget frequently distinguished three levels: failure, partial success, and success. In the final versions of the theory, development was viewed not as linear progression through the stages but as an open-ended spiral in which the differentiated forms and content at one level are reworked, restructured, integrated, or synthesized at the higher levels of the spiral.

Sensorimotor Stage

The six substages of this stage show the following developments: The infant exhibits (1) innate reflexes and an inability to think, have purpose, or distinguish himself or herself from the surroundings; (2) reflexes extended to repetitive actions; (3) the ability to reproduce fortuitous, pleasant, and interesting events; (4) increased coordination of ways to make the interesting things last; (5) discovery of new ways to produce interesting results; and (6) an ability to represent absent events symbolically. The principal accomplishments are the construction of coordinated movements, which have a grouplike mathematical structure; the construction of representation; the idea of permanent objects; and intentionality.

Preoperational Stage

This stage is often characterized more by what the child cannot do than by what the child can do. Thought seems rigidly captured by one aspect of a situation, often the child's own point of view (egocentrism), to the exclusion of other perspectives. Thought, besides being centered on a single salient feature of an event, seems to flow in sequences of simple juxtaposition rather than sequences of logical implication or physical causality. Children's reasons for their responses are often preposterous but lawful fabrications, or what Piaget called "justifications at any price."

Concrete Operational Stage

The errors the child makes during the preoperational stage are corrected in the following stage, but not uniformly or all at once. The solutions to problems are worked out separately in various domains. For example, the notion of invariance (conservation) is acquired separately and sequentially for the following domains and in the following order: number, length and mass, area, weight, time, and volume.

Formal Operational Stage

The young adolescent is able to consider all possibilities and to vary all but one in an analysis of a physical event. The ability to hypothetically vary all but one of the possible dimensions of a situation means that form can be considered and manipulated apart from its content and that reality can be conceptually subservient to possibility.

Neo-Piagetian Theory

Subsequent work by neo-Piagetian theorists has reinforced and expanded Piaget's constructivist stance and argued for ongoing intellectual development beyond adolescence that extended formal thought to new areas but based formal operations on structures that were less universal, more domain-specific, and associated with areas of schooled expertise. The course of development was taken to be more gradual, less punctuated, more socially and culturally dependent, and more integrated with other mental functions (like emotion and motivation) than in the field's interpretations of Piaget's initial formulations.

In addition, Piaget's theory of mental development has been used by contemporary scholars as an analytic tool to explicate features of many domains that have a developmental component, such as history (history of religion, science, art, drama, faith development, art history, and drama), evolution, and artificial intelligence.

SUGGESTED READINGS

Flavell, J. (1963). *The developmental psychology of Jean Piaget*. New York: D. Van Nostrand.

Vuyk, R. (1981). *Overview and critique of Piaget's genetic epistemology, 1965–1980* (2 vols.). New York: Academic Press.

FRANK B. MURRAY
University of Delaware

See also: **Cognitive Development; Intellectual Development**

PICK'S DISEASE

Pick's disease is a neurodegenerative dementing illness first described by Arnold Pick in 1892. Pick's original description, as reviewed by Kertsez (2007), was based on clinical cases of aphasia and behavioral abnormalities that corresponded to focal atrophy of the temporal and frontal lobes. The description of focal neurodegeneration was a new concept, as atrophy was felt to be a diffuse process at the time (Kertsez, 2007). Pick's original studies were limited to gross examination. Alois Alzheimer was the first to describe histological features of these patients in 1911 (Rossor, 2001). He found argyrophilic intraneuronal inclusion bodies, composed of the microfilament protein tau, in affected brain regions in these patients and "ballooned" achromatic cells, with relative sparing of the hippocampus and lack of neurofibrillary tangles or plaques (Rossor, 2001). These inclusion bodies, thought to be characteristic of all patients fitting Pick's original description, were named Pick bodies, and the degenerating neurons were

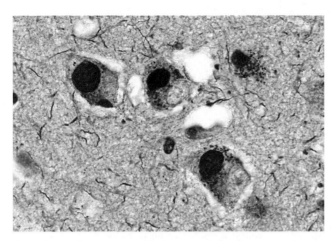

Figure 1. Cortical neurons displaying round intracellular tau inclusions (Pick bodies) in a PD patient. (Modified Bielschowsky silver stain 60x).

named Pick cells (see Figure 1). Onari and Spatz outlined criteria for diagnosis in 1926 with a strong emphasis on macroscopic features, including frontal atrophy and neuronal depletion in superficial cortical layers, with occasional presence of Pick bodies or Pick cells (Uchihara, Ikeda, & Tsuchiya, 2003). As it became apparent that not all clinical cases of Pick's disease contained the Pick bodies or Pick cells, characterization and nomenclature became problematic.

Nomenclature

Currently, Pick's disease refers only to cases of frontal and temporal atrophy combined with the presence of Pick bodies in postmortem examination. The term frontotemporal lobar degeneration (FTLD) refers to clinical cases of behavioral and executive dysfunction with atrophy in the frontal and/or anterior temporal lobes. While Pick's name is now limited to one pathological subtype of the clinical entity he originally described, some authorities have suggested the term Pick's complex (Kertsez, 2007) or Pick syndrome (Uchihara et al., 2003) to include all pathologic and clinical subtypes of FTLD to limit confusion. There are three clinical subtypes of FTLD corresponding to anatomically affected regions of the brain. The frontal variant (fvFTD or FTD) corresponds to bifrontal atrophy, whereas semantic dementia (SD) reflects a bilateral anterior temporal predominant type, and progressive nonfluent aphasia (PA or PNFA) refers to an asymmetric left frontotemporal predominant type (Neary et al., 1998).

Cairns and colleagues (2007) suggest an algorithm for pathologic diagnosis of FTD cases based on immunohistological staining of postmortem brain tissue. The main histological subtypes are based on the presence or absence of abnormal tau accumulations (tauopathies). FTLD tauopathies include Pick's disease; frontotemporal dementia with Parkinsonism (*MAPT* gene mutation on chromosome 17); corticobasal degeneration (CBD), an asymmetric Parkinsonian degenerative disease; and

progressive supranuclear palsy (PSP), another atypical Parkinsonian disease marked by axial rigidity and restricted eye movements. Nontauopathy forms (FTLD-U) display ubiquitinated inclusion bodies, which have recently been discovered to contain the DNA-binding protein TDP-43. A subset of FTLD-U patients have mutations in the gene for a growth factor, progranulin. Patients with amyotrophic lateral sclerosis (ALS) and frontal lobe dysfunction (FTD-MND) also display TDP-43 type reactivity. Finally, dementia lacking distinctive pathology (DLDH) displays similar gross degeneration without ubiquitin or tau reactive inclusions. It is intriguing that multiple protein substrates cause similar clinical manifestations, in some cases with associated motor disease.

Clinical Features

Patients with FTLD show variable expression of frontal lobe dysfunction (behavioral abnormalities and dysexecutive syndrome) and temporal lobe impairment (language problems including aphasia). Visuospatial skills and memory are relatively spared, as the medial temporal lobe is usually free of pathology. More specifically, involvement in the ventral median (orbitobasal) frontal lobe areas gives rise to symptoms of disinhibition, antisocial behavior, poor impulse control, stereotyped behaviors, aggressiveness, restlessness, and pressured speech (Boxer & Miller, 2005). Features of the Kluver-Bucy syndrome may be present late in the disease, including hyperorality and hypersexuality (Hodges, 2001).

Stereotypical behavior many times involves features of obsessive-compulsive disorder, and these patients often present first to psychiatric clinics. Symptoms of apathy and depression originate from the anterior cingulate gyrus and medial frontal lobes; involvement of the dorsal lateral prefrontal cortex is manifest in the dysexecutive syndrome (Hodges, 2001), which includes difficulty in planning, forming concepts, abstract thinking, reasoning, self-monitoring, and set-shifting (Boxer & Miller, 2005). Neuropsychological test batteries are effective in identifying these problems, including the Wisconsin Card Sorting Test, the Stroop Interference Test, the Verbal Fluency Test, and the Neuropsychiatric Inventory; the Folstein Mini-Mental State exam may not be sensitive to these cognitive domains (Hodges, 2001). These symptoms are the hallmark of the fvFTD variant but are also present in SD late in the course.

The SD variant is manifested by severe language disturbance. The main deficit is loss of semantic memory, the long-term memory component of knowledge of items in the environment and their relationships and meaning (Hodges, 2001). Patients are fluent but do not display an understanding of word meaning. Semantic paraphasias and phrase substitutions are common, and patients may have difficulty in identifying simple objects (Boxer &

Miller, 2005). These deficits correspond to anterior temporal lobe degeneration, more specifically in the inferior and middle temporal gyri (Neary et al., 1998). Patients with more right-sided pathology may develop difficulty in recognizing faces (proposagnosia) (Hodges, 2001). The Boston Naming Test and category fluency tasks are sensitive to abnormalities in this cognitive domain (Boxer & Miller, 2005). With increasing cognitive decline, patients progressively lose specific categories for objects.

Degeneration of the left perisylvian frontotemporal areas, including Brodman areas 44 and 45, produce a severe anomia and aphasia typical of the PA subtype (Boxer & Miller, 2005). These patients are not fluent in their speech and often progress to mutism (Hodges, 2001). Agrammatisms, problems with proper grammatical sentence construction; phenome paraphasias, the substitution of one sound for another; and apraxia of speech are also common (Boxer & Miller, 2005). Patients usually can comprehend speech well until late in the disease (Hodges, 2001). Behavioral abnormalities are minimal, and insight is usually preserved, leading to high rates of depression (Boxer & Miller, 2005). Neuropsychiatric testing of word rhyming and repetition uncovers deficits in these patients (Hodges, 2001).

Diagnosis

The main diagnostic dilemma is Alzheimer's disease (AD), but also included in the differential diagnosis are vascular dementia, Lewy body disease (LBD), mild cognitive impairment (MCI), Creutzfeldt-Jakob disease (CJD), depression, and psychiatric disorders. FTLD is the third most common dementia after AD and LBD (Neary et al., 1998) and may be more common in patients younger than age 60 (Boxer & Miller, 2005). The main differentiating features of FTLD from AD are presenile onset, lack of myoclonus, lack of amnesia or short-term memory loss, the presence of stereotypical behaviors, and carbohydrate craving (Hodges, 2001; Neary et al., 1998). Premorbid diagnosis rests on clinical evaluation, including a thorough neurological examination, neuropsychological testing as previously outlined, and neuroimaging. Magnetic resonance imaging (MRI) can yield important diagnostic information, as regions of gross brain atrophy can be identified. This is especially evident with the use of voxel measurements of brain regions. Functional imaging, including positron emission tomography (PET) and single photon emission computed tomography (SPECT), can also aid in diagnosis by using real-time measurements of brain metabolism.

Treatment

Treatment for FTLD and variants is limited. Current treatment strategies are based on neurotransmitter replacement rather than the pathogenesis of the disease (Huey, Putnam, & Grafman, 2006). In addition, a symptom-targeted approach can be beneficial (Boxer & Boeve, 2007). Serotonergic pathways are likely to be the most affected neurotransmitter system in FTLD. Most studies of the serotonin system in FTLD show a relative deficiency, which may account for the psychological features of the disease, including depression and compulsiveness (Huey et al., 2006). Serotonin-based treatment is most effective for the disinhibition, depression, and dietary changes seen in these patients, but personality changes and language function are very refractory to treatment (Boxer & Boeve, 2007). Lebert Stekke, Hasenbroekx, and Pasquier (2004) found the antidepressant trazodone to have a significant effect on adverse behaviors of FTLD through a double-blind placebo-controlled study, though its use may be limited because of the side effect of excessive fatigue (Boxer & Boeve, 2007; Huey et al., 2006). Meta-analysis showed an improvement in the neuropsychiatric inventory (NPI) scores of FTLD patients treated with serotonergic drugs (Huey et al., 2006), making this class of drug the first-line treatment for behavioral symptoms; symptoms not amenable to SSRI treatment may respond to atypical antipsychotics (Boxer & Boeve, 2007). As mentioned before, many cases of FTLD are associated with Parkinsonism and may be sensitive to the extrapyramidal side effects of these drugs (Boxer & Boeve, 2007). Methylphenidate, a stimulant that acts on dopaminergic, noradrenergic, and serotonergic transport, reduced risk-taking behavior in one double-blind placebo-controlled study (Rahman et al., 2006). The cholinergic system is relatively spared in this disease, and anticholinesterase agents are rarely effective in this patient population (Huey et al., 2006).

The behavioral disturbances can cause great functional impairment and stress on family. In addition, many long-term care nursing facilities are not equipped with adequate resources for behavioral modification therapy and the monitoring that these patients may require. An additional challenge is the younger age of onset compared with AD, making some patients difficult to place in long-term nursing care facilities. Newer treatments will focus on the pathogenesis of this disease and modify the disease course. Pick's original description has now expanded to include many different clinical and pathological subtypes as more links are discovered through advances in brain imaging, neuropsychiatric evaluation, immunohistochemistry, and genetic analysis.

REFERENCES

Boxer, A., & Boeve, B. (2007). Frontotemporal dementia treatment: Current symptomatic therapies and implications. *Alzheimer's Disease and Associated Disorders, 21*(4), s79–s87.

Boxer, A., & Miller, B. (2005). Clinical features of frontotemporal dementia. *Alzheimer's Disease and Associated Disorders, 19*(s1), s3–s6.

Cairns, N., Bigio, E., Mackenzie, I., et al. (2007). Neuropathologic diagnostic and nosologic criteria for frontotemporal lobar degeneration: Consensus of the consortium for frontotemporal lobar degeneration. *Acta Neuropathologica, 114,* 5–22.

Hodges, J. R. (2001). Frontotemporal dementia (Pick's disease): Clinical features and assessment. *Neurology, 56*(11s4), s6–s10.

Huey, E., Putnam, K., & Grafman, J. (2006). A systematic review of neurotransmitter deficits and treatments in frontotemporal dementia. *Neurology, 66*(1), 17–22.

Kertsez, A. (2007). Pick complex: Historical introduction. *Alzheimer's Disease and Associated Disorders, 21*(4), s5–s7.

Lebert, F., Stekke, W., Hasenbroekx, C., & Pasquier, F. (2004). Frontotemporal dementia: A randomized, controlled trial with trazodone. *Dementia and Geriatric Cognitive Disorders, 17*(4), 355–359.

Neary, D., Snowden, J., Gustafson, L., et al. (1998). Frontotemporal lobar degeneration: A consensus on clinical diagnostic criteria. *Neurology, 51*(6), 1546–1554.

Rahman, S., Robbins, T. W., Hodges, J. R., Mehta, M., Nestor, P. J., Clark, L., et al. (2006). Methylphenidate (Ritalin) can ameliorate abnormal risk-taking behavior in frontal variant of frontotemporal dementia. *Neuropharmacology, 31,* 651–658.

Rossor, M. N. (2001). Pick's disease: A clinical overview. *Neurology, 56*(11, s4), s3–s5.

Uchihara, T., Ikeda, K., & Tsuchiya, K. (2003). Pick body disease and Pick syndrome. *Neuropathology, 23,* 318–326.

SUGGESTED READINGS

Caselli R. J., & Yaari R. (2007) Medical management of frontotemporal dementia. *American Journal of Alzheimer's Disease and Other Dementias, 22*(6), 489–498.

Goldman, J. S., Adamson, J., Karydas, A., et al. (2007). New genes, new dilemmas: FTLD genetics and its implications for families. *American Journal of Alzheimer's Disease and Other Dementias, 22*(6), 507–515.

Hallam, B. J., Silverberg, N. D., Lamarre, A. K., et al. (2007). Clinical presentation of prodromal frontotemporal dementia. *American Journal of Alzheimer's Disease and Other Dementias, 22*(6), 456–467.

Rademakers, R., Baker, M., Gass, J., et al. (2007). An international initiative to study phenotypic variability associated with progranulin haploinsufficiency in patients with the common c.1477C>T (p.R493X) mutation. *Lancet Neurology, 6,* 857–868.

DAVID IRWIN
CAROL F. LIPPA
Drexel University College of Medicine

See also: **Dementia**

PITUITARY GLAND

The small gland beneath the brain's hypothalamus received the name *pituitary* in the early seventeenth century because of the mistaken notion that the structure made phlegm. Pituitary comes from the Latin *pituita,* which means "phlegm." The pituitary gland is also called the *hypophysis,* which is Greek for "undergrowth."

The pituitary is divided into two major parts or lobes: the anterior lobe or adenohypophysis and the posterior lobe or neurohypophysis. The structure is connected to the hypothalamus by the infundibulum or hypophyseal stalk. A schematic drawing of the gland is shown in Figure 1.

Anterior Lobe or Adenohypophysis

Because of its role in the control of other endocrine glands, the pituitary is often called the master gland of the body. This designation is more appropriately applied to the pituitary's anterior lobe, as the adenohypophysis manufactures and secretes hormones that regulate the body's most important glands (e.g., the adrenal glands, the thyroid gland, the gonads). In fact, the prefix *adeno-* means "of a gland."

The anterior lobe of the pituitary is derived from skin cells from the roof of the mouth, and the surgical approach to the pituitary is through the roof of the mouth, which should give you a better appreciation of the gland's location in your head. Although it is not in direct neural contact with the brain, the adenohypophysis is regulated by the hypothalamus, which secretes releasing factors that travel to the anterior lobe through blood vessels called the hypophyseal portal system. The releasing factors are peptides, and they modulate the secretion of anterior lobe hormones such as somatotropin, thyrotropin, adrenocorticotropin, lactogenic hormone, and the gonadotropins.

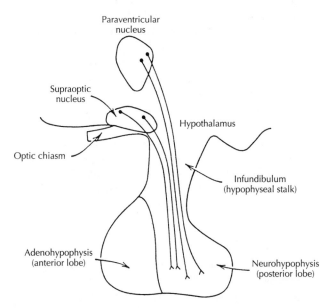

Figure 1. Schematic drawing showing the relationship of the posterior lobe (neurohypophysis) to the hypothalamus. The anterior lobe (adenohypophysis) is functionally connected to the hypothalamus by blood vessels (not shown).

Somatotropin (STH) is a growth-promoting hormone and, in fact, is usually called growth hormone. Its presence at appropriate developmental periods is essential for normal growth. Too much can produce a distorted growth problem called acromegaly; too little results in dwarfism.

Thyrotropin (TSH or thyroid-stimulating hormone) acts on the thyroid gland to promote the synthesis, storage, and release of the thyroid hormones thyroxine (T_4) and triiodothyronine (T_3). Thyroid hormones are involved in regulating the body's metabolism.

Adrenocorticotropin (ACTH or adrenocorticotropic hormone) stimulates the production and release of hormones by the adrenal cortex (the adrenal glands are above the kidneys). ACTH triggers the release of glucocorticoids (for example, cortisol), which are important in carbohydrate metabolism and in the body's resistance to stress. ACTH itself is released in response to physical or emotional stress.

Lactogenic hormone (LTH or prolactin) acts on the mammary glands to promote milk secretion. Prolactin also may be important for parental behaviors in vertebrates.

The gonadotropins (luteinizing hormone and follicle-stimulating hormone) act on the gonads. Luteinizing hormone (LH), for example, is necessary for ovulation in females. In males, LH acts on cells in the testes to cause them to produce testosterone.

Posterior Lobe or Neurohypophysis

Unlike the anterior lobe, which receives no direct neural innervation, the posterior lobe of the pituitary, or neurohypophysis, contains the axonic nerve terminals from two hypothalamic nuclei: the supraoptic and the paraventricular. The supraoptic nuclei predominantly synthesize vasopressin, known as antidiuretic hormone (ADH). ADH acts primarily on the kidneys to regulate water balance. Lack of ADH secondary to disease, trauma, or genetic vulnerability causes diabetes insipidus, a serious disorder characterized by excessive drinking and urination.

The paraventricular nuclei predominantly manufacture oxytocin, which is a smooth-muscle-contracting hormone. Oxytocin plays an important role in inducing the contractions of the uterine walls during the birth process; that is, oxytocin is responsible for labor pains. In addition, it is required for the release of milk in response to suckling. In males, oxytocin regulates prostate gland function.

SUGGESTED READINGS

Afifi, A. K., & Bergman, R. A. (1998). *Functional neuroanatomy.* New York: McGraw-Hill.

Klein, S. B., & Thorne, B. M. (2007). *Biological psychology.* New York: Worth.

B. MICHAEL THORNE
Mississippi State University

PLACEBO

A placebo is a substance that has little or no active pharmacological effect on the symptoms for which it is administered. The placebo effect occurs when inert substances, such as sugar pills, are given in place of active medications and the recipient's condition changes in the desired direction. Placebo treatments may also include the prescription of substances with known physiological effects but a mechanism of action that is unrelated to the patient's presenting problem (e.g., prescribing vitamins for a chronic pain condition). In this case, the placebo is given with the hope of promoting improved health through increased positive expectancies on the part of the patient. Because the recipient is not aware of the inactive nature of the placebo, the observed changes are often attributed to positive expectations about the treatment.

Prescribing placebo treatments was common in the United States until the middle of the twentieth century, when medications with known chemical mechanisms of action became available (Shapiro, 1971). Even though the placebo effect has been found in the treatment of a variety of ailments, including the common cold, diabetes, postoperative pain, arthritis, multiple sclerosis, headaches, and many others (Ross & Olson, 1981), the administration of placebo treatments today is an ethically controversial topic. Because the patient is unaware of the nature of the medication being given, these treatments and the physicians who administer them have been criticized for incorporating deceptive practices and violating the ethical principle of patient autonomy (i.e., the right of patients to make informed decisions about their treatment).

Advocates, however, cite the substantial improvement attributed to placebos in both clinical practice and randomized trials, and they argue that placebos can be administered without deceiving patients. A recent study of 679 internists and rheumatologists in the United States found that approximately half of the physicians surveyed routinely prescribe placebo treatments and that more than half find this practice ethically permissible. Furthermore, of the physicians who reported prescribing placebos, 68% stated that they tell patients the placebo is a medication that is not often used to treat the patient's condition but that might be beneficial, rather than explicitly telling the patient that the medication is a placebo (Tilburt, Emanuel, Kaptchuk, Curlin, & Miller, 2008).

In clinical trials, a placebo is often used as an alternative condition against which an active treatment is compared. One way to control for the placebo effect in pharmacological studies is to use a single- or double-blind experimental design. In a single-blind design, participants are not informed as to whether they are in an experimental or control condition, and hence they are unaware of which substance or procedure they are receiving; the researchers, however, are not blind to the participant's condition. In double-blind studies, both participants and experimenters are unaware of the participant's treatment condition. This helps to guard against experimenter expectancies and the intentional and unintentional influence these interactions may have on the dependent variables.

Even the administration of active drugs, however, carries an accompanying expectation of improvement, thereby presenting a potential confound to any research study. Relative improvement of the experimental group as compared with the placebo group (with both exhibiting expectation effects) is often attributed to the active drug. The problem, of course, is that very few studies incorporate a no-treatment condition, so it is very difficult to determine whether symptom improvement is truly due to (1) the active ingredient in the medication, (2) the positive expectancies that accompany both placebo and active treatments, (3) the natural course of the illness itself, or (4) other factors.

These research findings regarding placebos are problematic, as a multitude of clinical trials have found that patients report significant improvements in their illnesses following placebo treatment. This is a common criticism of studies of antidepressant medications (ADMs). For example, Kirsch, Moore, Scoboria, and Nicholls (2002) conducted a meta-analysis of ADM studies using the FDA database, which includes data from all studies conducted under FDA watch, rather than limiting their sample to only the studies in which medications were superior to placebos. They found an 18% difference between ADMs and placebo treatments based on a clinical interview assessing treatment outcome (an average of 2 points on the Hamilton Depression Scale); furthermore, they report that approximately 80% of the improvement seen in the medication group was also seen in the placebo group, leading the authors of this meta-analysis to question the clinical value of ADMs over placebos.

From another perspective, Hrobjartsson and Gotzsche (2001) conducted a meta-analysis comparing the placebo effect to a no-treatment control condition in a wide variety of illnesses (e.g., asthma, depression, pain, obesity, and insomnia). They found little evidence to support the claim that placebos exert substantive clinical effects. In addition, they note that the placebo effect was negatively correlated with sample size in the studies they examined. These authors conclude that "the use of placebo outside the aegis of a controlled, properly designed clinical trial cannot be recommended" (p. 1599). The discrepancies in findings between these two meta-analyses illustrate the depth of the gulf that exists between the poles of opinion on this topic. Unfortunately, as yet there is no easy answer for the consumer or the clinician, and further research is needed to more fully illuminate the role of the placebo in modern medicine.

Several theories have been proposed to explain the mechanisms of action underlying the placebo effect. One common hypothesis is that the administration of a placebo helps alleviate the patient's distress and anxiety, which in turn is related to symptom improvement. Another hypothesis is that placebos operate in much the same way as classically conditioned stimuli; that is, active agents are unconditioned stimuli and the instruments that are used for treatment administration (pills, syringes, etc.) are conditioned stimuli (Wickramasekera, 1980). Over time, several conditioning trials occur in which the two stimuli are paired during medical treatments. Eventually, the pills and syringes acquire the ability to independently elicit a curative response. A third possibility is that patients may simply report improvements because they believe this is what the experimenter desires, a phenomenon known as the good subject tendency.

In addition, it is important to consider the possibility that the placebo may actually evoke real somatic changes in the patient. One hypothesis regarding the physiological underpinnings of the placebo effect is that the expectation of improvement following placebo administration activates the endorphin system. Endorphins are often referred to as endogenous morphine, and they serve an important role in pain reduction. Levine, Gordon, and Fields (1978) investigated this hypothesis by using the opiate antagonist naloxone. As predicted, the administration of naloxone interfered with placebo analgesia in postoperative dental pain. These findings indicate that placebos may operate through activation of chemical neural circuits in addition to cognitive and emotional systems.

More recently, Mayberg and colleagues (2002) conducted a study using positron emission tomography (PET) to examine brain changes associated with placebo administration. In this study, depressed men received either fluoxetine (Prozac) or placebo in a double-blind 6-week trial, and all participants underwent pretreatment and posttreatment PET scanning. Half of the participants achieved symptom remission; notably, half of these remitters received fluoxetine, and the other half received placebo. Although fluoxetine response was associated with additional metabolic changes in the subcortical and limbic systems, investigators found considerable overlap in metabolic change in the cortical and paralimbic regions of the brain across both conditions. Hence, both interventions were associated with overlapping yet unique posttreatment neuroanatomical changes.

Bailar (2001) provides an apt metaphor for the myriad clinical and ethical complexities of the placebo effect. He invokes the story of *The Wizard of Oz*, in which each of the characters, through the power of positive expectation, got what they came for from the wizard. When Dorothy's dog, Toto, pulled back the curtain to reveal an ordinary man instead of a wizard, Dorothy and her friends realized that they had had the power to heal their own ailments all along and that the "wizard" had no special powers. The dilemma, however, is ever present: Would they have arrived at this conclusion on their own, had they never sought out the wizard in the first place?

REFERENCES

Bailar, J. C. (2001). The powerful placebo and the Wizard of Oz. *New England Journal of Medicine, 344*, 1630–1632.

Hrobjartsson, A., & Gotzsche, P. C. (2001). Is the placebo powerless? An analysis of clinical trials comparing placebo with no treatment. *New England Journal of Medicine, 344*, 1594–1602.

Kirsch, I., Moore, T. J., Scoboria, A., & Nicholls, S. S. (2002). The emperor's new drugs: An analysis of antidepressant medication data submitted to the U.S. Food and Drug Administration. *Prevention and Treatment, 5*, art. 23. Retrieved December 30, 2008, from http://journals.apa.org/prevention/volume5/pre0050023a.html.

Levine, J. D., Gordon, N. C., & Fields, H. L. (1978). The mechanism of placebo analgesia. *Lancet, 2*, 654–657.

Ross, M., & Olson, J. M. (1981). An expectancy–attribution model of the effects of placebos. *Psychological Review, 88*, 408–437.

Shapiro, A. K. (1971). Placebo effects in medicine, psychotherapy, and psychoanalysis. In A. E. Bergin & S. L. Garfield (Eds.), *Handbook of psychotherapy and behavior change: Empirical analysis.* New York: John Wiley & Sons.

Tilburt, J. C., Emanuel, E. J., Kaptchuk, T. J., Curlin, F. A., & Miller, F. G. (2008). Prescribing "placebo treatments": Results of national survey of U.S. internists and rheumatologists. *British Medical Journal, 337*, a1938.

Wickramasekera, I. (1980). A conditioned response model of the placebo effect: Predictions from the model. *Biofeedback and Self-Regulation, 5*, 5–18.

SUGGESTED READINGS

Beecher, H. K. (1955). The powerful placebo. *Journal of the American Medical Association, 159*, 1602–1609.

Guess, H., Engel, L., Kleinman, A., & Kusek, J. (Eds.). (2002). *Science of the placebo: Toward an interdisciplinary research agenda.* London: BMJ Books.

REBECCA Y. STEER
EMORY UNIVERSITY
LORIE A. RITSCHEL
Emory University School of Medicine

PLAY

The concept *play* is much like an inkblot, open to many different and quite varied interpretations. Nonetheless, the idea that play is a basic and vital human disposition has been recognized by a wide variety of writers. Philosopher Friedrich Schiller regarded play as crucial to the human experience (Schiller, 1967). For Schiller, play is the activity that allows humans to realize their highest aspirations and ideals. Johan Huizinga titled his book *Homo Ludens* (Huizinga, 1950) and argued that play was a defining human characteristic. Play, he contended, is the driving force in the evolution of civilization. Other writers on play make the case that it as a major dynamic in linguistics (Derrida, 2007), in literature (Wilson, 1990), and in game theory (Callois, 1961/2001). These diverse approaches to the meaning and purpose of play help to explain why psychologist Brian Sutton-Smith (Sutton-Smith, 1997) titled a book *The Ambiguity of Play.* The present article, however, will concern only those theories that have direct psychological implications and relevance.

Theories of Play

Psychologist and philosopher Herbert Spencer (Spencer 1896/1855) was very much taken by Darwin's theory of evolution. He proposed that play emerged as a by-product of evolving civilization. The higher the level of civilization, the less energy we need to expend to obtain the basic necessities of life. Our bodies, however, have not changed in accord with social progress. We remain biologically programmed to expend large amounts of energy to ensure survival. The growth of civilization means, therefore, that we have surplus energy. For Spencer, play is the means by which we discharge the surplus energy we once expended to meet our basic needs for food, shelter, and protection. In his view, modern children no longer need to struggle for survival and thus have a great deal of energy to spare. Children discharge this surplus energy through their play. The counterargument is, of course, that young animals, without higher civilization, still play.

Zoologist Karl Groos first studied play in animals (Groos, 1898) and then researched play in humans (Groos, 1901). As a result of his animal studies, Groos proposed the thesis that the play of young animals was a preparation for adult life. Through their play, the young of the species learn the survival skills they will require once they are fully grown. The young kitten pouncing on a ball of cotton thread was, Groos wrote, honing the skills it would need, as a grown cat, to catch a mouse. His study of human play led him to apply the same thesis to children. He maintained that when children are engaged in dramatic play—as doctor, teacher, nurse, and so forth—they, too, are learning the adaptive skills needed for survival in adult life. The analogy to children, however, really doesn't work. The skills a kitten learns in playing with a ball are, indeed, very much like the skills it will use when going after its prey as a grown cat. But children playing doctor, teacher, or nurse are not really practicing the skills employed by grown professionals in these occupations.

Italian educator Maria Montessori (Montessori, 1967) accepted and advocated the Groos theory of play. Montessori took Groos quite literally and believed that play should always serve a socializing purpose. She translated this thesis into her now famous dictum, "Play is the child's work." For Montessori, play was valuable only to the extent that it served an educational goal. Montessori's attitude toward play is perhaps best illustrated by her comment about imagination. Montessori wrote that "if children can imagine fairy tale kingdoms, they might better put this ability to use by imagining foreign countries like America" (Montessori, 1967). Montessori thus accepted the commonly held position that play and work are in opposition to one another. From this standpoint, work is hard and adaptive, while play is just having fun with few redeeming virtues. As described next, however, the identification of play and work runs counter to the theories and research of the two giants of psychology, Freud and Piaget.

Sigmund Freud did not regard play as a basic human drive, but he did believe it served an important therapeutic purpose. Freud likened play to the dream, "the life of the mind while asleep." Like the dream, play is the mind's way of realizing socially unacceptable thoughts, wishes, and desires in a disguised way. The disguising activity, the dream work, was carried out by primary process thinking. This is a form of thinking in which ideas are joined by their emotional valence rather than by rational linkages. In the dream, two fear-related events are joined because they were both fearful, despite happening at quite different times and places. Freud contrasted *primary process* affective thinking with *secondary process* rational thinking. The ego, the executive agent of the personality, uses the secondary process to adapt to the real world. It is necessarily logical and bounded by the limits of space, time, and causality. In outlining these two basic processes of mental functioning, Freud clearly distinguished between the processes utilized by play and those used for adaptation to the real world.

Psychoanalyst Ernst Kris (Kris, 1952) took Freud's theory further and argued that primary process thinking, when combined with rational thought, is the basis for imagination and creativity. He spoke of "regression in the service of the ego." In effect, creative artists take something from themselves (primary process) and something from the environment (secondary process) and create a product that cannot be reduced to either.

Swiss psychologist Jean Piaget has given us one of the most general theories of children's play (Piaget, 1951). Piaget, like Spencer, was very much a student of Darwin. His basic proposition was both simple and profound. Piaget contended that human intelligence—adaptive thinking and action—was an extension of our biological processes of adaptation. One of these processes is *assimilation*. Assimilation always involves a transformation of the world to meet the demands of the self. Piaget regarded play as one form of assimilation, a form involving the nonlogical processes of imagination and fantasy.

One way of defining play, therefore, is as the modification of experience as a result of behavior. Through play, children create new learning experiences that they could not encounter in any other way. Babbling is a case in point. No one teaches an infant to babble. However, through its nonrational babbling, the infant produces all the sounds it will need to learn its native language. Without playful babbling, the child would never learn spoken language. Piaget's idea of play is therefore comparable to Freud's description of primary process thinking.

Accommodation has to do with adapting ourselves to the demands of the environment. This is what we commonly define as learning and involves the modification of behavior as a result of experience. We make social accommodations when we learn to stop at red lights, stand in line, and pay our taxes. In many ways, this description parallels Freud's concept of socially adaptive, secondary (logical) process thinking. In Piaget's theory both assimilation and accommodation are present throughout life and grow in complexity with age and maturity. With respect to play, Piaget described the types of play that emerged sequentially in tandem with new levels of intellectual development, which are sensorimotor play, symbolic play, and games with rules.

Freud was once asked what was required for a full, happy, and productive life. He answered, "lieben and arbeiten"—to love and to work. Piaget was never asked the question, but he might well have answered "assimilation and accommodation." Play and work. If we join the thoughts of these two giants of psychology, we come up with the trilogy of love, play, and work as the necessary prerequisites to a full and happy life. Far from being in opposition to one another, it is only when all three operate in unison that we have the most enjoyable and productive life, whether at home, in school, or at work. When parents combine limit setting with love and play, their child rearing will be much more effective than if they do not. In the same way, if teachers combine limit setting with care and playful instruction, their students will achieve more than if they do not. Finally, in the workplace, if employers combine respect and care for employees with appropriate compensation and a playful work environment, their services and products will be of higher quality than if they do not.

Play, love, and work, then, are the basic human drives that power human thought and action throughout the human life cycle. Play is not a luxury, nor is it a waste of time; rather, it is an essential ingredient for a full, happy, and productive life.

REFERENCES

Callois, R. (1961/2001). *Man, play, and games*. Glencoe, IL: Free Press.

Derrida, J. (2007). *Basic writings of Jacques Derrida*. London: Routledge.

Groos, K. (1898). *The play of animals*. New York: D. Appleton.

Groos, K. (1901). *The play of man*. New York: D. Appleton.

Huizinga, J. (1950). *Homo ludens*. Boston: Beacon.

Kris, E. (1952). *Psychoanalytic explorations in art*. New York: International University Press.

Montessori, M. (1967). *The absorbent mind*. New York: Delta.

Piaget, J. (1951). *Play, dreams and imitation in childhood*. Melbourne: Heinemann.

Schiller, F. (1967). *On the aesthetic education of man in a series of letters*. Oxford: Clarendon Press.

Spencer, H. (1896/1855). *Principles of psychology*. New York: Appleton.

Sutton-Smith, B. (1997). *The ambiguity of play*. Cambridge, MA: Harvard University Press.

Wilson, R. R. (1990). *In Palamedes' shadow*. Boston: Northeastern University Press.

SUGGESTED READING

Elkind, D. (2007). *The power of play*. Cambridge, MA: DaCapo Press.

DAVID ELKIND
Tufts University

See also: **Child Psychology; Play Assessment; Play Therapy**

PLAY ASSESSMENT

Play assessment can tell us a great deal about a child's cognitive and emotional functioning. Pretend play is often a part of a clinical assessment, because play is such a natural form of expression for young children (age 4–10 years). Clinicians often infer much about a child's functioning from their observations of pretend play. Standardized play tasks and measures are being developed that can be used in a formal assessment battery. Play assessment can contribute to treatment planning and outcome evaluation.

Processes in Pretend Play

Children's pretend play is important in child development and in psychotherapy (Russ, 2004; Singer & Singer, 1990). Children's play provides a window into both cognitive and affective processes. Russ categorized several cognitive, affective, and interpersonal processes that can be observed and measured in play.

Cognitive Processes

Cognitive processes include organization, which is the ability to tell a story with a logical time sequence and indications of cause and effect; divergent thinking, which is the ability to generate a number of different ideas, story themes, and symbols; symbolism, which is the ability to transform objects (blocks, Legos) into representations of other objects (e.g., a block becomes a telephone); and fantasy and make-believe, which is the ability to engage in as-if play behavior or to pretend to be in a different time and space.

Affective Processes

Affective processes include expression of emotion, which is the ability to express positive and negative affect states and actual emotions in a pretend play situation; expression of affect themes, which is the ability to express affect content and images in play (a doll becomes a monster, which is aggressive or scary content, even if no emotion accompanies it); comfort and enjoyment in the play experience, which is the ability to be involved in play; and emotion regulation and modulation of affect in the play, which is the ability to contain the emotion within a narrative.

Interpersonal Processes

Interpersonal processes include empathy, which is the ability to express concern for others and to take the role of the other; communication, which is the ability to express ideas and emotions to others; and interpersonal schema, which is the capacity for self–other differentiation and trust in others.

Play processes relate to important areas of adaptive functioning in children. For example, play has been found to relate to creative problem solving, perspective taking, and coping (Russ, 2004). In child therapy, play is often used as a form of communication with the therapist. In addition, children use play for expression of thoughts and feelings and for working through and processing emotional material. Assessment of play skills can help to determine whether and how a child can use play in therapy.

Measures of Pretend Play

Several play measures have been developed that can be used in assessments for therapy. We describe a few of these measures here, and more detailed reviews are provided by Gitlin-Weiner, Sandgrund, and Schaefer (2000) and by Russ, Pearson, and Sacha (2006).

The Play Therapy Observation Instrument (PTOI) was developed by Howe and Silvern (1981) and adapted by Perry (Perry & Landreth, 1991) to assess children's play behavior in a way that would meaningfully inform diagnosis, treatment planning, and outcome measurement. This instrument assesses three areas of functioning: social inadequacy, emotional discomfort, and use of fantasy. The PTOI was designed to be used in rating 12-minute segments of a videotaped play therapy session. It has been found to discriminate adjusted from maladjusted children most strongly on the emotional discomfort subscale. There are some limitations to the PTOI, including the small number of published studies using the instrument and a lack of developmental norms and standardized administration.

The NOVA Assessment of Psychotherapy (NAP) was also designed to assess the play therapy process and outcome by capturing the components of the child's and therapist's behavior during play (Faust & Burns, 1991).

This scale includes a longer, comprehensive version to be used in research and a shorter, more convenient version for use in clinical settings. Some of the relevant aspects of the child's play that are coded are valence of affect expressed and cooperative and aggressive behavior. Case studies of the validity and reliability of the NAP suggest it may be useful in assessing affective and behavioral changes during treatment, but it is limited by a lack of published psychometric characteristics and normative data.

The Affect in Play Scale (APS) is a measure of pretend play that assesses both cognitive and affective play processes with a standardized play task, a set of instructions, and a coding system (Russ, 2004). The APS is appropriate for children from 6 to 10 years of age. The task consists of puppets and blocks, and children are asked to play with them any way they wish for 5 minutes. The play is videotaped and then coded on variables of organization of fantasy, imagination, comfort, amount of affect, and variety of affect content categories. There are six negative affect categories (e.g., aggression, sadness) and five positive affect categories (e.g., happiness, nurturance). Each unit of affect expression is scored. A detailed coding manual has been developed (Russ, 2004). Numerous validity studies have been carried out with the APS, and it has been related to theoretically relevant criteria such as creativity, coping, and emotional understanding. For example, the amount of affect in play has been found to be related to the amount of affect in descriptions of memories in first- and second-graders. This finding has implications for therapy, in that the expression of emotion in play is related to the ability to think about and describe emotional events in memory. Although a number of published studies with the APS present mean and standard deviation values for the measure, no comprehensive normative study of it has yet been carried out.

A version of the APS that used in vivo scoring would be user-friendly and should increase its use in research and with both clinical and research populations. A new version of the APS, the Affect in Play Scale–Brief Rating (APS-BR), does not require videotaping and uses a Likert rating scale to rate its cognitive and affective variables. The process of validating this new measure began with a study by Sacha Cordiano, Russ, and Short (2008). In this study, the validity of the APS-BR was assessed by comparing scores of play sessions using the original APS and the APS-BR in a sample of first- and second-grade children, by examining associations between scores on the APS-BR and scores on theoretically relevant criterion measures of divergent thinking and emotional memories, and by comparing the pattern of correlations between the APS-BR and criterion measures and the APS and the same criterion measures.

This study, which used existing videotapes of play observations from a previous study of the APS, produced encouraging results. Interrater reliability was high, and the APS-BR scores were highly correlated with their respective scores on the APS. Finally, significant correlations were found between the APS-BR and the criterion measures of divergent thinking and emotional memories. In addition, the patterns of correlations between the APS-BR and both criterion measures were similar in strength and direction to the patterns of correlations between the APS and these same measures. There is also a preschool version of the APS, the Affect in Play Scale–Preschool (APS-P), developed by Kaugars for children from 4–6 years of age. This version has been used in several studies and is beginning to show some validity.

Play Assessment of Atypically Developing Children

The Test of Playfulness (ToP; Bundy, 1997) was based on Neumann's definition of playfulness as involving internal control, intrinsic motivation, and freedom to suspend reality. It incorporates an observational assessment of structured and unstructured play. The ToP has demonstrated acceptable validity and reliability with children who have attention deficits and physical disabilities, and it has recently demonstrated adequate subject and item fit using Rasch analysis for children with autism.

The Structured Play Assessment (Ungerer & Sigman, 1981) is a videotaped 15- to 20-minute play interaction that has demonstrated excellent reliability and validity with typically developing children and children with autism, developmental delays, Down syndrome, and mental retardation. It has recently been used to assess functional and symbolic play as part of a randomized comparison of joint attention and play interventions for children with autism.

Play Assessment in Treatment Planning

Research from a variety of sources suggests that play helps reduce anxiety in children. For example, play prior to surgery has been found to reduce anxiety in children, and play has been found to reduce separation anxiety in preschoolers. Research also suggests that children who already have good fantasy and play skills are better able to use play to reduce anxiety. These and other research findings indicate that play should be considered for therapy if a child is experiencing anxiety around internal conflicts or external trauma and when the child has adequate play skills (see Russ, 2004). Play assessment can determine whether the child has play skills that are adequate for using play to process emotional material in therapy.

Next Steps

Regardless of which play assessment measure is being used, several next steps are important for play assessment to be more widely used in clinical and research settings. These include (1) a need for standardized administration and published psychometric properties of instruments with established norms; (2) a move away from videotaped observations, which can be inconvenient and decrease participation rates in research; (3) use of play assessment with clinical populations, including, but not limited to, children with autism, developmental delays, PTSD, anxiety, and/or depression; (4) use of play assessment within play intervention research for clinical populations, including, but not limited to, children with autism, developmental delays, PTSD, and anxiety; and (5) as more user-friendly and convenient measures of play assessment are developed, expanded use in settings such as museums, schools, and hospitals.

REFERENCES

Bundy, A. C. (1997). Play and playfulness: What to look for. In L. D. Parham & L. S. Fazio (Eds.), *Play in occupational therapy for children* (pp. 52–66). St. Louis, MO: Mosby-Year Book.

Faust, J., & Burns, W. J. (1991). Coding therapist and child interaction: Progress and outcome in play therapy. In C. E. Schaefer, K. Gitlin, & S. Sandgrund (Eds.), *Play therapy: Diagnosis and assessment* (pp. 663–689). New York: John Wiley & Sons.

Gitlin-Weiner, K., Sandgrund, A., & Schaefer, C. E. (2000). *Play diagnosis and assessment* (2nd ed.). New York: John Wiley & Sons.

Howe, P. A., & Silvern, L. E. (1981). Behavioral observation of children during play therapy: Preliminary development of a research instrument. *Journal of Personality Assessment, 45,* 168–182.

Perry, L., & Landreth, G. (1991). Diagnostic assessment of children's play therapy behavior. In C. E. Schaefer, K. Gitlin, & S. Sandgrund (Eds.), *Play therapy: Diagnosis and assessment* (pp. 643–660). New York: John Wiley & Sons.

Russ, S. W. (2004). *Play in child development and psychotherapy.* Mahwah, NJ: Lawrence Erlbaum.

Russ, S. W., Pearson, B. L., & Sacha Cordiano, T. J. (2006). Play assessment. In S. R. Smith & L. Handler (Eds.), *The clinical assessment of children and adolescents: A practitioner's handbook* (pp. 87–97). Mahwah, NJ: Lawrence Erlbaum.

Sacha Cordiano, T. J., Russ, S. W., & Short, E. J. (2008). Development and validation of the Affect in Play Scale–Brief Rating Version (APS-BR). *Journal of Personality Assessment, 90,* 52–50.

Singer, D. G., & Singer, J. L. (1990). *The house of make-believe: Children's play and the developing imagination.* Cambridge, MA: Harvard University Press.

Ungerer, J. A., & Sigman, M. (1981). Symbolic play and language comprehension in autistic children. *American Academy of Child Psychiatry, 20,* 318–337.

SANDRA W. RUSS
TORI SACHA CORDIANO
Case Western Reserve University

See also: **Behavioral Observation; Play Therapy; Psychological Assessment**

PLAY THERAPY

The term *play therapy* is employed in at least two ways to describe child psychotherapy. First, the term sometimes refers to particular child psychotherapy approaches that centrally emphasize children's play as a means of therapeutic communication and as a modality through which children's dilemmas can be solved (e.g., Davenport & Bourgeois, 2008; Landreth & Bratton, 2006; Schaefer, 1993). Second, the term *play therapy* is sometimes imprecisely employed to describe individual child psychotherapy generally, given that virtually all therapies rely on children's play at least as a mode of communication (Johnson, Rasbury, & Siegel, 1997). Child therapy approaches, however, do differ in whether play is considered relatively central versus relatively incidental to the process of change.

Various forms of play are useful in child psychotherapy. Even simple practice play (e.g., bouncing a ball) that develops very early can help a child relax and become comfortable with the therapist. In addition, playing games with rules (e.g., board games or cards), which takes skills that develop about age 7, can teach a child how to control impulses about competition and understand social roles. It is *symbolic* or *pretend play,* however, which dominates at about 3–6 years old, that is believed to be especially important for psychotherapy. Symbolic play expresses children's subjective, idiosyncratic experiences beyond their capacity to verbally explain themselves. Dougherty and Ray (2007) provided a summary of the stages of play development in regard to play therapy.

Symbolic play entails engaging in one activity with one object for the purpose of representing a different activity and a different object. Thus, a child might jump about while holding a broomstick, playing "horsie," in order to represent a cowboy riding a horse. Symbolic play can involve toys (e.g., dolls or action figures) or socio-dramatic scenes in which children join together to enact stories. Symbolic play represents and communicates children's personal viewpoints about real events as well as their personal reactions to those events (see Johnson et al., 1997; Schaefer, 1993).

For example, children cannot ride horsie on a broomstick unless they are familiar with the possibility of riding horses and have some wish to enact this activity. In fact, researchers find that children are especially likely to symbolically enact events and wishes that arouse their anxiety as well as their desire (Watson, 1994). Thus, symbolic play can reveal aspects of children's experience beyond the wishes and fears that they could otherwise articulate to themselves or others. Therefore, play therapy might be especially important to explore with children whose communication skills are especially limited. Landreth (2001) published a collection of illustrative efforts to employ play therapy with children whose communication skills are impaired because of developmental or physical disabilities.

Beyond providing information about children's internal lives, therapeutic orientations that place a very central value on play propose that engaging in symbolic play is inherently curative. Symbolic play sometimes provides children with an avenue to actually resolve the anxiety and dilemmas that are expressed symbolically (Schaefer, 1993; Watson, 1994). For example, play might provide relief by allowing a symbolic expression of experiences that would be too threatening to express directly (Johnson et al., 1997; Watson, 1994; Webb, 2007). Moreover, authorities of all orientations seem to agree that, while they are playing, children are in charge and experience the relief of being active and in control of situations and emotions that are symbolized through play, in contrast to the powerlessness they otherwise experience in threatening situations. That is, children can construct new ways of coping when they miniaturize or model dilemmas symbolically and then explore new solutions in terms of the models (e.g., Watson, 1994).

Although client-centered and existential therapists value uninterrupted play per se, these therapists further presume that such play is therapeutic insofar as it occurs in the context of an accepting, clarifying, and genuine therapeutic relationship (Ellinwood & Raskin, 1993; Landreth, 2002). Such relationships permit children to fully express and receive acceptance of their subjective experiences and impressions. Although other approaches to child therapy do not necessarily agree with client-centered and humanistic approaches that the accepting relationship is sufficient to bring about change, it is likely that the quality of the therapeutic relationship is crucially important to the success of all modalities (Shirk & Saiz, 1992).

In contrast to relying on unimpeded play, other play therapists actively intervene to alter the direction of the child's spontaneous play. For example, psychodynamic therapists intervene by providing children with interpretations about the meaning of the wishes, fears, and ways of coping that are represented symbolically. Such interpretations are intended to help children understand and express their experiences consciously, not only symbolically. Such awareness allows for increasingly adaptive coping. Moreover, some therapists emphasize the need to explicitly interpret connections between real, traumatizing events and the repetitive play through which children sometimes symbolize such traumas (Silvern, Karyl, & Landis, 1995).

Other therapeutic approaches give play a somewhat incidental role, rather than a central one. For example, play can be an adjunct to cognitive-behavioral therapy that has a primary goal of teaching new cognitions about the social world and new ways of coping with emotions and social interactions. Kendall and Braswell (1993) suggested that playing out problematic social interactions can reveal children's perspectives and their problematic cognitions that should be corrected. Similarly, Nims (2007) suggested integrating play with solution-focused therapy.

Whatever the particular approach, play therapy is ordinarily conducted in a therapeutic playroom. To facilitate the therapy process, the playroom is ideally equipped with materials that are suitable for children of different ages and ethnic/cultural backgrounds. Materials should be sufficiently varied to encourage enacting diverse themes and personal issues (Johnson et al., 1997). Unstructured materials, including sand, water, and clay, foster maximum freedom of self-expression. Structured materials such as cars or puppets are often introduced to elicit play about particular themes that deal with feelings, attitudes, and conflicts in family or peer relationships (Johnson et al., 1997). For example, some therapists introduce two dollhouses for children who are adjusting to having two homes after adoption or divorce (e.g., Kuhli, 1993). Similarly, toys that represent a classroom or medical equipment might be introduced for children who are facing difficulties in school or frightening medical procedures, respectively.

There is debate about whether including aggression-eliciting toys (toy guns, Bobo dolls, and the like) in the playroom ameliorates aggression or, instead, elicits further maladaptive aggression. At this time, no definitive research has resolved the issue. Given that there is a basis for concern, until an empirical answer becomes available, parents and therapists alike should either avoid or carefully monitor the impact of exposing aggressive children to aggression-eliciting toys in the playroom.

Although play therapy has traditionally been applied similarly for diverse problems, recently, specialized approaches have been developed for particular life problems. For example, specialized approaches have been developed for bereaved children, children undergoing medical procedures, and children with developmental or physical handicaps (Landreth, 2001; Webb, 2007), as well as aggressive children (Davenport & Bourgeois, 2008).

There has especially been emphasis on adapting play therapy for children who have been exposed to traumatizing events, such as natural disasters (e.g., Baggerley & Exum, 2008). Webb (2007) presented a collection of varied therapists' applications of play therapy to children who were traumatized by diverse circumstances, including bereavement, physical injuries, and child maltreatment. The most attention among traumatized children has apparently been given to the possible uses of play therapy either alone or in combination with other modalities for child abuse victims (Hetzel-Riggin, Brausch, & Montgomery, 2007; Silvern et al., 1995).

Hetzel-Riggin and colleagues (2007) conducted a meta-analysis of the effectiveness of play therapy among sexually abused children. This study was exceptionally useful, in that it compared play therapy to other modalities and also distinguished among specific symptoms that characterize molested children. Results revealed that psychotherapy was effective generally. More specifically, play therapy was significantly more effective than other modalities for improving children's social functioning. However, social-cognitive behavioral therapy, supportive therapy, and abuse-specific therapy were more effective than play therapy for ameliorating conduct problems. Other modalities were also more effective than play therapy for improving psychological distress and self-concept. There is a need for more research to identify the types of symptoms for which play therapy is and is not especially effective.

Recently, play has been integrated into family therapy (Baggerly & Exum, 2008) and parent training (Foote, Eyberg, & Schuhmann, 1998). Although parent training typically emphasizes discipline, empirical findings revealed that it is more effective to initially establish playful interactions between children and parents than to immediately focus on discipline (Foote et al., 1998). Similarly, there has been great interest in filial therapy, in which parents learn nondirective play therapy principles and skills that they employ with their children under the therapist's supervision. The goal is to foster child–parent attachment and warmth and to support the well-being of the individual parent and child (Bratton, Ray, Rhine, & Jones, 2005).

A recent meta-analysis of the results of 93 studies revealed that, overall, play therapy was significantly effective for highly diverse children and problems (Bratton et al., 2005). Given the existence of so many approaches to play therapy, however, it is important for parents to inquire about particular therapists' orientations and practices and their expertise with particular problems. By itself, the term *play therapy* reveals little about the characteristics of an individual therapist's treatment or its appropriateness for a given child.

REFERENCES

Baggerly, J., & Exum, H. A. (2008). Counseling children after natural disasters. *American Journal of Family Therapy, 36*(1), 79–93.

Bratton, S., Ray, D., Rhine, T., & Jones, L. (2005). The efficacy of play therapy with children: A meta-analytic review of treatment outcomes. *Professional Psychology: Research and Practice, 36*(4), 376–390.

Davenport, B. R., & Bourgeois, N. M. (2008). Play, aggression, the preschool child, and the family: A review of literature to guide empirically informed play therapy with aggressive preschool children. *International Journal of Play Therapy, 17*(1), 2–23.

Dougherty, J., & Ray, D. (2007). Differential impact of play therapy on developmental levels of children. *Journal of Play Therapy, 16*(1), 2–19.

Ellinwood, C. G., & Raskin, J. J. (1993). Client-centered/humanistic psychotherapy. In T. R. Kratochwill & R. R. Morris (Eds.), *Handbook of psychotherapy with children and adolescents* (pp. 264–375). Boston: Allyn & Bacon.

Foote, R., Eyberg, S., & Schuhmann, E. (1998). Parent–child interaction approaches to the treatment of child behavior problems. In T. H. Ollendick & R. J. Prinz (Eds.), *Advances in clinical child psychology* (Vol. 20, pp. 125–143). New York: Plenum.

Hetzel-Riggin, M. D., Brausch, A. M., & Montgomery, B. S. (2007). A meta-analytic investigation of therapy modality outcomes for sexually abused children and adolescents: An exploratory study. *Child Abuse & Neglect, 31*, 125–141.

Johnson, J. H., Rasbury, W. C., & Siegel, L. J. (1997). *Approaches to child treatment: Introduction to theory, research, and practice.* Boston: Allyn & Bacon.

Kendall, P., & Braswell, L. (1993). *Cognitive-behavioral therapy for impulsive children* (2nd ed.). New York: Guilford Press.

Kuhli, L. (1993). The use of two houses in play therapy. In C. E. Schaefer & D. M. Cangelosi (Eds.), *Play therapy techniques* (pp. 63–68). Northvale, NJ: Jason Aronson.

Landreth, G. L. (2001). *Innovations in play therapy: Issues, process, and special populations* (pp. 2570–270). Philadelphia: Taylor & Francis.

Landreth, G. (2002). *Play therapy: The art of the relationship* (2nd ed.). New York: Brunner-Routledge.

Landreth, G. L., & Bratton, S. C. (2006). *Child–parent relationship therapy (CPRT): A 10-session filial therapy model.* New York: Routledge, Taylor & Francis Group.

Nims, D. R. (2007). Integrating play therapy techniques into solution-focused brief therapy. *International Journal of Play Therapy, 16*(1), 54–68.

Schaefer, C. E. (1993). What is play and why is it therapeutic? In E. C. Schaefer (Ed.), *Therapeutic Powers of Play* (pp. 1–15). Northvale, NJ: Jason Aronson.

Shirk, S., & Saiz, C. C. (1992). Clinical, empirical, and developmental perspectives on the therapeutic relationship in child psychotherapy. *Development and Psychopathology, 4*, 713–728.

Silvern, L., Karyl, J., & Landis, T. (1995). Individual psychotherapy for traumatized children of abused women. In E. Peled, P. G. Jaffe, & J. L. Edelson (Eds.), *Ending the cycle of violence: Community responses to children of battered women* (pp. 43–76). Thousand Oaks, CA: Sage.

Strayhorn, J. M. (1994). Psychological competence-based therapy for young children and their parents. In C. W. LeCroy (Ed.), *Handbook of child and adolescent treatment.* New York: Free Press.

Watson, M. W. (1994). *Children at play: Clinical and developmental approaches to representation and meaning: The relation between anxiety and pretend play.* New York: Oxford University Press.

Webb, N. B. (2007). Play therapy with children in crisis: Individual, group, and family treatment (3rd ed.). New York: Guilford Press.

SUGGESTED READINGS

Bratton, S., Ray, D., Rhine, T., & Jones, L. (2005). The efficacy of play therapy with children: A meta-analytic review of treatment outcomes. *Professional Psychology: Research and Practice, 36*(4), 376–390.

Ellinwood, C. G., & Raskin, J. J. (1993). Client-centered/humanistic psychotherapy. In T. R. Kratochwill & R. R. Morris (Eds.), *Handbook of psychotherapy with children and adolescents* (pp. 264–375). Boston: Allyn & Bacon.

Landreth, G. (2002). *Play therapy: The art of the relationship* (2nd ed.). New York: Brunner-Routledge.

Webb, N. B. (2007). *Play therapy with children in crisis: Individual, group, and family treatment* (3rd ed.). New York: Guilford Press.

LOUISE SILVERN
BROOK MCCLINTIC
AMY K. NUTTALL
University of Colorado at Boulder

See also: **Family Therapy; Play Assessment**

PLEASURE PRINCIPLE

Sigmund Freud considered the pleasure principle, together with the reality principle, to be a basic regulatory principle of the mind. Influenced by Gustav Fechner, a German physicist considered to be the father of psychophysics, Freud theorized that conscious pleasure and unpleasure (discomfort) were experienced when mental stimulation became too intense. Freud proposed the term *pleasure principle* to denote an inferred mental process that regulates all stimuli impinging on the mind, whether from internal psychological or somatic sources or from external sources of any kind. This principle facilitates psychic processes that reduce or eliminate unpleasant extremes and, in this way, restore mental equilibrium. He later suggested that the mind, in accordance with this principle, develops an unconscious danger signal of anxiety to forewarn itself of impending overstimulation. This signal anxiety then triggers a variety of self-protective processes in the ego, including physical removal (flight from the anticipated danger) or the various ego defenses, which are the psychic equivalents of physical flight or avoidance (Shill, 2004).

The pleasure principle also serves to regulate libidinal gratification indirectly, because frustration of libidinal wishes and needs causes an unbearable increase in noxious stimulation. As their ego functions mature and develop, infants gradually learn that gratification is possible only through the agency of an external mothering person, and they consequently develop those specific innate capacities that facilitate securing gratification of basic human needs for nutrition and emotional care from important people (objects) in the environment. This is the influence of the reality principle, and Freud suggests that, in this manner, the necessity for dealing with the concrete external world as it is, rather than maintaining a fantasized world of pure pleasure, preserves the pleasure principle by regulating mental activity and action according to the demands of the external world, in order to secure gratification. Infants learn to use realistic ways of securing those resources, for example, from initially crying to the eventual verbalization of wishes and needs. Adherence to this reality principle facilitates the ego's ability to adapt the gratification of internal needs to accord with the external realities of available resources.

Freud observed further that people did not always engage in activities that produced pleasure but instead sometimes experienced rather severe mental or physical suffering. He coined the phrase "compulsion to repeat," commonly referred to as the repetition compulsion, to describe this human tendency, and he speculated that it evidenced the existence of a death instinct that counteracted the pleasure principle by directing human behavior toward self-deprivation and even annihilation (Freud, 1955). Although this pattern of behavior is universally acknowledged, its suggested origin in a hypothetical death instinct has been controversial and is not widely accepted. Freud subsequently supplemented this explanation by proposing the contribution to self-destructive behavior of masochism, sadism, and aggression emanating from an instinctual drive.

Freud did not always draw a sharp distinction between the pleasure principle as a hypothetical mechanism of mental regulation and the experience of subjective pleasure through the gratification of libidinal drives. In the end, he acknowledged that he had not settled this issue.

REFERENCES

Freud, S. (1955). Beyond the pleasure principle. In J. Strachey (Ed. & Trans.), *The standard edition of the complete psychological works of Sigmund Freud* (Vol. 18, pp. 3–64). London: Hogarth Press. (Original work published 1920)

Radford, P. (1970). Principles of mental functioning. In H. Nagera, A. Colonna, E. Dansky, E. First, A. Gavshon, A. Holder, et al. (Eds.), *Basic psychoanalytic concepts on metapsychology, conflicts, anxiety and other subjects* (pp. 47–76). London: Allen and Unwin.

Shill, M. A. (2004). Signal anxiety, defense, and the pleasure principle. *Psychoanalytic Psychology, 21,* 116–133.

MERTON A. SHILL
University of Michigan

See also: **Psychoanalytic Theories**

POLICE PSYCHOLOGY

Police psychology aims to assist law enforcement personnel and agencies in carrying out their functions and missions with optimal effectiveness, safety, health, and conformity to laws and ethics. Its nearly 100-year history dates back to Lewis Terman's testing of San Jose police applicants in 1916, although it was more than 50 years later that its modern era began. Two events in 1968 spurred police psychology's rapid development in America:

broad federal funding of hundreds of psychological studies and programs by the Law Enforcement Assistance Administration and the decision by the Los Angeles Police Department to hire Dr. Martin Reiser as the first full-time police psychologist in a major law enforcement agency. These events and the activities they spurred contributed to "the steady evolution of an expanding police psychology that has had a major influence on law enforcement" (Scrivner & Kurke, 1995, p. 6).

Today police psychology works to achieve its objectives through the application of the science and profession of psychology in four primary domains of practice (Corey et al., in press):

1. **Assessment.** Police psychologists working in this domain are charged with the development, validation, and implementation of assessment methods appropriate for preemployment and incumbent evaluation of suitability and emotional stability. These police psychological activities include job analyses, preemployment psychological evaluations of peace officer applicants, fitness-for-duty evaluations of incumbent officers, suitability evaluations for specialty assignments (e.g., hostage negotiators, tactical team members, and undercover officers), evaluations for promotional purposes, emergency consultations concerning the seriously mentally ill, test development, and related research, consultation, training, and supervision. Psychologists engaged in police assessment activities carry out their work largely in private practice settings, universities, or government agencies. Research regarding the validation of methods and procedures for preemployment psychological screening of police officers has produced a voluminous outcome literature. Although preemployment applicant screening is required in most states and jurisdictions, it is not a universal mandate.

2. **Clinical Intervention.** Police psychologists perform a wide range of clinical interventions with police officers and their families in the context of employee assistance counseling; individual counseling; group, couple, and family therapy; critical incident intervention; disability recovery; substance abuse treatment; mental attitude preparation; wellness programs; life coaching; and related research, consultation, training, and supervision. Clinical interventions for police personnel are typically designed as time-limited treatment modalities, emphasizing cognitive behavioral interventions, in order to promote accessibility, availability, efficiency, and effectiveness of such services to law enforcement organizations. Those who conduct clinical interventions are employed by the law enforcement agencies they serve, either full- or part-time as agency employees

or contract providers, in addition to those who work in more conventional private practice settings.

3. **Operational Support.** Police psychological services designed to support the mission of law enforcement officers and police units include forensic hypnosis, hostage negotiations, investigative interviewing techniques, criminal profiling, psychological autopsies, counterterrorism and counterintelligence, indirect assessments, and related training and consultation. Psychologists who provide operational support to police officers and agencies typically conduct their work in the field, such as when participating in a hostage negotiation, mediating conflict involving a person with serious mental illness, or performing a criminal profile. Operational psychology in law enforcement settings is in a relatively embryonic phase and borrows much from the military literature. In large part, the relative dearth of published outcome research in operational psychology, both in police and military settings, derives from the dynamic, consultative nature of the work in the field and the security issues that inhibit or preclude objective analysis. Nevertheless, an emerging body of literature is beginning to identify issues and methods common to this domain, and in the operational arenas with the longest history of activity and research (e.g., hostage negotiation), outcome studies clearly demonstrate psychology's effectiveness (Van Hasselt et al., 2006).

4. **Organizational Consultation.** Police psychologists engaged in organizational consulting focus on development of performance appraisal systems; consultation to supervisors, managers, and executives; team-building; leadership training; strategic planning; organizational development; process consultation; mediation; and other activities designed to address systemic issues, thereby maximizing police performance capabilities and effectiveness. When engaged in organizational consultation, police psychologists work within police settings, universities, and other settings common to industrial-organizational and consulting psychologists.

Police officers perform a unique and essential function in society with broad responsibility for protecting life and property and maintaining social order. Their unmatched civilian authority to use force, limit civil liberties, and access private property while performing their sworn duties and the chronic exposure to danger, trauma, and high psychological stress incurred by their work simultaneously demand from them extraordinary competence and enormous resilience. The nature of their work requires sustained vigilance to the possibility of a variety of threats to their own security, including violence, corruption, and intelligence breaches. Partly as a result of these threats, police personnel tend to operate in a comparatively insular way and often find it difficult to seek or accept help outside their own profession. In a comprehensive literature review, Woody (2005) documented and described the distinct subculture that often pushes law enforcement officers to accept unique cultural tenets that are quite different from those held by average citizens. Consequently, they tend to isolate themselves from commonplace family and social relationships, with the by-products of relationship problems as well as a variety of mental, physical, and behavioral problems.

As a result of these cultural and organizational demands, psychologists with particular knowledge of the issues, laws, challenges, ethical dilemmas, working conditions, stressors, missions, tactics, and roles inherent in police work are both more easily integrated into police operations and more welcomed by police professionals (Kurke & Scrivner, 1995). Indeed, police psychology requires distinctive knowledge of a wide range of subjects, depending on the domain of practice, including:

- The essential functions of police personnel
- The working conditions unique to various police positions
- Laws pertaining to the assessment of peace officers
- Confidentiality and testimonial privilege when treating law enforcement personnel
- Disability and workers' compensation
- The unique procedural rights of peace officers
- Labor–management rights and obligations
- Limitations on disclosure of confidential information when conducting employer-mandated evaluations
- Common and novel stressors inherent in police work (e.g., line-of-duty deaths, officer-involved shootings, witnessing multiple casualties, stressors unique to paramilitary organizations, and shift work)
- Differences between normal and abnormal adaptation to occupational trauma
- The research pertinent to enhancing resilience and recovery in police personnel

Police psychology is represented and advanced in the profession primarily by three national associations of police psychologists: (1) American Psychological Association, Division 18, Police & Public Safety Section; (2) International Association of Chiefs of Police (IACP), Police Psychological Services Section; and (3) Society for Police & Criminal Psychology (SPCP). Each provides a rich variety of continuing education opportunities conducted in conjunction with their respective annual meetings. IACP publishes a professional magazine, The Police Chief, in addition to guidelines pertinent to five practice areas: preemployment psychological evaluations, psychological fitness-for-duty evaluations, postshooting debriefing, peer counseling, and operational consulting. SPCP publishes the biannual Journal of Police & Criminal Psychology.

REFERENCES

Corey, D. M., Allen, S., Aumiller, G., Brewster, J., Cuttler, M., Gupton, H., et al. (in press). Police psychology core domains & competencies. The Police Chief.

Kurke, M. I., & Scrivner, E. M. (Eds.) (1995). Police psychology into the 21st century. Hillsdale, NJ: Lawrence Erlbaum.

Scrivner, E. M., & Kurke, M. I. (1995). Police psychology at the dawn of the 21st century. In M. I. Kurke & E. M. Scrivner (Eds.), Police psychology into the 21st century (pp. 3–30). Hillsdale, NJ: Lawrence Erlbaum.

Van Hasselt, V. B., Baker, M. T., Romano, S. J., Schlessinger, K. M., Zucker, M., Dragone, R., et al. (2006). Crisis (hostage) negotiation training: A preliminary evaluation of program efficacy. Criminal Justice and Behavior, 33(1), 56–69.

Woody, R. H. (2005). The police culture: Research implications for psychological services. Professional Psychology: Research and Practice, 36(5), 525–529.

DAVE COREY
Portland, Oregon, Police Bureau

AUDREY HONIG
Los Angeles County Sheriff's Department

See also: Forensic Psychology; Occupational Stress

POLITICAL PSYCHOLOGY

Political psychology is an interdisciplinary academic specialty focusing on the study of psychological processes that influence political behavior. Accordingly, a more precise label for the discipline might be the psychology of politics or psychological political science.

Contemporary political psychology draws from all cognate areas of psychology, with the strongest emphasis on social, cognitive, personality, and developmental psychology, motivation and emotion, and cognitive neuroscience. It also draws abundantly from its other parent discipline, political science, including the field of international relations. Furthermore, it has ties with political communication, economics, philosophy, sociology, and other related disciplines.

Development as an Organized Discipline

Scholarly interest in the impact of psychological processes on political behavior is as old as psychology itself. However, as an organized discipline—marked by the founding of the International Society of Political Psychology (ISPP) just three decades ago, in 1978—political psychology is comparatively young.

As stated on its web site (www.ispp.org), the ISPP is a nonprofit, nonpartisan, academic, scientific, and educational organization that aims "to establish a community of scholars and concerned individuals in universities, government, the communications media, and elsewhere who have scientific and practical interests in examining the relationship between political and psychological phenomena; to facilitate communication of scientific research, theory, and practice across disciplinary, national, and ideological boundaries; [and] to increase the theoretical and practical significance of political psychology both inside and outside academia."

The formal establishment of this emerging field was heralded by the *Handbook of Political Psychology,* edited by Jeanne N. Knutson (1973), founder of the ISPP. *The Psychology of Politics,* by William F. Stone (1974), represented the first attempt to produce a text specifically for courses in political psychology, although few such courses existed at the time. Today, courses in political psychology are offered at universities around the world. The ISPP journal, *Political Psychology,* "dedicated to the analysis of the interrelationships between psychological and political processes," was first published in 1980, further consolidating political psychology as a self-conscious academic enterprise. Landmark publications of the 1980s included *Political Psychology,* edited by Margaret G. Hermann (1986), and David O. Sears's (1987) article "Political Psychology" in the *Annual Review of Psychology.*

In 1991, the Ohio State University, with support from the ISPP, launched the first annual Summer Institute in Political Psychology (SIPP), an intensive program of study for graduate students, directed by Margaret G. Hermann. The program moved to Stanford University in 2005, under the direction of Jon A. Krosnick. In response to the burgeoning growth of political psychology in its first two decades, the ISPP formulated a "third decade plan" that included commissioning a new handbook for the psychology of politics, as well as a periodic volume to report theoretical advances, conceptual breakthroughs, and cutting-edge research. Consequently, the Oxford Handbook of Political Psychology was published in 2003, edited by David O. Sears, Leonie Huddy, and Robert Jervis, followed by the first issue of *Advances in Political Psychology,* edited by Margaret G. Hermann (2004).

Areas of Inquiry

As political psychology is an emerging field, its subject matter is still in a state of flux. However, a review of books in the field and the organizational framework of recent programs of the ISPP's annual scientific meeting reveal a common core of overlapping topics and subspecialties.

Cognition, Affect, and Motivation in Politics. Traditionally, much of the research in this area has focused on political decision making. A more recent trend is the growing interest in cognitive neuroscience and the role of emotion in politics.

Political Socialization. This area examines political development across the life span, including the development of political identity, ideological resonance, attitudes, and values.

Political Personality and Leadership. This domain of research focuses on what political scientists refer to as political elites. Areas of interest include psychodynamically oriented personality profiling and psychobiography; the analysis of personality or leadership styles, traits, and types; the motivational profiles of leaders; and structural and stylistic aspects of cognitive variables pertaining to the political behavior of individual leaders.

Political Participation. The focus of this area is the political behavior of ordinary citizens, referred to by political scientists as mass politics. It includes the study of political communication; impression formation; public opinion and the media; voting behavior; political cynicism, activism, and alienation; and political attitudes, values, and ideology.

Intergroup Relations. Topics at the forefront of this area include social identity, prejudice and stereotyping, intergroup conflict, and conflict resolution.

International Relations. This area, more closely related to political science than to psychology, examines psychological processes in foreign policy behavior, including topics such as perception (and misperception) in international politics, international negotiation, and more recently, globalization.

Political Stability and Change. This is a broad area of study, including topics such as democracy, civic engagement, social movements, collective action, social justice, war and peace, genocide, and terrorism.

REFERENCES

Hermann, M. G. (Ed.). (1986). *Political psychology.* San Francisco: Jossey-Bass.

Hermann, M. G. (Ed.). (2004). *Advances in political psychology* (Vol. 1). Amsterdam: Elsevier.

Knutson, J. N. (Ed.). (1973). *Handbook of political psychology.* San Francisco: Jossey-Bass.

Sears, D. O. (1987). Political psychology. *Annual Review of Psychology, 38,* 229–255.

Sears, D. O., Huddy, L., & Jervis, R. (Eds.). (2003). *Oxford handbook of political psychology.* New York: Oxford University Press.

Stone, W. F. (1974). *The psychology of politics.* New York: Free Press.

SUGGESTED READINGS

Deutsch, M., & Kinnvall, C. (2002). What is political psychology? In K. R. Monroe (Ed.), *Political psychology* (pp. 15–42). Mahwah, NJ: Lawrence Erlbaum.

Immelman, A. (2003). Personality in political psychology. In I. B. Weiner (Series Ed.), T. Millon, & M. J. Lerner (Vol. Eds.), *Handbook of psychology: Vol. 5. Personality and social psychology* (pp. 599–625). Hoboken, NJ: John Wiley & Sons.

Ward, D. (2002). Political psychology: Origins and development. In K. R. Monroe (Ed.), *Political psychology* (pp. 61–78). Mahwah, NJ: Lawrence Erlbaum.

AUBREY IMMELMAN
St. John's University, MN

POLYGRAPH (See Lie Detection)

PORTUGAL, PSYCHOLOGY IN

The roots of psychology in Portugal may be found within the work of some nineteenth-century professionals, primarily those in the medical sciences (psychiatry, neuropsychiatry) and philosophy. Some of the most prominent pioneers include Miguel Bombarda (1851–1910), Magalhaes de Lemos (1855–1931), Julio de Matos (1856–1922), Elysio de Moura (1877–1910), and Egaz Moniz (1874–1955). Silvio Lima (1904–1993) was the first author to write about the history of psychology in Portugal (Lima, 1950, as cited in Abreu, 2005). Lima, also a historical figure in the field, divided the history of psychology through 1950 into three different periods: the mid-nineteenth century to 1914, a period characterized by positivism; 1914 to 1941, a period marked by experimental methods; and 1941 to 1950, a period characterized by hermeneutic and humanistic approaches.

The 1960s were marked by the foundation of the first academic school in psychology (Institute for Applied Psychology [ISPA]) in 1962. The ISPA was a private school with a religious background that was approved by the Portuguese Education Ministry (Borges, 1986). During the 1970s and after the end of the dictatorship period, a movement toward the creation of psychology courses at public universities emerged. In 1976, three schools of psychology and educational sciences were created in the main Portuguese universities: Lisbon, Porto, and Coimbra. This was a major event in the history of psychology in Portugal, and it constituted a significant turning point in research, training, and professional practice. The first period of university training in psychology was markedly influenced by the French school and mostly oriented to educational sciences and clinical psychology and psychiatry. In a second phase, some newly graduated students in psychology followed an academic career in psychology and earned the PhD by training abroad, specifically in the United States (Nogueira, Saavedra, & Neves, 2006). Some of this second generation of academics were involved in the creation of new degrees in psychology at public universities. In 1991, Universiadade do Minho was created, and since then to the late 1990s, eight new public courses were established (ISCTE, Algarve, Evora, Beira Interior, Madeira, UTAD, Acores, and Aveiro). This exponential growth was even more evident in the implementation of private schools. Almost 30 years after the creation of the first private school of psychology (ISPA), a number of new private university programs were formed throughout the country. In 2007, more than 30 undergraduate programs in psychology (12 public and 21 private) were active and training more than 3,000 new students per year.

Organizations

There are four main professional associations in the field of psychology: the National Syndicate of Psychologists (SNP), founded in 1992 to defend the rights of professionals working in the field; the Portuguese Association of Psychology (APP), created in 1979 as a scientific society; the Portuguese Psychologists Association (APPORT), which played an important role in developing the first ethical code of psychologists in Portugal (1995); and the National Professional Body (APOP), created in 2002 with the final goal of creating legal regulation for the practice of psychology in Portugal. Besides these main associations, there are more than 30 scientific societies in specific subfields of psychology; these range from cognitive-behavioral therapy to criminal sexology.

Patterns of Education and Training

In the last few years, a major transformation within the structure of education and training in psychology has been taking place. Since 2006, most of the curricula for undergraduate and graduate degrees conform to the Bologna Declaration (1999) and the European Diploma in Psychology (2005). The European Federation of Psychologists' Associations (EFPA) adopted a document entitled "EuroPsyT—a Framework of Education and Training for Psychologists in Europe" (Lunt et al., 2001). The curricula resulting from the common framework were proposed in a three-phase program that would last for 6 years. These phases are as follows: (1) bachelor's degree, 3 years of training in basic knowledge on the major theories and techniques in psychology; (2) master's degree, 2 years aimed at preparing students for independent practice as psychologists within a specific area; and (3) supervised practice, 1 year of professional field training. The application of these criteria was relatively consensual among universities and professional organizations in Portugal.

Prominent Lines in Research

There are a few leading psychology research units in Portugal. Most of these units are linked to universities, are recognized by the Ministry of Science, and receive public funding from the Portuguese Science Foundation (FCT). In the most recent international evaluation (2003), 10 units were rated as good or above, the minimum criterion to be recognized by the FCT; two of them were classified as excellent, six as very good, and two as good. Most units are constituted of different groups or subunits in specific fields of basic and applied psychology (cognitive, experimental, developmental, clinical, educational, and social psychology), and they employ between 20 and 40 PhD investigators. There are also a number of units that conduct research in specific areas, such as clinical psychology, educational psychology, and social psychology.

Types of Applied Practice

In 2007, there were more than 13,000 licensed psychologists in Portugal, which is already above the optimal rate of one psychologist for each 1,000 inhabitants (Tikannen, 2004); the Portuguese population is around 10 million. This sharp increase in the number of psychologists is due to the boom of undergraduate courses in the last decade and the fact that psychology is one of the most popular courses among students in Portugal. This situation is, however, leading to major unemployment problems. Despite the need for psychologists in areas such as health care, education, and organizations, public services and major organizations are not prepared to integrate the increasingly higher number of psychologists finishing their degrees. Currently, most employed psychologists are working in one of the following fields: (1) clinical and health psychology, where these professionals work in health care organizations or private practice; (2) educational and school guidance, where these psychologists mostly work in public schools; and (3) work and organizational psychology, where these professionals work mostly within human resources departments. Aside from these three main areas of applied practice, some psychologists also work in forensic psychology, and a significant proportion conduct research and teach (mostly within universities).

Leading Journals

There are a few scientific journals in the field of psychology in Portugal. Most publications are related to universities: *Psychologica, Revista Portuguesa de Psicologia, Jornal de Psicologia, Psicologia: Teoria, Investigacao e Pratica,* and *Analise Psicologica.*

REFERENCES

Abreu, M. V. (2005). A sinopse de Sílvio Lima sobre "a Psicologia em Portugal" (1950): Fontes para uma história da psicologia em Portugal. *Iberpsicología: Revista Electrónica de la Federación española de Asociaciones de Psicología, 10,* 5.

Borges, M. I. P. (1986). História da psicologia em Portugal (VII): Antecedentes das faculdades de psicologia e ciências da educação. *Jornal de Psicologia, 5,* 1, 7.

Lunt, I., Bartram, D., Döpping, J., Georgas, J., Jern, S., Job, R., et al. (2001). *EuroPsyT—a framework for education and training for psychologists in Europe.* Available from EFPPA, Brussels.

Nogueira, C., Saavedra, L., & Neves, S. (2006). Critical (feminist) psychology in Portugal. Will it be possible? *Annual Review of Critical Psychology, 5.*

Tikannen, T. (2004). *The European diploma in psychology (EuroPsy) and the future of the profession in Europe.* EFPA publication.

PEDRO J. NOBRE
University of Trás-os-Montes e Alto, Douro, Portugal

POSITIVE PSYCHOLOGY

Although the concept of positive psychology may be traced back to the late nineteenth century, today the phrase is most often used in two ways. The first is associated with humanistic psychology and arose as a reaction against the reductionistic determinism of traditional psychoanalytic and behavioral psychology. From its beginning, humanistic psychology was concerned with exploring, understanding, and facilitating the development of positive human experience and behavior in an attempt to focus on the whole person.

For example, Abraham Maslow, one of the founding fathers of humanistic psychology, dedicated an entire chapter to outlining the major themes of a "positive approach to psychology" (1970). They include such things as researching wisdom, aesthetic perception, positive emotions, well-being, higher states of motivation, love, positive personal characteristics, self-actualization, healthy educational and organizational practices, and democracy. Another distinguishing feature of this approach to positive psychology, and to psychology in general, is that it advocates a diversity of research methods, especially qualitative techniques.

The second and more recent use of the phrase positive psychology describes an emerging school of thought in modern psychology that bears this name. Positive psychology, as it is called, also began as a reaction against certain aspects of traditional psychology, namely, its focus on negative and problematic human behavior, such as psychopathology and what is wrong or deficient in people. One of the first authoritative expressions of the basic goals, character, and methods of this field also included a most succinct definition of positive psychology: It is "a science of positive subjective experience, positive individual traits, and positive institutions" (Seligman & Csikszentmihalyi, 2000, p. 5). The distinguishing feature of this approach to positive psychology that separates it from the humanistic effort is the use of traditional psychological research methods, particularly a strong emphasis on the use of quantitative techniques.

The Field of Positive Psychology

Positive psychology's first focal area, positive subjective experience, is characterized by the study of such topics as well-being, personal happiness, life satisfaction, optimal human experience, exceptional performance, states of flow (total involvement), the importance of meaningful activity, and the good life. The second focus concerns the study of positive individual traits, and the field has already identified 24 "character strengths and virtues" (Peterson & Seligman, 2004). These positive individual qualities are generally divided into six major groups: wisdom (curiosity, learning, open-mindedness, originality, social intelligence, perspective), courage (valor, perseverance, integrity), humanity (kindness, love), justice (citizenship, fairness, leadership), temperance (self-control, prudence, humility), and transcendence (beauty, gratitude, hope, spirituality, forgiveness, playfulness, zest). This work includes the development of a set of criteria by which it may be determined whether a particular human quality or behavior is indeed such a positive strength or virtue.

A third concern of positive psychology aims at developing positive social processes and institutions, including healthy relationships, nurturing families, positive educational practices, healthy workplaces, good citizenship, and even positive political practices around the world. The University of Pennsylvania's Center for Positive Psychology is often identified as the epicenter of this approach.

A general goal of psychology and behavioral science is to help reduce suffering by developing methods to solve personal, organizational, and social problems. Thus, positive psychology aims at establishing a body of empirically supported positive practices in all three areas. One large-scale positive project, for instance, involves identifying and supporting the development of what are known as "signature strengths" (Peterson, 2006) or basic personality characteristics that are associated with mental health, personal well-being, and prosocial behavior.

Positive psychology also advocates the creation of positive therapeutic techniques and programs. In general, positive therapy involves emphasizing three aspects of the therapeutic process. One is the use of deep strategies, which includes employing the factors that are common to all good therapies, such as accurate empathy, genuineness in the relationship, mutual respect, and trust. However, a more distinguishing feature of positive therapy

is its strengths perspective, which emphasizes identifying and developing an individual's abilities and character strengths as an important part of the process. Finally, positive therapy often involves focusing on periods of well-being that people spontaneously experience and connecting these moments to the therapeutic process through such activities as journal writing. Many of these techniques are found in Fava's well-being therapy, which is often cited as an example of positive therapy (Linley & Joseph, 2004). Other forms of applied positive psychology are tailored to meet the characteristics and needs of educational, social, organizational, and institutional settings.

Both forms of positive psychology focus on similar goals and hopes for the future, especially understanding optimal functioning, fostering the good life, and creating healthy social institutions that facilitate well-being. However, it is very important to keep in mind that humanistic positive psychology and positive psychology differ greatly in regard to the scientific methods that each one employs to reach these ends. Although the humanistic approach is still very much concerned with its vision of positive psychology, this view reached a peak in the 1970s. In contrast, the newer positive psychology is undergoing a period of rapid growth and development.

For example, this approach has already produced a significant body of empirically based work on positive human phenomena (Snyder & Lopez, 2002), with much more on the horizon. Of course, neither school of positive psychology is without its critics, especially in regard to difficulties associated with researching many positive topics and the risk of becoming overly idealistic. Such criticisms notwithstanding, it is crucial to note that both forms of positive psychology are reminders that psychology must focus on human potential much more than has occurred in the past if it is to understand the human experience more completely.

REFERENCES

Linley, P. A., & Joseph, S. (2004). *Positive psychology in practice*. Hoboken, NJ: John Wiley & Sons.

Maslow, A. H. (1970). *Motivation and personality* (2nd ed.). New York: Harper & Row.

Peterson, C. (2006). *A primer in positive psychology*. Oxford, UK: Oxford University Press.

Peterson, C., & Seligman, M. (2004). *Character strengths and virtues: A handbook and classification*. Oxford, UK: Oxford University Press.

Seligman, M. E. P., & Csikszentmihalyi, M. (2000). Positive psychology: An introduction. *American Psychologist, 55*, 5–14.

Snyder, C. R., & Lopez, S. J. (2002). *Handbook of positive psychology*. Oxford, UK: Oxford University Press.

CHRISTOPHER J. MRUK
Bowling Green State University

POSITRON EMISSION TOMOGRAPHY (See Magnetic Resonance Imaging; Neuroimaging; Neuroscience)

POSTCONCUSSION SYNDROME

A concussion is a physiological disruption of brain function as a result of an external force to the head resulting in a loss or alteration of consciousness. Immediate postinjury objective signs of concussion are a person being dazed, confused, and disoriented, new onset of feeling nauseous or throwing up, or a period of loss of consciousness. Other postconcussion signs may include brief neurological impairments such as not being able to stand, walk, or converse sensibly immediately afterward. Acute subjective symptoms of concussion include feeling lightheaded, "seeing stars," having blurred vision, headaches, or experiencing ringing in the ears. Postconcussion syndrome (PCS), as the name suggests, is a characteristic complex of subjective symptoms that occurs subsequent to a concussion. In the vast majority of individuals these symptoms resolve within a time period ranging from minutes to 24–72 hours. Although some symptoms may last for days, approximately 90 percent or more of individuals who sustain a concussion are asymptomatic within a couple of weeks.

Brain concussions, along with penetrating brain injuries, are subsumed under the label of traumatic brain injury (TBI), and are classified as mild, moderate, or severe based on multiple factors, such as duration of loss of consciousness, duration of posttraumatic amnesia (i.e., the time period during which a person remains dazed, confused, and disoriented), and performance on a brief measure of basis cognitive status such as the Glasgow Coma Scale. The term "concussion" has become synonymous with a specific type and severity of injury that is most consistent with a mild TBI. However, a concussive mechanism of injury has the potential to result in damage across the range of TBI severity. Thus, although the concept of PCS, when originally described, was not intended to be limited to characterizing symptoms subsequent to a mild TBI, the two are now exclusively connected in both mainstream and medical communities.

Mild Traumatic Brain Injury

Mild TBI is the most common type of TBI with an estimated annual incidence of 1.2 million in the United States alone (Sosin, Sniezek, & Thurman, 1996). There is no doubt that a mild TBI is associated with acute disruption of brain functioning. The individual who sustains a mild TBI initially is at best dazed, confused, and temporarily disoriented and often has memory gaps for the injury itself and for some period of time thereafter (seconds to hours). At worst, the individual is clearly unconscious for up to 30 minutes and experiences a period of posttraumatic amnesia extending up to 24 hours. In addition, the circumstances resulting in the mild TBI frequently include other injuries and/or exposure to a potential psychologically traumatic event (e.g., motor vehicle accident).

PCS Diagnosis Criteria

Formal diagnostic criteria for PCS vary between the *Diagnostic and Statistical Manual of Mental Disorders* (DSM-IV-TR; 2000) and the *International Statistical Classification of Disease and Related Health Problems* (ICD-10; 1992). First, PCS is not an official diagnostic category in the DSM-IV-TR but is, rather, a set of proposed diagnostic criteria for investigation. In contrast, the description of PCS in the ICD-10 is not investigational but lacks specific criteria regarding the nature and severity of symptom complaints. A second significant difference between the two classification systems is that the DSM-IV-TR includes not only the subjective symptom complaints described earlier but also objective evidence of attention or memory difficulties upon formal testing, whereas ICD-10 criteria does not. Finally, the ICD-10 suggests that there may be a hypochondriacal preoccupation, while the DSM-IV does not discuss this possible presentation. Despite the differences, the complex of symptom complaints is quite similar between the two classification systems and include headaches, dizziness, fatigue, insomnia, cognitive complaints (e.g., difficulty with memory, attention, concentration, and thinking), reduced stress tolerance, irritability, emotional lability, and mood disturbance (e.g., depression or anxiety). DSM-IV-TR indicates that three symptoms must appear shortly after the injury and last at least three months, whereas the ICD-10 requires the presence of three symptoms but does not indicate duration of symptom persistence.

Factors in the Development of PCS

In most patients who have suffered a mild TBI or concussion, complete recovery is observed within a month or two (Dikmen, Machamer, & Temkin, 2001). However, in a small subset of patients (approximately 10–15%), physical and cognitive symptoms either persist or are misattributed to the mild TBI well beyond three months. It is this subset of patients, and the potential application of a PCS diagnosis therein, that serves as a source of much debate in the medical-legal community regarding the etiology and mechanism of persisting symptoms. There are some who contend that PCS reflects persisting subtle neurological dysfunction resulting from mild TBI; this dysfunction is beneath the detection threshold of routine diagnostic procedures such as CT, MRI, and EEG conducted shortly after injury (Hayes & Dixon, 1994). In contrast, others espouse that persistent complaints and difficulties reflect the role of psychological factors in the perpetuation of those symptoms. This perspective is reflected in the description of PCS in the ICD-10, which includes a statement regarding potential hypochondriacal tendencies in patients with PCS. Suggestions regarding specific psychological mechanisms implicated in negative outcomes in mild TBI not only include hypochondriasis, but also preexisting or concurrent psychological conditions such as depression and anxiety, lower levels of premorbid cognitive ability, lack of psychosocial support, and self-expectations regarding the likely effects of sustaining a mild TBI.

Resolution to the debate over PCS is likely some way off, if possible at all. The primary reason for the debate itself, as well as its unlikely resolution, rests in the very nature of the diagnosis and the symptoms that comprise it. Symptoms of PCS are quite common in normal individuals with base rates as high as 10–20% (Vanderploeg, Curtiss, Luis, & Salazar, 2007). In addition, the substantial overlap of PCS symptom clusters with a variety of medical and psychological conditions renders the entire concept of a postconcussion "syndrome" problematic. Finally, there is a substantial literature demonstrating significant contributions of gender, depression, anxiety, social-economic factors, and lower levels of intelligence or education to the development and perpetuation of the condition.

Implications and Future Directions of PCS

The fact that a clear resolution to the etiological and treatment debate regarding PCS is likely not on the near horizon does not diminish the urgency of gaining a greater understanding of the condition or the importance of efforts to assist those who suffer from its symptoms. Whether neurological, psychological, or both in nature, the impact of PCS can be profound, result in failure to return to work or other important social roles, and lead to a significant decrement in overall quality of life.

REFERENCES

American Psychiatric Association (2000). *Diagnostic and statistical manual of mental disorders* (4th ed., text rev.). Washington, DC: Author.

Dikmen, S., Machamer, J., & Temkin, N. (2001). Mild head injury: Facts and artifacts. *Journal of Clinical and Experimental Neuropsychology, 23*, 729–738.

Hayes, R. L., & Dixon, C. E. (1994). Neurochemical changes in mild head injury. *Seminars in Neurology, 14*, 25–31.

Sosin, D. M., Sniezek, J. E., & Thurman, D. J. (1996). Incidence of mild and moderate brain injury in the United States, 1991. *Brain Injury, 10*, 47–54.

Vanderploeg, R. D., Curtiss, G., Luis, C. A., & Salazar, A. M. (2007). Long-term morbidity and quality of life following mild head injury. *Journal of Clinical and Experimental Neuropsychology, 29*(6), 585–598.

World Health Organization. (1992). *International statistical classification of diseases and related health problems* (10th ed.). Geneva, Switzerland: World Health Organization.

SUGGESTED READING

McCrea, M. (2007). *Mild traumatic brain injury and postconcussion syndrome: The new evidence base for diagnosis and treatment.* New York: Oxford Press.

ERIC P. SPIEGEL
James A. Haley VAMC, Tampa, FL

RODNEY D. VANDERPLOEG
James A. Haley VAMC, Tampa, FL, and University of South Florida

POSTPARTUM DEPRESSION

For a diagnosis of postpartum depression to be made, the patient must meet the criteria for a major depressive disorder as specified in the *Diagnostic and Statistical Manual of Mental Disorders* (DSM-IV-TR; American Psychiatric Association, 2000). Furthermore, the onset of the episode of major depression should be within 4 weeks postpartum. That a woman with postpartum depression meets the criteria of a major depression means that she has five or more of the following symptoms (and at least one of these symptoms is 1 or 2): (1) a depressed mood most of the day, (2) a markedly diminished interest or pleasure in all or almost all activities most of the day, (3) significant weight loss or weight gain or a considerable decrease or increase in appetite, (4) insomnia or hypersomnia, (5) psychomotor agitation or retardation, (6) fatigue or loss of energy, (7) feelings of worthlessness or excessive guilt, (8) concentration problems, and (9) thoughts of death or suicide.

Apart from postpartum depression, the DSM-IV-TR also includes criteria for other postpartum mental disorders, such as manic, bipolar, and brief psychotic disorders. These disorders are not discussed here. Postpartum depression should be distinguished from postnatal blues. Postnatal blues, also known as baby blues, is a self-limiting condition that lasts a few days to 2 weeks and is accompanied by a depressed mood but generally does not require treatment.

Although the DSM-IV-TR requires an onset of the depressive episode within 4 weeks postpartum, it has also been suggested that a time frame of 3 months or even 1 year after birth would be more appropriate for defining postpartum depression. There is some controversy about whether the rates of depression increase after delivery, with some research showing that prevalence rates do indeed increase while others do not find support for this hypothesis. There is also controversy about whether postpartum depression should be considered a specific major depressive disorder. When women with postpartum depression meet all criteria for a major depression, then it is not necessary to consider it as a specific entity with a specific etiology. Giving birth to a child can be seen as a major stressor that triggers the onset of a depressive episode, and this is not necessarily different from other major life stressors that trigger the onset of depression.

Although postpartum depression is a maternal mental disorder, there is evidence that a considerable number of fathers also suffer from depression in the early postnatal period (Matthey, Barnett, Ungerer, & Waters, 2000). Paternal postpartum depression is closely related to maternal depression, with a 40% to 50% risk when the mother is depressed (Lee & Chung, 2007).

Consequences for Mother and Child

Although postpartum depression tends to remit spontaneously after 4–6 months in many cases, it has a considerable negative impact on the mother, the infant, and the family. Apart from the direct suffering caused by postpartum depression in the patient and the increased risk of hospitalization, several areas in the life of a patient can be adversely affected. Postpartum depression has been reported to result in an increased risk of marital stress and divorce, an increased risk of child abuse and neglect, and sometimes even in maternal suicide and infanticide.

Postpartum depression can also have serious consequences for the children of affected mothers, in the short term and in the long term. There is some evidence that mothers with postpartum depression are less affectionate toward their children and less responsive to their cries. These mothers have also been found to be more distant and to make fewer positive facial expressions and vocalizations with their infants. There are also indications that postpartum depression has negative effects on children. These possible negative effects include an increased risk of impaired mental and motor development, difficult temperament, poor self-regulation, low self-esteem, and long-term behavioral problems. It can also result in attachment insecurity, social interaction difficulties, and a negative influence on cognitive skills and expressive language development.

Prevalence, Incidence, and Risk Factors

About one in every seven new mothers is affected by postpartum depression, resulting in an overall prevalence rate of 13% (O'Hara & Swain, 1996). Postpartum mood disorders represent the most frequent form of maternal morbidity following delivery. However, there are also indications that the prevalence rates of postpartum depression are higher in some countries and lower to absent in other countries.

The causes of postpartum depression remain unclear, and most research suggests that it is caused by multiple, interacting biological and psychosocial factors. There is some evidence that genetic factors contribute to as much

as a third of the etiological variance of postpartum depression. Hormones, such as estrogen and progestogen, have commonly been suggested as potential biological causes, but studies in this field have not resulted in clear support of this. The strongest antenatal risk indicators for postpartum depression are antenatal depression, prenatal anxiety, recent stressful life events, lack of social support, and a history of depression (Robertson, Grace, Wallington, & Stewart, 2004). Other more modest risk indicators include a poor marital relationship and neuroticism. There are few indications that obstetric factors and low socioeconomic status are important risk indicators. Antenatal depression is by far the best predictor of postpartum depression. A substantial proportion of postpartum depression actually begins during pregnancy (Lee & Chung, 2007).

Prevention and Screening

Postpartum depression often goes undetected because of lack of proper screening and the shame and loneliness that often make a woman hide it from her surroundings. It is estimated that up to 50% of cases of postpartum depression are not detected. Untreated postpartum depression often remits spontaneously after 4–6 months, but it can in some cases last much longer and cause prolonged, serious suffering. Because it causes considerable distress and disruption to the women and their families, prevention and the delivery of effective treatment are generally considered a priority. Diagnosing and beginning treatment early could most likely prevent future suffering and disruption of the life of the individual, of family relations, and of the process of bonding and attachment with the baby.

Numerous studies have examined the possibility of preventing postpartum depression by offering a preventive intervention during the antenatal phase in high-risk women. The few studies that have examined prevention of postpartum depression with antidepressive medication have not resulted in clear outcomes. A meta-analysis of studies of psychosocial interventions also did not find definite evidence that prevention of postpartum depression is indeed possible (Dennis, 2005). However, this study did find an overall reduction of the incidence of postpartum depression of 19%, but this did not reach significance levels. Several of the studies in this area have not excluded women who were depressed during the antenatal phase. In a recent meta-analysis of 19 studies on prevention of the incidence of depressive disorders in general (Cuijpers, Van Straten, Smit, Mihalopoulos, & Beekman, in press), seven studies on prevention of postpartum depression were found that had excluded women who already had a depressive disorder. In this meta-analysis, it was found that the 19 studies significantly reduced the onset of depressive disorders by 22%, and there was a trend indicating that the seven studies on postpartum depression reduced the incidence by 35%. Most preventive interventions for post-partum depression are based on psychological treatments and especially cognitive behavior therapy and interpersonal psychotherapy.

Because of the low levels of detection of postpartum depression, routine periodic screening of new mothers is important. The most used screening instrument is the Edinburgh Postnatal Depression scale (EPDS; Cox, Holden, & Sagovsky, 1987). The EPDS is very brief (10 items) and easy to use, it takes only a few minutes to complete, it has been validated in many studies, it is translated into many languages, and it is superior to other, more general self-report questionnaires in the detection of postpartum depression (Boyd, Le, & Somberg, 2005).

Treatment

For the treatment of postpartum depression, a combination of antidepressant medication and psychosocial interventions is recommended (Altshuler et al., 2001). However, there is very limited evidence available on treatment with antidepressant medication to guide practice or policy recommendations (Hoffbrand, Howard, & Crawley, 2001). Furthermore, psychological interventions are usually preferred by mothers to antidepressant treatment, due to worries about safety issues with regard to breastfeeding. When the mother is breastfeeding, the uncertain neurobehavioral risks of antidepressant medication should be carefully considered.

Psychological and psychosocial treatments of postpartum depression have been studied better (Cuijpers, Brännmark, &Van Straten, 2008). Overall, these treatments have been found to result in a large reduction of depression (standardized mean effect size of 0.61). The best studied psychological treatment is cognitive behavior therapy. In this treatment, women learn how to restructure negative thoughts about themselves, the world, and their future. Cognitive behavior therapy and other psychotherapies are often combined with psychoeducation about postpartum depression, the consequences of having a child, and possibilities of changing their environment to reduce the risk of getting depressed. Apart from cognitive behavior therapy, interpersonal psychotherapy is gaining popularity as a psychological treatment of postpartum depression. In interpersonal psychotherapy for postpartum depression, disruptions in relationship are assumed to be a major cause of depression. Problems in these relationships are worked through during the therapy. Apart from cognitive behavior therapy and interpersonal psychotherapy, support groups are often used as a treatment. In support groups, women can talk about their problems with other women in the same situation and learn from each other. Usually, such groups are led by professional therapists, but in some cases by women who have recovered from postpartum depression by participating in a support group.

REFERENCES

Altshuler, L. L., Cohen, L. S., Moline, M. L., Kahn, D. A., Carpenter, D., Docherty, J. P., et al. (2001). The expert consensus guideline series. Treatment of depression in women [Special Issue]. *Postgraduate Medicine*, 1–107.

American Psychiatric Association. (2000). *Diagnostic and statistical manual of mental disorders* (4th ed., text rev.). Washington, DC: Author.

Boyd, R. C., Le, H. N., & Somberg, R. (2005). Review of screening instruments for postpartum depression. *Archives of Women's Mental Health, 8*, 141–153.

Cox, J. L., Holden, J. M., & Sagovsky, R. (1987). Detection of postnatal depression. Development of the 10-item Edinburgh Postnatal Depression Scale. *British Journal of Psychiatry, 150*, 782–786.

Cuijpers, P., Brännmark, J. G., & van Straten, A. (2008). Psychological treatment of postpartum depression: A meta-analysis. *Journal of Clinical Psychology, 64*, 103–118.

Cuijpers, P., van Straten, A., Smit, F., Mihalopoulos, C., & Beekman, A. (in press). Preventing the onset of depressive disorders: A meta-analytic review of psychological interventions. *American Journal of Psychiatry*.

Dennis, C. L. (2005). Psychosocial and psychological interventions for prevention of postnatal depression: Systematic review. *British Medical Journal, 331*(7507), 15.

Hoffbrand, S., Howard, L., & Crawley, H. (2001). Antidepressant treatment for post-natal depression. *Cochrane Database of Systematic Reviews 2001*, Issue 2. Art. No.: CD002018.

Lee, D. T. S., & Chung, T. K. H. (2007). Postnatal depression: An update. *Best Practice & Research Clinical Obstetrics and Gynaecology, 21*, 183–191.

Matthey, S., Barnett, B., Ungerer, J., & Waters, B. (2000). Paternal and maternal depressed mood during the transition to parenthood. *Journal of Affective Disorders, 60*, 75–85.

O'Hara, M., & Swain, A. (1996). Rates and risk of postpartum depression: A meta-analysis. *International Review of Psychiatry, 8*, 37–54.

Robertson, E., Grace, S., Wallington, T., & Stewart, D. E. (2004). Antenatal risk factors for postpartum depression: A synthesis of recent literature. *General Hospital Psychiatry, 26*, 289–295.

PIM CUIJPERS
VU University Amsterdam, The Netherlands

See also: **Culture and Depression; Lifespan Depression; Major Depressive Disorder**

POSTTRAUMATIC GROWTH

The view that the struggle with major challenges can lead to significant positive changes is present in ancient myths, is a theme in literature, and is reflected in some of the major world religions. Heroes encounter severe hardships and emerge transformed and better persons, and believers who suffer greatly are sanctified through their martyrdom. This theme is captured in the well-known Latin phrase, attributed to Seneca, the Younger, *per aspera ad astra*—by the harsh road to the stars. Although the idea is ancient, the systematic study of this phenomenon by social and behavioral scientists is recent.

The term *posttraumatic growth* first appeared in print in 1995 and is defined as the experience of significant positive change resulting from the struggle with a major life crisis. Before that date some scholars had already investigated some aspects of this phenomenon, and the idea that grappling with crisis can lead to positive psychological changes was part of the contributions of major scholars of the twentieth century, including Viktor Frankl, Gerald Caplan, and Irvin Yalom. Once researchers developed inventories to assess posttraumatic growth (e.g., Park, Cohen, & Murch, 1996; Tedeschi & Calhoun, 1996), systematic quantitative investigation became possible. Investigators in several countries have now administered these scales to people dealing with a wide variety of major life difficulties, including sexual assault, becoming physically handicapped as an adult, surviving an earthquake, coping with the birth of a medically fragile or severally handicapped baby, combat, the death of a loved one, cancer, and surviving the Holocaust. These studies have indicated that the phenomenon of posttraumatic growth is widespread and may be quite common (Linley & Joseph, 2004).

Although perhaps not exhaustive, the following five domains provide a good representation of the experience of posttraumatic growth (Morris, Shakespeare-Finch, Rieck, & Newbery, 2005; Tedeschi & Calhoun, 1996): the emergence of new possibilities in life, positive changes in relationships, a greater sense of personal strength, greater appreciation for life, and spiritual changes. New possibilities in life include the development of new interests and the establishment of a new path in life. For example, a woman who lost her child to cancer made the decision to become an oncology nurse to help other parents and children facing that disease. The encounter with life stressors can certainly lead to the loss of some relationships and damage to others, but many persons also report developing closer and more intimate relationships with important people in their lives, and there can also be an increase in compassion for others who suffer.

A traumatic event tells people very clearly that life can sometimes be unpredictable and uncontrollable, but individuals who face trauma often develop a greater sense of their own strength in the face of adversity; this change is reflected in the phrase *I now know I'm vulnerable, but I also know that I am stronger than I ever imagined.* Another domain of growth is the experience of a greater appreciation for one's life and for those things that are still possible and desirable, such as time with close friends, the smile on a toddler's face, a beautiful sunset, or perhaps something as simple as the pleasure of eating an ice cream cone. As a

father said, after almost having lost infant twins as the result of a hospital error, "I don't take any day for granted anymore; every day is precious."

A fifth area of growth is the spiritual or religious domain. Certainly, some people who encounter suffering lose faith and feel a loss of connection with, or lose any belief in, anything transcendent. But a characteristic of growth in this domain is the experience of a changed understanding and experience of existential, spiritual, or religious matters, in a way that is positive for the individual; the change is not necessarily toward greater faith or orthodoxy, but to understandings that are more personally meaningful and satisfying. The person has confronted major existential questions and has found new and more satisfying answers. In addition, as posttraumatic growth emerges from the person's struggle with very difficult situations, there may also be an accompanying change in two other areas. The process of change may also touch on people's broader understanding of the guiding narrative of their lives (Neimeyer, 2001) and may also be accompanied by an increase in wisdom (Baltes & Smith, 2008).

There may be occasions where the individual's report of growth reflects a somewhat distorted perception of circumstances (Zoellner & Maercker, 2006), but such distorted views are uncommon. Self-reports of growth are not related to the tendency to give socially desirable responses; respondents may actually underreport growth on quantitative measures, and self-reported growth is corroborated by others (Calhoun & Tedeschi, 2006). The current evidence suggests that, although there may be times when a person may report posttraumatic growth that is not matched by actual changes, such distortions do not explain the majority of reports of posttraumatic growth.

How common is the experience of posttraumatic growth? The answer varies, depending on what criteria are used to make the judgment about the presence and degree of growth. If the focus includes any of the five domains of growth described above, then the available evidence indicates that up to 90% of persons coping with major stressors report growth in at least one of those domains. If, on the other hand, the criteria are more stringent, requiring high levels of change in several domains, then the percentage of persons who can be said to have experienced growth is much lower. Some degree of posttraumatic growth, in at least some areas of life, tends to be experienced by a large proportion of persons exposed to major life crises (Calhoun & Tedeschi, 2006).

An unanswered question about posttraumatic growth is whether the experience of growth is accompanied by a commensurate reduction in psychological distress, for example, in symptoms of posttraumatic stress disorder. The evidence in this regard is currently mixed, with some studies showing no relationship, some a negative relationship (more growth and less distress), and a few reporting a positive relationship between growth and psychological symptoms. The point of view that currently makes the most sense about this possible relationship is to regard posttraumatic growth and psychological symptoms as essentially independent of each other. Patients with life threatening cancer, for example, might well be expected to experience anxiety about the potential course of the illness and sadness about the possibility of losing significant physical function, or even their lives; at the same time, however, they might experience a significant strengthening of intimate bonds with close family members and good friends, have a greater appreciation for the simple elements of everyday life, and perhaps even become more satisfied with their answers to the fundamental existential questions about life's meaning and purpose.

REFERENCES

Baltes, P. B., & Smith, J. (2008). The fascination of wisdom: Nature, ontogeny, and function. *Perspectives on Psychological Science, 3,* 56–64.

Calhoun, L. G., & Tedeschi, R. G. (Eds.). (2006). *Handbook of posttraumatic growth: research and practice.* Mahwah, NJ: Lawrence Erlbaum.

Linley, P. A., & Joseph, S. (2004). Positive change following trauma and adversity: A review. *Journal of Traumatic Stress, 17,* 11–21.

Morris, B., Shakespeare-Finch, J., Rieck, M., & Newbery, J. (2005). Multidimensional nature of posttraumatic growth in an Australian population. *Journal of Traumatic Stress, 18,* 575–585.

Neimeyer, R. (2001). *Meaning reconstruction and the experience of loss.* Washington, DC: American Psychological Association.

Park, C. L., Cohen, L., & Murch, R. (1996). Assessment and prediction of stress-related growth. *Journal of Personality, 64,* 645–658.

Tedeschi, R. G., & Calhoun, L. G. (1996). The posttraumatic growth inventory: Measuring the positive legacy of trauma. *Journal of Traumatic Stress, 9,* 455–471.

Zoellner, T., & Maercker, A. (2006). Posttraumatic growth in clinical psychology: A critical review and introduction of a two component model. *Clinical Psychology Review, 26,* 626–653.

SUGGESTED READINGS

Janoff-Bulman, R. (1992). *Shattered assumptions.* New York: Free Press.

Joseph, S., & Linley, P. A. (Eds.). (2008). *Trauma, recovery, and growth: Positive psychological perspectives on posttraumatic stress.* Hoboken, NJ: John Wiley & Sons.

Tedeschi, R. G., & Calhoun, L. G. (1995). *Trauma and transformation: Growing in the aftermath of suffering.* Thousand Oaks, CA: Sage.

LAWRENCE G. CALHOUN
RICHARD G. TEDESCHI
University of North Carolina Charlotte

POSTTRAUMATIC STRESS DISORDER

Posttraumatic stress disorder (PTSD) is a psychiatric disorder defined by symptoms reflecting disturbances in cognitive, behavioral, and physiological functioning that develop in the wake of exposure to a psychologically traumatic event. According to the *DSM-IV-TR* (American Psychiatric Association, 2000), the diagnosis applies to individuals who develop a requisite number of symptoms after experiencing, witnessing, or being confronted with an event that involved perceived or threatened loss of life, serious injury, or loss of physical integrity and that evoked fear, helplessness, or horror (e.g., military combat, sexual or physical assault, serious accidents, and major disasters). *DSM-IV-TR* organizes the symptoms of PTSD under three clusters: (1) reexperiencing (e.g., intrusive thoughts, nightmares, flashbacks, and psychophysiological reactivity to reminders of the trauma), (2) avoidance and emotional numbing (e.g., avoiding stimuli associated with the trauma and inability to experience a full range of emotions), and (3) hyperarousal (e.g., hypervigilance, exaggerated startle response, and sleep disruption). By definition, these symptoms must persist for more than 1 month after the trauma and produce clinically significant distress and/or impairment.

Prevalence and Etiology of Trauma and PTSD

Epidemiological studies suggest that 40–90% of the general population in the United States experiences a traumatic event meeting the PTSD stressor criterion at some point during their lifetimes. Males appear to be more likely to be exposed to a traumatic event than are females. The probability of developing PTSD after trauma exposure is estimated to be approximately 10% in the general population, with higher rates (i.e., closer to 25%) observed in association with traumatic events involving interpersonal violence, such as rape and military combat. Numerous factors contribute to the probability of developing the disorder, with the nature and severity of the event being the most important factor. In addition, psychosocial factors such as a family history of psychiatric illness, childhood trauma or behavior problems, and the presence of psychiatric symptoms prior to the trauma appear to increase the risk for the development of PTSD after trauma exposure.

Individual difference factors also play a role. After controlling for trauma exposure, the rate of PTSD among women in the general population of the United States is approximately twice as high as the rate for men (Breslau et al., 1998; Kessler, Sonnega, Bromet, Hughes, & Nelson, 1995). Research suggests that personality traits such as neuroticism/negative emotionality (Miller, 2003) represent vulnerabilities for the development of the disorder, whereas characteristics such as hardiness (King, King, Fairbank, Keane, & Adams, 1998) function as resilience factors.

Keane and Barlow (2002) adapted Barlow's model of anxiety and panic to promote an understanding of the variables involved in the development of PTSD. This conceptual model suggests that both biological and psychological vulnerabilities may underlie the development of PTSD. Each of these variables may exert independent effects or may interact to increase vulnerability to the disorder. From this standpoint, when an individual is exposed to a traumatic life event, a biological and psychological alarm occurs that leads to both conditioning of stimuli present at the time of the event and to cognitions involving anxious apprehension of a recurrence of the traumatic event. These emotionally charged stimuli then promote the development of avoidance strategies in order to effectively minimize the experience of aversive emotional reactions. The emergence of PTSD is a function of these variables, as well as of the strength of the social support system of the individual and the individual's coping abilities in the aftermath of trauma exposure.

Assessment of PTSD

A comprehensive clinical assessment of PTSD should include administration of structured diagnostic interviews, self-report psychometrics, and an evaluation of trauma across the life span (Keane, Brief, Pratt, & Miller, 2007; Keane, Silberbogen, & Weierich, 2008). Several structured interviews are available, and the Clinician-Administered PTSD Scale for the *DSM-IV* (Blake et al., 1990) and the PTSD module of the Structured Clinical Interview for the *DSM-IV* (First, Spitzer, Gibbon, & Williams, 1997) are standards in the field. Self-report instruments can also assist in diagnosis or provide efficient, low-cost methods for research and screening purposes. Of these, several were constructed specifically to assess PTSD (e.g., Mississippi Scale for Combat-Related PTSD; PTSD Checklist; PTSD Diagnostic Scale), whereas others were derived from existing items of major inventories such as the Minnesota Multiphasic Personality Inventory-2nd edition (MMPI-2) or the Symptom Checklist-90. Finally, instruments such as the Potential Stressful Events Interview and the Traumatic Stress Schedule are useful in evaluating trauma exposure across the life span. Virtually all of the available diagnostic measures of PTSD possess excellent psychometric properties (Keane et al., 2007; Wilson & Keane, 2004).

Treatment of PTSD

Treatment for PTSD typically involves psychotherapy, pharmacotherapy, or both. Of the psychotherapies, exposure-based approaches (e.g., systematic desensitization, prolonged exposure, imaginal and in vivo exposure) have received the most attention and empirical support to date (Foa, Keane, Friedman, & Cohen, in press). The central element of these techniques is the gradual exposure of the client to trauma-related cues to desensitize and extinguish problematic emotional and physiological reactions. The therapeutic mechanism has been conceptualized within the framework of classical conditioning: Repeated exposure to trauma-related cues (e.g., trauma-related images evoked from memory) in the absence of the feared negative consequences (e.g., the trauma itself) reduces the conditioned fear, anxiety, and avoidance characteristics of PTSD (Keane, Zimering, & Caddell, 1985).

A second promising category of empirically validated treatments for PTSD is cognitive restructuring therapies, such as cognitive processing therapy (Resick & Schnicke, 1993). Based on cognitive therapy principles, this approach was designed to identify and modify dysfunctional trauma-related beliefs and to teach specific behavioral and cognitively based coping skills. The treatment may also involve tasks that include an element of exposure, such as writing about or describing the trauma to disclose trauma-related cognitions.

Controlled studies that have directly compared treatments for PTSD provide strong evidence for the efficacy of these cognitive-behavioral therapies. One recent study compared prolonged exposure, cognitive processing therapy, and a wait-list condition in treating rape-related PTSD (Resick, Nishith, Weaver, Astin, & Feuer, 2002). The authors reported that the two treatments possessed comparable efficacy and that both were superior to the wait-list condition. This approach was also found to be effective in treating chronic combat-related PTSD in war veterans (Monson et al., 2006).

Pharmacological treatment of PTSD is primarily designed to treat symptom clusters of PTSD, rather than the entire syndrome or any underlying physiological dysregulation. Several classes of antidepressants have been found to be modestly effective, including monoamine oxidase inhibitors and tricyclics; selective serotonin reuptake inhibitors (SSRIs) have the strongest body of empirical support (Cooper, Carty, & Creamer, 2005). The SSRIs are currently the first choice of psychopharmacological treatment for PTSD. At present, studies are underway to examine the effectiveness of CBT and SSRIs when administered jointly. In addition, trials examining augmentation strategies to assess the efficacy of SSRIs with atypical antipsychotic medication are also underway to determine the relative efficacy of these medications in combination.

Controversies Involving the PTSD Diagnosis

Since its inclusion in the *DSM-III* in 1980, PTSD has been surrounded by considerable controversy. Critics have argued that the diagnosis (1) pathologizes the normal stress response and overshadows the fact that most individuals are resilient to or readily recover from the effects of psychological trauma; (2) requires clinicians to draw causal inferences about the influence of trauma exposure on the subsequent development of psychiatric symptoms, though in many cases this judgment may be difficult or impossible to make; and (3) promotes compensation-seeking and illness behavior while diminishing engagement in treatment. Controversy has also surrounded estimates of the prevalence of the disorder among the veteran population, the definition of trauma and types of experiences that are considered to be potentially traumatic, whether it is possible to repress traumatic memories only to recover them later, and the use of non-evidence-based treatments with individuals diagnosed with PTSD (Friedman, Resick, & Keane, 2007).

Although many challenges and questions remain, research in the field of PTSD has led to important advances in the understanding of the causes and consequences of the disorder, while also providing substantive support for the validity and clinical utility of the diagnosis. Cross-cultural studies have documented the occurrence of PTSD around the globe (e.g., Green et al., 2004), and investigators have identified personal and contextual factors that confer risk for the development of PTSD, as well as those that facilitate recovery (Vogt, King, & King, 2007). Finally, physiological and biological research demonstrates that individuals with the disorder can be differentiated from controls on the basis of autonomic response patterns and neurosteroid profiles; structural and functional brain-imaging studies also reveal abnormalities in hippocampal volume and amygdala and prefrontal cortex functioning in patients with the disorder (Neumeister, Henry, & Krystal, 2007).

REFERENCES

American Psychiatric Association. (2000). *Diagnostic and statistical manual of mental disorders* (4th ed., text rev.). Washington, DC: Author.

Blake, D. D., Weathers, F. W., Nagy, L. N., Kaloupek, D. G., Klauminzer, G., Charney, D. S., et al. (1990). A clinician ratings scale for assessing current and lifetime PTSD: The CAPS-1. *Behavior Therapist, 18,* 187–188.

Breslau, N., Kessler, R. C., Chilcoat, H. D., Schultz, L. R., Davis, G. C., & Andreski, P. (1998). Trauma and posttraumatic stress disorder in the community: The 1996 Detroit area survey of trauma. *Archives of General Psychiatry, 55,* 626–632.

Cooper, J., Carty, J., & Creamer, M. (2005). Pharmacotherapy for posttraumatic stress disorder: Empirical review and clinical recommendations. *Australian and New Zealand Journal of Psychiatry, 39,* 674–682.

First, M. B., Spitzer, R. L. Gibbon, M., & Williams, J. B. W. (1997). *Structured clinical interview for DSM-IV axis I disorders: Clinician version (SCID-CV).* Washington, DC: American Psychiatric Press.

Foa, E., Keane, T. M., Friedman, M. J., & Cohen, J. (in press). *Effective treatments for PTSD: Best practice guidelines from the International Society for Traumatic Stress Studies* (2nd ed.). New York: Guilford Press.

Friedman, M. J., Resick, P. A., & Keane, T. M. (2007). PTSD: Twenty-five years of progress and challenges. In M. J. Friedman, T. M. Keane, & P. A. Resick (Eds.), *Handbook of PTSD: Science and practice* (pp. 3–18). New York: Guilford Press.

Green, B. L., Friedman, M. J., de Jong, J. T. V. M., Solomon, S. D., Keane, T. M., Fairbank, J. A., et al. (Eds.). (2004). *Trauma interventions in war and peace: Prevention, practice, and policy.* Amsterdam: Kluwer Academic/Plenum Press.

Keane, T. M., & Barlow, D. H. (2002). Posttraumatic stress disorder. In D. H. Barlow (Ed.), *Anxiety and its disorders* (pp. 418–453) New York: Guilford Press.

Keane, T. M., Brief, D., Pratt, L., & Miller, M. W. (2007). Assessment of PTSD and its comorbidities in adults. In M. J. Friedman, T. M. Keane, & P. A. Resick (Eds.), *Handbook of PTSD: Science and practice* (pp. 279–305). New York: Guilford Press.

Keane, T. M., Silberbogen, A., & Weierich, M. (2008). Posttraumatic stress disorder. In J. Hunsley & E. Mash (Eds.), *A guide to assessments that work* (pp. 293–315). New York: Oxford University Press.

Keane, T. M., Zimering, R. T., & Caddell, J. M. (1985). A behavioral formulation of PTSD in combat veterans. *Behavior Therapist, 8,* 9–12.

Kessler, R. C., Sonnega, A., Bromet, E., Hughes, M., & Nelson, C. B. (1995). Posttraumatic stress disorder in the national comorbidity survey. *Archives of General Psychiatry, 52,* 1048–1060.

King, L. A., King, D. W., Fairbank, J. A., Keane, T. M., & Adams, G. A. (1998). Resilience-recovery factors in post-traumatic stress disorder among female and male Vietnam veterans: Hardiness, postwar social support, and additional stressful life events. *Journal of Personality and Social Psychology, 74,* 420–434.

Miller, M. W. (2003). Personality and the etiology and expression of PTSD: A three-factor model perspective. *Clinical Psychology: Science and Practice, 10,* 373–393.

Monson, C. M., Schnurr, P. P., Resick, P. A., Friedman, M. J., Young-Xu, Y., & Stevens, S. P. (2006). Cognitive processing therapy for veterans with military-related posttraumatic stress disorder. *Journal of Consulting and Clinical Psychology, 74,* 898–907.

Neumeister, A., Henry, S., & Krystal, J. H. (2007). Neurocircuitry and neuroplasticity in PTSD. In M. J. Friedman, T. M. Keane, & P. A. Resick (Eds.), *Handbook of PTSD: Science and practice* (pp. 151–165). New York: Guilford Press.

Resick, P. A., Nishith, P., Weaver, T. L., Astin, M. C., & Feuer, C. A. (2002). A comparison of cognitive-processing therapy with prolonged exposure and a waiting condition for the treatment of chronic posttraumatic stress disorder in female rape victims. *Journal of Consulting and Clinical Psychology, 70,* 867–879.

Resick, P. A., & Schnicke, M. K. (1993). *Cognitive processing therapy for rape victims: A treatment manual.* Newbury Park, CA: Sage.

Vogt, D. S., King, D. W., & King, L. A. (2007). Risk pathways for PTSD: Making sense of the literature. In M. J. Friedman,

T. M. Keane, & P. A. Resick (Eds.), *Handbook of PTSD: Science and practice* (pp. 99–115). New York: Guilford Press.

Wilson, J. P., & Keane, T. M. (2004) *Assessing psychological trauma and PTSD* (2nd ed.). New York: Guilford Press.

SUGGESTED READING

Friedman, M. J., Keane, T. M., & Resick, P. A. (Eds.). (2007). *Handbook of PTSD: Science and practice.* New York: Guilford Press.

Mark W. Miller
Brian P. Marx
Terence M. Keane
VA Boston Healthcare System and Boston University School of Medicine

POWER, STATISTICAL (See Statistical Power)

PREJUDICE AND DISCRIMINATION

Although often employed interchangeably and certainly related by laypersons and the media, the terms *prejudice* and *discrimination* possess distinct meanings for most social scientists. Prejudice denotes the possession of negative attitudes of a particular kind regarding members of a specific group or category. As commonly used in psychology, prejudice is not merely a statement of opinion or belief, but an attitude that includes feelings such as contempt, dislike, or loathing. Discrimination is a term applied to the negative actions that result from prejudicial attitudes and that are directed against the targets or victims of prejudice. Someone who is prejudiced may, in certain situations, practice discrimination. Prejudice, stereotyping, and discrimination often go hand-in-hand, but it is also possible to have one without the others.

More specifically, social scientists view prejudice as the possession of negative attitudes targeted at members of some particular group (religious, racial, ethnic, political)—attitudes that give rise to negative or unfavorable evaluations of individuals seen as belonging to that group. As an attitude, prejudice is seen as having a tripartite nature, with cognitive, affective, and behavioral components. A person's beliefs and expectations regarding a particular group are the cognitive component of the prejudicial attitude. The term *stereotypes* has come to designate networks or clusters of such beliefs and expectations. The basis of all stereotypes is that all those who belong to a specific category or group—ethnic, religious, racial, political, or any other classification—manifest similar behaviors and possess similar attitudes. The widespread application of stereotypes largely ignores human differences and individual differences.

The attitudinal nature of prejudice has generated measurement research modeled after much of the attitude literature. The cognitive, affective, and behavioral components of prejudice have been the subject of research directed at assessing the nature and extent of prejudice in the population at large (Inman & Baron, 1996). The cognitive or belief component of prejudice, the assessment of stereotypes, is generally tapped through a trait-selection procedure. Individuals are given a list of ethnic, religious, racial, and political categories and a list of traits, and they are asked to note which traits are associated with which group(s). Information on the affective or feeling component of prejudice is generally derived through the use of attitude scales engineered to measure the level of an individual's positive or negative feelings toward specific groups.

Individuals who are prejudiced against specific groups will tend to experience intense negative feelings when they come into contact with these groups, either directly or indirectly. The affective component of the prejudicial attitude comes into play here, with profound negative emotional feelings tending to accompany cognitive reactions to objects of prejudice. People who have prejudiced feelings are less likely to take in the context of the situation or the individual nature of the person belonging to the specific group. Instead, many assumptions are automatically made that link that person to the group.

The behavioral component of prejudice has engendered the most research interest. Here the concern is the tendency of prejudiced individuals to act in a negative manner toward targets of their prejudice. When such tendencies become manifest in overt behavior, discrimination is said to occur. Numerous constraints on behavior operate in everyday situations to prevent prejudicial feelings from being transformed into discriminatory behavior. If such obstacles are not present in a given instance, however, the prejudicial thought or tendency may find expression in the behavioral act, which may vary in intensity from the lowest level, mere social avoidance, to acts of extreme violence or even genocide.

Like prejudice, discrimination involves taking actions against people because they belong to a stereotyped group, ignoring personal merits or characteristics. However, discrimination usually stems from prejudicial attitudes and beliefs. Therefore, whereas prejudice is the mental set of beliefs that one may have, discrimination is the treatment or consideration based solely on a person's group membership status or assumptions about the person (Brehm, Kassin, & Fein, 2005). The social distance scale is an important tool in research into the behavioral component of prejudice. Subjects are presented with a series of hypothetical relationships between themselves and members of specific groups. The series of items represents increasing levels of closeness or intimacy between respondents and members of various groups (ranging from residing in the same country at the lowest level to intermarriage at the highest level), with the subjects being asked to indicate, for a given group, their willingness to accept individuals from that group into a given level of intimacy.

Prejudice and discrimination have also been linked together as "negative manifestations of integrative power." In this theoretical relationship, prejudice and discrimination imply some sort of relationship between people, albeit a negative one. In other words, when there is any relationship at all, there is some integration. Integration, in this case, is "achieved through hatred, fear, and the threat of a common enemy" (Boulding, 1989, p. 62). Some examples of this phenomenon on a large scale are the Balkans, Somalia, Sri Lanka, and the Middle East. However, it occurs on smaller scales as well, when one group holds negative stereotypes of another group and discriminates against members of that group based on those stereotypes.

REFERENCES

Boulding, K. E. (1989). *Three faces of power*. Thousand Oaks, CA: Sage.

Brehm, S. S., Kassin, S., & Fein, S. (2005). *Social psychology* (6th ed.). Boston: Houghton Mifflin.

Inman, M. L., & Baron, R. S. (1996). Influence prototypes on perceptions of prejudice. *Journal of Personality and Social Psychology, 70*, 727–739.

Florence L. Denmark
Pace University

PREMARITAL COUNSELING

The importance of marriage to family and individual functioning, and thus to society, is hard to overemphasize. As well as serving the economic and practical functions of nurturing the next generation, marriage in Western culture is expected to fulfill the emotional, sexual, and social needs of both partners, a very tall order. Thus, it is not surprising that many couples discover that their marital satisfaction deteriorates over the course of the first few years of marriage, and many eventually divorce. Through premarital counseling, mental health professionals work with couples to provide them with knowledge and skills, with the goal of preventing the development of marital distress and divorce and the accompanying pain and disruption in the family.

Comprehensive premarital counseling engages a couple in an exploration of expectations that the partners have for their future together, their relational styles, their understanding of each other, their match on important social and personality dimensions, their knowledge about the developmental stresses inherent in early marriage, their personal histories, and their readiness to manage the inevitable conflicts that will arise. The complex nature of marriage means that comprehensive premarital counseling may draw on many psychological theories and perspectives—attachment, social exchange, social learning, family systems, cognitive-behavioral, psychodynamic—each of which is particularly relevant to different aspects of a committed romantic relationship.

Valuable resources exist to assist counselors in assessing the extent of partners' knowledge and understanding of each other's personality, values, goals, and personal history and their risk for difficulties after marriage. Premarital assessment questionnaires are helpful in efficiently evaluating aspects of the premarital relationship that require exploration and work, although more research on marital outcomes in couples who complete these questionnaires as part of premarital preparation is needed (Halford, Markman, & Stanley, 2008). Questionnaires differ in terms of the content assessed, but common content dimensions include finances, sexuality, children, role expectations, support from family and friends, personality, and communication (see Larson, Newell, Topham, & Nichols, 2002, for a review of three such instruments). Results from these questionnaires not only identify potential areas of tension but also provide topics of varying difficulty on which to practice communication skills.

By providing education regarding the life cycle of marriage, premarital counseling can help to inoculate couples from the disappointment that comes from predictable difficulties. For example, in early marriage, the intense feelings of the courtship period mellow; as one manifestation, expressions of affection decrease dramatically over the first 2 years of marriage, even for couples who later report being happily married 13 years after their wedding (Huston, Caughlin, Houts, Smith, & George, 2001). Parenting adds new challenges, and many couples do not realize that marital satisfaction often declines with the increase in complexity and stress that children bring. Thus, education about the normative course of marriage can help couples understand the impact of important events, such as having a baby or moving, and this knowledge can help them attribute developmental stress to the situation instead of their partner.

In addition to education regarding the realities of modern marriage, most couples can benefit from training and coaching in relationship skills. The premarital counselor can receive training and certification in a number of established marriage preparation programs. Most well-known programs have many commonalities: they educate participants about relationships, teach positive communication skills and conflict management, and encourage adaptive relationship attitudes (Halford et al., 2008). Alternatively, the counselor may refer the couple to a retreat or series of sessions offered by established programs. Advantages of these programs are many: the content of well-established programs has been carefully crafted, couples may appreciate and enjoy working alongside other premarital couples, and research has demonstrated the short-term overall effectiveness of many of these programs (e.g., Carroll & Doherty, 2003).

Finally, as ongoing research adds to our understanding of marriage and intimate relationship processes, premarital counseling will evolve to incorporate new knowledge. For example, Fincham, Stanley, & Beach (2007) discuss transformational processes in current marital research that may provide new emphases for prevention in premarital counseling. These processes—such as commitment, forgiveness, sacrifice, and sanctification—emanate from deeply held values that give meaning to spouses' lives and have the potential to interact with communication between spouses in a way that naturally repairs marital dissatisfaction and distress. An understanding of these "deeper meaning" constructs may lead to the development of methods to foster self-repair and even self-transformation processes in couples as part of premarital counseling (Fincham et al., 2007). In a similar vein, Gordon and Christman (2008) believe that some at-risk premarital couples may benefit from an intervention model that combines relationship skills training with an exploration of how each partner's problematic communication behaviors may be motivated by attachment-related beliefs.

In sum, premarital counselors have the privilege of working with couples as they prepare to take the weightiest single step in their relationship, an extremely challenging and rewarding venture. As such, premarital counseling may facilitate different positive outcomes. Some couples may decide to terminate their relationship, probably preventing future disruption and pain and hopefully providing each partner with insight that will carry over into future intimate relationships. Other couples may decide to postpone their wedding as they gain insight into their relationship dynamics and work on strengthening their communication before tying the knot. Finally, for couples who continue with their wedding plans, premarital counseling can equip them with skills and knowledge to aid and gird them through inevitable rocky times, launching them on a positive path within the most important relationship of their adult lives.

REFERENCES

Carroll, J. S., & Doherty, W. J. (2003). Evaluating the effectiveness of premarital prevention programs: A meta-analytic review of outcome research. *Family Relations, 52,* 105–118.

Fincham, F. D., Stanley, S. M., & Beach, S. R. H. (2007). Transformative processes in marriage: An analysis of emerging trends. *Journal of Marriage and Family, 69,* 275–292.

Gordon, K. C., & Christman, J. A. (2008). Integrating social information processing and attachment style research with cognitive-behavioral couple therapy. *Journal of Contemporary Psychotherapy, 38*(3), 129–138.

Halford, W. K., Markman, H. J., & Stanley, S. (2008). Strengthening couples' relationships with education: Social policy and public health perspectives. *Journal of Family Psychology, 22*(4), 497–505.

Huston, T. L., Caughlin, J. P., Houts, R. M., Smith, S. E., & George, L. J. (2001). The connubial crucible: Newlywed years as predictors of marital delight, distress, and divorce. *Journal of Personality and Social Psychology, 80,* 237–252.

Larson, J. H., Newell, K., Topham, G., & Nichols, S. (2002). A review of three comprehensive premarital assessment questionnaires. *Journal of Marital & Family Therapy, 28*(2), 233–239.

SUGGESTED READINGS

Gottman, J. M., & Silver, N. (1999). *The seven principles for making marriage work.* New York: Three Rivers Press.

Napier, A. Y. (1988). *The fragile bond.* New York: HarperPerennial.

Wallerstein, J. S., & Blakeslee, S. (1995). *The good marriage.* New York: Houghton Mifflin.

Elizabeth A. Schilling
University of Connecticut Health Center

See also: **Marriage Counseling; Marital Discord**

PREMENSTRUAL SYNDROME

Premenstrual syndrome (PMS) is commonly understood to refer to a cluster of unpleasant physical and psychological symptoms that may be experienced prior to menstruation. Identified symptoms include bloating, breast tenderness, backache, muscle or joint pain, trouble with sleeping, acne, food cravings, irritability, mood swings, anxiety, and depression. The onset of menstruation is said to diminish symptom experience, and the cause of PMS is often described as related to the changing hormone levels of the menstrual cycle. The American Psychiatric Association (2000) includes premenstrual dysphoric disorder (PMDD) as a diagnostic category in the fourth edition of the *Diagnostic and Statistical Manual of Mental Disorders* (DSM-IV-TR) to refer to an extreme form of PMS, which is asserted to affect 3–8% of women.

In a recent comprehensive paper, Taylor (2006) traces the development of PMS as a "cultural entity and a medical concern" (p. 377). She notes that the earliest mention of PMS in the scientific literature was offered in 1843 by DeWeese, who referenced the "melancholies of menstruation" within the context of the nineteenth-century view that the uterus exerted control over women. Later, in the early 1900s, psychoanalytic theory reinforced the view that women were both physically and mentally debilitated because of their menstrual cycles, but it was Frank who, in 1931, based on his observations of 15 women, described what he called premenstrual tension (PMT) as varying degrees of discomfort prior to but relieved by the onset of menstruation. Frank and others prescribed various medical treatments for PMT; as Taylor points out, however, only doctors, and not the women undergoing treatment, were queried as to treatment effectiveness or side effects. It was not until the 1950s that the first placebo-controlled clinical trial was conducted to study the effects of various agents (e.g., diuretics, caffeine) on PMT severity, work output, and clinic visits.

In the 1960s, Katharina Dalton renamed PMT as PMS. Dalton, who treated women suffering from what she called progesterone-deficiency disease with supplemental progesterone at her PMS clinic in London, made her voice heard in the popular media, writing about the dangers to society of untreated PMS sufferers, nearly half, she claimed, of all women. Dalton's work, increased understanding of ovarian function, and advances in psychometrics prompted more empirical study of PMS and menstruation in the 1960s and 1970s. One important tool was the development of the Moos (1968) Menstrual Distress Questionnaire, which sought to specify the array and severity of menstrual-related symptomatology. Unfortunately, the Moos questionnaire permitted only exploration of negative symptomatology, within a research focus at the time on the debilitating effects of menstruation.

In the 1970s, critique of menstrual debilitation as the norm emerged. With respect to PMS, Dalton's work came under methodological scrutiny and was found wanting. Researchers were encouraged to explore premenstrual changes, as opposed to symptoms. This shift in the perspective of some researchers led to investigations of positive aspects of menstruation and, much later (in the 1990s), to a reexamination of PMS as a culture-bound rather than a medical syndrome (Chrisler, 1996). Nevertheless, the medicalization of PMS that began in the 1960s also continued. In the mid-1980s, professional medical organizations from the United States and Britain met to delineate PMS as a medical disease, and it was eventually listed in the *International Classification of Diseases Manual*. Subsequently, the continued attention from the psychiatric and psychological communities in the United States resulted in the inclusion of PMDD as a psychological disorder in the 1994 edition of the DSM-IV, in spite of an extensive literature review brought to bear during related deliberations that found little research supporting its existence (see Caplan, 2004).

Criticism of naming PMS and PMDD as physical or psychological disease entities is not limited to the lack of research supporting their existence but also includes the concern that such labeling renders premenstrual experience dysfunctional, thus reinforcing notions of women's biological inferiority and locating women's troubles in their biology rather than in social, contextual causes (see Nash & Chrisler, 1997). That women experience a range of physical and psychological changes associated with menstruation is not disputed. What is noted as problematic is viewing normative changes as a syndrome or mental disorder (disease entities) and the lack of specificity about when symptom experience is severe enough to warrant such labels.

Taylor (2006) reports that both earlier and recent robust studies of complex interactions between ovarian hormones and other body chemicals (e.g., prostaglandins, catecholamines) have not supported a primary endocrine abnormality as the etiology of PMS. She reports that one genealogical study of the interaction of menstrual cycle hormones and serotonin reveals no close etiological relationship between PMS and major depression, but she mentions other work suggesting that PMDD, as the extreme form of PMS, might have a different pattern of heritability. Finally, Taylor notes that whereas past research placed little focus on contextual factors (e.g., personality variables, cultural interpretations of menstrual experience) as contributing to premenstrual changes, current research is more likely to acknowledge these in interaction with biological factors. That said, Taylor concludes:

> The possibility that any single general theory can fully explain ... premenstrual symptoms for all women is now considered highly unlikely. Although severe PMS/PMDD has been predominantly regarded as a biologically-based illness, strong evidence now exists that variables such as life stress, response to stress, history of sexual abuse, and cultural socialization are important determinants of premenstrual symptoms. The prevailing view is that women with PMS are more sensitive to essentially normal hormonal shifts. The effects of these physiologic changes are different for each woman based on multiple psychosocial and cultural factors, creating a variety of distinct perimenstrual experiences. (p. 382)

Although the disease classification of PMS/PMDD continues to inform health care practice, Taylor (2006) notes improvements in empirical research methodology that have added women's experiences as an important part of the knowledge base. With regard to treatment, Taylor mentions that, prior to the mid-1980s, no specific treatments were recommended. In comparison, since the 1990s, numerous studies have been conducted to test the efficacy of a variety of nonmedical therapies, such as the use of herbs, nutritional substances, or lifestyle changes, in the reduction of symptoms. Some argue that the self-help treatment methods serve only to continue to problematize the menstrual cycle, but others point to the benefits of engaging women's sense of control in managing health issues, a strategy long acknowledged by health psychologists as useful in enhancing well-being and managing distressing symptoms. Notably, no one treatment, pharmacological or alternative, enjoys the status of a cure-all.

Advice from Caplan (2004) to health care practitioners who work with women who present with PMS symptoms includes the following: (1) Be aware of the stereotype that premenstrual women are out of control, (2) be prepared for women who have already diagnosed themselves as suffering from PMS or PMDD, (3) recommend a thorough medical workup to pinpoint any physiological problems that may not be immediately evident, and (4) become familiar with the biopsychosocial as well as the biomedical literature on the topics of PMS and PMDD and be willing to make this literature available and accessible to clients as appropriate.

REFERENCES

American Psychiatric Association. (2000). *Diagnostic and statistical manual of mental disorders* (4th ed., text rev.). Washington, DC: Author.

Caplan, P. J. (2004). The debate about PMDD and Sarafem: Suggestions for therapists. In J. Chrisler (Ed.), *From menarche to menopause: The female body in feminist therapy* (pp. 37–55). Binghamton, NY: Haworth.

Chrisler, J. C. (1996). PMS as a culture-bound syndrome. In J. C. Chrisler, C. Goldern, & P. D. Rozee (Eds.), *Lectures on the psychology of women* (107–121). New York: McGraw Hill.

Moos, R. H. (1968). The development of a menstrual distress questionnaire. *Psychosomatic Medicine, 30,* 853–867.

Nash, H. C., & Chrisler, J. C. (1997). Is a little (psychiatric) knowledge a dangerous thing? The impact of premenstrual dysphoric disorder on perceptions of premenstrual women. *Psychology of Women Quarterly, 21,* 315–322.

Taylor, D. (2006). From "it's all in your head" to "taking back the month": Premenstrual syndrome (PMS) research and the contributions of the Society for Menstrual Cycle Research. *Sex Roles, 54*(5–6), 377–391.

Margaret L. Stubbs
Chatham University, Pittsburgh, PA

PRESCRIPTION PRIVILEGES

In 2004, Louisiana became the second state (after New Mexico) to pass legislation authorizing psychologists to prescribe certain medications for the treatment of mental health disorders (Holloway, 2004). Previously, in 1998, the legislature in the territory of Guam provided the right of psychologists to prescribe under the supervision of psychiatrists. At that time, there were 16 psychologists in Guam. Sammons, Levant, and Page (2003) review the history of the prescriptive authority movement by noting that Senator Daniel K. Inouye (D-HI) proposed this to the Hawaii Psychological Association in 1984. He believed that this authority would fit nicely into their programmatic theme of transcending traditional boundaries.

Most of us are aware that physicians have prescriptive authority, and some of us know that dentists, optometrists, and podiatrists have more limited authority to prescribe. These practitioners can prescribe without physician involvement, but their practice tends to be restricted to conditions affecting certain body parts. For example, podiatrists tend to be restricted to conditions involving the feet, and optometrists are limited to conditions affecting the eyes. In addition, there are some professions that are considered to be physician extenders, who can prescribe under the authority of physicians. These include nurse practitioners, physician assistants, and pharmacists. As Fox and Sammons (1998) pointed out, nursing is moving toward independent status. Thus, advanced practice nurses (APNs) could prescribe drugs within their scope of practice by the year 2000, and nurse practitioners prescribe independently in 26 states.

Many of us assume that physicians have always had the right to prescribe. Sammons and colleagues (2003) note that prior to the twentieth century, nurses and pharmacists could order, compound, and dispense medications, and patients did not need to consult with physicians in order to obtain these medications. Medical education prior to 1920 was not particularly regulated, and not much background training was required, not even an undergraduate degree. The publication of a report by Abraham Flexner in 1910 did much to change that. This report urged the closing of substandard medical schools and recommended a standard curriculum that included clinical experience and a minimum of three years of training. As medical education improved and a research base was brought to the education of physicians, the status of medical practice changed and improved.

Psychologists themselves are not newcomers to the utilization of physical interventions. Biofeedback techniques, alarm bells for bedwetting, and polygraph assessments are relevant examples. Again, Senator Inouye came to the forefront by suggesting to the Assistant Secretary of Defense for Health Affairs that a pilot project be established that would permit psychologists to prescribe psychoactive drugs (Laskow & Grill, 2003). Despite considerable opposition from the Army Surgeon General's psychiatric advisers, the office of the Assistant Secretary of Defense for Health Affairs expressed willingness to continue with the project. This project (after numerous iterations) eventually resulted in permitting all of the participants who graduated from this pilot study to practice in an independent manner, as was intended by the program's designers.

The graduates of this program were permitted to prescribe from two classes of medications, which included psychotropic as well as adjunctive medications for drug-induced symptoms (Laskow & Grill, 2003). The outcome of this pilot project was positive. Despite fears about patient safety, no quality of care issues arose concerning the practice of the project graduates. In 1997, specific language in the Senate Appropriations Bill prevented the continuation of this pilot study. Numerous concerns about prescribing have been raised about prescriptive authority for psychologists. Although space does not permit a full discussion of these objections, the following topics that have surfaced can be addressed briefly: identity and political issues, training issues, financial concerns, liability, and overmedication issues.

With regard to political and identity issues, DeNelsky (1991) argues against the medicalization of psychology. He contends that the general public has accepted psychology as a mental health profession and views it differently from psychiatry. He further states that psychiatry made a conscious decision about 25 years ago to shift from a focus on psychotherapy toward an increase of administering psychotropic and other medications. But this has not increased its share of the mental health market. Psychology is the largest doctoral-level mental health discipline, and moving toward prescriptive authority is likely to affect psychology adversely. Many psychologists see prescription privileges as outside their knowledge base and outside the boundaries of their science (Brown, 2003).

In addition, prescriptive authority implies changing licensing laws, and making those changes opens the door to additional, often unwanted, changes. Furthermore, prescriptive authority is likely to increase animosity between psychiatry and psychology and result in continued fighting and posturing on both sides. Some of this has come to pass. Psychology has tried to gain prescriptive authority in a number of states, but in part due to opposition from organized psychiatry and, to some extent, from medicine, changes have been relatively slow to come.

There has been considerable debate concerning the nature of training needed by prescribing psychologists. Fox, Schwelitz, and Barclay (1992) describe a curriculum that requires undergraduate knowledge in biology and chemistry and preparation for graduate-level courses in biochemistry, physiological and biological aspects of drug interactions, and related courses, for a total of 39 semester hour credits. Some psychologists have raised a concern that there is already so much that needs to be learned in a graduate program in psychology that what used to take 3 to 4 years of graduate study now takes 6 to 7 years, plus an internship. Brown (2003) argues that an additional year of coursework would need to be added to the doctoral professional psychology curriculum. She wonders what would need to be deleted from the curriculum in order to provide prescriptive authority training. Some argue that the answer to all of this is continuing education, and there are a number of continuing education programs that aim to train individuals for an eventual examination for prescriptive authority. Others contend that the psychopharmacology curriculum leading toward prescriptive authority needs to be part of professional doctoral-level study in psychology.

Financial issues are another topic of concern. In most professional schools of psychology, stipends are limited, and tuition is quite high. The training costs for those seeking prescription privileges would probably increase substantially. Others express concern that malpractice insurance would increase markedly and worry that nonprescribing psychologists might have to share the burden of increased malpractice costs with those who do prescribe. Fox (1989) answered these concerns by stating that, in other professions, one can stipulate to not perform certain functions. He notes that surgeons pay higher premiums than do family practitioners; obstetricians and anesthesiologists pay higher premiums than do physicians who specialize in dermatology.

We have just touched on one aspect of liability under financial concerns. The larger issue, however, is the fact that prescribing is likely to increase insurance premiums for those psychologists who do prescribe. Consider the depressed patient to whom drugs are appropriately prescribed but who misuses the prescription to overdose and commit suicide. Also, some professionals who do prescribe are, at times, faced with patients who insist on obtaining medications. Some have argued that the right to prescribe includes the right not to prescribe. On the other hand, pharmaceutical companies are increasingly marketing psychotropic and other drugs to the public via television advertisements. It is also argued that there are many underserved individuals who receive little, if any, psychotherapy or other psychosocial treatments but are overmedicated. Some professionals worry that psychologists who prescribe will be more likely to give medications rather than psychotherapy, even if the latter is the preferred treatment. As we move more and more toward evidence-based treatments, others contend, that may become less of a problem.

In the previous edition of this encyclopedia, I noted that the overarching issue is the concern with political and identity matters. Many psychologists worried about becoming junior psychiatrists, and others worried about the battle with psychiatry and organized medicine. To some extent, that worry is ongoing. Further, the fear that confidence in psychosocial and psychotherapeutic methods will diminish remains a concern of practicing psychologists. However, as noted, psychology is not exclusively a mental health discipline (Fox, 1989) and deals with such topics as behavior change in health, learning, vocational functioning, aging, and rehabilitation. Psychology has made major advances in health psychology, behavior genetics, neuropsychology, and the application of knowledge gained from brain imaging. Prescriptive authority is one step in the education and training of psychologists in the twenty-first century.

REFERENCES

Brown, L. (2003). Doubts about prescribing. In M. Sammons, R. Levant, & R. Page (Eds.), *Prescriptive authority for psychologists.* Washington, DC: American Psychological Association.

DeNelsky, G. (1991). Prescription privileges for psychologists: The case against professional psychology. *Professional Psychology, 22,* 188–193.

Fox, R. (1989). Some practical and legal objections to prescription privileges for psychologists. *Psychotherapy and Private Practice, 6,* 23–29.

Fox, R., & Sammons, M. (1998). A history of prescription privileges. *APA Monitor,* 29.

Fox, R., Schwelitz, F., & Barclay, A. (1992). A proposed curriculum for psychopharmacology training for psychologists. *Professional Psychology: Research and Practice, 23,* 216–219.

Laskow, G., & Grill, D. (2003). The Department of Defense experiment: The psychopharmacology demonstration project. In M. Sammons, R. Levant, & R. Page (Eds.), *Prescriptive authority for psychologists.* Washington, DC: American Psychological Association.

Holloway, J. D. (2004). Louisiana becomes second state to enact prescription privileges law for psychologists. *Monitor on Psychology, 35.* Retrieved February 10, 2008, from http://www.apa.org/monitor/louisianarx.html.

Sammons, M., Levant, R., & Page, R. (2003). *Prescriptive authority for psychologists.* Washington, DC: American Psychological Association.

SUGGESTED READING

DeLeon, P., & Wiggins, J. (1996). Prescription privileges for psychologists. *American Psychologist, 41,* 225–229.

NORMAN ABELES
Michigan State University

PREVENTION OF MENTAL DISORDERS

The twentieth century witnessed major advances in the diagnosis and treatment of mental disorders. However, the alarming prevalence of many mental disorders, as well as their devastating consequences for individuals and communities, highlights the need for preventive interventions. Researchers have estimated that existing treatment methods are not sufficient to reduce the burden of depression, anxiety, and substance use by half, even assuming ideal conditions of treatment access, clinician competence, and patient compliance (Andrews & Wilkinson, 2002). Growing recognition of the importance of prevention has spurred research in this area, with considerable progress regarding methods and outcomes of preventive interventions over the past 15 years.

Defining Prevention

In the 1990s, the U.S. Congress charged the Institute of Medicine (IOM) to convene a Committee on Prevention of Mental Disorders. In their report (Mrazek & Haggerty, 1994), the IOM Committee proposed that the term *prevention* be reserved for interventions administered before the onset of a clinically diagnosable disorder. By contrast, *treatment* consists of interventions designed to ameliorate or cure a mental disorder that has already developed.

The IOM Report identified three levels of preventive interventions: *Universal preventive interventions* target an entire population group (e.g., public school elementary children). *Selective preventive interventions* target high-risk groups within a community (e.g., offspring of depressed parents). Risk status is determined on the basis of biological, psychological, or social factors known to be associated with the onset of a disorder, rather than individual risk profiles. *Indicated preventive interventions* target individuals with early signs or symptoms of a disorder who do not yet meet full diagnostic criteria (e.g., individuals with elevated depressive symptoms).

In general, the lower the cost and the fewer the possible ill effects of a preventive intervention, the more amenable it is for universal dissemination. Conversely, costlier and potentially risky or burdensome interventions should be reserved for use with individuals who have an indicated risk for the disorder. Nesting selective and indicated prevention approaches within universal prevention programs may increase the benefits of such programs. The nesting strategy provides a multitiered approach to prevention (Ialongo, Kellam, & Poduska, 2000; Kellam & Rebok, 1992), as exemplified by the parenting and classroom behavior management program developed by the Johns Hopkins University Preventive Intervention Research Center (JHU PIRC) to prevent mental health and substance abuse problems in youth (Ialongo et al., 2006).

The Nature and Scope of Prevention

Some disorders can be fully prevented by individual behavior. For example, alcohol, drug, and nicotine dependence are 100% preventable if an individual chooses not to use those substances. For other disorders, such as depression, individual strategies will reduce risk by some as yet unknown proportion. Similarly, prevention at the community level will reduce the incidence of disorders, rather than eliminating them completely. However, taken together, individual and community-level strategies can significantly lower rates of disorders. For instance, legal and other social interventions such as cigarette tax increases, antitobacco media campaigns, and laws prohibiting smoking indoors modify individual behavior and thus impact rates of smoking initiation and smoking cessation.

It is noteworthy that prevention efforts can be successful even when the causes of a disorder are poorly understood or cannot be modified directly. For instance, phenylketonuria (PKU) is a metabolic disorder resulting from genetic mutation. However, the severe mental retardation produced by PKU can be prevented via strict dietary control. Another example is the classic case of John Snow, who halted the nineteenth-century cholera epidemic in London by removing the handle of a Broad Street water pump, even though the specific agent that caused cholera was not yet known. Thus, although scientists do not yet fully comprehend the complex biological and social factors that produce mental disorders such as depression, the development of effective prevention strategies is nonetheless a feasible goal.

The IOM Committee identified as promising targets for prevention five disorders with heavy emotional and financial costs: conduct disorder, alcohol abuse/dependence, schizophrenia, Alzheimer's disease, and depressive disorders. A recent meta-analysis reviewed 13 randomized prevention trials to reduce the incidence of common mental disorders, including depression, anxiety, and psychosis (Cuijpers, Van Straten, & Smit, 2005). The overall relative risk of developing a mental disorder was significantly lower among experimental subjects than controls, suggesting that prevention of mental disorders is possible. The effect was particularly strong in cognitive behavioral preventive interventions for depressive and anxiety disorders.

Prevention of Depression as a Model of Preventive Intervention

As major depressive disorder arguably poses the most widespread risk of any mental disorder, both nationally and globally, and may be the most likely to be prevented first, it can serve as a model for the prevention of other disorders (Muñoz & Ying, 1993). The World Health Organization reported that major depression is the number one cause of disability in the world, and—with respect to the burden of disease in the world, taking into account both disability and mortality—major depression was the fourth most important disorder in 1990 and will become the second by 2020 (Murray & Lopez, 1996). Depression has been found to cause dysfunction that is equivalent to or worse than chronic physical illness, and it also contributes to major causes of death, such as smoking and drinking. With a problem of this magnitude, treatment is not sufficient to reduce prevalence (the total number of affected individuals); prevention of incidence (new cases) must be achieved.

To date, depression prevention interventions have been conducted with diverse populations and in varied settings, including adult primary care patients, pregnant women, adolescent children of depressed parents, and youth in school, and the evidence is promising both for preventing the onset of major depression (including postpartum depression) and for preventing relapse (Barrera, Torres, & Muñoz, 2007). These findings suggest prevention of major depressive episodes is a feasible goal because of two major advances. The first advance is the development of consistently successful means to identify groups at imminent risk for major depressive episodes. These methods,

primarily focusing on individuals who are not clinically depressed but score high on depression symptom scales, are yielding incidence rates of 25% or higher in the control groups. The second advance is the reduction in incidence reported in several randomized control trials from the 25% found in control groups to rates of 9–14% or lower in the experimental conditions, which works out to a reduction of 40% or better in new episodes of major depression. If we are able to consistently reduce 40% of new episodes of major depression, widespread availability of such preventive services could substantially reduce the burden of depression on our society.

Future Directions

Research has the potential to advance our ability to identify the most appropriate target groups for prevention efforts, a critical aspect of designing effective prevention strategies. Furthermore, well-designed prevention programs can and should inform our understanding of risk and protective factors key to the development of mental disorders, as well as elaborating our knowledge of developmental theory (Ialongo et al., 2006).

The mental health field will progress in the area of prevention of disorders as the general health care system moves toward parity in the treatment of mental and other disorders. Screening methods to identify cases of mental disorders in primary care settings will eventually be extended to the identification of individuals at risk. As preventive interventions receive empirical support, health care systems will be held accountable for providing those shown to be efficacious. Ultimately, as preventive interventions become more widespread, we will begin to see measurable drops in the incidence of targeted mental disorders, with a resulting decrease in their prevalence. This will be a major achievement both from the standpoint of lowering health care costs and, more important, reducing human suffering.

REFERENCES

Andrews, G., & Wilkinson, D. D. (2002). The prevention of mental disorders in young people. *Medical Journal of Australia, 177,* S97–S100.

Barrera, A. Z., Torres, L. D., & Muñoz, R. F. (2007). Prevention of depression: The state of the science at the beginning of the 21st century. *International Review of Psychiatry, 19,* 655–670.

Cuijpers, P., van Straten, A., & Smit, F. (2005). Preventing the incidence of new cases of mental disorders: A meta-analytic review. *Journal of Nervous and Mental Disease, 193,* 119–125.

Ialongo, N. S., Kellam, S., & Poduska, J. (2000). A developmental epidemiologic framework for clinical and pediatric psychology research. In D. Drotar (Ed.), *Handbook on pediatric and clinical psychology* (pp. 1–25). New York: Kluwer Academic/Plenum Press.

Ialongo, N. S., Rogosch, F. A., Cicchetti, D., Toth, S. L., Buckley, J., Petras, H., et al. (2006). A developmental psychopathology approach to the prevention of mental health disorders. In D. Cicchetti & D. J. Cohen (Eds.), *Developmental psychopathology* (2nd ed., pp. 968–1018). Hoboken, NJ: John Wiley & Sons.

Kellam, S. G., & Rebok, G. W. (1992). Building developmental and etiological theory through epidemiologically based preventive intervention trials. In J. McCord & R. E. Tremblay (Eds.), *Preventing antisocial behavior: Interventions from birth through adolescence* (pp. 162–195). New York: Guilford Press.

Mrazek, P., & Haggerty, R. (1994). *Reducing risks for mental disorders: Frontiers for preventive intervention research.* Washington, DC: National Academy Press.

Muñoz, R. F., & Ying, Y. (1993). *The prevention of depression: Research and practice.* Baltimore, MD: Johns Hopkins University Press.

Murray, C. J. L., & Lopez, A. D. (1996). *The global burden of disease: Summary.* Cambridge: MA: Harvard University Press.

SUGGESTED READINGS

Mendelson, T., & Muñoz, R. F. (2006). Prevention of depression in women. In C. L. M. Keyes & S. H. Goodman (Eds.), *Women and depression: A handbook for the social, behavioral, and biomedical sciences* (pp. 450–478). New York: Cambridge University Press.

Muñoz, R. F., Le, H. N., Clarke, G. N., Barrera, A. Z., & Torres, L. D. (in press). Preventing the onset of major depression. In I. H. Gotlib and C. L. Hammen (Eds.), *Handbook of depression* (2nd ed.). New York: Guilford Press.

RICARDO F. MUÑOZ
University of California, San Francisco

TAMAR MENDELSON
Johns Hopkins Bloomberg School of Public Health

See also: **Community Psychology; Tertiary Prevention**

PRIDE

Pride is a self-conscious emotion that fuels many of our most meaningful achievements, both everyday and life-changing. Like all self-conscious emotions, pride is experienced when individuals direct their attention inward and make a self-evaluation. As a positive emotion, pride occurs when these self-evaluations result in positive views of the self, that is, when individuals realize that their current self-representations fit with their goals for their identity—the kind of person they want to be. Thus, students experience pride after receiving a good grade, children after succeeding at a new task, and adults after finding a mate. Adults feel pride in response to a promotion at work, their child's first steps, or their partner's love. Indeed, pride seems to fuel several fundamental human pursuits: the desire to achieve, to attain power and status, to meet an attractive and intelligent romantic partner, to feel good about one's self and one's social group, and to raise successful and well-behaved children.

A Complex Emotion That Is "Plainly Expressed"

One of the major findings in the social sciences is that a small set of so-called basic emotions (anger, disgust, fear, happiness, sadness, and surprise) have distinct, universally recognized, nonverbal expressions (Ekman, 1992). Although the more complex self-conscious emotions (e.g., pride, shame, guilt) have historically been omitted from this elite set, Darwin himself suggested that, "of all the ... complex emotions, pride, perhaps, is the most plainly expressed.... A proud man exhibits his superiority over others by holding his head and body erect. He ... makes himself appear as large as possible; so that metaphorically he is said to be swollen or puffed up with pride" (1872, p. 263).

Consistent with Darwin's claim, recent studies suggest that pride is, in fact, associated with a universal nonverbal expression (see Tracy & Robins, 2007, for a review). The prototypical pride expression includes a small smile, expanded posture, head tilted slightly back, and arms akimbo with hands on hips or raised above the head with clenched fists (see Figure 1). This expression is reliably recognized and distinguished from similar emotions (e.g., happiness) by adults from several cultures and children as young as 4 years old. In fact, individuals from a highly isolated, preliterate society in Burkina Faso, West Africa, have been shown to reliably recognize the pride expression. Given that these individuals are unlikely to have learned about pride through exposure to Western media, their recognition suggests that the expression may be a human universal.

Other studies suggest that the recognizable pride expression is also spontaneously displayed when individuals experience pride. Children show it after a successful task completion (e.g., Stipek, Recchia, & McClintic, 1992), and athletes from a wide range of cultures show it after victory in the Olympic Games (see Tracy & Robins, 2007). Furthermore, blind athletes—including congenitally blind individuals who could not have learned the expression from seeing others show it—display pride in these same situations, suggesting that the pride expression may be a biologically innate behavioral response to success.

Together, these findings are consistent with the view that the pride expression is an evolved adaptation for securing and promoting social status and group inclusion. That is, individuals who show pride after success inform others that they merit increased status and group acceptance. In fact, studies have found that the pride expression implicitly signals high status and that pride is the only emotion that conveys this message (Shariff & Tracy, 2008). Thus, the reason for the pride expression's ubiquity across cultures, its high level of recognizability, and its apparent innateness in the behavioral repertoire may be that it

Expression B

Figure 1. *Prototypical pride expressions.* Expression A is slightly better recognized than Expression B, but both are reliably identified as pride. Reprinted from Tracy, J. L., & Robins, R. W. (2004). Show your pride: Evidence for a discrete emotion expression. *Psychological Science, 15,* 194–197.

has come to serve an essential function in human social groups: Proud individuals are automatically perceived as deserving high status—and may be granted status on this basis.

A Tale of Two Prides

Much as the pride nonverbal expression may be an evolved adaptation, the subjective emotional experience associated with pride also may fit within a Darwinian framework. Specifically, pride feelings may inform proud individuals of their increased level of status and acceptance (e.g., "I feel proud; I must have accomplished something that will make others like and respect me"). Such knowledge may, in turn, allow individuals to take advantage of the status boost their success has bought them. In addition, pride feelings function to reinforce and motivate the socially valued behaviors that elicited the emotion. We strive to achieve, to be a "good person," or to treat others well because doing so makes us proud of ourselves. Although we know cognitively that we should help others in need, it often takes the psychological force of an emotion like pride to make us act in altruistic ways. Individuals who perform such socially valued acts are, in turn, rewarded with social status and acceptance (Hardy & Van Vugt, 2006).

Yet, the pride experience is not a purely positive one. Ancient Greek and biblical thought condemned excessive pride, or hubris, and Dante referred to it as the deadliest of the seven deadly sins. In contrast, Western cultures tend to view pride as a virtue to be sought and rewarded. Reflecting these divergent perspectives, pride has been linked to both adaptive and maladaptive outcomes. Although pride in one's success promotes continued achievement-oriented behaviors, narcissistic pride may contribute to aggression, hostility, and interpersonal problems. In fact, several lines of research suggest that there are two conceptually and empirically distinct facets of pride: authentic and hubristic (Tracy & Robins, 2007).

Specifically, studies show that when asked to think about words relevant to pride, individuals consistently generate two very different categories of concepts. The first category (authentic pride) includes words such as *accomplished* and *confident,* whereas the second category (hubristic pride) includes words such as *arrogant* and *conceited.* Similarly, analyses of the feelings experienced in response to success demonstrate two relatively independent dimensions, which closely parallel the two semantic categories. Other studies suggest that these two dimensions of authentic and hubristic pride have highly divergent effects on personality, with authentic pride positively related to adaptive traits like extraversion, agreeableness, conscientiousness, and genuine self-esteem, whereas hubristic pride is more predictive of self-aggrandizing narcissism, aggression, and shame-proneness.

Finally, the dimensions also seem to have distinct cognitive antecedents. Attributing successes to internal, unstable (i.e., malleable), and controllable causes (e.g., one's own effort) tends to promote authentic pride, whereas attributing the same events to internal but stable (i.e., permanent) and uncontrollable causes (e.g., one's ability) is more likely to promote hubristic pride. Importantly, the two dimensions of pride are not distinguished by the kinds of events that elicit them; each occurs after successes in various domains (e.g., academics, romantic relationships). Rather, it is the way in which those successes are appraised—for example, whether they are attributed to stable versus unstable causes—that plays a role in determining which facet of pride is likely to occur.

One question this research raises is whether the two prides are, in fact, distinct emotions. In contrast to their divergent cognitive antecedents and personality correlates, they are both reliably associated with the *same* nonverbal expression, suggesting that, at least from a behavioral perspective, there is only one pride. However, this raises a perplexing question: If pride evolved to promote social status, why does it have a dark (i.e., hubristic) side?

One possibility is that the two dimensions evolved to solve unique adaptive problems regarding the acquisition of status. Recent studies suggest that authentic pride underlies the attainment of prestige, a form of high status that is granted on the basis of others' respect and desire to learn from the high-status individual. In contrast, hubristic pride seems to underlie the attainment of dominance, a form of high status granted on the basis of intimidation and others' fear of the high-status individual (Tracy, Cheng, & Shariff, 2008). Both forms of high status provide adaptive benefits, although dominance may have done so for a considerably longer time period in our evolutionary history (Henrich & Gil-White, 2001). In contemporary society, personality differences and situational contingencies are likely to determine whether a status-seeking individual makes the appraisals that lead to authentic pride and prestige, or those that lead to hubristic pride and dominance.

Over a century ago, Darwin (1872) included pride within his evolutionary model of emotions and emotion expressions. Empirical findings now support Darwin's view and demonstrate the significance of pride to research in social, personality, clinical, comparative, cultural, developmental, and biological psychology. Specifically, pride appears to be a core social emotion, central to the human need for status and acceptance.

REFERENCES

Darwin, C. (1872). *The expression of the emotions in man and animals* (3rd ed.). New York: Oxford University Press.

Ekman, P. (1992). An argument for basic emotions. *Cognition and Emotion, 6,* 169–200.

Hardy, C. L., & Van Vugt, M. (2006). Nice guys finish first: The competitive altruism hypothesis. *Personality and Social Psychology Bulletin, 32,* 1402–1413.

Henrich, J., & Gil-White, F. J. (2001). The evolution of prestige: Freely conferred deference as a mechanism for enhancing the benefits of cultural transmission. *Evolution and Human Behavior, 22,* 165–196.

Shariff, A. F., & Tracy, J. L. (2008). *Knowing who's boss: Implicit perceptions of status from nonverbal expressions of self-conscious emotions.* Manuscript submitted for publication.

Stipek, D., Recchia, S., & McClintic, S. (1992). *Self-evaluation in young children.* Monographs of the Society for Research in Child Development, *57,* Serial No. 226.

Tracy, J. L., Cheng, J., & Shariff, A. F. (2008). *A naturalist's view of pride.* Invited submission, in preparation.

Tracy, J. L., & Robins, R. W. (2007). The nature of pride. In J. L. Tracy, R. W. Robins, & J. P. Tangney (Eds.), *The self-conscious emotions: Theory and research* (pp. 263–282). New York: Guilford Press.

SUGGESTED READINGS

Tracy, J. L., & Robins, R. W. (2008). The nonverbal expression of pride: Evidence for cross-cultural recognition. *Journal of Personality and Social Psychology, 94,* 516–530.

Tracy, J. L., & Robins, R. W. (2007). The psychological structure of pride: A tale of two facets. *Journal of Personality and Social Psychology, 92,* 506–525.

Tracy, J. L., Robins, R. W., & Tangney, J. P. (2007). *The self-conscious emotions: Theory and research.* New York: Guilford Press.

JESSICA L. TRACY
University of British Columbia, Canada

PRIMARY MENTAL ABILITIES

One of the earliest accomplishments of the science of psychology was the objective measurement of mental abilities. In 1904, the British psychologist Charles Spearman argued that intelligence could be characterized as comprising a general factor (g), common to all meaningful activity, and of specific factors (s) that are unique to the different tasks used to measure intelligence. Binet and Simon (1905) in France and Terman (1916) in the United States introduced test instruments that applied the concept of general intelligence. However, American psychologists engaged in educational and occupational selection activities found the concept of general intelligence not very useful for predicting success in specific jobs or other life roles. In addition, the work of Thorndike and Woodworth (1901) on transfer of training had suggested that the notion of generalizability of a single ability dimension was not justified.

Soon there were efforts to determine whether human abilities could be described along a parsimonious number of distinct substantive dimensions. Initial work along these lines began with the publication of T. L. Kelley's *Crossroads in the Mind of Man* (1928), which advocated the determination of group factors representing distinct skills, such as facility with numbers, facility with verbal materials, spatial relationships, speed, and memory. These efforts were also aided by advances in the methods of factor analysis that allowed the determination of multiple factors, each representing a latent construct represented by sets of independently observed variables.

Most prominently associated with these developments was L. L. Thurstone (1935), who expounded the hope that a careful scrutiny of the relations among a wide array of assessment devices, developed to represent a given construct as purely as possible, would yield a limited number of dimensions that would reflect "the building blocks of the mind." He administered a battery of 56 simple psychological tests to a large number of children in Chicago schools and applied factor analysis to determine the latent basic ability dimensions represented by these tests. Given the procedures available at the time, he was reasonably successful in showing that fewer than 10 latent constructs were required to explain most individual differences' variance in his measures. The factors obtained in this work were consequently labeled primary mental abilities.

The most important factors identified by Thurstone that have subsequently been replicated in others' work are, in order of the proportion of individual differences explained, the following:

1. *Verbal Comprehension (V)*. This factor represents the scope of a person's passive vocabulary and is most often measured by multiple-choice recognition vocabulary tests.

2. *Spatial Orientation (S)*. The ability to visualize and mentally rotate abstract figures in two- or three-dimensional space. This ability is thought to be involved in understanding maps and charts and in assembling objects that require manipulation of spatial configurations. This may be a complex factor involving both visualization and the perception of spatial relationships.

3. *Inductive Reasoning (R or I)*. This is the ability to determine a rule or principle from individual instances, probably involved in most human problem solving. The ability is generally measured by a number or letter series that has several embedded rules; the subject is asked to complete the series correctly.

4. *Number (N)*. This is the ability to engage rapidly and correctly in a variety of computational operations. The simplest measure of this ability is a test checking sums for addition problems.

5. *Word Fluency (W)*. This factor represents a person's active vocabulary and is generally measured by free recall of words according to a lexical rule.

6. *Associative Memory (M)*. Found primarily in verbal tasks involving paired associates or list learning. It is not a general memory factor, evidence for which has not thus far been established.

7. *Perceptual Speed (P)*. This ability involves the rapid and accurate identification of visual details, similarities, and differences. This ability is usually measured by letter canceling, simple stimuli, or number comparison tasks.

Other organizational schemes to characterize multiple abilities have been developed by G. H. Thomson (1948) and P. E. Vernon (1960) in England and by J. P. Guilford (1967) in the United States. The last system actually classified tasks along a three-dimensional higher-order hierarchy in terms of content, product, and operations involved in each task, which resulted in a taxonomy of as many as 120 factors, many of which remain to be operationalized.

For purposes of educational application, L. L. Thurstone and T. G. Thurstone (1949) developed a series of tests at several difficulty levels, suitable from kindergarten to high school. These tests were designed to measure Thurstone's first five factors (V, S, R, N, and W). This battery was updated and revised by T. G. Thurstone in 1962. Measures of the other factors may be found in the kit of factor-referenced tests developed by the Educational Testing Service (Ekstrom, French, Harman, & Derman, 1976).

The primary mental abilities measures have had relatively little use in educational practice in recent years. However, these measures experienced a revival as a useful measurement instrument for charting the course of abilities in studies of adult development across the life span. A special version of the primary abilities tests particularly suitable for work with older adults is the Schaie-Thurstone Adult Mental Abilities Test (STAMAT; Schaie, 1985). Factorial invariance of six latent ability dimensions (inductive reasoning, spatial orientation, verbal ability, numeric ability, perceptual speed, and verbal memory) has been demonstrated in longitudinal samples across time and different birth cohorts, as well as across genders. The validity of the primary mental abilities in adults has also been examined with respect to its relation to measures of practical intelligence and subjective perception of competence, as well as to specific occupational outcomes (cf. Schaie, 2005).

REFERENCES

Binet, A., & Simon, T. (1905). Méthodes novelles pour le diagnostic du niveau intellectuel des anormaux. *L'Année Psychologique, 11,* 191.

Ekstrom, R. B., French, J. W., Harman, H., & Derman, D. (1976). *Kit of factor-referenced cognitive tests* (rev. ed.). Princeton, NJ: Educational Testing Service.

Guilford, J. P. (1967). *The nature of human intelligence.* New York: McGraw-Hill.

Kelley, T. L. (1928). *Crossroads in the mind of man: A study of differentiable mental abilities.* Stanford, CA: Stanford University Press.

Schaie, K. W. (1985). *Manual for the Schaie-Thurstone Adult Mental Abilities Test (STAMAT).* Palo Alto, CA: Consulting Psychologists Press.

Schaie, K. W. (2005). *Developmental influences on adult intelligence: The Seattle longitudinal study.* New York: Oxford University Press.

Spearman, C. (1904). "General intelligence": Objectively determined and measured. *American Journal of Psychology, 15,* 201–292.

Terman, L. M. (1916). *The measurement of intelligence.* Boston: Houghton, Mifflin.

Thomson. G. H. (1948). *The factorial analysis of human abilities* (3rd ed.). Boston: Houghton Mifflin.

Thorndike, E. L., & Woodworth, R. S. (1901). Influence of improvement in one mental function upon the efficiency of other mental functions. *Psychological Review, 8,* 247–262, 384–395, 553–564.

Thurstone, L. L. (1935). *Vectors of mind: Multiple-factor analysis for the isolation of primary traits.* Chicago: University of Chicago Press.

Thurstone, L. L., & Thurstone, T. G. (1949). *Examiner manual for the SRA Primary Mental Abilities Test.* Chicago: Science Research Associates.

Vernon, P. E. (1960). *The structure of human abilities* (rev. ed.). London: Methuen.

K. WARNER SCHAIE
Pennsylvania State University

See also: **Adult Intellectual Development; Intellectual Development; Intelligence**

PRIMARY MOTOR CORTEX

The primary motor cortex represents a principal component of sensory motor integration implemented in the brain. Motor cortex has the fundamental function to control voluntary movements, including integration of motor commands with the ongoing somatic sensory state of the body. To accomplish this function, primary motor cortex receives information from sensory, motor-related, and associative cortical and subcortical brain areas and sends massive output monosynaptically to the spinal cord, especially to alpha-motor neurons that couple to muscles. From classical perspectives, the primary motor cortex functions as the final cortical output for already processed movement commands, relaying signals from premotor cerebral cortical sites to the spinal cord. Recent evidence, however, indicates more complex and crucial roles for primary motor cortex in processing motor-related information.

In the past three decades, new concepts have emerged about the function and role of primary motor cortex in movement control. Instead of resembling an automatic piano player superimposed on spinal cord output, primary motor cortex appears to have significant functions related to movement planning and learning. The neural substrate for these higher-order functions of primary motor cortex probably relates to its distributed and plastic anatomical and functional organization.

Motor Cortical Organization

Primary motor cortex has three functional subdivisions, one each for the upper limb, the lower limb, and the head and neck; output from these subdivisions yields the motor commands that elaborate voluntary movement, though other motor-related brain regions, such as the premotor cortical areas in the frontal and parietal lobes, cerebellum, and basal ganglia, also have key roles in shaping motor output. Previous principles of primary motor cortex organization indicated a somatotopic pattern resembling a distorted but recognizable human body shape—the homunculus—represented on the surface of the primary motor cortex. A functional consequence of the homuncular arrangement could imply dedication of specific neural elements, such as a cortical column, to controlling one body part, perhaps a finger.

More recent evidence and a more complete and accurate reading of the historical record suggest that primary motor cortex does not have a regular and organized somatotopic pattern within each of the representations for a major body part. Instead, circuits in primary motor cortex exhibit a widely distributed, multiple, and overlapping representation plan of the different segments of the major body parts, though there remains separation between the leg, arm, and head representations. Thus, neural circuits in primary motor cortex related to finger movements are intermingled and may be shared with circuits for the more proximal movements, perhaps to create a substrate for coordinated actions. The intrinsic anatomical organization of primary motor cortex also would seem to support such a distributed substrate, insofar as patches of primary motor cortex send horizontal connections extensively throughout a major body representation; these horizontal connections do not appear to extend into other major body representations, at least not in nonhuman primates. Thus, within the arm representation, local zones have interconnections with many other local zones, thereby increasing interactions among local circuits that underlie control of the various individual joints that become involved in a coordinated multiple-joint action.

A parallel group of studies, done mostly with nonhuman primates, has attempted to reveal how neurons in primary motor cortex encode voluntary movement. Early approaches to this problem focused on single-joint movements, such as wrist flexion-extension, and described relationships of neural activity in primary motor cortex to limb position and exerted force. Subsequent work, recognizing that voluntary movements occur by coordinating multiple joints within and across limbs, examined so-called higher-order features of movement, particularly movement direction coding. Collectively, these studies found that neurons in primary motor cortex—and, indeed, most motor-related structures—have neuronal patterns that describe a "movement-field." By analogy to sensory receptive-fields, the movement-field of primary motor cortical neurons occupies a position, direction, or velocity (or combinations thereof) space in the three-dimensional space nearby the body. Whereas the organizational details of movement-fields in primary motor cortex appear to have a distributed pattern—much like that for individual movements—there also appears, as might be expected, a modest overrepresentation for movements directed forward and backward. Consideration of the temporal dynamics of movement control has yielded novel findings suggesting that individual neurons in primary motor cortex may "hold" a representation of movement fragments that becomes elaborated in time as movements become expressed. There also has been increasing recognition that motor-related areas near primary motor cortex—these areas also have corticospinal projections—might have crucial roles in shaping voluntary movement. In particular, portions of the premotor area may have particular specialization for reaching and grasping, and other portions of the premotor cortex may have a special role in movement planning and holding the plan in short-term memory, whereby the supplementary motor area might have a specialization for elaborating sequential movements.

Primary Motor Cortex: Plasticity and Cognition

Motor function has nearly infinite flexibility, including capabilities to learn new simple or complex tasks and to recover from central nervous system damage; these adaptations might occur because of changes in primary motor cortex internal processing. Flexibility of primary motor cortex output can be influenced by behavioral or physiological contexts. For example, changing a posture before moving modifies somatic sensory input to primary motor cortex that then can yield differing output from primary motor cortex. These effects may be explained by changes in central set by neural facilitation of primary motor cortex networks and probably is influenced by local synaptic interactions. Despite a propensity for functional plasticity, limits do seem to exist about the flexibility of primary motor cortex representations. In normal individuals, primary motor cortex sites retain functionality related to the represented movements, and in disease states, primary motor cortex function does not always recover following cerebral injury.

Possibly related to its flexible output, primary motor cortex has an important role in adapting and learning motor skills. Motor representations in human primary motor cortex exhibit modification following short-term or long-term experience, such as repeating a finger movement for a few minutes or over weeks. Learning a movement sequence changes the amount of functional activation in primary motor cortex or the coupling between primary motor cortex and target structures in the spinal cord. Primary motor cortex activation patterns also change when humans learn to associate arbitrary visual signals with already known motor skills.

Neural substrates in primary motor cortex may provide the basis for motor learning. Plasticity occurs between sites interconnected with internal, or horizontal, connections in primary motor cortex. Many of these horizontal connections exhibit short- and long-term synaptic plasticity, and this synaptic plasticity has been correlated with skill acquisition. Blockade of motor cortical synaptic plasticity reduces behavioral manifestations of motor learning or primary motor cortex output shifts. The coupling of functional studies on primary motor cortex relationships to motor learning and the new findings on synaptic reorganization of primary motor cortex suggest that it does have an important role in skill acquisition.

Primary motor cortex also has a role in higher-order motor functions, including cognition. Neurons in primary motor cortex have functional relationships with movement planning and appear to code for abstract movement features such as direction, movement goal, and target position. Furthermore, the activity neurons or circuits in primary motor cortex can be uncoupled from observable movements or neuronal excitability occurring within motor portions of the spinal cord, such as during mental rehearsal of movements. Recent results in humans using transcranial stimulation, which activates motor cortical output and neuronal recording in monkeys and humans, have indicated that primary motor cortex appears to participate in the movement mirror system. Mirror neurons, first described in ventral premotor cortex of monkeys, show increased activity during performance of a motor action and also when the actor observes another individual performing the same action. Several theories have emerged concerning the function of the mirror system; within motor-related structures and particularly within the primary motor cortex, it would appear that the mirror system represents a generalized system for mimicry to construct internal action plans, and this miming system could account for mirror neurons in brain movement-related areas.

In summary, primary motor cortex has complete and complex representations of the body. This neocortical area represents the major cortical output for sensory motor integration. Primary motor cortex does not function as a simple purveyor of already processed motor commands. It has a key role as a higher-order information processing structure and participates in many aspects of sensory motor integration.

SUGGESTED READINGS

Sanes, J. N. (2003). Neocortical mechanisms in motor learning. *Current Opinion in Neurobiology, 13,* 225–231.

Sanes J. N., & Donoghue, J. P. (2000). Plasticity and primary motor cortex. *Annual Review of Neuroscience, 23,* 393–415.

Scott, S. H. (2008). Inconvenient truths about neural processing in primary motor cortex. *Journal of Physiology, London, 586,* 1217–1224.

JEROME N. SANES
Alpert Medical School of Brown University

PRIMING

Priming is an implicit (nonconscious) long-term memory phenomenon that increases the processing efficiency (Schacter & Buckner, 1998) or tuning (Wiggs & Martin, 1998) that occurs as a consequence of a single repetition of an event. Consistent with the notion of increased efficiency or tuning, the neural signature of priming is a decrease in region-specific activation (i.e., repetition suppression) upon the repeated processing of studied material. This decreased activation contrasts with an increase in activation for explicit (conscious) retrieval for the same material.

Dissociations within priming are known to occur along processing distinctions. One distinction that has been widely demonstrated in studies of young subjects (Roediger & McDermott, 1993) and that has proven useful in understanding the brain basis of priming occurs on tasks that emphasize either perceptual (sensory-based) or conceptual (meaning-based) processing at retrieval. The neurobiological dissociations between explicit memory and priming, and between perceptual and conceptual priming, have been established in studies of normal subjects (Roediger & McDermott, 1993) and also in neuropsychological (Gabrieli, 1998; Fleischman, 2007), neuroimaging (Schacter & Buckner 1998), and neuropathological (Fleischman et al., 2005) studies.

Early studies demonstrated that persons with global amnesia due to bilateral hippocampal and/or diencephalic lesions could have a profound impairment in explicit memory but still be fully capable of demonstrating normal priming on the identical materials that they could neither recall nor recognize. This single dissociation suggested that explicit memory is dependent on the integrity of these regions, whereas priming is not. The double dissociation of explicit memory and priming with the integrity of neural structures within and outside these limbic regions eluded researchers for many years, however, until two case studies were published showing that posterior neocortical lesions impaired visual-perceptual priming but left explicit memory fully intact (Fleischman, 2007).

These studies established that these limbic regions were the critical neurobiological substrate underlying explicit memory ability, whereas priming was considered a cortical phenomenon. Studies of persons with Alzheimer's disease (AD) proved critical in further elucidating the neurobiological bases of priming. AD is characterized by degeneration of mesial-temporal structures, which, as in focal amnesia, results in profoundly impaired recall and recognition. Unlike focal amnesia, AD is additionally characterized by progressive and selective damage to association neocortices, which causes deficits in multiple cognitive domains as well as reduction or failure of some kinds of priming. Some kinds of priming remain robust in AD, and the pattern of preservation and loss in priming parallels the regional distribution of neuropathological change that occurs in the disease. Posterior cortical regions

are relatively preserved early in the course of AD, and so is perceptual priming, whereas anterior cortical regions are damaged in AD, and conceptual priming is impaired. These findings converge with findings from neuroimaging activation studies and focal lesion studies that have demonstrated a posterior cortical locus for visual perceptual priming and have implicated regions of the left frontal cortex and left frontal and temporal cortex in conceptual priming.

Twenty-five years of basic cognitive science research dedicated to the phenomenon of priming have yielded an abundance of information critical to furthering our understanding of the brain bases of human memory. In particular, great strides have been made in understanding the status of priming in aging and AD, and although this field has amassed numerous important findings, a handful stand out as being critical to the translation of this knowledge into ecologically valid interventions for memory impairment in aging and AD (Fleischman, 2007).

First, we now know that priming is not compromised in healthy aging. Second, when a mild reduction does appear in studies of healthy aging, it is probably attributable to individuals who are considered healthy but who are not aging as gracefully as their peers and who may be in the earliest stages of AD neuropathology deposition. Third, even in the face of devastated explicit memory, we know that islands of preservation in priming can occur, may be used to compensate for explicit memory loss, and thus may be the foundation on which process-specific cognitive retraining techniques can be developed. Fourth, we have a basic understanding of the mapping between particular processes in priming to particular neural regions, but this knowledge base is in need of further refinement in the service of developing biologically targeted interventions.

Future work in this area should endeavor to link the ability to benefit from repetition to known risk factors for developing clinically diagnosed AD, as well as to other important outcomes in aging, such as change in mobility and ability to carry out daily living activities. It is feasible that reduced efficiency in cognitive processing, measured by simple priming tasks, may provide a very early sign that an individual is at risk for cognitive, motor, and/or functional loss. If it can be shown that priming predicts cognitive, motor, and functional decline, and that priming can point to vulnerability in particular cognitive processing systems and/or neural regions early in the path of these declines, then this information can be used to guide cognitively and biologically targeted treatments to help maintain functional independence in aging and AD.

REFERENCES

Fleischman, D. A. (2007). Repetition priming in aging and Alzheimer's disease: An integrated review and future directions. *Cortex, 43,* 889–897.

Fleischman, D. A., Wilson, R. S., Gabrieli, J. D. E., Schneider, J. A., Bienias, J. L., & Bennett, D. A. (2005). Implicit memory and Alzheimer's disease neuropathology. *Brain, 128*, 2006–2015.

Gabrieli, J. D. E. (1998). Cognitive neuroscience of human memory. In J. T. Spence, J. M. Darley, & D. J. Foss (Eds.), *Annual review of psychology* (Vol. 49, pp. 87–115). Palo Alto, CA: Annual Reviews.

Roediger, H. L., & McDermott, K. B. (1993). Implicit memory in normal human participants. In H. Spinnler and F. Boller (Eds.), *Handbook of neuropsychology* (Vol. 8, pp. 63–131). Amsterdam: Elsevier.

Schacter, D. L., & Buckner, R. L. (1998). Priming and the brain. *Neuron, 20*, 185–195.

Wiggs, C. L., & Martin, A. (1998). Properties and mechanisms of visual priming. *Current Opinion in Neurobiology, 8*, 227–233.

SUGGESTED READINGS

Mitchell, D. B. (2006). Nonconscious priming after 17 years: Invulnerable implicit memory? *Psychological Science, 17*, 925–929.

Schacter, D. L., Wig, G. S., & Stevens, W. (2007). Reductions in cortical activity during priming. *Current Opinion in Neurobiology, 17*, 171–176.

DEBRA A. FLEISCHMAN
Rush University Medical Center, Chicago

PRINCIPAL COMPONENT ANALYSIS

Principal component analysis (PCA) is a data reduction technique formalized by Hotelling (1933) and later characterized statistically by Anderson (1963), although the concept goes back as far as Pearson (1901). PCA, as well as factor analysis, is used in the social sciences mainly to characterize underlying latent variables, or factors, that are represented as weighted combinations of the observed variables. The most common use of PCA in the social sciences is in the form of scale construction (psychometrics), although it can also be used to summarize any set of related variables and has more recently been applied to high-dimensional data problems in both imaging and genetics.

The basis of PCA is a mathematical manipulation of either the covariance or the correlation matrix of the data into independent components. The resulting components are sets of weights that can then be used to combine across the observed variables to create a smaller number of derived variables (scores) that retain a large proportion of the (co)-variance in the original data. Examination of the relative size of the raw and standardized weights gives evidence of each variable's contribution to the component. Thus, in its purest form, PCA makes no assumptions about the distribution of the data, and thus no formal statistical tests need be associated with it. In fact, if all derived components are retained, the data are recreated in their entirety, and no loss of information ensues. However, given that the ultimate goal is data reduction, in practice usually only the first few components are retained. If we make an additional assumption of multivariate normality of the observed variables, we then can test statistical hypotheses regarding the components.

The process of choosing the number of retained components comes in various forms, including (1) targeting a threshold of explained variance such as 80–90%, (2) choosing those PCs with eigenvalues greater than 1 (valid for correlation matrices only), and (3) observation of a scree plot to determine at what point the increase in the amount of variance explained becomes minimal. The choice of whether to use the covariance matrix or the correlation matrix is well debated, as they often result in different solutions. Although a case can be made for both, depending on the goals of the analysis, it is clear that, if the observed variables are not measured on the same scale, the interpretation of the covariance matrix is suspect, and the correlation matrix is preferred.

Although PCA and factor analysis have common goals, the techniques are different in that factor analysis is a formal statistical model, whereas PCA is not. More specifically, whereas PCA explains total variability, factor analysis partitions the total variability into that associated with the factors and that associated with random error. In addition, PCA consists of a unique solution, whereas factor analysis requires assumptions about the desired structure (e.g., number of factors) in order to obtain a solution. Solutions for both techniques can be further refined by using rotation, a transformation that results in a more easily interpretable structure.

REFERENCES

Anderson, T. W. (1963). Asymptotic theory for principal component analysis. *Annals of Mathematical Statistics, 34*, 122–148.

Hotelling, H. (1933). Analysis of a complex of statistical variables into principal components. *Journal of Educational Psychology, 24*, 417–441, 498–520.

Pearson, K. (1901). On lines and planes of closest fit to systems of points in space. *Philosophical Magazine, 2*, 559–572.

SUGGESTED READINGS

Bartholomew, D. J., Steele, F., Moustaki, I., & Galbraith, J. I. (2002). *The analysis and interpretation of multivariate data for social scientists.* New York: Chapman & Hall/CRC.

Jolliffe, I. T. (2002). *Principal component analysis* (2nd ed.). New York: Springer-Verlag.

MARY E. KELLEY
Emory University

See also: **Cluster Analysis; Factor Analysis**

PROBABILITY

Probability theory is important to psychology because it is the foundation on which statistics and statistical inference are based, and statistics are the tools for conducting empirical research. The basic notions of probability and chance have a very long history. Gambling, throwing dice, and randomization procedures such as drawing lots are very ancient, if not prehistoric. Although these concepts were vague by modern standards, it is surprising that even the simplest sort of probability calculus was not invented until relatively recent times. Why this did not take place much earlier is a matter of some mystery and controversy.

Systematic work leading to a formal appreciation of probability did not begin until around 1650, when the idea of relative frequencies and the likelihood of particular events based on gathered data began to take hold. Besides gaming, the primary motivation for the study of probability at this time was the establishment of actuarial tables based on local death records, initially compiled to keep track of the progress of the plague afflicting London late in the sixteenth century. In a sense, the origin of modern statistics and probability theory can be seen as a result of the plague, an idea that undoubtedly resonates with the feelings of many students beginning the study of statistics and probability!

Graunt (1620–1674) was the first to organize mortality records to make probabilistic inferences based on actual proportions and relative frequencies of events. For example, he argued in reasonably modern terms that one need not fear dying insane ("a Lunatick in Bedlam") because the odds against it were quite high (about 1,500 to 1). The analysis of "games of chance" provided the basis for further development of probability theory in the work of Pascal (1623–1662), Fermat (1601–1665), Huygens (1629–1695), and Bernoulli (1654–1705). This work saw the first development of a true mathematical foundation or theory of probability.

Early in the eighteenth century work on the binomial distribution was begun by Bernoulli and continued later by de Moivre (1667–1754). Bernoulli also developed the theorem that eventually became known as the "Law of Large Numbers," probably one of the most important events in the development of probability theory as it relates to statistical testing. The work of Laplace (1749–1827), a French astronomer and mathematician, was also significant. His two main treatises on the theory of probability and the "laws of chance," published in 1812 and 1814, provided the foundation on which probability theory is based. This work led eventually to the development of the method of least squares, the law of errors, and the normal distribution by Laplace, Gauss (1777–1855), and others early in the nineteenth century.

One of the first practical applications of this work was in astronomy. The problem was the necessity of fitting observations to theoretical distributions in order to be able to reject discrepant observations, not unlike many modern applications in the behavioral sciences. When astronomers became concerned with errors of measurement early in the nineteenth century, they eagerly seized on the work of Gauss. The oldest of the "exact" sciences, astronomy was ironically the first to systematically apply the principles of probability. Particularly interested in the work of Gauss was the Prussian astronomer Bessel (1784–1846), who in 1818 devised the concept of the "probable error," a precursor of the standard error and comparable, in modern terms, to a 50% confidence interval. Thus, many of the ingredients necessary for the development of statistical tests and statistical inference——probabilistic inference, distribution theory, methods of least squares, and the probable error——were all present before 1850.

The Belgian astronomer and mathematician, Quetelet (1796–1874), was the first to propose the use of the probable error in the biological and social sciences. Before Quetelet, it is fair to say that the word *statistics* retained its original meaning, referring primarily to descriptive data about the state, or "political arithmetic." Quetelet was the first to envision the utility of combining statistics with probability theory to develop a social science based on the Law of Large Numbers. The most famous example of Quetelet's work was his description of the frequency distribution of the heights of 100,000 French army conscripts. He noted that the distribution closely followed the normal curve, and he computed its probable error. Using this information, Quetelet calculated the number of conscripts expected in each height category and compared these to the observed numbers. He found the number of conscripts in the lowest category, just below the minimum height requirement, considerably exceeded the expected number, while the frequency in the category just above the cutoff was deficient by the same amount. He ascribed the discrepancy to fraud, asserting that such an occurrence could not have arisen through measurement error.

Quetelet's work greatly influenced the subsequent work of Galton (1822–1911) and, through Galton, had great impact on the founders of modern statistics early in the twentieth century. These founders included Karl Pearson (1857–1936) and Fisher (1890–1962). The influence of Quetelet's work was substantial because it was the first to present the principles of probability in terms accessible to nonmathematicians and to suggest specific applications for probability theory beyond the evaluation of measurement error in the physical sciences. Quetelet expounded the view that social phenomena were subject to quantitative laws, just as physical phenomena obeyed the laws of Newton and Kepler. He believed that the fusion of statistics and probability could reveal the underlying laws of nature governing human behavior, leading ultimately to his concept of *l'homme moyen*, the average man. Such a view nicely fit the mechanistic philosophy that resulted from the scientific revolution of the seventeenth century, the legacy of Newton and Descartes. Ironically, this philosophy was soon demolished in the physical sciences by the quantum revolution, but it became the dominant force in the developing science of human behavior and remains so today.

SUGGESTED READINGS

Agresti, A., & Finlay, B. (2009). *Statistical methods for the social sciences* (4th ed.). Upper Saddle River, NJ: Pearson Prentice-Hall.

David, F. N. (1962). *Games, gods, and gambling: A history of probability and statistical ideas*. Mineola, NY: Dover.

Meyers, J. L., & Well, A. D. (2003). *Research design and statistical analysis* (2nd ed.). Mahwah, NJ: Lawrence Erlbaum.

Newman, J. R. (1956). *The world of mathematics, Vol. 3*. New York: Simon & Schuster.

Stigler, S. M. (1986). *The history of statistics: The measurement of uncertainly before 1900*. Cambridge, MA: Belknap Press.

JOSEPH S. ROSSI
University of Rhode Island

PROBLEM SOLVING

A problem is a state of difficulty that needs to be resolved. For example, if you accidentally lock your car keys inside the car, the problem is how to get home or wherever you need to go without access to the car. Problem solving is the goal-driven process of changing one state of difficulty into a state that does not include the source of difficulty (Simon, 1999). The state without the source of difficulty is the desirable state. According to Sternberg and colleagues (e.g., Pretz, Naples, & Sternberg, 2003, pp. 4–5) and others (Bransford & Stein, 1993; Hayes, 1989), the problem-solving process can be described as a cycle of seven steps or events: (1) a problem is recognized or identified in the environment; (2) the problem is defined and represented mentally; (3) within the mental representation generated, a solution strategy is developed to solve the problem; (4) relevant knowledge about the problem is organized; (5) the physical and mental resources needed to solve the problem are distributed; (6) progress toward the goal of solving the problem is monitored; and (7) the solution is evaluated for meeting the goal of solving the problem.

Although many problems may require the execution of these seven steps in the order described, others may require the execution of these steps in a different order. Moreover, the successful solution of one problem may often entail the emergence of a host of new problems. For example, if you solve the problem of retrieving your car keys from the locked car by breaking a window, a new problem is how to fix the window in your car. Successful problem solvers are therefore flexible in how they apply problem-solving steps and also are able to anticipate new problems on the horizon. In the next three sections, we describe (1) classes of problems in the environment; (2) the key processes of problem recognition, definition, and representation; and (3) individual differences and environmental considerations in solving problems.

Two Classes of Problems

Psychologists have identified two classes of problems—well-defined and ill-defined problems. Well-defined problems are those that have a clear solution path. For example, trying to retrieve car keys from inside a locked car is a well-defined problem, because the solution is simply getting inside the car to retrieve the keys. The goal of a well-defined problem is evaluated directly. Often-cited examples of well-defined problems include mathematical problems, such as finding the product of two whole numbers. Such mathematical problems are well defined because they often involve applying an algorithm to reach a solution. Ill-defined problems are those that do not have a clear solution path. Many social and personal problems are ill defined, because they can be solved in many different ways. For example, what is the best way to encourage children to watch less television and play more outside? This problem is ill defined, because in principle, there are many methods of encouraging children to watch less television and play more outside, and whether the goal has been reached is a matter of deciding how much television watching has been reduced relative to outside play and whether the difference is acceptable.

Processes of Problem Recognition, Definition, and Representation

Recognition and Definition

The first step in problem solving is having a problem to solve. A problem can be recognized in the environment, or it can be created anew (Getzels, 1982). Alternatively, someone may give you a problem to solve. The presence of a problem requires definition or description if it is to be solved. Problem definition involves demarcating the scope of the problem and deciding what it means to solve the problem—that is, identifying the goal of problem solving. Defining the problem of how to retrieve your car keys from a locked car requires, in part, taking stock of whether your friend has a spare set of keys and whether he or she could find and deliver them to you. If your friend can do that, the problem of retrieving your keys from the locked car is suddenly smaller in scope than previously imagined.

Representation

Once a problem is defined, the individual then has to mentally organize the available knowledge about the problem and its solution. According to Newell and Simon (1972), a mental representation of a problem involves a description of the initial state of the problem (definition), a description of the goal for solving the problem, a set of allowable actions for moving from the initial state of the problem to the goal state, and a set of constraints that may impede the application of allowable actions. Allowable actions for solving a problem may include simple trial and error (i.e., heuristic), recall of information, or applying an algorithm. For example, the list of allowable actions for solving the problem of retrieving the keys from the locked car might include sliding a coat hanger through the driver door to pop the lock, trying to recall whether a friend has spare keys, or calling AAA. Often the process of mentally representing a problem leads to changes in the way a problem was originally defined.

Individual Differences and Environmental Considerations

There are individual differences in problem-solving performance (Beilock & DeCaro, 2007; Davidson & Sternberg, 2003). The variables that influence the success of individuals in their problem solving include knowledge, cognitive processes, working memory, motivation, mental sets, and environmental factors. First, individuals who possess greater knowledge about a domain (e.g., physics or chess) tend to generate better and more efficient problem representations than individuals who have less knowledge about the domain (Ericsson, 2006). Second, differences have been found in how well individuals use analogy, insight, and incubation periods to define and represent problems. Although the processes associated with insight and incubation periods are still debated, there is agreement that the use of analogical transfer can be highly useful in problem solving. Analogical transfer involves mapping the components of a problem that needs to be solved onto an already-solved problem.

Third, differences in working memory (WM) influence problem solving. WM is a theoretical construct proposed by cognitive psychologists to account for where in the brain individuals temporarily store and manipulate information. Individuals who have greater WM capacity have been found to be better problem solvers than those with less WM capacity, because they can generate more detailed problem representations and apply more complex algorithms as they solve problems (Beilock & DeCaro, 2007). Fourth, although a moderate level of arousal or motivation is conducive to problem solving, excessive arousal can interfere with a individual's capacity to monitor an adequate problem definition and representation. Fifth, a mental set can interfere with problem solving. For example, being fixated on a single way to solve a problem can potentially block better definitions and representations and thus keep an individual from searching for more efficient solutions.

Finally, the environment or social context in which problem solving occurs has a critical role. For example, the prevailing norms and attitudes of a social group may influence how an individual defines a problem and the types of solutions considered. The influence of the social environment is likely to be more relevant in ill-defined relative to well-defined problem-solving situations.

REFERENCES

Beilock, S. L., & DeCaro, M. S. (2007). From poor performance to success under stress: Working memory, strategy selection, and mathematical problem solving under pressure. *Journal of Experimental Psychology: Learning, Memory, and Cognition, 33*, 983–998.

Bransford, J. D., & Stein, B. S. (1993). *The ideal problem solver: A guide for improving thinking, learning, and creativity* (2nd ed.). New York: W. H. Freeman.

Davidson, J. E., & Sternberg, R. J. (Eds.). (2003). *The psychology of problem solving*. New York: Cambridge University Press.

Ericsson, K. A. (2006). Protocol analysis and expert thought: Concurrent verbalizations of thinking during experts' performance on representative tasks. In K. A. Ericsson, N. Charness, P. J. Feltovich, & R. R. Hoffman (Eds.), *The Cambridge handbook of expertise and expert performance* (pp. 223–241). New York: Cambridge University Press.

Getzels, J. W. (1982). The problem of the problem. In R. Hogarth (Ed.), *New directions for methodology of social and behavioral science: Question framing and response consistency*. San Francisco: Jossey-Bass.

Hayes, J. R. (1989). *The complete problem solver* (2nd ed.). Hillsdale, NJ: Lawrence Erlbaum.

Newell, A., & Simon, H. A. (1972). *Human problem solving*. Upper Saddle River, NJ: Prentice-Hall.

Pretz, J. E., Naples, A. J., & Sternberg, R. J. (2003). Recognizing, defining, and representing problems. In J. E. Davidson & R. J. Sternberg (Eds.), *The psychology of problem solving* (pp. 3–30). New York: Cambridge University Press.

Simon, H. A. (1999). Problem solving. In R. A. Wilson & F. C. Keil (Eds.), *The MIT encyclopedia of the cognitive sciences* (pp. 674–676). Cambridge, MA: MIT Press.

SUGGESTED READING

Ericsson, K. A., Charness, N., Feltovich, P. J., & Hoffman, R. R. (Eds.). (2006). *The Cambridge handbook of expertise and expert performance*. New York: Cambridge University Press.

Jacqueline P. Leighton
Oksana I. Babenko
University of Alberta, Canada

***See also:* Concept Formation; Intelligence; Memory Functions**

PROFILING (See Criminal Profiling)

PROGRESSIVE MUSCLE RELAXATION

Progressive muscle relaxation (PMR) is a fundamental form of stress management that was developed in the early 1920s by Edmund Jackson, an American physician, as a technique to help his patients reduce muscle tension. Jacobson's research demonstrated the connection between excessive muscle tension and a variety of physical and psychological disorders. Specifically, Jacobson's research revealed that muscle tension is always accompanied by a shortening of muscle fibers and that reducing muscle tension reduced central nervous system activity and promoted a relaxed state. That is, because muscle tension is associated with various types of psychological tension (e.g., anxiety), Jacobson hypothesized that anxiety could be reduced by learning to reduce muscle tension.

Jacobson essentially introduced the application of psychological principles to medicine and thus was a central figure in the development of psychosomatic medicine. In 1929 Jacobson presented the results of his research in the text *Progressive Relaxation.* Jacobson's primary popular work, *You Must Relax*, was published in 1934.

The Process of Progressive Muscle Relaxation

The process of progressive muscle relaxation is based on a basic principle of muscle physiology. Whenever a muscle is tensed, releasing the tension invariably creates relaxation in the muscle. Further, a muscle that is tensed and then relaxed does not only return to its pretension state, but in fact becomes even more relaxed, especially if it is allowed to rest.

The basic process of PMR is to focus on any voluntary muscle and in sequence tense and then relax the tension in that muscle. As the sequence of tensing and relaxing muscles progresses, other elements of the relaxation response follow naturally: breathing becomes slower and often deeper; heart rate and blood pressure decline; and vasodilatation occurs in the small capillaries of the extremities, creating comfortable warmth and a subjective sense of calmness and ease.

Although there are many specific muscle sequences that can be used for practicing PMR, there are some basic concepts and strategies in particular that promote its overall effectiveness. First, it is unnecessary and sometimes counterproductive to exert full tension when tensing a muscle. It appears that gradually tensing a muscle to approximately 75% of full tension is optimal. It is also essential to practice PMR in a quiet, comfortable setting protected from distraction for approximately 15 minutes. PMR can be practiced while seated or while lying down.

Assuming the role of an observer rather than that of a performer is also very helpful. Paradoxically, trying to make relaxation happen tends to hinder relaxing, whereas being an attentive observer of what is happening tends to promote a greater awareness of one's physical condition and also to create more relaxation. Being cognizant of the need to breathe as muscles are tensed and then relaxed greatly enhances the effect of PMR. In this vein, beginning PMR with a few moments of quiet abdominal breathing also greatly helps the initiation of the process.

The basic process of PMR consists of focusing on and contracting a specific muscle for 5 to 10 seconds. It is sometimes useful to contract a muscle while inhaling in order to encourage breathing. After contracting and inhaling, the muscle is then relaxed as one exhales. That muscle then remains relaxed for approximately 10 seconds. The process of tensing and relaxing is then repeated for that same muscle again. As the muscle is relaxing, it is important to focus on the specific sensations that occur, in order to become more aware of the relative tension or relaxation that exists in muscles at a particular time. In this sense, PMR is essentially a "physical mindfulness" exercise designed to increase awareness of one's bodily tension or relaxation, as well as to create relaxation.

This process of tensing and relaxing muscles is repeated in a particular sequence. Although there are a variety of muscle sequences that can be effective, most practitioners of PMR begin either with the feet and work upward or with the hands and work outward. The following is an example of this basic process and of one sequence.

> Begin by focusing on your right hand. Make your right hand into a fist and tense the muscles of your hand and wrist. Hold the tension (5–7 seconds). Now let go of the tension and let your hand relax—and notice the difference between the feeling of tension and the feelings of relaxation that is now in your hand (5–7 seconds).

This same process is then repeated, and then the process is then repeated with a focus on the left hand and then with directions focused on tensing other parts of the body: bring both fists toward shoulders (biceps); stretch out the arms and point the hands toward the ceiling at 90-degree angles (forearms); shrug shoulder toward ears (neck and shoulders); bend head toward chest as if trying to touch the chest (neck); arch back away from chair or floor (back and spine).

Then follow directions for the head and face: raise eyebrows toward forehead; close eyes tightly; purse lips; clench jaw. Then directions for the chest and trunk: inhale and hold breath and at the same time try to touch your shoulder blades together; pull in your stomach as if trying to touch your backbone. Then for the legs: with feet flat on the floor, press down on floor (thighs); raise right leg forward, repeat for left leg (thighs); bend your feet back and toward the ceiling (feet and ankles); complete by noticing and appreciating the nature of the relaxation.

Effectiveness and Applications

Chronic stress has been associated with a variety of psychological and physical disorders. An effective stress management approach includes changes in one's perspective, greater awareness of the events that trigger a stress response, and strategies to both avoid exposure to stress and to reduce stress that has been absorbed (Bracke & Thoresen, 1996; Bracke & Bugental 1995; Thoresen, & Bracke, 1993). PMR has been shown to be an effective approach to reducing the psychological arousal and symptoms that characterize chronic stress (e.g., hypertension, insomnia, gastrointestinal disorders) (Davis, McKay, & Eshelman, 1982).

REFERENCES

Bracke, P. E., & Thoresen, C. E. (1996). Reducing Type A behavior patterns: A structured-group approach. In R. Allan & S. Scheidt (Eds.), *Heart & mind* (pp. 255–290). Washington, DC: American Psychological Association.

Bracke, P. E., & Bugental, J. F. T. (1995). Existential addiction: A new conceptual model for Type A behavior and workaholism. In T. Pauchant (Ed.). *In search of meaning* (pp. 65–97). San Francisco: Jossey-Bass.

Davis M., McKay, M., & Eshelman, E. R. (1982). *The relaxation and stress reduction workbook.* Oakland, CA: New Harbinger Publications.

Thoresen, C. E., & Bracke, P. E. (1993). Reducing coronary recurrences and coronary prone behavior: A structured group approach. In J. Spira (Ed.). *Group therapy for the medically ill* (pp. 156–179). New York: Guilford Press.

PAUL E. BRACKE
Mountain View, CA

PROJECTIVE IDENTIFICATION

The term *projective identification* is the best known of Melanie Klein's (1946) concepts. Klein's view was that it refers to an unconscious belief (fantasy) that a part of the self or inner world, usually unwanted, may be disposed of by relocating it into the mental representation of another object. This is usually regarded as a primitive form of the mental mechanism of projection, but it is different in that it may involve actual behavior by people toward an object in a way that will allow them to confirm their omnipotent suppositions. This projectively identifying mechanism can be used for a variety of psychological purposes, including denial (disposing of undesirable elements) or controlling in fantasy the object. Or it may be a form of communication, as in the expression of disavowed anger or other unmetabolized affects.

Many psychoanalysts hold that projective identification is a fundamental and primary form of communication between mother and baby. In a direct analogy, it is often held to be the central link between patient and analyst. Bion (1984) asserts: "The link between patient and analyst, or infant and breast, is the mechanism of projective identification" (p. 106). It follows from this view that analysts must attend to their own responses to a patient's uses of projective identification—that is, to their countertransference—because it constitutes an important source of information about the patient's state of mind. This conception underlies the contemporary Kleinian model of the therapeutic action of psychoanalysis, inasmuch as the analyst's containment and interpretation of the patient's projective identifications are thought to have a progressive, transformative effect.

Some Kleinian psychoanalysts complain that the original intrapsychic meaning of projective identification has been obscured by its being used as a catchall term for much interpersonal experience (Spillius, 1988). A debate has taken place as to whether it is necessary to include another person in the concept, namely, someone who is emotionally affected by the use of projective identification. Most psychoanalysts now tend to use the term as representing both the subjective use of unconscious fantasy and involvement with another person in its identificatory deployment. The need for a relationship within which projective identification can achieve its aims is, therefore, currently implicit in most writings on the subject. This operational use of the concept, along with its foundation in fantasy, is established in analytic work in most regions of the world, including North America, Latin America, much of Europe, and, increasingly, Eastern Europe and Russia.

Projective identification as both a function of unconscious fantasy and as a medium of behavioral influence has been questioned by certain psychoanalysts in the United States, especially among self psychologists (e.g., Stolorow, Atwood, & Orange, 2002). These authors have argued that the communication of one's mental states to another person is an ordinary part of social interaction, whether those states are pleasant or unpleasant. Relying on intersubjectivist concepts like empathy, they thus reject the traditional idea that a theory of underlying fantasy must be invoked to explain how one person will come to know another person's experience. In doing so, they cite developmental research-based accounts of infant–parent dyads involved in rich and mutually informative patterns of interactionally regulated nonverbal exchange (Stern, 1985).

REFERENCES

Bion W. R. (1984). *Second thoughts: Selected papers on psycho-analysis.* London: Karnac Books. (Original work published 1967)

Klein, M. (1946). Notes on some schizoid mechanisms. *International Journal of Psychoanalysis 27*, 99–110.

Spillius, E. (1988). *Melanie Klein today* (2 vols.). London: Routledge.

Stern, D. (1985). *The interpersonal world of the infant.* New York: Basic Books.

Stolorow, R. D., Atwood, G. E., & Orange, D. M. (2002). *Worlds of experience: Interweaving philosophical and clinical dimensions in psychoanalysis.* New York: Basic Books.

SUGGESTED READINGS

Hinshelwood, R. D. (1991). Projective identification. In *A dictionary of Kleinian thought* (pp. 179–208). London: Free Association Books.

Sandler, J. (Ed.). (1987). *Projection, identification, projective identification.* New York: Guilford Press.

Seligman, S. (1999). Integrating Kleinian theory and intersubjective infant research: Observing projective identification. *Psychoanalytic Dialogues, 9*(2), 129–159.

PAUL WILLIAMS
Queens University Belfast, Northern Ireland

STEVEN SELIGMAN
University of California, San Francisco

See also: Object Relations Theory; Psychoanalytic Theories

PROJECTIVE TESTS (See Performance-Based Personality Measures)

PROPAGANDA

Propaganda is goal-oriented communication that employs (to one degree or another) deceptive tactics. The term derives from the Latin word *propagare,* meaning to spread plants to new locations. To spread propaganda originally meant to disseminate information in order to promote a cause, idea, or action (Rogers, 2007). In modern times, propaganda has taken on pejorative connotations: dishonest communication, factoids, rumors, misinformation, dirt, lies, distortions, deceit, manipulation, psychological warfare, and brainwashing (Jowett & O'Donnell, 1986).

Propaganda is first of all communication with a purpose (Jowett & O'Donnell, 1986). The goal may be laudable, as when government officials spread propaganda aimed at improving health practices among Mexicans in the late nineteenth and early twentieth centuries; the objectives were to increase personal hygiene, sanitation, vaccinations, and exercise (Agostini, 2006). More often, the objective serves the military, political, or pecuniary interests of the message sender at the expense of the recipient (Jowett & O'Donnell, 1986). Propaganda is also commonly synonymous with the deliberate and aggressive manipulation of images, symbols, and slogans that prey upon vulnerabilities—be they cognitive or emotional—in the human psyche (Pratkanis & Aronson, 2001). It slyly maneuvers recipients to accept a belief, adopt an attitude,

or perform an action as though they had come to these conclusions on their own. Characteristics of propaganda reflecting this deceptive methodology include censorship (the selective emphasis or exclusion of information), doctoring of data (purposeful misinformation for strategic objectives), and suggestion (circumvention of the reasoning process by impression formation or innuendo) (Rogers, 2007).

Propaganda differs from persuasion. The two may be distinguished on the basis of whose interests are being served. Propaganda is a "deliberate, systematic attempt to shape perceptions, manipulate cognitions, and direct behavior to achieve a response that furthers the desired intent of the propagandist" (Jowett & O'Donnell, 1986, p. 68), whereas persuasion is interactive and serves both the sender and the hearer. Similarly, propaganda hinders— and persuasion fosters—thoughtful deliberation of a matter (Pratkanis & Turner, 1996). Propagandistic communication is typically centralized and discourages feedback; persuasive communication encourages two-way and decentralized interactions. In propaganda campaigns, elites set the discussion agenda; in persuasion attempts, the agenda is collaboratively determined by group members. Perhaps most central to psychological distinctions between propaganda and persuasion is whether messages are processed in a mindless versus a thoughtful manner: propaganda tries to capitalize on peripheral processing paths (e.g., simple heuristics, emotional reactions), whereas persuasion attempts to employ the central route (e.g., effortful and systematic reasoning). In a word, the propagandist hopes you will not think too deeply, while the persuader appeals to your faculties of reasoning.

These characteristics vary according to the intensity of the propaganda: white propaganda is a relatively mild message in which the true source is identified and the message is accurate (e.g., Voice of America broadcasts during the Cold War; Rogers, 2007). White propaganda messages differ from neutral information in that they would not be sent without a considered aim (Jowett & O'Donnell, 1986). In gray propaganda, the source may or may not be identified, and message accuracy is uncertain (as when Voice of America denied U.S. involvement in the Bay of Pigs incident). Gray propaganda communiqués are competitive and include changing the subject, illogical arguments, card stacking (selective emphasis), exploiting common misperceptions, innuendo, equivocation, and marginalization of a target (Rogers, 2007).

Black propaganda is combative and unethical; the source of the message is misidentified, the message is false, and harm is intended (Rogers, 2007). Black propaganda tactics include demonization of the opposition, relentless attacks, falsified images, negative stereotypes, unsubstantiated atrocity stories, outrageous ("big") lies, planting false information to mislead the opposition, and baiting an action (Rogers, 2007). It sometimes takes the form of disinformation, which is the spreading of falsehoods by fake journalists (Jowett & O'Donnell, 1986). Black propaganda was exemplified when the tobacco industry created a supposedly independent scientific board—the Environmental Tobacco Smoke (ETS) Consultants Program—whose real objective was to reduce negative public opinion of ETS; these scientists were in fact paid and influenced by cigarette manufacturers (Muggli, Hurt, & Blanke, 2003).

Propaganda has been with us from ancient times. For example, Mayan leaders deliberately revised ancient texts so as to portray themselves in a favorable light (Pratkanis & Aronson, 2001). Greek sophists thought that the way to arrive at the best solution on a matter was through debate, so they developed methods of argumentation and persuasion. Aristotle thought these methods were not helpful in arriving at truth (only philosophy could attain that), but they were useful for convincing the masses of what was true (Pratkanis & Aronson, 2001). Regimes, reformers, and revolutionists from every era have all used propaganda (Jowett & O'Donnell, 1986).

In the late nineteenth and twentieth centuries, propaganda became institutionalized, as the means of mass communication grew. Pratkanis and Aronson (2001) select the opening of the first advertising agency, in Philadelphia in 1843, as the beginnings of our modern age of propaganda. Advertising and marketing ideas were later applied to the sale of political ideas, as when George Creel and his Committee on Public Information convinced Americans to engage in World War I. In modern times, propaganda is ubiquitous and potent; we live in a message-dense environment in which recipients typically have little time or training to analyze these communiqués.

Propaganda tactics are devices by which propagandists seek to influence recipients via peripheral routes of processing (Pratkanis & Aronson, 2001). These tactics employ a variety of psychological processes. Priming occurs when propagandists carefully choose words and images so as to set the agenda and activate cognitive structures in a way that favors their position (Pratkanis & Aronson, 2001). Analogies and metaphors also activate some cognitive structures and not others, as do message framing, the use of decoys to induce contrast effects, innuendo, and rumor. Propagandists encourage recipients to employ simple heuristics rather than careful reasoning, for example, as when products are described as "natural," and cues such as price, store image, brand name, message length, social consensus, and speaker self-confidence are used to imply product quality. Propagandists' use of vivid images and repetition make some ideas disproportionately more salient or familiar than others, and distraction may serve to draw attention away from the decision at hand.

Social psychologists have long known that credibility (i.e., perceived expertise in a given subject and trustworthiness) is a key factor in message acceptance; propagandists

seek to manufacture credibility in the eyes of the recipient (Pratkanis & Aronson, 2001). Perceptions of a message sender's credibility are disproportionately affected by peripheral characteristics, such as their attractiveness and likability, that take advantage of our desire to adopt beliefs and practices that boost our self-image. For example, teenage males were persuaded by Joe Camel advertisements to smoke cigarettes because of his machismo ("If I smoke Camel, I will also be macho"). Credibility is also enhanced by appearing to act against one's self-interest, as when a Democrat defends a Republican candidate, or when a message is "unintentionally" overheard. Whispering campaigns and word-of-mouth strategies capitalize on this process by paying people to spread favorable rumors—or unfavorable slander—by being overheard when conversing loudly in public settings.

Propagandists also capitalize on the psychology of emotion. The general strategy is to gain attention, stimulate emotion, and then offer a way to productively release that emotion by adopting the targeted position (Rogers, 2007). A sense of group identity and an emotional attachment to the group are remarkably easy to create; this attachment then leads to the ready adoption of group beliefs, standards, and rituals. Proponents of racist and isolationist ideology link group identity with hostility toward an outgroup and with separation (Finlay, 2007). The emotion of hate, which is useful in mobilizing support for war, acts of terrorism, and genocide, is fomented by propaganda stories portraying a perpetrator (them) and a victim (us; Sternberg, 2003). Crafted by cynical leaders, these stories spread because they increase depleted self-esteem or make sense of frustrating circumstances. Nazi arguments for exterminating Jews, set forth most strongly in word-of-mouth contexts and public meetings, alleged that Jews were trying to destroy Germany—the evidence for which was Theodore N. Kaufman's limited-circulation self-published book *Germany Must Perish!* (Bytwerk, 2005). The existence of this extremist manuscript was widely publicized by the Nazi propaganda machine to evoke defensive emotions, and subsequent complacency regarding the Holocaust, among German citizens.

Propaganda hinders effective democratic functioning and "results in the manipulation of the mob by the elite" (Pratkanis & Turner, 1996, p. 190). In contrast, deliberative persuasion leads to better solutions, greater group cohesion, and the meaningful incorporation of minority viewpoints. A number of principles can be employed to diminish the effects of propaganda and to encourage deliberative persuasion attempts. For example, forewarning can nullify the effect of a propagandistic message (Pratkanis & Aronson, 2001). Recipients can consider whether a message encourages the use of simple heuristics or provokes an emotional reaction in place of thoughtful consideration. Especially in our modern age, deliberative persuasion can be encouraged by regaining knowledge of persuasion and group participation skills.

REFERENCES

Agostini, C. (2006). Popular health education and propaganda in times of peace and war in Mexico City, 1890s–1920s. *American Journal of Public Health, 96,* 52–61.

Bytwerk, R. L. (2005). The argument for genocide in Nazi propaganda. *Quarterly Journal of Speech, 1,* 37–62.

Finlay, W. M. L. (2007). The propaganda of extreme hostility: Denunciation and regulation of the group. *British Journal of Social Psychology, 46,* 323–341.

Jowett, G. S., & O'Donnell, V. (1986). *Propaganda and persuasion.* Newbury Park, CA: Sage.

Muggli, M. E., Hurt, R. D., & Blanke, D. D. (2003). Science for hire: A tobacco industry strategy to influence public opinion on secondhand smoke. *Nicotine & Tobacco Research, 5,* 303–314.

Pratkanis, A. R., & Aronson, E. (2001). *Age of propaganda: The everyday use and abuse of persuasion* (rev. ed.). New York: W. H. Freeman.

Pratkanis, A. R., & Turner, M. E. (1996). Persuasion and democracy: Strategies for increasing deliberative participation and enacting social change. *Journal of Social Issues, 52,* 187–205.

Rogers, W. (2007). *Persuasion: Messages, receivers, and contexts.* Lanham, MD: Rowman & Littlefield.

Sternberg, R. J. (2003). A duplex theory of hate: Development and application to terrorism, massacres, and genocide. *Review of General Psychology, 7,* 299–328.

SUGGESTED READINGS

DiFonzo, N., & Bordia, P. (2007). *Rumor psychology: Social & organizational approaches.* Washington, DC: American Psychological Association.

Jowett, G. S., & O'Donnell, V. (Eds.). (2006). *Readings in propaganda and persuasion: New and classic essays.* Thousand Oaks, CA: Sage.

Pratkanis, A. R. (Ed.). (2007). *The science of social influence: Advances and future progress.* Philadelphia: Psychology Press.

NICHOLAS DIFONZO
Rochester Institute of Technology

See also: **Rumor**

PROPENSITY SCORES

A propensity score is the conditional probability of a unit being assigned to a condition, given a set of observed covariates. These scores can be used to equate groups on those covariates by using matching, blocking, weighting, or analysis of covariance. In theory, propensity score adjustments should reduce the bias that often accompanies nonrandom assignment, and the adjusted treatment effects should be closer to the effects that would have occurred had participants been randomly assigned to conditions.

Traditionally, statisticians have preferred the use of randomized experiments over quasi-experiments because they are known to yield unbiased estimates of effects when they are properly implemented and analyzed. The main idea behind propensity scores is to create a method for equating nonrandomized groups that mimics the equation of groups in randomized experiments. If that could happen, then it might be possible to obtain unbiased estimates from nonrandomized experiments. In a randomized experiment, a unit's true propensity score is the known probability of being assigned to either the treatment condition or the comparison condition. For instance, when using a coin toss to assign units equally to each of two conditions, the true propensity score would be $p = .5$ for every unit. In nonrandomized studies, we do not know the true probability of being in a condition because of selection bias; therefore, it must be estimated by using observed variables. Careful measurement of the predictors of selection into groups will improve the accuracy of the estimated propensity scores. All variables that play a role in the selection process (Rosenbaum & Rubin, 1984; Rubin & Thomas, 1996) and that are related to outcome should be used (Rubin, 1997).

Estimating Propensity Scores

Propensity scores are probabilities that range from 0 to 1, where scores above .5 indicate a propensity to be in the condition coded as 1 (typically the treatment group), and those below .5 indicate a propensity to be in the condition coded as 0 (typically the comparison group). Scores can be estimated with many methods. *Logistic regression* is the most common method for estimating propensity scores. In this method, a set of covariates is used in a logistic regression to predict the condition of assignment (treatment or control), and the propensity scores are the resulting predicted probabilities for each unit. The model may include nonlinear or interaction terms among the predictors. Typically, relevant predictors are included in a stepwise manner with liberal inclusion criteria (e.g., $p < .20$). *Classification and regression trees* are methods that predict membership in categories (in this case, treatment condition) from predictor variables through a sequence of hierarchical, binary splits. Each split is determined by the predicted probability that a unit will select into conditions based on a single predictor. With each dichotomous split, two branches result, and the splitting process continues for each new predictor until a certain number of nodes are obtained or all significant predictor variables are used. The result is a binary tree with terminal nodes (branches) representing groups of units with the same predicted condition. Each node has its own propensity score. *Bagging (bootstrap aggregation)* is a method that averages the results of many classification trees that are based on a series of bootstrap samples. In this case, random samples (with replacement) are drawn from the observed data set, and additional observations are simulated to mimic the observed distributions. A new classification tree is computed for each simulated data set. Bootstrapped trees are aggregated to form aggregated trees, resulting in a more stable prediction model. *Boosted modeling* is a method that, like bagging, uses an algorithm to create multiple models by using different predictors. Each model is weighted based on the strength of the model and aggregated to form a single, more stable model. It differs from bagging by (1) using the full, original sample for each model, whereas bagging uses bootstrap samples, and (2) weighting units based on how difficult they are to classify. Each iteration assesses how well each unit was correctly classified and then assigns a greater weight to that unit for the next iteration. Boosted modeling is used with either logistic regression procedures or classification trees.

Regardless of the method used to create propensity scores, the primary goal is not to optimally predict assignment to conditions but to balance the distributions of covariates over conditions. Tests for balance are a topic of much current development (e.g., Rubin, 2001). However, balance is a necessary but not sufficient condition for bias reduction. More important is the strong ignorability assumption, that assignment to treatment is orthogonal to pretest covariates once an adjustment for propensity scores is made. Unfortunately, no widely accepted test for strong ignorability is available.

Adjustments Using Propensity Scores

Once propensity scores are calculated, statistical adjustments can be made by using those scores. Typically, this is done by using matching, stratification, covariate adjustment, or weighting. Matching identifies similar cases from experimental and control groups based on the proximity of their propensity scores. Stratification divides the entire distribution into four to seven strata based on propensity scores, so observed variables are balanced for treated and control units within each stratum. Covariate adjustment uses propensity scores as covariates in an analysis of covariance in order to remove bias due to the covariates from the effect estimate. Weighting multiplies each observation by a function of its propensity scores before computing an average effect. Even when used properly, however, propensity scores cannot adjust for hidden bias, which occurs when nonredundant covariates that predict treatment and outcome are omitted from the propensity score model.

Empirical evidence about the effectiveness of propensity score analyses in removing bias has been mixed (e.g., Glazerman, Levy, & Myers, 2003), but the best designed of those tests are also the most supportive (e.g., Shadish, Clark, & Steiner, in press). However, that same evidence also suggests that propensity score analysis may not do better than other statistical adjustments like ordinary least squares regression on the covariates. It may be the case that the quality of the pretest covariate set is more important than the particular statistical adjustment technique.

REFERENCES

Glazerman, S., Levy, D. M., & Myers, D. (2003). Nonexperimental versus experimental estimates of earnings impacts. *Annals of the American Academy of Political and Social Science, 589,* 63–93.

Rosenbaum, P. R., & Rubin, D. B. (1984). Reducing bias in observational studies using subclassification on the propensity score. *Journal of the American Statistical Association, 79*(387), 516–524.

Rubin, D. B. (1997). Estimating causal effects from large data sets using propensity scores. *Annals of Internal Medicine 127,* 757–763.

Rubin, D. B. (2001). Using propensity scores to help design observational studies: Application to the tobacco litigation. *Health Services and Outcomes Research Methodology, 2,* 169–188.

Rubin D. B., & Thomas, N. (1996). Matching using estimated propensity scores: Relating theory to practice. *Biometrics, 52,* 249–264.

Shadish, W. R., Clark, M. H., & Steiner, P. M. (in press). Can non-randomized experiments yield accurate answers? A randomized experiment comparing random to nonrandom assignment. *Journal of the American Statistical Association.*

WILLIAM R. SHADISH
RODOLFO GALINDO
University of California, Merced

See also: **Logistic Regression; Probability; Randomized Control Trials**

PROSOCIAL BEHAVIOR

Of those aspects that distinguish humans from other species, the degree of cooperation, helping, and altruism among people is typically espoused as most important (Fehr & Fischbacher, 2003). Prosocial behavior, that is, behavior that has no obvious benefits for the responder but is beneficial to the recipient (i.e., actions that benefit another person without any expected reward for the self) (Eisenberg & Fabes, 1998), has traditionally been considered as the basis of human relationships. A significant number of studies have found evidence of concern for others beginning in infancy and developing throughout childhood and adolescence. Girls have generally been thought to be (or be capable of being) more prosocial than boys; however, the majority of research has not found appreciable gender differences in prosocial behavior. Both internal and external mechanisms have been proposed as determinants of prosocial behavior, as have genetic contributions (Knafo & Plomin, 2006a, 2006b).

The family and caretaker milieu have been suggested to be critical contributors as models and sources of specific standards of prosocial behavior. Parents and caretakers of children who exhibit prosocial behavior are typically prosocial in their own actions and seek to promote such actions. For example, they point out models of prosocial behavior and direct children toward stories, television programs, movies, and videos that illustrate cooperation, sharing, and empathy; and encourage generosity, helpfulness, and sympathy. These significant adults also employ inductive disciplinary methods as opposed to power-assertive practices. Interactions with siblings and peers also provide opportunities for trying out caring behavior and learning to see others' points of view, as well as offering models and reinforcers of prosocial behavior (Barry & Wentzel, 2006).

From middle childhood through adolescence, cognitive development relative to perspective taking—the capacity to imagine what others may be thinking and feeling—increases the potential to act prosocially. Although perspective taking can vary greatly among children and adolescents of the same age, cognitive maturity and interactions with adults and peers who explain their viewpoints and emotional experiences encourage noticing another's perspective. Interactions that provide practice in perspective taking have been shown to increase empathy and promote prosocial responding

Motives for prosocial behavior change with development of more mature moral reasoning. Young children tend to exhibit egocentric motives, such as the desire to earn praise and avoid disapproval. They weigh the benefits and costs to themselves and consider how they would like others to behave toward them. As moral reasoning develops, children become less self-centered and adopt societal standards of "being good," which eventually become internalized in the form of higher-level principles and values.

As individuals mature, they understand more, are better able to grasp the consequences of their behavior, and learn to accept and act upon general principles of morality. Cultures vary in the extent to which they foster prosocial behavior. Traditional collectivist cultures tend to inculcate prosocial values more than cultures that emphasize competition and individual achievement. External emphases have focused on situational determinants of prosocial behavior. Two major theoretical approaches for understanding prosocial behavior have stressed the importance of the situation or setting: a reinforcement explanation of why persons sometimes help others and a cognitive analysis of the manner in which perceptions and judgments can influence behavior. From the point of the view of some learning theorists, prosocial responses occur because they have been rewarded in the past. In addition to direct experiences, individuals are also influenced by their expectations about future rewards or punishments.

Among factors found to affect prosocial behavior are external determinants such as the presence of bystanders, as well as social exclusion. The presence of more than one bystander in an emergency situation tends to inhibit the responses of each person present. This bystander inhibition appears to be a function of individuals' uncertainty about the situation. People respond less when circumstances are ambiguous, when they are unfamiliar with the surroundings, and when they are unsure of the behavioral norms of a particular setting. Similarly, social exclusion has been found to decrease prosocial behavior (Twenge, Bartels, Baumeister, DeWall, & Ciarocco, 2007).

Internal factors found to affect prosocial behavior include such variables as the mood a person is experiencing. Helping behavior increases when individuals are in a positive mood. Prosocial behaviors enhance and prolong an already positive mood; positive moods promote thinking about the rewarding nature of prosocial behavior. Although prosocial behavior can offer a means to escape a negative mood, negative moods tend to encourage greater self-focus and thus decreased attention to others. Prosocial behavior also varies as a function of the relative balance of perceived costs and perceived rewards.

REFERENCES

Barry, C. M., & Wentzel, K. R. (2006). Friend influence on prosocial behavior: The role of motivational factors and friendship characteristics. *Developmental Psychology, 42*, 153–163.

Eisenberg, N., & Fabes, R. A. (1998). Prosocial development. In N. Eisenberg & W. Damon (Eds.), *Handbook of child psychology: Vol. 4. Social, emotional and personality development* (5th ed., pp. 701–778). New York: John Wiley & Sons.

Fehr, E., & Fischbacher, U. (2003, October 23). The nature of human altruism. *Nature, 425*, 785–791.

Knafo, A., & Plomin, R. (2006a). Parental discipline and affection and children's prosocial behavior: Genetic and environmental links. *Journal of Personality and Social Psychology, 90*, 147–164.

Knafo, A., & Plomin, R. (2006b). Prosocial behavior from early to middle childhood: Genetic and environmental influences on stability and change. *Developmental Psychology, 42*, 771–786.

Twenge, J. M., Bartels, M., Baumeister, R. F., DeWall, N., & Ciarocco, N. J. (2007). Social exclusion decreases prosocial behavior. *Journal of Personality and Social Psychology, 92*, 56–66.

SUGGESTED READINGS

Dovidio, J. F. Piliavin, J. A., Schroeder, D. A., & Penner, L. (2006). *The social psychology of prosocial behavior.* Mahwah, NJ: Lawrence Erlbaum.

Eisenberg, N. (2006). Prosocial behavior. In G. G. Bear & K. M. Minke (Eds.), *Children's needs III: Development, prevention, and intervention* (pp. 313–324). Washington, DC: National Association of School Psychologists.

Hey, D. F., & Cook, K. V. (2007). The transformation of prosocial behavior from infancy to childhood. In C. A. Brownell & C. B. Kopp (Eds.), *Socioemotional development in the toddler years: Transitions and transformations* (pp. 100–131). New York: Guilford Press.

CHARLES H. HUBER
New Mexico State University

See also: Altruism; Bystander Involvement; Modeling; Moral Development

PSEUDODEMENTIA

Brown (2005) raises the question as to whether the term *pseudodementia* is still valid and useful. He points out that many specialists have taken a second look at this diagnosis and have essentially abandoned it. With that in mind, it seems important to look at and see what this diagnosis is all about. Jenike (1988) points out that many elderly patients with depression show cognitive changes that include deficits in memory performance. The term *pseudodementia* (literally, "false dementia") is used to describe cognitive changes associated with depression that can be reversed with adequate treatment (p. 128). One should not assume, he warns, that cognitive disorders are necessarily a consequence of neurological disease. The danger appears to be that cognitively impaired patients can be viewed as hopelessly demented, warranting no further treatment for depressive symptoms. He suggests that although diagnosis is certainly important, the distinction between a psychiatric disorder and a neurological disorder may not be crucial, as long as one can determine that the course of the illness is not progressive.

The diagnostic categories in the *Diagnostic and Statistical Manual of Mental Disorders* (DSM-IV-TR; American Psychiatric Association, 2000) include Dementia of the Alzheimer's type and Vascular Dementia, among others. The diagnosis requires the existence of cognitive deficits, including (1) memory disturbances and (2) one or more additional cognitive disturbances (e.g., language, motor activities, planning, or organizing). Both of these criteria must cause significant impairment in social or occupational functioning and must represent a significant decline from prior functioning (p. 90). There is a caution listed, however, that the deficits are not due to other causes, including major depressive disorders, central nervous system conditions, substance abuse, and delirium.

With regard to depression, the DSM-IV-TR specifies that a diagnosis of major depression requires five or more symptoms, which can include the diminished ability to think or concentrate, indecisiveness, loss of energy, diminished interest in almost all activities, and feelings of fatigue. It is these types of symptoms that may mimic dementia or that may be present alongside depression. The issue for the diagnostician is whether treatment of these depressive symptoms can reverse or improve symptoms of dementia. Thus, pseudodementia refers to nonorganic factors that can account for symptoms of dementia. Initially, this was named depressive pseudodementia, under the assumption that depression will cause cognitive symptoms including memory impairment. Swihart and Pirozzolo (1988) pointed out, however, that pseudodementia is not well defined as a diagnostic category.

La Rue (1992) discusses neuropsychological findings in depressed older individuals and states that one in five severely depressed older patients experience severe cognitive losses, which she describes as "depressive pseudodementia" or "dementia syndrome of depression" (p. 269). She draws a distinction between milder cognitive problems and the more severe memory problems found in dementia syndrome of depression (DSD). There is clear evidence that a number of psychiatric disorders are accompanied by cognitive problems that may be severe enough to equal those caused by organic dementia. However, the most common cause of psychiatrically based dementia is depression, and that is why there is interest in the topic of pseudodementia or dementia syndrome of depression.

The primary feature of DSD is a cognitive disturbance that occurs at the time of a depressive episode, and these cognitive disturbances improve or disappear when the symptoms of depression are removed. La Rue (1992) insists that DSD can only be diagnosed post hoc, that is, after cognitive symptoms have returned to a normal baseline following a lifting of depression. She discusses a number of guidelines to help the clinician raise questions concerning the presence of DSD. However, she insists that these guidelines do not confirm its presence. She discusses several aspects of DSD and dementia. These include the history and clinical course, complaints and clinical behavior, and performance on cognitive tests. For example, the duration of DSD is short before help is sought, while seeking help for dementia may take a longer period of time. Also, prior psychiatric illness is common for DSD patients, although it is unusual for patients suffering from dementia. Diminished social skills are often prominent for DSD, whereas tthey are more often retained in dementia. Nocturnal accentuation is uncommon in DSD and common in dementia; attention and concentration on cognitive tests are often well preserved in DSD but are usually faulty in dementia and orientation testing, resulting in frequent "don't know's" for DSD, while obvious errors characterize dementia (p. 283).

Criteria for defining DSD have varied, according to La Rue, and systematic studies have been few in number. Also, not many studies have considered the long-term prognosis of DSD. Neuropsychological performance of patients suspected of having DSD is also not well established, and it is difficult to establish predictive values for such testing. Further neuropsychological assessments are also not likely to prevent misdiagnosis of DSD. La Rue notes that there did not appear to be any large-scale studies of DSD. She reviews a number of smaller studies and suggests that there may be differences between most depressed patients and those suspected of having DSD. Limited education and lower intelligence may contribute to the perception of DSD, as well as length of depressive illness. Antidepressants appear to be helpful in creating improvement, and DSD patients may require more assertive and longer treatment (p. 289).

A more recent discussion of pseudodementia by Lezak (2004) raises the question as to whether patients with Alzheimer's disease experience more depression than do organically intact patients. She suggests that patients diagnosed with both dementia and major depression may be a subset of patients who have significant subcortical impairment. On the other hand, there is no clear documentation concerning whether there is a greater incidence of psychiatric symptoms in patients with some type of cognitive deterioration (p. 219). She also states that some studies have not found memory problems in depressed patients, but those studies did not focus exclusively on major depression. Historical information may be helpful in separating out demented patients who are depressed from depressed patients who seem to be demented (Lezak, 2004). Because depressive symptoms can often be reversed with proper treatment, it is important to make an attempt at diagnosing reversible conditions, she suggests.

In a recent study of the long-term outcome of depressive pseudodementia in older adults (Saez-Fonseca, Lee, & Walker, 2007) in the United Kingdom, 182 patients suffering from moderate to severe depression were followed as inpatients or outpatients from 1997 through 1999. More than 70% of these patients were found to be demented at follow-up. The authors concluded that reversible cognitive impairment in these patients appeared to be a strong predictor of dementia.

As stated earlier, Brown (2005) argued that experts have been calling for the demise of the diagnosis of pseudodementia. Nevertheless, he points out, about 15% of patients with dementia had one of the reversible types of this disorder, and depression accounted for half of these findings. He argues that the original definition of pseudodementia as a false or factitious mental illness has been replaced by a narrower definition as a cognitive impairment that mimics forms of dementia and may be reversible if treated. He points out that cognitive impairment is part of depression. Brown further suggests that the term pseudodementia is part of the old organic-functional dichotomy in which dementia was considered an organic disorder, whereas schizophrenia and depression were considered to be functional disorders.

This distinction was dropped with the publication of DSM-IV. Brown submits that, in 20–40% of those diagnosed with dementia, a concurrent diagnosis of major depression is also given. Up to 70% of demented patients have some symptoms of depression, and there is usually responsiveness to treatment. Brown argues that pseudodementia as a label is simply politically incorrect (La Rue was probably sensitive to this, in that she preferred the use of the label dementia syndrome of depression). Brown believes that we should keep the concept, no matter what the label. Having it on the list of differential diagnoses reminds the clinician that patients complaining of memory loss may not be afflicted with dementia. The concept is also helpful in that it permits clinicians to concentrate on the depressive symptoms before doing an extensive workup on dementia. He believes it is helpful to tell patients and their families that depression can cause problems in thinking and that the first thing to do is to treat the depression. That certainly sounds like a helpful approach, although in my opinion it is important to do a dementia workup on older patients complaining about memory loss, because dementia itself can be held in check for a time with medications, even though dementia at this point in time appears to be incurable.

REFERENCES

American Psychiatric Association. (2000). *Diagnostic and statistical manual of mental disorders* (4th ed., text rev.). Washington, DC: Author.

Beers, M. (Ed.) (2000–2006). *Merck manual of geriatrics* (3rd ed.). White House Station, NJ: Merck.

Brown, W. (2005). Pseudodementia issues in diagnosis. *Applied Neurology, 1*, 40–43.

Jenike, M. (1988). Depression and other psychiatric disorders. In M. Albert & M. Moss (Eds.), *Geriatric neuropsychology*. New York: Guilford Press.

La Rue, A. (1992). *Aging and neuropsychological assessment*. New York: Plenum.

Lezak, M. (2004). *Neuropsychological assessment*. New York: Oxford University Press.

Saez-Fonseca, J., Lee, L., & Walker, Z. (2007). Long-term outcome of depressive pseudodementia in the elderly. *Journal of Affective Disorders, 101*, 123–129.

Swihart, A., & Pirozzolo, F. (1988). The neuropsychology of aging and dementia: Clinical issues. In H. A. Whitaker (Ed.), *Neuropsychological studies of nonfocal brain damage: Dementia trauma* (pp. 1–60). New York: Springer-Verlag.

SUGGESTED READING

Storandt, M., & VandenBos, G. (Eds). (1994). *Neuropsychological assessment of dementia and depression in older adults: A clinician's guide*. Washington, DC: American Psychological Association.

NORMAN ABELES
Michigan State University

See also: **Alzheimer's Disease; Dementia; Memory Functions**

PSI CHI

Psi Chi is the National Honor Society in Psychology, founded in 1929 for the purposes of encouraging, stimulating, and maintaining excellence in scholarship and advancing the science of psychology. Membership is open to graduate and undergraduate men and women who are making the study of psychology one of their major interests and who meet the minimum qualifications. Psi Chi is a member of the Association of College Honor Societies and is an affiliate of the American Psychological Association (APA) and the Association for Psychological Science (APS). Psi Chi's sister honor society is Psi Beta, the national honor society in psychology for community and junior colleges.

The purpose of Psi Chi is to encourage, stimulate, and maintain excellence in scholarship of the individual members in all fields, particularly in psychology, and to advance the science of psychology. Its mission is to produce well-educated, ethical, and socially responsible members committed to contributing to the science and profession of psychology and to society in general.

Psi Chi was founded on September 4, 1929, during the Ninth International Congress of Psychology held at Yale University. Shortly after Psi Chi's founding, a key was designed for the society, as well as a Psi Chi seal that features the key as its central element. Psi Chi's key is based on the Greek letters *psi* and *chi* that have been used for decades in the Psi Chi induction ritual to express the Greek words *psyche* and *cheires,* which in turn symbolize "mind" (particularly scholarship and the enrichment of the mind) and "hands" (a symbol of fellowship and cooperation in research).

Psi Chi publishes two quarterly publications, the *Eye on Psi Chi* magazine and the *Psi Chi Journal of Undergraduate Research.* Each year Psi Chi provides more than $300,000 in awards and grants in support of its members' research, as well as chapter activities. Eligible categories of awards and grants include those that support undergraduates, graduate students, faculty advisers, and chapters.

With its national headquarters in Chattanooga, Tennessee, Psi Chi functions as a federation of chapters located at more than 1,000 senior colleges and universities in the United States and Canada. Membership in Psi Chi is open to those who are making the study of psychology one of their major interests and who are students or faculty members in an institution where a chapter is located. The total number of memberships registered at the national office is now more than 500,000 lifetime members. Many of these members have gone on to distinguished careers in psychology. Distinguished members of Psi Chi include Albert Bandura, Guillermo Bernal, Jerome Bruner, Florence Denmark, Diane Halpern, Elizabeth Loftus, B. F. Skinner, Robert Sternberg, and Philip Zimbardo.

More information about Psi Chi is available at its web site (http://www.psichi.org).

ALVIN WANG
University of Central Florida

PSYCHOANALYSIS

Psychoanalysis is a theory of the mind and a method derived from that theory to treat mental disturbances. It had its origins in the discoveries and formulations developed over some 50 years by its creator, Sigmund Freud, a neurologist, neuroanatomist, and neuropathologist living in Vienna, who had an inquiring mind about the nature of mental processes. Freud was born in 1856. During a travel grant at the famous Salpetriere Clinic in Paris for 4 months in 1885–1886, under the noted French neurologist Charcot, the young physician came to learn from his mentor, via now-classic experiments in hypnosis, that ideas can instill and then remove and abolish the central features of hysteria.

Previously, an older colleague, Josef Breuer, had informed Freud of a patient with a double personality, consisting of alternating states of normalcy and multiple hysterical symptoms coming on around the death of her father. The patient would induce auto-hypnotic states during which she would speak to Breuer of distressing events around the origins of each symptom, after which the symptoms would disappear one at a time. The patient herself called these treatments the "chimney sweep" or "talking cure." Breuer then induced daily hypnoses, thus facilitating this process and furthering the birth of the cathartic method, part of the treatment armamentarium today.

Breuer had stopped this treatment abruptly as his own emotional involvement with the patient and the unusual intimacy of the process threatened his personal life. When the patient then suddenly became worse, demonstrating vividly the symptoms of pseudocyesis (false pregnancy), Breuer left "in a cold sweat" and the next day took his wife on a second honeymoon trip to Venice. The patient, known as Anna O., later became the first social worker in Germany and one of the first in the world.

Freud had expressed great interest in Breuer's experience, which he put together with what he had learned from Charcot in Paris. On his return to Vienna, seeing patients with complex symptoms without neurological or other organic findings to explain them, he continued this experimental process, honing himself, however, to develop an objective scientific attitude toward emotional and mental life. This was the first necessary step if the goal was to develop a method of treatment under the rubric of science. A brief trial with hypnosis, followed by actively urging the patient to speak, then the method of asking the patient to say whatever comes to mind, without censoring, evolved into the free association technique now so familiar to the public.

The accumulated results of this type of investigation, by Freud and a cadre of early pioneers, came to constitute the clinical data of psychoanalysis. But this was only one source. Freud's monumental *The Interpretation of Dreams,* published in 1900, brought in more ordinary, universal mental products (Freud, 1900/1953). These went on to jokes, slips of the tongue, and evidences of mental distortions in everyday life. The analysis of symptoms led to the analysis and understanding of character. The abnormal was seen to merge with the normal. A science of the mind began to take shape.

During the first third of what became known as the century of Freud, Freud and many early adherents constructed a comprehensive and coherent theory of mental functioning to encompass and make comprehensible the vast body of accumulating data. As dreams, hitherto elusive and mysterious, came to be seen as subject to rational forces and to have meanings in everyday life, new veins of hidden meaning and purpose were applied and extracted from all of human mental products, which came to include art, literature, music, poetry, and every aspect of human culture.

The new theory evolved piece by piece, as an explosion of discoveries and insights into the operation of the human mind exceeded what had been known in all previous history. At the base of the new theoretical structure was a postulated unconscious layer of mental functioning, unknown to consciousness, which was a major determinant of external human behavior. Among many new formulations and perspectives that evolved under the new theory, instinctual drives are defended against and conflicts repressed, while compromise formations lead to mental constellations and behavior that emerge into conscious life.

In a book on the subject of anxiety, probably second in importance only to his work on dreams, Freud refers to anxiety as "the fundamental phenomenon and main problem of neurosis" (1926/1959, p. 144). Later, anxiety was seen by Ernest Jones as the most frequent single symptom perhaps in all of medicine. Among other central concepts are the importance of childhood in future mental development and a new role of sexuality in childhood that altered previous thinking. The Oedipus complex, the name of which derived from the Greek myth, occurring at the age of 4 or 5, is the peak period of "the infantile neurosis," an internal psychic conflict during a crucial developmental phase of individual growth. It is from the type and degree of resolution of this childhood conflict that much of future mental life devolves.

To characterize the analytic process, Freud named two special mechanisms as central to the therapeutic procedure. One was the presence and analysis of transference and the transference neurosis, which come about as the patient displaces repressed conflicts onto the person of the analyst. The other is the analysis of resistances, which are obstacles to insight that point to inner defenses, also operative in the unconscious, that keep forbidden wishes and thoughts from becoming conscious. A third therapeutic path is the special interest in dreams, which early in the history of the field became "the royal road" to the unconscious.

A number of "principles of mental functioning" were described that reign over large swaths, if not all, of psychic functioning (Freud, 1911/1958). These include the pleasure–pain principle, the reality principle, and five metapsychological "points of view" (Freud, 1915/1957), which later became six, that represent converging approaches to the understanding of any psychic phenomenon. These are the dynamic, topographic, genetic, economic, and structural approaches of Freud, and the adaptive approach added later by others. The structural approach, which describes three psychic systems conducting the conflicts and also nonconflictual issues that course through life, became dominant and pathognomonic symbols for psychoanalysis. These three systems—the ego, the id, and the superego—have become part of language throughout the civilized world.

Spawning a veritable new industry, the total theoretical system, as it evolved and was applied, struck receptive chords in multitudes of people and became the intellectual signature of the twentieth century, known as "the century of Freud." Psychoanalysis, theory and method, spread rapidly throughout the Western world. From Vienna, it centered quickly in Zurich, Berlin, and Budapest. Ernest Jones brought it to England, and A. A. Brill brought it to the United States.

Not unexpectedly, the new or expanded view of the psychology of humans met with a mixed reception, ranging from strong advocacy to aversion. This is no different in the wider society than it is in the treatment of an individual. Conflicts that the conscious ego prefers to keep unconscious are lifted into conscious vision with varying degrees of acceptance, from readiness to rejection.

The history of development within the profession itself has similarly forked. Along with the steady development of the mainstream theory over the century has been the growth of many alternative and parallel theories, all supported as under the rubric of psychoanalysis. Such a tendency toward dissension was characteristic of the field from the beginning, resulting in such early names as Jung, Adler, Rank, and Ferenczi, each espousing a different center of theory or method.

Some of the suggested new directions of influence today include a focus on an earlier phase in life, from postnatal to the first year or two, in preference to the oedipal period (Klein); objects, or attachment to others, rather than drives, as the main inner source of motivation (Fairbairn, 1954); interpersonal (Sullivan, 1953) and cultural (Horney, 1937) factors playing more of a role in etiology than intrapsychic conflicts; self-preservation and maintenance of cohesion of the whole (Kohut, 1971) as the main source of anxiety, rather than specific fears of mutilation and separation; and on the side of technique, the use of empathy and reassurance rather than insight as the major curative factor.

The field is currently divided into two general orientations. One holds a pluralistic view that the existence of these many alternative theories is the best solution to differing views that are equivalent in their scientific validity and therapeutic methods. The other, probably a minority view, is that all valid additions and discoveries can be grafted onto a single group of enduring findings, the trunk of the theoretical tree, for a coherent unitary theory that includes and can sustain the infinite number of variations that constitute humankind (Rangell, 2007). All alternative theories either borrow from this trunk or, if not, are questionably psychoanalytic.

REFERENCES

Fairbairn, W. R. D. (1954). *An object-relations theory of the personality.* New York: Basic Books.

Freud, S. (1953). The interpretation of dreams. In J. Strachey (Ed. & Trans.), *The standard edition of the complete psychological works of Sigmund Freud* (Vols. 4–5). London: Hogarth Press. (Original work published 1900)

Freud, S. (1957). Papers on metapsychology. In J. Strachey (Ed. & Trans.), *The standard edition of the complete psychological works of Sigmund Freud* (Vol. 14, pp. 109–258). London: Hogarth Press. (Original work published 1915)

Freud, S. (1958). Formulations on the two principles of mental functioning. In J. Strachey (Ed. & Trans.), *The standard edition of the complete psychological works of Sigmund Freud* (Vol. 12, pp. 218–226). London: Hogarth Press. (Original work published 1911)

Freud, S. (1959). Inhibitions, symptoms and anxiety. In J. Strachey (Ed. & Trans.), *The standard edition of the complete psychological works of Sigmund Freud* (Vol. 20, pp. 87–172). London: Hogarth Press. (Original work published 1926)

Horney, K. (1937). *The neurotic personality of our time.* New York: Norton.

Kohut, H. (1971). *The analysis of the self.* New York: International Universities Press.

Rangell, L. (2007). *The road to unity in psychoanalytic theory.* New York: Jason Aronson.

Sullivan, H. S. (1953). *The interpersonal theory of psychiatry.* New York: Norton.

SUGGESTED READINGS

Fenichel, O. (1945). *The psychoanalytic theory of neurosis.* New York: Norton.

Hartmann. H. (1939). *Ego psychology and the problems of adaptation.* New York: International Universities Press, 1958.

Klein, M. (1948). *Contributions to psychoanalysis.* London: Hogarth Press.

LEO RANGELL
University of California, Los Angeles

See also: Insight-Oriented Psychotherapy; Psychoanalytic Theories; Psychodynamic Psychotherapy

PSYCHOANALYTIC THEORIES

Psychoanalytic theory is a continually evolving body of knowledge, but the so-called genetic or developmental point of view, which regards current functioning as a consequence of developmentally prior phases, has always been central. The notion that mental disorders could be best understood as residues of childhood experiences and primitive modes of mental functioning was key to Freud's thinking (Freud, 1905/1961), and a developmental approach to psychopathology has been the traditional framework of psychoanalysis. Each theory described here focuses on particular aspects of development or specific developmental phases and delineates a model of normal personality development based on clinical experience.

Freud's Psychoanalytic Theory

It was Freud who first linked mental disorders to childhood experiences and occurrences in the developmental process. One of the most important aspects of Freud's theory was his recognition of infantile sexuality. Freud countered idealized perceptions of childhood innocence. He viewed childhood as a period during which children struggle to achieve control over their biological needs and to make them acceptable to society through the microcosm of the family. Freud understood pathology as a failure of this process. Childhood conflict was thought to create a persistence of the problem, aggravated by current life pressures and generating significant anxieties that could only be resolved by so-called neurotic compromise: partially succumbing to infantile sexual demands, while simultaneously engaging in a self-punishing struggle against these demands. Freud's final model went beyond sexual concerns and posited aggressive or destructive motives independent of sexual drives. These motives confront children with a further developmental task of accommodation: having to gradually tame natural destructiveness in order to protect against long-term psychic pain. Freud and many of his followers considered genetic predisposition to be a crucial factor in abnormal reactions to socialization experiences.

Beyond Freud: Some General Comments

The post-Freudian models of development that dominated the second half of the past century of psychoanalytic thinking fall into three broad categories. In the United States, ego psychology broadened Freud's most complex model of the mind—the structural theory of id, ego, and superego—to incorporate a concern with adaptation to the social world in addition to the intrapsychic world. In Europe, particularly in the United Kingdom, object-relations theories were primarily concerned with internal representations of the parental figures and the fantasies that individuals can have about their relationships with these internally represented objects. In the United States, both approaches have recently given way to an interpersonalist tradition that is principally concerned with the observable infant–caregiver relationship and the vicissitudes of the social construction of subjective experience. Such approaches are generally referred to as relational theories.

Ego Psychology

Heinz Hartmann

Ego psychologists concentrated on the development of the adaptive capacities that children bring to bear on their struggle with their biological needs. Hartmann's model (Hartmann, Kris, & Loewenstein, 1949) aimed to link drives and ego functions and to reveal how negative interpersonal experiences could disrupt the development of the psychic structures necessary for adaptation. He also showed that regression (the reactivation of earlier structures) was the most significant constituent of psychopathology. Hartmann was one of the earliest theorists to emphasize the complexity of the developmental process, maintaining that the reasons that a particular behavior persists are likely to be different from the reasons it originally occurred.

Ego psychologists are also important for their identification of the omnipresence of intrapsychic conflict throughout development and for their recognition that genetic endowment, as well as interpersonal experiences, may be crucial in determining a child's developmental path (an idea that is partially reflected in the developmental psychopathological concept of resilience).

Anna Freud

Ego psychologists were among the earliest to investigate development by means of direct observations of children. Child analysts discovered that children's personality traits and symptoms are rarely consistent across childhood, revealing that symptomatology is a dynamic phenomenon that overlays and is interwoven with a basic developmental process. Anna Freud's developmental theory arose from her studies of disturbed and healthy children in situations of intense social stress. She identified many of the characteristics that would subsequently be linked to resilience. Her research showed that children in concentration camps could ensure their physical and psychological survival by the social support that they gave one another. Similarly, it showed that children's distress levels during the London Blitz were predicted by their caregivers' anxieties and that these children were typically more fearful of the threat represented by separation from their parents than of objective danger. Her emphasis on the protective power of social support and the detrimental effect of parental pathology in the context of coping with threat or danger has been substantiated by recent research with children experiencing severe trauma.

Anna Freud was also one of the first theorists to recognize the importance of an equilibrium between developmental processes (Freud, 1965). Her research helps to explain why children deprived of certain capacities by environment or constitution are at increased risk of psychological disturbance. She was the first psychoanalyst to place the process and mechanisms of development at the center of psychoanalytic thinking. Her approach defined abnormal functioning in terms of its deviation from normal development, while at the same time using the understanding gained from clinical cases to elucidate the process of normal development. In this sense, her approach is very much one of developmental psychopathology. It is a logical extension of her work to explore the therapeutic process in developmental terms, too.

Margaret Mahler

Margaret Mahler was a pioneer of developmental observation in the United States. Her observations of the ambitendency of children in their second year of life threw light on chronic problems of consolidating individuality. Mahler highlighted the paradox of self-development: that developing a separate identity involves forfeiting a gratifying closeness with the caregiver (Mahler, 1968). Mahler's model stresses the importance of the caregiver in facilitating separation. The pathogenic potential of withdrawal of the mother, when confronted with the child's wish for separateness, helps to account for the transgenerational aspects of psychological disturbance.

Joseph Sandler

In the United Kingdom, the most successful integration of the developmental perspective with psychoanalytic theory is Joseph Sandler's development of Anna

Freud's and Edith Jacobson's work. Sandler's framework allowed developmental researchers to integrate their findings within a psychoanalytic formulation that clinicians could also use. Central to his formulation is the representational structure containing both reality and distortion, which is the driving force of psychic life. Sandler was innovative in positing affects, as opposed to drives, as the organizers of human motivation. Crucial to his theory is the concept of background of safety (Sandler, 1987): the idea that the individual's primary aim is to experience a feeling of security, meaning that circumstances that are familiar will often feel safer, even if they are objectively adverse.

Object-Relations Theories

Melanie Klein

The developmental model constructed by Melanie Klein initially occasioned severe criticism, because of its apparently excessive assumptions about the cognitive capacities of infants. However, developmental research appears surprisingly consistent with some of Klein's claims concerning perception of causality and causal reasoning. Kleinian developmental concepts have gained popularity because they provide powerful descriptions of the clinical interaction between both child and adult patients and their psychoanalyst. Post-Kleinian psychoanalysts such as W. R. Bion have emphasized the impact of emotional conflict on the development of cognitive capacities.

W. R. D. Fairbairn and D. W. Winnicott

Studies of severe character disorders by the object-relations school of psychoanalysts in Britain have shown early relationships with caregivers to be a crucial factor in personality development. W. R. D. Fairbairn focused on the individual's need for the other (Fairbairn, 1952), instigating a shift in the focus of psychoanalytic attention that culminated in the self emerging as a central part of the psychoanalytic model, notably in the work of Winnicott (1971). Winnicott's notion of a self-defensive caretaker or false self that may emerge as a response to a trauma occurring at the stage of absolute dependency has become a crucial developmental construct. His notions of primary maternal preoccupation, transitional phenomena, the holding environment, and the mirroring function of the caregiver provided a clear research focus for developmentalists interested in individual differences in the development of self structure (Fonagy, Gergely, Jurist, & Target, 2002). Winnicott emphasized the traumatic effects of early maternal failure and the importance of maternal sensitivity for the establishment of a secure relationship. Developmental studies of psychopathology have continued to validate these claims in many respects

and have consistently affirmed the significance of the parent–child relationship.

Heinz Kohut

Heinz Kohut's theories relied heavily on his investigations of narcissistic disorders. His work represents one of many attempts by North American theorists to integrate object-relations ideas into models that retain facets of structural theories. Perhaps his most significant contribution to developmental psychology was his assertion of the need for an understanding caregiver to counterbalance the infant's sense of helplessness in its biological striving for mastery. Indeed, Kohut asserted that understanding objects was important throughout life, a claim that is bolstered by increasing evidence from epidemiological studies of the protective effect of social support. In Kohut's theory—which borrowed freely though largely without acknowledgment from Winnicott and British object-relations theorists—the mirroring object becomes a self-object, and the need for empathy drives development, culminating in the attainment of a cohesive self. Drive theory becomes secondary to self theory, in that the failure to attain an integrated self-structure both leaves room for and generates aggression and isolated sexual fixation.

Otto Kernberg

Kernberg's contribution to psychoanalysis is unsurpassed in recent history. His systematic integration of structural theory and object relations theory (Kernberg, 1987) is probably the most frequently used psychoanalytic developmental model, particularly in relation to personality disorders. His understanding of psychopathology is developmental insofar as personality disturbance is understood to reflect the individual's failure to develop adequate means of addressing intrapsychic conflict, beyond the most primitive defenses of early childhood. Kernberg's exceptional commitment to operationalizing his ideas distinguishes his models from many psychoanalytic theories and has rendered them open to empirical investigation.

Beyond Object Relations

Relational Theories

The opening up of psychoanalysis to psychologists and other nonmedically qualified professionals and the declining influence of ego psychology cleared the way for a new intellectual approach to theory and technique. The relational approach is arguably rooted in work by Harry Stack Sullivan and Clara Thompson in the United States and John Bowlby in the United Kingdom. The former gave rise to the interpersonalist approach (Mitchell, 1988). This approach challenges traditional conceptions of the relationship between analyst and subject, as based on the doctor–patient structure, envisaging it instead as a relationship between equals. This approach emphasizes the interpersonal character of the sense of self and stresses the influence this characteristic has on the therapeutic process. The insistence of many interpersonalists that enactments by the analyst within the therapy are almost as inevitable as those by the patient in the transference has been particularly controversial. This tradition has lacked a significant developmental approach until recently.

John Bowlby

Bowlby's cognitive-systems model of the internalization of interpersonal relationships (internal working models) has been highly influential. His work developed the emphasis of object-relations theories on the importance of the security of early relationships. His theory holds that children's expectations regarding a caregiver's behavior and their own behavior develops from their understanding of experiences of previous interaction. The child's behavior with the attachment figure (and, by extension, with others) is shaped by these expectations. Bowlby's developmental model highlights the intergenerational transmission of internal working models, and a growing body of empirical research has confirmed this phenomenon.

Numerous theories have drawn heavily on the developmental research tradition, combining attachment theory ideas with psychoanalytic conceptions within a general systems theory frame of reference. A book by Daniel Stern (1985) has been among the most significant in this regard. More recently, Peter Fonagy and colleagues have proposed a developmental model in the relational tradition that has its origins in attachment theory but is also heavily influenced by object-relations theories (Fonagy et al., 2002). Mentalization-based theories emphasize the emergence of the self as an experiential agent of change rather than as a representation. They suggest that, before the self is experienced as a thinking and feeling entity, there exists an intersubjective self that acquires understanding of its own functioning through the reactions of the caregiver. A secure, playful relationship with attuned caregivers who have the child's mind in their mind enables the child to arrive at mentalization, which involves thinking of the other and the self as motivated by mental states. If this relationship is disrupted (for example, by maltreatment or the child's constitutional problems), mentalization will not be fully achieved, resulting in severe attachment-related personality problems.

All psychoanalytic formulations assume a causal link between psychopathology and developmentally prior phases. In recent years, psychoanalytic theories have been criticized for depending too much on single case studies and for the deficit in reliable empirical evidence to back up their assertions. However, cognitive and neuropsychological research has produced a rapidly increasing body of information with relevance for psychoanalysis. We have reached a time when the appropriateness of many psychoanalytic ideas may well become more evident, as we discover more about brain function.

However, changes in the way psychoanalytic knowledge is gained must occur if psychoanalysis is to have a future role in the mind sciences. Psychoanalysis must limit the assumptions it makes about normal development, while simultaneously enhancing the effectiveness of its interface with other relevant disciplines. Should psychoanalysis succeed in meeting the challenges that integration with cognitive psychology and neuroscience would involve, then it could prove to be of great value to developmental psychopathology. This is particularly true of the fundamental psychoanalytic developmental assumption that the representations of unconscious beliefs and affects that individuals construct in early life help to shape their later behavior and experiences. Psychoanalytic theory remains relevant, and its capacity to enhance our understanding of development and psychopathology has yet to be fully exploited.

REFERENCES

Fairbairn, W. R. D. (1952). *An object-relations theory of the personality*. New York, Basic Books.

Fonagy, P., Gergely, G., Jurist, E., & Target, M. (2002). *Affect regulation, mentalization and the development of the self*. New York: Other Press.

Freud, A. (1965). *Normality and pathology in childhood: Assessments of development*. Madison, CT: International Universities Press.

Freud, S. (1961). Three essays on the theory of sexuality. In J. Strachey (Ed. & Trans.), *The standard edition of the complete psychological works of Sigmund Freud* (Vol. 7, pp. 123–230). London: Hogarth Press. (Original work published 1905)

Hartmann, H., Kris, H., & Loewenstein, R. (1949). Notes on the theory of aggression. *Psychoanalytic Study of the Child, 3–4*, 9–36.

Kernberg, O. F. (1987). An ego psychology-object relations theory approach to the transference. *Psychoanalytic Quarterly, 51*, 197–221.

Mahler, M. (1968). *On human symbiosis and the vicissitudes of individuation*. New York: International Universities Press.

Mitchell, S. A. (1988). *Relational concepts in psychoanalysis: An integration*. Cambridge, MA: Harvard University Press.

Sandler, J. (1987). *From safety to the superego: Selected papers of Joseph Sandler*. New York: Guilford Press.

Stern, D. N. (1985). *The interpersonal world of the infant: A view from psychoanalysis and developmental psychology*. New York: Basic Books.

Winnicott, D. W. (1971). *Playing and reality*. London: Tavistock.

SUGGESTED READINGS

Bronstein, C. (Ed.). (2001). *Kleinian theory: A contemporary perspective*. London: Whurr.

Cooper, A. M. (Ed.). (2006). *Contemporary psychoanalysis in America: Leading analysts present their work.* Washington, DC: American Psychiatric Press.

Fonagy, P., & Target, M. (2003). *Psychoanalytic theories: Perspectives from developmental psychopathology.* London: Routledge.

PETER FONAGY
University College London, United Kingdom

See also: Ego Psychology; Object Relations Theory; Personality, Psychodynamic Models of

PSYCHODRAMA

Psychodrama is a method of group and individual psychotherapy in which people are helped to explore their psychosocial issues by using sensitively guided enactment and a wide range of action-based techniques. During a psychodrama session, the person in focus recreates significant events, relationships, or internal processes in order to explore their impact, integrate new responses, and gain insight, healing, and growth.

Psychodrama is holistic in the sense that it takes into account the whole person—one's thoughts, feelings, behavior, physical being and sensations, relationships, social context, and history, and also the emotional and spiritual dimensions of well-being. In psychodrama, people are helped to enhance their own capacity for psychological healing by expressing their own true feelings and rediscovering their natural spontaneity, creativity, and imagination. It is a method for helping individuals explore their own truth through active processes and practice more effective living without being punished for making mistakes.

Origins

Psychodrama was devised in the 1930s by psychiatrist Jacob Levy Moreno (1889–1974) and further developed in collaboration with his wife, Zerka Toeman Moreno, who continues to teach and demonstrate psychodrama to this day. Moreno was born in Romania and spent his formative years in Vienna during its renowned period of cultural ferment. Psychodrama grew out of his interest in philosophy, theater, and group interactions. As a young physician, Moreno was among the first to recognize the healing power of groups, including the importance of self-help groups.

Moreno first became interested in the healing potential of spontaneity and creativity when watching children play in the parks of Vienna and joining them as a storyteller. He observed that children often appeared able to solve their conflicts with play and without adult intervention. He also noted that children who repeatedly took the same roles in their play had more difficulty in showing creativity. With encouragement to try new roles, the children became more spontaneous and vital in their interactions.

After emigrating to the United States in the 1920s, Moreno further developed his insights into the importance of spontaneity and creativity for mental and social well-being. These insights became central tenets of psychodrama. Moreno also developed widely influential methods and concepts such as sociometry, sociodrama, the theater of spontaneity, role play, group psychotherapy, and the principle of the encounter. Many later developments in interactive and improvisational theater, applied drama, and forms of therapy like Gestalt and self-help groups have their origins in the ideas and work of Moreno. His broad influence is a reminder that Moreno's concept of human beings is that we are all, in his terms, co-creators of the world around us, with vast reserves of untapped creative power. His far-reaching therapeutic vision was that all people should be helped to increase their spontaneity and creativity in order to help themselves and become cocreators of their society.

Psychodrama in Practice

Psychodrama is notably different from talk-based therapy, because in psychodrama all aspects of life are not only discussed but also recreated, worked through in action, and integrated in the here-and-now of the therapy session. This active involvement can deepen learning, recovery, and growth. The scenes enacted may be based on defining events in a person's life, current or past relationships, unfinished situations, desired roles, inner thoughts, self-doubts, or deep-rooted beliefs and conflicts. A psychodrama often begins with a scene examining a current problem or difficulty, and it may trace it back to earlier life situations. Here, the participant may have the chance to experience what was missing but needed at that time. The enactment then returns to the present, where new learning can be integrated and put into practice.

An important aspect of psychodrama is that the people in focus are part of the action. They play the role of themselves and also have the opportunity to reverse roles to better understand the perspective of other people. Volunteers from the group take roles in the drama as needed. Psychodrama allows for the safe expression of strong feelings and, for those who need it, the practice of containing emotions. As participants move from talking about things into action, opportunities arise to heal the past, express and integrate blocked thoughts and emotions, clarify the present, experience new roles, and practice new skills. These scenes may include finally saying good-bye to a loved one, revisiting a painful time to express previously forbidden emotions, or trying out a new, successful role. Here are some examples:

The psychodrama of a man who has suffered a string of relationship breakdowns: During the drama, he is helped to trace his difficulties back to his early relationship with his mother, which was cold and distant. Speaking to a group member who is in the role of his mother, the man expresses his unmet need for love and care from her. He then has the opportunity, within the drama, to experience a different kind of mothering. Following this, he is given time to practice a new way of being in relationships, drawing from this experience of attuned parenting.

The psychodrama of a woman who chooses a group member to represent the child she never had: In the drama, she holds the child she always wanted but could not have for physical reasons. She expresses her grief and longing, while gently stroking the child's hair and face. After a long and sensitive encounter with this much-wanted child, she is helped to explore ways in which she can still carry out this vital role of mothering with her nieces and nephews and in her community.

The psychodrama of a man who, as a boy, had been raped and strangled nearly to death by a neighbor who had befriended him: Twenty years later, he is still terrified by the memory of this event. In the session, the man finally manages to summon up his rage about the abuse and takes back the ability to say No! as he accuses his abuser and sees him brought to justice in a psychodramatic courtroom.

The psychodrama of a woman who cannot face an upcoming family reunion, where she will see her sister after many years: During the psychodrama, she explores scenes from their childhood, where they were highly competitive and she felt bullied by her sister. She reverses roles with her sister and gains insight into the reasons for her sister's behavior. She realizes that they were both growing up in a highly competitive environment and being bullied by their parents. She ends the drama by finding new ways of behaving toward her sister at the upcoming reunion.

Elements of Psychodrama

There are five elements present in a psychodrama session: (1) the protagonist, who is the person whose story or issue is the primary focus of the session; (2) the auxiliary egos, who are group members who assume the roles of significant others in the drama and may include significant people, objects, or even aspects of the self or a person's internal world, for example, "my optimistic self" or "my negative thoughts"; (3) the audience, consisting of group members who witness the drama and who may become involved as protagonists or in auxiliary roles and whose emphasis is on creating a safe and supportive environment

where each person is a potential therapeutic agent for the others; (4) the stage, which is the physical space in which the drama is conducted and may be an actual stage or simply a designated space; and (5) the director, who is the trained therapist who guides participants through each phase of the session.

Structure of a Session

The structure of a typical psychodrama session includes the following elements:

Warm-up. This typically takes the form of structured group activities around a given theme. The group members are helped to develop trust, cohesion, and energy, while also warming up to the psychodrama.

Protagonist selection. Usually there is a process where one or more potential protagonists emerge, and there may be a group selection to choose a protagonist for that session.

The presenting scene. This is the first scene of the drama. Typically, this is a current or recent troubling issue, event, or internal conflict. During this early phase of the drama, the director will often take time to establish a working contract and build up or reinforce the protagonist's strengths and resilience before proceeding further.

Scenes establishing the pattern of response. One or more scenes from the recent past or further in the past are enacted, where the pattern of response is further elaborated.

Tracing the response or belief back to its roots. During this phase of the drama, the role or the behavioral or emotional response is traced back to earlier life situations and often to its time and place of origin. This may be a scene from early in life and may include a traumatic event. In some cases, for example, where there has been unresolved trauma through the generations, the trauma may be traced back through three or more generations.

Emotional catharsis. At this point in the drama, the protagonist is given the opportunity to feel and express what has often been a forbidden feeling or response. Typically the emotions of anger, fear, or sadness are expressed during this phase of the drama.

Surplus reality. This was a term devised by Moreno. It describes the part of the psychodrama where protagonists have the chance to experience what was missing but needed at that time in their lives. This might be a scene of rescue, repair, taking back power, obtaining justice, or being heard, validated, or comforted by a significant other person. For example, in psychodramas addressing childhood suffering, this is the point in the drama when the once silenced child is allowed to speak his or her truth, to feel, and to recover knowledge that was once blocked from understanding.

Integration. The enactment then returns to the present, where new learning can be integrated and put into practice. The new perceptions and experiences are integrated and developed into new roles and new responses. In some cases, future projection and role play may be used to practice the new response in anticipated situations from the future.

Sharing. At the conclusion of the drama, the participants speak about what they share in common with the theme of the drama. This may include personal experiences or emotional responses. Witnessing and participating in each others' personal stories and sharing sensitively afterwards often generates feelings of deep understanding, satisfaction, and trust among group members.

This is a general outline; each psychodrama is unique and will include variations of these elements.

Influence and Applications of Psychodrama

Conceptually, psychodrama encompasses the perspectives of varied branches of psychotherapy, including the humanistic, integrative, existential, psychodynamic, body-oriented, cognitive, solution-focused, and person-centered traditions. Psychodrama has been applied in every type of therapeutic and mental health setting, and it is also used in personal development, relationship and marital counseling, community building, professional training, and business and industry. Some of psychodrama's central techniques, such as role reversal, the empty chair, role play, and doubling, have been widely influential and adapted by many other treatment modalities. In many countries, psychodrama is seen as a treatment of choice in helping people with difficulties in relationships, self-management, and social and emotional functioning. This is especially the case when individuals' difficulties are complex (including the combination of several problems at once), and they feel that their issues cannot be addressed sufficiently through talk-based therapies. Psychodrama is also particularly useful for helping people experiencing unresolved loss, trauma, or mood disorders, such as anxiety or depression. Psychodrama has also been used to good effect with people who have been diagnosed with personality disorders and a wide range of other mental health conditions, including psychosis.

Today, psychodrama is practiced throughout the world. There are many thousands of practitioners, psychodrama training schools, and national and regional accrediting organizations throughout North and South America, Europe, Russia, Australia, New Zealand, and increasingly in Asia.

SUGGESTED READINGS

Baim, C., Burmeister, J., & Maciel, M. (Eds.). (2007). *Psychodrama: Advances in theory and practice.* London: Routledge.

Blatner, A. (1997). *Acting in: Practical applications of psychodramatic methods* (3rd ed.). New York: Springer.

Dayton, T. (2005). *The living stage: A step-by-step guide to psychodrama, sociometry and experiential group therapy.* Deerfield Beach, FL: Health Communications.

Fox, J. (Ed.). (1987). *The essential Moreno: Writings on psychodrama, group method, and spontaneity, by J. L. Moreno.* New York: Springer.

Horvatin, T., & Schreiber, E. (Eds.). (2006). *The quintessential Zerka: Writings by Zerka Toeman Moreno on psychodrama, sociometry and group psychotherapy.* London: Routledge.

Marineau, R. (1989). *Jacob Levy Moreno, 1889–1974.* London: Routledge.

Moreno, J. L. (1934). *Who shall survive? A new approach to the problem of human interrelations.* Washington, DC: Nervous and Mental Disease Publishing.

Moreno, J. L. (1946–1969). *Psychodrama* (3 vols.; last two with Z. T. Moreno). Beacon, NY: Beacon House.

CLARK BAIM
Birmingham Institute for Psychodrama, Birmingham, United Kingdom

See also: **Group Therapy**

PSYCHODYNAMIC DIAGNOSTIC MANUAL

The *Psychodynamic Diagnostic Manual* (*PDM*; PDM Task Force, 2006) is the first psychological diagnostic classification system that considers the whole person in various stages of development. A task force of five major psychoanalytic organizations and leading researchers, under the guidance of Stanley I. Greenspan, Nancy McWilliams, and Robert Wallerstein, came together to develop the *PDM*. The resulting nosology goes from the deep structural foundation of personality to the surface symptoms that include the integration of behavioral, emotional, cognitive, and social functioning.

The *PDM* improves on the existing diagnostic systems by considering the full range of mental functioning. In addition to culling years of psychoanalytic studies of etiology and pathogenesis, the *PDM* relies on research in neuroscience, treatment outcome, infant and child development, and personality assessment.

The *PDM* does not look at symptom patterns described in isolation, as do the *International Classification of Diseases* (*ICD*) and the *Diagnostic and Statistical Manual* of the American Psychiatric Association (*DSM*). Research on brain development and the maturation of mental processes suggests that patterns of behavioral, emotional, cognitive, and social functioning involve many areas working together rather than in isolation. Although it is based on psychodynamic theory and supporting research, the *PDM* is not doctrinaire in its presentation. It may be used in conjunction with the *ICD* or *DSM*. The PDM Task Force made an effort to use language that is accessible to all the schools of psychology. It was developed to be particularly useful in case formulation that could improve the effectiveness of any psychological intervention.

The *PDM* has received very favorable reviews from mostly the psychoanalytic community (Clemens, 2007; Ekstrom, 2007; Migone, 2006; Silvio, 2007). However, even nonpsychodynamic psychologists who were introduced to the *PDM* as part of MMPI-2 and ethics and risk-management workshops have reacted positively to the new diagnostic system. Ninety percent of 192 psychologists surveyed (65 self-identified as psychodynamic, 76 as cognitive behavioral, and 51 as family systems, humanistic-existential, or eclectic in orientation) rated the *PDM* as favorable to very favorable (Gordon, 2008).

Classification of Adult Mental Health Disorders

Personality Patterns and Disorders—P Axis

The *PDM* covers the full range of human development: adults, adolescents, children, and infants. The adult diagnostic section begins with personality. The P axis, personality patterns and disorders, has been placed first in the *PDM* system because of the accumulating research finding that symptoms cannot be understood or well treated in the absence of an understanding of the deeper personality traits of the adult who has the symptoms.

The P axis takes into account two areas. We are first asked to consider the person's level of personality organization or severity of personality disorder. This continuum goes from a mainly healthy personality (absence of a personality disorder) to a mainly neurotic-level personality disorder and, at the most severe end, a mainly borderline-level personality disorder. *Borderline* is used by the *PDM* as a level of severity and not as a specific personality disorder, as it is in the *DSM*.

The levels of personality organization (healthy, neurotic, or borderline) are determined by assessing a person's capacities in six respects: identity maturation, the ability to form stable satisfying relationships, affect tolerance and regulation, moral reasoning, reality testing, and the ability to respond to and recover from stress.

After determining the overall level of personality organization, we identify the P axis personality patterns (which may be adaptive and cause minimum if any impairment) and any more pervasive personality disorders (which repeatedly cause pain to ourselves or to others). The personality patterns or disorders to consider are the following: schizoid; paranoid; psychopathic (antisocial), with subtypes passive-parasitic and aggressive; narcissistic, with subtypes arrogant-entitled and depressed-depleted; sadistic, with an intermediate manifestation of sadomasochistic; masochistic (self-defeating), with subtypes moral masochistic and relational masochistic; depressive, with subtypes introjective, anaclitic, and converse manifestation hypomanic; somatizing; dependent, with passive-aggressive versions and converse manifestations of counterdependent; phobic (avoidant), with converse manifestations of counterphobic; anxious; obsessive-compulsive, with subtypes obsessive and compulsive; hysterical (histrionic), with subtypes inhibited and demonstrative or flamboyant; dissociative; and mixed/other.

Then the *PDM* P axis considers each personality disorder in terms of temperamental, thematic, affective, cognitive, and defense patterns. The psychopathic (antisocial) personality, for example, has aggressiveness and a high threshold for emotional stimulation as part of the temperamental or contributing constitutional-maturational factors. The main thematic or central tension or preoccupation is manipulating and being manipulated. The central affects are rage and envy. The characteristic pathogenic belief about the self is "I can make anything happen." The characteristic pathogenic belief about others is "Everyone is selfish, manipulative, and dishonest." The central ways of defending involve reaching for omnipotent control over others.

The *PDM* does not consider disorders as being artificially isolated and distinct. For example, depression can be a mood disorder on the symptom axis, and also a personality disorder on the P axis with different traits. The *PDM* classifies a depressive personality disorder with the subtypes of introjective (self-critical), anaclitic (high reactivity to loss and rejection), and the converse manifestation of hypomanic personality disorder (high energy, counterdepressive, fear of closeness). The *PDM* also makes treatment suggestions when there are sufficient data to support them. The introjective type tends to respond better to interpretations and insight, whereas the anaclitic type tends to respond better to the actual therapeutic relationship. The hypomanic type often flees from commitment and therefore does not stay long enough in treatment. The *PDM* suggests emphasizing that the commitment to the treatment is important to improvement. People with hypomanic personality disorders are most likely to be at the borderline level and favor such defenses as idealization of self and the devaluation of others, whereas those with depressive personalities favor such defenses as devaluation of self and the idealization of others.

Profile of Mental Functioning—M Axis

The second *PDM* dimension is the M axis, mental functioning, which takes a detailed look at the capacities that contribute to an individual's personality and overall level of psychological health or disturbance. These include the capacity for regulation, attention, and learning; the capacity for relationships (including depth, range, and consistency); the quality of internal experience (level of confidence and self-regard); the capacity for affective experience, expression, and communication; the level of defensive patterns; the capacity to form internal representations; the capacity for differentiation and integration; the self-observing capacities (psychological-mindedness); and the capacity for internal standards and ideals, that is, a sense of morality.

Symptom Patterns: The Subjective Experience—S Axis

Last, the *PDM* considers the S axis, manifest symptoms and concerns. These are the *DSM-IV-TR* symptom patterns, but with an emphasis on the patient's subjective experience of the symptoms. The patient may evidence a few or many patterns, which may or may not be related. The *PDM* does not regard them as highly demarcated biopsychosocial phenomena. These symptom patterns should be seen in the context of the person's personality (P axis) and mental functioning (M axis).

Classification of Child and Adolescent Mental Health Disorders

Profile of Mental Functioning for Children and Adolescents—MCA Axis

The classification of child and adolescent disorders begins with the MCA axis, profile of mental functioning for children and adolescents. This axis addresses the adequacy of a child or adolescent's mental functions in dealing with such experiences as relationships, emotions, and anxiety.

Child and Adolescent Personality Patterns and Disorders—PCA Axis

Next, the *PDM* looks at the PCA axis, child and adolescent personality patterns and disorders, which involve emerging patterns of personality tendencies and styles that may change or remain relatively stable throughout the course of life. As with adults, we are asked to first assess the level of severity: "normal" emerging personality patterns, moderately dysfunctional emerging personality patterns, and severely dysfunctional emerging personality patterns. Then the *PDM* asks us to consider several specific dysfunctional personality patterns: fearful of closeness and intimacy (schizoid); suspicious and distrustful; sociopathic (antisocial); narcissistic; impulsive or explosive; self-defeating; depressive; somatizing; dependent; avoidant or constricted, with a subtype counterphobic; anxious; obsessive-compulsive; histrionic; dysregulated; and mixed/other.

Child and Adolescent Symptom Patterns: The Subjective Experience—SCA Axis

Finally, the *PDM* considers the SCA axis, child and adolescent symptom patterns, with attention to how they are experienced subjectively. The SCA axis looks at symptom patterns in a developmental, dynamic context and regards each child's subjective experience of his or her symptoms as unique. This approach includes discerning healthy responses, developmental crises, situational crises, and disorders of affect. The main symptom categories used are the following: anxiety disorders, somatization (somatoform) disorders, affect and/or mood disorders (including prolonged mourning or grief reaction, depressive disorders, bipolar disorders, and suicidality), disruptive behavior disorders, reactive disorders (including psychic trauma and posttraumatic stress disorder), disorders of mental functioning (including psychotic disorders and neuropsychological disorders), psychophysiologic disorders, developmental disorders, and other disorders.

The Classification of Mental Health and Developmental Disorders in Infancy and Early Childhood

The *PDM* classification of infant and early childhood disorders is unique and appropriate to this age group. The primary diagnoses include the interactive disorders that involve symptom patterns like anxiety, depression, and disruptive behaviors; the regulatory-sensory disorders that involve such symptoms as inattention, overreactivity and underreactivity, and sensory seeking; and neurodevelopmental disorders of relating and communicating, including the autism spectrum disorders.

Research Foundations for the *PDM*

The *PDM* devotes the latter half of the book to the "Conceptual and Research Foundations for a Psychodynamically Based Classification System for Mental Health Disorders." These are valuable articles and references on the concepts and research that support the *PDM* classification system. These articles can also inform researchers with respect to using constructs and designs based on the *PDM* formulations of the whole person that would improve external validity.

REFERENCES

Clemens, N. A. (2007). The *Psychodynamic Diagnostic Manual*: A review. *Journal of Psychiatric Practice, 13*(4), 258–260.

Ekstrom, S. (2007). Review of *Psychodynamic Diagnostic Manual*. *Journal of Analytical Psychology, 52*(1), 111–114.

Gordon, R. M. (2008). *Early reactions to the PDM by psychodynamic, CBT and other non-psychodynamic psychologists*. Manuscript submitted for publication.

Migone, P. (2006). La diagnosi in psicoanalisi: Presentazione del *PDM* (*Psychodynamic Diagnostic Manual*) [The psychoanalytic diagnosis: Presentation of the *Psychodynamic Diagnostic Manual* (*PDM*)]. *Psicoterapia e scienze umane, 40*(4), 765–774.

PDM Task Force. (2006). *Psychodynamic diagnostic manual.* Silver Spring, MD: Alliance of Psychoanalytic Organizations.

Silvio, J. R. (2007). Review of *Psychodynamic Diagnostic Manual. Journal of the American Academy of Psychoanalysis and Dynamic Psychiatry, 35*(4), 681–685.

ROBERT M. GORDON
Allentown, Pennsylvania

PSYCHODYNAMIC PSYCHOTHERAPY

The term "Psychodynamic Psychotherapy" is a generic label that is applied to a large group of psychotherapies that are derived theoretically and technically from clinical psychoanalysis. The term usually is understood as being synonymous with the terms "Psychoanalytic Psychotherapy" or "Psychoanalytically Oriented Psychotherapy." These psychotherapies share certain commonalities with regard to their approaches to understanding psychopathology, their psychological change strategies, and interventions that mark them as descendants of traditional or classical psychoanalysis, but they also differ from classical psychoanalysis and from each other in numerous ways, both theoretically and clinically.

Most psychoanalytic authors distinguish Psychodynamic Psychotherapy from psychoanalysis by comparing the two forms of psychotherapy on certain extrinsic factors, such as frequency of sessions, the use of the couch by the patient and the corresponding abstinent or silent role on the part of the therapist, and the length of the treatment. Most versions of Psychodynamic Psychotherapy are conducted on a once- or twice-weekly basis for a period of a few months to a few years. In fact, among the more exciting recent developments in this field has been the emergence of psychodynamic therapies that are designed to be short-term (Binder, 2004). Typically, patient and therapist sit face to face, and the patient's verbalizations are guided to some degree by the therapist's commentary and inquiry. These factors stand in contrast to the features of psychoanalysis proper, which is conducted on a more intensive and frequent schedule of sessions for periods of many years, and which utilizes free association on the part of the patient, often while reclining on a couch out of sight of the analyst, and infrequent comments and interventions on the part of the analyst.

Gill (1994) attempted to differentiate psychoanalysis from psychodynamic psychotherapy by referring to what he called intrinsic criteria, which are more descriptive of the ways in which psychotherapies are practiced. He suggested reserving the label "Psychoanalysis" for those therapies that focus exclusively on the exploration of, interpretation of, and resolution of the unconscious transference-countertransference relationship between therapist and patient. He argued further that "Psychodynamic Psychotherapy" could be understood to refer to any form of psychological treatment that conceptualized the development of psychopathology by relying on traditional psychoanalytic theoretical concepts of unconscious motivation and conflict. In these therapies the impact of such unconscious variables is explored most frequently through patients' reports of their ongoing relationships, and the interpretation of the unconscious aspects of the therapeutic interaction are less of a focus. It is this differentiation on the basis on intrinsic clinical factors that most clearly separates the variety of psychodynamic psychotherapies from their common ancestry in classical psychoanalysis.

The variation among the individual forms of Psychodynamic Psychotherapy is determined largely by the specific version of psychoanalytic theory on which the therapy is based and by the specific theory of change that guides therapeutic intervention in each model. These theoretical issues are discussed next.

Psychodynamic Theories of Psychopathology

Current psychodynamic theories are the inheritors of more than a century of conceptualizing human behavior in terms of unconscious motivation, conflict, and defense. All versions of psychodynamic theory share this emphasis on the unconscious determination of conscious cognition, affect, and behavior. However, there are important differences in the ways each theory sees such processes emerging during the course of psychological development. Those theorists who remain identified with more traditional Freudian models tend to emphasize biological determinism of intrapsychic conflicts and to downplay the role of the interpersonal environment in shaping people and their psychological difficulties.

These theories tend to posit universal and fixed developmental stages that can give rise to conflict and to fixation, the latter referring to the idea that the person unknowingly returns or regresses to these points of conflict in later life. Symptoms like anxiety, depression, or obsessive ideas and rituals are considered to be symbolic of one or more unacknowledged conflicts and also to be the outcome of a compromise between the person's wish to express the unconscious desire and the defensive mechanisms that keep the wish outside of consciousness. Freud's (1953) description of the stages of infantile sexuality, and of the adult manifestations of the unconscious sexual conflicts that emerge during childhood, are the prototype of this type of theorizing.

In contrast to these models, many contemporary psychodynamic theories rely heavily on interpersonal and environmental factors to explain psychological distress, while retaining the traditional emphasis on unconscious processes. These theories, which lately have been grouped under the rubric of "Relational Psychoanalysis," tend to produce formulations of psychological development that are more individualized and specific to the individual patient's childhood experiences with his or her parents, siblings, and other significant persons. These early interpersonal interactions are considered to be central to the development of psychological structures, emotional and motivational conflicts, and permanent images or representations of the self and of others. Such experiences, if they were colored by indifference, inconsistency, abandonment, neglect, abuse, or trauma, are avoided or disowned but are stored in the patient's memory, usually unconsciously, and their influences and consequences continue to be felt in adult daily life. These representations and their associated emotions and thought processes then become the templates for new experiences and relationships, often skewing and distorting the patients' view of the world and making them vulnerable to psychological symptoms and to the repetition of these experiences in adult life. Relational theories and their impact on psychodynamic psychotherapy are described by Greenberg and Mitchell (1983).

Psychodynamic Theories of Change

Most if not all psychodynamic psychotherapies consider insight to be a central, if not the most important, change factor in psychotherapy. Insight refers to an expansion of patients' awareness of those psychological processes that are crucial to their distress and disturbance, about which they have been previously unknowing. Insight usually is the result of a complex and difficult process of exploration of a patient's memories, feelings, fantasies, dreams, and current experiences. As the stuff of his or her life is perused, certain repetitive themes, images, feelings, and memories will tend to re-occur. Sometimes insight occurs spontaneously as a patient discusses his or her life, but more typically patients change and expand their self-knowledge after the therapist has interpreted the meaning of these communications. Interpretation refers to the provision by the therapist of a tentative explanation for some psychological or interpersonal experience on the part of the patient.

If interpretations resonate with patients, they may become aware of some conflictual and painful combination of feelings, desires, memories, and events that have been unwittingly impacting on their psychological life. If this process is considered to be complete, then patients will also become aware of those defense mechanisms and personality traits through which they have been keeping those issues out of their awareness, and they will also admit into

consciousness those anxieties, painful affects, self-images, and anticipated interpersonal consequences that led to the original need to exclude them from consciousness. As these feeling states and structures become more accessible to consciousness, they seem to lose their ability to influence the patient's experiences and behavior, and often are revised into more neutral and benign forms. Acceptance of the emotions that accompany such conflictual psychological material is known as abreaction, and this is crucial to therapeutic process. Expanded intellectual understanding of one's psychodynamic makeup without abreaction is a sterile and therapeutic useless experience (Gold, 2002).

A second psychodynamic theory of change focuses on the ameliorative effects of learning new patterns of relating to others. This hypothesized mechanism of change is often referred to as a "corrective emotional experience" (Alexander & French, 1946). Such learning can occur in a number of different ways and in at least two venues: in patients' ongoing interactions with the important people in their life, and in patients' interaction with their therapist. Psychodynamic therapists who view this type of learning as important usually argue that patients will engage most of the important persons in their life, including the therapist, in negative patterns of behavior that unconsciously re-create those interactions that were central to the creation of their difficulties. As patients become aware of these repetitive interactions and of their connections to the past, they may be able to make new behavioral choices. The new experiences that can accrue from these novel patterns of relating allow a patient to come into contact with the memories, emotions, and images that unconsciously remained active as the sources of the disruptive interpersonal patterns. Thus, insight and intrapsychic change can result from new learning and new interactions. Certain psychodynamic therapists argue that the interaction between therapist and patient is a critically important source of new, corrective experiences. In this perspective, as therapists learn about the ways in which patients were treated by their parents, they deliberately try to engage them in new ways that will counter and correct their expectations. For example, with a patient who was treated coldly and distantly by his or her father, the therapist might decide to be particularly warm and close to further the distinction between past and present.

Therapeutic Process in Psychodynamic Psychotherapy

As might be apparent from the preceding discussion, Psychodynamic Psychotherapy is an experiential learning process during which patient and therapist mutually explore the workings of the patient's mind and the impact of his or her developmental experiences on that mind. Although different varieties of these therapies may emphasize one set of experiences or change mechanisms over another, virtually all psychodynamic psychotherapies share this exploratory, investigative framework. Some clinicians may separate psychotherapy from an initial diagnostic or assessment phase, but in practice, assessment and psychotherapy are being conducted continually and coincidentally. Psychodynamic psychotherapy begins with shared ignorance: patients are unaware of much of what makes them the person they are, while the therapist knows little about them at all. Through the intensive exploration of all aspects of psychological life, patient and therapist come to formulate an ever-evolving series of hypotheses, or narrative explanations, about the patient's psychology. This narrative is conveyed to the patient through the therapist's questions, interpretations, and style of interacting, and it is often formulated by the patient individually. When the treatment is successful, patients emerge with greatly enhanced self-awareness, a more complex pallet of emotional experience, and greater freedom from the conflicts and hurts of their past.

REFERENCES

Alexander, F., & French, T. (1946). *Psychoanalytic therapy*. New York: Ronald Press.

Binder, J. (2004). *Key competencies in brief dynamic therapy*. New York: Guilford Press.

Freud, S. (1953). Three essays on the theory of sexuality. In J. Strachey (Ed. and Trans.), *The standard edition of the complete psychological works of Sigmund Freud, Vol. 7* (pp. 1–130). London: Hogarth Press. (Original work published in 1905)

Gill, M. M. (1994). *Psychoanalysis in transition*. New York: Basic Books.

Gold, J. (2002) Insight in treatment. In E. Ervin (Ed.), *The Freud encyclopedia* (pp. 392–394). Miami: Garland Press.

Greenberg, J., & Mitchell, S. (1983). *Object relations in psychoanalytic theory*. Cambridge, MA: Harvard University Press.

SUGGESTED READINGS

Singer, E. (1965). *Key concepts in psychotherapy*. New York: Basic Books.

Unsano, R., Sonnenberg, S., & Lazar, S. (2004). *Concise guide to psychodynamic psychotherapy*. Washington, DC: American Psychiatric Publishing.

Wachtel, P. L. (2008). *Relational theory and the practice of psychotherapy*. New York: Guilford Press.

JERRY GOLD
Adelphi University

PSYCHOLINGUISTICS

Most would agree that modern psycholinguistics began after Noam Chomsky's review of *Verbal Behavior* by B. F. Skinner (1959), which rejected the book's behaviorist explanation of language development and use. Acquisition could not be explained by simple input–output relations, Chomsky wrote, because the input was not consistent or comprehensive enough (the "poverty of the stimulus" argument). The only way to explain language was to understand and explain the internal, cognitive representations that mediate input and output. Psycholinguistics brings psychologist cognitive scientists and linguists together in the study of the cognitive processes that underpin the acquisition, representation, production, perception, and comprehension of language. This article focuses on behavioral research and identifies comprehensive texts on psycholinguistics in the references. The relevance to psycholinguistics of bilingualism (see Kroll & De Groot, 2005), neuropsychology (see Caplan, 1996), and neuroscience (Hartley, 2001; Gaskell, 2007) are not included in this presentation.

What is the relationship between language and thought? The Sapir-Whorf hypothesis (Whorf, 1956), also known as *linguistic relativity*, states that because language categorizes our experience (e.g., the things we name), it affects the way we think: Speakers of different languages will think differently from each other. Strong versions of this hypothesis, known as *linguistic determinism*, predict that we are bound by the language we speak, so that, for example, speakers of a language with 4 or 5 color terms will perceive colors differently from speakers of a language with 20 color terms. There has been a resurgence of work on linguistic relativity, and there is agreement that language and thought have a close relationship and that language can shape cognitive processes (particularly when language is necessary for the task). However, cognition and categorization are remarkably flexible, so linguistic determinism is not supported.

Elsewhere, there are two recurring questions that frame a number of debates in psycholinguistic research. The first of these questions is whether language is unique or innate to human beings and what this means for how it is represented. Noam Chomsky views language and particularly syntax as a specialist innate module, largely independent from other cognitive processes; alternatively, language and syntax can be seen to interact more closely with cognition and semantic categorization. There have been several attempts to teach primates language, and although there is certainly acquisition of vocabulary, the evidence for receptive or expressive syntax is inconclusive, which suggests that the human ability is specialized.

In language development, is there a critical period during infancy when innate language faculties are switched on, and beyond which language learning is not possible or severely limited? Typical acquisition of language occurs rapidly between birth and 5 years. First words appear around 1 year, two-word utterances at 2 years, and more complex syntactic and morphological features by age 3 or 4. This ability is reduced after puberty, but children need to be exposed to language to learn it at all, and they need to have social interaction to learn it well (possibly because of motivation). However, damage to the language-dominant left hemisphere in childhood does not necessarily lead to language impairment, suggesting a neural and cognitive flexibility that argues against strict hardwiring. However, there does appear to be a weak critical period for the acquisition of phonology and syntax (Hartley, 2001; Owens, 2007), just as there are critical periods in the development of other biological systems. We must ask, "What exactly is innate?". Are there specific syntactic rules and representations that are activated (i.e., the "universal grammar" of Noam Chomsky; Aitchison, 1998), or do we have a remarkable suite of cognitive systems that learn from the environment and become specialized for language (i.e., innate processes; Steinberg & Sciarini, 2006)?

The second recurring question is whether language processes are modular (autonomous and independent from other cognitive processes and each other) or interactive (with feedback and two-way relationships between different processes). The interactive-modular debate and related questions arise in almost every area of psycholinguistic research, largely because of the advent of connectionist models that propose interactive, parallel, and distributed processes in contrast to modular, serial, and localist processing. An important construct is that information cascades from one stage of processing to the next (i.e., incremental pieces of information are made available to the next stage before processing is completely finished at the first stage), and a typical theoretical contrast is between bottom-up (feed-forward from lower or earlier to higher or later processes) versus top-down (feedback from higher or later to lower or earlier stages).

The lexicon is the cognitive store of lexical (word) information. It includes the semantic and phonological information for each word (the word form and its meaning), and for some theorists, it also includes syntactic information (e.g., noun or verb), although this is debated. Key ideas are whether words are represented as holistic, localist units (a lemma represents each word in one space) or distributed as a pattern across features (e.g., animals that share semantic features such as "has legs" or "has eyes"); distributed featural theories currently dominate. It is widely agreed that when a word meaning is accessed, there is spreading activation from that word to other related words. This explains semantic priming (when "mouse" is preceded by "rat," we respond quicker than if it is preceded by "boy"). Recent embodied theories have stressed the importance of sensory and motor information; for example, the meaning of the word *kick* may be stored primarily in motor systems (Hartley, 2001; Gaskell, 2007).

When we speak and produce words, it is generally agreed that we do so in stages: (1) The preverbal message is generated, and concepts are retrieved to express it; (2) lexico-semantic representations (words) are selected to express the concepts, and syntactic information is retrieved to generate sentence structure; and (3) phonological representations are retrieved that map onto the selected words. All models assume cascading of information from conceptual to lexico-semantic representations, which allows multiple words to be activated for a particular concept (e.g., *couch, sofa,* or *divan*). Syntactic structure is held to be somewhat independent of individual words because of syntactic priming (the tendency to repeat the same syntactic structures). Debates center around whether the system is interactive with feedback from later phonological levels to earlier processes involved in lexical selection (Wheeldon, 2000).

The recognition of spoken words is an incremental process with three phases: (1) perceptual processes that segment an acoustic signal into speech sounds, with segmental (speech sounds) and supra-segmental (e.g., stress or the probability of particular sound sequences) sources of information used to disambiguate the input; (2) the activation of multiple competing candidates that could correspond to the input; and (3) the resolution of competition, leading to recognition of an individual item. Models differ as to whether the input is matched to abstract, symbolic representations of phonemes, to multiple traces of prior perceptual experience of a phoneme, or to both. There is debate as to whether phonemes are represented prelexically in order to access the lexicon or constructed after recognition, how candidates are generated from the input, and whether lexical activation feeds back to bias early perceptual processes. For example, the language you speak affects your recognition of words. However, bottom-up mechanisms may be fully optimized without the need for feedback (Gaskell, 2007; Hartley, 2001).

For visual word recognition operations, information does not unfold over time. Orthography (graphemes or written forms of words) is often a representation of phonology (spoken word forms), and for alphabetic writing systems, at least there is a systematic and strong connection between them. Writing systems are "shallow" if there is complete consistency between spelling and sound (e.g., Italian) and "deep" when the relationship is more opaque (e.g., English). Children take longer to learn reading and writing for deep languages. Inconsistent spelling to sound relationships (e.g., *yacht* vs. *lot*) produce processing costs (i.e., longer reaction times and more errors in certain tasks). Visual word recognition has three basic processes: (1) Primitive features of graphemes map onto abstract letter representations, (2) the relative position of individual letters is established, and (3) input maps onto word representations for recognition. Models typically posit a triangular relationship between orthographic, phonological, and semantic information, with two-way connections so that each form of information can influence the other. There are debates over the strength of these connections (e.g., how important phonology is for visual word recognition), whether certain processes operate incrementally and serially (e.g., mapping from orthography to phonology in word naming), and whether words are represented as holistic units or distributed features (Gaskell, 2007).

In sentence comprehension, the focus is on the correct syntactic interpretation (or parse). Consider the classic garden path sentence, "The horse raced past the barn fell" (i.e., the horse that was raced past the barn fell). The ambiguity arises because we initially parse *raced* as a verb (the horse raced), rather than a past participle (that was raced). This shows us that parsing is incremental and that decisions are made even when input is ambiguous. Parsing might operate serially, with modular syntactic information used first for an initial parse and other semantic information used subsequently for revisions (as needed in garden paths) and a final decision. Alternatively, constraint-based accounts have parallel interactive processes that consider multiple possibilities at once and prioritize them according to various constraints (e.g., frequency of the syntactic structure, plausibility). Initial parallelism can quickly become serial as information discounts contextually improbable parses (Garrod & Pickering, 1999). When we comprehend discourse or narrative, it is widely held that we construct a mental model or situation model of the described scene, events, and actors.

In morphology (the internal structure of words), there are long-running arguments over regular and irregular forms of the past tense (e.g., *talk* and *talked* vs. *think* and *thought*). Is there a dual system with syntactic rules, such as "add *ed* to all regular forms" or a unified system with whole forms that differ in phonology only? Syntactic rules support a specialized syntactic module versus a unified system that depends on interactions between phonology and semantics (Gaskell, 2007; Hartley, 2001).

REFERENCES

Aitchison, J. (1998). *The articulate mammal: An introduction to psycholinguistics* (4th ed.). Oxford, UK: Routledge.

Caplan, D. (1996). *Language: Structure, processing and disorders.* Cambridge, MA: MIT Press.

Chomsky, N. (1959). Review of "Verbal Behavior" by B. F. Skinner. *Language, 35,* 26–58.

Garrod, S., & Pickering, M. (Eds.). (1999). *Language processing.* Hove, England: Psychology Press.

Gaskell, M. G. (Ed.). (2007). *The Oxford handbook of psycholinguistics.* Oxford, UK: Oxford University Press.

Hartley, T. (2001). *The psychology of language: From data to theory* (2nd ed.). Hove, UK: Psychology Press.

Kroll, J. F., & De Groot, A. M. B. (Eds.). (2005). *Handbook of bilingualism: Psycholinguistic approaches.* New York: Oxford University Press.

Owens, R. E. (2007). *Language development: An introduction* (7th ed.). London: Allyn & Bacon.

Steinberg, D. D., & Sciarini, N. V. (2006). *An introduction to psycholinguistics* (2nd ed.). London: Pearson, Longman.

Wheeldon, L. R. (Ed.). (2000). *Aspects of language production.* Hove, UK: Psychology Press.

Whorf, B. (1956). *Language, thought, and reality: Selected writings of Benjamin Lee Whorf* (J. Carroll, Ed.). Cambridge, MA: MIT Press.

LOTTE METEYARD
University College London, United Kingdom

See also: Language Acquisition; Morphology

PSYCHOLOGICAL ASSESSMENT

Psychological assessment consists of a variety of procedures for evaluating characteristics of people. Psychological assessment has sometimes been equated with psychological testing, but the assessment process goes beyond merely giving tests. Psychological assessors integrate information obtained not only from test protocols, but also from interviews, behavioral observations, collateral reports, and historical documents. This article describes these sources of information and the applications of assessment information in clinical, educational, health care, forensic, and industrial/organizational settings.

Sources of Assessment Information

Psychological assessments typically begin with an interview in which people are asked about (1) their understanding of the purpose for which they are being evaluated; (2) the nature and history of any psychological problems they have been having; (3) their developmental background, including their family and cultural heritage, their education, their work experience, and their medical history; and (4) their current life circumstances with respect to family, friends, employment, preferred activities, usual habits, future outlook, and the like. Most commonly, these interviews are semistructured in nature, which means that they include requests for specific items of information (e.g., "Who is in your family?") and also relatively open-ended inquiries (e.g., "What was growing up like for you?"). What is learned in interviews helps assessors decide whether formal standardized testing is needed to provide additional information for the purposes of the evaluation and, if so, whether measures of intellectual ability, personality characteristics, neuropsychological status, or specific kinds of psychopathology (e.g., depression, posttraumatic stress disorder) would be advantageous to include in the test battery.

When psychological assessments do include formal testing, the tests used are of two types: self-report inventories and performance-based measures. Self-report inventories ask people directly about matters related to the purpose of the evaluation (e.g., "Do you often lose your temper?" answered "Yes" or "No"; "Do you feel anxious or uncomfortable when you're in a crowd of people?" answered "Always," "Often," "Seldom," or "Never"). Because of their directness, and because they comprise a standard set of items that elicit only a few types of direct responses (e.g., Yes or No), self-report inventories are relatively easy to administer, score, and validate, and they are also likely to yield dependable information. As a limitation of self-report inventories, however, the information they yield consists only of what people are able and willing to say about themselves. This can be problematic, because everyone has personal characteristics and underlying feelings and attitudes of which they are not fully aware, and most people know things about themselves that they are reluctant to admit, especially during a psychological evaluation that may influence some decision that will be made about them. As a consequence, self-reports may tell a dependable story, provided the respondent is not deliberately being dishonest, but they may not tell the whole story about an individual's attitudes, attributes, and life experiences.

Performance-based measures, unlike self-report inventories, are based not on what people are able and willing to say about themselves, but instead on how they perform certain tasks they are given to do. Tests of intelligence and of neurocognitive functioning are performance-based measures. Assessors do not directly ask a person "How smart are you?" or "How good is your memory?" because very few people have adequate benchmarks for answering such questions accurately. Moreover, people who have concerns about their level of intelligence or the status of their memory functions may be in denial of limited intelligence or memory, or they may be disinclined to acknowledge such shortcomings, as in answering "I'm smart enough" or "My memory is just fine." With performance-based assessment, the speed and accuracy with which people can respond to standard tests of intelligence and memory indicate their functioning level relative to other people (e.g., an IQ score in the average range) or relative to themselves (e.g., lower memory test scores than they earned on a previous testing or that they would be expected to earn given their educational or occupational accomplishments).

In performance-based personality assessment, people are asked to perform tasks in which there is some degree of ambiguity or lack of structure in the test stimuli or the instructions they are given. In the four most widely used types of performance-based personality measures, for example, respondents are asked what they see in a series of inkblots (e.g., the Rorschach Inkblot Method); to make up stories about pictures of people or scenes (e.g., the Thematic Apperception Test); to draw figures of people and objects; and to write out full sentences to complete brief phrases (as in "My greatest fear is _____"). The manner in which people go about these tasks and the content of what they say, draw, or write provide considerable information about their personality style, their current mental and emotional state, and their underlying attitudes and concerns, including some of which they may not be fully aware or would not be inclined to report if asked about them directly.

Because of these respects in which performance-based personality measures differ from self-report inventories, they help examiners identify features of people that might otherwise not come to light. Additionally, because of the indirect nature of performance-based assessment, people being examined usually have little awareness of the interpretive implications of their responses. It is consequently more difficult for people to tailor their performance-based responses in an effort to mislead the examiner than it is on the more direct self-report inventories, in which the implications of many items are quite clear (e.g., "Are your feelings easily hurt?"). On the other hand, because of the relatively indirect nature of performance-based personality assessment measures, their interpretation is often more inferential and speculative than conclusions based on direct self-reports. Moreover, the conclusions derived from performance-based personality measures are more likely than the implications of a self-report to consist of alternative possibilities rather than any single fairly certain implication. In view of these differences between self-report inventories and performance-based measures, there is a broad consensus that psychological testing as part of an assessment process should consist of a multifaceted battery that integrates findings from both types of tests, thereby retaining the merits of both while getting around the limitations of each.

Turning to the other three sources of information in psychological assessments, behavioral observations are an integral part of conducting interviews and administering psychological tests. In each of these situations, assessors can learn about the people they are evaluating from observing how they behave both in giving their responses (e.g., fluently or haltingly) and in how they relate to the assessor (e.g., assertively or deferentially). In some kinds of psychological assessments, situations may be created specifically for the purpose of observing and evaluating how people behave in them. Two common examples of such behavioral assessment are observing a parent and child interact in a play setting and observing patterns of interaction among members of a family who are instructed to arrive at a consensus solution to some problem.

Collateral reports consist of information provided by people who are well acquainted with the individual being assessed. In evaluations of young people, talking with their parents or primary caregivers is almost always an essential component of a psychological assessment. Similarly, for adults who are seriously impaired by mental disorder (e.g., psychosis, dementia), a spouse, adult child, or sibling can often provide important assessment information that would otherwise not be available. Finally, when people are for some reason unable or unwilling to give accurate accounts of events in their lives, historical documents, especially medical and school records, can prove valuable in understanding their nature as a person and addressing the questions that led to their request or referral for evaluation.

Applications of Assessment Information

The assessment process culminates in the utilization of descriptions of psychological characteristics and behavioral tendencies to formulate conclusions and recommendations. These recommendations are based on translating the assessment information into its implications for various types of decisions, and the overall purpose and eventual goal of psychological assessment can be conceived as a way of facilitating decisions about classification, selection, placement, diagnosis, and treatment of people being evaluated. Psychological assessment is most widely applied in clinical settings, where it is undertaken mainly to address questions of differential diagnosis and treatment planning. By clarifying the nature and extent of psychological disorder in persons being evaluated, a good assessment guides decisions about how best to provide treatment for these people.

In educational settings, psychological assessments can help to indicate school readiness, determine class placement, and identify needs for counseling or special educational services for students with conduct or learning problems. In health care settings, psychological assessments can help to identify psychological aspects of physical illness, monitor adaptation to chronic illness or disability, estimate tolerance for surgical procedures, and reveal the sources of an unhealthy life style or poor compliance with prescribed treatment. In forensic cases, assessed indications of mental impairment can contribute in criminal cases to determinations of competence and sanity. In civil cases, assessment findings related to psychological dysfunction or incapacity are often relevant in adjudicating personal injury and disability claims. In family law, assessment information about the personal qualities and psychological adjustment of children and their parents is commonly considered in mediating child custody and visitation disputes. In organizational settings, psychological assessment can prove useful in evaluating candidates for employment or promotion, and assessment findings can help determine the fitness-for-duty of persons who have become psychologically impaired or who have behaved in ways that raised concern about their potential for violence.

SUGGESTED READINGS

Archer, R. P. (Ed.). (2006). *Forensic uses of clinical assessment instruments*. Mahwah, NJ: Lawrence Erlbaum.

Heilbrun, K. (2001). *Principles of forensic mental health assessment*. New York: Kluwer Academic/Plenum.

Hersen, M. (Ed.-in-Chief). (2004). *Comprehensive handbook of psychological assessment* (4 vols.). Hoboken, NJ: John Wiley & Sons.

Hersen, M., & Turner, S. M. (Eds.). (2003). *Diagnostic interviewing* (3rd ed.). New York: Kluwer Academic/Plenum.

Maruish, M. E. (Ed.) (2004). *The use of psychological testing for treatment planning and outcome assessment* (3 vols.). Mahwah, NJ: Lawrence Erlbaum.

Meyer, G. J., Finn, S. E., Eyde, L. D., Kay, G. G., Moreland, K. L., Dies, R. R., et al. (2001). Psychological testing and psychological assessment: A review of evidence and issues. *American Psychologist, 56*, 128–165.

IRVING B. WEINER
University of South Florida

See also: Assessment Psychology; Interview Assessment; Performance-Based Personality Measures; Self-Report Inventories

PSYCHOLOGICAL AUTOPSY

Approximately five decades ago, the term *psychological autopsy* first appeared in the mental health literature. The methodology is most often associated with cases of completed suicide and involves constructing a psychological profile of the deceased during the time immediately prior to death. By conducting interviews with significant individuals, reviewing records, and investigating events that appear to bear directly on the deceased's emotional state, investigators seek to determine the motivation or circumstances that may have contributed to the death. Initially, it was utilized as a clinical tool to assist coroners and medical examiners in determining the cause of death in equivocal cases (Clark & Horton-Deutsch, 1992), but the technique has evolved over the years to become a recognized research, clinical, and forensic tool. Yet despite this general acceptance, the methodology still has many critics and a number of legitimate shortcomings that severely limit its utility in some settings (Pouliot & De Leo, 2006) while offering promise in others (Aufderheide, 2000).

The Psychological Autopsy as a Research Tool

The obvious catch-22 for suicide researchers is that they never have direct contact with their subjects. To get around this problem, early researchers employed standardized protocols to review completed suicides and assess the link between suicide and previously unknown factors such as physical and mental illness, childhood and family history, and pivotal life events. The reliability of these research studies, however, has been criticized for having inadequate control subjects, being influenced by intervening variables, and most important, lacking standardized data collection protocols, which make comparisons between studies difficult when conflicting findings are reported. Although these methodological problems do not totally negate the findings that have been reported to date, they have, unfortunately, limited the scope and utility of those investigations.

The Psychological Autopsy as a Clinical Tool

It is perhaps as a clinical tool to establish the cause of an individual death where the psychological autopsy is most vulnerable to criticism. With no standardized methodology for collecting information, there cannot be meaningful differences in the data available for consideration. This creates the potential for subjective bias, and even misrepresentation (Selkin & Loya, 1979), in the conclusions drawn. In fact, it can be argued that relying on the soft, correlational indices that are typically collected almost guarantees that the findings will be open to alternative explanations because it is impossible to know if the real cause of the death was actually identified.

The Psychological Autopsy as a Forensic Tool

Despite the preceding criticisms, the psychological autopsy has been introduced in both civil and criminal courts to support or refute death determinations in individual cases. As a forensic tool, however, it has experienced minimal acceptance, particularly in federal court, where there are objective standards for presenting and accepting scientific evidence. This standard, termed the Daubert Standard, requires that evidence be founded on scientific knowledge that has been (1) technically tested, (2) peer-reviewed, (3) standardized in its application, and (4) widely accepted in the scientific community. These requirements have proven to be a very high standard for any retrospective analysis to meet (White, 2002).

Because methodology is neither universally accepted nor standardized, introducing the findings in court often depends on the experience and academic credentials of the practitioner using it. This makes sense because courts recognize that any testimony provided retrospectively by a mental health expert will rely on subjective opinion resulting from the collection of imperfect, uncertain, and often incomplete information. Therefore, given its questionable reliability, it is understandable why the courts are reluctant to accept the results of a psychological autopsy at face value without critically evaluating the expertise of the person presenting the findings.

The Psychological Autopsy as a Risk Management Tool

As we have seen, the psychological autopsy has limitations as a research, clinical, or forensic tool. However, the methodology has considerable potential as an investigative instrument in institutional settings as part of a risk management program for suicide prevention. In most institutional environments where suicides occur, the question concerning cause of death (i.e., was this a suicide?) is typically much less equivocal than the circumstances for which the methodology was initially developed. As such, the primary goal of the review can focus less on understanding the motivation for the act (which is still important) and more on conducting an administrative analysis to determine how future suicides can be prevented.

Using a standardized data collection protocol, institution-based investigators can collect a large number of clinical, demographic, environmental, and policy variables associated with suicide deaths and can track them over an extended period of time. If the protocol is comprehensive, is applied in all cases of suicide, and is conducted in a standardized manner, and if the organization ensures adequate management oversight and follow-up, then the psychological autopsy can be an invaluable management tool. At a minimum, it can be critical for evaluating the adequacy of policy, compliance with policy, the development of screening and assessment instruments, the need for targeted training efforts, and the effectiveness of individual treatment regimens.

Clearly, some of the criticisms raised here also apply in the risk management context, and additional intra-agency impediments can arise when reviewing, and potentially criticizing, the actions of superiors and peers. Nevertheless, the benefits outweigh the potential problems. For example, many data collection inconsistencies can be mitigated in institutional environments, where access to relevant individuals and relevant medical and mental health records, as well as the ability to track the activities of individuals, is less restricted than in the community. The mandatory use of standardized protocols can ensure reliability over time, and the generalizability of the data is less important when used for internal administrative review than when it is used for broader research or courtroom applications. Finally, despite the potential internal disruptions that may accompany a critical review of a suicide death, the benefit to the system that accrues by identifying problems and correcting them typically outweighs the political downside.

With institution-specific modifications, the basic methodology has widespread applicability in many health care settings. Aufderheide (2000) suggests that correctional settings offer a good environment for conducting a psychological autopsy. This is understandable, given the amount of control those reviewers have over every aspect of the autopsy process. However, similar advantages also exist in medical and psychiatric hospitals, as well as in other residential care centers where the adequacy of care or suicide prevention programs must be assessed.

REFERENCES

Aufderheide, D. (2000). Conducting the psychological autopsy in correctional settings. *Journal of Correctional Health Care, 7*(1), 5–36.

Clark, D. C., & Horton-Deutsch, S. L. (1992). Assessment in absentia: The value of the psychological autopsy method for studying antecedents of suicide and predicting future suicides. In R. W. Maris & A. L. Berman (Eds.), *Assessment and prediction of suicide* (pp. 144–182). New York: Guilford Press.

Pouliot, L., & De Leo, D. (2006). Clinical issues in psychological autopsy studies. *Suicide and Life-Threatening Behavior, 36*(5), 491–510.

Selkin, J., & Loya, F. (1979). Issues in the psychological autopsy of a controversial public figure. *Professional Psychology, 10*, 77–82.

White, T. (2002). Improving the reliability of expert testimony in suicide litigation. *Journal of Psychiatry and Law, 30*, 331–353.

SUGGESTED READINGS

Snider, J. E., Hane, S., & Berman, A. (2006). Standardizing the psychological autopsy: Addressing the Daubert Standard. *Suicide and Life-Threatening Behavior, 36*, 511–518.

Selkin, J. (1994). Psychological autopsy: Scientific psychohistory or clinical intuition? *American Psychologist, 49*, 74–75.

THOMAS W. WHITE
Training and Counseling Services,
Shawnee Mission, KS

PSYCHOLOGICAL HEALTH

All psychotherapeutic systems have a vision of psychological health rooted in and stemming from their view of human nature. The goal of therapy is to develop interventions that, based on each orientation's personality theory, remove obstacles and barriers and develop awareness, insights, skills, and abilities that enhance a person's psychological health (Shapiro, 1983).

Historically, mainstream psychology has been pathology-based, viewing psychological health as the absence of symptoms, from the time of Freud to the advent of the *Diagnostic and Statistical Manual of Mental Disorders*. Expanding this view, investigation into positive states of psychological health took root in the 1950s with humanistic psychologists like Carl Rogers and Abraham Maslow. More recently, researchers have further developed and empirically investigated models of positive health (e.g., Seligman, 1998), including non-Western models (e.g., Wallace & Shapiro, 2006).

These investigations suggest that elimination of pathology may give us the concept of the average or normal rather than a concept of optimal psychological health.

This paradigm shift regarding optimal health is reflected in the recent development of the field of positive psychology, which asserts that there has been too great a focus on what makes people sick rather than a more holistic view of health, which also includes the strengths and positive qualities that help people flourish. Further, scholarship is currently underway to link positive psychology to an emerging field of positive sociology, which expands the concept of individual positive health to include and encompass communities, families, and organizational life—that is, societal health (J. D. Shapiro, 2007).

Five Views of Human Nature and Psychological Health

There are five main views of human nature, each with its own perspectives on psychological health and the goals of therapy. As described next, these are the biomedical, psychodynamic, behavioral/cognitive-behavioral, humanistic/existential, and transpersonal approaches.

Biomedical Approach

View of Human Nature. The biomedical paradigm, which guides modern medicine and psychiatry, views human nature as determined in large part by physiological processes. An example can be seen in the biomedical approach to depression: assessment leads to a precise diagnosis for which an organic cause is identified (e.g., lack of serotonin), and then a treatment specific to the pathology is prescribed (e.g., selective-serotonin reuptake inhibitor [SSRI]).

Goal of Therapy. The goal of therapy in this approach is to alleviate undesired symptoms via medication, restore biochemical homeostasis, and thereby achieve psychological health.

Psychodynamic Approach

View of Human Nature. Classical psychodynamic psychology views human nature as the product of unconscious conflicting needs, forces, and impulses. In Freud's terms, humans are "lived by unknown and uncontrolled forces," which originate in the amoral id. The id harbors primitive instincts and drives such as sex (libido), love, aggression, and death. The superego is the internal agent of authority, the conscience that determines the ideal to be achieved. And last, the ego, the conscious self, attempts to realistically satisfy the demands of the other two. From this view, psychological health is achieved when the ego is successful at satisfying the repressed id impulses in a socially acceptable manner as enforced by the superego. Mental illness, or neurosis, results when tension arising between these psychic forces creates emotional distress like anxiety or depression and sometimes physical symptoms.

Goal of Therapy. From a psychodynamic view of human nature, psychological health is sought by uncovering the repressed facets of the self "to make the unconscious conscious." Psychological health is achieved when repressed desires, fears, and depressions are made conscious and brought under control: "Where id was, ego shall be" (Freud, 1961, pp. 57–58).

Behavioral/Cognitive-Behavioral Approach

View of Human Nature. The cognitive-behavioral approach views human nature as a tabula rasa, a blank slate. The individual is not motivated by the intrapsychic forces of ego and id, but instead by environmental stimuli and social interactions (or cognitive representations of the two). Therefore, psychological maladjustment is a likely consequence of maladaptive learning, reinforcement patterns, or cognitive distortions.

Goal of Therapy. A cognitive-behavioral approach, founded by Albert Ellis and Aaron Beck (1976), teaches clients to identify and reinterpret the illogical notions that underlie their distressing symptoms. Since cognitions, feelings, and behaviors are causally interrelated, cognitive-behavioral approaches alter the maladaptive cognitions in an attempt to bring about behavioral and affective change. Psychological health is achieved when maladaptive patterns (cognitive and behavioral) are recognized and changed, consequently alleviating undesired symptoms.

Humanistic/Existential Approach

View of Human Nature. The humanistic/existential approach views the individual as controlled by neither a genetic amoral id nor by external stimuli. The humanistic approach instead views the individual as constantly changing or becoming, with the capacity for full conscious awareness. "The organism has one basic tendency in striving—to actualize, maintain, and enhance the experience of the organism" (Rogers, 1951). The existential approach argues that there is no innate self-actualizing nature; in other words, existence precedes essence, and therefore a person must create his or her authentic self (Yalom, 1980). The unhealthy person, from the humanistic/existential viewpoint, is one who restricts the task of openly discovering and making sense of his or her existence, turns away from the responsibility of creating choices, and fails to relate with others and the world authentically in the present moment.

Goal of Therapy. The goal of humanistic/existential therapy is to foster what Maslow called self-actualization, allowing the client to assume full responsibility for developing his or her identity. Ultimately, this entails authentically encountering the human environment, the inevitability of isolation and mortality, and realizing that, as Rollo May and Victor Frankl have noted, if one cannot choose one's fate, one can nevertheless choose one's own attitude toward it.

Transpersonal Approach

View of Human Nature. The transpersonal approach views human nature as having an impulse toward ultimate states that are positive and motivated by values that transcend the self. Further, the transpersonal approach sees humans as having an interconnected essence (Walsh & Vaughan, 1994).

Goal of Therapy. From the transpersonal tradition, the goal of therapy is to extend the identity or sense of self beyond the narrow self so that individuals realize their connection with others and the world. The qualities of the healthy person include realizing the limits of ego identity, developing compassion, opening to peak experiences, and being aware of unified consciousness, ultimate values, and meaning.

Toward an Integrative View of Psychological Health

As can be seen from the preceding overview, each of the five traditions has different assumptions and beliefs about human nature, and their views of psychological health are based on that perspective and paradigmatic viewpoint. Those views, in turn, determine how each approach then evolves and develops techniques of intervention.

Given the increased sophistication of recent psychological research into the multiple influences on human nature (genetic, environmental-social, personal, and cultural), as well as a broader understanding of health that includes both sociological and cross-cultural knowledge, it appears that a more complete view of psychological health may need to integrate the unique perspectives offered by multiple approaches. The time may be past when each tradition can claim it has the one and only true view of human nature and therefore of psychological health.

One way to seek such integration is developmental. For example, Wilber (1977), following in the tradition of Maslow, Erickson, Piaget, and Kohlberg, proposes that each of the major schools of psychology has historically addressed the issues and pathologies of particular developmental/hierarchical levels. Therefore, each is true for that level but is explaining only a part of the spectrum of the whole of human development. Such a multilevel, integrative view of psychological health is complementary, rather than exclusive, and can have clinical and therapeutic implications. For example, meditation can be seen as a self-regulation intervention for stress management (e.g., from a behavioral approach), a technique for gaining increased awareness of the self (e.g., from a humanistic approach), a means to create regression in the service of the ego (psychodynamic approach), and an opportunity for going beyond the ego and developing selfless service (e.g., from a transpersonal approach) (cf. Shapiro, 1980).

Integration of approaches can also occur on a clinical level. For example, a comprehensive treatment plan for depression may include addressing biochemical imbalances (biomedical), learning coping strategies to handle environmental stressors and to develop external mastery (behavioral), interpreting cognitive distortions and learning more internal self-control of thoughts and feelings (cognitive), overcoming lack of trust in oneself (humanistic), examining unconscious intrapsychic conflict (psychodynamic), exploring the effect of interpersonal and social situations, organizations, and communities on the person (social psychological, sociological), and exploring meaning and ultimate spiritual questions (transpersonal). Depending on the patient, an intervention open to all levels may be helpful in increasing psychological health (Shapiro & Astin, 1998).

A comprehensive view of psychological health also needs to explore the vision of healthy development across the life span and in multiple domains (cf. Ryff, 1989). This would include measures such as positive affect, life satisfaction, positive sense of control, self-determination, optimism, resilience, and self-acceptance. It would involve looking at how humans can successfully address different developmental tasks.

This includes the building tasks of being sensitive to the body and its needs (physical well-being), developing a strong purpose and identity in life (ego well-being), increasing depth in friendships and loving relationships (interpersonal well-being), and being a productive and contributing member of society (societal well-being).

It also would include the yielding tasks: learning the limits of ego identity, becoming increasingly nondefensive, recognizing and coping with interpersonal loss of relationships and loved ones, and addressing mortality, impermanence, and the limits of the physical body within a personally meaningful understanding and belief system. Clearly, the task of both defining and then seeking to achieve psychological health is not an easy one. Cooperative efforts among psychological schools and insights from our medical, anthropological, and sociological colleagues, as well as from our spiritual and wisdom traditions, may all be important to evolve a systemic, multilevel, and integrative definition of psychological health. Though not a simple undertaking, such a broad, multidisciplinary approach has the potential to considerably benefit both clinical therapeutic practice and even society at large.

REFERENCES

Beck, A. (1976). *Cognitive therapy and the emotional disorders*. New York: International Universities Press.

Freud, S. (1961). *Civilization and its discontents*. New York: W. W. Norton.

Rogers, C. R. (1951). *Client-centered therapy*. Cambridge, MA: Houghton Mifflin.

Ryff, C. D. (1989). Happiness is everything, or is it? Explorations on the meaning of psychological well-being. *Journal of Personality and Social Psychology, 57*(6), 1069–1081.

Seligman, M. (1998, April 29). Opening remarks (testimony) congressional briefing on prevention. Washington, DC: U.S. Congress.

Shapiro, D. H. (1980). *Meditation: Self-regulation strategy and altered state of consciousness*. New York: Aldine de Gruyter.

Shapiro, D. H. (1983). A content analysis of Eastern and Western, traditional, and new age approaches to psychotherapy, health, and healing. In R. N. Walsh & D. H. Shapiro, *Beyond health and normality: Explorations of exceptional psychological well-being* (pp. 433–491). New York: Van Nostrand.

Shapiro, D. H., & Astin, J. A. (1998). *Control therapy: An integrated approach to psychotherapy, health, and healing*. New York: John Wiley & Sons.

Shapiro, J. D. (2007). *The case for positive sociology*. Paper presented at the University of California, San Diego, Department of Sociology.

Wallace, A., & Shapiro, S. L. (2006). Mental balance and well being: Building bridges between Buddhism and Western psychology. *American Psychologist, 61*(7), 690–701.

Walsh, R. N., & Vaughan, F. (Eds.). (1994). *Paths beyond ego*. Los Angeles: Tarcher.

Wilber, K. (1977). *Spectrum of consciousness*. Wheaton, IL: Quest.

Yalom, I. D. (1980). *Existential psychotherapy*. New York: Basic Books.

DEANE H. SHAPIRO
University of California, Irvine

CRAIG SANTERRE
VA Puget Sound Health Care System, Seattle Division

SHAUNA L. SHAPIRO
Santa Clara University

JOHN A. ASTIN
California Pacific Medical Center, San Francisco

JOSH D. SHAPIRO
University of California, San Diego

JENA HUSTON
Argosy University, Phoenix

See also: **Abnormality; Positive Psychology; Psychopathology**

PSYCHOLOGICAL MEASUREMENT, BIAS IN

The issue of reliable and valid assessment of mental health status has been faced in clinical practice since the inception of efforts to evaluate intelligence, dating at least to Spearman's theory of general intelligence. G-theory, as it became known, presumed that individuals possess an overall intelligence, as opposed to more varied intelligences in diverse areas, as later expressed by Thurstone (1927), and more recently rearticulated by Gardner (1983). Unfortunately, efforts to develop psychological assessment instruments have historically focused and been standardized on white middle-class males. Little or no consideration was given to the diversity of the U.S. population with respect to gender, race, ethnicity, religiosity, or any other relevant demographic characteristic. Even within the United States, various verbal expressions are unclear or uninterpretable among some native born Americans in all parts of the country.

An exemplar of how assessment can be seriously biased is illustrated in one of the most commonly used scales to measure depression (Center for Epidemiological Depression Scale, CES-D). The CES-D is a brief scale that is used both in research and in clinical practice to screen for depressive symptomatology. One item inquires, "Have you felt blue?" To most nonminorities this is a rather simple question to answer. In Spanish, however, blue is translated to the color "azul." Putting such a question to an unacculturated Hispanic person in a clinical or research setting can be confusing to a person being assessed and perhaps lead to a misperception of the person by the interviewer. Similar issues persist with attempts to apply any assessment instruments that do not take culture into account when working with ethnic and racial groups other than those on whom the instruments have been standardized.

Three decades ago, Marcos (1976) performed seminal studies showing how speaking English, without the presence of a clinically trained translator, can lead to misdiagnosis of a disorder in persons for whom English is not their primary language. Marcos's work, however, was based on small samples of patients encountered in his clinical practice; hence, despite the insightfulness of his work, its generalizability may be questionable. Simply translating an English and culturally mainstream-oriented instrument into a second language does not solve this problem. As a personal anecdote, being in a bilingual household, my sons often have diametrically opposed interpretations of conversations that occur among our family members. Emotions may erupt as a result, which at home are readily resolved. In clinical setting, however, emotional outbreaks can invoke misinterpreted clinical readings.

Among more recent attempts to establish so-called unbiased assessment has been the development of the TEMAS (Tell-Me-A-Story) test, by Costantino and his associates (Costantino, Malgady, & Rogler, 1988). The TEMAS test is colorful and pictorial, unlike the Thematic Apperception Test, and it depicts both Hispanic and African American children interacting in conflict-provoking situations. For instance, one TEMAS picture shows two children, one helping an elderly woman to carry her groceries from a local store, and the other, in the same "split scene" picture, attempting to steal the groceries from the woman. The person taking the test then tells a story about what he or she sees in the

picture: who are the characters, what happened before the event, how are the characters feeling, and ultimately how the scenario will be resolved. The TEMAS test is scored on a variety of dimensions, such as reality testing, anxiety, depression, self-concept, and the like, in order to create a personality profile. Scoring is performed by trained clinicians, who rate the stories according to the level of adaptive behavior as opposed to psychopathology of the children's answers. Needless to say, a child siding with the helping side of the picture receives a healthy evaluation, while one opting for the negative side is rated on the pathological side of the scale.

Extensive psychometric data have been compiled on the TEMAS. These data document impressive internal consistency and test-retest reliability for the pictures, as well as criterion-related validity as indicated by correlations with other instruments, including the CES-D and the Spielberger State-Trait Anxiety Scale. Subsequently, TEMAS has been adopted by numerous school districts throughout the country, including New York City, Miami, and Los Angeles, as a standard for psychological assessment in special educational referrals and clinical decision-making. In addition, other research has shown that TEMAS can be used in therapeutic settings with ethnic minority children, as a way of enhancing evidence-based treatment outcomes.

Some years ago, Rogler, Malgady, Costantino, and Blumenthal (1987) defined three levels of cultural sensitivity: translation, adaptation to culture, and culture-specific development of new assessment instruments. Since then, cultural sensitivity has been referred to as cultural responsiveness and cultural competence (American Psychological Association, Guidelines for Culturally Competence Care). The three levels incline incrementally toward the directness of connection with the culture of the client.

Most recently, Malgady and Colon-Malgady (2008) have discussed the topic of building community norms for ethnic minority populations. Hispanics have now exceeded African Americans in census reports on minority group representation in this county. Hispanic diversity is a particularly challenging issue in assessment due to a variety of differences in immigration status, socioeconomic status, income, and access to and willingness to seek mental health care. School districts routinely refer troubled children to their resident school psychologists, who may or may not administer a battery of psychological tests. To the extent that these tests are not relevant to the troubled child's culture or have simply been translated from English into some other language, they undermine our commitment to serve the growing immigrant and diverse populations that are populating today's schools.

Malgady and Zayas (2005) also defined various levels of assessment bias. The first of these consists of using white middle-class based norms to make educational and psychological or psychiatric decisions about ethnic minorities. Norms of one population, depending upon the assessment device, do not necessarily provide a basis for inferring the status of other ethnic groups. Norms actually derive from the ancient Greek way of measuring time of day. A "gnomon" was a column that cast a shadow across a disk to tell the time of day. Few of us would argue about the time of day, despite slight variations in our watches. Others would argue more vehemently about the accuracy of psychological assessments.

Differences among ethnic group test scores, widely published both in the literature and in the media, identify some controversial issues. Can we measure all ethnic groups with the same time clock? Can each ethnic group have a different time clock? The consequences of such simpleminded questions have ramifications for test developers and unacculturated clinicians as well. One cannot tell the "time" from the "watch" of another ethnic group.

With respect to their reliability and validity, especially in predicting treatment outcomes, few tests have been assessed for their applicability to different ethnic groups. If an assessment is biased, the clinical inferences drawn from it can lead to ineffective or negative outcomes. This refers not only to referral for a particular psychological treatment modality, but also to pharmacological interventions selected by psychiatrists or suggested by other primary health care providers involved in case dispositions.

With the issue of reliability aside, validity of assessment in the service of treatment disposition is the most important consideration. A recent review by Suzuki and Ponterotto (2007) in the *Handbook of Multicultural Assessment* indicates that there is little evidence of acculturative assessment, that treatment providers are largely untrained by our universities on the topic, and that the consequences of cultural insensitivity and incompetence are dire. For example, a minority client suffering from long-term depression who does not seek treatment, which is not uncommon (Rogler, Malgady, & Rodriguez, 1989), may develop schizophreniclike symptoms. The medication and treatment prescribed could be entirely inappropriate in such scenarios. As the immigration clock ticks, more and more ethnic minorities are being disserved as well as underserved.

Some ways to construct culturally appropriate instruments for ethnic minorities are qualitative. These include conducting focus group interviews with residents of minority communities and clients in mental health centers. Cortes, Rogler, and Malgady (1994) conducted a study of randomly selected residents in the Bronx, New York, and a major medical center serving the largely Hispanic community in the Bronx. Items were constructed from the interview and visitation data through qualitative content analysis. Nearly 500 surveys were delivered to respondents who agreed to informed consent procedures. Major themes that emerged included anger and distress. The meaningfulness of this survey may lie less in the importance of the statistical outcomes than in the approach to developing items for assessing minorities in a culturally appropriate manner. Asked their health concerns in a noninvasive manner, Hispanics in this survey readily disclosed a wealth of information about their well-being and health care.

Returning to the language of interview or item development issue for minorities, a study by Malgady, Costantino, and Rogler followed earlier-cited research to interview with items asked in English only, Spanish only, or bilingually. Not surprisingly, the greatest response rate and more accurate diagnoses of clinical participants occurred with bilingual interviews, as judged by an independent panel of psychologists blinded to interview disposition.

Bias in assessment can be introduced by numerous factors. Ethnic match of the pair certainly facilitates the process. Setting of the interview is important, be it at home, or in a clinical setting. The preferred language of the respondent is critical in order to avoid misinterpretation, even at an idiomatic level. Most crucial, however, is direct contact with the ethnic group of interest to create and revise inquiries that are pertinent to the purpose of either clinical intervention or research.

REFERENCES

Cortes, D. E., Rogler, L. R., & Malgady, R. G. (1994). Biculturality among Puerto Rican adults in the United States. *American Journal of Community Psychology, 22,* 707–721.

Costantino, G., Dana, R., & Malgady, R. G. (2007). *TEMAS (Tell-Me-A-Story) assessment in multicultural societies.* Mahwah, NJ: Lawrence Erlbaum.

Costantino, G., Malgady, R. G., & Rogler, L. R. (1988). *TEMAS (Tell-Me-A-Story) test manual.* New York: Western Psychological Services.

Gardner, H. (1983). *Frames of mind: The theory of multiple intelligences.* New York: Basic Books.

Malgady, R. G., & Colon-Malgady, G. (2008). Constructing test norms for ethnic minority populations. In L. A. Suzuki & J. G. Ponterotto (Eds.), *Handbook of multicultural assessment: Clinical, psychological, and educational applications* (3rd ed.). San Francisco: Jossey-Bass.

Malgady, R. G., & Zayas, L. (2005). Cultural considerations in psychodiagnosis with Hispanics. In F. J. Turner (Ed.), *Social work diagnosis in contemporary practice.* New York: Oxford University Press.

Marcos, L. R. (1976). Bilinguals in psychotherapy: Language as an emotional barrier. *American Journal of Psychotherapy 30,* 552–569.

Rogler, L. H., Malgady, R. G., Costantino, G., & Blumenthal, R. (1987). What do culturally sensitive services mean? The case of Hispanics. *American Psychologist, 42,* 565–570.

Rogler, L. H., Malgady, R. G., & Rodriguez, O. (1989). *Hispanics and mental health: A framework for research.* Malabar, FL: Krieger.

Suzuki, L. A., & Ponterotto, J. G. (Eds.). (2007). *Handbook of multicultural assessment of multicultural assessment: Clinical, psychological, and educational implications* (3rd ed.). San Francisco: Jossey-Bass.

SUGGESTED READINGS

Bogner, M. S. (1994). *Human error in medicine*. Mahwah, NJ: Lawrence Erlbaum.

Suzuki, L. A., & Penterotto, J. G. (2008). *Handbook of multicultural assessment*. San Francisco: Jossey-Bass.

ROBERT G. MALGADY
Touro College, New York, NY

PSYCHOLOGICAL MINDEDNESS

Psychological mindedness (PM) is the ability to process information with reference to a psychological system. Hatcher and Hatcher (1997) explain that different psychological systems may lead to different conceptualizations of PM. Fundamentally, however, PM requires identifying some data as psychological (rather than biological, religious, economic, etc.) and finding psychological meaning in the data. Therefore, the psychologically minded person is capable of making psychological rather than purely biological, religious, economic, or any other nonpsychological attributions for behavior. For example, a psychologically minded person might explain an aggressive outburst by saying, "I did it because I was angry," rather than "The devil made me do it" or "I have a chemical imbalance."

Viewed broadly, PM is at the heart of psychology. Teachers, researchers, and clinicians attack problems by defining them in psychological terms and then by thinking psychologically about them; they all attempt to get their respective audiences to think psychologically about those problems as well. Therefore, PM is a core concept—perhaps *the* core concept—in psychology, when defined broadly.

As a term of art, however, PM was first used in a narrower sense. The concept of PM developed within an American psychoanalytic framework to describe patients who could understand and profit from interpretation, a key intervention in psychodynamic psychotherapy that relies on elucidating psychological patterns and is expected to lead to insight. Writing within a psychoanalytic framework, Appelbaum (1973) provided an early and influential definition of PM as "a person's ability to see relationships among thoughts, feelings, and actions, with the goal of learning the meanings and causes of his experiences and behavior."

Dollinger, Greening, and Tylenda (1985) understood PM as both an ability and an interest in "reading between the lines" of human experience. Highly psychologically minded individuals were seen as sagacious, insofar as they know what to look for and seem to do this without explicit training. Dollinger's definition highlights the strong social-cognitive facets of PM.

Conte and colleagues (1990) define PM as "an attribute of an individual that presupposes a degree of access to one's feelings that leads, through discussion of one's problems with others, to an ability to acquire insight into the meaning and motivation of one's and others' thoughts, feelings, and behavior, and to a capacity for change." They claim atheoretical status for their definition of the construct, but they acknowledge that it describes a method of meaning-making that is of particular value to the psychoanalytic intellectual tradition.

McCallum and Piper (1990) describe PM as an ability to appreciate intrapsychic dynamics and to apply that understanding to one's difficulties. The authors regard the psychologically minded person as one who draws upon a hierarchically organized set of psychodynamic assumptions involving recognition of internal experience, conflict, and defense.

Hatcher and Hatcher (1997) wrote that PM is a complex set of cognitive and emotional skills that unfold according to a particular developmental sequence. Three distinct lines of development were discerned: "(a) the growing understanding of internal, individual sources of motivation, (b) the developing ability to recognize the simultaneous presence of several, often conflicting motivations, and (c) the awareness of the use of self-deception to protect oneself against painful self-awareness."

Measurement

The two most recent measures of PM were published in 1990 by Conte and colleagues and by McCallum and Piper. In the Psychological Mindedness Assessment Procedure (PMAP; McCallum & Piper, 1990), participants view a standardized clinical vignette, as portrayed by actors, and are asked to provide a narrative description of the "patient's" problems. These descriptions are then coded for nine levels of PM. Conte and colleagues (1990) developed a 45-item, self-report measure of PM (PM Scale) that assesses individual differences on scales for Avoidance of Insight, Openness to New Ideas, and Access to One's Feelings.

Research Findings

Personality

In psychoanalytic terms, PM is a function of the ego, and it should therefore correlate with measures of ego development and ego strength. Helson and Roberts (1994) report that PM scores in late adolescence in fact predicted level of ego development at age 43 in a longitudinal study. Furthermore, the PM Scale was significantly and positively associated with ego strength, as measured by the Dynamic Personality Inventory and the Self-Evaluation Questionnaire in psychiatric outpatients (Conte, Buckley, Picard, & Karasu, 1995).

Recent research has linked PM to a variety of healthy psychological characteristics, including extraversion, openness, ambiguity, tolerance, internal locus of control, mindfulness, and cognitive and affective aspects of empathy. Positive empirical associations have also been found between PM and attachment to peers and adjustment to college in university students (Beitel & Cecero, 2003; Beitel, Ferrer, & Cicero, 2004, 2005; Cecero, Beitel, & Prout, 2008). These associations secure the place of PM as a construct within the field of positive psychology.

Psychopathology

Psychological mindedness has failed repeatedly to correlate with pretreatment psychiatric symptomatology or level of functioning (Conte et al., 1990; McCallum & Piper, 1990). However, PM is significantly negatively correlated with alexithymia as measured by the Toronto Alexithymia Scale (Bagby, Taylor, & Parker, 1994). PM has also been inversely related to neuroticism, magical thinking, and self-consciousness (Beitel & Cecero, 2003; Beitel, Ferrer, & Cecero, 2004). More recently, Cecero, Beitel, and Prout (2008) have discovered negative relations between PM and a variety of early maladaptive schemas.

Psychotherapy

Psychological mindedness is an important patient variable in monitoring and predicting the outcome of psychotherapy. High PM predicted positive outcome in four modalities of time-limited psychotherapy (Piper, Debbane, Bienvenu, & Garant, 1984). Conte and colleagues (1990) found that the construct has predicted the number of psychotherapy sessions attended. PM has also predicted increased global functioning and decreased psychosocial symptoms and problems as assessed by patients, treating therapists, and independent raters (Conte et al., 1990).

Although a psychologically minded orientation has many benefits, there are costs as well. Farber and Golden (1997) noted that highly psychologically minded people are at risk for observing and reflecting to the exclusion of experiencing life events. Farber (1989) stated that "the highly psychologically-minded person is wiser but sadder." There are also times when a psychologically minded approach is insufficient to promote a positive treatment response, as in cases when biological factors (e.g., brain lesion) are driving psychopathology (Farber & Golden, 1997; Dollinger, 1997).

Psychological mindedness is a core psychological construct that holds tremendous promise for research and practice. Although the term developed within the psychoanalytic tradition, its broad definition makes it readily available to many other schools of psychological thought. It is at once social and cognitive, with clearly specified developmental pathways. Therefore, PM should be of great interest to basic scientists in cognitive, social,

and developmental psychology. PM as a pattern recognition process may also be interesting to basic researchers. In addition, PM should be included under the umbrella of positive psychology, given its associations with mental health and well-being. Hopefully, its utility will take the construct far beyond its current domains of personality and clinical psychology.

REFERENCES

Appelbaum, S. A. (1973). Psychological mindedness: Word, concept and essence. *International Journal of Psychoanalysis, 54,* 35–46.

Bagby, M. R., Taylor, G. J., & Parker, J. D. (1994). The twenty-item Toronto Alexithymia Scale: II. Convergent, discriminant, and concurrent validity. *Journal of Psychosomatic Research, 38,* 33–40.

Beitel, M., & Cecero, J. J. (2003). Predicting psychological mindedness from personality style and attachment security. *Journal of Clinical Psychology, 59,* 163–172.

Beitel, M., Ferrer, E., & Cecero, J. J. (2004). Psychological mindedness and cognitive style. *Journal of Clinical Psychology, 60,* 567–582.

Beitel, M., Ferrer, E., & Cecero, J. J. (2005). Psychological mindedness and awareness of self and others. *Journal of Clinical Psychology, 61,* 739–750.

Cecero, J. J., Beitel, M., & Prout, T. (2008). Exploring the relationships among early maladaptive schemas, psychological mindedness, and adjustment to college. *Psychology and Psychotherapy: Theory, Research, and Practice, 81,* 105–118.

Conte, H. R., Buckley, P., Picard, S., & Karasu, T. B. (1995). Relations between psychological mindedness and personality traits and ego functioning: Validity studies. *Comprehensive Psychiatry, 36,* 11–17.

Conte, H. R., Plutchik, R., Jung, B. B., Picard, S., Karasu, T. B., & Lotterman, A. (1990). Psychological mindedness as a predictor of psychotherapy outcome: A preliminary report. *Comprehensive Psychiatry, 31,* 426–431.

Dollinger, S. J., (1997). Psychological mindedness as "reading between the lines." In M. McCallum & W. E. Piper (Eds.), *Psychological mindedness: A contemporary understanding* (pp. 169–187). Mahwah, NJ: Lawrence Erlbaum.

Dollinger, S. J., Greening, L., & Tylenda, B. (1985). Psychological-mindedness as "reading between the lines": Vigilance, locus of control, and sagacious judgment. *Journal of Personality, 53,* 603–625.

Farber, B. A. (1989). Psychological mindedness: Can there be too much of a good thing? *Psychotherapy, 26,* 210–217.

Farber, B. A., & Golden, V. (1997). Psychological mindedness in psychotherapists. In M. McCallum & W. E. Piper (Eds.), *Psychological mindedness: A contemporary understanding* (pp. 211–235). Mahwah, NJ: Lawrence Erlbaum.

Hatcher, R. L., & Hatcher, S. L. (1997). Assessing the psychological mindedness of children and adolescents. In M. McCallum & W. E. Piper (Eds.), *Psychological mindedness: A contemporary understanding* (pp. 59–75). Mahwah, NJ: Lawrence Erlbaum.

Helson, R., & Roberts, B. W. (1994). Ego development and personality change in adulthood. *Journal of Personality and Social Psychology, 66*, 911–920.

McCallum, M., & Piper, W. E. (1990). The Psychological Mindedness Assessment procedure. *Psychological Assessment, 2*, 412–418.

Piper, W. E., Debbane, E. G., Bienvenu, J. P., & Garant, J. (1984). A comparative study of four forms of psychotherapy. *Journal of Consulting and Clinical Psychology, 52*, 268–279.

SUGGESTED READING

McCallum, M., & Piper, W. E. (Eds.). (1997). *Psychological mindedness: A contemporary understanding.* Mahwah, NJ: Lawrence Erlbaum.

MARK BEITEL
Yale University School of Medicine

See also: Insight

PSYCHOLOGICAL SCIENCE

Psychological science connotes the application of scientific methods and rationales to the study of psychological issues to produce a utilizable body of knowledge called, appropriately, psychological science. To make the story complete, the brief discussion here characterizes psychological content, explicates relevant scientific method and practice, details some historical developments and insights that made this conflation of psychology and science possible, and mentions in passing the relationship of psychological science to the vast arena of scientific endeavor.

Historians of science tend to recognize the beginning of the sixteenth century as the start of a period in which major advances were made in cosmology, biology, chemistry, and physics. This was a period in which major suppositions about the nature of real-world phenomena dating back to Aristotle were overthrown. This rejection of authority as a criterion for validity of knowledge was part of a more general reexamination of basic beliefs and their support that has been termed the Age of Enlightenment. What changed all this was the development of empiricism, the doctrine that truth should be obtained from nature rather than from presumably infallible authorities whose knowledge was obtained by contemplation and logical but potentially fallible thinking. The world itself and what could be found out about it from observation became an increasingly potent alternative source of judgment and truth. Science based upon systematic, controlled observations of the world and its phenomena emerged.

Through much of the time period after the beginnings of the scientific revolution, the term psychological science would have had the status of an oxymoron. Science and psychology, until recently a branch of philosophy, played in different ballparks; they were philosophically contradictory. Science dealt with real, palpable, empirical objects and events, while psychology's concern was with immaterial, private, ephemeral entities and states like minds or souls. Because of the subjective quality of psychology's interest in mind and its nature, psychological issues or entities, according to the philosopher Immanuel Kant, were private events not open to public scrutiny and measurement and could not be described mathematically. Therefore, psychology could not be an empirical science in the sense that science was understood at the time. Things change.

Historically, a concern for mental events and their relationship to action, to the social and physical environment, and to the anatomical body has roots that go back at least to the Greeks. Traditionally, speculation about these matters has been included in a subfield of philosophy that was called psychology. Psychological issues, by consensus, included mind and conscious experience and a host of identifiable associated processes like memory, thinking, emotion, learning, deciding, mental development in children, and perception. These were studied by using the time-honored philosophic method of deep, thoughtful analysis while seated in the proverbial armchair. At this point in time, Kant's evaluation was correct. But by the nineteenth century, scientific methodology and, in particular, the experimental method had developed.

In psychology, Weber demonstrated that although we might not be able to measure conscious experience directly—Kant's objection—we could certainly observe the behavioral results of presumed mental functions, results such as verbal statements by judges comparing the relative weights of two physical objects. Weber found that the weight difference between two objects judged to be just noticeably different was proportional to the weight of the objects—the heavier the weights, the greater the size of the weight difference between two different weights judged to be just noticeably different. This fundamental insight—that we can produce evidence of what mental processes do in others, even if we cannot observe the processes directly—was elaborated upon by Fechner and subsequently has been the basis of the historical development of psychological science. It was soon applied to learning by Ebbinghaus, to the study of intelligence by Binet, to perception by the Gestalt school, and to learning and action by the behaviorists and was adopted by cognitive psychologists in the past 50 years. Typical objective data from such experimental treatments include reaction times, error rates, scaled judgments, response rates, and physiological recordings of neurological processes.

Psychological science, as with other sciences, has the goals of description, explanation, and application. The goal of description is to develop an empirically based, coherent account of a set of related phenomena and the factors that produce them. Initially, an attempt is made to determine the factors that affect a particular psychological phenomenon and the manner in which these factors or variables interact with one another and relate to the observed results. The description may take the form of a mathematical relationship among the variables, although much psychological research is much less ambitious and seeks only to determine whether a particular variable has an expected effect, often couched in terms of statistical significance. So-called clinical trials of drugs are of this nature. A variation on this strategy is to determine just what is affected by or related to a particular treatment. For example, brain scans are done to determine which brain structures seem implicated in various psychological functions or processes.

Explanation is of a different character. This *why* question does not simply involve the determination of an empirical relationship among variables or factors, as does the *what* question. Explanation deals with fundamental issues of causation—fundamental because it is not explanation to state that a lightbulb lights because a switch on the wall is pushed. That fact is merely a description of the empirical relationship between two factors: the light and the switch. The fundamental explanation itself is embedded in a context of known relationships involving physical properties of materials and the related laws of electricity, among other things, by means of which the relationship between the push on the switch and the lighting of the bulb makes sense. The ultimate goal of psychological science is to develop an analogous context of known relationships among psychological, physiological, and environmental factors by means of which psychological phenomena are explained or implied, perhaps by reducing them to physiological laws.

This explanatory connection is called a theory. In essence, a theory consists of a set of assumptions taken to be true and procedures for generalizing from these assumptions to a particular set of empirical circumstances. A theory in this sense can vary widely in comprehensiveness and complexity from a hypothetical-deductive framework with formal axioms and logical rules as proposed by the logical positivists to, at the other extreme, a more metaphorical inspiration, such as "memory decays over time." The value of theories is that they suggest or imply derived results called hypotheses that predict what the outcome of an empirical process, an observation or an experiment, should be if the theoretical framework adequately describes the real world. If the predicted result emerges from the experimental procedure, it is taken to be evidence in favor of the theory and contributes to an even deeper understanding of the phenomenon being studied. If the result is negative, the falsity of the hypothesis may be demonstrated.

Popper has pointed out that hypotheses, in order to be scientific, must be capable of predicting empirical events that may not occur—the hypothesis must be falsifiable.

Negative events must not simply be explained away; they have theoretical consequences. Questions about the scientific value of psychoanalysis or creationism, for example, have been raised on the basis of a lack of falsifiability.

One view of scientific theories is that they are simply social constructions applicable to a real world that we can never fully know or understand. In this sense, theories are never fully complete statements but only approximations that make sense given a limited empirical understanding of the world. Kuhn was one of the first philosophers of science to point out that in the history of science there are numerous examples of scientific theories that accumulate fact and explanatory principles over time but then collapse under the weight of accumulated negative evidence. What may emerge from such a scientific revolution is a new framework involving different organizational principles, what Kuhn has called a paradigm shift. Psychological science arguably is in an early developmental stage of this continuing process.

The third goal of any science is utilization. Scientific knowledge, as we have seen, consists of empirical facts about the dependence of real-world events upon the stipulated circumstances that create them. If we are to have control over real-world events, we must make use of these known relationships; we must know what affects what. We must diagnose real-world problems in terms of the known factors that control and influence aspects of the problem, and we must develop prescriptive regimens of known controlling factors that lead to the desired result. Psychological science has had significant contributions to make in many problem areas involving human thought, action, and emotion, including equipment design, education, alleviation of mental health and emotional problems, and the like.

SUGGESTED READINGS

Bechtel, W. (1988). *Philosophy of science: An overview for cognitive science*. Hillsdale, NJ: Lawrence Erlbaum.

Fechner, G. T. (1965). On Fechner's law. In R. J. Herrnstein & E. G. Boring (Eds.), *A sourcebook in the history of psychology* (pp. 66–75). Cambridge, MA: Harvard University Press. (Original work published 1860)

Kuhn, T. S. (1970). *The structure of scientific revolutions* (2nd ed.). Chicago: University of Chicago Press.

Popper, K. R. (1965). *Conjectures and refutations: The growth of scientific knowledge* (2nd ed.). New York: Harper & Row.

Weber, E. H. (1965). On Weber's law. In R. J. Herrnstein & E. G. Boring (Eds.), *A sourcebook in the history of psychology* (pp. 64–66). Cambridge, MA: Harvard University Press. (Original work published 1834)

C. ALAN BONEAU
George Mason University

See also: **Experimental Psychology; Hypothesis Testing; Scientific Method**

PSYCHOLOGICAL SYSTEMS

A psychological system is a way of conceptualizing and organizing the basic phenomena of psychology. It is similar to what in advanced sciences Kuhn (1962) called a paradigm. Like a paradigm, a psychological system subsumes under a single umbrella theories that are based on similar assumptions and use a similar language to describe phenomena. Over the history of psychology, four distinct systems have emerged: cognitive, psychodynamic, behavioral, and humanistic psychology (Pear, 2007). Although other classifications have been proposed, the one used here is the most parsimonious.

Four Psychological Systems

Cognitive Psychology

In the cognitive system, features of the external world are represented in the mind. Precursors of the cognitive system are found in writings of ancient Greek philosophers and subsequent Western and Eastern philosophers. Two of the most notable European philosophers who adopted this view were Descartes, who postulated how external stimulation is transmitted through the nervous system, and Kant, who believed that the world external to the mind is essentially unknowable and beyond our ability to conceptualize.

Throughout history, various philosophers and scientists have attempted to understand the mechanisms by which representations (symbols) relate to the external world and how they function in the mind. Philosophers known as the British empiricists theorized how representations of external objects or ideas become associated with each other. The cognitive system was also evident in the early days of scientific psychology, which focused on consciousness as its primary interest. In Europe, Wilhelm Wundt used a form of introspection to analyze consciousness into its elements, whereas Franz Brentano advocated an alternative form based on the concept of intentionality (the tendency of objects of consciousness to point to something beyond). In the United States, William James emphasized the functional aspects of consciousness.

As it became clear that there were serious problems with introspective methodology, cognitive theories (e.g., Gestalt psychology) shifted away from classical introspection. Overshadowed for a time by behaviorism, the cognitive system was rejuvenated in the 1950s by the rise of computers, which provided an information-processing model for the mind (Mandler, 2002; Miller, 2003). Linking cognitive psychology to computer science countered the charge that cognitive psychology was unscientific because of its focus on an intangible entity—namely, the mind—which cognitive psychologists now conceptualize as the software of the brain.

One criticism of the cognitive system concerns the computer analogy, which seems to require a homunculus to correspond to the computer user. This introduces the problem of accounting for the cognition of the homunculus, which leads to an infinite regress. An argument in response to this criticism is that postulating a number of relatively simple homunculi avoids this problem. Another criticism is that the cognitive system does not give much attention to motivation and emotion. Cognitive psychologists, however, point out that there is no reason that motivation and emotion could not be conceptualized as segments of a computer program that are run in specific situations, in the same manner that processing occurs with other forms of information.

Psychodynamic Psychology

The psychodynamic system stresses unconscious or hidden motivation, which is assumed to be a powerful determinant of such processes as conscious motivation, perception, memory, psychopathology, and conduct. A precursor of the psychodynamic system is Plato's allegory of the soul (psyche) as a chariot pulled by two powerful horses. One horse is ignoble and seeks only the gratification of base desires, whereas the other is noble and seeks lofty ends. The charioteer tries to steer them in such a way as to keep them from going in different directions.

Later precursors of the psychodynamic system were Western European philosophers who stressed a person's will as a major aspect of the human personality. Nietzsche is of particular note, with his strong denunciation of all forms of hypocrisy and his emphasis on hidden motives that often underlie our actions. The philosophy of intentionality or "aboutness" developed by Brentano is another noteworthy precursor, in the sense that all psychological acts have reference or meaning. It is interesting that both the cognitive and the psychodynamic systems have roots in intentionality. The ways in which symbols are manifested in the two systems, however, are different. In the cognitive system, symbols are the tools of thought; in the psychodynamic system, they are manifestations that potentially reveal hidden thought processes. Thus, in the psychodynamic system, symbols can appear in dreams, verbal slips, artistic works, and culturally significant designs or patterns, as well as in everyday actions.

The psychodynamic approach burst on the psychological scene with the writings of Sigmund Freud. Interestingly, at the time when the majority of scientific psychology was stressing consciousness as the key to understanding psychological phenomena, Freud stressed a dynamic unconscious. The motivating force was the libido, which constitutes sexual motivation broadly conceived.

Disaffected followers—most famously, Alfred Adler and Carl Jung—broke with Freud primarily regarding the underlying motivating force. Adler stressed striving for self-esteem and social interest (*Gemeinschaftsgefuhl*), whereas Jung stressed a need for the integration of diverse aspects of the personality as the primary motivational forces. Subsequent generations of psychodynamic theorists have tended more toward Freudian concepts, but with substantial modifications. Thus, there are a number of distinct forms of the psychodynamic system and a number of overlapping versions. All forms, however, are characterized by their emphasis on unconscious motivation expressed through symbolic representations.

The founders of the psychodynamic system were trained as physicians, whereas most psychologists of their day had educational backgrounds in philosophy. This led to a difference in their approach to research methodology. Whereas most psychologists attempted to follow a Galilean approach of manipulating independent variables and observing their effects on dependent variables, the founders of the psychodynamic system adopted a research approach involving case studies of individual patients being treated for psychological disorders.

A major criticism of the psychodynamic approach is that it is based almost totally on interpretation and conjecture, with vague criteria for determining which interpretation is correct. Added to this problem is the heavy focus on case studies under conditions that critics would say manifest questionable scientific reliability. There are, however, studies using standard methodology that tend to support certain aspects of the psychodynamic approach (Fonagy, 2002; Westen, 1998). Moreover, within the psychodynamic system, there is growing awareness of the need to address the criticisms of it through epistemology and sound methodology (Summers, 2008).

Behavioral Psychology

Precursors to the behavioral system are found in ancient writings that do not postulate an inner agent of the body, that is, a mind or soul. These writings include most of the Hebrew Bible (Old Testament) and the New Testament of the Christian Bible, as well as Buddhist writings. It also includes some writings of the ancient Greeks, especially those of Aristotle and Theophrastus. More recent precursors of the behavioral system are Ivan Pavlov and Vladimir Bekhterev, both of whom stressed conditioned or association reflexes as the fundamental units or constituents of psychological processes. They measured behavior and did not postulate an inner entity (soul or mind) that was distinct from behavior.

Behaviorism burst into psychology with John B. Watson's famous statement:

> Psychology as the behaviorist views it is a purely objective experimental branch of natural science. Its theoretical goal is the prediction and control of behavior. Introspection forms no essential part of its methods, nor is the scientific value of its data dependent upon the readiness with which they lend themselves to interpretation in terms of consciousness. The behaviorist, in his efforts to get a unitary scheme of

animal response, recognizes no dividing line between man and brute. The behavior of man, with all of its refinement and complexity, forms only a part of the behaviorist's total scheme of investigation. (Watson, 1913, p. 158)

Following Watson, behaviorists focused on animal as well as human behavior. Animal behavior can often be studied more conveniently than human behavior, and the findings can be generalized to humans because of the continuity of species. Behaviorists emphasize Pavlovian and operant conditioning processes because these are powerful and reliable behavior-control methods with wide generality.

In the period known as the behavioral revolution, behaviorism became the predominant system in academic psychology. After Watson left academic psychology, behaviorism bifurcated into strands called radical and methodological behaviorism (Skinner, 1945). Radical behaviorism maintains that psychological concepts should be expressed exclusively in behavioral terms. The existence and scientific importance of private behavior (e.g., thoughts, images) are not denied, but private behavior is not given a special causative status. It is less studied because it is less accessible—although advances in technology are expected to alter this limitation. Like radical behaviorism, methodological behaviorism rejects introspection as a predominant scientific methodology for psychology and focuses on observable behavior as the primary datum of psychology. Methodological behaviorism, however, does use external behavior as a basis for speculating or theorizing about hypothetical or real internal processes (i.e., the interest is not on behavior per se, but on what behavior can tell us about processes that cannot be directly observed). Thus, methodological behaviorism overlaps with cognitive psychology in focusing on hypothetical inner determinants of overt behavior.

The primary criticisms of behaviorism are that behavioral language and rigorous behavioral definitions are too cumbersome to describe complex mental processes and that they may be too narrow and restrictive to ever fully capture the most interesting and important properties of the human psyche. Behaviorists respond that scientific language often seems cumbersome in part because of its unfamiliarity, but that a precise operational language is necessary in order for a science to advance.

Humanistic Psychology

The humanistic system questions traditional Western scientific methods and theories that neglect the unique significance of human beings. Precursors occurred during the Renaissance, when Western science began to develop as part of the growing reaction to the domination of intellectual activities by the Catholic Church. The emphasis thereby shifted from revealed truth to observation of nature, and from the Divine to humans as ultimate source of value (Moss, 2001). This concept harks back to the ancient Greek philosopher Protagoras' dictum that "man is the measure of all things." Pursuit of natural philosophy (science) as human activity replaced the view of the church as the holder of all truth with the idea that individuals could find truth for themselves through "reading the book of nature" and using their own intellects. However, extending the same scientific thinking to humans as that applied to the rest of nature met with deep philosophical resistance. Two prominent schools of thought that developed in opposition to the straightforward application of Western science to human behavior were phenomenology and existentialism, with their stress on consciousness and self-determination. Interestingly, these influences are traceable to Brentano and Nietzsche, who also influenced the psychodynamic system previously outlined.

From the early 1900s through to the 1950s, behaviorism and psychoanalysis were the dominant approaches within academic psychology. Both systems attempted to follow their respective versions of a traditional scientific approach to human thought and behavior. Humanistic psychology arose as a reaction to this domination of behaviorism and psychoanalysis, and for this reason, it was originally called third-force psychology (Bugental, 1964). There was an initial opposition to the term *humanistic* by some of the founders, because of its seemingly antireligious and antispiritual stance. The term *humanistic psychology* was eventually adopted, because the founders saw the behavioral and psychodynamic systems as tending to be dehumanizing. When cognitive psychology overtook behaviorism, humanistic psychologists saw it as being just as mechanistic as behaviorism.

Tageson (1982), in a systematic treatise, identified the following themes that are emphasized by humanistic psychology: phenomenology, holism, self-determination, teleology, self-actualization, authenticity, and spirituality (also see Bugental, 1964). Because of its rejection of determinism and reductionism, humanistic psychologists often eschew standard psychological research designs. Somewhat ironically, Carl Rogers, one of the founders of humanistic psychology, was instrumental in promoting research in clinical psychology to determine the effectiveness of humanistic psychotherapy.

The chief criticisms of humanistic psychology are that it is self-indulgent and value laden and that its rejection of standard research methodology cannot lead to a science of psychology. Humanistic psychologists argue that it is important to recognize the values inherent in any scientific system, as well as to appreciate humans from a positive perspective.

Other Potential Systems

There are other approaches to psychology that one might want to call systems. For example, neuroscience, evolutionary psychology, positive psychology, and transpersonal psychology might be considered by some to be psychological systems. However, none of these approaches provides a distinct language that encompasses all psychological phenomena of interest. Moreover, each of the four systems discussed here addresses the concepts and phenomena encompassed by these approaches.

REFERENCES

Bugental, J. F. T. (1964). The third force in psychology. *Journal of Humanistic Psychology, 4,* 19–25.

Fonagy, P. (Ed.). (2002). *An open door review of outcome studies in psychoanalysis* (2nd ed.). London: International Psychoanalytical Association.

Kuhn, T. S. (1962). *The structure of scientific revolutions.* Chicago: University of Chicago Press.

Mandler, G. (2002). Origins of the cognitive (r)evolution. *Journal of the History of the Behavioral Sciences, 38,* 339–353.

Miller, G. A. (2003). The cognitive revolution: A historical perspective. *Trends in Cognitive Sciences, 7,* 141–144.

Moss, D. (2001). The roots and genealogy of humanistic psychology. In K. J. Schneider, J. F. T. Bugental, & J. F. Pierson (Eds.), *The handbook of humanistic psychology: Leading edges in theory, research, and practice* (pp. 5–20). Thousand Oaks, CA: Sage.

Pear, J. J. (2007). *A historical and contemporary look at psychological systems.* Mahwah, NJ: Lawrence Erlbaum.

Skinner, B. F. (1945). The operational analysis of psychological terms. *Psychological Review, 52,* 270–277; Rejoinders and second thoughts, 278–294.

Summers, F. (2008). Theoretical insularity and the crisis of psychoanalysis. *Psychoanalytic Psychology, 25,* 413–424.

Tageson, C. W. (1982). *Humanistic psychology: A synthesis.* Homewood, IL: Dorsey Press.

Watson, J. B. (1913). Psychology as the behaviorist views it. *Psychological Review, 20,* 158–177.

Westen, D. (1998). The scientific legacy of Sigmund Freud: Toward a psychodynamically informed psychological science. *Psychological Bulletin, 124,* 333–371.

SUGGESTED READINGS

Brennan, J. F. (Ed.). (1995). *Readings in the history and systems of psychology* (2nd ed.). Upper Saddle River, NJ: Prentice-Hall.

Smith, N. W. (2001). *Current systems in psychology: History, theory, research, and applications.* Belmont, CA: Wadsworth.

JOSEPH J. PEAR
University of Manitoba, Canada

See also: **Humanistic Psychotherapies; Psychoanalytic Theories; Radical Behaviorism**

PSYCHOLOGICAL TESTING (See Psychological Assessment)

PSYCHOLOGICAL TRAUMA (See Disaster Psychology; Posttraumatic Stress Disorder; Trauma Psychology)

PSYCHOLOGY AND PHILOSOPHY

Concerns that are now typically part of contemporary psychology—What is the nature of the mind? What causes human happiness? How do humans come to believe or know?—were, until the end of the nineteenth century, the concerns only of philosophers. In the latter part of the nineteenth century, investigators such as Wilhelm Wundt took an experimental approach to these questions, or at least certain aspects of these questions, and contemporary scientific psychology was born. Although empirical and experimental methods allow psychologists to address questions commonly outside the scope of philosophy (e.g., What is the incidence of depression?), philosophical concerns continue to influence these empirical pursuits. One clear example of such influence is the general agreement among psychologists that research takes place within a context of philosophical assumptions: What is science? What counts as evidence? What inferences are legitimate to make given the data? What are morally permissible research or clinical methodologies? Relatedly, analytic philosophers often engage in conceptual explication, and psychologists are often still puzzled by their concepts, for example, What is intelligence? What is clinical depression? Ludwig Wittgenstein (1953), in his *Philosophical Investigations,* famously wrote the following:

> The confusion and barrenness of psychology is not to be explained by calling it a "young science"; its state is not comparable with that of physics, for instance, in its beginnings. (Rather with that of certain branches of mathematics. Set theory.) For in psychology there are experimental methods and conceptual confusion . . . . The existence of the experimental method makes us think we have the means of solving the problems which trouble us; though problem and method pass one another by.

Thus, to the extent one worries about the slow progress of psychological science, this suggests a metaproblem for psychology, one that is typically seen in the philosophy of science: Is psychology using the right methods to discover knowledge?

Naturalized Epistemology

Arguably, the central philosophical metaproblem within psychology is the problem of knowledge. Psychologists want to gain and use knowledge, and they seek to construct epistemologically sound methods for doing so. Thus, of central concern in contemporary psychology is the question, "What method(s) can be used to gain knowledge

about a particular subject matter?" It is central for three reasons: (1) Scientific psychology has made slow progress, and it is difficult not to blame this at least partially on the limitations of its research methods; (2) the phenomena studied by psychologists may be sufficiently different from the phenomena studied by other natural scientists that the wholesale adoption of the methods of natural science for use in psychology may be inappropriate; and (3) psychology empirically investigates learning, that is, the acquisition of knowledge, and therefore may inform our conceptions of epistemology. Such approaches to epistemology are referred to as *naturalized* epistemology and are endorsed not only by psychologists but also by prominent philosophers such as W. V. Quine and Karl Popper. Popper, trained as a psychologist but best known as a philosopher of science, has advocated *evolutionary* epistemology, which explains the capabilities and limits of human learning through evolutionary mechanisms.

The Good Life

Psychologists are increasingly drawn into the domain of ethics, a domain previously relegated to clergy and philosophers. Ethics has to do with the good life, asking questions such as "What is the good?" "How ought I act?" and "Is happiness the ultimate goal in life?" Psychological research, particularly work done by clinical and social psychologists, is viewed by some as providing insight into these important questions. Psychological well-being, for example, is a collection of positive attributes that might be comparable to what philosophers refer to as virtues. Psychologists and philosophers alike agree that variables like good health, positive outlook, quality friends, social networks, and a developed sense of self are all implicated in humans' ability to flourish. In addition, thinking accurately about one's life and its circumstances may be related to the good life. This is the focus of cognitive therapy, for example. As with epistemology, there are those who believe that empirical evidence can provide answers to ethical questions. Although most thinkers agree that empirical findings can help people more effectively realize their goals, it is a matter of great controversy as to whether such findings can help to define what is good or virtuous.

Philosophy of Mind

Otherwise known as the mind–body problem, the problematic nature of this field of inquiry is typically traced to Descartes's (in)famous articulation of substance dualism (although both Plato and Aristotle weighed in on the issue). Two broadly constructed solutions have been proposed to the mind–body problem, which has changed significantly since Descartes's time, being construed now as the problem of consciousness, but the various solutions to this problem suggested by thinkers throughout history still address the same fundamental issue.

Substance dualism is the thesis that there is an essential difference between minds (mental phenomena) and bodies (physical phenomena); that is, mind is an essentially thinking substance, and body is an essentially extended substance. Given this bifurcation of reality into two separate and unconnected domains, subsequent thinkers have developed theories aimed at ameliorating the difficulties associated with our commonsense intuition that the mind and body do in fact interact. Psychophysical interactionism stipulates that bodily (brain) states cause corresponding mental states that, in turn, are capable of causally instantiating subsequent bodily states. Epiphenomenalism is the thesis that bodily (brain) states cause corresponding mental states, but that these mental states are causally inefficacious with respect to bringing about subsequent body states. As such, epiphenomenalism is a one-way interaction: body to mind, but not the other way around. Psychophysical parallelism avoids the problem of interaction altogether by claiming that mental and physical states run parallel to one another, like two clocks each showing the same time, but do not interact.

Monism is the thesis that all of the objects of reality are of one kind. As such, monism is the explicit denial of the dualistic claim that mind and body are essentially different. Given our predilection toward discussing the topic in terms of the mental and the physical, monistic theories are devoted to describing how one of these terms is reducible, or identical, to the other. Idealism is a kind of monism that states "all things are essentially mental or, at least, depend upon the mind for their existence." Materialism is a kind of monism that states "all things are physical"; that is, the mind is just the brain. Phenomenalism is a less popular variety of monism that stipulates that all empirical statements (including, but not limited to, statements about mental and physical states) are reducible to actual or possible phenomenal appearances. In general, any monistic theory that reduces both mind and body to another, more fundamental reality or substance is labeled a *dual aspect theory*.

Free Will and Determinism

As psychological explanations of human behavior become more precise, belief in free will becomes more difficult to entertain. One who maintains that humans are free agents claims (at least implicitly) that (1) our psychological understanding of the causes of human behavior underdetermines the actual range and complexity of observed behavior and that (2) no future scientific advances will eventuate in a theory that adequately accounts for the full range of human behavior. Those psychologists who adopt a deterministic position, such as Sigmund Freud and B. F. Skinner, need not necessarily claim that current psychological theory does, in fact, account for the entire range of human behavior. Rather, the determinist need only

stipulate that such an all-embracing scientific account of human behavior is possible.

Political Philosophy

Increasingly psychologists, and particularly the American Psychological Association, weigh in on key political issues facing the nation (e.g., abortion, war, affirmative action, sexual rights, military interrogations). There are key questions concerning whether psychologists have sufficient data to inform these debates and key questions regarding whether this is just an expression of psychologists' political philosophies.

REFERENCE

Wittgenstein, L. (1953). *Philosophical investigations* (E. M. Anscombe, Ed. & Trans.). Oxford, UK: Blackwell.

SUGGESTED READINGS

Grunbaum, A. (1984). *The foundations of psychoanalysis: A philosophical critique*. Berkeley: University of California Press.

O'Donohue, W., & Kitchener, R. F. (Eds.). (1996). *The philosophy of psychology*. London: Sage.

Popper, K. R. (1965). *The logic of scientific discovery*. New York: Harper and Row.

Quine, W. V., & Ullian, J. S. (1978). *The web of belief* (2nd ed.). New York: Random House.

WILLIAM O'DONOHUE
University of Nevada, Reno

See also: **Logical Positivism**

PSYCHOLOGY AND RELIGION (See Religion and Psychology)

PSYCHOLOGY AND THE LAW

The field of psychology and law first began to develop within the last century and is currently experiencing a period of growth and expansion. The interaction between the disciplines of psychology and law has greatly increased over the past few decades in three overlapping areas: forensic psychology, legal psychology, and psychological jurisprudence. In forensic psychology, psychologists act as experts, practitioners, researchers, and/or consultants with respect to legally relevant clinical areas (such as competency to stand trial, insanity, or civil commitment to psychiatric hospitals). Legal psychology uses applied and empirical research methods to study a range of issues of importance to the legal system (e.g., eyewitness accuracy, police selection, procedural justice, jury decision making, and legal assumptions about human behavior relevant to the rights of defendants, victims, children, and mental patients). Finally, psychological jurisprudence is that area of the field in which the main focus involves efforts to develop a philosophy of law and justice based on psychological values.

The growth of psychology and the law is evident in the publication of numerous books and the creation of book series in psychology and law; journals and periodicals specifically targeted toward psychology and legal issues; the establishment of the American Psychology-Law Society, the American Academy of Forensic Psychology, and the American Board of Forensic Psychology; and the development and expansion of educational and internship experiences. Many graduate programs have developed degree programs in which a specialization or concentration in psychology and law can be obtained, and a number of universities have established joint degree programs in psychology and law in which both a PhD and a law degree can be obtained (Bersoff et al., 1997). The following provides a broad overview of the major areas in which psychologists in the field of psychology and law are engaged. Psychologists are often asked to testify in court, both about psychological evaluations of individuals and about research findings that may be applicable to a specific criminal or civil court case (see Brodsky, 2004; Ceci & Hembrooke, 1998, for discussion of the role of expert witnesses).

Psychology and law can be conceptualized as encompassing both sides of the justice system (civil and criminal), as well as two broad aspects of psychology (clinical and experimental). Professionals who practice mainly within the civil-clinical area of the field focus on clinical activities within the civil justice system, including conducting evaluations for civil commitment or evaluations of risk for violence among psychiatric patients or providing psychological treatment for these issues. In addition, researchers working within this area of the field focus their efforts on the development and evaluation of treatment programs or the development and validation of assessment instruments for the evaluation of these civil issues. Professionals who work mainly within the civil-experimental area of the field focus on studying and researching topics at the intersection of psychology and the civil justice system. Examples of such issues include civil commitment criteria, policies, and practices; the right to refuse treatment; and mental health law and policy implications.

Professionals who practice mainly within the criminal-clinical area of the field focus on clinical issues relevant to the criminal justice system and the defendants within this system. Such clinical issues might include evaluations of competency to stand trial, mental state at the time of the offense (criminal responsibility, insanity), mitigation at sentencing, or risk for future offending, as well as the treatment of offenders (for an overview, see Melton, Petrila, Poythress, & Slobogin,

2007). Researchers within this area of the field focus on the development and validation of instruments for the various types of evaluations (e.g., Roesch, Zapf, & Eaves, 2006) or on developing and evaluating treatment programs for various types of offenders or issues (e.g., Heilbrun & Griffin, 1999).

Professionals who work mainly in the criminal-experimental area of the field focus on conducting research and advancing knowledge with respect to various aspects of the criminal justice system, such as eyewitness testimony and accuracy, jury deliberations and decision making, police selection, criminal investigation techniques, or punishment and sentencing.

One area that has had increased attention in both research and practice is the assessment of and communication about violence potential. Research has provided substantial insights into the risk and protective factors that are associated with violent behavior, and this research has changed how we approach risk assessment. Indeed, psychologists have shifted from trying to predict dangerousness to the assessment of risk, which involves thinking about and assessing those factors that will increase or decrease the probability that an individual will become violent in the future. Instead of attempting to make a prediction about a particular individual and whether he or she is dangerous, the focus changed to an examination of those situational and dispositional factors that increase or decrease the probability that a particular individual will become violent. Several risk assessment instruments have been developed to guide evaluators through a consideration of particularly important and empirically derived variables for both adults and juveniles (e.g., Corrado, Roesch, Hart, & Gierowski, 2002; Kropp, Hart, Webster, & Eaves, 1995; Webster, Douglas, Eaves, & Hart, 1997).

The preceding categorization is, obviously, very broad and simplistic. Many professionals within the field of psychology and law perform multiple activities that include but are not limited to teaching, research, supervision, expert testimony, consultation, evaluation, and treatment and that span more than one of the categories described here.

The discipline of psychology has begun to make an impact on the discipline of law, and continued research and practice is crucial to furthering our understanding of how psychology and the law interact with respect to particular issues. Experts within the field of psychology and law need to continue to conduct research and provide testimony and evidence with respect to policy recommendations and suggested improvements to the legal systems, both criminal and civil.

The field of psychology and law will no doubt continue to grow and expand in the years to come. It will be important for well-trained professionals to continue to teach, consult, testify, evaluate, treat, supervise, and conduct research in all the various aspects of this field in order to continue to expand and refine the field of psychology and law.

REFERENCES

Bersoff, D. N., Goodman-Delahunty, J., Grisso, J. T., Hans, V. P., Poythress, N. G., & Roesch, R. G. (1997). Training in law and psychology: Models from the Villanova conference. *American Psychologist, 52,* 1301–1310.

Brodsky, S. L. (2004). *Coping with cross-examination and other pathways to effective testimony.* Washington, DC: American Psychological Association.

Ceci, S. J., & Hembrooke, H. (Eds.). (1998). *Expert witness in child abuse cases: What can and should be said in court.* Washington, DC: American Psychological Association.

Corrado, R. R., Roesch, R., Hart, S. D., & Gierowski, J. K. (2002). *Multi-problem violent youth: A foundation for comparative research on needs, interventions, and outcomes.* NATO Science Series. Amsterdam: IOS Press.

Heilbrun, K., & Griffin, P. (1999). Forensic treatment: A review of programs and research. In R. Roesch, S. D. Hart, & J. R. P. Ogloff (Eds.), *Psychology and law: The state of the discipline* (pp. 241–274). New York: Kluwer Academic/Plenum Press.

Kropp, P. R., Hart, S. D., Webster, C. D., & Eaves, D. (1995). *Manual for the Spousal Assault Risk Assessment guide* (2nd ed.). Vancouver, British Columbia, Canada: British Columbia Institute against Family Violence.

Melton, G. B., Petrila, J., Poythress, N. G., & Slobogin, C. (2007). *Psychological evaluations for the courts: A handbook for mental health professionals and lawyers* (3rd ed.). New York: Guilford Press.

Roesch, R., Zapf, P. A., & Eaves, D. (2006). *Fitness interview test—revised: A structured interview for assessing competency to stand trial.* Sarasota, FL: Professional Resource Press.

Webster, C. D., Douglas, K. S., Eaves, D., & Hart, S. D. (1997). *HCR-20: Assessing risk for violence* (version 2). Burnaby, British Columbia, Canada: Mental Health, Law, and Policy Institute, Simon Fraser University.

SUGGESTED READINGS

Bersoff, D. (1999). Preparing for two cultures: Education and training in law and psychology. In R. Roesch, S. D. Hart, & J. R. P. Ogloff (Eds.), *Psychology and law: The state of the discipline* (pp. 375–401). New York: Kluwer Academic/Plenum Press.

Goldstein, A. M. (Ed.). (2007). *Forensic psychology: Emerging topics and expanding roles.* Hoboken, NJ: John Wiley & Sons.

Slobogin, C. (2006). *Proving the unprovable: The role of law, science, and speculation in adjudicating culpability and dangerousness.* New York: Oxford University Press.

Zapf, P. A., & Roesch, R. (2005). Competency to stand trial: A guide for evaluators. In I. B. Weiner & A. K. Hess (Eds.), *Handbook of forensic psychology* (3rd ed., pp. 305–331). Hoboken, NJ: John Wiley & Sons.

RONALD ROESCH
Simon Fraser University

PATRICIA A. ZAPF
John Jay College of Criminal Justice

See also: **Civil Competence; Competency to Stand Trial; Criminal Responsibility; Expert Testimony; Forensic Psychology**

PSYCHOLOGY, HISTORY OF

The subject matter of psychology captured the human imagination long before psychology became a science. Throughout antiquity, Chinese, Babylonian, Egyptian, Indian, Hebraic, and Persian scholars explored psychological topics ranging from sensation, emotion, and cognition to education, personality, and mental disorders. In ancient Greece, many enduring figures, including Thales, Anaximander, Anaximenes, Pythagoras, Parmenides, Heraclitus, Leucippus, and Democritus, made contributions important to Western intellectual history. Rejecting popular supernatural explanations, Hippocrates (c. 460–c. 377 B.C.E.) introduced a naturalistic approach to medicine that encompassed both physical and mental illness. He also formulated the first classification system of mental disorders.

During the Golden Age of Greece, Socrates (c. 470–c. 399 B.C.E.) rebelled against prevailing assumptions about human nature while asserting that reason was the basis of true knowledge. His student Plato (c. 428–c. 347 B.C.E.) made profound insights about the formal abstract nature of truth, considered the role of memory and sensation in human nature, and proposed an early conflict model of mental illness. As a student of Plato, Aristotle (384–322 B.C.E.) shifted away from the teachings of his mentor and moved toward an early psychology founded on experience rather than reasoning. His restless interests tackled the study of biopsychology, memory, learning, imagination, dreams, and comparative psychology. By establishing a foundation for logic and launching a comprehensive view of causality, Aristotle laid the cornerstone for early scientific thought.

Psychology in the Modern Era of Philosophy

Early interest in human and animal psychology evolved over time, stretching from the Roman era to the Middle Ages to the Renaissance. Seventeenth-century philosophy confronted the task of combating skepticism and restoring faith in human knowledge. In the tradition of Aristotle, a movement based on empiricism stressed the importance of personal experience and observation in all sciences and laid the groundwork for later developments in psychology. British philosopher of science Francis Bacon (1561–1626) constructed an empirical philosophy built on a critical empirical-inductive method, and he called for a close examination of the problem of knowledge. Following Bacon, John Locke (1632–1704) argued that mind at birth is like a blank slate devoid of characters or ideas. He was a powerful advocate for the centrality of experience and learning. His work increased public interest in universal education and childrearing. Over the next two centuries, philosophies of experience flourished in Europe, especially in England. A host of scholars promoted empiricism alongside the related fields of associationism and utilitarianism. Notable figures who advocated such philosophies included George Berkley (1685–1753), David Hartley (1705–1757), David Hume (1711–1776) Etienne Bonnot de Condillac (1715–1780), Jeremy Bentham (1748–1832), Mary Wollstonecraft (1759–1797), James Mill (1773–1836), John Stuart Mill (1806–1873), and Alexander Bain (1818–1903).

Around the same time that empiricism shaped modern notions about philosophy and psychology, rationalism offered a persuasive counterpoint on the problem of knowledge. The rationalists wrote thoughtful works that tackled theoretical and practical questions and emphasized a priori knowledge, deduction, and the concept of an active mind that selectively organizes sensory data. The French rationalist René Descartes (1596–1650) is often credited with founding modern philosophy. In original and innovative work, Descartes developed an early scientific methodology and provided rich and often testable hypotheses about the relationship between behavior and physiology. Following the Cartesian legacy, several key figures made contributions to modern rationalism, with some even attempting to reconcile the conflicting claims of empiricism and rationalism. Thinkers such as Baruch Spinoza (1632–1677), Gottfried Wilhelm Leibniz (1646–1716), Christian von Wolff (1679–1754), Thomas Reid (1710–1796), and Immanuel Kant (1724–1804) contributed to the intellectual and cultural context from which psychology as a formal discipline was born.

Naturalism and Humanitarian Reform

Arising from the Victorian era, modern evolutionary theory was rooted in the idea of naturalism, the doctrine that scientific procedures and laws are applicable to all phenomena. Based on meticulous data collection, Charles Darwin (1809–1882) formulated a theory of evolution that stressed the mechanism of natural selection. He applied his interests in evolution to psychological topics, ranging from the study of developmental processes in small children to the facial expressions of psychotic patients. Darwinian thought brought a new emphasis on functional, developmental, and comparative processes of human and animal behavior. At the same time, the rise of social statistics offered an important tool that would shape the quantification of later psychological research.

In the nineteenth century, naturalistic beliefs about mental and emotional disturbances sparked radical reform in the treatment and care of people with psychiatric disorders. Born in an age of social agitation for reform, the movement to provide humanitarian care for people with mental illness contributed to an intellectual climate supportive of a new helping profession.

The Formal Founding of Psychology

In the eighteenth century, psychology emerged as a formal discipline, giving rise to a diversity of organized schools or systems (Heidbreder, 1933). Psychophysics and physiology invigorated a dedicated band of German and American scientists who forged ahead toward the creation of a new science. The emerging field of psychophysics fueled interest in the relationship between the properties of stimuli as measured by a physical scale and the psychological impressions of those stimuli. Ernst Heinrich Weber (1795–1878) and Gustav Theodor Fechner (1801–1887) set forth a systematic approach to psychophysics that helped lay the conceptual and methodological foundations for the new discipline of psychology.

The formal beginnings of experimental psychology can be traced to the year 1879, when the University of Leipzig recognized a psychological laboratory founded by Wilhelm Wundt (1832–1920). More than any other person, Wundt is regarded as the founding figure of modern psychology. Wundt also advanced the first systematic vision of psychology, known as voluntarism. Under his direction, psychology flourished in a prolific stream of publications that emerged from the laboratory in Leipzig. Based on the introspective reports of his participants, Wundt's research focused on sensation, perception, and reaction time, although additional studies were conducted on associationism, emotion, word associations, attention, and dreams. The breadth of Wundt's (1919) vision is revealed in his *Volkerpsychologie,* a sociocultural psychology that encompassed social psychology, anthropology, personality, psycholinguistics, forensic psychology, and the psychology of religion.

Structuralism

The formal founding of psychology at Leipzig galvanized a new generation of psychologists. It did not take very long for new lecture courses, laboratories, and degree programs to spring up in Europe and the United States. After a brief time working with Wundt, Edward Bradford Titchener (1867–1927) brought his brand of psychology to the United States in the form of structuralism, a school of psychology modeled on chemistry and other established sciences. Relying on data culled through introspection, the structuralists' goal was to chronicle the elements of consciousness. They were further inspired to determine the rules that govern the combining of mental elements.

Outside of structuralism, several European scientists were significant in establishing psychology after its founding. Hermann Ebbinghaus (1850–1909) was a pioneer in the experimental study of memory and forgetting. Other key figures of the period include Franz Brentano (1838–1917), Carl Stumpf (1848–1936), Georg Elias Muller (1850–1934), and Oswald Kulpe (1862–1915).

Functionalism

Rebelling against structuralism, American scholars took psychology in bold new directions with the founding of functionalism, a loose-knit system that underscored broad methodologies drawn from basic and applied problems associated with experience and behavior. The venerable psychologist and philosopher William James (1842–1910) reigned as the founding spirit of American psychology. James (1890), in his seminal two-volume *Principles of Psychology*, established a fluid, commonsense psychology that set the stage for his later philosophical works on pluralism, pragmatism, and radical empiricism. James's dedicated belief in free will and individual experience framed his memorable discussions of habit, thought, emotion, memory, and selfhood. Never afraid to challenge conventional thinking, he brought a vitality and enthusiasm to the discipline that offered a stark contrast with his contemporaries in structuralism. Before shifting from psychology to philosophy, James forged a legacy that left an enduring imprint on the discipline.

Under James's direction, G. Stanley Hall (1844–1924) earned the first doctoral degree in psychology at Harvard in 1878. Emerging from the considerable shadow that James cast over the discipline, Hall took on the role of expanding the boundaries of psychology during the heady early years of American psychology. As a founder and first president of the American Psychological Association, he established a visible organizational identity that broadened interest in psychology. A tireless worker, Hall was a prominent university administrator, the editor of multiple journals, and a prolific author who blazed new academic trails, most notably in the study of developmental psychology (Hall, 1891, 1904). His colleague John Dewey (1859–1952) was a key figure in the functionalist school of thought. Dewey argued for a process-oriented psychology that stressed the role of adaptation in human experience. Like Hall, Dewey was a pioneer in the child-study movement, a perspective that bolstered interest in the psychology of children.

In the same functionalist tradition, James Rowland Angell (1869–1949) argued that psychology should accent mental operations rather than the "stuff of experience." Hugo Munsterberg (1863–1916) was a German-American psychologist and an advocate for applied psychology, with research on forensic, clinical, and industrial psychology. Mary Whiton Calkins (1863–1930) served as the first female president of the American Psychological Association and advocated a reconciliation of functionalism with structuralism. Psychologist and educator Leta Stetter Hollingworth (1886–1939) enlarged the functionalist spirit with work on gender bias and gifted children, among other topics. Subjecting gender differences to rigorous experimental activity, her work exposed several nineteenth-century myths regarding the psychology of women.

Behaviorism

Despite the breadth and influence of the American school of functionalism, a rival school emerged that challenged the basic assumptions of a psychology built on the study of mental phenomena. E. L. Thorndike (1874–1949), a pioneer in the experimental investigation of animal behavior, advanced an influential learning theory known as connectionism. His practical work focused on behavior, and he can be considered a forerunner of behaviorism. Inspired by Russian psychologists and reflexologists, including Ivan Sechenov (1829–1905), Ivan Pavlov (1849–1936), and Vladimir Bekhterev (1857–1927), the American school of behaviorism proposed a tough new agenda for psychology. Rejecting the study of mind and consciousness as unscientific, the behaviorists demanded a discipline that focused on objective and observable behavior. At the forefront of the revolution, a brash young psychologist named John B. Watson (1878–1958) assailed the psychology of his day. In his landmark article, "Psychology as the Behaviorist Views It," Watson (1913) rejected the work of his contemporaries as sentimental and subjective. As the founder of American behaviorism, Watson placed an extreme emphasis on the environment in shaping behavior. With an unswerving belief in determinism and materialism, Watson argued that complete prediction and control of behavior could be achieved only by a psychology that found identity with the natural sciences.

Despite a chilly early reception, behaviorism gained a foothold and, in time, became the dominant system in twentieth-century American psychology. In the years following Watson, a host of diverse figures rounded out a movement of neobehaviorism. One of the most influential behaviorists, Clark L. Hull (1884–1952) advanced a mathematical-deductive approach to the study of animal and human behavior. As set forth in his classic book, *Principles of Behavior* (1943), Hull developed his theory in terms of quasi-mathematical postulates and corollaries that lent themselves to experimental procedure. Never a strident behaviorist, Edward Chase Tolman (1886–1959) emphasized the purposive nature of behavior, finding a way to combine behaviorism with disparate perspectives (such as Gestalt psychology) that gave a greater role to cognition. In doing so, Tolman's work is regarded as one of the precursors of cognitive psychology.

Arguably, B. F. Skinner (1904–1990) was the foremost behaviorist of the twentieth century. Drawing inspiration from Thorndike more than Watson, Skinner argued that scientific psychology must concern itself with the analysis of behavior rather than the study of cognition. In his seminal book, *The Behavior of Organisms*, Skinner (1938) established an experimental analysis of behavior that featured operant conditioning as the centerpiece. Though initially uninterested in the applications of operant conditioning, Skinner's later work generalized his ideas from the domain of the laboratory to the complexity of the social world.

Gestalt Psychology

Due to dissatisfaction with a perceived narrowness in the elementary dimensions of Wundt's psychology, Gestalt psychology emerged in the early twentieth century as a complex and radical psychology that stressed a broader worldview. As structuralism faded into history, the Gestalt school raged against American behaviorism. Opposing the reductionistic approaches of structuralism and behaviorism, the Gestalt psychologists insisted that the quality of the whole is radically different from the sum of its parts. As the brainchild of Max Wertheimer (1880–1943), the Gestalt movement was envisioned as a new way of thinking about human and animal psychology. Beginning with early research on apparent motion and problem solving among indigenous people, Wertheimer initiated a bold new approach to the study of perception, learning, and thinking, among other areas. Wertheimer's book, *Productive Thinking* (1982), was the culmination of a life's work: an attempt to study thinking that resulted in new ideas, breakthroughs, or insights that make a difference (Wertheimer, 1945/1982).

Wertheimer's colleague, Wolfgang Köhler (1887–1967), emerged as a rising star at the University of Berlin, a position of status that made him a visible opponent of the Nazi regime after Adolf Hitler came to power in 1933. Köhler's (1925/1976) landmark research on primate problem solving demonstrated insightful new methods for studying animal cognition in ways that challenged traditional behaviorist explanations. As the unofficial spokesman of Gestalt psychology, Köhler assimilated other sciences, especially physics, into a broad systematic approach to psychology. The most prolific of the three founding members, Kurt Koffka (1886–1941) contributed to the literature on perception and pointed toward a Gestalt model of development. Wertheimer, Köhler, and Koffka inspired Kurt Lewin (1890–1947) to extend the Gestalt vision to other subdisciplinary branches of psychology, including motivation, personality, social psychology, and conflict resolution.

A second generation of Gestalt psychologists offered refreshing new work in the tradition of their mentors, but they faced great challenges with the death grip that the Nazi party held on German science. Consequently, many principal figures in this school fled their native country and emigrated to the United States and England, bolstering interest in their work on a broader international scale.

Psychoanalysis

As the founder of psychoanalysis, Sigmund Freud (1856–1939) articulated a vision of psychology that was both a major system of psychology and a prominent method of psychotherapy. An unapologetic determinist, Freud believed that irrational unconscious motives influence the conscious mind, a troubling challenge to our cherished belief in human rationality. In classic works such as *Civilization and Its Discontents* (Freud, 1930/1961), he outlined a system that delved into a facet of the human mind that was untapped in the psychologies of his day. Aside from the clinical aspects of his work, Freud conceptualized a system of psychology that came to grips with issues relating to personality, motivation, developmental psychology, and social psychology. Despite generating a great deal of controversy along the way, the psychodynamic school became an influential force in the twentieth century, connected with many fields including literature, philosophy, art, religion, and history.

As with many of the other systems, psychoanalysis inspired devotion as well as derision. In some cases, dissent came from within as psychoanalysis became a house divided. Having once been a dedicated follower, Alfred Adler (1870–1937) broke with Freud to found a system of psychological thought known as individual psychology. Adler emphasized the importance of overcoming early feelings of inferiority. He focused on the purposive or goal-directed nature of behavior and on the capacity of the individual to identify with the goals of society at large. Although Freud had proclaimed Carl Gustav Jung (1875–1961) as his successor, the two men broke after a once-productive relationship turned volatile. As the founder of analytic psychology, Jung drew inspiration from a disparate source of disciplines, including alchemy, religion, art, mythology, and literature. Jung investigated both the personal and collective dimensions of the unconscious mind while accentuating the role that spirituality and transformation play in the human experience. As with Adler and Jung, Karen Danielsen Horney (1885–1952) initially found value in Freud's ideas before growing dissatisfied with psychoanalysis. She challenged Freud's ideas about gender development, human sexuality, neurosis, and therapy. As a result, she enlarged the domain of psychoanalysis with a more sociocultural perspective.

Psychology in the Postsystem Era

As the classic schools of psychology began to wane, new perspectives emerged in experimental and applied psychology. After World War II, an explosion of interest in clinical psychology fostered growth in the field. Humanistic psychologists argued for a broader subject matter of psychology, one that would include topics such as growth, joy, suffering, wisdom, meaning, authenticity, dignity, and peak experiences. Abraham Maslow (1908–1970) conceptualized his broad humanistic school as a third force in American psychology, alongside psychoanalysis and behaviorism. Carl R. Rogers (1902–1987) placed a radical emphasis on the person in his nondirective psychotherapy, stressing the values of empathy, congruence, and unconditional positive regard (Rogers, 1951). At the same time, an existential movement emphasized the centrality of experience, the role of freedom in human life, and the quest for authenticity in the face of all of the absurdities and forces that threaten human dignity. Later, three distinct waves of psychotherapy emerged in modern clinical psychology, giving rise to behavior therapy, cognitive therapy, and mindfulness-based treatments.

Advances in experimental psychology offered a staggering breadth of perspective as psychology became more interdisciplinary than ever before in its history. Innovations in methodology and technology invigorated several key disciplines. Cognitive science made critical inroads with an emphasis on such higher mental operations as sensation and perception, memory, learning, problem solving, language, judgment, and decision making. Drawing on advances in technology, behavioral neuroscience witnessed profound growth in research on the central nervous system and inspired development of associated areas in psychopharmacology, behavioral genetics, and psychoneuroimmunology. In less than a century-and-a-half since its formal founding, psychology has undergone unprecedented expansion that broadened the conceptual and methodological foundation of the discipline.

REFERENCES

Freud, S. (1961). Civilization and its discontents. In J. Strachey (Ed. & Trans.), *The standard edition of the complete psychological works of Sigmund Freud* (Vol. 21, pp. 55–145). London: Hogarth Press. (Original work published 1930)

Hall, G. S. (1891). The contents of children's minds on entering school. *Pedagogical Seminary, 1*, 139–173.

Hall, G. S. (1904). *Adolescence.* New York: Appleton-Century-Crofts.

Heidbreder, E. (1933). *Seven psychologies.* New York: Appleton-Century-Crofts.

Hull, C. L. (1943). *Principles of behavior.* New York: Appleton-Century-Crofts.

James, W. (1890). *The principles of psychology.* New York: Henry Holt.

Köhler, W. (1976). *The mentality of apes.* New York: Liveright. (Original work published 1925).

Rogers, C. R. (1951). *Client-centered therapy.* Boston: Houghton Mifflin.

Skinner, B. F. (1938). *The behavior of organisms: An experimental analysis.* New York: Appleton-Century-Crofts.

Watson, J. B. (1913). Psychology as the behaviorist views it. *Psychological Review, 20*, 158–177.

Wertheimer, M. (1982). *Productive thinking.* M. Wertheimer (Ed.). Chicago: University of Chicago Press. (Original work published 1945)

Wundt, W. (1919). *Elements of folk psychology* (E. L. Schaub, Trans.). New York: Macmillan.

SUGGESTED READINGS

Boring, E. G. (1950). *A history of experimental psychology* (2nd ed.). Englewood Cliffs, NJ: Prentice Hall.

King, D. B., Viney, W., & Woody, W. D. (2009). *A history of psychology: Ideas and context* (4th ed.). Boston: Allyn & Bacon.

Scarborough, E., & Furumoto, L. (1987). *Untold lives: The first generation of American women psychologists.* New York: Columbia University Press.

D. Brett King
University of Colorado at Boulder

PSYCHOLOGY OF MEN

The study of sex and gender differences in psychology has a long and distinguished history. However, a field of psychology explicitly devoted to the study of the psychology of men is a relatively recent development. Beginning as a response to the feminist critique of traditional gender roles that gained prominence in the late 1960s, the psychology of men is now an established specialization within developmental, clinical, and counseling psychology. The American Psychological Association has established a division, the Society for the Psychological Study of Men and Masculinity, devoted to this psychology of men. In addition, a number of national organizations, such as the National Organization of Men against Sexism, have sections and interest groups devoted to issues pertaining to the psychology of men.

The psychology of men has roots in the feminist analysis of traditional gender roles. Social scientists and psychologists interested in the psychology of men followed the lead of feminist researchers and studied the restrictive and detrimental effects of male gender role socialization. Some of these effects included difficulties in intimate emotional relationships, inhibitions on male–male friendships, restriction of emotional expression, excessive devotion to work and competition, drug and alcohol problems, and interpersonal violence.

In institutions of higher education, psychologists studied restrictive gender role socialization as it related to both men and women. As these researchers disseminated their findings through conferences and publications, a subarea of gender psychology devoted to the psychology of men began to develop. Psychologists working in this subarea began to build scientific support for the assertions of feminist-inspired critiques of traditional gender roles as applied to boys and men. The development and use of psychological assessment instruments to measure the negative impact of this restrictive masculine gender role socialization further enhanced the scientific credibility of the emerging field of the psychology of men.

Scholars studying the psychology of men have documented the existence of psychological stress associated with adherence to traditional masculine gender roles. Historically, traditional masculine gender roles have been defined as an overvaluing of competition and toughness, a devaluing of emotional expression, and an aversion to behaviors and attitudes associated with femininity. Research demonstrated that attempts by men to adhere to these aspects of the masculine gender role were associated with restricted emotional expression, value conflicts between occupational or vocational achievement and devotion to family, inhibitions on affection between men, and excessive preoccupations with power, competition, and control. Men who experienced conflict in these aspects of their lives also experienced increased levels of stress, anxiety, depression, physical problems, and a host of other detrimental psychological symptoms.

As academic psychologists researched aspects of strain associated with adherence to the traditional masculine gender role, practicing psychologists began to develop networks of men and women who were devoted to challenging the social problems that resulted from adherence to traditional aspects of masculine gender role socialization. At least three distinct men's movements emerged from these efforts. First, a movement called the mythopoetic men's movement, spearheaded by the poet Robert Bly, was marked by the publication of his popular book *Iron John* in 1990. This movement was devoted to supporting men as they examined the personal meaning of masculinity in their lives. This movement utilized a number of different venues to achieve its goals, including workshop formats, weekend retreats, individual psychotherapy, and at times men's counseling groups specifically dedicated to this endeavor. A second men's movement, called the men's rights movement, emerged from networks of men working together to fight what were perceived to be inequities in the judicial system. Problems that some men associated with divorce or child custody proceedings were an impetus for the advancement of the men's rights movement. Finally, the profeminist men's movement was organized to address issues of social justice that were largely based on the feminist critique of American culture. Aspects of this critique include the discrepancy in pay between men and women, violence directed toward women by men, and other aspects of oppression perceived to be a result of traditional masculine ideology and socialization.

Today, researchers in the psychology of men have extended their inquiry into specific problem areas for men, such as depression in men, violence, suicide, and men's health problems. In addition, a number of psychologists are examining why boys tend to perform poorly in school settings and why boys are more frequently diagnosed with behavior and learning problems in these settings. Research has demonstrated that over the span of a typical educational experience, boys tend to perform much more poorly than girls on a number of achievement and outcome measures.

On a more practical note, a number of clinical and counseling psychologists have been developing specific assessment and intervention methods that are geared toward helping male clients in educational, hospital, and clinic settings. Some of these methods include the use of all-male psychotherapy groups and masculine-specific counseling and therapy methods designed to reduce the stigma many men feel when they seek help for personal problems. An important benefit of such efforts may be that more men will seek help for the stresses associated with efforts to conform to the traditional masculine gender role.

SUGGESTED READINGS

Levant, R. F., & Pollack, W. S. (Eds.). (1995). *A new psychology of men*. New York: Basic Books.

Pleck, J. H. (1981). *The myth of masculinity*. Cambridge, MA: MIT Press.

SAM V. COCHRAN
University of Iowa

See also: **Gender Differences; Gender Roles; Masculinity**

PSYCHOLOGY OF WOMEN

The psychology of women is a subdiscipline of the field of psychology with the primary goal of understanding and improving the lives of girls and women through improved research, methods of practice, and dissemination of knowledge about sex and gender. The psychology of women does not encompass all theory and research about women; instead, it includes only that which is undertaken from the epistemological perspectives and principles of feminism. This area of psychology was spurred by serious limitations in psychological theory and research that date back to the inception of psychology in the late 1890s. During these early years of psychology, male pioneers in the field, such as Francis Galton and William James, held firm opinions of the temperamental and intellectual inferiority of women (Rosenberg, 1982). Along with most of the general public at the time, these early psychologists presumed that gender differences were large in magnitude, inherited, and immutable. To further illustrate misogyny within the field, women were excluded from many educational and professional opportunities in the early decades of psychology. In one striking example, Mary Whiton Calkins was denied a doctorate from Harvard even though she achieved all requirements for the degree, and she went on to have a distinguished research and teaching career.

It was in this climate of androcentric bias and misogyny that Helen Thompson Woolley studied neurology and philosophy at the University of Chicago and received her degree in 1900. Thompson Woolley recognized the deficiencies and biases inherent in psychology at the time and, in response to notions of women's mental inferiority, developed the first methodologically sound laboratory study of gender differences in mental capacity. Her findings revealed very large intrasex differences, with much smaller differences between men and women (Rosenberg, 1982). This study can be considered the first in the study of psychology of women. Thompson Woolley was a strong influence on other female psychologists at the time, and her work had some general influence; however, strong biases about women and gender differences persisted in the field for several decades. Research was designed to confirm prejudices, and when empirical findings did not fit expectations, they were ignored or distorted to fit preconceived notions (Tavris, 1992).

In response to the continued androcentric nature of psychology and other academic disciplines, and with the impetus of the second wave of the women's movement in the late 1960s and 1970s, the women's studies movement was born. This university-based movement included feminist researchers, teachers, and practitioners primarily in the disciplines of the social sciences and humanities. The first women's studies program was established in the United States in 1970, and since then, more than 700 women's studies programs have been instituted nationally, as well as others around the world (Stake, 2006). The initial aims of the women's studies movement, including the psychology of women, were to research and disseminate new knowledge about women and gender to accomplish the following: replace prevailing biases and assumptions, develop approaches to applied problems that recognize the particular issues and challenges faced by women and girls, and develop and implement pedagogy consistent with feminist principles. The women's studies movement flourished because of an influx of young women scholars who were influenced by the women's studies movement and because of strong interest among college students for more knowledge about women and gender; this had previously been missing from the college curriculum.

The characteristics of the psychology of women field, which parallel those of other women's studies disciplines in many ways, have evolved to some extent over time. A primary focus in the early years was to determine the nature, extent, and causes of differences between males and females through scientifically sound research and, thus, to debunk prevailing myths of sex differences. Maccoby and Jacklin (1974) published a highly influential review of available research on gender differences that revealed that most differences are small, do not always favor males, and just as Thompson had reported from her study three-quarters of a century earlier, intrasex differences were far greater than any intersex differences. This review was followed by a plethora of new studies that examined possible sex differences and investigated

factors that may explain them. Meta-analytic approaches have allowed a more precise and objective approach to the review process and have confirmed that, even in areas in which women and men have been assumed to be quite disparate, sex differences are generally nonexistent or small. For example, Hyde, Fennema, and Lamon's (1990) meta-analysis of mathematics performance variables revealed small differences between girls and boys, some of which favored girls.

Psychology of women scholars have focused on those topics of special interest and concern to women—topics that had been ignored by other psychology researchers. Partially because of prevailing and unsubstantiated beliefs about women and reproduction, much attention has been given to reproductive and life cycle issues. Specific topics that have been investigated include emotional and behavioral correlates of stages of the menstrual cycle, the process of menopause, and mothers' postnatal adjustment. Related topics of interest include the physical and mental health implications of marriage for women and men, as well as changes in gender differences at later life stages.

The early scholars in the field of the psychology of women were primarily middle-class and European American. These researchers and teachers focused primarily on women as a homogeneous group, failing to note the importance for many women of other identities. Far more attention has been given in recent years to the interlocking identities associated with ethnic group, social class, age, status and social role, sexual orientation, and the unique experiential implications of occupying such intersections of identity. Psychology of women scholars recognize and emphasize the diversity of women's experiences; they seek to understand how woman are affected by and cope with the multiple oppressions that stem from sexism, racism, homophobia, ageism, and other biases.

Gender attitudes have been an ongoing focus for individuals studying the psychology of women. Special efforts have been made to study attitudes about women who display behaviors that are contrary to traditional expectations (e.g., interest in a traditionally male occupation) or who occupy roles that are untraditional for women (e.g., leader). A variety of gender attitude scales have been developed over the years to investigate aspects of gender attitudes and their effects on the treatment of women (e.g., Glick & Fiske, 2001). A closely related topic of continuing interest is sexual harassment in educational and work settings. Included in this definition is a range of noxious behaviors ranging from negative statements about women to coercion for sexual favors. Recent investigations continue to reveal that these problems are widespread and carry serious costs for the girls and women who are targets of harassment (e.g., Chan, Lam, Chow, & Cheung, 2008).

Violence has become an increasingly well-researched area in the psychology of women in recent years. Unacceptable violence against women and girls has been redefined, largely through the efforts of feminist researchers and activists, to include not only stranger rape, physical domestic violence, and child abuse but also verbal domestic abuse and date and marital rape. Much current work is focused on understanding how best to prevent all types of violence against women and how to determine which women are most at risk for victimization or revictimization. For example, researchers have examined attitudes, such as myths about men's and women's sexuality, that correlate with the acceptance of sexual violence.

Another recent strong interest among psychology of women researchers has been the influence of the cultural standards for body image and size on girls and women. As the cultural ideals for females have become increasingly unobtainable for most girls and women, the incidence of body dissatisfaction, eating disorders, and unhealthy dieting has escalated. The theory of body objectification (Fredrickson & Roberts, 1997) has provided a conceptual frame for understanding the links between cultural pressures (particularly exposure to the media), the internalization of cultural standards, and negative mental health outcomes. A related issue is the increased sexualization of girls in our present-day culture, a significant concern with widespread implications for the ultimate welfare of girls and women (see APA Task Force, 2007).

Throughout the history of the psychology of women, scholars have been attentive to the social context within which gender-related behaviors are embedded. From this context-specific perspective, much of what has been interpreted to be essential, static, and natural in women and men is created by influences in the social environment. Thus, psychology of women scholars treat gender as a socially constructed phenomenon that comes about through such social mechanisms as reinforcement patterns, modeling, and proximal situational cues for traditionally gendered behavior. This perspective has evolved further for many psychology of women scholars to a full social constructivist stance that holds that the researcher's hypotheses, design of research studies, and interpretation of findings are influenced by qualities in the researcher that are themselves determined by social forces. Thus, most psychology of women scholars depart from the logical positivist tradition of psychology in recognizing the subjective nature of the scientific enterprise and the dangers of assuming ultimate truths.

Division 35 of the American Psychological Association (later renamed the Society for the Psychology of Women, SWP) was established in 1973 to provide an organization for teachers, researchers, and practitioners interested in the psychology of women. Goals of the organization include the promotion of feminist scholarship, social advocacy toward public policies that promote equality and social justice, and the empowerment of women for community, national, and global leadership. Membership is open to all who are interested in the psychology of women, including students and those who are not members of APA. More information about SPW may be obtained from the organization Web site (http://www.apa.org/divisions/div35/).

REFERENCES

American Psychological Association Task Force on the Sexualization of Girls. (2008). *Report of the APA task force on the sexualization of girls.* Retrieved June 11, 2008, from http://www.apa.org/pi/wpo/sexualization.html.

Chan, D. K., Lam, C. B., Chow, S. Y., & Cheung, S. F. (2008). Examining the job-related, psychological, and physical outcomes of workplace sexual harassment: A meta-analytic review. *Psychology of Women Quarterly, 32,* 362–376.

Fredrickson, B. L., & Roberts, T. (1997). Objectification theory: Toward understanding women's lived experiences and mental health risks. *Psychology of Women Quarterly, 21,* 173–206.

Glick, P., & Fiske, T. (2001). An ambivalent alliance: Hostile and benevolent sexism as complementary justifications for gender inequality. *American Psychologist, 56,* 109–118.

Hyde, J. S., Fennema, E., & Lamon, S. (1990). Gender differences in mathematics performance: A meta-analysis. *Psychological Bulletin, 107,* 139–155.

Maccoby, E. E., & Jacklyn, C. N. (1974). *The psychology of sex differences.* Stanford, CA: Stanford University Press.

Rosenberg, R. (1982). *Beyond separate spheres: The intellectual roots of modern feminism.* New Haven, CT: Yale University Press.

Stake, J. S. (2006). Pedagogy and student change in the women's and gender studies classroom. *Gender and Education, 18,* 199–212.

Tavris, C. (1992). *The mismeasurement of women.* New York: Simon & Schuster.

JAYNE E. STAKE
University of Missouri–St. Louis

PSYCHOMETRICS

The field of psychometrics generally considers the data from educational and psychological tests and assessments from a quantitative perspective. Such data normally emerge from test responses, although they may come from a wide variety of measurement instruments. Two divisions might be identified within psychometrics: theoretical and applied psychometrics. Psychometric theory (as portrayed by Embretson & Reise, 2000; Lord, 1980; McDonald, 1999; Nunnally, 1978) provides researchers and psychologists with mathematical models to be used in considering responses to individual test items, entire tests, and sets of tests. Applied psychometrics is the implementation of these models and their analytic procedures to test data (e.g., Thorndike, 1982).

The four primary areas of psychometric consideration are norming and equating, reliability, validity, and item analysis. There are both theoretical formulations regarding these four categories and actual procedures to be performed in estimating the usefulness of a test in a specific instance.

Norming and Equating

Both norming and equating procedures relate to developing test score reporting systems. Norming tests is part of test standardization and generally involves administering the examination to a representative sample of individuals, determining various levels of test performance, and translating the raw test scores to a common metric. There are two scoring models that are generally used in norming: linear transformations and nonlinear transformations. Linear transformations change the mean and standard deviation of the raw test scores but maintain all other aspects of the raw score distribution; the relative positions of examinees are unchanged. The purpose of linear transformations is typically to provide test results on scales with which psychologists are familiar and, hence, to increase the amount of information and meaning carried in a score. Common scales, for example, with their means and standard deviations are standard or z scores (0.00, 1.00), t scores (50, 10), IQ scales (100, 15; the Wechsler tests and the Stanford-Binet), and the College Entrance Examination scale (500, 100).

Three nonlinear transformations are common; these are normalization transformations, percentile equivalents, and developmental norms. Normalization transformations fit the test score distribution to a normal curve while maintaining the original rank-ordering of the examinees. Percentile equivalents express each score as the proportion of examinees falling at or below that test score. Developmental norms are converted scores that express test performance relative to normal development, typically as either years of age or schooling. Age equivalents, such as mental age, describe test performance in terms of behavior typical for children of various ages. Grade equivalents are commonly used on educational achievement tests and express scores in terms of performance typical of school grade. Age and grade equivalent scores are often used in educational and clinical contexts, but while they have descriptive value, they have extreme psychometric and interpretative problems. (See Anastasi & Urbina, 1997; Thorndike, 1982.)

Tests are sometimes equated when there are numerous forms of the same test and linked if the test forms are similar but not identical. Although all forms should measure the same attribute with equal precision, raw scores from different forms invariably have varying percentile equivalents. Equating brings all forms to a common scale (see Kolen & Brennan, 2004, for a comprehensive introduction). A number of basic equating strategies exist. In the first, each test form is administered to an equivalent (e.g., randomly sampled) group of examinees, and scores on the various forms are adjusted so that equal scores have equal percentile ranks (the same proportion falling at or below the score). In a costlier and more precise method, all examinees take all forms of the test, and equations are used to estimate the score equivalencies among the various forms. A third, frequently used method involves the administration of a common test or fraction of a test to all examinees. This common assessment serves as a bridging test that permits all measurements to be placed on a single scale; on many multiform examinations, a few anchor items are placed on each form to serve as the bridging test. Descriptions of these three methods are found in Dorans, Pommerich, and Holland (2007); Kolen and Brennan (2004); and Thorndike (1982). A relatively recent psychometric family of models of test scores called item response theory (IRT) models has made equating more feasible. The Rasch model is a useful and relatively simple IRT model; it permits scaling tests and test items by using methods presumably independent of the population from which the test data emerge. The Rasch model considers only the difficulty of test items; more complex IRT models include item discrimination and the chance of success without requisite knowledge (i.e., guessing). These methods are explained by Hambleton, Swaminathan, and Rogers (1991); Lord (1980); and Thorndike (1982).

Norming and equating have taken on new importance with recent events in testing, the greatly increased use of tests to make high-stakes decisions. Such tests have been required by the No Child Left Behind legislation, to help make high school graduation decisions, to be used as admissions and employment measures, and to use as certification examinations to permit entry into various occupations and professions. The determination of a passing mark for each of these examinations is a norming decision, and employing multiple forms of examinations to make these decisions indicates equating.

At the turn of the millennium, one change in standardized testing has been rapidly impacting both norming and equating: the use of computer-adaptive tests. Such tests are administered by computer, and a test taker's responses to initial questions affects the questions administered subsequently, with an aim of reducing testing time with a level of accuracy similar to that of paper-and-pencil standardized tests. The computer programs that control the administration of such tests need to make estimates of test taker ability after each response, so that an appropriate next question is administered. Many in educational and certification testing believe that the future of standardized testing involves computer administration, where the test adapts to the performance of the test taker.

Reliability

Both reliability and validity refer to the generalizability of test scores—the determination of what inferences about test scores are reasonable (Cronbach, Gleser, Nanda, & Rajaratnam, 1972). Reliability concerns inferences made about consistency of measurement. Consistency is defined by tradition as a family of relationships: temporal stability, similarity among tests proposed to be equivalent, homogeneity within a single test, and comparability of assessments made by raters. A procedure called the test–retest method is used to establish the reliability of a test by administering the test and then waiting a short period (e.g., 2 weeks) before administering the same test again to the same group. The two sets of scores are then compared to determine how similar they are. In the alternate-forms method, two parallel measures are developed, and both are administered to a sample of examinees. These methods use the correlation coefficient between the two sets of measurements as the reliability coefficient, an index that ranges from .00 to 1.00 and denotes the percentage of test variance that is reliable. Using raters essentially as parallel forms is called interrater reliability and is often used when expert judgments are needed.

Each of these procedures flows from what has been called the classical or parallel testing model of reliability (Nunnally, 1978). In this model, each test score is perceived as the sum of two independent components: true score and error. True scores may be thought of as either perfect measurement of the attribute in question, were such assessment possible, or the average of an infinite number of testings. Error is defined as randomly occurring deviations from true score. Because error is random, it neither correlates with itself nor correlates with true score. Under these conditions, it follows that when two sets of purportedly parallel measurements are correlated with one another, the resultant correlation coefficient is equal to the proportion of the individual differences resulting from the test that are due to true score differences—statistically, the ratio of true score variance to the variance of obtained scores. The classical model does not specify whether the parallel measurements may be made at the same time or how equivalent parallel measurements need to be.

An alternate model to the parallel testing model is the domain sampling model. This model requires that a test constructor must define the universe of behaviors of interest. If it were possible to measure an individual on all aspects of the universe, the resultant performance would equal that individual's universe score. Reliability is then defined as the ability of the given test to predict that universe score. This model allows psychometricians to estimate the reliability of tests under the condition that items or tests are essentially randomly selected from the population of possible items or tests. Among the reliability estimation procedures that emanate from this model are various internal consistency formulations. These procedures estimate the correlation between the test and the universe from the average correlations between items on the test. Among these formulas are coefficient alpha (for all tests) and various Kuder-Richardson formulas (for items scored correct or incorrect). Under this model, reliability is maximized by including as many items as possible and by having items that intercorrelate highly with one another.

A third model, the generalizability model (Cronbach et al., 1972) is a step beyond the domain sampling model; it assumes that one may generalize over dissimilar conditions as well as similar conditions. Thus, in the domain sampling model, a researcher may estimate the reliability between two PhD-level psychologists, whereas in the generalizability model, one could estimate the extent we may generalize from a PhD-level psychologist to a psychiatrist or a social worker. Thus, one can generalize from one set of test scores or observations to another at another time or another collected under somewhat different conditions, and so forth. Clearly, generalizability bridges the gap between reliability and validity.

Validity

Validity refers to the quality with which scores resulting from a measurement procedure provide the desired inferences. Because psychologists make a number of different kinds of inferences by using tests and measurements, there have traditionally been several kinds of validity: criterion-related, content, and construct validity. Criterion-related validity has been used to assess the ability of measurement devices to infer success on the job or in advanced education. Typically, the predictive measure is correlated with some quantified subsequent assessment of job or school success, called a criterion. The resultant correlation coefficient is called the predictive validity coefficient. Psychometricians often adjust these coefficients: when the range of criterion scores is narrow or when the criterion is unreliable, for example (see Cronbach, 1971; Thorndike, 1982). Sometimes researchers do not wait to collect criterion data; when these data are collected at essentially the same time as the predictor, the study is said to be a concurrent validity study. Furthermore, since a single instrument is often not able to predict a criterion as well as would be desired, multiple predictors are used, often with the statistical procedure of multiple regression. This procedure weights the various predictive tests to achieve maximal prediction of the criterion. A methodology has also developed to ensure that predictions from tests do not favor one group or bias another. In general, findings of such differential validity have been quite rare.

When the purpose of a test is to assess mastery of skills within some behavioral domain, content validity is often involved. The content validity of a test is typically judged by determining how well the domain has been covered. Such judgments are generally made by those who are expert in the test domain. Careful and detailed description of the domain prior to test construction and implementation of procedures to ensure adequate sampling from all aspects of the domain are critical for content validity.

In recent years, it has become accepted that construct validity subsumes predictive and content validity (Geisinger, 1992). The critical question asked with construct validity is how well a given test measures the trait(s) it is supposed to be measuring. The construct validity of a test is rarely determined by a single study; rather, it is the gradual accumulation of evidence that provides conclusions regarding construct validity. Experts may make judgments regarding the nature of the test and the relationship of test tasks to the construct. Empirical procedures, however, are normally employed. A test may be correlated with other measures that seem to measure the same attribute (evidence of convergent validity), experimental procedures that purportedly affect the trait may be implemented and their effect upon the test scores studied, or groups that would appear to differ on the attribute can be tested and their scores compared. Discriminant validity is demonstrated by low correlations in studies where tests do not correlate with variables with which they should not. Evidence from content validity and criterion-related validity research may be used as part of the evidence needed for construct validation.

One part of validity, as acknowledged by many test theorists (e.g., Messick, 1989), relates to test fairness. If a test is valid, then it should not lead to scores that differ inappropriately among groups as divided by various racial, ethnic, or sexual lines, among others. Considerable effort has been advanced over the past 25 years to help psychologists and others develop and use psychological measures fairly (Sandoval, Frisby, Geisinger, Scheunemann, & Grenier, 1998).

Item Analysis

The present discussion includes only an overview of item analysis procedures; detailed descriptions are found in McDonald (1999) and Thorndike (1982). In general, most classical item analysis procedures either (1) look at the number of examinees answering the item correctly and incorrectly, (2) correlate individual items with other variables, or (3) check items for bias. IRT analyses provide comparable information. The proportion of examinees answering an item correctly is perhaps inappropriately called the item difficulty. Selecting items that correlate highly with total test score maximizes internal consistency reliability in a test; selecting items that correlate highly with an external criterion maximizes predictive validity. A descriptive IRT analog of these correlations, known as the item characteristic curve, is a graph that plots the proportion of examinees answering a question correctly against their total test scores (or some other estimate of their ability level). For effective items, these

graphs are positively ascending lines that do not descend as ability increases. The steeper the slope, the higher the item correlated with the underlying trait. The last set of item analysis procedures presented here, those concerned with item bias, attempt to identify items that are differentially difficult for various groups and are so-called differential item functioning analyses (Cole & Moss, 1989; Holland & Wainer, 1993), indicating that the item operates differently for different groups. In other words, these procedures control for overall differences in tested ability and then search for items that are differentially difficult for minority groups. The aim is that if these items are eliminated from subsequent forms of the test, the test will be considered fair. At present, these procedures are being subjected to initial scrutiny and are of yet undetermined value.

This presentation has of necessity avoided numerical concepts, but psychometrics is a quantitative discipline, as perusing the references demonstrates. The aim of the four quantitative concepts presented here is to improve the quality of data in psychology. Item analysis procedures are generally employed in test construction and refinement with the purpose of selecting items to maximize a test's utility. The use of norms makes test scores communicate information more effectively; equating tests makes scores from varying forms of the same examination comparable. In general, the value of any psychological measuring device is defined by its validity, and the reliability of a measurement procedure limits the validity of the device. Thus, psychometrics is a discipline that employs numbers, but it is also a subdiscipline that evaluates itself quantitatively.

REFERENCES

Anastasi, A., & Urbina, S. (1997). *Psychological testing* (7th ed.). Upper Saddle River, NJ: Prentice Hall.

Cole, N. S., & Moss, P. A. (1989). Bias in test use. In R. L. Linn (Ed.), *Educational measurement* (3rd ed., pp. 201–220). New York: American Council on Education/Macmillan.

Cronbach, L. J. (1971). Test validation. In R. L. Thorndike (Ed.), *Educational measurement* (2nd ed., pp. 443–507). Washington, DC: American Council on Education.

Cronbach, L. J., Gleser, C. C., Nanda, N., & Rajaratnam, N. (1972). *The dependability of behavioral measurements*. New York: John Wiley & Sons.

Dorans, N. J., Pommerich, M., & Holland, P. W. (Eds.). (2007). *Linking and aligning scores and scales*. New York: Springer.

Embretson, S. E., & Reise, S. P. (2000). *Item response theory for psychologists*. Mahwah, NJ: Lawrence Erlbaum.

Geisinger, K. F. (1992). The metamorphosis in test validation. *Educational Psychologist, 27*, 197–222.

Hambleton, R. K., Swaminathan, H., & Rogers, H. J. (1991). *Fundamentals of item response theory*. Newbury Park, CA: Sage.

Holland, P. W., & Wainer, H. (Eds.). (1993). *Differential item functioning*. Hillsdale, NJ: Lawrence Erlbaum.

Kolen, M. J., & Brennan, R. L. (2004). *Test equating: Methods and practices* (2nd ed.). New York: Springer.

Lord, F. M. (1980). *Applications of item response theory to practical testing problems*. Hillsdale, NJ: Lawrence Erlbaum.

McDonald, R. P. (1999). *Test theory: A unified approach*. Mahwah, NJ: Lawrence Erlbaum.

Messick, S. (1989). Validity. In R. L. Linn (Ed.), *Educational measurement* (3rd ed., pp. 12–104). New York: American Council on Education/Macmillan.

Nunnally, J. C. (1978). *Psychometric theory* (2nd ed.). New York: McGraw-Hill.

Sandoval, J., Frisby, C. L., Geisinger, K. F., Scheunemann, J. D., & Grenier, J. R. (Eds.). (1998). *Test interpretation and diversity*. Washington, DC: American Psychological Association.

Thorndike, R. L. (1982). *Applied psychometrics*. Boston: Houghton Mifflin.

Kurt F. Geisinger
University of Nebraska–Lincoln

See also: Item Analysis; Reliability; Validity

PSYCHONEUROENDOCRINOLOGY

Psychoneuroendocrinology is the study of endocrine functions ultimately controlled by the brain. In turn, many brain processes underlying mood and cognition are influenced by the hormonal products of the various endocrine organs. The main endocrine functions of the body organize development and growth, reproduction, homeostasis (temperature, fluids, minerals, and energy balance), and immunity. Although endocrine dysfunctions are often produced by direct organic disorders, many endocrine disorders have been traced to abnormal brain processes. Thus, the discipline of psychoneuroendocrinology focuses on an exploration of the relationships between mind, brain, and endocrine systems. The following account briefly describes the major constituents of the neuroendocrine system and focuses on how the brain, moods, and cognition regulate, and are regulated by, hormones.

General Principles

Most vital endocrine functions in humans are directly influenced by a relatively small brain region—the hypothalamus (roughly 0.003% of the entire brain mass). The neurosecretory cells that regulate the pea-size pituitary (master) gland at the base of the brain are mostly located in the middle third of the hypothalamus. The important neuroendocrine cell groups in this region consist of the paraventricular and arcuate nuclei. Different groups of cells in these nuclei are responsible for the direct release of some hormones into the bloodstream. These hypothalamic influences are mediated by direct axonal projections through the infundibular stalk to the posterior lobe of the pituitary. They control functions such as water balance through the release of antidiuretic hormone (vasopressin) and uterine contraction and milk production and ejection in pregnant and lactating women, respectively, through the release of the hormone oxytocin.

However, the majority of hormones or releasing hormones are synthesized and released by the anterior lobe of the pituitary, through the secretion of special hypothalamic peptides termed tropic or releasing factors. Upon their secretion, these tropic factors enter capillaries at the level of the median eminence that coalesce to form portal vessels that run through the infundibular stalk and terminate in vascular sinuses in the anterior lobe of the pituitary. The range of functions associated with anterior pituitary products include maturation and growth, immunity, reproduction, pain modulation, energy, and metabolism, broadly defined. Thus, although the pituitary gland is responsible for the release of many hormones and tropic peptides acting on body tissues and end organs, it is admirably enslaved by the hypothalamus and by the negative feedback effects of the released hormones. Negative feedback inhibition is an important regulatory mechanism whereby hormone release acts at several levels, including the pituitary, hypothalamus, and even brain areas that project to the hypothalamus, to reduce its own further release and thus help reduce deviations from optimal set points that are detrimental to organisms. The hypothalamus and the brain circuits associated with its activity play a critical role in endocrine functions, and in turn, endocrine status has a significant impact on brain processes subserving affect and cognition.

Hormones, Mood, and Cognition

Most hormones play a significant role in affect and cognition. Take, for instance, cortisol, which is secreted by the adrenal cortex under the influence of the anterior pituitary peptide adrenocorticotropin hormone (ACTH). Cortisol hypersecretion, such as in Cushing's disease, produces several psychological changes ranging from hyperphagia through insomnia, euphoria, anxiety, panic, and unipolar and bipolar disorders. On the other hand, a significant number of individuals diagnosed with major depression present signs of adrenal hypertrophy and increased circulating levels of cortisol. The mechanisms hypothesized to mediate increased cortisol levels in clinically depressed patients have implicated increased activity at the level of the hypothalamus and dysregulation of brain serotonergic-containing systems. A reduction of circulating cortisol levels, observed in patients with Addison's disease (adrenal atrophy and insufficiency) is itself correlated with irritability, apprehension, mild anxiety, and inability to concentrate. Thus, low or high circulating cortisol levels produce some of the same affective problems. The mechanisms whereby low cortisol levels affect mood and other cognitive functions are ill understood. Normalization of cortisol levels usually improves the psychological profiles of these patients, and a variety of antidepressant treatments also lead to cortisol normalization in depressed patients. Learning is influenced by circulating cortisol levels, and evidence of poor memory with either too much or too little cortisol has been documented.

Similar observations are reported with thyroid hormones (T_3 and T_4), which are crucial for normal brain development and functions. Hypothyroidism during fetal life (a condition known as cretinism) produces short stature, sexual immaturity, and severe mental defects in afflicted individuals. In adulthood, hypothyroidism is often associated with depression, bipolar disorder, low energy, appetite and sleep changes, poor concentration, memory impairments, and apathy. The similarity of these symptoms to clinical depression routinely prompts clinicians to test thyroid functions to distinguish between the two conditions. The reverse interaction between affective illnesses, particularly major depression, and thyroid hypofunction, has also been documented recently. As with cortisol, hyperthyroidism (as in Graves' disease) presents with several psychiatric symptoms, including insomnia, irritability, agitation, major depression, attention-deficit disorder, paranoia, and most often, generalized anxiety disorder. Exactly how thyroid hormone dysregulation produces affective disorders, particularly major depression and rapid-cycling bipolar disorder, is mostly unknown. Lower thyroid hormone levels have been suggested to reduce β-adrenergic receptor activity and central serotonin activity, states often associated with a variety of affective disorders.

Growth hormone (GH; also known as somatotropin) dysregulation similarly has a variety of interactions with affect and cognition. Perhaps one of the most famous phenomena associated with GH hyposecretion in children is psychosocial dwarfism, a state of short stature sustained by parental abuse. GH deficiency in adults is associated with higher incidence of affective disorders, lack of energy, and impaired self-control. GH hypersecretion can also result in affective disorders, increased appetite, and loss of drive and libido, without observable changes in intelligence or memory functions. Treatments that normalize GH levels ameliorate the psychological symptoms produced by GH dysregulation. A similar picture emerges with sex hormones, which are believed to be responsible for disturbances in memory retrieval, anger, moodiness, and anxiety associated with premenstrual syndrome (PMS) in 30% of cycling women, and major depression is often associated with childbirth and menopause. Elimination of ovarian cycling in PMS, or estrogen replacement at menopause, can be effective treatments in these conditions. On the other hand, several affective illnesses, and physical and psychological stress, are well known to interfere with sexual functions in general and with their associated hormones and cycles.

Finally, this article would be incomplete without an overview of recent investigations on food intake, energy balance, and metabolic control in view of the near-epidemic levels of obesity worldwide. Obesity-associated pathologies include metabolic syndrome (of which diabetes mellitus or type II is a subcomponent), hypertension, cardiovascular disease, some cancers, and oftentimes, comorbid anxiety and depressive symptomatology. A flurry of research in this field followed the discovery of leptin in 1994 (from the Greek word *leptos*, meaning "thin"), which turned out to be the product of the *ob* gene, responsible for the grossly obese phenotype in mice (*ob/ob*) lacking this gene. Leptin was the first of several hormones shown to be synthesized and released from fat cells or adipocytes in a pulsatile manner, being entrained by the sleep-wake cycle (highest levels in late night and early morning hours) and meal timing. Blood leptin concentration is directly proportional to the amount of body fat tissue; other factors such as sex (higher in women), fat distribution (visceral vs. subcutaneous), other hormones (e.g., insulin, glucocorticoids), and immune-related cytokines (e.g. tumor necrosis factor α—TNFα, interleukin1) also influence circulating leptin levels. The release of leptin and other adipokines (adiponectin, resistin, visfatin, plasminogen activator inhibitor 1, and so on) is incompletely understood, although the circulation's nutritional and energy content, including insulin and glucose, regulate these hormones' production, storage, and release.

Once in the circulation, these hormones interact with specific receptors throughout the body, including many brain regions (especially in the hypothalamus). Caloric deprivation induced by sustained and strenuous training (competitive athletes), anorexia nervosa, and highly stressful lifestyles is readily associated with lower circulating leptin levels responsible for amenorrhea in women, low testosterone levels in men, reduced thyroid hormone levels, and increased circulating glucocorticoid levels. These abnormalities can often be improved by long-term treatment with exogenous recombinant human leptin (r-metHuLeptin). The initial high hopes that dysfunctional leptin signaling would be the main culprit in overweight and obese individuals quickly faded, however. It is now widely believed that leptin and other adipokines and gut-related peptides (ghrelins, cholecystokinin, PYY, and so on) have primarily evolved to maximize energy stores, and not so much to limit such mechanisms. Of particular relevance, leptin interacts with a number of specific cognitive and affective functions in higher brain regions (food-associated sensory processing, memory, reward, stress) that may be associated with its reported anxiolytic and antidepressive characteristics. In addition, known anatomical projections from higher brain areas, such as the amygdala and prefrontal cortex, to endocrine motor areas of the hypothalamus are likely to be responsible for overriding hypothalamic adipokine-induced satiety signals, especially in humans.

There are thus clear psychological outcomes associated with endocrine imbalances that are ameliorated with hormonal normalization in most instances. Likewise, psychiatric conditions encompassing several mood disorders have a significant impact on most endocrine functions. These observations suggest intimate two-way connections between the brain and the control of body-wide endocrine systems, which essentially remain to be clearly defined.

SUGGESTED READINGS

Akil, H., Campeau, S., Cullinan, W. E., Lechan, R. M., Toni, R., Watson, S. J., et al. (1999). Neuroendocrine systems I: Overview—Thyroid and adrenal axes. In M. J. Zigmond, F. E. Bloom, S. C. Landis, J. L. Roberts, & L. R. Squire (Eds.), *Fundamental neuroscience*. San Diego, CA: Academic Press.

Badman, M. K., & Flier, J. S. (2007). The adipocyte as an active participant in energy balance and metabolism. *Gastroenterology, 132*, 2103–2115.

Campeau, S. (2002) Psychoneuroendocrinology. In V. S. Ramachandran, (Ed.), *Encyclopedia of the human brain*. San Diego, CA: Academic Press.

Frohman, L., Cameron, J., & Wise, P. (1999). Neuroendocrine system II: Growth, reproduction, and lactation. In M. J. Zigmond, F. E. Bloom, S. C. Landis, J. L. Roberts, & L. R. Squire (Eds.), *Fundamental neuroscience*. San Diego, CA: Academic Press.

McEwen, B. S. (1994). Endocrine effects on the brain and their relationship to behavior. In G. J. Siegel, B. W. Agranoff, R. W. Albers, & P. B. Molinoff (Eds.), *Basic neurochemistry*. New York: Raven Press.

Nemeroff, C. B. (1992). *Neuroendocrinology*. Boca Raton, FL: CRC Press.

Nemeroff, C. B. (1999). *The psychiatric clinics of North America: Psychoneuroendocrinology* (Vol. 21, no. 2). Philadelphia: W. B. Saunders.

Schulkin, J. (1999). *The neuroendocrine regulation of behavior*. Cambridge, UK: Cambridge University Press.

Zheng, H., & Berthoud, H.-R. (2007). Eating for pleasure or calories. *Current Opinion in Pharmacology, 7*, 607–612.

SERGE CAMPEAU
University of Colorado at Boulder

See also: **Pituitary Gland**

PSYCHONEUROIMMUNOLOGY

Psychoneuroimmunology (PNI) can be defined as the study of adaptive interactions among the behavioral, neurological, endocrinal, and immunological systems. PNI emerged from the realization that the immune system does not operate autonomously, as had been assumed by those who had conceptualized it as a closed system. This former perspective assumed the immune system was driven by challenges from foreign substances (antigens) and was regulated by soluble products that were produced and released by immune cells (e.g., lymphokines, cytokines, monokines). Although antigens do initiate immune responses, and cytokines (such as interleukin-1) do regulate immune processes, data now demonstrate that there are bidirectional communication pathways between the immune system and the central nervous system (CNS), with each providing important regulatory control over the other (Maier, Watkins, & Fleshner, 1994).

The general function of the immune system is to identify and eliminate antigens that enter the body, that is, pathogenic microorganisms (bacteria, viruses), fungi, parasites, tumors, and toxic chemicals. It also acts as a regulatory, repair, and surveillance infrastructure that prevents its components from turning against each other and assists in tissue repair after injury.

The most important cells in the immune system are the thymus (or T) cells. They are a special type of leukocyte or white blood cell, of which there are three major categories: granulocyte cells, monocytes (called macrophages when they mature), and lymphocytes. Lymphocytes include T cells as well as bone marrow (or B) cells. B cells are responsible for the production and secretion of antibodies.

Cells involved in immunity can be grouped into two categories: innate immunity cells (including natural killer cells) and adaptive immunity cells (including T cells and antibody-secreting B cells). Natural killer (NK) cells destroy virally infected cells and certain tumors; they are also lymphocytes but are not T cells. There are two general types of T cells: Cytotoxic T cells are capable of destroying target cells (and are known as CD8+ cells); helper T cells enhance the immune response (and are known as CD4+ cells). The latter cells are the primary, but not exclusive, targets of the human immunodeficiency virus (HIV). A tumor cell can be attacked by macrophages after being covered with antibodies, or it can be killed directly by NK cells. As a result, innate immune mechanisms operate as a first line of defense against invading pathogens.

One branch of the adaptive immune system can be referred to as the antibody-generating system, which operates through the bloodstream by means of antibodies produced by B cells. When activated by an antigen, B cells produce any of five known types of antibodies; for example, type IgE tends to increase during stress and is responsible for allergic reactions (e.g., wheezing and sneezing as reactions to pollen or house dust). In general, the antibody system is directed toward infectious organisms outside cells. Other cell types, such as macrophages, present the antigen to the B cell to initiate its activities.

The CD8+ cells belong to the immune system's other branch, the cell-mediated immunity system. They tend to target infected or tumorous cells. Helper T cells facilitate the function of the killer T cells and the B cells.

All of these activities are coordinated through the production of messenger substances (e.g., cytokines, lymphokines, monokines) that are the means by which these cells communicate with each other. The array of messages that are sent may tell cells to relocate to another area of the body, to self-destruct, to proliferate (clonally expand), or to attack a foreign organism.

Immune function can require global alterations involving the entire organism as well as local processes. The CNS can be a major player in orchestrating the widespread outcomes in a coordinated fashion. Thus, the CNS must be able to exert control over some aspects of the immune response. One aspect of this activity is through the hypothalamic-pituitary-adrenal axis that results in interactions between the immune, neural, and endocrine systems.

Conversely, in order to accomplish this function, the CNS must receive information about events in the body, such as infectious agents that have penetrated the skin, pain signals, and the status of the immune processes. Hence, the immune system exerts control over the neural function, and the CNS exerts control over the immune system. These neural-immune interactions permit psychological events to enter the matrix. If neural processes regulate immune processes, then potentially they can impact behavior, emotion, and cognition. PNI studies these complex interactions.

In addition, the immune system is influenced by neuroendocrine outflow from the pituitary gland. Two pathways link the brain and the immune system: the autonomic nervous system (ANS) and the pituitary-mediated neuroendocrine outflow. Both routes provide biologically active molecules capable of interacting with cells of the immune system.

The potential interactions between neuroendocrine processes and immune processes are demonstrated by observations that immune cells activated by immunogenic stimuli are capable of producing neuropeptides (Ader, Cohen, & Felten, 1995).

A laboratory example of CNS involvement in the modulation of immunity is the classical Pavlovian conditioning of antibody-immune responses and cell-mediated immune responses. When a distinctly flavored drinking solution (the conditioned stimulus) is paired with injection of an immunosuppressive drug (the unconditioned stimulus), the subsequent antibody response is attenuated in conditioned animals reexposed to the conditioned stimulus (Ader & Cohen, 1991). Pavlov's dogs were conditioned to salivate when their caretaker appeared, even when he did not bring food. More recently, rats were given a beverage at the same time they were injected with a drug. Eventually, the rats displayed a reaction to the drug when they were given only the beverage.

In Pavlovian terms, an antigen can be thought of as an unconditioned stimulus that elicits an immune response.

These data may assist the understanding of how immune activity may decrease as a result of exposure to stimuli that are not ordinarily immunosuppressive. For example, women who had undergone a number of chemotherapy treatments of ovarian cancer displayed immunosuppression after simply returning to the hospital for additional treatment. In other words, their immune functions were suppressed when they reentered the hospital because the hospital itself had become the conditioned stimulus.

When a transplant reaction occurs, it is a result of the cell-mediated immune response. Cell-mediated immunity is also responsible for delayed types of allergy or hypersensitivity. A person sensitive to tuberculin as a result of exposure to tuberculosis will develop an area of reddening and hardness of the skin shortly after the skin injection. PNI studies also implicate psychosocial factors in the predisposition to, and the initiation and progression of, diseases involving somatization (Wickramasekera, 1998). The exact chain of psychophysiological events has not been firmly established, but changes in several components of both antibody-mediated and cell-mediated immunity have been associated with naturally occurring and experimentally induced behavioral and emotional states. For example, the degree of students' loneliness can moderate their immune reactions (Kiecolt-Glaser, 1999). Students' immune systems appear to function poorly once they experience feelings of loneliness for an extended period of time.

PNI has triggered a paradigm shift in the understanding of immunoregulatory functions. This new systems-oriented, mind–body paradigm may provide an understanding of the means by which psychosocial factors and emotional states influence development and progression of infectious autoimmune and neoplastic diseases. It may also demonstrate how behaviorally conditioned immune responses can be utilized to decrease the amount of medication needed for patients to regain or regulate homeostasis. However, most studies have measured only one measure of immunity at one point in time with a circumscribed sample. A considerable amount of research is needed to distill general principles from these specific findings.

REFERENCES

Ader, R., & Cohen, N. (1991). The influence of conditioning on immune responses. In R. Ader, D. L. Felten, & M. Cohen (Eds.), *Psychoneuroimmunology* (2nd ed., pp. 611–646). San Diego, CA: Academic Press.

Ader, R., Cohen, N., & Felten, D. (1995). Psychoneuroimmunology: Interactions between the nervous system and the immune system. *Lancet, 345*, 99–103.

Freeman, L. (2004). Psychoneuroimmunology and conditioning of immune function. In L. Freeman, *Mosby's complementary & alternative medicine: A research-based approach* (2nd ed., pp. 69–97). Philadelphia: Mosby.

Kiecolt-Glaser, J. K. (1999). Stress, personal relationships, and immune functioning: Health implications. *Brain, Behavior, and Immunity, 13*, 61–72.

Maier, S. F., Watkins, L. R., & Fleshner, M. (1994). Psychoneuroimmunology: The interface between behavior, brain, and immunity. *American Psychologist, 49*, 1004–1017.

Wickramasekera, I. (1998, Spring). Out of mind is not out of body: Somatization, the high risk model, and psychophysiological psychotherapy. *Biofeedback, 32*, pp. 8–11.

SUGGESTED READINGS

Ader, R. (2004). An expert speaks. In L. Freeman, *Mosby's complementary & alternative medicine: A research-based approach* (2nd ed., pp. 91–93). Philadelphia: Mosby.

Pert, C. (1997). *Molecules of emotion: The science behind mind-body medicine*. New York: Scribner.

STANLEY KRIPPNER
Saybrook Graduate School, San Francisco

See also: Homeostasis; Pavlovian Conditioning

PSYCHONOMIC SOCIETY

The objective of the Psychonomic Society (http://www.psychonomic.org) is to promote the communication of scientific research in psychology and allied sciences. It achieves this goal through two main mechanisms: (1) an annual meeting devoted to the presentation of scientific papers and (2) the publication of scholarly journals in a variety of domains relating to cognition.

Annual Meeting

A four-day meeting for the presentation of scientific papers is held each November and attended by approximately 2,000 researchers. The meeting features more than 900 papers and posters, selected symposia on cutting-edge themes, and a keynote address by a world-renowned research psychologist. Several satellite conferences are also held in conjunction with the annual meeting, including Comparative Cognition Society; Judgment and Decision-Making (JDM); Object, Perception, Attention, and Memory (OPAM); Society for Computers in Psychology (SCiP); and Women in Cognitive Science (WiCS). The society celebrated its 50th annual meeting in Boston in 2009.

Publications and Publication Office

Consistent with its main function of disseminating original research, the Psychonomic Society publishes six well-known journals spanning central topics in cognition: *Behavior Research Methods; Cognitive, Affective, & Behavioral Neuroscience; Learning & Behavior; Memory & Cognition; Attention, Perception, & Psychophysics;* and *Psychonomic Bulletin & Review.*

Membership

The society currently has approximately 1,850 members and 650 associate members. To be eligible for membership, a person must hold the PhD degree or equivalent and must have published significant psychological research beyond the doctoral dissertation. Candidates for membership must be nominated by a member of the society and elected by the membership committee of the governing board. These selections are made twice a year. To be eligible for associate membership, a person must hold the PhD degree or equivalent and must be nominated by a member of the society.

Governing Board, Officers, and Committees

The governing board is responsible for general supervision over the affairs of the society. It consists of 12 members of the society elected for staggered terms of six years each and, ex-officio, the secretary-treasurer, and convention manager. The governing board meets once a year at the annual meeting. There are also three standing committees: the publications committee, the membership committee, and the finance committee, each chaired by a member of the governing board. The chairperson of the governing board is elected by the members of the governing board for a single one-year term.

History

The Psychonomic Society was founded by a group of experimental psychologists during a meeting in Chicago in December 1959. The main goal was to create a society that would support open communication about psychological science with minimal structure. An interesting article about the society's inception and history can be found in a 1995 article by Dewsbury and Bolles, "The Founding of the Psychonomic Society," published in the *Psychonomic Bulletin & Review* (vol. 2, pp. 216–233).

Advocacy and Affiliations

The governing board maintains associations with organizations that seek to promote the advancement of behavioral research, serving as representatives to the Council of Scientific Society Presidents and the Federation of Behavioral, Psychological, and Cognitive Sciences. Through these associations, the society is represented in political lobbying efforts and is able to contribute to the shaping of the national scientific research agenda.

LAURA A. CARLSON
University of Notre Dame

PSYCHOONCOLOGY

The set of diseases known collectively as cancer represents the second most common cause of death in the United States. About 565,650 Americans were expected to die from cancer in 2008, accounting for 25% of deaths. An estimated 1.4 million new cases were diagnosed in 2008, with prostate and breast cancers being most frequent in men and women, respectively, followed by lung cancer, which is the most lethal, then colorectal cancers (American Cancer Society, 2008). The lifetime risk for cancer in men is 1 in 2, and in women, 1 in 3. Because of improvements in prevention and medical care, the 5-year relative survival rate for all cancers diagnosed from 1996 to 2003 has increased to 66%; in children, it has increased to 80%. Although death rates from cancer are declining, incidence rates of many cancers continue to rise. African Americans and people of low socioeconomic status have the highest rates of new cancers and cancer deaths.

Psychooncology, or psychosocial oncology, is the subfield of psychology that generally addresses the following issues: (1) the role that psychological and behavioral variables play regarding cancer risk and survival; (2) the impact of cancer on the psychological functioning of a patient, as well as on his or her family; and (3) the development and evaluation of efficacious psychosocial interventions aimed at improving the cancer patient's quality of life (Holland, 1998).

Risk Factors

Behavioral risk factors refer to various lifestyle activities that can increase the likelihood a person will develop cancer. Such factors, accounting for 75–80% of cancer cases and deaths, include tobacco use, poor nutrition, inactivity, obesity, infectious agents, certain medical treatments, overexposure to sunlight, and various cancer-causing agents. Smoking is the single most preventable cause of death, accounting for 30% of all deaths and 87% of lung cancer deaths. It increases an individual's risk for 15 different cancers, as well as other diseases. Lack of physical activity and poor nutrition cause a third of cancer deaths, making them important modifiable determinants of cancer risk for nonsmokers. The American Cancer Society (2008) suggests maintaining a healthy weight, being physically active, consuming a healthy diet, limiting alcohol consumption, and avoiding overexposure to ultraviolet radiation related to indoor and outdoor tanning. Because many cancers can be prevented by changes in lifestyle activities, one aspect of psychooncology research involves identifying ways to change such behaviors (e.g., reduce smoking, lose weight, increase exercise), as well as ways to increase the likelihood that at-risk individuals get medical checkups (e.g., breast exams) in order to allow early detection and preventive measures.

Psychological Impact of Cancer

Being diagnosed with cancer often engenders fear, anxiety, and depression. Moreover, the actual cancer treatments themselves can lead to a significant amount of psychological distress. Cancer patients often describe the various medical treatments (e.g., surgery, radiation, chemotherapy, bone marrow transplants) as worse than the disease itself. The physical side effects of treatment (e.g., scarring from surgery; loss of hair, nausea, diarrhea, and fatigue from chemotherapy and radiation) can be very taxing, and the psychological consequences can also be severe. Reactions can include uncertainty about the outcome of treatment, fear of recurrence, feelings of loss of control, sexual difficulties, embarrassment, and overall poor quality of life.

If fortunate to respond well to physical treatment, cancer survivors and their families are faced with living with the significant physical and psychological challenges often associated with suffering from a chronic disease (Nezu, Nezu, Felgoise, & Zwick, 2003). For example, a third of cancer patients experience significant distress, with frequency and severity increasing in advanced stages of the illness. Actual psychopathology rates range from 23% to 66% across cancer populations, the most prevalent being adjustment disorders with depressed or anxious mood. Major depression affects about 25% of cancer patients. Risk factors associated with depression include higher levels of physical disability, advanced stages of disease, poor premorbid coping skills, social isolation, family history of cancer and depression, personal history of depression, alcohol or other substance abuse, socioeconomic pressures, and the presence of pain. Side effects of medication and treatment are also thought to contribute to depression. Cancer survivors also report posttraumatic stress disorder symptoms, showing somatic vigilance, recurrent recollection of events, and major concerns about the future. In addition, estimates of suicide among cancer patients range from 2 to 10 times greater than the general public.

Success of coping with cancer-related distress often varies with tumor type, treatment, diagnosis, and quality of life prior to illness (Nezu, Nezu, Felgoise, & Zwick, 2003). How one copes can influence adaptation and moderate the negative impact of cancer on social, physical, and emotional functioning. An optimistic style of coping, often referred to as a fighting spirit, has been associated with positive psychological adjustment and less distress. Social problem solving is another psychosocial variable found to be important when people are attempting to manage and adapt to stressful situations, including those involved in dealing with cancer. Another psychosocial factor influencing the impact of cancer is social support, whereby a patient's perception of the quality of support available can influence that patient's sense of well-being.

Psychological Interventions for Coping with Cancer

Various psychological interventions have been developed to help cancer patients and their families cope more effectively in order to improve their overall quality of life. Such clinical interventions can help reduce patients' distress and enhance their sense of control. Cognitive behavior therapy (CBT) interventions are effective approaches that address a variety of cancer-related psychological issues, including reducing anticipatory nausea and vomiting, decreasing overall distress, and improving a patient's quality of life. For example, cognitive-behavioral stress management has been found to be highly effective in improving a breast cancer patient's ability to cope with cancer-related stressors, reduce moderate depression, improve benefit finding (i.e., the belief that cancer had made a positive contribution to one's life), and enhance one's general sense of optimism (e.g., Antoni et al., 2006). Problem-solving therapy, one form of CBT, has also been found to be highly effective in decreasing clinically high levels of depression, anxiety, and general distress among adults across cancer diagnoses (Nezu, Nezu, Felgoise, McClure, & Houts, 2003). Psychological treatments have also been developed and found to be effective for caregivers and family members of cancer survivors, both in terms of fostering their caregiver skills and in terms of ameliorating caregiver burden and distress.

A current controversy in the field of psychooncology is the ability of psychological interventions to actually have an impact on mortality, that is, improve survival rates after cancer remission. Although the literature includes a small number of studies that demonstrate that psychosocial interventions do extend the lives of cancer patients, an almost equal number failed to show this specific effect (Nezu, Nezu, Felgoise, McClure, et al., 2003). Such a discrepancy in findings may, in part, be due to methodological problems associated with the research design of such studies (see Coyne & Lepore, 2006).

REFERENCES

American Cancer Society. (2008). *Cancer facts and figures* (57th ed.). Atlanta, GA: American Cancer Society.

Antoni, M. H., Lechner, S. C., Kazi, A., Wimberly, S. R., Sifre, T., Urcuyo, K. R., et al. (2006). How stress management improves quality of life after treatment for breast cancer. *Journal of Consulting and Clinical Psychology, 74,* 1143–1152.

Coyne, J. C., & Lepore, S. J. (2006). Rebuttal: The black swan fallacy in evaluating psychological interventions for distress in cancer patients. *Annuals of Behavioral Medicine, 32,* 115–118.

Holland, J. C. (1998). *Psycho-oncology.* New York: Oxford University Press.

Nezu, A., Nezu, C., Felgoise, S., & Zwick, M. (2003). Psychosocial oncology. In A. M. Nezu, C. M. Nezu, & P. A. Geller (Eds.), *Health psychology* (pp. 267–292). New York: John Wiley & Sons.

Nezu, A. M., Nezu, C. M., Felgoise, S. H., McClure, K. S., & Houts, P. S. (2003). Project genesis: Assessing the efficacy of problem-solving therapy for distressed adult cancer patients. *Journal of Consulting and Clinical Psychology, 71,* 1036–1048.

SUGGESTED READINGS

Baum, A., & Andersen, B. L. (Eds.). (2001). *Psychosocial interventions for cancer.* Washington, DC: American Psychological Association.

Feuerstein. M. (Ed.). (2007). *Handbook of cancer survivorship.* New York: Springer.

ARTHUR M. NEZU
LAUREN M. GREENBERG
CHRISTINE MAGUTH NEZU
Drexel University

PSYCHOPATHIC PERSONALITY

Because of its important social impact, psychopathic personality (psychopathy) is one of the most studied personality disorders. Psychopathy is characterized by distinctive emotional (shallow affect, lack of remorse or shame, callousness), interpersonal (charm, grandiosity, deceitfulness, manipulativeness), and behavioral features (impulsivity, irresponsibility, norm-violating acts). Antisocial personality disorder (APD) comprises a related, but distinguishable syndrome. The diagnostic criteria for APD include extensive coverage of behavioral deviancy in childhood and adulthood but limited coverage of affective and interpersonal features.

Historic Conceptualizations

The origins of psychopathy can be traced to French physician Philippe Pinel, who applied the term *manie sans delire* ("insanity without delirium") to individuals who exhibited impulsively violent behavior while otherwise appearing sound in mind. However, modern conceptualizations derive from American psychiatrist Hervey Cleckley's classic book, *The Mask of Sanity* (1976). Based on his experiences with psychopathic hospital patients, Cleckley sought to clarify and narrow the scope of the diagnosis, which had expanded since Pinel to encompass a diverse array of conditions. Cleckley described psychopathy as a deep-rooted emotional pathology masked by an outward appearance of robust mental health. Unlike other psychiatric patients who appear obviously disturbed, psychopaths present initially as confident, personable, and psychologically well adjusted, but they reveal their underlying disturbance over time through their attitudes and actions. Cleckley identified 16 specific criteria for the disorder, consisting of

Table 1. Cleckley's (1976) 16 diagnostic criteria for psychopathy, grouped by conceptual category

Conceptual Category	Criterion Number and Label
Positive adjustment	
	1. Superficial charm and good intelligence
	2. Absence of delusions and other signs of irrational thinking
	3. Absence of "nervousness" or psychoneurotic manifestations
	14. Suicide rarely carried out
Chronic behavioral deviance	
	4. Unreliability
	7. Inadequately motivated antisocial behavior
	8. Poor judgment and failure to learn by experience
	13. Fantastic and uninviting behavior with drink and sometimes without
	15. Sex life impersonal, trivial, and poorly integrated
	16. Failure to follow any life plan
Emotional-interpersonal deficits	
	5. Untruthfulness and insincerity
	6. Lack of remorse or shame
	9. Pathologic egocentricity and incapacity for love
	10. General poverty in major affective reactions
	11. Specific loss of insight
	12. Unresponsiveness in general interpersonal relations

indicators of positive psychological adjustment, behavioral deviance, and emotional unresponsiveness and impaired social relatedness (Table 1).

Cleckley did not characterize psychopathic patients as explosively violent, predatory, or deliberately cruel. Rather, he viewed the harm they did to others as a by-product of their shallow, feckless natures. Along with ne'er-do-wells and petty criminals, Cleckley's case histories included examples of "successful psychopaths" with careers as physicians, scholars, or businessmen. In contrast, other influential writers of Cleckley's time who focused on psychopathy in criminal offenders emphasized coldness, viciousness, and exploitativeness. For example, McCord and McCord (1964) identified lovelessness (inability to form deep attachments) and guiltlessness (absence of remorse) as the essence of the disorder. Thus, Cleckley and his contemporaries differed in the emphasis they assigned to boldness (venturesomeness, emotional stability) versus meanness (predatory aggressiveness, cruelty) in conceptualizing psychopathy, while similarly emphasizing disinhibition (deficient impulse control).

Modern Conceptualizations

Psychopathy in Adult Offender Samples

Hare (2003) developed an interview-based inventory, the Psychopathy Checklist–Revised (PCL-R), for assessing psychopathy as described by Cleckley in offender samples. The PCL-R's 20 items refer extensively to criminal acts and attitudes and capture the affective-interpersonal

and behavioral deviancy features identified by Cleckley, but not the positive adjustment features. Most notably, absence of nervousness and anxiety or mood disorder symptomatology are not part of the PCL-R definition. High overall scores on the PCL-R are associated with impulsive and aggressive tendencies, low affiliation, low empathy, Machiavellianism, and persistent violent offending. This picture is more in line with the mean and disinhibited conception of criminal psychopathy advanced by Cleckley's contemporaries than with Cleckley's own portrayal of psychopathic inpatients as bold and disinhibited.

Although developed to index psychopathy as a unitary syndrome, the PCL-R nonetheless contains distinctive item subsets, or factors: an affective-interpersonal factor (divisible into affective and interpersonal facets) and an antisocial deviancy factor (divisible into impulsive-irresponsible and antisocial behavior facets). Reflecting the unitary conception of psychopathy that guided the PCL-R's development, the two factors and their constituent facets show moderate correlations with one another. Factor 1 is associated with pathological tendencies including high narcissism, low empathy, and use of instrumental aggression (Hare, 2003). Controlling for overlap with Factor 2, PCL-R Factor 1 also shows some relations with adaptive tendencies (e.g., low fearfulness, distress/anxiety, depression; Hicks & Patrick, 2006). In contrast, Factor 2 is mainly associated with deviant tendencies, including high impulsivity, general sensation seeking, and aggressiveness (in particular, reactive aggression); early and persistent antisocial deviance; and alcohol and drug problems.

Psychopathy in Adult Noncriminal Samples

The best-known measures for assessing psychopathy in noncriminal samples are self-report inventories. Most of these emphasize measurement of the antisocial deviancy (Factor 2) component of psychopathy. A notable exception is the Psychopathic Personality Inventory (PPI; see Lilienfeld & Fowler, 2006), which is designed to comprehensively index personality traits embodied in Cleckley's description. Like the PCL-R, the PPI measures psychopathy in terms of two broad factors, one (PPI-I) reflecting dominance, stress immunity, and fearlessness and the other (PPI-II) reflecting impulsivity and aggressiveness. Benning, Patrick, Blonigen, Hicks, and Iacono (2005) labeled these factors *fearless dominance* and *impulsive antisociality*.

In contrast with the PCL-R, the two factors of the PPI are uncorrelated. PPI-I can be viewed as indexing a purer, more benign expression of underlying temperamental fearlessness (termed "boldness") than Factor 1 of the PCL-R, which can be viewed as tapping "meanness" more so than boldness (Patrick, in press). Scores on PPI-I are associated with positive adjustment (e.g., higher well-being; lower anxiousness and depression), as well as tendencies toward narcissism, low empathy, and thrill seeking. Scores on PPI-II are generally indicative of deviancy, including impulsivity and aggressiveness, child and adult antisocial behavior, substance problems, high negative affect, and suicidal ideation (Benning et al., 2005).

Psychopathy in Conduct-Disordered Youth

Various inventories have been developed to assess psychopathy in children and adolescents. The most widely researched of these is the Antisocial Process Screening Device (APSD; see Frick & Marsee, 2006), which is designed for use with children age 6–13 who exhibit behavioral problems. The APSD was patterned after the PCL-R and includes 20 items that are completed by parents or teachers. Its items index two distinctive factors: a Callous-Unemotional (CU) factor reflecting emotional insensitivity and interpersonal callousness and an Impulsive/Conduct Problems (I/CP) factor reflecting impulsiveness, behavioral deviancy, and inflated self-importance. High I/CP children with low scores on the CU factor show diminished intellectual ability, high anxiety and negative emotional reactivity, and frequent reactive (but not instrumental-premeditated) aggression (Frick & Marsee, 2006). In contrast, children high in CU as well as I/CP tendencies appear intellectually normal, are attracted to activities entailing novelty and risk, score lower on anxiety and neuroticism measures, and are less reactive to distressing stimuli and learn less readily from punishment. They also exhibit high levels of both proactive and reactive aggression and engage more persistently in violent behavior across time. Thus, along with the PCL-R (and in contrast with the PPI), the APSD can be viewed as indexing meanness and disinhibition in its measurement of the psychopathy construct.

Roots of Psychopathy: Causal Factors Contributing to Disinhibition, Boldness, and Meanness

Three prominent themes are evident in the aforementioned conceptualizations of psychopathy: disinhibition, boldness, and meanness (Patrick, in press). Recent twin studies point to differing causal factors underlying the disinhibition component as compared with the boldness and meanness components. In terms of brain mechanisms, disinhibition or externalizing (reflecting poor planfulness, impaired regulation of affect, and deficient behavioral restraint) can be viewed as arising from impairments in the functioning of higher brain systems—including the prefrontal cortex and anterior cingulate cortex—that operate to guide and inhibit behavior and regulate emotional responses. As a result, high externalizing individuals operate in the present moment and fail to moderate their actions and reactions as a function of past experiences or anticipated future outcomes.

In contrast, boldness (entailing a capacity to remain calm under pressure and recover quickly from stressors, high social efficacy, and a tolerance for unfamiliarity and danger) can be conceptualized as an adaptive phenotypic expression of an underlying fearless disposition (genotype). Deviations in responsiveness of lower brain structures including the amygdala have been posited to play a role in this underlying disposition. In addition, it seems likely that other factors (e.g., superior functioning of affective-regulatory circuitry in the brain; parental influences that promote competence and mastery) also contribute to phenotypic boldness.

The third thematic construct, meanness, entails deficient empathy, disdain for and lack of close attachments with others, rebelliousness, excitement seeking, exploitativeness, and empowerment through cruelty. The external correlates of the APSD CU factor (low anxiety/neuroticism, diminished responsiveness to stressors, heightened tolerance for unfamiliarity and risk) point to low dispositional fear as one substrate for meanness. However, meanness represents a pathological expression of low fear—one involving a profound lack of social connectedness. From this perspective, factors that contribute to interpersonal detachment would be expected to shape fearlessness in the direction of meanness as opposed to boldness. Environmental influences likely to promote meanness include punitive parenting and early exposure to physical or sexual abuse. There are probably distinctive constitutional-genetic influences that contribute as well.

Successful versus Unsuccessful Psychopathy

A comparatively less studied concept is the notion of the successful psychopath, that is, an individual who possesses the core underlying disposition of a psychopath but who refrains from serious antisocial conduct (Cleckley, 1976; Lykken, 1995). Most research to date has focused on incarcerated offenders or noninstitutionalized individuals who exhibit salient antisocial-externalizing traits. The concept of psychopathy as aggressive externalizing (i.e., meanness + disinhibition) emphasized in research of this kind is likely to be less relevant to an understanding of successful psychopathy than the construct of boldness. The availability of measures such as the PPI that index the boldness component of psychopathy separately from its meanness and disinhibition components opens the door toward investigation of aspects of psychopathy that may be consistent with (or even contribute to) success as opposed to failure in society.

REFERENCES

Benning, S. D., Patrick, C. J., Blonigen, D. M., Hicks, B. M., & Iacono, W. G. (2005). Estimating facets of psychopathy from normal personality traits: A step toward community-epidemiological investigations. *Assessment, 12,* 3–18.

Cleckley, H. (1976). *The mask of sanity* (5th ed.). St. Louis, MO: Mosby. (Original edition published 1941)

Frick, P. J., & Marsee, M. A. (2006). Psychopathy and developmental pathways to antisocial behavior in youth. In C. J. Patrick (Ed.), *Handbook of psychopathy* (pp. 353–374). New York: Guilford Press.

Hare, R. D. (2003). *The Hare Psychopathy Checklist–Revised* (2nd ed.). Toronto, Ontario: Multi-Health Systems. (Original edition published 1991)

Hicks, B. M., & Patrick, C. J. (2006). Psychopathy and negative affectivity: Analyses of suppressor effects reveal distinct relations with trait anxiety, depression, fearfulness, and anger-hostility. *Journal of Abnormal Psychology, 115,* 276–287.

Lilienfeld, S. O., & Fowler, K. A. (2006). The self-report assessment of psychopathy: Problems, pitfalls, and promises. In C. J. Patrick (Ed.), *Handbook of psychopathy* (pp. 107–132). New York: Guilford Press.

Lykken, D. T. (1995). *The antisocial personalities.* Hillsdale, NJ: Lawrence Erlbaum.

McCord, W., & McCord, J. (1964). *The psychopath: An essay on the criminal mind.* Princeton, NJ: Van Nostrand.

Patrick, C. J. (in press). Conceptualizing the psychopathic personality: Disinhibited, bold, or just plain mean? In D. R. Lynam & R. T. Salekin (Eds.), *Handbook on child and adolescent psychopathy.* New York: Guilford Press.

SUGGESTED READING

Patrick, C. J. (2006). *Handbook of psychopathy.* New York: Guilford Press.

CHRISTOPHER J. PATRICK
UMA VAIDYANATHAN
University of Minnesota

See also: Antisocial Personality Disorder; Psychopathy Checklist

PSYCHOPATHOLOGY

Psychopathology is a term derived from the Greek roots *psych* (meaning "mind" or "soul"), *path* (referring to "feeling" or "suffering"), and *ology* ("the study of"). Thus, one can define the term most broadly as the study of the suffering of the mind. More specifically, psychopathology can be defined as the study of mental illness or the understanding of behaviors and experiences that may indicate mental illness or impairment.

The conceptualization of psychopathology has undergone numerous iterations through history. The concept of psychopathology began within a religious framework. In antediluvian times, most believed that abnormal behaviors were caused by evil spirits, later escalating to the belief that these individuals were possessed by demons. In turn, exorcisms and burnings at the stake were performed among many of these so-called possessed persons. For hundreds of years, these ideas were prominent, until the early 1800s, when these aberrant behaviors began to be considered manifestations of mental illness.

Several professions may be involved in some way or another with psychopathology, including, but not limited to, clinical psychologists, psychiatrists, neurologists, social workers, and nurses. Clinical psychologists focus primarily on research into the causes of mental illness, as well as research and practice of psychological treatments. Neurologists focus on the brain structures involved in mental illness. Psychiatrists focus on the neurochemistry and pharmacological treatment of mental illness, whereas nurses and social workers provide psychotherapy. Thus, many different disciplines contribute to the science and treatment of psychopathology.

The official handbook for the classification of psychopathology in the United States is the *Diagnostic and Statistical Manual of Mental Disorders* (*DSM;* American Psychiatric Association, 2000). The *DSM* uses a multiaxial system to note the primary mental disorder (Axis I), as well as broader factors that may influence symptoms and course. Other axes include personality disorders and mental retardation (Axis II), general medical conditions (Axis III), psychosocial and environmental problems (Axis IV), and global functioning (Axis V). In all, the *DSM-IV-TR* contains nearly 300 diagnostic categories, including 25 culture-bound syndromes (those likely to be present in specific regions). Thus, the *DSM* allows diagnosticians to formally classify psychopathology, aiding both treatment and research of mental illness.

For each disorder, the *DSM* provides a set of symptoms to be identified in making diagnoses. To be diagnosable, behaviors must cause distress or impairment in some way. Nearly 50% of people will experience a psychological disorder in their lifetime, with anxiety disorders (28.8%), impulse-control disorders (24.8%), and mood disorders (20.8%) having the highest lifetime prevalence (Kessler, Berglund, Demler, Jin, & Walters, 2005). Much of the research in psychopathology focuses on the causes and treatments of disorders.

Genetic and Biological Factors

Studies of the concordance of psychological disorders between family members provide information about the heritability of psychopathology, particularly when monozygotic (identical) and dizygotic (fraternal) twins are studied. Because the effects of environment and biology can be more clearly separated, adoption studies yield the most accurate evidence of etiology. A calculation of the degree of genetic transmission among family members is referred to as a heritability coefficient, with 1.0 indicating 100% heritability. Some disorders, such as schizophrenia, bipolar disorder, and autism, have heritability estimates as high as .75, whereas many other disorders have heritability estimates well below .50, such as depression and conduct disorder (cf. Kendler, 2001).

It is believed that genes increase risk for disorder by changing the functioning of brain structures and neurotransmitters. For example, depression may be related to deficits in several neurotransmitter systems—including serotonin and norepinephrine—whereas anxiety disorders may be related to GABA, norepinephrine, and serotonin functioning. Researchers in schizophrenia have also found decreased volume of various structures of the brain in those with the disorder (e.g., Suddath et al., 1990).

There are several issues related to genetic and biological findings that must be mentioned. For one, traumas may occur during brain development within the womb. In addition, dysregulation of certain biological systems has been linked to mental illness, including the cortisol system in depression (Garbutt et al., 1994). Research in the areas of genetics and biology should take these findings into account. Nonetheless, studying genetics and biology is invaluable in understanding the etiology of these disorders.

Psychological and Sociocultural Factors

Early on in the development of the field, the role of psychosocial factors was dominated by Sigmund Freud's theories of psychoanalysis, in which unconscious conflicts determined much of one's mental distress. Although some of his work is still influential in understanding psychopathology to this day, most of Freud's theories have not been supported empirically. In the mid-twentieth century, an emphasis on behaviorism, or learning theory, emerged.

Behaviorism involves the role of learning in psychopathology. Classical conditioning refers to learned associations (e.g., the pairing of a dog bite with intense fear). Operant conditioning refers to reinforcement and punishment contingencies that shape behavior (e.g., the behavior of avoiding dogs decreases anxiety and is thus reinforced). Both types of conditioning appear to influence the etiology and maintenance of psychological disorders, with particular support in understanding anxiety disorders.

Models concerning cognition and personality have also become quite prominent in understanding risk for psychological disorders. For example, Beck (1967) proposed the triad theory of depression: The self, the world, and the future are viewed in an overly negative light, contributing to both the etiology and the maintenance of depression. And in terms of personality, neuroticism, defined as a tendency to react to events with frequent and intense negative affect, tends to be higher in those at risk for developing depression and anxiety.

The effects of socioeconomic status, culture, gender, and age may all have profound influences on the expression of psychopathology. For example, twice as many women as men are afflicted with major depression, and many more men than women experience externalizing disorders such as conduct disorder and substance abuse (Kessler et al., 2005). Psychopathology may be experienced quite similarly around the world, but researchers have shown that the presentation of these disorders may vary depending on one's race and ethnicity. For example, schizophrenia is likely to have a more positive outcome in Nigeria, India, and Colombia than in the United States, perhaps because of stronger family values of caretaking (Sartorius et al., 1986). Hence, it is important to consider personal context in psychopathology.

Although both biological and psychological factors may increase vulnerability to disorders, symptoms are often triggered by stressors. Common examples of stressors include traumatic life events such as loss of employment, death of a family member, or a natural disaster. Indeed, in one study, a major stressful life event preceded the onset of a major depressive episode in 80% of participants (Hammen, Ellicott, Gitlin, & Jamison, 1989). In another study, those with a certain type of serotonin transporter gene were much more likely to develop depression following a stressful life event than those with another type of serotonin transporter gene (Caspi et al., 2003). Thus, the interaction of stress and predisposition to psychopathology—not just one factor by itself—contributes to the expression of a mental disorder.

Treatment

The treatment of mental illness has come a long way in the last 50 years. Most recently, serious efforts have been made to critically examine the efficacy of various treatments. Standards in treatment research now encourage the random assignment of participants to a treatment or control group, careful description of the diagnostic status of participants in a study, the use of a treatment manual, and the use of reliable and valid measures of outcome. These standards are not free from controversy, as some studies exclude many potential participants.

Nonetheless, findings have supported the efficacy of several treatments, with the clearest evidence in support of cognitive-behavioral treatments. In addition, recent research is focusing on beneficial factors that are common to most treatments, such as the quality of the therapist–client relationship.

Future Directions

The field of psychopathology is quite young, and there is much work to be done. Unfortunately, discrimination in employment and social avenues is still quite common. Indeed, the economic consequences of severe mental illness often sadly result in homelessness for the untreated. Thus, better understanding of mental illness and care of those experiencing disorder is needed. In addition, efforts to increase public understanding and the availability of treatment are vital.

REFERENCES

American Psychiatric Association. (2000). *Diagnostic and statistical manual of mental disorders* (4th ed., text rev.; *DSM-IV-TR*). Washington, DC: Author.

Beck, A. T. (1967). *Depression: Clinical, experimental and theoretical aspects*. New York: Harper & Row.

Caspi, A., Sugden, K., Moffitt, T. E., Taylor, A., Craig, I. W., Harrington, H., et al. (2003). Influence of life stress on depression: Moderation by a polymorphism in the 5-HTT gene. *Science, 301*(5631), 386–389.

Garbutt, J. C., Mayo, J. P., Little, K. Y., Gillette, G. M., Mason, G. A., Dew, B., et al. (1994). Dose–response studies with protirelin. *Archives of General Psychiatry, 51*, 875–883.

Hammen, C., Ellicott, A., Gitlin, M., & Jamison, K. R. (1989). Sociotropy/autonomy and vulnerability to specific life events in patients with unipolar depression and bipolar disorders. *Journal of Abnormal Psychology, 98*(2), 154–160.

Kendler, K. S. (2001). Twin studies of psychiatric illness. *Archives of General Psychiatry, 58*, 1005–1014.

Kessler, R. C., Berglund, P., Demler, O., Jin, R., & Walters, E. E. (2005). Lifetime prevalence and age-of-onset distributions of *DSM-IV* disorders in the National Comorbidity Survey replication. *Archives of General Psychiatry, 62*, 593–602.

Sartorius, N., Jablensky, A., Korten, A., Ernberg, G., Anker, M., Cooper, J. E., et al. (1986). Early manifestations and first-contact incidence of schizophrenia in different cultures: A preliminary report on the initial evaluation phase of the WHO Collaborative Study on Determinants of Outcome of Severe Mental Disorders. *Psychological Medicine, 16*, 909–928.

Suddath, R. L., Christison, G. W., Torrey, E. F., Casanova, M. F., Weinberger, D. R., et al. (1990). Anatomical abnormalities in the brains of monozygotic twins discordant for schizophrenia. *New England Journal of Medicine, 322*, 789–793.

SUGGESTED READINGS

Jamison, K. R. (1995). *An unquiet mind*. New York: Vintage Books.

Kring, A. M., Davison, G. C., Neale, J. M., & Johnson, S. L. (2007). *Abnormal psychology* (10th ed.). Hoboken, NJ: John Wiley & Sons.

Spitzer, R. L., First, M. B., Williams, J. B. W., & Gibbon, M. (1994). *DSM-IV casebook: A learning companion to the Diagnostic and Statistical Manual of Mental Disorders*. Arlington, VA: American Psychiatric Publishing.

DANIEL FULFORD
SHERI L. JOHNSON
University of Miami

See also: **Abnormality; Emotional Disturbances**

PSYCHOPATHY CHECKLIST

The Hare Psychopathy Checklist–Revised (PCL-R; Hare, 1991, 2004) is a standardized psychological test of lifetime psychopathic (antisocial) personality disorder symptoms intended for use with adult correctional offenders and forensic psychiatric patients. It has proved to be particularly useful in forensic mental health evaluations and is in wide use, both in the original English and in numerous foreign language translations. The PCL-R is administered most often as part of comprehensive assessments of risk and treatability for sentencing, civil commitment, institutional classification, and release decision making.

The PCL-R is a 20-item observer rating scale. Each item reflects a different symptom or characteristic of psychopathy. Information used to make ratings comes from personal interviews and collateral sources, including official records. Ratings are made on a 3-point scale (0 = Absent, 1 = Present to a limited extent, 2 = Present and severe). Items are omitted if insufficient information is available to rate them. Items are summed (and prorated, if necessary) to yield a total score that can range from 0 to 40. Scores of 30 and higher are generally considered diagnostic of psychopathy. Alternatively, total scores can be interpreted dimensionally, relative to norms from a variety of reference groups presented in the test manual. Items also can be summed to yield scores on two superordinate factors and four subordinate factors, called facets, although these are used primarily for research purposes.

The psychometric properties of the PCL-R have been evaluated extensively within the framework of classical test theory. Its structural reliability is good to excellent: Item adequacy, as indexed by corrected item–total correlation, is typically .40–.50; item homogeneity, as indexed by mean interitem correlation, is typically .20–.30; and internal consistency, as indexed by Cronbach's α, is typically .85–.90. It also has good to excellent interrater reliability: For items, the intraclass correlation coefficient

(ICC) is typically .60–.80; for total scores, the ICC is typically.80–.90; and for categorical diagnoses, interrater agreement, as indexed by the kappa coefficient (κ), is typically .50–.75. The test–retest reliability of the total score and diagnosis has been examined infrequently but appears to be good to excellent over periods of 1 week to 1 month and at least fair over periods of 6 months to 2 years. More recent evaluations within the framework of item response theory indicate that most PCL-R items have good discriminating power with respect to the underlying latent trait. There is some evidence of small but statistically significant metric bias across dominant cultures but no evidence of metric bias between ethnic majority versus minority groups within dominant cultures.

PCL-R total scores have good concurrent validity. Correlations with clinical diagnoses and self-report measures of psychopathy are moderate to large. With respect to predictive validity, PCL-R total scores are reliably associated with serious antisocial behavior, including violence, in both institutional and community settings. The construct-related validity of the PCL-R is supported by a large body of clinical and experimental research on the etiology, course, comorbidity, and treatment of psychopathy.

REFERENCES

Hare, R. D. (1991). *Manual for the Hare Psychopathy Checklist–Revised*. Toronto, Ontario: Multi-Health Systems.

Hare, R. D. (2003). *Manual for the Hare Psychopathy Checklist–Revised* (2nd ed.). Toronto, Ontario: Multi-Health Systems.

Patrick, C. J. (Ed.). (2006). *Handbook of psychopathy*. New York: Guilford Press.

STEPHEN D. HART
Simon Fraser University, Canada

See also: **Antisocial Personality Disorder; Psychopathic Personality**

PSYCHOPHARMACOLOGY

Psychopharmacology, from the Greek *psyche* meaning "soul," *pharmakon* meaning "drug," and *logos* meaning "knowledge," is the study of drugs that affect mood, cognition, and behavior. The field encompasses a range of topics including drug composition, properties, effects, interactions, toxicity, and therapeutic application (Stahl & Muntner, 2008). Two fundamental divisions of basic research in psychopharmacology are pharmacokinetics, what the body does to medication, and pharmacodynamics, what medication does to the body (Tozer & Rowland, 2006). Understanding these actions and the functions controlled by the affected neurotransmitter systems has advanced the field of psychopharmacotherapy, the clinical application of psychopharmacology for the treatment of mental and emotional problems (Janicak, Davis, Preskorn, Ayd, & Pavuluri, 2006).

Pharmacokinetic studies include processes involved in the absorption, distribution, metabolism, and excretion of drugs from the body. Absorption is the process through which a substance is taken into the body and made bioavailable to its tissues and organs. Distribution refers to the process through which the drug is carried through the bloodstream to bodily tissues and organs. Metabolism is the process through which the initial parent compound is broken down into metabolites, primarily through the action of liver enzymes. Excretion refers to the removal of compounds and their metabolites from the body through, for example, urine, feces, and exhalation.

Pharmacodynamic studies have investigated the biochemical and physiological effects of drugs on the body, generally, and the nervous system, specifically. These studies explore mechanisms of action and the relationship between a drug's concentration and its effects. Advances in the understanding of neurotransmission (i.e., how nerve cells communicate with each other) have facilitated growth in the understanding of how drugs affect thoughts, feelings, and actions. Neurotransmitters that have been studied include acetylcholine (voluntary movement of the skeletal muscles), norepinephrine (wakefulness or arousal), dopamine (motivation, desire, and pleasure), serotonin (memory, emotion, sleep and wakefulness), and GABA (inhibition of motor neurons). Receptor binding studies, which investigate the processes and effects of drug binding to nerve cell receptors, have found that upon binding, drugs may mimic normal action (agonist), block normal action (antagonist), or produce an action opposite the normal action (inverse agonist). Studies of toxicity have increased the understanding of the degree to which drugs are able to produce illness or damage to an organism.

In the United States, clinical investigations of a previously untested drug are generally divided into three phases. Phase 1 studies involve the initial introduction of a new investigational drug into humans. These studies are usually conducted with fewer than 100 healthy volunteer participants. They are designed to determine the metabolic and pharmacological actions of the drug in humans, any side effects associated with increasing doses, and if possible, early evidence of efficacy. Phase 2 studies include initial controlled clinical trials conducted to obtain preliminary data on the efficacy of the drug for a particular indication or indications in patients with the disease or condition. This phase of testing also helps determine the common short-term side effects and risks associated with the drug. Phase 2 studies typically involve several hundred people who meet criteria for the disorder being targeted. Phase 3 studies are intended to gather all additional information on safety and effectiveness of the drug to evaluate its overall benefit–risk profile. Phase 3 studies should also provide an adequate basis for extrapolating the results to the general population and transmitting that information to the physician through labeling. Phase 3 studies usually include several hundred to several thousand patient-participants.

Through this investigational process, several classes of medications have been identified and approved for the treatment of specific mental disorders. For example, drugs used to treat clinically distressing or disabling fears and anxieties include benzodiazepines, selective serotonin reuptake inhibitors (SSRIs), and serotonin-norepinephrine reuptake inhibitors (SNRIs) and have been approved for use in generalized anxiety disorder, panic disorder, obsessive-compulsive disorder, posttraumatic stress disorder, and social anxiety disorder. Antidepressant drugs such as SSRIs, SNRIs, tricyclics, and monoamine oxidase inhibitors (MAO inhibitors) are used to treat features of depression such as sadness, loss of interest, sleep or appetite disturbance, and suicidality. Atypical and conventional antipsychotics are used to treat severe mental disorders that typically include delusions, hallucinations, or disorganized thought processes, such as mania, schizophrenia, and depression with psychotic features.

In using medications to treat mental disorders, prescribing psychopharmacotherapists invoke knowledge from multiple disciplines, including basic neuroanatomy and neurophysiology, physiology, general clinical medicine, psychiatric diagnostics, and general pharmacology. Although psychiatrists are specialist physicians licensed to practice psychopharmacotherapy, other medical doctors and psychiatric advanced practice nurses also have prescription privileges. Recently, psychologists have sought prescription privileges. Although approval for those privileges has been legislated in some states, the effort has been met with active resistance from physician groups and remains controversial even among psychologists (see Lavoie & Barone, 2006, for a review).

A major focus of current work in applied psychopharmacology is improving the selectivity of pharmacological agents, thereby reducing side effects and potentially increasing efficacy. The promise of identifying receptor subtype-specific drugs and other specific agents is growing with advances in the field of pharmacogenetics (Weber, 2008). Pharmacogenetics explores the use of molecular genetics in predicting the likelihood of an individual's response and risk for toxicity to medications prior to their being taken by an individual. Recent advances in the cloning, sequencing, and expression of genes that encode receptors for neurotransmitters have permitted the identification of novel receptor subtypes that were undetected by traditional pharmacological approaches. For example, it is now possible, through genetic manipulation, to knock out

certain receptor or receptor systems to study the effects of these or other related receptor systems. Molecular modeling holds the promise of identifying precise drug-binding sites that would allow the development of new compounds tailored to these sites.

REFERENCES

Janicak, P. G., Davis, J. M., Preskorn, S. H., Ayd, F. J., & Pavuluri, M. N. (2006). *Principles and practice of psychopharmacotherapy* (4th ed.). Baltimore: Williams & Wilkins.

Lavoie, K. L., & Barone, S. (2006). Prescription privileges for psychologists: A comprehensive review and critical analysis of current issues and controversies. *CNS Drugs, 20*(1), 51–66.

Stahl, S. M., & Muntner, N. (2008). *Stahl's essential psychopharmacology: Neuroscientific basis and practical applications* (3rd ed.). New York: Cambridge University Press.

Tozer, T. N., & Rowland, M. (2006). *Introduction to pharmacokinetics and pharmacodynamics: The quantitative basis of drug therapy.* Philadelphia: Lippincott Williams & Wilkins.

Weber, W. (2008). *Pharmacogenetics.* New York: Oxford University Press.

SUGGESTED READINGS

Meyer, J. S., & Quenzer, L. F. (2005). *Psychopharmacology: Drugs, the brain, and behavior.* Sunderland, MA: Sinaeur Associates.

Schatzberg, A. F., & Nemeroff, C. B. (2004). *The American psychiatric publishing textbook of psychopharmacology* (3rd ed.). Washington, DC: American Psychiatric Publishing.

Timothy J. Bruce
Peter Alahi
*University of Illinois College of Medicine,
Peoria, IL*

See also: **Prescription Privileges**

PSYCHOPHYSICS

Psychophysics is the quantitative study of the relation between stimulus and sensation or sensory response. As such, it is concerned with the following questions: (1) How much stimulation is required to produce a sensation or sensory response? (2) How much must a stimulus be changed for the change to be detected? (3) In what way or ways must a stimulus be changed to be perceptually equivalent to another? (4) How does the sensation or sensory response change with changes in stimulus magnitudes? Answers to these questions (among others) are provided by psychophysical methods. These consist of the three classical methods—limits, adjustment, and constant stimuli—that were advanced, but not originated, by Gustav T. Fechner

(1801–1887) for use in determining thresholds, for numerous suprathreshold psychophysical scaling methods used for deriving measures of sensation magnitude, and for signal detection theory methods used in providing measures of basic sensory sensitivity, minimally contaminated by motivational and attitudinal biases. Although employed primarily with human subjects, several of the psychophysical methods have been adapted for studying nonhuman sensitivity (Stebbins, 1970).

Classical Psychophysics

"By psychophysics," wrote Gustav T. Fechner (1966/1860) in his *Elements of Psychophysics,* "I mean a theory which, although ancient as a problem, is new here insofar as its formulation and treatment are concerned; in short, it is an exact theory of the relation of body and mind." Specifically, Fechner attempted to devise a precise and quantitative way of measuring the mind by providing a measure of sensation magnitude. The idea that strong stimuli generate strong sensations and weak stimuli generate weak sensations was not new.

The task was to determine how strong the corresponding sensation was for a given stimulus. Quantitative attempts to do this date back at least to the time of the Greek astronomer Hipparchus of Nicaea (ca. 190–ca. 120 B.C.E.), who invented the stellar magnitude scale that categorized stars into six categories from faintest (sixth magnitude) to brightest (first magnitude). This scale was subsequently found to be approximated by a logarithmic function and consequently was redefined as a logarithmic scale by the British astronomer N. R. Pogson (1829–1891). The concept of a faintest visible star suggests that there may be even fainter and invisible stars. Correspondingly, other stimulus dimensions could be divided into perceptible and imperceptible parts. The concept of such a division was incorporated into psychology by Johann Friedrich Herbart (1776–1841) and was influential in Fechner's analysis. But once into consciousness, how intense is the resulting sensation? This is the basic question of psychophysics. Fechner proposed one answer: $R = k \log (I/I_0)$. The sensation magnitude (R) in Fechner's law varies directly with the logarithm of the stimulus intensity-to-threshold (I/I_0) ratio. An alternative formulation was proposed by the Belgian physicist J. A. F. Plateau (1801–1883), who arrived at a power function to describe the sensation of brightness. This formulation has been advanced for other senses as well as vision by S. S. Stevens (1906–1973) in a large number of experiments and theoretical articles that are summarized in his published *Psychophysics: Introduction to Its Perceptual, Neural, and Social Prospects* (Stevens, 1975). The general equation for Stevens's power function is $R = cI^n$, where the sensation magnitude (R) varies directly with the stimulus magnitude (I) raised to a power (n). The value of n depends upon which sense is being stimulated but is considered to be relatively constant over time and across (normal) observers. The constant (c) in the equation is determined by the measurement units used.

These two theoretical formulations—Fechner's law and Stevens's law—describe differently the way the sensation magnitude, R, changes with stimulus intensity. Although both state that R increases monotonically with stimulus intensity, different predictions are made about the amount of the increase. Much experimental work has been done using numerous psychophysical methods in an attempt to determine which fits the data better. For example, by using the method of magnitude estimation (which has the observer assign numbers proportional to the perceived stimulus magnitudes), results consistent with Fechner's law would appear as a line when graphed in semilogarithmic coordinates, whereas those consistent with Stevens's law would be a line in log-log coordinates. Findings have largely supported Stevens's law over Fechner's law, particularly for power functions for which the exponent is 1.0 or larger (e.g., length, duration, electric shock) and for which the predicted results clearly diverge. In those cases for which the exponent is small (e.g., brightness of an extended source or loudness of a sound), data variability may mask the smaller difference in predictions made by the two laws.

Signal Detection Theory

Motivation, expectation, and attitude are biases possessed by the observer in psychophysical threshold determinations. On trials in which no stimulus is presented (catch trials), yes responses occur (indicating perception of a nonexistent stimulus). This circumstance in signal detection theory (SDT) is called a false alarm. Correct detection of the stimulus (responding with yes when the stimulus is present) is termed a hit. Changes in motivation, expectation, or attitude can increase the hit rate, but at the expense of elevating the false alarm rate. Classical psychophysics attempted to keep the false alarm rate low so that false alarms could safely be ignored in threshold determinations. Signal detection theory gives equal consideration to both hit and false alarm rates in determining an alternative index of sensitivity, which is designated d'. The details for computing d' depend upon the SDT procedure used, and alternative sensitivity indices are used (e.g., percent correct). The motivational, expectancy, and attitudinal biases are collectively treated as the observer's criterion, which is estimated from the false alarm rate (Green & Swets, 1966). The criterion can be manipulated by changing the proportion of signal trials (and so informing the observer), by instructing the observer to be more lenient or strict, or by changing the payoffs for different decisions. When data are plotted with the hit rate along the ordinate and the false alarm rate along the abscissa, different levels for the observer's criterion yield different data points along what is called a receiver operating characteristic (ROC) curve. Different ROC curves are generated by different signal levels, but all points on the same ROC curve represent the same level of detectability. Thus sensory and nonsensory factors can be separately identified.

Applications

Psychophysical theory and methods have found application not only in the analysis of basic sensitivity to stimuli but also in screening for sensory deficits (where an individual's threshold is compared with known normal values), in the design of equipment and signaling devices in engineering psychology, in the study of memory by using signal detection techniques, and in the comparative evaluation of medical imaging and clinical diagnostic tests (Swets, 1996).

REFERENCES

Fechner, G. T. (1966). *Elements of psychophysics*. D. H. Howes & E. G. Boring (Eds.); H. E. Adler (Trans.) New York: Holt, Rinehart and Winston. (Original work published 1860).

Green, D. M., & Swets, J. A. (1966). *Signal detection theory and psychophysics*. New York: John Wiley & Sons.

Stebbins, W. C. (Ed.). (1970). *Animal psychophysics: The design and conduct of sensory experiments*. New York: Appleton-Century-Crofts.

Stevens, S. S. (1975). *Psychophysics: Introduction to its perceptual, neural, and social prospects*. New York: John Wiley & Sons.

Swets, J. A. (1996). *Signal detection theory and ROC analysis in psychology and diagnostics: Collected papers*. Mahwah, NJ: Lawrence Erlbaum.

SUGGESTED READINGS

Baird, J. C. (1997). *Sensation and judgment: Complementarity theory of psychophysics*. Mahwah, NJ: Lawrence Erlbaum.

Macmillan, N. A., & Creelman, C. D. (2005). *Detection theory: A user's guide* (2nd ed.). Mahwah, NJ: Lawrence Erlbaum.

Marks, L. E., & Gescheider, G. A. (2002). Psychophysical scaling. In H. Pashler (Ed. in Chief) & J. Wixted (Vol. Ed.), *Stevens' handbook of experimental psychology: Vol. 4. Methodology in experimental psychology* (pp. 91–138). New York: John Wiley & Sons.

GEORGE H. ROBINSON
University of Alabama

PSYCHOPHYSIOLOGY

Psychophysiology, the study of the interaction of psychological and physiological variables, is relatively new as a separate discipline. The formal development of psychophysiology began in the 1950s, when a group composed mainly of psychologists met informally under the leadership of R. C. Davis. In 1960 this group organized the Society for Psychophysiological Research, with Chester Darrow as the first president. Research communications among this group were initiated in 1955, when Al Ax began a newsletter dealing with research and instrumentation in psychophysiology. In 1964 this newsletter developed into the journal *Psychophysiology,* with Ax as the editor, and became the official publication of the Society for Psychophysiological Research. However, the subject matter of psychophysiology—the interaction of mind and body—has been studied for centuries by people trained as philosophers, physicists, physicians, physiologists, and, most recently, psychologists.

John Stern (1995) defined the work of psychophysiology as " ... any research in which the dependent variable is a physiological measure and the independent variable a behavioral one." For example, if subjects are shown pictures, some of landscapes and some of car accident scenes, and the subjects' heart rates are recorded, we have an example of a psychophysiological experiment according to Stern's definition. The dependent variable is heart rate and the independent variable is type of slide, landscape, or car accident scene. This study would exemplify the typical psychophysiological experiment from the 1960s and 1970s in which something was done to subjects and their peripheral physiological responses were recorded. Rather than viewing pictures, the subject might have been solving problems, experiencing an embarrassing situation or provocative motion, or watching a radar screen for signs of enemy planes. Rather than heart rate, the peripheral physiological response recorded might have been sweating; a change in blood pressure, muscle potentials, or cortisol levels in saliva; a change in the size of the pupil of the eye; alterations in EEG activity, respiration, stomach motility, or penis size; or any of several other bodily changes.

Stern's definition of psychophysiology is not wrong; but with the passage of time it has become too limiting. The type of research he was defining, as just described, examined the physiological changes that accompanied certain psychological or behavioral manipulations. More recent experiments conducted by psychophysiologists show that it is equally tenable to manipulate physiological variables and examine behavioral changes. In a study typical of this type of research, the heart rate of subjects would be modified by biofeedback and their ability to withstand pain measured. The dependent variable in this case is a behavioral one: the indication of how much pain the person can tolerate. The independent variable is a physiological one: the person's heart rate.

The other large change in the nature of psychophysiological research has been the shift in emphasis from the recording of peripheral, mostly autonomic nervous system measures, to recording central nervous system activity of humans, made possible by the availability of brain-imaging equipment. This change in emphasis can be seen clearly if one compares the table of contents of a 1964 issue of the journal *Psychophysiology*, where most articles describe changes in autonomic activity, and a recent issue. The table of contents of the March 2008 issue of the journal indicates that 13 of the 15 articles describe changes in brain activity, whereas only one describes a study that measures autonomic activity.

Psychophysiologists are not the only group of behavioral scientists who study the relationship of physiological and psychological variables. Psychophysiologists are a subset of a larger group of behavioral scientists who were referred to as physiological psychologists in the past and are now referred to as biological psychologists, psychobiologists, or behavioral neuroscientists. Other biological psychologists usually study the effects of their manipulation of the brain or other parts of the nervous system on some aspect of behavior. The independent variable might be destruction of a part of the brain, while the dependent variable might be eating behavior. Obviously such research must be conducted on nonhuman animals and only rarely on human beings. Most psychophysiologists, on the other hand, study the responses of humans rather than of nonhuman animals and, therefore, must limit their methods of data collection to the surface recording of bioelectric signals and/or brain imaging techniques. Harmless electrodes are attached to the skin over the organ of interest or noninvasive brain imaging techniques are used. The techniques of psychophysiology have the advantage of not greatly interfering with normal behavior.

Today commercially available equipment for conducting psychophysiological research is excellent and extremely reliable. With less emphasis on required electronic skills, the psychophysiologist has more time to devote to theoretical and empirical work related to the interaction of psychological and physiological factors.

REFERENCE

Stern, J. A. (1964). Towards a definition of psychophysiology. *Psychophysiology, 1*, 90–91.

SUGGESTED READINGS

Andreassi, J. L. (2006). *Psychophysiology: Human behavior and physiological response* (5th ed.). Hillsdale, NJ: Lawrence Erlbaum.

Cacioppo, J. T., Tassinary, L. G., & Berntson, G. G. (Eds.). (2007). *Handbook of psychophysiology* (3rd ed.). Cambridge, UK: Cambridge University Press.

Hugdahl, K. (1995). *Psychophysiology: The mind-body perspective*. Cambridge, MA: Harvard University Press.

Stern, R. M., Ray, W. J., & Quigley, K.S. (2001). *Psychophysiological recording* (2nd ed.). New York: Oxford University Press.

ROBERT M. STERN
Pennsylvania State University

PSYCHOSEXUAL STAGES

In Sigmund Freud's (1938) personality theory, development is described in terms of stages defined by the specific expression of sexual, or libidinal, urges. Those areas of the body—the erogenous zones—that give rise to libidinal pleasure at specific ages are identified as the focus of each developmental stage. Thus the pleasure derived from sucking liquids and mouthing foods is the focus of the first developmental period, the oral stage. The satisfaction surrounding the retaining and expelling of feces defines the second, the anal stage. The phallic stage refers to the period in which the young child begins to explore and derive pleasure from the genitals. These three stages, called the pregenital stages, span, respectively, the first year of life, the second 2 years, and the years from 3 to 5, roughly.

The pregenital stages are followed by a period of supposed psychosexual quiescence, the latency period, which lasts until the onset of puberty. Puberty, however, brings with it a resurgence of the pregenital urges, which now focus specifically on the pleasures deriving from the genital organs; thus the name of this final developmental period is the genital stage.

Libidinal urges in Freudian theory are not equatable with genital sexuality. For example, three of the psychosexual stages are "pregenital." The term *libido* is meant to define a broad concept of mental sexual energy occurring even in infancy. Nor do the stages refer only to male sexuality, despite the masculine language. For example, the phallic stage refers to the last pregenital stage of both sexes.

Oral Stage. The oral stage of development is characterized by a need for nurturance and by pleasure derived primarily from activities of the mouth and lips, such as the sucking, mouthing, and swallowing of food, as well as, later, the biting and chewing of food. These early gratifications are said to be the precursors of the development of later character traits. Thus, the two main sources of oral pleasure, oral incorporation and biting (seen as aggressive), may be the prototypes for later habits and personality traits. Oral incorporation as a predominant trait may lead to the acquisition of material things and acquisitiveness in personal relationships. An oral aggressive style may include such behavior traits as biting sarcasm, chewing out an opponent, and spewing out an invective. Dependency and need for approval are seen as main components of the oral character. Some evidence for this relationship was established by Masling, Weiss, and Rothschild (1968), who found that conforming college students gave significantly more oral-dependent responses on the Rorschach test than less conforming subjects.

Anal Stage. The anal stage extends approximately from 1 year of age to 3, when bowel and bladder control is a primary task and the pleasure and pain derived from expelling and retaining feces are the main libidinal outlet.

The toddler in the anal period is growing in independence and self-assertion. Freud saw the events surrounding the task of toilet training as crucial for later character formation. A child who is harshly trained and severely punished for accidents before acquiring control may express rage by defecating at will at inappropriate times or by being selfish and stingy (anal retentive). Conversely, the child who is rewarded and praised for control efforts becomes the generous (anal expulsive) and often creative individual. Freud may well have been reacting to the fact that in his day, children were toilet trained at a young age, even as young as 6 months. Salkind (2004, p. 127) speculates that Freudian theory (as well as the invention of the washing machine) may have led to less strict parenting practices in the twentieth century.

Phallic Stage. Between 3 and 5 years of age, the child begins more active body exploration. The locus of erotic pleasure shifts from the anus to the genitals as the young child discovers the pleasurable effects of masturbation. One of the main tenets of Freudian theory, the Oedipus complex, has its origins in this stage. Named for the mythical Greek king of Thebes who killed his father and married his mother, the Oedipus complex refers to the child's incestuous desire for the opposite-sex parent. In the boy, the simultaneous pleasure from autoerotic activity, coupled with a desire for the mother and a rivalry with his father, generates anger in his father, which the boy perceives as a threat. Since the erotic pleasure emanates from the genitals, the boy assumes that the father may destroy them. Freud called this perceived threat castration anxiety.

The resolution of the Oedipus complex in girls is not so clear in Freudian theory. Since castration to the girl appears to be a fait accompli, she blames her mother, whom she sees as sharing her plight, and envies the male for his organ and favored position and power. Freud's term for this condition was penis envy. The girl gradually gives up her attachment to her father and begins to identify with her mother. The imbalance between these two aspects of the phallic stage, castration anxiety for boys and penis envy for girls, has led some to criticize Freud's theory as sexist (Salkind, 2004, pp. 128–129). Notice that even the term used to designate this stage—that is, *phallic,* the adjectival form of *phallus,* another word for penis—is entirely masculine.

Genital Stage. After a period of psychosexual quiescence, termed latency, puberty brings with it a resurgence of the phallic strivings and more realistic capabilities for their expression. Once again, masturbation becomes a source of erotic satisfaction, and appears so nearly universal and urgent that Freud called this adolescent impulse the onanism of necessity. Armed with full adult genitals and sexual drives, the growing adolescent shifts his or her affection from parents to peers, first of the same sex (a brief homosexual phase, just after puberty), and then of the opposite sex. In the fully integrated adult, the psychosexual urges most often find expression in activity with an opposite-sex partner of roughly the same age. More important, these urges no longer are purely narcissistic, as they were in the pregenital stages. The psychosexual urges now extend and generalize to altruism, friendship, sharing, and loving of a more adult nature.

REFERENCES

Asch, S. E. (1956). Studies of independence and conformity: I. A minority of one against a unanimous majority. *Psychological Monographs, 70*(9, Whole No. 416), 1–70.

Freud, S. (1969/1938/1935/1920). *A general introduction to psychoanalysis.* New York: Pocket Books.

Masling, J., Weiss, L., & Rothschild, B. (1968). Relationships of oral imagery to yielding behavior and birth order. *Journal of Consulting and Clinical Psychology, 32,* 89–91.

Salkind, N. (2004). *An introduction to theories of human development.* Thousand Oaks, CA: Sage.

JOHN PAUL McKINNEY
Michigan State University

See also: **Child Psychology; Psychoanalytic Theories**

PSYCHOSOMATIC DISORDERS (See Somatoform Disorders)

PSYCHOSTIMULANT TREATMENT FOR CHILDREN

Psychostimulants are the most widely used and efficacious treatments currently available for children with Attention-Deficit/Hyperactivity Disorder (ADHD). Recent estimates by the Center for Disease Control indicate that 2.5 of the 4.4 million children with ADHD residing in the United States between 4 and 17 years old are prescribed medication, and in most cases, are given one of the available psychostimulants. Table 1 lists available psychostimulant formulae according to their release format (extended, intermediate, immediate), and the typical dosing schedule, onset of effect, and peak/duration of behavioral effects for each formula.

An estimated 50–96% of children following a daily psychostimulant regimen evidence positive treatment effects across a wide breadth of domains. These include classroom attention and academic performance; parent/teacher ratings of social deportment; performance on a wide range of neurocognitive, vigilance, and memory tests; peer relationships/interpersonal behavior; and extracurricular activities (for a review, see Rapport & Kelly, 1991; Rapport, Kofler, Alderson, & Raiker, 2008). Treatment

Table 1. Prescription Psychostimulants for ADHD

	Generic Name	Brand Name	Dosing Schedule	Onset of Action	Peak behavioral effect	Duration of behavioral effect
Extended Release	Mixed Salts of Amphetamine	Adderall XR	q A.M.	60–120 minutes	Bimodal	10–12 hours
	Dexmethylphenidate Hydrochloride	Focalin XR	q A.M.	60 minutes	Bimodal	6–8 hours
	Methylphenidate Hydrochloride	Concerta	q A.M.	30–120 minutes	Bimodal	12 hours
	Lisdexamfetamine Dimesylate	Vyvanse	q A.M.	NA	NA	12 hours
	Methamphetamine Hydrochloride	Desoxyn (also in IR)	q A.M. – b.i.d	NA	NA	NA
	Methylphenidate Transdermal System	Daytrana	q A.M.	60–120 minutes	NA	12 hours
Intermediate Release	Methylphenidate Hydrochloride	Metadate CD	q A.M.	30–120 minutes	Bimodal	6–8 hours
		Metadate ER	q A.M.	60–90 minutes	5 hours	4–8 hours
		Ritalin SR	b.i.d.	60–90 minutes	5 hours	4–8 hours
		Ritalin LA	q A.M.	30–120 minutes	Bimodal	6–8 hours
	Dextroamphetamine	Dexedrine Spansule	b.i.d.	60–90 minutes	8 hours	6–8 hours
Immediate Release	Methylphenidate	Ritalin	b.i.d. to t.i.d.	20–60 minutes	2 hours	3–6 hours
		Methylin	b.i.d. to t.i.d.	20–60 minutes	2 hours	3–6 hours
	Dexmethylphenidate Hydrochloride	Focalin	b.i.d. to t.i.d.	20–60 minutes	2 hours	4 hours
	Mixed Salts of Amphetamine	Adderall	b.i.d. to t.i.d.	30–60 minutes	1–2 hours	4–6 hours
	Dextroamphetamine	Dextrostat	b.i.d. to t.i.d.	20–60 minutes	2 hours	4–6 hours
		Dexedrine	b.i.d. to t.i.d.	20–60 minutes	3 hours	4–6 hours

q A.M.= once daily in the morning; b.i.d = twice a day; t.i.d = three times a day; IR = immediate release.

response rates vary considerably among research studies and depend on what constitutes a positive response and on the outcome variables used to gauge effectiveness. For example, 94% of children with ADHD show significantly improved classroom deportment, whereas only 53% evidence improved academic performance based on statistically derived normative comparison scores (Rapport, Denney, DuPaul, & Gardner, 1994).

Psychostimulants have also proven more effective than alternative treatments—such as behavioral interventions and traditional community care—in the largest, multisite controlled clinical trial conducted to date (MTA Cooperative Group, 1999), and these effects were maintained over 14 months. The study results also revealed that the combination of behavioral management and psychostimulant treatment was no more effective than psychostimulant treatment alone for most children who continued with the medication regimen. From a cost-effective perspective, these results are encouraging because behavioral interventions are difficult to initiate and maintain over time across multiple domains and individuals.

Prescription Practices and Titration

A child's primary physician typically prescribes a trial psychostimulant regimen, with the initial starting dose or dosage based on established practice guidelines (Physicians' Desk Reference [PDR], 2007). Some physicians factor in a child's gross body weight when deciding on the initial dosage and strive to approximate the 0.3 mg/kg dosage previously recommended in the PDR as the dosage most likely to optimize a child's learning and cognitive function. Height, weight, heart rate, and blood pressure are monitored routinely during ensuing office visits, and parents are queried about the medication's effectiveness and presence of potential side effects. Dosage is titrated (adjusted) upwards weekly or biweekly as warranted based on parent reports concerning the medication's effectiveness and a lack of serious or persistent side effects. Some physicians also ask the child's primary classroom teacher to complete a brief rating scale or submit a written note concerning the child's behavior over the past week(s).

Several factors complicate what otherwise appears to be a relatively straightforward endeavor. The implicit assumption that heavier children require a larger dose relative to lighter-weight children is based on the drug profile of other medicines whose distribution is related to the number or size of fat molecules in the body. None of the psychostimulants relies on this mechanism for distribution, and studies by independent investigative teams reveal no significant relationship between children's body weight and psychostimulant response (e.g., Rapport & Denney, 1997). A more complicated issue concerns the dose-response nature of psychostimulants. For example, a common belief perpetuated in earlier versions of the PDR is that different behavioral domains are optimized at widely discrepant dosage levels in children—viz., that lower doses optimize cognitive performance, whereas high doses optimize classroom behavior and manageability. Comprehensive literatures reviews (Rapport & Kelley, 1991) and direct observations of children receiving psychostimulant treatment while working in classroom or laboratory environments do not support this contention. Classroom deportment and cognitive performance (including academic performance) are affected at similar dosage levels, and typically within the middle to higher range (Rapport et al., 1994). These results, however, are based on average responses of groups of children, and the optimal dosage for a particular child must be determined in the context of a controlled medication trial.

Asking parents to judge their child's response to a psychostimulant is fraught with difficulties. The demands for extended periods of concentration and scholarly effort are typically much greater at school than at home. Furthermore, the effectiveness of many psychostimulant formulas is expended or diminished significantly by the time a child returns home from school (see *duration of behavioral effect* in Table 1).

Requesting the classroom teacher to complete a rating scale at each week's conclusion is also problematic. Most commercially available rating scales require classroom teachers to rate children on several descriptive behavioral items, most of which reflect behaviors that fall under the *Comatose Rule* or CR. The CR holds that if a comatose individual could receive a desirable score on a rating scale designed to assess therapeutic effectiveness, the scale is unlikely to assess important adaptive changes in children's behavior or performance. Exemplars include items such as *excitable/impulsive, restless or overactive, disturbs other children,* and *constantly fidgeting*—a comatose individual would receive a perfect score on these items and not be engaged in scholarly activities and learning. Conversely, improved academic functioning nearly always coincides with improved behavior. The essence of this finding is that children's academic performance in the classroom (rather than improved behavior) should serve as the primary target for titrating psychostimulants in children. This domain can be easily assessed by having the classroom teacher complete a valid and treatment-sensitive index of a child's academic performance.

Treatment Emergent (Side) Effects

The most commonly occurring side effects associated with psychostimulant therapy fall into three broad categories: cardiovascular effects (i.e., increased heart rate, blood pressure), physical effects (i.e., reduced appetite and corresponding weight loss/slowed growth), and physical/behavioral complaints. Cardiovascular and physical effects associated with psychostimulant therapy are usually transient, dose dependent, readily resolved by discontinuing therapy, and fail to remain significant in long-term follow-up studies. The physical/behavioral complaints typically reported by or observed in children prescribed a psychostimulant regimen include decreased appetite, increased irritability or nervousness, sleep disturbance, abdominal discomfort, headache, dry mouth, and itchy skin. These symptoms, however, need to be distinguished from the commonly reported physical and behavioral complaints reported in the general child population before attributing them to a medication regimen (cf. Rapport, Kofler, Coilo, et al., 2008).

A more serious potential emergent symptom associated with psychostimulant therapy reported by parents is "zombie-like behavior," wherein the child becomes excessively quiet and withdrawn with an accompanying loss of processing speed and spontaneity. The condition is nearly always associated with a dosage regimen that is too high for the child and referred to technically as *over-focused phenomenon* or *cognitive restriction.* One method of assessing whether the effect represents an over-focused state or significantly improved and adaptive attention is to monitor the child's academic work during the week. Positive medication effects are associated with increased daily completion of academic assignments and usually improved accuracy (e.g., fewer careless errors, improved handwriting). If a child's accuracy remains high with a corresponding decrease in productivity, it may signal some degree of cognitive restriction.

The use of psychostimulants as a therapeutic regimen to treat children with ADHD remains a controversial topic. A majority of children derive clear and sustained benefit from this therapeutic modality, although most experienced clinicians and researchers concur that neither this nor any treatment regimen used alone adequately addresses the multifaceted difficulties associated with ADHD. It is also important to recognize that psychostimulants and behavioral interventions for ADHD are maintenance therapies rather than cures, as neither has any proven lasting therapeutic efficacy once active therapy terminates.

REFERENCES

MTA Cooperative Group. (1999). A 14-month randomized clinical trial of treatment strategies for attention-deficit/hyperactivity disorder. *Archives of General Psychiatry, 56,* 1073–1086.

Physicians' Desk Reference, 62nd ed. (2007). Montvale, NJ: Thomson PDR.

Rapport, M. D., & Denney, C. B. (1997). Titrating methylphenidate in children with attention-deficit/hyperactivity disorder: Is body mass predictive of clinical response? *Journal of the American Academy of Child and Adolescent Psychiatry, 36*, 523–530.

Rapport, M. D., Denney, C. B., DuPaul, G. J., & Gardner, M. J. (1994). Attention deficit disorder and methylphenidate: Normalization rates, clinical effectiveness, and response prediction in 76 children. *Journal of the American Academy of Child and Adolescent Psychiatry, 33*, 882–893.

Rapport, M. D., & Kelly, K. L. (1991). Psychostimulant effects on learning and cognitive function: Findings and implications for children with attention-deficit hyperactivity disorder. *Clinical Psychology Review, 11*, 61–92.

Rapport, M. D., Kofler, M., Alderson, M., & Raiker, J. S. (2008). Attention-deficit/hyperactivity disorder. In M. Hersen & D. Reitman (Eds.), *Handbook of psychological assessment: Case conceptualization and treatment, Vol. 2: Children and adolescents* (pp. 349–404). Hoboken, NJ: John Wiley & Sons.

Rapport, M. D., Kofler, M. J., Coiro, M. M., Raiker, J. S., Sarver, D. E., & Alderson, R. M. (2008). Unexpected effects of methylphenidate in ADHD reflect decreases in core/secondary symptoms and physical complaints common to all children. *Journal of Child and Adolescent Psychopharmacology, 18*, 237–247.

SUGGESTED READINGS

DuPaul, G. J., Rapport, M. D., & Perriello, L. M. (1991). Teacher ratings of academic performance: The development of the Academic Performance Rating Scale. *School Psychology Review, 20*, 284–300.

Solanto, M., Arnsten, A., & Castellanos, F. X. (2000). *Stimulant drugs and ADHD: Basic and clinical neuroscience.* New York: Oxford University Press.

MARK D. RAPPORT
JOSEPH S. RAIKER
University of Central Florida

PSYCHOSURGERY

Psychosurgery is the surgical removal or destruction of healthy brain tissue for relief of severe, persistent, and debilitating psychiatric symptomatology. Cranial surgery can be traced back, with early archaeological evidence of trepanation, to around 7300–6220 B.C. (Lillie, 1998). However, the first widespread application of psychosurgery procedures to psychiatric patients began in the late 1930s, reached its peak in the 1960s, and began to decline in the 1970s (Weingarten & Cummings, 2001).

In the first half of the twentieth century, the most frequently used technique was the frontal lobotomy, wherein fibers in the frontal lobes were cut bilaterally to destroy the fiber tracts connecting the frontal lobes to the rest of the brain. A rod with a retractable wire loop was inserted and rotated through a burr hole drilled in the skull to create a cavity in the neural tissue (Mashour, Walker, & Martuza, 2005). Modifications allowed closed procedures by placing and rotating a leukotome (cutting instrument) into 1-cm burr holes drilled through the bony arch at the outer border of the eye socket. The transorbital lobotomy was introduced in 1946; this procedure was performed with an instrument resembling an ice pick inserted through the bony orbits above the eyes and then swept across the prefrontal cortex (Heller, Amar, Liu, & Apuzzo, 2006).

Precise placement of lesions became possible in the late 1950s with the invention of a stereotaxic instrument that held the head in a fixed position; a knife or electrode could then be lowered into the brain at a point predetermined by a set of three-dimensional coordinates as defined by an atlas (anatomical map) and x-rayed reference points in the brain. The use of knife cuts was gradually replaced by the use of electric currents or radio-frequency waves delivered through electrodes. Some neurosurgeons have also used cryoprobes, radioisotopes, proton beams, ultrasound, and thermocoagulation (Weingarten & Cummings, 2001).

Emotional changes occur in a variety of neurological disorders, including epilepsy, stroke, movement disorders, and trauma. Clinically, it has been noted that lesions in distinctly different areas of the brain will disrupt emotional processing at different levels or stages. Therefore, a common feature shared by theories of emotional dysfunction is that multiple brain systems are involved (Barbas, Saha, Rempel-Clower, & Ghashghaei, 2003; Oscar-Berman & Bowirrat, 2005). The theories may be classified into those stressing asymmetrical contributions of the two cerebral hemispheres and those emphasizing frontal-cortical-subcortical system connections. Damage to different frontal lobe circuits and their projections to cortical and subcortical regions can result in behavioral abnormalities, impaired emotional processing, and dysregulation (Weingarten & Cummings, 2001).

Disruption of the dorsolateral prefrontal circuit results in impaired executive functioning, perseveration, and inability to shift strategies. Lateral orbitofrontal circuit dysfunction results in disinhibition, irritability, and inappropriate behavior. Disruption of the anterior cingulate circuit can result in profound apathy, minimal emotional response to pain, and akinetic mutism. The basal ganglia are a major target for these frontal circuits; thus patients with Parkinson's disease present with disruption of emotional processing (Clark, Oscar-Berman, Shagrin, & Pencina, 2007).

The most effective early targets for relief of psychiatric symptoms involve the medial and ventral areas of the frontal lobes bilaterally. Other regions with well-defined connections to specific frontal areas have been targeted for psychosurgery. These regions are part of the frontal-subcortical circuitry and include the cingulum, amygdala, several areas in the thalamus and hypothalamus, and anterior portions of the internal capsule (to interrupt frontothalamic projections). Tractotomy is the interruption of fiber tracts connecting frontal areas with lower brain centers, and it has been used to treat major depression, anxiety, and obsessive-compulsive disorder. Cingulotomy is the lesioning of the anterior cingulate area for treatment of severe anxiety and/or depression. Limbic leukotomy involves both tractotomy and cingulotomy, and the lesions are part of both the medial and lateral circuits of the limbic system. Amygdalotomy has been effective in a majority of patients with aggressive behaviors associated with temporal lobe epilepsy. Pallidotomy or thalamotomy for patients with severe Parkinson's disease has restored motor function to normal levels, but these beneficial effects may not be permanent (Kiss et al., 2003).

Because psychosurgery is most often performed on apparently normal brain tissue, its practice has generated considerable controversy. In his 1986 book *Great and Desperate Cures,* Valenstein exposed many factors leading to the abuse of psychosurgery in the mid-twentieth century, including the absence of psychotropic medications, overcrowded psychiatric asylums, poorly defined clinical indications, and sparse patient follow-up records. The National Commission for the Protection of Human Subjects of Biomedical and Behavioral Research supported several intensive investigations on the use and efficacy of psychosurgery (http://www.bioethics .gov/reports/past_commissions/index.html). Opponents of psychosurgery have compared it with the abuses of human subjects in biomedical experiments carried out in Germany during World War II. Those in favor of psychosurgery have argued that its prohibition would rob patients of their right to effective medical treatment by limiting the scope of procedures available.

Currently, the number of procedures in the classic sense of ablation of healthy tissue has dropped significantly, on account of the use of pharmacologic agents and a number of minimally invasive techniques purported to produce less damage and fewer adverse effects. Such procedures include transcranial magnetic stimulation (TMS) to brain areas associated with emotional regulation, deep brain stimulation (DBS) for modulation of subcortical regions associated with Parkinson's disease, and vagal nerve stimulation to treat epilepsy and major depression (Heller et al., 2006). Vagal nerve stimulation was approved in 2005 for treatment of refractory major depression; however, its use for treatment of epilepsy warrants further investigation.

The term *psychosurgery* has become less popular as neurosurgeons, psychiatrists, and cognitive neuroscientists develop and redefine psychosurgical procedures to include a combination of treatment modalities. To date, *neuromodulation* is a common term that includes a variety of surgical, electrical, and pharmacological approaches, as well as gene therapy and stem cell transplantation, to treat severe chronic illness due to pain, movement disorders, epilepsy, and specific psychiatric disorders. The present state of psychosurgery necessitates a potential redefinition of functional neurosurgery to encompass neuromodulation techniques for a variety of ethical, legal, and scientific concerns.

REFERENCES

Barbas, H., Saha, S., Rempel-Clower, N., & Ghashghaei, T. (2003). Serial pathways from primate prefrontal cortex to autonomic areas may influence emotional expression. *BMC Neuroscience, 4,* 25–37.

Clark, U. S., Oscar-Berman, M., Shagrin, B., & Pencina, M. (2007). Alcoholism and judgments of affective stimuli. *Neuropsychology, 21,* 346–362.

Heller, A. C., Amar, A. P., Liu, C. Y., & Apuzzo, M. L. J. (2006). Surgery of the mind and mood: A mosaic of issues in time and evolution. *Neurosurgery, 59,* 720–739.

Kiss, Z. H. T., Wilkinson, M., Krcek, J., Suchowersky, O., Hu, B., Murphy, W. F., et al. (2003). Is the target for thalamic deep brain stimulation the same as for thalamotomy? *Movement Disorders, 18,* 1169–1175.

Lillie, M. C. (1998). Cranial surgery dates back to the Mesolithic. *Nature, 391,* 854 .

Mashour, G. A., Walker, E. E., & Martuza, R. L. (2005). Psychosurgery: Past, present, and future. *Brain Research Reviews, 48,* 409–419.

Oscar-Berman, M., & Bowirrat, A. (2005) Genetic influences in emotional dysfunction and alcoholism-related brain damage. *Neuropsychiatric Disease and Treatment, 1,* 1–19.

Valenstein, E. S. (Ed.). (1986). *Great and desperate cures: The rise and decline of psychosurgery and other radical treatments for mental illness.* New York: Basic Books.

Weingarten, S. M., & Cummings, J. L. (2001). Psychosurgery of frontal-subcortical circuits. In D. L. Lichter & J. L. Cummings (Eds.), *Frontal-subcortical circuits in psychiatric and neurological disorders* (pp. 421–435). New York: Guilford Press.

SUGGESTED READINGS

Appleby, B. S., Duggan, P. S., Regenberg, A., & Rabins, P. V. (2007). Psychiatric and neuropsychiatric adverse events associated with deep brain stimulation: A meta-analysis of ten years' experience. *Movement Disorders, 22,* 1722–1728.

Fins, J. J., Rezai, A. R., & Greenberg, B. D. (2006). Psychosurgery: Avoiding an ethical redux while advancing a therapeutic future. *Neurosurgery, 59,* 713–715.

Rossini, P. M., & Rossi, S. (2007) Transcranial magnetic stimulation, diagnostic, therapeutic and research potential. *Neurology, 68,* 484–488.

MARLENE OSCAR-BERMAN
MARY M. VALMAS
Boston University School of Medicine and Department of Veterans Affairs Healthcare System, Boston Campus

PSYCHOTHERAPY

What is psychotherapy? Although originally defined as one-on-one sessions of a patient and therapist with the intent of changing the inner workings of the patient's psychological life, over the past several decades, psychotherapy has broadened in its formats, participants, procedures, and focus (there are now more than 250 different forms of psychotherapy), so that any definition of psychotherapy must be far-ranging enough to encompass the full spectrum of different psychotherapies. What relaxation therapy, family therapy, cognitive therapy, group therapy, insight-oriented therapy, play therapy (with children), and exposure therapy—to name a few—have in common is a set of psychological or behavioral procedures, delivered by one or more therapists, designed to change the thoughts, feelings, somatic symptoms, or behaviors of one or more participants who are seeking help.

Although the practice of psychotherapy is not regulated, it is generally delivered by psychologists, psychiatrists, social workers, family therapists, psychiatric nurses, pastoral counselors, or addiction counselors. National surveys have found that about 3.6% of the U.S. population have made at least one visit to a mental health specialist during the past year (Olfson, Marcus, Druss, & Pincus, 2002). People who seek psychotherapy do so for a variety of reasons, including treatment for an ongoing psychiatric disorder such as agoraphobia or depression, difficulty in coping with recent stressful life events, or desire for more success or satisfaction with life.

History

Psychotherapy in its modern form can be traced to Sigmund Freud in the late nineteenth century. Psychoanalysis was developed as a long-term treatment designed to bring repressed unconscious conflicts to the patient's awareness. Despite the large number of brands of psychotherapy today, only a few general schools have continued to be influential. The psychodynamic, or psychoanalytic, school continued to develop over the twentieth century. Under the influence of Sandor Ferenczi, Otto Rank, Franz Alexander, and Thomas French, the psychoanalytic school shifted toward shorter-term treatments that included increased therapist activity. Modern psychodynamic therapy evolved in the 1970s under the influence of Malan, Mann, Sifneos, and Davanloo, who encouraged a focal treatment that explored patients' maladaptive interpersonal styles within the context of time limits. In the 1980s, Luborsky (1984) and Strupp and Binder (1984) published manuals for implementing short-term dynamic psychotherapy. These treatments focus mainly on the interpretation of maladaptive relationship patterns as they influence the patient's current relationships and functioning in the context of a supportive therapeutic relationship.

Closely related to dynamic treatments, the interpersonal school was first described by Harry Stack Sullivan. Sullivan focused on interpersonal relationships as they influenced the development of the patient's personality. In 1984, Klerman and colleagues published a manual for interpersonal psychotherapy (Klerman, Weissman, Rounsaville, & Chevron, 1984). This treatment emphasizes the patient's current interpersonal relationships. Unlike dynamic treatments, developmental factors and maladaptive relationship patterns as they are expressed in the therapeutic relationship are not given direct attention.

Carl Rogers developed the client-centered school of psychotherapy. This approach focuses on the psychological climate created by the therapist. An environment characterized by genuine acceptance, sensitive understanding, and empathic understanding is believed to foster within a patient the ability to reorganize her or his personality. Unlike dynamic therapy, the climate of the therapeutic relationship alone is believed to foster the patient's gains.

The behavioral school of psychotherapy has also been influential. Behavior therapy has its base in learning theory. The model postulates that symptoms are a result of learned behaviors that are subject to direct manipulation by contingency management and classical conditioning. Techniques focus on modifying behavior through positive and negative reinforcement and exposure (desensitization).

Versions of a cognitive approach to psychotherapy were developed separately by Albert Ellis and Aaron Beck in the 1950s. In Ellis's rational emotive therapy, problems are seen as a result of faulty expectations and irrational thoughts. The goal of this treatment is to teach patients to modify their thinking patterns (Ellis & MacLaren, 2005). Beck's cognitive therapy focuses on identifying, testing the validity of, and correcting the dysfunctional beliefs that underlie the patient's cognitions (Beck, Rush, Shaw, & Emery, 1979).

These types of psychotherapy are applied in both individual and group formats. In individual therapy, the therapist works one-on-one with the patient, whereas group formats may include groups of strangers, couples, or families brought together to work on a specific topic. The family systems approach to psychotherapy focuses on each family member as coequal in importance. The therapist helps the members identify problems in the family system and reorganize themselves as an effective family unit.

A recent trend to emphasize the common factors across the various schools of psychotherapy has paved the way for a movement toward integration of different approaches. Many practitioners find it useful to borrow techniques from multiple schools to maximize patient benefit. Cognitive and behavioral techniques are often used in conjunction and seen as important complements to each other in the therapeutic process. One new modification of cognitive-behavioral therapy involves incorporating so-called mindfulness techniques into the therapy (Segal,

Teasdale, & Williams, 2002). These techniques teach patients to identify their thoughts from moment to moment without judging the thoughts in any way.

Another important trend has been toward brief, rather than long-term, treatment (Olfson et al., 2002). This trend has been influenced in part by research conducted on brief therapy and also because of the need to contain health care costs (i.e., most insurance companies will pay for only a limited number of sessions of psychotherapy).

Research on Psychotherapy

Although many are skeptical of psychotherapy as a treatment, it has been investigated in research studies more than any other medical procedure, with many more than 1,000 studies of psychotherapy performed to date. Extensive reviews of the research literature have concluded that, broadly speaking, psychotherapy works. Research is now directed toward more specific questions, such as finding out what type of psychotherapy procedure works best with identified types of patient problems or disorders and developing new techniques for enhancing treatment benefits. Other research examines psychotherapy as it is delivered in the community—its effectiveness, cost, and dose–response relationships. Still yet another form of psychotherapy research (process studies) looks at what actually happens during psychotherapy sessions and attempts to unravel the relationship between actions of the therapist in sessions and changes in the patient(s).

Research on specific treatment procedures for different problems and disorders has led to recommendations about which psychotherapy procedures have sufficient empirical support. These recommendations are based largely upon the results of studies in which patients are randomly assigned to psychotherapy versus a control group (e.g., a waiting list or a psychological or pill placebo). Specific psychotherapies have received strong empirical support as treatments of obsessive-compulsive disorder, major depressive disorder, panic disorder, agoraphobia, and generalized anxiety disorder (Nathan & Gorman, 2007). For these disorders, the relative effectiveness of psychotherapy compared with psychotropic medication, or the combination of medication and psychotherapy, is of high public health significance and a topic of much ongoing research. One specific finding has been that patients with a diagnosis of major depressive disorder who receive a brief course of cognitive therapy have lower rates of relapse following treatment than patients who have a course of antidepressant medications and then stop their medications (Hollon et al., 2005).

Studies of psychotherapy as it is practiced in the community have yielded important data on the number of treatment sessions that are necessary to help patients achieve a recovery from their symptoms. For 50% of patients to recover, about 16 sessions of psychotherapy are required (Hansen & Lambert, 2003). Although brief psychotherapy may be help to many, longer-term psychotherapy may still be needed for other patients to reach full recovery. Other community-based studies of psychotherapy examine the extent to which treatments developed and tested under ideal conditions in academic settings can be exported to the types of therapists and patients who participate in psychotherapy in community settings.

Although medications have increasingly been used to treat mental health problems, the advantages of psychotherapy in regard to documented efficacy, the relative lack of side effects, and the potential to prevent relapses support a continuing role for psychotherapy as part of an overall approach to the alleviation of symptoms of psychiatric disorders and improving overall functioning and quality of life.

REFERENCES

Beck, A. T., Rush, A. J., Shaw, B. F., & Emery, G. (1979). *Cognitive therapy of depression*. New York: Guilford Press.

Ellis, A., & MacLaren, C. (2005). *Rational emotive behavior therapy: A therapist's guide* (2nd ed.). Atascadero, CA: Impact.

Hansen, N. B., & Lambert, M. J. (2003). An evaluation of the dose–response relationship in naturalistic treatment settings using survival analysis. *Mental Health Services Research, 5,* 1–12.

Hollon, S. D., DeRubeis, R. J., Shelton, R. C., Amsterdam, J. D., Salomon, R. M., O'Reardon, J. P., et al. (2005). Prevention of relapse following cognitive therapy vs. medications in moderate to severe depression. *Archives of General Psychiatry, 62,* 417–422.

Klerman, G. L., Weissman, M. M., Rounsaville, B. J., & Chevron, E. S. (1984). *Interpersonal psychotherapy of depression*. New York: Basic Books.

Luborsky, L. (1984). *Principles of psychoanalytic psychotherapy: A manual for supportive-expressive treatment*. New York: Basic Books.

Nathan, P., & Gorman, J. (2007). *Treatments that work* (3rd ed.). New York: Oxford University Press.

Olfson, M., Marcus, S. C., Druss, B., & Pincus, H. A. (2002). National trends in the use of outpatient psychotherapy. *American Journal of Psychiatry, 159,* 1914–1920.

Segal, Z., Teasdale, J., & Williams, M. (2002). *Mindfulness-based cognitive therapy for depression*. New York: Guilford Press.

Strupp, H. H., & Binder, J. L. (1984). *Psychotherapy in a new key: A guide to time-limited dynamic psychotherapy*. New York: Basic Books.

SUGGESTED READINGS

Barlow, D. H. (Ed.). (2001). *Clinical handbook of psychological disorders: A step-by-step treatment manual* (3rd ed.). New York: Guilford Press.

Lambert, M. J. (Ed.). (2004). *Bergin and Garfield's handbook of psychotherapy and behavior change* (5th ed.). Hoboken, NJ: John Wiley & Sons.

PAUL CRITS-CHRISTOPH
MARY BETH CONNOLLY GIBBONS
University of Pennsylvania

PSYCHOTHERAPY, EFFECTIVE ELEMENTS OF

In the last three decades a strong and empirically supported consensus has emerged that psychotherapy is effective. Therefore one might expect that the question "Which elements in psychotherapy therapy are responsible for its effectiveness?" would have straightforward answers supported by reasonable consensus in the profession. This, however, is not the case.

The Search for Effective Ingredients (EI)

Up to the middle of the twentieth century, claims for effectiveness in psychotherapy were based on theoretical arguments supported by anecdotal case notes. The situation took a turn when Eysenck (1952) published a data-based article in which he concluded that therapies, apart from behavioral therapy, are not efficacious (Eysenck was a proponent of behavioral treatment). The ensuing controversy provided a strong impetus for applying scientific research principles to the evaluation of the effects of psychotherapy. Better-designed outcome studies proliferated, but they were inconclusive, with researchers using different measures and contrasts coming up with opposing claims.

In 1977, Smith and Glass published a meta-analysis (a procedure to combine data based on diverse measurements) that summarized the results of all the research done on therapy effectiveness to that time. The results of this important study were both reassuring and challenging. Over-all, psychotherapy in all of its different forms and across all the treatments and problems investigated was demonstrated to be significantly effective. The challenging part of the Smith and Glass conclusions was that few reliable differences in effectiveness were found among the great variety of treatments based on different theories of what is effective in therapy. This result became known as the "Dodo Bird verdict" (in *Alice in Wonderland*, after the "race," the Dodo Bird declares, "Everybody has won, and all must have prizes"). The original Smith and Glass meta-analysis has been criticized, reanalyzed, and replicated, and the results have been remarkably consistent.

The "Dodo Bird verdict" has strongly influenced the way the search for the "effective ingredients" has been pursued. Most researchers agree that over-all effectiveness cannot be claimed for any theory or treatment as such. However, there are two distinct interpretations of what the verdict implies. One side argues that the effective ingredients must be factors common to all treatments, whereas another side thinks that the Dodo Bird got it wrong and that the equivalence of effectiveness on such broad scale is an artifact. Instead, from this second perspective, effective ingredients of therapy are realized in specific interventions, but these effects are only evident when the efficacious intervention is paired with the psychological problem it was designed to address.

The Case for Specific Therapy Ingredients

Since 1995 Division 12 (Clinical Psychology) of the American Psychological Association has made a strong effort to identify clearly articulated therapies for specific problems (Empirically Supported Treatments [EST]) that have been validated using randomized clinical trials or similar research designs. It was hoped that finding specifically efficacious treatments for particular problems, apart from providing the public with trustworthy treatments, would lead to the identification of important specific therapy ingredients (STIs). Over 130 treatment/problem combinations have received various levels of EST support (Chambless & Ollendick, 2001); however, the question of what are the effective ingredients in these therapies has not been resolved. Each EST contains a number of proposed effective components, and it cannot easily be determined which one(s) may be responsible for client change. In addition, there are a number of different ESTs with diverse STIs that have proven effective for the major categories of psychological problems (e.g., psychodynamic, cognitive, and emotion-focused treatments are efficacious for depression).

An even stronger approach to locate STIs has involved component studies, in which two similar treatments are administered, but in one the STI is removed. If the study with the particular STI shows better results than the one without it, the ingredient has proved effective. Overall, the results of component studies do not support the STI position; if both versions of the treatment are provided competently, the results are neither statistically nor clinically different (Ahn & Wampold, 2001). There may, however, be some exceptions to this finding (e.g., Siev & Chambless, 2007).

Although the search for STIs has yielded few reliable results, there is reasonable consensus that, at the level of treatments, therapies that incorporate one or more of the following elements can provide effective relief for a range of psychological problems: cognitive restructuring, in-vivo desensitization, modeling/rehearsal, insight, and focusing/deepening emotional (re)experiencing. The caveat in identifying these elements as effective ingredients of psychotherapy is that the effect of each of these interventions can only be observed within the context of a complex therapy environment involving many other potentially significant elements (e.g., relationship, therapist quality, contextual, and problem variables). Which of these combinations yields effective results is not yet resolved. To summarize, then, the goal of isolating effectiveness at the level of therapy ingredients is tempting, and the top candidates just noted have some empirical support, but the jury is out on how we can isolate what is effective in which situations and on whether we should think of these ingredients as effective or synergistic.

The Case for Common Factors

There is near unanimous support for the therapeutic alliance as a common factor in all forms of psychotherapy (Horvath & Bedi, 2002). A good alliance also appears to increase the effectiveness of psychoactive medications (Krupnick et al., 1996). This means that, for treatment to succeed, it is important to develop a collaborative relationship with the client; a kind of "the two of us together against the problem" stance, which includes the client's trust and confidence in the therapist and endorsement of the therapeutic activities involved. There are some indications that the development of a good alliance and the successful management of its ups and downs, or ruptures, is therapeutic in and of itself (Safran, Muran, Samstag, & Stevens, 2001), but this effect may be specific to therapies in which the emphasis is on the relationship.

Good circumstantial evidence supports the notion that a cogent psychological rationale for the cause of the client's problems together with a reasonable (to the client) explanation of how the ritual of therapy will lead to positive change is a necessary, and thus effective, ingredient in psychotherapy. This evidence is circumstantial, insofar as what has been documented is that placebo, that is, therapies without these elements, produce significantly poorer results (Wampold, 2007). However, these sham placebo treatments are often missing several additional components present in real treatments, and hence the conclusion, although eminently logical, awaits further and more direct investigation.

The effect of therapists is very difficult to disentangle from the treatments they deliver and the context of the treatment. However, recent developments in multilevel statistical procedures have permitted the reanalysis of some very good research data. There is a converging consensus that the quality of the therapist, within a particular therapy regimen, accounts for a significant portion of the variance in outcomes that can be attributed to the therapy (Lambert & Ogles, 2004). One of the paths of impact proposed is that therapists who are able to develop and maintain a good alliance will be more successful in producing positive outcome across their patient caseload than therapists who are not as able in this respect. However, the possibility that there are other therapist qualities

or actions that directly or indirectly influence therapy outcome cannot be eliminated.

There are several client characteristics that have documented links to therapy outcome. Although these characteristics are important from the perspective of determining who are the clients most likely to benefit from psychotherapy, they are not effective ingredients of therapy in the sense that we have been exploring this issue. The exception is a client/therapy matching factor: specifically, there is evidence that clients who drop out of therapy often do so because they do not find some aspect of the treatment compatible. In this sense, a good match between clients (including their expectations, prior beliefs, and relational capacities), their therapy, and their therapist might well be an effective ingredient of psychotherapy.

In summary, the available empirical evidence indicates strong support for the common factor elements as effective ingredients, but the case should not be considered closed. The effort to isolate TSIs has been handicapped by imprecision of diagnosis as well as by difficulties and limitations in implementing the type of research needed to validate the exact match hypotheses in the context of psychotherapy. The likely convergence between neuropsychology and therapy may yet change the landscape, in that more precise distinctions among diagnostic categories as well as the identification, or at least cortical localization, of how different interventions are processed and retained by clients should help to resolve the STI controversy.

Importantly, therapy occurs in a complex social context, and in the real world common factors and specific interventions are inseparable. Researchers need to put observations in categories and create artificial distinctions. Once this artifact is taken into account, it appears likely that the effective common factors we can document are but a facet of the complex interdependent geometry that includes the ability of the therapist to tailor the therapy to the expectations and capacities of the client, to select treatment methods that fit with this rationale, to intervene in ways that address the problematic cognitive and emotional processes of the client, and to adjust all of these elements to fit the social context within which therapy occurs. This hypothesis is consistent with the model of therapy put forward by Frank and Frank (1991), who suggested that effective psychotherapy must include an intense and emotionally charged relationship with a "socially sanctioned healer," a cogent treatment rationale that introduces elements of hope, and a coherent treatment routine in harmony with the rationale.

REFERENCES

Ahn, H., & Wampold, B. E. (2001). Where oh where are the specific ingredients? A meta-analysis of component studies in counseling and psychotherapy. *Journal of Counseling Psychology, 48*(3), 251–257.

Chambless, D. L., & Ollendick, T. H. (2001). Empirically supported psychological interventions: Controversies and evidence. *Annual Review of Psychology, 52,* 685–716.

Eysenck, H. J. (1952). The effects of psychotherapy: An evaluation. *Journal of Consulting Psychology, 16,* 319–324.

Frank, J. D., & Frank, J. B. (1991). *Persuasion and healing: A comparative study of psychotherapy* (3rd ed.). Baltimore, MD: Johns Hopkins University Press.

Horvath, A. O., & Bedi, R. P. (2002). The alliance. In J. C. Norcross (Ed.), *Psychotherapy relationships that work* (pp. 37–70). New York: Oxford University Press.

Krupnick, J. L., Sotsky, S. M., Simmens, S., Moyer, J., Elkin, I., Watkins, J., et al. (1996). The role of the therapeutic alliance in psychotherapy and pharmacotherapy outcome: Findings in the National Institute of Mental Health Treatment of Depression Collaborative Research Program. *Journal of Consulting and Clinical Psychology, 64*(3), 532–539.

Lambert, M. J., & Ogles B. M. (2004). The efficacy and effectiveness of psychotherapy. In M. J. Lambert (Ed.), *Bergin and Garfield's handbook of psychotherapy and behavior change* (5th ed., pp. 139–193). Hoboken, NJ: John Wiley & Sons.

Safran, J. D., Muran, J. C., Samstag, L. W., & Stevens, C. (2001). Repairing alliance ruptures. *Psychotherapy: Theory, Research, Practice, Training, 38*(4), 406–412.

Siev, J., & Chambless, D. L. (2007). Specificity of treatment effects: Cognitive therapy and relaxation for generalized anxiety and panic disorders. *Journal of Consulting and Clinical Psychology, 75*(4), 513–522.

Wampold, B. E. (2007). Psychotherapy: The humanistic (and effective) treatment. *American Psychologist, 62*(8), 857–873.

SUGGESTED READINGS

Chambless, D. L. (2002). Beware the dodo bird: The dangers of overgeneralization. *Clinical Psychology: Science and Practice, 9*(1), 13–16.

Norcross, J. C. (Ed.). (2002). *Psychotherapy relationships that work: Therapist contributions and responsiveness to patients.* New York: Oxford University Press.

Wampold, B. E. (2001). *The great psychotherapy debate.* Mahwah, NJ: Lawrence Erlbaum.

ADAM O. HORVATH
Simon Fraser University, Canada

PSYCHOTHERAPY, EFFECTIVENESS OF

The effectiveness of psychotherapy has been the subject of study since the 1930s. The activities that characterize psychotherapy practice have evolved over time and today consist of hundreds of established procedures based on psychological theories aimed at reducing the symptoms of psychopathology. In this brief summary, some of the most notable findings are reviewed and their implications highlighted.

Psychotherapy Is Effective

Hundreds of studies have now been conducted on the effects of psychotherapy, including research on psychodynamic, humanistic, behavioral, cognitive, and variations and combinations of these approaches. Reviews of this research, both qualitative and quantitative, have shown that about 75% of those who enter treatment show *some* benefit (Lambert & Ogles, 2004). This pronounced positive effect occurs across a wide range of disorders, with the exception of primarily biologically based disturbances, such as bipolar disorder and the schizophrenias, where the impact of psychological treatments is secondary to psychoactive medications (American Psychological Association, 2006). Within disorders, there is variability, such that some disorders yield to treatment more easily (e.g., phobias, panic) than others (e.g., obsessive-compulsive disorder), and some require longer and more intense interventions. For the most part, psychological interventions surpass the effects of medication for psychological disorders and should be offered prior to medications (except with the most severely disturbed patients), because they are less dangerous and less intrusive, or at the very least, in addition to medications, because they reduce the likelihood of relapse once medications are withdrawn (Thase & Jindal, 2004). Among the important factors that determine outcome, the particular therapist and the patient–therapist relationship loom large (Norcross, 2002).

The Effects of Psychotherapy Are More Powerful Than Informal Support and Placebo Controls

Numerous studies and reviews of the literature have been conducted in which researchers designed experiments where patients were randomly assigned to a no-treatment control group, a placebo control group, or a psychotherapy treatment group. These experimental designs allowed researchers to narrow the causes of improvement while isolating and ruling out competing factors that could account for the positive effects of psychotherapy. It can be observed that patients who do not get psychotherapy improve, probably as a result of seeking support from friends, family, clergy, and the like. Patients who enter a placebo control group fare even better than untreated patients, probably as a result of having contact with a therapist, the expectation of being helped created by the experimental procedures, and the reassurance and support they received during the study. In contrast, a greater portion of patients who enter psychotherapy return to a state of normal functioning.

The Outcomes of Psychotherapy Are Substantial

Those who have studied psychotherapy have been rigorous in defining and measuring important factors of individual functioning. Methods for measuring outcome have included patient reports, physiological changes, expert judge ratings, and ratings by family members, friends and coworkers, as well as employment, medical, and legal standing (e.g., arrest, incarceration). These rating sources tap a variety of areas of functioning, mainly symptoms of distress (e.g., anxiety, depression, anger), interpersonal functioning (e.g., family conflict, loneliness, intimacy), and social role performance (e.g., conflict at work, absenteeism, employment status). These factors are of considerable importance to the patient, the patient's family, and society at large. In addition, much recent effort has been expended to define what a normal state of functioning is and how to assess which patients have attained this normative state at the end of treatment. We can conclude that 40–60% of patients who receive 12–14 sessions of psychotherapy return to a normal state of functioning (Hansen, Lambert, & Forman, 2002), a remarkable outcome when one considers the degree of suffering that is associated with psychological disorders.

The Outcomes of Therapy Tend to Be Maintained

Numerous follow-up studies have tracked patients after leaving treatment, for periods ranging from 6 months to more than 5 years. These studies are fairly consistent in demonstrating that treatment effects are enduring. For example, gains following treatment for depression commonly endure for at least 2 years (Lambert & Ogles, 2004).

Psychotherapy Is Relatively Efficient

Research on psychotherapy has studied the speed with which patients improve over the course of treatment. Studies have examined the length of treatment and outcome by using numerous research designs. This has important practical as well as social policy implications. It appears that the more psychotherapy, the greater the probability of improvement, with diminishing returns after about 6 months of weekly psychotherapy. Thus, the power of treatment is most apparent early in the process. Lambert (2007), summarizing the relation of the number of treatment sessions and improvement, collected data from large samples of patients undergoing treatment who rated their symptoms, interpersonal relations, life functioning, and quality of life on a weekly basis before each treatment session. Thus, their outcome was assessed from the beginning of treatment until it was completed or they withdrew. About a third of patients recovered by the 10th session, 50% by the 20th session, and 75% by the 55th session of therapy. This means that if session limits are set by insurance companies, institutions, and government agencies,

half of those coming for treatment will be underserved with a benefit that is less than 20 sessions. For about 25% of patients, even 50 sessions will not be sufficient to bring them back into the ranks of normal functioning.

Psychotherapy Is for Better and for Worse

Despite the overall positive findings, a portion of patients who enter treatment are worse off when they leave treatment than when they entered. Lambert and Ogles (2004) estimated that about 5–10% of patients deteriorate during treatment, and an additional 15–25% show no measured benefit. This finding supports the need for regulation by state licensing boards, legislatures, and professional associations. This rate of deterioration can be reduced if these governing bodies move to maintain high standards of practice by keeping untrained persons from providing services that require professional judgment and the highest level of ethical practice. As disheartening as it is to know that psychotherapy may be harmful for a small portion of patients and impotent with many others, it also points to the need for quality assurance mechanisms that reduce these occurrences to their lowest possible levels.

Harmon and colleagues (2007) have shown that if patient progress is tracked on a weekly basis, and decision support tools are used to identify patients who are not responding to treatment in the first three sessions, then providing feedback to therapists about this fact improves outcome and decreases patient deterioration. Outcome management systems are being developed, and these systems are likely to enhance outcomes for the failing patient. These authors also reported that the use of such systems was cost-effective because therapists who received feedback tended to terminate cases who had improved rapidly after fewer sessions (75% of cases), while retaining for more sessions patients who were ifdentified as failing. This proved to be satisfying to all involved (therapists, administrators, and patients), but the data also indicated that many of the difficult patients were still in need of further, additional, or different treatment. Nevertheless, monitoring patient progress and providing feedback to therapists promises to make behavioral health care efforts self-correcting and, ultimately, more effective.

It is clear from the hundreds of studies that have been completed and published that psychotherapy is effective, efficient, and lasting. A variety of treatments have a promising future as the intervention of choice for psychologically based disorders—reducing suffering and returning patients to levels of functioning characteristic of their undisturbed peers.

REFERENCES

American Psychological Association. (2006). Evidence-based practice in psychology. *American Psychologist, 61*(4), 271–285.

Bauer, S., Lambert, M. J., & Nielsen, S. L. (2004). Clinical significance methods: A comparison of statistical techniques. *Journal of Personality Assessment, 82*, 60–70.

Hansen, N. B., Lambert, M. J., & Forman, E. M. (2002). The psychotherapy dose–response effect and its implications for treatment delivery services. *Clinical Psychology: Science and Practice, 9*, 329–343.

Harmon, S. C., Lambert, M. J., Smart, D. W., Hawkins, E. J., Nielsen, S. L., Slade, K., et al. (2007). Methods of enhancing patient outcome for potential treatment failures: The use of therapist/client feedback and clinical support tools. *Psychotherapy Research, 17*, 379–392.

Lambert, M. J. (2007). Presidential address: A program of research aimed at improving psychotherapy outcome in routine care: What we have learned from a decade of research. *Psychotherapy Research, 17*, 1–14.

Lambert, M. J., & Ogles, B. M. (2004). The efficacy and effectiveness of psychotherapy. In M. J. Lambert (Ed.), *Bergin and Garfield's handbook of psychotherapy and behavior change* (5th ed., pp. 139–193). Hoboken, NJ: John Wiley & Sons.

Norcross, J. C. (Ed.). (2002). *Psychotherapy relationships that work.* New York: Oxford University Press.

Thase, M. E., & Jindal, R. D. (2004). Combining psychotherapy and psychopharmacology for treatment of mental disorders. In M. J. Lambert (Ed.), *Bergin and Garfield's handbook of psychotherapy and behavior change* (5th ed., pp. 743–766). Hoboken, NJ: John Wiley & Sons.

SUGGESTED READING

Wampold, B. (2001). *The great psychotherapy debate: Models, methods and findings.* Mahwah, NJ: Lawrence Erlbaum.

MICHAEL J. LAMBERT
Brigham Young University

PSYCHOTHERAPY, EFFICACY OF

Two methods have been utilized to conduct scientific evaluations of psychotherapy. Efficacy and effectiveness research are both important and provide distinct information about how psychotherapy works. Although both methods are used, to date efficacy studies have dominated the field. As a result, most of what we know about how well psychotherapy works comes from efficacy rather than effectiveness research.

Efficacy studies tests psychotherapy in a tightly controlled experimental design and typically utilize a structured, manualized session format that is delivered in a fixed number of sessions. Patients are selected with care, with the bulk of patients carrying single, uncomplicated diagnoses, being in specific age ranges, and meeting other strict inclusion and exclusion criteria. Patients are randomly assigned to different treatments and, ideally, the treatment being studied is also compared to a placebo control. The strict experimental design in efficacy studies provides strong internal validity and thereby enables researchers to be confident that the treatment under investigation causes the observed effect. However, because of this tightly controlled format, efficacy studies are associated with weaker external validity, suggesting that obtained findings may not generalize to the clinical populations for whom they are ultimately intended.

Effectiveness studies, by contrast, evaluate the outcome of therapy directly on these clinical populations; in doing so, however, they sacrifice the rigors of efficacy research. Effectiveness research is conducted as psychotherapy, but it is actually delivered in the field, in a variety of settings that include hospital clinics, schools, inpatient units, and private practice offices. Patients are heterogeneous, typically have multiple diagnoses, and are not randomly assigned to treatment groups. The choice of specific treatments or therapists is often determined by patients themselves, manuals are typically not utilized, and the length of treatment is often not fixed. Treatment is usually terminated once the therapist or patient determine that progress has occurred or as a function of insurance constraints. As a result, effectiveness research, although not as internally rigorous as efficacy research, provides information about how well treatment works when it is carried out in clinical practice.

Efficacy Research on Psychotherapy

Comprehensive reviews have identified psychotherapies that have been specified in a manual, have specific criteria for training and competence evaluations, and have supporting data from controlled clinical trials (e.g., Chambless et al., 1998; Nathan & Gorman, 1998; Weissman, Markowitz, & Klerman, 2000). Chambless and Ollendick (2001) completed the most extensive of these reviews in which they integrated the efforts of eight workgroups from the United States, the United Kingdom, and Canada that focused on identifying empirically supported treatments (EST). Although the criteria used to define ESTs were not the same for each workgroup, they were all conservative in nature. For a treatment to be defined as empirically supported by any of the workgroups, support from at least one rigorous randomized clinical trial was necessary. Based on Chambless and Ollendick's (2001) review of reviews, it is accurate to say that at least one EST and sometimes several exist for a broad spectrum of psychiatric disorders and adjustment problems, including anxiety and stress, agoraphobia and panic disorders with agoraphobia. blood injury phobia, generalized anxiety disorder, geriatric anxiety, obsessive-compulsive disorder, panic disorder, posttraumatic stress disorder, public speaking anxiety, social phobia, specific phobia, chemical abuse and dependence, alcohol abuse and dependence, benzodiazepine withdrawal, cocaine abuse, opiate dependence, depression, bipolar disorder, geriatric depression, major depression, anorexia, binge-eating disorder, borderline personality disorder, bulimia, chronic pain disorder, irritable-bowel syndrome, marital discord, migraine headache, obesity, schizophrenia, smoking cessation, and sexual dysfunction.

ESTs are not efficacious for all conditions. For example, interpersonal psychotherapy (IPT) has been shown to be ineffective in two clinical trials with opiate abusers. Additionally, ESTs may be differentially effective across conditions. Westen and Morrison's (2001) comprehensive meta-analysis of studies published on the efficacy of manualized psychotherapies revealed that long-term outcomes for panic disorder were superior to those for depression or generalized anxiety disorder. Further, ESTs may be similarly effective when compared to other psychotherapies for the same condition. For example, with the exception of interpersonal psychotherapy, which was somewhat more efficacious, a recent meta-analysis by Cuijpers, van Straten, Andersson, and van Oppen (2008) found few differences in the efficacy of psychotherapies for mild to moderate depression in adults.

Although reviews reflect variability in the efficacy of ESTs across conditions, research suggests that ESTs may be as effective as psychotropic interventions for several disorders (e.g., panic disorder, major depression, and bulimia nervosa). Thus, having psychotherapy available as an alternative to medication is important for patients who do not want to take medication (e.g., pregnant or lactating women), who cannot tolerate medications (e.g., side effects, adverse reactions), or who are not responsive to medications. For other disorders, psychotherapy is an invaluable adjunct (but not a solo treatment) to medication (e.g., bipolar disorder, schizophrenia) that enhances compliance, reduces residual symptoms, and decreases relapse.

In this section we highlight data on the efficacy of specific EST for several commonly occurring psychiatric disorders, described in the following sections.

Depression

Current psychotherapy treatments for depression target one or more of the following: behavioral passivity, pessimism, negative perceptions of self, others, and the world, a ruminative cognitive style, and interpersonal disruptions (McGinn & Sanderson, 2001). Both IPT (Weissman et al., 1979; Elkin et al., 1989) and Cognitive Behavioral Therapy (CBT; Butler, Chapman, Forman & Beck, 2006; DeRubeis et al, 2005; cf. Glaoguen, Cottraux, & Cucherat, 1998; Elkin et al., 1989) have been shown to be as effective in reducing symptoms as psychotropic medication for acute treatment of major depression (Dimidjian et al., 2006; Depression Guideline Panel, 1993). However, the onset of action is slower for psychotherapy. An amalgam of CBT and IPT (cognitive behavioral analysis system of psychotherapy) has been shown to be effective in the

treatment of chronic depression, and when combined with medication, increased the response rate from 55% to 85% (Keller et al., 2000).

Depression is associated with a high relapse rate. When administered less intensively (approximately once a month) following an acute phase of weekly treatment, both IPT and CBT have been shown to decrease the rate of relapse and recurrences (Frank et al., 1990; Harkness et al., 2002; Jarrett, Basco, & Risser, 1998). In addition, CBT has been shown both alone, and in combination with light therapy to effectively treat depression among individuals with seasonal affective disorder (Rohan, et al., 2007).

Although not as extensive, controlled trials have also supported the use of IPT and CBT for the treatment of adolescent depression (Brent et al., 1997; Mufson, Moreau, Weissman, & Klerman, 1993; Rosello & Bernal, 1996, 1999), and late-life depression (Reynolds et al., 1999a, 1999b; Sloane et al., 1985). In addition, psychotherapy has been shown to be an efficacious treatment for depression secondary to other problems. For example, CBT has been shown to decrease depressive symptoms in patients diagnosed with multiple sclerosis and major depressive disorder (Mohr, Boudewyn, Goodkin, Bostrom, & Epstein, 2001), and both IPT and CBT have been shown to reduce depression among depressed HIV-positive patients (Markowitz et al., 1995; Safren et al., 2009), and among patients with marital dysfunction (Foley et al., 1989; O'Leary & Beach, 1990).

Preliminary research suggests that a new generation of CBT treatments (Ma & Teasdale, 2003; Hayes et al., 2004) that emphasize mindfulness and experiential acceptance may be also be effective, particularly in preventing relapse among individuals with chronic depression (Ma & Teasdale, 2003).

Bipolar Disorder

CBT and IPT for bipolar disorder target (1) mediating mechanisms (such as distorted cognitions, disrupted circadian rhythms) and/or (2) social/interpersonal events that may be triggers or consequences of bipolar episodes (e.g., interpersonal disputes). For example, bipolar patients may be prone to overly optimistic explanatory biases in the manic phase of their illness and pessimistic styles in the depressive phases of their illness (Johnson, 2005), which have been targeted through the use of cognitive restructuring techniques. Lam et al. (2003) found that, when compared with routine care (medication alone), cognitive therapy (CT) targeting relapse prevention in conjunction with mood stabilizers demonstrated superior outcomes at 1 year in terms of relapse, hospitalizations, social functioning, and medication adherence. Although days spent in depressive episodes and depressive severity scores were initially lower among CT patients, these differences were not maintained at 30 months (Lam, Hayward, Watkins, Wright, & Sham, 2005). Similarly, Ball et al. (2006) reported that although patients in CT had lower depression scores at 6 months and longer periods to depressive relapses over 18 months, the benefits of CT on depression lessened over time, implying the need for maintenance treatment.

A social rhythm regulation component was added to standard IPT (Interpersonal and Social Rhythm Therapy [IPSRT]) to address the specific issues in treating bipolar patients (Basco & Rush, 1996; Frank et al., 2005; Miklowitz & Goldstein, 1997). These treatments are considered adjuncts in combination with medication (e.g., Lam et al., 2000). Frank et al. (2005) conducted a single-center clinical trial of IPSRT which provided support for treatment efficacy; when compared to patients assigned to clinical management in the acute phase, patients treated with IPSRT had longer periods of symptom improvement during the maintenance phase of the study. Furthermore, additional analyses revealed that IPSRT decreased the likelihood of depressive recurrence in bipolar I patients (Frank, 1999).

In addition to CBT and IPSRT, research has demonstrated some promising findings for psychoeducational programs in a variety of modalities (see Miklowitz, 2008 for a review).

Anxiety Disorders

Treatment manuals based upon the principles of CBT exist for each of the anxiety disorders. Treatment strategies focus on addressing self-perceived overestimations of danger, underestimations of ability to cope, maladaptive coping strategies and increased physiological arousal, and include several common components: psychoeducation, cognitive restructuring, relaxation strategies, and exposure and response prevention (Sanderson & McGinn, 1997). These strategies are tailored to address the specific psychopathology associated with each disorder. There is a considerable body of evidence from controlled studies supporting the efficacy of CBT for the range of anxiety disorders (cf. Nathan & Gorman, 1998 for a comprehensive review): agoraphobia (e.g., Chambless, Foa, Groves, & Goldstein, 1979), generalized anxiety disorder (e.g., Barlow, Rapee, & Brown, 1992; Covin, Ouimet, Seeds, & Dozois, 2008; Gosselin, Ladouceur, Morin, Dugas, & Baillargeon, 2006; Mitte, 2005; Stanley et al., 2003), obsessive-compulsive disorder (e.g., Fals-Stewart, Marks, & Schafer, 1993; Foa et al., 2005; Whittal, Robichaud, Thordarson, & McLean, 2008), panic disorder (e.g., Barlow, Gorman, Shear, & Woods, 2000; Kenardy et al., 2003; Craske & Barlow, 2008; Mitte, 2005), social phobia among children (e.g., Beidel, Turner, Young, & Paulson, 2005; Kendall, Hudson, Gosch, Flannery-Schroeder, & Suveg, 2008), social phobia among adults (Clark et al., 2006;

Heimberg et al., 1998; Hofman, Schulz, Meuret, Moscovitch, & Suvak 2006), posttraumatic stress disorder (e.g., Bisson, Ehlers, Matthews, Pilling, Richards, & Turner, 2007; Foa et al., 2005; Foa, Rothbaum, Riggs, & Murdock, 1991; McDonagh et al., 2005), and with severe mental illness and posttraumatic stress disorder (Mueser et al., 2008). New generations of CBT treatments for anxiety disorders are still in the early stages of development and have yet to undergo thorough empirical scrutiny. However, preliminary data suggests that these approaches, which emphasize mindfulness and experiential acceptance rather than control/avoidance attempts, may be successful, especially when combined with cognitive-behavioral techniques (Evans et al., 2007; Koszyck, Benger, Shlik, & Bradwejn, 2007; Roemer and Orsillo, 2007).

Schizophrenia

Efficacy studies of psychotherapy for schizophrenia typically compare two or more treatments in patients who are also receiving antipsychotic medication. Psychotherapy is seen as an adjunct to medication. The focus of outcome is relapse prevention rather than symptom reduction at posttreatment. CBT of schizophrenia can best be viewed as attempts to decrease the patient's vulnerability to relapse by remediating deficits (e.g., social skills training); increasing medication compliance (e.g., providing patients with skills to discuss side effects with their doctor rather than just discontinuing medication), and reducing stress in the family (e.g., decreasing expressed emotion, providing problem solving strategies for resolving family conflicts). Social skills training can lower relapse rates in patients with schizophrenia. In a study by Hogarty, Anderson, and Reiss (1986), patients being treated with medication who received social skills training had a significantly lower relapse rate than those who received individual supportive psychotherapy (20% versus 41%). Overall, when compared to treatment as usual, behavioral, supportive, and systems based family intervention strategies were efficacious in reducing relapse rates in patients with schizophrenia (e.g., Falloon, et al., 1985; Leff, Kuipers, Berkowitz, & Sturgeon, 1985; Schooler et al., 1997). In a study by Tarrier et al. (1998), patients who received cognitive behavior therapy (i.e., strategies for coping with symptoms, problem-solving training, and relapse prevention strategies) showed improvement in psychotic symptoms when compared with routine care alone, while those assigned to supportive counseling fell in an intermediary position. Interestingly, at the 2-year follow-up, CBT and supportive therapy demonstrated convergence on measures of positive and negative symptoms and clinical improvement, and both were superior to routine care (Tarrier et al., 2000).

Researchers have also examined whether cognitive therapy techniques, when added to treatment as usual, can be used to improve the positive symptoms (hallucinations, delusions) of acute schizophrenia and the negative symptoms (blunted affect, low motivation) of chronic schizophrenia. Studies revealed that CBT techniques can produce impressive effects in terms of the number and severity of positive symptoms, and can lessen general psychopathology and distress associated with hallucinations and delusions (see Rector and Beck, 2001 for a review; see also Zimmerman, Favrod, Trieu, & Pomini, 2005 who report more modest effect sizes). In addition, research has demonstrated a beneficial impact of CBT techniques for negative symptoms; for example, Rector, Seeman, and Segal (2003) found that CBT led to a significant reduction in negative symptoms at the 6-month follow-up (67% deemed 'responders' versus 31% in the control group). Importantly, Turkington et al.'s (2007) five-year follow-up study revealed that the beneficial impact of CBT on overall symptom severity and negative symptoms is durable, supporting the justifiability of the added cost of adjunctive CBT treatment. Finally, Rathod, Kingdon, Weiden, and Turkington (2008) recently argued that CBT is an effective addition to antipsychotic medication in the treatment of "medication resistant" symptomatology.

Various family interventions (behavioral, supportive, and systems) also appear to be effective and a direct comparison of two evidence-based family interventions found that supportive family therapy and behavioral family therapy were equivalent in efficacy (Baucom, Shoham, Mueser, Daiuto, & Stickle, 1998). These findings are not surprising considering the family intervention strategies across the three theoretical orientations share many common essential treatment components (Baucom et al., 1998). There is evidence that family therapy involving the use of insight-oriented techniques and focusing on the past is not beneficial in reducing relapse (Kottgen, Sonnichsen, Mollenhauer, & Jurth, 1984) and can be associated with negative outcomes (McFarlane, Link, Dushay, Marchal, & Crilly, 1995). Research shows, however, that family psychoeducation has a consistent positive impact on patient outcome in schizophrenia (McFarlane, Dixon, Lukens, & Lucksted, 2003), and a recent study revealed that positive therapeutic alliance with patients' relatives was associated with a decreased likelihood of prodromal signs of relapse and rehospitalization during a 2-year follow-up period (Smerud & Rosenfarb, 2008).

Effectiveness

The next challenge is determining how well these treatments generalize to clinical practice where patients often do not have a single diagnosis, where practitioners in the community must be used, and where training programs must be simple and cost-efficient (effectiveness research). While effectiveness research is in its infancy the existing data generated thus far support the use of CBT in clinical practice (Antonuccio, Thomas, & Danton, 1997;

Franklin, Abramowitz, Kozac, Levitt, & Foa, 2000; Friedman et al. 2003; Otto, Pollack, & Maki, 2000; Sanderson, Raue, & Wetzler, 1998; Tuschen-Caffier, Pook, & Frank, 2001; Wade, Treat, & Stuart, 1998; Warren and Thomas, 2001). A recent review conducted by Hunsley and Lee (2007) reveals that, despite methodological limitations, effectiveness studies are demonstrating comparable treatment completion and improvement rates to those reported for randomized trials of treatment efficacy. Indeed, findings for both adults (e.g., Addis et al., 2004; Minami et al., 2008) and children (e.g., Mufson et al., 2004) support the generalizability of treatments with proven efficacy to clinical settings.

REFERENCES

Addis, M. E., Hatgis, C., Krasnow, A. D., Jacob, K., Bourne, L., & Mansfield, A. (2004). Effectiveness of cognitive-behavioral treatment for panic disorder versus treatment as usual in a managed care setting. *Journal of Consulting and Clinical Psychology, 72,* 625–635.

Antonuccio, D. A., Thomas, M., & Danton, W. G. (1997). A cost–effectiveness analysis of cognitive behavior therapy and fluoxetine in the treatment of depression. *Behavior Therapy, 28,* 187–210.

Ball, J. R., Mitchell, P. B., Corry, J. C., Skillecorn, A., Smith, M., & Malhi, G. S. (2006). A randomized controlled trial of cognitive therapy for bipolar disorder: focus on long–term change. *Journal of Clinical Psychiatry, 67,* 277–286.

Barlow, D. H., Gorman, J. M., Shear, M. K., & Woods, S. W. (2000). Cognitive-behavioral therapy, imipramine, and their combination in panic disorder. *Journal of the American Medical Association, 283,* 2529–2536.

Barlow, D. H., Rapee, R., & Brown, T. (1992). Behavioral treatment of generalized anxiety disorder. *Behavior Therapy, 23,* 551–570.

Basco, M. R. & Rush, A. J. (1996). *Cognitive-behavioral therapy for bipolar disorder.* New York: Guilford Press.

Baucom, D. H., Shoham, V., Mueser, K. T., Daiuto, A. D., & Stickle, T. R. (1998). Empirically supported couple and family interventions for marital distress and adult mental health problems. *Journal of Consulting and Clinical Psychology, 66,* 53–88.

Beidel, D. C., Turner, S. M., Young, B., & Paulson, A. (2005). Social effectiveness therapy for children: Three-year follow-up. *Journal of Consulting and Clinical Psychology. 73,* 721–725.

Bisson, J. I., Ehlers, A., Matthews, R., Pilling, S., Richards, D., & Turner, S. (2007). Psychological treatments for chronic post–traumatic stress disorder: Systematic review and meta-analysis. *British Journal of Psychiatry, 190,* 97–104.

Brent, D. A., Holder, D., Kolko, D., Birmaher, B., Baugher, M., Roth, C., et al. (1997). A clinical psychotherapy trial for adolescent depression comparing cognitive, family, and supportive treatments. *Archives of General Psychiatry, 54,* 877–885.

Butler, A. C., Chapman, J. E., Forman, E. M., & Beck, A. T. (2006). The empirical status of cognitive-behavioral therapy: A review of meta-analyses. *Clinical Psychology Review, 26,* 17–31.

Chambless, D. L., Baker, M. J., Baucom, D., Beutler, L. E., Calhoun, K. S., Crits-Christoph, P., et al. (1998). Update on empirically validated therapies II. *The Clinical Psychologist, 51,* 3–16.

Chambless, D. L., Foa, E. B., Groves, G. A., & Goldstein, A. J. (1979). Flooding with Brevital in the treatment of agoraphobia: Countereffective? *Behavior Research and Therapy, 17,* 243–25.

Chambless, D. L. & Ollendick, T. H. (2001). Empirically supported psychological interventions: Controversies and evidence. *Annual Review of Psychology, 52,* 685–716.

Clark, D. M., Ehlers, A., Hackmann, A., McManus, F., Fennell, M., Grey, N., et al. (2006). Cognitive therapy versus exposure and applied relaxation in social phobia: A randomized controlled trial. *Journal of Consulting and Clinical Psychology. 74,* 568–578.

Covin, R., Ouimet, A. J., Seeds, P. M., & Dozois, D. J. A. (2008). A meta-analysis of CBT for pathological worry among clients with GAD. *Journal of Anxiety Disorders, 22,* 108–116.

Craske, M. G. & Barlow, D. H. (2008). Panic disorder and agoraphobia. In D. H. Barlow (Ed.), *Clinical handbook of psychological disorders,* (4th ed., pp. 1–64). New York: Guilford Press.

Cuijpers, P., van Straten, A., Andersson, G., & van Oppen, P. (2008). Psychotherapy for depression in adults: A meta-analysis of comparative outcome studies. *Journal of Consulting and Clinical Psychology, 76,* 909–922.

Depression Guideline Panel. (1993). Depression in Primary Care, Volume 2. Treatment of Major Depression. *Clinical Practice Guideline, Number 5.* Rockville, MD. (Department of Health and Human Services, Public Health Service, Agency for Healthcare Policy and Research. AHCPR Publication No. 93–0551). Washington, DCUS Government Printing Office.

Dimidjian, S., Hollon, S. D., Dobson, K. S., Schmaling, K. B. Kohlenberg, R. J., Addis, M. E., et al. (2006). Randomized trial of behavioral activation, cognitive therapy, and antidepressant medication in acute treatment of adults with major depression. *Journal of Consulting and Clinical Psychology, 74,* 658–670.

Elkin, I., Shea, M. T., Watkins, J. T., Imber, S. D., Sotsky, S. M., Collins, J. F., et al. (1989). National Institute of Mental Health treatment of depression collaborative research program. *Archives of General Psychiatry, 46,* 971–982.

Evans, S., Ferrando, S., Findler, M., Stowell, C., Smart, C., & Haglin, D. (2007). Mindfulness-based cognitive therapy for generalized anxiety disorder. *Journal of Anxiety Disorders, 1,* 1–6.

Falloon, I. R. H., Boyd, J. L., McGill, C. W., Williamson, M., Razani, J., Moss, J. B., et al. (1985). Family management in the prevention of morbidity in schizophrenia: Clinical outcome of a two year longitudinal study. *Archives of General Psychiatry, 42,* 887–896.

Fals-Stewart, W., Marks, A. P., & Schafer, J. A. (1993). A comparison of behavioral group therapy and individual behavior therapy in treating obsessive-compulsive disorder. *Journal of Nervous & Mental Disease, 181,* 189–193.

Foa, E. B., Hembree, E. A., Cahill, S. P., Rauch, S. A. M., Riggs, D. S. ; Feeny, N. C., et al. (2005). Randomized trial of prolonged exposure for posttraumatic stress disorder with and without cognitive restructuring: Outcome at academic and community clinics. *Journal of Consulting and Clinical Psychology, 73,* 953–964

Foa, E. B., Liebowitz, M., Kozak, M., Davies, S., et al. (2005). Randomized, placebo-controlled trial of exposure and ritual prevention, clomipramine, and their combination in the treatment of obsessive compulsive disorder. *American Journal of Psychiatry, 162,* 151–161.

Foa, E. B., Rothbaum, B. O., Riggs, D. S., & Murdock, T. B. (1991). Treatment of post-traumatic stress disorder in rape victims. *Journal of Consulting and Clinical Psychology, 59,* 715–723.

Foley, S. H., Rounsaville, B. J., Weissman, M. M., Sholomaskas, D. & Chevron, E. (1989). Individual versus conjoint interpersonal therapy for depressed patients with marital disputes. *International Journal of Family Psychiatry, 10,* 29–42.

Frank, E. (1999). Interpersonal and social rhythm therapy prevents depressive symptomatology in bipolar I patients. *Bipolar Disorder, 1* (Suppl. 1), 13.

Frank, E., Kupfer, D. J., Perel, J. M., Cornes, C., Jarret, D. B., Mallinger, A. G., et al. (1990). Three-year outcomes for maintenance therapies in recurrent depression. *Archives of General Psychiatry, 47,* 1093–1099.

Frank, E., Kupfer, D. J., Thase, M. E., Mallinger, A. G., Swartz, H. A., Fagiolini, A. M., et al. (2005). Two-year outcomes for interpersonal and social rhythm therapy in individuals with bipolar I disorder. *Archives of General Psychiatry, 62,* 996–1004.

Franklin, M. E., Abramowitz, J. S., Kozak, M. J, Levitt, J. T., & Foa, E. B. (2000). Effectiveness of exposure and response prevention for obsessive-compulsive disorder. Randomized compared with nonrandomized samples. *Journal of Consulting and Clinical Psychology, 68,* 594–602.

Friedman, S., Smith, L., Halpern, B., Levine, C., Paradis, C., et al., 2003. Obsessive-compulsive disorder in a multi-ethnic urban outpatient clinic: Initial presentation and treatment outcome with exposure and response prevention. *Behavior Therapy, 34,* 397–410.

Glaoguen, V., Cottraux, J., & Cucherat, M. (1998) A meta-analysis of the effects of cognitive therapy in depressed patients. *Journal of Affective Disorders, 49,* 59–72.

Goisman, R. M., Rogers, M. P, Stekettee, G. S., Warshaw, M. G., Cuneo, P., & Keller, M. B. (1993). Utilization of behavioral methods in a multi-center anxiety disorders study. *Journal of Clinical Psychiatry, 54,* 213–218.

Gosselin, P., Ladouceur, R., Morin, C. M., Dugas, M. J., & Baillargeon, L. (2006). Benzodiazepine discontinuation among adults with GAD: A randomized trial of cognitive-behavioral therapy. *Journal of Consulting and Clinical Psychology. 74,* 908–919.

Harkness, K. L., Frank, E., Anderson, B., Houck, P. R., Luther, J., & Kupfer, D. J. (2002). Does interpersonal psychotherapy protect women from depression in the face of stressful life events? *Journal of Consulting and Clinical Psychology. 70,* 908–915.

Hayes, S. C., Masuda, A., Bissett, R., Luoma, J., & Guerrero, L. F. (2004). DBT, FAP, and ACT: How empirically oriented are the new behavior therapy technologies? *Behavior Therapy, 35,* 35–54.

Heimberg, R. G., Liebowitz, M. R., Hope, D. A., Schneier, F. R., Holt, C. S., Welkowitz, L. A., et al. (1998). Cognitive behavioral group therapy versus phenelzine therapy for social phobia: 12–week outcome. *Archives of General Psychiatry, 55,* 1133–1141.

Hofmann, S. G., Schulz, S. M., Meuret, A. E., Moscovitch, D. A., & Suvak, M. (2006). Sudden gains during therapy of social phobia. *Journal of Consulting and Clinical Psychology, 74,* 687–697.

Hogarty, G. E., Anderson, C. M., & Reiss, D. J. (1986). Family psychoeducation, social skills training and maintenance chemotherapy in the aftercare treatment of schizophrenia. *Archives of General Psychiatry, 43,* 633–642.

Hunsley, J., & Lee, C. M. (2007). Research-informed benchmarks for psychological treatments: Efficacy studies, effectiveness studies, and beyond. *Professional Psychology: Research and Practice, 38,* 21–23.

Jarrett, R. B., Basco, M. R., & Risser, R. (1998). Is there a role for continuation phase cognitive therapy for depressed outpatients? *Journal of Consulting and Clinical Psychology, 66,* 1036–1040.

Johnson, S. L. (2005). Life events in bipolar disorder: Towards more specific models. *Clinical Psychology Review, 25,* 1008–1027.

Keller, M. B., McCullough, J. P., Klein, D. N., Arnow, B., Dunner, D. L., Gelenberg, A. J., et al. (2000). A comparison of nefazodone, the cognitive behavioral analysis system of psychotherapy, and their combination for the treatment of chronic depression. *New England Journal of Medicine, 342,* 1462–1470.

Kenardy, J. A., Dow, M. G. T., Johnston, D. W., Newman, M. G., Thomson, A., Taylor, C., et al. (2003). A Comparison of Delivery Methods of Cognitive-Behavioral Therapy for Panic Disorder: An International Multicenter Trial. *Journal of Consulting and Clinical Psychology, 71,* 1068–1075.

Kendall, P. C., Hudson, J. L., Gosch, E., Flannery-Schroeder, E., & Suveg, C. (2008). Cognitive-behavioral therapy for anxiety disordered youth: A randomized clinical trial evaluating child and family modalities. *Journal of Consulting and Clinical Psychology, 76,* 282–297.

Koszyck, D., Benger, M., Shlik, J., & Bradwejn, J. (2007). Randomized trial of a meditation-based stress reduction program and cognitive behavior therapy in generalized social anxiety disorder. *Behavior Research and Therapy, 45,* 2518–2526.

Kottgen, C., Sonnichsen, I., Mollenhauer, K., & Jurth, R. (1984). Group therapy with the families of schizophrenic patients. Results of the Hamburg Camberwell Family Interview Study III. *International Journal of Family Psychiatry, 5,* 84–94.

Lam, D. H., Bright, J., Jones, S., Hayward, P., Schuck, N., Chisholm, D., et al. (2000). Cognitive therapy for bipolar illness: A pilot study of relapse prevention. *Cognitive Therapy and Research, 24,* 503–520.

Lam, D. H., Hayward, P., Watkins, E. R., Wright, K., & Sham, P. (2005). Relapse prevention in patients with bipolar disorder: Cognitive therapy outcome after 2 years. *American Journal of Psychiatry, 162,* 324–329.

Lam, D. H., Watkins, E. R., Hayward, P., Bright, J., Wright, K., Kerr, N., et al. (2003). A randomized controlled study of cognitive therapy of relapse prevention for bipolar affective disorder: Outcome of the first year. *Archives of General Psychiatry, 60,* 145–152.

Leff, J., Kuipers, L., Berkowitz, R. & Sturgeon, D. (1985). A controlled trial of social intervention in the families of schizophrenic patients: Two year follow-up. *British Journal of Psychiatry, 146,* 594–600.

Ma, S. H., & Teasdale, J. (2003). Mindfulness-Based cognitive therapy for depression: Replication and exploration of differential relapse prevention effects. *Journal of Consulting and Clinical Psychology, 72,* 31–40.

Markowitz, J. C., Klerman, G. L., Clougherty, K. F., Spielman, L. A., et al. (1995). Individual psychotherapies for depressed HIV-positive patients. *American Journal of Psychiatry, 152,* 1504–1509.

McDonagh, A., Friedman, M., McHugo, G., Ford, J., Sengupta, A., Mueser, K., et al. (2005). Randomized trial of cognitive-behavioral therapy for chronic posttraumatic stress disorder in adult female survivors of childhood sexual abuse. *Journal of Consulting and Clinical Psychology, 73,* 515–524.

McFarlane, W. R., Dixon, L., Lukens, E., & Lucksted, A. (2003). Family psychoeducation and schizophrenia: A review of the literature. *Journal of Marital and Family Therapy, 29,* 223–246.

McFarlane, W. R., Link, B., Dushay, R. Marchal, J. & Crilly, J. (1995). Psychoeducational multiple family groups: Four-year outcome in schizophrenia. *Family Process, 34,* 127–144.

Miklowitz, D. J. (2008). Adjunctive psychotherapy for bipolar disorder: State of the evidence. *American Journal of Psychiatry, 165,* 1408–1419.

Miklowitz, D. R., Goldstein, M. J. (1997). *Bipolar Disorder: A Family-Focused Treatment Approach.* New York: Guilford Press.

Minami, T., Wampold, B. E., Serlin, R. C., Hamilton, E. G., Brown, G. S. & Kircher, J. C. (2008). Benchmarking the effectiveness of psychotherapy treatment for adult depression in a managed care environment: A preliminary study. *Journal of Consulting and Clinical Psychology, 76,* 116–124.

Mitte, K. (2005). Meta-analysis of cognitive-behavioral treatments for generalized anxiety disorder: A comparison with pharmacotherapy. *Psychological Bulletin, 131,* 785–795.

Mohr, D. C., Boudewyn, A. C., Goodkin, D. E., Bostrom, A., & Epstein, L. (2001) Comparative outcomes for individual cognitive-behavior therapy, supportive-expressive group psychotherapy, and sertraline for the treatment of depression in multiple sclerosis. *Journal of Consulting and Clinical Psychology, 69,* 942–949.

Mueser, K. T., Rosenberg, S. D., Xie, H., Jankowski, M. K., Bolton, E. E., Lu, W., et al. (2008). A randomized controlled trial of cognitive-behavioral treatment for posttraumatic stress disorder in severe mental illness. *Journal of Consulting and Clinical Psychology, 76,* 259–271.

Mufson, L., Dorta, K. P., Wickramaratne, P., Nomura, Y., Olfson, M., & Weissman, M. M. (2004). A randomized effectiveness trial of interpersonal psychotherapy for depressed adolescents. *Archives of General Psychiatry, 61,* 577–584.

Mufson, L., Moreau, D., Weissman, M. M. & Klerman, G. L. (1993). *Interpersonal psychotherapy for depressed adolescents.* New York: Guilford Press.

Nathan, P. E., & Gorman, J. M. (Eds.). (1998). *A guide to treatments that work.* New York: Oxford University Press.

O'Leary, K. D. & Beach, S. R. H. (1990). Marital therapy: A viable treatment for depression and marital discord. *American Journal of Psychiatry, 147,* 183–186.

Otto, M. W., Pollack, M. H., & Maki, K. M. (2000). Empirically supported treatments for panic disorder: Costs, benefits, and stepped care. *Journal of Consulting and Clinical Psychology, 68,* 556–563.

Rathod, S., Kingdon, D., Weiden, P., & Turkington, D. (2008). Cognitive-behavioral therapy for medication-resistant schizophrenia: A review. *Journal of Psychiatric Practice, 14,* 22–33.

Rector, N. A., & Beck, A. T. (2001). Cognitive behavioural therapy of schizophrenia: An empirical review. *Journal of Nervous & Mental Disease, 189,* 278–287.

Rector, N. A., Seeman, M. V., & Segal, Z. V. (2003). Cognitive therapy for schizophrenia: A preliminary randomized controlled trial. *Schizophrenia Research, 63,* 1–11.

Reynolds, C. F., Frank, E., Perel, J. M., Imber, S. D., Cornes, C., Miller, M. D., et al. (1999). Nortriptyline and interpersonal psychotherapy as maintenance therapies for recurrent major depression: A randomized controlled trial in patients older than 59 years. *Journal of the American Medical Association, 281,* 39–45.

Reynolds, C. F., Miller, M. D., Pasternak, R. E., Frank, E., Perel, J. M., Cornes, C., et al. (1999). Treatment of bereavement–related major depressive episodes in later life: A controlled study of acute and continuation treatment with nortriptyline and interpersonal psychotherapy. *American Journal of Psychiatry, 156,* 202–208.

Rohan, K. J., Roecklein, K. A., Tierney Lindsey, K., Johnson, L. G., Lippy, R. D., Lacy, T. M., et al., (2007). A randomized controlled clinical trial of cognitive–behavioral therapy, light therapy, and their combination for seasonal affective disorder. *Journal of Consulting and Clinical Psychology, 75,* 489–500.

Rosello, J. & Bernal, G. (1999). The efficacy of cognitive-behavioral and interpersonal treatments for depression in Puerto Rican adolescents. *Journal of Consulting and Clinical Psychology, 67,* 734–745.

Rosello, J. & Bernal, G. (1996). Adapting cognitive-behavioral and interpersonal treatments for depressed Puerto Rican adolescents. In E. D. Hibbs and P. S. Jensen, (Eds.). *Psychosocial treatments for child and adolescent disorders.* Washington, DC: American Psychological Association, 157–185.

Safren, S. A., O'Cleirigh, C., Tan, J. Y., Raminani, S. R., Reilly, L. C., Otto, M. W., et al. (2009). A randomized controlled trial of cognitive behavioral therapy for adherence and depression (CBT-AD) in HIV-infected individuals. *Health Psychology, 28,* 1–10.

Sanderson, W. C. & McGinn, L. K. (1997). Psychological treatments of anxiety disorder patients with comorbidity. In Wetzler, S, & Sanderson, W. C. (eds.): *Treatment strategies of patients with comorbidity.* New York: Wiley.

Sanderson, W. C. & McGinn, L. K. (2001). Cognitive behavior therapy of depression. In M. W. Weissman (Ed.) *Treatment of Depression: Bridging the 21st Century,* 249–280.

Sanderson, W. C., Raue, P. J., & Wetzler, S. (1998). The generalizability of cognitive behavior therapy for panic disorder. *Journal of Cognitive Psychotherapy, 12,* 323–330.

Schooler, N. R., Keith, S. J., Severe, J. B., Mathews, S. M., Bellack, A. S., Glick, I. D., et al. (1997). Relapse and rehospitalization during maintenance treatment of schizophrenia. The effects of dose reduction and family therapy. *Archives of General Psychiatry, 54,* 453–463.

Sloane, R. B., Staples, F. R., Schneider, L. S., et al., (1985). Interpersonal therapy versus nortriptyline for depression in the elderly. In: G. D. Burrows, T. R. Norman and L. Dennerstein, Editors, *Clinical and Pharmacological Studies in Psychiatric Disorders,* London: John Libbey, 344–346.

Smerud, P. E., & Rosenfarb, I. S. (2008). The therapeutic alliance and family psychoeducation in the treatment of schizophrenia: An exploratory prospective change process study. *Journal of Consulting and Clinical Psychology, 76,* 505–510.

Stanley, M. A., Beck, J. G., Novy, D. M., Averill, P. M., Swann, A. C., Diefenbach, G. J., et al. (2003). Cognitive-behavioral treatment of late-life generalized anxiety disorder. *Journal of Consulting and Clinical Psychology, 71,* 309–319.

Tarrier, N., Kinney, C., McCarthy, E., Humphreys, L., Wittkowski, A., & Morris, J. (2000). Two-year follow-up of cognitive-behavioral therapy and supportive counseling in the treatment of persistent symptoms in chronic schizophrenia. *Journal of Consulting and Clinical Psychology, 68,* 917–922.

Tarrier, N., Yusupoff, L., Kinney, C., McCarthy, E., Gledhill, A., Haddock, G., et al., (1998). A randomised controlled trial of intensive cognitive behaviour therapy for chronic schizophrenia. *British Medical Journal, 317,* 303–307.

Turkington, D., Sensky, T., Scott, J., Barnes, T. R. E., Nur, U., Siddle, R., et al. (2007). A randomized controlled trial of cognitive-behavior therapy for persistent symptoms in schizophrenia: A five-year follow-up. *Schizophrenia Research, 98,* 1–7.

Tuschen-Caffier, B., Pook, M., & Frank, M. (2001). Evaluation of manual-based cognitive-behavioral therapy for bulimia nervosa in a service setting. *Behaviour Research and Therapy, 39,* 299–308.

Wade, W. A., Treat, T. A., & Stuart, G. L. (1998). Transporting an empirically supported treatment for panic disorder to a service clinic setting: A benchmarking strategy. *Journal of Consulting and Clinical Psychology, 66,* 231–239.

Warren, R. & Thomas, J. C., (2001). Cognitive behavior therapy obsessive-compulsive disorder in private practice: An effectiveness study. *Journal of Anxiety Disorders, 15,* 277–285.

Weissman, M. M., Markowitz, J. C., & Klerman, G. L. (2000). *Comprehensive guide to interpersonal therapy.* New York: Basic Books.

Weissman, M. M., Prusoff, B. A., DiMascio, A., Neu, C., Goklaney. M., & Klerman, G. L. (1979). The efficacy of drugs and psychotherapy in the treatment of acute depressive episodes. *American Journal of Psychiatry, 136,* 555–558.

Westen, D., & Morrison, K. (2001). A multidimensional meta-analysis of treatments for depression, panic, and generalized anxiety disorder: An empirical examination of the status of empirically supported therapies. *Journal of Consulting and Clinical Psychology, 69,* 875–899.

Whittal, M. L., Robichaud, M, Thordarson, D. S., & McLean, P. D. (2008). Group and individual treatment of obsessive-compulsive disorder using cognitive therapy and exposure plus response prevention: A 2-year follow-up of two randomized trials. *Journal of Consulting and Clinical Psychology, 76,* 1003–1014.

Zimmermann, G., Favrod, J., Trieu, V. H. & Pomini, V. (2005). The effect of cognitive behavioral treatment on the positive symptoms of schizophrenia spectrum disorders: A meta-analysis. *Schizophrenia Research, 77,* 1–9.

LATA K. McGINN
Albert Einstein College of Medicine, Yeshiva University

WILLIAM C. SANDERSON
Hofstra University

JENNIFER STEINBERG
Cognitive and Behavioral Consultants of Westchester, White Plains, NY

PSYCHOTHERAPY INTEGRATION

Although a substantial number of psychotherapists identify themselves as eclectic or integrative (Norcross & Goldfried, 2005), the acceptance of psychotherapy integration was a process that evolved over several decades. A seed for psychotherapy integration was first planted by French in his address of the 1932 meeting of the American Psychiatric Association (later published as French, 1933), in which he drew parallels between psychoanalysis and Pavlovian conditioning. Subsequently, the potential for psychotherapy integration received attention from only a handful of authors between 1932 and 1960 (e.g., Dollard & Miller; Rosenzweig), and did not emerge as a theme until the 1960s and 1970s, beginning with Frank's (1961) *Persuasion and Healing.*

Frank's book addressed commonalities cutting across varying attempts at personal influence and healing in general. Soon after, the important concept of "technical eclecticism" was introduced in 1967 by Lazarus, who argued that clinicians could use techniques from various therapeutic systems without necessarily accepting the theoretical underpinnings associated with these approaches. By this time, many clinicians were coming to recognize that no one single theoretical system could adequately address the diversity of clients and their presenting problems. For example, in 1975, Wachtel maintained that many instances of relapse following behavior therapy might possibly be linked to the client's maladaptive patterns that might more readily be identified when reviewed from within a psychodynamic framework.

With these developments, psychotherapy integration became a bona fide movement in the 1980s. An important contribution was made in a seminal paper by Goldfried (1980), who argued that a fruitful level of abstraction at which such a comparative analysis across therapies might take place would be somewhere between the specific techniques and theoretical explanations for the potential effectiveness of these techniques. He maintained that it is at this intermediate level of abstraction—the level of clinical strategy or principle—that potential points of overlap may exist.

Another significant event in the history of psychotherapy integration was the formation of an international organization specifically devoted to this endeavor. Formed in 1983, the Society for the Exploration of Psychotherapy Integration (SEPI) was established as a way of bringing together the growing number of professionals interested in this area. The 1990s witnessed a continued growth of writing on psychotherapy integration, as well as a continued trend toward more therapists identifying themselves as eclectic/integrative. In 1991, SEPI began publishing its own journal, *Journal of Psychotherapy Integration.* The first edition of the *Handbook of Psychotherapy Integration* (edited by Norcross and Goldfried) was published in 1992, followed by Stricker and Gold's *Comprehensive Handbook of Psychotherapy Integration* in 1993.

For a more comprehensive review of the history of psychotherapy integration, as well as references to the works just cited, see Norcross and Goldfried (2005).

Factors Contributing to Psychotherapy Integration

Despite being a topic of discussion for several decades, psychotherapy integration has only developed into a defined area of interest within the past 20 years. Norcross (2005) has suggested mutually reinforcing factors that have fostered the accelerated interest in psychotherapy integration in recent decades: (1) confusion from the proliferation of therapies; (2) no single approach working for all cases; (3) socioeconomic contingencies (e.g., managed health care); (4) growth of problem-focused treatments; (5) opportunity to observe other approaches; (6) the importance of therapeutic commonalities (e.g., the working alliance); (7) research evidence on treatments that work; and (8) existence of a professional network for integration (i.e., SEPI).

What Is Meant by Psychotherapy Integration?

There are a number of routes to psychotherapy integration: technical eclecticism, theoretical integration, common factors or principles, and assimilative integration.

Technical Eclecticism

The least theoretical of these pathways is technical eclecticism, which seeks to select the best intervention for the person and the problem based on the best available data. Thus, the foundation is more pragmatic than theoretical.

Examples of technical eclecticism include Lazarus' multimodal therapy and Beutler and colleagues' systematic treatment selection and prescriptive psychotherapy, descriptions of which may be found in Norcross and Goldfried (2005). Technical eclectics utilize interventions from different sources without necessarily identifying with the theories that generated them.

Theoretical Integration

The most theoretical of these pathways is theoretical integration, which seeks to integrate two or more therapies with the intention of developing an overlapping theoretical system that is better than the constituent therapies alone. There is an emphasis on integrating the underlying theories, along with their theory specific techniques into an overarching framework. Examples of this approach include Wachtel and colleagues' effort to integrate psychoanalytic and behavioral theories and Ryle's cognitive-analytic therapy (see Norcross & Goldfried, 2005). More macro systems have been constructed to integrate most of the major theoretical schools of psychotherapy, such as Prochaska and DiClemente's transtheoretical approach, also described by Norcross and Goldfried (2005). This form of integration seeks to accomplish more than simply highlighting complementarities between different theories; rather, it seeks to develop a new theory that is greater than the sum of its parts. As noted by Norcross (2005) "the primary distinction between technical eclecticism and theoretical integration is that of empirical pragmatism and theoretical flexibility" (p. 9).

Common Principles

Stemming from the work of Frank (1961), Garfield (1980) and Goldfried (1980), a common principles approach seeks to elucidate the core ingredients that different therapies share in common. Although factors that are considered to be unique to a specific therapy are still considered important, it is the commonalities across approaches that are thought to be most important in accounting for treatment outcomes. This method is predicated on accumulating research on commonalities across treatments that may be important in accounting for psychotherapy outcome (e.g., the working alliance).

Assimilative Integration

Assimilative integration was defined by Messer (2001) as "the incorporation of attitudes, perspectives, or techniques from an auxiliary therapy into a therapist's primary, grounding approach" (p. 1). This form of integration calls for a firm grounding in one system of psychotherapy with a willingness to incorporate practices and views from other systems. Assimilative integration may be conceptualized as a bridge between technical eclecticism and theoretical integration, and it may be accomplished through the lens of common principles.

It is important to note how techniques, theory and principles interrelate. One who is technically eclectic cannot disregard theory, just as one who is a theoretical integrationist cannot disregard techniques, and common change principles would not be possible in the absence of either. Indeed, techniques may be viewed as parameters of principles of change. For example, empathy may be seen as a way to implement the common principle involving the importance of a therapeutic alliance. Further, the delineation of change principles—which are derived by grouping techniques according to their function—can be used to develop a theory of change.

Integration in Clinical Practice

Whereas integrationism is the modal theoretical orientation for American psychologists, a variety of eclectic/integrative systems exist in practice (Norcross & Goldfried, 2005). In an early survey of eclectic psychotherapists, Garfield and Kurtz (1977) found that the integration of psychoanalytic and learning theory was the most common. Norcross, Karpiak, and Lister (2005) more recently surveyed self-identified eclectic/integrative therapists and found that, with regard to their preferred integration pathway, 27.5% of respondents identified with theoretical integration, 27.5% identified with common change principles, 26% identified with assimilative integration, and 19% identified with technical eclecticism. When asked to provide a rationale for their adoption of an integrative approach, the majority of therapists noted the importance of tailoring the treatment to the needs of the client.

Research on Integration

Despite psychotherapy integration being the focus of a large theoretical and clinical literature, empirical research on it has been slow to progress. However, evidence has begun to accumulate in recent years for factors that support or contribute to integration and for treatments that fall under most of the major categories of psychotherapy integration (see Norcross & Goldfried, 2005).

For example, in terms of eclecticism, the work of Beutler and colleagues has provided useful evidence-based guidelines for prescribing specific types of interventions for certain types of clients (e.g., clients with high versus low level of reactance). Examples of theoretically driven integrative treatments with empirical support consist of Ryle's cognitive analytic therapy, Prochaska and DiClemente's transtheoretical model that focuses on stages of change (precontemplative, contemplation, preparation, action, and maintenance), and Linehan's dialectic-behavior therapy (DBT) for borderline personality disorder.

Rather than focusing on specific techniques or theory, Castonguay and Beutler (2006) drew on the work of a task force that gathered research findings of principles of change, the results of which are summarized in *Principles of Therapeutic Change That Work*. From an assimilative integration perspective, Castonguay and colleagues designed and tested an integrative treatment for depression that uses techniques from humanistic and interpersonal therapies to help repair alliance ruptures in cognitive therapy. Another example that has been studied is McCullough's cognitive-behavioral analysis system of psychotherapy (CBASP), an integrated approach to treating chronic depression. A comprehensive review of research on integrated approaches may be found in the Schottenbauer, Glass and Arnkoff chapter in Norcross and Goldfried (2005).

Education and Training

Historically, psychotherapists have been trained exclusively in a single orientation. More recently, however, beginning therapists are receiving training in several theoretical orientations, or are at least exposed to a variety of approaches throughout their training. Training in psychotherapy integration is a complex enterprise. An integrative approach to training attempts to take into account the complexity of change and the reality that no one single approach is effective for all clients and clinical problems. However, thinking and practicing from an integrative framework requires a solid foundation in a variety of treatment approaches, which can place more pressure on students and programs that attempt to coordinate this into their clinical training.

In a study that surveyed APA-accredited internships and counseling psychology graduate programs, Lampropoulos and Dixon (2007) found that training directors held positive attitudes toward psychotherapy integration. Approximately 31% of all programs offered mandatory or optional training in five major psychotherapy theories, and 90% reported teaching psychotherapy integration in their programs as part of one or more courses. Training in psychotherapy integration can take many forms. A common thread in many of these models is an early emphasis on training students in fundamental relationship and communication skills. Interpersonal skills are important in that they allow therapists to gain competency in establishing, repairing, and maintaining the therapeutic alliance.

A second step usually entails exposing trainees to multiple major theoretical systems and promoting openness to the specific strengths and weakness inherent in any single approach. Proposed models typically begin to diverge from one another as students progress through their coursework and begin their practica, depending on several factors, including the type of integration, expectations regarding competency, and timing (i.e., integration from the outset or after a certain level of mastery of one or more approaches). Despite disagreement regarding the proper route toward integration in education and training, training programs appear to have become more committed to psychotherapy integration.

Future Directions

A strong, if not greater, number of clinicians will likely continue to identify themselves as integrative. Unlike previous integrative therapists who were predominately trained in a single orientation and eventually came to identify with an integrative framework, more beginning therapists are likely to identify themselves as integrative earlier on in their training, which speaks to the importance of developing and testing evidence-based integrative training models. This, in turn, will have consequences for psychotherapy integration in everyday clinical practice.

Research on psychotherapy integration is in its relative infancy, and continued research will be necessary if it is to remain a force in psychology and psychotherapy. This, of course, goes beyond testing the relative efficacy of integrative treatments. Although this information will no doubt be important, the development of effective integrative treatment strategies has been, and should continue to be, informed by psychotherapy process research, with an emphasis on variables (technique, participant and relationship) that are both unique and cut across different theoretical orientations, resulting in clinically useful principals of change (see Castonguay & Beutler, 2006). Similarly, emphasis should be placed on the empirical test, refinement, and dissemination of core clinical principles.

REFERENCES

Castonguay, L. G., & Beutler, L. E. (Eds.) (2006). *Principles of therapeutic change that work*. New York: Oxford University Press.

Frank, J. D. (1961). *Persuasion and healing: A comparative study of psychotherapy*. New York: Schocken Books.

French, T. M. (1933). Interrelations between psychoanalysis and the experimental work of Pavlov. *American Journal of Psychiatry*, *89*, 1165–1203.

Garfield, S. L. (1980). *Psychotherapy: An eclectic approach*. New York: Wiley.

Garfield, S. L., & Kurtz, R. (1977). A study of eclectic views. *Journal of Consulting and Clinical Psychology*, *45*, 78–83.

Goldfried, M. R. (1980). Toward the delineation of therapeutic change principles. *American Psychologist*, *35*, 991–999.

Lampropoulos, G. K., & Dixon, D. N. (2007). Psychotherapy integration in internships and counseling psychology doctoral programs. *Journal of Psychotherapy Integration*, *17*, 185–208.

Messer, S. B. (2001). Introduction to the special issue on assimilative integration. *Journal of Psychotherapy Integration*, *11*, 1–4.

Norcross, J. C., & Goldfried, M. R. (2005). A primer on psychotherapy integration. In J. C. Norcross and M. R. Goldfried (Eds.), *Handbook of psychotherapy integration* (2nd ed.) (pp. 3–23). New York: Oxford University Press

Norcross, J. C., & Goldfried, M. R. (Eds.) (2005). *Handbook of psychotherapy integration* (2nd ed.). New York: Oxford University Press

Norcross, J. C., Karpiak, C. P., & Lister, K. M. (2005). What's an integrationist? A study of self-identified integrative and (occasionally) eclectic psychologists. *Journal of Clinical Psychology. 61*, 1587–1594.

Stricker, G., & Gold, J. R. (1993). *Comprehensive handbook of psychotherapy integration.* New York: Plenum Press.

JAMES F. BOSWELL
Pennsylvania State University

MARVIN R. GOLDFRIED
Stony Brook University

See also: Psychotherapy, Effective Elements of; Psychotherapy Research; Psychotherapy Training

PSYCHOTHERAPY, PHILOSOPHY OF

Psychotherapy is often considered to be an applied science consisting of a compendium of techniques or approaches validated by empirical research. Alternately, it is viewed as an art form requiring a creative, intuitive, and individualistic approach to clients and their problems. Psychotherapy, however, can also be regarded as a philosophically influenced practice whose underpinnings transcend its scientific, human engineering, or artistic dimensions.

Examples of some of these domains are (1) our possessing a priori categories of understanding that are part of therapeutic work, such as certain assumptions about reality, and underlying narrative structures; (2) the inevitability of value-laden issues in therapy; (3) the presence of societal and cultural influences on the practice of psychotherapy, as well as the effect of psychotherapy on the terms in which people in our society view themselves; and (4) the importance of regarding clients as having ethical and legal standing as well as being free agents, quite apart from their status as the objects of scientific understanding and healing (Messer & Woolfolk, 1998; Woolfolk & Murphy, 2004). We will take up each of these areas in turn.

A Priori Categories of Understanding

Every intellectual endeavor has a starting point that is prior to empirical investigation. Without our possessing the conceptual categories that are prior to experience, we could not organize the world into objects and events. When we look at the world, we do so through particular lenses or conceptual schemes that influence what we see.

Philosophical analysis is a tool for making the properties of these lenses explicit, helping us to understand the concepts that underlie our thinking.

One aspect of the philosophical and cultural a priori is referred to by contemporary philosophers as "the Background." It contains the taken-for-granted knowledge and norms that are implicit in our practical and theoretical activities. For example, our clients have a certain cultural background, which we most often share. To understand how much we take this common cultural understanding for granted, imagine the practice of psychotherapy in a different culture—say, Japan. When individuals seek psychotherapy in Japan, it is frequently not to reduce their own distress, which is the norm in Western culture, but because they believe they possess traits that may cause discomfort to others (Bankart, 1997). With such clients, who are not imbued with such Western ideals as individualism, autonomy, and self-realization, the entire project of psychotherapy is viewed very differently. What one means by such therapeutic goals as interpersonal effectiveness and emotional maturity are no longer so obvious and straightforward. (For other ways in which culture influences psychotherapy, see Hoshmand, 2006.)

Consider, too, as an example of the background, the contrasting narrative themes underlying different forms of treatment, which often go unrecognized. One typology of narratives describes four such "visions" or viewpoints: romantic, tragic, ironic, and comic (Frye, 1957). From the romantic viewpoint, life is an adventure or quest, a drama of the triumph of good over evil, virtue over vice, and light over darkness. It idealizes individuality and authentic self-expression. The romantic vision underpins humanistic approaches to psychotherapy (e.g., client-centered, existential, experiential), which stress the value of and possibilities for spontaneity, authenticity, and creativity.

The ironic vision, by contrast, encompasses an attitude of detachment and suspicion, of keeping things in perspective, and of recognizing the fundamental ambiguity and mystery of every issue that life presents. Whereas behavioral and cognitive therapists tend to take client complaints at face value, and humanistic therapists accept most client feelings as authentic expression, psychoanalytic therapists are more likely to look for hidden meanings, paradoxes, and contradictions. This puts them more squarely in the ironic mode.

The tragic vision is an acceptance of the limitations in life—not all is possible, not all is redeemable, not all potentialities are realizable. The clock cannot be turned back, death cannot be avoided, and human nature cannot be radically perfected. Many aspects of psychoanalysis fall within the tragic vision. People are determined by events of their early childhood, which are subject to repression and beyond their conscious purview. The outcome of psychoanalytic treatment is not unalloyed happiness or all obstacles overcome, but rather the fuller recognition and acceptance of what one's struggles are about, and the conditions and limitations of life.

By contrast, within the comic vision, the direction of events is from bad to better or even best. Obstacles and struggles are ultimately overcome. Harmony and unity, progress and happiness prevail. Cognitive-behavior therapy holds out the promise of finding greater happiness through the application of scientific principles of healing; humanistic approaches emphasize the substantial possibility for gratification. These underlying visions profoundly affect both the process and desired outcomes of these different forms of treatment. For their application to psychotherapy, taking each into account, see Messer (2006).

Psychotherapy and Values

Virtually all of the innovators who made significant contributions to psychotherapy, such as Freud, Rogers, Wolpe, Perls, and Beck, considered themselves to be discoverers of morally neutral, scientific knowledge and viewed psychotherapy as an objective application of that knowledge to the goal of psychological health. By contrast, philosophical analysis helps us see how values often establish, albeit covertly, the criteria for intervention, influence patterns of therapeutic exploration, and promote standards for client conduct.

For example, a man comes to a therapist announcing that he is considering leaving his wife for a much younger, recently married woman and wants help making the decision (Messer, 2001). A therapist operating within the values of liberal, secular individualism would stress the happiness and contentment of the individual above all else and above all others, encouraging him to explore the issue in these self-directed (some might say "selfish") terms. One who holds to communitarian values might be more inclined to address how the client's decision to leave his wife will cause others to suffer, such as spouses, children, and other family members. Yet another therapist, hewing to religious values such as the sanctity of marriage, might emphasize the psychological and moral consequences of breaking marital vows

Despite claims to the contrary, there is no value-free psychotherapy. For a discussion of how the moral dimension of psychotherapy has gotten transformed and disguised by medical and technological language and concepts, see Miller (2004). He argues that the field of psychotherapy would be more successful in alleviating human suffering were it to bring to light the moral dimensions of practice.

The Intersection of Psychotherapy with Societal and Cultural Worldviews

The institution of psychotherapy is a significant source of, and influence on, contemporary customs, values, and worldviews and is constantly incorporating them in its purview (Gurman & Messer, 2003; Woolfolk & Murphy, 2004). For example, all societies need mechanisms that establish what behavior is to be promoted and what is to be proscribed. Although we most often think of clinicians as healers, they also function as agents of social control. The clinician is granted responsibility for many bizarre, incapable, or destructive individuals whom the rest of society will not or cannot tolerate.

Psychotherapy and its related theory and language are also cultural phenomena that have affected how people think about themselves. For example, laypeople refer to Freudian slips, defenses, guilt complexes, conditioned responses, existential angst, identity crises, or discovering their true selves—all terms related to the activity of psychotherapy. Similarly, when they explain their problems in terms of childhood occurrences such as parental neglect or harsh criticism, repressed memories, or learned associations, they demonstrate that psychotherapy is far more than a scientific or technical endeavor. Its language constitutes the very belief systems that people employ to make sense out of their lives.

The Client as a Person with Agency

In addition to understanding and treating clients based on science, psychotherapists must recognize that their clients have legal and ethical standing as persons. In discussing with clients the scheduling of appointments, setting a fee, establishing therapeutic goals, or assessing whether the benefits of a course of therapy are commensurate with its costs, the ground rules come from ethics and practical reason, not science. Psychotherapists regard clients in these discussions not as objects of science, but as parties to a contract, as free agents, as consumers with the prerogative to decide and choose.

In summary, psychotherapy is not only a scientific, medical, or technical enterprise but is undergirded by philosophical assumptions, many of which are covert. Given its role as a guide for living, psychotherapy is influenced by the prevailing sociocultural milieu, its customs, and its values. In turn, psychotherapy has had a profound effect on our very definition of who and what we are and that to which we aspire.

REFERENCES

Bankart, C. P. (1997). *Taking care: A history of Western and Eastern psychotherapies*. Pacific Grove, CA: Brooks/Cole.

Frye, N. (1957). *Anatomy of criticism*. Princeton, NJ: Princeton University Press.

Gurman, A. S., & Messer, S. B. (2003). Contemporary issues in the theory and practice of psychotherapy: A framework for comparative study. In A. S. Gurman & S. B. Messer (Eds.), *Essential psychotherapies: Theory and practice* (2nd ed., pp. 1–23). New York: Guilford Press.

Hoshmand, L. (Ed.). (2006). *Culture, psychotherapy and counseling: Critical and integrative perspectives.* Thousand Oaks, CA: Sage.

Messer, S. B. (2001). Empirically supported treatments: What's a non-behaviorist to do? In B. D. Slife, R. N. Williams, & S. H. Barlow (Eds.), *Critical issues in psychotherapy: Translating new ideas into practice* (pp. 3–19). Thousand Oaks, CA: Sage.

Messer, S. B. (2006). Psychotherapy integration using contrasting visions of reality. In G. Stricker & J. Gold (Eds.), *A casebook of psychotherapy integration* (pp. 281–291). Washington, DC: American Psychological Association Press.

Messer, S. B., & Woolfolk, P. L. (1998). Philosophical issues in psychotherapy. *Clinical Psychology: Science and Practice, 5,* 251–263.

Miller, R. B. (2004). *Facing human suffering: Psychology and psychotherapy as moral engagement.* Washington, DC: American Psychological Association Press.

Woolfolk, R. L., & Murphy, D. (2004). Axiological foundations of psychotherapy. *Journal of Psychotherapy Integration, 14,* 168–191.

SUGGESTED READINGS

Slife, B. D., Williams, R. N., & Barlow, S. H. (Eds.). (2001). *Critical issues in psychotherapy: Translating new ideas into practice.* Thousand Oaks, CA: Sage.

Woolfolk, R. L. (1998). *The cure of souls: Science, values and psychotherapy.* San Francisco, CA: Jossey-Bass.

STANLEY B. MESSER
ROBERT L. WOOLFOLK
Rutgers University

See also: Psychotherapy

PSYCHOTHERAPY RESEARCH

Psychotherapy research is primarily concerned with the evaluation of the impact and process of psychological interventions for clinical disorders (e.g., depression, anxiety), problems of living (e.g., marital discord), and medical conditions (e.g., chronic pain). It is also concerned with characteristics of the client and therapist as they relate to treatment process and outcome. Most psychotherapy research has focused on individual treatment. However, numerous investigations have also been conducted on couples, family, and group therapy.

Psychotherapy Outcome

With regard to outcome, more than 60 years of research have shown that psychotherapy works: It is more effective than the absence of treatment and placebo treatments (Lambert & Ogles, 2004). Psychotherapy has been demonstrated to be beneficial not only in research under controlled conditions (i.e., *efficacy* research) but also in naturalistic environments (i.e., *effectiveness* research). Guided by the American Psychological Association (Division 12) Task Force on empirically supported treatments (ESTs), researchers have been able to identify a large number of effective psychosocial interventions for specific clinical problems experienced by adults, adolescents, and children (see Nathan & Gorman, 2002). Although by no means all of them (e.g., interpersonal and emotion-focused therapies for depression), most of the current ESTs are cognitive-behavioral—in part because cognitive-behavioral therapists have devoted more energy to empirically assessing the outcomes of their interventions than have therapists from other orientations. However, with the exception of a number of specific problems (e.g., panic disorder, phobias, childhood aggression, psychotic behaviors, health-related behaviors) for which CBT currently stands as the treatment of choice, comparative outcome research suggests that the impact of different forms of psychotherapy tends to be equivalent (Lambert & Ogles, 2004). As noted by Kopta, Lueger, Saunders, and Howard (1999), differences between therapists appear to explain more of the outcome variance than differences between treatments (see also Wampold, 2001). Outcome research (i.e., dose–effect studies) has also demonstrated that clients' improvement tends to follow consistent patterns across a variety of psychotherapeutic approaches, with (1) early sessions resulting in more change than later sessions and (2) acute distress improving faster than chronic distress, which in turn improves faster than characterological symptoms (see Kopta et al., 1999).

Although psychotherapy works, there are clear limitations to its impact. Treatment efficacy for a number of clinical problems, such as various personality disorders, remains to be firmly established. Moreover, numerous clients terminate treatment prematurely, others do not respond to therapy, others respond but subsequently relapse, and some even deteriorate (Garfield, 1994; Lambert & Ogles, 2004). This state of affairs clearly indicates that there is room for improvement in therapy outcome. As a strategy to increase the beneficial impact of therapy, therapists have attempted to integrate, combine, or selectively prescribe techniques associated with different therapeutic orientations. Although such integrative and/or eclectic efforts have received empirical attention, more research needs to be conducted to support the promising clinical and theoretical contributions of the integration movement.

Psychotherapy Process

Whereas outcome research focuses on whether psychotherapy works, process research investigates *how* it works (or why it fails to work for everyone). Researchers have studied process variables related to the following: (1) the *therapist* (e.g., competence or skills, adherence to treatment manuals, use of specific techniques or principles of change, focus of intervention, verbal and nonverbal activity, response modes, goals and intentions, expectations, emotions, self-disclosure, self-acceptance, self-congruence), (2) the *client* (e.g., aims, expectations, suitability to treatment, concerns, intentions, verbal and nonverbal activity, content of dialogue, response modes, self-exploration, emotional experience, voice quality, perception of therapist actions or intentions, identification with or internalization of the therapist, description and explanations of change, openness versus defensiveness, cooperation versus resistance), (3) the *client–therapist relationship* (e.g., working alliance, mutual influence, affiliative and disaffiliative patterns of interaction), and (4) the *structure of treatment* (e.g., duration of therapy, stages of treatment, frequency of sessions, fees, client role preparation, stability of the therapeutic arrangements, the use of supervision, procedures for termination). These variables have been studied either by investigating a single form of therapy or by comparing different approaches.

One goal of process research is to describe what happens during therapy. For example, several studies have shown that therapists can adhere to treatment protocols and that different forms of treatment can be differentiated based on the therapist's use of prescribed techniques (DeRubeis, Hollon, Evans, & Bemis, 1982). However, studies have also demonstrated that there are important differences between what therapists do and what they say they do (or what their theoretical orientation prescribes them to do). For example, supportive interventions that are typically associated with CBT (e.g., persuading the phobic client to enter the phobic situation, prescription of daily activities, altering interactions with significant others) have been found to be present in different modalities of psychodynamic treatment, including classical psychoanalysis (Wallerstein & Dewitt, 1997). A study by Truax (1966) has also suggested that rather than being nondirective, the interventions of Carl Rogers followed a process of operant conditioning.

Above and beyond its purely descriptive function, another goal of process research is to identify the factors that facilitate or interfere with clients' improvement. Several process variables, identified within different dimensions of psychotherapy, have been positively linked with outcome (Orlinsky, Ronnestad, & Willutzki, 2004). As demonstrated by two recent APA task forces (Castonguay & Beutler, 2005; Norcross, 2002), a number of these variables are related to the client–therapist relationship. In particular, the quality of the therapeutic alliance has been shown to be a robust predictor of improvement. According to Lambert (1992), common factors (such as alliance) and placebo effects account for approximately 45% of the variance in therapy outcome. Process research has

also provided support for the therapeutic importance of variables assumed to be unique to particular approaches. Clients' emotional experiences have related to outcome in humanistic treatment (Hill, 1990). Furthermore, the use of homework and other specific techniques has been linked to improvement in cognitive therapy (CT; Feeley, DeRubeis, & Gelfand, 1999). On the other hand, other CT-prescribed techniques have been found to be either unrelated to outcome (Jones & Pulos, 1993) or negatively associated with improvement (Castonguay, Goldfried, Wiser, Raue, & Hayes, 1996). Similarly, the technique of transference is not always linked with positive change in psychodynamic therapy (Schut et al., 2005). Researchers at Vanderbilt University also found that along with an increased adherence to a treatment manual, psychodynamic therapists showed a higher level of disaffiliative communications (e.g., hostile messages toward clients) following a training program that was in part designed to reduce therapists' hostile interaction with difficult clients. Such disaffiliative communication patterns were associated with poor outcome in another study conducted within that research program (see Henry & Strupp, 1994).

It should be noted that the methods and statistical analyses typically used in process–outcome studies are not always adequate to capture the complexity of the process of change (Stiles, 1988). For instance, correlational strategies (which assume a linear relationship between the frequency of the process variable and outcome) cannot provide information concerning the context within which a process variable takes place. Because such strategies are based on the assumption that the more one uses a therapeutic intervention, the better it is for the client, correlational strategies fail to take into consideration the fact that the therapist will use an effective technique more or less frequently based on the client's needs. The timing or appropriateness of a technique, in other words, is more important than the frequency with which it is used (Stiles, 1988). Thus, several investigators have developed new ways of conducting process research (e.g., task analysis, interpersonal process recall) in order to provide contextual and finer-grained analyses of interaction patterns between participants, especially during significant (i.e., helpful or detrimental) therapeutic episodes (Rice & Greenberg, 1984). Furthermore, sophisticated longitudinal analyses (e.g., hierarchical linear modeling, structural equation modeling) have been more frequently applied to the examination of treatment moderators, mediators, and complex change processes over time (Laurenceau, Hayes, & Feldman, 2007).

Client and Therapist Characteristics

Psychotherapy researchers have also been interested in examining characteristics of clients and therapists. In fact, as for client–therapist relationship variables, several of these characteristics have been the focus of the two most recent APA task forces mentioned previously (Castonguay & Beutler, 2005; Norcross, 2002). Various demographic variables have been investigated (e.g., age, gender, social class, and ethnicity), but none of them appears to account for a significant part of the outcome variance (Clarkin & Levy, 2004). Professional characteristics of therapists, such as profession (e.g., clinical psychology, social work, psychiatry), training level, and experience, have also failed to reliably predict client improvement (Beutler et al., 2004; Lambert & Ogles, 2004).

A number of personal characteristics of both client and therapist, however, appear to be related to psychotherapy process and outcome. For example, the client's pretreatment level of perfectionism has been negatively related to outcome in different forms of psychotherapy, and the presence of a personality disorder also seems to be a poor prognostic indicator for a number of Axis I disorders such as depression, anxiety disorders, and eating disorders (Clarkin & Levy, 2004). Furthermore, studies suggest that clients with interpersonal problems (e.g., hostility) have difficulty establishing a therapeutic alliance (Kopta et al., 1999). In addition, the therapist's emotional well-being has been linked with positive change (Beutler et al., 2004), and the therapist's negative introject (i.e., hostile and controlling way of relating toward self) has been found to predict negative interpersonal patterns in the client–therapist relationship (Henry & Strupp, 1994).

Studies have also examined whether matching client and therapist variables could improve the impact of therapy; matching demographic variables has not led to significant results. A large number of studies have also investigated the potential interaction between client characteristics and types of therapy. With few exceptions, this research has lead to a paucity of reliable findings. Among these exceptions is the work of Beutler and colleagues (1991), who demonstrated that clients with an externalized coping style (those who react to stress by acting out and blaming others) improved more in a symptom-oriented treatment (e.g., cognitive therapy [CT]) than clients with an internalized style of coping (those who tend to ruminate and self-blame when confronted with stress). On the other hand, internalizing clients responded most to an insight-oriented treatment (e.g., supportive/self-directive therapy [S/SD]). Beutler and colleagues (1991) have also found that whereas clients high in reactance level (those who resist being controlled by others) fare better in a nondirective treatment (e.g., S/SD) than in directive therapies (e.g., focused-expressive therapy and CT), clients low in reactance respond more to CT than to S/SD.

Research has offered considerable information with regard to the impact of psychotherapy, the mechanisms of change, and the characteristics of the client and therapist that are related to the outcome and process of different approaches. Recent efforts have been made to promote the implementation of evidence-based practice, emphasizing the availability of knowledge derived from different research methodologies (Norcross, Beutler, & Levant, 2006). At this time, however, it is fair to say that psychotherapy research has had a limited impact on clinical practice. For example, although the current ESTs represent, for many researchers, the ultimate embodiment of the scientific practitioner model, they are perceived by many clinicians as irrelevant academic efforts, if not major threats to valid clinical practice. Fortunately, efforts to bridge the gap between researchers and clinicians have begun to emerge. Among them, the creation of practice research networks seems particularly promising, as they are based on an active collaboration between clinicians and researchers to develop and implement scientifically rigorous and clinically relevant research. Without efforts of this and other sorts to solidify and actualize the scientific practitioner model, it is more than likely that future attempts to improve the effect of psychotherapy and to understand the process of change will be seriously hampered.

REFERENCES

Beutler, L. E., Engle, D., Mohr, D., Daldrup, R. J., Bergan, J., Meredith, K., et al. (1991). Predictors of differential response to cognitive, experiential, and self-directed psychotherapeutic procedures. *Journal of Consulting and Clinical Psychology, 59,* 333–340.

Beutler, L. E., Malik, M., Alimohamed, S., Harwood, T. M., Talebi, H., Noble, S., et al. (2004). Therapist variables. In M. J. Lambert (Ed.), *Bergin and Garfield's handbook of psychotherapy and behavior change* (5th ed., pp. 227–306). Hoboken, NJ: John Wiley & Sons.

Castonguay, L. G., & Beutler, L. E. (Eds.). (2005). *Principles of therapeutic change that work.* New York: Oxford University Press.

Castonguay, L. G., Goldfried, M. R., Wiser, S., Raue, P. J., & Hayes, A. H. (1996). Predicting outcome in cognitive therapy for depression: A comparison of unique and common factors. *Journal of Consulting and Clinical Psychology, 64,* 497–504.

Clarkin, J. F., & Levy, K. N. (2004). The influence of client variables on psychotherapy. In M. J. Lambert (Ed.), *Bergin and Garfield's handbook of psychotherapy and behavior change* (5th ed., pp. 194–226). Hoboken, NJ: John Wiley & Sons.

DeRubeis, R. J., Hollon, S. D., Evans, M. D., & Bemis, K. M. (1982). Can psychotherapies for depression be discriminated? A systematic investigation of cognitive therapy and interpersonal therapy. *Journal of Consulting and Clinical Psychology, 50,* 744–756.

Feeley, M., DeRubeis, R. J., & Gelfand, L. A. (1999). The temporal relation of adherence and alliance to symptom change in cognitive therapy for depression. *Journal of Consulting and Clinical Psychology, 67,* 578–582.

Garfield, S. L. (1994). Research on client variables in psychotherapy. In A. E. Bergin & S. L. Garfield (Eds.), *Handbook of psychotherapy and behavior change* (4th ed.). New York: John Wiley & Sons.

Henry, W. P., & Strupp, H. H. (1994). The therapeutic alliance as interpersonal process. In A. O. Horvath & L. S. Greenberg (Eds.), *The working alliance: Theory, research, and practice*. New York: John Wiley & Sons.

Hill, C. E. (1990). Explanatory in-session process research in individual therapy: A review. *Journal of Consulting and Clinical Psychology, 58*, 288–294.

Jones, E. E., & Pulos, S. M. (1993). Comparing the process in psychodynamic and cognitive-behavioral therapies. *Journal of Consulting and Clinical Psychology, 61*, 306–316.

Kopta, S. M., Lueger, R. J., Saunders, S. M., & Howard, K. I. (1999). Individual psychotherapy outcome research: Challenges leading to greater turmoil or a positive transition. *Annual Review of Psychology, 50*, 441–469.

Lambert, M. J. (1992). Psychotherapy outcome research: Implications for integrative and eclectic therapists. In J. C. Norcross & M. R. Goldfried (Eds.), *Handbook of psychotherapy integration* (pp. 94–129). New York: Basic Books.

Lambert, M. J., & Ogles, B. M. (2004). The efficacy and effectiveness of psychotherapy. In M. J. Lambert (Ed.), *Bergin and Garfield's handbook of psychotherapy and behavior change* (5th ed., pp. 139–193). Hoboken, NJ: John Wiley & Sons.

Laurenceau, J-P., Hayes, A. M., & Feldman, G. C. (2007). Some methodological issues in the study of change processess in psychotherapy. *Clinical Psychology Review, 27*, 682–695.

Nathan, P. E., & Gorman, J. M. (Eds.). (2002). *A guide to treatments that work* (2nd ed.). New York: Oxford University Press.

Norcross, J. C. (Ed.). (2002). *Psychotherapy relationships that work: Therapist contributions and responsiveness to patient needs*. New York: Oxford University Press.

Norcross, J. C., Beutler, L. E., & Levant, R. F. (Eds.). (2006). *Evidence-based practices in mental health: Debate and dialogue on fundamental questions*. Washington, DC: American Psychological Association Books.

Orlinsky, D. E., Ronnestad, M.H., & Willutzki, U. (2004). Fifty years of psychotherapy process–outcome research: Continuity and change. In M. J. Lambert (Ed.), *Bergin and Garfield's handbook of psychotherapy and behavior change* (5th ed., pp. 307–389). Hoboken, NJ: John Wiley & Sons.

Rice, L. N., & Greenberg, L. S. (1984). *Patterns of change: Intensive analysis of psychotherapy process*. New York: Guilford Press.

Schut, A. J., Castonguay, L. G., Bedics, J. D., Smith, T. L., Barber, J. P., Flanagan, K. M., et al. (2005). Therapist interpretation, patient–therapist interpersonal process, and outcome in psychodynamic psychotherapy for avoidant personality disorder. *Psychotherapy: Theory, Research, Practice, and Training, 42*, 494–511.

Stiles, W. B. (1988). Psychotherapy process–outcome correlations may be misleading. *Psychotherapy, 25*, 27–35.

Truax, C. B. (1966). Reinforcement and non-reinforcement in Rogerian psychotherapy. *Journal of Abnormal Psychology, 71*, 1–9.

Wallerstein, R. S., & DeWitt, K. N. (1997). Intervention modes in psychoanalysis and in psychoanalytic psychotherapies: A revised classification. *Journal of Psychotherapy Integration, 7*, 129–150.

Wampold, B. E. (2001). *The great psychotherapy debate: Models, methods and findings*. Mahway, NJ: Lawrence Erlbaum.

SUGGESTED READING

Lambert, M. J. (Ed.). (2004). *Bergin and Garfield's handbook of psychotherapy and behavior change* (5th ed.). Hoboken, NJ: John Wiley & Sons.

Louis G. Castonguay
Samuel S. Norberg
Alexander J. Schut
Michael J. Constantino
Pennsylvania State University

PSYCHOTHERAPY TRAINING

The story of psychotherapy training reaches back to antiquity. Perhaps a devoted student accompanied the medicine man, shaman, or priest and helped alleviate mental anguish. This student apprenticed or modeled the rituals, prescriptions, and incantations while providing sympathetic care to the afflicted. In more contemporary times, the art and science of psychotherapy and its training or supervision dates back to the late nineteenth century. Bernheim, Charcot, and Janet demonstrated hysteria and hypnotic phenomena to their eager students, one of whom was Freud. Freud formally systematized many of the ideas of the time into a unified theory including developmental states, unconscious phenomena, the continuity of abnormal and normal people, and the combination of scientific and humane treatment for the mental disorders. He conferred with his senior colleague, Breuer, and eventually formed his Wednesday evening groups whereby psychoanalytic theory, clinical cases, and the scientific methodology of psychoanalysis were reviewed, debated, and revised.

Major Theories

Psychoanalytic

Freudian institutes followed Freud's lead by developing three types of analysis, each with complementary goals. Training analysis enables clinicians to unearth their own blind spots and empathically understand the demands of the psychoanalytic task on the analysand. As Caligor stated, "The analyst as the analyzing instrument must understand the process from the insides" (1985, p. 120). Similarly, within interpersonal theory, Thompson examined "the role of the analyst's personality therapy," one of the chapter titles in *Interpersonal Psychoanalysis,* a greatly undervalued collection of her papers (Green, 1964).

Control analysis refers to the controlled supervision of at least two analytic cases by which students' views of the case and of the theoretical and personal disposition that go into their interpretations are acutely examined. Self-discovery is the goal of control analysis, consonant with the expectation of that control analysis is a lifelong activity.

Personal analysis shows trainees, from within the psychoanalytic framework, the benefit in their own analysis and allows students to experience demands made on the patient or analysand. This realization should be metabolized and affect one's practice with patients. One untoward consequence of this system of training (i.e., control and personal analysis) is that the psychotherapy of students becomes the focus of some supervisors' efforts, rather than educating the student, imparting skills, and achieving learning structures. This is seen clearly when a trainee has a problem with a case and the supervisor turns the problem into an inquiry into the trainee's psyche, rather than considering this inquiry as a teaching opportunity. The second major implication of Freud's view of training is that he claimed medical education could impede a therapist's analytic skills because "an arduous and circuitous way of approaching the profession of analysis ... burdens him with too much else of which he can never make us ... diverting interest and whole mode of thought from the understanding of physical phenomena" (Gay, 1989, citing Freud's "Question of Lay Analysis" from 1926). Freud favored a curriculum "from psychology, the history of civilization and sociology, as well as anatomy, biology, and the study of evolution. Psychoanalysis is part of psychology: not of medical psychology in the old sense, not of the psychology of morbid processes, but simply of psychology" (Gay, 1989, p. 680). The import of this view countered the American psychoanalytic institutes' eight-decade-long refusal to train anyone but psychiatrists, and it was cited in an antitrust suit that finally broke the hegemony against the training of psychologists, social workers, and other nonphysicians as psychoanalysts.

Behavioral Approaches

Behavioral psychotherapists take an entirely different tack toward educating clinicians. Behavioral techniques are seen as learned skills, with the supervisor reinforcing positive skills and extinguishing inappropriate behaviors. The skill sets are intended to accomplish identifiable clinical tasks that the supervisor helps define, apply, and refine. These tasks are seen as no more or less plastic or refractory than any other learning task. Both behavioral clinical techniques and the teaching of clinicians are based on learning principles. This system is both economical and based on a solid century of research findings on learning processes.

Behaviorists downplay the traditional key ingredients of therapist training, including knowing when a patient is ready for an intervention and knowing how to gauge patient trust in a psychotherapist. Skilled behaviorists,

however, share this sensitivity with clinicians of other orientations and teach such judgment to their students, extratheoretically.

Existential-Humanistic

If possible, this approach is even more resolute than psychoanalysis in seeing the clinician as the instrument of personality change. Rogers describes "the excitement of our learning as we clustered about the machine which enabled us to listen to ourselves, playing over and over some puzzling point at which the interview clearly went wrong, or those moments in which the client moved significantly forward" (1975, p. 3). If the clinician established unconditional positive regard for the client, empathic regard for others, and congruence of experiencing, then necessary conditions for effecting client growth were present. If training could instill those attitudes or awaken these capacities in the clinician, then growth, healing, and actualization were not only possible but inevitable. The training task centered on refining the listening, empathy, and congruence skills in the student. The student was valued or prized, and the client then would be similarly valued or prized. The central tenet, then, is as follows: People who feel valued grow and accomplish, be they patients or clinicians.

Boulder: Scientist-Practitioner

During World War II, psychologists contributed to the war effort principally in selecting, classifying, and training personnel. Diagnosing, conducting research on, and treating combat neurosis (now known as posttraumatic stress disorder) opened opportunities both in the military and on the civilian front. The flood of returning soldiers seeking education under the GI Bill added to the impetus to building graduate programs. The Veterans Administration and the U.S. Public Health Administration, needing a way to ascertain competent treatment for the war-injured, worked with the American Psychological Association to develop an accreditation system for clinical doctoral programs (Baker & Benjamin, 2000). Based on David Shakow's (1942) model, by which a person is trained in assessment, psychotherapy, and research skills, a 15-day conference held at Boulder, Colorado, in 1949 established a curriculum and system of program accreditation. This model has prevailed for decades and is now most frequently referred to as the scientist-practitioner model. A number of training model conferences followed (e.g., Northwestern, Chicago, Thayer, Vail, and Salt Lake City) that addressed various issues arising in the years after the Boulder conference (Cohen, 1992).

Recent Issues

A number of changes and pressures both within the profession and in society resulted in a spate of recent issues affecting psychotherapy training. These include:

1. the establishment of the PsyD, or professional degree, as an option to the PhD (analogous as an MD or DDS degree would be to a biology PhD)
2. the growth of university versus proprietary and free-standing doctoral programs
3. the strains between the clinical and research missions in clinical psychology training
4. the hybrid nature of psychology, involving both humanistic and scientific thrusts
5. extending training to include a postdoctoral year before licensure
6. a growing movement toward competence assessment in response to the forces pulling at the Boulder model
7. the bottom-line imposition of managed care and third-party payments

All these issues created tensions that led to a splintering of the basic Shakow training model. Responses to the issues include a proliferation of free-standing, non-university-based, proprietary schools, often with portions of the course work conducted online and practica that are not supervised by faculty but by local adjunct faculty. This loosening of the psychotherapy training from a research base led a set of universities to form an academy of clinical sciences that promotes a research focus. Their clinical science program's goal is to produce researchers who can empirically find effective psychotherapies for particular problems.

As a result of both the clinical sciences approach and the third-party payer's goal to reduce health care costs, two systems of psychotherapy have been deemed as evidence-based treatments. Cognitive-behavioral and interpersonal approaches were recognized as evidence based, but what specific elements define each approval and their curative elements await further investigation.

Amid these forces, the student seeking clinical training is well advised to examine graduate psychology programs carefully to see what that program emphasizes both in name and practice (Norcross, Sayette, & Mayne, 2008; Walfish & Hess, 2001). A knowledgeable adviser is invaluable because he or she can help clarify what a program offers and how the student can plan a course of education and training amid this ferment. Similarly, a person seeking psychotherapy will be well advised to seek a person who is clinically skilled to assess and work with the person in competently creating change and also someone who is caring and personally skilled.

REFERENCES

Baker, D. B., & Benjamin, L. T. (2000). The affirmation of the scientist-practitioner: A look back at Boulder. *American Psychologist, 35,* 241–247.

Caligor, L. (1985). On the psychoanalytic training (as symposium). On training analysis or sometimes analysis in the service training. *Contemporary Psychoanalysis, 21,* 120–129.

Cohen, L. D. (1992). The academic department. In D. K. Freedheim (Ed.), *History of psychotherapy: A century of change* (pp. 731–764). Washington, DC: American Psychological Association.

Gay, P. (1989). *The Freudian reader.* New York: Norton.

Green, M. R. (Ed.). (1964). *Interpersonal psychoanalysis: Papers of Clara M. Thompson.* New York: Basic Books.

Hess, A. K. (2008). Psychotherapy supervision: A conceptual review. In A. K. Hess, K. D. Hess, & T. H. Hess (Eds.), *Psychotherapy supervision: Theory, research, and practice* (2nd ed., pp. 3–22). New York: John Wiley & Sons.

Norcross, J., Sayette, M., & Mayne, T. (2008). *Insider's guide to graduate programs in clinical and counseling psychology* (2008/2009 ed.). New York: Guilford Press.

Rogers, C. R. (1975). Empathic: An unappreciated way of being. *Counseling Psychology, 5,* 2–9.

Shakow, D. (1942). The training of the clinical psychologist. *Journal of Counseling Psychology, 2,* 227–288.

Walfish, S., & Hess, A. K. (Eds.). (2001). *Succeeding in graduate school: The career guide for the psychology student.* Mahwah, NJ: Lawrence Erlbaum.

SUGGESTED READINGS

Bernard, J. M., & Goodyear, R. K. (2004). *Fundamentals of clinical supervision* (3rd ed.). Boston: Allyn & Bacon.

Falendar, C. A., & Shafranske, E. P. (2004). *Clinical supervision: A competency-based approach.* Washington, DC: American Psychological Association.

Watkins, Jr., C. E. (Ed.). (1997). *The handbook of psychotherapy supervision.* New York: John Wiley & Sons.

ALLEN K. HESS
Auburn University at Montgomery

See also: **Counseling; Psychotherapy; Psychotherapy Research**

PSYCHOTIC DISORDERS

Psychosis refers to a breakdown in the ability to recognize external reality. Symptoms of psychosis include hallucinations, delusions, and disorganization of thought or behavior. Hallucinations entail the perception of something that is not present, and they can occur in auditory, visual, tactile, olfactory, and gustatory modes. Delusions are characterized by a fixed, false belief, and they vary across a spectrum from plausible to bizarre. Thought disorder can range in severity from subtle disorganization to total incoherence.

A psychotic disorder refers to any mental disorder that is primarily characterized by psychotic symptoms. Nonetheless, psychosis can reflect multiple diagnostic entities and can result from many causes. Therefore, it is extremely important that patients presenting with psychotic symptoms are thoroughly assessed before a diagnosis is made. In the *Diagnostic and Statistical Manual* (*DSM-IV*; 1994) and the *DSM-IV Text Revision* (*DSM-IV-TR*; 2000), nine disorders are grouped together under the classification of psychotic disorders. These include schizophrenia, schizophreniform disorder, schizoaffective disorder, delusional disorder, brief psychotic disorder, shared psychotic disorder, psychotic disorder due to a general medical condition, substance-induced psychotic disorder, and psychotic disorder not otherwise specified (NOS).

Because of its chronic course, relative frequency (about 1% of the population), and profoundly disabling impact, schizophrenia is among the most common diagnoses seen in psychiatric settings. Schizophrenia is characterized by two or more of the following symptoms: delusions, hallucinations, disorganized speech, grossly disorganized or catatonic behavior, and negative symptoms. The last refers to deficits in energy, emotion, and initiative. These symptoms must substantially interfere with everyday functioning, not be due to substance abuse or a medical disorder, and have persisted for at least 6 months (or less if successfully treated). Schizophreniform disorder is diagnosed when schizophrenic symptoms have lasted less than 6 months. Schizoaffective disorder is diagnosed when a mood disorder, either depression or mania, is present alongside schizophrenic symptoms, although psychotic symptoms must also persist in the absence of mood symptoms. Delusional disorder refers to delusions without prominent hallucinations or thought disorder. Brief psychotic episodes are quite rare, but are occasionally found in people with either strong trauma histories or borderline personality disorder. Although the symptoms may be florid, they resolve quickly, and the person can return to normal levels of functioning. Shared psychotic disorder, also known as folie à deux, is diagnosed when two or more people share delusional ideation. When the psychotic symptoms can be attributed to a known medical disorder, psychotic disorder due to a general medical condition is diagnosed. Substance abuse can also cause psychotic symptoms. It is often difficult to determine the cause of psychotic symptoms in a substance-using patient. Nevertheless, substance-induced psychosis generally resolves soon after the substance is stopped. Finally, psychotic disorder NOS is used for any psychotic disorder that does not meet criteria for another diagnosis.

There are, however, additional sources of psychotic symptoms, including mood disorders, neurological illness, and medication side effects. Moreover, psychosis can be confused with delirium, a marked impairment of attention, and other cognitive functions related to an acute medical condition. As delirium may reflect a life-threatening illness, differential diagnosis of delirium and psychosis is critical. Finally, malingering, or faking illness for intended gain, is not infrequent, particularly in settings where there is a clear incentive for such behavior. Malingering is particularly common in forensic cases or in inpatient psychiatry services that provide room and board for mentally ill patients.

When assessing psychosis, collateral history is particularly important. Psychotic patients, by definition, are not reliable historians. History from family and treating clinicians can corroborate (or contradict) the patient's story and fill in missing data. Clinicians should inquire about the onset of symptoms (abrupt vs. gradual), previous psychiatric treatment, and the prior level of social and occupational functioning. Clinicians should also evaluate the degree of disorganization of thought and behavior, the bizarreness and fixity of delusions, and the complexity and modality of hallucinations. Negative symptoms, interpersonal relatedness, emotional expression, and mood should be noted as well. A medical workup is often necessary, particularly following an acute change of mental status. The consistency between self-reported symptoms and observable behavior is another central piece of data. Gross discrepancies between self-report and observable behavior can suggest either underreporting or overreporting of symptoms.

The first line of treatment is antipsychotic medication. Psychotherapy, although not the first line of treatment, can be helpful for associated conditions or symptoms. For example, supportive psychotherapy can help patients adjust to life with their illness. Social skills training has been shown to benefit schizophrenic patients, as has group therapy.

The two primary classes of medications are the typical and atypical antipsychotics. Typicals refer to an earlier class of drugs and work primarily on the dopaminergic neurotransmitter system. These drugs include haloperidol (Haldol), fluphenazine (Prolixin), chlorpromazine (Thorazine), and thioridazine (Mellaril). Typical drugs can have high or low potency. High-potency drugs (haloperidol, fluphenazine) carry a risk of extrapyramidal symptoms (EPS), which involve tremors and other abnormal involuntary movements. The low-potency drugs (chlorpromazine, thioridazine) carry a risk of anticholinergic symptoms, such as dry mouth and blurred vision. Atypical antipsychotic medications were developed much more recently. Atypicals act on multiple neurotransmitters, including dopamine, serotonin, and norepinephrine. Although their side effect profiles differ from those of the typicals, many of these medications carry an increased risk of metabolic disorders, such as weight gain and diabetes. The first atypical, clozapine (Clozaril), is extremely effective but carries a small risk of agranulocytosis, a potentially fatal disorder of the white blood cells. Thus, patients taking clozapine need close monitoring. Additional atypical antipsychotics include risperidone (Risperdal), olanzapine

(Zyprexa), quetiapine (Seroquel), ziprasidone (Geodon), and aripiprazole (Abilify).

It was widely assumed that the newer atypicals were more effective than the older typicals until a landmark study, published in 2005, showed no difference in efficacy between three atypical antipsychotic medications (quetiapine, risperidone, ziprasidone) and perphenazine (Trilafon), a mid-potency typical antipsychotic. Although olanzapine proved superior to perphenazine, it also had the highest rates of metabolic side effects.

REFERENCES

American Psychiatric Association. (1994). *Diagnostic and statistical manual of mental disorders* (4th ed.). Washington, DC: Author.

American Psychiatric Association. (2000). *Diagnostic and statistical manual of mental disorders* (4th ed., text rev.). Washington, DC: Author.

Andreasen, N. C. (1985). Positive and negative symptoms in schizophrenia: A critical evaluation. *Schizophrenia Bulletin, 11,* 380–389.

Buchanan, R. W., Breier, A., Kirkpatrick, B., Ball, P., & Carpenter, W. T. (1998). Positive and negative symptom response to clozapine in schizophrenic patients with and without the deficit syndrome. *American Journal of Psychiatry, 155,* 751–760.

Lieberman, J. A., Stroup, T. S., McEvoy, J. P., Swartz, M. S., Rosenheck, R. A., Perkins, D. O., et al., for the Clinical Antipsychotic Trials of Intervention Effectiveness (CATIE) Investigators. (2005). Effectiveness of antipsychotic drugs in patients with chronic schizophrenia. *New England Journal of Medicine, 353,* 1209–1223.

Sadock, B. J., & Sadock V. A. (2003). *Synopsis of psychiatry: Behavioral sciences/clinical psychiatry* (9th ed.). Philadelphia: Lippincott Williams & Wilkins.

SUGGESTED READINGS

Fujii, D., & Ahmed, I. (2007). *The spectrum of psychotic disorders: Neurobiology, etiology & pathogenesis.* New York: Cambridge University Press.

Kopelowicz, A., Liberman, R. P., & Zarate, R. (2006). Recent advances in social skills training for schizophrenia. *Schizophrenia Bulletin, 32*(Suppl. 1), 12–23.

LISA J. COHEN
Beth Israel Medical Center and Albert Einstein College of Medicine

PSYCHOTROPIC MEDICATIONS (See Antianxiety Medications; Anticonvulsant Medications; Antidepressant Medications; Antipsychotic Medications; Mood Stabilizing Medications; Psychostimulant Treatment for Children)

PTSD (See Posttraumatic Stress Disorder)

PUBERTY

Puberty is the period of development when sexual, reproductive maturity is reached. The span of puberty covers the approximate ages of 9–15 in girls and 10–16 in boys. Why is this predictable, biological event surrounded by so much psychological turmoil for some adolescents? The significance of puberty as a psychological event for adolescents is that it entails major neuroendocrine and structural brain changes as well as a period of growth that is exceeded in rapidity only during infancy. These neuroendocrine and structural brain changes putatively alter cognition, emotions, and potentially social roles, yet all of these changes are essential for the healthy development of adolescents. Changes in the behavior of adolescents, in turn, affect the functioning of the family as adolescents and families develop within a close system of dynamic and coordinated relationships. Furthermore, pubertal-age adolescents and their families experience these major changes within a culture that continues to harbor the impression that puberty is synonymous with adolescence, a period negatively characterized as one in which there is risky sexuality, delinquency, and psychopathology. This section will discuss the neuroendocrine processes responsible for the onset and progression of puberty, the measurement of puberty, and the problem behaviors associated with off-time pubertal development.

Advances in the technology to examine neuroendocrine changes at puberty now allow for a precise description of the brain and gonadal changes that are responsible for reproductive maturity and growth. The brain undergoes extensive remodeling at puberty and these changes are at the core of reproductive maturation (Sisk & Foster, 2004). Much of what is known about the human gonadotropin releasing hormone (GnRH) pulse generator and the onset of puberty is based on primate animal models, primarily the rhesus monkey (see Plant, 2000; Knobil, 1988). The neuroendocrine processes consist of reactivation of the hypothalamic-pituitary-gonadal (HPG) axis, referred to as gonadarche, which is held in check from infancy until the beginning of puberty (Plant, 2008). Reactivation of GnRH via the GnRH pulse generator is the primary component of the neurobiology of puberty. GnRH is secreted in a pulsatile fashion by specialized neurons in the median eminence of the hypothalamus. GnRH in the hypothalamus stimulates the pituitary to secrete gonadotropins, luteinizing hormone (LH), and follicle stimulating hormone (FSH). LH and FSH travel via peripheral circulating blood to stimulate target cells in the testes in males and ovaries in females to secrete testosterone and estradiol, respectively. Vital to reproduction, gonadal hormones assist in the regulation of ovulation and spermatogenesis in females and males, respectively.

The specific neural signal regulating GnRH reactivation is not known in spite of decades of research. Sisk and Zehr (2005) suggest that permissive signals that reactivate GnRH cannot fully explain the onset of reproductive competence as such signals are not unique to puberty. The onset of puberty likely results from an innate developmental clock that senses the unfolding of primary genetic programs that produce signals that, in turn, determine responses to endogenous and exogenous signals (e.g., the environment) that bring about high-frequency GnRH pulses (Sisk & Zehr, 2005). In addition, males and females differ in the permissive signals responsible for the onset of puberty with most of the triggers in women related to energy balance. A master regulatory gene may allow for expression of multiple permissive genes, but to date this master gene remains elusive.

Secondary sex characteristics also appear during puberty: breast and pubic hair development in girls and genital and pubic hair development in boys. These characteristics are stimulated by estrogen and testosterone as well as by adrenal androgens. It is the appearance of secondary sexual characteristics that are assumed to alter reactions to adolescents by family, peers, teachers, and adolescents themselves.

Measurement of Puberty in Psychological Research

Including a measure of pubertal development may be a key associative or explanatory factor in psychological research with adolescents. Since puberty is considered a process, there are a number of measures that reflect puberty (see Dorn et al., 2006) including measures of physical growth in height, staging of sexual maturity by physical exam, hormone concentrations, testicular volume, and age at menarche. The "gold standard" of determining pubertal stage is by physical examination using Tanner criteria for breast development in girls, genital development in boys, and pubic hair in both (Marshall & Tanner, 1969; 1970). Self-report of pubertal stage has frequently been used by either having adolescents view photographs or line drawings of the five stages of pubertal development or responding to the Pubertal Development Scale (PDS; Petersen et al., 1988) wherein the adolescent reports on the degree of change in pubertal characteristics (e.g., height, facial hair, voice change).

The two most common indices of pubertal development used in psychological research are pubertal stage and pubertal timing. Pubertal stage refers to the degree of external, reproduction-related physical development, generally referred to as the development of secondary sexual characteristics (e.g. breast, genital, pubic hair growth). Pubertal timing indicates the degree of pubertal maturation relative to that of same-age peers and timing is often referred to as early, on-time, or late.

Two questions are of primary concern in assessment of pubertal maturation. First, what is the appropriate measure of puberty to include? The answer lies with the research question. For example, in most cases if one is examining a physiological outcome (e.g., drug metabolism, brain development), then it is likely that the choice should be the gold standard of pubertal stage by physical exam. Alternatively, if one is asking how puberty might influence body image or psychopathology, then perhaps a self-report measure may be adequate. The second primary concern lies with what is the reliability and validity of that measure? Oftentimes inadequate concern is paid to the methodology of pubertal assessment with resulting threats to reliability and validity.

Timing of Puberty and Psychological Development

Both early and late timing of puberty have been linked to adjustment problems such as early sexual activity, substance use, delinquency, behavior problems, depression, low self-esteem, and poor body image (e.g., Ge, Brody, Conger, Simons, & McBride-Murray, 2002; Graber, Lewinsohn, Seeley, & Brooks-Gunn, 1997; Kaltiala-Heino, Kosunen, & Rimpela, 2003). Overall, most studies show that early timing is detrimental for females. For males, some studies have found associations between early timing and depression, but others find that early and late timing is associated with delinquency. Thus, pubertal timing effects appear to vary by the outcome being examined. Additionally, there are other influences that affect the strength and direction of these relations. For example, harsh parenting, neighborhood disadvantage, deviant peers, or stressful life events amplify the effect of early pubertal timing. Additionally, timing effects vary based on race; early maturing African-American girls are less likely to have poor body image than early maturing Caucasian girls. In general, overwhelming evidence shows that pubertal timing affects the behavior and mental health of developing adolescents. Therefore, it is important to include measures of timing of puberty in studies of mental health and behavior problems during the pubertal years.

In conclusion, puberty is a period in the life span characterized by neuroendocrine changes and sometimes the emergence of disruptive behavior and psychopathology. The endocrine changes provide the signals for physical growth changes and changes in body shape and proportions. The timing of the endocrine and growth change is associated with behavior problems and changes in emotions. Progress has been made in the last two decades on mapping the biological changes of puberty and emotion and behavior in boys and girls. To date, there are virtually no studies that show the direct links between neuroendocrine brain changes and psychological development. Nonetheless, with the availability of new imaging technologies, these connections will become more transparent in the future.

REFERENCES

Dorn, L. D., Dahl, E., Woodward, H. R., Biro, F. (2006). Defining the boundaries of early adolescence: A user's guide to assessing pubertal status and pubertal timing in research with adolescents. *Applied Developmental Science, 10,* 30–56.

Ge, X., Brody, G. H., Conger, R. D., Simons, R. L., & McBride-Murray, V. (2002). Contextual amplification of pubertal transitional effect on African American children's problem behaviors. *Developmental Psychology, 38,* 42–54.

Graber, J. A., Lewinsohn, R. M., Seeley J. R., & Brooks-Gunn, J. (1997). Is psychopathology associated with the timing of pubertal development? *Journal of the American Academy of Child & Adolescent Psychiatry, 36,* 1768–1776.

Kaltiala-Heino, R., Kosunen, E., & Rimpela, M. (2003). Pubertal timing, sexual behaviour and self-reported depression in middle adolescence. *Journal of Adolescence, 26,* 531–545.

Knobil, E. (1988). The hypothalamic gonadotropic hormone releasing hormone (GnRH) pulse generator in the rhesus monkey and its neuroendocrine control. *Human Reproduction, 3,* 29–31.

Marshall, W. A., & Tanner, J. M. (1969). Variations in patterns of pubertal change in girls. *Archives of Disease in Childhood, 44,* 291–303.

Marshall, W. A. and Tanner, J. (1970). Variations in the pattern of pubertal change in boys. *Archives of the Disabled Childhood, 45:* 13–23.

Petersen, A. C., Crockett, L., Richards, M., & Boxer, A. (1988). A self-report measure of pubertal status: Reliability, validity, and initial norms. *Journal of Youth and Adolescence 17,* 117–133.

Plant, T. (2008). Hypothalamic control of the pituitary-gonadal axis in higher primates: Key advances over the last two decades. *Journal of Neuroendocrinology, 20,* 719–726.

Sisk, C. L., & Foster, D. L. (2004). The neural basis of puberty and adolescence. *Nature Neuroscience, 7,* 1040–1047.

Sisk, C. L., & Zehr, J. L. (2005). Pubertal hormones organize the adolescent brain and behavior. *Frontiers in Neuroendocrinology, 26,* 163–174.

ELIZABETH J. SUSMAN
Pennsylvania State University

SONYA NEGRIFF
LORAH D. DORN
Cincinnati Children's Hospital Medical Center

PYGMALION EFFECT

The term *Pygmalion effect* refers broadly to the effects of interpersonal expectations, that is, the finding that what one person expects of another can come to serve as a self-fulfilling prophecy. These effects of interpersonal self-fulfilling prophecies have come to be called Pygmalion effects in general, and especially so when the interpersonal expectancy effects occur in an educational context.

Early Laboratory Experiments

The earliest studies of Pygmalion effects were conducted with human participants. Experimenters obtained ratings of photographs of stimulus persons from their research participants, but half of the experimenters were led to expect high photo ratings and half were led to expect low photo ratings. In the first several such studies, experimenters expecting higher photo ratings obtained substantially higher photo ratings than did experimenters expecting lower photo ratings.

To investigate the generality of these interpersonal expectancy effects in the laboratory, two studies were conducted with animal subjects. Half of the experimenters were told that their rats had been specially bred for maze (or Skinner box) brightness, and half were told that their rats had been specially bred for maze (or Skinner box) dullness. In both experiments, when experimenters had been led to expect better learning from their rat subjects, they obtained better learning from their rat subjects (Rosenthal, 1976).

Pygmalion Effects in the Classroom

Researchers hypothesized that if rats became brighter when expected to by their experimenters, then perhaps children could become brighter when expected to by their teachers. Accordingly, all of the children in one study were administered a nonverbal test of intelligence, which was disguised as a test that would predict intellectual blooming. The test was labeled The Harvard Test of Inflected Acquisition. There were 18 classrooms in the school, three at each of the six grade levels. Within each grade level, the three classrooms were composed of children with above average ability, average ability, and below average ability, respectively. Within each of the 18 classrooms, approximately 20% of the children were chosen at random to form the experimental group. Each teacher was given the names of the children from his or her class who were in the experimental condition. The teachers were told that these children's scores on the Harvard Test of Inflected Acquisition indicated that they would show surprising gains in intellectual competence during the next 8 months of school. The only difference between the experimental group and the control group children, then, was in the mind of the teacher.

At the end of the school year, 8 months later, all the children in the school were retested with the same nonverbal test of intelligence. The children from whom the teachers has been led to expect greater intellectual gain showed a significantly greater gain than did the children in the control group (Rosenthal & Jacobson, 1992).

Domains Investigated

A dozen years after the Pygmalion effect classroom study was completed, the research literature on interpersonal expectancy effects had broadened to include 345 experiments that could be subsumed under one of eight domains of research: human learning and ability, animal learning, reaction time, psychophysical judgments, laboratory interviews, person perception, inkblot tests, and everyday situations (Rosenthal, 1991). After another dozen years,

Table 1. Summary of Four Factors in the Mediation of Teacher Expectancy Effects

Factor	Brief Summary of the Evidence
Central Factors	
Climate (affect)	Teachers appear to create a warmer socioemotional climate for their "special" students. This warmth appears to be at least partially communicated by nonverbal cues. (Estimated effect size $r = .29$)
Input (effort)	Teachers appear to teach more material and more difficult material to their "special" students. (Estimated effect size $r = .27$)
Additional Factors	
Output	Teachers appear to give their "special" students greater opportunities for responding. These opportunities are offered both verbally and nonverbally (e.g., giving a student more time to answer a teacher's question). (Estimated effect size $r = .17$)
Feedback	Teachers appear to give their "special" students more differentiated feedback, both verbal and nonverbal, as to how these students have been performing. (Estimated effect size $r = .10$)

Note: Even the smallest effect size r listed here reflects a difference in performance levels of 55% versus 45%; the larger effect size rs listed here reflect a difference in performance levels of 64% versus 36%.

the overall mean effect size of the 479 studies was found to be an r of .30. An r of that magnitude can be thought of as the effects of interpersonal expectations changing the proportion of people performing above average from 35% to 65% (Rosenthal & Rosnow, 2008).

The Four-Factor Theory

A considerable amount of research has been summarized, employing meta-analysis, that suggests how teachers may treat differently those children for whom they have more favorable expectations. Table 1 summarizes these differences as four factors, two that are primary and two that are somewhat smaller in their magnitude of effect (Harris & Rosenthal, 1985).

More Recent Research

The effects of interpersonal expectancies have been studied in an ever widening circle of contexts. Pygmalion effects in management, courtrooms, nursing homes, and a variety of classrooms have been investigated. It has been shown that organizational effectiveness can be increased by raising leaders' expectations, that juries' verdicts of guilty can be increased by assigning them judges (to instruct them) who believe the defendant to be guilty, that the depression levels of nursing home residents can be reduced by raising the expectation levels of caretakers, and that teacher expectations can serve as self-fulfilling prophecies in other countries and for more than simply intellectual tasks. In all these cases, the mediating variables are receiving special attention, with rapidly growing evidence that much of the mediation is occurring by means of unintended nonverbal behavior (Ambady & Rosenthal, 1992; Babad, 1992; Eden, 1990, Rosenthal, 2002).

REFERENCES

Ambady, N., & Rosenthal, R. (1992). Thin slices of expressive behavior as predictors of interpersonal consequences: A meta-analysis. *Psychological Bulletin, 111*, 256–274.

Babad, E. (1992). Teacher expectancies and nonverbal behavior. In R. S. Feldman (Ed.), *Applications of nonverbal behavioral theories and research* (pp. 167–190). Hillsdale, NJ: Lawrence Erlbaum.

Eden, D. (1990). *Pygmalion in management: Productivity as a self-fulfilling prophecy.* Lexington, MA: D. C. Heath.

Harris, M. J., & Rosenthal, R. (1985). Mediation of interpersonal expectancy effects: 31 meta-analyses. *Psychological Bulletin, 97*, 363–386.

Rosenthal, R. (1976). *Experimenter effects in behavioral research* (enlarged ed.). New York: Irvington. (Original work published 1966)

Rosenthal, R. (1991). *Meta-analytic procedures for social research* (rev. ed.). Newbury Park, CA: Sage.

Rosenthal, R. (2002). Covert communication in classrooms, clinics, courtrooms, and cubicles. *American Psychologist, 57*, 839–849.

Rosenthal, R., & Jacobson, L. (1992). *Pygmalion in the classroom.* New York: Irvington. (Original work published 1968.)

Rosenthal, R., & Rosnow, R. L. (2008). *Essentials of behavioral research: Methods and data analysis* (3rd ed.). Boston: McGraw-Hill.

SUGGESTED READINGS

Rosenthal, R. (2002). The Pygmalion effect and its mediating mechanisms. In J. Aronson (Ed.), *Improving academic achievement* (pp. 25–36). New York: Academic Press.

Rosenthal, R. (2003). Covert communication in laboratories, classrooms, and the truly real world. *Current Directions in Psychological Science, 12*, 151–154.

ROBERT ROSENTHAL
University of California, Riverside, and Harvard University

See also: **Classroom Behavior**

PYROMANIA (See Firesetting)

Q-METHODOLOGY

Q-methodology embraces, and is particularly suited for, the study of human subjectivity. Commonly (though incompletely) known as the Q-sorting technique, Q-methodology encompasses a unique set of psychometric and operational principles that, when combined with specialized statistical applications of correlational and factor-analytical techniques, provides psychological researchers with an organized and rigorously quantitative means for examining subjective impressions (McKeown & Thomas, 1988). It allows complex naturalistic data to be reliably rated and examined. From the standpoint of Q-methodology, the subjectivity inherent in many areas of psychology is not problematic; it is merely regarded as points of view on any matter to be researched. In fact, it is only subjective judgments that are at issue in Q-methodology, and although they are typically improvable, they can nevertheless be reliably and intersubjectively observed, and they can be shown to have structure and form. Q-methodology is employed to test whether subjective phenomena are intersubjectively observable and co-occur; this is done by assessing their relationships through rigorous quantitative means (Jones, 2000).

Q-Methodology in Psychology

Psychology has traditionally relied heavily on self-report inventories because these self-reports provide invaluable (and quick) information. Other methods and modalities of data collection, however, provide researchers with additional knowledge about a given construct. Moreover, self-report inventories can be insufficient in their coverage and often are distorting. The respondent may be deliberately deceptive, unwittingly defensive, or insufficiently self-observant or insightful (Block, 2008).

In Q-methodology, observer ratings (e.g., completed by a mental health clinician) rather than self-report (e.g., completed by a client or patient) are the key source of information. Surprisingly, until recently, little research had combined clinical observations with statistical aggregation (Westen & Shedler, 2007). Q-methodology can be especially useful in capturing and quantifying information about subtle aspects of clinical phenomena (e.g., personality, psychopathology, or psychotherapy process) that are not readily assessed via self-report (Block, 2008).

An important feature of Q-methodology is its applicability with both ipsative and normative measurement. Although the scoring procedure is ipsative (see later), the resulting data can be treated as normative data (e.g., for measuring individual differences). Therefore, Q-methodology is appropriate for identifying the relative importance of characteristics within an individual as well as across individuals. Historically, psychology researchers have been pulled between these two paradigmatic directions in the pursuit of cultivating a more comprehensive understanding of human beings. Q-methodology has been offered by its proponents as a methodological approach that can facilitate simultaneous exploration into the idiographic position, which emphasizes the unique aspects of a given individual's psychology, and the nomothetic position, which emphasizes general laws and probabilities across individuals.

Q-Sorting Procedure

In Q-methodology, researchers seek to enable clinical judges to model their viewpoints on a matter of subjective importance through the operational medium of a Q-sort (McKeown & Thomas, 1988). Q-sorting is a process wherein subjects model their point of view by systematically rank-ordering a purposively sampled set of stimulus items along a continuum in a forced-choice format. The assessor must assign a specified number of items to each score category that approximates a normal distribution. Paired comparisons in a forced normal distribution result in ranking most items of the phenomena being rated as essentially neutral, placing in greater relief the most uncharacteristic and most characteristic items at the two ends of the distribution. All Q-items are ranked in comparison with each other rather than rated independently of each other, as is the case with Likert-type scaling.

This forced-choice rating system used in Q-methodology ensures multiple evaluations of items and attenuates response set biases (e.g., halo effects) that are often present with Likert-type scaling (Ablon & Jones, 1998). With Likert-type scaling, some raters naturally gravitate toward extreme values, others toward moderate values, and some use the entire scale range. Thus, differences in scores could reflect not only differences between the individuals assessed but also differences in the response tendencies of the raters (Westen & Shedler, 2007).

The Q-sort rankings are correlated and then factor-analyzed to discover the groupings of opinions as expressed among the respondents. No definitions are assumed beforehand; rather, they are inferred from the location of statements provided by respondents as they are distributed along the Q-sort continuum. In Q-methodology, the presence of several orthogonal factors is evidence of different points of view in the person-sample. An individual's positive loading on a factor indicates his or her shared subjectivity with others on that factor; negative loadings, on the other hand, are signs of rejection of that factor's perspective (McKeown & Thomas, 1988). Further, each respondent's factor loading indicates the degree of association between that respondent's individual Q-sort and the underlying composite attitude or perspective of that factor.

Differences between Q-Methodology and R-Methodology

Q-methodology has many significant differences with conventional R-methodological approaches to the measurement and study of subjective phenomena (e.g., opinions, attitudes, and values). In contradistinction to R-methodological practice, phenomena under study are not assumed to have a priori meaning independent of the respondent's self-reference. Having no inherent meaning or status as facts, individual items in a Q-sample are assigned meaning and significance, first in Q-sorting by the respondent, and second, in factor interpretation by the researcher (McKeown & Thomas, 1988).

Categorical definitions (e.g., scores on single-continuum adherence or fidelity scales) embraced by R-methodological approaches are avoided in Q-methodology because they always carry the risk of missing or misinterpreting meaning from the respondent's frame of reference. Context and meaning are critical when investigating subjective psychological phenomena; variables are not sufficiently understood in isolation from the rest. The principle of contextuality is tied to the premise of Q as a method of subjective impression, as opposed to expression, which lies at the heart of the difference between Q- and R-methods (McKeown & Thomas, 1988). Again, the choice of method depends on the topic under investigation. Generally speaking, when capabilities or objective behavioral performance is at issue, methods of expression (R-methodology) are in order, and when the focus is on human subjectivity, methods of impression (Q-methodology) are indicated.

Q-Methodology: Examples

Q-methodology has existed for many years in the study of normal personality (Block, 2008), psychopathology (Westen & Shedler, 2007), and psychotherapy process (Ablon & Jones, 1998; Jones, 2000).

Personality

The California Q-Sort procedure (CQ; Block, 2008) is a method for portraying, in a comprehensive, articulated, and commensurate configurational form, the subjective evaluation of a person formulated by a competent observer. The CQ attempts to provide a standard language and way of encoding complex, configural descriptions of persons in a form suitable for communication, quantitative comparison, and statistical evaluation. It is purposed to capture the character of a person as it is subjectively comprehended by an interested appraiser. This Q-sort was introduced as a way of transforming an observer's informal subjective impressions or evaluation of a person into an explicit, quantifiable form (Block, 2008).

Psychotherapy Process

Psychotherapy process research (i.e., the emergent moment-to-moment properties of patient–therapist interaction within the therapy session) plays an integral role in the development and utilization of evidence-based practice. Utilizing Q-methodology, psychotherapy process studies are generally nonintrusive and add to our cumulative understanding of the psychotherapy endeavor by providing information about the effective ingredients of therapeutic change.

The Psychotherapy Q-Set (PQS; Jones, 2000) consists of 100 items; the items provide a pantheoretical language and rating procedure for the comprehensive description, in clinically relevant terms, of the therapist–patient interaction in a form that is suitable for quantitative comparison and analysis (Jones, 2000). The items describe the following: patient attitudes, behaviors, or experience; the therapist's actions and attitudes; and the nature of their interaction. Entire psychotherapy sessions are coded to extract, describe, and define the almost infinite complexity of therapist–patient interaction.

Further, Q-methodology is appropriate for psychotherapy research questions at very different levels of discourse, as evidenced by its utility with (1) large-scale nomothetic evaluations of patterns among various types of treatments and their relative efficacy with different types of clinical problems and (2) clinical or idiographic evaluations, which focus on identifying processes of change in particular therapeutic dyads (Blatt, 2005).

Psychopathology

The Shedler-Westen Assessment Procedure (SWAP) is a dimensional personality assessment instrument developed for use by clinically experienced interviewers, and it is designed to maximize both psychometric precision and clinical utility (Westen & Shedler, 2007). This Q-sort instrument includes 200 descriptive statements describing pathological and healthy aspects of personality. To date, The SWAP has been used to (1) refine and dimensionalize existing *Diagnostic and Statistical Manual of Mental Disorders* (DSM–IV-TR; American Psychiatric Association, 2000) diagnostic categories and criteria, (2) empirically identify diagnostic groupings without presupposing the DSM–IV-TR typology of personality disorders (PDs), and (3) identify factors or trait dimensions relevant to describing personality pathology.

Q-methodology has the promise of demonstrating the usefulness of commensurable observer evaluations in clinical, research, personnel, or other contexts (Block, 2008), though some have raised concerns about its effectiveness (Wood, Garb, Nezworski, & Koren, 2007).

As with the field of psychology, Q-methodology has been said to have had a long history and a short past. Q-methodology has been frequently used since the 1930s in the social sciences. Despite its long history, the last two decades have seen an increase in the utilization of Q-methodology by psychological researchers. In psychology, it has been used in the study of normal personality, psychopathology, and psychotherapy process. Though sparingly used in the area of psychotherapy training and supervision, the years to come may find it more frequently in use in this manner.

REFERENCES

Ablon, J. S., & Jones, E. E. (1998). How expert clinicians' prototypes of an ideal treatment correlate with outcome in psychodynamic and cognitive-behavioral therapy. *Psychotherapy Research, 8*(1), 71–83.

Blatt, S. (2005). Commentary on Ablon and Jones. *Journal of the American Psychoanalytic Association, 53*(2), 569–578.

Block, J. (2008). *The Q-Sort in character appraisal: Encoding subjective impressions of persons quantitatively.* Washington, DC: American Psychological Association.

Jones, E. E. (2000). *Therapeutic action: A guide to psychoanalytic psychotherapy.* Northvale, NJ: Aronson.

McKeown, B., & Thomas, D. (1988). *Q-methodology. Quantitative methodology in the social sciences, No. 66.* Thousand Oaks, CA: Sage.

Stephenson, W. (1935). Technique of factor analysis. *Nature, 136,* 297.

Stephenson, W. (1953). *The study of behavior: Q-technique and its methodology.* Chicago: University of Chicago Press.

Westen, D., & Shedler, J. (2007). Personality diagnosis with the Shedler-Westen Assessment Procedure (SWAP): Integrating clinical and statistical measurement and prediction. *Journal of Abnormal Psychology, 116*(4), 810–822.

Wood, J. M., Garb, H. N., Nezworski, M. T., & Koren, D. (2007). The Shedler-Westen Assessment Procedure-200 as a basis

for modifying *DSM* personality disorder categories. *Journal of Abnormal Psychology, 116*(4), 823–836.

MICHAEL BAMBERY
University of Detroit Mercy

JOHN PORCERELLI
Wayne State University Medical School

QUALITATIVE RESEARCH METHODS

Qualitative psychological research addresses people who are living through particular situations. Findings are presented discursively (descriptively) or through listed interrelated themes. Examples of studied phenomena are the experiences of being criminally victimized, being joyful, awaiting biopsy results, and the formation of white-space Rorschach responses as described by clients. Two related forms of qualitative research, conversation analysis and discourse analysis, identify people's interactive ways of gaining or maintaining influence. Examples of these studies are interdisciplinary team meetings with patients in a psychiatric facility, marital discussions, and psychotherapy sessions. These situations as lived by participants are not amenable to experimental methods, which require manipulation and measurement in terms of predetermined categories. Hence, qualitative—descriptive—methods have been developed to access situations as they unfold in the life world. Qualitative research is not opposed to categorical, quantitative research, which historically has been essential to psychology's becoming scientific and has provided our ever-evolving body of knowledge. Qualitative research is in the beginning stages of providing an empirical body of understanding.

Long before qualitative research was known by that term, it was practiced by cultural anthropologists like Ruth Benedict and Margaret Mead as ethnography. Today, researchers from many disciplines conduct similar participant observation studies of a setting (with extensive notes and figures) in order to be aware of context before conducting any kind of research in that setting. Other ethnographic researchers focally study subcultures such as New York subway culture or the culture of physicians' waiting rooms. Early psychologists conducted qualitative research without a label, for example, Frederick Bartlett's 1930s descriptions of memory. For decades, industrial and organizational psychologists have conducted marketing research, often in a format that is a forerunner of current focus groups.

Among the social sciences and related disciplines, psychology, because of its strong identification with natural science traditions and its historical grounding in logical positivism, has been the last to regard qualitative research as indeed being research. Sociology led the way and was readily followed by education, nursing, and counseling psychology. Qualitative research is scientific but not in the same manner as experimental, mathematical research. It is a sister science with related but different criteria for rigor and validity. It assumes that we can know the world only in human ways, which necessarily involve researchers' background, context, interests, and purposes. Qualitative research does not attempt to approximate truth independent of humans' descriptive efforts. This is a distinctly different approach to science than realism and positivism, both of which have been bypassed by contemporary physicists.

Because of the time-intensive labor of studying texts, many qualitative studies formally analyze a small number of events or texts, often as few as 6 to 10. However, reports typically present what was found for all cases (no probability levels). Researchers assume that similar findings will occur in related studies, but they await those empirical studies to see what might differ in other contexts. The data that are analyzed are empirical—usually typescripts of participants' descriptions and interviews, sometimes along with field notes. These data, as well as research procedures, are available for examination by research colleagues and other interested persons.

Researchers explicitly specify in advance of the study what they know of their interests in the subject matter, and they note assumptions and values that have emerged during the study. These assumptions and values are then either dropped from the analyses or kept and specified. Data are read, reread, and reread again as the researcher (re-searcher) seeks to describe what is common to the texts and is essential to the studied situation. Authors assume that readers of the research report will offer more felicitous wording here and there, connections with still more literature, and nuances that were not specified. The rigor of qualitative research lies in careful, evocative, holistic representation (description) of the phenomenon, as well as in well-considered design and in open, reflexive, and reflective analysis. Validity criteria include specification of consensus checks: review of procedures, data, and findings by others; coherence of the findings, with no gaps, contradictions, or anomalies; resonance with readers' experience; and meaningful touch points with theory and research literature.

In general, the data for qualitative research fall into three main forms (with many variations): (1) ethnographic, descriptions of a culture or subgroup through direct observation; (2) first-person reports, descriptions usually followed by interviews of research participants; and (3) observations and/or recordings of dyadic, group, or cultural interactions. Claims to qualitative research status are false when the basis of the claim is merely the absence of statistical data or when survey data have been summarized impressionistically.

Methodology is the study of approaches to research, in which the choice of a qualitative or quantitative approach or both is discussed, perhaps along with the specific research procedures (methods). The first qualitative procedures, which emerged in the 1960s, were grounded theory, introduced by the sociologists B. Glasser and A. Struass, and empirical phenomenology, introduced by A. Giorgi and the Duquesne University Psychology Department. Among the classic procedures not already mentioned are narrative, focus groups, constructivist, intuitive inquiry, and the researcher group procedures dialogical and conceptual encounter. Although "mixed methods" typically refers to combining qualitative and quantitative procedures, just as traditional research design may include many kinds of statistical analysis, so qualitative research projects increasingly combine and vary established procedures, depending on the subject matter. Denzin and Lincoln (2005) have chronicled developments in diverse procedures through their detailed handbooks. Fischer (2006) combined down-to-earth discussion of qualitative method with 13 full reports of qualitative studies written by a range of researchers. Smith (2003), among others, has presented brief, readable, characterizations by authors of their established procedures. Both philosophical foundations and procedures continue to evolve.

REFERENCES

Denzin, N. K., & Lincoln, Y. S. (Eds.). (2005). *The Sage handbook of qualitative research*. Thousand Oaks, CA: Sage.

Fischer, C. T. (2006). *Qualitative research methods for psychologists: Introduction through empirical studies*. San Diego, CA: Academic Press.

Smith, J .A. (2003). *Qualitative psychology: A practical guide to research methods*. Thousand Oaks, CA: Sage.

SUGGESTED READINGS

Churchill, S. C., & Wertz, F. J. (2001). An introduction to phenomenological research in psychology: Historical, conceptual, and methodological foundations. In K. S. Schneider, J. R. T. Bugental, & J. F. Pierson (Eds.), *The handbook of humanistic psychology: Leading edges in theory, research, and practice*. Thousand Oaks, CA: Sage.

Corbin, J., & Straus, A. C. (2008). *Basics of qualitative research: Techniques and procedures for doing grounded theory*. Thousand Oaks, CA: Sage.

CONSTANCE T. FISCHER
Duquesne University

See also: **Behavioral Observation; Participant Observation**

QUALITY OF LIFE

Quality of life has become a popular concept that is used by politicians, marketing executives, media and sports personalities, and members of the public. There is an extensive scientific literature of books, theoretical articles, and empirical studies on the subject by health practitioners, psychologists, sociologists, economists, geographers, social historians, and philosophers. Scholars in ancient China and Greece were interested in quality of life several millennia ago, and renewed interest occurred in times of enlightenment in the centuries that followed. In more recent history, quality of life emerged as a political entity in the United States in the mid-1950s and in Europe in the 1960s. In presidential commissions and in their speeches, U.S. presidents such as Eisenhower, Johnson, and Nixon popularized the term. The focus on quality of life in the last half century has increased, as there has been a general recognition that the health of countries must be judged by something more than gross economic factors and that the health of individuals is something beyond the absence of illness.

The economic focus led to the development of social indicators directed at objectively measuring the quality of life of populations at large. In 1970, the Organization for Economic Cooperation and Development (OECD) encouraged member countries to develop and report measures of social well-being for their constituents. This resulted in a number of countries reporting such social indicators as the number of schools per person, the number of hospital beds per person, and the number of health care professionals per person. It soon became apparent that, although social indicators provided information about cultural entities (towns, states, countries), they provided little or no information about the quality of life of individuals within these entities. This led researchers in a number of countries, including the United States, Canada, Australia, and parts of Europe, to assess the subjective or perceived quality of life of population samples within their countries.

Perhaps the earliest such study was by Bradburn (1969), who surveyed two samples ($N = 2,787$ and $N = 2,163$) from several metropolitan areas in the United States. He employed as his measure the affect balance score, which was based on ratings of positive and negative affect and was assumed to be indicative of quality of life. A second landmark study in the United States was carried out by Campbell, Converse, and Rogers (1976), who sampled 2,160 individuals selected to be representative of the national population. Participants were asked to rate their satisfaction in a number of life domains and with their lives as a whole. Subsequent to these early cross-sectional studies, the methods of assessing quality of life in the population at large have become more complex, and there is a greater emphasis on longitudinal studies.

In 1947, the World Health Organization promulgated a definition of health that suggested that health was not just the absence of illness but was also a state of physical, psychological, and social well-being. This definition provoked health professionals, particularly the researchers among them, to begin viewing the impact of interventions in a broader context than just symptom recovery. Thus, in the last 30 years there has been a proliferation of what have come to be known as health-related quality of life (HRQOL) measures. Perhaps the earliest HRQOL measure was the Karnofsky Index, which has been used in numerous studies since its introduction more than 50 years ago (Karnofsky & Burchenal, 1949). Global and specific HRQOL measures have been developed in most branches of health care, including cardiology, cancer, epilepsy, urology, psychiatry, and internal medicine, to name just a few.

One of the most ambitious projects is that of the World Health Organization Quality of Life Group (1998), who have developed global health measures of quality of life that can be employed with people from differing cultures worldwide. The initial work of the group was directed toward developing the WHOQOL-100, a culturally valid assessment of well-being. Subsequently, the 26-item WHOQOL-BREF was developed for use when time is restricted and respondent burden must be minimized (Skevington, Lofty, & O'Connell, 2004). The development of the WHO measures has facilitated numerous studies of factors associated with quality of life across cultures and nations.

Despite the popular and scientific interest in quality of life, there continues to be little agreement on what is meant by the term. As Evans (1994) noted, quality of life has been used interchangeably with well-being, psychological well-being, subjective well-being, happiness, life satisfaction, positive and negative affect, and the good life. There is, in fact, a high degree of similarity among many of these measures, and factor analyses with samples of the general population indicate that measures of life satisfaction, positive and negative affect, and quality of life are highly related to each other and form a single factor (Evans & Kazarian, 2001). Most researchers in the field argue that quality of life is a multidimensional concept, and there is fair agreement as to the majority of subdomains within the construct. There is some disagreement concerning the method by which measures in each of the subdomains should be aggregated to form an overall measure of quality of life.

Because of the way interest in the field has evolved, the area of quality of life research has an abundance of measures and a paucity of theoretical models. Two prominent models are the bottom-up and top-down models of quality of life. Proponents of the top-down model argue that our general quality of life influences quality of life in the specific domains of our life and therefore that the focus of research should be on these global measures. Those who advocate the bottom-up model propose that our quality of life in each life domain affects our overall quality of life, and thus the specific domains should be the focus of research. Another current line of research is the identification of factors that influence an individual's quality of life. There is increasing evidence that personality dimensions like self-esteem, locus of control, extraversion, neuroticism, and hardiness, to name but a few, influence an individual's quality of life. This network of relationships could form the basis for a more elegant theory in the field.

Emphasis in the future will be on the development of theoretical models of quality of life. This research will in turn impact many of the measurement issues that are extant at present. Another area of research that is developing is the measurement and comparison of quality of life in various cohorts across the life span (Halvorsrud & Kalfoss, 2007). As might be expected with the emergence of the field of positive psychology, interest has focused on intervention strategies to enhance quality of life. Frisch (2006) has discussed the theory behind quality of life therapy (QOLT), outlining the core techniques in QOLT and describing area-specific interventions using QOLT. Evans and Kazarian (2001) have described a model that integrates principles of health, quality of life, and health promotion that can inform health promotion strategies across cultures, and they provide a range of examples of these programs.

REFERENCES

Bradburn, N. M. (1969). *The structure of psychological well-being.* Chicago: Aldine.

Campbell, A., Converse, P. E., & Rogers, W. L. (1976). *The quality of American life.* New York: Russell Sage Foundation.

Evans, D. R. (1994). Enhancing quality of life in the population at large. *Social Indicators Research, 33,* 47–88.

Evans, D. R., & Kazarian, S. S. (2001). Health promotion, disease prevention, and quality of life. In S. S. Kazarian & D. R. Evans (Eds.), *Handbook of cultural health psychology* (pp. 85–112). San Diego, CA: Academic Press.

Frisch, M. B. (2006). *Quality of life therapy: Applying a life satisfaction approach to positive psychology and cognitive therapy.* Hoboken, NJ: John Wiley & Sons.

Halvorsrud, L., & Kalfoss, M. (2007). The conceptualization and measurement of quality of life in older adults: A review of empirical studies published during 1994–2006. *European Journal of Ageing, 4,* 229–246.

Karnofsky, D. A., & Burchenal, J. H. (1949). The clinical evaluation of chemotherapeutic agents in cancer. In C. M. Macleod (Ed.), *Evaluation of chemotherapeutic agents* (pp. 191–205). New York: Columbia University Press.

Skevington, S. M., Lofty, M., & O'Connell, K. A. (2004). The World Health Organization's WHOQOL-BREF quality of life assessment: Psychometric properties and results of the international field trial. A report from the WHOQOL Group. *Quality of Life Research, 13,* 299–310.

The World Health Organization Quality of Life Group. (1998). WHOQOL user manual. Geneva, Switzerland: Division of Mental Health, World Health Organization.

SUGGESTED READINGS

Bognar, G. (2005). The concept of quality of life. *Social Theory and Practice, 31,* 561–580.

Hughes, M. (2006). Affect, meaning, and quality of life. *Social Forces, 85,* 611–629.

Ring, L., Höfer, S., McGee, H., Hickey, A., & O'Boyle, C. A. (2007). Individual quality of life: Can it be accounted for by psychological or subjective well-being? *Social Indicators Research, 82,* 443–461.

DAVID R. EVANS
University of Western Ontario, Canada

See also: **Happiness; Positive Psychology**

QUASI-EXPERIMENTAL DESIGN

Like all experiments, quasi-experiments manipulate treatments to determine their effects. Quasi-experiments differ from randomized experiments in that units are not randomly assigned to conditions. Instead, units are assigned to conditions using such nonrandomized ways as permitting units to choose conditions or assigning them based on presumed need or merit. Lacking random assignment, quasi-experiments may not yield unbiased estimates, threatening the validity of inferences about treatment effects.

Basic Types of Quasi-Experiments

Quasi-experimental designs include, but are not limited to, the following, in order from strongest to weakest. In *regression discontinuity designs,* the only quasi-experimental design that can yield an unbiased effect, the experimenter uses a cutoff score from a continuous variable to determine assignment to treatment and comparison conditions. An effect is observed if the regression line of the assignment variable on outcome for the treatment group is discontinuous from that of the comparison group at the point of the cutoff. In *interrupted time series designs,* many (100 or more) consecutive observations over time are available on an outcome; treatment is introduced in the midst of those observations to determine its impact on the outcome as evidenced by a disruption in the time series after treatment. A variant of the latter is *single-group* or *single-case designs,* in which one group or unit is repeatedly observed over time while the scheduling and dose of treatment are manipulated to demonstrate that treatment affects outcome. In *nonequivalent control group designs,* probably the most common quasi-experimental design, the outcomes of two or more treatment or comparison conditions are studied, but the experimenter does not control assignment to conditions. In a *one-group posttest-only designs,* only one group is given a treatment and observed for effects by using one posttest observation.

Validity and Threats to Validity

In 1963, Campbell and Stanley created a validity typology, including threats to validity, to evaluate the quality of causal inferences made using quasi-experimental designs. The threats are common reasons why researchers may be incorrect about the inferences they draw from cause-probing studies. Campbell and Stanley described only two types of validity, internal validity and external validity; Cook and Campbell (1979) later added statistical conclusion validity and construct validity. Of the four types of validity, internal validity is the most crucial to the ability to make causal claims from quasi-experiments. Internal validity concerns the validity of inferences that the relationship between two variables, A (the presumed treatment) and B (the presumed effect), is causal from A to B. Random assignment reduces the plausibility of most threats to internal validity. Lacking randomization, quasi-experimenters must pay particular attention to the following threats, showing that they cannot explain the results:

1. *Ambiguous temporal precedence,* the inability to determine which variable occurred first, preventing the ability to establish which variable is the cause or effect.
2. *Selection,* systematic differences between unit characteristics in each condition that could affect the outcome.
3. *History,* events that occur simultaneously with the treatment that could affect the outcome.
4. *Maturation,* natural development over time that could affect the outcome.
5. *Regression,* when units are selected from their extreme scores, they may have less extreme scores on other measures, appearing as if an effect occurred.
6. *Attrition,* when units who drop out of the experiment are systematically different in their responses than those who remain.
7. *Testing,* when repeatedly exposing units to a test may permit them to learn the test, appearing as if a treatment effect occurred.
8. *Instrumentation,* changes in the instrument used to measure responses over time or conditions may appear as if an effect occurred.
9. *Additive and interactive threats to internal validity,* the impact of a threat can be compounded by, or may depend on the level of, another threat.

Campbell and his colleagues discussed three other validity types. *Statistical conclusion validity* addresses inferences about how well the presumed cause and effect covary. *Construct validity* addresses inferences about higher-order constructs that research operations represent. *External validity* addresses inferences about whether the relationship holds over variation in persons, settings, treatment variables, and measurement variables. A set of threats exists for each of these three validity types (see Shadish, Cook, & Campbell, 2002).

Design Features

To prevent a threat from occurring, researchers can manipulate certain features within a design, thereby improving the validity of casual inferences made by using quasi-experiments (Shadish et al., 2002). Examples include the following: (1) adding observations over time before or after treatment to examine whether trends over time before treatment can explain an apparent treatment effect, (2) adding more than one comparison group to serve as a source of inference about what would have happened to treatment participants if they did not receive treatment, (3) varying the application of treatment by removing or varying it, and (4) better controlling assignment by using a regression discontinuity design or matching. All quasi-experiments are combinations of such design features, ideally chosen to diagnose or minimize the plausibility of threats to validity in a particular context.

Statistical Adjustments

Although Campbell emphasized the importance of good design in quasi-experiments, many other researchers sought to resolve problems in making causal inferences from quasi-experiments through statistical adjustments, such as propensity scores, selection bias modeling, and the use of structural equation modeling. A great deal of empirical research has been devoted to studying the effectiveness of these statistics, often comparing adjusted results from quasi-experiments to randomized results from similar studies. Results suggest such adjustments can be useful when a nonrandomized experiment contains a rich set of pretest covariates that predict both treatment assignment and outcome (e.g., Shadish, Clark, & Steiner, 2008). The best causal inferences from quasi-experiments are likely to be obtained when they are well designed to begin with, so that the amount of bias that needs to be adjusted statistically is already low.

The last three decades have seen enormous progress in the design, implementation, and statistical analysis of quasi-experiments (Shadish & Cook, in press). Although randomized experiments are still preferred when they are feasible and ethical, that progress makes high-quality quasi-experiments a more viable option.

REFERENCES

Campbell, D. T., & Stanley, J. C. (1963). *Experimental and quasi-experimental designs for research.* Chicago: Rand-McNally.

Cook, T. D., & Campbell, D. T. (1979). *Quasi-experimentation: Design and analysis issues for field settings*. Chicago: Rand-McNally.

Shadish, W. R., Clark, M. H., & Steiner, P. (2008). Can nonrandomized experiments yield accurate answers? A randomized experiment comparing random to nonrandom assignment. *Journal of the American Statistical Association, 103*, 1334–1343.

Shadish, W. R., & Cook, T. D. (in press). The renaissance of field experimentation in evaluating interventions. *Annual Review of Psychology*.

Shadish, W. R., Cook, T. D., & Campbell, D. T. (2002). *Experimental and quasi-experimental designs for generalized causal inference*. Boston: Houghton-Mifflin.

WILLIAM R. SHADISH
RODOLFO GALINDO
University of California, Merced

See also: **Propensity Scores; Validity**

QUESTIONNAIRES

Questionnaires are inventories used by researchers to gather various kinds of information from responding individuals. Questionnaires are typically self-administered, so-called self-report devices. As such, they are similar to interviews conducted face-to-face or over the telephone. In fact, some or all of the individuals who do not choose to complete a survey are often contacted and interviewed by a researcher so that their opinions and information may be included in the study data. Among the advantages of questionnaires are their relatively low cost as a means of gathering data, a general freedom from bias on the part of an interviewer, the large number of individuals who can be asked to respond, the sense of anonymity that respondents may feel, the temporal flexibility afforded the respondent, the possibility of directly linking research questions and survey results, and the ease of data coding and analysis for interpretation of the results (Judd, Smith, & Kidder, 1991).

A major disadvantage of questionnaires relates to return rates; frequently, only a small fraction of those originally provided the questionnaire complete it. Moreover, those who complete it are generally not representative of the entire population. Respondents also may not be honest or may permit subtle biases to influence their responses. Another disadvantage of questionnaires is that sometimes individuals provide vague or incomplete answers; in an interview, a skilled interviewer may probe further to elicit the proper response. Furthermore, many individuals are still unable to read and write well enough to complete a questionnaire. All of these may lead to biases in the results.

Questionnaires are used in both basic psychological research and applied research and in either experimental or correlational research. For example, many psychologists who investigate personality use survey questionnaires to gain insights about personal functioning. In applied research, questionnaires are often used in program evaluations, job analyses, needs assessments, and market research. They may also be used as dependent variables in experiments. Questionnaires should not generally be called tests because the term *test* holds the connotation that there is a correct answer to a given question. Rather, most behaviors elicited by self-report questionnaires are of typical behavior; these include personality variables, attitudes, values, beliefs, interests, and descriptions of past and present behavior. Furthermore, because most questionnaire research is correlational, causal attributions are, for the most part, inappropriate, although it is the experimental design, rather than the nature of the variable per se, that dictates the ability to make causal statements.

Types of Questionnaires

Questionnaires are traditionally instruments that have been printed but increasingly are administered via the computer, often over the Internet. Responses may either be placed on the survey itself or on a separate answer sheet if the survey is printed; for computerized administration of questionnaires, respondents enter their answers on the computer. Most questionnaires are composed of numerous questions and statements. Statements are frequently used to determine the extent to which respondents agree or disagree with a given thought, concept, or perspective. This agree-disagree format has become formalized and is often referred to as Likert scales, after the industrial psychologist Rensis Likert, who pioneered their use and analysis.

Questions may be of two general types: free response or response selection. Free response questions are often called open-ended questions; response selection questions are also known as close-ended or fixed-alternative questions. A chief advantage of response selection questions is that responses may be easily analyzed. Answers to free response questions, on the other hand, must be first categorized, scored, and coded. Since the scoring and coding process often demands the knowledge and understanding of a professional, the process is inevitably time-consuming as well as expensive. Some computer scoring of written responses is also occurring. Furthermore, respondents may find the work required of them to detail their answers in writing laborious and therefore choose not to respond or to give short, largely inadequate responses.

Constructing a Questionnaire

There are a number of steps involved in performing a study involving a questionnaire. An example listing of these steps follows.

1. Specifying the objectives of the study
2. Designing the questionnaire itself
3. Drafting the questionnaire
4. Editing the questionnaire
5. Developing instructions for administering the questionnaire
6. Pretesting the questionnaire
7. Revising the questionnaire
8. Developing a sampling plan for administering the questionnaire
9. Executing the survey or data collection
10. Data analysis
11. Reporting the results

Several of these steps are discussed here. It is essential that the goals of the study are carefully detailed; such work may lead to the elimination of unnecessary items from the questionnaire and result in a higher response rate. These objectives are operationalized in an outline of the questionnaire. Once topics for questions are provided, decisions as to best item formats may be made (e.g., free response or response selection questions).

Bouchard (1976) reported that while questionnaire construction is still primarily an art form, there are various rules of thumb based on both research and experience that may improve the decision making at this stage. These suggestions include involving the respondent population in as many stages of the construction process as possible; avoiding ambiguity at all costs; limiting questions to a single idea and thus keeping items as short as possible; writing questions using a level of language appropriate for the respondent population; avoiding negatively worded sentences and, even more, the use of double negatives; avoiding words with negative connotations; avoiding conditional clauses; wherever possible, using response selection questions rather than free response questions; and implementing procedures to reduce the influence of social desirability (described later) and other response sets (such as agreeing with all items). Editing should be performed by specialists in questionnaire construction as well as members of the respondent population. Readability checks can ensure that the wording is appropriate to the educational level of the respondents. The ordering of questions within the survey is important and must be performed with care.

Both introductions and instructions are advisable. Good introductions have been shown to increase the rate of returned questionnaires. Some researchers send postcards to potential respondents in advance of the survey to advise them that it is coming. Explaining the purpose and importance of the questionnaire is strongly recommended. Instructions on the questionnaire should be clear and as simple as possible. If the survey is to be returned in the mail, a stamped, addressed envelope should be included.

Pretesting the questionnaire is essential. Interviews with or written comments from these respondents may highlight potential difficulties that may be avoided. Occasionally, when many respondents specify "other" responses to certain response selection questions, new options can be added. Data-analytic issues cannot be detailed in a brief recitation such as this one. However, analyses used with other psychological measures (interitem correlations, reliability and validity studies) are frequently appropriate for questionnaires.

Two recurring problems in questionnaire research are response biases and nonrespondents. In many studies, respondents either avoid threatening questions or try to make themselves look good; this latter response style is known as social desirability. Bradburn, Sudman, and Associates (1980) make a number of recommendations to reduce this effect. Long, explanatory introductions to threatening questions help, as do promises of confidentiality. Permitting respondents to write sensitive answers rather than simply checking an answer is also beneficial. A potentially useful strategy is asking respondents to describe friends or "people like themselves," rather than them personally.

Increasingly, questionnaires are being used in cross-cultural research. In many such cases, more than one language becomes involved, and the translation of a questionnaire from one language to another is required. Cautions are necessary in such instances, especially because language and culture must both be addressed (Geisinger, 1994).

Achieving an adequate and unbiased sample is perhaps the biggest problem in questionnaire research. The nonresponse problem is twofold. First, many individuals do not respond to surveys. Furthermore, these nonrespondents frequently differ from respondents. Strategies to increase return rates include appeals for help and offers of small rewards, for example. Another strategy is to interview a random sample of nonrespondents.

Because of their relative ease, low cost, and low intrusion value, questionnaires are frequently used as data-collection devices in psychology. Solutions to problems such as those mentioned here are likely to continue to be sought. Even if good solutions are found, however, it is unlikely that experimental methodology will relinquish its preeminent status in psychology in that causal relationships are more easily discerned with it. Nonetheless, questionnaire use is increasing, and this growth will probably continue, especially with computer administration and scoring.

REFERENCES

Bouchard, T. J., Jr. (1976). Field research methods: Interviewing, questionnaires, participant observation, systematic observation, unobtrusive measures. In M. D. Dunnette (Ed.), *Handbook of industrial and organizational psychology* (pp. 363–413). Chicago: Rand McNally.

Bradburn, N. M., Sudman, S. O., & Associates. (1980). *Improving interview method and questionnaire design.* San Francisco, CA: Jossey-Bass.

Bradburn, N. M., Sudman, S. O., & Wansink, B. (2004). *Asking questions: The definitive guide to questionnaire design—for market research, political polls, and social and health questionnaires.* Hoboken, NJ: John Wiley & Sons.

Geisinger, K. F. (1994). Cross-cultural normative assessment: Translation and adaptation issues influencing normative interpretation of assessment instruments. *Psychological Assessment, 6,* 304–312.

Judd, C. M., Smith, E. R., & Kidder, L. H. (1991). *Research methods in social relations.* Fort Worth, TX: Holt, Rinehart & Winston.

SUGGESTED READINGS

Dillman, D. A. (2000). *Mail and internet surveys: The tailored design method.* New York: John Wiley & Sons.

Sudman, S., Bradburn, N. A., & Schwartz, S. (1995). *Thinking about answers: The application of cognitive processes to survey methodology.* New York: John Wiley & Sons.

KURT F. GEISINGER
University of Nebraska–Lincoln

See also: Interview Assessment